THE ST. MARTIN'S
HANDBOOK

Second Edition

THE ST. MARTIN'S HANDBOOK

Andrea Lunsford
OHIO STATE UNIVERSITY

Robert Connors
UNIVERSITY OF NEW HAMPSHIRE

ST. MARTIN'S PRESS

NEW YORK

ANNOTATED INSTRUCTOR'S EDITION

Cheryl Glenn
OREGON STATE UNIVERSITY

Roger C. Graves
UNIVERSITY OF WATERLOO

R. Gerald Nelms
SOUTHERN ILLINOIS UNIVERSITY

Dennis Quon
UNIVERSITY OF WATERLOO

English Editor Karen Allanson
Associate Editor Edward Mitchell-Hutchinson
Project Manager Denise Quirk
Production Supervisor Katherine Battiste

Manufactured in the United States of America.
65432
fedcba

For information, write:
St. Martin's Press, Inc.
175 Fifth Avenue
New York, NY 10010

ISBN: 0-312-05808-X

The text of this book has been printed on recycled paper.

Preface to Annotated Instructor's Edition

When we began this annotated edition, we hoped to create an efficient and accessible resource for instructors. Our first thought was of everyday classroom needs—teaching suggestions, answers to the exercises, and so on. As we began work, however, we came upon materials and ideas for teaching that have, we think, expanded our original horizons, providing not only the *what* to teach but, more importantly, the *how* and the *why*. Our experience mirrors the recent history of composition scholarship. In the past twenty years, the *what* has changed from a product-oriented approach to what is typically referred to as a process approach. Our teaching no longer focuses entirely upon the final text; we now intervene in the course of student writing, and try to embrace the overall procedure as well as the final product. Accompanying this shift in *what* has been increasingly sophisticated pedagogy and research, the *how,* and greater justification, the *why.* In our experience, the *what* cannot be separated from the *how* and the *why.* Without explaining *why* we teach what we do, the *what* remains simply dogma. By not providing information about *how* to teach it, the *what* remains merely abstraction.

Each chapter in this instructor's edition, therefore, contains various kinds of annotations that respond not only to everyday classroom needs but also to broad pedagogical concerns. First come *Background* sections, which present useful historical and theoretical information. *Teaching Practices* offer specific classroom and assignment strategies. *Optional Exercises* supplement the exercises in the student text with additional opportunities for writing practice. Citations of *Useful Readings* refer interested readers to books and articles that explore issues presented in each chapter. And sprinkled throughout are brief quotations from professional writers that can generate discussion, illuminate the subject at hand, or simply entertain.

This edition also includes two new kinds of annotations. *For Collaborative Work* builds on the first edition's *Writing Together* notes to provide an expanded set of suggestions for group work, and *For the Writing Log* offers specific ideas and assignments for log or journal work. Also new to this edition are a master bibliography of the *Useful Readings* and a name index to the annotations.

Users of the first edition may notice the absence here of the essays that provided an introduction to rhetorical theory and the teaching of writing. We refer interested instructors to *The St. Martin's Guide to Teaching Writing,* Second Edition, by Robert Connors and Cheryl Glenn, which collects a number of essays that will ground that volume's many practical suggestions in theoretical and historical discussion. On the very practical side, we include here, as before, sample syllabi for semester- and quarter-length courses to help you use *The St. Martin's Handbook.*

Creating this annotated edition has offered us a rich opportunity to practice what we so often preach. Throughout this project, we have tested the materials we were creating in the crucible of our classrooms, thereby making the necessary if not always successful connection between theory and practice. Similarly, we have found ourselves collaborating in the same ways we ask our students to do—again making that connection between theory and practice. And like our students, we have ourselves struggled with the concept of audience, attempting to address both beginning and experienced instructors of composition.

Our collaboration on this project includes number of friends and colleagues to whom we are indebted. At St. Martin's Press, we wish to thank Jean Smith, Mark Gallaher, Edward Mitchell-Hutchinson, Marilyn Moller, Denise Quirk, and Richard Steins, who have supplied support and encouragement. Carrie Shively Leverenz, of Ohio State University, has made invaluable contributions to this edition; our special thanks to her and to Heather Graves and Cinthia Gannett. Several reviewers shared suggestions that have helped to improve this edition: Toni-Lee Caposella, Stonehill College; Brooke Horvath, Kent State University; Dawn Hubbell-Staeble and Deepika Karle, both of Bowling Green State University. We are especially grateful to those good friends and generous colleagues who provided clerical support, research assistance, and generous, always valuable criticism: Melinda Bako, Doug Brent, Beverly Bruck, Lorraine Carlat, Heather Graves, Sue Lape, Jaime Mejia, Roxanne Mountford, Marcia Nelms, Jon Olson, Mike Rose, Cindy Selfe, Kimberly Town, Kelly Vezdos, and Tracy Vezdos. In an important sense, however, this group extends to include all the teachers to whom this book is addressed. Everything in this book is written for you—but in fact much, perhaps most, of it has been inspired by you.

Andrea Lunsford   Cheryl Glenn
Robert Connors   Roger C. Graves
                                             R. Gerald Nelms
                                             Dennis Quon

Contents

CONTENTS

Useful Readings

This bibliography compiles all of the *Useful Reading* citations listed in this instructor's edition. Abbreviations used are: *CCC—College Composition and Communication; CE—College English; EJ—English Journal; EQ—English Quarterly; RTE—Research in the Teaching of English.*

Achtert, Walter S. and Joseph Gibaldi. *The MLA Handbook for Writers of Research Papers.* 3rd ed. New York: MLA, 1985.

Aitchison, Jean. *Language Change: Progress or Decay?* Suffolk, England: Fontana, 1981.

Altick, Richard D. and Andrea A. Lunsford. *Preface to Critical Reading.* 6th ed. New York: Holt, 1984.

Anderson, Kristen F. "Using a Spelling Survey to Develop Basic Writers' Linguistic Awareness: A Response to Ann B. Dobie." *Journal of Basic Writing* 6 (1987): 72–78.

Anderson, Paul V. "What Survey Research Tells Us about Writing at Work." *Writing in Nonacademic Settings.* Ed. Lee Odell and Dixie Goswami. New York: Guilford, 1985.

Anson, Chris M., ed. *Writing and Response: Theory, Practice, and Research.* Urbana: NTCE, 1989.

Barnett, Marva T. *Writing for Technicians.* Albany: Delmar, 1982.

Baron, Dennis. *Grammar and Gender.* New Haven: Yale UP, 1986.

———. *Declining Grammar and Other Essays on the English Language.* Urbana, IL: NCTE, 1989.

Bartholomae, David. "Inventing the University." *When a Writer Can't Write: Studies in Writer's Block and Other Composing Process Problems.* Ed. Mike Rose. New York: Guilford, 1985: 134–165.

———. "The Study of Error." *CCC* 31 (1980): 253–69.

Bartholomae, David, and Anthony Petrosky. *Facts, Artifacts, and Counterfacts: Theory and Method for a Reading and Writing Course.* Upper Montclair, NJ: Boynton, 1986.

Baugh, Albert C., and Thomas Cable. *A History of the English Language,* 3rd ed. Englewood Cliffs: Prentice, 1978.

Bazerman, Charles. *The Informed Writer: Using Sources in the Disciplines.* 2nd ed. Boston: Houghton, 1985.

Bean, John C., Dean Drenk, and F. D. Lee. "Microtheme Strategies for Cognitive Skills." *New Directions for Teaching and Learning: Teaching Writing in the Disciplines.* Ed. C. W. Griffen. San Francisco: Jossey, 1982.

Berlin, James. *Rhetoric and Reality: Writing Instruction in American Colleges 1900–1985.* Carbondale: Southern Illinois UP, 1987.

Booth, Wayne. "The Rhetorical Stance." *CCC* 14 (1963): 139–45.

Braddock, Richard. "The Frequency and Placement of Topic Sentences in Expository Prose." *RTE* 8 (1974): 287–302.

Brannon, Lil, Melinda Knight, and Vera Neverow-Turk. *Writers Writing.* Upper Montclair, NJ: Boynton, 1983.

Bruffee, Kenneth. "Collaborative Learning and the 'Conversation of Mankind.' " *CE* 46 (1984): 635–52.

Burke, Kenneth. "Lexicon Rhetoricae." *Counter-Statement.* 1931. Berkeley and Los Angeles: U of California P, 1968. 123–68.

Carpenter, Carol. "Exercises to Combat Sexist Reading and Writing." *CE* 43 (1981): 293–300.

The Chicago Manual of Style. 13th ed. Chicago: U of Chicago P, 1982.

Christensen, Francis. "A Generative Rhetoric of the Sentence." *Rhetoric and Composition.* Ed. Richard L. Graves. Upper Montclair, NJ: Boynton, 1984. 110–18.

Coe, Richard. *Toward a Grammar of Passages.* Carbondale: Southern Illinois UP, 1988.

Comrie, Bernard. *Aspect.* Cambridge: Cambridge UP, 1976.

Connors, Robert J. "*Actio:* A Rhetoric of Manuscripts." *Rhetoric Review* 2 (1983): 64–73.

———. "The Rise and Fall of the Modes of Discourse." *CCC* 32 (1981): 444–55.

Corbett, Edward P. J. *Classical Rhetoric for the Modern Student.* 3rd ed. New York: Oxford UP, 1990.

———. *The Elements of Reasoning.* New York: Macmillan, 1991.

Daiute, Colette. *Writing and Computers.* Reading, MA: Addison, 1985.

Daly, Mary, and Jane Caputi. *Webster's First New Intergalactic Wickedary of the English Language.* Boston: Beacon 1987.

D'Angelo, Frank. "The Topic Sentence Revisited." *CE* 37 (1986): 431–41.

Dinitz, Susan, and Jean Kiedaisch. "The Research Paper: Teaching Students to be Members of the Academic Community." *Exercise Exchange* 31 (1986): 8–10.

Dobie, Ann B. "Orthographical Theory and Practice, or How to Teach Spelling." *Journal of Basic Writing* 5 (1986): 41–48.

———. "Orthography Revisited: A Response to Kristen Anderson." *Journal of Basic Writing* 7 (1988): 82–83.

Ede, Lisa S., and Andrea A. Lunsford. "Audience Addressed/Audience Invoked: The Role of Audience in Composition Theory and Pedagogy." *CCC* 35 (1984): 155–71. Rpt. in Tate and Corbett, *The Writing Teacher's Sourcebook.*

Elbow, Peter. *Writing without Teachers.* New York: Oxford UP, 1973.

———. *Writing with Power.* New York: Oxford UP, 1981. 59–77.

Emig, Janet. *The Web of Meaning: Essays on Writing, Teaching, Learning, and Thinking.* Ed. Dixie Goswami and Maureen Butler. Upper Montclair, NJ: Boynton, 1983.

———. "Writing as a Mode of Learning." *CCC* 28 (1977): 122–28. Rpt. in Tate and Corbett, *The Writing Teacher's Sourcebook.*

Faigley, Lester. "Competing Theories of Process: A Critique and a Proposal." *CE* 48 (1986): 527–42.

Faigley, Lester, and Stephen Witte. "Analyzing Revision." *CE* 32 (1981): 400–14.

Finnegan, Edward. *Attitudes Toward English Usage.* New York: Teachers College P, 1980.

Flesch, Rudolph. *The ABC of Style: A Guide to Plain English.* New York: Harper, 1964.

Francis, W. Nelson, and Henry Kucera. *Frequency Analysis of English Usage.* Boston: Houghton, 1982.

Flower, Linda. "Writer-based Prose: A Cognitive Basis for Problems in Writing." *CE* 41 (1979): 19–37.

Fowler, H. W. *A Dictionary of Modern English Usage.* 2nd ed. Rev. and ed. Sir Ernest Gowers. New York: Oxford UP, 1965.

Fulwiler, Toby, ed. and intro. *The Journal Book.* Portsmouth: Heinemann, 1987.

Gannett, Cinthia. *Gender and the Journal: Diaries and Academic Discourse.* Albany: SUNY P, 1992.

Gebhardt, Richard. "Initial Plans and Spontaneous Composition: Toward a Comprehensive Theory of the Writing Process." *CE* 44 (1982): 620–27.

Graves, Richard L. "Symmetrical Form and the Rhetoric of the Sentence." *Essays on Classical Rhetoric and Modern Discourse.* Ed. Robert J. Connors, Lisa S. Ede, and Andrea A. Lunsford. Carbondale,: Southern Illinois UP, 1984.

Halliday, M. A. K. *System and Function in Language.* Ed. Gunther Kress. London: Oxford UP, 1976.

Halliday, M. A. K., and Rugaiya Hasan. *Cohesion in English.* London: Longman, 1976.

Halpern, Jeanne, and Sarah Liggett. *Computers & Composing: How New Technologies Are Changing Writing.* Carbondale: Southern Illinois UP, 1984.

Hartwell, Patrick. "Grammar, Grammars, and the Teaching of Grammar." *CE* 47 (1985): 105–27.

Hashimoto, Irwin. "Pain and Suffering: Apostrophes and Academic Life." *Journal of Basic Writing* 7 (1988): 91–98.

Havelock, Eric A. "The Character and the Content of the Code." *The Literate Revolution in Speech and Its Cultural Consequences.* Princeton: Princeton UP, 1982.

Heath, Shirley Brice. *Ways with Words.* Cambridge: Cambridge UP, 1983.

Herndon, Jeanne H. *A Survey of Modern Grammars.* New York: Holt, 1976.

Highet, Gilbert. "Ciceronianism and Anti-Ciceronianism." *Prose Style: A Historical Approach through Studies.* San Francisco: Chandler, 1971.

Homan, C. Hugh. *Handbook to Literature.* 4th ed. Indianapolis: Bobbs, 1980.

Jeske, Jeff. "Borrowing from the Sciences: A Model for the Freshman Research Paper." *Writing Instructor* 6 (Winter 1987): 62–67.

Johnson, Samuel. "Preface to a Dictionary of the English Language." Rpt. in Bertrand H. Bronson, *Samuel Johnson: Rasselas, Poems, and Selected Prose.* 3rd ed. New York: Holt, 1971.

Keene, Michael L. "Technical Information in the Information Economy," Rpt. in *Perspectives on Research and Scholarship in Composition.* Ed. Ben W. McClelland and Timothy R. Donovan. New York: MLA, 1985.

Kennedy, Mary Lynch. "The Composing Process of College Students Writing from Sources." *Written Communication* 2 (1985): 434–56.

Kinneavy, James. "The Basic Aims of Discourse." *CCC* 20 (1969): 297–304.

Kline, Charles R., and W. Dean Memering. "Formal Fragments: The English Minor Sentence." *RTE* 11 (Fall, 1977): 97–110. Rpt. in *Rhetoric and Composition: A Sourcebook for Teachers and Writers.* Ed. Richard L. Graves. Upper Montclair, NJ: Boynton, 1984.

Kneupper, Charles W. "Teaching Argument: An Introduction to the Toulmin Model." *CCC* 29 (1978): 237–41.

Kolln, Martha. "Closing the Books on Alchemy," *CCC* 32 (1981): 139–51.

Krishna, Valerie. "The Syntax of Error." *Journal of Basic Writing* 1 (1975): 43–49. Rpt. in *Rhetoric and Composition: A Sourcebook for Teachers and Writers.* Ed. Richard L. Graves. Upper Montclair, NJ: Boynton, 1984. 128–32.

Kroll, Barry M. "How College Freshmen View Plagiarism." *Written Communication* 5 (1988): 203–21.

———. "Writing for Readers: Three Perspectives on Audience." *CCC* 35 (1984): 172–85.

Laib, Nevin. "Conciseness and Amplification." *CCC* 41 (1990): 443–59.

Lamb, Catherine. "Beyond Argument in Feminist Composition." *CCC* 42 (1991): 11–24.

Langer, Judith. "Learning through Writing: Study Skills in the Content Areas." *Journal of Reading* 29 (1986): 400–06.

Lanham, Richard A. *Analyzing Prose.* New York: Scribner, 1983.

———. *Style: An Anti-Textbook.* New Haven: Yale UP, 1977.

Larson, Richard L. "The 'Research Paper' in the Writing Course: A Non-Form of Writing." *CE* 44 (1982): 811–16. Rpt. in Tate and Corbett, *The Writing Teacher's Sourcebook.*

———. "Structure and Form in Non-Narrative Prose." *Ten Bibliographic Essays.* Ed. Gary Tate. Fort Worth: Texas Christian UP, 1987.

Lauer, Janice. "Issues in Rhetorical Invention." *Essays on Classical Rhetoric and Modern Discourse.* Ed. Robert J. Connors, Lisa S. Ede, and Andrea A. Lunsford. Carbondale: Southern Illinois UP, 1984.

Lindemann, Erika. *A Rhetoric for Writing Teachers.* 2nd ed. New York: Oxford UP, 1987.

McCartney, Robert. "The Cumulative Research Paper." *Teaching English in the Two-Year College* 12 (1985): 198–202.

McCrum, Robert, William Cran, and Robert MacNeil. *The Story of English.* New York: Penguin, 1987.

Macrorie, Ken. *Telling Writing.* 2nd ed. Rochelle Park, NJ: Hayden, 1970.

Markels, Robin Bell. *A New Perspective on Cohesion in Expository Paragraphs.* Carbondale: Southern Illinois UP, 1984.

Matthews, Mitford M. "The Freshman and His Dictionary." *About Language.* Ed. William H. Robert and Gregoire Turgeon. Boston: Houghton, 1986.

Mencken, H. L. *The American Language.* New York: Knopf, 1937.

Morris, William, and Mary Morris. *Harper Dictionary of Contemporary Usage.* New York: Harper, 1975.

Murray, Donald. *Learning by Teaching.* Upper Montclair, NJ: Boynton, 1982.

———. "Teaching the Other Self: The Writer's First Reader." *CCC* 33 (1982): 140–47.

Nilsen, Aileen Pace. "Winning the Great 'He'/'She' Battle." *CE* 46 (1984): 151–57.

Noguchi, Rei R. *Grammar and the Teaching of Writing: Limits and Possibilities.* Urbana, IL: NCTE, 1991.

O'Hare, Frank. *Sentence Combining: Improving Student Writing without Formal Grammar Instruction.* Urbana, IL: NCTE, 1973.

Ong, Walter. "Historical Backgrounds of Elizabethan and Jacobean Punctuation Theory." *PMLA* 59 (1944): 349–60.

———. *Orality and Literacy.* London: Methuen, 1982.

Orwell, George. "Politics and the English Language." *Shooting an Elephant and Other Essays.* New York: Harcourt, 1974.

Ottens, Allen J. *Coping with Academic Anxiety.* New York: Rosen, 1984.

Palacas, Arthur L. "Parentheticals and Personal Voice." *WC* 6 (1989): 506–27.

Perelman, Chaim. "The Premises of Argumentation" in *The Realm of Rhetoric.* Notre Dame: U of Notre Dame P, 1982.

Period Styles: A History of Punctuation. New York: The Herb Lubalin Study Center of Design and Typography in the Cooper Union for the Advancement of Science and Art, 1988.

Perl, Sondra. "The Composing Processes of Unskilled College Writers." *RTE* 13 (1979): 5–22.

———. "Understanding Composing." *CCC* 31 (1980): 363–69.

Philips, Martin. "CALL in Its Educational Context." *Computers in English Language Teaching and Research.* London: Longman, 1986.

Pianko, Sharon. "A Description of the Composing Processes of College Freshman Writers." *RTE* 13 (1979): 5–22.

Powell, Alfred. "A Chemist's View of Writing, Reading, and Thinking across the Curriculum." *CCC* 36 (1985): 414–18.

Price, Gayle, "A Case for a Modern Commonplace Book." *CCC* 31 (1980), 175–82.

"Printing, Typography, and Photoengraving." *The New Encyclopaedia Britannica: Macropaedia.* 1987.

Pyles, Thomas and John Algeo. *The Origins and Development of the English Language.* 3rd ed. New York: Harcourt, 1982.

Quantic, Diane. "Insights into the Research Process from Student Logs." *Journal of Teaching Writing* 5 (1986): 221–25.

Redish, Janice C., Robbin M. Battison, and Edward S. Gold. "Making Information Accessible to Readers." *Writing in Nonacademic Settings.* Ed. Lee Odell and Dixie Goswami. New York: Guilford, 1985.

Rico, Gabriel L. *Writing the Natural Way.* Los Angeles: Tarcher, 1983.

Schwartz, Helen J. and Lillian S. Bridwell-Bowles. "A Selected Bibliography on Computers in Composition: An Update." *CCC* 38 (1987): 453–57.

Selfe, Cynthia L. *Computer-Assisted Instruction in Composition: Create Your Own.* Urbana, IL: NCTE, 1986.

The Sentence and the Paragraph. Urbana, IL: NCTE, 1963.

Shamoon, Linda K. and Robert A. Schwegler. "Sociologists Reading Student Tests: Expectations and Perceptions." *Writing Instructor* 7 (Winter 1988): 71–81.

Shaughnessy, Mina P. *Errors and Expectations: A Guide for the Teacher of Basic Writing.* New York: Oxford UP, 1977.

Sherrard, Carol. "Summary Writing: A Topographical Study." *WC* 3 (1986): 324–43.

Sommers, Nancy. "Revision Strategies of Student Writers and Experienced Adult Writers." *CCC* 31 (1980): 378–88.

Taylor, Karl K. and Ede B. Kidder. "The Development of Spelling Skills from First Grade through Eighth Grade." *WC* 5 (1988): 222–44.

Teall, Edward N. *Meet Mr. Hyphen and Put Him in His Place.* New York: Funk, 1937.

Thomas, Lewis. "Notes on Punctuation." *New England Journal of Medicine* 296 (1977): 1103–05.

Toulmin, Stephen. *The Uses of Argument.* New York: Cambridge UP, 1964.

Traugott, Lee, Elizabeth Closs, and Mary Louise Pratt. *Linguistics for Students of Literature.* New York: Harcourt, 1980.

Tufte, Virginia. *Grammar as Style*. New York: Holt, 1971.

Weathers, Winston. "Grammars of Style: New Options in Composition." *Freshman English News*. 4 (Winter 1976): 1–4, 12–18. Rpt. in *Rhetoric and Composition: A Sourcebook for Teachers and Writers*. Ed. Richard L. Graves. Upper Montclair, NJ: Boynton, 1984.

Weaver, Richard M. "Ultimate Terms in Contemporary Rhetoric." *Language Is Sermonic: Richard M. Weaver on the Nature of Rhetoric*. Ed. Richard L. Johannesen et al. Baton Rouge: Louisiana State UP, 1970.

Webb, Robert A. *The Washington Post Deskbook on Style*. New York: McGraw, 1978.

Whitelock, Dorothy. *Sweet's Anglo-Saxon Reader in Prose and Verse*. Oxford: Oxford UP, 1967.

Williams, Joseph M. *Origins of the English Language: A Social and Linguistic History*. New York: Free Press, 1975. 265–74.

———. "The Phenomenology of Error." *CCC* 32 (1981): 152–68.

———. *Style: Ten Lessons in Clarity and Grace*. 3rd ed. Glenview, IL: Scott, 1989.

Winterowd, Ross. "The Grammar of Coherence." *CE* 31 (1970): 328–35.

Witte, Stephen P. and Lester Faigley. "Coherence, Cohesion, and Writing Quality." *CCC* 32 (1981): 189–204.

Woodson, Linda. *A Handbook of Modern Rhetorical Terms*. Urbana, IL: NCTE, 1979.

Young, Art, and Toby Fulwiler. *Writing across the Disciplines: Research into Practice*. Upper Montclair, NJ: Boynton, 1986.

Sample Syllabi

SAMPLE SYLLABUS FOR FIFTEEN-WEEK SEMESTER

Structure of the Course

One of the best ways to learn to write is by writing, and for that reason students in this course will be asked to do a lot of inventing, drafting, and revising—that's what writing is. Sharing work with others, either in peer-response sessions, writing groups, or collaborative efforts, promotes learning about writing by widening the response writers get to their work. Finally, texts can help in learning to write by answering questions students may have or suggesting ways of going about the business of writing. Because each of these three principles operates powerfully in the classroom, they form the basis of the course schedule outlined below. To provide practice writing and sharing those writings, often the class will be devoted to writing workshops. These writing workshops give students the chance to see how other students have handled writing assignments, to practice editing skills by helping other students edit their own work, and to draft essays. Many class days will involve a class discussion of a student essay that demonstrates how the writing being done might best be handled. In addition, many classes will open with a short writing assignment, freewrite, or writing log entry. Each week the class will read sections from *The St. Martin's Handbook* that address issues about writing, guide students in their understanding of those issues, and suggest ways for them to broaden their knowledge and apply that knowledge to their writing.

Written Assignments

Students write five essays during the term. An acceptable draft of each essay must be turned in by the final due date for each essay. At any time during the term, a final grade may be assigned to the draft that each student judges to be his or her final effort on each essay. At least one week before the end of the term, students turn in four of five final drafts for final evaluation. Before the last day of classes, students turn in the fifth essay for a final grade. All final drafts must be typed or computer-generated.

Since students can suspend final evaluation of their progress until the end of the semester, this grading system provides students with the opportunity to have their best work evaluated.

Attendance

Because much of each student's most important work will take place in class, attendance in class should be mandatory. (Warn chronically late students once; after that, count each late appearance as an absence.)

Final Course Grades

Final course grades will be arrived at by combining grades for the five graded papers, class attendance, participation, and conferences with the teacher in the following manner:

—portfolio of final, graded essays (4 × 15%)   60%
—research essay (fourth essay)   20%
—attendance   10%
—conferences, writing logs   10%

Course Schedule

Week	Topics/Focus

1   Introduction: briefly outline the course; identify learning objectives from your perspective and ask the students to add some of their own; present guidelines for grading, plagiarism, late essays, attendance. Diagnostic writing sample.
Writing, reading, and research (Chapter 1); considering purpose and audience (Chapter 2); rewrite diagnostic test to demonstrate drafting, learning through writing. Assign the first essay: identify the task clearly, provide models of successful attempts, link the assignment to learning objectives, suggest ways for students to use the assignment to learn about something that interests them.

2   Invention techniques: mapping, brainstorming (Chapter 3); research as invention (Chapter 39). Apply invention methods to first assignment. Draft of first essay due; peer-response in class; teacher response: read for overall direction, scope, and suitability for your course and first assignment.
Revising and editing the draft (Chapter 4). Compare writing log entries.

3   Second draft of first essay due; peer-response in class; constructing paragraphs (Chapter 6).
Confer with students individually either during office hours or classroom writing workshops. Identify specific error patterns you have noticed; conduct mini-lectures for students who share error patterns (the specific chapters you will need to refer to will emerge from the class' needs: see Chapters 7–18 and 29–38).

4   First essay due.
Assign the second essay: identify the task clearly, provide models of successful attempts, link the assignment to learning objectives, suggest ways for students to use the assignment to learn about something that interests them. Repeat invention techniques used for the first essay; repeat freewriting sessions and exchange freewrites to share ideas, approaches to the assignment.

5   Draft of the second essay due; peer-response in class, teacher response to focus and questions to promote further research or development. Constructing effective sentences (Chapter 19); Creating coordinate and subordinate structures (Chapter 20).
Writing workshop and/or individual conferences. Second draft of second essay due.

6   Understanding diction; enriching vocabulary; building common ground (Chapters 26–28). Confer with students individually either during office hours or classroom writing workshops. Identify specific error patterns you have noticed; conduct mini-lectures for students who share error patterns (the specific chapters you will need to refer to will emerge from the needs of the class: see Chapter 7–18 and 29–38).

7   Second essay due.
Assign the third essay: identify the task clearly, provide models of successful attempts, link the assignment to learning objectives, suggest ways for students to use the assignment to learn about something that interests them. Repeat invention techniques used for the second essay; add tagmemic heuristic or clustering. Recognizing and using arguments (Chapter 5).

8   Draft of the third essay due; peer-response in class, teacher response to focus and questions to spur research or development.
Creating parallel sentence structures (Chapter 21); varying sentence structures (Chapter 22).
Confer with students either individually in class or during office hours.

9   Identify specific error patterns you have noticed; conduct mini-lectures for students who share error patterns (the specific chapters you will need to refer to will emerge from the class' needs: see Chapter 7–18 and 29–38).

10   Third essay due.
Assign the fourth essay (a research essay: identify the

task clearly, provide models of successful attempts, link the assignment to learning objectives, suggest ways for students to use the assignment to learn about something that interests them).

Becoming a researcher (Chapter 39); conducting research (Chapter 40); using dictionaries (Chapter 25).

11   Research file due: a list of all sources consulted so far; notes; photocopies of relevant readings; summaries; quotations.

Using sources (Chapter 41); Writing a research essay (Chapter 42).

12   Draft of research essay due; confer individually with students; devote class time to writing workshops.

Creating memorable prose (Chapter 23).

13   Second draft of research essay due; peer-response in class.

Documenting sources (Chapters 43–44).

14   Final draft of research essay due.

Fifth assignment: rewrite or revise an essay from: 1) a course in the student's major, 2) a discipline that interests him or her, or 3) this course.

Writing in different disciplines (Chapter 45); writing professional and business correspondence (Chapter 47).

Due: a description of the conventions of the student's discipline; a description of the style of his or her field.

Due: typed, final drafts of first four papers for final grading.

15   Draft of the fifth assignment due; peer-response in class, teacher response through individual conferences in class or during office hours; writing workshops in class.

Final draft of fifth essay due.

Course evaluations.

SAMPLE SYLLABUS FOR TEN-WEEK QUARTER

Structure of the Course

One of the best ways to learn to write is by writing, and for that reason students in this course will be asked to do a lot of inventing, drafting, and revising—that's what writing is. Shar-

ing work with others, either in peer-response sessions, writing groups, or collaborative efforts, promotes learning about writing by widening the response writers get to their work. Finally, texts can help in learning to write by answering questions students may have or suggesting ways of going about the business of writing. Because each of these three principles operates powerfully in the classroom, they form the basis of the course schedule outlined below. To provide practice writing and sharing those writings, often the class will be devoted to writing workshops. These writing workshops give students the chance to see how other students have handled writing assignments, to practice editing skills by helping other students edit their own work, and to draft essays. Many class days will involve a class discussion of a student essay that demonstrates how the writing being done might best be handled. In addition, many classes will open with a short writing assignment, freewrite, or writing log entry. Each week we will read sections from *The St. Martin's Handbook* that address issues about writing, guide us in our understanding of those issues, and suggest ways for us to broaden our knowledge and apply that knowledge to our writing.

Written Assignments

Students write four essays during the term. An acceptable draft of each essay must be turned in by the final due date for each essay. At any time during the term, a final grade may be assigned to the draft that each student judges to be his or her final effort on each essay. At least one week before the end of the term, students turn in three of four final drafts for final evaluation. Before the last day of classes, students turn in the fourth essay for a final grade. All final drafts must be typed or computer-generated.

Since students can suspend final evaluation of their progress until the end of the semester, this grading system provides them with the opportunity to have their best work evaluated.

Attendance

Because much of each student's most important work will take place in class, attendance in class should be mandatory. (Warn chronically late students once; after that, count each late appearance as an absence.)

Final Course Grades

Final course grades will be arrived at by combining grades for the four graded papers, class attendance, participation, and conferences with the teacher in the following manner:

—final, graded essays (4 × 20%):   80%
—attendance   10%
—conferences, writing logs   10%

Course Schedule

Week   *Topics/Focus*

1   Introduction: briefly outline the course; identify learning objectives from your perspective and ask the students to add some of their own; present guidelines for grading, plagiarism, late essays, attendance.
Diagnostic writing sample.
Writing, reading, and research (Chapter 1); considering purpose and audience (Chapter 2); rewrite diagnostic test to demonstrate drafting, learning through writing.
Assign the first essay: identify the task clearly, provide models of successful attempts, link the assignment to learning objectives, suggest ways for students to use the assignment to learn about something that interests them.

2   Invention techniques: mapping, brainstorming (Chapter 3); research as invention (Chapter 39). Apply invention methods to first assignment.
Draft of first essay due; peer-response in class; teacher response: read for overall direction, scope, and suitability for your course and first assignment.
Revising and editing the draft (Chapter 4).
Compare writing log entries.

3   Second draft of first essay due; peer-response in class; constructing paragraphs (Chapter 6).

Confer with students individually either during office hours or classroom writing workshops. Identify specific error patterns you have noticed; conduct mini-lectures for students who share error patterns (the specific chapters you will need to refer to will emerge from the class' needs: see Chapters 7–18 and 29–38).

4   First essay due.
Assign the second essay: identify the task clearly, provide models of successful attempts, link the assignment to learning objectives, suggest ways for students to use the assignment to learn about something that interests them. Repeat invention techniques used for the first essay; repeat freewriting sessions and exchange freewrites to share ideas, approaches to the assignment.

5   Draft of the second essay due; peer-response in class, teacher response to focus and questions to promote further research or development. Constructing effective sentences (Chapter 19); creating coordinate and subordinate structures (Chapter 20).
Writing workshop and/or individual conferences. Second draft of second essay due.

6   Understanding diction; enriching vocabulary; building common ground (Chapters 26–28). Confer with students individually either during office hours or classroom writing workshops.
Identify specific error patterns you have noticed; conduct mini-lectures for students who share error patterns (the specific chapters you will need to refer to will emerge from the needs of the class' needs: see Chapter 7–18 and 29–38).

7   Second essay due.
Assign the third essay: identify the task clearly, provide models of successful attempts, link the assignment to learning objectives, suggest ways for students to use the assignment to learn about something that interests them. Repeat invention techniques used for the second essay; add tagmemic heuristic or clustering.
Recognizing and using arguments (Chapter 5).

8   Draft of the third essay due; peer-response in class, teacher response to focus and questions to spur research or development.
Creating parallel sentence structures (Chapter 21); varying sentence structures (Chapter 22).

Confer with students either individually in class or during office hours.

Identify specific error patterns you have noticed; conduct mini-lectures for students who share error patterns (the specific chapters you will need to refer to will emerge from the class's needs: see Chapters 7–18 and 29–38).

9   Third essay due.

Assign the fourth essay: rewrite or revise an essay from: 1) a course in the student's major, 2) a discipline that interests him or her, or 3) this course.

Writing in different disciplines (Chapter 45); writing professional and business correspondence (Chapter 47).

Due: a description of the conventions of the student's discipline; a description of the style of his or her field.

Due: typed, final drafts of first three papers for final grading.

10   Draft of the fourth assignment due; peer-response in class, teacher response through individual conferences in class or during office hours; writing workshops in class.

Final draft of fourth essay due.

Course evaluations.

THE ST. MARTIN'S HANDBOOK

Second Edition

THE ST. MARTIN'S HANDBOOK

Andrea Lunsford

OHIO STATE UNIVERSITY

Robert Connors

UNIVERSITY OF NEW HAMPSHIRE

ST. MARTIN'S PRESS

NEW YORK

Editor of The St. Martin's Handbook   Marilyn Moller
English Editor   Karen Allanson
Project Manager   Denise Quirk
Manuscript Editor   John Elliott
Development Associate   Kristin Bowen
Editorial Assistant   Amy Horowitz
Production Supervisor   Katherine Battiste
Text Design   Anna George
Cover Design   Nadia Furlan-Lorbek

Library of Congress Catalog Card Number: 90−71646
Manufactured in the United States of America.
65432
fedcba

For information, write:
St. Martin's Press, Inc.
175 Fifth Avenue
New York, NY 10010

ISBN: 0-312-05367-3

ACKNOWLEDGMENTS

Maya Angelou. "I Dared to Hope," copyright 1991 by the New York Times Company. Reprinted by permission.
"Chicken Soup: It Might Help Your Memory." From *Newsweek,* December 1, 1986 © 1986, Newsweek, Inc. All rights reserved. Reprinted by permission.

Acknowledgments and copyrights are continued at the back of the book on page 778, which constitutes an extension of the copyright page.

 The text of this book has been printed on recycled paper.

Preface

The story of *The St. Martin's Handbook* stretches back to 1983, when in the course of investigating the history of writing instruction, we came across some information that led us to a series of compelling questions. We discovered, for example, that in the late nineteenth century, professors at Harvard perceived that their students had great difficulty distinguishing between the use of *shall* and *will,* and that in the 1930s, American students persistently misused *would* for the simple past. How quaint, we thought; look at how much student writing problems have changed.

But what exactly were these changes? This question took on greater significance as we focused our investigation on the history and development of composition textbooks. As part of that research, we found that the first edition of John C. Hodges's *Harbrace College Handbook* (1941) was based on an analysis of over twenty thousand student papers written in the 1930s. So, we reasoned, that book reflected the writing problems of students of the time, problems that were decidedly different from how to use *shall* and *will.* How might the problems faced by our students have changed?

With something of a shock, we realized that we didn't know. Further investigation showed us not only that Hodges's research seemed to be the last serious effort of that kind but that his handbook was still organized exactly as it had been in 1941. Since subsequent college handbooks had necessarily responded to that book, we realized with some surprise that the world of composition handbooks was still being tacitly guided by conceptions of error patterns that were half a century old.

We set out, then, to discover what patterns of error actually characterize student writing today, and which of these patterns seem most important to their instructors. To answer this question, we gathered a nationwide sample of over twenty thousand marked student essays and carefully analyzed a scientifically stratified sample of them, eventually identifying the twenty error patterns most characteristic of student writing today. We got some provocative results.

Most intriguing to us was how many of these errors related in some way to visual memory—wrong words, wrong or missing verb endings, missing or misplaced possessive apostrophes, even the *its/it's* confusion—which suggests that students today are less familiar with the visible aspects of writing than students once were. Part of the effect of an oral, electronic culture seems to be, then, that students do not automatically bring with them the visual knowledge of writing conventions that text-wise writers possess and use effortlessly.

This problem of visualization was most pronounced in terms of spelling errors, which occur—by a factor of 300 percent—more frequently than any other error. Interestingly enough, the words students most often misspell are homonyms, thus further suggesting that the visual aspect of spelling is particularly important, that in a world of secondary orality we need to find ways to help students visualize their language.

Our research also revealed that many errors are governed not so much by hard and fast rule as by rhetorical decisions involving style, tone, and rhythm. Among others, such errors include omitted commas after an introductory element, inappropriate shifts in verb tense, and misused commas with restrictive and nonrestrictive elements. This finding suggested to us that students need help writing prose that is not only mechanically correct but rhetorically effective as well. Doing so, we believe, demands that they view the tools of writing—grammar, punctuation, mechanics—as having rhetorical force and as being based on choices they must learn to make.

Armed with this information, we set out to create a textbook that would address the needs of students at the end of the twentieth century. The result was *The St. Martin's Handbook*. In many ways it was a traditional handbook, but in other important respects, it charted new territory, moving in directions new to the handbook tradition.

Distinguishing features

The most important new direction has been its constant **attention to writing**, not just to correctness. Our research and experience convince us that students need practice in *writing,* not only in revising incorrect sentences. Like all composition handbooks, this book provides guidance in checking and revising for correctness. Unlike most others, however, it also offers ample opportunity for student writing, in guided-writing and imitation exercises that get students to stretch their writing muscles as well as in revision exercises that send them back into their own writing.

This attention to writing informs every chapter in the book, including those dealing with grammar and mechanics. The chapter on adjectives and adverbs, for instance, asks students to focus not only on how to use adjectives and adverbs correctly but also on the more compelling question of why and in what circumstances to use them at all. The end punctuation chapter provides rules for using periods, question marks, and exclamation points, and, in addition, it asks students to try revising a piece of their own writing for sentence variety, using declarative, interrogatory, and exclamatory structures. In other words, we have tried to present grammar and mechanics as tools to use for a writing purpose, not simply to use "correctly."

The St. Martin's Handbook has broken other new ground in its **systematic attention to reading**. Because we see writing and reading as inextricably linked, we have included reading instruction throughout the text. Not only do we offer extensive guidance to help students read observantly and critically—whether evaluating a draft, an argument, a paragraph, or a source—but we also present reading as one more tool that can help improve writing skills. The first chapter offers guidelines for reading, and almost every subsequent chapter includes a special exercise asking students to "read with an eye for" some structure or element they are learning to use as writers—verbs, semicolons, hyphens, and so on. These exercises ask them to study passages from famous essays (and sometimes, poems) or from drafts of their own or other student work. In addition to the benefits of studying expert use of basic rhetorical elements, such exercises will, we hope, help build students' visual knowledge of writing and writing conventions. Many of these exercises ask students then to imitate something in the passage—in other words, to step from their reading into writing.

And since many of you use a handbook along with a reader, we have deliberately taken many passages from essays often included in composition readers—that is, from the essays your students are likely to be reading. These examples serve as models for imitation, as prompts for writing, or as occasions for readerly response. Such passages will of course serve as memorable examples; more important, however, they will provide the larger rhetorical context so often missing in most other handbooks.

Finally, the first edition of *The St. Martin's Handbook* attempted to provide **practical guidelines for recognizing, understanding, and revising each of the twenty most common errors**. In presenting these errors, we tried to give a clear message about "correctness" *along with* realistic discussion of actual usage. Without oversimplification, our goal was to help students know *what to do*. Most important, we presented errors as opportunities for improving skills, as something to be examined in rhetorical context and learned from rather than as blots to be eradicated. We asked students not simply to amass information about errors but to analyze the sources and consequences of those errors in their own writing—to build, if you will, a theory about how to improve their writing based on a close study of the errors that they make.

New to this edition

Response to the first edition of *The St. Martin's Handbook* reaffirmed our commitment to its innovative emphasis on writing instruction, on reading, and on the rhetorical nature of all writing choices, including those which result in errors of convention. In preparing the second edition, therefore, we wanted to expand these features while building on our original research base. To do so, we decided to pursue another research question, one that had been tugging at our mental apronstrings ever since we began this project in 1983. If we now could say with some assurance what errors characterize student writing today, what could we say about student use of larger rhetorical elements? To put our question in the discourse of rhetoric, having focused so intently on the third canon—style—what could we discover about the first and second canons—invention and arrangement?

To explore this question, we turned to another stratified sample of the marked twenty thousand essays. This time, however, we looked not at errors but at content and organization. Again, we got some provocative results. We found, for instance, that these aspects of the composing process are as important to readers today as they were over 2,000 years ago, when Aristotle said that the two responsibilities of any orator were to (1) state a claim clearly and (2) prove it. The use of good reasons, proof, evidence, and examples—the rhetorical tools of invention—elicited most consistent commentary from teachers, followed closely by commentary on the ways in which such materials were arranged or organized.

These findings strongly suggest that readers are interested in the *what* as well as the *how* of student writing. More specifically, they suggest that student writers need to master methods of logical analysis and patterns of development not simply to demonstrate that they can recognize the difference between classification and division, for example, but rather to gain the understanding and assent of their readers. In fact, 77 percent of the papers we examined contained comments about large rhetorical issues, a finding that in itself challenges the claim sometimes heard that teachers do little with student papers except mark errors.

An emphasis on readers and the role they play in creation of powerful writing underlies both our research and every chapter of the second edition of *The St. Martin's Handbook*. This focus results in two emphases: making students aware of the effect their choices (of arguments, examples, methods of organization, sentence structure, word choices) are likely to have on readers; and helping them become careful and critical readers of their own writing. These two goals, we hope, are realized in the following new features:

A framework to help students take charge of their own writing. An expanded introduction, called "Taking a Writing Inventory," offers a systematic way for students to identify the strengths and weaknesses in their own writing and set out concrete plans for individual improvement. By showing them how to analyze their use of the elements our research has demonstrated to be most important—broad content issues (or those of *invention*); organization and presentation (those of *arrangement*); the twenty most common surface errors (those of *style*)—this chapter will, we hope, challenge and guide students to take charge of their own development as writers. This system for "taking charge" continues throughout the book, as each chapter ends with an exercise inviting students to take inventory of some particular aspect of their writing. The introduction serves, in addition, as an index, with cross-references to all the places in the book where students can find more help on each topic. Especially helpful, we hope, will be the step-by-step guidelines in almost every chapter that show students how to check—and revise—their own drafts for common problems.

A new diction chapter on building common ground.   Chapter 28 rests on two major assumptions: that writers will wish to address readers whose backgrounds, values, and perspectives not only will be different from their own but also will vary widely from reader to reader; and that language offers a primary means of acknowledging and respecting such differences and of bridging them by establishing common ground among readers and writers. Based on Kenneth Burke's theories of identification and division in language use, this chapter asks students to take a close look at how the words they use can work to include—or exclude—their readers. Special guidelines help students think carefully and concretely about the language they choose to refer to others and to recognize that these choices have very real consequences. Emphasis throughout the chapter is on how such language choices can make connections with others.

A new design highlighting materials for quick reference.   As we worked on this book, we spoke with hundreds of colleagues about handbooks. Among the many concerns we found was one very common one—that a handbook must be accessible, that it has to be easy to get in and out of quickly. To this end, we have put many of the most useful guidelines in charts and lists, and we've placed them in light blue boxes for easy reference. A new three-color design uses blue to mark materials for quick reference and reddish brown for the major divisions of the book. Our goal here is for users of this book to be able to use it easily and quickly. Our greatest hope is that our readers will spend less time with our text and, as a result, have more time to contemplate their own.

A special chapter on audience and purpose.   A concern for audience runs throughout this book, and Chapter 2 asks students to consider what they know—and need to know—about their readers and about their own purposes and rhetorical stances. In short, the chapter asks students to gather available information about "real-life" audiences—where they come from, how old they are, and so on—*and* to examine their own assumptions about an audience as they *imagine* them to be—that they are all middle class, say, or all of one race. Such assumptions are often revealed in language. For example, use of the pronoun *we* assumes that an imagined audience will identify with this "we." If they do not, however, the writer is likely to exclude—in other words, lose—them as readers. Thinking about audience in this dual way helps students determine whether their writing is likely to achieve its purposes and reach its intended readers.

A look at language in everyday use. Our experience as teachers tells us that students use most of the patterns and structures discussed in this text intuitively in their everyday discourse. To help students see language in this way, each chapter includes a brief boxed vignette on the everyday use of that chapter's subject—agreement, say, or adjectives—and asks them to look for additional examples, providing, we hope, another opportunity for them to become keen observers of language. Used systematically, these brief studies of everyday language use offer students and teachers a way to build a bridge between the conventions of college writing and the broader communities in which we all live.

Six chapters on research writing. Nowhere do students need more thorough instruction in how to move back and forth between reading and writing than in the writing they do based on sources. For this reason, *The St. Martin's Handbook* concentrates not simply on helping students produce a "research paper," but on how they might use research for many writing purposes, showing students how to approach all sources with a questioning eye and how to assess source materials critically, not just to find them and use them. Step-by-step guidelines on synthesizing data and drawing inferences are designed to help students use their research in support of their own written arguments. New to this edition are more extensive guidelines on using quotations, summaries, and paraphrases; many more documentation models (now in two separate chapters—43 on MLA style, 44 on APA and other styles); and special tips throughout the book on using sources.

Expanded instruction on writing about literature. We now present three critical stances a writer might adopt in interpreting literature: a *text-based stance,* focusing mainly on textual features; a *context-based stance,* focusing on historical materials or conditions to illuminate the text; and a *reader-based stance,* bringing in personal experience and reflection to interpret the text. These approaches are illustrated by three examples of student work—a full-length paper on a novel, an excerpt from an essay on a drama, and a lengthy journal entry on a poem.

A special look at three writers. Woven through the book are examples from the work of three highly respected and often anthologized writers: Maya Angelou, Lewis Thomas, and Eudora Welty. For instructors who wish to highlight one or more of these authors or to use this handbook in conjunction with one of their works, we include a brief appendix with brief introductions and a list of their major works.

Attention to the needs of basic writers. Several features of this edition are especially appropriate for basic writers. The focus on reading not only provides instruction and practice in critical reading but also offers practice drawing conclusions or inferences from their reading— practice that is particularly valuable for basic writers. In addition, the focus on their own writing and on making plans for their own writing development helps basic writers to make a crucial link between their first-year writing course and the academic writing they must master for all their college work. Finally, the use of actual student sentences and essays throughout the book and the emphasis on everyday uses of language in every chapter invite students— and particularly basic writing students—to link the language of this handbook and the classrooms it is used in with their experiences outside of school.

An expanded ancillary program. Several useful resources accompany *The St. Martin's Handbook.* All have been revised for this second edition and are available free of charge to instructors. The workbook is available for students to purchase. Instructors are authorized to make copies of the software for their students and may order, free of charge, the CLAST and TASP guides and the *Pocket Guide to Library Research.*

CLASSROOM RESOURCES

Annotated Instructor's Edition, with background information, teaching suggestions, and additional classroom activities.

The St. Martin's Guide to Teaching Writing, by Robert Connors and Cheryl Glenn, with advice about day-to-day issues in teaching writing, a detailed survey of current rhetorical and pedagogical theories and practices, and an anthology of journal articles.

Assigning, Responding, Evaluating: A Writing Teacher's Guide, by Edward M. White.

STUDENT RESOURCES

The St. Martin's Workbook, Second Edition, by Lex Runciman
The St. Martin's Pocket Guide to Library Research and Documentation
Preparing for the CLAST with The St. Martin's Handbook
Preparing for the TASP with The St. Martin's Handbook

SOFTWARE

The St. Martin's Invention and Revision Software
The St. Martin's Hotline, a pop-up reference system.
The St. Martin's Documentation Hotline, a pop-up reference to the four major documentation styles.
The Exercise Tutor, including Authorkit, which allows instructors to create their own exercises on disk.

Acknowledgments

The St. Martin's Handbook remains a collaborative effort in the best and richest sense of the word. We are particularly indebted to Marilyn Moller of St. Martin's Press, whose efforts as editor on this project have been above and beyond the call of any duty we have ever known; for her friendship, guidance, and sheer intellectual verve, we are deeply grateful. Jean Smith continues to support our work and to make the efforts made by St. Martin's on our behalf possible. Throughout preparations for this new edition, we have relied on the extraordinarily valuable contributions of Denise Quirk, who has worked so hard and on so many aspects of this project that we simply could not get along without her. In particular, we are indebted to her expertise in all matters of research and documentation. In addition, John Elliott has provided extensive editorial help, which has guided and instructed us at every turn, while Amy Horowitz and Kristin Bowen offered thoughtful assistance in many matters, large and small. For the elegant and accessible design of this edition, we are indebted to Anna George. And for providing us with careful response to the text and astute analyses of its usefulness to teachers, we are grateful to the St. Martin's sales representatives; they are, in our experience, simply the best.

The St. Martin's Handbook is accompanied by an imaginative and highly practical set of ancillary materials. For their assistance in editing these materials, we are most grateful to Mark Gallaher, who orchestrated the entire endeavor, as well as to Elayna Browne, Edward Mitchell-Hutchinson, Kim Richardson, Susanne Rosenberg, and Sam Sebren.

Special thanks for colleagues Lex Runciman, who wrote *The St. Martin's Workbook,* Edward M. White, who wrote the evaluation and diagnostic booklet, *Assigning, Responding, Evaluating,* and Cheryl Glenn, who made significant contributions to *The St. Martin's Guide to Teaching Writing.*

We are also more than grateful to the many instructors and students on whose work we continue to depend. Among our own students, Laura Brannon, Leah Clendening, Tisha Clevinger, Amy Dierst, Sean Finnerty, Jennifer Gerkin, Amy Lewis, Faye Purol, Chris Reeves, Julie Slater, Daniel Taffe, and Tracy Vezdos all provided essays and other writing samples. For this edition, we wish especially to thank those teachers and students whose campuses we have visited for their generous criticism of our work; this text owes a great deal to their wise advice and counsel. In addition, we are most appreciative of the colleagues—both instructors and students—who have painstakingly reviewed our manuscript and its several revisions and shared their thoughts on our efforts. Their incisive comments, queries, criticisms, and suggestions have improved this book immeasurably: Jean Aston, Community College of Allegheny; Rise Axelrod, California State University, San Bernardino; Valerie Balester, Texas A&M University; Robert Barrier, Kennesaw State College; Deborah Boyd, Winthrop College; Richard Bullock, Wright State University; Toni-Lee Caposella, Stonehill College; Karen Carney, University of Illinois, Urbana; Donna Cheney, Weber State College; Brenda Cox, University of Georgia; Christine Cozzens, Agnes Scott College; Jerry Craven, West Texas State University; Carol David, Iowa State University; Kitty Chen Dean, Nassau Community College; Ruth Fischer, George Mason University; Irene Gale, University of South Florida; Sherri Geller, Columbia University; Andrew Harnack, Eastern Kentucky University; Sue Ellen Holbrook, Southern Connecticut State University; Mary Huffer, Lake-Sumter Community College; Deepika Karle, Bowling Green State University; Judith Kohl, Dutchess Community College; Carolyn Kropp, Southern Illinois University, Edwardsville; Jo Ann Little, Pima County Community College, Downtown Campus, and University of Arizona; Patricia McAlexander, University of Georgia; Mary Sue MacNealy, Memphis State University; Michael Miller, Longview Community College; Mike Moran, University of Georgia; Pat Murray, California State University, Northridge; Robert Newman, SUNY Buffalo; Cheryl Piper, Lorain County Community College; Mary Ellen Pitts, Memphis State University; Kirk Rasmussen, Utah Valley Community College; Ken Risdon, University of Minnesota, Duluth; Mike Rose, University of California, Los Angeles; Jennifer Rosti, Roanoke College; Jacqueline Jones Royster, Spelman College; Cary Ser, Miami-Dade Community College, South Campus; John S. Shea, Loyola University, Lake Shore Campus; Paul Sladky, Augusta College; Janet Smart, Jacksonville State University; Carolyn Smith, University of Florida; Jane Stanhope, American University; Susan Swan, Lane Community College; Douglas Tedards, University of the Pacific; George Trail, University of Houston; Richard Tubbs, Community College of Aurora; Keith Walters, University of Texas, Austin; Angela Weisl, Columbia University; Deanna White, University of Texas, San Antonio; and Linda Woodson, University of Texas, San Antonio.

We'd like to give special thanks to the following students, all users of the first edition of *The St. Martin's Handbook,* who shared with us their thoughts and suggestions about what worked well and what didn't. Many of the improvements in the second edition come inspired—or suggested—by

John Howell, Ohio State University; Ruth Jenners, Southern Illinois University; Sanford Macmillan, Bowling Green State University; Julie Pardue, University of Georgia; and Judy Anne Peters, Bowling Green State University.

We also wish to acknowledge and express our gratitude to the many users of the first edition who took the time to respond to a detailed questionnaire and whose many comments and criticisms helped us see what to expand and what to trim, what to fix and what to leave alone as we revised this book. We thank Kathryn Murphy Anderson, Boston University; Norbert Artzt, Miami-Dade Community College; Patricia Truxter Atkins, Westminster College of Salt Lake City; Bobbye Au, Roanoke College; Charles Ballard, University of Nebraska, Lincoln; Martha Bartter, Ohio State University, Marion Campus; Beth Ann Bassein, University of South Colorado; Anna Battigelli, SUNY Plattsburgh; Arthur Bennett, Ferris State University; Nicholas Boden, San Bernardino Valley College; Reed Bonadonna, Boston University; Duane Bruce, University of Hartford; Catherine Chalmers, Western State College of Colorado; David Chapman, Samford University; Chris Coates, University of Florida; Frank Coffman, College of Du Page; Marilyn Cozad, Morningside College; Walter Creed, University of Hawaii; Teresa Daniel, USAF Academy; Robert Denham, Roanoke College; Bonnie Devet, College of Charleston; Ron Dooley, North Park College; Chris Ellery, Angelo State University; John F. Eveland, Iowa State University; Christopher Fahy, Boston University; Pat Fite, Incarnate Word College; Craig A. Gannon, Sterling College; Lynn Garland, Mira Costa College; Cheryl Glenn, Oregon State University; Priscilla Groseclose, Bowling Green State University; Elree Harris, Westminster College of Salt Lake City; Beth Harrison, Berea College; Susan Morrison Hebble, Loyola University, Lake Shore Campus; Robert Heron, Northeastern University; Kurt Hild, The Master's College; Margaret Hisrich, Kent State University, Tuscarawas Campus; David Hoehner, University of Utah; Victoria Holmsten, San Juan College; Marilyn Hurley-Valentine, Quinsigamond Community College; Carla Johnson, Saint Mary's College, Indiana; Norman Katz, Harvard University; Brent Keetch, California Polytechnic State University, San Luis Obispo; Edward Kline, University of Notre Dame; Robbie Knott, North Carolina State University; Cynthia Lanier, Memphis State University; Robert Loughridge, Genesee Community College; Thomas Mantey, Ohio University; Katherine Maynard, Rider College; William McCarron, East Texas State University; Patricia MacDonald, Palomar College; A. L. McCleod, Rider College; Judy Merrell, Community College of Allegheny County, Boyce Campus; Michael Miller, Longview Community College; William Mitchell, Oklahoma Baptist University; Margaret Nettles, Athens Area Vocational Technical School; Jane Parks, Dalton College; Marcia Peabody, Mira Costa College; Barbara Reese, Casper College; Kris Robinson, Westminster College of Salt Lake City; Rosalyn

Rosignol, Mira Costa College; Jennifer Rosti, Roanoke College; Zelda Rouillard, Western State College of Colorado; Anne Salvatore, Rider College; Brenda Serotte, CUNY, Herbert Lehman College; Thomas Sharpe, Washington State Community College; George Sibley, Western State College of Colorado; Caryl Sills, Monmouth College; Gary Simmers, Dalton College; Haskel Simonowitz, California State University, Los Angeles; Dennis Slattery, Incarnate Word College; Karl Smart, Michigan State University; Mark Smith, Northern Michigan University; Louis Suarez, Lorain County Community College; Suzanne Swiderski, Loyola University, Chicago; Cynthia Taylor, University of Southern Colorado; Lee Roger Taylor, Jr., Western Wyoming College; Kimberly Town, Ohio State University; Mary Truitt, College of William and Mary; Anita Turpin, Roanoke College; Carla Valley, University of Wisconsin, La Crosse; June Verbillion, Northeastern Illinois University; Loius Volpe, Rider College; Nancy Ward, University of Pittsburgh; Eileen Ward, College of Du Page; Edward White, California State University, San Bernardino; Harriett Williams, University of South Carolina, Columbia; and Amy Winokur, La Roche College.

Finally, we welcome a special new collaborator, Aillinn Maebh Connors, born August 19, 1991, and say thanks to some very special friends: Keith Walters, whose keen eye and brilliant teacherly insights continue to challenge and instruct us; Lorraine Carlat, whose organizational skill and infinite patience continue to amaze and gratify us; Suzanne Clark, whose theoretical and practical insights have helped us think more imaginatively about students writing about literature; Jamie Barlowe, Beverly Bruck, Suellynn Duffey, Cinthia Gannett, Cheryl Glenn, Mary Kuhner, Donna LeCourt, Beverly Moss, Kim Spinnazola, Jonathan Temez, Monica Trader, Eric Walborn, and, most especially, Carrie Leverenz, Heather Graves, and Patricia Kelvin, who have cheerfully provided more support than we have had any right to expect; the faculty and graduate students at Ohio State University who helped us to organize and analyze a second three-thousand-paper sample; David Frantz, Murray Beja, and Micheal Riley, administrators who have supported our research throughout; and—always—Lisa Ede, critical reader and friend extraordinaire.

We could go on and on and on and on, for we are fortunate (beyond our wildest dreams, as our mentor Ed Corbett would say) to be part of a unique scholarly and academic community, one characterized by compassion, by commitment to students, by a celebration of learning. We are grateful to be among you.

Andrea Lunsford
Robert Connors

A Note to Students

Our goal in writing *The St. Martin's Handbook* has been to produce a book that will guide you to becoming competent and compelling writers, a book that you can use easily and efficiently throughout—and beyond—your college years.

We first began work on this book by examining a scientifically selected sample of more than twenty thousand essays written by students from all areas of the country—students probably at least a little like you. We discovered the kinds of writing errors you are most likely to make and studied the twenty most common error patterns in detail. Throughout this book you will find guidance on those patterns. Then for the second edition of this text, we examined another carefully selected sample of the twenty thousand papers, this time looking at broad content issues and at issues of organization and presentation. By focusing in particular on teachers' comments about these larger writing issues, we hoped to gain some insight into which ones are especially important in helping readers grasp your meaning.

The introductory chapter of this book, "Taking a Writing Inventory," is our attempt to respond to our research findings, to provide you with a tool for analyzing your use of the writing patterns and strategies most college students need to practice. The introduction—and indeed, the entire book—offers a plan for building on strengths and eliminating weaknesses in your own writing.

Throughout this text, we thus ask that you become accustomed to carefully analyzing your own prose. In almost every chapter, we will not only provide explanations and opportunity for practice but also we will be asking you to apply the principles presented directly to your own writing. If you follow our directions, they will guide you in becoming a systematic self-critic—and a stronger writer. And since writing and reading in many ways go hand in hand, many chapters will also offer you a chance to read with an eye for various logical or stylistic or conventional aspects of writing, often in the work of some of the finest American and English writers. Sometimes you will be asked to try to imitate their sentences. As your writing improves, so will your reading.

Chapters 1–6 will guide you through the process of expository and argumentative essays—from your first choice of a topic to your final typed essay. Chapters 7–38 provide thorough discussion of writing conventions—grammar, punctuation, and mechanics. These chapters provide examples and practice to guide you in mastering such conventions and in learning to use them appropriately and effectively.

Next come chapters that will help you understand, carry out, and use research in your writing; examine the writing of your chosen discipline; practice taking essay examinations; and produce job application letters and résumés.

The book has been designed to make its information as easy as possible to find and use. You can find what you are looking for by consulting the table of contents, the subject index, or the index of authors and titles. Once you find the correct chapter, you can skim the many headings. If your instructor uses our codes in marking your essays, you can find the code symbols at the top of each page. Even the exercises can be "used" easily, for we include at the end of the book answers to many of them, to allow you to check your understanding as you work.

Because we assume you will be consulting this book regularly when you are revising your drafts, we wish to call to your attention the many sections designed to help you *check* various elements and structures. Especially notable are guidelines to assist you to check—and revise—your own drafts; to make these easy to find, these are in light blue boxes marked with a blue arrow.

For those who compose on a computer, we offer a complimentary pop-up reference system, invention and revisions software, and a pop-up documentation reference, all available for IBM-compatible and Macintosh systems. These are available to instructors, who are authorized to make copies for students.

Finally, we'd like to call your attention to a feature you might use in taking inventory of your writing: a writing log. We urge you to keep a log as a repository of materials from and for your writing—notable anecdotes, exemplary phrases, memorable images, troublesome words or structures. Procedures for keeping a log are described on p. 7, and exercises at the end of every chapter suggest materials to add to it. Keeping a log can help you to examine and contemplate—and thus improve—your own writing.

We hope that this book will prove to be a useful reference. But in the long run, a book can be only a guide. You are the one who will put such guidance into practice, as you work to become a precise, a powerful, and a persuasive writer. Why not get started on achieving that goal right now?

Andrea Lunsford
Robert Connors

Contents

*The > symbol marks quick-reference guidelines.

Taking a Writing Inventory

What do we mean by a "writing inventory"? And why do we begin this book by suggesting that you take one? The word *inventory* comes from a Latin word meaning "find," and in reference to writing, taking inventory carries the familiar meaning of taking stock—finding and looking closely at items in your stock of writing, cataloging and describing those items—much as you might take inventory of the records in your old LP collection or as a store manager might take inventory of items on hand. But taking inventory also carries another sense of "find," one we more often associate with the words *invent* and *invention*. In this sense, taking inventory means to discover new things about your writing and thus to produce improvements in it that will, in turn, become part of the stock of your inventory.

This dual sense of what it means to take inventory runs throughout *The St. Martin's Handbook,* asking you to look closely and analytically at your own writing—and helping you to produce stronger and stronger pieces of new writing, which can then serve as material for further analysis. This chapter aims to get you started on a full inventory of your writing by asking you to identify a representative sample of your written work and then to analyze its features. Then, throughout this book, you will find that the last exercise in each chapter provides an opportunity for you to add to your inventory.

How might you identify those features of your writing most important for an inventory? That question has been one of many questions guiding research conducted for this book. In an analysis of a representative sample taken from twenty thousand freshman and sophomore essays from colleges and universities across the United States, we found that the features that readers most often comment on fall into three categories:

1. Broad content issues
2. Organization and presentation
3. Surface errors

BACKGROUND

Surprisingly few studies have been done on the nature of teachers' written comments on student writing, and no studies have looked at large numbers of essays commented on by large numbers of teachers. For this edition of *The St. Martin's Handbook,* Lunsford and Connors analyzed teachers' global comments on three thousand student essays, a stratified sample of twenty-one thousand marked student essays gathered from teachers throughout the United States. Of the three thousand essays, 77 percent carried global comments—those that address issues of rhetoric, organizational structure, longitudinal writing development, mastery of content, and so on. This finding suggests that teachers care a great deal about such matters and that, contrary to popular opinion, they comment on them rather than only pouncing on every surface error. The most commonly used form of global comment is one that begins positively, with praise for some element in the essay, and then details the negative points.

USEFUL READING

Anson, Chris M., ed. *Writing and Response: Theory, Practice, and Research.* Urbana, IL: NCTE, 1989.

Lindemann, Erika. *A Rhetoric for Writing Teachers.* 2nd ed. New York: Oxford UP, 1987. Lindemann provides background material for the teaching of writing, including a history of rhetoric, a survey of linguistics, and a useful bibliography.

Shaughnessy, Mina. *Errors & Expectations: A Guide for the Teacher of Basic Writing.* New York: Oxford UP, 1977. Since the publication of this book, every scholarly work on error has referred to it.

Sommers, Nancy. "Responding to Student Writing," *CCC* 33 (1982), 148–56.

BACKGROUND

The overlapping terms *journal, log, diary,* and *daybook* refer to a wide range of writing practices whose origins may be as old as writing itself. Until the Renaissance, most journals were essentially public or semipublic documents, such as daily accounting or business records, chronicles of public bodies or historical events, and travel journals. With the intellectual and social changes of the Renaissance and Reformation, however, we see the beginnings of what we now think of as the journal, or "the book of the self." Thus, while we may think of the journal as a relatively new pedagogical instrument, introduced in the 1960s as an aid to prewriting, it actually has a much longer affiliation with education. Schoolchildren from the Tudor Era right up through the early twentieth century have kept commonplace books filled with observations, facts, and quotations from their reading as a source of ideas. Journals or logs have also been kept to monitor or track the development of a specific skill or the whole intellect, as the locus of prewriting or drafting, as a place to develop fluency and to experiment with language, and as a place to connect and explore the public and private selves.

These research findings suggest that readers evaluate the effectiveness of your writing by how well you use and control these features of it and that you can benefit from organizing an inventory of your own writing according to these three major categories. Following are some guidelines for doing so.

≫ Taking a writing inventory

1. If you are using this chapter in a writing course, assemble copies of the first two or three pieces of writing you do, making sure to select pieces to which either your instructor or other students have responded.
2. Read through this writing, adding your own comments about its strengths and weaknesses.
3. Examine the instructor and peer comments very carefully, and compare them with your own comments.
4. Group all the comments into the categories discussed in this chapter—broad content issues, organization and presentation, and surface errors.
5. Make an inventory of your own strengths and weaknesses in each category.
6. Identify the appropriate sections of this book for more detailed help in areas where you need it.
7. Make up a priority list of three or four particular problems you have identified, and write out a plan for eliminating them.
8. Note at least two strengths you want to build on in your writing.

Keeping a writing log

One very good way to keep track of your writing strengths and weaknesses is by establishing a **writing log**, a notebook or folder in which you can record observations and comments about your writing—from instructors, other students, or yourself. This book will offer you frequent opportunities to make entries in a writing log, beginning with this chapter. As you take inventory of some of your writing, you will be gathering information about how readers respond to various features of it—broad content issues, organization and presentation, and surface errors. This information can serve as the data for an opening entry in your writing log. Here is an example of one such entry, made by Tamara Washington, an undergraduate at Ohio State University.

ENTRY 1 WRITING INVENTORY

I've taken a first look at the essay I wrote on the second day of class, one my response group and the teacher read. Here's what I've found so far:

	Strengths	Weaknesses
Broad content issues	lots of good examples	ideas not in logical order
Organization, presentation	great title! (Everyone loved it.)	paragraphs too short to make my points (Two are only one sentence long.)
Surface errors	semicolons used correctly—I was worried about this!	one unintentional sentence fragment *Its/it's* mistake(!) (See p. 471, and *never* make this mistake again!!)

ASSESSING BROAD CONTENT ISSUES

As a writer, you are in some ways like the supervisor of a large construction job or the conductor of an orchestra: you must orchestrate all the elements of your writing into a persuasive performance, assemble all the ideas, words, evidence, and so on into one coherent structure. Doing so calls on you to attend carefully to several big questions: what is the purpose of your writing? what points does it make? does it fully develop, support, or prove those points? to whom is it addressed? does this writing reflect your full powers as a writer? Answering such questions as part of your writing inventory is important, for readers expect your purpose to be clear, your points to be fully established, and so on. They expect, in short, that you are a good writer, and they look to you to guide them skillfully to an understanding of your meaning.

Our research indicates that readers comment most often on the following broad content issues in student writing:

1. Use of supporting evidence
2. Use of sources
3. Achievement of purpose
4. Attention to audience
5. Overall impression

Use of supporting evidence

According to Aristotle, an effective speaker needs to do two basic things: make a claim and prove it. Readers, too, expect that a piece of writing

TEACHING PRACTICE

If you want students to take a full inventory of their writing, you might consider working through the beginning of a hypothetical inventory with them. To do so, distribute copies of a student essay (from your files or from another class) and ask the students to work with you to identify the three categories of features dealt with in this section: broad content issues, organization and presentation, and surface errors. Practicing such categorization in class should help students carry out an analysis of their own writing.

TEACHING PRACTICE

If you want to give students practice in taking writing inventory on a more detailed level, ask them to examine a piece of writing for some specific feature—looking for every organizational "clue," for instance, or every transitional word or phrase. They can do this part of the assignment particularly well in groups. Then ask them to reflect on their findings and to draw one or more conclusions—about their use of organizational cues, transitions, or whatever feature they have looked for. Such an exercise asks students to move from observation to generalization, to "metadiscourse" about their own writing, or to what Shirley Brice Heath calls building theories about their own language use. The more students are able to make such mental moves, the better they will be at monitoring their own learning.

TEACHING PRACTICE

Ask students to look at essays or assignments written recently for instructors' comments on the logic or use of evidence and support. Ask them to bring examples of such comments to class for discussion.

USEFUL READING

Fulwiler, Toby, ed. and intro. *The Journal Book*. Portsmouth: Heineman, 1987. The most current anthology of theoretical and pedagogical articles on the uses of the academic journal. Includes "Guidelines for Using Journals in School Settings," Sharyn Lowenstein on the history of the journal, and Ann Berthoff on the double-entry journal, as well as many practical applications for the journal.

Gannett, Cinthia. *Gender and the Journal: Diaries and Academic Discourse*. Albany: SUNY P, 1992. History and development of journal and diary traditions both as literature and as literacy practices, the gendering of the diary as a feminized literacy practice, current issues and applications for education.

Price, Gayle. "A Case for a Modern Commonplace Book." *CCC* 31 (1980), 175–82. Connects earlier commonplace book traditions with newer ideas about academic journal keeping.

---

will make one or more points clearly and illustrate or support those points with ample evidence—good reasons, examples, or other details, Effective use of such evidence helps readers understand a point, makes abstract concepts concrete, and offers "proof" that what you are saying is sensible and worthy of attention and assent. In fact, this element is the one readers in our research commented on *most often,* accounting for 56 percent of all comments we analyzed. These readers tended to make statements like these:

> This point is underdeveloped.
> I like the way you back this claim up.
> The details here don't really help me see your point.
> Good use of proofs.
> I'm not convinced—what's your authority?
> The three reasons you offer are very persuasive.
> Good examples.

Any inventory of your writing should include a close look at how well you use supporting evidence.

 For more discussion of the use of good reasons, see 5c; of examples and details, see 5d–f. For more on providing such support in paragraphs, see 6d.

Use of sources

One special kind of supporting evidence for your points comes from source materials. Choosing possible sources, evaluating them, and using the results of your research effectively in your writing not only supports your claim but also builds your credibility as a writer, demonstrating that you understand what others have to say about a topic and that you are fully informed about varying perspectives on the topic. But finding enough sources, judging their usefulness, and deciding when to quote, when to summarize, and when to paraphrase—and then doing so accurately and working the results smoothly into your own writing—is a skill that takes considerable practice, one you should develop throughout your college writing career. You can begin sharpening that skill now by taking a close look at how well you use sources in your writing. The readers whose responses we studied commented regularly on such use of sources. Here are some of their remarks:

> Your list of sources is extraordinarily thorough—impressive reading!
> Only two sources? You need at least several more.
> Who said this?

Nice use of Sagan's main argument!

One of the clearest paraphrases I've seen of this crucial passage.

Your summary leaves out three of the writer's main points.

Your summary is just repetition—it doesn't add anything new.

This quotation beautifully sums up your argument.

Why do you quote at such length here? Why not paraphrase?

You cite only sources that support your claim—citing one or two with differing views would help show me you've considered other opinions.

 For more discussion of choosing, reading, and evaluating sources, see 41a–b; of quoting, paraphrasing, and summarizing, see 41c; and of incorporating source materials in your text, see 42d.

Achievement of purpose

Purposes for writing vary widely—from asking for an appointment or a job interview to sending greetings or condolences to summarizing information for a test to tracing the causes of the Second World War for an essay. In college writing, your primary purpose will often be directly related to the assignment you receive. As a result, you need to pay careful attention to what an assignment asks you to do, noting particularly any key terms in the assignment such as "analyze" or "argue" or "define" or "summarize." Such words are important in meeting the requirements of the assignment, staying on the subject, and thus achieving your purpose.

Readers' responses can often reveal how well you have achieved your primary purpose. Here are some comments responding to purpose:

Why are you telling us all this?

What is the issue here, and what is your stand on it?

Very efficient and thorough discussion! You explain the content very clearly and thus reveal your understanding of the article.

What is your purpose here? What do you want to happen as a result of your argument ?

You simply give a plot summary here, one that does little to analyze character development.

Your writing will profit from some time spent identifying the purposes of several pieces of writing you have done and thinking about how well you achieved those purposes.

 For guidelines on considering purposes, see 2c.

USEFUL READING

Bitzer, Lloyd F. "The Rhetorical Situation." *The Rhetoric of Western Thought.* 3rd ed. Ed. James Golden, Goodwin F. Berquist, and William E. Coleman. Dubuque, IA: Kendall, 1983. A brief and pointed analysis of the components of the rhetorical situation including the exigence, the audience, and the constraints.

Booth, Wayne C. "The Rhetorical Stance." *Now Don't Try to Reason with Me: Essays and Ironies for a Credulous Age.* Chicago: U of Chicago P, 1970. Booth posits a carefully balanced tripartite division of rhetorical appeals including "the available arguments about the subject itself, the interests and peculiarities of the audience, and the voice, the implied character, of the speaker" (27).

USEFUL READING

Lunsford, Andrea A., and Lisa S. Ede. "Audience Addressed/Audience Invoked: The Role of Audience in Composition Theory and Pedagogy." *The Writing Teacher's Sourcebook*. 2nd ed. Ed. Gary Tate and Edward P. J. Corbett. New York: Oxford UP, 1988. Ede and Lunsford point out the limitations of two prominent concepts of audience, that of "audience addressed," which emphasizes the concrete reality of the writer's audience, and that of "audience invoked," which focuses on the writer's construction of an audience. They argue that a writer's audience may be both addressed and invoked.

Kirsch, Gesa, and Duane H. Roen. *A Sense of Audience in Written Communication*. Newbury Park, CA: Sage, 1990. A collection of sixteen essays with a broad interdisciplinary focus on audience from historical to theoretical to empirical points of view.

TEACHING PRACTICE

Peter Elbow reminds us that it is characteristic of good teachers to *like* student writing, even though they see its weaknesses or failures. Elbow urges teachers to cultivate their enjoyment of student writing by: (1) looking for "strengths, both real and potential"; (2) practicing "conscious, disciplined, positive reinforcement"; and (3) getting to know students through conferences, journals, and free topic choices. Elbow concludes,

> It's not improving our writing that leads us to like it, but rather our liking it that leads us to improving it. Liking writing makes it easier to criticize it—and makes criticism easier to take and to learn from. (Lecture delivered at Bread Loaf School of English, July 17, 1991.)

Attention to audience

All writing is written to be read, if only by the writer. Most college writing is addressed to instructors and other students, though you may sometimes write to another audience—a political figure, a prospective employer, a campus administrator. The most effective writing is that which is sensitive to readers' backgrounds, values, and needs. Such writing, for example, takes time to define terms readers may not know, to provide necessary background information, to consider readers' perspectives on and feelings about a topic. Here are some reader comments on audience:

> This doesn't sound like something written for fourth-graders.
> Careful you don't talk down to your readers.
> You've left me behind here. I can't follow.
> Your level of diction is perfect for relating to the Board of Trustees.
> I'm really enjoying reading this!
> Don't assume everyone shares your opinion about this issue.

 For guidelines on considering your audience, see 2e.

Overall impression

When friends or instructors read your writing, they may often give you information about the overall impression it makes, perhaps noting the ways in which it seems to be improving or in which you may be lapsing back into bad habits. As a writer, you will do well to note such responses carefully. In particular, you need to make such comments as concrete as you can by trying to determine, for instance, exactly what has caused some improvement or weakness in your writing. Setting up a conference with the instructor is one way to explore these general responses. Before doing so, however, carry out your own analysis of what the comments mean, and then find out what your instructor thinks.

In the sample of twenty thousand essays we examined, readers tended to give their overall impression most often in a note at the very beginning or the very end of an essay, saying things like the following:

> I was looking for more critical analysis from you, and I've found it!
> Much improved over your last essay.
> Your grasp of the material here is truly impressive.
> What happened here? I can't understand your point in this essay.
> I know you can do a much better job of summarizing than this shows.
> You have the capacity to become a fine writer. I'm pleased with this!

For more specific ways of assessing the overall impression your writing creates, see the final exercise in every chapter of this book. These exercises are set up to help you take inventory of your use of the topics in each chapter.

EXERCISE I.1

Begin your writing inventory by recording the results of a careful look at broad content issues in at least one piece of your own writing. (1) First, list all comments your instructors and classmates have made about your use of supporting evidence, use of sources, achievement of purpose, attention to audience, and overall progress. If you find other large-scale issues referred to, include them in your list. (2) Then, look over your writing your own critical eye, using the guidelines in this introduction to evaluate your handling of broad content elements. (3) After examining the lists, summarize your major areas of strength and those areas in which you need to improve. (4) If you are keeping a writing log, enter this inventory there.

FOR COLLABORATIVE WORK

After students have begun their inventories, ask them to work in groups to compare their findings, and to respond to one another's "top priority" lists of ways to improve their writing.

ASSESSING ORGANIZATION AND PRESENTATION

The most important or brilliant points in the world will have little effect on readers if they are presented in a way that makes them hard to recognize, read, or follow. Indeed, research for this book confirms that readers depend on writers to organize and present their material—sections, paragraphs, sentences, arguments, details, source citations—in ways that provide aids to understanding. After use of supporting evidence, the features of student writing most often commented on had to do with organizational issues. In addition to clear and logical organization of information, readers appreciate careful formatting and documentation of sources. Although you can't always "tell a book by its cover," our research suggests that the "cover" of your writing—its physical format—can offer an important aid to readers and help to establish your credibility as a conscientious writer. Careful attention to the conventions of source documentation can produce the same result. Because organizational and presentational features of writing give important signals to your readers, they are well worth including in your writing inventory. Here are those features most often commented on in the student writing we examined:

1. Overall organization
2. Sentence structure and style
3. Paragraph structure
4. Format
5. Documentation

USEFUL READINGS

Lanham, Richard A. *Analyzing Prose.* New York: Scribner's, 1983. Lanham applies Aristotelian classifications of style (such as noun and verb styles, parataxis and hypotaxis, periodic and running styles) in order to provide both a descriptive and evaluative approach to analyzing modern prose style.

Williams, Joseph M. *Style: Ten Lessons in Clarity and Grace.* 3rd ed. Glenview, IL: Scott, 1989. Intended as a how-to manual for writers, this book outlines four principles of effective style: clarity, cohesion, emphasis, and concision. Williams also discusses punctuation and usage as matters of style.

Overall organization

Readers expect a writer to provide organizational patterns and signals that will help them follow the thread of what the writer is trying to say. Sometimes such organizational cues are simple. If you are giving directions, for example, you might give chronological cues (first you do A, then B, and so on), and if you are describing a place, you might give spatial cues (at the north end is A, in the center is B, and so on). But complex issues often call for complex organizational patterns, and you might find yourself needing to signal readers that you are moving from a problem to several possible solutions, for example, or that you are moving through a series of comparisons and contrasts. Because the organizational patterns you choose provide crucial signals for readers, you can profit by taking a close look at the organizational strengths and weaknesses of some of your writing. Readers responded in the following ways to organizational features:

> I'm confused here—what does this point have to do with the one before it?
>
> Your most important point is buried here in the middle. Why not move it up front?
>
> Organization here is chronological rather than topical; as a result, you write synopsis, not analysis.
>
> How did we get here? You need a transition.
>
> Very clear, logical essay. A joy to read.
>
> I'm lost: this sentence seems totally out of place.
>
> You need to reorganize the three details: son, friend, *then you.*

 For more discussion of overall organization, see 4e and 5g. For more on organizational methods of development, see 3d; on transitional signals that aid organization, see 6c; and on ways of linking paragraphs, see 6f.

Sentence structure and style

Effective sentences form the links in a chain of writing, guiding readers in ways that aid reading and understanding. If you have never taken a close look at how your sentences work (or don't work) to help organize your writing and guide readers, a little time and effort now will provide an overview. How long do your sentences tend to be? Do you use strings of short sentences that make the reader work to fill in the connections between them? Do any long sentences confuse the reader or wander off the topic? How do your sentences open? How do you link them logically? Answering these questions provides additional data for your writing inventory. Here are some comments the readers in our research made about sentences:

The pacing of your sentences here really keeps me reading—excellent variation of length and type.

Combine sentences to make the logical connection explicit here.

Your use of questions helps clarify this complex issue.

This is not effective word order for a closing sentence—I've forgotten your main point.

These sentences all begin with nouns—the result is a kind of dull clip-clop, clip-clop, clip-clop.

Too many short, simple sentences here. This reads like a grocery list rather than an explanation of a complex issue.

This sentence goes on forever—how about dividing it up?

 For guidelines on checking sentences, see p. 176. For detailed discussion of sentence types, see 7d; of sentence effectiveness, see Chapter 19; and of sentence variation, see Chapter 22.

Paragraph structure

Just as overall organization can help follow the thread of thought in a piece of writing, so too can paragraph structure. You may tend to paragraph by feel, so to speak, without spending much time thinking about structure. In fact, the time to examine your paragraphs should generally be *after* you have completed a draft. Since paragraphs play such a major role in making your writing coherent and clear, however, you can profit by examining them carefully now. Begin by studying any readers' comments that refer to your paragraphs. Here are some of the kinds of comments you might find:

The sentences in this paragraph don't follow in a logical order.

Why the one- and two-sentence paragraphs? Elaborate!

Your introductory paragraph immediately gets my attention and gives an overview of the essay—good!

I can't follow the information in this paragraph.

This paragraph is not unified around one main idea.

Very effective ordering of details in this paragraph.

This paragraph skips around two or three points. It has enough ideas for three paragraphs.

 For guidelines on checking paragraphs, see p. 135. For detailed information on paragraph development in general, see Chapter 6.

Format

Readers depend on the format of a piece of writing to make their job as pleasant and efficient as possible. Therefore, you need to pay very close attention to how your materials are physically presented and to the visual effect they create. Because format guidelines vary widely from discipline to discipline, even from assignment to assignment, part of your job as a writer is always to make certain you know what format is most appropriate for a particular course or assignment.

In the research conducted for this book, readers made the following kinds of comments about format:

> You need a title, one that really works to get across your meaning.
>
> This tiny single-spaced type is almost impossible to read.
>
> The table of contents here is very clear and helpful.
>
> Number pages—these were not in the right order!
>
> Your headings and subheadings helped me follow this report.
>
> Never turn in a computer-printed essay without separating the pages and tearing off the tractor holes.

 For more thorough discussion of format, see Chapter 49.

Documentation

Any writing that uses source materials requires careful documentation—parenthetical citations, endnotes, footnotes, lists of works cited, bibliographies—to guide readers to your sources and let them know you have carried out accurate research. A close look at your writing may reveal that you have internalized certain documentation rules—listing authors last name first, for instance—but that you don't understand others at all. While very few writers, even strong writers, carry all these documentation guidelines around in their heads, they do know where to look to find them. Here are some readers' comments that focus on documentation:

> I checked my copy of *Emma* and this quotation's not on the page you list.
>
> Footnote numbers should come at the *end* of quotations.
>
> What are you paraphrasing here? Your introduction merely drops readers into the middle of things. *Introduce the material paraphrased.*
>
> What are you summarizing here? Where do these ideas come from?
>
> I can't tell where this quotation ends.
>
> Keep your parenthetical citations as simple as possible—see 43a.

Why aren't works listed in alpha order?

This is *not correct* MLA citation style. Check your book!

What is the date of this publication?

 For more information on documenting sources, MLA style, see Chapter 43; APA and other styles, see Chapter 44.

EXERCISE I.2

Continue your writing inventory by analyzing the five features of organization and presentation described above in at least one piece of your writing. (1) Chart your instructor's comments, and consider asking a classmate whose opinions you value to comment on your use of these features. (2) Then, add your own observations about your use of these features. (3) On the basis of these analyses, summarize what you take to be your major areas of strength as well as those areas in which you need to improve. (4) If you are keeping a writing log (see I–2), enter the results of your analysis there.

LEARNING FROM YOUR SURFACE ERRORS

Whereas readers may notice your handling of broad content issues and your organization and presentation either because these provide stepping stones for following your meaning or because they create stumbling blocks to such understanding, your spelling, grammar, punctuation, word choice, and other small-scale matters will seldom draw attention or comment unless they look wrong. Because such surface errors disrupt communication between writers and readers, they are an important source of information about your writing.

What can we tell you about the kinds of surface errors you are likely to find in your writing and the response they elicit from readers? Our study of student writing reveals, first of all, that—even with word processors and spell checkers—spelling errors are *by far the most common,* by a factor of more than three to one. (A list of the words most often misspelled can be found in Chapter 24.) Second, readers are not disturbed by all surface errors, nor do instructors always mark all of them. In fact, whether your instructor comments on an error in any particular assignment will depend on his or her judgment about how serious and distracting it is and what you should be dealing with at the time. Finally, not all surface errors are even consistently viewed as errors. In fact, some of the patterns identified in our research are considered errors by some instructors but stylistic options by others.

FOR COLLABORATIVE WORK

After students have completed this part of their inventory, ask them to work in groups of three to compare findings and plans for improvements.

BACKGROUND

The greater the writer's fixation on error, the greater the difficulty that writer will have writing. The more the instructor focuses on error, the more the student will worry about error. In *The Concept of the Mind* (1949), British philosopher Gilbert Ryle wrote that "errors are exercises in competence." And this new concept of error as "portals to discovery" became the mainstay of Mina Shaughnessy's study of basic writing (1977). By 1981, Isabella Halsted was writing that errors are "*not* Sin, not Crime punishable by F." Errors are simply mistakes that we are all capable of, given the wrong circumstances: lack of sleep, deadline pressure, unfamiliarity with formal English. Halsted describes her own attitude toward error:

> Like soot on the pane, Error is something that gets in the way of the clear vision. . . . Error on all levels is distracting, annoying, obstructive. Error is inexcusable ultimately, yes, [but] not because it is Wrong *per se.* . . . In plain pragmatic terms, the absence of Error is useful; but when our students take pains to avoid it—by writing short sentences, by sticking to one tense, by writing as little as possible—I doubt very much that they do so in order to better communicate with a reader, but rather to play safe, to avoid the red marks.

*Give me a fruitful error any time, full of seeds,
bursting with its own corrections.*

—VILFREDO PARETO

USEFUL READING

Epes, Mary. "Tracing Errors to their Sources: A Study of the Encoding Processes of Adult Basic Writers." *Journal of Basic Writing* 4 (Spring 1985): 4–33. Epes makes a cogent argument for grammatical instruction that reflects Edited American English.

Finegan, Edward. *Attitudes Toward English Usage.* New York: Teachers College P, 1980. Charts the war between prescriptivists and descriptivists.

Halsted, Isabella. "Putting Error in Its Place." *Journal of Basic Writing* 1 (Spring 1975): 72–86. Rpt. in *The Writing Teacher's Sourcebook.* Ed. Gary Tate and Edward P. J. Corbett. New York: Oxford, 1981. 244–56.

Hartwell, Patrick. "Grammar, Grammars, and the Teaching of Grammar." *CE* 47 (1985): 105–27. Definitions and purposes of the various grammars.

Kolln, Martha. "Closing the Books on Alchemy." *CCC* 32 (1981): 139–51. While no direct relation exists between grammar instruction and *writing* improvement, there are other important reasons for studying grammar—to analyze, to build shared vocabulary and conceptual frameworks.

While many people may tend to think of "correctness" as absolute, based on hard and fast, unchanging "rules," instructors and students know better. We know that there are "rules," all right, but that the rules change all the time. "Is it okay to use *I* in essays for this class?" asks one student. "My high school teacher wouldn't let us." "Will more than one comma error flunk an essay?" asks another. These questions show that rules clearly exist, but they also suggest that these rules are always shifting and thus constantly need to be explored.

Our research shows some of the shifts that have occurred in the last century alone. Mechanical and grammatical questions that no longer concern most people used to be perceived as extremely important. In the late nineteenth century, for instance, instructors at Harvard said that the most serious writing problem their student had was an inability to distinguish between the proper uses of *shall* and *will*. Similarly, split infinitives seemed to many instructors of the 1950s a very serious problem, but at least since the starship *Enterprise* set out "to boldly go" where no one has gone before, split infinitives have wrinkled fewer brows.

These examples of shifting standards do not mean that there is no such thing as "correctness" in writing—only that *correctness always depends on some context*. Correctness is not so much a question of absolute right or wrong as it is a question of the way the choices a writer makes are perceived by readers. As writers, we are all judged by the words we put on the page. We all want to be regarded as competent and careful, and errors in the writing we produce work against that impression. The world judges us by our control of the conventions we have agreed to use, and we all know it. As Robert Frost once said of poetry, trying to write without honoring the conventions and agreed-upon rules is like playing tennis without a net.

A major assumption this book makes is that you want to understand and control not only the broad content issues and organizational features of writing but the surface conventions of academic writing as well. Since you already know the vast majority of these conventions, the most efficient way to proceed is to focus on those that are still unfamiliar or puzzling. Achieving this practical focus means identifying, analyzing, and overcoming patterns of surface error in your writing.

Why not decide right now to take charge of your own writing by charting and learning from your errors? This effort need not mean becoming obsessed with errors to the exclusion of everything else in your writing. Perfectly correct writing is, after all, a limited and limiting goal. You want to aim for a perfectly persuasive and enlightening piece of writing—that also happens to be correct.

To aid you in producing writing that is conventionally correct, we have identified the twenty most common error patterns (other than misspelling) among United States college students in the late 1980s. Here they are, listed in the order of occurrence.

 The twenty most common errors

1. Missing comma after an introductory element
2. Vague pronoun reference
3. Missing comma in a compound sentence
4. Wrong word
5. Missing comma(s) with a nonrestrictive element
6. Wrong or missing verb ending
7. Wrong or missing preposition
8. Comma splice
9. Missing or misplaced possessive apostrophe
10. Unnecessary shift in tense
11. Unnecessary shift in pronoun
12. Sentence fragment
13. Wrong tense or verb form
14. Lack of agreement between subject and verb
15. Missing comma in a series
16. Lack of agreement between pronoun and antecedent
17. Unnecessary comma(s) with a restrictive element
18. Fused sentence
19. Dangling or misplaced modifier
20. *Its / it's* confusion

Statistically, these twenty are the errors most likely to cause you trouble. A brief explanation and examples of each one are given in this chapter, and each error pattern is cross-referenced to at least one place elsewhere in this book where you can find more detail or additional examples.

Missing comma after an introductory element

When a sentence opens with an introductory word, phrase, or clause, readers usually need a small pause between the introductory element and the main part of the sentence. Such a pause is most often signaled by a comma.

BACKGROUND

Perhaps an outgrowth of Renaissance attitudes toward the use of "correct" or Ciceronian Latin, prescriptive attitudes toward English grammar developed in the eighteenth century and have dominated language study ever since. Prescriptive grammar holds that there are inherently correct and incorrect grammatical forms, while descriptive grammar holds that no language or variety of language (dialect) is superior to any other in a *linguistic* sense. For the descriptivist, no grammar is to be preferred except for *nonlinguistic* reasons.

In *Grammar and Good Taste: Reforming the American Language* (New Haven: Yale UP, 1982), Dennis E. Baron posits that the association of grammatical correctness with moral virtue and social prestige in the United States grew out of patriotic attempts during the post-Revolutionary period to distinguish American English from British English. He goes on to note that this association of grammar and morality fostered the anxiety over grammatical correctness that the public feels even today.

OPTIONAL EXERCISE

Here are twenty passages taken from the group of student essays on which Lunsford and Connors's research was based. Each passage contains one of the twenty most common student writing errors, and they are numbered to correspond with the "top twenty" list as presented here. These may be used in at least three different ways: (1) You might reproduce this list and use it as a diagnostic test early in the semester to see how practiced your students are at recognizing these errors; (2) You might use them as a review test at the end of the semester or after concluding your class's study of this introduction; (3) You may simply want to use them as examples of the top twenty errors, supplementing those given in the text.

1. The Beast, which is one of the biggest roller coasters, has a thunderous ride of steep hills and turns. As you race down the first and biggest hill your coaster is engulfed by a tunnel at the end of the hill.

2. Once you find where other surfers are, you can set up your camp. This entails claiming your own territory. You do this by laying out your oversized beach towel and by turning your radio on loud enough to mark your domain without disturbing anyone else. This should help you blend in with the locals.

3. I was gaining speed and feeling really good but when I looked back he wasn't there. I panicked. I saw him and my parents down at the other end of the street and forgot to look forward. When I finally did turn forward I saw that I was rapidly closing in on my neighbor's car. How ironic, I was about to hit the car of the man who was trying to teach me how to ride a bike.

4. Assateague is perfect for those who want to simply lay out in the sun, go swimming, and walk along the coast. But for those who crave a little more excitement, Ocean City is just a few minutes away by car. Ocean City hosts all the hotels, restaurants, and gift shops one could desire.

5. The knights with armor and horses beautifully decorated participate in battles of jousting, target shooting with spears, archery, and duals of strategy and strength using swords and shields. During the evening, there is a break from the fighting and a beautiful ceremony of marriage is acted out.

6. I decided to begin searching for an outfit while the rollers in my hair cooled. I began throwing everything out of my closet. Nothing seemed to fitting my mood and not one thing caught my eyes as it fell on the bed. I had no idea what I was even looking for since I didn't know where I was going.

INTRODUCTORY WORD

Frankly‸ we were baffled by the committee's decision.

INTRODUCTORY PHRASE

In fact‸ the Philippines consist of more then eight thousand islands.

To tell the truth‸ I never have liked the Mets.

Because of its isolation in a rural area surrounded by mountains‸ Crawford Notch doesn't get many visitors.

INTRODUCTORY CLAUSE

Though I gave detailed advice for revising‸ his draft became only worse.

Short introductory elements do not always need a comma. The test is whether the element seems to need a pause after it. The following sentence, for example, would at first be misunderstood if it did not have a comma—readers would think the introductory phrase was *In German nouns,* rather than *In German*. The best advice is that you will rarely be wrong to add a comma after an introductory element.

In German‸ nouns are always capitalized.

 For guidelines on checking commas after introductory elements, see page 451. For more on commas and introductory elements in general, see 7c, 22b, and 29a.

2

Vague pronoun reference

A pronoun like *he, she, it, they, this, that,* or *which* should refer clearly to a specific word (or words) elsewhere in the sentence or in a previous sentence. When readers cannot tell for sure whom or what the pronoun refers to, the reference is said to be vague. There are two common kinds of vague pronoun reference. The first occurs when there is more than one word that the pronoun might refer to; the second, when the reference is to a word that is implied but not explicitly stated.

POSSIBLE REFERENCE TO MORE THAN ONE WORD

Before Mary Grace physically and verbally assaulted Mrs. Turpin, ~~she~~ was
the latter
a judgmental woman who created her own ranking system of people and

used it to justify her self-proclaimed superiority.

Transmitting radio signals by satellite is a way of overcoming the problem
the airways
of scarce airwaves and limiting how ~~they~~ are used.

REFERENCE IMPLIED BUT NOT STATED

The troopers burned an Indian camp as a result of the earlier attack. This
destruction of the camp
was the cause of the war.

They believe that a zygote, an egg at the moment of fertilization, is as
such an assertion
deserving of protection as the born human being, but ~~it~~ cannot be proven

scientifically.

 For guidelines on checking for vague pronoun reference, see 13c. For
more on pronoun reference, see Chapter 13.

3

Missing comma in a compound sentence

A compound sentence is made up of two (or more) parts that could
each function as an independent sentence. If there are only two parts, they
may be linked by either a semicolon or a coordinating conjunction (*and, but,
so, yet, nor, or, for*). When a conjunction is used, a comma should usually be
placed before it to indicate a pause between the two thoughts.

The words "I do" may sound simple, but they mean a complex

commitment for life.

We wish dreamily upon a star, and then we look down to see that we have

stepped in the mud.

7. You should also think about how far you
want to walk to class from your apartment.
You may want to live in an apartment that
is a shorter walking distance between
campus. Or you may not mind the longer
distance.

8. Chips and sauces are not the only thing
that you get free refills on, you also get free
refills on all non-alcoholic beverages, such
as soda and tea. The servers are very good
about getting you more of both things
when you need refills, usually you do not
even have to ask.

9. What I'm trying to get at is that because of
this persons immaturity, many people have
suffered. This persons lack of responsibility has turned peoples lives upside down.

10. The good thing about its location is that it
is right off the main highway, very easy to
spot. There are also plenty of road signs
pointing you in the direction of the park.
And if you got extremely lost, pulling off
and asking would be the easiest way to get
on track.

11. After deciding to begin your college career,
many students are then faced with the
predicament of where to live. This is not
such a problem for students from out of
town, but it is if you live in the same city or
area in which you chose a school.

12. When I got to half court, the guy that was
playing center on my team stood between
the defensive player and me. As I dribbled
around the center, he stopped the defensive player. Not by using his hands but by
his big body. This is a strategy used to get
a player open for a shot.

13. I thought about all of the work we had
done this quarter in English. I had not
done well on my spelling tests even when I
had cheated on them. I did my reading
assignments with other people so I never
answered the question by myself completely.

14. Their hands are folded and it seems as though they are mumbling to themselves. They try to get the person's attention but never does what they planned to do.

15. I was driving along behind an older Volkswagen Jetta, following closely, but not close enough that I couldn't see eveything that was going on around. My eyes were watching the break lights the curbs the side walks, and the path of the car in front of me.

16. On the other hand, what if you don't care for your partner—or even worse—they don't care for you? You know now that it is still okay to separate without the problem of obtaining a divorce. Many divorces that take place within the first years of marriage might have been avoided if the couple had lived together before marrying.

17. There is also a stand up roller coaster called, The King Kobra, which goes upside down in the first loop, with plenty of tossing and turning. Like I said previously, King's Island also keeps the people with weaker stomachs in mind; there are rides all throughout the park which are a little slower paced.

18. I felt someone's hand shaking my shoulder. I lifted my head up to see my best friend Stephanie looking down at me. "That must have been some dream. Come on the bell rang class is over."

19. Trying to keep parents happy is a constant effort made by kids to keep in good standing with mom and dad. After all, it is they who will support us until we are capable of living on our own with things like money, food, and clothes.

20. You can not just decide to have a party and have it the same day. You have to prepare for it. All the things that you do before, during, and after the party determines it's success. The better you prepare for it, the better time everyone will have.

In *very* short sentences, this use of the comma is optional if the sentence can be easily understood without it. The following sentence, for example, would be misunderstood if it did not have a comma—readers would think at first that Meredith was wearing her feet. The best advice is to use the comma before the coordinating conjunction because it will always be correct.

Meredith wore jeans‚and her feet were bare.

 For guidelines on checking for commas in compound sentences, see p. 451. For further discussion and examples, see 7dl and 29b.

4

Wrong word

"Wrong word" errors range from simple lack of proofreading, like using *should* for *would,* to mistakes in basic word meaning, like using *prevaricate* when you mean *procrastinate,* to mistakes in shades of meaning, like using *sedate* when you mean *sedentary.* Many errors marked "wrong word" are *homonyms,* words that are pronounced alike but spelled differently, like *their* and *there.*

A knowledge of computers is ~~inherent~~ assumed in his office.

Mark noticed the ~~stench~~ fragrance of roses as he entered the room.

Paradise Lost contains many ~~illusions~~ allusions to classical mythology.

 For guidelines on checking a draft for wrong words, see 27b. For additional, more detailed information about choosing the right word for your meaning, see 27a and c. For discussion of choosing respectful words see Chapter 28.

5

Missing comma(s) with a nonrestrictive element

A nonrestrictive element is a word, phrase, or clause that gives additional information about the preceding part of the sentence but does not restrict or limit the meaning of that part. A nonrestrictive element is not essential to the sentence; it can be deleted without changing the sentence's basic meaning. As an indication that it is not essential, it is always set off from the rest of the sentence with a comma before it and, if it is in the middle of the sentence, after it as well.

Marina‚who was the president of the club‚was first to speak.

Louis was forced to call a session of the Estates General‚which had not met for 175 years.

The bottom of the pond was covered with soft brown clay‚a natural base for a good swimming hole.

 For guidelines on checking for commas with nonrestrictive elements, see p. 451. For additional explanation, see 29c.

6

Wrong or missing verb ending

The verb endings -s or (-es) and -ed (or -d) are important markers in standard edited English. It is easy to forget these endings in writing because they are not always pronounced clearly when spoken. In addition, some dialects do not use these endings in the same way as standard edited English.

uses
Eliot ~~use~~ feline imagery throughout the poem.

I runs a mile every morning before breakfast.

dropped
The United States ~~drop~~ two atomic bombs on Japan in 1945.

imagined
Nobody ~~imagine~~ he would actually become president.

An -s (or -es) ending must be added to present-tense indicative verbs whose subjects are singular nouns; *he, she,* and *it;* and most indefinite pronouns (such as *anyone, each, everybody, nobody, nothing, someone*). The ending is not added to verbs whose subjects are plural nouns; *I, you, we,* and *they;* and indefinite pronouns that have a plural meaning (such as *both* and *few*). The past-tense and past-participle forms of most verbs must end in *-ed* (or *-d*).

 For guidelines on checking for verb endings, see p. 194 and 198. For more on verb endings, see pp. 192–95, 9b, 9c, and 10a.

Grammar is a piano I play by ear. All I know about grammar is its power. —JOAN DIDION

Any fool can make a rule and every fool will mind it. —HENRY DAVID THOREAU

You can be a little ungrammatical if you come from the right part of the country. —ROBERT FROST

But enough of these errors. The good writer masters grammar in order to control his words, and meaning is his target. —KEN MACRORIE

USEFUL READING

Williams, Joseph M. "The Phenomenology of Error." *CCC* 32 (1981): 152–68. Williams argues that we need to view errors as simply socially inappropriate, easily remedied behavior.

7

Wrong or missing preposition

Many words in English are regularly used with a particular preposition to express a particular meaning; for example, throwing a ball *to* someone is different from throwing a ball *at* someone. The first ball is thrown to be caught; the second, to hurt someone. Using the wrong preposition in such expressions is a common error. Because most prepositions are so short and are not stressed or pronounced clearly in speech, they are also often left out accidentally in writing.

The bus committee is trying to set a schedule that will meet the needs of most people who rely ~~in~~ on public transportation.

Nixon compared the United States ~~with~~ to a "pitiful, helpless giant."

Finally, she refused to comply ~~to~~ with army regulations.

In his moral blindness Gloucester is similar ~~with~~ to Lear.

Hilary is absolutely enamored ~~with~~ of Barbie.

 For guidelines on checking a draft for wrong or missing prepositions, see 27b. For additional information about choosing the correct preposition, see 7b6.

8

Comma splice

A comma splice occurs when two (or sometimes more) clauses that could each stand alone as a sentence are written with only a comma between them. Such clauses must be either clearly separated by a punctuation mark stronger than a comma—a period or semicolon—or clearly connected with a word like *and* or *although,* or else the ideas they state should be combined into one clause.

Westward migration had passed Wyoming by; even the discovery of gold in nearby Montana failed to attract settlers.

for

I was strongly attracted to her, she had special qualities.

Having

~~They always had~~ roast beef for Thanksgiving, ~~this~~ was a family tradition.

 For guidelines on checking for comma splices, see p. 265. For additional information about ways to avoid or revise comma splices, see Chapter 15.

9

Missing or misplaced possessive apostrophe

To show that one thing belongs to another, either an apostrophe and an *-s* or an apostrophe alone is added to the word representing the thing that possesses the other. An apostrophe and *-s* are used for singular nouns (words that refer to one thing, such as *leader* or *Chicago*); for indefinite pronouns (words like *anybody, everyone, nobody, somebody*); and for plural nouns (words referring to more than one thing) that do not end in *-s*, such as *men* and *women*. For plural nouns ending in *-s*, such as *creatures* or *fathers*, only the apostrophe is used.

                                         child's

Overambitious parents can be very harmful to a ~~childs~~ well-being.

                       Yankees'

Ron Guidry was once one of the ~~Yankee's~~ most electrifying pitchers.

 For discussion and guidelines on checking for possessive apostrophes, see 32a.

10

Unnecessary shift in tense

An unnecessary shift in tense occurs when the verbs in a sentence or passage shift for no reason from one time period to another, such as from past to present or from present to future. Such tense shifts confuse the reader, who must guess which tense is the right one.

                          cries

Joy always laughs until she ~~cried~~ at that episode of *Dynasty*.

                                        slipped   fell

Lucy was watching the great blue heron take off when she ~~slips~~ and ~~falls~~

into the swamp.

Each team of detectives is assigned to three or four cases at a time. They ~~will~~ investigate only those leads that seem most promising.

The senator had begun his speech when a young man in jeans ran up to the podium. He ~~shoves~~ a cream pie in the senator's face.

⫸ For guidelines on checking for unnecessary shifts in tense, see 14a. For more on using verb tenses in sequences, see 9g.

11

Unnecessary shift in pronoun

An unnecessary pronoun shift occurs when a writer who has been using one kind of pronoun to refer to someone or something shifts to another for no reason. The most common shift in pronoun is from *one* to *you* or *I*. This shift often results from an attempt at a more formal level of diction, which is hard to maintain when it is not completely natural.

When one first sees a painting by Georgia O'Keeffe, ~~you are~~ impressed by a sense of power and stillness.

If we had known about the ozone layer, ~~you~~ could have banned aerosol sprays years ago.

⫸ For guidelines on checking a draft for unnecessary pronoun shifts, see 14d.

12

Sentence fragment

A sentence fragment is a part of a sentence that is written as if it were a whole sentence, with a capital letter at the beginning and a period, question mark, or exclamation point at the end. A fragment lacks one or both of the two essential parts of a sentence, a subject and a complete verb; or else it begins with a subordinating word, which means that it depends for its meaning on another sentence.

LACKING SUBJECT

Marie Antoinette spent huge sums of money on herself and her favorites.
Her extravagance helped
~~Helped~~ bring on the French Revolution.
∧

LACKING COMPLETE VERB

was
The old aluminum boat sitting on its trailer.
∧

BEGINNING WITH SUBORDINATING WORD

, where
We returned to the drugstore, ~~Where~~ we waited for the rest of the gang.
∧

≫ For guidelines on checking for sentence fragments, see p. 274. For additional, more detailed information on sentence fragments, see Chapter 16.

13

Wrong tense or verb form

Errors that are marked as being the wrong tense or verb form include using a verb that does not indicate clearly that the action or condition it expresses is (or was or will be) completed—for example, using *walked* instead of *had walked* or *will go* instead of *will have gone*. In some dialects of English, the verbs *be* and *have* are used in ways that differ significantly from their use by most native speakers; these uses may also be labeled as the wrong verb form. Finally, many errors of this kind occur with verbs whose basic forms for showing past time or a completed action or condition do not follow the regular pattern, like *begin, began, begun* and *break, broke, broken*. Errors may occur when a writer confuses the second and third forms or treats these verbs as if they followed the regular pattern—for example, using *beginned* instead of *began* or *have broke* instead of *have broken*.

had
Ian was shocked to learn that Joe died only the day before.
∧

is   *has*
The poet ~~be~~ looking at a tree when she ~~have~~ a sudden inspiration.
∧   ∧

broken
Florence Griffith Joyner has ~~broke~~ many track records.
∧

built   *took*
The Greeks ~~builded~~ a wooden horse that the Trojans ~~taked~~ into the city.
∧   ∧

For guidelines on checking verb tenses, see p. 206. For additional, more detailed information about verb tenses and forms, see 7b1, Chapter 9, and Chapter 10.

14

Lack of agreement between subject and verb

A subject and verb must agree, or match. In many cases, the verb must take a different form depending on whether the subject is singular (one) or plural (more than one): *The old man is angry and stamps into the house* but *The old men are angry and stamp into the house.* Lack of agreement between the subject and verb is often just a matter of leaving the -s ending off the verb out of carelessness and failure to proofread, or of transcribing a dialect form that does not have this ending (see Errors 6 and 13). Sometimes, however, it results from particular kinds of subjects of sentence constructions.

When other words come between subject and verb, a writer may mistake a noun nearest to the verb for the verb's real subject. In the following sentence, for example, the subject is the singular *part,* not the plural *goals.*

A central part of my life goals ~~have~~ *has* been to go to law school.

Other problems can arise from subjects made up of two or more parts joined by *and* or *or;* subjects like *committee* or *jury,* which can take either singular or plural verb forms depending on whether they are treated as a unit or as a group of individuals; and subjects like *mathematics* and *measles,* which look plural but are singular in meaning.

My brother and his friend Larry commutes every day from Louisville.

The committee ~~was~~ *were* taking all the responsibility themselves.

Measles ~~have~~ *has* become much less common in the United States.

Pronoun subjects cause problems for many writers. Most indefinite pronouns, like *each, either, neither,* or *one* take singular verb forms. The relative pronouns, *who, which,* or *that* take verbs that agree with the word the pronoun refers to.

Each of the items in these designs ~~coordinate~~ *coordinates* with the others.

Johnson was one of the athletes who ~~was~~ *were* disqualified.

Finally, some problems occur when writers make the verb agree with a word that follows or precedes it rather than with the grammatical subject. In the following sentences, for example, the subjects are *source* and *man*.

His only source of income ~~were~~ *was* his parents.

Behind the curtains ~~stand~~ *stands* an elderly man producing the wizard's effects.

 For guidelines on checking for subject-verb agreement, see p. 226. For additional, more detailed information about subject-verb agreement, see Chapter 10.

15

Missing comma in a series

A series consists of three or more parallel words, phrases, or clauses that appear consecutively in a sentence. Traditionally, all the items in a series are separated by commas. Many newspapers and magazines do not use a comma before the *and* or *or* between the last two items, and some instructors do not require it. Check your instructor's preference, and be consistent in either using or omitting this comma.

Sharks eat mostly squid,shrimp,crabs,and other fish.

You must learn to talk to the earth,smell it,squeeze it in your hands.

 For guidelines on checking a draft for series commas, see p. 451. For more on parallel structures in a series, see 21a, or on using commas in a series, see 29d.

16

Lack of agreement between pronoun and antecedent

Most pronouns (words like *I, it, you, him, her, this, themselves, someone, who, which*) are used to replace another word (or words), so that it does not have to be repeated. The word that the pronoun replaces or stands for is called its antecedent. Pronouns must agree with, or match, their antecedents in gender—for example, using *he* and *him* to replace *Abraham Lincoln* and *she* and *her* to replace *Queen Elizabeth*. They must also agree with their antecedents in referring to either one person or thing (singular) or more than one (plural)—for example, using *it* to replace *a book* and *they* and *them* to replace *fifteen books*.

Most people have few problems with pronoun-antecedent agreement except with certain kinds of antecedents. These include words like *each, either, neither,* and *one,* which are singular and take singular pronouns; antecedents made up of two or more parts joined by *or* or *nor;* and antecedents like *audience* or *team,* which can be either singular or plural depending on whether they are considered a single unit or a group of individuals.

Every one of the puppies thrived in ~~their~~ _its_ new home.

Neither Jane nor Susan felt that ~~they~~ _she_ had been treated fairly.

The team frequently changed ~~its~~ _their_ positions to get varied experience.

The other main kind of antecedent that causes problems is a singular antecedent (such as *each* or *an employee*) that could be either male or female. Rather than use masculine pronouns (*he, him,* and so on) with such an antecedent, a traditional rule that excludes or ignores females, a writer should use *he or she, him or her,* and so on, or else rewrite the sentence to make the antecedent and pronoun plural or to eliminate the pronoun.

Every student must provide his _or her_ own uniform.

~~Every student~~ _All students_ must provide ~~his~~ _their_ own ~~uniform~~ _uniforms_.

Every student must provide ~~his own~~ _a_ uniform.

 For guidelines on checking for pronoun-antecedent agreement, see p. 233. For additional, more detailed information about pronoun-antecedent agreement, see Chapter 11.

17

Unnecessary comma(s) with a restrictive element

A restrictive element is a word, phrase, or clause that restricts or limits the meaning of the preceding part of the sentence; it is essential to the meaning of what precedes it and cannot be left out without changing the sentence's basic meaning. Because of this close relationship, it is *not* set off from the rest of the sentence with a comma or commas.

An arrangement, for orchestra, was made by Ravel.

Several groups, opposed to the use of animals for cosmetics testing, picketed the laboratory.

People, who wanted to preserve wilderness areas, opposed the plan to privatize national parks.

The vice president succeeds, if and when the president dies or becomes incapacitated.

Shakespeare's tragedy, *Othello*, deals with the dangers of jealousy.

In the last examples above, the appositive is essential to the meaning of the sentence because Shakespeare wrote more than one tragedy.

≫ For guidelines on checking for unnecessary commas with restrictive elements, see p. 452. For additional, more detailed information about restrictive phrases and clauses, see 29c and 29j1.

18

Fused sentence

Fused sentences (sometimes called run-on sentences) are created when two or more groups of words that could each be written as an independent sentence are written without any punctuation between them. Such groups of words must be either divided into separate sentences, by using periods and capital letters, or joined in a way that shows their relationship, by either adding words and punctuation or by rewriting completely.

The current was swift. He he could not swim to shore.

Klee's paintings seem simple, but they are very sophisticated.

She doubted the value of meditation; nevertheless she decided to try it once.

For guidelines on checking for fused sentences, see p. 265. For more detailed information about ways to revise fused sentences, see Chapter 15.

19

Misplaced or dangling modifier

A misplaced modifier is a word, phrase, or clause that is not placed close enough to the word if describes or is related to. As a result, it seems to modify some other word, phrase, or clause, and readers can be confused or puzzled.

They could see the eagles swooping and diving, with binoculars,

He had decided he wanted to be a doctor, when he was ten years old,

Slowly and precisely, I watched the teller count out the money,

The architect only wanted to use pine paneling for decoration.

Rising over the trees, the campers saw a bright red sun,

A dangling modifier is a word, phrase, or elliptical clause (a clause from which words have been left out) that is not clearly related to any other word in the sentence. The word that it modifies exists in the writer's mind, but not on paper in the sentence. Such a modifier is called "dangling" because it hangs precariously from the beginning or end of the sentence, attached to nothing very solid.

A doctor should check your eyes for glaucoma every year if *you are* over fifty.

Looking down the stretch of sandy beach, *one sees* people ~~are~~ lying face down trying to get a tan.

As a male college student, many people are surprised *that I,* at my support ~~for~~ the draft.

For guidelines on checking for misplaced and dangling modifiers, see p. 289. For additional, more detailed information on misplaced and dangling modifiers, see 17a and 17c.

20

Its / It's confusion

The word *its,* spelled without an apostrophe, is the possessive form of *it,* meaning "of it" or "belonging to it." The word *it's,* spelled with an apostrophe, is a shortened from of *it is* or *it has.* Even though with nouns an apostrophe often indicates a possessive form, the possessive form of a pronoun in this case is the one *without* the apostrophe.

The car is lying on it's side in the ditch.

Its a white 1986 Buick.

Its been lying there for two days.

 For guidelines on checking *its* and *it's,* see 32b. For more on *its* and *it's,* see 24b.

EXERCISE I.3

Take time now to continue your writing inventory by analyzing the surface errors as well as "surface strengths" in at least one piece of your writing. (1) Go through your writing, noting down every instance in which your instructor or classmates have marked an error or made a comment, either positive or critical, in such areas as spelling, grammar, punctuation, capitalization, and other issues like those discussed in the section above. (2) Then go through once more, using the guidelines on the twenty most common errors in this introduction, to add your own observations about strengths and areas that need improvement. (3) Finally, compile a list of both strengths and weaknesses, and decide which areas you plan to work on first. (4) If you are keeping a writing log, enter the results of your writing inventory there.

FOR COLLABORATIVE WORK

Ask students to work in groups of three to compare findings and plans for improvement.

Part One

The Writing Process

———————— ⟨⟩ ————————

1

Writing, Reading, and Research

TEACHING PRACTICE

The job of teaching writing is a complex blending of two purposes: first, to help students see that they have a voice and to help them become comfortable with developing a writing process that can express it; second, to introduce them to the conventions of academic discourse, with its genres, levels of expertise, different tones, and sense of audience.

In your class are many students who know exactly what you expect of them: flawlessly executed, fully developed essays. They are sure that you write without anxiety, false starts, or dictionaries, for you are an English instructor. Therefore, you might start by asking students how they think experienced writers work. Then discuss your writing process as well as theirs.

Your students will benefit from comparing their writing habits: how (and if) they gather their thoughts first, whether they add new information as they move through the writing assignment, if they prefer quiet or background

Chances are that you have been a writer, reader, and researcher since you were a small child. When you first began trying to write your name, for instance, you were also learning to read what you had written. And you were, in addition, doing research—making observations, asking questions, proceeding by trial and error, and probably also taking cues from the response your newfound skills evoked from admiring relatives. In fact, throughout your life, whether you've been aware of it or not, the processes of writing, reading, and researching have been closely interrelated. Certainly, a significant part of your college education will involve these activities, for they are the primary means of creating and sharing academic knowledge.

1a

Considering the process of writing

No one can complete college without doing a lot of writing, and more and more people in education, business, and the professions now realize the crucial importance of being able to write effectively. In fact, research shows that writing encourages and enhances certain kinds of learning, and even that some kinds of complex thinking may be impossible without it. Writing, then, is not a mysterious artistic talent that only a lucky few are born with, but an essential and powerful means of discovering what you know and of communicating that knowledge with others. As one author says:

> . . . writing is foremost a mode of thinking and, when it works well, an act of discovery. I write to find out what I believe, what seems logical and sensible to me, what notions, ideas, and views I can live with.
>
> — JOSEPH EPSTEIN

Writers, then, are simply people who create and explore observations and ideas on paper and who care about the ways that their readers respond to their written words. In order to write successfully, however, it helps to understand how the writing process works and how to develop a method that works for you. Looking carefully at the way you go about writing, at your processes of writing, should help you view your own writing with a critical eye and determine how to make the kinds of changes that will lead to better pieces of writing and greater intellectual rewards. Because the writing process is directly related to the quality of the finished piece of writing, the next several chapters will focus on the various parts of that process.

The mental activities that actually accompany the writing process are tremendously complex. They are, moreover, so subtle and so lightning-fast that we are only now beginning to learn how they all interact. But we do know that writers always set and shift and reset a series of goals as they write. These goals range from those as large as "try to make the reader laugh here" or "explain this concept" to ones as small as "use a semicolon instead of a period here to make this section flow more smoothly."

Researchers often describe the process of writing as seamless and **recursive**, meaning that its goals or parts are constantly flowing into and influencing one another, without any clear break between them. This shifting set of goals may focus one moment on deciding how to organize a paragraph and the next moment on using knowledge gained from that decision to revise the wording of a sentence. Repetitive, erratic, and often messy, writing does not proceed in nice, neat steps: first an idea; then a plan; then an introduction, body, and conclusion. In fact, these "steps" often take place simultaneously, in a kind of spiraling sequence, with exploring, drafting, and revising all taking place throughout the process of writing. A writer may get an idea for a conclusion while drafting the introduction, or may plan one paragraph while revising the previous one.

Everyday use

Deciding which college to attend and going through the process of applying and enrolling called on you to do some important reading, writing, and researching. You may remember doing some research on possible colleges, poring over catalogs to determine which schools would be appropriate, and writing up the final applications. Think for a moment about how you have used reading, writing, and research in other decisions you've made recently— what computer to buy, where to vacation, and so on.

---

noise, what time of day they do their best writing, how soon before the deadline they begin their assignments, and, most important, what kind of writing they do.

By discussing your students' writing processes, you will help them accomplish three goals: (1) They will listen and talk to one another, not just to you, thereby fostering a classroom atmosphere that lends itself to collaborative writing practices. (2) They will realize that you, too, have a unique writing process. (3) They will see that because writing is a recursive process consisting of planning, drafting, and revising, they can concentrate on one step at a time.

USEFUL READING

Perl, Sondra. "Understanding Composing." *CCC* 31 (1980): 363–69. Rpt. in *Rhetoric and Composition: A Sourcebook for Teachers and Writers*. 2nd ed. Ed. Richard L. Graves Arguing that "throughout the process of writing, writers return to substrands of the overall process, or subroutines," Perl attempts to identify the features of this recursiveness.

Emig, Janet. *The Web of Meaning: Essays on Writing, Teaching, Learning, and Thinking*. Ed. Dixie Goswami and Maureen Butler. Upper Montclair, NJ: Boynton, 1983. Emig argues, among other things, that there is no one formula for teaching writing, that writing processes are recursive, and that writing "is as often a preconscious or unconscious roaming as it is a planned and conscious rendering of information and events" (141).

Emig, Janet. "Writing as a Mode of Learning." *CCC* 28 (1977): 122–28. Rpt. in *The Writing Teacher's Sourcebook*. Ed. Gary Tate and Edward P. J. Corbett. New York: Oxford UP, 1988. Emig argues that writing represents a unique mode of learning, noting that it is inherently reinforcing, that it uses both hemispheres of the brain, and that it provides immediate feedback.

BACKGROUND

In "Pre-writing: The Stage of Discovery in the Writing Process," D. Gordon Rohman challenged the field of composition studies by arguing that writing is a learnable process. He begins his essay, published in *CCC* (16 [1965]: 106–12), by positing the following:

Writing is usefully described as a process, something which shows continuous change in time like growth in organic nature. Different things happen at different stages in the process of putting thoughts into words and words onto paper. In our Project English experiment, we divided the process at the point where the "writing idea" is ready for the words and the page: everything before that we called "Pre-Writing," everything after "Writing" and "Re-Writing."

USEFUL READING

Bartholomae, David. "Inventing the University." *When a Writer Can't Write: Studies in Writer's Block and Other Composing Process Problems.* Ed. Mike Rose. New York: Guilford Press, 1985: 134–65. Bartholomae argues that in order to succeed in college, students need to learn to speak the language of the university, "to try on the particular ways of knowing, selecting, evaluating, reporting, concluding, and arguing" that are valued by various academic discourse communities.

In any case, writers seldom pay conscious attention to these constantly shifting goals and recursive patterns. Ideally, writing can be a little like riding a bicycle; with practice the process becomes more and more automatic. As you become more practiced as a writer, more and more of the goal-juggling you do will become automatic. Like an experienced cyclist, you will be able to pay attention to the big things—oncoming traffic, the view, the route you're taking—without thinking too consciously about changing gears or moving your feet.

It is useful to think of the writing process as a series of recursive activities: **considering purpose and audience**, during which the writer determines the purposes the piece of writing is intended to accomplish and thinks carefully about those to whom it is addressed; **exploring, planning, and drafting**, during which the writer gathers information, develops a tentative thesis and organization, and puts down on paper a version of the piece of writing; **revising, editing, and proofreading**, during which the writer works with the draft to improve it and polishes it to its final form. But these activities seldom if ever occur in a linear sequence, with one completed step rigidly following another. Rather, most writers move back and forth—considering the assignment, exploring the topic, thinking about audience, gathering more information, planning, drafting, revising, drafting another section, revising again, planning a little more, focusing more sharply on audience, revising yet again, editing and proofreading—until the writing is complete. Though the following sections discuss the various parts of the process in the order presented in the list above, in any actual writing task these activities are almost always interwoven.

1

Considering purpose and audience

In most of your college work, the writing process will begin with an assignment for a course. Whether the topic is specified by the instructor or left up to you, you will do well to begin by thinking carefully about the assignment itself, making sure you understand what it is asking you to do and, if necessary, clarifying it with your instructor.

As you think about the assignment carefully, you will want to decide what major purposes you hope to accomplish in the piece of writing. In addition to presenting yourself well and demonstrating your skill as a writer, you will intend for the writing to accomplish some goal—to persuade your readers to take a certain action, to explain some event or phenomenon to them, and so on. And because specific purposes can be fulfilled only in relation to specific readers, you will want to think carefully about your audience, those readers to whom your piece of writing is addressed. (Purpose and audience are examined in detail in Chapter 2.)

2
Exploring

Writing worth reading usually starts with a nagging question or puzzle or idea that calls for some exploration—thinking about what you already know, coming up with a working thesis, gathering information if necessary. While this kind of "exploring" continues throughout the writing process, it is often the way a writer begins.

Depending on the writing task, exploring can last a few minutes or several months. If you have to write a one-page essay in class about a member of your family, you will probably jot down a few notes and start writing very quickly. If, on the other hand, you have six weeks to prepare a fifteen-page paper on U.S.-Soviet relations, you need to do some research and explore the topic thoroughly before planning what you want to say. (Strategies for exploring a writing topic are presented in Chapter 3.)

3
Planning

Exploring is closely connected to planning, which involves deciding how to organize your writing. Sometimes a possible organizational plan will occur to you at an early stage and help shape your thesis and direct any research you need to do. More often, perhaps, a plan will grow out of the thesis or your search for information. However your plan develops and however tentative it is, it will act as a guide as you produce a first draft. Your thesis and organization may well shift as you draft, but just having them there will help you keep on course, or at least remember where you are headed. (Organizing and planning are discussed in Chapter 3.)

4
Drafting

Drafting is the central part of writing—the one element in the process that can never be skipped or avoided. As one student put it, drafting is that point "where the rubber meets the road," the time when you try your ideas out in writing. As much as anything, drafting serves as a continuation of the process of exploration. The British writer E. M. Forster once wrote, "How can I know what I think until I see what I say?" Indeed, no matter how thoroughly you may already have explored your topic, you will discover more about it while drafting. Sometimes these new insights will cause you to turn back—to change your organizational plan, to bring in more information, to approach the subject from a new angle, to rethink the way you appeal to your audience, or even to reconsider your purpose. Drafting, then, is *not* just "putting your ideas down on paper." More often than not, it also involves coming up with new ideas or completely reshaping your concept of what you are trying to achieve in the essay.

Because writing out the actual draft is just one part of this recursive activity, many experienced writers report that they rarely try to make their writing come out perfectly the first time. Rather, they view drafting as just that—the process of working out a *first draft,* during which they explore thoughts and try out arguments and examples. The goal of drafting is not to produce a final copy, or even a version good enough to show anyone else. Smooth sentences, the ideal word choice, and the right punctuation can come later; in your first draft, just get your thoughts down, and keep drafting until you run out of ideas to explore. (See Chapter 3 for more on drafting.)

5

Revising

With your first draft, you have a version of your essay before you, and the rest of your work will be devoted to making sure it says what you want it to say. Doing so requires careful rereading and analysis of the draft with an eye toward establishing a systematic plan for revising.

Re-vision means literally "seeing again." It means looking at a draft with a critical eye—seeing it anew and deciding if it accomplishes your original goals. You may have assumed before now that revising is simply a matter of correcting misspellings, inserting missing commas, and typing up the result. Although such tasks are important, true revision is something more. It means examining the draft to reassess the main ideas, the organization, the structure of paragraphs, the variety of sentences, the choice of words, the attitudes shown toward the topic and the audience, the thoroughness with which the topic is developed. It means polishing to achieve smooth phrasing and memorable prose. It may mean writing new sentences, moving paragraphs, eliminating whole sections, doing additional research, or even choosing a new topic and starting all over again. In fact, because it can be extensive, revising often closely resembles drafting.

Getting responses from others

In addition to your own analysis of the draft's strengths and weaknesses, you may want to get responses from other people. The analysis you do on your own is important, of course, because no one knows as well as you what you are trying to say. But most writing assumes an audience larger than the writer alone; and revising can be made easier and more productive if you can actually make use of such an audience, be it your friends, your classmates, or your instructor. Getting comments and criticisms from others is a way of seeing your work through new eyes, and it is a helpful part of any writer's revision process. (See Chapter 4.)

Writing and rewriting are a constant search for what it is one is saying. —JOHN UPDIKE

I have never thought of myself as a good writer. Anyone who wants reassurance of that should read one of my first drafts. But I'm one of the world's great rewriters. —JAMES A. MICHENER

The main thing I try to do is write as clearly as I can. Because I have the greatest respect for the reader, and if he's going to the trouble of reading what I've written—I'm a slow reader myself and I guess most people are—why, the least I can do is make it as easy as possible for him to find out what I'm trying to say, trying to get at. I rewrite a good deal to make it clear. —E. B. WHITE

6
Editing and proofreading

After you have received any critical responses to your draft and have revised thoroughly, the tasks of editing and proofreading begin. Editing involves making what you have written ready for the world, which means making it meet those conventions of written form known as "correctness." Sentence structure, spelling, mechanics, punctuation—all must meet conventional standards. Even editing may lead you to reconsider an idea, a paragraph, a transition, or an organizational pattern—and you may find yourself planning or drafting once again. When all editing is complete and you have produced a final manuscript, you then must proofread to catch and correct any typographical errors. (See Chapter 4.)

7
Taking inventory of your own writing

Although you may not have thought very much about how you go about producing a piece of writing, you probably already have your own characteristic writing process. One of the best ways to improve this process is to make the effort to analyze it from time to time. You can do this most systematically by keeping a **writing log**, a notebook in which you jot down your thoughts about a writing project while you are working on it or after you have completed it. Studying these notes will help you identify patterns of strength and weakness in your writing, and sharing the writing log with your instructor or your classmates may yield some helpful advice on how you can write more efficiently and effectively. (For more on keeping a writing log and a sample entry from one student's log, see p. I–2.)

To get started on thinking about and evaluating your own writing process, answer the following questions. If you are keeping a writing log, record your answers there.

Examining your own process of writing

1. How do you typically go about preparing for a writing assignment? Describe the steps you take, including rereading the assignment, asking questions about it, talking to instructors or friends, jotting down ideas, gathering information, and so on. How far in advance of the due date do you usually begin working on the assignment?
2. When and where do your best ideas often come to you?
3. Where do you usually do your writing? Describe this place. Is it a good place to write? Why, or why not?
4. When you write, are you usually physically alone? Is there usually music, conversation, or other noise in the background?

TEACHING PRACTICE
Grading the students' writing logs may discourage them from analyzing their writing processes. The logs, however, can tell you what help your students need.

An ungraded essay is a good way for you and your students to assess their current approach to composition. Assign the students to write a brief description of someone they knew well during childhood. Their essays should enable the reader to picture the person clearly and to understand how the writer felt about the subject. You may want to use this diagnostic essay as the basis for future assignments.

After they have completed their essays, ask the students to answer the questions in the text. Then consider the following questions as you read their writing logs to determine how they might improve their writing.

1. Could the student spend more time in preparation?
2. Is the essay aimed at a particular audience?
3. Is the purpose for writing evident?
4. Did the student do any revising at all? What kind(s)?
5. Do you and the student agree on the strengths of the essay?

Now is a good time to assure your students that you will help them improve their writing in specific ways, building on their strengths and concentrating on one problem at a time.

FOR COLLABORATIVE WORK
Divide the class into groups of three and ask the members of each group to discuss their writing processes and practices, and their own answers to the above questions. Then have them work together to write a one- or two-page description on the findings of their group, first describing, then comparing and contrasting the writing strategies of group members.

USEFUL READING

Murray, Donald M. "Teaching the Other Self: The Writer's First Reader." *CCC* 33 (1982): 140–47. According to Murray, all writers have an "other self" that is capable of reading a piece of writing in progress and giving advice to the writer about how the writing should proceed. Murray argues that the teacher should teach a student's "other self" by giving the writer's "other self" the chance to speak in teacher-student conferences and in small and large workshops with other writers.

5. What materials do you use? pen or pencil, note pad, loose-leaf paper, index cards, typewriter, word processor? What do you find most (and least) helpful or appealing about these materials?

6. What audience do most assignments ask you to address? the instructor? classmates? a wider audience? How much thought do you typically give to the audience as you work on the assignment?

7. What strategies do you typically use to explore a topic?

8. How do you typically go about writing a first draft? Do you finish it in one sitting, or do you prefer to take breaks?

9. How do you typically go about revising, and what does your revising include? Do you write out complete revised drafts or simply insert, delete, or move material in the previous draft? How many drafts or stages of revision do you usually go through before the final version? Why? What are the things you think about most as you revise?

10. If you "get stuck" while writing, what do you usually do to get moving again?

11. What would you say is most efficient and effective about your writing process? What is most enjoyable? What is least efficient and effective about your writing process? What is least enjoyable?

12. What specific steps could you take to improve your writing process?

EXERCISE 1.1   Taking Inventory: Your Writing Process

Take a few moments to remember all of the writing you did when you were applying to college: the letters you wrote, the forms you completed, and so on. In a brief paragraph, describe this writing and speculate on how it may have helped you be accepted by the college(s) that did so. Using the guidelines in 1a7, try to recall the process you followed.

Considering the process of reading

If you have ever read a book or seen a movie about Helen Keller, you will remember the electrifying moment when she first learns to "read," when she first realizes that the symbols traced in her palm contain meanings. Through these symbols, she begins to "see" a new world in her imagination. And so it is with all readers, for all of us build imaginative worlds of meaning from words. The words themselves, after all, are just marks on a page or screen; it takes an active reader to construct meaning from them. You will recognize this principle if you think of a time when you were reading along and suddenly realized that you were not getting any meaning, that you were just looking at words. Only when you went back, engaged those words actively, and puzzled them out were you really *reading*.

1

Reading to write

Reading is closely related to writing, if only because writers need to be able to read their own work with a careful eye. Indeed, one good way to improve your writing is by paying close attention to what you read, taking tips from writers you especially admire. In the words of William Faulkner, "Read, read, read. Read everything—trash, classics, good and bad, and see how they do it." Throughout this handbook, we will be examining the work of well-known writers to "see how they do it," to see what they do with the strategies and structures you yourself will be practicing.

In addition, most chapters include exercises asking you to read a passage with an eye for some element in the writing—adjectives, subordination, dashes, and so on. These exercises are designed to help you learn to use these elements in your own work—and they can lead you to insights about how you can make your own writing more accurate and powerful.

2

Reading with a critical eye

The writer Anatole Broyard once cautioned readers about the perils of "just walking through" a book. A good reader, he suggested, "stomps around" in a book—underlining passages, scribbling in the margin, noting any questions or comments. Following are some guidelines that can help you do more than just "walk through" your reading.

 Some guidelines for reading

> **PREVIEWING**
>
> - Determine your purpose for reading—to gather information for a writing assignment? to determine whether a source will be useful for a research project? to study for an examination? to prepare for class discussion?
> - Consider the title. What does it tell you about what is to come?
> - Think about what you already know about the subject. What opinions do you hold on this subject? What major topics do you anticipate? What do you hope to learn? *(Continued)*

BACKGROUND

The interconnection between reading and writing has received a great deal of attention during the last decade. It has become clear that writing teachers are doing far more than teaching sentence structure—we are helping socialize students into a kind of discourse that many of them are unfamiliar with. Academic discourse is more than just correctness; it is a style of presentation that involves awareness of audience, grasp of subject, and confidence in the writer's own ethos and abilities. As David Bartholomae says in "Inventing the University,"

> Every time a student sits down to write for us, he has to invent the university for the occasion—invent the university, that is, or a branch of it, like history or anthropology or economics or English. The student has to learn to speak our language, to speak as we do, to try on the peculiar ways of knowing, selecting, evaluating, reporting, concluding and arguing that define the discourse of our community. . . . The student has to appropriate (or be appropriated by) a specialized discourse, and he has to do this as though he were easily and comfortably one with his audience, as though he were a member of the academy or an historian or an anthropologist or an economist; he has to invent the university by assembling and mimicking its language while finding some compromise between idiosyncracy, a personal history, on the one hand, and the requirements of convention, the history of a discipline, on the other. He must learn to speak our language (134–35).

In order to become part of the conversation of academic discourse, students must be exposed to it. Readings in a writing course assist the socialization process in several ways: they provide models of good writing (as well, sometimes, as models of writing to be avoided); they provide content issues that can be discussed; analyses of the decisions that writers have made can illuminate the composing process. We will be using all of these elements in the reading exercises and the examples from works by Eudora Welty, Lewis Thomas, and Maya Angelou throughout the handbook.

- What do you know about the author? What expertise does he or she have in this subject? What biases might he or she have?
- Look at how the text is structured. Are there subdivisions? Read over any headings. Skim the opening sentences of each paragraph.
- Decide what you think the main point or theme of the text will be.

READING AND ANNOTATING

- Read carefully, marking places that are confusing or that you want to reread.
- Identify key points or arguments, important terms, recurring images, and interesting ideas, either by underlining them in the text or making notes in the margin.
- Note any statements that you disagree with or question and any counterevidence or counterarguments that occur to you.
- Note any sources used in the text.

SUMMARIZING

- Summarize the main points. Do they match your expectations?
- Jot down any ideas you want to remember, questions you want to raise, and ideas for how you may use this material.

ANALYZING

- Identify evidence that supports the main argument or illustrates the main point, as well as any that seems to contradict it.
- Decide whether sources used are trustworthy.
- Identify the writer's underlying assumptions about the subject as well as any biases revealed in the text. (See 41d.)

REREADING

- Reread quickly to be sure you have understood the reading.
- Identify the author's purpose. Was that purpose accomplished?
- Determine whether all questions you had during the first reading have been answered.

RESPONDING

- Think about the reading as a whole. What did you like best about it? What puzzled or irritated you? Were your expectations met? If not, why not? What more would you like to know about the subject?
- Note what you have learned about effective writing from this reading. If you keep a writing log, record these notes there.

EXERCISE 1.2

Following the guidelines in 1b, read one of the assigned essays from your course text or, if you are not using a text, the student essay in Chapter 4 or Chapter 5 of this book. Summarize the reading briefly, and note down any thoughts you have about your reading process (in your writing log, if you keep one).

1c

Doing research

Writing something "out of your head," based entirely on your own ideas and opinions, can be highly satisfying and pleasurable. But as the French novelist Marcel Proust wrote, "Any mental activity is easy if it need not take reality into account." Most writing, certainly most of the writing you will do for college, does require that you "take reality into account"; and that requirement helps to explain why research is a basic tool for writers. Few of us command enough knowledge of the "reality" of any topic to be able to write confidently about it without at least looking up a few items of information in a reference book or making a few direct observations to check a pattern.

For many writing assignments, of course, you will need to do much more extensive research for broader purposes: to get a better understanding of the topic, to see how your thoughts and perceptions about it compare with those of others, to determine which aspects of it you can and would like to investigate or discuss, to find evidence or examples. Even if you know the topic very well, however, your research is important for establishing credibility with your audience, and thus gaining their agreement. (Chapters 39–44 provide detailed discussion of research strategies.)

1d

Benefiting from collaboration

Philosopher Hannah Arendt once remarked that "for excellence, the presence of others is always required." Nowhere is Arendt's observation more accurate than in the college community. As mentioned earlier, your college coursework will call on you to read, write, and research a vast amount of material. But you will not—or need not—do all that reading, writing, and researching alone. Far from it. Instead, you can be part of a

BACKGROUND

In contrast to the narrow view of "student research," which confines it to a few weeks of hurried library activity at the end of a semester, this book sees the concept of research in a hermeneutic way: research is the process of understanding, interpreting, and applying new information *of all kinds*. We are all always engaged in research, some of which results in writing and much of which does not. Every essay a student writes is a research paper, and though some may require more library reading and correlation of information than others, it is impossible to write without having done research—even if that research is just into the shifting world of personal memories.

BACKGROUND

Recent works in philosophy and literary theory have undercut the concept of the "solitary creator and interpreter," who strives alone to read and write and to make sense of the world. One of the most important facts to have come out of recent research into writing is that most real-world writing is done collaboratively. As Lisa Ede and Andrea Lunsford explain:

> People in a range of professions regularly write as parts of teams or groups, and their ability to participate successfully in such collaborative writing efforts is essential both to their productivity and job satisfaction. . . . In an effort to determine just how many people in the "real world" write collaboratively, we surveyed 1200 randomly selected members of six professional associations. . . . Of the 1200 members surveyed, 530 persons (or almost 50% of our sample) completed the questionnaire. And of these 530 respondents, 87% reported that they have written as part of a team or group.

Collaborative work in composition classes, then, is not merely a good idea pedagogically; it is also important preparation for the writing tasks that students will find when they leave the classroom. The emphasis this book puts on collaboration will help use class time more efficiently, and it will also get students used to learning together in ways that reflect how reading, writing, and research work together.

Bruffee, Kenneth. "Collaborative Learning and the 'Conversation of Mankind.'" *CE* 46 (1984): 635–52. Bruffee outlines a rationale for collaborative learning and relates that rationale to classroom practice. He argues that collaborative learning is an effective pedagogy because it illustrates that knowledge is socially constructed. For a practical application of Bruffee's theories see his *A Short Course in Writing* (Cambridge, MA: Winthrop, 1980.)

Lunsford, Andrea, and Lisa Ede. *Singular Texts/Plural Authors: Perspectives on Collaborative Writing.* Carbondale: Southern Illinois UP, 1990. Lunsford and Ede trace the development of the idea of "the author" and demonstrate through extensive research that collaborative writing is quite common in business, government, and other major institutions, including the academy. They describe two modes of collaborative writing, *hierarchical* and *dialogic,* and offer guidelines and specific suggestions for incorporating collaboration in classrooms.

Elbow, Peter. *Writing without Teachers.* New York: Oxford UP, 1973. Elbow offers practical advice about setting up a writing group, including advice about how group members should respond to each other's writing.

FOR COLLABORATIVE WORK

Setting up study groups is one of the most important things you can help students accomplish. These guidelines can help students work in their groups, but you may need to form the groups and assign their early tasks.

It is important in setting up and using these groups that a few conscientious and enthusiastic students do not do all of the work. Change the membership of the groups occasionally and assign rotating roles to students when you assign tasks, so that one student will be a researcher, then a group coordinator, then a reporter to the class, etc.

broad conversation that includes all the texts you read; all the writing you produce; all the discussions you have with teachers, friends, family members, and classmates; all the observations and interviews you conduct. It is this conversation we have in mind when we stress the importance of collaboration to you as a student seeking to achieve excellence in college and throughout your life.

Collaboration can play an important part in all the writing you do, first if you talk with others about your topic and your plans for approaching it, then if you seek responses to your draft and gather suggestions for improving it. In much the same way, reading can be done "with others" —first by entering into mental conversation with the author, then by comparing your understanding of the text with that of other readers and using points of agreement or disagreement as the basis for further analysis.

For this term at least, the most immediate and valuable of your collaborators may be the members of the class in which you are using this book. Indeed, you can learn a great deal by listening carefully not only to your instructor but to all of your classmates. You can profit even more by talking over issues with them, by comparing notes and ideas with them, and by using them as a first and very important audience for your writing; for they will inevitably offer you new perspectives, new ways of seeing and knowing. Here are some tips for working in a group.

Establishing a study group

1. Set up a group with an odd number of members, such as three or five.
2. Trade phone numbers and schedules, and set a regular meeting time.
3. Set an agenda for each meeting. If, for instance, you want to work on introductions to an essay, agree to bring several versions for each member of the group to evaluate. If you intend to read and critique entire drafts, make arrangements to distribute copies to each member ahead of time.
4. Use the group to work through difficult readings, assignments, or problems. If an assignment is long, have each member take one section to explain, illustrate, and "teach" to the others. If you as a group cannot understand or solve something, seek out an instructor for help.
5. Give every member an opportunity to contribute.
6. Listen carefully to what each person says. If discussion lags or if disagreements arise, try paraphrasing what each person has said to see if all members are hearing the same things.
7. Establish regular times to assess how effective the group is, making individual notes on the following questions: What has the group accomplished so far? What has it been most helpful with? What has it been least helpful with? What have I contributed to it? What has each of the others contributed? How can we make the group more effective?

2

Considering Purpose and Audience

Effective writers share at least one thing in common with expert jugglers: they are able to attend to a number of important elements all at once, to keep, as it were, a lot of balls in the air. Among the most important and pervasive of the elements a writer must "juggle" are those concerning *purpose* and *audience*. As a writer, you will have occasion to write for many purposes and to address many audiences—to amuse your friends, to reassure your parents that you are still alive and well, to inform a credit-card company about an error in your bill, to explain a sales campaign to employees, to persuade your local government to lower its assessment of the value of your house, and so on. As a careful and effective writer, you will want to understand as much as possible about your purposes for writing and about those readers you're addressing. This chapter will get you started thinking about these crucial elements in any writing process.

2a

Deciding to write

Because purpose and audience are such important considerations in effective writing, you should start thinking about them at an early stage, as soon as you make the decision to write.

In a general sense, of course, this decision is often made for you. You must take an essay examination at 10 A.M.; your editor sets a Tuesday deadline for your newspaper story; a professor announces that a research paper will be due next month; your employer asks for a full report on a complex issue by the next management meeting.

But even in such situations, consciously *deciding to write* is important. Experienced writers report that making up their minds to begin a writing

It is well to understand as early as possible in one's writing life that there is just one contribution which every one of us can make; we can give unto the common pool of experience some comprehension of the world as it looks to each of us. —DOROTHEA BRANDE

I am convinced that all writers are optimists whether they concede the point or not. . . . How otherwise could any human being sit down to a pile of blank sheets and decide to write? —THOMAS COSTAIN

find out? How can I best arrange my information and ideas? How much time do I have? How long should the composition be?

As soon as you make a writing assignment, encourage your students to respond to these questions by "thinking with a pencil in hand," jotting down ideas in their writing logs. Unlike experienced writers, students tend to spend little time prewriting. You might want to remind your students that almost all writers, even experienced ones, dread the blank page. Many authors say that the quickest way to face that challenge is to cover the blank page with writing, allowing anything to find its way onto the page.

Your students will soon understand the importance of prewriting to their success as writers. They will not only develop their own prewriting techniques but will come to depend upon them.

TEACHING PRACTICE

Most student writers will, initially, prefer to be assigned a topic. However, British researcher James Britton has shown that inexperienced writers have more difficulty accepting an assigned topic than one they have chosen themselves (*The Development of Writing Abilities, 11–18* [London: Macmillan, 1975]). Still, many students need practice at finding ways to generate topics. The activities below may help them get started.

Collaborative Brainstorming: Use small groups to generate 10–20 possible topics or questions for several subject areas, such as interesting people, current controversies, cultural trends, problems on campus, scientific discoveries we'd like to know more about, possibilities for progress or decay, and so on. Students can use

task represents a big step toward actually getting the job done. You can use this insight to your advantage, determining not to put off a writing assignment but to meet it head-on by consciously deciding to get to work on it.

When a topic is not specified but left open, many of us put off getting started because we have trouble thinking of or deciding on one. Experienced writers tell us that the best way to choose a topic is literally to let the topic choose you. That is to say, those subjects that compel you—that puzzle, intrigue, or even irritate you—are likely to engage your interests and hence encourage your best writing. Even with assigned topics, you can often find some aspect that is particularly compelling. Once you start to *wonder* about a topic, you are at the point of having something to write about.

EXERCISE 2.1

Think back to a recent writing assignment. What helped you finally decide to write? Once you had decided to write, what exactly did you do to get going? In a paragraph or two, describe your situation and answer those questions. Then compare your description with those of two or three classmates.

Understanding writing assignments

Most on-the-job writing addresses specific purposes, audiences, and topics: a group of scientists produces a report on food additives for the federal government; an editorial assistant composes a memo for an editor

---

Everyday use

You can probably remember a time when something you wrote failed to achieve your purpose or, worse yet, backfired on you. Even a fairly routine thank-you note calls for careful thinking about its audience and its purpose: such a note sent to a grandparent for a birthday present will differ considerably from a letter thanking a prospective employer for an interview or a club for help on a group project. Take a moment now to think about thank-you letters you have either sent or received. How do such letters differ according to different purposes and audiences?

summarizing the problems in a new manuscript; a team of psychologists prepares video scripts intended to help companies deal with alcoholism among employees. These writers all have one thing in common: specific goals. They know exactly why, for whom, and about what they are writing.

College writing assignments, in contrast, may seem to appear out of the blue, with no specific purposes, audiences, or topics. In extreme cases, they may be only one word long, as in a theater examination that consisted of the single word "Tragedy!" At the opposite extreme come assignments in the form of fully developed cases, often favored in business and engineering courses. Such cases are very specific: you could, for example, be asked to assume the role of a civil engineer who is to evaluate various proposals for constructing a bridge and report the results of your evaluation to your superiors.

In between the one-word exam and the fully developed case lies a wide spectrum of assignments. You may get assignments that specify purpose but not audience—to write an essay arguing for or against capital punishment, for example. Or you may be given an organizational pattern to use—to compare and contrast two of the novels you have read in a course, for example—but no specific topic. Because each assignment is different, and because comprehending a topic is crucial to your success in responding to it, you should always make sure you understand the assignment as fully as possible.

 Analyzing an assignment

- *What, exactly, does the assignment ask you to do?* Look for words like *analyze, classify, compare, contrast, describe, discuss, define, explain,* and *survey.* These are key terms, and you should be sure you understand what task they set. Remember that these words may differ in meaning among disciplines—*analyze* might mean one thing in literature and something rather different in biology.

- *What knowledge or information do you need?* Do you need to do any research? (See 3a and 3c for ways of assessing your own knowledge and gathering additional information.)

- *How can you limit—or broaden—the topic or assignment to make it more interesting?* Is there any particular aspect of the topic in which you have special interest or knowledge? Be sure to check with your instructor if you wish to redefine the assignment in any way.

- *What are the assignment's specific requirements?* Consider length, format, organization, and deadline. Being sure of such things will

(Continued)

these topics or questions as starters for pre-writing activities (see 3a), which may lead directly to an essay draft.

Using the Writing Log: Ask your students to keep a section in their writing logs dedicated to compiling essay topics on subjects that interest them. The log can also be a place to store ideas, intriguing facts, observations, provocative quotations from public figures or from students' reading (academic or otherwise). Organizing these entries under general subject headings (of the teacher's suggestion or the writer's invention) can provide some initial development of the topics.

TEACHING PRACTICE

Three to five pages is an appropriate page length for most composition-course essays. Most essays of fewer than three typed, double-spaced pages are inadequate in ways other than length. Three- to five-page papers demand development of a topic beyond simple description of a problem or a narration of an event, yet they are short enough to require significant narrowing of the topic.

Consider assigning due-dates for drafts. A day or two after introducing invention strategies, assign an exploratory draft. A couple of days later, schedule conferences with your students to discuss their work. Within the next few days, have them bring their revisions—along with all their planning notes and earlier drafts—to class. Setting deadlines for drafts reinforces the importance of starting early.

help you not only respond properly to the assignment but also know the scope expected. Your instructor is not likely to expect library research for a paper due in twenty-four hours, for example. If no length is designated, you should ask for some guideline.

- *What is your purpose as a writer in this assignment?* Do you need to demonstrate knowledge of a certain body of material, or do you mainly need to show the ability to express certain ideas clearly? (See 2c for a discussion of ways to assess purpose.)
- *Who is the audience for this piece of writing?* Does the writing task tell you to *assume* a particular readership besides your instructor? (See 2e for a discussion of ways to assess your audience.)

Throughout the next two chapters, we will follow the work of Jennifer Gerkin on an essay for her first-year English course at Ohio State University. Her class was given the following assignment: "Examine the effects of prejudice on your life, and discuss your efforts to deal with those effects."

Jennifer saw that the assignment was broad enough to allow her to focus on something that interested her, and she knew that the key word *examine* invited her to describe—and analyze—situations concerning prejudice in her life. Her instructor said to assume that he and members of the class would be the primary audience.

EXERCISE 2.2

The following assignment was given to an introductory psychology class: "Discuss in an essay the contributions of Jung and Freud to modern clinical psychology." What would you need to know about the assignment in order to respond successfully? Using the questions in 2b, analyze this assignment.

2c

Deciding on purposes

The writing of college essays, reports, and other papers almost always involves multiple purposes. On one level, you are writing to establish your credibility with your instructor, to demonstrate that you are a careful thinker and effective writer. Fulfilling this purpose means considering your

---

BACKGROUND

The earliest rhetoricians spoke of the aims or purposes of rhetoric in primarily active terms: to inform, to move, to delight. Sometime during the eighteenth and nineteenth centuries, the focus shifted from active purpose to static form—exposition (to inform), argumentation (to move), description and narration (to delight). Later, such strategies as process, comparison and contrast, division, and classification were added to lists of methods of development, lists derived from the classical *topoi*.

In actual practice, no such thing as a purely descriptive essay or a comparison-and-contrast essay exists outside of the classroom. To teach these techniques as discourse structures is to confuse means with ends.

instructor's expectations very carefully, a concern addressed in detail in 2e. But good college writing also accomplishes some other, more individual purposes that the writer has in mind. In fact, the best writing you do in college will be writing that in some way achieves a goal or goals of your own, that says as clearly and forcefully as possible what you think about a topic, and what you have to say to readers about this topic.

For example, if you are writing an essay about abortion, your purposes might be to share your knowledge of the topic with your readers, to persuade them to support or oppose legalized abortion, or even to clarify in your own mind the medical information about abortion or the moral debate over it. If you are writing a profile of your eccentric grandfather, you might be trying to amuse your readers at the same time that you are paying tribute to someone who was important to you.

In ancient Rome, the great orator Cicero noted that a good speech generally fulfilled one of three major purposes: to delight, to teach, or to move. Although the world has changed mightily in the two thousand years since Cicero, our purposes when we communicate with one another remain pretty much the same: we seek to *entertain* (delight), to *inform and explain* (teach), and to *persuade or convince* (move).

Most of the writing you do in college will address one or some combination of these purposes, and it is thus important for you to be able to recognize the overriding purpose of any piece of writing. If, for example, an American history professor asks you to explain the web of causes that led up to the 1964 Civil Rights Act (primary purpose: to explain) and you respond by writing an impassioned argument that the act was needed (primary purpose: to persuade), you have misunderstood the purpose of the assignment.

For most college writing, you should think in terms of *purposes* rather than one single purpose. Specifically, you should consider purpose in terms of the *assignment,* in terms of the *instructor's expectations,* and in terms of *your own goals.*

 Considering purposes

> ■ *The assignment.* Is the primary purpose of the assignment to entertain, to explain, to persuade—or some other purpose? What does the primary purpose suggest about the best ways to achieve it? If you are unclear about the primary purpose, have you talked with your instructor or classmates about it? Are there any secondary purposes to keep in mind?
>
> *(Continued)*

USEFUL READING

Connors, Robert. "The Rise and Fall of the Modes of Discourse." *CCC* 32 (1981): 444–55. Charts the history of the teaching of writing, especially the teaching of formal divisions of discourse.

Kinneavy, James. "The Basic Aims of Discourse." *CCC* 20 (1969): 297–304. A distilled version of Kinneavy's *Theory of Discourse,* in which he divides discourse into referential, persuasive, literary, and expressive, each emphasizing a particular element in the exchange between writer and audience about the subject of the discourse.

- *The instructor's expectations.* What are the instructor's purposes in giving this assignment—to make sure you have read certain materials? to determine whether you understand certain materials? to evaluate your thinking and writing abilities? to determine whether you can evaluate certain materials critically? How can you fulfill these expectations?
- *Your own goals.* What are your purposes in carrying out this assignment—to respond to the topic adequately and accurately? to meet the instructor's expectations? to learn as much as possible about a new topic? to communicate your ideas as clearly and forcefully as possible? How can you achieve these goals?

As she considered the assignment, Jennifer Gerkin saw that her primary purpose was to explain the effects of prejudice on her life, but she recognized some other purposes as well. Because this essay was assigned early in the term, she wanted to get off to a good start; thus one of her purposes was to write as well as she could, to demonstrate her ability to her classmates and her instructor. In addition, she decided that she wanted to find out something new about herself and to use this knowledge to get her readers to think about themselves.

EXERCISE 2.3

Choose one of the following assignments, and describe its various purposes. At the discretion of your instructor, this exercise may be done in small-group discussions, with one group member taking notes and reporting to the rest of the class.

1. Compare two book-length biographies of Emily Dickinson.
2. Discuss the controversies surrounding the use of genetic engineering to change characteristics of unborn children.
3. Write about a person who has been important in your life, and describe why he or she has affected you strongly.
4. Support or attack proposals for a compulsory national civilian service for young Americans who do not join the military.
5. Analyze the use of headlines in a group of twenty advertisements.
6. Describe a favorite spot in your hometown.
7. Explain the concept of virtual reality.
8. Read two poems by e. e. cummings, and decide which one you like better. Write an essay explaining why you prefer the one you do.

EXERCISE 2.4

Consider a writing assignment you are currently working on. What are its purposes, in terms of the assignment, the instructor, and you, the writer?

2d

Considering your rhetorical stance

"Where do you stand on that?" is a question often asked, particularly of those running for office or already occupying positions of authority—a police chief, a college president, a company manager. But as writers, it is important to ask the question of ourselves as well. "Where you stand" on your topic, your **rhetorical stance**, is important to your writing; and an understanding of this stance is closely related to an understanding of your purposes for writing and of your intended audience. Thinking about your stance will help you examine the feelings you have on any topic and thus help you address the topic fully. And knowing your own stance well will help you see in what way that stance might differ from those held by members of your audience.

A student writing a proposal for increased disability services, for instance, knew that her stance on this topic was profoundly influenced by the fact that she had a brother with Down's syndrome. She knew, therefore, that she brought an intense interest to this topic that she couldn't count on her audience having. She would need to work hard, then, on finding ways to get her audience to understand—and share—her stance.

 Considering your rhetorical stance

- What is your overall attitude toward the topic? approval? dislike? curiosity? indifference? How strong are your feelings?
- How much do you know about the topic? What questions do you have about it?
- What interests you *most* about the topic? Why?
- What interests you *least* about it? Why?
- What seems important (or unimportant) about the topic?
- What preconceptions, if any, do you have about it?
- What do you expect to conclude about the topic?

BACKGROUND

The idea of the "rhetorical stance" was first put forward by Wayne Booth in a *CCC* article of the same name (*CCC* 14 [1963]: 139–45). A good rhetorical stance, said Booth, was the result of an effective balance between the three Aristotelian forms of proof: ethos, pathos, and logos. Too much emphasis on ethos, the wonderfulness of the writer, would result in an imbalance Booth called the entertainer's stance. Too much emphasis on pathos, playing to the desires of the audience, would result in the advertiser's stance. And too much emphasis on logos, the message in itself, would result in the imbalance Booth called the pedant's stance. Keeping these three elements at work but not allowing any one to predominate was the work of the successful writer.

2e

Focusing on your audience

Understanding others means being able to "talk their language," or "walk a mile in their shoes." Philosopher Kenneth Burke notes that *language* is our primary means of making such a meeting of minds possible, of identifying with other people. We know that skilled writers consider their audiences carefully; in fact, one of the characteristic traits of a mature writer is the ability to write for a variety of audiences, using language, style, and evidence all appropriate to particular readers.

The key word here is *appropriate*: just as a funeral director would hardly greet a bereaved family with "So, what can I do for you?," neither would you be likely to sprinkle jokes through an analysis of child abuse written for a PTA group. Why not? Because such behavior would be wildly inappropriate in that context and because your good sense would lead you to consider the nature of your audience and to address them in an appropriate way.

For much of your college writing, an instructor may serve as the primary audience. You may, however, sometimes find yourself writing for others: lab reports addressed to your class, business proposals addressed to a hypothetical manager, or in one American history class, a letter to a seventeen-year-old living in the year 1775. Every writer can benefit from thinking carefully about who the audience is, what the audience already knows or thinks, and what the audience needs and expects to find out.

 Considering your audience

- What group of people do you most want to reach? your boss? other college students? scientists? people already sympathetic to your views? people unsympathetic to your views? potential voters? members of a group you belong to—or don't belong to?

- How much do you know about your intended audience? In what ways may its members differ from you? from one another? Think in terms of level of education, geographical region, age, sex, occupation, social class, ethnic and cultural heritage, politics, religion, marital status, sexual orientation, and so on. (See Chapter 28.)

- What assumptions do you make about your audience? What might they value? Think in terms of qualities such as brevity, originality, conformity, honesty, security, adventure, wit, seriousness, thrift, generosity, and so on. What goals and aspirations do they have?

- What is your audience's stance toward your topic? What are they likely to know about it? What preconceived views might they have?
- What do you need to be sensitive to in your audience's background?
- What is your relationship to the audience? Is it student to instructor? friend to friend? subordinate to superior? superior to subordinate? citizen to community? something else?
- What is your attitude toward the audience? friendly? hostile? neutral? admiring? impatient?
- What attitudes will the audience expect you to hold? What attitudes might disturb or offend them?
- What kind(s) of response(s) do you want to evoke?

In addition to her instructor, Jennifer Gerkin's audience included the members of her writing class. Thinking about her classmates, she saw that they were mostly her age; that they were almost all the same race, Caucasian; that they were all from the Midwest.

1

Addressing specific audiences

Thinking systematically about your audience can help you in a number of ways in making decisions about a writing assignment. For example, it can help you decide what sort of organizational plan to follow (which one would be easiest for a particular audience to understand, for example), what information to include or to exclude, and even what specific words to choose. If you are writing an article for a magazine for nurses about a drug prescribed to prevent patients from developing infections from intravenous feeding tubes, you will not need to give much information about how such tubes work or to define many terms. But if you are writing about the same topic in a pamphlet for patients, you will have to give a great deal of background information and define (or avoid) technical terms.

EXERCISE 2.5

To experiment with how considerations of appropriateness for a particular audience affect what you write, describe one of your courses to three audiences: to your best friend, to your parents, then to a group of high school students attending an open house at your college. Then describe the differences in content, organization, and wording that the differences in audience led you to make.

USEFUL READING

Kroll, Barry M. "Writing for Readers: Three Perspectives on Audience." *CCC* 35 (1984): 172–85. Kroll examines three prominent views of audience—the "rhetorical," the "informational," and the "social." For each view he offers an analysis of its theoretical assumptions, its pedagogical implications, and its limitations.

Ede, Lisa and Andrea Lunsford. "Audience Addressed/Audience Invoked: The Role of Audience in Composition Theory and Pedagogy." *CCC* 35 (1984): 155–71. Rpt. in *The Writing Teacher's Sourcebook*. Ed. Gary Tate and Edward P. J. Corbett. New York: Oxford UP, 1988. Ede and Lunsford point out the limitations of two prominent concepts of audience, that of "audience addressed," which emphasizes the concrete reality of the writer's audience, and that of "audience invoked," which focuses on the writer's construction of an audience. To think exclusively of the "audience addressed" is to overemphasize the audience and underestimate the writer; to think exclusively of the "audience invoked" is to overemphasize the power of the writer and undervalue that of the reader. Ede and Lunsford argue that a writer's audience may be both addressed and invoked, and they propose a model of audience which takes into consideration the shifting relationships between writer and reader.

TEACHING PRACTICE

Dealing with questions of audience is one of the most complex problems facing any writer, and one that face-to-face oral communication doesn't completely prepare students for. You can use the questions listed in 2e for oral or written practice in getting students more comfortable with writing for a more distant or diverse audience than they may be used to. Try asking students to do some preparation for the same writing task addressed to two different audiences. For each audience they should answer the questions on the list. For instance, ask students to prepare to write an essay describing the college health service's policies on distribution of birth control information. They should answer the questions on the list for two audiences: a women's student group at another college and a religiously based scholarship committee. This exercise can be done either individually or in groups, and in either case the writing is followed by class discussion on the kinds of problems each audience presents to a writer.

TEACHING PRACTICE

Ask each student to bring in an article, editorial, or column from the newspaper and to circle elements in the writing that deliberately include or exclude certain kinds of audiences. Ask students to read the circled excerpts and talk about whether the writer seemed to be aware of or in control of his or her effects, and how and why the writer made the choices he or she made concerning the inclusion or exclusion of audiences.

2

Appealing to your whole audience

All writing aims to appeal to some audience, and writers need to pay careful attention to the ways in which their writing can make readers participate as part of the audience, or can leave them out. One small example may help to illustrate this point. Look at the following sentence:

> As every schoolchild knows, the world is losing its rain forests at the rate of one acre per second.

The writer here gives a clear message about who is—and who is not—part of the audience: if you know what "every schoolchild knows," you can consider yourself part of this audience. But what if you don't know this "fact" at all? Then you may feel that you are *not* part of this writer's audience: the writing does not invite you to participate.

As a writer, there are various things you can do to make readers feel they are part of your audience. Things to be especially careful with include the pronouns you use, the assumptions you make, and the kind of support you offer for your ideas.

Using appropriate pronouns

The pronouns you use can either include or exclude readers. Writers sometimes use *we,* for example, in a way that asks readers to join or identify with a particular group. Study the following example:

> As all of us are quick to agree, we have an absolute constitutional right to bear arms.

In this case, notice how the language either allows you—or does not allow you—to become part of the audience. The sentence implies that all of "us" agree that "we" have the right to carry guns. But what if you are *not* in favor of this proposition? Then you are excluded from this writer's audience, and you may feel irritated or even antagonistic as a result.

As a writer, you need to be particularly attentive to the ways in which your writing can include or exclude certain people from your audience. If you use *we* to include your readers, make sure that those you are addressing really fall into this group.

Making no unfounded assumptions

Be careful about any assumptions you make about your readers and their views, especially about language that may unintentionally exclude readers you want to include. Use words like *naturally* or *of course* carefully, for what seems "natural" to you—that English should be the official U.S. language, for instance, or that tobacco should be outlawed—may not seem at all natural to others you may wish to include in your audience.

The best advice about any audience you wish to address is to take nothing about them for granted. Think as carefully as you can about the individuals who you wish to be part of your audience, and use language that includes rather than excludes them. (See also Chapter 28.)

Offering appropriate evidence

The examples and other evidence you offer in support of your arguments can help draw in your readers. The student mentioned in 2d writing about disability services, for example, might find that personal anecdotes about a particular disabled person could bring the topic "to life" for readers without any personal experience or interest in the topic. By actually asking readers to imagine themselves "in a wheelchair, trying to enter a building with steps but no ramp," she would with her writing be clearly inviting them to be a part of her audience, and helping them to accept her ideas. Such strategies can also, however, leave readers out. Statistical evidence might well appeal to public policy planners but may not appeal to—or could even leave out—ordinary citizens. The point is that you should carefully choose supporting evidence that is most likely to invite your readers to see themselves as part of your audience.

Using sources
Considering their purpose and stance

Awareness of purpose and audience can help you evaluate sources, from the textbooks you are assigned to the materials you may draw on in doing research. You can begin to examine sources carefully by asking questions such as these:

> What does the writer want to accomplish here?
> Why does the writer want to accomplish this purpose?
> What does the writer believe about this topic?
> What should I take the writer's word about?
> What should I be skeptical about?
> Whom does the writer seem to be addressing?
> What does the writer want readers to do, and why?

(See 41d for more information on evaluating sources.)

EXERCISE 2.6   Reading with an Eye for Purpose and Audience

Advertisements provide good examples of writing that is tailored carefully for specific audiences. Find two ads for the same product that appeal to different audiences. You might compare ads in a men's magazine to those in a women's magazine to see what differences there are in the message and photography. Or you could look at products that seem to appeal to men (Marlboro cigarettes, perhaps) next to those that are marketed to women (such as Virginia Slims). What conclusions can you draw about ways of appealing to specific audiences?

EXERCISE 2.7   Taking Inventory: Purpose and Audience

Consider something you have written or are working on right now.

1. Can you state its purpose(s) clearly and succinctly? If not, what can you do to clarify its purpose(s)?
2. What other purposes for this piece of writing can you imagine? How would fulfilling some other purpose change the writing?
3. Can you tell from reading the text who the intended audience is? If so, what in your text clearly aims to relate to that audience? If not, what can you add that will help you appeal to this audience?
4. What other audiences can you imagine? How would the writing change if you were to address some different audience?

If you are keeping a writing log, enter any conclusions you can make about purpose and audience in your own writing.

TEACHING PRACTICE

Students may have trouble coming up with a succinct statement of purpose for a piece of writing they are currently working on. Often their purpose will be little more than a simple statement like "My purpose is to tell the story of how I felt after I wrecked my Dad's Buick," or "My purpose is to describe how stupid it is to shoplift." Try pushing students beyond these simple statements into purpose statements that include some effect on the audience, since audience and purpose are always linked. The intended audience for most first drafts is usually either "people in the class," or "you, the teacher." Again, asking students to go beyond audiences that are immediately available will increase their repertoire of abilities. In talking with or writing to the student, keep asking the question in Exercise 2.7 about how the writing would change if written for some other audience. That is the key issue.

3

Exploring, Planning, Drafting

Lewis Thomas, one of America's leading essayists, began writing essays when he was invited to contribute a monthly column for the *New England Journal of Medicine*. A scientist and medical doctor, Thomas at first tried various methods of planning and organizing his columns, including meticulous outlines. Nothing seemed to work. After producing several of what Thomas himself considered "dreadful" essays, therefore, he shook off all attempts at detailed planning and plunged right in, thinking about and developing his ideas by simply writing as fast as he could.

Like Thomas, you may do best by diving right into your writing projects, exploring your topics as you draft. Or you may work more effectively by doing extensive exploration and producing detailed blueprints before you ever begin drafting. As this example suggests, there are many productive ways to go about exploring, planning, and drafting. This chapter takes a close look at some of the ways these activities work in practice.

3a

Exploring a topic

The point is so simple that we often forget it: we write best about topics we know well. One of the most important parts of the entire writing process, therefore, is exploring your topic, surveying what you know about it and then determining what you need to find out about it.

You may already have a good system for exploring topics you wish to write about. If so, use it and share it with friends and members of your class. If you have no particular personal system, however, this chapter provides a brief description of strategies that can be very useful in getting you started in your thinking about a topic and in helping you determine what you

BACKGROUND

Classical rhetoric consisted of five canons: *inventio* (invention), *dispositio* (arrangement), *elocutio* (style), *memoria* (memory), and *pronunciatio* (delivery). Just as the classical orators appreciated the fluidity of these elements, modern writers realize that the ebb and flow of "prewriting," "writing," and "revising" aids in the composing process.

The process of discovery implied by the Latin *inventio* and the Greek *heuresis* (eureka!) parallel our modern concept of "prewriting," which is also called rhetorical "invention." Since "prewriting" is often used to refer both to "invention" and to "planning," your students might want to think of "invention" as discovering what to say about a topic; of "planning" as the choices of what, when, and how to say it; and of "prewriting" as the first stage in the writing process, when "invention" and "planning" most often occur.

already know—and indeed in helping you solve problems that crop up later in the actual writing. The strategies include brainstorming, freewriting, looping, clustering, and questioning.

1

Brainstorming

Used widely in business, industry, and engineering, **brainstorming** involves tossing out ideas—often with several other people—in order to find new ways to approach a topic. You can easily adapt brainstorming to writing, however. All you need is a pen or pencil and a blank sheet of paper with which to carry out the following steps:

1. Give yourself a time limit—five or ten minutes, perhaps—and write down in list form *every* word or phrase that comes into your mind about your topic. Just put down key words and phrases, not sentences. No one has to understand the list but you. Don't worry about whether something will be useful or not. Just get it *all* down.

2. If nothing much seems to occur to you, try "thinking the opposite." If you are trying, for instance, to think of reasons to reduce tuition at your college and are coming up blank, try concentrating on reasons to *increase* tuition. Once you start generating ideas in one direction, you can move back to exploring the other side of the topic.

Everyday use

If you have ever written a serious love letter, you probably know all about exploring a topic and working hard on a draft. You might have spent days, weeks, even months, exploring the ideas you wanted to convey, thinking over what exactly to say, and considering the effects your language would have. And you may have drafted, torn up the draft, and then drafted some more, searching for just the right words to express something deeply felt and equally difficult to put into words.

Thank goodness few writing tasks are as demanding as a love letter, but most of the writing you do will call on you to give some serious thought to what you want to say and to how you want to say it. Take a moment to think of other occasions outside of school when you have had to think long and hard about something you needed to write—a letter to a friend asking for a special favor, a personal statement to accompany a job application, or something else. How, exactly, did you go about exploring your topic and planning what to say?

FOR COLLABORATIVE WORK

The brainstorming exercise works particularly well with groups of three to five students, but it generates even more energy when conducted with the entire class. Whether you or your students suggest the topic is not as important as getting started. Appoint two students to record ideas as they are suggested by the rest of the class. After about ten minutes, break the class into groups of four and ask each group to choose an idea and to develop a thesis from it.

To get started, I will accept anything that occurs to me. —WILLIAM STAFFORD

How do I know what I think until I see what I say? —E. M. FORSTER

USEFUL READING

Lauer, Janice M. "Issues in Rhetorical Invention." *Essays on Classical Rhetoric and Modern Discourse.* Ed. Robert J. Connors, Lisa S. Ede, and Andrea A. Lunsford. Carbondale: Southern Illinois UP, 1984. 127–39. Various prewriting techniques imply various assumptions about the composing process. Lauer distinguishes prewriting methods according to such factors as "the genesis of writing, exploratory acts and their relationship to judgment, and the province of invention."

3. When the time is up, stop and read over your list. If anything else comes to you, add it to the list. Then reread the list, looking for patterns, clusters of interesting ideas, or one central idea.

Brainstorming by yourself can work well, but it is particularly effective with a group of three to five people. You may want to get together with several members of your class to brainstorm about one another's topics.

2

Freewriting

Freewriting is a method of exploring a topic by writing about it—or whatever else it brings to mind—for a period of time *without stopping*. Here is the way to do it:

1. Set a time limit of no more than ten minutes. Begin by thinking about your topic, and then simply let your mind wander and write down everything that occurs to you, in complete sentences as much as possible. Don't stop for anything; if necessary, write "I can't think of what to write next" over and over until something else occurs to you.

2. When the time is up, stop and look at what you've written. You are sure to find much that is unusable, irrelevant, or nonsensical. But you may also find important insights and ideas that you didn't even know you had.

3

Looping

Looping is a form of directed freewriting that narrows or focuses a topic in five-minute stages, or "loops." As in freewriting, you first write whatever comes to mind about your topic, basically following the free flow of your thoughts. Then you follow a central thread of those thoughts wherever it leads you. Here is how to do looping:

1. With your topic in mind, spend five minutes freewriting *without stopping*. This is your first loop.

2. Look back at what you have written. Find the strongest or most intriguing thought. This is your "center of gravity," which you should summarize in a single sentence; it will become the starting point of your next loop.

3. Starting with the summary sentence from your first loop, spend another five minutes freewriting. This second loop circles around the center of gravity in the first loop, just as the first loop circled around your topic. Look for a center of gravity within this second piece of freewriting, which will form the basis of a third loop.

4. Keep this process going until you have discovered a clear angle on your topic or something about it you can pursue in a full-length essay.

BACKGROUND

James Moffett (*Teaching the Universe of Discourse*) and Janet Emig (*The Composing Processes of Twelfth Graders*) posit that freewriting not only increases verbal fluency but also provides a means for discovering ideas. In *Writing without Teachers* (New York: Oxford UP, 1973), Peter Elbow writes:

> The habit of compulsive, premature editing doesn't just make writing hard. It makes writing dead. Your voice is damped out by all the interruptions, changes, and hesitations between the consciousness and the page. (6)

Freewriting eliminates the beginning writer's most frustrating habit: focusing on correctness rather than content. During final drafting, your students will need to focus on correctness—but not until then.

FOR THE WRITING LOG

Elbow suggests in *Writing without Teachers* that students who sincerely want to improve their writing keep a freewriting diary:

> Just ten minutes a day. Not a complete account of your day; just a brief mind sample for each day. You don't have to think hard or prepare or be in the mood: without stopping, just write whatever words come out—whether or not you are thinking or in the mood. (9)

You might suggest that students keep a section of their logs dedicated to such a diary.

USEFUL READING

Elbow, Peter. "The Loop Writing Process." *Writing with Power*. New York: Oxford UP, 1981. 59–77. Elbow offers a refinement of freewriting which he calls loop writing— "a way to get the best of both worlds: both control and creativity" (59).

4

Clustering

Clustering is a way of generating ideas using a visual scheme or chart. It is especially useful for understanding the relationships among the parts of a broad topic or for developing subtopics. Clustering is done as follows:

1. Write down your topic in the middle of a blank piece of paper, and circle it.
2. Write down what you see as the main parts of the topic in a ring around the topic circle. Circle each one and draw a line from it to the topic in the center.
3. Think of any ideas, examples, facts, or other details relating to each main part. Write each of these down near the appropriate part, circle it, and draw a line from it to the part.
4. Repeat this process with each new circle until you can't think of any more details to add. Some of these trails may lead to dead ends, but you will end up with various trains of thought to follow and many useful connections among ideas.

(You can see an example of clustering in 3a6.)

5

Questioning

The strategies presented thus far for exploring topics are all informal and based on freewheeling association of ideas. But there are more formal and structured strategies that involve asking—and answering—particular questions. The following are several widely used sets of questions designed to help you explore your topic. Of course, you can also make up your own questions to use.

Questions to describe a topic

Originally developed by Aristotle, the following questions can help you explore any topic by carefully and systematically describing it.

1. *What is it?* What are its characteristics, dimensions, features, and parts? What does it look like?
2. *What caused it?* What changes occurred to create your topic? How is it changing? How will it change? What part of a changing process is your topic? What may it lead to in the future?
3. *What is it like or unlike?* What features differentiate your topic from others? What analogies does your topic support?

BACKGROUND

The questions in this section are meant to stimulate the writer's thinking and are based on various *heuristics* (prompts for thinking that involve questioning and other guides for investigation). Ultimately, all such heuristics derive from the *topoi,* the "topics" or "commonplaces" of classical rhetoric.

In *Classical Rhetoric for the Modern Student,* Edward P. J. Corbett writes that the "topics constitute a method of probing one's subject in order to discover possible ways of developing that subject" (24). Special topics are those classes of argument appropriate to particular kinds of discourse: judicial, ceremonial, or political. Aristotle names the common topics, those that could be used for any occasion, as "definition," "comparison," "relationship," "testimony," and "circumstance."

Like the questioning strategies in this section, the *topoi* were a way to find something to say about a subject.

4. *What is it part of?* What larger system is your topic a part of? How is your topic related to this larger system?

5. *What do people say about it?* What reactions does your topic arouse in people? What about the topic causes those reactions?

Questions to explain a topic

This is the well-known question set of *who, what, when, where, why,* and *how.* Widely used in news reporting, these questions are especially useful to help you explain a topic.

1. *Who* is doing it?
2. *What* is at issue?
3. When does it begin? *When* does it end?
4. *Where* is it taking place?
5. *Why* does it occur?
6. *How* is it done?

Questions to persuade

When your purpose is to persuade or convince, answering the following questions developed by the philosopher Stephen Toulmin can help you think analytically about your topic.

1. What *claim* are you making about your topic?
2. What *good reasons* support your claim?
3. What *underlying assumptions* support the reasons for your claim?
4. What *backup evidence* do you have or can you find to add further support to your claim?
5. What *refutations* of your claim can be made?
6. In what ways is or should your claim be *qualified*?

6

Looking at one student's exploratory work

Jennifer Gerkin, the student whose work we began following in the previous chapter, tried two strategies to explore her topic: brainstorming and clustering. Here are her brainstorming notes:

Some prejudice in everyone
Where does it come from?
Learned—we aren't born with it
Examples: against some races
against some ways of thinking
against some ways of dressing

USEFUL READING

Corbett, Edward P. J. *Classical Rhetoric for the Modern Student.* 3rd ed. New York: Oxford UP, 1990. This comprehensive text introduces both teacher and student to the theory and practice of classical rhetoric, including chapters on invention, arrangement, style, delivery, and memory.

Brainstorming helped her to get an idea of what she might have to say about prejudice. In order then to find out whether she really wanted to pursue this angle on her topic, she decided to try clustering. Here is what she produced:

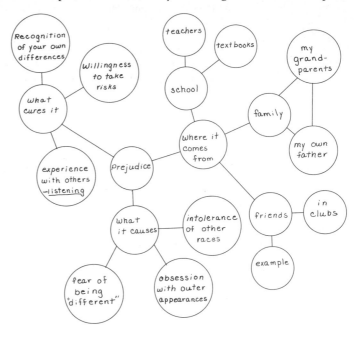

EXERCISE 3.1

Choose a topic that interests you, and explore it by using two of the strategies described in 3a. When you have generated some material, you might try comparing your results with those of other members of the class to see how effective or helpful each strategy was. If you have trouble choosing a topic, use one of the working theses in Exercise 3.2.

3b

Establishing a working thesis

A **thesis** states the main idea of a piece of writing. Most kinds of college writing contain a thesis statement, often near the beginning, which functions as a promise to the readers, letting them know what will be discussed. Though you will probably not have a finished thesis when you begin to write, you should establish a tentative **working thesis** early on in your writing process.

The word *working* is important here, as the working thesis may well be clarified or otherwise changed as you write. In spite of the fact that it will probably change, a working thesis is important for two main reasons: (1) it focuses your thinking, research, and investigation on a particular point about the topic and thus keeps you on track; and (2) it provides concrete questions to ask about purpose, audience, and your rhetorical stance (helping you see, for example, what you must do to design a thesis for a particular audience).

A working thesis should have two parts: a topic part and a comment part. The **topic** part states the topic, while the **comment** part makes an important point about the topic. Here are two examples.

┌─────── TOPIC ───────┐ ┌─────────── COMMENT ───────────┐
Recent studies of depression suggest that it is much more closely related

to physiology than scientists had previously thought.

┌─────── TOPIC ───────┐ ┌─────────── COMMENT ───────────┐
The current health care crisis can be traced to three major causes.

A successful working thesis has three characteristics. It should

1. Be potentially *interesting* to your intended audience
2. Be as *specific* as possible
3. Limit the topic enough to be *manageable*

You can evaluate a working thesis by checking it against each of these criteria. For example:

PRELIMINARY WORKING THESIS

Theories about "global warming" are being debated around the world.

INTEREST The topic itself holds interest, but it seems to have no real comment attached to it. The thesis merely states a bare fact, and there seems no place to go from here except to more bare facts.

SPECIFICITY The thesis is fairly clear, but not very specific. Who is debating these theories? What is at issue in this debate?

MANAGEABILITY The thesis is not manageable: it would require research in many countries and in many languages and would be beyond the capacities and time limits of most if not all students.

ASSESSMENT This thesis is too general and needs to be narrowed by a workable comment before it can be useful. Also, the field for investigation is too large and vague. This preliminary thesis can be narrowed into the following working thesis.

WORKING THESIS

Scientists from several different countries have challenged "global warming" theories and claimed that they are more propaganda than science.

For her essay, Jennifer Gerkin produced this preliminary working thesis: "Prejudice is learned." When Jennifer subjected this thesis to the tests of interest, specificity, and manageability, she decided that it was interesting but not very specific or manageable. Instead of prejudice in general, therefore, she decided to focus on a specific kind of prejudice and to adopt this working thesis: "Obsession with appearances has been part of my life since the day I was labeled 'the smart one.'"

EXERCISE 3.2

Choose one of the following preliminary working theses, and, after specifying an audience, evaluate the thesis in terms of interest, specificity, and manageability. Revise it as necessary to meet these criteria.

1. Drug abuse presents Americans with a big problem.
2. Abortion is a right.
3. Othello is a complex character whose greatest strength is, ironically, also his greatest weakness.
4. The Persian Gulf War created worse problems in the Middle East than the ones it solved.
5. White-collar crime poses greater danger to the economy than more obvious forms of street crime.
6. An educated public is the key to a successful democracy.

EXERCISE 3.3

Using the topic of the assignment you chose in Exercise 3.1, write a preliminary working thesis. Evaluate it in terms of interest, specificity, and manageability, and then revise it as necessary to create a satisfactory working thesis.

FOR COLLABORATIVE WORK

Exercise 3.3 can be extended to include peer responses. After your students have critiqued their own work, ask them to exchange their preliminary working theses and then evaluate them, using questions such as the following:

1. Does the thesis arouse your interest? What is the "so what?" of the thesis?
2. Is the thesis clear and specific? Can you make it more so?
3. Does the thesis seem manageable within the limits of time and length? Does the author promise to do too much? Can you help narrow the thesis?

The value of this additional exercise is greater perspective. What is patently obvious to the writer may not be so discernible to a reader, whose information is limited to the text.

3c

Gathering information

Many of your writing assignments will call for some research. Your instructor may specify that you research your topic and cite your sources, or you may find that you do not know enough about your topic to write about it effectively without doing some research. You may need to do research at various stages of the writing process—early on, to help you understand or define your topic, or later on, to find additional examples in support of your thesis. But once you have defined a working thesis, consider what additional information you might need.

If you find it necessary to do research, you should probably begin with those resources closest to hand: your instructor, who can help you decide what kind of research to do, and your textbooks, which may include a bibliography or list of references. Basically, you can do two kinds of research: library research, which includes nonprint sources as well as books and periodicals, and field research, which includes personal observation, interviews, surveys, and other means of gathering information directly. Detailed discussion of how to conduct both kinds of research is given in Chapter 40. If you determine you need to research your topic further, turn to that chapter for detailed guidelines.

3d

Organizing information

Exploring a topic and gathering information can provide essential data for an essay, but the data are raw—and not very helpful—until they are organized. Even as you are finding information on your topic, therefore, you should be thinking about how you will group or organize that information in your writing in a way that will make it accessible and persuasive to your readers.

The ways you group your information will ultimately depend on your topic, purpose, and audience. At the simplest level, however, writers can group information according to three different principles:

1. **Space**—*where* bits of information occur
2. **Time**—*when* bits of information occur, usually chronologically
3. **Logic**—*how* bits of information are related

TEACHING PRACTICE

Many students—including juniors and seniors—have little experience with research projects or familiarity with a campus library. You might consider holding a class in the library and asking a reference librarian to describe the general resources of the library and to explain their location and usefulness.

USEFUL READING

Larson, Richard L. "The 'Research Paper' in the Writing Course: A Non-Form of Writing." *CE* 44 (1982): 811–16. Rpt. in *The Writing Teacher's Sourcebook*. Ed. Gary Tate and Edward P. J. Corbett. New York: Oxford UP, 1988. Larson argues against teaching the "research paper" as a generic form on the basis that such an approach misleads students about the nature of research and its presentation. According to Larson, instructors should teach students to view research broadly—as more than just the recording of information from library books—and to conduct it imaginatively.

1

Organizing information spatially

If the information you have gathered is *descriptive,* you may choose to organize it spatially (see 3a5 for questions that help you describe a topic). Using **spatial organization** allows the reader to "see" your information, to fix it in space. A report on a college library's accessibility to students in wheelchairs, for example, might well group information spatially. In describing the spaces in the library that are most often used and evaluating their accessibility to a student in a wheelchair, the writer would most certainly present information spatially—one room or space or area at a time. In this case, the description of the student's progress through various library spaces might even be accompanied by a map. (See 6c for examples of information organized spatially.)

2

Organizing information chronologically

You are probably already very familiar with **chronological organization**, since it is the basic method used in stories, cookbooks, and instructions for assembling or using various products. All of these kinds of writing group information according to when it occurs in some process or sequence of events. Reports of laboratory studies and certain kinds of experiments also use chronological ordering of information.

A student studying the availability of motorcycle parking in a campus lot ordered his information chronologically to show the times when motorcycles entered and exited the lot and thus to identify peak periods of demand for parking spaces. This student chose to present this information in narrative (story) form, using chronological order to build tension as the minutes tick by and the lot gets more and more crowded, the cyclists more and more frustrated. If you choose to use a narrative or story form for presenting information, you will probably use chronological order. But reversing that order—or starting in the middle or at the end and then skipping back to the beginning, using a kind of flashback technique—can provide effective methods of organizing data as well.

Chronological order is especially useful in **explaining a process**, step by step by step. A biology report, for instance, might require describing a frog's process of circulation. An essay for an anthropology class might include an explanation of the initiation rituals in a native American culture. If you decide to organize information about a process in chronological order, you can test whether your explanation is clear and precise by asking a fellow student to read the explanation and report how easy (or hard) it is to follow the steps of the process.

3

Organizing information logically

In much of the writing you do in college, you will find it appropriate to organize information according to some set of logical relationships. The most commonly used **logical patterns** include *illustration, definition, division/classification, comparison/contrast, cause-effect,* and *problem-solution.* (See 6c for examples.)

Illustrating a point

Often much of the information you gather will serve as examples to **illustrate a point.** An essay discussing how one novelist influenced another might cite a number of examples from the second writer's books that echo themes, characters, or plots from the first writer's works. An appeal for donating money to the Red Cross might be organized around a series of examples of how such money will be used. If you use illustration in writing intended to persuade or convince, arrange the examples in order of increasing importance, for maximum effect.

Defining terms

Many topics can be developed by **definition**: by saying what something is—or is not—and perhaps by identifying the characteristics that distinguish it from things that are similar or in the same general category. A magazine article about poverty in the United States, for example, would have to define very carefully what it meant by poverty—what level of personal income, household assets, or other measure defined a person, family, or household as poor. A student essay about Pentecostalism for a religion class might develop the topic by explaining what characteristics separate Pentecostalism from related religious movements, such as fundamentalism or evangelicalism.

Dividing and classifying

Division means breaking a single item into its parts; **classification** means grouping many separate items according to their similarities. Dividing a topic involves beginning with one object or idea and discussing each of its components separately. An essay about the recruiting policies of the United States military, for instance, might be organized by dividing the military into its different branches—army, air force, and so on—and then discussing how each branch recruits volunteers. Classifying involves putting items or pieces of information into categories. If you have been reading histories of the eighteenth century in preparation for an essay on women's

FOR COLLABORATIVE WORK

Ask your students to read and comment on one another's drafts, looking first at organizational patterns in individual paragraphs and then throughout the entire paper. Ask them to write in the margin the type of paragraph organization. Toward the end of class, call on several students to read paragraphs that illustrate different forms of organization. Some paragraphs may defy classification because of the ingenuity of the writer or the rough condition of the draft.

roles in that time, and you have accumulated dozens of pages of notes in the process, you could begin to organize this mass of undigested information by classifying it: information related to women's education, women's occupations, women's legal status, and so on.

Comparing and contrasting

Comparison focuses on the similarities between two things while **contrast** highlights their differences, but the two are often used together. Asked to read two chapters in a philosophy text (one on Plato and the other on Aristotle), to analyze the information, and to write a brief response, you might well use an organizational framework based on comparison and contrast. You could then organize the response in one of two ways: by presenting all the information on Plato in one section and all on Aristotle in another *(block comparison)* or by alternating back and forth between Plato and Aristotle, looking at particular characteristics of each *(alternating comparison)*.

Analyzing causes and effects

Cause-effect analysis either examines why something happens or happened by looking at its causes, or looks at a set of conditions and explains what effects result or are likely to result from them. An environmental-impact study of the probable consequences of building a proposed dam, for instance, suggests moving from causes to effects. On the other hand, a newspaper article on the breakdown of authority in inner-city schools might well be organized by focusing on the effects of the breakdown and then tracing those effects back to their causes.

Considering problems and solutions

Moving from a **problem** to a **solution** presents a natural and straightforward way of organizing certain kinds of information. The student studying motorcycle parking, in fact, decided to structure the overall organization of his data in just this way: he identified a problem (the need for more parking) and then offered two possible solutions. Many assignments in engineering, business, and economics call for a similar organizational strategy. One economics professor asked students to gather information on the latest slide in the stock market and to use that information to give advice to investors who lost money. The information students gathered first defined the problem the investors faced and then formed the basis for potential solutions.

EXERCISE 3.4

Using the topic you chose in Exercise 3.1, identify the most effective means of organizing your information. Write a brief paragraph explaining why you chose this particular method (or methods) of organization.

EXERCISE 3.5

Identify which method or methods of organization you would recommend for students who are writing on the following topics—and why.

1. the need for a new undergraduate library
2. the autobiographical elements in Virginia Woolf's *To the Lighthouse*
3. why voting rates in U.S. elections are declining
4. education to prevent the spread of AIDS
5. the best places to study on campus

Writing out a plan

A writer who has carefully organized information is one who already has a plan for a draft, a plan that should then be written down. The student who wrote about the motorcycle parking shortage organized all his data and developed the following plan. Notice that his plan calls for several organizational strategies within an overall problem-solution framework:

INTRODUCTION

give background to problem (use *chronological order*)
give overview of problem (use *division*)
state purpose—to offer solutions

BODY

present proof of problem in detail (use *illustration*)
present two possible solutions (use *comparison*)

CONCLUSION

recommend against first solution because of cost and space
recommend second solution and summarize benefits of doing so

. . . *content determines form, yet content is discovered only in form.* —DENISE LEVERTOV

In any work that is truly creative, the writer cannot be omniscient in advance about the effects that he or she proposes to produce. The suspense . . . is not just in the reader, but in the writer, who is intensely curious about what will happen. —MARY McCARTHY

TEACHING PRACTICE

Even the most proficient pre-draft outliners need to know that outlines are not unalterable or absolute; they are merely guides. Outlines must conform to the paper—not the paper to the outline. Outlines, like the papers they help organize, must be revisable.

If you require an unchangeable, formal outline, your students may not be able to adhere to it. Instead, ask them to prepare a "writing plan," a backbone for the body of the paper. Then allow them to develop their papers as much by their drafting processes, which reveal form, as by their plan. Another possibility is to suggest that they write each idea on a notecard. They can then easily rearrange their ideas and experiment with various orders. They will also learn that some ideas are expendable.

Preparing a formal outline

While an informal plan worked well for this writer, you may wish to prepare a more formal outline. A formal outline is a double-edged sword. On the one hand, it allows you to see before drafting exactly how all the main parts of your essay will fit together—how your ideas relate, how abstract your ideas are, what the overall structure of your argument will be. On the other hand, a full formal outline can be devilishly hard to write before you've considered your material in some less formal way.

Most formal outlines follow a conventional format of numbered and lettered headings and subheadings using roman numerals, capital letters, arabic numbers, and lowercase letters to show the levels of importance of the various ideas and their relationships. Each new level is indented to show its subordination to the preceding level. For example:

Thesis statement
  I. First main topic
     A. First subordinate idea
        1. First supporting idea
        2. Second supporting idea
        3. Third supporting idea
     B. Second subordinate idea
        1. First supporting idea
        2. Second supporting idea

 II. Second main topic
     A. First subordinate idea
        1. First supporting idea
        2. Second supporting idea
     B. Second subordinate idea
        1. First supporting idea
        2. Second supporting idea
           a. First supporting detail
           b. Second supporting detail

Each level contains at least two parts, so there is no A without a B, no 1 without a 2. Comparable items are placed on the same level—all capital letters, for instance, or all arabic numbers. Each level develops the idea before it—1 and 2 under A, for example, include the points that develop, explain, or demonstrate A. Headings are stated in parallel form—either all sentences, or all topics that are grammatically parallel.

Formal outlining requires logical thought and careful evaluation of your ideas, which is precisely why it is a valuable effort. Charting out such an outline allows you to see the skeleton of an essay, making sure that all the "bones" are in the right and logical places, that all the relationships make sense. A full-sentence outline will make those relationships most clear, so if you want to give your organization the most rigorous test of its structure, try working it into a full-sentence outline. If the logical relationships seem fully established to you, a topic outline will provide the necessary test of coherence. Remember, however, that an outline is at best a means to an end, not an end in itself. New ideas will almost surely occur as you write, and you should not feel bound to the ideas on your outline. Though an outline serves, on one level, as a plan for your essay, it can also serve to stimulate altogether new thoughts and plans, ones you should feel free to consider and pursue. Many instructors require a formal outline, particularly with a research essay. An example of a formal outline that accompanied a student's final essay appears in 43d.

Whatever form your organizational plan takes, you may want or need to change it as you begin drafting. Writing has a way of stimulating thought, and the process of drafting may bring new ideas to pursue. Or you may find that you need to go back and reexamine some information or gather more information.

EXERCISE 3.6

Write out a plan for an essay supporting the working thesis you developed in Exercise 3.3.

3f

Producing a draft

Most of us are in some sense "producing a draft" the moment we begin thinking about a topic. One writer reports that his best ideas for opening essays almost always come to him in the shower, another that she "practices" writing versions of paragraphs or sentences in her head while driving to and from work. At some point, however, we sit down with pen, typewriter, or word processor to attempt an actual version of a draft.

1

Be flexible

No matter how good your planning, investigating, and organizing have been, chances are that you will want and need to do more of them as you draft. This fact of life leads to the first principle of successful drafting: be flexible. If you see that your organizational plan is not working, do not

Just get it down on paper, then we'll see what to do with it. —MAXWELL PERKINS

Get black on white! —GUY DE MAUPASSANT

I have rewritten—often several times—every word I have ever published. My pencils outlast their erasers. —VLADIMIR NABOKOV

BACKGROUND

Remind your class that first drafts are never perfect. One of the many scholars and researchers who believe that first drafts are rarely directed toward an audience, Linda Flower has listed the features of what she calls "writer-based prose." According to Flower, this stage of writing is

1. Typically narrative or chronological in structure
2. Usually filled with private terms that may not be meaningful to another reader
3. Sometimes elliptical
4. Filled with unclear referents and causal relations
5. Frequently loaded with self-referents such as "I believe," "I feel," "in my opinion"

Flower views writer-based prose as a natural stage in the composing process, one that allows for discovery and growth and that should not be criticized because it is not yet "reader-based."

Often, proficient writers can skip the stage of writer-based prose and move directly to reader-based prose. These writers seem to internalize their writer-based drafts, unlike many beginning writers.

hesitate to alter it. If some information now seems irrelevant, leave it out, even if you went to great lengths to obtain it. Throughout the drafting process, you may need to go back to points you have already been through. You may learn that you need to do more research, or that your whole thesis must be reshaped, or that your topic is too broad and should be narrowed. The writing process is primarily a learning process, and you will continue planning, investigating, and organizing throughout that process.

2

Knowing your best writing situation

Definite principles of drafting are hard to come by, because we actually know very little about how writers produce drafts. What we do know suggests that there may be almost as many ways to produce a successful draft as there are people to do it. Nevertheless, you can profit by learning as much as possible about what kind of situation is likely to help you produce your best writing. *Where* and *when* are you most comfortable and productive writing? *What conditions* do you prefer—complete quiet? music? Do you have any *rituals* that help—exercising beforehand? making a pot of coffee? Once you determine the atmosphere most conducive to your best writing, make every effort to do your drafting in that atmosphere.

 Some guidelines for drafting

- *Have all your information close at hand and arranged according to your organizational plan.* Stopping to search for a piece of information can break your concentration or distract you.

- *Try to write in stretches of at least twenty to thirty minutes.* Writing can provide its own momentum, and once you get going the task becomes easier.

- *Don't let small questions bog you down.* As you write, questions will come up that need to be answered. But unless they are major ones, just put a mark in the margin or make a tentative decision and move on.

- *Remember that a first draft need not be perfect.* In order to keep moving and get a draft done, you often must sacrifice some fine points of writing at this stage. Concentrate on getting all your ideas down on paper, and don't worry about anything else.

- *Stop writing at a place where you know exactly what will come next.* Doing this will help you get started easily when you return to the draft.

Here is Jennifer Gerkin's first draft.

Prejudice in My Life

''Your daughter is absolutely beautiful!'' the
woman gushed as she talked to my father. She was a
friend of his from work, and had heard much about my
sister Tracy and I, but had never met us before. I
could tell that she was one of those blunt, elderly
ladies, the type that pinches cheeks, because as soon as
she finished appraising my sister, she turned to me with
a <u>deductive</u> look in her eye. Her face said it all. Her
beady brown eyes traveled slowly from my head to my toe
as she sized me up and said rather condescendingly,
''Oh, and she must be the smart one.'' I looked down at
my toes as I rocked nervously back and forth. Then,
looking at my sister I realized for the first time that
she was very pretty, and I was, well, the smart one.

1

The incident, which occurred when I was six and
my sister was seven, has changed me in many ways.
Primarily, as a result of the harsh appraisal my
father's acquaintance gave me, I have always been very
concerned about my appearance. Conceivably, a concern
about my appearance can be beneficial, however, at times
it is a bit of an obsession. I have become overly
critical of my own appearance, but even more critical of
the appearance of those around me. I instantly judge a
person by the way he or she looks, a prejudice that
includes everyone, not just minorities.

2

Certainly, there are many men and women who are
obsessed with their appearance. Although my obsession
over my own appearance has relaxed dramatically over the
past few years, especially since I've been in college,
it is still a problem that affects my life in many ways.
I can remember exactly what I wore for every first day
of school since eighth grade, or on any other important

3

day of my life. Granted, this simply may mean that I have a good memory, but I can also remember what a majority of my friends wore on the first day of school, and describe each garment with amazing speed and accuracy, right down to the last accessory.

Similarly, I used to take two to two and a half hours to get ready for school, church, shopping, or simply to walk the dog. Fortunately, I have cut my ''primping time'' down and can now get ready in a thrifty half an hour.   4

My obsession with my appearance is something I can   5
overcome, or at least control, but as I mentioned before, my critical eyes are always turned towards others. The minute I see someone, I assess them by their appearance. For example, if I see a person who is dressed shabbily, I instantly assume they are poor and unintelligent. If I see someone with fancy clothes and nice jewelry, I usually assume that they are rich and snobbish. For a more concrete example, on one of the first few days of class, a young man walked into my English class with a bandanna on his head and blue lipstick on his lips. I immediately thought, ''What a weirdo!'' Later, after talking to this classmate, I found that he was a very interesting, intelligent member of society that I respect very much. I am ashamed that I judge people so hastily, and I try very hard to overcome my prejudice.

I include everyone in my hasty assessment of   6
people by their appearance. So in a way, I guess I am extremely prejudiced. The only difference between my assessment of whites and of ethnic minorities is that the latter includes a few stereotypes, as well as ''surface judgments.'' Hence, I have two hurdles to overcome; traditional stereotyping, and my own ''personal stereotyping.''

I have taken major steps to overcome my harsh
judgement of people. Several years ago, I would have
let the fact that a classmate had blue lipstick and a
bandanna on deprive me of meeting an interesting
individual. Now I never let my first judgement of
people be the one that counts; I find out how the person
really is inside. This has widened my horizons to
include many people that I may have never had the
pleasure to meet had I maintained my original judgement.

I feel that many people are preoccupied with
appearances. When we overcome this shallow perception
of our brothers and sisters, prejudice will vanish. I
am waiting anxiously for the important day when we will
no longer judge each other according to what is on the
outside, but for what is on the inside. And when this
day finally arrives, I promise to all mankind that I
will not remember what I was wearing.

EXERCISE 3.7

Write a draft of an essay from the plan you produced in Exercise 3.6.

3g

Reflecting on your writing process

Once you finish a draft, make a point of reflecting a bit on your writing
process and of noting your thoughts in your writing log if you are keeping
one (see 1a7). With the experience of writing still fresh in your mind, you
can note down what went well, what gave you problems and why, what you
would like to change or improve.

When Jennifer Gerkin reflected on her writing process, she discovered
that her brainstorming and clustering had been the most fruitful for
generating ideas and supporting examples, and that answering the questions
for explaining a topic hadn't added much. She recognized as well that she

felt very comfortable with her classmates and her professor (her audience), which made writing about something quite personal relatively easy. In addition, she saw that she'd worked extra hard to make her essay interesting, wanting to impress an audience she liked and respected so much. The main weaknesses, she decided, were in grammar, punctuation, organization, and diction. As for the strengths, Jennifer saw that by using her own personal experiences she made a serious topic quite approachable, even entertaining.

 Reflecting on your writing process

1. How did you arrive at your specific topic?
2. When did you first begin to think about the assignment?
3. What type of exploring or planning did you do?
4. How long did it take to complete your draft (including the time spent gathering information)?
5. Where did you write your draft? Briefly describe the setting.
6. How did awareness of your particular audience help to shape your draft?
7. What have you learned from your draft about your own rhetorical stance on your topic?
8. What do you see as the major strengths of your draft?
9. What do you see as the major weaknesses of your draft?
10. What would you like to change about your drafting process?

EXERCISE 3.8   Taking Inventory: Your Own Writing Process

Using the questions in 3g, reflect on the process you went through as you prepared for and wrote the draft of your essay in Exercise 3.7. Make your answers an entry in your writing log, if you are keeping one.

4

Revising and Editing

There's only one person a writer should pay attention to. . . . It's the reader. And that doesn't mean any compromise or sell-out. The writer must criticize his or her own work *as a reader*.   — WILLIAM STYRON

Learn to trust your own judgment, learn inner independence, learn to trust that you will sort the good from the bad. . . .   — DORIS LESSING

These two experienced writers know firsthand the power that self-criticism and self-confidence bring to the task of revising. If you have analyzed your own process of writing, you probably know whether you tend to revise extensively and when you tend to make any revisions. Perhaps you also know what kinds of revisions you typically make. And a careful look at any piece of writing you have submitted to an instructor will reveal how well you edited the paper. You may, however, have thought of revising and editing as one and the same thing; after all, both involve changes in a draft. The distinction between the processes of revising and editing, however, is one that will be useful as you become a more powerful and efficient writer.

Revising involves reenvisioning your draft—taking a fresh look at how clearly your thesis is stated and how persuasively it is developed, how logical your organization is, how varied your sentences are, how appropriate and memorable your choice of words is. In each case, you will be rethinking your aims and methods in terms of your original purpose and audience and of all you have learned during work on the piece of writing. Revising may call for changes both large and small. You may need to reshape sentences, rethink sections, gather more information to support a point, perhaps even do some further exploratory writing.

Editing, on the other hand, involves fine-tuning your prose, attending to details of grammar, usage, punctuation, and spelling. You might think of editing as the dress rehearsal for a written "performance" to make your writing ready for public presentation. This chapter will explore the processes

"I never have time to rewrite; I always wait until the night before."

"How can I improve my first draft when I don't know whether it's good?"

"I don't care about what I'm writing. I just want to get it over with."

"I'm such a bad writer that I hate to read my own writing."

"If I can't get it right the first time, I must be stupid."

Such typical attitudes toward revision support Erika Lindemann's claim that "for most students, *rewriting* is a dirty word." Students tend to view rewriting as an indication of failure, as punishment, or as simply a "filler" for classroom time. Because students have often been trained to outline carefully or to follow the format of a five-paragraph essay, revising means nothing more than making their words "prettier" or moving from handwriting to type or whiting-out misspelled words and mispunctuated sentences. In fact, many student writers are under the misapprehension that "real" writing is perfectly formed and flows onto the page at the touch of the Muse's hand. It is important for them to realize that almost all experienced writers revise their work repeatedly.

TEACHING PRACTICE

Since students often confuse revising (making changes in content) with editing (correcting mechanical errors), you may wish to clarify the difference between these two steps. To reinforce this important distinction:

1. Try to observe the distinction yourself.
2. Discuss revising and editing on separate days, as separate class topics.
3. Plan separate practice exercises for revising and editing.

of revising and editing and provide you with a systematic plan for making the best use of these processes in your own writing.

4a

Getting distance before revising

The ancient Roman poet Horace advised aspiring writers to get distance from their work by putting it away for nine years. If such advice seemed impractical to the Romans, it seems just about impossible to those writing in the late twentieth century. You have schedules to follow, deadlines to meet, examinations to take, graduation ceremonies to qualify for. Nevertheless, Horace's advice holds a germ of truth: the more time and distance you give yourself between the writing of a draft and its final revision, the more objectivity you will gain and the more options you will have as a writer. Even putting the draft away in a folder for a day or two will help clear your mind and give you some distance from your writing.

4b

Rereading your draft

After giving yourself—and your draft—a rest before revising, review the draft by rereading it carefully for meaning, by recalling your purpose, and by considering your audience.

1

Rereading for meaning

Effective writers are almost always effective readers, particularly of their own writing. You can best begin revising, then, by rereading your draft carefully. For this reading, don't worry about small details. Instead, concentrate on your meaning and how clearly you have expressed it. If you see places where meaning seems unclear, note them in the margin.

2

Remembering your purpose

After rereading, quickly note the main purpose of the piece of writing and decide whether it matches your original purpose. You may want to go back to your original assignment to see exactly what it asks you to do. If the

---

Everyday use

We revise and edit all the time, even in our conversations. Directions to a child on how to measure ingredients for cupcakes may have to be revised on the spot, for instance, if the child isn't understanding, or a story may be revised in the telling to get the sequence of events right. You may well remember a time when you consciously edited what you were saying in order to be tactful or considerate of another person's feelings. For example, a woman seeing a new baby for the first time was stuck for what to say to the proud parents—for the baby struck her as anything but cute. Revising and editing rapidly in her head, she stumbled on what she hoped was a tactful as well as an honest response. "What a baby!" she exclaimed. "What a baby!"

Set aside some portion of a day to listen carefully for revising and editing in conversations you hear or conduct yourself. Then analyze what kinds of revisions you heard and what was most interesting to you about them.

---

assignment asks you to "prove" something, make sure you have done so. If you intended to propose a solution to a problem, check to make sure you have indeed set forth a well-supported solution rather than, for instance, an analysis of the problem. (See 2b and 2c.)

3

Considering your audience

Gaining some distance from your draft should help you think clearly about how appropriate the essay is for your audience. Have you thought carefully about how your audience's experiences and expectations may be different from yours and taken such differences into consideration? (See 2e.) Is the language formal or informal enough for these readers? Will they be interested in and able to follow your discussion? Have you defined any terms readers may not know? What objections might they raise?

EXERCISE 4.1

Take twenty to thirty minutes to look critically at the draft you prepared in Exercise 3.7, rereading it carefully, checking how well the purpose is accomplished, and considering how appropriate the draft is for the audience. Then write a paragraph about how you would go about revising it.

USEFUL READING

Brannon, Lil, Melinda Knight, and Vera Neverow-Turk. *Writers Writing*. Upper Montclair, NJ: Boynton, 1983. Arguing that writing and revising should not be considered two separate stages in the writing process, the authors provide examples of successive drafts by both student writers and professional writers.

Faigley, Lester, and Stephen Witte. "Analyzing Revision." *CE* 32 (1981): 400–14. The authors distinguish between surface revision (usually at the phrase or word level) and text-based revision (at the structural level).

Flower, Linda. "Writer-Based Prose: A Cognitive Basis for Problems in Writing." *CE* 41 (1979): 19–37. Flower suggests that early drafts are frequently directed not to readers, but to the writer. A significant part of revision is the movement from writer-based to reader-based prose.

Murray, Donald. *Learning by Teaching*. Upper Montclair, NJ: Boynton, 1982. A collection of essays written by the former director of the freshman writing program at the University of New Hampshire. Of the several essays on revising, especially important is "Teaching the Motivating Force of Revision," in which Murray argues that revision, as a process of discovery, can actually become its own motivating force for students.

FOR COLLABORATIVE WORK

Having students respond to each other's work is probably the most common type of collaboration in composition classes. Peer-responding helps students (1) move beyond an exclusive focus on the teacher as audience; (2) learn to accept and use constructive criticism; (3) practice analyzing written texts, including their own; and (4) acquire the vocabulary of composition.

Nevertheless, many students are reluctant to share their writing with one another. They may regard the instructor as the only one qualified to give advice or criticism; hence, time spent with peers is time wasted. Some students are embarrassed to show what they fear is poor writing to peers who will judge them personally. Moreover, they lack experience in offering constructive criticism. To help your students overcome these obstacles, you may want to try some of the following cooperative writing activities:

1. At the beginning of the term, have groups of students read and comment on one another's writing. You may wish to suggest a number of your own questions as well as those in the text to help them respond to what they read.

2. Your students may need help in learning how to respond to another's work—how to temper aggressiveness with tact, how to balance *what* has been said with *how* it has been said, both in terms of the writer's text and the reader's comments. In this way they will learn how to respond to drafts and how to trust and help one another, both vital aspects of a productive composition course.

3. Using an anonymous, imperfect model draft, provide at least one or two practice sessions before the class undertakes its first peer-responding session. During these preliminary discussions, check their responses and help students who have trouble offering comments.

4c

Getting critical responses to your draft

In addition to your own critical appraisal, you may want to get responses from friends or classmates. Although you may trust them to do a thorough job for you, remember that they probably don't want to hurt your feelings by criticizing your writing. You can help by convincing them that constructive criticism is what you need, that trying to protect you by not mentioning problems does you no good.

But even honestly critical readers need to know where to focus their responses. In some cases, you may get exactly the advice you need by asking a quick, direct question: "What do you see as my thesis?" Be sure to pose questions that require more than yes/no answers. Ask readers to tell you in detail what they see, and then compare their reading to what you see. Merely asking "Is my thesis clear?" will not tell you nearly so much as "Would you paraphrase my thesis so I can see if it's clear?"

Following are some questions for evaluating a draft. They can be used to respond to someone else's draft or one of your own. When you ask someone else to evaluate your draft, be sure that person knows your assignment, intended audience, and major purposes.

 Reviewing a draft

1. *Assignment:* Does the draft carry out the assignment? What could the writer do to better fulfill the assignment?

2. *Title and introduction:* Does the title tell the reader what the draft is about? Does it catch the reader's interest? What does the opening accomplish? How does it catch the reader's attention? How else might the writer begin? (See 4f.)

3. *Thesis and purpose:* Paraphrase the thesis as a promise: "In this paper I will . . ." Does the draft fulfill that promise? Why, or why not? Does it fulfill the writer's major purposes? (See 4b and 4d.)

4. *Audience:* How does the draft capture the interest of and appeal to the intended audience? (See 4b.)

5. *Rhetorical stance:* Where does the writer stand on the issues involved in the topic? Is the writer an advocate or a critic?

6. *Supporting points:* List the main points, in order of presentation. Then number them in order of interest to you. Review them one by one. Do any need to be explained more fully or less fully? Should any be eliminated? Are any confusing or boring to you? Do any

make you want to know more? How well are the main points supported by evidence, examples, or details? (See 4d.)

7. *Organization:* What kind of overall organizational plan is used—spatial, chronological, or logical? Are the points presented in the most useful order? What, if anything, might be moved? Can you suggest ways to make connections between paragraphs clearer and easier to follow? (See 4e.)

8. *Paragraphs:* Which paragraphs are clearest and most interesting to read, and why? Which ones are well developed, and how are they developed? Which paragraphs need further development? What kinds of information seem to be missing? (See 4g.)

9. *Sentences:* Choose the three sentences you consider the most interesting or the best written—stylistically effective, entertaining, or memorable for some other reason. Then choose three sentences you see as weak—confusing, awkward, or simply uninspired. Are sentences varied in length, in structure, and in their openings? (See 4g.)

10. *Words:* Mark words that are particularly effective—those that draw vivid pictures or provoke strong responses. Then mark words that are weak, vague, or unclear. Do any words need to be defined? Are verbs active and vivid? Are any words potentially offensive, to the intended audience or anyone else? (See 4g.)

11. *Tone:* What dominant impression does the draft create—serious, humorous, satiric, persuasive, passionately committed, highly objective? Mark specific places where the writer's voice comes through most clearly. Is the tone appropriate to the topic and the audience? Is it consistent throughout? If not, is there a reason for varying it? (See 4g.)

12. *Conclusion:* Does the draft conclude in a memorable way, or does it seem to end abruptly or trail off into vagueness? If you like the conclusion, tell why. How else might it end? (See 4f.)

13. *Final thoughts:* What are the main strengths and weaknesses in the draft? What surprised you—and why? What was the single most important thing said?

4. To encourage group discussion, you may wish to share one of your preliminary drafts or examples of work in progress and have your students comment on it.

5. Remind your students that the goal of discussion is to improve, not merely approve, their writing.

6. Ask your students to keep a record of peer responses to their work. Do certain problems recur? As they become increasingly aware of their writing profiles, your students will develop self-critical faculties which they can apply to their own writing. What they can do today in group discussion with peers, they will be able to do individually and by themselves in the future.

FOR THE WRITING LOG

Have students write a journal entry (freewriting or listing) on their perceptions of the advantages and disadvantages of peer-response. Have them share their entries in small groups or put together a class list of the possibilities and potential problems. Knowing their concerns will allow you to explain the nature of peer-response more fully and thus alleviate many of their initial concerns. Then you can more easily model/introduce collaborative writing activities such as the ones listed above.

TEACHING PRACTICE

To make sure that your students are offering more than yes or no comments to the response questions, consider collecting and evaluating their responses. Reinforce specific responses that quote a word or phrase or that refer to a specific paragraph or line. Your interest will underscore the value of peer response.

Some responses to Jennifer Gerkin's draft

TISHA CLEVINGER'S RESPONSE

Assignment: You do what we were asked to do: "investigate the effect of prejudice on your life."

Introduction: I like it. . . . It's a dramatic scene that catches the reader's interest. Also, it manages to make the reader feel for the author. . . .

Having worked in groups, your students could have as many as four or five sets of responses to their writing. Lest they be overwhelmed by so many suggestions and questions, assure them that they need not heed all the advice, just weigh it. However, if several comments point in the same direction, the writer should take them seriously.

When students are faced with conflicting advice, they will naturally turn to you for the "right" answer. Because this is an impossible request, you will have to encourage them to reach their own decisions. Have them ask other students to respond to their particular problems. Ask about their original writing choices and about the potential effect of suggested changes. Using others' comments to make independent decisions should be a goal of every writer.

Ideally, peer-responding sessions will be so effective, profitable, and stimulating that your students will initiate sessions outside the classroom. Realistically, however, they will probably hesitate to ask others who have no peer-responding experience or training. Therefore, you may want to provide them with several questions or statements for introducing a session:

1. "Would you mind telling me what you think of this?"

2. "The point I want to make in this paper is _____."

3. "How well did I succeed?"

4. "What do you think of my support?"

5. "I had trouble with this part. Does it make sense to you? What can I do to improve it?"

At least once during the term, have each of your students initiate a responding session with someone other than a classmate. Ask them to report on their success.

I like beginning quotations because they get the reader involved in the paper immediately, if only to find out what will come next.

Thesis: "In this paper I will describe how this incident has caused me to be very critical of myself and those around me, solely on the basis of looks." The paper fulfills the thesis by showing specific examples to illustrate the point.

Audience: Well, we are your audience, along with Dr. Walters. You got my attention right away. . . . I didn't feel like you ever "talked down" to us.

Paragraphs: Paragraphs 1 and 5 are the most interesting because you tell the reader about your own experiences. Paragraphs 3 and 4 follow in a close second. Paragraphs 5 and 6 could possibly be combined. . . . They may be stronger as one.

Words: Words and phrases I find effective: *beady, harsh appraisal, thrifty,* and *horizons.* I have difficulty with *deductive.* Try to find some other words for *appearance.* You use it excessively.

Conclusion: Memorable. The righteous and heavy tone of the last paragraph is lightened by the humor of the final sentence. I agree with you about the importance of changing attitudes and I feel that you needed to say it, but I'm glad you ended the paper humorously.

CHRIS REEVES'S RESPONSE

Rhetorical stance: You take a very strong stand against prejudice, especially your own. It's clear that you are mostly criticizing yourself. Does this change a little at the end though?

Supporting points: (1) Original cause of obsession; (2) obsession over your own appearance; (3) obsession and judgment of others' appearances; (4) realization of ramifications of judging by appearance; (5) benefits. All of these points are necessary in the essay. Each point was interesting, but I'd like to see the part about your blue-lipsticked classmate developed more.

Organization: The essay as a whole is organized in a cause-effect analysis. You show what causes your obsession with appearance and its effect on you. This is a good way to organize. . . . The transitions are smooth.

Sentences: I liked sentence 3 because it is very descriptive; I could picture the lady standing there. The last sentence was interesting and made me remember the paper. Sentence 29 could be reworded so that it reads more smoothly.

Tone: Serious and highly objective. This tone is appropriate because prejudice is a serious topic, and it is important to be objective about oneself. The last sentence is humorous in tone. This tone shift shows that you are taking the topic seriously, but taking yourself lightly.

Conclusion: The last sentence is very memorable. You sound almost apologetic, which shows that you were able to recognize a fault in yourself, admit it, and take steps to overcome it. The essay could also end by saying something about the woman in paragraph 1.

SEAN FINNERTY'S RESPONSE

Introduction: . . . Another way you could have begun would have been to present your first encounter with the unnamed young man in the bandanna and then use a flashback to explain the cause of the prejudice you felt.

Thesis: One problem with the draft that hit me very early was the apparent lack of a thesis statement.

Paragraphs: To my reading, paragraph 1 is your clearest one and 3 and 4 were the most interesting to read. However, paragraph 3 begins very awkwardly. Perhaps you could save the statement about how you have "relaxed" your prejudice until paragraph 7, where it would fit in better. Paragraph 8 seems to belong more to your conclusion than to the body of your draft.

Words: I like the descriptive words you use in your first paragraph with the exception of *deductive.* . . . *Primarily* seems unnecessary in the second paragraph. And your draft becomes more believable without *dramatically* in paragraph 3; "relaxed some" sounds more genuine.

Final thoughts: The main strength of the paper is your ability to keep the reader's attention.

As these responses demonstrate, different readers may react in very different ways to the same piece of writing. They do not always agree on what is strong or weak, effective or ineffective; they may not even agree on what the thesis is. In addition, you may find that you simply do not agree with their advice. As the author, the authority on what you want to say, you must decide what advice to follow and how best to do so. In examining responses to your writing, you can often proceed efficiently by looking first for areas of agreement ("everyone was confused by this sentence—I'd better revise it") or strong disagreement ("one person said my conclusion was 'perfect' and someone else said it 'didn't conclude'—better look carefully at that paragraph again").

THE INSTRUCTOR'S RESPONSE

Jennifer Gerkin also got some advice from her instructor, Keith Walters, in the form of marginal comments on her draft. Here are excerpts from these comments:

> The incident, which occurred when I was six and   2
>
> my sister was seven, has changed me in many ways.
>
> Primarily, as a result of the harsh appraisal my
>
> father's acquaintance gave me, I have always been very
>
> concerned about my appearance. <u>Conceivably</u>, a concern ?

about my appearance can be beneficial, however, at times
it is a bit of an obsession. I have become overly
critical of my own appearance, but even more critical of
the appearance of those around me. I instantly judge a
person by the way he or she looks, a prejudice that
includes everyone, not just minorities. *Such judgments are not a prejudice, but*

for parallelism *a practice that may be a basis for prejudice.*

Similarly, I used to take two to two and a half
hours to get ready for school, church, shopping, or
simply to walk the dog. Fortunately, I have cut my *ing*
''primping time'' down and can now get ready in a
thrifty half an hour. *Why a 2-sentence paragraph?*

I feel that many people are preoccupied with
appearances. When we overcome this shallow perception
of our brothers and sisters, prejudice will vanish. I
eagerly?
am waiting anxiously for the important day when we will
by? no longer judge each other according to what is on the
outside, but for what is on the inside. And when this
day finally arrives, I promise to all mankind that I
will not remember what I was wearing. *Many writers now use humankind or people.*
a great ending!

In addition, he suggested that she reconsider how well her examples
work, and add more concrete detail to make it easier for readers to imagine
them. On the basis of the responses she received, she decided on the
following changes: (1) to state her thesis more explicitly; (2) to provide
concrete examples of her own biases; and (3) to reconsider her conclusion.

EXERCISE 4.2

Using the questions listed in 4c as a guide, analyze the draft you wrote in
Exercise 3.7.

USEFUL READING

Horwath, Brooke K. "The Components of Written Response: A Practical Synthesis of Current Views." *Rhetoric Review* 2 (1984): 136–56. Horvath attempts to summarize and synthesize current literature on responding to student writing by identifying seven types of "formative" response—response that treats the text as part of an ongoing process rather than as a finished product. His categories include responses that correct, that emote, that suggest, that question, that remind, and that assign. Horvath also provides an eighty-one-item annotated bibliography of books, articles, and ERIC documents that treat response to student writing.

Sommers, Nancy. "Revision Strategies of Student Writers and Experienced Adult Writers." *CCC* 31 (1980): 378–88. Rpt. in *The Writing Teacher's Sourcebook.* Ed. Gary Tate and Edward P. J. Corbett. New York: Oxford, 1988. Based on her case studies of freshman writers and experienced adult writers, Sommers concludes that during revision, inexperienced writers focus almost exclusively on rewording whereas experienced writers focus on finding the structure of their argument and on accommodating their anticipated readers. What inexperienced writers need, according to Sommers, is a sense of writing and revising as a process of discovery.

4d

Evaluating the thesis and its support

Once you have received advice on your draft from all sources available to you and have studied the responses, reread the draft once more, paying special attention to your thesis and its support. Check to make sure your thesis sentence contains a clear statement of the *topic* that you will discuss and a *comment* explaining what is particularly significant or noteworthy about the topic. As you continue to read, ask yourself how each paragraph relates to or supports the thesis and how each sentence develops the paragraph topic. Such careful rereading can help eliminate irrelevant sections or details or identify sections needing further details or examples.

Be particularly careful to note what kinds of evidence, examples, or good reasons you offer in support of your major points. If some points need more support, look back at your exploratory work and at suggestions from your readers. Jennifer Gerkin, for example, saw that one of her readers had asked for further development of paragraph 6, and thus added two examples. If necessary, take time to gather more information and to do further exploration (see 3a and 3c).

EXERCISE 4.3

After rereading the draft you wrote in Exercise 3.7, evaluate the revised working thesis you produced in Exercise 3.3, and then evaluate its support in the draft. Identify points that need further support, and list those things you must do to provide that support.

4e

Analyzing organization

One good way to check the organization of a draft is by outlining it. You may have written an outline *before* the draft, but drawing up an outline *after* it is finished allows you to evaluate the organizational plan as it actually exists in the draft. After numbering paragraphs in the draft, read through each one, jotting down its main idea or topic in a sentence or phrase. Then examine your list, and ask yourself the following questions:

- What organizational strategies are used? spatial? chronological? logical? Are they used effectively?

Ask your students to locate a story, an article, or a book they especially enjoyed. Either in class or as homework, have them analyze the organization of the piece by answering the following questions and citing examples:

1. Why do you suppose the author started here? Is there a flashback? a provocative question? a description?

2. Does the author "hook" you? If so, how?

3. At what point in the piece did you become interested and decide to go on?

4. How is the piece held together? Find appropriate transitional devices, repetition of key words, or repetitive sentence structures.

5. How does the author prepare you for the information in the middle and the end of the piece?

6. What would you like to ask the author?

7. Was the ending satisfying to you? predictable? surprising?

8. How does the author end the piece?

9. Look at the title. Does it seem appropriate to you now that you've finished the piece? Did it when you started? Can you improve upon it or provide an alternative?

A good title should be like a good metaphor: it should intrigue without being too baffling or too obvious.   —E. B. WHITE

A title is the writer's stamp of approval on her or his work.   —SUE V. LAPE

- Do the main points clearly relate to the thesis and to one another? Are any of them irrelevant?
- Can you identify any confusing leaps from point to point? Do you need to provide transitions?
- Can you identify clear links between paragraphs and ideas? Do any others need to be added?
- Have any important points been left out?

EXERCISE 4.4

Draw up a brief outline of Jennifer Gerkin's first draft (in 3f), and evaluate its organization. Begin by answering the questions given in 4e.

EXERCISE 4.5

Check the paragraph transitions in Jennifer Gerkin's first draft. Did you find any others that were weak or missing? If so, suggest at least two ways of strengthening or adding any.

Reconsidering the title, introduction, and conclusion

First and last impressions count. In fact, readers remember the first and last parts of a piece of writing better than anything else. For this reason, it is wise to pay careful attention to three important elements—the title, the introduction, and the conclusion.

1

The title

A good title gives readers information, draws them into the piece of writing, and even gives an indication of the writer's view of the topic. It is an important device for defining what the writer is seeking to do. Jennifer Gerkin's original title, "Prejudice in My Life," was accurate enough but not vivid or particularly intriguing. Following a discussion of this draft, she produced a new draft and chose as its title "The Smart One." This revision piques readers' curiosity and leads up to the startling statement that ends paragraph 1, though it does not really let readers know what the essay will be about.

2

The introduction

A good introduction accomplishes two important tasks: first, it draws readers into the piece of writing, and second, it presents the topic and makes some comment on it. It contains, in other words, a strong lead, or "hook," to attract readers' interest and often an explicit thesis as well. The most common kind of introduction opens with a general statement about the topic and then goes into more detail, leading up to a statement of the specific thesis at the end. A writer can also begin an introduction effectively with a vivid statement of the problem that led to the thesis or with an *intriguing quotation,* an *anecdote,* a *question,* or a *strong opinion.* The rest of the introduction then develops this beginning item into a more general or detailed presentation of the topic and the thesis. (See 6e for a fuller discussion and examples of various kinds of introductions.)

In many cases, especially when the writer begins with a quotation or anecdote, the introduction consists of two paragraphs, the first providing the "hook" and the second an explanation of its significance. Jennifer Gerkin followed this pattern in her introduction, whose first paragraph contains a very strong "hook," an anecdote from her childhood that immediately appeals to readers. The second paragraph then explains how this experience at a young age led to the obsession with appearance that is her topic. Although she considered the suggestion of one of her respondents that she shift the order of paragraphs and open with paragraph 2, in order to make the topic clear immediately, she decided that the dramatic opening paragraph made the introduction more effective as it was.

3

The conclusion

Like introductions, conclusions present special challenges to a writer. If a good introduction captures readers' attention, sets the topic, and signals what is to come, a good conclusion leaves readers satisfied that a full discussion has taken place. Often a conclusion will begin with a restatement of the thesis and then end with more general statements that grow out of it; this pattern reverses the common general-to-specific pattern of the introduction. Writers can also draw on a number of other ways to conclude effectively, including a *provocative question,* a *quotation,* a *vivid image,* a *call for action,* or a *warning.* (See 6e for a fuller discussion and examples of various kinds of conclusions.)

Jennifer Gerkin's concluding paragraph clearly restates her thesis, and the final sentence packs just the punch she wanted. But the first three sentences are all general, and two of her respondents described them as "too idealistic" and "righteous and heavy." She decided therefore to qualify her statements in the second sentence and thus make the conclusion more realistic:

> When we overcome this shallow perception of our brothers and sisters, prejudice ~~will vanish.~~ *may not disappear, but will certainly diminish.*

EXERCISE 4.6

Review Jennifer Gerkin's draft in 3f, and compose an alternative conclusion, perhaps by taking the advice of one of her respondents to "end by saying something about the woman in paragraph 1." Then write a paragraph commenting on the strengths and weaknesses of the conclusion she actually used.

4g

Examining paragraphs, sentences, words, and tone

In addition to the large-scale task of examining the logic, organization, and development of their writing, effective writers look closely at the smaller elements: paragraphs, sentences, and words. Many writers, in fact, look forward to this part of revising because its results can often be very dramatic. Turning a bland, forgettable sentence into a memorable one—or finding just exactly the right word to express a thought—can yield great satisfaction and confidence.

1

Examining paragraphs

Paragraphing serves the reader by visually breaking up long expanses of writing and by signaling a shift in focus. Readers expect a paragraph to develop an idea or topic, a process that almost always demands several sentences or more (see 6a). The following guidelines can help you evaluate your paragraphs as you revise:

USEFUL READING

Williams, Joseph M. *Style: Ten Lessons in Clarity and Grace.* 3rd ed. Glenview, IL: Scott, 1989. A practical guide for revising, with special attention given to the sentence. Individual chapters deal with such problems as overuse of nominalization and passive voice, prose sprawl, and lack of coherence and emphasis.

1. Look for the topic or main point of each paragraph, whether it is stated or merely implied. Then check to see that every sentence expands or supports the topic.

2. Check to see how each paragraph is organized—spatially, chronologically, or by some logical relationship such as cause-effect or comparison-contrast. Then determine whether the organization is appropriate to the topic of the paragraph and if it is used fully to develop the paragraph. (See 6c and 6d.)

3. Count the number of sentences in each paragraph, noting paragraphs that have only a few. Do these paragraphs sufficiently develop the topic of the paragraph?

See also the guidelines for checking paragraphs at the end of Chapter 6.

In paragraph 4 of her draft, Jennifer Gerkin counted only two sentences, which actually illustrated a point made in paragraph 3. She decided, therefore, to combine the two paragraphs and to elaborate on sentence 1 in the original paragraph 4.

> Similarly, I used to take two to two and a half
>
> hours to get ready for school, church, shopping, or
>
> simply to walk the dog. Fortunately, I have cut my
>
> ''primping time'' down and can now get ready in a
>
> thrifty half an hour. For example, I might try on five different outfits (and five different shades of lipstick), none of which would satisfy my demanding eyes.

EXERCISE 4.7

Choose two other paragraphs in Jennifer Gerkin's draft in 3f, and evaluate them using the guidelines listed above. Write a brief paragraph in which you suggest ways to improve the development or organization of these paragraphs.

2

Examining sentences

Good sentences operate like a well-practiced marching band, each one moving forward in an orderly and impressive way that keeps readers engaged and ready for more. As with life, variety is the spice of sentences. You can add variety to the life of your sentences by looking closely at their length, structure, and opening patterns. (See the guidelines for checking sentences at the end of Chapter 7.)

Varying sentence length

Too many short sentences, especially one after another, can sound like a series of blasts on a car horn—or like an elementary school textbook—while a steady stream of long sentences may tire or confuse readers. Most writers aim for some variety of length, then, breaking up a series of fairly long sentences with a very brief one, for example.

In looking at her second paragraph, Jennifer Gerkin found that all of its five sentences were almost exactly the same length: nineteen, twenty-two, nineteen, twenty, and twenty-two words. In revising, she decided to shorten the second sentence to make the comparison more dramatic and to extend the last sentence to thirty-six words:

> The incident, which occurred when I was six and my sister was seven, has changed me in many ways. One Primarily, as a result of ~~the~~ harsh appraisal that has been ~~my~~ an extreme concern for ~~father's acquaintance gave me, I have always been very concerned about~~ my appearance. Conceivably, a concern about my appearance can be beneficial; however, at times it is a bit of an obsession. I have become overly critical of my own appearance, but even more critical of the appearance of those around me. I instantly judge a practice that is the basis for prejudice and one that person by the way he or she looks, ~~a prejudice that~~ limits my appreciation of myself as well as of others. ~~includes everyone, not just minorities.~~

Varying sentence structure

The simple sentence is the most common kind of sentence in modern English, but using all simple sentences can sound very dull. On the other hand, constant use of compound sentences may result in a singsong or repetitive rhythm, while long strings of complex sentences may sound, well, overly complex. The best rule is to strive to vary your sentences; see 22c.

Varying sentence openings

If anyone has ever noted that your writing seemed "choppy," the cause of the problem probably lay in unvaried sentence openings. Most sentences in English follow subject-predicate order and hence open with the subject of an independent clause, as does the sentence you are now reading. But opening too many sentences in a row this way results in a jerky, abrupt, or "choppy" rhythm. You can vary sentence openings by beginning with a dependent clause, a phrase, an adverb, a conjunctive adverb, or a co-ordinating conjunction. (See 22b for more information on ways of opening sentences.)

Jennifer Gerkin's opening paragraph provides vivid description and imaginative use of dialogue, but it can be improved by varying sentence openings. Note how revising some of the openings improves the flow and makes the entire paragraph easier to read and more memorable:

''Your daughter is absolutely beautiful!'' the

woman gushed as she talked to my father. ~~She was~~ a
                           she

friend of his from work, ~~and~~ had heard much about my

sister Tracy and I, but had never met us before. I

could tell that she was one of those blunt, elderly

ladies, the type that pinches cheeks, because as soon as

she finished appraising my sister she turned to me with

a deductive look in her eye. Her face said it all. ~~Her~~
                     traveling

beady brown eyes ~~traveled~~ slowly from my head to my toe

~~as~~ she sized me up and said rather condescendingly,

''Oh, and she must be the smart one.'' I looked down at

my toes as I rocked nervously back and forth. Then,

looking at my sister I realized for the first time that

she was very pretty, and I was, well, the smart one.

Checking for sentences opening with *it* and *there*

As you go over the sentences of your draft, look especially carefully at the ones beginning with *it* or *there* followed by a form of *be.* Sometimes such a construction can be used to create a special emphasis, as in "It was a dark and stormy night . . ." But such structures can easily be overused or misused. You don't know what *it* means, for instance, unless the writer has already pointed out exactly what *it* stands for (see 13c). A more subtle problem with these openings, however, is that they may be used to avoid taking responsibility for a statement. Look at the following two sentences:

> It is necessary to raise student fees.
>
> The university must raise student fees.

The first sentence avoids responsibility by beginning with the weak *It is*—and fails to tell us *who says* it is necessary.

Many writers use *it is, there is,* and similar openings not to avoid responsibility but just because they are easy ways of getting a sentence going. But they are often unnecessary, and using them gives the important opening spot of a sentence to a vague, weak word (*it* or *there*) and the most overused verb in the English language (*be*). Usually a sentence will be much stronger if it is rewritten to begin another way. For example, *It is known that radon causes cancer* can be rewritten as *Radon is known to cause cancer.*

OPTIONAL EXERCISE

After your students have written two versions of each of the "there are" and "it is" sentences in Exercise 4.8, ask them to see how many variations they can achieve as a class. Have your class examine these sentences according to the questions on diction in 4g3.

EXERCISE 4.8

Here are two sentences from Jennifer Gerkin's draft that feature either *it is* or *there are.* Find at least two ways to rewrite each one to eliminate these constructions.

1. Certainly, there are many men and women who are obsessed with their appearance.
2. Conceivably, a concern about my appearance can be beneficial; however, at times it is a bit of an obsession.

EXERCISE 4.9

Find a paragraph of your own writing that lacks variety of sentence length, sentence structure, or sentence openings. Then write a revised version of your paragraph.

3

Examining words

Even more than paragraphs and sentences, word choice, or diction, offers writers an opportunity to put their personal stamp on a piece of writing. As a result, writers often study their diction very carefully, making sure they get the most mileage out of each word. Because word choice is highly individual, general guidelines are hard to define. Nevertheless, the following questions should help you become aware of the kinds of words you most typically use.

1. Are the nouns primarily abstract and general or concrete and specific? Too many abstract and general nouns can create boring prose. To say that you bought a new car is much less memorable or interesting than to say you bought a new convertible or a new Nissan. (See Chapter 27.)

2. Are there too many nouns in relation to the number of verbs? The *effect* of the *overuse* of *nouns* in *writing* is the *placing* of too much *strain* on the inadequate *number* of *verbs* and the resultant *prevention* of *movement* of the *thought.* In the preceding sentence, one tiny form of the verb *be* (*is*) has to drag along the entire weight of all those nouns. The result is a heavy, boring sentence. Why not say instead, *Overusing nouns places a big strain on the verbs and consequently slows down the prose?*

3. How many verbs are forms of *be*? If *be* verbs account for more than about a third of your total verbs, you are probably overusing them. (See Chapter 9.)

4. Are verbs *active* whenever possible? Passive verbs are harder to read and remember than active ones. Although the passive voice has many uses (see Chapter 9), often your writing will be stronger, more lively and energetic, if you use active verbs.

Jennifer Gerkin made a number of changes in diction on the basis of her classmates' responses, her instructor's comments, and her own critical analysis. In the first paragraph, for example, her use of the word *deductive* drew a puzzled response from several people. After checking the dictionary, she decided she had chosen the wrong word and substituted *judgmental.* In addition, she replaced overly general words in several places, changing *looked* to *stared* in paragraph 1 and *fancy* to *stylish* and *nice* to *expensive* in paragraph 5. Finally, in the last sentence, she took her instructor's suggestion and substituted *humankind* for *mankind,* which many people object to as sexist.

4

Examining tone

Word choice is closely related to tone, the attitude toward the topic and the audience that the writer's language conveys. In examining the tone of your draft, you need to consider the nature of the topic, your own attitude toward it, and that of your intended audience. Check for connotations of words as well as for slang, jargon, emotional language, and the level of formality to see whether they create the tone you want to achieve (humorous, serious, impassioned, and so on) and whether that tone is an appropriate one given your audience and topic. You may even discover from

TEACHING PRACTICE

Joseph Williams in *Style* points out that avoiding passives and agentless constructions will usually make one's style "more vigorous and direct" (22). He gives these examples for comparison:

Patient movement to less restrictive methods of care may be followed by increased probability of recovery.

If we treat patients less restrictively, they may recover faster.

However, as Williams points out, "often we don't say who is responsible for an action, because we don't know or don't care, or because we'd just rather not say:

Between July 2 and July 9, over five thousand brochures *were printed.*

If a person *is found* guilty of negligence, he or she *can be sued.*

Valuable records *should always be kept* in a fireproof safe. (24)

After giving students these examples, have them select one page of a current draft and highlight every passive construction they can locate. They can work individually, in pairs, or in small groups to determine if each instance of the passive is justified or not.

your tone that your own attitude toward the topic, your rhetorical stance, is different from what you originally thought. (See Chapter 27.)

Since Jennifer Gerkin's respondents and instructor praised her draft highly for its combination of humor, seriousness, and objectivity, she felt that her general tone needed no major changes. As mentioned earlier, however, she did revise her conclusion somewhat to "tone down" its excessive idealism and "righteous and heavy" quality.

EXERCISE 4.10

Turn to 3f, and read Jennifer Gerkin's paragraphs 3, 4, and 5. Describe the tone you think she achieves. Does the tone seem appropriate to the audience she was writing to—classmates in a first-year college writing course—and to the topic she chose? Assume that these paragraphs are intended instead for a group of third-graders. What would you do to alter the tone for this audience?

4h

Editing

Because readers expect, even demand, a final copy that is clean and correct in every way, and because you want to put your very best foot forward in any formal writing you do, you need to make time for thorough and careful editing. You can make editing somewhat systematic by keeping a personal checklist of editing problems. All writers have personal trouble spots, problems that come up again and again in their writing. You may already be aware of some of your own trouble spots and will probably have others pointed out to you by instructors. Paying attention to the *patterns* of editing problems you find in your writing can help you overcome errors.

An editing inventory

After identifying any typical trouble spots in your writing and getting advice on editing from this handbook, organize the information you have gathered in a systematic way. To begin, list all the errors or corrections marked on the last piece of writing you did. Then note the context of the sentence in which each error appeared. Finally, try to derive a guideline to spot future errors of the same kind. You can broaden these guidelines as you begin to find patterns of errors, and you can then add to your inventory every time you write and edit a draft. Here is an example of such a checklist.

MARKED ERRORS	IN CONTEXT	LOOK FOR
wrong preposition	*to* for *on*	*to*
spelling	*to* for *too*	*to* before adjectives, adverbs
fragment	starts with *when*	sentences beginning with *when*
spelling	*a lot*	*alot*
missing comma	after *however*	sentences opening with *however*
missing apostrophe	*Michael's*	all names
missing apostrophe	*company's*	all possessive nouns
tense shift	*go* for *went*	use of present tense
spelling	*sacrifice*	*sacrafice*
comma	after *for example*	*for example*

This writer has begun to isolate patterns, like her tendency to write sentence fragments beginning with subordinating conjunctions (*when* and *while*) and to leave out apostrophes in possessives (*company's* and *Michael's*) and commas after introductory elements.

Some errors, such as the use of wrong words or misspellings, may seem so unsystematic that you may not be able to identify patterns in them. (If spelling presents a special problem for you, keeping a separate spelling checklist as explained in Chapter 24 can help, or you may want to get a program that checks spelling as part of a word processor package.) But keeping an editing checklist will gradually allow you to identify most of the characteristic problems that trouble you. And because keeping up your checklist takes only a few minutes for each piece of writing, doing so is well worth the time.

EXERCISE 4.11

Using several essays you have written, establish your own editing checklist based on the one shown in 4h.

4i

Proofreading the final draft

As a writer, you need to make your final draft *errorless*. You can do so by taking time for one last, careful proofreading, which means reading to correct any typographical errors or other slips, such as inconsistencies in spelling and punctuation. To proofread most effectively, read through the copy *aloud,* making sure that punctuation marks are used correctly and consistently, that all sentences are complete, and that no words are left out. Then go through again, this time reading *backwards* so that you can focus on each individual word and its spelling. This final proofreading aims to make your written product letter-perfect, something you can be proud of.

You have already seen and read about a number of the revisions Jennifer Gerkin made in her first draft. Following is the edited and proofread version she turned in to her instructor. If you compare her final draft with her first draft, you will notice a number of additional revisions and changes made in editing and proofreading. For example, she corrected *I* to *me* in sentence 2, made the spelling of *judgment* consistent, made several pronouns singular to agree with their antecedents in paragraph 4, and deleted unnecessary commas. What other improvements and corrections can you spot?

                    The Smart One
    ''Your daughter is absolutely beautiful!'' the   1
woman gushed to my father. A friend of his from work,
she had heard much about my sister Tracy and me but had
never met us before. I could tell that she was one of
those blunt elderly ladies, the type that pinches
cheeks, because as soon as she finished appraising my
sister, she turned to me with a judgmental look in her
eye. Her face said it all. Beady brown eyes traveling
slowly from my head to my toes, she sized me up and said
rather condescendingly, ''Oh, and she must be the smart
one.'' I stared down at my toes as I rocked nervously
back and forth. Then, looking at my sister, I realized
for the first time that she was very pretty and I was,
well, the smart one.

        This incident, which occurred when I was six and my   2
sister was seven, has affected me in many ways. One
result of that harsh appraisal has been an extreme
concern for my appearance. Although some concern about
how one looks can be beneficial, at times it has become
a bit of an obsession with me. I have become not only

overly critical of my own appearance but even more
critical of the appearance of those around me. I
instantly judge a person by the way he or she looks, a
practice that is the basis of most kinds of prejudice
and one that limits my appreciation of myself and of
others.

    Although many men and women are preoccupied with
their appearance, my particular obsession has affected
my life to an extent that now seems incredible to me. I
can remember exactly what I have worn on the first day
of school every year since eighth grade and on every
other important day of my life. Often, I attempt to
attribute these amazing recollections to the fact that I
have a good memory. However, additional evidence
confirms that an obsession with appearance better
accounts for my behavior. I can also recall what a
majority of my friends wore on the first day of school
and describe each garment with amazing speed and
accuracy right down to the last accessory, whereas I
remember almost nothing about the day's events.
Similarly, I used to take more than two hours to get
ready for school, church, shopping, or even walking the
dog. I would, for example, frantically try on five
different outfits and five different shades of lipstick,
none of which would satisfy my demanding eyes.
Fortunately, since coming to college I have cut down my
''primping time'' and can now get ready in a thrifty
half hour.

    My obsession with my own appearance is something I
have managed to overcome or at least control, but it
affects my relationships as well: my critical eyes are
always turned towards others. The minute I see someone,
I assess him or her on the basis of appearance. For
example, if I see a person who is dressed shabbily, I

instantly assume that she is poor and unintelligent. If
I see someone with stylish clothes and expensive
jewelry, I usually assume that he is rich and snobbish.
More specifically, on one of the first few days of this
quarter, a young man walked into my English class
wearing a bandanna on his head and blue lipstick. I
immediately thought, ''What a weirdo!'' Later, after
talking to this classmate, I have come to realize that
he is a very interesting, intelligent person whom I
respect very much.

I include everyone in my hasty assessment of people
by their appearance. The only difference between my
assessment of my fellow whites and that of ethnic
minorities is that my assessment of minorities includes
a few traditional stereotypes, as well as ''surface
judgments'' based on appearances. For example, when I
see a woman wearing the traditional Muslim veil, I
instantly assume she is meek and subservient to men;
when I see an Amish family in a black horse-drawn buggy,
I assume that their lives are dull and emotionally
repressed. Hence, I have two hurdles to overcome:
traditional stereotyping and my own ''personal
stereotyping.''

I am ashamed that I judge people so hastily, and I
try very hard to overcome my prejudice because I realize
it limits me. Several years ago, I would have let the
fact that a classmate wore blue lipstick and a bandanna
deprive me of meeting an interesting individual. Now, I
try never to let my first judgment of people be the one
that counts; I make the effort to find out how the
person really is inside. I have widened my horizons to
include many delightful people whom I might have never
had the pleasure to meet had I maintained my original
judgment.

I know, however, that many people in our society 7
remain preoccupied with appearances. When this shallow
perception of our brothers and sisters is overcome,
prejudice may not disappear, but it will certainly
diminish. Eagerly, I await the important day when we no
longer judge each other according to what is on the
outside but pay attention instead to what is on the
inside. And when this day finally arrives, I promise
all humankind that I will not remember what I--or anyone
else--was wearing.

EXERCISE 4.12 Reading with an Eye for Revision

Using the guidelines in 4c, read the draft you wrote in Exercise 3.7 with an eye for revising. Try to do this at least a day after the time you finished the draft. List the things you need or want to address in your revision. At this point, you may want to exchange drafts with some classmates and share responses.

EXERCISE 4.13

Revise, edit, and proofread the draft you wrote in Exercise 3.7.

EXERCISE 4.14 Taking Inventory: Your Own Revising Process

1. How did you begin revising?
2. What kinds of comments on or responses to your draft did you have? How helpful were they and why?
3. How long did revising take? How many drafts did you produce?
4. Were the revisions that you tended to make mostly additions? deletions? replacements of one word, example, and so on, by another? transfers of material from one place to another?
5. What kinds of changes did you tend to make—in organization, paragraphs, sentence structure, wording, adding or deleting information?
6. What gave you the most trouble as you were revising?
7. What pleased you most? What would you most like to change about your process of revising, and how do you plan to go about doing so?

FOR COLLABORATIVE WORK

Even writing that has reached "final draft" stage can be revised, and often very effectively. Have students choose two paragraphs from Jennifer Gerkin's final draft on pp. 64–67 and, working with two or three other students, plan and carry out a further revision. They should begin by reading the paragraphs aloud once or twice and jotting down items in three columns: a "plus" column for words, phrases, or ideas they especially like; a "minus" column for words, phrases, or ideas they *don't* like, and a "question" column for words, phrases, or ideas that seem unclear or somehow questionable. Then they can compare notes all around and, together, draft a revision. Finally, have them compare their revisions with the original paragraphs and report to the class, explaining the changes and describing what they have done to improve the paragraphs.

OPTIONAL EXERCISE

Revising styles vary considerably, depending on the purpose of the writing or on the field the writing is in. Ask students to choose someone in a field they are interested in (a professor in a major they might elect, for example) and set up an interview with that person. Using the revising and editing guidelines in this chapter, ask them to draw up a list of questions they'd like to ask the resource person about revising and editing in his or her field. (See Chapter 40 for tips on how to conduct interviews.) Finally, based on the notes they take during the interview, ask them to compare the resource person's revising style to their own.

5

Recognizing and Using Argument

BACKGROUND

Aristotle, in his *Politics,* defined humans as "political animals," imbued with ethical and emotional concerns, but basically rational. The classical period in Greece was long thought of as being characterized by stable values, social cohesion, and a unified cultural ideal, and thus for many years our conception of classical rhetoric held that it was primarily concerned with reasonable appeals made within a rational culture.

More recent scholarship has shown that the classical period was not nearly as complacent and rational a world as earlier scholars thought, and that our view of classical rhetoric was only a partial one. Following some of the ideas of that group of early Greek thinkers known as the sophists, many contemporary rhetoricians view humankind as "symbol-using animals" who live in a fragmented world mediated by and through language. In *A Rhetoric of Motives* (Berkeley and Los Angeles: U of California P, 1969), philosopher and critic Kenneth Burke refers to that society when he writes that "rhetoric is concerned with Babel after the Fall" (23) and goes on to substantiate the modern goal of rhetoric as "communication," differing from the traditional goal of combative or coercive "persuasion": "Wherever there is persuasion, there is rhetoric. And wherever there is 'meaning,' there is 'persuasion' " (127).

Some 2,400 years ago, Aristotle noted that we need to understand the art of language use (which he called rhetoric) in order to create meaning, to express meaning clearly, and to defend ourselves against others who would use language to manipulate us. These needs are no less pressing as we approach the twenty-first century than they were for Aristotle and the Greeks in the fourth century B.C. In fact, written language surrounds us more than ever before, and this language—in advertisements, news stories, memos, and reports—not only competes for our attention but argues for our agreement.

Even supposedly abstract and seemingly "factual" subjects like mathematics depend to a large extent on successful **argument**: language whose purpose is to persuade. As two professors point out in a recent book, the common idea that mathematics represents some unchanging and absolute truth is in fact a myth. "Mathematics in real life is a form of social interaction," the authors note, in which "proving" anything involves a mixture "of calculations and casual comments, of convincing argument and appeals to the imagination."* As in mathematics, issues in medical and other scientific research often are resolved more through argumentation and interpretation of data than through reference to just "the facts."

Since argument so pervades our lives, we need to understand and be able to recognize and use it effectively. Fortunately, Aristotle also provided us with the essential elements of using argument when he said the writer must do two basic things: (1) make a claim, and (2) prove it. These two things are easier said than done, of course. In this chapter, you will practice the "survival arts" of recognizing, understanding, and using written arguments.

---

*Philip J. Davis and Reuben Hersh, *Descartes' Dream: The World According to Mathematics* (Boston: Houghton, 1988).

5a

Recognizing argument

In a way, all language use has an argumentative "edge." Even when you greet someone warmly, you wish to convince the person that you are genuinely glad to see him or her, that you value his or her presence. In this sense we are immersed in argument the way we are immersed in air. Advertisements argue that we should buy certain products; clothing argues that we should admire or respect the people inside; our friends argue— through their actions, their language, even their personal style—that we should accept and value them.

Even apparently objective news reporting has strong argumentative overtones. By putting a particular story on the front page, for example, a paper "argues" that this subject is more important than others; or by using emotional language and focusing on certain details in reporting an event, a newscaster tries to persuade us to view the event in a particular way. What one reporter might call *a massive demonstration,* for example, another might call *a noisy protest,* and yet another, *an angry march.* We could find this argumentative "edge," therefore, wherever we find meaning in language.

As we saw in the last three chapters, for example, Jennifer Gerkin's primary purpose in her essay "The Smart One" is to explain the roots of her own prejudice. Yet her essay clearly has an argumentative edge: to persuade readers to guard against their own biases. In this essay, therefore, explanation plays the major role and argument a secondary role. This chapter, in contrast, will look at writing whose *primary purpose* is argument, and specifically at ways to provide convincing support for a claim.

Everyday use

Perhaps the most pervasive form of argument we face in our everyday lives is advertising. From the cereal box at breakfast to the posters on the bus to a few minutes of television before bed, advertisements call out to us to buy some product, vote for some candidate, behave in some particular way. To get a sense of how much advertising comes into your everyday life, keep a notebook or piece of paper with you for one whole day and simply put down a mark every time you see or hear an advertisement. Count up your total at the end of the day and compare your count with those of others in your class. Where did you encounter advertising most often? Which of the advertisements were particularly powerful, and why?

BACKGROUND

In *Modern Dogma and the Rhetoric of Assent* (Chicago: U of Chicago P, 1974), Wayne Booth posits that good rhetoric is

> the art of discovering good reasons, finding what really warrants assent because any reasonable person ought to be persuaded by what has been said. (xiv)

Although good reasons *ought* to guarantee assent, sometimes they do not, for each person finds a reason to believe or not. Sometimes, the reason is not a rational one. However, in *Classical Rhetoric for the Modern Student,* Edward P. J. Corbett echoes Aristotle, reminding us that

> Rationality is humanity's essential characteristic. It is what makes people human and differentiates them from other animals. Ideally, reason should dominate all of people's thinking and actions, but actually, they are often influenced by passions and prejudices and customs. To say that people often respond to irrational motives is not to say that they never listen to the voice of reason. We must have faith not only that people are capable of ordering their lives by the dictates of reason but that most of the time they are disposed to do so. (37)

USEFUL READING

Corbett, Edward P. J. *Classical Rhetoric for the Modern Student.* 3rd ed. New York: Oxford UP, 1990. This text provides a thorough, cogent, and readable exposition of Aristotelian rhetoric and a brief history of rhetoric.

1

Knowing when argument is appropriate

Of course, argument is not always necessary. If everyone can agree on the truth of a statement, no argument is needed. For instance, saying that personal ownership of computers in North America has increased in the last twenty years makes a factual statement that should not produce an argument. On the other hand, saying that computers pose dangers to mental health presents an arguable assertion that must be convincingly supported before readers will accept it.

In many important areas of our lives, widespread agreement seldom exists. Is nuclear power generation necessary? Should we take one job or another, live in one location or another, marry one person or another, or marry at all? Should our town increase taxes for schools? Should we risk job security by protesting a policy we feel to be unethical? Is a new building an architectural masterpiece or an eyesore? Is the use of pesticides threatening the lives of farm workers? Such arguable questions are often at the center of our lives, and in most instances they fall into that area where absolute knowledge or truth is simply unavailable.

To acknowledge that we can seldom find *absolute* answers to moral, political, and artistic questions, however, is not to say that we cannot move toward agreement on such questions by thinking clearly about them. In fact, this is precisely the way we gain most human knowledge: by arguing through and, sometimes, coming to agreement on crucial issues.

In much of your work in college, you will be asked to participate in this process by taking a position and arguing for that position—whether to analyze a trend or explain a historical event or prove a mathematical equation. Such work will usually require you to make an arguable statement, to make a claim based on the statement, and finally to present *good reasons* in support of the claim.

2

Checking whether a statement can be argued

The first step in the process of argument is to make a statement about a topic and then to check that the statement can, in fact, be argued. An arguable statement should have three characteristics:

- It should attempt to convince readers of something, change their minds about something, or urge them to do something.
- It should address a problem for which no easily acceptable solution exists or ask a question to which no absolute answer exists.
- It should present a position that readers could disagree with realistically.

USEFUL READING

Corbett, Edward P. J. *The Elements of Reasoning.* New York: Macmillan, 1991. A short, practical summary of common strategies of argumentation—definition, cause and effect, evaluation, proposal—based on classical rhetoric. Includes chapters on the appropriate arena of argument, on forms of argument, and on logical fallacies.

Lamb, Catherine. "Beyond Argument in Feminist Composition." *CCC* 42 (1991): 11–24. Lamb describes teaching a feminist approach to argument, one that emphasizes the use of negotiation and/or mediation in order to resolve a disagreement in a mutually satisfying way.

EXERCISE 5.1

Using the three guidelines in 5a2, decide which of the following statements are arguable and which are not.

1. *Raging Bull* was the best movie of the 1980s.
2. The climate of the earth is gradually getting warmer.
3. The United States must drastically reduce military spending in order to balance the budget.
4. Shakespeare died in 1616.
5. Marlowe really wrote the plays of Shakespeare.
6. Water boils at 212 degrees Fahrenheit.
7. Van Gogh's paintings are the work of a madman.
8. The incidence of lung cancer has risen in the last ten years.
9. Abortion denies the fetus's inherent right to life.
10. The national 55-mile-per-hour speed limit was responsible for lower accident rates.

5b

Formulating an argumentative thesis

Once you have an arguable statement, you need to make a claim about the statement, one you will then work to persuade readers to accept. Your claim becomes the working thesis for your argument. For example, look at the following statement:

The use of pesticides endangers the lives of farm workers.

This statement is arguable—it aims to convince, it addresses an issue with no easily identifiable answer, and it can realistically be disputed.

Although it does make a kind of claim—that pesticides threaten lives—the claim is just a factual statement about *what is*. To develop a claim that can become the working thesis for an argument, you usually need to direct this kind of statement toward some action; that is, your claim needs to move from *what is* to *what ought to be*:

| STATEMENT ABOUT WHAT IS | Pesticides endanger the lives of farm workers. |
| CLAIM ABOUT WHAT OUGHT TO BE | Because pesticides endanger the lives of farm workers, their use should be banned. |

EXERCISE 5.1: Suggested Answers

1. Arguable
2. Arguable, depending on the acceptance of scientific data
3. Arguable
4. Not arguable
5. Arguable
6. Not arguable, unless students want to discuss boiling temperatures at different air pressures
7. Arguable
8. Arguable, depending on the acceptance of statistical reports
9. Arguable
10. Arguable, although some studies continue to show correlations between reduced speed and lower accident rates. More readily verifiable is the correlation between speed limit and mortality rate.

Failure to sharply define one's subject is the chief cause of fuzzy, disunified discourse. Vague beginnings invite chaotic endings. The audience for a discourse . . . can achieve no firmer grasp of the thesis than the writer or speaker . . . has. —EDWARD P. J. CORBETT

An essay is only as good as its thesis. —ANONYMOUS

The art of writing has for backbone some fierce attachment to an idea. —VIRGINIA WOOLF

OPTIONAL EXERCISE

Have your students test the following thesis statements for purpose, audience, position, and support:

(1) My paper will deal with the issue of drug use by college athletes. My audience is made up of coaches and administrators, and I want to point out that it is their insistence on perfection and on winning at all costs that often causes athletes to turn to drugs to stimulate performance, to relieve stress, and to relax.

(2) In this essay, I will argue that this university discriminates against people who live off campus and who must drive to school. I know this is true because I am a commuter and can never find a parking spot. If there's a blizzard, the university doesn't close because students can walk to class. The university schedules two or three hours between classes for commuter students and then doesn't provide them with any place to go except the library, where you can't even get a coke.

How can these statements be improved?

EXERCISE 5.2: Answers will vary.

EXERCISE 5.3: Suggested Answers

1. The Arab-Israeli conflict can be managed but not solved. Thesis: The U.S. government should not attempt to solve the Arab-Israeli conflict because (1) it is essentially religious, not political; (2) neither side has a tradition of compromise; (3) both sides will accept nothing less than possession of the same territories.

This claim becomes your argumentative thesis. Like any working thesis, this one contains two elements, a topic (the statement about what is) and a comment (the claim about what ought to be). See 3b for more discussion of how to formulate a thesis.

┌──────────── TOPIC ────────────┐
Because pesticides endanger the lives of farm workers,

┌──────── COMMENT ────────┐
their use should be banned.

Recognizing implied theses

In some fields, such as literature or history, you will usually be making a claim that urges readers not to take action, but to interpret something in a certain way, to see part of the world of information as you see it. Doing so calls on you first to offer readers your interpretation as clearly as possible and then to support your interpretation in a way that will bring readers to share your view.

In such cases, the claim about what ought to be will usually be implied rather than stated directly. For example, a history report that makes the claim that moral opposition to slavery was the major underlying cause of the Civil War is in effect arguing that readers should view the Civil War in this light—that they should accept this particular interpretation of its cause—rather than seeing the cause as a constitutional struggle over states' rights or an economic conflict between Northern industrialists and Southern planters. Or if you are asked on an art history examination to argue the claim that Van Gogh's paintings are the works of a madman, you are in effect trying to persuade your instructor that he or she ought to view Van Gogh's works as unconscious products of a disordered mind rather than the result of conscious rational decisions.

EXERCISE 5.2

Using two arguable statements from Exercise 5.1 or two that you create, formulate two working argumentative theses, identifying the topic and the comment for each one.

EXERCISE 5.3

Formulate an arguable statement and create a working argumentative thesis for two of the following general topics.

1. the Arab-Israeli conflict
2. mandatory testing of prison inmates for HIV
3. free access to computers for all students on campus
4. a new federal student loan program
5. surrogate motherhood

5c

Formulating good reasons

In his *Rhetoric,* Aristotle discusses the various ways one can argue a point. Torture, he notes, makes for a very convincing argument, but not one that reasonable people would resort to. A pointed gun is no substitute for good reasons, and today we still rely on the three types of good reasons named by Aristotle—those that establish credibility, those that appeal to logic, and those that appeal to emotion.

5d

Establishing credibility

To make your argument convincing, you must first gain the respect and trust of your readers, or **establish your credibility** with them. Your character is embodied in your words, and the way this character is perceived by others largely influences how credible you and your arguments will be. The ancient Greeks called this particular kind of character appeal *ethos* and valued it highly. The little boy who cried "Wolf!" when there really was no wolf approaching was very quickly mistrusted by his townspeople. His was essentially a problem of *ethos:* he lost credibility because he could not be trusted to tell the truth.

In general, writers can establish credibility in three ways:

1. By being knowledgeable about the topic at hand
2. By establishing common ground with the audience, in the form of respect for their points of view and concern for their welfare
3. By demonstrating fairness and evenhandedness

Let us now look at each element of credibility more closely.

2. Prison inmates retain basic human rights, including the right not to be tested for HIV. Thesis: Mandatory testing of prisoners for HIV is wrong because it would infringe on their basic right to privacy.
3. Free access to computers is an unrealistic goal. Thesis: Students should not have free access to computers because (1) the cost would be prohibitive; (2) they don't have equal access to other facilities such as study carrells, musical instruments, practice fields, and sports equipment.
4. The new federal student loan program is a step in the right direction. Thesis: The new federal student loan program should be supported because (1) it ensures access to higher education for many more people; (2) it does not add substantially to the budget deficit because the funds will be repaid; and (3) its success may encourage the government to develop other useful programs.
5. Surrogate motherhood is another name for baby selling. Thesis: Women should not be allowed to act as surrogate mothers because (1) legalizing this practice justifies selling a human life; (2) a surrogate mother is not a factory but is in some sense "one" with the baby; and (3) the children of surrogates may be psychologically traumatized when they find out the truth about their birth.

1

Demonstrating knowledge

A writer can establish credibility first by establishing his or her credentials. You can, for instance, show that you have some personal experience with the subject, as Jennifer Gerkin did in the opening of her essay (see p. 64). In addition, showing that you have thought about the subject carefully or researched it can establish a confident tone. In doing so, your point is not to boast or show off. Rather, you are assuring your audience that the position you hold is based on adequate knowledge and has been systematically thought out.

To determine whether you can effectively present yourself as knowledgeable enough to argue an issue, consider the following questions:

- Can you provide information about your topic from sources other than your own knowledge?
- What are the sources of your information?
- How reliable are your sources?
- Do any sources contradict each other? If so, can you account for or resolve the contradictions?
- If you have personal experience relating to the issue, is this experience directly applicable to your claim?

These questions will help you probe your own stock of knowledge and assess your own credibility in making a claim, and they may help you see what other work you need to do to establish credibility. They may well show that you must do more research, check sources, resolve contradictions, refocus your working thesis, or even change your topic.

2

Establishing common ground

Many arguments between people or groups are doomed to end without resolution because the two sides occupy no common ground, no starting point of agreement. They are, to use an informal phrase, coming from completely different places. Such has often been the case, for example, in arms-control talks in which the beginning positions of the Soviet Union and the United States were so far apart that no resolution could ever be reached.

Lack of common ground also dooms many arguments closer to our everyday lives. If you and your roommate cannot seem to agree on how often to clean the apartment, for instance, the difficulty may well be that your definition of a clean apartment conflicts radically with your roommate's. If

BACKGROUND

Argumentation, persuasion, rhetoric—these terms may bring to mind images of hostility, manipulation, deception, and of overpowering, overmastering, outmaneuvering. In *A Rhetoric of Motives* (Berkeley and Los Angeles: U of California P, 1969), Kenneth Burke postulates that the image of persuasion should not be bellicose, but rather that

> a speaker persuades an audience by the use of stylistic identifications; his act of persuasion may be for the purpose of causing the audience to identify itself with the speaker's interests; and the speaker draws on identification of interests to establish rapport between himself and his audience. (46)

Identification, Burke reminds us, occurs when people share some principle in common—that is, when they establish common ground. Persuasion should not begin with absolute confrontation and separation but with the establishment of common ground, from which differences can be worked out. (See Chapter 28 of the handbook.)

you and a classmate cannot agree on how to work together on a joint assignment, you may find that your very different cultural backgrounds lead you to approach the job in two compellingly different ways. You may find, in fact, that you will not be able to resolve such issues until you can establish common definitions on which to base the arguments. In this way, common ground provides a necessary starting point, one that can turn a futile quarrel into a constructive argument. (For a more thorough discussion of how language can help establish common ground between you and your readers, see Chapter 28.)

Common ground is just as important in written arguments as it is in diplomatic negotiations or personal disputes. Because topics and writers and audiences are so individual and varied, no foolproof or absolute guidelines exist for a writer to establish common ground with an audience. Following are some questions, however, that can help you find common ground in presenting an argument:

- What are the differing perspectives on this issue?
- What common ground can you find—aspects of the issue on which all sides agree?
- How can you express such common ground clearly to all sides?
- How can you discover—and consider—opinions on this issue that differ from your own?

If you turn back to Jennifer Gerkin's essay in 4i, you will see that she attempted to establish common ground with readers by relating her experience to theirs and by demonstrating her openness to change. If you can establish common ground on an issue, you will have taken a giant step toward demonstrating goodwill toward your readers. We are inclined, after all, to listen with interest and attention to those we believe to have our best interests at heart. On the other hand, we are naturally suspicious of those who seem to want to further only their *own* interests.

3

Demonstrating fairness

In arguing a position, writers must demonstrate fairness toward opposing arguments. Audiences are more inclined to give credibility to writers they believe to be fairly considering and representing their opponents' views than to those who seem to be ignoring or distorting such views. We have all experienced unfair arguments: a co-worker loses his temper and blames you for a decision that was largely his idea, or a clever politician avoids a tough question at a news conference by giving an answer that ignores the questioner's point and then calling on someone else. Such

FOR COLLABORATIVE WORK

Your students will better understand the concept of "common ground" if you provide them with an opportunity to demonstrate how opposing parties can reach agreement. Divide the class into pairs of students who hold opposing views and ask each pair to establish a first principle of agreement, their common ground. Use frustrating situations the students experience as well as the following rhetorical situations:

1. Your roommate keeps an annoying schedule. (For example, if an earlybird and a night owl are roommates, they may keep antagonistic schedules. Yet when they discuss their unhappiness, both agree that they each need quiet for sleeping and studying and noise for relaxing. They have thus established common ground, a starting point for working out their differences.)
2. Your English teacher doesn't accept late papers.
3. You show your parents your 2.0 average.
4. You'd like permission (and money) to go to Florida during spring break.
5. Your roommate constantly borrows your belongings.
6. You need help with child care or household duties.

USEFUL READING

Perelman, Chaim. "The Premises of Argumentation." *The Realm of Rhetoric*. Notre Dame: U of Notre Dame P, 1982. 21–32. Discusses common ground, the starting point of agreement for any discourse.

tactics seem unfair, and to the extent that we recognize them we condemn them. It goes without saying, then, that to be an effective writer, you need to avoid such tactics and establish yourself as open-minded and evenhanded. Following are some questions that can help you discover ways of doing so in arguing your position:

- Can you show that you are taking into account all significant points of view? How?
- Can you demonstrate that you understand and sympathize with points of view other than your own? How?
- What can you do to show that you have considered evidence carefully, even that which does not support your position?

4

Recognizing ethical fallacies

Some arguments focus not on establishing the credibility of the writer but on destroying the credibility of an opponent. At times such attacks are justified: if a nominee for the Supreme Court has acted in unethical ways in law school, for example, that information is a legitimate argument against the nominee's confirmation. Many times, however, someone attacks a person's character in order to avoid dealing with the issue at hand. Be extremely careful about attacking an opponent's credibility, for doing so without justification can harm your own credibility. Such unjustified attacks are called **ethical fallacies**. They take two main forms: *ad hominem* charges and guilt by association.

Ad hominem (Latin for "to the man") charges directly attack someone's character rather than focusing on the issue under discussion, suggesting that because something is "wrong" with this person, then whatever he or she says must also be wrong.

> Molly Yard is just a hysterical feminist. We shouldn't listen to her views on abortion. [Labeling Yard "hysterical" and linking that label with "feminist" focuses on Yard's character rather than on her views on the issue at hand.]

Guilt by association attacks someone's credibility by linking that person with a person or activity the audience considers bad, suspicious, or untrustworthy.

> Senator Fleming does not deserve reelection; one of her assistants turned out to be involved with the Mafia. [Is there any evidence that the senator knew about the Mafia involvement?]

EXERCISE 5.4

Study carefully the following advertisement for the environmental group Greenpeace, and then list the ways in which the copywriters demonstrate knowledge, establish common ground, and demonstrate fairness. Do you think they succeed or fail in establishing credibility?

HELP US MAKE WAVES!

You can help keep the world's most unusual fleet in action...

We go into action without force. Without violence. But we *do* make waves. We're Greenpeace.

From the North Atlantic to the South Pacific, on the Great Lakes or in the near-frozen bays of Antarctica, Greenpeace is fighting for a cleaner environment and a more peaceful earth. You've heard about our campaigns to intercept renegade whalers on the high seas... to confront the nuclear superpowers in their contaminated testing zones... to block the dumping of toxic wastes into our water.

Greenpeace fights to *save* life and preserve our environment. And now *you* can be part of our worldwide campaigns to stop the slaughter of whales, dolphins and other animals... to prevent the spread of toxic pollution... to halt further testing of nuclear weapons and rid the oceans of nuclear-armed warships... to protect wilderness and wildlife from industrial and military exploitation.

Dangerous work? Yes. But we're willing to face the risks.

Over the past 15 years, Greenpeace's nonviolent navy has taken on the U.S. Department of Defense, the Soviet Navy, the Norwegian Coast Guard and the Royal Canadian Mounted Police. Our flagship, the *Rainbow Warrior*, was blown up by French secret service operatives, killing a member of her crew. Our activists have been threatened, arrested and beaten. They've had explosive harpoons shot over their heads and barrels of radioactive waste dropped on their boats.

But tough challenges bring dramatic victories. As a result of just some of Greenpeace's campaigns: the International Whaling Commission voted to end all commercial whaling; 37 years of dumping radioactive waste into the Atlantic Ocean was stopped; the annual slaughter of harp seals in Canada is virtually over; the French ceased atmospheric testing of nuclear weapons.

You can help Greenpeace meet tomorrow's challenges — help win tomorrow's victories.

Greenpeace needs you.

Greenpeace depends on the financial support of thousands of citizens around the world — people like you who care about the future of our planet — to keep our fleet in action. Your tax-deductible contribution today will help pay for the supplies and equipment we must have to take on those who poison our seas and slaughter our marine life.

You benefit as well.

When you support Greenpeace, you'll have the satisfaction of knowing that every Greenpeace victory for the environment is a victory *you* have helped make possible. And, for your contribution of $15 or more, you will receive our colorful, informative magazine, *Greenpeace*, to keep you up to date on our worldwide actions to protect our planet. Make some waves today!

EXERCISE 5.5

Using a working argumentative thesis you drafted in Exercise 5.2 or 5.3, write a paragraph or two describing how you would go about establishing your credibility in arguing that thesis.

5e

Appealing to logic

While the character we present in writing always exerts a strong appeal (or lack of appeal) in an argument, our credibility alone cannot and should not carry the full burden of convincing a reader. Indeed, we are

---

EXERCISE 5.4: Answers

The copywriters work to establish credibility by:

1. Demonstrating knowledge (of nuclear testing, toxic pollution).
2. Appealing to logical judgment (saving a life, preserving the environment).
3. Demonstrating fairness (putting knowledge and experience in the public domain).
4. Establishing common ground (we both care about the future of our planet; we'll both benefit from the organization's success).

EXERCISE 5.5: Answers will vary.

TEACHING PRACTICE

Ask your students to look again at the misleading ads, editorials, or columns they brought to class, this time analyzing them for logical appeals. Often unfair text is based on emotional rather than logical or ethical appeals.

inclined to view the **logic of the argument**—the reasoning behind it—as more important than the character of the person presenting the case. In truth, the two are usually inseparable and thus of equal importance. Nevertheless, strong logical support characterizes most good arguments. This section will examine the most effective means of providing logical support for a written argument: examples and precedents, testimony and authority, and causes and effects.

1

Providing examples and precedents

Just as a picture can sometimes be worth a thousand words, so can a well-conceived **example** be extremely valuable in arguing a point. No one in recent years has used the example to greater effect than President Ronald Reagan, who often employed a homespun example from his childhood or even from one of his movies to drive home a point. This paragraph, in fact, has used Reagan as an example in making its point: that examples are one of the staples of everyday argument.

Examples are used most often to support generalizations or to bring abstractions to life. For instance, a *Newsweek* review of the movie *Star Trek IV* made the general statement that the movie contained "nutty throwaway lines that take a minute to sink in" and then illustrated the generalization with this example:

> When the crew, flying the Klingon warship they inherited . . . , land in Golden Gate Park, they fan out to different corners of the city. . . . Kirk's parting command, spoken like a PTA mother at the county fair: "Everybody remember where we parked."

The generalization would have meant little without the example.

Examples can also help us understand abstractions. "Famine," for instance, may be difficult for us to think about in the abstract—but a graphic description of a drought-stricken community, its riverbed cracked dry, its people listless, emaciated, and with stomachs bloated by hunger, speaks directly to our understanding.

Precedents are particular kinds of examples taken from the past. The most common use of precedent occurs in law, where an attorney may argue a case by citing the precedent of past decisions. A judge may be asked to rule that a defendant was negligent, for example, because the Supreme Court upheld a ruling of negligence in an almost identical case ten years earlier.

Precedent appears in everyday arguments as well. If you urge your best friend to work your shift for you on the basis that the last time she needed some time off you worked her shift, you are arguing on the basis of precedent. Or if as part of a proposal for increased lighting in the library

BACKGROUND

In 466 B.C., when a democracy was established in the ancient Greek colony of Syracuse, an art of rhetoric was formulated by the Sicilian Corax, an art that was later transmitted to Greece by Corax's pupil Tisias. Rhetoric began as a practical art, a part of civic life in the democracy of Syracuse. An immediate consequence of the establishment of a democracy was a mass of litigation on claims to property, urged by democratic exiles who had been dispossessed. Their claims, going back many years, often required stating and arranging a complicated series of details. Without documents to prove ownership, the litigants were forced to rely on inferential reasoning; without lawyers to plead their cases, they were left to plead their own cases—hence the need for professional advice, and hence Corax's custom-designed art of rhetoric.

Throughout the classical period, Corax's art of inferential reasoning proved to be more persuasive than other forms of testimony. Today, however, jurors place a great deal of emphasis on testimony, while judges and attorneys are often still persuaded by inferential reasoning. In our writing, we expect both citations of authority and good reasoning.

parking garage you point out that the university has increased lighting in four similar garages in the past year, you are again arguing on the basis of precedent.

In research writing, you usually must list your sources for any examples or precedents not based on your own knowledge (see 41d).

Following are some questions for checking any use of example and precedent:

- How representative are the examples?
- Are they sufficient in strength or number to lead to a generalization?
- In what ways do they support your point?
- How closely does the precedent relate to the point you're trying to make? Is the situation really a similar one?
- How timely is the precedent? What would have been good to do in 1520 is not necessarily good today.

2

Citing authority and testimony

Another way to support an argument logically is to cite **authority**. As young children we were easily swayed by authority; it was right to do something simply because our parents (the authorities) said so. In recent years the use of authority has figured prominently in the antismoking movement. Many older Americans will remember, for instance, the dramatic impact of the U.S. surgeon general's 1963 announcement that smoking is hazardous to health. At the time, many people quite smoking, largely convinced by the authority of the person offering the evidence. Authority has been used in a similar way in the more recent effort to control drug use and abuse in the United States.

But as with other strategies for building support for an argumentative claim, citing authorities demands careful consideration. Following are some questions you might consider to be sure that you are using authorities effectively:

- Is the authority timely? (To argue that the United States should pursue a policy just because it is one supported by Thomas Jefferson will probably fail because Jefferson's times were so radically different from ours.)
- Is the authority qualified to judge the topic at hand? (To cite a biologist in an essay on linguistics is not likely to strengthen your argument.)
- Is the authority likely to be known and respected by readers? (To cite an unfamiliar authority without some identification would lessen the impact of the evidence given.)

Authorities are commonly cited in research writing (treated in Part Eight), which relies on the findings of other people. In addition, you can cite authorities in answering essay examination questions (treated in Chapter 46) or in an assignment that asks you to review the literature in any field (treated in Chapter 45).

Testimony—the evidence an authority presents in support of a claim—is a feature of much contemporary argument. Most familiar are the testimonials found in advertisements—a television personality promoting dog food, or a star athlete speaking for cereal. In fact, we are so inundated with the use of testimonials in television advertising that we may be inclined to think of them only in terms of *misuse*. But if the testimony is timely, accurate, representative, and provided by a respected authority, then it, like authority itself, can add powerful support to an argument. In an essay for a literature class, for example, you might argue that a new edition of a literary work will open up many new areas of interpretation. You could strengthen this argument by adding a quotation from the author's biographer noting that the new edition carries out the author's intentions much more closely than the previous edition did.

In research writing, you should list your sources for authority and testimony not based on your own knowledge (see 42d).

3

Establishing causes and effects

Showing that one event is the cause—or the effect—of another can sometimes help to support an argument. To take an everyday example, suppose you are trying to explain, in a petition to change your grade in a course, why you were unable to take the final examination. In such a case you would most naturally try to trace the **causes** of your failure to appear—the death of your grandmother followed by the theft of your car, perhaps—so that the committee reading the petition would change your grade. In identifying the causes of a situation, you are implicitly arguing that the **effect**—your not taking the examination—should be given new consideration.

Tracing causes often lays the groundwork for an argument, particularly if the effect of the causes is one we would like to change. Recent figures from the U.S. Department of Education, for example, indicate that the number of high school dropouts is rising. If we can identify and understand the causes of this increase—for example, a decline in reading skills—we may be able to make an argument for policies aimed at reversing the trend by affecting the causes in some way—such as hiring more teachers to provide remedial reading instruction.

TEACHING PRACTICE

Cause-and-effect relationships are often complex: what appears at first glance to be the obvious cause of an event turns out to be only a secondary influence, sometimes an influence that obscures the primary cause and effect relationship. For example, one student felt sure that her migraine headaches were brought on by stress, air pressure, and certain food allergies; only after several seizures was she convinced otherwise: she had a small brain tumor. Encourage your students to persevere in finding the real connections between events and their causes.

In college writing, you may often be asked to show causes and effects. In an environmental science class, for example, a student may argue that a national law regulating smokestack emissions from utility plants is needed because (1) acid rain on the East Coast originates from emissions at utility plants in the Midwest, (2) acid rain kills trees and other vegetation, (3) midwestern states have been prevented by utility lobbying from passing strict laws controlling emissions from such plants, and (4) in the absence of such laws, acid rain will destroy most eastern forests by 2020. In this case, the first point is that the emissions cause acid rain; the second, that acid rain causes destruction of eastern forests; and the third, that states have not acted to break the cause-effect relationship established by the first two points. The fourth point ties all of the previous points together to provide an overall argument from effect: "unless X, then Y."

In fact, a cause-effect relationship is often extremely difficult to establish. Scientists and politicians continue to disagree, for example, over the extent to which acid rain is responsible for the so-called dieback of many eastern forests. If we can show that X definitely causes Y, though, we will have a powerful argument at our disposal. That is why so much effort has gone into establishing a definite link between smoking and cancer and between certain dietary habits and heart disease; if the causal link can be established, it will argue most forcefully that we should alter our behavior in certain clear-cut ways.

4

Using inductive and deductive reasoning

Traditionally, logical arguments are classified as using either inductive or deductive reasoning, which almost always work together. **Inductive reasoning**, most simply, is the process of making a generalization based on a number of specific instances. If you find you are ill on ten occasions after eating seafood, for example, you will likely draw the inductive generalization that seafood makes you ill. It may not be an absolute certainty that the seafood was the culprit, but the *probability* lies in that direction.

We all use such inductive reasoning for simple everyday discussions, but induction can be quite complex, as demonstrated by the medical response to the sudden outbreak of an apparently new illness in the mid-1970s. This illness, later named Legionnaires' disease, resulted in many deaths. Medical researchers used a painstaking and time-consuming process of inductive elimination, examining every case in great detail to determine what the patients had in common, before they were able to generalize accurately about the cause of the disease.

Deductive reasoning, most simply, reaches a conclusion by assuming a general principle (known as a **major premise**) and then applying that

BACKGROUND

One of Aristotle's greatest contributions to rhetorical theory was the use of deductive as well as inductive logic: he used the enthymeme, whose essential difference from the syllogism in logic is not so much that one of the premises is left unstated as that the argument is based on premises that are probably true rather than absolutely true and that the opening premise is agreed on by speaker and audience.

principle to a specific case (the **minor premise**). In practice, this general principle is usually derived from induction. The inductive generalization "seafood makes me ill," for instance, could serve as the major premise for the deductive argument "since all seafood makes me ill, the plate of it just put before me is certain to make me ill."

The fictional detective Sherlock Holmes was famous for using deductive reasoning to solve his cases. Beginning, for instance, with the major premise "watchdogs always bark at strangers," Holmes applied that premise to the case of a stolen racehorse and reasoned that because the watchdog did not bark when the horse was stolen, the thief was not a stranger but someone the dog knew.

Deductive arguments like these have traditionally been analyzed as **syllogisms**, three-part statements containing a major premise, a minor premise, and a conclusion:

MAJOR PREMISE	All people die.
MINOR PREMISE	I am a person.
CONCLUSION	I will die.

Syllogisms may work for technical logical purposes, but rarely do they prove useful in the kind of arguments you are likely to write. They are simply too rigid and absolute to serve in arguments about questions that have no absolute answers, and they often lack any appeal to an audience. From Aristotle came a simpler alternative, the **enthymeme**, which calls on the audience to supply the implied major premise. For example:

This bridge is carrying twice as much traffic as it was built for, so we need to build a new bridge or restrict traffic on this one.

You can analyze this enthymeme by restating it in the form of two premises and a conclusion:

MAJOR PREMISE	Bridges should carry only the amount of traffic for which they were built.
MINOR PREMISE	This bridge is carrying twice the traffic for which it was built.
CONCLUSION	We need to build a new bridge or restrict traffic on this one.

Note that the major premise is one the writer can count on an audience agreeing to or supplying: safety and common sense demand that bridges carry only the amount of traffic for which they are built. By thus inspiring audience "participation," an enthymeme actually gets the audience to *contribute* to the argument.

Jennifer Gerkin's essay in 4i rests on an enthymeme whose implied major premise she assumes her readers will accept: "Prejudice is harmful to all of us." She goes on to demonstrate her own prejudice and to show how that prejudice has harmed her as well as others.

Whether it is expressed as a syllogism or an enthymeme, a deductive conclusion is only as strong as the premises on which it is based. The citizen who argues that "Ed is a crook who shouldn't be elected to public office" is arguing deductively, based on an implied major premise: "No crook should be elected to public office." In this case, most people would agree with this major premise. So the issue in this argument rests on the minor premise—that Ed is a crook. Only if that premise can be proven satisfactorily are we likely to accept the deductive conclusion that Ed shouldn't be elected to office.

While we may well agree with some unstated major premises (such as that no crook should be elected), at other times the unstated premise may be more problematic. The person who says, "Don't bother to ask for Jack's help with physics—he's a jock" is arguing deductively on the basis of an implied major premise: "jocks don't know anything about physics." In this case, careful listeners would demand proof of the unstated premise. Because bigoted or prejudiced statements often rest on this kind of reasoning, writers should be particularly alert to it. (See Chapter 28 for a discussion of language that labels people in prejudicial ways.)

5

Recognizing logical fallacies

Logical fallacies are formal errors in reasoning. Though they cannot stand up to analysis, they are commonplace enough and, indeed, can often convince audiences. Sharp readers will detect fallacious appeals, however—and may even reject an otherwise worthy argument that relies on them. Your time will be well spent, therefore, in learning to recognize—and to avoid—these fallacies. Common logical fallacies include begging the question, *post hoc,* non sequitur, either/or, hasty generalizations, and oversimplification.

Begging the question is a kind of circular argument that treats a question as if it has already been answered.

> That television news provides accurate and reliable information was demonstrated conclusively on last week's *60 Minutes*. [This statement says in effect that television news is accurate and reliable because television news says so.]

The *post hoc fallacy,* from the Latin *post hoc ergo propter hoc,* which means "after this, therefore caused by this," assumes that just because B happened *after* A, it must have been *caused* by A.

> We should not rebuild the town docks because every time we do a big hurricane comes along and damages them. [Does the reconstruction cause hurricanes?]

A **non sequitur** (Latin for "it does not follow") attempts to tie together two or more logically unrelated ideas as if they *were* related.

> If we can send a spacecraft to Mars, then we can discover a cure for cancer. [These are both scientific goals, but do they have anything else in common? What does achieving one have to do with achieving the other?]

The **either/or fallacy** asserts that a complex situation can have only two possible outcomes, one of which is necessary or preferable.

> If we do not build the new aqueduct system this year, residents of the Tri-Cities area will be forced to move because of lack of water. [What is the evidence for this claim? Do no other alternatives exist?]

A **hasty generalization** bases a conclusion on too little evidence or on bad or misunderstood evidence.

> I couldn't understand the lecture today, so I'm sure this course will be impossible. [How can the writer be so sure of this conclusion based on only *one* piece of evidence?]

Oversimplification of the relation between causes and effects is another fallacy based on careless reasoning.

> If we prohibit the sale of alcohol, we will get rid of the problem of drunkenness. [This claim oversimplifies the relation between laws and human behavior.]

EXERCISE 5.6

The following sentences contain deductive arguments based on implied major premises. Identify each of the implied premises.

1. A dream is not an accurate picture of reality, because it is heavily influenced by our subjective feelings.
2. In a recent national survey, a majority of Americans said they either smoke marijuana or do not care if others do; therefore, smoking marijuana should be legalized.
3. Active euthanasia is morally acceptable when it promotes the best interests of everyone concerned and violates no one's rights.

EXERCISE 5.6: Suggested Answers

1. Subjective feelings distort our pictures of reality.
2. Activities should not be illegal that are overtly or covertly approved of by the majority of Americans.
3. Whatever promotes the best interests of all concerned and violates no one's rights is morally acceptable.
4. Women should not be exposed to a higher risk of death.
5. Only those who can talk can feel pain.

4. Women soldiers should not serve in combat positions because doing so would expose them to a much higher risk of death.

5. Animals can't talk, so therefore they can't feel pain as humans do.

EXERCISE 5.7

The following brief article from *Newsweek* raises some provocative questions about causes and effects, and in doing so it uses example and authority. Read the article, and assess it in terms of the questions that follow.

Mom always told you chicken noodle soup could cure a cold. But could it prevent a disabling disease like Alzheimer's? That's what researchers are asking about a new chicken soup under development by Thomas J. Lipton Co. Inc. The still-to-be-named soup is enriched with purified lecithin, a nutrient undergoing testing as an Alzheimer's treatment. In accordance with Food and Drug Administration regulations, Lipton stops short of attaching medical claims to its new product. But the company may introduce it simply as "chicken soup with lecithin" sometime next year.

The soup is the brainchild of MIT Prof. Richard Wurtman and Harvard neurologist John Growden. Wurtman and Growden approached Lipton after discovering that purified lecithin could affect the chemistry of the brain. The purified lecithin, which is more concentrated than that sold in health-food stores, raises blood levels of choline, which, in turn, may aid memory.

Whether the new soup could benefit the general population is still unclear. But Wurtman and Growden are studying the product's effect on memory and fatigue. Says Lipton spokesman Larry Hicks, "The market may be much larger than we now know."

1. What is the cause-effect argument?
2. Is the link between cause and effect fully established?
3. What evidence would be required to establish that link more fully?
4. Does the use of authority or testimony help establish the link? Why, or why not?
5. What example is used in the introduction—and is it effective in illustrating the point?
6. Can you identify any logical fallacies?

EXERCISE 5.8

Analyze the advertisement in Exercise 5.4 for the use of examples and precedents; authority and testimony; causes and effects; induction and deduction; and logical fallacies.

EXERCISE 5.7: Answers

1. (i) Purified lecithin may help aid memory.
   (ii) This soup has purified lecithin in it.
   (iii) This soup may help aid memory.

2. No: *may, could* are conditional.

3. Studies showing that lecithin improves memory in Alzheimer's patients; studies that show a similar improvement in people who do not have Alzheimer's.

4. Authority helps establish the inference of causation: MIT and Harvard are so highly respected that if their professors show interest in this possibility, there must be a connection.

5. In family folklore, chicken noodle soup is thought to cure colds. Its effectiveness is in the suggestion that contemporary research has proved that Mother was right.

6. Begs the question of whether lecithin helps; *non sequitur:* just because chicken soup prevents colds doesn't mean that chicken soup with lecithin will do more and just because lecithin changes brain chemistry doesn't mean that the change will be discernable.

EXERCISE 5.8: Suggested Answers

The success of this advertisement is based on its use of deductive arguments supported with examples and precedents. Consider the following: "Greenpeace fights to *save* life and preserve the environment," followed by these examples: "to stop the slaughter of whales, dolphins, and other animals"; "to prevent the spread of toxic pollution"; "to halt further testing of nuclear weapons and rid the oceans of nuclear-armed warships"; "to protect wilderness and wildlife from industrial and military exploitation."

The advertisement declares that their activists are willing to face danger, supporting their claim with the following statements: they have "taken on the U.S. Department of Defense, the

Soviet Navy, the Norwegian Coast Guard and the Royal Canadian Mounted Police." They go on to say that their flagship "was blown up" and that their activists have been killed, "threatened, arrested and beaten." "They've had explosive harpoons shot over their heads and barrels of radioactive waste dropped on their boats."

The only authority cited in the advertisement is the organization's unselfish and high-minded *ethos* and its appeals to their readers, "people like you who care about the future of our planet." In fact, the word *you* or *your* is used at least twelve times in the advertisement.

These activists risk a *post hoc* fallacy when they claim that only their efforts have resulted in ending all commercial whaling, radioactive waste dumping in the Atlantic Ocean, the annual slaughter of harp seals in Canada, and French testing of nuclear weapons.

EXERCISE 5.9: Answers will vary.

TEACHING PRACTICE

Although they may deny it at first, many of your students read descriptions for their own sake. Even after they know the scores, for example, they read the play-by-play account of ball games. They read cookbook accounts of recipes for familiar dishes. After looking at a picture of a house or an apartment, they read on for its written description in the classified ads.

Discuss the reading of description with your students, asking them what kinds of appeals, pleasure, and information they get from the descriptions.

Ask your students about wheelchair accessibility on campus. What kind of additional infor-

EXERCISE 5.9

Using your working argumentative thesis from Exercise 5.2 or 5.3, write a paragraph describing the logical appeals you would use to support the thesis.

5f

Appealing to emotion

Most successful arguments appeal to our hearts as well as to our minds. Good writers, therefore, supplement appeals to logic and reason with those designed to **enlist the emotional support** of their readers. This principle was vividly demonstrated a few years ago when Americans began hearing about a famine in Africa. Facts and figures (logical appeals) did indeed convince many Americans that the famine was both real and serious. What brought an outpouring of aid, however, were not the facts and figures but the arresting photographs of children, at once skeletal and bloated, dying of starvation. In this case, the emotional appeal of those photographs spoke more powerfully than did the logical statistics. Writers can gain similarly powerful effects through the use of description, concrete language, and figurative language.

1

Using description

Vivid **description** provides one of the most effective means of appealing to emotions. Travel articles and advertisements draw heavily on this principle: think of all the descriptions of sunny beaches that appear in newspapers during the dreary winter months. Description can work just as effectively in your written arguments. Using strong, descriptive details can bring a moving immediacy to any argument.

The student described in Chapter 3 who was at work on a proposal to make the library more accessible to students in wheelchairs had amassed plenty of facts and figures, including diagrams and maps, illustrating the problem. But her first draft seemed dry and lifeless in spite of all her information. She decided, therefore, to ask a friend who used a wheelchair to accompany her to the library—and she revised her proposal to open with a detailed description of that visit and the many frustrations her friend encountered.

2

Using concrete language

Concrete language stands at the heart of effective description and hence helps build emotional appeal. The student urging improved wheelchair access to the library, for instance, could have said simply that her friend "had trouble entering the library." Such a general statement, however, has little impact; it does not appeal to readers' emotions or allow them to imagine themselves in a similar position. The revised version, full of concrete description, does so: "Maria inched her heavy wheelchair up the narrow, steep entrance ramp, her small arms straining to pull up the last twenty feet, her face pinched with the sheer effort of getting into Main Library." (See 27c.)

3

Using figurative language

Figurative language, or figures of speech, can also help paint a detailed and vivid picture. They do so by making striking comparisons between something you are writing about and something else that is easier for a reader to visualize, identify with, or understand.

Figures of speech include metaphors, similes, and analogies (see 27d). **Metaphors** compare two things directly: *Richard the Lion-Hearted; old age is the evening of life*. **Similes** make comparisons using *like* or *as: Richard is as brave as a lion; old age is like the evening of life*. **Analogies** are extended metaphors or similes that compare an unfamiliar concept or process to a more familiar one to help the reader understand the unfamiliar concept:

> The most instructive way I know to express this cosmic chronology is to imagine the fifteen-billion-year lifetime of the universe (or at least its present incarnation since the Big Bang) compressed into the span of a single year. Then every billion years of Earth history would correspond to about twenty-four days of our cosmic year, and one second of that year to 475 real revolutions of the Earth about the sun.
>
> – CARL SAGAN, "The Cosmic Calendar"

Metaphors, similes, and analogies can all make an abstract or otherwise difficult concept understandable in terms of more concrete, everyday experience. James Watson and Francis Crick, who won the Nobel Prize for their work on the structure of DNA, used the metaphor of a zipper to describe how two strands of molecules could separate during cell division. In the same way, a student arguing for a more streamlined course registration process may find good use for an analogy, saying that the current process makes students feel like laboratory rats in a maze. This

mation and explicit description could they expect if they took a wheelchair user to their library? Would the person have problems retrieving books from the stacks or simply getting into the stacks? Could he or she get by the entrance turnstile? Could he or she reach the circulation desk? What appeals would be implicit in such a description—ethical, emotional, rational?

analogy, which suggests manipulation, helpless victims, and a clinical coldness, creates a vivid description and hence adds emotional appeal to the argument. For an analogy to work effectively, however, it must be supported by evidence. In this case, the student would have to show that the current registration process has a number of similarities to a laboratory maze, such as uncaring officials overseeing the process and confused students wandering through complex bureaucratic channels and into dead ends.

4

Shaping your appeal to your audience

As with appeals to credibility and to logic, appealing to emotions is effective only insofar as it moves your particular audience. Of course, you can't predict absolutely any audience's emotional response, but you can consider your topic and assess its probable emotional effects. A student arguing for increased lighting in campus parking garages, for instance, might consider the emotions such a discussion will potentially raise (fear of attackers, anger at being subjected to such danger, compassion for victims of such attacks), decide which emotions would be most appropriately appealed to, and then look for descriptive and figurative language to carry out such an appeal.

In a leaflet to be distributed on campus, for example, the student might describe the scene in a dimly lighted garage as a student parks her car and then has to walk to an exit alone through shadowy corridors and staircases. Parking in the garage might be compared to running the gauntlet in a fraternity hazing or venturing into a jungle with dangerous animals lurking behind every tree.

In a proposal to the university administration, on the other hand, the student might describe past attacks on students in campus parking garages and the negative publicity and criticism these provoked among students, parents, alumni, and other groups. For the administration, the student might compare the lighting in the garages to high-risk gambling, arguing that the university is taking a significant chance with the current lighting conditions and that increased lighting would lower the odds against future attacks.

5

Recognizing emotional fallacies

Appeals to the emotions of an audience constitute a valid and necessary part of argument. Unfair or overblown emotional appeals, however, attempt to overcome the reasonable judgment of readers. The most common kinds of these **emotional fallacies** include bandwagon appeal, flattery, in-crowd appeal, veiled threats, and false analogies.

There are only three things, after all, that a [piece of writing] must reach: the eye, the ear, and what we may call the heart or mind. It is most important of all to reach the heart of the reader. —ROBERT FROST

. . . when Einstein was looking for relativity, he did so because he had an emotional feeling that the universe has unity and sense. He believed this before he discovered the theory of relativity. It was a very strong feeling in him; then he discovered the theory of relativity. which proved his feeling. . . . The point is not to get rid of those emotions but simply to know them for what they are. —SUSAN GRIFFIN

Bandwagon appeal suggests that a great movement is under way and that the reader will be a fool or a traitor not to join it.

> Voters are flocking to candidate X by the millions, so you'd better cast your vote the right way. [Why should you jump on this bandwagon? Where is the evidence to support this claim?]

Flattery tries to persuade readers to do something by suggesting that they are thoughtful, intelligent, or perceptive enough to agree with the writer.

> We know you have the taste to recognize that an investment in an Art-Form ring will pay off in the future. [*How* will it pay off?]

In-crowd appeal, a special kind of flattery, invites readers to identify with an admired and select group.

> Want to know a secret that more and more of Middletown's successful young professionals are finding out about? It's Mountainbrook Manor, the condominiums that combine the best of the old with the best of the new. [Who are these "successful young professionals," and will you become one by moving to Mountainbrook Manor?]

Veiled threats try to frighten readers into agreement by hinting that they will suffer adverse consequences if they don't argree.

> If Public Service Electric Company does not get an immediate 15 percent rate increase, its services to you, its customers, may be seriously affected. [How serious is this possible effect? Is it legal or likely?]

False analogies make misleading comparisons between two situations that are *not* alike in most or important respects.

> If the United States gets involved in a land war in the Middle East, it will turn out just like Vietnam. [Is there any point of analogy except that they are both wars? This example was written in 1988. The Persian Gulf War that has taken place since then demonstrates well the weaknesses of such analogies.]

EXERCISE 5.10

Make a list of the common human emotions that might be attached to the following topics, and suggest appropriate ways to appeal to those emotions in a specific audience you choose to address.

1. prohibiting smoking on campus
2. capital punishment
3. nuclear power generation
4. television evangelism
5. competency testing for teachers

BACKGROUND

People suspect the emotional appeal as being somehow unethical or undignified, as being a poor substitute for logical reasoning. They feel duped if they have succumbed to an emotional appeal, the kind of appeal that can be easily abused. Since emotional appeals cannot be avoided, however, they ought to be reasonably made and relate logically to the action desired. An emotional appeal without a logical base is, perhaps, an unjustified appeal.

EXERCISE 5.10: Suggested Answers

1. Concern over harm to the environment and to smokers and nonsmokers as well; concern over basic human rights if banned.

2. Moral indignation as culpable citizen of a state that puts people to death; pity for condemned; gratification that criminals are punished within the full extent of the law; fear of being put to death.

3. Fear of radiation leakage; anger at the government for putting innocent citizens in danger; pride in technological achievement; distress at increased electricity bills to pay for new power plant.

4. Joy over the rebirth of overt religious conviction; distaste with the perceived abuse of emotional appeals and misuse of money; amusement by others' gullibility.

5. Fear of failure; belief that it is a waste of time, money, and energy; sympathy for the tested; belief in favorable consequences.

EXERCISE 5.11: Answers will vary.

EXERCISE 5.11

Jennifer Gerkin's essay in Chapter 4 argues that people shouldn't judge others on the basis of appearance. Read the essay carefully, underlining emotional appeals, including descriptive passages, concrete language, and figurative language.

EXERCISE 5.12: Answers will vary.

EXERCISE 5.12

Read the following paragraph, and then write a paragraph evaluating its use of description and figurative language.

In 1973, all American women became legally entitled to have abortions performed in hospitals by licensed physicians. Before they were legal, abortions were frequently performed by persons who bore more resemblance to butchers than they did to doctors. The all-too-common result was serious complications or death for the woman. Since 1989, states have been able to restrict where and when abortions are performed. Even if the 1973 Supreme Court decision is completely reversed, abortion will not end. Instead, women will again resort to illegal abortions, and there will be a return to the slaughterhouse. Since abortions are going to take place no matter what the law says, why not have them done safely and legally in hospitals instead of in basements, alleys, or dirty compartments in some killing shed? The decision to have an abortion is not an easy one to make, and I believe that a woman who makes it deserves to have her wish carried out in the very safest way possible. Critics of abortion stress the importance of the unborn child's life. At the very least, they should also take the woman's life and safety into consideration.

EXERCISE 5.13: Answers will vary.

EXERCISE 5.13

Using a working argumentative thesis you formulated in Exercise 5.2 or 5.3, make a list of the emotional appeals most appropriate to your topic and audience. Then spend ten to fifteen minutes brainstorming, looking for descriptive and figurative language to carry out the appeals.

Using sources
Finding support for your argument

When you are constructing a written argument, it is almost essential to use sources. Even if your assignment doesn't specify that you must consult outside sources, there is no better way to find support for your argument. The key to convincing people to accept your argument is good reasons, and the most effective way of finding and establishing these reasons is with the help of appropriate sources. You cannot, after all, expect people to simply "take your word" for something. You need to offer evidence from others in support of your claim. Sources can be especially helpful for:

- demonstrating knowledge
- citing authority and testimony
- providing background information
- finding opinions that differ from your own
- demonstrating fairness

Organizing an argument

Once you have assembled good reasons in support of an argumentative thesis, you must organize your material in order to present the argument convincingly. While there is no ideal or universally favored organizational framework for an argumentative essay, you may find it useful to try the classical five-part system that was often followed by ancient Greek and Roman orators. The speaker began with an *introduction,* which stated the thesis, then gave the *background* information. Next came the different *lines of argument,* and then the *refutation of opposing arguments.* A *conclusion* both summed up the argument and made an emotional appeal to the audience. You can adapt this format to written arguments as follows:

1. *Introduction*
   gains readers' attention and interest
   establishes your qualifications to write about your topic
   establishes common ground with readers
   demonstrates fairness
   states or implies your thesis
2. *Background*
   presents any necessary background information
3. *Lines of argument*
   present good reasons (including logical and emotional appeals) in
      support of your thesis
   generally present reasons in order of importance
   demonstrate ways your argument may be in readers' best interest
4. *Refutation of opposing arguments*
   considers opposing points of view
   notes both advantages and disadvantages of opposing views

FOR COLLABORATIVE WORK

Divide the class in small groups, and ask your students to develop arguments. Have them speculate on what subtopics might be created to support these arguments, write out the working thesis, and then work to construct a set of rough notes for each argument.

They can use the topics in Exercise 5.10, come up with their own topics, or use one of the following:

1. the smoking ban on airplanes
2. two-career marriages
3. "returning" students
4. some topic of current import on campus

OPTIONAL EXERCISE

Have students choose one of the following statements and make notes regarding any personal experience they have that supports or refutes it. Then have them, using library sources, gather as much additional evidence as possible. Finally, ask them to use this information and notes on personal experiences to write a short essay arguing either for or against this statement.

1. Vegetarians have a lower incidence of heart attacks than meat-eaters.
2. College degrees mean higher incomes.
3. To succeed, college students must resort to various forms of dishonesty.
4. Students should graduate from college if only to be four years older and wiser when they join the job market.
5. Exercise relieves stress.
6. We are returning to the moral standards of the fifties.
7. AIDS is the worst disease the United States has ever known.
8. Student loans, grants, and scholarships are becoming scarce.

5. *Conclusion*
 may summarize the argument
 elaborates on the implication of your thesis
 makes clear what you want readers to think or do
 makes a strong ethical or emotional appeal

Asked to write an argumentative essay addressed to fellow students about an issue of current interest on her campus, Tracy Vezdos decided to write about the movement to put warning labels about "explicit lyrics" on record albums. Her thesis: "As a form of censorship, the labeling of record albums has no place in American society." Following is her essay, which is organized according to the five-part classical system. The parts are labeled in the margin. Notice that because the thesis is stated in a negative form, arguing *against* labeling, most of the essay is devoted to refuting the arguments in favor of labeling. Also notice that a source citation is given for a piece of information that the writer considered specific enough to need it (see 42d).

```
            It's Only Rock 'n' Roll
      Devil worship, premarital sex, drugs,
violence, suicide--can rock music really
promote all these detriments to today's
youth?   ''Yes,'' says Tipper Gore of the
Parents' Music Resource Center (PMRC).
''Absolutely not,'' responds the Musical
Majority, a group formed in opposition to
PMRC's campaign to have warning label
placed on rock records.   While parents
are understandably concerned about rock
songs that seem to glorify promiscuous
sex, drugs, and other vices, this impres-
sion is often misleading.
      In fact, song lyrics can invoke many
varying interpretations, just as other
kinds of language can.   In recent years,
Mark Twain's most famous novel, The Adven-
tures of Huckleberry Finn, has been banned
from literature courses in many high
```

INTRODUCTION GAINS READERS' ATTENTION

DEMONSTRATES FAIRNESS

PROVIDES AN EXAMPLE TO SUPPORT THE FOLLOWING GENERALIZATIONS schools—including yours, perhaps—because it contains the word <u>nigger</u>.   Critics view this term as evidence that the novel should be interpreted as racist.   Those who are against banning <u>Huckleberry Finn</u>, however, note that a careful reading of it shows that Twain does not promote racism but denounces it as ignorant and immoral.

As in the realm of literature, arguments over interpretation are at the heart of the record labeling controversy.   Part of the controversy almost certainly rests on differences in age.   Teenagers know only too well how often things we like or do can be interpreted by adults in ways very different from ours.   We also know **BUILDS COMMON GROUND** that efforts to challenge our interpretations or to control access to these things we want to do or read or listen to only make them more attractive.   In any case, *ENTHYMEME BASED ON IMPLIED MAJOR PREMISE "CENSORSHIP IS HARMFUL"* efforts to control what we can read or what we can listen to are essentially efforts at censorship.   And as a form of censorship, the labeling of record albums **THESIS** has no place in American society.

The PMRC campaign began in the **BACKGROUND** mid–1980s when Gore, the wife of Senator Albert Gore of Tennessee, and a number of other wives of prominent national politicians began lobbying record companies and performers to label records that the group considered too ''explicit.''   In September 1985, the Senate Commerce Committee held hearings into the issue, and soon

OPTIONAL EXERCISE
Have students study Tracy Vezdos's use of authority and testimony and decide how exactly it helps her (or does not help her) to argue her point. Then send them to look at something they've written recently, and see whether they use authority or testimony to good effect. If not, how might they?

afterward the twenty-two major record companies that are members of the Recording
Industry Association of America accepted a
system of voluntary labels. As is currently the case with the labeling of movies, the companies themselves decide which
records need labels. If the recording
artist agrees, the label <u>Explicit</u> <u>lyrics--
parental</u> <u>advisory</u> is placed on the album
cover.

    The effects of labeling are already
becoming obvious in smaller record stores:
a decline in sales of labeled records and
the refusal of some stores to carry them,
for fear of being known as a ''pornrock''
store. Do the record companies and artists who permit their albums to be labeled
feel their freedom of expression will remain safe despite this first, major step-
toward censoring their material? Already,
PMRC has moved on to the music television
channel (MTV), where it wants to have editing done on what it deems explicitly
sexual or violent videos. PMRC claims
that it does not advocate government censorship. While it may not advocate such
censorship directly, it seems likely that
the group would support congressional efforts to label television programming, especially those programs intended for young
people. Advertisers might withdraw their
sponsorship of ''explicit content'' programs, causing networks to cancel them and
to avoid programming similar material.

LINES OF
ARGUMENT

ESTABLISHES
CAUSE-EFFECT
RELATIONSHIP

LINES OF
ARGUMENT

PRESENTS GOOD
REASON:
LABELING IS
INDIRECT
CENSORSHIP, MAY
ENCOURAGE
MORE DIRECT
CENSORSHIP

The final result may well be that no
Americans—including those of us of college age—will be able to listen to certain songs or see certain shows that the
PMRC considers ''too explicit.''

One of the problems I personally have
with PMRC involves its use of the word <u>ex-</u>
<u>plicit</u>. My dictionary defines <u>explicit</u>
as ''clearly stated or expressed, with
nothing implied; definite.'' Lyrics for
almost any song could fall under this
broad definition, even those of many of
the ''classics.'' Perhaps not surprisingly, then, the main targets of PMRC are
not heavy metal bands such as Motley Crue
and Black Sabbath, who adorn their album
covers with scantily dressed women and
sing rebellious, anti-authority songs.
Most of the artists with songs on the
''Filthy Fifteen,'' a list compiled by
PMRC of the most ''harmful'' songs of
1986, are mainstream performers such as
Madonna, Bruce Springsteen, and Cyndi
Lauper.

CONSIDERS OPPOSING VIEW: "EXPLICIT" LYRICS ENCOURAGE "HARMFUL" BEHAVIOR

Madonna's ''Papa, Don't Preach,''
about a pregnant teenager who wants to get
married and keep her baby, was particularly repugnant to the PMRC, who felt that
the song would encourage teenage pregnancy. A careful listening to the lyrics, however, reveals that the pregnant
girl attempts to gain her father's acceptance and guidance—not to rebel against
his authority. This case of misinterpre-

REFUTES OPPOSING VIEW WITH EVIDENCE THAT LYRICS ARE MISINTERPRETED AND HAVE LITTLE INFLUENCE

tation is not an isolated one.   At the
Senate Commerce Committee hearings, John
Denver testified that his song ''Rocky
Mountain High'' had been banned from many
radio stations because station managers
interpreted the tune as advocating the use
of drugs.   The lyrics, however, indicate
that the ''high'' Denver feels comes from
the Colorado mountains, not marijuana.

The PMRC's concern about lyrics seems
unnecessary in any case.   A survey of 266
junior high and high school students that
was reported in <u>Newsweek</u> showed that the
lyrics have very little or no influence on
teenagers who listen to them.   In fact,
37 percent of the students could not even
describe what their three favorite songs
were about--they just liked them.   As for
Satanism, sex, drugs, and violence, only 7
percent of the 622 songs that were mentioned contained these elements, according
to the students (''So Who Understands'').

The PMRC admits that it finds only a
small minority of rock lyrics offensive.
But it argues that labeling of records
with these lyrics is justified in order to
give parents information about what their
children are listening to and to discourage teenagers from buying--and being influenced by--records that seem to promote
harmful and immoral activities.   Many
people can agree with these goals, and in
some cases record labeling may help to ac-

CONSIDERS
OPPOSING VIEW,
ACKNOWLEDGES
ITS ADVANTAGES

complish them.   But more often, labeling
will probably increase teenagers' exposure
to the very lyrics the PMRC considers
harmful.   We all know the thrill of
sneaking into an R-rated movie or of looking up the bawdy parts of Chaucer's <u>Can-
terbury</u> <u>Tales</u> (those not printed in our
literature textbooks).   In the same way,
an <u>Explicit</u> <u>lyrics</u> label may draw teenagers' attention and challenge their curiosity.   Even if parents can prevent their
children from buying a labeled record, the
young people may be all the more eager—
and likely—to listen to the album at a
friend's.   Instead of encouraging better
communication and understanding between
parents and children, labels may well only
result in more friction.

REFUTES
OPPOSING VIEW,
ARGUING THAT
ITS ADVANTAGES
ARE ILLUSORY

To find out how those of us who are
slightly older feel about the issue, I
took a random survey of Ohio State students, asking whether records should be
labeled and why or why not.   The majority
said ''No,'' on the grounds of freedom of
speech.   Surprisingly enough, a large minority favored labels as a guide for parents.   One answer I received, however,
completely dispels the parental guide argument: ''We should make our children safe
for ideas, not ideas safe for our children. . . .   Only naive fools would say
'yes'—a record album should carry a warning about explicit material—and actually

OFFERS GOOD
REASON:
LABELING IS
ABRIDGMENT OF
FREE SPEECH

believe that the social control that they
have imposed on themselves . . . will not
grow.''

    I agree. Parents have an awesome   CONCLUSION
responsibility in raising their children,
and part of that responsibility includes
monitoring the material their children are
exposed to and, more important, helping
them interpret such materials. Record
companies and singers should not have   SUMMARIZES
                                                                ARGUMENT
to perform these services for parents,
and a group of politically influential
people should not try to make them do so.

    In the long run, we teenagers must   ELABORATES ON
                                                                IMPLICATIONS
learn to judge for ourselves what is ac-   OF THESIS
ceptable and how best to interpret all the
language that surrounds us. We have to
take an honest look at ourselves and our   ASKS READERS
                                                                TO EXAMINE
friends to recognize the many profound   THEIR VIEWS
problems we have to deal with, problems
that are much more complex and frightening
than the words on a record album. After
all, as Mick Jagger proclaimed, ''It's
only rock 'n' roll.''

References

So who understands rock lyrics, anyway.
    (1986, July). <u>Newsweek</u>, p. 71.

EXERCISE 5.14: Answers will vary.

EXERCISE 5.14

Using the classical system, draft an argument in support of one of the theses you formulated in Exercise 5.2 or 5.3.

EXERCISE 5.15

Another useful system of argument was developed by the philosopher Stephen Toulmin. Essentially a modern elaboration of the system first put forth by Aristotle, the Toulmin system is presented in 3a5 as a way of generating material for an argumentative essay but might also be used as follows for organizing or analyzing such an essay:

1. State the claim or thesis.
2. Qualify the claim in any way necessary.
3. Present the good reasons to support the claim.
4. Discuss any underlying assumptions that support these reasons.
5. Give any evidence that might add support to the claim (facts, statistics, testimony, etc.).
6. Acknowledge and respond to any counterarguments your readers might make.

Suppose you were writing an essay about smoking. Your claim might be that smoking should be banned. You could qualify this claim by suggesting that the ban be limited to your campus. As reasons in support of the claim, you might say that smoking causes heart disease and lung cancer and that nonsmokers are endangered by others' smoke. Your underlying assumption would be that people are entitled to protection from harmful actions by others. As evidence you could cite statistics about lung and heart disease and perhaps quote the U.S. surgeon general as an authority on the subject. One possible counterargument you could anticipate would be that smokers have rights too; you could respond by reminding readers that you are suggesting only an on-campus ban and that they would be free to smoke *off* campus.

Use the Toulmin system to draft an argument in support of one of the theses you formulated in Exercise 5.2 or 5.3. If you wish, you can write on the same topic you wrote on in Exercise 5.14.

5h

Analyzing an argument

Guidelines for organizing an argument can also be used to advantage in analyzing a draft of an argument to judge how effective it is. Here are some questions, based on the classical system explained in 5g, that you can use to analyze an argument.

EXERCISE 5.15: Answers will vary.

USEFUL READING

Kneupper, Charles W. "Teaching Argument: An Introduction to the Toulmin Model." *CCC* 29 (1978): 237–41. An introduction to Toulmin logic.

Toulmin, Stephen. *The Uses of Argument.* New York: Cambridge UP, 1964. According to Toulmin, the persuasiveness of our arguments (i.e. "claims") depends upon both the general principles ("warrants") that underlie our interpretations of data and the reasons we provide for them.

> *Analyzing an argument*

1. What have you done to gain readers' interest? (See 5g.)

2. How have you established your qualifications to write about your topic? Have you shown personal experience with it? Do you cite authoritative sources to support your claim? (See 5d.)

3. What have you done in your introduction to establish common ground with your audience? Have you acknowledged various perspectives on your topic and demonstrated fairness to opposing viewpoints? (See 5d2, 5d3.)

4. Have you stated your thesis? If not, will readers be able to recognize it? Is the thesis sufficiently focused? (See 5b.)

5. What background information have you presented? Is it sufficient to support your thesis? (See 5d1.)

6. What good reasons have you presented to support your thesis? Have you shown examples? cited precedents or authorities? quoted testimony? established a cause-effect relationship? How have you appealed to your readers' emotions? (See 5e, 5f.)

7. Have you committed any fallacies? (See 5d4, 5e5, 5f5.)

8. Have you dealt adequately with opposing points of view? Have you noted both their advantages and disadvantages? (See 5d3.)

9. How do you conclude? Have you summarized your argument? elaborated on the implications of your claim? ended with some kind of ethical or emotional appeal? Have you made clear what you want your readers to think or do? (See 5g.)

EXERCISE 5.16

Using the six categories in the Toulmin system described in Exercise 5.15, try analyzing the argument implicit in the advertisement for Greenpeace in Exercise 5.4. Write out your analysis in a page or so.

EXERCISE 5.17   Reading with an Eye for Argument

In this excerpt from an opinion essay in the *New York Times*, Maya Angelou considers the African-American community's debate over Clarence Thomas's nomination to the Supreme Court—and her own eventual decision to support him. Identify her major claim. What ethical, logical, and emotional appeals does she offer to support that claim? How effective are these appeals in answering other possible viewpoints?

EXERCISE 5.16: Suggested Answers

1. Claim: Greenpeace works successfully on behalf of the environment.

2. Qualifications: Whatever its past successes, Greenpeace can continue to be effective only if the reader supports it.

3. Reasons: The first two paragraphs include specific examples of the kinds of environmental campaigns waged by Greenpeace.

4. Underlying assumptions: The advertisement assumes the reader cares about the environment, wants to stop the hunting of endangered species, wants an end to toxic waste dumping and nuclear testing, etc.

5. Evidence: The ad lists examples of Greenpeace's successes throughout, especially in the fourth paragraph.

6. Counterargument acknowledged: The work Greenpeace does is often dangerous. Response: Greenpeace is willing to undertake it.

Judge Thomas has given his adversaries every reason to oppose and distrust him. Many of his audacious actions as chairman of the Equal Employment Opportunity Commission were anti-affirmative action, anti-busing and anti-other opportunities to redress inequality in our country. . . .

Judge Thomas, a poor black from Pinpoint, Ga., has reached proximity to America's highest court because of the very laws his forefathers fought to have written and enforced, and which he has treated so cavalierly.

It follows then that many African-Americans ask, how can we advance if one we have sent forth in the vanguard ignores our concerns?

In these bloody days and frightful nights when an urban warrior can find no face more despicable than his own, no ammunition more deadly than self-hate and no target more deserving of his true aim than his brother, we must wonder how we came so late and lonely to this place.

In this terrifying and murderous season, when young women achieve adulthood before puberty, and become mothers before learning how to be daughters, we must stop the rhetoric and high-sounding phrases, stop the posing and preening and look to our own welfare.

We need to haunt the halls of history and listen anew to the ancestors' wisdom. . . . How were our forefathers able to support their weakest when they themselves were at their weakest? How were they able to surround the errant leader and prevent him from being co-opted by forces that would destroy him and them? How were they, lonely, bought separately, sold apart, able to conceive of the deep, ponderous wisdom found in "walk together, children . . . don't you get weary."

The black youngsters of today must ask black leaders: If you can't make an effort to reach, reconstruct and save a black man who has graduated from Yale, how can you reach down here in this drug-filled, hate-filled cesspool where I live and save me?

I am supporting Clarence Thomas's nomination, and I am neither naïve enough nor hopeful enought to imagine that in publicly supporting him I will give the younger generation a pretty picture of unity, but rather I can show them that I and they come from a people who had the courage to be when being was dangerous, who had the courage to dare when daring was dangerous—and most important, had the courage to hope.

Because Clarence Thomas has been poor, has been nearly suffocated by the acrid odor of racial discrimination, is intelligent, well trained, black and young enough to be won over again, I support him.

The prophet in "Lamentations" cried, "Although he put his mouth in the dust . . . there is still hope."

EXERCISE 5.18 Taking Inventory: Your Own Arguments

Using the guidelines in 5h, analyze the argument in something you've recently written or in the draft you wrote in Exercise 5.14. Decide what you need to do to revise your argument, and write out a brief plan for your revision.

6
Constructing Paragraphs

BACKGROUND

Earlymanuscriptsranwordstogetherlikethis

Words were not considered individual entities; rather they formed the continuum of oral language. Later manuscripts, however, began to sacrifice precious paper by leaving space between the words and special marks in the margin as an aid to the reader. Often the marginalia were a series of alphabetized letters or pictorial signs that aided the copyist, the reader, and the memorizer alike in keeping their place. The *para graphos* (¶) was a common marginal mark, nor a unit of discourse at all.

In fact, the paragraph as we know it today—with its qualities of consecutiveness and loose order of propositions—did not begin to emerge until the late seventeenth century and did not attain full codification until the eighteenth. Not until the mid-nineteenth century did the first systematic formulation of paragraph theory appear, in Alexander Bain's *English Composition and Rhetoric* (1866).

BACKGROUND

In his "Structure and Form in Non-Narrative Prose" (*Ten Bibliographic Essays,* ed. Gary Tate [Fort Worth: Texas Christian UP, 1987]),

The hero of the Rex Stout mysteries, Nero Wolfe, once solved a case by identifying the paragraph structure of a particular writer/murderer. A person's style of paragraphing, Wolfe was later to claim, serves even more reliably than do fingerprints as a stamp of identity. Like Stout's character, you probably already have a characteristic way of paragraphing, one you can learn to understand and use to advantage.

Paragraphs provide an essential way for writers to guide their readers' understanding. These important elements of prose have, in fact, existed for as long as people in the Western world have been writing. Long before the age of the printing press, sections of text were set off from one another by marks in the margin. In Greek, *para graphos* means "mark beside," and these marks looked like this: ¶. With the invention of movable type, printers had to fit lines of type into frames. Because they could no longer use the margins easily, they began marking a paragraph by indenting its first line, as we still do today. The old name stuck, however, and so we call these units *paragraphs.*

Most simply, a **paragraph** is a group of sentences or a single sentence set off as a unit. Usually the sentences in a paragraph all revolve around one main idea. When a new idea comes up, a new paragraph begins. Within this rather broad general guideline, however, paragraph structure can be highly flexible, allowing writers to create many different individual effects for various writing purposes.

Paragraphing for readers

Numerous studies indicate that readers come to any piece of writing with certain conventional expectations. In terms of paragraphs, readers usually have the following expectations:

- That the beginnings and ends of paragraphs contain important guiding information
- That the opening sentence provides direction and lets readers know what the paragraph is about
- That the middle of the paragraph develops what the paragraph is about
- That the end of the paragraph may sum up the paragraph's contents, bringing the discussion of an idea to a close in anticipation of the paragraph that follows
- That the paragraph "makes sense" as a whole, its words and sentences clearly related
- That the paragraph relates in some clear way to the paragraphs around it

EXERCISE 6.1

The following passage consists of a series of paragraphs, run together, from an essay by scientist Lewis Thomas. Read the passage carefully, and decide how you would divide it into paragraphs. Bring your paragraphed passage to class for discussion and comparison with those of your classmates.

My parents' house had an attic, the darkest and strangest part of the building, reachable only by placing a stepladder beneath the trapdoor, and filled with unidentifiable articles too important to be thrown out with the trash but no longer suitable to have at hand. This mysterious space was the memory of the place. After many years, all the things deposited in it became, one by one, lost to consciousness. But they were still there, we knew, safely and comfortably stored in the tissues of the house. These days most of us live in smaller, more modern houses or in apartments, and attics have vanished. Even the deep closets in which we used to pile things up for temporary forgetting are rarely designed into new homes. Everything now is out in the open, openly acknowledged and displayed, and whenever we grow tired of a memory, an old chair, a trunkful of old letters, they are carted off to the dump for burning. This has seemed a healthier way to live, except maybe for the smoke—everything out to be looked at, nothing strange hidden under the roof, nothing forgotten because of no place left in impenetrable darkness to forget. Openness is the new life-style, no undisclosed belongings, no private secrets. Candor is the rule in architecture. The house is a machine for living, and what kind of a machine would hide away its worn-out, obsolescent parts? But it is in our nature as human beings to clutter, and we hanker for places set aside, reserved for storage. We tend to accumulate and outgrow possessions at the same time, and it is an endlessly discomforting mental task to keep sorting out the ones to get rid of. We might, we think, remember them later and find a use for them, and if they are gone for good, off to the dump, this is a source of nervousness. I think it may be one of the reasons we drum our fingers so much these days.
— LEWIS THOMAS, "The Attic of the Brain"

Richard Larson explains what he sees as the three categories of paragraph theory: (1) paragraphs as expanded sentences, governed by comparable syntactical forces; (2) as self-contained units of writing with their own unique principles; (3) and as parts of the overall discourse, informed by the strategies a writer chooses for the overall piece.

EXERCISE 6.1: Suggested Answers

Thomas' paragraphs are as follows:

Paragraph 2 begins with sentence 5.

Paragraph 3 begins with sentence 7.

Paragraph 4 begins with sentence 8.

Paragraph 5 begins with sentence 12.

Note that paragraph 3 is one sentence.

USEFUL READING

The Sentence and the Paragraph. Urbana, IL: NCTE, 1963. An important collection comprising essays by Francis Christensen on the generative rhetoric of the sentence and the paragraph. Also includes Alton L. Becker's "A Tagmemic Approach to Paragraph Analysis" and a symposium on the paragraph by Francis Christensen, A. L. Becker, Paul C. Rodgers, Jr., Josephine Miles, and David H. Karrfalt.

Everyday use

Of all the paragraphs in a piece of writing, none is more important than the first. Outside of classroom assignments, in fact—in job applications, newspaper articles, fund-raising appeals—the quality of the opening paragraph often determines whether readers even bother to read further. One high-school student, Ted Frantz, found himself concentrating hard on his opening paragraph as he worked on an essay describing his "major academic interest" to accompany his college application. Here is the paragraph he came up with to get his readers' attention and introduce his subject:

Picture a five-year-old boy with a stack of cards in his hands, not baseball cards, but presidential flash cards. He would run around asking anybody to question him about presidents; this kid knew incredible facts and could name every president in the correct order from Washington to Ford. I was this little boy, and ever since I was five, I have had a passion for studying history.

Take some time to look at some opening paragraphs in the reading you normally do: newspapers or magazines, textbooks, "junk mail." How well do such paragraphs get and hold your attention? Bring the paragraphs you find to class for discussion.

BACKGROUND

Students often have problems with paragraphing—with development and cohesion. And their problems are often diagnosed in various ways. For instance, George Goodin and Kyle Perkins argue that because students fail to subordinate effectively, their writing is replete with digressions and afterthoughts ("What Makes a Text Coherent?" *CE* 34 [1983]: 417–30). Betty Bamberg argues that cohesion comes with the successful movement from "writer-based" to "reader-based" prose. "Writer-based" prose often consists of elliptical expressions, sentences that have meaning for the writer but that omit information necessary for the reader's understanding ("Discourse Analysis and the Art of Coherence." *CE* 44 [1982]: 57–63).

Successful prewriting may be the best cure for both of these paragraphing problems. By planning ahead what to say and how to say it, writers can better stay on course. Therefore, reaffirm the need for prewriting as you introduce paragraphing. Adequate prewriting will result in a more orderly text, one more easily paragraphed during drafting or revision.

6a

Constructing unified, coherent, and well-developed paragraphs

Let us look now at the specific elements that make up a well-written paragraph—one that makes a point in a way that is easy for readers to understand and follow. Consider the following paragraph:

I never knew anyone who'd grown up in Jackson without being afraid of Mrs. Calloway, our librarian. She ran the Library absolutely by herself, from the desk where she sat with her back to the books and facing the stairs, her dragon eye on the front door, where who knew what kind of person might come in from the public? SILENCE in big black letters was on signs tacked up everywhere. She herself spoke in her normally commanding voice; every word could be heard all over the Library above a steady seething sound coming from her electric fan; it was the only fan in the Library and stood on her desk, turned directly onto her streaming face.
– EUDORA WELTY, *One Writer's Beginnings*

This paragraph begins with a general statement of the main idea: that everyone who grew up in Jackson feared Mrs. Calloway. All the other sentences then give specific details about why she inspired such fear. This example demonstrates the three qualities essential to most successful paragraphs: **unity**, **coherence**, and **development**. It focuses on one main idea (unity); its parts are clearly related (coherence); and its main idea is supported with specifics (development).

Making paragraphs unified: focusing on a main idea

To be readable and effective, paragraphs generally focus on one main idea. One good way to achieve such paragraph **unity** is to state the main idea clearly in one sentence and relate all the other sentences in the paragraph to that idea. The sentence that presents the main idea is called the **topic sentence**. Like the thesis for an essay, the topic sentence includes a topic and some comment on that topic (see 3b). In the above paragraph by Eudora Welty, the topic sentence opens the paragraph. Its topic is Mrs. Calloway; its comment, that those who grew up in Jackson were afraid of her.

1

Positioning a topic sentence

Although a topic sentence usually appears at the beginning of a paragraph, it may appear anywhere in the paragraph—or it may not appear at all, but rather be implied.

Topic sentence at the beginning

If you want readers to see your point immediately, open with the topic sentence. Such a strategy can be particularly useful in essay examinations (Chapter 46), in memos (Chapter 47), or in argumentative writing (Chapter 5). The following paragraph opens with a clear topic sentence on which subsequent sentences build.

> *Our friendship was the source of much happiness and many memories.* We danced and snapped our fingers simultaneously to the soul tunes of the Jacksons and Stevie Wonder. We sweated together in the sweltering summer sun, trying to win the championship for our softball team. I recall the taste of pepperoni and sausage pizza as we discussed the highlights of our team's victory. Once we even became attracted to the same young man, but luckily we were able to share his friendship.

BACKGROUND

The notion that one sentence in every paragraph should announce the topic of that paragraph was derived from the fourth law of Alexander Bain's "seven laws" for creating paragraphs: "Indication of theme: The opening sentence, unless obviously preparatory, is expected to indicate the scope of the paragraph" (*English Composition and Rhetoric,* 1866).

Since Bain, the "topic sentence" has remained controversial in composition theory. Although most compositionists agree with Bain that every paragraph should have a unifying theme or purpose, not all agree that it should be announced by a topic sentence. In his study of professional writers, Richard Braddock found that topic sentences are used far less than we have traditionally believed; his research calls into question the teaching of topic sentences. On the other hand, Frank D'Angelo argues that despite Braddock's findings, the use of topic sentences improves the readability of a paragraph; therefore, all writers—and especially beginning writers—should use topic sentences.

OPTIONAL EXERCISE

If your class uses a reader, have students turn to *any* essay in it and see whether they can find a topic sentence in each paragraph. (1) What is the placement of the topic sentence? (2) What are the key terms in that topic sentence? (3) How does the information in that paragraph relate to those key words?

The topic sentence announces the main topic of the paragraph (a friendship) and comments on it (as the source of happiness and memories). The next four sentences elaborate on the topic by giving specific examples and concrete physical descriptions to show the reader how the happiness and memories were created.

Topic sentence at the end

When specific details lead up to a generalization, putting the topic sentence at the end of the paragraph makes good sense. In the following paragraph, the last sentence is a general statement that sums up and accounts for the specifics that have preceded it.

> During the visit, Dee takes the pictures, every one of them, including the one of the house that she used to live in and hate. She takes the churn top and dasher, both whittled out of a tree by one of Mama's uncles. She tries to take Grandma Dee's quilts. Mama and Maggie use these inherited items every day, not only appreciating their heritage but living it too. *Dee, on the other hand, wants these items only for decorative use, thus forsaking and ignoring their* real *heritage.*

In this instance, the concluding topic sentence brings the paragraph to its climax by explaining the significance of the things Dee takes.

Topic sentence at the beginning and end

Sometimes you will want to state a topic sentence at the beginning of the paragraph and then refer to it in a slightly different form at the end. Such an "echo" of the topic sentence adds emphasis, pointing up the importance you attach to the idea. In the following paragraph, the writer begins with a topic sentence announcing a problem.

> *Many of the difficulties we experience in relationships are caused by the unrealistic expectations we have of each other.* Think about it. Women are expected to feel comfortable doing most of the sacrificing. They are supposed to stay fine, firm, and forever twenty-two, while doing double duty in the home and in the workplace. The burden on men is no easier. They should be tall, handsome, and able to wine and dine the women. Many women go for the glitter and then expect these men to calm down once in a relationship and become faithful, sensitive, supportive, and loving. Let's face it. Both women and men have been unrealistic. *It's time we develop a new sensitivity toward each other and ask ourselves what it is we need from each other that is realistic and fair.*

The last sentence restates the topic sentence as a proposal for solving the problem. This echo of the topic sentence is especially appropriate, for the essay goes on to specify how the problem might be solved.

USEFUL READING

Braddock, Richard. "The Frequency and Placement of Topic Sentences in Expository Prose." *Research in the Teaching of English* 8 (Winter 1974): 287–302. After analyzing the use of topic sentences by professional writers, Braddock concludes that topic sentences are used far less than textbooks claim. We should not deceive our students on the subject.

D'Angelo, Frank. "The Topic Sentence Revisited." *CE* 37 (1986): 431–41. Citing work in psycholinguistics, D'Angelo argues that the use of topic sentences improves readability, which justifies teaching them.

Markels, Robin Bell. *A New Perspective on Cohesion in Expository Paragraphs.* Carbondale: Southern Illinois UP, 1984. Investigating paragraph cohesion from a perspective that focus both on semantics and structural (syntactic) cohesiveness, Markels offers useful alternative backgrounding to the grammatical concept of unity.

Topic sentence implied but not stated

Occasionally, a topic will be so obvious that no topic sentence is necessary at all. Here is an example of such a paragraph, from an essay about working as an airport cargo handler.

> In winter the warehouse is cold and damp. There is no heat. The large steel doors that line the warehouse walls stay open most of the day. In the cold months, wind, rain, and snow blow across the floor. In the summer the warehouse becomes an oven. Dust and sand from the runways mix with the toxic fumes of fork lifts, leaving a dry, stale taste in your mouth. The high windows above the doors are covered with a thick, black dirt that kills the sun. The men work in shadows with the constant roar of jet engines blowing dangerously in their ears.
>
> – Patrick Fenton, "Confessions of a Working Stiff"

Here the implied topic sentence might be stated as *Working conditions in the warehouse are uncomfortable, dreary, and hazardous to health and hearing.* But the writer does not have to state this information explicitly, because we can gather it easily from the examples and specific details that he provides. The description of "wind, rain, and snow" blowing across the floor in the winter, of "dust and sand" mixed with "toxic fumes" in an "oven" in summer, and of "thick, black dirt that kills the sun" and "the constant roar of jet engines" makes the general unpleasantness and danger of this workplace vividly clear.

Though implied topic sentences are common, especially in descriptions, they may be viewed as weaknesses in some college writing.

EXERCISE 6.2

Choose an essay you have written, and identify the topic sentence of each paragraph, noting where in the paragraph each topic sentence appears and whether any is implied rather than stated. Experiment with one paragraph, positioning its topic sentence in at least two different places. What difference does it make? If you have any implied topic sentences, try stating them explicitly. Is the paragraph easier to read?

EXERCISE 6.2: Answers will vary.

2

Relating each sentence to the main idea

Whether the main idea of a paragraph is stated in a topic sentence or is only implied, you have to make sure each sentence relates or contributes to the main idea. Look, for example, at the following paragraph, which opens an essay about black music:

When I was a teenager, there were two distinct streams of popular music: one was black, and the other was white. The former could only be heard way at the end of the radio dial, while white music dominated everywhere else. This separation was a fact of life, the equivalent of blacks sitting in the back of the bus and "whites only" signs below the Mason-Dixon line. Satchmo might grin for days on "The Ed Sullivan Show" and certain historians hold forth *ad nauseam* on the black contribution to American music, but the truth was that our worlds rarely twined.
— MARCIA GILLESPIE, "They're Playing My Music, but Burying My Dreams"

Sentence one announces the topic (two streams of popular music: black and white). Sentence two relates the topic to the respective positions of "black" and "white" music on the radio dial, and sentence three expands on this notion of musical separation by comparing it to the separate seats for blacks on buses or their exclusion from certain "public" places. The last sentence rephrases the topic sentence in a much more pointed way: though black music might appear regularly on television and people might write volumes about how much blacks have contributed to American music, the two worlds of black and white music at one time remained separate. Each sentence clearly relates to the topic, and the paragraph as a whole is unified.

EXERCISE 6.3

The following paragraph lacks unity. Identify the topic sentence, and revise the paragraph by deleting any sentence unrelated to the topic.

According to advertisers, one side of every woman's personality is sensual, knowing, experienced, worldly, unshockable, well-versed in the art of love: in short, a woman in every sense of the word. The opposing side is shy, sweet, trusting, innocent, untried: a maiden totally immersed in her own purity. Many argue that men possess a split personality, too. This is exactly how I feel as a woman: forever pushed, pulled, jostled, teased, and finally lured into treading a fine thread between blatant maturity and subtle innocence. No wonder so many women begin to feel like a Dr. Doolittle "Push-me, Pull-you," the animal with two heads facing in opposite directions, each vying for its own desires and neither budging an inch.

EXERCISE 6.4

Choose one of the following topic sentences, and spend some time exploring the topic (see 3a). Then write a paragraph that includes the topic sentence, making sure that each of the other sentences relates to it. Assume that the paragraph will be part of a letter you are writing to an acquaintance.

1. I found out quickly that college life was not quite what I had expected.
2. Being part of the "in crowd" used to be of utmost importance to me.
3. My work experience has taught me several important lessons.
4. Until recently, I never appreciated my parents fully.
5. I expect my college education to do more than simply assure me of a job.

EXERCISE 6.5

Choose an essay you have written recently, and examine the second, third, and fourth paragraphs. Does each have a topic sentence or strongly imply one? Do all the other sentences in the paragraph focus on its main idea? Would you now revise any of these paragraphs—and if so, how?

EXERCISE 6.5: Answers will vary.

6c

Making paragraphs coherent: fitting details together

A paragraph has coherence if its details fit together clearly in a way that readers can easily follow. You can achieve paragraph coherence in three simple ways: by organizing ideas; by repeating key terms or phrases; by using parallel structures.

1

Organizing ideas

If you take every fourth sentence of an essay and arrange them together, one after another, in paragraph form, you will *not* end up with a paragraph. Why not? Because the sentences will have only a haphazard relationship to one another. Though they may well be connected to the same topic, the lack of any organizational relationship will result in incoherence. Clear organization of ideas goes a long way toward creating coherence. The following discussion will review the most common means of organizing a paragraph—spatial order, chronological order, and logical order.

Using spatial order

Paragraphs organized in **spatial order** take a "tour" of something, beginning at one point and moving, say, from near to far, left to right, north to south. Especially useful in **descriptive** paragraphs, spatial order allows a writer to direct readers' attention in an orderly way to various elements of

USEFUL READING

Halliday, M. A. K., and Rugaiya Hasan. *Cohesion in English*. London: Longman, 1976. A classification of cohesive ties in paragraphs and essays: reference, substitution, ellipsis, conjunction, and lexical ties.

Witte, Stephen P., and Lester Faigley. "Coherence, Cohesion, and Writing Quality." *CCC* 32 (1981): 189–204. Using an adjusted version of Halliday and Hasan's classifications, the authors conclude that cohesion is connected to our perceptions of how well the text fits to its context.

something in physical space. A topic sentence may be unnecessary in such a paragraph, because the paragraph's organization will be obvious to the reader. Sometimes, however, a topic sentence at the beginning of the paragraph helps set the scene or tell the reader what is going to be described. Note the movement from ceiling to walls to floor in the following paragraph.

> The professor's voice began to fade into the background as my eyes wandered around the classroom in the old administration building. The water-stained ceiling was cracked and peeling, and the splitting wooden beams played host to a variety of lead pipes and coils. My eyes followed these pipes down the walls and around corners, until eventually I saw the electrical outlets. I thought it strange that they were exposed, and not built in, until I realized that there was probably no electricity when the building was built. Below the outlets the sunshine was falling in bright rays across the hardwood floor, and I noticed how smoothly it was worn. Time had certainly taken its toll on this building.

Using chronological order

Paragraphs organized in **chronological order** arrange a series of events according to time, putting earliest events first, followed in sequence by later events, one at a time. Chronological order is used frequently in **narrative** paragraphs, which basically tell a story. Rarely do they require a topic sentence, because the main idea is obvious in the action. The following paragraph uses careful chronology to tell a story and also to build suspense: we want to know what the last event in the sequence will be. The words expressing time help build this suspense: *all of a sudden, three months, a year later,* and so on.

> The experience of Lloyd S., an Oregon businessperson, is one of the most convincing cases for taking vitamins. For his first forty years, Lloyd was healthy and robust. He owned a thriving nursery and loved to hike, fish, and camp. All of a sudden, he started feeling fatigued. A loss of appetite and weight soon followed, and in three months he was transformed from a ruddy, muscular man into a pallid, emaciated one. Lloyd had cancer of the pancreas. After he was given a prognosis of six months to live, his family and friends were devastated, but Lloyd was a fighter. When the conventional treatments of drugs and chemotherapy did not help, he turned to a holistic approach, which emphasized a change in diet and life style—and large doses of vitamins. After a series of blood tests to discover every possible nutritional deficiency, Lloyd was given concentrated vitamin and mineral supplements to ensure maximum cell efficiency and growth so that his body could attempt to heal itself. At the end of six months, Lloyd not only was alive but also showed improvement. A year later he was free of cancer and began the long battle to regain his original vitality. Coincidence? Perhaps. To Lloyd and me, however, his

recovery became a powerful demonstration of how the world's most intricate machine, the human body, performs—if only we supply it with the needed nutrients.

Chronological order is also commonly used in **explaining a process**. Paragraphs that explain how something happens or how something is done proceed in chronological order: first one step, then the next, then the next. You are already very familiar with process as a means of organizing information. After all, every set of directions, every recipe, every user's manual, presents a series of steps that make up a process someone wants to learn or to follow. Here is an example:

> Before trying to play the flute, figure out how to put it together. The flute is divided into three parts: the mouthpiece, the main body, and the end piece. First remove the main body (the longest part) from the case, and set it down with the keys facing up and the openings away from you. Now, pick up the mouthpiece (the piece with one hole), and attach it to the hole at the far left end of the main body by gently twisting it from side to side, in a manner similar to jiggling a door knob. Repeat the same process in attaching the end piece to the other end of the main body, taking care not to twist or smash the keys. The keys on the end piece should be lined up with those on the main body.

In college writing, you will probably use process paragraphs less often to tell readers how to do something than to explain how a process occurs in general—for example, how a bill becomes law or how aerosol sprays destroy the ozone layer of the atmosphere.

Using logical order

Paragraphs organized in **logical order** arrange details to reflect certain logical relationships. Explanations and examples of some of these relationships—illustration, definition, division/classification, comparison/contrast, cause-effect, and problem-solution—are given in 6d. Two other logical patterns commonly used in paragraphs are *general-to-specific* and *specific-to-general*.

Paragraphs organized in a **general-to-specific** pattern usually open with a topic sentence presenting a general or abstract idea, followed by a number of more specific points designed to substantiate or prove or elaborate on the generalization.

GENERAL-TO-SPECIFIC

> We have surely all cheated at least one time in our lives. People cheat in dozens of ways, ranging from small-scale things like writing notes on their hands for tests to the monumental deception of having an affair.

GENERAL TOPIC

SPECIFICS

OPTIONAL EXERCISE

Have students practice using logical order by writing a paragraph describing their possessions—academic/personal; from home/from school; old/new; personal/public. They may want to look around their rooms as they write.

Did they start out or end up with a controlling idea? What is it? Do they have a topic sentence?

We cheat when we pass the speed limit. Powerful families and corporations cheat their way out of legal binds with the help of highly paid lawyers. Businesspeople record activities, such as dining out, as business-related so they will not have to pay for the expense personally. Dieters are always cheating, and if we really think about it, people cheat when they use makeup or fashion to cover up or disguise features they find unattractive. Even my grandmother cheats by taking short cuts in her prescribed daily walks.

Paragraphs can also follow a **specific-to-general** organization, first providing a series of specific examples or details and then tying them together with a general conclusion.

SPECIFIC-TO-GENERAL

At 8:01 A.M. on Saturday morning, the bright images hawk cereal: Fruit Loops, Frosted Flakes, Captain Crunch. At 8:11, it's toy time, as squads of delighted children demonstrate the pleasures of owning Barbie, Ken, or G. I. Joe. By 8:22, Coca-Cola is quenching thirsts everywhere, and at 8:31, kids declare devotion to their Nikes, insuring that every child tuned in will want a pair. And so goes Saturday morning children's programming: one part "program" (and that exclusively cartoons) to three parts advertising. "Children's television" today is simply a euphemism for one long, hard sell, an initiation rite designed to create more and more American consumers.

SPECIFIC POINTS

GENERAL TOPIC

EXERCISE 6.6: Answers will vary.

EXERCISE 6.6

Choose one of the following topic sentences, or create one of your own; and try writing two different paragraphs on the topic, using a different organizational pattern for each. Then explain, in writing, why you used the organizational patterns you did and how effective and coherent each one was.

1. I remember very clearly the first time I ever experienced great satisfaction.
2. Explaining _____ to my parents was the hardest thing I've ever done.
3. People who are extremely vain about their looks often go to ridiculous lengths to keep up their appearance.
4. My classes this term can, with understatement, be described as demanding.
5. Many people share one basic fear: public speaking.

2

Repeating key words and phrases

A major means of building coherence in paragraphs is through **repetition**. Weaving in repeated references to key words and phrases not only links sentences but also alerts readers to the importance the words or phrases hold in the larger piece of writing. Notice in the following example how the repetition of the key words *shopping, market(s), shoppers, bargain(ing), customers, shop(s), buy, price, store,* and *item* helps hold the paragraph together.

> Over the centuries, *shopping* has changed in function as well as in style. Before the Industrial Revolution, most consumer goods were sold in open-air *markets, customers* who went into an actual *shop* were expected to *buy* something, and *shoppers* were always expected to *bargain* for the best possible *price*. In the nineteenth century, however, the development of the department *store* changed the relationship between buyers and sellers. Instead of visiting several *market* stalls or small *shops, customers* could now *buy* a variety of merchandise under the same roof; instead of feeling expected to *buy,* they were welcome just to look; and instead of *bargaining* with several merchants, they paid a fixed *price* for each *item*. In addition, they could return an *item* to the *store* and exchange it for a different one or get their money back. All of these changes helped transform *shopping* from serious requirement to psychological recreation.

Notice also that the cluster of other terms related to shopping helps make the paragraph hang together: *consumer goods, buyers, sellers, merchandise, money.*

EXERCISE 6.7

Read the following paragraph. Then identify the places where the author repeats key words and phrases, and explain how they bring coherence to the paragraph.

> "Thirty-nine fifty for one textbook! You've got to be kidding," I mumbled as I dragged myself slowly toward the checkout stand. I did not know how I was going to pay for tuition, housing, phone bills, and groceries if all my textbooks cost me that much. "I might as well join the army," I thought. At least it would pay my tuition and give me army rations. Right now, army chow sounded considerably better than boiled pages from a psychology text. I stood there full of resentment; I had no intention of spending all my hard-earned money on textbooks. Yet I had no choice. This was a book I had to have, whatever the cost.

BACKGROUND

Repetition of key words and phrases is an age-old technique for pulling together thematically related units; moreover, the rhythm of such verbal/visual echoing effectively holds the audience's attention. We are all familiar with various repetitive devices:

Single Word

> Vanity of vanities, saith the preacher, vanity of vanities; all is vanity.
> —ECCLESIASTICUS 1:1

Syntactic Structure

> The thoughts are but overflowings of the mind, and the tongue is but a servant of the thought.
> —PHILIP SIDNEY

> Blood hath bought blood, and
>   blows have answer'd blows;
> Strength match'd with strength,
>   and power confronted power.
> —SHAKESPEARE

Anaphora (Initial Repetition)

> [W]e shall defend our island, whatever the cost may be, we shall fight on the beaches, we shall fight on the landing grounds, we shall fight in the fields and in the streets, we shall fight in the hill; we shall never surrender.
> —WINSTON CHURCHILL

> Say that I was a drum major for justice. Say that I was a drum major for peace. That I was a drum major for righteousness. And all of the other shallow things will not matter.
> —MARTIN LUTHER KING, JR.

EXERCISE 6.7: Suggested Answers

Repeated key words include: textbook; pay; tuition; cost; army.

3
Using parallel structures

Parallel structures—structures that are grammatically similar—provide another effective way of bringing coherence to a paragraph. They emphasize the connection between related ideas or events in different sentences. For example:

> William Faulkner's "Barn Burning" tells the story of a young boy trapped in a no-win situation. If he betrays his father, he loses his family. If he betrays justice, he becomes a fugitive. In trying to free himself from his trap, he does both.

In this paragraph, the writer skillfully uses the parallel structures *if he does x, he does y,* in order to give the effect of a "no-win situation." At the end of the paragraph, we are prepared for the last sentence in the parallel sequence: *In doing x, he does y.* As readers, we feel pulled along by the force of the parallel structures in the paragraph. (See Chapter 21 for detailed discussion of ways to use parallel structure to create various effects.)

EXERCISE 6.8

Read the following paragraph from a famous essay by a woman who wants a "wife," and identify every use of repetition and parallel structures. In a brief paragraph of your own, explain how the writer uses these structures to build coherence in this paragraph.

I would like to go back to school so that I can become economically independent, support myself, and, if need be, support those dependent upon me. I want a wife who will work and send me to school. And while I am going to school I want a wife to take care of my children. I want a wife to keep track of the children's doctor and dentist appointments. And to keep track of mine, too. I want a wife to make sure my children eat properly and are kept clean. I want a wife who will wash the children's clothes and keep them mended. I want a wife who is a good nuturant attendant to my children, who arranges for their schooling, makes sure that they have an adequate social life with their peers, takes them to the park, the zoo, etc. I want a wife who takes care of the children when they are sick, a wife who arranges to be around when the children need special care, because, of course, I cannot miss classes at school. My wife must arrange to lose time at work and not lose the job. It may mean a small cut in my wife's income from time to time, but I guess I can tolerate that. Needless to say, my wife will arrange and pay for the care of the children while my wife is working.
　　　　　　　　　　　　　　　　　— JUDY BRADY, "I Want a Wife"

4

Using pronouns

Writers also achieve coherence in a paragraph through the use of **pronouns**. Because pronouns usually refer back to nouns or other pronouns, they act as natural coherence devices, leading readers naturally from sentence to sentence (see Chapter 13). The following paragraph, from an essay on old age, uses pronouns effectively in linking sentences to one another. Note how much slower and more awkward the paragraph would be if each pronoun were replaced with the noun it stands for. Also note that the writer uses the name when he first introduces each new artist—and then uses pronouns thereafter to refer to that person. (Italics added for emphasis.)

> For such [old] persons, every new infirmity is an enemy to be outwitted, an obstacle to be overcome by force of will. *They* enjoy each little victory over *themselves,* and sometimes *they* win a major success. Renoir was one of *them. He* continued painting, and magnificently, for years after *he* was crippled by arthritis; the brush had to be strapped to *his* arm. "You don't need your hand to paint," *he* said. Goya was another of the unvanquished. At 72 *he* retired as an official painter of the Spanish court and decided to work only for *himself. His* later years were those of the famous "black paintings" in which *he* let *his* imagination run (and also of the lithographs, then a new technique). At 78 *he* escaped a reign of terror in Spain by fleeing to Bordeaux. *He* was deaf and *his* eyes were failing; in order to work *he* had to wear several pairs of spectacles, one over another, and then use a magnifying glass; but *he* was producing splendid work in a totally new style. At 80 *he* drew an ancient man propped on two sticks, with a mass of white hair and beard hiding *his* face and with the inscription "*I* am still learning." — MALCOLM COWLEY, *The View from 80*

EXERCISE 6.9

Analyze three paragraphs from something you've written recently for pronoun use. How do the pronouns bring coherence to the paragraphs? Is it clear what noun or pronoun each of the pronouns refers back to? How could different or additional pronoun use improve the coherence of these paragraphs?

5

Using transitional devices

Transitions are words and phrases that help bring coherence to a paragraph by signaling relationships between and among sentences. In acting as signposts from one idea to the next, transitions such as *after all, for*

My first aim will be to *clean down* . . . Moor House from chamber to cellar; my next to rub it up with beeswax, oil, and an indefinite number of cloths, till it glitters again; my third, to arrange every chair, table, bed, carpet with mathematical precision; afterwards I shall go near to ruin you in coals and peat to keep up good fires in every room; and lastly, the two days preceding that on which your sisters are expected will be devoted by Hannah and me to such a beating of eggs, sorting of currants, grating of spices, compounding of Christmas cakes, chopping up of materials for mince-pies, and solemnizing of other culinary rites, as words can convey but an inadequate notion of to the uninitiated like you. My purpose, in short, is to have all things in an absolutely perfect state of readiness for Diana and Mary before next Thursday; and my ambition is to give them a beau-ideal of a welcome when they come. (Chapter xxxiv)

FOR THE WRITING LOG

Have your students locate a paragraph from anything they have been reading which makes obvious or interesting use of transitions and copy it or clip it into their writing log. Have them mark all the transitions and note the functions they perform.

FOR COLLABORATIVE WORK

Have students break into groups and trade drafts of current essays. As they read one another's papers, have them draw arrows between or circles around key terms, ideas, and pronouns, and mark transitional phrases with heavy underlining and parallelism with //sm. Simply stopping to analyze prose might help them better understand elements of unity and coherence.

example, indeed, so, and *thus* help readers follow the progression of a paragraph. *Finally* indicates that a last point is at hand; *likewise,* that a similar point is about to be made; and so on. To get an idea of how important transitions are in directing readers, try reading the following paragraph, from which all transitional devices have been removed:

A PARAGRAPH WITH NO TRANSITIONS

In "The Fly," Katherine Mansfield tries to show us the "real" personality of "the boss" beneath his exterior. The fly helps her to portray this real self. The boss goes through a range of emotions and feelings. He expresses these feelings on a small but determined fly, whom the reader realizes he unconsciously relates to his son. The author basically splits up the story into three parts, with the boss's emotions and actions changing quite measurably. With old Woodifield, with himself, and with the fly, we see the boss's manipulativeness. Our understanding of him as a hard and cruel man grows.

We can, if we work at it, figure out the relationship of these ideas to one another, for this paragraph is essentially unified by one major idea. But the lack of transitions results in an abrupt, choppy rhythm that lurches from one idea to the next, dragging the confused reader behind. See how much easier the passage is to read and understand with transition added:

THE SAME PARAGRAPH, WITH TRANSITIONS

In "The Fly," Katherine Mansfield tries to show us the "real" personality of "the boss" beneath his exterior. The fly *in the story's title* helps her to portray this real self. *In the course of the story,* the boss goes through a range of emotions and feelings. *At the end,* he *finally* expresses these feelings on a small but determined fly, whom the reader realizes he unconsciously relates to his son. *To accomplish her goal,* the author basically splits up the story into three parts, with the boss's emotions and actions changing quite measurably *throughout. First* with old Woodifield, *then* with himself, and *last* with the fly, we see the boss's manipulativeness. *With each part,* our understanding of him as a hard and cruel man grows.

Note how the writer carefully leads us through the points of her paragraph. Most of the transitional devices here point to movement in time, helping us follow the chronology of the story being discussed: *in the course of the story; at the end; finally; throughout; first; then; last.*

It is important to note that transitions can only clarify connections between thoughts; they cannot create connections. As a writer, you must choose transitions that fit your meaning and not expect a transition to *provide* meaning. If you open a sentence with *therefore,* for example, be sure that the thought expressed by the rest of the sentence really follows logically from the previous sentences.

Commonly used transitions

TO SIGNAL SEQUENCE

again, also, and, and then, besides, finally, first . . . second . . . third, furthermore, last, moreover, next, still, too

TO SIGNAL TIME

after a bit, after a few days, after a while, afterward, as long as, as soon as, at last, at length, at that time, before, earlier, immediately, in the meantime, in the past, lately, later, meanwhile, now, presently, shortly, simultaneously, since, so far, soon, then, thereafter, until, when

TO SIGNAL COMPARISON

again, also, in the same way, likewise, once more, similarly

TO SIGNAL CONTRAST

although, but, despite, even though, however, in contrast, in spite of, instead, nevertheless, nonetheless, notwithstanding, on the contrary, on the one hand . . . on the other hand, regardless, still, though, yet

TO SIGNAL EXAMPLES

after all, even, for example, for instance, indeed, in fact, of course, specifically, such as, the following example, to illustrate

TO SIGNAL CAUSE AND EFFECT

accordingly, as a result, because, consequently, for this purpose, hence, so, then, therefore, thereupon, thus, to this end

TO SIGNAL PLACE

above, adjacent to, below, beyond, closer to, elsewhere, far, farther on, here, near, nearby, opposite to, there, to the left, to the right

TO SIGNAL CONCESSION

although it is true that, granted that, I admit that, it may appear that, naturally, of course

TO SIGNAL SUMMARY, REPETITION, OR CONCLUSION

as a result, as has been noted, as I have said, as we have seen, as mentioned earlier, in any event, in conclusion, in other words, in short, on the whole, therefore, to summarize

For a discussion of transitional devices to link paragraphs, see 6f.

EXERCISE 6.10: Suggested Answers

Transitional devices include: like that of; also; Some years ago; Today; particularly; of course; For many years; for instance; but.

EXERCISE 6.11: Suggested Answers

Here is the paragraph as published.

(3) And in the next year the drought hit. (5) My mother and father trudged from the well to the chickens, the well to the calf pasture, the well to the barn, and from the well to the garden. (1) The sun came out hot and bright, endlessly, day after day. (6) The crops shriveled and died. (2) They harvested half the corn, and ground the other half, stalks and all, and fed it to the cattle as fodder. (7) With the price at four cents a bushel for the harvested crop, they couldn't afford to haul it into town. (4) They burned it in the furnace for fuel that winter.

EXERCISE 6.12: Suggested Answers

I must make, I must confess, I have been, I have almost; first; confessions/confess; white moderate, White Citizen's Counciler, white moderate; who is more devoted, who prefers, who constantly says, who paternalistically believes, who lives, who constantly advises; to "order" that to justice, a negative peace which

EXERCISE 6.10

Read the following paragraph, and identify all transitional devices. Then read the paragraph with these words or phrases left out, and briefly describe, in writing, the difference the transitional devices make.

The popularity of the various regional styles of American costume, like that of the various national styles, is also related to economic and political factors. Some years ago modes often originated in the Far West and the word "California" on a garment was thought to be an allurement. Today, with power and population growth shifting to the Southwestern oil-producing states, Wild West styles—particularly those of Texas—are in vogue. This fashion, of course, is not new. For many years men who have never been nearer to a cow than the local steakhouse have worn Western costume to signify that they are independent, tough and reliable. In a story by Flannery O'Connor, for instance, the sinister traveling salesman is described as wearing "a broad-brimmed stiff gray hat of the kind used by businessmen who would like to look like cowboys"—but, it is implied, seldom succeed in doing so.

—ALISON LURIE, *The Language of Clothes*

EXERCISE 6.11

The following sentences are shown in the following paragraph out of the original order. Look for pronouns, transitional words and phrases, and other clues to coherence. Then rearrange the sentences so that the paragraph is once again coherent.

(1) The sun came out hot and bright, endlessly, day after day. (2) They harvested half the corn, and ground the other half, stalks and all, and fed it to the cattle as fodder. (3) And in the next year the drought hit. (4) They burned it in the furnace for fuel that winter. (5) My mother and father trudged from the well to the chickens, the well to the calf pasture, the well to the barn, and from the well to the garden. (6) The crops shriveled and died. (7) With the price at four cents a bushel for the harvested crop, they couldn't afford to haul it into town.

— DONNA SMITH-YACKEL, "My Mother Never Worked"

EXERCISE 6.12

Identify each of the devices—repetition of key words or phrases, parallel structures, pronouns, transitional expressions—that make the following paragraph coherent.

I must make two honest confessions to you, my Christian and Jewish brothers. First, I must confess that over the past few years I have been gravely disappointed with the white moderate. I have almost reached the regrettable conclusion that the Negro's great stumbling block on his stride toward freedom is not the White Citizen's Counciler or the Ku Klux Klanner, but the white moderate, who is more devoted to "order" than to justice; who prefers a negative peace which is the absence of tension to a positive peace which is the presence of justice; who constantly says, "I agree with you in the goal you seek, but I cannot agree with your methods of direct action"; who paternalistically believes he can set the timetable for another man's freedom; who lives by a mythical concept of time and who constantly advises the Negro to wait for a "more convenient season." Shallow understanding from people of good will is more frustrating than absolute misunderstanding from people of ill will. Lukewarm acceptance is much more bewildering than outright rejection.

– MARTIN LUTHER KING, JR., "Letter from Birmingham Jail"

6d

Developing paragraphs fully: providing details

In addition to being unified and coherent, a paragraph must hold readers' interest and explore its topic fully, using whatever details, evidence, and examples are necessary. Without such **development**, a paragraph may seem lifeless and abstract.

Most good writing does two things: it presents generalized ideas and explanations, and it backs up these generalities with specifics. This balance, the shifting between general and specific, is especially important at the paragraph level. If a paragraph contains nothing but specific details, with no explanation of how they should be viewed as a whole, readers may have trouble following the writer's meaning. If, on the other hand, a paragraph contains only abstract ideas and general statements, readers will soon become bored or will fail to be convinced by it. General statements or conclusions thus rest on specific, concrete pieces of knowledge and sensory details. Well-developed paragraphs include examples and reasons that demonstrate such knowledge and details. Consider the following poorly developed paragraph:

A POORLY DEVELOPED PARAGRAPH

No such thing as "human nature" compels people to behave, think, or react in certain ways. Rather, from the time of our infancy to our death, we are constantly being taught by the society that surrounds us, the customs, norms, and mores of our distinct culture. Everything in culture is learned, not genetically transmitted.

This paragraph is boring. Although its main idea is clear, and its sentences hold together, it fails to gain our interest, hold our attention, or convince us

is the absence of tension to a positive peace which is the presence of justice; I agree with you, but I cannot agree with; timetable, mythical concept of time, "more convenient season"; Shallow understanding from people of good will, absolute understanding from people of ill will; Lukewarm acceptance, outright rejection.

OPTIONAL EXERCISE

Here is another paragraph for the same kind of analysis performed in Exercise 6.12.

After this display, however, Walters must state a punishment for the affluence she has just eyed so worshipfully. Most often, Walters will, after a little fawning, suddenly confront the subject with a very rude personal question, just as a child or imbecile would. At these moments, the interviewer actively personifies the viewing audience at its nosiest. It is, in fact, her genius to intuit the wonderings of the tactless oaf within each one of us and then to become that oaf, speaking its "mind" right in the star's home, right in the star's face.

—MARK CRISPIN MILLER,
"Barbara Walters' Theater of Revenge"

Too much noise deafens us; too much light dazzles us; too much distance or too much proximity impedes vision; too much length or too much brevity of discourse obscures it.

– BLAISE PASCAL

Then said I, Lord, how long?

–ISAIAH 6:11

because it lacks any concrete illustrations. Now look at the paragraph revised to include needed specifics:

THE SAME PARAGRAPH, REVISED

> Imagine a child in Ecuador dancing to salsa music at a warm family gathering, while another child in the United States is decorating a Christmas tree with bright, shiny red ornaments. Both of these children are taking part in their country's cultures. It is not by instinct that one child knows how to dance to salsa music, nor is it by instinct that the other child knows how to decorate the tree. No such thing as "human nature" compels people to behave, think, or react in certain ways. Rather, from the time of our infancy to our death, we are constantly being taught by the society that surrounds us, the customs, norms, and mores of our distinct culture. A majority of people feel that the evil in human beings is "human nature." However, the Tasaday, a "Stone Age" tribe who were discovered not long ago in the Philippines, do not even have equivalents in their language for the words *hatred, competition, acquisitiveness, aggression,* and *greed.* Such examples suggest that everything in culture is learned, not genetically transmitted.

Though both paragraphs argue the same point, only the second comes to life. It does so by bringing in specific details *from* life. We *want* to read this paragraph, for it appeals to our senses (a child dancing; bright, shiny red ornaments) and our curiosity (who are the Tasaday?).

Almost every paragraph can be improved by making sure that its general ideas rest on enough specific detail. You can, of course, add too many details, pushing examples at the reader when no more are needed. For every writer who has to chop back jungles of detail, however, there are five whose greatest task is to irrigate deserts of generality.

EXERCISE 6.13

Rewrite the following undeveloped paragraphs by adding concrete supporting details, examples, and reasons to them.

1. *The introduction to an essay tentatively titled "A Week on $12.80"*
   Nothing is more frustrating to a college student than being dead broke. Not having money for enough food or for the rent, much less for entertainment, is not much fun. And of course debts for tuition and books keep piling up. No, being broke is not to be recommended.

2. *The introduction to a humorous essay contrasting cats and dogs*
   Have you threatened your cat lately? If not, why not? Why not get a *real* pet—a dog? Dogs, after all, are better pets. Cats, on the other hand, are a menace to the environment.

EXERCISE 6.13: Suggested Answers

(1) Nothing is more frustrating to a college student than being dead broke. As though studying, doing written homework, taking exams, and performing lab experiments aren't enough, most students also have to worry about money. Not having money for enough food or for the rent, much less for entertainment, is not fun. Food and shelter are not comfort enough for the student who spends her days and nights in her schoolwork. She also needs to unwind, but going to the movies, out for pizza or beer, takes money.

(2) Have you threatened your cat lately? If not, why not? Threaten your cat with another pet, a real pet, a better pet—a dog. While your cat lounges around the house, scattering its hair all over your favorite chair, ignoring all your requests to move, to eat, to go out, a dog will anticipate your every command. A dog will leap out of your chair when it sees you come, will lap up its food, and will scratch at the door when you reach for its leash. In addition to its good nature, a dog offers you loyalty and protection.

FOR COLLABORATIVE WORK

Have students break into groups to focus and expand the information in the two paragraphs in Exercise 6.13, revising them completely. Then, have them share their revisions and identify their topic sentences.

1
Using logical patterns of development

The **logical patterns** presented in 3d for organizing essays can also serve as a means of developing paragraphs. These patterns include illustrating, defining, dividing and classifying, comparing and contrasting, exploring causes and effects, and considering problems and solutions or questions and answers.

Illustrating a point

Illustrating a point is one of the most useful ways of developing the main idea of a paragraph. You can illustrate a point with concrete examples or with good reasons.

A SINGLE EXAMPLE

> The Indians made names for us children in their teasing way. Because our very busy mother kept my hair cut short, like my brothers', they called me Short Furred One, pointing to their hair and making the sign for short, the right hand with fingers pressed close together, held upward, back out, at the height intended. With me this was about two feet tall, the Indians laughing gently at my abashed face. I am told that I was given a pair of small moccasins that first time, to clear up my unhappiness at being picked out from the dusk behind the fire and my two unhappy shortcomings made conspicuous. — MARI SANDOZ, "The Go-Along Ones"

SEVERAL REASONS

> But I did not want to shoot the elephant. I watched him beating his bunch of grass against his knees, with that preoccupied grandmotherly air that elephants have. It seemed to me that it would be murder to shoot him. At that age I was not squeamish about killing animals, but I had never shot an elephant and never wanted to. (Somehow it always seems worse to kill a large animal.) Besides, there was the beast's owner to be considered. Alive, the elephant was worth at least a hundred pounds; dead, he would only be worth the value of his tusks, five pounds, possibly. But I had got to act quickly. I turned to some experienced-looking Burmans who had been there when we arrived, and asked them how the elephant had been behaving. They all said the same thing: he took no notice of you if you left him alone, but he might charge if you went too close to him.
> — GEORGE ORWELL, "Shooting an Elephant"

Defining

You will often have occasion to develop an entire paragraph by **defining** a word or concept. Some college courses, particularly ones that deal with difficult abstractions, require writing that often calls for this strategy. A

BACKGROUND

As we have said earlier in these notes, no such thing as a pure definition or division-and-classification or comparison-and-contrast essay exists outside of the classroom, and to teach or assign these techniques as discourse structures is to confuse means with ends. Discourses are, perhaps without exception, motivated by multiple aims. However, we can identify primary aims and primary organizing principles in order to construct essays using dynamic and reciprocal notions of function and form.

FOR THE WRITING LOG

Encourage students to take note of professional writers' use of these strategies in their reading for this and their other courses, and to clip or copy some effective uses of each into a section in their writing logs. Emphasize, though, that these strategies can be "effective" only within a context of larger intentions by having them add some notes on what the writer's overall purposes were and how using these strategies contributed to a larger rhetorical aim.

philosophy exam, for instance, might require you to define concepts such as *truth* or *validity*. Often, however, you will find it necessary to combine definition with other methods of development. You may need to show examples or draw comparisons or divide a term you are defining into two parts. In the following paragraph, Tom Wolfe defines *pornoviolence,* a word he has coined, by contrasting it first with "accumulated slayings and bone crushings" and then with violence seen from the point of view of "the hero."

> It is not the accumulated slayings and bone crushings that make [this TV show into] pornoviolence, however. What makes pornoviolence is that in almost every case the camera angle, therefore the viewer, is with the gun, the fist, the rock. The pornography of violence has no point of view in the old sense that novels do. You do not live the action through the hero's eyes. You live with the aggressor, whoever he may be. One moment you are the hero. The next you are the villain. No matter whose side you may be on consciously, you are in fact with the muscle, and it is you who disintegrate all comers, villains, lawmen, women, anybody. On the rare occasions in which the gun is emptied into the camera—i.e., into your face—the effect is so startling that the pornography of violence all but loses its fantasy charm. There are not nearly so many masochists as sadists among those little devils whispering into one's ears.
>
> — TOM WOLFE, "Pornoviolence"

Dividing and classifying

Dividing breaks a single item into parts. **Classifying,** which is actually a form of dividing, groups many separate items according to their similarities. You could, for instance, develop a paragraph evaluating a history course by dividing the course into several segments—textbooks, lectures, assignments—and examining each one in turn. Or you could use classification in developing a paragraph giving an overview of history courses at your college, grouping the courses in a number of ways—by the time periods or geographic areas covered, by the kinds of assignments demanded, by the numbers of students enrolled, or by some other criterion.

DIVIDING

> We all listen to music according to our separate capacities. But, for the sake of analysis, the whole listening process may become clearer if we break it up into its component parts, so to speak. In a certain sense we all listen to music on three separate planes. For lack of a better terminology, one might name these: (1) the sensuous plane, (2) the expressive plane, (3) the sheerly musical plane. The only advantage to be gained from mechanically splitting up the listening process into these hypothetical planes is the clearer view to be had of the way in which we listen.
>
> — AARON COPLAND, *What to Listen for in Music*

TEACHING PRACTICE

As a way of introducing the idea of classifying, consider asking the class to answer the following series of questions:

> What are your strengths and weaknesses as a writer?
>
> Is your writing process linear or recursive?
>
> How do you learn in this class: from writing? from taking notes? from reading and responding to your friends' work?
>
> What are your reasons for taking this course?

Use their answers to these questions to classify students into different groups. (Not only does this exercise demonstrate classification, it also forces students to become aware of the circumstances or context of this course. In *Teaching the Universe of Discourse,* James Moffett calls such awareness "meta-awareness," a consciousness of abstraction.) Then have students draft a paragraph presenting the results of your classification.

CLASSIFYING

Two types of people are seduced by fad diets. Those who have always been overweight turn to fad diets out of despair; they have tried everything, and yet nothing seems to work. The second group who succumb are those who appear perfectly healthy but are baited with slogans such as "look good, feel good." These slogans prompt self-questioning and insecurity—do I *really* look good and feel good?—and as a direct result, many of these people also fall prey to fad diets. With both types of people, however, the problems surrounding fad diets are numerous and dangerous. In fact, these diets provide neither intelligent nor effective answers to weight control.

Comparing and contrasting

You can develop some paragraphs easily and effectively by comparing and contrasting various aspects of the topic or by comparing and contrasting the topic with something else. **Comparing** things highlights their similarities; **contrasting**, their differences. Whether used alone or together, comparing and contrasting both act to bring the topic at hand more clearly into focus (we can better understand an unknown, for example, by comparing it to something we know well) or to help us evaluate the items compared and contrasted.

You can structure comparison/contrast paragraphs in two basic ways. One way is to present all the information about one item, then all the information about the other item (block method). The other possibility is to alternate back and forth between the two items, focusing in turn on particular characteristics of each (alternating method).

BLOCK METHOD

You could tell the veterans from the rookies by the way they were dressed. The knowledgeable ones had their heads covered by kerchiefs, so that if they were hired, tobacco dust wouldn't get in their hair; they had on clean dresses that by now were faded and shapeless, so that if they were hired they wouldn't get tobacco dust and grime on their best clothes. Those who were trying for the first time had their hair freshly done and wore attractive dresses; they wanted to make a good impression. But the dresses couldn't be seen at the distance that many were standing from the employment office, and they were crumpled in the crush.

– Mary Mebane, "Summer Job"

ALTERNATING METHOD

Malcolm X emphasized the use of violence in his movement and employed the biblical principle of "an eye for an eye and a tooth for a tooth." King, on the other hand, felt that blacks should use nonviolent

FOR COLLABORATIVE WORK

Ask students to break into groups to discuss the contrasts between high school and college or between life with and life without children. Students should keep notes, then write a short essay on one of the topics.

civil disobedience and employed the theme "turning the other cheek," which Malcolm X rejected as "beggarly" and "feeble." The philosophy of Malcolm X was one of revenge, and often it broke the unity of black Americans. More radical blacks supported him, while more conservative ones supported King. King thought that blacks should transcend their humanity. In contrast, Malcolm X thought they should embrace it and reserve their love for one another, regarding whites as "devils" and the "enemy." King's politics were those of a rainbow, but Malcolm X's rainbow was insistently one color—black. The distance between Martin Luther King, Jr.'s thinking and Malcolm X's was the distance between growing up in the seminary and growing up on the streets, between the American dream and the American reality.

EXERCISE 6.14: Answers will vary.

EXERCISE 6.14

Outline the paragraph on Martin Luther King, Jr., and Malcolm X, noting its alternating pattern. Then rewrite the paragraph using block organization: the first part of the paragraph devoted to King, the second to Malcolm X. Finally, write a brief paragraph analyzing which of the two paragraphs seems more coherent and easy to follow and why.

Exploring causes and effects

Certain topics will require you to consider the process of **cause and effect**, and you can often develop paragraphs by detailing the causes of something or the effects that something leads to. A geology study question, for instance, may lead you to write a paragraph describing the major causes of soil erosion in the Midwest—or the effects of such erosion. The following paragraph discusses the effects of television on the American family.

> Television's contribution to family life has been an equivocal one. For while it has, indeed, kept the members of the family from dispersing, it has not served to bring them *together*. By its domination of the time families spend together, it destroys the special quality that distinguishes one family from another, a quality that depends to a great extent on what a family *does*, what special rituals, games, recurrent jokes, familiar songs, and shared activities it accumulates.
>
> — MARIE WINN, *The Plug-in Drug: Television, Children, and the Family*

Considering problems and solutions

Paragraphs developed by the **problem-solution pattern** open with a statement of a problem, usually the topic sentence, and then offer a solution in the sentences that follow, as in this paragraph:

Since World War II, voting participation in the United States has declined to the point that barely half of those eligible to vote do so even in presidential elections. The voting rate in elections for other offices is even lower. To reverse this dangerous trend, I would like to see legislation making voting compulsory in presidential elections, with fines for those who neglect this responsibility. A voting requirement for presidential elections would bring almost all citizens into an essential part of the political process in this country. In addition, it would motivate more people to become active in presidential campaigns so that when they have to vote, they will have had some influence in the selection of candidates. Although voting in nonpresidential elections would not be compulsory, the turnout for these elections would undoubtedly increase too as people became accustomed to taking a more active political role.

Similar to the problem-solution pattern is the **question-answer pattern** of development, which does just what its name suggests: the first sentence poses a question, and the rest of the paragraph provides the answer. Beginning with a question provides a means of getting—and focusing—readers' attention.

Combining patterns

As you might expect, many paragraphs combine these methods of development. In the following paragraph, the writer divides a general topic (the accounting systems used by American companies) into two subtopics (the system used to summarize a company's overall financial state and the one used to measure internal transactions) and then develops the second subtopic through illustration (the assessment of costs for a delivery truck shared by two departments) and cause-effect (the system produces some disadvantages).

Most American companies have basically two accounting systems. One system summarizes the overall financial state to inform stockholders, bankers, and other outsiders. That system is not of interest here. The other system, called the managerial or cost accounting system, exists for an entirely different reason. It measures in detail all of the particulars of transactions between departments, divisions, and key individuals in the organization, for the purpose of untangling the interdependencies between people. When, for example, two departments share one truck for deliveries, the cost accounting system charges each department for part of the cost of maintaining the truck and driver, so that at the end of the year, the performance of each department can be individually assessed, and the better department's manager can receive a larger raise. Of course, all of this information processing costs money, and furthermore may lead to arguments between the departments over whether the costs charged to each are fair.
— WILLIAM OUCHI, "Japanese and American Workers: Two Casts of Mind"

EXERCISE 6.15: Suggested Answers

1. comparison /contrast, illustration, specifics
2. illustration

EXERCISE 6.16–26: Answers will vary.

EXERCISE 6.15

Identify the specific method of development used in each of the following paragraphs, and explain why you think each paragraph is or is not effectively developed using that method.

1.   Other differences I saw between Florida and Germany were the scenery and the culture. Florida's scenery consisted of one-story houses and green lawns. Palm trees and occasional garbage could be seen along the road. In Germany, houses were weirdly shaped with small lawns, if any. Buildings were very close to the road, and very little garbage could be found on the streets. Driving in Germany could be hazardous as compared with driving in Florida, because in Germany there are no speed limits. Cultural differences, such as the time of day you eat and the food you eat, were apparent between Germany and Florida. Communications were obviously different, with the German language being spoken in Germany.

2.   According to Hollywood, the Indian was always the liar, the thief, the cold-blooded, ruthless killer with no compassion. For example, in many movies a wild band of Indians surround a helpless family and, for absolutely no reason at all, slaughter the whole family. The Indians depicted by Hollywood also make sneak attacks on a sleeping town, killing the townspeople and pillaging every inch of the town. In other films, the Indians rustle cattle and horses from farmers and, of course, slay the farmers. This picture of the "Old West" is one of the greatest fallacies of all time.

EXERCISE 6.16

Choose two of the following topics or two others that interest you, and brainstorm or freewrite about each one for ten minutes (see 3a). Then use the information you have produced to determine what method(s) of development would be most appropriate for each topic.

1. the pleasure a hobby has given you
2. 2 Live Crew's image and M.C. Hammer's image
3. an average Saturday morning
4. why Monopoly is an appropriate metaphor for U.S. society
5. the best course you've ever taken

EXERCISE 6.17

Refer to the argument you drafted in Exercise 5.14, and study the ways you have developed each paragraph. For one paragraph, write a brief evaluation of its development. How would you expand or otherwise improve the development?

2

Determining paragraph length

While the paragraph has existed as a unit of writing for a long, long time, it has changed over the years. If you look at Edward Gibbon's *Rise and Fall of the Roman Empire* (published in the late eighteenth century), for instance, you will see paragraphs longer than most written today. In general, both paragraphs and sentences have gotten shorter over the last two hundred years. Newspapers and magazines, with their narrow columns, are partially responsible for this shift in paragraph length, for they have accustomed readers to short lines and paragraphs.

Though writers must keep the expectations of readers firmly in mind, paragraph length must be determined primarily by content and the writer's purpose. Paragraphs should develop an idea, create any desired effects (such as suspense, humor, or enthusiasm), and advance the piece of writing. Fulfilling these aims will sometimes call for short paragraphs, sometimes for long ones. For example, in an argumentative essay, you may want to put all your lines of argument or all the evidence for your claim into one long paragraph to create the impression of a solid, overwhelmingly convincing thesis. In a narrative about an exciting event, on the other hand, a series of short paragraphs may help to create suspense, as the reader keeps reaching the end of a paragraph and rushing to the following one to find out what happened next.

An important point to remember is that a new paragraph signals for the reader a pause or a break in thought. Just as timing can make a crucial difference in telling a joke, or a dramatic pause in telling a piece of news or gossip, so the pause signaled by a paragraph can raise readers' anticipation for what is to follow or give them a moment to "digest" mentally the material presented in the previous paragraph.

Reasons to start a new paragraph

- To turn to a new idea
- To emphasize something (such as a point or an example)
- To change speakers (in dialogue)
- To lead readers to pause
- To break up lengthy text (often to take up a subtopic)
- To start the conclusion

EXERCISE 6.18

Go through some of your favorite books, looking for two paragraphs—a very long one and a very short one—that impress you as particularly effective. What

USEFUL READING

Christensen, Francis. "A Generative Rhetoric of the Paragraph." *CCC* 16 (1965): 144–56. Exemplifies the view that paragraphs are determined by forces similar to those that determine sentences and explains the three principal kinds of paragraphs: coordinate, subordinate, and a mixture.

Larson, Richard. "Structure and Form in Non-Narrative Prose." *Ten Bibliographic Essays.* Ed. Gary Tate. Fort Worth: Texas Christian UP, 1987. 39–82. An exposition of his own paragraph theory as well as an overview of contemporary theory.

TEACHING PRACTICE

As discussed in Chapter 3, lead "hooks" draw readers in and then quickly announce what they can expect from the essay. Ask your students to look for the "hook" of any selection in their anthology.

Of a good beginning cometh a good end.
　　　　　　　　　　　　–JOHN HEYWOOD

It is in the hard, hard rock-pile of seeking to win, hold, or deserve a reader's interest that the pleasant agony of writing comes in.
　　　　　　　　　　　–JOHN MASON BROWN

main idea does each develop? What effects does each create? How does each advance the piece of writing it is a part of?

EXERCISE 6.19

Examine the paragraph breaks in something you have written recently. Explain briefly in writing why you decided on each of the breaks. Would you change any of them now? If so, how and why?

6e

Composing special-purpose paragraphs

Some paragraphs serve specialized functions. These include opening paragraphs, concluding paragraphs, transitional paragraphs, and dialogue paragraphs.

1

Opening

Even a good piece of writing may remain unread if it has a weak opening paragraph. In addition to announcing your topic (usually in a thesis statement), therefore, an introductory paragraph must engage the readers' interest and focus their attention on what is to come next. At their best, introductory paragraphs function as hors d'oeuvres, whetting the appetite for following courses or, as the title sequences in a film, carefully setting the scene and establishing themes. Writers often leave the *final* drafting of the introduction until last, because its focus may change over the process of writing.

One common kind of opening paragraph follows a general-to-specific pattern, ending with the thesis. In such an introduction, the writer opens with a general statement and then gets more and more specific, concluding with the most specific sentence in the paragraph—the thesis. The following paragraph illustrates such an opening.

> The United States has seen many changes in its economy during the last hundred years. Among these changes is the organization of workers. Unions were formed in the late nineteenth and early twentieth centuries to battle against long work hours and bad   GENERAL STATEMENT MOVE TO SPECIFICITY

working conditions. It was not uncommon then for a worker to be required to work twelve or more hours a day, six days a week, in hazardous and often deadly conditions. The workers organized against their employers and won their battles. Today, it is very uncommon to find such oppressive conditions in the workplace. Why, then, do unions still exist today? When we examine many of the labor battles of recent years, we find that unions exist mostly as bargaining units through which workers can gain higher wages—at any cost.   THESIS

In this paragraph, the opening sentence introduces a general subject, changes in the U.S. economy; subsequent sentences focus more specifically on unionization; and the last sentence presents the thesis, which the rest of the essay will develop. Other ways of opening an essay include quotations, anecdotes, questions, or opinions.

Opening with a quotation

"Go back to hell where you came from, you old wart hog," says Mary Grace, an unattractive girl from a Massachusetts college, to Mrs. Ruby Turpin, a hypocritical Southern woman, in Flannery O'Connor's "Revelation." Mary Grace's words sting poor Mrs. Turpin, who is not used to criticism. Mary Grace's message is that Mrs. Turpin is not better than the people she thinks badly of, and her attack causes Mrs. Turpin to stop and scowl in a moment of uncharacteristic self-doubt.

Opening with an anecdote

"Your daughter is absolutely beautiful!" the woman gushed to my father. A friend of his from work, she had heard much about my sister Tracy and me but had never met us before. I could tell that she was one of those blunt elderly ladies, the type that pinches cheeks, because as soon as she finished appraising my sister, she turned to me with a judgmental look in her eye. Her face said it all. Beady brown eyes traveling slowly from my head to my toes, she sized me up and said rather condescendingly, "Oh, and she must be the smart one." I stared down at my toes as I rocked nervously back and forth. Then, looking at my sister, I realized for the first time that she was very pretty and I was, well, the smart one.
— JENNIFER GERKIN, "The Smart One"

Opening with a question

Why is the American population terrified of turning to nuclear power as a future source of energy? People are misinformed, or not informed at all, about its benefits and safety. If Americans would take time to learn about what nuclear power offers, then their apprehension and fear might be transformed into hope.

Opening with an opinion

Exploitation in America is as common as the common cold. Since its beginning, this nation has thrived on economic exploitation, and the problem became especially widespread during the period from 1900 to 1920. During this time many children, as well as adults, were forced to work fourteen to fifteen hours a day for pennies. It did not take long for people to realize they were being exploited, but there was little they could do about it. Some people went on strike, but they accomplished little. Besides being taken advantage of economically, many people were exploited socially and sexually. John Dos Passos's *1919* and E. L. Doctorow's *Ragtime* both deal with economic, social, and sexual exploitation during this period. However, Dos Passos's treatment of this theme is pessimistic, while Doctorow's is optimistic.

EXERCISE 6.20

Refer once more to the argument you drafted in Exercise 5.14. Examine your introduction carefully, trying to identify the strategy you have used. Then choose a different strategy from among those discussed above, and write an alternate introduction. Finally, write a paragraph evaluating which introduction is most effective and why.

2

Concluding

A good conclusion wraps up a piece of writing in a meaningful and memorable way. If a strong opening paragraph whets the appetite of readers or arouses their curiosity, a strong concluding paragraph satisfies them that the job the writer set out to do is indeed completed, that their expectations have been met. In doing so, a strong conclusion reminds readers of the thesis of the essay and leaves them feeling that they know a good deal more than when they began. The concluding paragraph provides the last opportunity for you to impress your message on your readers' minds and to create effects you desire. As such, it is well worth your time and effort.

One of the most common strategies for concluding uses the specific-to-general pattern, often beginning with a restatement of the thesis (but *not* a word-for-word repetition of it) and moving to several more general statements. The following paragraph moves in such a way, opening with a final point of contrast, specifying it in several sentences, and then ending with a much more general statement.

> Lastly, and perhaps greatest of all, there was the ability, at the end, to turn quickly from war to peace once the fighting was over. Out of the way these two men behaved at Appomattox came the possibility of a peace of reconciliation. It was a possibility not wholly realized, in the years to come, but which did, in the end, help the two sections to become one nation again . . . after a war whose bitterness might have seemed to make such a reunion wholly impossible. No part of either man's life became him more than the part he played in this brief meeting in the McLean house at Appomattox. Their behavior there put all succeeding generations of Americans in their debt. Two great Americans, Grant and Lee—very different, yet under everything very much alike. Their encounter at Appomattox was one of the great moments of American history.
>
> — BRUCE CATTON, "Grant and Lee: A Study in Contrasts"

Other effective strategies for concluding include questions, quotations, vivid images, calls for action, or warnings.

Concluding with a question

> All so-called "permanent" antifreeze is basically the same. It is made from a liquid known as ethylene glycol, which has two amazing properties: It has a lower freezing point than water, and a higher boiling point than water. It does not break down (lose its properties), nor will it boil away. And every permanent antifreeze starts with it as a base. Also, just about every antifreeze has now got antileak ingredients, as well as antirust and anticorrosion ingredients. Now, let's suppose that, in formulating the product, one of the companies comes up with a solution that is pink in color, as opposed to all the others, which are blue. Presto—an exclusivity claim. "Nothing else looks like it, nothing else performs like it." Or how about, "Look at ours, and look at anyone else's. You can see the difference our exclusive formula makes." Granted, I'm exaggerating. But did I prove a point?
>
> — PAUL STEVENS, "Weasel Words: God's Little Helpers"

Concluding with a quotation

> Despite the celebrity that accrued to her and the air of awesomeness with which she was surrounded in her later years, Miss Keller retained an unaffected personality, certain that her optimistic attitude toward life was justified. "I believe that all through these dark and silent years God has been using my life for a purpose I do not know," she said. "But one day I shall understand and then I will be satisfied."
>
> — ALDEN WHITMAN, "Helen Keller: June 27, 1880–June 1, 1968"

Concluding with a vivid image

It is, in any case, finally you that I end up having to trust not to laugh, not to snicker. Even as you regard me in these lines, I try to imagine your face as you read. You who read "Aria," especially those of you with your theme-divining yellow felt pen poised in your hand, you for whom this essay is yet another "assignment," please do not forget that it is my life I am handing you in these pages—memories that are as personal for me as family photographs in an old cigar box.

— RICHARD RODRIGUEZ, from a postscript to "Aria"

Concluding with a call for action

It is now almost 40 years since the invention of nuclear weapons. We have not yet experienced a global thermonuclear war—although on more than one occasion we have come tremulously close. I do not think our luck can hold forever. Men and machines are fallible, as recent events remind us. Fools and madmen do exist, and sometimes rise to power. Concentrating always on the near future, we have ignored the long-term consequences of our actions. We have placed our civilization and our species in jeopardy.

Fortunately, it is not yet too late. We can safeguard the planetary civilization and the human family if we so choose. There is no more important or more urgent issue.   — CARL SAGAN, "The Nuclear Winter"

Concluding with a warning

Because propaganda is so effective, it is important to track it down and understand how it is used. We may eventually agree with what the propagandist says because all propaganda isn't necessarily bad; some advertising, for instance, urges us not to drive drunk, to have regular dental checkups, to contribute to the United Way. Even so, we must be aware that propaganda is being used. Otherwise, we will have consented to handing over our independence, our decision-making ability, and our brains.

— ANN McCLINTOCK, "Propaganda Techniques in Today's Advertising"

EXERCISE 6.21

Choose an essay you have recently written, and examine the conclusion carefully, trying to identify what strategy you have used. Then choose a different strategy from among those discussed above, and write a new conclusion, striving for the maximum effect on readers. Finally, describe and evaluate the techniques you used in your revision.

3

Using transitional paragraphs

On some occasions, you may need to call your readers' attention very powerfully to a major transition between ideas. To do so, consider using an entire short paragraph to signal that transition, as in the following example from an essay on "television addiction." The opening paragraphs of the essay characterize addiction in general, concluding with the paragraph about its destructive elements. The one-sentence paragraph that follows arrests our attention, announcing that these general characteristics will now be related to television viewing.

> Finally a serious addiction is distinguished from a harmless pursuit of pleasure by its distinctly destructive elements. A heroin in addict, for instance, leads a damaged life: his increasing need for heroin in increasing doses prevents him from working, from maintaining relationships, from developing in human ways. Similarly an alcoholic's life is narrowed and dehumanized by his dependence on alcohol.
>
> Let us consider television viewing in the light of the conditions that define serious addictions.
>
> — MARIE WINN, *The Plug-in Drug: Television, Children, and the Family*

4

Using paragraphs to signal dialogue

Paragraphs of dialogue can bring added life to almost any sort of writing. The traditional way to set up dialogue in written form is simple: start a new paragraph each time the speaker changes, no matter how short each bit of conversation is. Here is an example.

> Whenever I brought a book to the job, I wrapped it in newspaper—a habit that was to persist for years in other cities and under other circumstances. But some of the white men pried into my packages when I was absent and they questioned me.
>
> "Boy, what are you reading those books for?"
>
> "Oh, I don't know, sir."
>
> "That's deep stuff you're reading, boy."
>
> "I'm just killing time, sir."
>
> "You'll addle your brains if you don't watch out."
>
> — RICHARD WRIGHT, *Black Boy*

EXERCISE 6.22

Go through some of your favorite books, articles, or essays to find an opening or concluding paragraph that you consider particularly effective. Try to analyze what makes the paragraph so effective. Then, choosing a topic of great interest to you, try to write an opening or concluding paragraph that matches the paragraph you admire—the structure of its sentences, the pattern of its development, its use of particular devices such as quotations, questions, and so on. Then compare the two paragraphs, and decide how effective your own is.

6f

Linking paragraphs

The same methods that can be used to link sentences and create coherent paragraphs can be used to link paragraphs themselves together so that a whole piece of writing flows smoothly and coherently. Some reference to the previous paragraph, either explicitly stated or merely implied, should occur in each paragraph after the introduction. As in linking sentences, you can create this reference by repeating or paraphrasing key words and terms and by using parallel structures, pronouns, and transitional expressions.

Repeating key words

. . . In fact, human offspring remain *dependent on their parents* longer than the young of any other species.

Children are *dependent on their parents* or other adults not only for their physical survival but also for their initiation into the uniquely human knowledge that is collectively called culture. . . .

Using parallel structure

. . . Kennedy made an effort to assure non-Catholics that he would respect the separation of church and state, and most of them did not seem to hold his religion against him in deciding how to vote. Since his election, *the church to which a candidate belongs* has become less important in presidential politics.

The region from which a candidate comes remains an important factor. . . .

Using pronouns

Singer's tale is of a pathetic Polish Jew, Gimpel, who because of *his* strong faith believes everything *he* is told. At the beginning of the tale, we learn that Gimpel has had a gruesomely cruel life. *He* is an orphan, and all *his* life *he* has been teased and tormented for believing everything *he* hears.

Even the most ridiculous and far-fetched tales take *him* in. For example, when *he* is told that the messiah has come and *his* parents have risen from the dead, *he* goes out to search for *them*! In *his* seemingly foolish search, *he* is berated by the townsfolk.

Using transitional expressions

. . . While the Indian, in the character of Tonto, was more positively portrayed in "The Lone Ranger," such a portrayal was more the exception than the norm.

Moreover, despite this brief glimpse of an Indian as an ever-loyal sidekick, Tonto was never accorded the same stature as the man with the white horse and silver bullets. . . .

Checking the paragraphs in your own writing

1. What is the topic sentence of each paragraph? Is it stated or implied? If stated, where in the paragraph does it fall? Should it come at some other point? Would any paragraph be improved by deleting or adding a topic sentence? (6b1)

2. Which sentences, if any, do not relate in some way to the topic sentence? Is there any way to justify their inclusion? (6b2)

3. What is the most general sentence in each paragraph? If it is not the topic sentence, should it remain or be omitted?

4. Is each paragraph organized in a way that is easy for readers to follow? By what means are sentences linked? Do any more links need to be added? Do any of the transitional expressions try to create links that do not really exist between ideas? (6c)

5. How completely does each paragraph develop its topic sentence? What methods of development are used, and are they effective? What other methods might be used? Does the paragraph need more material? (6d and 6d1)

6. Does the first sentence in each paragraph let readers know what the paragraph is about? Does the last sentence in some way conclude that paragraph's discussion? If not, does it need to?

7. How long is each paragraph? Are paragraphs varied in length? Does any paragraph seem too long or too short? Is there anything that might be given strong emphasis by a one-sentence paragraph? (6d2 and 6e3)

(Continued)

8. By what means are the paragraphs linked together? Do any more links need to be added? Do any of the transitional expressions try to create links that do not really exist between ideas? (6f)

9. How does the introductory paragraph catch the interest of readers? How exactly does it open—with a quotation? an anecdote? a question? a strong statement? How else might it open? (6e1)

10. How does the last paragraph draw the essay to a conclusion? What lasting impression will it leave with readers? How exactly does it close—with a question? a quotation? a vivid image? a warning or call for action? How else might it conclude? (6e2)

EXERCISE 6.23

Look at the essay you drafted in Exercise 3.7 or the argument you drafted in Exercise 5.14, and identify the ways your paragraphs are linked together. Identify each use of repetition, parallel structures, pronouns, and transitional expressions, and then evaluate how effectively you have joined paragraphs.

EXERCISE 6.24　Revising for Paragraphs

The following long paragraph is from an essay in which a student attempts to assess the "American dream" after reading an essay by Joan Didion, "Some Dreamers of the Golden Dream." Read the paragraph, and decide whether or not it should be broken up into two or more paragraphs and where any new paragraphs should begin. Then explain your reasons for any changes you make and what effects are created by the new paragraphing.

When I think of the "American dream," I visualize a white and blue two-story Colonial house, complete with a two-car garage, white picket fence, happily married husband and wife, two children (one boy, one girl), a dog, and family vacations across the state in the Ford station wagon. I'm not really sure where I received my information on this subject; I have just learned through the years that this is the type of life I should strive for and look forward to. The traditional "American dream" is apparently changing, though. The white and blue two-story house is now a three-story mansion embedded in the cliffs of Malibu overlooking the Pacific Ocean; the happily married husband and wife have usually known the same happiness in three prior marriages; the family vacations are now two weeks in Hawaii with the Mercedes station wagon waiting for them in the Los Angeles airport parking lot. This new and extreme version of the fairy tale is rapidly becoming everyone's new goal, according to Joan Didion's essay "Some Dreamers of the Golden Dream." Didion speaks of

Southern California and states that people have derived their new ideal from newspapers and movies, not from reality. I find this statement very true to life, for most people do receive the majority of their ideas about how they should live from newspapers and movies. Therefore, if the movies present an image of gorgeous beachside mansions and expensive imported cars, then that is exactly what most people will strive for. This type of life style may not be right for every individual, though, and many people realize this fact too late. They spend their lives working and striving to become successful in society's eyes. Then, once they have reached their goal, they realize they are not truly happy, for they gained wealth and status for all the wrong reasons.

EXERCISE 6.25   Reading with an Eye for Paragraphs

Think of a writer you admire, and read something he or she has written. Find one or two paragraphs that impress you in some way, and analyze them using the guidelines on pp. 135–36. Try to decide what makes them effective as paragraphs.

EXERCISE 6.26   Taking Inventory: Paragraphs

Examine two or three paragraphs you have written, using the guidelines on pp. 135–36 to evaluate the unity, coherence, and development of each one. Identify the topic of each paragraph, the topic sentence (if one is explicitly stated), any methods of development, and any means used to create coherence. Decide whether or not each paragraph successfully guides your readers, and explain your reasons. Then choose one paragraph and revise it.

Part Two

Sentences: Making Grammatical Choices

7
Constructing Grammatical Sentences

BACKGROUND

Although closely related, rhetoric and grammar have always maintained themselves as separate disciplines. Rhetoric, nearly as old as Greek culture itself, formed the basis of the *trivium,* the Greek educational system that also included grammar and dialectic (philosophical logic). For some 1,700 years, from late antiquity to the Middle Ages, the *trivium* remained the centerpiece of education, keeping grammar allied with rhetoric. But today, grammar is more closely connected with other fields of language study—with linguistics, composition studies, and stylistics—that make constant reference to grammatical terms. The relationship of grammar to composition studies has always been controversial: how to teach grammar in writing courses—indeed, whether to teach it at all—remains a topic much disputed. Few teachers have been willing to dispense entirely with instruction in grammar; most of us teach it without any conclusive evidence that teaching grammar in any way improves the writing of our students. In his impressive meta-analysis, *Research on Written Composition* (Urbana, IL: NCTE, 1986), George Hillocks reports that "[n]one of the studies reviewed . . . provides any support for teaching grammar as a means of improving composition skills" (138). Yet we continue to teach our students about grammar, perhaps because we feel that to be the most effective

Outside of school, you may not have thought very much about grammar, the main subject of this chapter. Indeed, you may agree in principle with the fifteenth-century Holy Roman Emperor Sigismund, who answered a question about his Latin grammar by saying, "I am the Roman emperor and am above grammar."

In one sense, all native speakers of a language are, like Sigismund, "above" grammar. All speakers, that is, learn the grammar of their language naturally as they learn to speak. This intuitive knowledge of grammar leads us to say, "The bright red cardinal surprised me," rather than "Cardinal bright the surprised me red"—without even thinking about it. This ability to arrange words into meaningful patterns comes, in fact, very early to each of us and accounts for the fact that young children often produce sophisticated sentences out of the blue, without having to study or "learn" a system by which to produce them.

But in another sense, none of us, including an emperor, is above grammar. As the sentence about the cardinal demonstrates, we are bound by certain patterns or "rules" in producing sentences. And breaking those "rules" moves a speaker from sense to nonsense, from being easily understood to being completely misunderstood.

If we learn the basic grammar of language as we learn to speak, then why bother to study it? In the first place, though all speakers know the *basic* grammatical "rules," these rules can generate a very broad range of sentences, some of which will be much more artful and effective than others. As someone who uses written language, you want not simply to write, but to write skillfully and effectively, and understanding grammatical structures can help you do so.

Furthermore, within the basic "rules" of English grammar, wide latitude exists. Not everyone, for instance, grows up speaking with precisely the same set of grammatical rules. Knowledge of the differences can help you produce sentences that are not only grammatical but appropriate to a particular situation. The "rules" that allow a speaker to say "Hey, man, this be one *fine* set of wheels" in one situation, for example, are not quite the same as those that lead him or her to say "Yes, sir, this car is completely acceptable" in another. If you understand grammar, you will not only understand both statements but also know when and why to use one and when the other. Finally, because language is so closely related to thought, studying our language patterns, our grammar, can give us insight into our own ways of thinking. If in some important sense we *are* what we say (and write), then examining the principles through which we express our meanings can help us understand ourselves as well as others.

This chapter takes a look at the basic units of grammar—those elements that allow us to produce meaningful sentences.

writers, they need to learn certain grammatical conventions. As William Irmscher writes, "The relation of grammar and writing is one of the enduring controversies of English studies . . ." *Teaching Expository Writing* (New York: Holt, 1979, 16).

EXERCISE 7.1

Think of a writer whose work you enjoy, and read something by him or her. Write down some sentences you find pleasing, and try to determine what makes them memorable: the pacing and rhythm? the pictures they bring to mind? Reading them aloud is one good way to focus your attention on their rhythm and structure. Then try writing some sentences of your own, imitating the structure of the professional writer's sentences as best you can.

EXERCISE 7.1: Answers will vary.

This exercise lends itself very well to inclusion in the writing log.

Everyday use

Perhaps more than any other subject we'll ever study, grammar comes to us almost automatically, without our thinking about it or even being aware of it. Listen in, for instance, on this conversation between two six-year-olds:

Charlotte: My new bike that Grandma got me has a red basket and a loud horn, and I love it.

Anna: Can I ride it?

Charlotte: Sure, as soon as I take a turn.

This simple conversation features sophisticated grammatical constructions—subordination of one clause to another, a compound object, a series of adjectives—all used effortlessly. Take a few minutes to listen in on some spoken conversation, and transcribe a few sentences as we've done here. Then, using this chapter, see what kinds of grammatical structures the conversation contains.

USEFUL READING

Noguchi, Rei R. *Grammar and the Teaching of Writing: Limits and Possibilities.* Urbana, IL: NCTE, 1991. Noguchi streamlines the teaching of grammar by focusing on the writing problems most responsive to grammar-based instruction, by drawing on students' unconscious understanding of their native language, and by relating grammar to style, content, and organization.

BACKGROUND

When students face grammar lessons, they often feel that their language has become suddenly foreign—that they don't know any grammar. Oh, but they do. They completely mastered the grammar of their native tongue long ago. They may be comforted to know that there is a difference between what they know about their language—their *competence*—and how they use their language—their linguistic *performance*. Unlike certain "speaking" animals, which can only imitate what they have heard before, your students know the rules for combining the elements of their native language—words, ideas, and sentences—and have the *competence* to say things that have never been said before and to create purposeful and meaningful discourse. If one of your students says, "Yesterday, I seen a horrible fight," you know exactly what she means. Her *competence* is perfect, though her *performance*—by the standards of Edited American English—may not be. She makes sense. But if she says, "A yesterday saw fight I horrible," you cannot understand her. The words themselves are correct, but not the grammar. Your student will be able to tell you that the second string of words is ungrammatical and that it doesn't make sense. Her *competence* with her language, her knowledge of grammar, gives her this ability. However, an "ungrammatical" sentence such as "Yesterday, I seen that we was almost out of gas" is a matter of *performance*.

EXERCISE 7.2: Answers

The subject is set in italics; the predicate is set in boldface.

1. *We* **set out for the gallows.**
2. *He* **was an army doctor, with a gray toothbrush moustache and a gruff voice.**
3. *The rest of us, magistrates and the like,* **followed behind.**
4. *The dog* **answered the sound with a whine.**
5. *The hangman, a gray-haired convict in the white uniform of the prison,* **was waiting beside his machine.**

7a

Understanding the basic grammar of sentences

Put most simply, a **sentence** is a grammatically complete group of words that expresses a thought. To be grammatically complete, a group of words must contain two major structural components—a subject and a predicate. The **subject** identifies what the sentence is about, and the **predicate** says or asks something about the subject or tells the subject to do something.

SUBJECT	PREDICATE
We	shall overcome.
I	have a dream.
California	is a state of mind.
You	can't touch this.
The rain in Spain	stays mainly on the plain.
Puff, the magic dragon,	lived by the sea.

Some brief sentences have one-word subjects and predicates (for example, *Time passes*) or even a one-word predicate with an implied or "understood" subject (for example, *Stop!*). Most sentences, however, contain additional words that expand the basic subject and predicate. In the example above, for instance, the subject might have been simply *Puff;* the words *the magic dragon* say more about the subject. Similarly, the predicate of that sentence could grammatically be *lived;* the words *by the sea* expand the predicate by telling us where Puff lived.

EXERCISE 7.2

The following sentences are taken from "A Hanging," an essay by George Orwell. Identify the subject and predicate in each sentence, underlining the subject once and the predicate twice. Example:

> *One prisoner* <u>had been brought out of his cell</u>.

1. We set out for the gallows.
2. He was an army doctor, with a gray toothbrush moustache and a gruff voice.
3. The rest of us, magistrates and the like, followed behind.
4. The dog answered the sound with a whine.
5. The hangman, a gray-haired convict in the white uniform of the prison, was waiting beside his machine.

7b

Recognizing the parts of speech

If the basic sentence parts are subjects and predicates, the central elements of subjects and predicates are nouns and verbs. For example:

```
 ┌── SUBJECT ──┐┌─────── PREDICATE ───────┐
        NOUN     VERB
 A solitary figure waited on the platform.
```

Nouns and verbs are two of the eight **parts of speech**, one set of grammatical categories into which words may be classified. The other six parts of speech are pronouns, adjectives, adverbs, prepositions, conjunctions, and interjections. Many English words can function as more than one part of speech. Take the word *book*, for instance: when you *book a plane flight*, it is a verb; when you *take a good book to the beach*, it is a noun; and when you *have book knowledge*, it is an adjective.

The system of categorizing words by part of speech comes to English from Latin. The differences between Latin and English are many, of course, and the parts-of-speech system is thus not as precise for English as it is for Latin. Many grammarians argue that students of English grammar should focus less on the parts of speech and more on the parts of a sentence. Even so, the parts of speech remain an important part of our grammatical vocabulary, and all dictionaries use them to label their entries. In this chapter, we will see how the various parts of speech are used in sentences.

1

Recognizing verbs

The word *verb* comes from the Latin *verbum*, which simply means "word." As their derivation suggests, **verbs** are among the most important words, for they move the meaning of sentences along by showing action (*glance, jump*), occurrence (*become, happen*), or a state of being (*be, live*). Verbs change form to show *time, person, number, voice,* and *mood*.

TIME	we *work*, we *worked*
PERSON	I *work*, she *works*
NUMBER	one person *works*, two people *work*
VOICE	she *asks*, she *is asked*
MOOD	we *see*, if we *saw*

Auxiliary verbs (also called **helping verbs**) combine with other verbs (often called **main verbs**) to create *verb phrases*. Auxiliaries include the

USEFUL READING

Aitchison, Jean. *Language Change: Progress or Decay?* Suffolk, Engl.: Fontana, 1981. See chapter one, "The Ever-Changing Wheel," 26–31.

Bartholomae, David. "The Study of Error." *CCC* 31 (1980): 253–69. Argues that learning formal written discourse amounts to learning a second language, and so English-as-a-Second-Language (ESL) techniques apply.

Baugh, Albert C., and Thomas Cable. *A History of the English Language.* 3rd ed. Englewood Cliffs, NJ: Prentice, 1978. A highly readable history of our language.

Hartwell, Patrick. "Grammar, Grammars, and the Teaching of Grammer." *CE* 47 (1985): 105–27. Definitions and purposes of the various grammars.

TEACHING PRACTICE

Read aloud the following passage, asking your students to record every main verb.

Nuns go by as quiet as lust, and drunken men and sober eyes sing in the lobby of the Greek hotel. Rosemary Villanucci, our next-door friend who lives above her father's cafe, sits in a 1939 Buick eating bread and butter. She rolls down the window to tell my sister Frieda and me that we can't come in. We stare at her, wanting her bread, but more than that wanting to poke the arrogance out of her eyes and smash the pride of ownership that curls her chewing mouth. When she comes out of the car we will beat her up, make red marks on her white skin and she will cry and ask us do we want her to pull her pants down. We will say no. We don't know what we should feel or do if she does, but whenever she asks us, we know she is offering us something precious and that our own pride must be asserted by refusing to accept.

–TONI MORRISON, *The Bluest Eye*

forms of *be, do,* and *have,* which are also used as main verbs, and the words *can, could, may, might, must, shall, should, will,* and *would.*

> You *must get* some sleep tonight!
> I *could have danced* all night.
> She *would prefer* to take Italian rather than Spanish.

See Chapter 9 for a complete discussion of verbs and 10a for more on how verbs change form to show person and number.

EXERCISE 7.3

Identify and underline each verb or verb phrase in the following sentences. Example:

Charlie <u>should do</u> fine in Saturday's tennis match.

1. His future does look bright.
2. The ice cream ran all over the table and the floor.
3. Over the next few days, I tapped about seventy maple trees.
4. One person can collect sap, a second might run the evaporator, and a third should finish the syrup.
5. A trip to Florida would be great.
6. At a glittering ceremony, they announced the winner.
7. The deer population rose drastically in the early twentieth century, after the disappearance of the cougar and the wolf.
8. The bookcase will extend from floor to ceiling.
9. Relatives of the veterans had brought flags to the cemetery.
10. The dormitory kitchen smelled like old fish.

2

Recognizing nouns

The word *noun* comes from the Latin *nomen,* which means "name." That is what **nouns** do: they name things. Nouns can name persons (*aviator, child*), places (*lake, library*), things (*truck, suitcase*), or concepts (*happiness, balance*). **Proper nouns** name specific persons, places, things, or concepts: *Bill, Iowa, Supreme Court, Buddhism.* Proper nouns are capitalized. (See 35b.) **Collective nouns** name groups: *team, flock, jury.* (See 10d.)

Most nouns can be changed from **singular** (one) to **plural** (more than one) by adding -*s* or -*es: horse, horses; kiss, kisses.* Some nouns, however,

---

EXERCISE 7.3: Answers

1. does look
2. ran, ran over (two-word verb)
3. tapped
4. can collect; might run; should finish
5. would be
6. announced
7. rose
8. will extend
9. had brought
10. smelled

TEACHING PRACTICE

A verb is the key to a sentence: the starting point for any translation, the pivot of action, the movement. We tend to emphasize verbs in our teaching because so few writers use them effectively, and those that do, produce lively, often powerful, prose. We usually begin to learn a language, however, by building up our repertoire of nouns—in much the way multiply disabled Helen Keller rose to a new level of consciousness when she learned her first word—a noun—with the help of Annie Sullivan. Read aloud the following exerpt from *The Story of My Life* in which Keller relates that magical event:

> We walked down the path to the well-house, attracted by the fragrance of the honeysuckle with which it was covered. Someone was drawing water and my teacher placed my hand under

have irregular plural forms: *woman, women; alumnus, alumni; mouse, mice; deer, deer.* (See 24e.) **Mass nouns** cannot be made plural because they name something that cannot easily be counted: *dust, peace, prosperity.*

Nouns can also take a possessive form to show ownership. A writer usually forms the possessive by adding an apostrophe plus -*s* to *a singular noun or just an apostrophe to a plural noun: the horse's owner, the boys' department.* (See 32a.)

Nouns are often preceded by one of the **articles** *a, an,* or *the: a rocket, an astronaut, the launch.* Articles are also known as **noun markers** or **determiners.**

EXERCISE 7.4

Identify the nouns, including possessive forms, and the articles in each of the following sentences. Underline the nouns once and the articles twice. Example:

The <u>Puritans' hopes</u> *were dashed when* <u>Charles II</u> *regained his* <u>father's throne.</u>

1. Nightlife begins in Georgetown even before the sun goes down.
2. Although plagiarism is dishonest and illegal, it does occur.
3. Thanksgiving is a grim season for turkeys.
4. Henderson's story is a tale of theft and violation.
5. In the front row sat two people, a man with slightly graying hair and a young woman in jeans.

3

Recognizing pronouns

Pronouns function as nouns in sentences and often take the place of specific nouns, serving as short forms so that we do not have to repeat a noun that has already been mentioned. A specific noun that a pronoun replaces or refers to is called the **antecedent** of the pronoun. (See Chapters 11 and 13.) In the following example, the antecedent of the pronoun *she* is *Caitlin.*

Caitlin refused the invitation even though *she* wanted to go.

You are already familiar with pronouns; we could scarcely speak or write without them. (The preceding sentence, for instance, includes the pronouns *you, we,* and *them.*) Look now at all the categories of pronouns: personal, reflexive, intensive, indefinite, demonstrative, interrogative, relative, and reciprocal.

the spout. As the cool stream gushed over one hand, she spelled into the other the word *water,* first slowly then rapidly. I stood still, my whole attention fixed upon the motion of her fingers. Suddenly I felt a misty consciousness as of something forgotten—a thrill of returning thought; and somehow the mystery of language was revealed to me. I knew then that "w-a-t-e-r" meant the wonderful cool something that was flowing over my hand. That living word awakened my soul, gave it light, hope, joy, set it free! . . . I left the well-house eager to learn. Everything had a name, and each name gave birth to a new thought. As we returned to the house every object which I touched seemed to quiver with life. That was because I saw everything with the strange, new sight that had come to me. . . . [M]other, father, sister, teacher were . . . words that were to make the world blossom for me. . . .

EXERCISE 7.4: Answers

Nouns are set in italics; articles are set in boldface.

1. *Nightlife; Georgetown;* **the;** *sun*
2. *plagiarism*
3. *Thanksgiving;* **a;** *season; turkeys*
4. *Henderson's story;* **a;** *tale; theft; violation*
5. **the;** *row; people;* **a;** *man; hair;* **a;** *woman; jeans*

Personal pronouns refer to specific persons or things. Each has several different forms (for example, *I, me, my, mine*) depending on how it functions in a sentence. (See Chapter 8.)

> I, you, he, she, it, we, they
> After the scouts made camp, *they* ran along the beach.

Reflexive pronouns refer back to the subject of the sentence or clause in which they appear. They end in *-self* or *-selves.*

> myself, yourself, himself, herself, itself, oneself, ourselves, yourselves, themselves
> The seals sunned *themselves* on the warm rocks.

Intensive pronouns have the same form as reflexive pronouns. They are used to emphasize their antecedents.

> He decided to paint the apartment *himself.*

Indefinite pronouns do not refer to specific nouns, although they may refer to identifiable persons or things. They express the idea of a quantity—"all," "some," "any," or "none"—or an unspecified person or thing—"somebody," "any book." Indefinite pronouns are one of the largest categories of pronouns; following is a partial list:

> all, anybody, both, each, everything, few, most, none, one, some
> *Somebody* screamed when the lights went out.

Demonstrative pronouns identify or point to specific nouns.

> this, that, these, those
> *These* are Peter's books.

Interrogative pronouns are used to ask questions.

> who, which, what
> *Who* can help to set up the chairs for the meeting?

Relative pronouns introduce dependent clauses and "relate" the dependent clause to the rest of the sentence (see 7c4).

> who, which, that, what, whoever, whichever, whatever
> Margaret owns the car *that* is parked by the corner.

The interrogative pronoun *who* and the relative pronouns *who* and *whoever* have different forms depending on how they are used in a sentence. (See Chapter 8.)

Reciprocal pronouns refer to the individual parts of a plural antecedent.

each other, one another
The business failed because the partners distrusted *each other*.

EXERCISE 7.5

Identify the pronouns and any antecedents in each of the following sentences, underlining the pronouns once and the antecedents twice. Example:

As identical <u><u>twins</u>, <u>they</u> really do understand <u>each other</u>.

1. She thanked everyone for helping.
2. The crowd that greeted the pope was the largest one I have ever seen.
3. Who knows better than Mark himself what he should do?
4. They have only themselves to blame.
5. People who are extremely fastidious often annoy those who are not.

EXERCISE 7.5: Answers

Pronouns are set in italics; antecedents are set in boldface.

1. *She*; **everyone**
2. **crowd**; *that*; *one*; *I*
3. *Who*; **Mark**; *himself*; *what*; *he*
4. *They*; *themselves*
5. **People**; *who*; *those*; *who*

4

Recognizing adjectives

Adjectives modify (limit the meaning of) nouns or pronouns, usually by describing, identifying, or quantifying those words.

The *red* Corvette ran off the road. [describes]
It was *defective*. [describes]
That Corvette needs to be repaired. [identifies]
We saw *several* Corvettes race by. [quantifies]

Most adjectives, like *red* in the examples above, are used to describe. In addition to their basic forms, most descriptive adjectives have other forms that are used to make comparisons: *small, smaller, smallest; foolish, more foolish, most foolish, less foolish, least foolish*.

This year's attendance was *smaller* than last year's.
This year's attendance was the *smallest* in ten years.

Many of the pronouns in 7b3 can also function as adjectives when they are followed by a noun.

That is a dangerous intersection. [pronoun]
That intersection is dangerous. [adjective]

Who would succeed in the world should be wise in the use of pronouns. Utter the You twenty times, when you once utter the I. —JOHN HAY

FOR COLLABORATIVE WORK

Have students break into groups and work to transform the following ordinary statements into powerful messages—expanding them with adjectives and adverbs. Then, have them share their messages with the rest of the class.

1. Candidates travel across the nation.
2. The spider went up the waterspout.
3. A stir was audible in the hall.
4. Fifi gets angry.
5. The prisoner dozed off and was wakened.
6. The boy entered the line.

Pronouns that can be used as adjectives include personal (*her* idea), interrogative (*which* model should we buy?), relative (we're not sure *which* model we should buy), demonstrative (*this* book), and indefinite (*every* item). Other kinds of adjectives that identify or quantify are articles (*a, an, the*) and numbers (*three, sixty-fifth, five hundred*).

Proper adjectives are adjectives formed from or related to proper nouns (*French, Emersonian*). Proper adjectives are capitalized. (See 35b.)

Chapter 12 provides a complete discussion of adjectives.

5

Recognizing adverbs

Adverbs modify verbs, adjectives, other adverbs, or entire clauses. You can recognize many adverbs by their *-ly* ending, though some adverbs do not have such an ending (*always, never, very well*) and some words that end in *-ly* are not adverbs but adjectives (*friendly, lovely*). One of the most common adverbs is *not*.

Allegra and Sam *recently* visited New Orleans. [modifies the verb *visited*]

They had an *unexpectedly* exciting trip. [modifies the adjective *exciting*]

They *very* soon discovered the French Quarter. [modifies the adverb *soon*]

Frankly, they would have liked to stay another month. [modifies the independent clause that makes up the rest of the sentence]

Adverbs often answer one of the following questions: *how? when? where? why? to what extent?* In the first example above, for instance, *recently* answers the question *when?* In the third sentence, *very* answers the question *to what extent?*

Many adverbs, like many adjectives, have different forms that are used in making comparisons: *forcefully, more forcefully, most forcefully, less forcefully, least forcefully.*

The senator spoke *more forcefully* than her opponent.

Of all the candidates, she speaks the *most forcefully.*

Conjunctive adverbs modify an entire clause and express the connection in meaning between that clause and the preceding clause (or sentence). Examples of conjunctive adverbs include *however, furthermore, therefore,* and *likewise.* (See 7b7.)

The most movable of all parts of speech, adverbs can often be placed in different positions in a sentence without changing or disrupting the meaning of the sentence. Notice in the following examples how placement creates only slight differences in emphasis.

Reluctantly, Eduardo gave up the trophy.

Eduardo *reluctantly* gave up the trophy.

Eduardo gave up the trophy *reluctantly.*

Chapter 12 provides a complete discussion of adverbs.

EXERCISE 7.6

Identify the adjectives and adverbs in each of the following sentences, underlining the adjectives once and the adverbs twice. Remember that articles and some pronouns are used as adjectives. Example:

<u>Luckily</u>, <u>each</u> day brought <u>new</u> challenges.

1. We were ready to leave when our dog suddenly became slightly snappish.
2. Anxiously, I took my place in the long line to register for classes.
3. The aromas from the pantry were rather mysterious, and our stomachs grumbled hungrily.
4. Twenty Italian flags snapped in the strong breeze.
5. Ms. Peters was the most inspirational of the three instructors.
6. That dealer agreed too easily to our first offer.
7. Never did I expect to move to a small town in Texas.
8. After the election the president spoke more pessimistically.
9. The biggest factor in homelessness is a drop in federal aid for housing.
10. Some say that the personal life of a political candidate should not be discussed in the media.

EXERCISE 7.7

Expand each of the following sentences by adding appropriate adjectives and adverbs. Delete *the* if need be. Example:

The veterinarians examined the patient.

Then, *the* three *veterinarians* thoroughly *examined the* nervous *patient.*

1. A corporation can fire workers.
2. The heroine marries the prince.
3. In the painting a road curves between hills.
4. Candles gleamed on the tabletop.
5. Feminists have staged demonstrations against the movie.

EXERCISE 7.6: Answers

Adjectives are set in italics; adverbs are set in boldface.

1. *ready; our;* **suddenly; slightly;** *snappish*
2. **Anxiously;** *my; the; long*
3. *The; the;* **rather;** *mysterious; our;* **hungrily**
4. *Twenty; Italian; the; strong*
5. *the;* **most;** *inspirational; the; three*
6. *That;* **too; easily;** *our; first*
7. **Never;** *a; small*
8. *the; the;* **more; pessimistically**
9. *the; biggest; a; federal*
10. *the; personal; a; political;* **not;** *the*

EXERCISE 7.7: Suggested Answers

1. A multinational corporation can fire undependable workers.
2. The beautiful, athletic heroine marries the charming, bookish prince.
3. In the pastoral painting a dirt road curves between the rolling hills.
4. The tall, white candles gleamed brightly on the well-scrubbed tabletop.
5. Ardent feminists have staged impressive demonstrations against the obscenely violent movie.

BACKGROUND

Besides connecting nouns and pronouns to other words, prepositions also have important semantic dimensions, serving as the most important words in certain sentences.

> Watch that crazed killer *behind* you.
> Tie that artery *below* his ear.

Until the late Middle Ages, relationships among words were indicated by inflectional endings. But by 1300, when only the possessive (-'s) and plural (-s) endings remained, prepositions were used to signal relationships. Chaucer was the first to use the preposition *during* (c. 1385), while the *Piers Plowman* poet was the first to use the prepositions *concerning* and *except* (c. 1377).

6

Recognizing prepositions

Prepositions are important structural words that express relationships—in space, time, or other senses—between nouns or pronouns and other words in a sentence.

> We did not want to leave *during* the game.
>
> The contestants waited nervously *for* the announcement.
>
> Drive *across* the bridge, go *down* the avenue *past* three stoplights, and then turn left *before* the Gulf station.

Some common prepositions

about	at	down	near	since
above	below	during	of	through
across	before	except	off	toward
after	behind	for	on	under
against	beneath	from	onto	until
along	beside	in	out	up
among	between	inside	over	upon
around	beyond	into	past	with
as	by	like	regarding	without

SOME COMPOUND PREPOSITIONS

according to	except for	instead of
as well as	in addition to	next to
because of	in front of	out of
by way of	in place of	with regard to
due to	in spite of	

If you are in doubt about which preposition to use, consult your dictionary. Frederich Wood's *English Prepositional Idioms* is a dictionary devoted to prepositions.

A *prepositional phrase* is made of a preposition together with the noun or pronoun it connects to the rest of the sentence. (See 7c3.)

EXERCISE 7.8: Answers

1. of; through; on
2. through; across; into
3. past; at
4. During; down; between
5. by; to; by; of

EXERCISE 7.8

Identify and underline the prepositions. Example:

> *In the dim interior of the hut crouched an old man.*

1. A gust of wind blew through the window, upsetting the vase on the table.
2. He ran swiftly through the brush, across the beach, and into the sea.

3. A few minutes past noon, the police arrived at the scene.
4. During our trip down the river, a rivalry developed between us.
5. The book, by Anne Morrow Lindbergh, describes the flight the Lindberghs made to the Orient by way of the Great Circle Route.

7

Recognizing conjunctions

Conjunctions connect words or groups of words to one another. There are four kinds of conjunctions: coordinating conjunctions, correlative conjunctions, subordinating conjunctions, and conjunctive adverbs.

Coordinating conjunctions

Coordinating conjunctions join equivalent structures—two or more nouns, pronouns, verbs, adjectives, adverbs, prepositions, conjunctions, phrases, or clauses. (See 20a.)

COORDINATING CONJUNCTIONS			
and	or	nor	so
but	for	yet	

T. S. Eliot wrote poems *and* plays.

A strong *but* warm breeze blew across the desert.

Please print *or* type the information on the application form.

Her arguments were easy to ridicule *yet* hard to refute.

Nor, for, and *so* can connect independent clauses only.

He did not have much money, *nor* did he know how to get any.

The student glanced anxiously at the clock, *for* only twenty minutes remained in the exam period.

Ellen worked two shifts on Thursday, *so* she was tired that night.

Correlative conjunctions

Correlative conjunctions also join equivalent elements. They come in pairs.

TEACHING PRACTICE

To give your students practice in thinking about the relationships between words and ideas, you may want to present them a conjunction-less passage, asking them to insert the appropriate conjunctions. With the italicized conjunctions left out, present the following passage:

> *If* my mother was in a singing mood, it wasn't so bad. She would sing about hard times, bad times, *and* somebody-done-gone-and-left-me times. *But* her voice was so sweet *and* her singing-eyes so melty I found myself longing for those hard times, yearning to be grown without "a thin di-i-ime to my name." I looked forward to the delicious time *when* "my man" would leave me, *when* I would "hate to see that evening sun go down . . ." 'cause *then* I would know "my man has left this town." Misery colored by the greens *and* blues in my mother's voice took all of the grief out of the words *and* left me with a conviction that pain was *not only* endurable, it was sweet.   —TONI MORRISON, *The Bluest Eye*

CORRELATIVE CONJUNCTIONS	
both . . . and	neither . . . nor
either . . . or	not only . . . but also
just as . . . so	whether . . . or

Both W. H. Auden *and* William Carlos Williams wrote poems about Bruegel's *Fall of Icarus.*

Jeff *not only* sent a card *but also* visited me in the hospital.

Subordinating conjunctions

Subordinating conjunctions introduce adverb clauses and signal the relationship between the adverb clause and another clause, usually an independent clause. For instance, in the following sentence the subordinating conjunction *while* signals a time relationship, letting us know that the two events in the sentence happen simultaneously.

Sweat ran down my face *while* I frantically searched for my child.

SOME COMMON SUBORDINATING CONJUNCTIONS		
after	if	though
although	in order that	unless
as	once	until
as if	since	when
because	so that	where
before	than	while
even though	that	

Unless sales improve dramatically, the company will soon be bankrupt.

My grandmother began traveling *after* she sold her house.

Conjunctive adverbs

Conjunctive adverbs connect independent clauses. As their name suggests, conjunctive adverbs can be considered both adverbs and conjunctions because they modify the second clause in addition to connecting it to the preceding clause. Like many other adverbs and unlike other conjunctions, they can be moved to different positions in a clause. For example:

The cider tasted bitter; *however,* each of us drank a tall glass of it.

The cider tasted bitter; each of us, *however,* drank a tall glass of it.

The cider tasted bitter. Each of us drank a tall glass of it, *however.*

SOME CONJUNCTIVE ADVERBS

also	indeed	now
anyway	instead	otherwise
besides	likewise	similarly
certainly	meanwhile	still
finally	moreover	then
furthermore	namely	therefore
however	nevertheless	thus
incidentally	next	undoubtedly

Independent clauses connected by a conjunctive adverb must be separated by a semicolon or a period, not just a comma (see 15c).

> Some of these problems could occur at any company; *however,* many could happen only here.

EXERCISE 7.9

Underline the coordinating, correlative, and subordinating conjunctions as well as the conjunctive adverbs in each of the following sentences. Example:

> *David used his sleeping bag <u>even though</u> the cabin was furnished with sheets <u>and</u> blankets.*

1. When we arrived at the pond, we saw many of the neighborhood children playing there.
2. Pokey is an outside cat; nevertheless, she greets me at the front door each night as I arrive home.
3. The colt walked calmly, for he seemed to know he would win the race.
4. The shops along the waterfront were open, but business was slow.
5. The Environmental Protection Agency was once forced to buy an entire town because dioxins had rendered it uninhabitable.
6. The story was not only long but also dull.
7. I did not know whether to laugh or cry after I realized my mistake.
8. Exhausted men and women worked the pumps until their arms ached.

EXERCISE 7.9: Answers

1. when
2. nevertheless; as
3. for
4. but
5. because
6. not only . . . but also
7. whether . . . or; after
8. until
9. although; as if
10. neither . . . nor; therefore

9. Although I live in a big city, my neighborhood has enough trees and raccoons to make me feel as if I live in the suburbs.

10. Neither Henry nor Rachel could understand the story; therefore, they did not recommend it.

8
Recognizing interjections

Interjections express surprise or emotion: *oh, ouch, ah, hey.* Interjections often stand alone, as fragments. Even when they are included in a sentence, they are not related grammatically to the rest of the sentence. They are used mostly in speaking; in writing they are used mostly in dialogue.

"Yes! All right!" The fans screamed, jumping to their feet.

The problem suggested, *alas,* no easy solution.

7c

Recognizing the parts of a sentence

The parts-of-speech system helps us understand the way words can be used. In addition, we need to look at the parts of the sentence, for every sentence has a grammatical pattern or structure, in which words function. Look at the word *book.* In 7b we saw that *book* can function as various parts of speech—as a noun, an adjective, and a verb.

NOUN
A book is always a welcome gift.

ADJECTIVE
Henry has more book knowledge than wisdom.

VERB
How can I book a flight to Fort Worth?

Notice that *book* has exactly the same form for each part of speech. It would be impossible to recognize its meaning without the context of a particular sentence. In fact, even within a sentence, a word that can be categorized as a certain part of speech can function in more than one way.

SUBJECT
This book describes the ecology of the Everglades.

DIRECT OBJECT
I need a book about the ecology of the Everglades.

Book is a noun in both of these sentences, yet in the first it serves as the subject of the verb *describes,* while in the second it serves as the direct object of the verb *need.* Knowing the word's part of speech tells only part of the story; we have to recognize the part it plays in the pattern or structure of a particular sentence.

 Basic sentence patterns

---

1. SUBJECT/VERB

   S   V

Babies cry.

2. SUBJECT/VERB/SUBJECT COMPLEMENT

   S   V   SC

Babies seem fragile.

3. SUBJECT/VERB/DIRECT OBJECT

   S   V   DO

Babies drink milk.

4. SUBJECT/VERB/INDIRECT OBJECT/DIRECT OBJECT

   S   V   IO   DO

Babies give grandparents pleasure.

5. SUBJECT/VERB/DIRECT OBJECT/OBJECT COMPLEMENT

   S   V   DO   OC

Babies make parents proud.

This section examines the essential parts of a sentence—subjects, predicates, objects, complements, phrases, and clauses—and provides practice in using them to construct sentences of various kinds.

1

Recognizing subjects

As explained in 7a, almost every sentence has a stated subject, which identifies whom or what the sentence is about. The **simple subject** consists of one or more nouns or pronouns; the **complete subject** consists of the simple subject with all its modifiers. Depending on the number and kinds of modifiers, subjects can be as plain as one word or far more complex. The following examples show the complete subjects in italics, with the simple subjects labeled *ss.*

Those who are learning to compose and arrange their sentences with accuracy and order are learning, at the same time, to think with accuracy and order. —HUGH BLAIR

BACKGROUND

In reaction to the purely formal, static quality of the terms *subject* and *predicate,* various linguists developed a theory linking the binary form of the sentence with the functions of those major divisions. As described by William J. Van de Kopple in "Something Old, Something New: Functional Sentence Perspective" (*Research in the Teaching of English* 17 [Feb. 1983]: 85–99):

> In brief, for Functional Sentence Perspectivists a sentence conveys its message most effectively if its two major parts, the topic and comment, perform specific semantic and communicative tasks. In English, the topic usually includes the grammatical subject and its adjuncts. The comment usually includes the verb and objects or carries primary sentence stress.

> For each part the theorists posit slightly different but often corresponding communicative functions. They claim that the topic should express either the theme of the sentence, the elements with the least communicative dynamism . . . the least important information, or the old information. They assert that the comment should express either information about the theme, the elements with the most communicative dynamism, the most important information, or the new information.

ss
Baseball is a summer game.

ss
Sailing over the fence, the ball crashed through Mr. Wilson's window.

ss
Stadiums with real grass are hard to find these days.

ss
Those who sit in the bleachers have the most fun.

A *compound subject* contains two or more simple subjects joined with a coordinating conjunction (*and, but, or*) or a correlative conjunction (*both . . . and, either . . . or, neither . . . nor, not only . . . but also*).

Baseball and softball developed from cricket.
Both *baseball and softball* developed from cricket.

The simple subject usually comes before the predicate, or verb, but not always. Sometimes writers reverse this order for effect.

Up to the plate stepped *Casey*.
Great was the *anticipation* among Mudville fans.

In imperative sentences, which express requests or commands, the subject *you* is almost always implied but not stated.

(*You*) Keep your eye on the ball.

In questions and certain other constructions, the subject usually appears between the auxiliary verb and the main verb.

Did *Casey* save the game?
Never have *I* known greater disappointment.

In sentences beginning with *there* or *here* followed by a form of the verb *be* (*is, are, was, were, have been, will be,* and so on), the subject always follows the verb. *There* and *here* are never the subject.

Here is the sad *ending* of the poem.
There was no *joy* in Mudville.

EXERCISE 7.10

Identify the complete subject and the simple subject in each of the following sentences. Underline the complete subject once and the simple subject twice. Example:

EXERCISE 7.10: Answers

Complete subjects are set in italics; simple subjects are set in boldface.

1. *The* **novels** *of F. Scott Fitzgerald*
2. *a two-foot* **snowfall**
3. *three startling* **examples**
4. *A* **house** *that faces west*
5. *Some* **women** *worried about osteoporosis*

A *fresh, moist* <u><u>breeze</u></u> *kicked up at just the right time.*

1. The novels of F. Scott Fitzgerald depict the Jazz Age.
2. Was a two-foot snowfall unexpected?
3. Here are three startling examples.
4. A house that faces west gets the afternoon sun.
5. Some women worried about osteoporosis take calcium supplements.

2

Recognizing predicates

In addition to a subject, every sentence has a predicate, which asserts or asks something about the subject or tells the subject to do something (see 7a). The "hinge" or key word of most predicates is a verb. As we saw in 7b1, a verb can include auxiliary verbs (as in this sentence, where *can* is an auxiliary and *include* is the main verb). The **simple predicate** of a sentence is the main verb and any auxiliaries; the **complete predicate** also includes any modifiers of the verb and any objects or complements and their modifiers. In the following examples, the complete predicates are italicized and the simple predicates are labeled *sp*.

My roommate *⌐SP⌐ seems wonderful.*

She *⌐SP⌐ offered me the use of her word processor.*

Both of us *⌐——SP——⌐ are planning to major in history.*

A **compound predicate** contains two or more verbs that have the same subject, usually joined by a coordinating or correlative conjunction.

Charles *shut the book, put it back on the shelf, and sighed.*

The Amish *neither drive cars nor use electricity.*

On the basis of how they function in predicates, verbs can be divided into three categories: linking, transitive, and intransitive.

Linking verbs

A **linking verb** links, or joins, a subject with a **subject complement**, a word or word group that identifies or describes the subject. If it identifies the subject, the complement is a noun or pronoun (and is sometimes called a predicate noun). If it describes the subject, the complement is an adjective (and is sometimes called a **predicate adjective**). In the following examples, *a single mother* is a predicate noun and *exhausted* is a predicate adjective.

┌───S───┐ V ┌───SC───┐
Christine is a single mother.

S V SC
She is exhausted.

The forms of *be,* when used as main verbs rather than as auxiliary verbs, are linking verbs (like *are* in this sentence). Other verbs, such as *appear, become, feel, grow, look, make, seem, smell,* and *sound,* can also function as linking verbs, depending on the sense of the sentence.

┌──────────S──────────┐ ┌───V───┐ ┌───SC───┐
The abandoned farmhouse had become dilapidated.

S V ┌───SC───┐
It looked ready to fall down.

Transitive and intransitive verbs

If a verb is not a linking verb, it is either transitive or intransitive. A **transitive verb** expresses action that is directed toward a noun or pronoun, called the direct object of the verb.

S ┌───V───┐ ┌───DO───┐
I will analyze three poems.

A direct object identifies what or who receives the action of the verb. In the preceding example, the subject and verb alone do not express a complete thought: *what* will I analyze? The direct object completes the thought.

A direct object may be followed by an **object complement**, a word or words that describe or identify the direct object. Object complements may be adjectives, as in the first example below, or nouns, as in the second example.

S ┌─V─┐ ┌──────DO──────┐ ┌──OC──┐
I consider Marianne Moore's poetry exquisite.

┌──────────S──────────┐ ┌─V─┐ ┌─DO─┐ ┌──OC──┐
Her poems and personality made Moore a celebrity.

A transitive verb may also be followed by an **indirect object**, which tells to whom or what, or for whom or what, the verb's action is done. You might say that the indirect object is the recipient, or beneficiary, of the direct object.

BACKGROUND

Verbs that take an object are *transitive,* from the Latin *transire,* "pass over." Transitive verbs cannot express their meaning without passing over to a complement.

> We *bounced* our *ball* in Waterford Gallery.
> We *bounced* our *ideas* off one another.
> We *bounced* the *pickpocket* out of the restaurant.

Intransitive, that is, "not passing over," verbs are capable of expressing themselves without a complement to complete their meaning.

> Oz *has spoken.*
> Jorge *slunk* past the mission.
> The ball *bounced* over my head.

Sometimes, transitive verbs take an indirect object as well as a direct object, as in:

> Christiana gave Alfred (i.o.) a black eye (d.o.).

> Aurelia sent Joe (i.o.) a Christmas card (d.o.).

These classifications, transitive and intransitive, vary from one sentence to another, depending on how a particular verb is used. A few words (*ignore*) are only transitive, while others (*shine, die*) are only intransitive.

Dictionaries label verbs as *v.t.* (transitive verb) or *v.i.* (intransitive verb), according to use.

Moore's poems about the Dodgers give me considerable pleasure.

Brooklyn owes Marianne Moore something.

An **intransitive verb** expresses action that is not directed toward an object. Therefore, an intransitive verb does not have a direct object.

The Red Sox persevered.

Their fans watched helplessly.

In the preceding sentences, the action of the verb *persevered* has no object (it makes no sense to ask *persevered what?* or *persevered whom?*), and the action of the verb *watched* is directed toward an object that is implied but not expressed.

Some verbs that express action can be only transitive or only intransitive, but most such verbs can be used both ways, with or without a direct object.

A maid wearing a uniform opened the door. [transitive]

The door opened silently. [transitive]

EXERCISE 7.11

Identify and underline the predicate in each of the following sentences. Then identify and label each verb as linking, transitive, or intransitive. Finally, identify and label all subject and object complements and all direct and indirect objects. Example:

We *considered city life unbearable*.

1. California is dry in the summer.
2. The U.S. Constitution made us a nation.
3. A round of applause seemed appropriate.
4. Rock and roll will never die.
5. Advertisers promise consumers the world.

USEFUL READING

Halliday, M. A. K. *System and Function in Language.* Ed. Gunther Kress. London: Oxford UP, 1976. An enlightening, nontraditional grammarian's perspective on transitive verbs, their function and form.

EXERCISE 7.11: Answers

Predicates are set in italics.

1. *is dry in the summer:* lnkg-is; sc-dry
2. *made us a nation:* trans-made; do-us; oc-nation
3. *seemed appropriate:* lnkg-seemed; sc-appropriate
4. *will never die:* intrans-will . . . never die
5. *promise consumers the world:* trans-promise; io-consumers, do-world

3

Recognizing and using phrases

A **phrase** is a group of words that lacks either a subject or a predicate or both. Phrases function in useful ways to add information to a sentence or shape it effectively. Look at the following sentence:

The new law will restrict smoking *in most public places.*

The basic subject of this sentence is a noun phrase, *the new law;* the basic predicate is a verb phrase, *will restrict smoking.* Additional information is provided by the prepositional phrase *in most public places.* The prepositional phrase functions here as an adverb, telling *where* smoking will be restricted. This section will discuss the various kinds of phrases: noun, verb, prepositional, verbal, absolute, and appositive.

Noun phrases

Made up of a noun and all its modifiers, a **noun phrase** can function in a sentence as a subject, object, or complement.

— SUBJECT —
Delicious, gooey peanut butter is surprisingly healthful.

— OBJECT —
Dieters prefer *green salad.*

— COMPLEMENT —
A tuna sandwich is *a popular lunch.*

Verb phrases

A main verb and its auxiliary verbs make up a **verb phrase**, which functions in a sentence in only one way: as a predicate.

Frank *had been depressed* for some time.

His problem *might have been caused* by tension between his parents.

Prepositional phrases

A **prepositional phrase** includes a preposition, a noun or pronoun called the **object of the preposition**, and any modifiers of the object. Prepositional phrases function as either adjectives or adverbs.

ADJECTIVE	Our house *in Maine* was a cabin.
ADVERB	*From Cadillac Mountain* you can see the northern lights.

EXERCISE 7.12

Following are some sentences written by the sports columnist Red Smith. Identify and underline all the prepositional phrases. Then choose two of the sentences, and write sentences that imitate their structures. Example:

> He glanced *about the room* *with a cocky, crooked grin.*
> The cat stalked *around the yard* *in her quiet, arrogant way.*

1. In those days the Yankees always won the pennant.
2. Fear wasn't in his vocabulary and pain had no meaning.
3. Coaching in Columbus is not quite like coaching in New Haven.
4. He stepped out of the dugout and faced the multitude, two fists and one cap uplifted.
5. The old champ looked fit, square of shoulder and springy of tread, his skin clear, his eyes bright behind the glittering glasses.

EXERCISE 7.13

Combine each of the following pairs of sentences into one sentence by making the second sentence into one or more prepositional phrases. Example:

> *over*
> The Greeks won a tremendous victory~~. They were fighting~~ the Persians.

1. Socrates was condemned. His fellow citizens made up the jury that condemned him.
2. Socrates faced death. He had no fear.
3. The playwright Aristophanes wrote a comedy. Its subject was Socrates.
4. Everyone thought Socrates was crazy. Only a few followers disagreed.
5. Today Socrates is honored. He founded Western philosophy.

Verbal phrases

Verbals are verb forms that do not function as verbs in sentences. Instead, they function as nouns, adjectives, and adverbs. There are three kinds of verbals: participles, gerunds, and infinitives.

The **participle** functions as an adjective in sentences. The **present participle** is the *-ing* form of a verb: *dreaming, being, seeing.* The **past participle** of most verbs ends in *-ed: dreamed, watched.* But some verbs have an irregular past participle: *been, seen, hidden, gone, set.* (See 9b.)

EXERCISE 7.12: Answers

1. In those days
2. in his vocabulary
3. in Columbus; in New Haven
4. of the dugout
5. of shoulder; of tread; behind the glittering glasses

Imitations of these sentences will vary.

EXERCISE 7.13: Suggested Answers

1. Socrates was condemned by a jury of his fellow citizens.
2. Without fear, Socrates faced death.
3. Aristophanes wrote a comedy about Socrates.
4. Except for a few of his followers, everyone thought Socrates was crazy.
5. Today Socrates is honored as the founder of Western philosophy.

His kiss awakened the *dreaming* princess.

The cryptographers deciphered the *hidden* meaning in the message.

The **gerund** has the same form as the present participle but functions in sentences as a noun.

SUBJECT	*Writing* takes practice.
OBJECT	The organization promotes *recycling*.

The **infinitive** is the *to* form of a verb: *to dream, to be, to see*. An infinitive can function in a sentence as a noun, adjective, or adverb.

NOUN	She wanted *to write*.
ADJECTIVE	They had no more time *to waste*.
ADVERB	The corporation was ready *to expand*.

A verbal can never stand alone as the verb of a sentence because it is a **nonfinite**, or "unfinished," **verb**. Take the present participle *barking,* for instance. *The terrier barking* is not a sentence; to make it a sentence you need to add one or more auxiliary verbs: *The terrier is barking* or *The terrier had been barking*. The verb phrases *is barking* and *had been barking* are **finite verbs**, which do not need any other auxiliary to function as verbs.

Verbal phrases are made up of a verbal and any modifiers, objects, or complements. Let us turn now to examine the forms and functions of the various kinds of verbal phrases.

PARTICIPIAL PHRASES

Participial phrases consist of a present participle or past participle with any modifiers, objects, or complements. Participial phrases always function as adjectives in sentences.

Irritated by the delay, Louise complained.

A dog *howling at the moon* kept me awake.

Notice that many participial phrases may appear in different places in a sentence, as long as it is clear which word they modify (see Chapter 17). Decisions about where to place participial phrases must usually be made within the larger context of a piece of writing. The choice often depends on the rhythm or emphasis the writer wants to achieve.

Fearing that I would be left alone, I quickly followed the group.

I quickly followed the group, *fearing that I would be left alone.*

GERUND PHRASES

Gerund phrases consist of a gerund with any modifiers, objects, or complements: *hoping for a victory, critical thinking.* In sentences, gerund phrases function as nouns—as a subject, a subject complement, a direct object, an indirect object, or an object of a preposition.

Opening their eyes to the problem [S] was not easy.

His downfall was *relying too much on his computer.* [SC]

They suddenly heard *a loud wailing from the sandbox.* [DO]

The critics gave *Pavarotti's singing* [IO] their enthusiastic approval.

In addition to *being confused,* [OBJ OF PREP] she was alone.

INFINITIVE PHRASES

Infinitive phrases consist of an infinitive with any modifiers, objects, or complements: *to be happy, to go to a movie tonight.* They can function as nouns, adjectives, or adverbs.

My goal is *to be a biology teacher.* [NOUN/SC]

A party would be a good way *to end the semester.* [ADJECTIVE]

To perfect a draft, [ADVERB] always proofread carefully.

Notice that infinitive phrases used as adverbs, like the last example above, may appear in different places in a sentence as long as it is clear which word they modify (see Chapter 17). For example, *To perfect a draft* could be moved to the end of its sentence. As with participial phrases, placement should depend on the effect it creates within the larger context.

EXERCISE 7.14

Identify each participial phrase, gerund phrase, and infinitive phrase, and specify which part of speech it functions as in the sentence. Example:

Pacing the hall with impatience, [PARTICIPIAL-ADJ] I wished my friends would arrive.

EXERCISE 7.14: Answers

1. gerund-Buying his first Corvette: n, subj
2. gerund-careful saving: n, object of prep
3. inf-to renovate the house: n, subj compl
   inf-to sell it: n, subj compl
4. part-Raised in Idaho: adj, modifying "I"
   part-exploring nature: adj, obj compl
5. part-Sitting by the window and listening to the wind: adj, modifying I
   part-blowing through the trees: adj, obj compl
   inf-to be alive: adv

TEACHING PRACTICE

Consider using sentence-combining techniques to reinforce the effective compression that can be achieved with absolute and appositive phrases. For instance, *I jumped into the car and took off, the tires screeching in protest* combines at least three simpler sentences:

> I jumped; (I jumped) into the car.
> I took off.
> The tires were screeching in protest.

Write these sentences on the board and work with your students to delete repetitive elements to form a combined sentence with an absolute element. You can do the same exercise to achieve an appositive phrase:

> Maya Angelou will appear on campus tonight.
> Maya Angelou is a celebrated novelist and (Maya Angelou is a celebrated) essayist.

FOR THE WRITING LOG

Have students choose any full page from a current draft and identify all the types of phrases (participial, gerund, infinitive, appositive, absolute, and prepositional) they have used. Then have them write a log entry describing the range and pattern of phrasal constructions they have employed and setting out a plan to improve their use of phrases.

1. Buying his first Corvette was the happiest moment in Ron's life.
2. After four years of careful saving, he got his car.
3. Our plan was to renovate the house and then to sell it.
4. Raised in Idaho, I spent plenty of time exploring nature.
5. Sitting by the window and listening to the wind blowing through the trees, I feel happy and lucky to be alive.

Absolute phrases

An **absolute phrase** usually consists of a noun or pronoun and a participle. It modifies an entire sentence rather than a particular word. Absolutes may appear almost anywhere in a sentence and are usually set off from the rest of the sentence with commas. (See 29a.)

> I stood on the deck, *the wind whipping my hair.*
> *My fears laid to rest,* I climbed into the plane for my first solo flight.

When the participle is *being,* it is often omitted.

> The ambassador, *her head (being) high,* walked out of the room.

Appositive phrases

A noun phrase that renames the noun or pronoun that immediately precedes it is called an **appositive phrase.**

> The report, *a hefty three-volume work,* included 150 recommendations.
> We had a single desire, *to change the administration's policies.*
> Maya Angelou, *the celebrated writer,* will appear on campus tonight.

EXERCISE 7.15

Read the following sentences, and identify and label all of the prepositional, verbal, absolute, and appositive phrases. Notice that one kind of phrase may appear within another kind. Example:

> ┌─────ABSOLUTE─────┐
> *His voice breaking with emotion, Ed thanked us for the award.*
> └──PREP──┘

1. Approaching the rope, I suddenly fell into the icy pond.
2. To listen to Bruce Springsteen is sheer delight.

3. The figure outlined against the sky seemed unable to move.

4. Floating on my back, I ignored my practice requirements.

5. Jane stood still, her fingers clutching the fence.

6. Bobby, a sensitive child, was filled with a mixture of awe and excitement.

7. Shocked into silence, they kept their gaze fixed on the odd creature.

8. Basking in the sunlight, I was lost in reminiscence of birch trees.

9. Susan, the leader of the group, was reluctant to give up any authority.

10. His favorite form of recreation was taking a nap.

Using phrases to shape and expand sentences

Phrases provide valuable tools for shaping or expanding sentences. They bring in additional information, and they can help you emphasize certain parts of a sentence and deemphasize others. In this way, they help distinguish the main idea from the extra details. Look, for instance, at the following sentence:

> Jupiter crashed through the tomato vines with the remains of a felt hat in his mouth.
> — JOHN CHEEVER, "The Country Husband"

Cheever might have expressed the ideas in this sentence in many other ways. For instance:

> Jupiter crashed through the tomato vines. He had the remains of a felt hat in his mouth.

> Crashing through the tomato vines, Jupiter held the remains of a felt hat in his mouth.

In the first possibility, turning some of the prepositional phrases into a second sentence separates the statement into two parts and thus weakens or at least changes the impact it has on readers—perhaps because we see the crash and the torn hat at a greater chronological distance from each other. In the second possibility, turning the verb of the original sentence into a participle puts greater emphasis on what was in the dog's mouth than on his crash through the vines and thus describes a slightly different scene.

Following are some examples of how some student writers used various kinds of phrases to shape and expand particular sentences.

NOUN PHRASE

That car will never win the race.

That battered, valveless, bent-up bone-shaker will never win the race.

USEFUL READING

Christensen, Francis. "A Generative Rhetoric of the Sentence." *Rhetoric and Composition.* Ed. Richard Graves. Upper Montclair, NY: Boynton, 1984. 110–18. The idea for expanding sentences by adding and manipulating modifying phrases derives largely from Francis Christensen, who maintained that students can achieve syntactic fluency by adding modifiers at the beginning, middle, and end of their sentences. He focuses on the cumulative sentence and demonstrates how writers can add final free modifiers to main clauses to expand sentences.

PARTICIPIAL PHRASE

The expressway looked like a long parking lot. It was jammed with traffic that was crawling into the city.

Jammed with traffic crawling into the city, the expressway looked like a long parking lot.

ABSOLUTE PHRASE

The dictator's long period of totalitarian rule was over, and he stepped into his limousine.

His long period of totalitarian rule over, the dictator stepped into his limousine.

Positioning phrases

As noted earlier, many phrases can be placed either at the beginning, in the middle, or at the end of a sentence. For example:

Calling on every ounce of energy, Jo sprinted toward the finish line.

Jo, *calling on every ounce of energy,* sprinted toward the finish line.

Jo sprinted toward the finish line, *calling on every ounce of energy.*

The phrase in these examples is a participial phrase that modifies *Jo.* While changing its placement does not alter the basic meaning of the sentence, it affects rhythm and emphasis, most notably in the third example by changing the important concluding words of the sentence.

Prepositional, infinitive, and absolute phrases can also occupy more than one sentence position. There are no absolute guidelines for placement, but three tips may help: (1) be sure the phrase clearly modifies any word it should modify (see Chapter 17); (2) read the sentence in the context of the surrounding sentences to see which placement seems most effective to you (see 22b); and (3) decide what you want to emphasize (or not emphasize), and place phrases accordingly. Putting phrases at the beginning or end of a sentence gives more emphasis than putting them in the middle.

EXERCISE 7.16

Use prepositional, participial, infinitive, gerund, absolute, or appositive phrases to expand each of the following sentences. Example:

The apples dropped from the limb.

In response to my vigorous shake, *the apples dropped from the limb.*

1. Nancy jogged down Willow Street.
2. She looked healthy when he saw her the second time.

FOR COLLABORATIVE WORK

Have students share the results of their survey of the kinds of phrases they use. Then have students work together to expand or revise selected sentences from each others' drafts to incorporate new types of phrases, and discuss the effects of their revisions.

EXERCISE 7.16: Suggested Answers

1. Dressed in her brand new running shoes, Nancy jogged down Willow Street, hoping to cover more distance than she had yesterday, when she was running in worn-out sneakers.

2. After soaking up the sun and eating good food, she looked healthy when he saw her the second time.

3. Richard had lost almost all of his hair.
4. The Sunday afternoon dragged.
5. Teresa looked at her mother.
6. The candidates shook hands with the voters.
7. We were uncertain what to do.
8. Ben often thought regretfully about the past.
9. The letter lay on the desk.
10. They lived in a trailer.

EXERCISE 7.17

Use a participial, infinitive, gerund, absolute, or appositive phrase to combine each of the following pairs of sentences into one sentence. Example:

His constant complaining
~~He complained constantly. This habit~~ irritated his co-workers.

1. David Klein performed a monologue. He is an actor and comedian.
2. We waited to go through customs. Our passports were clutched in our hands.
3. She bought a new camera. This purchase lifted her spirits.
4. Michael had his ear pierced. He did this because it annoyed his parents.
5. The protesters were carrying their banners. They headed down the street.

4

Recognizing and using clauses

A **clause** is a group of words containing a subject and a predicate. There are two kinds of clauses: independent and dependent. **Independent clauses** (also known as **main clauses**) can stand alone as complete sentences.

The window is open.
The batter swung at the ball.

Pairs of independent clauses may be joined with a coordinating conjunction and a comma (see 7b7).

The window is open, *so* we'd better be quiet.
The batter swung at the ball, *and* the umpire called her out.

3. Because he had taken such strong medication, Richard had lost almost all his hair.
4. The Sunday afternoon dragged to an absolute halt.
5. Teresa looked at her mother, her eyes searching for the familiar face that now seemed so old.
6. In addition to kissing babies, posing for pictures, and eating boiled chicken, the candidates shook hands with the voters.
7. Having thoughtlessly locked ourselves out while the bathtub filled with water, we were uncertain what to do.
8. A late bloomer, Ben often thought regretfully about the past.
9. Unopened, the letter lay on the desk in its gleaming white envelope looking very inviting.
10. A young couple and their children, they lived in a trailer, crowded together like sardines.

EXERCISE 7.17: Suggested Answers

1. An actor and comedian, David Klein performed a monologue.
2. Waiting to go through customs, we clutched our passports in our hands.
3. To lift her spirits, she bought a new camera.
4. To annoy his parents, Michael had his ear pierced.
5. Carrying their banners, the protesters headed down the street.

Like independent clauses, **dependent clauses** (also known as **subordinate clauses**) contain a subject and a predicate. They cannot stand alone as complete sentences, however, for they begin with a subordinating word—a subordinating conjunction (see 7b7) or a relative pronoun (see 7b3). The subordinating word connects the dependent clause to an independent clause. Each of the following sentences, for instance, consists of one brief independent clause.

> The window is open.
> The room feels cool.

You might choose to combine these two independent clauses with a comma and coordinating conjunction: *The window is open, and the room feels cool.* But you could also combine the two clauses by turning one into a dependent clause.

> *Because the window is open,* the room feels cool.

In this combination the subordinating conjunction *because* transforms the independent clause *the window is open* into a dependent clause. In doing so, it indicates a causal relationship between the two clauses.

Dependent clauses function in sentences as nouns, adjectives, or adverbs.

Noun clauses

Noun clauses can function as subjects, direct objects, subject complements, or objects of prepositions. Thus they are always contained within another clause rather than simply attached to it, as adjective and adverb clauses are. They usually begin with a relative pronoun (*that, which, what, who, whom, whose, whatever, whoever, whomever, whichever*) or with *when, where, whether, why,* or *how.*

> $\overset{\llcorner\quad\quad S\quad\quad\lrcorner}{\text{That he had a college degree}}$ was important to her.

> She asked $\overset{\llcorner\quad\quad DO\quad\quad\lrcorner}{\text{where he went to college.}}$

> The real question was $\overset{\llcorner\quad\quad SC\quad\quad\lrcorner}{\text{why she wanted to know.}}$

> She was looking for $\overset{\llcorner\quad\quad OBJ\ OF\ PREP\quad\quad\lrcorner}{\text{whatever information she could get.}}$

Notice that in each of these sentences the noun clause is an integral part of the independent clause that makes up the sentence; for example, in the second sentence the independent clause is not just *She asked* but *She asked where he went to college.*

Adjective clauses

Adjective clauses modify nouns and pronouns in another clause. Usually, they follow immediately after the words they modify. Most adjective clauses begin with the relative pronouns *who, whom, whose, that,* or *which.* Some begin with *when, where,* or *why.*

The surgery, *which took three hours,* was a complete success.

It was performed by the surgeon *who had developed* the procedure.

The hospital was the one *where I was born.*

Sometimes the relative pronoun introducing an adjective clause may be omitted, as in the following example.

That is one book [that] I intend to read.

Adverb clauses

Adverb clauses modify verbs, adjectives, or other adverbs. They begin with a subordinating conjunction (see 7b7). Like adverbs, they usually tell why, when, where, how, under what conditions, or to what extent.

We hiked *where there were few other hikers.*

My backpack felt heavier *than it ever had.*

I climbed as swiftly *as I could under the weight of my backpack.*

Like adverbs, adverb clauses can usually be placed in different positions in a sentence without affecting the meaning.

If you look up from the valley, you will see Half Dome.
You will see Half Dome *if you look up from the valley.*

EXERCISE 7.18

Identify the independent and dependent clauses and any subordinating conjunctions and relative pronouns in each of the following sentences. Example:

┌──────DEPENDENT CLAUSE──────┐
If I were going on a really long hike, I would carry a lightweight stove.
[*If* is a subordinating conjunction.]

EXERCISE 7.18: Answers

1. ind-The driver was driving a tan Pontiac; dep-who won the race; rel-who

2. dep-As a potential customer entered the store; sub conj-As; ind-Tony nervously attempted to retreat to the safety of the back room

3. ind-The names still haunt me; dep-they called my grandmother

4. dep-When she was deemed old enough to understand; sub conj-when; ind-she was told the truth; ind-she finally knew why her father had left home; rel-why

5. dep-Though most of my grandfather's farm was wooded; sub conj-Though; ind-there were also great expanses of green lawns and quiet, trickling streams

6. ind-I decided to bake a chocolate cream pie; dep-which was Lynn's favorite; rel-which

7. dep-If Keats had lived longer; sub conj-If; ind-he might have written even greater poems; ind-his early death is perhaps part of his appeal

8. ind-The trip was longer; dep-than I had remembered; rel-than

9. dep-After she finished the painting; sub conj-After; ind-Linda cleaned the brushes

10. ind-I could see that he was very tired; rel-that; ind-I had to ask him a few questions

USEFUL READING

Williams, Joseph. *Style: Ten Lessons in Clarity and Grace.* 3rd ed. Glenview, IL: Scott, 1989. Williams provides methods for both streamlining and enriching sentences.

1. The driver who won the race was driving a tan Pontiac.

2. As a potential customer entered the store, Tony nervously attempted to retreat to the safety of the back room.

3. The names they called my grandmother still haunt me.

4. When she was deemed old enough to understand, she was told the truth, and she finally knew why her father had left home.

5. Though most of my grandfather's farm was wooded, there were also great expanses of green lawns and quiet, trickling streams.

6. I decided to bake a chocolate cream pie, which was Lynn's favorite.

7. If Keats had lived longer, he might have written even greater poems, but his early death is perhaps part of his appeal.

8. The trip was longer than I had remembered.

9. After she finished the painting, Linda cleaned the brushes.

10. I could see that he was very tired, but I had to ask him a few questions.

Using clauses to shape and expand sentences

Like phrases, clauses are an important means of shaping sentences in particular ways or expanding sentences into more varied or interesting ones. For example, look at the following sentences, each of which consists of one independent clause expressing one idea:

Tei's parents disliked Ken. She was determined to marry him.

Now look at how clauses can be used to combine these ideas in one sentence.

1. Although her parents disliked Ken, Tei was determined to marry him.

2. Tei's parents disliked Ken, whom she was determined to marry.

3. Tei's parents disliked Ken, but she was determined to marry him.

In sentence 1, putting the information about the parents' dislike of Ken into a dependent adverb clause gives less emphasis to that idea and more emphasis to the idea expressed in the subject and predicate—Tei's determination to marry him. In sentence 2, on the other hand, the idea of Tei's determination is deemphasized by being placed in a dependent adjective clause. Finally, in sentence 3, the two ideas are given equal emphasis by being expressed in two independent clauses connected by the coordinating conjunction *but.*

As you write sentences, and especially when you are revising a draft, pay attention to how you can use clauses to add details or emphasis to your ideas (see Chapters 19–23). Following are examples of how some student writers used various kinds of clauses to shape and expand particular sentences.

NOUN CLAUSE

Charles later learned the truth.

Charles later learned *what Vinnie had known for years.*

ADJECTIVE CLAUSE

Everything was swept away.

Everything *that he valued most in life* was swept away.

My childhood seemed entirely happy. I grew up on a large farm.

My childhood, *which was spent on a large farm,* seemed entirely happy.

ADVERB CLAUSE

Some people opposed the war, but they supported the troops.

Although some people opposed the war, they supported the troops.

Positioning clauses

Like many phrases, most adverb clauses can be placed at the beginning, in the middle, or at the end of a sentence.

If nothing goes wrong, the furniture will be delivered tomorrow.

The furniture, *if nothing goes wrong,* will be delivered tomorrow.

The furniture will be delivered tomorrow *if nothing goes wrong.*

Changing the position of the adverb clause *if nothing goes wrong* does not affect the basic meaning of the sentence, but it affects the rhythm and the emphasis by highlighting or downplaying the possibility that something could go wrong. (See 17a and 22b.)

EXERCISE 7.19

Expand each sentence below by adding at least one dependent clause. Be prepared to explain how your addition improves the sentence. Example:

The books tumbled from the shelves.

As the earth continued to shake, *the books tumbled from the shelves.*

1. The last guests left.
2. The German government dismantled the Berlin Wall.
3. The new computer made a strange noise.

EXERCISE 7.19: Suggested Answers

1. The last guests, who had stayed much later than we expected, finally left.
2. After many changes and upheavals, the German government dismantled the Berlin wall, which had become a symbol of oppression.
3. The new computer, which had been programmed by an employee who had long since left the company, made a strange noise.
4. Rob, who was a collector of jazz records, always borrowed money from his friends.
5. The streets that the graduate students had overtaken were ringing with loud music.
6. We stood outside for an hour while the opening band played.
7. The history seminar, which foregrounds the scientific achievements of women, begins tomorrow.
8. Because she was willing to stay home on weekends and study, Erin won the translation contest.
9. Before the drought hit, a river flowed through the forest.
10. A man, whose memorial plaque hangs in the lobby, was killed in that mill in 1867.

EXERCISE 7.20: Answers

(The entire sentences are, of course, independent clauses.)

1. dep (rel) cl-that Professor Strunk omitted needless words; prep p-at a glance; n p-Professor Strunk; n p-a glance

2. prep p-in our bare skins; n p-our bare skins

3. prep p-beyond recall; n p-the word

4. prep p-in a zoo; n p-a zoo; n p-the ticket; prep p-for some animals and birds; n p-some animals and birds

5. prep p-of encountering a Perelman piece; prep p-in a magazine; n p-the pleasures and satisfactions; n p-a Perelman piece; n p-a magazine

6. inf p-to read Thoreau; inf p-to enjoy him; n p-his enthusiasms; n p-his acute perception

7. dep cl-When I start a book; np-a book; dep (rel) cl-what my characters are going to do; n p-my characters; v p-are going; inf p-to do; prep p-for their eccentric behavior; n p-their eccentric behavior

8. n p-no sensible writer; inf p-to develop; n p-a style; v p-do have; n p-distinguishing qualities; n p-very evident; dep cl-when you read the words; n p-the words

9. v p-was rendering; n p-an account; dep cl-When I wrote "Death of a Pig"; prep p-of a Pig; prep p-of what actually happened; prep p-on my place; n p-my place; prep p-to my pig; n p-my pig; dep (rel) cl-who died; prep p-to me; dep (rel) cl-who tended him; prep p-in his last hours; n p-his last hours

10. prep p-of Charlotte's descendants; v p-still live; prep p-in the barn; n p-Charlotte's descendants; n p-the barn; dep cl-when the warm days of spring arrive; n p-the warm days; prep p-of spring; n p-tiny spiders; part p-emerging into the world; n p-the world

Imitation sentences will vary.

4. Rob always borrowed money from friends.

5. The streets were ringing with loud music.

6. We stood outside for an hour.

7. The history seminar begins tomorrow.

8. Erin won the translation contest.

9. A river flowed through the forest.

10. A man was killed in that mill in 1867.

EXERCISE 7.20

Following are some sentences from the letters of E. B. White. Read each one carefully, focusing on the phrases and clauses. Underline any dependent clauses once and any phrases twice. Finally, choose two sentences, and use them as a model to write sentences of your own, imitating White's structure phrase for phrase and clause for clause. Example:

> I was born in 1899 and expect to live forever, searching for beauty and raising hell in general.
>
> Sarah was hired in May and plans to work all summer, living at home and saving money for law school.

1. You can see at a glance that Professor Strunk omitted needless words.

2. Either Macmillan takes Strunk and me in our bare skins, or I want out.

3. I regard the word *hopefully* as beyond recall.

4. Life in a zoo is just the ticket for some animals and birds.

5. I recall the pleasures and satisfactions of encountering a Perelman piece in a magazine.

6. The way to read Thoreau is to enjoy him—his enthusiasms, his acute perception.

7. When I start a book, I never know what my characters are going to do, and I accept no responsibility for their eccentric behavior.

8. No sensible writer sets out deliberately to develop a style, but all writers do have distinguishing qualities, and they become very evident when you read the words.

9. When I wrote "Death of a Pig," I was simply rendering an account of what actually happened on my place—to my pig, who died, and to me, who tended him in his last hours.

10. A good many of Charlotte's descendants still live in the barn, and when the warm days of spring arrive there will be lots of tiny spiders emerging into the world.

7d

Classifying sentences

Like words, sentences can be classified in several different ways: grammatically, functionally, or rhetorically. Grammatical classification groups sentences according to how many and what types of clauses they contain. Functional classification groups them according to whether they make a statement, ask a question, issue a command, or express an exclamation. Rhetorical classification groups them according to where in the sentence the main idea is located. These methods of classification can help you analyze and assess your sentences as you write and revise.

1

Classifying sentences grammatically

Grammatically, sentences fall into one of the following types: *simple sentences, compound sentences, complex sentences,* and *compound-complex sentences.* You have already seen most of these types in the section on clauses.

Simple sentences

A **simple sentence** consists of one independent clause and no dependent clause. The subject or the predicate, or both, may be compound.

The trailer is surrounded by a wooden deck.

Both my roommate and I had left our keys in the room.

At the country club, the head pro and his assistant give lessons, run the golf shop, and try to keep the members content.

Compound sentences

A **compound sentence** consists of two or more independent clauses and no dependent clause. The clauses may be joined by a comma and a coordinating conjunction, by a comma and a correlative conjunction, or by a semicolon. (See Chapters 15, 20, 29, and 30.)

Occasionally, a car goes up the dirt trail, and dust flies everywhere.

Just as we decorate our houses with paintings and other attractive objects, so birds bring colorful or shiny materials back to their nests.

Alberto is obsessed with soccer; he eats, breathes, and lives the game.

BACKGROUND

In a series of essays, Francis Christensen demonstrated a way to map sentences and paragraphs according to levels of generality and modification. According to Christensen, *periodic* sentences are those that delay or postpone announcing the general main clause until the very end, leading into the topic with supporting or modifying details. This kind of sentence forces a reader to hold the subject in mind until the very end and keeps syntactic tension high. In the hands of skilled writers, periodic sentences can keep readers alert for what is to come and make the main idea, when it finally does appear, all the more impressive.

Although structures using various degrees of periodicity can be very effective in challenging and interesting readers, they do not constitute the most frequently used pattern in modern English. Rather, the *cumulative* structure, which adds details after the main clause or announcement of the topic, is the more dominant. Christensen writes in "A Generative Rhetoric of the Sentence" (*CCC* 14 [1963]: 156),

> The main clause, which may or may not have a sentence modifier before it, advances the discussion; but the additions move backwards, as in this clause, to modify the statement of the main clause or more often to explicate or exemplify it, so that the sentence has a flowing and ebbing movement, advancing to a new position and then pausing to consolidate it, leaping and lingering as the popular ballad does.

Because the main clause is presented at or near the beginning of the sentence, cumulative structures do not require readers to hold the subject in suspense until the end. In one sense, then, these sentences may be easier to read than periodic ones, yet the skillful writer can position the most important piece of information at the end. But Christensen warns that "the cumulative sentence in unskilled hands is unsteady, allowing a writer to ramble on, adding modifier after modifier, until the reader is almost overwhelmed, because the writer's central idea is lost" (*Notes Toward a New Rhetoric,* 1978).

Using exclusively periodic or cumulative sentences, of course, would be desperately monotonous. And so the best writers mingle structures—short and long, periodic and cumulative—though never forgetting that the most important ideas naturally deserve the most prominent positions.

TEACHING PRACTICE

Before your students turn in their papers, ask them to identify by type each of the sentences in their papers. (You may want to review with them the definitions and constructions of each sentence type.) Then, ask them to tally each type (simple, compound, complex, compound-complex, cumulative, periodic). They should use the results to answer the following questions: possibly in their writing logs. What kinds of sentences do they use most often? Do they use all kinds of sentences or rely on just a couple? What effect does their choice of sentence structures have on their prose? Do they recognize or know how to construct all the sentence types? If any students express interest in doing so, you may want to give them an opportunity to revise these papers before they hand them in.

Like everything metaphysical the harmony between thought and reality is to be found in the grammar of language.
          –LUDWIG WITTGENSTEIN

Complex sentences

A **complex sentence** consists of one independent clause with at least one dependent clause.

```
       ┌────DEPENDENT CLAUSE────┐
Many people believe that anyone can earn a living.
     ┌────DEPENDENT CLAUSE────┐
Those who do not like to get dirty should not go camping.
   ┌────DEPENDENT CLAUSE────┐
As I awaited my interview, I sat with other nervous candidates.
```

Compound-complex sentences

A **compound-complex** sentence consists of two or more independent clauses and at least one dependent clause.

```
   ┌───IND CL───┐ ┌─────DEP CL─────┐      ┌───IND CL───┐
I complimented Joe when he finished the job, and he seemed pleased.
```

Sister Lucy tried her best to help Martin, but he was an undisciplined boy who drove many teachers to despair.

2

Classifying sentences functionally

In terms of function, sentences can be classified as **declarative** (making a statement), **interrogative** (asking a question), **imperative** (giving a command), or **exclamatory** (expressing strong feeling).

DECLARATIVE	Julia plays oboe for the Cleveland Orchestra.
INTERROGATIVE	How long has she been with them?
IMPERATIVE	Get me a ticket for her next performance.
EXCLAMATORY	What a talented musician she is!

3

Classifying sentences rhetorically

In addition to permitting functional and grammatical classifications, some sentences can be classified rhetorically as either cumulative or periodic sentences. Such a classification is important because the two patterns create very different rhythms and emphases.

Cumulative sentences

Cumulative sentences begin with the subject and predicate containing the main thought and then build on this foundation with a series of phrases or clauses. When they are constructed skillfully, cumulative sentences create a strong rhythm and make for easy, often exciting, reading. Look at the following examples (the second example includes two cumulative sentences):

> The old man sat, waiting, watching, never tiring of his self-appointed task of keeping track of all who passed, his hat pulled tightly over his forehead, hiding eyes that missed nothing.

> I could still feel the way I'd moved with the horse, the ripple of muscle through both the striving bodies, uniting as one. I could still feel the irons round my feet, the calves of my legs gripping, the balance, the nearness to my head of the stretching brown neck, the mane blowing in my mouth, my hands on the reins.
> — DICK FRANCIS

Periodic sentences

Periodic sentences save the subject and verb of the independent clause until the end, building toward them and making the reader wait for the full meaning or significance to emerge.

> Pulling my tie off and flinging it haphazardly onto the sofa, stretching out to read the paper, listening to the crickets chirp, I felt the tensions of the workday disappear.

> Though we long for the easy answer, the simple solution, the quick rationalization, only the harsh truth can set us free.

Although cumulative sentences are more common in most modern prose than are periodic sentences, the ability to construct both will give you stylistic options that will strengthen your writing. (See 22c.)

EXERCISE 7.21

Classify each of the following sentences as simple, compound, complex, or compound-complex. In addition, note any sentences that could be classified as cumulative or periodic or as imperative, interrogative, or exclamatory.

1. Solve your problems yourself.
2. The screen door creaked and banged when she ran into the house.

EXERCISE 7.21: Answers

1. simple, imperative
2. complex, declarative, periodic
3. compound, interrogative
4. simple, declarative, cumulative
5. compound, exclamatory
6. complex, declarative
7. simple, imperative, periodic
8. compound-complex, declarative
9. compound-complex, declarative
10. complex, declarative, periodic

3. Should he admit his mistake, or should he keep quiet and hope to avoid discovery?

4. People go on safari to watch wild animals in their natural habitat.

5. What a risk they took, but what a prize they won!

6. When I first arrived at college and was exposed to the diversity of lifestyles there, I became confused about where I fit in and who my role models should be.

7. Keeping in mind the terrain, the weather, and the length of the hike, decide what you need to take.

8. Dreams are necessary, but they can be frustrating unless you have the means to attain them.

9. Retail sales declined as consumers cut back on discretionary spending, and many small businesses failed.

10. Wandering in the stockroom, searching for pairs of shoes that I would swear were not there and finally meekly asking my co-workers to help me find them, I wasted countless hours during my first week on the job.

 Checking the sentences in your own writing

A good way to examine your own sentences is by studying two or three examples of your own writing. Classifying each sentence—grammatically, as simple, compound, complex, or compound-complex (7d1); functionally, as declarative, interrogative, imperative, or exclamatory (7d2); rhetorically, as cumulative or periodic (7d3). Perhaps keep a tally of how many of each type of sentence you write, and then look for patterns.

1. Are your sentences varied, or do you rely heavily on one or two sentence patterns?

2. If you write mainly simple sentences, see if combining some to make compound or complex sentences makes your writing flow more smoothly.

3. If you have many compound sentences, see if revising some as complex sentences makes your writing easier to read.

4. If your sentences are all declarative, see if there's one you'd like to emphasize and try rephrasing it as a question or exclamation.

5. If you find several short sentences in a row, try combining them into one cumulative sentence.

EXERCISE 7.22 Revising for Sentence Construction

The following paragraph is adapted from a speech once given by Adlai Stevenson. The sentences have been simplified greatly. Try revising the paragraph by using phrases and clauses to combine some of the sentences. You might find it necessary to add or drop words. There is no one "correct" way to revise the paragraph; the object of the exercise is simply to practice using the various structures presented in this chapter.

America is much more than an economic fact. It is much more than a geographical fact. It is a political fact. It is a moral fact. It is the first community in which men set out in principle to institutionalize freedom. It is the first community in which men set out to institutionalize responsible government. It is the first community in which they set out to institutionalize human equality. And we love it for this audacity! Jefferson and Lincoln saw in this vision "the last, best hope of man." How easy it is, contemplating this vision, to see in it "the last, best hope of man." To be a nation founded on an ideal in one sense makes our love of country a vital force. It is a more vital force than any instinctive pieties of blood. It is a more vital force than any instinctive pieties of soil.

EXERCISE 7.23 Reading with an Eye for Sentences

The following sentences come from the openings of well-known works. Read each sentence carefully, and identify the independent clauses and dependent clauses. Then choose one sentence, and write a sentence that imitates its structure clause for clause and phrase for phrase. Example:

She is an open and trusting child, unprepared for and unaccustomed to the ambushes of family life, and perhaps it is just as well that I can offer her little of that life.   — JOAN DIDION, "On Going Home"

Those were long and desperate years, filled with and burdened by the pain of multiple loss, yet now it is clear to me that they gave me strength for the future.

1. Most people who bother with the matter at all would admit that the English language is in a bad way, but it is generally assumed that we cannot by conscious action do anything about it.
   — GEORGE ORWELL, "Politics and the English Language"

2. We observe today not a victory of party but a celebration of freedom, symbolizing an end as well as a beginning, signifying renewal as well as change.   — JOHN F. KENNEDY, Inaugural Address

3. Once in a long while, four times so far for me, my mother brings out the metal tube that holds her medical diploma.
   — MAXINE HONG KINGSTON, "Photographs of My Parents"

EXERCISE 7.22: Suggested Answers

America is much more than an economic or geographical fact. It is a political and moral fact—the first community in which men set out in principle to institutionalize freedom, responsible government, and human equality. And we love it for this audacity! How easy it is, contemplating this vision, to see in it—as Jefferson or Lincoln saw in it—"The last, best hope of man." To be a nation founded on an ideal in one sense makes our love of country a more vital force than any instinctive pieties of blood and soil.

EXERCISE 7.23: Answers

The dependent clauses are:

1. who bother with the matter at all; that the English language is in a bad way; that we cannot by conscious action do anything about it

3. that holds her medical diploma

Imitations of the sentences will vary.

4. Moths that fly by day are not properly to be called moths; they do not excite that pleasant sense of dark autumn nights and ivy blossom which the commonest yellow underwing asleep in the shadow of the curtain never fails to rouse in us.　　— Virginia Woolf, "The Death of the Moth"

5. When Ulysses S. Grant and Robert E. Lee met in the parlor of a modest house at Appomattox Court House, Virginia, on April 9, 1865, to work out the terms for the surrender of Lee's Army of Northern Virginia, a great chapter in American life came to a close, and a great new chapter began.
　　　　— Bruce Catton, "Grant and Lee: A Study in Contrasts"

EXERCISE 7.24　Taking Inventory: Sentences

Look at one or two paragraphs of something you have written recently, and classify the sentences, using the guidelines for checking sentences on p. 176. Does your classification reveal that you vary the types of sentences you use, or do you tend to write primarily one type of sentence? If you find that you depend primarily on one type, revise to include other types—for example, if you write mainly simple sentences, try combining some of them to make compound or complex sentences. If you keep a writing log, you might record this work there along with any observations you have about sentence variation.

8

Understanding Pronoun Case

The grammatical term *case* may be unfamiliar to you (since it comes, like many such terms, from Latin), but the concept it represents is one you will recognize immediately. Take a look, for example, at the italicized pronouns in the following excerpt.

> *I* want a wife who will care for *me* when *I* am sick and sympathize with *my* pain. . . . *I* want a wife who will keep *my* clothes clean, ironed, mended, replaced when need be, and who will see to it that *my* personal things are kept in their proper place. . . .
> —Judy Brady, "I Want a Wife"

Most of us know intuitively when to use *I,* when to use *me,* and when to use *my.* Our choices reflect differences in case, the form a pronoun takes to indicate its function in a sentence. The italicized words in the excerpt show the singular first-person pronoun in three different cases: the subjective case (*I*), the objective case (*me*), and the possessive case (*my*). As this example demonstrates, pronouns functioning as subjects are in the subjective case; those functioning as objects are in the objective case; and those functioning as possessives are in the possessive case.

SUBJECTIVE PRONOUNS

I/we	you	he/she/it	they	who/whoever

OBJECTIVE PRONOUNS

me/us	you	him/her/it	them	whom/whomever

POSSESSIVE PRONOUNS

my/our mine/ours	your yours	his/hers/its his/hers/its	their theirs	whose

BACKGROUND

When a pronoun follows a pronoun's nature, a pronoun substitutes for a noun; the noun then becomes the pronoun's antecedent.

Thanks to the existence of pronouns, we are able to avoid such redundancy and write, instead:

When a pronoun follows its nature, it substitutes for a noun that becomes its antecedent.

The most highly inflected parts of speech in present-day English, pronouns are nearly as complex and informational as their Latinate counterparts. Compare:

As Dennis delivered Dennis's inaugural address, Dennis nervously looked out into the freezing crowd only to see Dennis's mother smiling beatifically at Dennis.

As *he* delivered *his* inaugural address, Dennis nervously looked out into the freezing crowd only to see *his* mother smiling beatifically at *him.*

Although *Dennis* is the antecedent of *he, his,* and *him,* the pronoun form changes. English pronouns are specific in terms of person, gender, and number. In fact, our pronouns often carry as much information as their antecedents. *I, you,* and *he* tell us about person; *he, she,* and *it* tell us about gender; *I, we, she,* and *they* tell us about number.

TEACHING PRACTICE

If you have students who speak languages other than English, ask them to explain the pronoun system of those languages, in terms of person, number, and gender.

BACKGROUND

The pronoun *you* gives no information other than number—second person. Except for context, there is no way to tell if *you* is singular or plural, masculine or feminine. Such was not always the case. Until the thirteenth century, English used different forms of second-person pronouns: the *th*-forms, indicating singular (*thee, thy, thou*); and the *y*-forms, indicating plural (*ye, you, your*).

With the influence of the French language, the *th*-forms came to denote intimacy and were used with close friends, family, and children; the *y*-forms, to denote a measure of formality or respect, used with everyone else. These two forms corresponded with the *tu* and *vous* forms of French.

Everyday use

During the 1991 NCAA tournament, two members of a winning team were being interviewed on CBS. The reporter asked whether the players had "felt a win coming on." One of them responded this way: "Marcus and me—or Marcus and I, I should say—we definitely knew we could win. All we had to do was play our own game." This player certainly would have been understood by the TV audience had he stuck with "Marcus and me," but he corrected himself because he realized that I, rather than me, should be used as a subject.

The player's near misuse of pronoun case is a common one, especially in casual conversation. Make a point of listening for pronoun case—perhaps in conversation, or in radio or TV interviews—and then look for examples in printed conversations or interviews. Do you find that pronoun case is used differently in talk than in print? If so, how?

8a

Using the subjective case

A pronoun should be in the **subjective case** when it is a subject of a clause, a subject complement, or an appositive renaming a subject or subject complement. (See 7b and 7c.)

SUBJECT OF AN INDEPENDENT CLAUSE

They could either fight or face certain death with the lions.
We felt that Betty was enthusiastic and wanted to learn the material.
My brother and *I* adored our grandparents.
Who wrote "Araby"?
You must be kidding.

SUBJECT OF A DEPENDENT CLAUSE

Before *they* could get to the front, the war ended.
Roberto told the story to Carla, *who* told all her friends.
Give credit to the ones *who* did the work.
Our group appealed to *whoever* was willing to listen.

SUBJECT COMPLEMENT

Even though pronouns used as subject complements should, grammatically, be in the subjective case, Americans often use the objective case, especially in conversation: "Who's there?" "It's *me*." To many speakers of English, "it's me" sounds preferable to "it's I." Nevertheless, you should use the subjective case for all formal writing.

The first person to see Monty after the awards was *she*.

The main supporters of recycling were Jean and *I*.

It is *he* who brings life and spirit to the class.

If I were *she*, I would worry about other things.

If you find the subjective case for a subject complement stilted or awkward, try rewriting the sentence using the pronoun as the subject.

She was the first person to see Monty after the awards.

APPOSITIVE RENAMING A SUBJECT

Three students—Peter, Richard, and *she*—worked on the report.

APPOSITIVE RENAMING A SUBJECT COMPLEMENT

The finalists were two dark horses, Michael and *I*.

Using the objective case

A pronoun should be in the **objective case** when it functions as a direct or indirect object (of a verb or verbal), a subject of an infinitive, an object of a preposition, or an appositive renaming an object. (See 7b3 and 7c3.)

OBJECT OF A VERB

The professor surprised *us* with a quiz. [direct object of *surprised*]

The grateful owner gave *him* a reward. [indirect object of *gave*]

Presidents usually rely on advisors *whom* they have known for years. [direct object of *have known*]

OBJECT OF A VERBAL

The Parisians were wonderful about helping *me*, and I ended the year speaking fluent French. [direct object of gerund]

Wishing *her* luck, the coach stepped back to watch the performance. [indirect object of participle]

Leonard offered to show *him* around town. [direct object of infinitive]

SUBJECT OF AN INFINITIVE

The objective case is also used in sentences like the following, where the pronoun is preceded by a verb and followed by an infinitive. Though the pronoun in such constructions is called the subject of the infinitive, it is in the objective case because it is the object of the sentence's verb.

Writing helps *me* to know myself better.

The student campaigners convinced his wife and *him* to vote in favor of the school bond.

The trip led *us* to appreciate how much California owes to Mexico.

OBJECT OF A PREPOSITION

Several of my friends went with *me*.

Alice planned a surprise party for *them*.

APPOSITIVE RENAMING AN OBJECT

We selected two managers, Joan and *her*, to attend the seminar.

8c

Using the possessive case

A pronoun should be in the **possessive case** when it shows possession or ownership. Notice that there are two forms of possessive pronouns: adjective forms, which are used before nouns or gerunds (*my, your, his, her, its, our, their, whose*), and noun forms, which take the place of a noun (*mine, yours, his, hers, its, ours, theirs, whose*). (See 30a.)

ADJECTIVE FORMS

Many of Hitchcock's movies put viewers on the edge of *their* seats.

Whose life is it, anyway?

The sound of *his* hammering echoed through the corridor.

NOUN FORMS

The responsibility is *hers*.

"It's *mine!*" declared the child, clutching the golf club.

Whose is this blue backpack?

Using possessive pronouns before gerunds

A pronoun that appears before a gerund should be in the possessive case (*my/our, your, his/her/its, their*). **Gerunds** are *-ing* forms of verbs that function as nouns (*writing, sailing*).

I remember *his* singing.

What can be tricky is distinguishing gerunds from present participles, for both are *-ing* forms of verbs. **Present participles**, however, function as adjectives, and modify the pronouns, which are in the objective case (*me/us, you, him/her/it, them*).

I remember *him* singing.

Notice the difference in meaning in the two examples about the singer. In the first, the memory is of *singing,* which is a gerund, modified by the possessive pronoun *his.* In the second, the memory is of *him,* which is a direct object of *remember* and thus is in the objective case; *singing* is a present participle modifying *him.*

EXERCISE 8.1

The following passage comes from "University Days," James Thurber's classic essay about his years as a student at Ohio State University. Most of its pronouns have been removed. Put a correct pronoun in each blank, labeling each one as subjective, objective, or possessive case.

Another course that I didn't like, but somehow managed to pass, was economics. _____ went to that class straight from the botany class, which didn't help _____ to understand either subject. _____ used to get them mixed up. But not as mixed up as another student in _____ economics class who came there direct from a physics laboratory. _____ was a tackle on the football team, named Bolenciecwcz. At that time Ohio State University had one of the best football teams in the country, and Bolenciecwcz was one of _____ outstanding stars. In order to be eligible to play it was necessary for _____ to keep up in _____ studies, a very difficult matter, for while _____ was not dumber than an ox _____ was not any smarter. Most of _____ professors were lenient and helped _____ along. None gave _____ more hints in answering questions or asked _____ simpler ones than the economics professor, a thin, timid man named Bassum. One day when _____ were on the subject of transportation and distribution, it came Bolenciecwcz's turn to answer a question. "Name one means of transportation," the professor said to _____. No light came into the big tackle's eyes. "Just any means of transportation," said the professor. Bolenciecwcz sat staring at _____. "That is," pursued the professor, "any medium, agency, or method of going from one place to another." Bolenciecwcz had the

EXERCISE 8.1: Answers

Another course that I didn't like, but somehow managed to pass, was economics. I went to that class straight from the botany class, which didn't help me to understand either subject. I used to get them mixed up. But not as mixed up as another student in my economics class who came there direct from a physics laboratory. He was a tackle on the football team, named Bolenciecwcz. At that time Ohio State University had one of the best football teams in the country, and Bolenciecwcz was one of its outstanding stars. In order to be eligible to play it was necessary for him to keep up in his studies, a very difficult matter, for while he was not dumber than an ox he was not any smarter. Most of his professors were lenient and helped him along. None gave him more hints in answering questions or asked him simpler ones than the economics professor, a thin, timid man named Bassum. One day when we were on the subject of transportation and distribution, it came Bolenciecwcz's turn to answer a question. "Name one means of transportation," the professor said to him. No light came into the big tackle's eyes. "Just any means of transportation," said the professor. Bolenciecwcz sat staring at <u>him</u>. "That is," pursued the professor, "any medium, agency, or method of going from one place to another." Bolenciecwcz had the look of a man <u>who</u> is being led into a trap. "You may choose among steam, horse-drawn, or electrically propelled vehicles," said the instructor. "I might suggest the one which <u>we</u> commonly take in making long journeys across land." There was a profound silence in which everybody stirred uneasily, including Bolenciecwcz and Mr. Bassum. Mr. Bassum abruptly broke this silence in an amazing manner. "Choo-choo-choo," <u>he</u> said, in a low voice, and turned instantly scarlet. <u>He</u> glanced appealingly around the room. All of <u>us</u>, of course, shared Mr. Bassum's desire that Bolenciecwcz should stay abreast of the class in economics, for the Illinois game, one of the hardest and most important of the season was just a week off. "Toot, toot, too-toooooot!" some student with a deep voice moaned, and <u>we</u> all looked encouragingly at Bolenciecwcz. Somebody else gave a fine imitation of a locomotive letting off steam. Mr. Bassum himself rounded off the little show. "Ding, dong, ding, dong," <u>he</u> said, hopefully. Bolenciecwcz was staring at the floor now, trying to think, <u>his</u> great brow furrowed, <u>his</u> huge hands rubbing together, <u>his</u> face red.

OPTIONAL EXERCISE

See p. 429 for another exercise related to this passage from Thurber.

EXERCISE 8.2: Answers

1. your
2. hers
3. our
4. his
5. Whose

look of a man _____ is being led into a trap. "You may choose among steam, horse-drawn, or electrically propelled vehicles," said the instructor. "I might suggest the one which _____ commonly take in making long journeys across land." There was a profound silence in which everybody stirred uneasily, including Bolenciecwcz and Mr. Bassum. Mr. Bassum abruptly broke this silence in an amazing manner. "Choo-choo-choo," _____ said, in a low voice, and turned instantly scarlet. _____ glanced appealingly around the room. All of _____, of course, shared Mr. Bassum's desire that Bolenciecwcz should stay abreast of the class in economics, for the Illinois game, one of the hardest and most important of the season, was only a week off. "Toot, toot, too-toooooot!" some student with a deep voice moaned, and _____ all looked encouragingly at Bolenciecwcz. Somebody else gave a fine imitation of a locomotive letting off steam. Mr. Bassum himself rounded off the little show. "Ding, dong, ding, dong," _____ said, hopefully. Bolenciecwcz was staring at the floor now, trying to think, _____ great brow furrowed, _____ huge hands rubbing together, _____ face red.   —JAMES THURBER, "University Days"

Now write a paragraph or two about your own least—or most—favorite class. When you are finished, underline all the personal pronouns you used, and label each one for case.

EXERCISE 8.2

Insert a correct possessive pronoun in the blank in each sentence. Example:

<u>My</u> eyes ached after studying for ten hours.

1. Your parents must be pleased about _____ going back to college.
2. Ken's dinner arrived quickly, but Rose waited an hour for _____ .
3. We agreed to pool _____ knowledge.
4. Even many supporters of Lincoln opposed _____ freeing the slaves.
5. _____ responsibility should it be to teach moral values?

Using *who, whoever, whom,* and *whomever*

A common problem with pronoun case is deciding whether to use *who* or *whom*. In speech and even in some informal writing, *whom* has become a rarely used word. Even when traditional grammar requires *whom,* many Americans use *who* instead. Nevertheless, in formal written English, which includes most of the writing you do at college, the case of the pronoun should properly reflect its grammatical function. *Who* and *whoever* are the subjective case forms and should be used when the pronoun is a subject or subject complement. *Whom* and *whomever* are the objective case forms and should be used when the pronoun is a direct or indirect object or the object of a preposition.

Most writers find that two particular situations can lead to confusion with *who* and *whom:* when they begin a question and when they introduce a dependent clause. In a dependent clause, you may also have to choose between *whoever* and *whomever.* (See 7c4.)

1

Beginning a question with *who* or *whom*

You can determine whether to use *who* or *whom* at the beginning of a question by answering the question using a personal pronoun. If the answer is in the subjective case, use *who;* if it is in the objective case, use *whom.*

Who wrote the story? [*She* wrote the story. *She* is subjective; thus *who* is correct.]

Whom did you visit? [I visited *them. Them* is objective; thus *whom* is correct.]

If the *who/whom* clause is interrupted by another expression (such as *did you say* or *does she think*) answering the question using a personal pronoun will still tell you the right case to use.

Who do you think wrote the story? [I think *she* wrote the story. *She* is subjective; thus *who* is correct.]

2

Beginning a dependent clause with *who, whoever, whom,* or *whomever*

Pronoun case in a dependent clause is determined by its function in the clause, no matter how that clause functions in the sentence. If the pronoun acts as a subject or subject complement in the clause, use *who* or *whoever.* If the pronoun acts as an object, use *whom* or *whomever.* (See 7c4.)

The new president was not *whom* she had expected. [*Whom* is the object of the verb *had expected* in the clause *whom she had expected.* Though the clause as a whole is the complement of the subject *president,* the pronoun should be in the objective case.]

The schoolmarm . . . continues the heroic task of trying to make her young charges grasp the difference between who *and* whom. *Here, alas, the speechways of the American people seem to be again against her. The two forms of the pronoun are confused magnificently in the debates in Congress, and in most newspaper writing, and in ordinary discourse the great majority of Americans avoid* whom *diligently, as a word full of snares. When they employ it, it is often incorrectly, as in "*Whom *is your father?" and "*Whom *spoke to me?" Noah Webster, always the pragmatic reformer, denounced it as usually useless so long ago as 1783. Common sense, he argued, was on the side of "*Who *did he marry?" Today such a form as "*Whom *are you talking to?" would seem very affected to most Americans; they might write it, but they would never speak it. . . . A shadowy line often separates what is currently coming into sound usage from what is still regarded as barbarous.* –H. L. MENCKEN

The center is open to *whoever* wants to use it. [*Whoever* is the subject of the clause *whoever wants to use it*. Though the clause as a whole is the object of the preposition *to,* the pronoun should be in the subjective case.]

Richard feels like a knight *who* is headed for great adventure. [*Who* is the subject of the clause *who is headed for great adventure.*]

Whomever the party suspected of disloyalty was executed. [*Whomever* is the object of the verb *suspected* in the clause *Whomever the party suspected of disloyalty*. Though the clause as a whole is the subject of the sentence, the pronoun should be in the objective case.]

If you are not sure which case to use, try separating out the dependent clause from the rest of the sentence and looking at it in isolation. Rewrite the clause as a new sentence with a personal pronoun instead of *who(ever)* or *whom(ever)*. If the pronoun is in the subjective case, use *who* or *whoever;* if it is in the objective case, use *whom* or *whomever*.

Anyone can hypnotize a person (*who/whom*) wants to be hypnotized. [Separate out the clause *who/whom wants to be hypnotized*. Substituting a personal pronoun gives you *he wants to be hypnotized. He* is subjective case; thus: Anyone can hypnotize a person *who* wants to be hypnotized.]

The minister grimaced at (*whoever/whomever*) made any noise. [Separate out the clause *whoever/whomever made any noise*. Substituting a personal pronoun gives you *they made any noise. They* is subjective case; therefore: The minister grimaced at *whoever* made any noise.]

The minister smiled at (*whoever/whomever*) she greeted. [Separate out the clause *she greeted whoever/whomever*. Substituting a personal pronoun gives you *she greeted them. Them* is objective case; therefore: The minister smiled at *whomever* she greeted.]

If the dependent clause is interrupted by an expression such as *he thinks* or *she says,* delete the expression when you separate out the clause.

The minister grimaced at (*whoever/whomever*) she thought made any noise. [Separate out the clause *whoever/whomever made any noise,* deleting the interrupting expression *she thought*. Substituting a personal pronoun gives you *they made any noise. They* is subjective case; therefore: The minister grimaced at *whoever* she thought made any noise.]

EXERCISE 8.3

Insert *who, whoever, whom,* or *whomever* correctly in the blank in each of the following sentences. Example:

She is someone <u>who</u> will go far.

1. _____ shall I say is calling?
2. _____ the voters choose faces an almost impossible challenge.
3. The manager promised to reward _____ sold the most cars.
4. Professor Quiñones asked _____ we wanted to collaborate with.
5. _____ will the new tax law benefit most?

8e

Using the correct case in compound structures

Most problems with case of personal pronouns occur when the pronoun is part of a compound subject, complement, or object. Each part of a compound structure should be in the same case as it would if used alone. That is, pronouns in compound subjects and compound subject complements should be in the subjective case; pronouns in compound objects should be in the objective case.

SUBJECTS

Mrs. Wentzel and *I* simply could not exist in the same classroom.
When *Zelda* and *he* were first married, they lived in New York.

SUBJECT COMPLEMENTS

The winners of the competition were *Renata* and *he*.
The next two speakers will be *Philip* and *she*.

OBJECTS OF VERBS

The boss invited *her* and *her family* to dinner. [direct object]
They offered *Gail* and *her* a summer internship. [indirect object]

OBJECTS OF PREPOSITIONS

This morning saw yet another conflict between *my sister* and *me*.
My aunt put me in the room once shared by *my uncle* and *her*.

If you are unsure whether to use the subjective or the objective case in a compound structure, make each part of the compound into a separate sentence.

Come to the park with my roommate and (*I/me*). [Separating the compound structure gives you *come to the park with my roommate* and *come to the park with me*; thus: Come to the park with my roommate and *me*.]

8f

Using the correct case in appositives

Pronoun case in an appositive is determined by the word that the appositive renames. If the word functions as a subject or subject complement, the pronoun should be in the subjective case; if it functions as an object, the pronoun should be in the objective case.

> All three panelists—Arlene, Tony, and *I*—were stumped by the question. [*Panelists* is the subject of the sentence, so the pronoun in the appositive *Arlene, Tony, and I* should be in the subjective case.]

> The poker game that night produced three big winners, my grandmother, Aunt Rose, and *me*. [*Winners* is the direct object of the verb *produced*, so the pronoun in the appositive *my grandmother, Aunt Rose, and me* should be in the objective case.]

8g

Using the correct case in elliptical constructions

Elliptical constructions are those in which some words are understood but left out. In comparisons with *than* or *as*, we often leave words unsaid: *I see Elizabeth more often than* [*I see*] *her sister*. When sentences with such constructions end in a pronoun, the pronoun should be in the case it would be in if the construction were complete.

> His brother has always been more athletic than *he* [is].

In some constructions like this, the case of the pronoun depends on the meaning intended.

ELLIPTICAL	Willie likes Lily more than *she*.
COMPLETE	Willie likes Lily more than *she* [likes Lily].
ELLIPTICAL	Willie likes Lily more than *her*.
COMPLETE	Willie likes Lily more than [he likes] *her*.

As these examples demonstrate, use the subjective case if the pronoun is actually the subject of an omitted verb; use the objective case if it is an object of an omitted verb.

8h

Using *we* and *us* correctly before a noun

When the first-person plural pronoun is used with a noun, the case of the pronoun depends on the way the noun functions in the sentence. If the noun functions as a subject or subject complement, the pronoun should be in the subjective case (*we*). If the noun functions as an object, the pronoun should be in the objective case (*us*).

> *We* fans never give up hope. [*Fans* is the subject.]
> The Orioles depend on *us* fans. [*Fans* is the object of a preposition.]

If you are unsure about which case to use, recasting the sentence without the noun will give you the answer. Use whichever pronoun would be correct if the noun were omitted: *We never give up hope. The Orioles depend on us.*

EXERCISE 8.4

Choose the appropriate pronoun from the pair in parentheses in each of the following sentences. Example:

> *The fear of* (them/their) *taking advantage of him never entered his mind.*

1. The relationship between (*they/them*) and their brother was often strained.
2. When I was young, I had a friend (*who/whom*) I idolized.
3. This love for children probably began because there were three children younger than (*I/me*) in my family.
4. The only candidates left in the race were (*he/him*) and Dukakis.
5. I am getting more and more interested in (*him/his*) accompanying me on the next trip.
6. When Carol and (*she/her*) first met, they despised each other.
7. The two people closest to me, (*he/him*) and my mother, expected me to return home after graduation.
8. Soap operas appeal to (*whoever/whomever*) is interested in intrigue, suspense, joy, pain, grief, romance, infidelity, sex, or violence.
9. Later (*we/us*) "rejects" were taken to watch the taping of the show.
10. The only mother and father (*who/whom*) they know are the people (*who/whom*) raised them and took care of them.

EXERCISE 8.4: Answers

1. them
2. whom
3. I
4. he
5. his
6. she
7. he
8. whoever
9. we
10. whom, who

EXERCISE 8.5: Answers

1. her and me⟶she and I
2. I⟶me
3. who⟶whom
4. correct
5. him⟶his (or omit pronoun)
6. him⟶he
7. correct
8. me⟶I
9. correct
10. whomever⟶whoever

EXERCISE 8.5

Edit each of the following sentences to correct errors in pronoun case. (Not all sentences contain errors.) Example:

Of the group, only ~~her~~ ^{she} and I finished the race.

1. The readers, her and me, agreed that the story was very suspenseful.
2. Just between you and I, this course is a disaster!
3. The people who Jay worked with were very cold and unsociable.
4. Who would have thought that twenty years later he would be king?
5. Roderigo becomes involved in the plot without him knowing it.
6. Only him, a few cabinet members, and several military leaders were aware of the steady advance Japan was making toward Pearl Harbor.
7. All of the job candidates were far more experienced than I.
8. As out-of-towners, my buddy and me did not know too many people.
9. I never got to play that role in front of an audience, but I am one of the few performers who really did "break a leg."
10. Constance always lent money to whomever asked her for it.

 Checking your own use of case

1. Are all pronouns after forms of the verb *be* in the subjective case? "It's *me*" is common in spoken English, but in writing it should be "It is *I*." (8a)

2. To check for correct use of *who* and *whom* (and *whoever* and *whomever*), especially those that begin a question or dependent clause, try substituting *he* or *him*. If *he* is correct, use *who* (or *whoever*); if *him*, use *whom* or *whomever*. (8d)

3. In compound structures, make sure any pronouns are in the same case they would be in if used alone. (*She* [and Jake] were living in Spain.)(8e)

4. When a pronoun follows *than* or *as*, complete the sentence mentally. If the pronoun is subject of an unstated verb, it should be in the subjective case (I like her better than *he* [likes her].) If the pronoun is object of an unstated verb, put it in the objective case (I like her better than [I like] *him*. (8g)

5. Circle all the pronouns to see if you rely too heavily on any one pronoun or case. Check especially for overuse of *I*.

EXERCISE 8.6 Reading with Attention to Case

The poet e.e. cummings often broke the standard rules of grammar and word order to create particular effects in his poetry. Read the following poem, and note the function of each pronoun. Then rearrange the words of the poem so that they follow as closely as possible the normal order they would take in an ordinary sentence. How does pronoun case give you a clue to this arrangement?

> Me up at does
>
> out of the floor
> quietly Stare
>
> a poisoned mouse
>
> still who alive
>
> is asking What
> have i done that
>
> You wouldn't have   — e. e. cummings

EXERCISE 8.7 Taking Inventory: Pronoun Case

Research shows that one of the most overused words in any language is the word for *I*. Whenever you write anything that includes your own opinions, you probably rely to some degree on first-person pronouns, singular and plural. Read over the paragraph(s) you wrote in Exercise 8.1 with attention to your use of pronouns. Do you find any patterns? If you find that you rely heavily on any one case—that half your sentences begin with *I*, for example—decide whether your writing seems at all monotonous as a result. If so, try revising, paying attention to pronoun case. See, in other words, whether revising some sentences to change *I* to *me* (or vice versa) brings greater variety to your writing. If you keep a writing log, you might enter your work into it, noting what you have learned about your use of pronoun case.

EXERCISE 8.6: Suggested Answers

A poisoned mouse who is still alive does quietly stare up at me out of the floor asking What have i done that you wouldn't have

9

Using Verbs

BACKGROUND

English has the most varied and flexible verb forms of all the modern languages: its six tenses can fall in the indicative, subjunctive, or imperative mood; its verbs can be in active or passive voice, in present, continuous, or emphatic form, in completed or progressive aspect. English verbs can stand alone or work together, or they can transform themselves into nouns and adjectives.

Such plasticity arose from Scandinavian, German, and French influences. In fact, Old English verbs were Germanic in nature: they distinguished between only two simple tenses, present and past, and signified all other information (number, person, gender, mood, voice) by inflectional endings. Old English verbs were more often strong than weak, or more often *irregular* than *regular*: strong verbs (*sing, sang; bind, bound; choose, chosen*) have the power to indicate tense by transforming their medial vowels, not by merely adding a feeble *-ed* inflectional ending (*kick, kicked, kicked*).

The Norman Invasion greatly influenced Middle English, infusing it with the vocabulary and grammar of the French- and Latin-speaking ruling class. One significant influence was the linguistic regularization of the verbs: more than half of the strong (irregular) verbs became weak (regular), using *-ed* inflectional

When used skillfully, verbs can be called the heartbeat of prose, moving it along, enlivening it, carrying its action. Verbs are extremely flexible and can change form to mark grammatical agreement with the subject (see Chapter 10) or to indicate *tense, voice,* or *mood.*

CHANGE IN TENSE	The runner *skims* around the track. [present tense] The runner *skimmed* around the track. [past tense]
CHANGE IN VOICE	She *savors* every step. [active voice] Every step *is savored.* [passive voice]
CHANGE IN MOOD	She *is* completely content. [indicative] If she *were* not content, she would not be smiling. [subjunctive]

This chapter explores in detail the way verbs work, with attention to form, tense, voice, and mood.

VERB FORMS

Except for *be,* all English verbs have five possible forms.

BASE FORM	PAST TENSE	PAST PARTICIPLE	PRESENT PARTICIPLE	-S FORM
talk	talked	talked	talking	talks
adore	adored	adored	adoring	adores
jog	jogged	jogged	jogging	jogs

The **base form** is the one listed in the dictionary. For all verbs except *be,* it is the form used to indicate action that takes place in the present when the subject is a plural noun or the pronoun *I, you, we,* or *they.*

> In the ritual, the women *go* into trances.
> The men *take* knives and *point* them at their chests.

The **past tense** is used to indicate action that took place entirely in the past. For most verbs, it is formed by adding *-ed* or *-d* to the base form. Some verbs, however, have irregular past-tense forms (see 9b). *Be* has two past-tense forms, *was* and *were.*

> The Globe *served* as the playhouse for many of Shakespeare's works.
> In 1613, it *caught* fire and *burned* to the ground.
> We *were* in England last year.

The **past participle** is used to form perfect tenses (see 9d–f), passive voice (p. 210), and adjectives. It usually has the same form as the past tense, though some verbs have irregular past participles (see 9b). The past participle cannot function alone as a predicate but must be used with the auxiliary verbs *have* or *be.*

> She *had accomplished* the impossible. [past perfect]
> No one *was injured* in the explosion. [passive voice]
> *Standardized* tests usually require *sharpened* pencils. [adjective]

The **present participle** is constructed by adding *-ing* to the base form. Like the past participle, it cannot function alone as a predicate but must be used with auxiliary verbs to indicate continuing action. The present participle can also function as an adjective or as a noun, called a gerund. (See 7c.)

endings rather than internal transformation to indicate tense. This impulse to regularize verbs was checked by the rise of English on the social scale and the stabilizing effect of printing. Now, even the native-born English speaker must memorize the strong or irregular verb forms.

USEFUL READING

Aitchison, Jean. *Language Change: Progress or Decay.* Suffolk, Engl. Fontana, 1981. Written from a sociolinguist's perspective, this work explains the implementation, causes, and developmental features of language change. The entire discussion is accessible and straightforward; Chapter 3 specifically discusses verb forms and the inherent causes of their change.

Many students *are competing* in the race. [continuing action]

He tried to comfort the *crying* child. [adjective]

Climbing the mountain took all afternoon. [noun/gerund]

Except for *be* and *have*, the **-s form** consists of the base form plus *-s* or *-es*. This form indicates the present tense for third-person singular subjects. All singular nouns; *he, she,* and *it;* and many indefinite pronouns (such as *everyone* or *someone*) are third-person singular.

The dog *snaps* at people who try to pet it.

She usually *takes* the shortcut across campus.

No one *believes* his story.

It is very important to note that the *-s* form occurs *only* in the third-person singular of the present tense.

	SINGULAR	PLURAL
FIRST PERSON	I wish	we wish
SECOND PERSON	you wish	you wish
THIRD PERSON	he/she/it wishes	they wish
	Joe wishes	children wish
	someone wishes	

Some dialects occasionally use the base form instead of the *-s* form with a third-person singular subject. In addition, some people skip over the *-s* form in speech and then, as a result, often tend to forget the *-s* or *-es* in writing. For college writing, be sure to use the *-s* or *-es* endings.

DIALECT	She *live* in a high-rise apartment.
ACADEMIC	She *lives* in a high-rise apartment.

The third-person singular forms of *be* and *have* are *is* and *has*.

The second stage of the ritual *is* the so-called liminal stage.

A whale *has* lungs instead of gills.

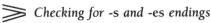 *Checking for -s and -es endings*

> If you tend to leave off the *-s* and *-es* verb endings, you should check for them systematically when proofreading.
>
> 1. Underline every verb, and then circle all those in the present tense.

2. Find the subject for every verb you circle.

3. If the subject is a singular noun; *he, she,* or *it;* or most indefinite pronouns, be sure the verb ends in *-s* or *-es.* If it is not third-person singular, the verb should not have an *-s* or *-es* ending.

4. Be careful when you see auxiliary verbs such as *can* or *may* (9a). Auxiliaries that *sound* like the present tense (*She can help.*) are used with the base form, never the *-s* or *-es* form.

Forms of be

Be has three forms in the present tense (*am, is, are*) and two in the past tense and two in the past tense (*was, were*).

Present tense

	SINGULAR	PLURAL
FIRST PERSON	I *am*	we *are*
SECOND PERSON	you *are*	you *are*
THIRD PERSON	he/she/it *is*	they *are*
	Jane *is*	children *are*
	somebody *is*	some *are*

Past tense

	SINGULAR	PLURAL
FIRST PERSON	I *was*	we *were*
SECOND PERSON	you *were*	you *were*
THIRD PERSON	he/she/it *was*	they *were*
	Jane *was*	children *were*
	somebody *was*	some *were*

Although some dialects sometimes use the base form *be* in place of *am, is,* and *are* and the base form *have* in place of *has,* you should always use *am, is, are,* or *has* in college and other formal writing.

DIALECT	She *be* the oldest member of the family.
ACADEMIC	She *is* the oldest member of the family.
DIALECT	She *have* ten great-grandchildren.
ACADEMIC	She *has* ten great-grandchildren.

EXERCISE 9.1: Answers will vary.

BACKGROUND

The term *auxiliary* comes from the Latin *auxiliaris,* meaning "help." Hence, auxiliary verbs help to make some form of another verb. In *is eating,* the auxiliary verb *is* helps to make a form of the verb *eat*; in *have seen* and *will have brought,* the auxiliary verbs *have* and *will have* help to make forms of *see* and *bring,* respectively.

Your students should be aware that other words sometimes intervene between the auxiliary and the main verb as in *I have already given you the money.*

FOR THE WRITING LOG

To practice and highlight the use of modals and auxiliaries, ask the students to write an entry in their writing log about hopes and dreams, a stream-of-consciousness list of what could or should be, or what could, should, or might have been.

The exercise will work best if they write on several hopes rather than focusing on just one. (By focusing, they may shift tenses and stop using the modal auxiliaries that you will soon be calling to their attention.) Then, ask them to exchange their writing logs, read one another's entries, and mark the auxiliaries. Discuss their effective and their questionable uses of auxiliaries.

EXERCISE 9.1

Write a paragraph or two about a past event in your life—a visit, a ceremony, a job, anything you remember and wish to write about. Then take a close look at the verbs. How many different verbs do you use? how many different verb tenses? Which verbs might you like to improve?

9a

Using auxiliary verbs

Sometimes called helping verbs, **auxiliary verbs** are used with a base form, present participle, or past participle to create verb phrases. The base form or participle in a verb phrase is called the main verb. The most common auxiliaries are forms of *have, be,* and *do,* which are used to indicate completed, continuing, or future actions; passive voice; emphasis; questions; and negative statements.

> We *did consider* all viewpoints. [completed action]
>
> The college *is building* a new dormitory. [continuing action]
>
> They *will explain* the procedure. [future action]
>
> We *were warned.* [passive voice]
>
> I *do respect* this viewpoint. [emphasis]
>
> *Do* you *know* the answer? [question]
>
> He *does* not *like* wearing a tie. [negative]

Modal auxiliaries—*can, could, might, may, must, ought to, should, would*—show possibility, necessity, obligation, and so on.

> You *can see* three states from the top of the mountain. [possibility]
>
> I *must try* harder to go to bed early. [necessity]
>
> She *should visit* her parents more often. [obligation]

Although some dialects use the base form *be* as an auxiliary instead of *am, is,* or *are,* the standard forms should be used in college writing.

DIALECT	They *be* working to earn money for tuition.
ACADEMIC	They *are working* to earn money for tuition.
DIALECT	I *be* scheduled to take biology next semester.
ACADEMIC	I *am* scheduled to take biology next semester.

In making a negative statement, some dialects use *don't* with a third-person singular subject. In academic writing, use *doesn't* in such constructions.

| DIALECT | The character *don't* seem true to life. |
| ACADEMIC | The character *doesn't* seem true to life. |

Some dialects use past or present participles without an auxiliary verb as the predicate of a sentence. Many writers also leave out the auxiliary accidentally. In academic writing, a participle must have an auxiliary verb attached to it in order to function as a predicate. (See Chapter 16.)

DIALECT	They *planning* to fix up that old house.
ACADEMIC	They *are planning* to fix up that old house.
DIALECT	My roommate *gone* to her seminar.
ACADEMIC	My roommate *has gone* to her seminar.

EXERCISE 9.2

Edit the following sentences so that all verb forms are acceptable in formal written English. (Some of the sentences do not require any change.) Example:

Although Joe ~~seem~~ *seems* in control, his actions ~~making~~ *make* me wonder.

1. When the dance begin, a man in costume appears.
2. The man have long fingernails and a mask.
3. All of the people in the village participate in the ceremony.
4. The doctor works two nights a week at a clinic.
5. A hot shower always relax me.
6. The thought of nuclear war be terrifying to most people.
7. New mothers often suffers from depression.
8. He don't know whether to try again or to give up.
9. The deposit refunded if the customer don't buy the equipment.
10. Mayor Burns running for reelection this fall.

9b

Using regular and irregular verbs

A verb is **regular** when its past tense and past participle are formed by adding *-ed* or *-d* to the base form.

TEACHING PRACTICE

Because everyone has a tendency to regularize, or generalize, the English language, even native speakers need to memorize the irregular verb forms. Until we incorporate those irregular forms of our language, we overgeneralize the regular forms. As children, we overgeneralize both the plural form (*dogs, mouses,* and *sheeps*) and the verb form (*hummed, runned, shaked,* and *catched*). You may want to review these verb paradigms with your students.

BASE FORM	PAST TENSE	PAST PARTICIPLE
love	loved	loved
honor	honored	honored
obey	obeyed	obeyed

 Checking for -ed or -d endings

> Speakers sometimes skip over the *-ed* or *-d* endings in conversation and thus may forget to include them in writing. If you tend to make this mistake, you should make a point of systematically checking for it when proofreading. Underline all the verbs, and then underline a second time any that are past tense or past participles. Check each of these for an *-ed* or *-d* ending. Unless the verb is irregular (see below), it should end in *-ed* or *-d*.

Irregular verbs

A verb is **irregular** when it does not follow the *-ed* or *-d* pattern. The past tense and past participle of irregular verbs are most often formed by changing an internal vowel: *begin, began, begun*. In some such verbs, *-en* or *-n* is also added to the past participle: *break, broke, broken*. Other verbs change form more radically: *go, went, gone*. Still others do not change at all: *hurt, hurt, hurt*. If you are uncertain about the correct verb form, consult your dictionary, which lists any irregular forms under the entry for the base form.

 Some common irregular verbs

BASE FORM	PAST TENSE	PAST PARTICIPLE
arise	arose	arisen
be	was/were	been
bear	bore	borne, born
beat	beat	beaten
become	became	become
begin	began	begun
bite	bit	bitten
blow	blew	blown
break	broke	broken
bring	brought	brought
broadcast	broadcast	broadcast

TEACHING PRACTICE

For review, write the present tense of ten or twelve irregular verbs on the chalkboard and call on volunteers to provide the past tense and past participle forms.

Then have your students write entries in their logs, using only verbs from the list on pp. 198–200. Ask several of the students to read their work aloud, noting the irregular forms they have used properly.

BASE FORM	PAST TENSE	PAST PARTICIPLE
build	built	built
burn	burned, burnt	burned, burnt
burst	burst	burst
buy	bought	bought
catch	caught	caught
choose	chose	chosen
come	came	come
cost	cost	cost
cut	cut	cut
dig	dug	dug
dive	dived, dove	dived
do	did	done
draw	drew	drawn
dream	dreamed, dreamt	dreamed, dreamt
drink	drank	drunk
drive	drove	driven
eat	ate	eaten
fall	fell	fallen
feel	felt	felt
fight	fought	fought
find	found	found
fly	flew	flown
forget	forgot	forgotten, forgot
freeze	froze	frozen
get	got	gotten, got
give	gave	given
go	went	gone
grow	grew	grown
hang (suspend)[1]	hung	hung
have	had	had
hear	heard	heard
hide	hid	hidden
hit	hit	hit
keep	kept	kept
know	knew	known
lay	laid	laid
lead	led	led
leave	left	left
lend	lent	lent
let	let	let
lie (recline)[2]	lay	lain

[1] *Hang* meaning "execute by hanging" is regular: *hang, hanged, hanged.*
[2] *Lie* meaning "tell a falsehood" is regular: *lie, lied, lied.*

FOR COLLABORATIVE WORK

After the class has divided into groups, have the students compose two sentences for each of twelve verbs either of your own choosing or from the list on pp. 198–200. In one sentence they should use the past tense form; in the second they should use the past participle form.

These exercises will help your students recognize the comparative differences in usage and sense between the two forms. At the same time, the students will also develop an ear for which auxiliaries sound best with which past participles.

Let the students share their sentences with the rest of the class so they can see the range of possible combinations.

BACKGROUND

By today's standards, even Shakespeare sometimes chose the "incorrect" verb form:

> Then, Brutus, I have much mistook your passion. —*JULIUS CAESAR*

> Have you chose this man? —*CORIOLANUS*

> When they are fretten with the gusts of heaven. —*MERCHANT OF VENICE*

BASE FORM	PAST TENSE	PAST PARTICIPLE
lose	lost	lost
make	made	made
mean	meant	meant
meet	met	met
pay	paid	paid
prove	proved	proved, proven
put	put	put
read	read	read
ride	rode	ridden
ring	rang	rung
rise	rose	risen
run	ran	run
say	said	said
see	saw	seen
send	sent	sent
set	set	set
shake	shook	shaken
shoot	shot	shot
show	showed	showed, shown
shrink	shrank	shrunk
sing	sang	sung
sink	sank	sunk
sit	sat	sat
sleep	slept	slept
speak	spoke	spoken
spend	spent	spent
spread	spread	spread
spring	sprang, sprung	sprung
stand	stood	stood
steal	stole	stolen
strike	struck	struck, stricken
swim	swam	swum
swing	swung	swung
take	took	taken
teach	taught	taught
tear	tore	torn
tell	told	told
think	thought	thought
throw	threw	thrown
wake	woke, waked	waked, woken, woke
wear	wore	worn
win	won	won
wind	wound	wound
write	wrote	written

EXERCISE 9.3

Complete each of the following sentences by filling in each blank with the past tense or past participle of the verb listed in parentheses. Remember that a past participle cannot function by itself as a verb; for a past participle to fit in a blank, one or more auxiliary verbs must precede it. Example:

We had not *eaten* (eat) since lunch, yet we *felt* (feel) no hunger.

1. Clearly, this short story would not have _____ (be) as effective if it had been _____ (write) in the third person.
2. Once she had _____ (come) to this realization, she _____ (find) that she was no longer afraid of change.
3. The process of hazing _____ (begin) soon after fraternities were formed.
4. Hearns _____ (lose) control of the fight, and Hagler _____ (take) advantage of this loss.
5. On the Saturdays before Geiberger and Langer _____ (win) their respective tournaments, each had _____ (shoot) a sixty-eight.
6. People think that we _____ (grow) up together because we are practically inseparable.
7. I painfully _____ (draw) ninety-five dollars from my wallet and _____ (set) the money on the counter.
8. It would have been helpful if someone had _____ (meet) me at the airport and had _____ (take) me to the hotel.
9. As the boat _____ (sink), the passengers _____ (put) on their life preservers and _____ (say) their prayers.
10. When I first _____ (meet) her, I _____ (think) that she was the most unpleasant person I had ever _____ (know).

EXERCISE 9.4

Where necessary, edit the following sentences to eliminate any inappropriate verb forms. Example:

began
She ~~begin~~ the examination on time.

1. Socrates drank the hemlock calmly and died a few hours later.
2. The band had sang its last song before the fight begun.
3. When the battle was over, the rebels had been beat badly.
4. By the mid-1970s, New York had almost went bankrupt.
5. The lake freezed early this year.

EXERCISE 9.3: Answers

1. been, written
2. come, found
3. began
4. lost, took
5. won, shot
6. grew
7. drew, set
8. met, taken
9. sank; put; said
10. met, thought, known

After your students have completed this exercise, review their answers in class. Ask them why they chose certain forms. Indicators of appropriate forms were:

Use of auxiliary, indicating past participle form (sentences 1, 2, 8, 10)

The tense of verb in other clauses, indicating tense of missing verb (sentences 2, 3)

Other indications of time in the sentence (sentence 5: past, indicated by "Saturdays"; sentence 6: past, semantically indicated)

Those sentences that require context of situation to determine form (sentences 4, 7, 9)

EXERCISE 9.4: Answers

1. correct
2. sang⟶sung; begun⟶began
3. beat⟶beaten
4. went⟶gone
5. freezed⟶froze

Using *lie* and *lay, sit* and *set, rise* and *raise*

Three pairs of verbs—*lie* and *lay, sit* and *set*, and *rise* and *raise*—cause problems for many writers because the two verbs in each pair have similar-sounding forms and somewhat related meanings. In each pair one of the verbs is **transitive**, meaning that it takes a direct object; the other is **intransitive**, meaning that it does not take an object. The best way to avoid confusing the two is to memorize their forms and meanings—or to use synonyms. All of these verbs except *raise* are irregular.

BASE FORM	PAST TENSE	PAST PARTICIPLE	PRESENT PARTICIPLE	-S FORM
lie	lay	lain	lying	lies
lay	laid	laid	laying	lays
sit	sat	sat	sitting	sits
set	set	set	setting	sets
rise	rose	risen	rising	rises
raise	raised	raised	raising	raises

Lie is intransitive and means "recline" or "be situated." *Lay* is transitive and means "put" or "place." This pair is especially confusing because *lay* is also the past-tense form of *lie*.

INTRANSITIVE	He *lay* on the floor unable to move.
TRANSITIVE	I *laid* the package on the counter.

Sit is intransitive and means "be seated." *Set* usually is transitive and means "put" or "place."

INTRANSITIVE	She *sat* in the rocking chair daydreaming.
TRANSITIVE	She *set* the vase on the table.

Rise is intransitive and means "get up" or "go up." *Raise* is transitive and means "lift" or "cause to go up."

INTRANSITIVE	He *rose* from the bed and left the room.
TRANSITIVE	He *raised* himself to a sitting position.
INTRANSITIVE	The price of coffee is *rising*.
TRANSITIVE	The store is *raising* the price of coffee.

TEACHING PRACTICE

As a mnemonic device, you might point out to students that, in each of these three troublesome pairs, the *i* word (lie, sit, rise) is the intransitive one.

OPTIONAL EXERCISE

For a quick review exercise, have your students complete each of the following sentences with a form of either *raise* or *rise*.

1. She suddenly *(rose)* up and spoke.
2. Yeast causes bread to *(rise)*.
3. We all know to *(raise)* our hand before we speak in class.
4. Some say that Jesus *(raised)* Lazarus from the dead.

EXERCISE 9.5

Choose the appropriate verb form in each of the following sentences.

1. Sometimes she just (*lies/lays*) and stares at the ceiling.
2. I (*lay/laid*) my books down just as the telephone rang.
3. The doctor asked the patient to (*lie/lay*) on his side for an injection.
4. He used whatever was (*lying/laying*) around the house.
5. Doctors urge us to (*sit/set*) aside fad diets once and for all.
6. I (*sat/set*) back, closed my eyes, and began to meditate.
7. (*Sitting/Setting*) in the sun too long can lead to skin cancer.
8. The Federal Reserve Bank is planning to (*rise/raise*) interest rates.
9. When the temperature (*rises/raises*), the humidity usually declines.
10. We (*rose/raised*) every morning at six and went jogging.

VERB TENSES

Tenses show when the action expressed by the verb takes place. We characteristically think of time in terms of present, past, and future; and the three *simple tenses* are the present tense, the past tense, and the future tense.

PRESENT TENSE	I jump
PAST TENSE	I jumped
FUTURE TENSE	I will jump

More complex aspects of time relationships, such as ongoing or completed actions or conditions, are expressed through *progressive, perfect,* and *perfect progressive forms* of the simple tenses. Although such terminology sounds complicated in the abstract, you regularly use all these forms. Here are all the tense forms of one verb, *ask.*

SIMPLE PRESENT	she *asks*
SIMPLE PAST	she *asked*
SIMPLE FUTURE	she *will ask*
PRESENT PERFECT	she *has asked*
PAST PERFECT	she *had asked*
FUTURE PERFECT	she *will have asked*

EXERCISE 9.5: Answers

1. lies
2. laid
3. lie
4. lying
5. set
6. sat
7. sitting
8. raise
9. rises
10. rose

BACKGROUND

The concept of tense can be especially confusing to those students who try to correlate it directly with actual time. Grammatical tense gives us the mechanical forms of verbs, forms that follow definite rules of construction, but it does not always represent actual time in the past, present, or future.

For example, *present tense* can indicate an action or existence taking place in the present, past, or future:

His feet hurt. (taking place right now—present)

Water boils at 212°F. (a fact in the past, present, future)

My roommate drinks iced tea every morning. (habitual action—past, present, future)

We are having turkey for Thanksgiving. (intended future action)

Huckleberry Finn is a resourceful, sensitive boy. (historical present, giving vividness to a past event)

I hear that Jaime spoke to the new students. (*hear* gives the past action a present connection)

PRESENT PROGRESSIVE	she *is asking*
PAST PROGRESSIVE	she *was asking*
FUTURE PROGRESSIVE	she *will be asking*
PRESENT PERFECT PROGRESSIVE	she *has been asking*
PAST PERFECT PROGRESSIVE	she *had been asking*
FUTURE PERFECT PROGRESSIVE	she *will have been asking*

The simple tenses locate an action only within the three basic time frames of present, past, and future. The perfect form of each tense expresses the idea of a *completed* action in the present, past, or future; and the progressive form expresses the idea of a *continuing* action. Finally, the perfect progressive form expresses the idea of an action that *continues up to some point* in the present, past, or future.

Using the present tense forms

The **simple present** indicates actions occurring at the time of speaking, as well as those occurring habitually and those considered to be general truths or scientific facts. In addition, with appropriate time expressions, the simple present can be used to indicate a scheduled future event.

They *are* very angry about the decision.

I *eat* breakfast every day at 8:00 A.M.

Love *conquers* all.

Water *freezes* at 0 degrees Celsius.

Residents of Greenland *endure* bitter cold for most of the year.

Classes *begin* next week.

The simple present is also used in discussing literary and artistic works created in the past that exist in our experience. For example, a literary character such as Ishmael in *Moby Dick,* created by Herman Melville over a century ago, exists in our present time as well.

Ishmael slowly *comes* to realize all that *is* at stake in the search for the white whale.

The **present progressive** indicates actions that are ongoing or continuous in the present.

> Yolanda *is applying* for a scholarship.

The present progressive is typically used to describe an action that is happening at the moment of speaking, in contrast to the simple present, which more often indicates habitual actions.

PRESENT PROGRESSIVE	You *are driving* too fast.
SIMPLE PRESENT	I always *drive* carefully.

With an appropriate expression of time, the present progressive can also be used to indicate a scheduled event in the future.

> We *are having* friends over for dinner tomorrow night.

The **present perfect** indicates actions begun in the past and either completed at some unspecified time in the past or continuing into the present.

> Uncontrolled logging *has destroyed* many tropical forests.
> Anti-abortion activists *have tried* to reverse the decision.

The **present perfect progressive** indicates an ongoing action begun in the past and continuing into the present.

> The two sides *have been trying* to settle the case out of court.

9e

Using the past tense forms

The **simple past** indicates actions that occurred at a specific time and do not extend into the present.

> She *felt* better as soon as her exams were over.
> Germany *invaded* Poland on September 1, 1939.

The **past progressive** indicates continuing actions in the past, often with specified limits.

> Lenin *was living* in exile in Zurich when the tsar was overthrown.
> In the 1980s, many of the baby boomers *were becoming* parents.

The **past perfect** indicates actions that were completed by a specific time in the past or before some other past action occurred.

USEFUL READING

Comrie, Bernard. *Aspect.* Cambridge, Engl.: Cambridge UP, 1976. A study of *aspect*, which differs from tense in that it refers to the duration or continuation of an action in time, rather than its occurrence in relation to the present moment.

Williams, Joseph M. *Origins of the English Language: A Social and Linguistic History.* New York: Free Press, 1975. 265–74. Williams describes and traces the historical development of the two aspects: progressive (*He was imitating his mother*) and perfect (*He has fixed the car*).

BACKGROUND

In the early seventeenth century, the rules of English usage were codified according to the Latin model by John Wallis, who prescribed that *shall* and *will* could not be considered synonymous. Simple future expectation was to be indicated by *shall* in first person and by *will* in second or third person:

> I *shall* meet Jens in the morning, then we *shall* review his money-market account.

> Although you *will* gasp when you see her tattoo, Delphine *will* be delighted that you noticed.

According to Wallis (and all prescriptivists since), determination, desire, willfulness, or promise on the part of the speaker is represented by just the opposite paradigm—*will* in the first person and *shall* in second or third person:

> Tomorrow, I *will* return and defeat you.

> Of course, we *will* go to the funeral, whatever the weather.

> You *shall* remain in my will, no matter whom you marry.

> Before they return to the Republic of China, Meimei is determined that both she and Sheng *shall* finish medical school and their internships.

Despite the three-hundred-year crusade to establish this distinction, most English speakers have successfully expressed futurity and determination without it.

TEACHING PRACTICE

Students claim that they never use the word *shall* in any locution, that *shall* is rare, hence "formal." Ask your students to think a minute about the use of *shall*. What examples can they offer? Which uses seem most natural to them? "*Shall* questions," which imply a certain amount of jointness, and "*shall* injunctions" are not so rare as the class might think. Consider the following examples:

> By the fourth century, Christianity *had become* the state religion.
> Homesteaders found that speculators *had* already *taken* the best land.

The **past perfect progressive** indicates continuing actions in the past that began before a specific time in the past or before some other past action began.

> They *had been living* beyond their means for years before they went bankrupt.
> Carter *had been planning* a naval career until his father died.

Using the future tense forms

The **simple future** indicates actions that have yet to begin.

> The exhibition *will come* to Washington in September.
> I *shall graduate* the year after next.

The **future progressive** indicates continuing actions in the future.

> The loans *will be coming* due in the next two years.
> A team of international observers *will be monitoring* the elections.

The **future perfect** indicates actions that will be completed by or before some specified time in the future.

> If no one shows up, all our work *will have been* futile.
> In ten years, the original investment *will have doubled.*

The **future perfect progressive** indicates continuing actions that will be completed by some specified time in the future.

> By the time the session ends, the negotiators *will have been working* for ten hours without a break.
> In May, I *will have been living* in Tucson for five years.

 Checking verb tenses

Errors in verb tenses take several forms. Some are errors in verb form: writing *seen* for *saw,* for example, which is an instance of confusing the standard participle and past tense forms. Others are errors in tense: using the simple past (*Uncle Charlie arrived*) when meaning requires the present perfect (*Uncle Charlie has arrived*). Still others result from using dialect (*we be going*) in situations requiring standard edited English (*we are going*).

If you have trouble with verb tenses, the best thing you can do is to keep a log of your errors and then to look for patterns. Once you can identify specific problems, you can make a point of routinely proofreading for them.

EXERCISE 9.6

Complete each of the following sentences by filling in the blank with an appropriate form of the verb listed in parentheses. Since more than one form will sometimes be possible, be prepared to explain reasons for your choices.

1. In spite of the poor turnout in today's referendum, local officials _____ (expect) the bond issue to pass.
2. Ever since the first nuclear power plants were built, opponents _____ (predict) disaster.
3. Thousands of Irish peasants _____ (emigrate) to America after the potato famine of the 1840s.
4. The newspaper _____ (arrive) late every day this week.
5. The committee _____ (meet) again next week.
6. President Kennedy was shot while he _____ (ride) in a limousine.
7. By eleven o'clock this morning, stock prices _____ (fall) fifteen points.
8. By the time a child born today enters first grade, he or she _____ (watch) thousands of television commercials.
9. In "The Road Not Taken," the poet _____ (come) to a fork in the road.
10. The supply of a product _____ (rise) when the demand is great.

EXERCISE 9.7

Read the following passage from a conversation with Maya Angelou, and identify the tenses of each italicized verb. Then, write a paragraph or two describing your own morning routine, and identify the tense of the verbs you use.

I *wake* usually about six and *get* immediately out of bed. Then I *begin* to wonder why. . . . I *make* very strong coffee and *sit* in the sunroom with the newspaper, the *Winston-Salem Journal*, the only paper in town.

Shall I pick you up at six?

What *shall* we drink? (first person—request)

You *shall* not take the name of the Lord in vain.

You *shall* regret your evil ways. (second person—moral injunction)

The vendor *shall* maintain the equipment in good repair.

The athlete *shall* maintain a 2.5 grade point average. (third person—legal or commercial usage; specifications or requirements)

Who *shall* decide when doctors disagree? (third person—literary usage)

EXERCISE 9.6: Answers

1. expect—present; are expecting—present progressive
2. have predicted/have been predicting—action begun in past continues
3. emigrated—completed action
4. arrived/has arrived—started in past, may continue today
5. will meet/will be meeting—future (continuing) action
6. rode/was riding—past action, completed
7. had fallen—in past, before other action
8. will have watched—future action, completed by a certain time
9. comes—literary work
10. rises—general truth

EXERCISE 9.7: Suggested Answers

All verbs are simple present except for *(a)re doing* (present progressive); *(h)ave met, has been, has suggested* (all present perfect); *was* (simple past), *(h)ave got* (present perfect); and *will take* (simple future).

I *love* to read the letters to the editor. I *like* to see what *angers* people: only one in a hundred says "I *love* what you*'re doing*"; the other ninety-nine *say* they *hate* the paper or this *is* nonsense or that *is* absolutely wrong. I *feel* as if I*'ve* just *met* eight people, little human vignettes. . . .

At about 8:30 I *start* looking at the house because the housekeeper *arrives* at nine and I*'m* still too well brought-up to *offer* Mrs. Cunningham a house in too much disarray so I *straighten* up before she comes in. She *has been* my housekeeper for six years now—my sister *has suggested* that in another life she *was* a staff-sergeant. I *give* to her and she *gives* to me and we *live* together with a lot of laughter. My secretary, Mrs. Garris, also *comes* at nine and that's when real life *begins*. Mrs. Garris *is* a lovely Southern black lady with efficiency and grace vying for dominance in her spirit. She *says*, "Ms. Angelou, you*'ve got* to sign this, send that, agree to that, deny this . . ." and I *say*, "Mrs. Garris, I *will talk* to you in an hour."   —A LIFE IN THE DAY OF MAYA ANGELOU

9g

Using verb tenses in sequences

Because tense is crucial to our understanding of when actions occur and because time relationships can be very complex, careful and accurate use of tenses is important to clear writing. Even the simplest narrative describes actions that take place at different times; using particular tenses for particular actions allows readers to follow such time changes readily.

The relationship between the tense of the verb in the independent clause of a sentence and the tense of a verb in a dependent clause or a verbal is called the **sequence of tenses**. In general, the verb in a dependent clause may be in any tense form required for your meaning. The only limitation is that the relationship between the forms in the independent and dependent clauses make sense. For example, all of the following make sense and are acceptable grammatically.

He *lent* her the money because he *is* a generous man. [past/present]

He *lent* her the money because he *loved* her. [past/past]

He *lent* her the money because she *will invest* it wisely. [past/future]

Even though in general you can use almost any sequence of tenses, in a particular sentence the tense of the verb in the dependent clause may be limited by the meaning. For example, it makes no sense to say *He lent her the money because he will love her* or *He lent her the money because she had invested it wisely.*

1

Verb sequence with infinitives

An infinitive is *to* plus the base form (*to go, to be*). Use the **present infinitive** to indicate actions occurring at the same time as or later than the action of the predicate verb.

> I *wanted to swim* in the ocean last summer. [The wanting and the swimming occurred at the same time in the past.]
>
> I *expect to swim* in the ocean next summer. [The expecting is present; the swimming is in the future.]

Use the **perfect infinitive** (*to have* plus the past participle) to indicate actions occurring before the action of the predicate verb.

> She *seems to have become* a recluse. [The condition of becoming a recluse took place before the "seeming."]
>
> He *was reported to have left* his fortune to his cat. [The leaving of the fortune took place before the reporting.]

2

Verb sequence with participles

Use the **present participle** (base form plus *-ing*) to indicate actions occurring at the same time as that of the predicate verb.

> *Seeking* to relieve unemployment, Roosevelt *established* several public works programs. [Both the seeking and the establishment of the programs occurred simultaneously in the past.]

Use the **present perfect participle** to indicate action occurring before that of the predicate verb. The present perfect participle consists of *having* plus the past participle: *having gone, having been.*

> *Having crushed* all opposition at home, he *launched* a war of conquest. [He launched the war after he crushed the opposition.]

Use the **past participle** to indicate action occurring either before or at the same time as that of the predicate verb.

> *Flown* by an expert pilot, the passengers *felt* completely secure. [The flying and the feeling were simultaneous.]
>
> *Flown* to the front, the troops *joined* their hard-pressed comrades. [The flying occurred before the joining.]

TEACHING PRACTICE

Ask your students to look at their most recent piece of writing—an essay or a writing log entry—and note how they naturally balanced the sequence of tenses in their prose.

3

Verb sequence and habitual actions

One common error in verb usage occurs when indicating repeated or habitual actions. In conversation, we all hear people use *will* or *would* to describe habitual actions; in writing, however, you should stick to the present and past tenses.

UNEDITED	When my editor is happy with an article, she *will pass* it on to the typesetter.
EDITED	When my editor is happy with an article, she *passes* it on to the typesetter.
UNEDITED	While their parents sat on the porch, the children *would play*.
EDITED	While their parents sat on the porch, the children *played*.

EXERCISE 9.8

Edit each of the following sentences to create the appropriate sequence of tenses between the verb in the predicate and the participle or infinitive. Example:

He needs to ~~send~~ in his application before today. [*have sent* written above *send*]

1. When he was twenty-one, he wanted to have become a millionaire by the age of thirty.
2. Leaving England in December, the settlers arrived in Virginia in May.
3. They hoped to plant their garden by now.
4. Cutting off all contact with family, he did not know whom to ask for help.
5. Having sung in the shower, he did not hear the doorbell.

VOICE

Voice is the feature of transitive verbs that tells whether the subject is acting (*he questions us*) or being acted upon (*he is questioned*). When the subject is acting, the verb is in the **active voice**; when the subject is being acted upon, the verb is in the **passive voice**. The passive voice is formed, as in this sentence, by using the appropriate form of the auxiliary verb *be* followed by the past participle of the main verb.

EXERCISE 9.8: Answers

1. When he *was* twenty-one, he *wanted to become* a millionaire by the age of thirty.
2. *Having left* England in December, the settlers *arrived* in Virginia in May.
3. They *had hoped* to plant their garden by now.
4. *Having cut off* all contact with family, he *did* not *know* whom to ask for help.
5. *Singing* in the shower, he *did* not *hear* the doorbell.

USEFUL READING

Williams, Joseph M. *Style: Ten Lessons in Clarity and Grace*. 3rd ed. Glenview, IL: Scott, 1989. For an advanced discussion of the stylistic virtues of active and passive voice, see pp. 9–14.

	ACTIVE VOICE	PASSIVE VOICE
PRESENT	He *questions* us.	He *is questioned.*
PAST	He *questioned* us.	He *was questioned.*
FUTURE	He *will question* us.	He *will be ques tioned.*
PRESENT PERFECT	He *has questioned* us.	He *has been questioned.*
PAST PERFECT	He *had questioned* us.	He *had been questioned.*
FUTURE PERFECT	He *will have questioned us*	He *will have been questioned.*

Most contemporary writers use the active voice as much as possible because it makes prose more *active,* more lively. To say that "the mail was opened" (passive voice) does not give the sense of action or immediacy that "Lorraine opened the mail" (active voice) does. In the passive construction, the mail is just there—being opened, by no one or nothing in particular. Even adding "by Lorraine" does not do much to enliven the passive version. When passive-voice verbs pile up in a passage, that passage will generally be harder to understand and remember.

The most problematic use of the passive voice occurs when writers seek to avoid taking responsibility for what they have written. A university president who announces that "it is recommended that fees be raised substantially" skirts a number of pressing questions: recommended by whom? raised by whom?

In spite of such questionable uses, however, the passive voice can work to good advantage in some situations. Much scientific writing uses the passive voice effectively to highlight the object or phenomenon being studied rather than the person or persons doing the studying. Look at the following example, from an essay describing brain surgery:

> A curved incision was made behind the hairline so it would be concealed when the hair grew back. It extended almost from ear to ear. Plastic clips were applied to the cut edges of the scalp to arrest bleeding. The scalp was folded back to the level of the eyebrows. Incisions were made in the muscle of the right temple, and three sets of holes were drilled near the temple and the top of the head because the tumor had to be approached from directly in front. The drill, powered by nitrogen, was replaced with a fluted steel blade, and the holes were connected. The incised piece of skull was pried loose and held out of the way by a large sponge.
> – ROY C. SELBY, JR., "A Delicate Operation"

Reporters often use the passive voice to protect the confidentiality of their sources, as in the familiar phrase *it is reported that,* or when the performer of an action is unknown or less important than the recipient. When Tom Wicker submitted his article on the assassination of President Kennedy to the *New York Times,* he began this way:

DALLAS, Nov. 22 — President John Fitzgerald Kennedy was shot and killed by an assassin today.

He died of a wound in the brain caused by a rifle bullet that was fired at him as he was riding through downtown Dallas in a motorcade.

Vice President Lyndon Baines Johnson, who was riding in the third car behind Mr. Kennedy's, was sworn in as the 36th President of the United States 99 minutes after Mr. Kennedy's death.

— TOM WICKER, *New York Times*

Wicker's article uses the passive voice with good reason: he wants the focus of the sentences on Kennedy, not on who killed him, and on Johnson, not on who swore him in.

Writers, then, must decide for themselves when the passive voice is appropriate and when it is not. If you find that you use the passive a great deal, practice shifting your sentences to active voice. To do so, convert the subject of the verb into a direct or indirect object, and make the performer of the action into the subject. (See 14c and 23b.)

PASSIVE	The test administrator *was told* to give the student an electric shock each time a wrong answer *was given*.
ACTIVE	Researchers *told* the test administrator to give the student an electric shock each time he or she *gave* a wrong answer.
PASSIVE	I *was awakened* promptly at seven by the alarm clock.
ACTIVE	The alarm clock *awakened* me promptly at seven.

EXERCISE 9.9

Convert each of the following sentences from active to passive voice or from passive to active, and note the differences in emphasis these changes make. Example:

Machiavelli advises the prince to gain the friendship of the people.

The prince is advised by Machiavelli to gain the friendship of the people.

1. Huge pine trees were uprooted by the storm.
2. Marianne avoided such things as elevators, subways, and closets.
3. For months, the baby kangaroo is protected, fed, and taught how to survive by its mother.
4. The lawns and rooftops were covered with the first snow of winter.
5. Flannery O'Connor employs the images of both a boxcar and a swinging bridge to show the inconsistencies between Mrs. Turpin's classification of people and God's classification of people.

EXERCISE 9.9: Answers

1. The storm *uprooted* huge pine trees.
2. Such things as elevators, subways, and closets *were avoided* by Marianne.
3. For months, the mother kangaroo *protects, feeds,* and *teaches* her baby to survive.
4. The first snow of winter *covered* the lawns and rooftops.
5. To show the inconsistencies between Mrs. Turpin's classification of people and God's classification of people, images of both a boxcar and a swinging bridge *are employed* by Flannery O'Connor.

EXERCISE 9.10

Look at several essays you have written recently or pieces of writing by others that you particularly like, and find examples both of the active voice and the passive voice. Convert each of the examples to the other voice, and note the difference in emphasis and rhythm the changes make.

EXERCISE 9.10: Answers will vary.

MOOD

The **mood** of a verb indicates the attitude of the writer toward what he or she is saying or writing. Different moods are used to express a fact, opinion, or inquiry (indicative mood); a command or request (imperative mood); or a wish, requirement, or condition contrary to fact (subjunctive mood). Compare, for example, the three sentences that follow.

INDICATIVE | I *ate* the plums.
IMPERATIVE | *Eat* the plums.
SUBJUNCTIVE | If I *were to eat* the plums, I would be sick.

Most frequent is the **indicative mood**, the one for stating facts or opinions or for asking questions.

The Frisbees *soar* through the air.
People *should recycle* their garbage.
Where *are* you *going*?

The **imperative mood** is used for giving commands and instructions or making requests. It is the base form of the verb. Sentences with the imperative mood in the main clause almost always omit the subject (*you*). In these cases, the subject is said to be "understood."

Take the appropriate wrench, and *loosen* the plug counterclockwise.
Sit down at once!
Help!

The **subjunctive mood** expresses wishes, conditions that are contrary to fact, requests, or demands. It is used primarily in dependent clauses beginning with *that* or *if*.

If I *were* in charge, things *would be* different.

TEACHING PRACTICE

In *A Room of One's Own,* Virginia Woolf employs the subjunctive mood:

> [I]t is unthinkable that any women in Shakespeare's day *should have had* Shakespeare's genius. For genius like Shakespeare's is not born among laboring, uneducated, servile people. It was not born in England among the Saxons and the Britons. It is not born today among the working classes. How, then, *could* it *have been* born among women whose work began, . . . almost before they were out of the nursery, who were forced to it by their parents and held to it by all the power of law and custom? Yet genius of a sort *must have existed* among women as it *must have existed* among the working classes.

Discuss how Woolf's use of the subjunctive affects the tone and meaning of this passage. How does this mood help her make an ironic point?

9h

Using the subjunctive

The present tense of the subjunctive uses the base form.

PRESENT

It is important that children *be* psychologically ready for a new sibling.

The only requirement is that the relationship between forms in the two clauses *make* sense.

The past tense of the subjunctive is the same as the past indicative except for the verb *be,* which uses *were* for all subjects.

PAST

He spent money as if he *had* infinite credit.

If the store *were* better located, it would attract more customers.

Because the subjunctive can create a rather formal tone, many people today tend to substitute the indicative in informal conversation.

INFORMAL	If I *was* a better typist, I would type my own papers.
FORMAL	If I *were* a better typist, I would type my own papers.

Nevertheless, formal writing still requires the use of the subjunctive in the following kinds of dependent clauses.

1

Those expressing a wish

I wish I *were* with you right now.

He wished that his mother *were* still living nearby.

2

Those beginning with *if* and expressing a condition that does not exist

If the federal government *were* to ban the sale of tobacco, tobacco companies and distributors would suffer a great loss.

If no one *were allowed* to ignore the rules, language would stagnate.

One common error is to use the subjunctive in both clauses. Notice the proper verb sequence: use the subjunctive in the *if* clause and the conditional (*would*) in the main clause.

| UNEDITED | If I *would have played* harder, I would have won. |
| EDITED | If I *had played* harder, I would have won. |

3

Those beginning with *as if* and *as though*

He cautiously started down the trail as if he *were walking* on thin ice.

During the 1920s Americans speculated in Florida real estate as though it *were* a risk-free investment.

4

Those beginning with *that* and expressing a demand, request, requirement, or suggestion

It is requested that each member *contribute* ten dollars.

The job demands that the employee *be* in good physical condition.

EXERCISE 9.11

Revise any of the following sentences that do not use the appropriate subjunctive verb forms required in formal writing. Example:

I saw how carefully he moved, as if he ~~was~~ *caring for an infant.*

                  were

1. Her stepsisters treated Cinderella as though she was a servant.
2. Hamlet wishes he was not responsible for avenging his murdered father.
3. Freud recommended that an analyst use dreams as a means of studying the human personality.
4. If more money was available, we would be able to offer more scholarships.
5. It is necessary that the manager knows how to do any job in the store.

EXERCISE 9.12

The poem below is a famous example of nonsense verse, one that plays games with words—and freely *invents* words. Read the poem out loud, and then underline all the verbs, whether actual English words (like *bite*) or made-up ones (like *outgrabe*). How do you know which made-up words are verbs?

> 'Twas brillig, and the slithy toves
>   Did gyre and gimble in the wabe;
> All mimsy were the borogoves,
>   And the mome raths outgrabe.

"Beware the Jabberwock, my son!
    The jaws that bite, the claws that catch!
Beware the Jubjub bird, and shun
    The frumious Bandersnatch!"

He took his vorpal sword in hand;
    Long time for manxome foe he sought—
So rested he by the Tumtum tree,
    And stood awhile in thought.

And, as in uffish thought he stood,
    The Jabberwock, with eyes of flame,
Came whiffling through the tulgey wood,
    And burbled as it came!

One, two! One, two! And through and through
    The vorpal blade went snicker-snack!
He left it dead, and with its head
    He went galumphing back.

"And hast thou slain the Jabberwock?
    Come to my arms, my beamish boy!
O frabjous day! Callooh! Callay!"
    He chortled in his joy.

'Twas brillig, and the slithy toves
    Did gyre and gimble in the wabe;
And mimsy were the borogoves,
    And the mome raths outgrabe.
            — LEWIS CARROLL, "Jabberwocky"

 Checking the verbs in your own writing

1. Circle all forms of *be, do,* and *have.* Decide in each case if you can substitute a stronger, more specific verb.

2. Check all uses of the passive voice for appropriateness. (pp. 210–13)

3. Double-check forms of *lie* and *lay, sit* and *set, rise* and *raise.* Decide if you need a transitive or intransitive verb, and see that you use the correct one. Then see that the word you use has your intended meaning. (9c)

4. If you have trouble with verb endings, check for them using the guidelines on p. 194–95 for *-s/-es* and p. 198 for *-ed/-d.*

5. If you have problems with verb tenses, use the guidelines in 9f to check over your verbs.

6. Check all verbs that introduce sources (quotations, paraphrases, and summaries). Do you rely on the most general verbs (*say, write,*

ask, for instance)? If so, try replacing these with more vivid, specific verbs (*claim, insist, wonder,* for instance). See pp. 590–91 for a list of verbs to use for incorporating source materials.

Using sources
Choosing verbs to integrate sources

When you paraphrase, quote, or summarize other sources, you should choose your verbs carefully. Though you can almost always use the most general verb, *say* or *write* ("as Mary Gordon writes"), you can usually find other verbs that convey your source's stance more precisely (such as Gordon "comments," "counters," "suggests"). Is your source commenting on something, disagreeing with someone, making a suggestion? On pp. 590–91 is a list of verbs appropriate for incorporating source materials into your own writing.

EXERCISE 9.13   Reading with an Eye for Verbs

Some years ago a newspaper in San Francisco ran the headline "GIANTS CRUSH CARDINALS, 3–1," provoking the following friendly advice from John Updike about the art of baseball-headline verbs:

> The correct verb, San Francisco, is "WHIP." Notice the vigor, force, and scorn obtained. . . . [These examples] may prove helpful: 3–1—WHIP, 3–2—SHADE, 2–1—EDGE. 4–1 gets the coveted verb "VANQUISH." Rule: Any three-run margin, *provided the winning total does not exceed ten,* may be described as a vanquishing.

Double-digit scores, Updike continues, merit such verbs as "ANNIHILATE," "OBLITERATE," and "HUMILIATE." (Thus, "A's ANNIHILATE O's, 13–2.") And if the home team is on the short end of the score, "SHADE" should become "SQUEAK BY." Finally, Updike advises, use of "BOW" can allow the home team, while losing, "to be given the active position in the sentence and an appearance of graciousness as well."

Take the time to study a newspaper with an eye for its verbs. Copy down several examples of strong verbs as well as a few examples of weak or overused verbs. For the weak ones, try to come up with better choices.

EXERCISE 9.14   Taking Inventory: Verbs

Three of the most overused verbs in the English language are *be, do,* and *have.* Writing that relies too heavily on these verbs almost always bores readers. Look now at the description you wrote in Exercise 9.1, or at anything else you've written recently, to see if you rely too heavily on these verbs. Revise accordingly.

EXERCISE 9.13: Answers will vary.

TEACHING PRACTICE

Using a recent piece of writing, have your students identify the kinds of verbs they used: auxiliary, modal auxiliary, regular, and irregular.

Ask the students to choose a portion of text and make all the verbs (except the verb *be* and auxiliary verbs) monosyllabic, then recopy the same piece replacing all the verbs with polysyllabic ones of similar meaning. As they read to themselves or aloud, can they hear a difference in style and tone, simply from the change in verbs? Is one version stuffier? clearer? more academic? reader friendly?

10

Maintaining Subject-Verb Agreement

BACKGROUND

The English language, even in its earliest stages, is extremely redundant: such redundancy is a type of "agreement" in terms of person, number, gender, and tense. One needs only the most basic facility with language to make meaning out of the following passage, written in modern English:

> The wolf stood in the pit, so hungry that he was crazy. He was really cursing the one who brought him there.

Look how much help we get with tense: *stood, was, was cursing.* We are provided with three times the information, the agreement, we need to know that this passage is in past tense. Now, look at the information telling us that there is only one wolf: *wolf* has no plural marker *(-s);* the *was* and *was cursing* are in the third-person-singular form, and the pronouns referring to the wolf are singular *(he* and *him).*

From the source of the above passage, *The Fox and the Wolf,* we can see the redundancy or agreement that even in A.D. 1200 wove a safety net for the reader:

> þe wolf in þe putte stod,
> A fingret so þat he ves wod.
> Inou he cursede þat þider him broute!
>
> (ll. 257–59)

In ordinary language, agreement refers to an accord or a correspondence between ideas or actions: you reach an *agreement* with your boss about salary; the United States and the Soviet Union negotiate an *agreement* about nuclear arms. This ordinary meaning of *agreement* covers its grammatical use as well. When subjects and verbs match each other in person and in number, we say that they "agree." This chapter takes a close look at the conventions governing such agreement.

A verb must agree with its subject in number (singular or plural) and in person (first, second, or third).

Maya Angelou comes from Stamps, Arkansas. [third-person singular]

We very much *want* to visit her hometown. [first-person plural]

Scenes from Arkansas *appear* in her works. [third-person plural]

In practice, only a very few subject-verb constructions cause confusion, so we will look at those constructions in greater detail.

10a

Making verbs agree with third-person singular subjects

English once used a complex system of verb endings to reflect the person, number, and gender of the subject. Over the centuries, however, most such endings have disappeared from use. Today the main kinds of subjects requiring a special verb form are third-person singular subjects: singular nouns and third-person singular pronouns. To make a present-tense verb agree with a third-person singular subject, we normally add -s or -es to the base form.

> A vegetarian diet *lowers* the risk of heart disease.
>
> She *misses* her friends from high school.

The only two verbs that do not follow this -s or -es pattern for third-person singular subjects in the present tense are *have* and *be*. *Have* changes to *has*; *be* has different forms for both the first and third persons and for both the present and past tense. (See 9b.)

Notice that although an -s or -es ending indicates a plural noun, the same kind of ending indicates a "singular" verb form. If the subject is a *plural* noun, the verb form does *not* take the -s or -es.

> A car *needs* regular maintenance.
>
> Cars *need* regular maintenance.

Some dialects do not consistently use the -s or -es ending with a third-person singular subject, and many people forget to use it in writing because it is often not stressed or pronounced clearly in speech. Always use the ending, however, in college or professional writing. If you have trouble with this particular pattern of subject-verb agreement, you should proofread especially for it; see p. 194–95.

10b

Making the subject and verb agree when separated by other words

When the simple subject is separated from the verb by other structures, such as a prepositional phrase, make the verb agree with the subject and not with another noun that is closer to the verb.

> s   v
>
> A *vase* of flowers *makes* a room attractive.
>
> s   v
>
> Many *books* on the best-seller list *have* little literary value.

Many writers forget to maintain agreement when a plural noun falls between a singular subject and the verb, as in the first example above, or when a singular noun falls between a plural subject and the verb, as in the second example. In the first sentence, notice that the simple subject is *vase,* not *flowers,* which is the object of the preposition *of.* In the second sentence, the simple subject is *books,* not *list,* which is the object of the preposition *on.*

Here, we are given the same three clues, in verb forms that look vaguely familiar, that the passage is in past tense: *stod, ves, cursede;* and nearly the same information regarding the singleness of the wolf: *wolf* (without the single marker -s); and the singular verb *ves.*

TEACHING PRACTICE

If your students speak languages in addition to English, ask them to explain the agreement necessary in those languages. Spanish, for example, extends agreement to the gender and number of adjectives; Black English Vernacular, French, and many other languages call for negative concord whereas English rejects it; Chinese languages do not use agreement, depending instead on word order to relate words in sentences.

BACKGROUND

In "Agreement," an important chapter in *Errors & Expectations,* master diagnostician Mina Shaughnessy writes:

> The idea of agreement—that is, of certain words in sentences being formally linked to others so as to reinforce or repeat some kinds of meaning rather than others—is common to many languages. What is arbitrary in each language is what that language chooses to reinforce. Standard English, for example, is laced by forms that reinforce number. . . , a time frame . . . gender and person. (136)

One of the most common student errors, error of agreement grows out of all the possibilities for agreement in our language. Shaughnessy saw such errors as "exercises in competence" and knew that students who have trouble with agreement need to become *habituated* in, to develop an "ear for," the conventions of their language.

Everyday use

Subjects and verbs are at work in almost every statement you make, and you make them "agree" effortlessly most of the time. Look, for instance, at three sentences taken from a recent broadcast of a baseball game. The subjects and verbs are not italicized.

Guzman powers *another blistering curve ball over the plate.*

The Yanks *move* on to Milwaukee tomorrow.

The duel *of the no-hitters* continues *into the eighth.*

Take time to listen to someone reporting an event—a play-by-play announcer, perhaps, or an on-the-scene reporter. Note down some of the subject-verb combinations. Do you find any that don't sound right, that might not "agree"?

Also be careful when a simple subject is followed by a phrase beginning with *as well as, along with, together with, in addition to,* or other prepositions. Make the verb agree with the simple subject, not with a noun in the intervening phrase.

>   s   v
> The *president,* along with many senators, *opposes* the bill.
>
>   s   v
> A *passenger,* as well as the driver, *was injured* in the accident.

Some writers think it awkward to use a singular verb form when the complete subject, including the intervening phrase, expresses a plural idea. If sentences like the ones above strike you as awkward, try making the subject plural and using a plural verb form (see 10c). Consider these possible revisions for the sentences above.

> The president and many senators *oppose* the bill.
>
> Both the driver and a passenger *were injured* in the accident.

If you know that you have problems with subject-verb agreement when the simple subject and the verb are separated by other words, identify the simple subject and the verb and then mentally delete any intervening words to make sure that the subject and verb agree in number and person.

EXERCISE 10.1

"Visiting relatives is/are treacherous." Either of these verbs makes a grammatically acceptable sentence, "agreeing" with a subject, yet they result in two very

---

EXERCISE 10.1: Suggested Answers

1. Visiting relatives *is* treacherous. ["Visiting" is the subject.]

2. Visiting relatives *are* treacherous. ["relatives" is the subject.]

different statements. Complete the sentence by choosing one of the verbs, and write out a brief statement of the two possible meanings. Then write a paragraph or two about visiting relatives. Finally, study your passage for its use of subjects and verbs. Do you have any questions about subject-verb agreement?

EXERCISE 10.2

Underline the appropriate verb form in each of the following sentences. Example:

> *The benefits of family planning* (is/<u>are</u>) *not apparent to many peasants.*

1. It (*pains/pain*) me to see so much misery in the world.
2. I, together with my sister, (*am/is/are*) planning a surprise party for him.
3. Walls of glass (*characterizes/characterize*) much modern architecture.
4. The system of sororities and fraternities (*supplies/supply*) much of the social life on some college campuses.
5. The buck (*stops/stop*) here.
6. The soldiers, along with their commanding officer, (*was/were*) cited for bravery beyond the call of duty.
7. In many species, the male, as well as the female, (*cares/care*) for the offspring.
8. He (*holds/hold*) a controlling interest in the company.
9. The author of those stories (*writes/write*) beautifully.
10. Current research on AIDS, in spite of the best efforts of hundreds of scientists, (*leaves/leave*) serious questions unanswered.

10c

Making verbs agree with compound subjects

Two or more subjects joined by *and* generally require a plural verb form.

> Tony and his friends *commute* every day from Louisville.
> A backpack, a canteen, and a rifle *were issued* to each recruit.

When subjects joined by *and* are considered a single unit or refer to a single person or thing, they take a singular verb form.

EXERCISE 10.2: Answers

1. pains
2. am
3. characterize
4. supplies
5. stops
6. were
7. cares
8. holds
9. writes
10. leaves

TEACHING PRACTICE

Traditionally, sentence diagramming has been the way students identified the subject and verb of a sentence. Although such close syntactical analysis will help *some* students determine subject-verb or pronoun-antecedent agreement, most of our students just don't have the technical command of grammar to diagram or parse a sentence.

To help your students develop their ear for agreement, ask them to bring in or create sentences that seem confusing. Then ask them to come up with ways of determining the information that separates the subject from the verb.

For example, try these sentences orally with your students:

1. To see so many people here is/*are* gratifying.
2. The problems with the house is/*are* overwhelming.
3. Every one of the details *was*/were perfect.
4. It is/*are* the fault of the citizens.
5. Pizza with pepperoni, mushrooms, and green peppers is/*are* delicious.

Habit is habit, and not to be flung out of the window by any man, but coaxed downstairs a step at a time.   —MARK TWAIN

Drinking and driving *remains* a major cause of highway fatalities.

Fried ham and grits *is* Duane's idea of a great breakfast.

His closest friend and political ally *was* his brother.

If the word *each* or *every* precedes singular subjects joined by *and,* the verb form is singular.

Each boy and girl *chooses* one gift to take home.

Every city, town, and hamlet *has* a Main Street.

For compound subjects whose parts are joined by *or* or *nor,* the verb agrees in number and person with the part closest to the verb.

Laws, rules, or convention *governs* most of our everyday decisions.

Neither my roommate nor my parents *plan* to vote.

Neither Maria nor you *were* among the finalists.

Either you or I *am* wrong.

To avoid awkwardness with compound subjects made up of both singular and plural parts, place a plural part closest to the verb.

AWKWARD   Either the witnesses or the defendant *is* lying.

REVISED   Either the defendant or the witnesses *are* lying.

10d

Making verbs agree with collective-noun subjects

Collective nouns, such as *family, team, audience, group, jury, crowd, band, class, flock,* and *committee,* are singular in form but refer to a group of individual persons or things. When used as subjects, collective nouns can take either singular or plural verb forms, depending on the context. When they refer to a group as a single unit, they take a singular verb form.

The team wearing red and black *controls* the ball.

Waving banners frenetically, the crowd *screams* its support.

When they refer to the individual members of a collective, however, they take a plural verb form.

The family of ducklings *scatter* when the cat approaches.

The committee *have* not agreed on many points.

The meaning of a sentence as a whole is your guide to whether the collective noun refers to a unit or to the separate parts of a unit.

> After deliberating, the jury *reports* its verdict. [as a single unit]
>
> The jury still *disagree* on a number of counts. [as separate individuals]

10e

Making verbs agree with indefinite-pronoun subjects

Indefinite pronouns are those that do not refer to specific persons or things. Most take singular verb forms.

> *Common indefinite pronouns*

another	each	much	one
any	either	neither	other
anybody	everybody	nobody	somebody
anyone	everyone	no one	someone
anything	everything	nothing	something

Of the two jobs, neither *holds* much appeal.

Each of the plays *depicts* a hero undone by a tragic flaw.

Some indefinite pronouns take plural verb forms: *both, few, many, others,* and *several.*

> Though many *apply,* few *are* chosen.

Several indefinite pronouns—*all, any, enough, more, most, none, some*—can be singular or plural, depending on the noun they refer to.

SINGULAR	All of the cake *was* eaten.
PLURAL	All of the candidates *promise* to improve the schools.

(See 11c for a discussion of indefinite pronoun–antecedent agreement.)

OPTIONAL EXERCISE

The following sentences contain compound and collective-noun subjects. Have your students edit them for subject-verb agreement.

1. Every week, Sharma, Julio, and Richard attends/*attend* a group total of fifty hours of school.
2. Crosby, Stills, Nash, and Young *was*/were one of the hottest groups in the early seventies.
3. Neither the president nor his administration *claims*/claim to know anything about arms shipment to the Middle East.
4. Mike and his friends is/*are* going to decorate your yard with crepe paper after the game.
5. The composition class plan/*plans* to celebrate Valentine's Day at the professor's house.
6. The professor or her assistant *is*/are always in the office.
7. The couple *vow*/vows to have and hold until death.

10f

Making verbs agree with relative-pronoun subjects

When the relative pronouns *who, which,* or *that* act as the subject of a dependent clause, the verb in the clause should agree in number with the antecedent of the pronoun.

> Fear is an ingredient that *goes* into creating stereotypes. [*That* refers to *ingredient;* hence the singular verb form *goes.*]

> Guilt, jealousy, and fear are ingredients that *go* into creating stereotypes. [*That* refers to *ingredients;* hence the plural verb form *go.*]

When the phrase *one of the* precedes the relative pronoun, you have to be especially careful to determine whether the pronoun refers to the word *one* or to another word. Look at the following sentence:

> Alex is one of the *employees* who always *work* overtime.

In this sentence, a number of employees always work overtime, and Alex is among them. Thus *who* refers to *employees,* and the verb form is plural. Now look at the following sentence:

> Alex is the only *one* of the employees who always *works* overtime.

In this sentence, only one employee always works overtime, and that employee is Alex. Thus *one* and not *employees* is the antecedent of *who,* and the verb form is singular.

10g

Making linking verbs agree with their subjects, not complements

A linking verb should agree with its subject, which precedes it, not with the subject complement, which follows it (see 7c2).

> The signings of three key treaties *are* the topic of my talk. [The subject is *signings.*]

> Nero Wolfe's passion *was* orchids. [The subject is *passion.*]

10h

Making verbs agree with subjects that are plural in form but singular in meaning

Some nouns that seem plural in form (such as *mathematics* and *measles*) are singular in meaning and take singular verb forms.

Mathematics *is* not always an exact science.

Measles still *strikes* many Americans.

Other nouns of this kind (such as *statistics* and *politics*) may be either singular or plural. In the first sentence below, *statistics* refers to a single course of study; hence it takes a singular verb form. In the second sentence, *statistics* refers to a number of figures; hence it takes a plural verb form.

Statistics *is* a course I really dread.

The statistics in that study *are* highly questionable.

Data, the plural form of the word *datum,* is often used informally as singular, but is grammatically plural and should, in college and other formal writing, be used with a plural verb.

| INFORMAL | The data *is* all in. |
| FORMAL | The data *are* all in. |

10i

Making verbs agree with subjects that follow them

In English, verbs usually follow subjects. When this order is reversed, it is easy to become confused. Make the verb agree with the subject, not with a noun that happens to precede it.

Beside the barn *stand* silos filled with grain. [The subject is *silos.*]

Another common inversion of subject-verb order occurs in sentences beginning with *there is* or *there are* (or *there was* or *there were*). *There* serves only as an introductory word, or expletive (see 23a1); the subject follows the verb.

There *are* five basic positions in classical ballet. [The subject is *positions.*]

10j

Making verbs agree with titles and words used as words

When the subject is the title of a book, film, or other work of art, the verb form is singular even if the title is plural in form.

> *One Writer's Beginnings describes* Eudora Welty's childhood.

Similarly, a word referred to as a word requires a singular verb form even if the word itself is plural.

> *Steroids* is a little word that packs a big punch in the world of sports.

 Checking for subject-verb agreement

> Underline each finite verb. Then identify the subject that corresponds to the verb. Put the two together to see if they agree. For example, the sentence *The players on our side is sure to win* can be stripped down to a simple subject-verb *players is.* Bringing together the subject and verb in this way helps some writers to recognize agreement problems; here the verb should be *are: players are.* Check especially the following kinds of subjects.
>
> 1. *Compound subjects.* Those joined by *and* usually take a plural verb. With those joined by *or* or *nor,* however, the verb agrees with the part of the subject closest to the verb. (10c)
> 2. *Collective-noun subjects.* These take a singular verb when they refer to a group as a single unit, a plural verb when they refer to individual members of a group. (10d)
> 3. *Indefinite-pronoun subjects.* Most take a singular verb (see list in 10e); *both, few, many, others,* and *several* take a plural verb. (10e)

EXERCISE 10.3

Revise any of the following sentences as necessary to establish subject-verb agreement. (Some of the sentences do not require any change.) Example:

> *darts*
> Into the shadows ~~dart~~ the frightened raccoon.

1. Every check and money order cost 50 cents.

2. Talking and getting up from my seat was my crime.
3. If rhythm and blues is your kind of music, try Mary Lou's.
4. His merry disposition and his recognized success in business make him popular in the community.
5. *The vapors* were a Victorian term for hypochondria.
6. Neither the lighting nor the frame display the painting well.
7. In the foreground is two women playing musical instruments.
8. Most of the voters support a reduction in nuclear weapons.
9. Each of the players are dealt five cards to start the game.
10. Either his phony smile or his bragging seem to fool many people.
11. The team needs time to learn to cooperate with one another.
12. Her grandmother is the only one of her relatives who still goes to church.
13. *Our Tapes* were one of Fitzgerald's earlier titles for *Tender Is the Night*.
14. Sweden was one of the few European countries that was neutral in 1943.
15. Politics have been defined as the art of the possible.

5. were ——→was; a word referred to as a word is singular
6. display ——→displays; "neither/nor"
7. is ——→are; "two women" is the plural subject
8. correct; "most" refers to a quantity
9. are ——→is; "each" is singular
10. seem ——→seems; "either/or" calls for a singular verb
11. needs ——→need; must be plural because of "one another"
12. correct; "only one" is singular
13. were ——→was; *Our Tapes* is singular, a title
14. was (second verb) ——→were; "that" refers to "countries"
15. have ——→has; "politics" is a collective noun

EXERCISE 10.4

Underline the appropriate verbs in parentheses in the following passage about the Iks, a tribe in Uganda.

The solitary Ik, isolated in the ruins of an exploded culture, (*has/have*) built a new defense for himself. If you (*live/lives*) in an unworkable society, you can make up one of your own, and this (*is/are*) what the Iks (*has/have*) done. Each Ik (*has/have*) become a one-man tribe on its own, a constituency.

Now everything (*fall/falls*) into place. This is why they do (*seems/seem*), after all, vaguely familiar to all of us. We've seen them before. This is precisely the way groups of one size or another, ranging from committees to nations, (*behaves/behave*). It is, of course, this aspect of humanity that (*have/has*) lagged behind the rest of evolution, and this is why the Ik (*seem/seems*) so primitive. In his absolute selfishness, his incapacity to give anything away, no matter what, he (*is/are*) a successful committee. —LEWIS THOMAS, "The Iks"

EXERCISE 10.4: Answers

has; live; is; have; has; falls; seem; behave; has; seems; is

EXERCISE 10.5 Reading with an Eye for Subject-Verb Agreement

The following passage, from a 1990 essay questioning suggestions that our society is returning to more traditional values, especially marriage, includes several instances of complicated subject-verb agreement. Read the passage, paying close attention to the subjects and verbs and noting the rules governing subject-verb agreement in each case.

EXERCISE 10.5: Suggested Answers

none of these assumptions about marriage *add up*; plural, *none* refers to *assumptions*

Between the public statistic and the private reality *lies* a sea of contradiction; singular, subject is *sea*

Marriage *seems* to me; *Marriage* is singular

the divorce rate—with or without new babies in the house—*remains* constant; *divorce rate* is singular

The fabric of men-and-women-as-they-once-were *is* so thin; *fabric* is singular

no amount of patching *can weave* that cloth together; *amount* is singular

The longing for connection may *be* strong; *longing* is singular

but even stronger *is* the growing perception; singular, subject is *perception*

that only people who *are* real to themselves; plural, *who* refers to *people*

that only people who are real to themselves *can connect; people* is plural

Two shall be as one *is* over; singular, *Two shall be as one* is an expression that forms a singular subject

no matter how lonely we *get; we* is plural

For me, none of [these assumptions about marriage] add up. Between the public statistic and the private reality lies a sea of contradiction in which these pronouncements drown. Marriage seems to me more conflict-ridden than ever, and the divorce rate—with or without new babies in the house—remains constant. The fabric of men-and-women-as-they-once-were is so thin in places no amount of patching can weave that cloth together again. The longing for connection may be strong, but even stronger is the growing perception that only people who are real to themselves can connect. Two shall be as one is over, no matter how lonely we get.

—Vivian Gornick, "Who Says We Haven't Made a Revolution?"

EXERCISE 10.6 Taking Inventory: Subject-Verb Agreement

Return to the passage you wrote for Exercise 10.1. Using the information in this chapter, especially the guidelines in 10j, examine each subject and its verb. Have you maintained subject-verb agreement throughout? Revise to correct any errors you find, and then look for any patterns in your writing. If you find any, make a note to yourself (in a writing log, if you keep one) of things to look for routinely as you revise your writing.

11

Maintaining Pronoun-Antecedent Agreement

"Pronouns are tricky rather than difficult," says H. W. Fowler in *A Dictionary of Modern English Usage*. The "trickiness" Fowler notes comes primarily from the fact that pronouns always stand in for another word, a noun or some other pronoun, called the *antecedent*. Making sure that the pronoun and its antecedent match up, or "agree," is a task every writer faces.

Like a verb with its subject, a pronoun must agree with its antecedent in person and number. In addition, a third-person singular pronoun must agree with its antecedent in *gender*—masculine, feminine, or neuter. (See 7a3.) Study two examples from Maya Angelou:

> The English teacher spoke with deliberation, as if *she* were testing the taste of the words. [third-person singular, feminine]

> I would never again work to make *people* smile inanely and would take on the responsibility of making *them* think. [third-person plural]

EXERCISE 11.1

Take a moment to think of some memorable object from your life—a special toy, perhaps, or a now dog-eared favorite book—anything you remember well. Picture it as clearly as you can, and then write a paragraph or two describing it: what it looks like, how you use or used it, how you feel about it or remember it. Then look over your description, identifying every pronoun. Can you find clear antecedents for each one?

EXERCISE 11.1: Answers will vary.

11a

Making pronouns agree with compound antecedents

A compound antecedent whose parts are joined by *and* requires a plural pronoun.

> My parents and I tried to resolve *our* disagreement.
>
> Keith, Molly, and Jane hid behind Dad's chair, and nobody saw *them.*

When a compound antecedent is preceded by *each* or *every,* however, it takes a singular pronoun.

> Every plant and animal has *its* own ecological niche.

A compound antecedent that refers to a single person or thing also takes a singular pronoun.

> The producer and director invested all of *her* savings in the film.

With a compound antecedent whose parts are joined by *or* or *nor,* the pronoun agrees with the nearest antecedent. This kind of sentence, however, can be awkward and may need to be revised if the parts of the antecedent are of different genders or persons.

> AWKWARD   For us to win the meet, you or Charlyce must win *her* next dive.
>
> REVISED   For us to win the meet, you must win *your* next dive, or Charlyce must win *hers.*

With compound antecedents containing both singular and plural parts, the sentence may sound awkward unless a plural part comes last.

> AWKWARD   Neither the radio stations nor the newspaper would reveal *its* sources.
>
> REVISED   Neither the newspaper nor the radio stations would reveal *their* sources.

11b

Making pronouns agree with collective-noun antecedents

When a collective-noun antecedent (*herd, team, audience*) refers to a single unit, it requires a singular pronoun.

The audience fixed *its* attention on center stage.

Finally, our team scored *its* first victory.

When such an antecedent refers to the individual parts of the unit, however, it requires a plural pronoun.

The crew divided the loot among *themselves*.

The director chose this cast because *they* had experience in the roles.

Remember that collective nouns referring to single units require not only singular pronouns but also singular verb forms. Collective nouns referring to separate individuals in a unit, on the other hand, require plural pronouns and plural verb forms.

Each generation *has its* own slang. [*generation* as single unit]

That generation *have* sold *their* souls for money. [*generation* as separate individuals]

11c

Making pronouns agree with indefinite-pronoun antecedents

A pronoun whose antecedent is an indefinite pronoun should agree with it in number. Indefinite pronouns may be always singular (as with *one*)

Everyday use

Take the Interstate until you come to Exit 3 and then 313. Go past it, and take the next exit, which will be Broadway.

The above directions, intended to lead an out-of-towner to her friend's house, provide a good example of the importance of maintaining pronoun-antecedent agreement. The little word it *in this example is very important. Does* it *mean Exit 3, or does* it *mean 313—or are they perhaps the same thing? If the visitor doesn't already know, or if the exit and 313 aren't both clearly marked, she could have difficulty finding her way.*

Make a point of looking—or listening—for pronouns in some everyday situation. Directions, perhaps for using an appliance or finding a destination, are a good place to look. It might be interesting to compare written and spoken directions, to see whether pronouns are used differently. Are writers more careful than speakers?

BACKGROUND

The adjectives *every* and *each* and the pronouns *everyone, no one, anyone, anybody* are generally regarded as singular, regardless of the sentence construction. These words cause difficulty for students, not so much because of their indefiniteness, but because of the agreement problem inherent in third-person-singular nouns and verbs: should agreement be reached in number or gender?

In the following sentence, should you pair *every* with *his* and perpetuate sexist language? Or should you pair the singular *every* with the plural *their,* a practice that is falling into general usage?

Every driver takes *his/her/its/their* lives into *his/her/its/their* own hands.

Or should you recast the entire sentence into the plural?

All drivers take *their* lives into *their* own hands.

Current convention prefers the singular for *everybody* even when a contextual and common sense analysis shows that *everybody* refers to more than one person:

On Saturday mornings, *everybody* meets at Shauna's place before heading to the ball diamond. Beth, Cindi, and Robert always show up first. Tim and Matt usually arrive last.

or plural (as with *many*), or their number may depend on their context. (See 10e.)

One of the ballerinas lost *her* balance. [singular]

Many in the audience jumped to *their* feet. [plural]

Some of the furniture was showing *its* age. [singular meaning for *some*]

Some of the farmers abandoned *their* land. [plural meaning for *some*]

11d

Checking for sexist pronouns

One somewhat complicated problem in pronoun-antecedent agreement involves a pronoun referring to a singular antecedent that may be either male or female. Look at the following passage:

> . . . the Country Club pool was small. One diving board, no spinning top. But its size only seemed to me to be a measure of its exclusiveness. *Whoever* had laid out plans for the Country Club was an entrepreneur with an eye for the one beautiful, rolling and wooded piece of land outside Ames. *He* must have known immediately that such an acreage had to be saved; *he* had a true aristocrat's instinct and converted it into a private preserve. — Susan Allen Toth, "Swimming Pools"

Notice that although the author apparently does not know who laid out the plans for the Country Club, she uses the pronoun *he* to refer to this person. In traditional English grammar, writers used masculine pronouns, known as the generic *he,* in such cases. In recent decades, however, many people have pointed out that such wording ignores or even excludes females—and thus should be avoided. There are several ways of doing so.

 Ways of avoiding generic use of he, his, *or* him

Look at the following sentence.
Every citizen should know *his* rights under the law.

Now consider three ways to express the same idea without *his*.

1. Revising to make the antecedent plural
   All citizens should know *their* rights under the law.
2. Revising the sentence altogether
   Everyone should have some knowledge of basic legal rights.

BACKGROUND

The use of a plural pronoun with an indefinite antecedent has a long history in educated usage:

> Everyone in the house were in their beds.
> —HENRY FIELDING

> A person can't help their birth.
> —WILLIAM THACKERAY

> It's enough to drive anyone out of their senses.
> —GEORGE BERNARD SHAW

This lineage notwithstanding, it is now apt to be considered incorrect by many readers. However, because it provides a simple solution to many problems of sexist usage, it is becoming more and more widely accepted in academic and formal writing. For the moment, it is probably most prudent to counsel students to seek out other alternatives to the generic use of masculine pronouns.

USEFUL READING

Baron, Dennis. *Grammar and Gender.* New Haven: Yale UP, 1986. Baron offers a critical history of the relationship between sexism and the development of the English language. Chapter 10 focuses on attempts to solve the problem of pronoun agreement with the third-person singular.

Nilsen, Aileen Pace. "Winning the Great 'He'/ 'She' Battle." *CE* 46 (1984): 151–57. Nilsen uses an examination of manuscripts submitted to *English Journal* to demonstrate the complexities of using "sex-fair" language. She then offers four principles intended to guide such usage.

3. Using both masculine and feminine pronouns

    Every citizen should know *his or her* rights under the law.

    The last option, using both masculine and feminine pronoun, can be awkward, especially when repeated several times in a passage. Be careful not to overuse it.

When an antecedent is an indefinite pronoun, such as *anybody* or *each,* you can avoid the generic *he* by using a plural pronoun. For example:

Everybody had *their* own theory about Nancy's resignation.

You will probably hear—and perhaps use—such sentences in conversation, but be careful about using them in writing. Although this usage—*everybody* with the plural pronoun *their*—is now gaining some acceptance, many readers will consider it excessively informal or even incorrect. *Everybody* is grammatically singular and hence calls for a singular pronoun. See 10e for a list of indefinite pronouns and 28a for more discussion of ways to avoid sexist language.

 Checking for pronoun-antecedent agreement

Circle all pronouns, and then identify the antecedent of each one. Check to see that the pronoun agrees in person and number with its antecedent; if it does not, revise the pronoun accordingly. Look especially carefully at any compound antecedents (11a), indefinite-pronoun antecedents (10e and 11c), and collective-noun antecedents (11d) to see that the pronouns agree in both person and number.

EXERCISE 11.2

Revise the following sentences as necessary to create pronoun-antecedent agreement and to eliminate the generic *he* and any awkward pronoun references. Some of the sentences can be revised in more than one way, and some of them do not require any change. Example:

Every graduate submitted his diploma card.

Every graduate submitted his *or* her *diploma card.*

All *graduates submitted* their *diploma cards.*

1. With tuition on the rise, a student has to save money wherever they can.

2. Not everyone gets along with his roommate, but the two can usually manage to tolerate each other temporarily.

3. Congress usually resists presidential attempts to encroach on what they consider their authority.

4. Either Tom or Teresa would be willing to lend us her car.

5. If his own knowledge is all the reader has to go by, how can he identify one source as more reliable than another?

6. Every house and apartment has their advantages and their drawbacks.

7. Neither the scouts nor their leader knew their way out of the forest.

8. Our team no longer wears their red and white uniforms.

9. To create a positive impression, a candidate attempts to flood the media with favorable publicity about themselves.

10. I often turn on the fan and the light and neglect to turn it off.

EXERCISE 11.3 Reading with an Eye for Pronouns

Following is the opening paragraph from *Democracy in America,* Alexis de Tocqueville's classic critique of American institutions and culture, which was first published in 1835. Read the paragraph with an eye for pronouns. Does the use of the masculine pronoun to refer to both men and women seem odd to you? Revise the paragraph to eliminate this generic use of masculine pronouns.

> After the birth of a human being, his early years are obscurely spent in the toils or pleasures of childhood. As he grows up, the world receives him, when his manhood begins, and he enters into contact with his fellows. He is then studied for the first time, and it is imagined that the germ of the vices and the virtues of his maturer years is then formed. This, if I am not mistaken, is a great error. We must begin higher up; we must watch the infant in his mother's arms; we must see the first images which the external world casts upon the dark mirror of his mind, the first occurrences which he witnesses; we must hear the first words which awaken the sleeping powers of thought, and stand by his earliest efforts,—if we would understand the prejudices, the habits, and the passions which will rule his life. The entire man is, so to speak, to be seen in the cradle of the child.
> — ALEXIS DE TOCQUEVILLE, *Democracy in America*

EXERCISE 11.4 Taking Inventory: Pronoun-Antecedent Agreement

In a paragraph or two, describe some "typical" person—a typical student at your school, a typical citizen in your hometown, a typical new parent, whatever. You might begin with the sentence "The typical _____ is. . . ." Then analyze your description for agreement between pronouns and their antecedents.

EXERCISE 11.3: Suggested Answers

After the birth of human beings, their early years are obscurely spent in the toils or pleasures of childhood. As they grow up, the world receives them, when their adulthood begins, and they enter into contact with their fellows. They are then studied for the first time, and it is imagined that the germ of the vices and the virtues of their maturer years are then formed. This, if I am not mistaken, is a great error. We must begin higher up; we must watch infants in their mothers' arms; we must see the first images which the external world casts upon the dark mirror of their minds, the first occurrences which they witness; we must hear the first words which awaken the sleeping powers of thought, and stand by their earliest efforts,—if we would understand the prejudices, the habits, and the passions which will rule their lives. The entire human being is, so to speak, to be seen in the cradle of the child.

TEACHING PRACTICE

Ask students to look for other examples of writing that uses pronouns to refer to both men and women. Suggest that they look for both sexist and nonsexist examples, and have them bring their examples to class for discussion. You might want to read a few of them aloud and then put one sexist example up on the board for the class to revise.

12

Using Adjectives and Adverbs

As words that describe other words, adjectives and adverbs add liveliness and color to the flat gray surface of writing, helping writers *show* rather than just tell. Adjectives and adverbs allow us to show readers what we want them to see—to help them visualize objects, scenes, or even abstractions. See, for instance, how much Dorothy West relies on adjectives and adverbs in the following description.

> With a *long blackened fireplace* stick Mama *carefully* tilted the lid of the *three-legged* skillet to see if her cornbread was *done*. . . . *Gently* she let the lid drop. . . .
> — DOROTHY WEST, *The Living Is Easy*

West could have said simply, "Mama checked to see if her cornbread was done." But we would not be able to picture the scene as we do in the passage above. Adjectives such as *blackened* and *three-legged* and adverbs such as *carefully* and *gently* create a vivid image of Mama and evoke a definite impression of West's own attitude about her subject.

But if adjectives and adverbs can create many dramatic effects, they can also "betray" a writer who uses them inappropriately. Like any other part of a sentence, they must follow certain rules and conventions. This chapter discusses some of these rules and conventions and common problems that writers have with adjectives and adverbs.

12a

Distinguishing adjectives from adverbs

Although adjectives and adverbs both modify other words, each modifies different parts of speech. **Adjectives** modify nouns and pronouns, answering the questions *which, how many,* or *what kind?* Many adjectives are formed by adding the suffixes *-able, -ful, -ish, -less,* or *-y* to nouns and verbs.

BACKGROUND

In early English, many adverbs were formed from adjectives by adding *e: bright,* the adjective, became *brighte,* the adverb. In time, the *e* was dropped, but the adverbial use was kept. Hence, from a false analogy, many adjectives (such as *excellent*) that could not form adverbs by adding *e* were used as adverbs. Shakespeare freely used such a construction:

> Which the false man does *easy*.
> —*MACBETH* 2.3.143

> Thou didst it *excellent*.
> —*TAMING OF THE SHREW* 1.1.89

> Grow not *instant* old.
> —*HAMLET* 1.5.94

> 'Tis *noble* spoken.
> —*ANTONY AND CLEOPATRA* 2.2.99

And he used both forms of the adverb side by side:

> She was *new* lodged and *newly* deified.
> — *LOVER'S COMPLAINT* 84.

In function, adjectives and adverbs alike modify other parts of speech, and their differences in spelling and pronunciation have been conflated in the linguistic tendency toward regularization. Like that of Shakespeare's day, today's informal conversation often makes no distinction between an adjective and an adverb in constructions such as *Come quick!* and *The* moon *shines bright* that omit the *-ly* adverb suffix. In their enthusiasm to be correct, some speakers even add the *-ly* suffix to words that function as adjectives, such as: *I feel badly that you've lost your job.* Since *feel* is a linking verb, the speaker should use the adjective *bad* rather than the adverb *badly*.

BACKGROUND

Many well-known writers on style, heirs of Hemingway and Orwell, counsel in the strictest terms against any but the most "necessary" adjectives and adverbs. William Zinsser calls the overuse of modifiers "clutter" and advises writers to "strip every sentence to its cleanest components:"

> . . . Every word that serves no function . . . [and] every adverb that carries the same meaning that's already in the verb, . . . weaken the strength of a sentence.

According to Zinsser, carefully chosen nouns and verbs resonate with connotative meaning. These words rarely need modifiers: *friend* does not need *personal*; *mope* does not need *dejectedly* (*On Writing Well.* 4th ed. [New York: HarperCollins, 1990].

On the other hand, Francis Christensen, in "A Generative Rhetoric of the Sentence," argues that a mature and interesting prose style lies in the use of adjectives and adverbs, which enables students to express complicated thoughts in complicated ways (*Rhetoric and Composition: A Sourcebook for the Teacher* [Upper Montclair, NJ: Boynton, 1984], 110–18).

BACKGROUND

In the chapter "Vocabulary" in *Errors & Expectations*, Mina Shaughnessy describes the vocabulary features of three groups of writers (basic, intermediate, and advanced), including their use of adjectives and adverbs. Basic writers commonly use only a few, already-overused adverbs (*too, very, really, quite, hardly*) and just twenty-one or so adjectives.

Helpless customers wrote *angry* letters to *the* company.

His one comfortable chair is covered in *a colorful Spanish* fabric.

Participles and infinitives can also function as adjectives. (See 7c3.)

The *perplexed* clerk looked at me with a *questioning* expression.

Sandra could not decide which job *to take.*

Although adjectives usually precede the words they modify, they sometimes follow instead. An adjective can also appear after a linking verb as a subject complement modifying the subject (see 7c2 and 12b).

Butler found the Victorian family *stifling.*

Chocolate is *irresistible* to Lee.

Adverbs modify verbs, adjectives, and other adverbs; they answer the questions *how?, when?, where?,* or *to what extent?* Many adverbs are formed by adding *-ly* to adjectives.

The children ran *outdoors.* [modifies the verb *ran*]

He was *not* content to wait. [modifies the adjective *content*]

The shack leaned *slightly* backward. [modifies the adverb *backward*]

Adverbs can also modify an entire clause.

Fortunately, the rain had ended before the wedding.

Infinitives can function as adverbs. (See 7c3.)

The news was almost too good *to believe.* [modifies the adjective *good*]

Everyday use

Adjectives and adverbs often serve as instant identifiers: for those who remember the early days of television, a "really big show" instantly signaled Ed Sullivan. Today the material girl has to be Madonna; the bad boys of basketball, the Detroit Pistons; "I am the greatest" still evokes Muhammad Ali; and "Let's get busy!" means Arsenio Hall is here. Look for some examples of adjectives and adverbs that work as labels in this way. Then think of an adjective or adverb to characterize something or someone in your life.

While adjectives usually are closely tied to the words they modify, adverbs that modify verbs or clauses can often be in various places.

Connor *gleefully* tore open his presents.

Connor tore open his presents *gleefully*.

Gleefully, Connor tore open his presents.

Since adjectives and adverbs both act as modifiers, often have similar forms, and in some cases can occupy the same positions in sentences, sometimes the only way of identifying a word as one or the other is to identify its function in the sentence. Remember: adjectives modify nouns and pronouns; adverbs modify verbs, adjectives, and other adverbs.

EXERCISE 12.1

Read the following passage, noting the adjectives and adverbs (all italicized).

In our *hellbent* earnestness to romanticize the cowboy we've *ironically* dis-esteemed his *true* character. . . . Instead of the *macho, trigger-happy* man our culture has *perversely* wanted him to be, the cowboy is *more apt* to be *convivial, quirky,* and *softhearted*. . . .
— GRETEL EHRLICH, "About Men"

Think of a group you might like to write a thumbnail sketch of, as Ehrlich does in her passage about cowboys. Then try writing one or two sentences that characterize this group. Check over your sketch, noting the words that do the most to paint a picture of your subject. Using this chapter as a guide, see how many of them are adjectives and adverbs.

EXERCISE 12.2

Read the following paragraph with an eye for the adjectives and adverbs. Identify each one, and determine which word each modifies.

The peacock does most of his serious strutting in the spring and summer when he has a full tail to do it with. Usually he begins shortly after breakfast, struts for several hours, desists in the heat of the day, and begins again in the late afternoon. Each cock has a favorite station where he performs every day in the hope of attracting some passing hen; but if I have found anyone indifferent to the peacock's display, besides the telephone lineman, it is the peahen. She seldom casts an eye at it. The cock, his tail raised in a shimmering arch around him, will turn this way and that, and with his clay-colored wing feathers touching the ground, will dance forward and backward, his neck curved, his beak parted, his eyes glittering. Meanwhile the hen goes about her business, diligently searching the ground as if any bug in the grass were of more importance than the unfurled map of the universe which floats nearby.
— FLANNERY O'CONNOR, "The King of the Birds"

Intermediate writers, she claims, use -ly adverbs (*adequately, fluently,* for example) and adjectives more "informative" than *good, bad, important;* these include *hostile, honest, monstrous, impatient.* Shaughnessy encourages teachers to work with writers of all levels, building their academic vocabulary in three ways: learning about words, learning words, and learning a sensitivity to words.

EXERCISE 12.1: Answers will vary.

EXERCISE 12.2: Answers

[a, an, the = articles; his = possessive pronoun; this/that = demonstrative pronouns]

serious——→strutting; full——→tail; usually——→begins; after——→begins; shortly——→after; several——→hours; again——→begins; late——→afternoon; each——→cock; favorite——→station; every——→day; some passing——→hen; indifferent——→anyone; seldom——→casts; raised ——→tail; shimmering——→arch; around——→raised; clay-colored wing——→feathers; touching——→feathers; forward/backward——→will dance; curved——→neck; parted——→beak; glittering——→eyes; diligently——→searching; searching——→business; any——→bug; more ——→importance; unfurled——→map; nearby ——→floats

Using adjectives after linking verbs

Be careful to use adjectives, not the corresponding *-ly* adverbs, after linking verbs. The most frequently used linking verbs are forms of *be,* but they also include sensory verbs—such as *look, appear, seem, sound, feel, smell,* and *taste*—and verbs of becoming such as *become, grow, prove,* and *turn.* (See 7c2.) When they function as linking verbs, they are always followed by adjectives (or nouns). Most of these verbs, however, can also be used to express action. When they express action, they can be followed by adverbs.

> The dog looked *hungry.* [linking verb with adjective]
> The dog looked *hungrily* at the steak. [action verb with adverb]

Using adverbs to modify verbs, adjectives, and adverbs

Be careful to use adverbs, not adjectives, to modify verbs, adjectives, and other adverbs.

NOT	She always dresses *casual.*
BUT	She always dresses *casually.*

Good *and* well, bad *and* badly

The modifiers *good, well, bad,* and *badly* cause problems for many writers because the distinctions between *good* and *well* and between *bad* and *badly* are often not observed in conversation and because *well* can function as either an adjective or an adverb. Be careful to use the appropriate word in college writing.

Good and *bad* are adjectives, and both can be used after a linking verb.

> The weather looks *good* today.
> I feel *bad* for Jason.

Do not use *good* or *bad* to modify a verb, an adjective, or an adverb; use *well* or *badly* instead.

| NOT | He plays the trumpet *good* and the trombone not *bad*. |
| BUT | He plays the trumpet *well* and the trombone not *badly*. |

Badly is an adverb and can be used to modify a verb, an adjective, or another adverb. Do not use it after a linking verb; use *bad* instead.

In her first recital, the soprano sang *badly*.

| NOT | The clams tasted *badly*. |
| BUT | The clams tasted *bad*. |

Well can be either an adjective (meaning "in good health") or an adverb.

| ADJECTIVE | After a week of rest, Julio felt *well* again. |
| ADVERB | He cooks *well* enough to be a chef. |

Real *and* really

Be careful also to observe the distinction between *real* and *really*. In conversation, the adjective *real* is often used in place of the adverb *really*, but in college writing, use the adverb form. And take care not to overuse *really*.

| INFORMAL | The spectators were *real* disappointed by the show. |
| FORMAL | The spectators were *really* disappointed by the show. |

EXERCISE 12.3

Revise each of the following sentences to maintain correct adverb and adjective use. Then identify each adjective or adverb that you have revised, and point out the word each modifies.

         shockingly
Their ~~shocking~~ bad behavior annoyed us.

1. Honest lawyers are not complete obsessed with status or money.
2. He acts negative to her, and in the next episode he proposes marriage!
3. Hypochondriacs call a doctor whenever they feel badly.
4. Christmas Day was real cold, and it was raining heavy.
5. A politician's wardrobe is often careful chosen.
6. When fully grown, the silkworm stops eating good and spins its cocoon.
7. One soldier was wounded bad in the chest.
8. Computers have sure made a difference in Americans' lives.
9. On the new stereo, many of the records sounded differently.
10. They brought up their children very strict.

Laughter is the sensation of feeling good all over, and showing it principally in one spot.

—JOSH BILLINGS

EXERCISE 12.3: Answers

1. completely——→obsessed
2. negatively——→acts
3. bad——→feel
4. really——→cold
5. carefully——→chosen
6. well——→eating
7. badly——→wounded
8. surely——→have made
9. different——→sounded
10. strictly——→brought up

12d

Using comparatives and superlatives

In addition to their simple or positive form, many adjectives and adverbs have two other forms, the **comparative** and **superlative**, that are used for making comparisons.

POSITIVE	COMPARATIVE	SUPERLATIVE
large	larger	largest
early	earlier	earliest
careful	more careful	most careful
happily	more happily	most happily

Canada is *larger* than the United States.

He promised to be *more careful* with his money.

They are the *most happily* married couple I know.

As these examples suggest, the comparative and superlative of most short (one-syllable and some two-syllable) adjectives are usually formed by adding the endings *-er* and *-est. More* and *most* are also used with short adjectives, however, and can sometimes create a more formal tone. The only ways to form the comparative and superlative of longer adjectives—three syllables or more—and of most adverbs is with *more* and *most.* If you are not sure whether an adjective or adverb has *-er* and *-est* forms, consult the dictionary entry for the simple form, where any *-er* and *-est* forms are usually listed.

1

Recognizing irregular forms

Some adjectives and adverbs have irregular comparative and superlative forms. Here is a list of them.

POSITIVE	COMPARATIVE	SUPERLATIVE
Adjectives		
good	better	best
well	better	best
bad	worse	worst
ill	worse	worst
little (quantity)	less	least
many	more	most
some	more	most
much	more	most

BACKGROUND

Not the product of a set of rules, the common irregular adjectives and adverbs originated from different Old English words. For example, *good* came from the Old English *god,* which is related to the German *gut.* Both words are derived from the Indo-European root *ghedh-,* "unite, join together, be suitable." *Better* and *best* come from the Old English *betera* and *betst,* both of which are derived from the Indo-European *bhad-,* "good."

Bad is not derived from the Old English word for bad or evil, *yfel.* Instead, it comes from the Old English *baedan,* "compel, afflict." *Worse* and *worst* come from their Old English synonyms, *wiersa* and *wyrsta.*

POSITIVE	COMPARATIVE	SUPERLATIVE
Adverbs		
well	better	best
ill	worse	worst
badly	worse	worst

2

Distinguishing between comparatives and superlatives

The comparative is used to compare two things, the superlative to compare three or more.

Rome is a much *older* city than New York.

Damascus is one of the *oldest* cities in the world.

In conversation, you will often hear the superlative form used even when only two things are being compared: *Of those two suits, the black one is the most becoming.* In college writing, however, use the comparative: *Of those two suits, the black one is the more becoming.*

3

Checking for double comparatives and superlatives

Double comparatives and superlatives unnecessarily use both the *-er* or *-est* ending and *more* or *most.* Occasionally, they can act to build a special emphasis, as in the title of Spike Lee's movie *Mo' Better Blues.* In college writing, however, make sure not to use *more* or *most* before adjectives or adverbs ending in *-er* or *-est.*

INCORRECT	Paris is the *most loveliest* city in the world.
REVISED	Paris is the *loveliest* city in the world.
INCORRECT	Rome lasted *more longer* than Carthage.
REVISED	Rome lasted *longer* than Carthage.
OR	Rome lasted *much longer* than Carthage.

4

Checking for incomplete comparisons

In speaking, we sometimes use incomplete comparisons—ones that specify only one of the things being compared—because the context makes the rest of the comparison clear. If, after comparing an essay of yours with

BACKGROUND

In *The American Language,* H. L. Mencken points out that some double comparatives may actually have a logic to their usage: "more better," for instance (463). One day we feel better than the day before; the next day, we feel completely well. Hence, we can report that we are "even better" or "still better" or, colloquially, "more better."

OPTIONAL EXERCISE

Ask students to rewrite the following incomplete comparisons, making them clear and explicit by providing a situation and a revised, complex form:

1. You're taller!
2. No, you're more than I am.
3. She's happier.
4. They cheat more.
5. Mine are the most.
6. Mostly red ones.

a classmate's, you say "Yours is better," the context makes it clear that you mean "Yours is better *than mine.*" In writing, that context may not exist. So take time when editing to check for incomplete comparisons—and to complete them if they are unclear.

INCOMPLETE	The patients taking the drug appeared *healthier.*
COMPLETE	The patients taking the drug appeared *healthier than those receiving a placebo.*
INCOMPLETE	I consider Mozart *the greatest.*
COMPLETE	I consider Mozart *the greatest of all composers.*

EXERCISE 12.4

Choose three of the following numbered words, and write a brief passage that uses the simple, comparative, and superlative forms of each one. Example:

frisky   *friskier*   *friskiest*

George adopted a small, *frisky* puppy named Brutus. Quickly, Brutus became even *friskier,* chasing neighbors and jumping on children. He was at his *friskiest* the day Aunt Victoria came to visit.

1. loudly
2. well (adverb)
3. wholesome
4. some
5. little
6. rare
7. good
8. thirsty
9. heavily
10. sarcastically

12e

Using nouns as modifiers

Sometimes a noun can function as an adjective by modifying another noun, as in the following examples:

chicken soup	space station	law school
money supply	atom bomb	rye bread
control center	day care	

In familiar terms such as those listed above, we have no trouble understanding the meaning. In fact, a phrase like *chicken soup* is the most succinct and direct way of expressing the idea of soup made from chicken. If noun modifiers pile up, however, they can obscure meaning and should thus be revised.

EXERCISE 12.4: Answers will vary.

BACKGROUND

"The long compound noun phrase" is a common stylistic habit, according to Joseph Williams. In *Style: Ten Lessons in Clarity and Grace,* Williams provides perfect examples of overnominalization:

> *Early childhood thought disorder misdiagnosis* often occurs as a result of unfamiliarity with recent *research literature* describing such conditions. This paper is a review of seven recent studies in which are findings of particular relevance to *preteen hyperactivity diagnosis* and to *treatment modalities* involving *medication maintenance level evaluation procedures.* (33)

Although piling up nominalizations is acceptable and is, in fact, considered economical in some scientific and technical circles, it has the potential for ambiguity and confusion. In Williams's term, it is "graceless." To unpack such phrases, he says, begin with the last noun and reverse the order, turning the packed phrase into a string of prepositional phrases. Better yet is to look for verbs that have been nominalized such as *misdiagnosis;* used as verbs, those words can put new life into a sentence. Watch, too, for possessive nouns that can be rewritten as prepositional phrases.

AWKWARD   The cold war–era Rosenberg espionage trial and execution continues to arouse controversy.

REVISED   The Rosenbergs' trial and execution for espionage during the cold war era continues to arouse controversy.

Here the string of nouns is broken up by turning *Rosenberg* into a possessive and *espionage* and *era* into objects of prepositions.

EXERCISE 12.5

Revise each of the following sentences to use modifiers correctly, clearly, and effectively. Many of the sentences can be revised in more than one way. Example:

He is sponsoring a housing project finance plan approval bill.

He is sponsoring a bill to approve a financial plan for the housing project.

1. In the Macbeths' marriage, Lady Macbeth is presented as the most ambitious of the two.
2. The article argued that walking is more healthier than jogging.
3. St. Francis made Assisi one of the famousest towns in Italy.
4. Most of the elderly are women because women tend to live longer.
5. Minneapolis is the largest of the Twin Cities.
6. A University of Arizona Lunar and Planetary Laboratory research scientist agrees that mining asteroids may well prove economically important.
7. My graduation day will be the most happiest day of my life.
8. The student cafeteria is operated by a college food service system chain.
9. Japanese cars captured much of the American market because American consumers found they were more reliable.
10. I think *Oedipus Rex* is a successfuler play than *The Sandbox*.

≫ Checking adjectives and adverbs

1. Identify all the adjectives and adverbs, and scrutinize each one carefully to see whether it's the best word possible. Considering one or two synonyms for each one might help you to decide.
2. Is each adjective and adverb really necessary? See if a more specific noun would do away with the need for an adjective (*mansion* rather than *enormous house,* for instance); do the same with verbs and adverbs.

                                               (Continued)

EXERCISE 12.5: Suggested Answers

1. Of the two Macbeths, Lady Macbeth is presented as the more ambitious.
2. According to the article, walking is more healthful [not healthy] than jogging.
3. St. Francis made Assisi one of the most famous towns in Italy.
4. Women tend to live longer than men; hence, more of the elderly are women.
5. Minneapolis is the larger of the Twin Cities.
6. A research scientist from the Lunar and Planetary Laboratory, University of Arizona, argues that mining asteroids may well prove economically important.
7. My graduation day will be the happiest day of my life.
8. The student cafeteria is operated by a college food service, part of a chain.
9. Because Americans found they were more reliable, Japanese cars captured much of the American car market.
10. I think *Oedipus Rex* is a more successful play than *The Sandbox.*

3. Look for places where you might make your writing more vivid or specific by adding an adjective or adverb.

4. Be sure that adjectives modify nouns or pronouns and that adverbs modify verbs, adjectives, or other adverbs. (12a)

5. Check for proper use of *good* and *well, bad* and *badly, real* and *really.* Be sure you don't overuse *really.* (12c)

6. Check all comparisons to see that they're complete. (12d4)

Using sources
Quoting passages with effective adjectives

To quote, summarize, or paraphrase? Sometimes it can be difficult to decide how exactly to incorporate materials from outside sources in your own writing. Adjectives can help you decide: if your source uses adjectives that are especially vivid or apt—ones you would *not* wish to replace—you should consider quoting the passage directly.

EXERCISE 12.6   Reading with an Eye for Adjectives and Adverbs

Find some examples of adjectives and adverbs that you consider noteworthy. You might look anywhere—in essays, short stories, newspapers, your own journal. Copy down five examples, and comment in writing on why they impress you as so effective. What do they add to the larger piece of writing? What would be lost if they were removed?

EXERCISE 12.7   Taking Inventory: Adjectives and Adverbs

Think of something you can observe or examine closely, and take a few minutes to study it. In a paragraph or two, describe your subject for someone who has never seen it. Using the guidelines on pp. 243–44, check your use of adjectives and adverbs and revise your paragraphs. How would you characterize your use of adjectives and adverbs—do you overuse them? Put these thoughts in your writing log if you keep one.

EXERCISE 12.6: Answers will vary.

FOR COLLABORATIVE WORK

Have students bring their responses to Exercise 12.6 to class, and put them up on the board. Ask for comments about what the adjectives and adverbs add in each case. Ask students to suggest synonyms that might be substituted, and consider the effectiveness of the different versions. Try removing the adjectives and adverbs altogether, and consider the result. Finally, ask students which version they prefer, and why.

Part Three

Sentences: Making Conventional Choices

———————— ◇ ————————

13

Maintaining Clear Pronoun Reference

BACKGROUND

Two speakers immersed in conversation can be somewhat ambiguous about their pronoun references because they are speaking in an immediate context. They can rely more on their physical signals and close proximity than on their actual syntax. Each listener has opportunities to interrupt and question anything that seems unclear, or to look perplexed.

The audience of a public speech and the reader of written discourse, however, have little chance to interrupt or question the speaker or author. The rules of etiquette and the varying degrees of formality produce this distance and its demand for clarity of references. Members of an audience rarely interrupt a speaker to ask a question. Readers rarely telephone authors to clarify their pronoun references.

A piece of oratory or writing often creates its own context that clarifies potentially confusing pronoun references. Take, for example, the last sentence of the above paragraph: *Readers rarely telephone authors to clarify their pronoun references.* Taken out of context, *their* could confuse us, but we know that only authors create pronoun references—a fact made clear in the context.

One of your key responsibilities to your readers is making sure that any pronouns refer clearly to their antecedents. Clear pronoun reference oils the wheels of good prose, helping avoid unnecessary repetition and moving a passage along easily. See, for example, the effect pronouns have in the following paragraph.

> *He* was crude, certainly, my Uncle Jake; *he* was coarse, of course; gross, it goes without saying; uncouth, beyond question. But was *he* vulgar? I don't think *he* was. For one thing, *he* was good-hearted, and it somehow seems wrong to call anyone vulgar who is good-hearted. But more to the point, I don't think that if you had accused *him* of being vulgar, *he* would have known what the devil you were talking about. To be vulgar requires at least a modicum of pretension, and this Uncle Jake sorely lacked.
> — Joseph Epstein, "What Is Vulgar?"

If you read the paragraph again, repeating *Uncle Jake* in place of every *he* and *him,* you can see for yourself how useful these pronouns can be. Now look what happens if another uncle is added to the story:

> *He* was crude, certainly, my Uncle Jake, and my Uncle Alfred was sloppy; *he* was coarse, of course. . . .

In this instance, the reference for the first *he* is clear, because it is followed by *Uncle Jake.* But what about the second *he*—does it refer to Uncle Jake, or to Uncle Alfred?

This chapter will alert you to ways of avoiding such problems in your own writing by maintaining clear pronoun reference. Doing so is a fairly simple matter—of identifying each pronoun, finding the word it substitutes for, and making sure the pronoun cannot mistakenly refer to any other word as well.

Everyday use

Those little words that are pronouns can carry a lot of weight in conversation. Speakers of English rely constantly on clear pronoun choices to help communicate effectively in a wide range of situations: explaining to the service person what it is your computer will not do; describing to an insurance agent precisely the kinds of coverage you need; telling a mechanic about the strange noise your car is making. A driver we know recently faced this challenge:

Mechanic:	So what's the problem?
Driver:	On rainy days, it really acts weird.
Mechanic:	It won't start on rainy days?
Driver:	Sometimes it won't start. But there are other problems too. All those little lights on the dashboard light up at once. That white needle goes all the way over, and the little gauge there jiggles around nervously.
Mechanic:	Hmmm. Does it crank?
Driver:	The little gauge?
Mechanic:	The car. The engine.

This conversation shows pronoun reference in use. The one "break-down" in communication occurs because the driver assumes that the mechanic's question—"Does it crank?"—refers back to the last thing the driver mentioned—"the little gauge." The mechanic, however, is using it *to refer to the* car, *not the gauge. Can you think of times when unclear pronoun reference has made for confusion?*

EXERCISE 13.1

Turn back to the passage about Uncle Jake that opens this chapter. Think of two uncles (or two aunts or two other relatives) you might describe, and do so in a brief paragraph. Look then at your passage to see how you've used pronouns.

13a

Matching pronouns to their appropriate antecedents

If more than one possible antecedent for a personal pronoun appears in a sentence or passage, the pronoun should refer clearly and unambiguously to only *one* of them. Notice, in the following passage, how Eudora

BACKGROUND

In their *Frequency Analysis of English Usage* (Boston: Houghton, 1982) W. Nelson Francis and Henry Kucera studied the frequency with which words appear in Edited American English. Pronouns are among the most frequently used words, as the following chart indicates:

Word	Rank
he	7
it	11
they	13
I	15
we	23
she	24
you	30
who	35

The authors also note that personal, reflexive, singular pronouns (*myself, herself, himself*) occur much more frequently in imaginative prose than in informative prose. Conversely, plural forms of these reflexive, personal pronouns (*ourselves, themselves*) occur much more frequently in informative prose than in imaginative prose (544). While Francis and Kucera offer no explanation for this relationship, pronoun use seems to indicate that imaginative prose tends to focus on individuals, while transactional or informative prose tends to focus on groups of people.

EXERCISE 13.1: Answers will vary.

OPTIONAL EXERCISE

Ask students to spend five minutes interviewing two friends or classmates about the courses they are currently taking. Have them take notes and try to get down the interviewee's exact words. Then have them write up a brief summary of their interviews. Have them note how they have used pronouns in their summaries—and make sure that each pronoun refers accurately to the person they intend.

Welty uses pronouns carefully to help readers tell which of two male characters, Sonny and Bowman, she is referring to. The passage describes Sonny frisking Bowman for a concealed gun.

> Sonny came over and put *his* hands on *him.* Bowman felt *them* pass (*they* were professional too) across *his* chest, over *his* hips. *He* could feel Sonny's eyes upon *him* in the dark.
>
> — EUDORA WELTY, "Death of a Traveling Salesman"

In the following sentences, however, from an essay about the same story, the pronoun does not refer clearly to only one antecedent.

AMBIGUOUS	The meeting between Bowman and Sonny makes *him* compare *his* own unsatisfying domestic life with one that is emotionally secure.
CLEAR	The meeting between Bowman and Sonny makes *Bowman* compare *his* own unsatisfying domestic life with one that is emotionally secure.
CLEAR	Meeting Sonny makes *Bowman* compare *his* own unsatisfying domestic life with one that is emotionally secure.
CLEAR	After meeting Sonny, whose domestic life is emotionally secure, *Bowman* finds *his* own domestic life unsatisfying.

In the ambiguous sentence, readers cannot determine whether Bowman or Sonny is the antecedent of *him* and *his.* All three revisions make the reference clear. The first does so by replacing a pronoun (*him*) with a noun (*Bowman*), but it requires repeating the noun. The second eliminates one pronoun, and the third recasts the sentence altogether.

If you are reporting what someone said to someone else, check carefully for ambiguous pronoun reference. Reporting their words directly, in quotation marks, is one sure way to eliminate ambiguity.

AMBIGUOUS	Kerry told Ellen she should be ready soon.
CLEAR	Kerry told Ellen to be ready soon.
CLEAR	Kerry told Ellen, "I should be ready soon."
CLEAR	Kerry told Ellen, "You should be ready soon."

13b

Keeping pronouns and antecedents close together

If a pronoun is too far from its antecedent, readers will have trouble making the connection between the two.

CONFUSING   The right-to-life coalition believes that a *zygote,* an egg at the moment of fertilization, is as deserving of protection as is the born human being, and thus that abortion is as much murder as is the killing of a child. The coalition's focus is on what *it* will become as much as on what *it* is now.

CLEAR   The right-to-life coalition believes that a *zygote,* an egg at the moment of fertilization, is as deserving of protection as is the born human being, and thus that abortion is as much murder as is the killing of a child. The coalition's focus is on what *the zygote* will become as much as on what *it* is now.

EXERCISE 13.2

Revise each of the following items to clarify pronoun reference. All of the items can be revised in more than one way. If a pronoun refers ambiguously to more than one possible antecedent, revise the sentence in at least two different ways, reflecting each possible meaning. Example:

While Melinda was away, Sheila found the ring she had lost.
Sheila found Melinda's lost ring while Melinda was away.
Sheila found her lost ring while Melinda was away.

1. Anna smiled at her mother as she opened the birthday package.
2. Lear divides his kingdom between the two older daughters, Goneril and Regan, whose extravagant professions of love are more flattering than the simple affection of the youngest daughter, Cordelia. The consequences of this error in judgment soon become apparent, as they prove neither grateful nor kind to him.
3. In many cases of child abuse, especially when the parents totally ignore their children, they eventually become criminals.
4. New England helped shape many aspects of American culture, including education, religion, and government. As New Englanders moved west, they carried its institutions with them.
5. Ira told Ed he needed a vacation.
6. James told Allen that his mother was ill.
7. After Ed hired Paul, he felt relieved.
8. When drug therapy is combined with psychotherapy, the patients relate better to their therapists, are less vulnerable to what disturbs them, and are more responsive to them.
9. Not long after the company set up the subsidiary, it went bankrupt.
10. If guns cause crimes, outlaw them.

EXERCISE 13.2: Suggested Answers

1. As Anna opened her birthday gift, she smiled at her mother. As her mother opened her birthday gift, Anna smiled at her.
2. Lear divides his kingdom between the two older daughters, Goneril and Regan, whose extravagant professions of love are more flattering than the simple affection of the youngest daughter, Cordelia. The consequences of this error in judgment soon become apparent, as the older daughters prove neither grateful nor kind to him.
3. Abused children, especially those totally ignored by their parents, often become criminals. Parents who totally ignore their children often become guilty of child abuse.
4. New England helped to shape many aspects of American culture, including education, religion, and government. As New Englanders moved west, they carried their institutions with them.
5. Ira told Ed, "You need a vacation." Ira told Ed, "I need a vacation."
6. James told Allen that his own mother was ill. James told Allen that Allen's mother was ill.
7. Ed felt relieved after he hired Paul. Paul felt relieved after Ed hired him.
8. When drug therapy is combined with psychotherapy, the patients relate better and are more responsive to their therapists, and they are less vulnerable to what disturbs them.
9. Not long after the company set up the subsidiary, the subsidiary (the company) went bankrupt.
10. If guns cause crimes, outlaw guns.

13c

Recognizing troublesome pronoun reference

Matching a pronoun to one specific antecedent and keeping pronouns and antecedents close together will take you a long way toward establishing clear pronoun reference. A few pronouns, however, cause particular problems for writers. The sections that follow provide practice in checking to see that these pronouns are used clearly and properly.

1

Checking for vague and ambiguous use of *it, this, that,* and *which*

Writers are often tempted to use *it, this, that,* or *which* as a kind of shortcut, a quick and easy way of referring to something mentioned earlier. But such shortcuts can often cause confusion. Make sure that these pronouns refer clearly to a specific antecedent.

VAGUE	When they realized the bill would be defeated, they tried to postpone the vote. However, *it* failed. [What does *it* refer to—the bill, the attempt to postpone a vote on it, or perhaps both?]
CLEAR	When they realized the bill would be defeated, they tried to postpone the vote. However, *the attempt* failed.
VAGUE	Today has been wonderful: I've finished my last paper, gotten an A on my art final, and registered for graduation. Because of *this,* I intend to celebrate. [Does *this* refer only to the graduation? Or are all the events reason for the celebration?]
CLEAR	Today has been wonderful: I've finished my last paper, gotten an A on my art final, and registered for graduation. Because of *these successes,* I intend to celebrate.
AMBIGUOUS	She read a review of the book, *which* was confusing. [What does *which* refer to: the review or the book?]
CLEAR	She read a review of the book, *a work* that was confusing.
CLEAR	She read a review of the book, but *the review* was confusing.

If *that* or *which* opens a clause that refers to a specific noun, put *that* or *which* directly after the noun, if possible.

AMBIGUOUS	We worked all night on the float for the Rose Parade *that* our club was going to sponsor. [Does *that* refer to the float or the Rose Parade?]
CLEAR	We worked all night on the float *that* our club was going to sponsor for the Rose Parade.

USEFUL READING

Williams, Joseph M. *Style: Ten Lessons in Clarity and Grace.* 3rd ed. Glenview, IL: Scott, 1989. See p. 136 on summative modifiers, illustrated by the following: "I am taking a course in Romantic poetry, a kind of literature which has been . . ."

2

Checking for appropriate use of *who, which,* and *that*

Be careful to use the relative pronouns *who, which,* and *that* appropriately. *Who* refers primarily to people or to animals with names. *Which* refers to animals or to things, and *that* refers to animals, things, and occasionally to anonymous or collective groups of people.

> Stephen Jay Gould, *who* has won many awards for his writing about science, teaches at Harvard.

> The whale, *which* has only one baby a year, is subject to extinction because it reproduces so slowly.

> Laboratories *that* use animals for experimentation have become controversial.

3

Checking for indefinite use of *you* and *they*

In conversation, we frequently use *you* and *they* in an indefinite sense, as in such expressions as *you never know* and *on television they said*. In college and professional writing, however, such constructions are inappropriately informal. Be careful to use *you* only to mean "you, the reader," and *they* only to refer to a clear antecedent.

INAPPROPRIATE	Television commercials try to make *you* buy without thinking.
REVISED	Television commercials try to make *viewers* buy without thinking.
INAPPROPRIATE	In France *they* allow dogs in most restaurants.
REVISED	Most restaurants in France allow dogs.

4

Checking for adjectives or possessives used as antecedents

Pronouns should not refer to adjectives or possessives as antecedents. Though an adjective or possessive may clearly imply a noun antecedent, it does not serve as a clear antecedent.

INAPPROPRIATE	In Welty's story, *she* characterizes Bowman as a man unaware of his own isolation.
REVISED	In her story, Welty characterizes Bowman as a man unaware of his own isolation.
REVISED	In Welty's story, Bowman is characterized as a man unaware of his own isolation.

≫ *Checking for unclear pronoun reference*

1. Find all the pronouns in your draft, and then identify the specific noun that is the antecedent of each one.

2. If you cannot find a noun antecedent, replace the pronoun with a noun or supply an antecedent to which the pronoun clearly refers.

3. Next, look to see if the pronoun could be misunderstood to refer to a noun other than its antecedent. If so, replace the pronoun with the appropriate noun, or revise the sentence so that the pronoun can refer to only one possible antecedent.

4. Finally, look at any pronoun that seems far from its antecedent. If a reader might have trouble relating the pronoun to its antecedent, replace the pronoun with the appropriate noun.

EXERCISE 13.3

Revise the following sentences to establish clear and appropriate pronoun reference. Most of the sentences can be revised in more than one way. Example:

~~It~~ says | *in the newspaper* | to expect rain today.

1. On the turnpike, they charge very high prices for gasoline.
2. In Texas, you often hear about the influence of big oil corporations.
3. They said on the radio that somebody had won the lottery.
4. A friend of mine recently had a conversation with a veteran that changed his view of the Persian Gulf War.
5. She dropped off a friend which had gone to the party with her.
6. Not only was the chair delivered three weeks late, but the store also told me this was normal.
7. I take care not to get too bundled up in the winter because it will be too hot when you are indoors.
8. Company policy prohibited smoking, which many employees resented.
9. Didion's essay "Goodbye to All That" describes how she left New York.
10. In Tom Jobim's lyrics, he often describes the beaches of Rio.

EXERCISE 13.3: Suggested Answers

1. Gas stations on the turnpike charge very high prices.
2. Texans often hear about the influence of big oil corporations.
3. The lottery winner was announced on the radio.
4. After recently having a conversation with a veteran, my friend saw the Persian Gulf War differently.
5. She dropped off a friend who had gone to the party with her.
6. The chair was delivered three weeks late, which, according to the store management, is a normal practice.
7. I take care not to get too bundled up in the winter because I get too hot when I go indoors.
8. Many employees resented smoking, so the company policy prohibited it.
9. In her essay "Goodbye to All That," Didion describes how she left New York.
10. In his lyrics, Tom Jobim often describes the beaches of Rio.

EXERCISE 13.4 Revising to Clarify Pronoun Reference

Revise to establish a clear antecedent for every pronoun that needs one.

In Paul Fussell's essay "My War," he writes about his experience in combat during World War II, which he says still haunts his life. Fussell confesses that he joined the infantry ROTC in 1939 as a way of getting out of gym class, where he would have been forced to expose his "fat and flabby" body to the ridicule of his classmates. However, it proved to be a serious miscalculation. After the United States entered the war in 1941, other male college students were able to join officer training programs in specialized fields that kept them out of combat. If you were already in an ROTC unit associated with the infantry, though, you were trapped in it. That was how Fussell came to be shipped to France as a rifle platoon leader in 1944. Almost immediately they sent him to the front, where he soon developed pneumonia because of insufficient winter clothing. He spent a month in hospitals; because he did not want to worry his parents, however, he told them it was just the flu. When he returned to the front, he was wounded by a shell that killed his sergeant, which had been with him since basic training.

EXERCISE 13.5 Reading with Attention to Pronoun Reference

The following poem depends on its title to supply the antecedent for the pronouns that follow and that knit the poem together. Read the poem out loud, and then provide its one-word title. How did you know what the title should be? Then try writing a poem of your own (perhaps three or four verses) like this one, using pronouns and other words to give "clues" to your title.

> His art is eccentricity, his aim
> How not to hit the mark he seems to aim at,
>
> His passion how to avoid the obvious,
> His technique how to vary the avoidance.
>
> The others throw to be comprehended. He
> Throws to be a moment misunderstood.
>
> Yet not too much. Not too errant, arrant, wild,
> But every seeming aberration willed.
>
> Not to, yet still, still to communicate
> Making the batter understand too late.   — ROBERT FRANCIS

EXERCISE 13.6 Taking Inventory: Pronoun Reference

Turn to something you've written, and analyze your use of pronouns. Do any pronouns not refer clearly and directly to the correct antecedent? Could any antecedents be ambiguous? Using the guidelines in 13c, revise as necessary. Note any patterns in your pronouns—in a writing log, if you keep one.

EXERCISE 13.4: Suggested Answers

In his essay "My War," Paul Fussell writes about his experience in combat during World War II, which he says still haunts his life. Fussell confesses that he joined the infantry ROTC in 1939 as a way of getting out of gym class, where he would have been forced to expose his "fat and flabby" body to the ridicule of his classmates. However, his decision to join the infantry ROTC proved to be a serious miscalculation. After the United States entered the war in 1941, other male college students were able to join officer training programs in specialized fields that kept them out of combat. If any students were already in an ROTC unit associated with the infantry, though, they were trapped in it. That was how Fussell came to be shipped to France as a rifle platoon leader in 1944. Almost immediately he was sent to the front, where he soon developed pneumonia because of insufficient winter clothing. Fussell spent a month in hospitals; because he did not want to worry his parents, however, he told them he had the flu. When he returned to the front, he was wounded by a shell that killed his sergeant, who had been with him since basic training.

EXERCISE 13.5: Answer

"The Pitcher"

14

Recognizing Shifts

A **shift** in writing is, most simply, an abrupt change of some sort that results in inconsistency. Consider, for example, the very famous opening lines of *The Adventures of Huckleberry Finn:*

> You don't know about me without you have read a book by the name of *The Adventures of Tom Sawyer;* but that ain't no matter. That book was made by Mr. Mark Twain, and he told the truth, mainly. There was things which he stretched, but mainly he told the truth.

Now replace the last sentence with this one: *In a few instances Mr. Twain may have exaggerated slightly; however, for the most part he showed proper respect for factuality.* As readers we would be jolted and no doubt confused by such a shift in tone, from exaggerated informality to almost straitlaced formality.

Such a shift, because it is so blatant, is hard to miss. This chapter will help you recognize shifts that are a bit more subtle and will offer strategies for revising to eliminate them. These include shifts in the tense, mood, and voice of verbs; in the person and number of pronouns; from direct to indirect discourse; and in tone and diction. If you have had such shifts pointed out in your writing, checking for them should become a regular part of your writing process.

EXERCISE 14.1: Answers will vary.

EXERCISE 14.1

Look at the passage from *Huckleberry Finn* above. Now imagine a very different Huck Finn, one in a suit, bow tie, and starched shirt, introducing the story to, say, Queen Victoria. How might such a formal and serious Huck write the passage? Write such a passage, and then have a look at those done by two or three classmates. Compare notes on how you each accomplished the shift in tone.

14a

Recognizing shifts in tense

If the verbs in a sentence or passage refer to actions occurring at different times, they may require different tenses: *Mac started the kennel because he had always loved dogs.* Be careful, however, not to change tenses unnecessarily or in a way that does not make sense. Look, for instance, at this sentence: *Clarissa yowled until her owner looks up.* The shift in tenses from past to present confuses readers, who are left to guess which tense is the correct one.

INCONSISTENT	A very few countries *produce* almost all of the world's illegal drugs, but drug addiction *affected* many more countries.
REVISED	A very few countries *produce* almost all of the world's illegal drugs, but drug addiction *affects* many more countries.
INCONSISTENT	Some people never really *settle* down to a profession. In fact, such people *have found* jobs only when they *needed* food or shelter.
REVISED	Some people never really *settle* down to a profession. In fact, such people *find* jobs only when they *need* food or shelter.

(See Chapter 9 for a complete discussion of verb tense.)

 Checking for unnecessary shifts in tense

> Because we deliberately—and necessarily—shift back and forth among tenses all the time, it can be difficult to spot those tense shifts that are not logically consistent. If you have problems with tense shifts, the following strategies might help.
>
> 1. Circle all the verbs in your draft.
> 2. Look at the verbs in sequence, and check that any shift from one tense to another is logically consistent. Check for consistency both within a sentence and between sentences. You might even find it helpful to make a timeline charting the various tenses used.
> 3. If you find any illogical shifts in tense, revise to eliminate them.

EXERCISE 14.2: Suggested Answers

1. The day is hot, stifling, and typical of July, a day when no one willingly *ventures* out onto the burning asphalt.

2. Then, suddenly, the big day *arrived*. The children were still a bit sleepy, for their anticipation had kept them awake.

3. The importance of music to society is evident throughout the entire magazine. A good example *is* the first advertisement.

4. A cloud of snow powder rose as skis and poles *flew* in every direction.

5. After fitness became popular in the 1970s, all of a sudden there *were* fewer and fewer fleshy Americans parked in front of their television sets. By the early 1990s, that trend had changed as couch potatoes multiplied.

TEACHING PRACTICE

Help your students identify mood by using the following passages from Martin Luther King, Jr.'s "I Have a Dream."

Indicative: used in making a statement of fact.

> It is obvious today that America has defaulted on this promissory note insofar as her citizens of color are concerned. Instead of honoring this sacred obligation, America has given the Negro people a bad check; a check which has come back marked "insufficient funds." But we refuse to believe that the bank of justice is bankrupt. We refuse to believe that there are insufficient funds in the great vaults of opportunity of this nation. So we have come to cash this check—a check that will give us upon demand the riches of freedom and the security of justice.

Imperative: expresses a command or an entreaty.

> Go back to Mississippi, go back to Alabama, go back to South Carolina, go back to Georgia, go back to Louisiana, go back to the slums and ghettos of our northern cities, knowing that somehow this situation can and will be changed. Let us not wallow in the valley of despair.

Everyday use

Dramatic or even outrageous shifts are a staple of comedians and humor writers. Here is columnist Dave Barry: "I would have to say that the greatest single achievement of the American medical establishment is nasal spray." Part of Barry's humor comes from his tendency to shift tone, from the serious (the American medical establishment) to the ridiculous (nasal spray). If you have a favorite comedian or comic strip, look for such shifts in tone. What role do they play in making you laugh?

EXERCISE 14.2

Revise any of the following sentences in which you find unnecessary shifts in verb tense. Most of the sentences can be revised in more than one way. Example:

> *The local newspaper covers campus events, but it* ~~did~~ does *not appeal to many student readers.*

1. The day is hot, stifling, and typical of July, a day when no one willingly ventured out onto the burning asphalt.

2. Then, suddenly, the big day arrives. The children were still a bit sleepy, for their anticipation had kept them awake.

3. The importance of music to society is evident throughout the entire magazine. A good example was the first advertisement.

4. A cloud of snow powder rose as skis and poles fly in every direction.

5. After fitness became popular in the 1970s, all of a sudden there are fewer and fewer fleshy Americans parked in front of their television sets. By the mid-1990s, that trend will change as couch potatoes multiply.

14b

Recognizing shifts in mood

Be careful not to shift from one mood to another without reason. The mood of a verb can be indicative (*He closes the door*), imperative (*Close the door*), or subjunctive (*If the door were closed, . . .*). (See 9h.)

INCONSISTENT	*Keep* your eye on the ball, and you *should bend* your knees. [shift from imperative to indicative]
REVISED	*Keep* your eye on the ball, and *bend* your knees.

INCONSISTENT	I asked that Rhonda *tutor* the Laotian children in English and that she *teaches* them some American games as well. [shift from subjunctive to indicative]
REVISED	I asked that Rhonda *tutor* the Laotian children in English and that she *teach* them some American games as well.

EXERCISE 14.3

Revise the following sentences to eliminate any unnecessary shifts in mood. Example:

Walk over to the field house, and then~~you should~~ get in line.

1. Place a test strip on the subject area; you should expose the test strip to light and develop it for two and a half minutes.
2. I think it is better that Grandfather die painlessly, bravely, and with dignity than that he continues to live in terrible physical pain.
3. Whether women be homemakers or are executives, they deserve respect.
4. The consultant recommended that the candidates tell more jokes and that they smile more during their speeches.
5. Say no to drugs, and you should consider alcohol a drug, too!

14c

Recognizing shifts in voice

Do not shift unnecessarily between the active voice (*She sold the furniture*) and the passive voice (*The furniture was sold*). Sometimes a shift in voice is perfectly justified. In the sentence *I am known for being unpredictable and adventurous, but I consider myself a practical person*, the shift from passive (*am known*) to active (*consider*) allows the writer to keep the emphasis on the subject *I*. Making both verbs active (*People know me as an unpredictable and adventurous person, but I consider myself a practical person*) changes the focus of the sentence. Often, however, shifts in voice merely confuse readers. (See Chapter 9.)

INCONSISTENT	Although she confessed to the crime, her accomplice was not identified by her.
REVISED	Although she confessed to the crime, she did not identify her accomplice.

Subjunctive: makes a conditional statement, expresses a wish, or indicates doubt and uncertainty.

> I have a dream that one day every valley shall be exalted, every hill and mountain shall be made low, the rough places will be made plain, and the crooked places will be made straight, and the glory of the Lord shall be revealed, and all flesh shall see it together.

EXERCISE 14.3: Suggested Answers

1. Place a test strip on the subject area; then *expose* the test strip to light and develop it for two and a half minutes.
2. I think it better that Grandfather die painlessly, bravely, and with dignity than that he *continue* to live in terrible pain.
3. Whether women *are* homemakers or executives, they deserve respect.
4. The consultant recommended that the candidates tell more jokes and *smile* more during their speeches.
5. Say no to drugs, and *consider* alcohol a drug, too!

| INCONSISTENT | Four youngsters approached him, and he was asked to buy a raffle ticket. |
| REVISED | Four youngsters approached him and asked him to buy a raffle ticket. |

EXERCISE 14.4: Suggested Answers

1. I call it smooth, but my parents *see* it as sneaky and devious.
2. No change
3. When someone says "roommate" to a high school senior bound for college, that senior *conjures up* thoughts of no privacy and potential fights.
4. The first thing *we see* as we start down the slope is a large green banner.
5. The physician moves the knee around to observe the connections of the cartilage and ligaments, and *injects* a fluid into the joint.

TEACHING PRACTICE

Because many students have been told never to use *I* in their papers, they frequently alternate between *I* and *you* within a single piece of writing.

> *I* went to the fair and couldn't find any of my friends. So *I* was really bored. *You* want to be with *your* friends, but *you* can't find them, and *you* don't see anyone *you* know to ride the ferris wheel with. So *I* went to the beer garden, ordered a beer, sat down, and waited to see if *I* would see anybody *I* know.

To help make students aware of their shifts in pronoun, ask them to circle all their uses of *I* and *you* in one of their essays. Then, ask them to exchange essays and let their partner help them find appropriate alternatives to the constant shift.

EXERCISE 14.4

Revise each of the following sentences that contains an unnecessary shift in voice. One of the sentences does not require any change. Example:
                                                she prefers jazz.
Although she enjoys rock music, jazz is preferred by her.

1. I call it smooth, but it is seen as sneaky and devious by my parents.
2. Once these shells housed creatures; now they are crushed by the waves.
3. When someone says "roommate" to a high school senior bound for college, thoughts of no privacy and potential fights are conjured up.
4. The first thing that is seen as we start down the slope is a green banner.
5. The physician moves the knee around to observe the connections of the cartilage and ligaments, and a fluid is injected into the joint.

14d

Recognizing shifts in person and number

Do not shift unnecessarily between first person (*I, we*), second person (*you*), and third person (*he, she, it, one,* or *they*) or between singular and plural. Such shifts in person and number create confusion.

INCONSISTENT	*One* can do well in college if *you* budget *your* time carefully.
REVISED	*One* can do well in college if *one* budgets time carefully.
REVISED	*You* can do well in college if *you* budget *your* time carefully.
INCONSISTENT	*Nurses* are paid much less than doctors, even though *a nurse* has the primary responsibility for the daily care of patients.
REVISED	*Nurses* are paid much less than doctors, even though *nurses* have the primary responsibility for the daily care of patients.

Many shifts in number are actually problems with pronoun-antecedent agreement (see 11a–11d).

INCONSISTENT	I have difficulty seeing another *person's* position, especially if *their* opinion contradicts mine.
REVISED	I have difficulty seeing other *people's* positions, especially if *their* opinions contradict mine.
REVISED	I have difficulty seeing another *person's* position, especially if *his or her* opinion contradicts mine.

 Checking for unnecessary pronoun shifts

> 1. Circle all the pronouns in your draft.
> 2. Draw a line from pronoun to pronoun looking for shifts, especially among *I, you,* and *one.*
> 3. If any of the shifts are logically inconsistent, revise to eliminate them.

EXERCISE 14.5

Revise each of the following sentences to eliminate any unnecessary shifts in person or number. Some sentences can be revised in more than one way. Example:

> *When a person goes to college, you face many new situations.*
> *When a person goes to college, he or she faces many new situations.*
> *When people go to college, they face many new situations.*

1. Suddenly we heard an explosion of wings off to our right, and you could see a hundred or more ducks lifting off the water.
2. Workers with computer skills were in great demand, and a programmer could almost name their salary.
3. I liked the sense of individualism, the crowd yelling for you, and the feeling that I was in command.
4. New parents often find it hard to adjust to having a baby around; you can't just get up and go someplace.
5. A person needs to feel that they are respected by others to perform well in a leadership position.

BACKGROUND

Mina Shaughnessy suggests that problems in pronoun shifts stem from the writer's "unstable sense of the writer-audience relationship, with the shift to 'you' signifying a more direct sense of audience" (113). She identifies three additional general sources of pronoun-shift errors: (1) students' tendency "to reduce complexity without impairing communication"; (2) the problem of remembering which pronouns have been used; and (3) the problem of learning the differences among descriptive, narrative, and analytic writing (*Errors & Expectations* [New York: Oxford UP, 1977], Chapter 4: "Common Errors").

TEACHING PRACTICE

To illustrate how shifts in person (and in tense) can be used effectively, read aloud Martin Luther King, Jr.'s "I Have a Dream." Make a special point of focusing on paragraphs 7, 8, and 11–18, discussing King's rhetorical purpose.

EXERCISE 14.5: Suggested Answers

1. Suddenly, we heard an explosion of wings off to our right, and *we* could see a hundred or more ducks lifting off the water.
2. Workers with computer skills were in great demand, and a programmer could almost name *his or her* salary.
3. I liked the sense of individualism, the crowd yelling for *me,* and the feeling that I was in command.
4. New parents often find it hard to adjust to having a baby around; *they* can't just get up and go someplace.
5. *People need* to feel that they are respected by others to perform well in a leadership position.

BACKGROUND

Indirect discourse is often preceded by the word *that,* and both pronouns and verb tenses are often different from those used in direct discourse. Generally, if the introducing verb is past, it doesn't affect the verb in a direct quotation. However, a signal verb in past tense will ordinarily shift the verbs in indirect discourse one step back into the past:

> *Direct discourse*
> The president said, "*I have* no knowledge of those events."

> *Indirect discourse*
> The president said that *he had* no knowledge of those events.

When questions appear in direct discourse, they are followed by a question mark *(The instructor confronted us, asking "What do you think you are doing?").* When reported in indirect discourse, questions often include *who, if, why, whether, what,* or *how*—and they omit the question mark *(The instructor confronted us, asking <u>what</u> we thought we were doing.).*

Recognizing shifts between direct and indirect discourse

When you quote someone's exact words, setting them off in quotation marks, you are using **direct discourse**. When, on the other hand, you report what someone says without repeating the exact words, you are using **indirect discourse**.

DIRECT	Ambrose Bierce defined *love* as "a temporary insanity curable by marriage."
INDIRECT	Ambrose Bierce said that love is a momentary madness that can be taken care of by marriage.

Shifting between direct and indirect discourse in the same sentence can cause problems, especially with questions.

INCONSISTENT	Bob asked what could he do to help?
DIRECT	Bob asked, "What can I do to help?"
INDIRECT	Bob asked what he could do to help.

Using sources
Direct and indirect discourse

When weaving a source's words into your own prose, be careful not to shift awkwardly, or ungrammatically, from direct to indirect discourse (or the reverse). For instance:

INCONSISTENT	Chief Seattle *said* that one nation *followed* another "like the waves of the sea" and therefore "regret *is* useless." [Shifting from indirect to direct discourse results in inconsistent verb sequence.]
DIRECT	Chief Seattle said that "nation follows nation, like the waves of the sea" and that therefore "regret is useless."
INDIRECT	Chief Seattle said that nations come and go, like everything in nature, and that therefore feeling sad is useless.

In general, you should use direct discourse for words that are memorable or otherwise important and use indirect discourse when the exact words are less important than their content. In the previous example, direct quotation is probably more appropriate, for Chief Seattle's words are poetic and memorable. In some contexts, however, a writer might want to paraphrase his words, as in the indirect example—for instance, if Chief Seattle is already quoted in many other places in the same work.

EXERCISE 14.6

Revise each of the following sentences to eliminate the shifts between direct and indirect discourse by putting the direct discourse into indirect form. Example:

> Nathaniel Hawthorne once stated that there was nothing he preferred to ~~my~~ his own solitude.

1. Loren Eiseley feels an urge to join the birds in their soundless flight, but in the end he knows that he cannot, and "I was, after all, only a man."
2. According to the article, the ozone layer is rapidly dwindling, and "we are endangering the lives of future generations."
3. The instructor told us, "Please read the next two stories before the next class" and that she might give us a quiz on them.
4. Oscar Wilde wrote that books cannot be divided into moral and immoral categories, and "books are either well-written or badly written."
5. Richard Rodriguez acknowledged that intimacy was not created by a language; "it is created by intimates."

14f

Recognizing shifts in tone and diction

Tone in writing refers to the way the writer's attitude toward the topic and/or audience comes across to the audience. (See 4g4.) Tone is closely related to **diction**, or word choice—not only the choice of individual words, but the overall level of formality, technicality, or other effects created by the individual words. Within a sentence, a paragraph, or an entire piece of writing, be careful not to change your tone or level of diction unless you have a reason for doing so.

Tone

When they are used for emphasis or humor, shifts in tone can be effective. Mark Twain was a master of such shifts. In the following passage,

Alas, poor Yorick! How surprised he would be to see how his counterpart of today is whisked off to a funeral parlor and is in short order sprayed, sliced, pierced, pickled, trussed, trimmed, creamed, waxed, painted, rouged and neatly dressed—transformed from a common corpse into a Beautiful Memory Picture. This process is known in the trade as embalming and restorative art.
—JESSICA MITFORD,
"Behind the Formaldehyde Curtain"

FOR COLLABORATIVE WORK

To illustrate shifts in tone, you may want to provide your class with copies of both Lincoln's Gettysburg Address and Mencken's "Gettysburg Address in Vulgate." To highlight the change in tone, read them aloud. Then ask the class to identify the phrases and words Mencken uses in place of Lincoln's terms. Discuss how the connotations of words control the "meaning" of a piece of writing.

To give students practice in identifying tone, break them into groups, asking each group to describe the characteristics of one Gettysburg Address. You can use Lincoln's version, Mencken's, and the five versions reprinted in *Preface to Critical Reading,* 6th ed., by Richard D. Altick and Andrea A. Lunsford (NY: Holt, 1984, 104–07).

BACKGROUND

Shifts in tone and diction can be justified. In the following excerpt, a parody of college catalogs, the diction shifts from formal, sometimes technical, language to much less formal, colloquial language, and finally to slang.

Economic Theory: A systematic application and critical evaluation of the basic analytic concepts of economic theory, with an emphasis on money and why it's good. Fixed coefficient production functions, cost and supply curves, and nonconvesity comprise the first semester, with the second semester concentrating on spending, making change, and keeping a neat wallet. The Federal Reserve System is analyzed, and advanced students are coached in the proper method of filling out a deposit slip. Other topics include: Inflation and Depression—how to dress for each. Loans, interest, welching.
—WOODY ALLEN, "Spring Bulletin"

he presents a mock graduation address, "Advice to Youth," beginning with a serious tone and then shifting at the beginning of the second paragraph to characteristic humor.

Being told I would be expected to talk here, I inquired what sort of a talk I ought to make. They said it should be something suitable to youth—something didactic, instructive, or something in the nature of good advice. Very well. I have a few things in my mind which I have often longed to say for the instruction of the young; for it is in one's tender early years that such things will best take root and be most enduring and most valuable. First, then, I will say to you, my young friends—and I say it beseechingly, urgingly—

Always obey your parents, when they are present. This is the best policy in the long run, because if you don't they will make you. Most parents think they know better than you do, and you can generally make more by humoring that superstition than you can by acting on your own better judgment.
— MARK TWAIN, "Advice to Youth"

Unintended shifts in tone, on the other hand, confuse readers and leave them wondering what the writer's real attitude is. In the following passage, the tone shifts in the last sentence.

INCONSISTENT

The question of child care forces a society to make profound decisions about its economic values. Can most families with young children actually live adequately on only one salary? If some conservatives had their way, June Cleaver would still be stuck in the kitchen baking cookies for Wally and the Beaver and waiting for Ward to bring home the bacon, except that with only one income the Cleaver family would be lucky to afford hot dogs.

The first two sentences of this passage set a serious, formal tone, discussing child care in fairly general, abstract terms, but in the third sentence the writer shifts suddenly to a sarcastic attack based on references to television characters of an earlier era. Readers cannot tell whether the writer is presenting a serious analysis of the child care issue or a passionate argument about a hotly debated topic. See how the passage was revised to make the tone consistent.

REVISED

The question of child care forces a society to make profound decisions about its economic values. Can most families with young children actually live adequately on only one salary? Some conservatives believe that women with young children should not work outside the home, but many are forced to do so for financial reasons.

Diction

Like shifts in tone, inappropriate shifts in level of diction can confuse readers. In general, diction may be classified as technical (*Araucaria araucana* instead of *monkey puzzle tree*), informal or colloquial (*Give me a ring if there's anything I can do*), formal (*Please inform me if I can be of further assistance*), or slang (*He used to be a real jock, but now he's a couch potato*). In the following sentences, the diction shifts from formal to highly informal, giving an odd, disjointed feeling to the passage.

INCONSISTENT

Since taking office, Prime Minister Cresson has been bombarded with *really gross* news, including *tons of* strikes, record unemployment, several scandals, and even *bitching* from colleagues in her own party.

REVISED

Since taking office, Prime Minister Cresson has been bombarded with unrelenting bad news, including a wave of strikes, record unemployment, several scandals, and even sniping from colleagues in her own party.

EXERCISE 14.7   Reading with an Eye for Shifts

The following paragraph includes several *necessary* shifts in person and number. Read the paragraph carefully, marking off all such shifts. Notice how careful the author must be as he shifts back and forth among pronouns.

It has been one of the great errors of our time to think that by thinking about thinking, and then talking about it, we could possibly straighten out and tidy up our minds. There is no delusion more damaging than to get the idea in your head that you understand the functioning of your own brain. Once you acquire such a notion, you run the danger of moving in to take charge, guiding your thoughts, shepherding your mind from place to place, *controlling* it, making lists of regulations. The human mind is not meant to be governed, certainly not by any book of rules yet written; it is supposed to run itself, and we are obliged to follow it along, trying to keep up with it as best we can. It is all very well to be aware of your awareness, even proud of it, but never try to operate it. You are not up to the job.
— LEWIS THOMAS, "The Attic of the Brain"

EXERCISE 14.8   Taking Inventory: Shifts

Find an article about a well-known person you admire. Then write a paragraph or two about him or her, making a point of using both direct and indirect discourse. Using the suggestions in 14e, check your writing for any inappropriate shifts between direct and indirect discourse, and revise as necessary.

FOR THE WRITING LOG

Encourage students to record examples of tone and diction shift—including ones that are either intentionally or unintentionally humorous. Some students may enjoy fashioning deliberately humorous sentences containing such shifts, modeled after the examples by Woody Allen in the previous Background and Dave Barry on p. 256.

EXERCISE 14.7: Suggested Answers

third-person singular (It has been . . .)⟶ first-person plural (our time . . .)⟶third-person singular (There is no delusion . . .)⟶second-person singular (your head . . .)⟶third-person singular (The human mind . . .)⟶first-person plural (and we are obliged . . .)⟶third-person singular (It is all very well . . .)⟶second-person singular (your awareness . . .)

(Note the shift in mood from the indicative to the imperative in the second last sentence.)

15

Identifying Comma Splices and Fused Sentences

In their attempts to recapture the "stream of consciousness," both James Joyce and William Faulkner experimented freely with comma splices and fused sentences. Molly's soliloquy in Joyce's *Ulysses* is one of the most famous of these attempts:

> why cant you kiss a man without going and marrying him first you sometimes love to wildly when you feel that way so nice all over you you cant help yourself I wish some man or other would take me sometime when hes there and kiss me in his arms theres nothing like a kiss long and hot down to your soul almost paralyses you[.]

Joyce deliberately used comma splices and fused sentences for purpose and effect. But when student writers use them, they usually do so unknowingly. When they combine two independent clauses without appropriately signaling the combination, they produce a *comma splice* (often called a *comma fault*) or a *fused sentence* (often called a *run-on sentence*). Student writers often defend their *comma splices* in terms of their closely connected ideas or logical progression.

> Anna came in from the tennis court absolutely famished, she opened the freezer, took out the chocolate mocha ice cream, and dug in.

Because it indicates how the two independent clauses are to be separated, the *comma splice*

The terms *comma splice* and *fused sentence* grow out of metaphors based on the words *splice* and *fuse*. In grammatical terms, a **comma splice** occurs when two independent clauses are joined with only a comma; a **fused sentence**, when two independent clauses are joined with no punctuation or connecting word between them.

SPLICE	It was already spring, the tulips were in bloom.
FUSED	It was already spring the tulips were in bloom.

Comma splices and fused sentences appear frequently in literary and journalistic writing, for like many other structures we commonly identify as "errors," each can be used to powerful effect. In the following passage, see how comma splices create momentum and build to a climax.

> Golden eagles sit in every tree and watch us watch them watch us, although there are bird experts who will tell you in all seriousness that there are NO golden eagles here. Bald eagles are common, ospreys abound, we have herons and mergansers and kingfishers, we have logging with percherons and belgians, we have park land and nature trails, we have enough oddballs, weirdos, and loons to satisfy anybody.
>
> — ANNE CAMERON

In the second sentence, six independent clauses are spliced together with commas. The effect is a rush of details, from the rather oddball birds to the oddball people, and finally to the *loons,* a word that can apply to either birds or people.

In your college writing, you will seldom if ever wish to focus attention on sentences in this particular way. In fact, doing so will almost always be identified not as a means of creating emphasis or special effect but as an error. This chapter aims to help you learn to recognize comma splices and fused sentences in your own writing and provides five methods of revising to eliminate them.

Everyday use

While we certainly pause as we speak in order to mark off our thoughts or to add emphasis, we do not "speak" punctuation. In fact, excited conversation may contain many comma splices, which then appear in dialogue to represent the rhythms of speech. For example:

"What about Tom?"
"We can tell your father and Billy that Tom's mother called, he was sick, his grandmother died, anything, just so we don't have to bring him with us." – THOMAS ROCKWELL, *How to Eat Fried Worms*

The comma splices in this dialogue are effective because they convey the speech patterns of two ten-year-old boys; they would not, however, be appropriate (or effective) in most college writing. Try revising the above dialogue to make it sound more adult. You may see some ways—and reasons— to keep comma splices out of your own writing.

EXERCISE 15.1

If you listen carefully, you may well "hear" comma splices and fused sentences in conversations around you. Try to transcribe a few minutes of conversation among two or three friends. Look for comma splices or fused sentences, using the guidelines that follow.

 Checking for comma splices and fused sentences

1. Underline every independent clause in your draft. (7c4)
2. Look for places where independent clauses fall one after another, and look at what comes between them.
3. If you find no punctuation, you have identified a fused sentence.
4. If you find only a comma without *and, but, or, for, so,* or *yet,* you have identified a comma splice.
5. Look to see if any clauses are linked by conjunctive adverbs— words like *however, then,* or *therefore* (see 7b7 for a list)—and then make sure that a semicolon precedes any conjunctive adverb. If not, you have a comma splice.
6. Revise any fused sentences or comma splices using one of the five methods listed below.

above is easier to read than the following *fused sentence:*

Anna came into her room to find her cat prancing around on her dresser her jewelry box was lying sideways on the floor her jewelry all sprawled out.

Although these sentence-level "errors" often indicate closely connected ideas, they just as often reflect hurried writing or typing and little or no proofreading.

BACKGROUND

As important as sentence pattern (syntax) is word choice (semantics). In his or her mind and experience, the writer may understand the relationship between two sentences, but the reader may have to struggle to determine the writer's meaning:

I was strongly attracted to him. He talked like no man I had ever heard before.

In this example, the writer likely wants to say that he or she was attracted to him because of the extraordinary brilliance or melodiousness of his speech. The addition of *because* or *for* would indicate the positive causal connection between the two clauses. On the other hand, perhaps the man talked like a robot, or used the most vulgar language the writer had ever heard; in this case, *although* or *however* would more accurately convey the writer's meaning—probably.

EXERCISE 15.1: Answers will vary.

Five methods of eliminating comma splices and fused sentences

- Separating clauses into two sentences (15a)
- Linking clauses with a comma and a coordinating conjunction (15b)
- Linking clauses with a semicolon (15c)
- Recasting two clauses as *one* independent clause (15d)
- Recasting one independent clause as a dependent clause (15e)

As a writer, you must decide which method to use in revising—or avoiding—comma splices and fused sentences. The choice requires looking at the sentences before and after the ones you are revising in order to determine how a particular method will affect the rhythm of the passage and perhaps reading the passage aloud to see how the revision will sound.

15a

Separating the clauses into two sentences

The simplest way to revise comma splices or fused sentences is to separate them into two sentences.

COMMA SPLICE	Emma encourages Harriet to reject a proposal from a young farmer and to expect one from Mr. Elton, her interference soon leads to embarrassment.
FUSED SENTENCE	Emma encourages Harriet to reject a proposal from a young farmer and to expect one from Mr. Elton her interference soon leads to embarrassment.
REVISED	Emma encourages Harriet to reject a proposal from a young farmer and to expect one from Mr. Elton. Her interference soon leads to embarrassment.

Although this method may be the simplest, it is not always the most appropriate. In the preceding example, choosing to divide the two independent clauses into two separate sentences makes good sentence sense. The combined sentences contain twenty-four words and, dividing them into two sentences of eighteen and six words adds emphasis to the last six words by putting them in a sentence of their own. If the two spliced or fused clauses are very short, however, dividing them into two separate sentences may not succeed so well.

COMMA SPLICE	Emma gives Harriet advice about marriage proposals, she soon regrets having done so.

USEFUL READING

Weathers, Winston. "Grammars of Style: New Options in Composition." *Freshman English News* 4 (Winter 1976): 1–4. Rpt. in *Rhetoric and Composition: A Sourcebook for Teachers and Writers.* Ed. Richard L. Graves. Upper Montclair, NJ: Boynton, 1984. 133–47. Weathers points out that although teachers think they are giving students a wide range of stylistic options, they are, in fact, subscribing to a rather limited "grammar of style." He offers a description of marginalized styles that teachers should consider, including a style he calls the "labyrinthine sentence."

| FUSED SENTENCE | Emma gives Harriet advice about marriage proposals she soon regrets having done so. |
| REVISED | Emma gives Harriet advice about marriage proposals. She soon regrets having done so. |

Here the two short sentences in a row, both opening with the subject, sound abrupt and overly terse, and some other method of revision would probably be preferable. (See Chapter 22.)

15b

Linking the clauses with a comma and a coordinating conjunction

For comma splices and fused sentences in which the two clauses are fairly closely related and equally important, another alternative for revision is to use a comma and a coordinating conjunction: *and, but, or, nor, for, so,* or *yet*. Using a coordinating conjunction helps indicate what kind of link exists between the ideas in the two clauses. For instance, *but* and *yet* signal opposition or contrast (*I am strong, but she is stronger*); *for* and *so* signal cause-effect relationships (*The cabin was bitterly cold, so we built a fire*).

COMMA SPLICE	I could use the money for tuition, I could use it to buy a new car.
FUSED SENTENCE	I could use the money for tuition I could use it to buy a new car.
REVISED	I could use the money for tuition, *or* I could use it to buy a new car.

In the preceding example, the two clauses represent alternatives, so *or* is an appropriate conjunction to link them. (See 20a for more on using coordinating conjunctions to write more varied and interesting sentences.)

15c

Linking the clauses with a semicolon

If the ideas in the two independent clauses in a comma splice or fused sentence are closely related and you want to give them equal emphasis, link them with a semicolon.

COMMA SPLICE	This photograph is not at all realistic, it even uses dreamlike images to convey its message.
FUSED SENTENCE	This photograph is not at all realistic it even uses dreamlike images to convey its message.
REVISED	This photograph is not at all realistic; it even uses dreamlike images to convey its message.

Here, the second independent clause elaborates on the statement in the first independent clause, offering evidence that the photograph is not at all realistic. Because the two independent clauses are closely related and of equal importance, linking them with a semicolon makes sense.

Punctuating clauses linked with a conjunctive adverb or a transitional phrase

Be careful when linking clauses with conjunctive adverbs (words like *however, thus, also;* see 7b7) or transitional phrases (*in fact, in contrast, in addition;* see 6c5). Such words and phrases must be used with a semicolon, a period, or a coordinating conjunction.

COMMA SPLICE	Most Third World countries have very high birthrates, therefore most of their citizens are young.
FUSED SENTENCE	Most Third World countries have very high birthrates therefore most of their citizens are young.
REVISED	Most Third World countries have very high birthrates; therefore, most of their citizens are young.
REVISED	Most Third World countries have very high birthrates. Therefore, most of their citizens are young.
REVISED	Most Third World countries have very high birthrates; most of their citizens, therefore, are young.
REVISED	Most Third World countries have very high birthrates, and therefore most of their citizens are young.

As you can see, any of the three methods discussed thus far can be used to revise a comma splice or fused sentence that uses a conjunctive adverb or transitional phrase inappropriately. The context of the passage can help you decide which method to choose. Notice that conjunctive adverbs and transitional phrases can appear in various positions in the clause. These words and expressions are usually set off from the rest of the clause by commas (see 29a).

Recasting the two clauses as a single independent clause

Sometimes two independent clauses that are spliced or fused together can be reduced to a single independent clause.

COMMA SPLICE	Many people complain that a large part of their mail is advertisements, most of the rest is bills.
FUSED SENTENCE	Many people complain that a large part of their mail is advertisements most of the rest is bills.
REVISED	Many people complain that most of their mail is advertisements and bills.

The revision combines the phrases *a large part of their mail* and *most of the rest* into the phrase *most of their mail* and connects the words *advertisements* and *bills* with the conjunction *and*. These changes reduce the two independent clauses to a single clause that is more direct and succinct. (See 19b for more ways to avoid needless repetition.)

Recasting one of the independent clauses as a dependent clause

Another option for revising two spliced or fused independent clauses is to convert one of them to a dependent clause. This method is most appropriate when the meaning or effect of one clause is dependent on the other or when one is less important than the other.

COMMA SPLICE	Zora Neale Hurston is regarded as one of America's major novelists, she died in obscurity.
FUSED SENTENCE	Zora Neale Hurston is regarded as one of America's major novelists she died in obscurity.
REVISED	*Although* Zora Neale Hurston is regarded as one of America's major novelists, she died in obscurity.

In the preceding example, the first clause stands in contrast to the second one: in contrast to Hurston's importance today (she is held in high esteem) are the circumstances of her death (obscurity). In the revision, the writer chose to emphasize the second clause and to make the first one into a dependent clause by adding the subordinating conjunction *although*. (For a list of subordinating conjunctions, see 7b7.)

COMMA SPLICE	The Arts and Crafts movement called for handmade objects, it reacted against mass production.
FUSED SENTENCE	The Arts and Crafts movement called for handmade objects it reacted against mass production.
REVISED	The Arts and Crafts movement, *which reacted against mass production,* called for handmade objects.

In this example, both clauses discuss related aspects of the Arts and Crafts movement. In the revision, the writer chose to emphasize the first clause, the one describing what the movement advocated, and to make the second clause, the one describing what it reacted against, into a dependent clause by adding the relative pronoun *which*. (For a list of relative pronouns, see 7b3.)

Notice that dependent clauses must often be set off from the rest of the sentence with commas (see Chapter 29). See also 22a2 and 22b2 about using dependent clauses to write more varied and effective sentences.

EXERCISE 15.2

Revise to correct the comma splice or fused sentence using *two* of the methods in this chapter. Use each of the methods at least once. Example:

> *I had misgivings about the marriage, I did not attend the ceremony.*
> *I had misgivings about the marriage, so I did not attend the ceremony.*
> *Because I had misgivings about the marriage, I did not attend the ceremony.*

1. I was sitting on a log bridge, the sun sank low in the sky.
2. Reporters today have no choice they must use computers.
3. I couldn't answer some questions, these are the ones that stick in my mind.
4. My mother taught me to read my grandmother taught me to *love* to read.
5. *David Copperfield* was written as a serial it is ideal for television.
6. Lincoln called for troops to fight the Confederacy, four more Southern states seceded as a result.
7. The mother eagle called twice the young eagle finally answered.
8. Jim grew beautiful tulips, however he had less success with strawberries.
9. Vaclav Havel was once imprisoned as a dissident, still he eventually became president of Czechoslovakia.
10. The music lifted her spirits she stopped sighing and began to sing.

EXERCISE 15.2: Suggested Answers

1. While I was sitting on a log bridge, the sun sank low in the sky.
2. Reporters today have no choice but to use computers.
3. I couldn't answer some questions. These are the ones that stick in my mind.
4. My mother taught me to read, but my grandmother taught me to *love* to read.
5. Because *David Copperfield* was written as a serial, it is ideal for television.
6. Lincoln called for troops to fight the Confederacy; as a result, four more Southern states seceded.
7. The mother eagle called twice before the young eagle finally answered.
8. Jim grew beautiful tulips; however, he had less luck with strawberries.
9. Vaclav Havel was once imprisoned as a dissident; still, he eventually became president of Czechoslovakia.
10. As the music lifted her spirits, she stopped sighing and began to sing.

EXERCISE 15.3

Revise the following paragraph, eliminating all comma splices by using a period or a semicolon. Then revise the paragraph again, this time using any of the other methods in this chapter. Comment on the two revisions. What differences in rhythm do you detect? Which version do you prefer, and why?

My sister Mary decided to paint her house last summer, thus, she had to buy some paint. She wanted inexpensive paint, at the same time, it had to go on easily and cover well, that combination was unrealistic to start with. She had never done exterior painting before, in fact she did not even own a ladder. She was a complete beginner, on the other hand, she was a hard worker and was willing to learn. She got her husband, Dan, to take a week off from work, likewise she let her two teenage sons take three days off from school to help. Mary went out and bought the "dark green" paint for $6.99 a gallon, it must have been mostly water, in fact, you could almost see through it. Mary and Dan and the boys put one coat of this paint on the house, as a result, their white house turned a streaky light green. Dan and the boys rebelled, declaring they would not work anymore with such cheap paint. Mary was forced to buy all new paint, even so, the house did not really get painted until September.

EXERCISE 15.4 Revising for Comma Splices and Fused Sentences

Revise the following paragraph, eliminating the comma splices and fused sentences using any of the methods discussed in this chapter. Then revise the paragraph again, this time eliminating each comma splice and fused sentence by a *different* method. Decide which paragraph is more effective, and why. Finally, compare the revision you prefer with the revisions of several other students, and discuss the ways in which the versions differ in meaning.

Gardening can be very satisfying, it is also hard work people who just see the pretty flowers may not realize this. My mother spends long hours every spring tilling up the soil, she moves many wheelbarrow-loads of disgusting cow manure and chicken droppings, in fact, the whole early part of gardening is nauseating. The whole garden area has to be rototilled every year, this process is not much like the ad showing people walking quietly behind the Rototiller, on the contrary, my father has to fight that machine every inch of the way, sweating so much he looks like Hulk Hogan after a hard bout. Then the planting all must be done by hand, my back aches, my hands get raw, my skin gets sunburned. I get filthy whenever I go near that garden my mother always asks me to help, though. When harvest time comes the effort is *almost* worth it, however, there are always extra zucchinis I give away at school everybody else is trying to give away zucchinis, too. We also have tomatoes, lettuce, there is always more than we need and we feel bad wasting it wouldn't you like this nice bag of cucumbers?

EXERCISE 15.3: Answers will vary.

EXERCISE 15.4: Answers will vary.

EXERCISE 15.5: Answers will vary.

FOR COLLABORATIVE WORK

Ask your students to read this passage by Gertrude Stein and then write a short paragraph describing the effects Stein achieves with her comma splices. As a class, share your insights in a discussion. Then ask your students to rewrite the passage to achieve different effects, such as short, choppy sentences or a stream-of-consciousness narration.

> Think of all the detective stories everybody reads. The kind of crime is the same, and the idea of the story is very often the same, take for example a man like Wallace, he always has the same theme, take a man like Fletcher he always has the same theme, take any American ones, they too always have the scene, the same scene, the kind of invention that is necessary to make a general scene is very limited in everybody's experience, every time one of the hundreds of times a newspaper man makes fun of my writing and of my repetition he always has the same theme, always having the same theme, that is, if you like, repetition, that is if you like repeating that is the same thing, but once started expressing this thing, expressing any thing there can be no repetition because the essence of that expression is insistence, and if you insist you must each time use emphasis and if you use emphasis it is not possible while anybody is alive that they should use exactly the same emphasis.

EXERCISE 15.5 Reading with an Eye for Special Effects

E. M. Forster is known as a careful and correct stylist, yet he often deviates from the "correct" to create special effects. Look, for example, at the way he uses a comma splice in the following passage:

One of the evils of money is that it tempts us to look at it rather than at the things that it buys. They are dimmed because of the metal and the paper through which we receive them. That is the fundamental deceitfulness of riches, which kept worrying Christ. That is the treachery of the purse, the wallet and the bank-balance, even from the capitalist point of view. They were invented as a convenience to the flesh, they have become a chain for the spirit.

– E. M. FORSTER, "The Last Parade"

Forster uses a comma splice in the last sentence to emphasize parallel ideas; any conjunction, even *and,* would change the causal relationship he wishes to show. The effect is to stop us in our tracks as readers—because the grammar is unexpected, it attracts just the attention that Forster wants for his statement.

Look through some stories or essays to find some comma splices and fused sentences. Copy down one or two, including enough of the surrounding text to show context, and comment in writing on the effect they create.

EXERCISE 15.6 Taking Inventory: Comma Splices and Fused Sentences

Go through some essays you have written, checking for comma splices and fused sentences. Revise any you find, using one of the methods in this chapter. Comment on your chosen methods—in your writing log, if you are keeping one.

16

Recognizing Sentence Fragments

Sentence fragments are groups of words punctuated as sentences but lacking some element grammatically necessary to a sentence, usually either a subject or a finite verb. We see them sometimes in literary works used to add dramatic emphasis, to speed up rhythm, or to create realistic dialogue. For example:

> The history of England is the history of the male line, not of the female. Of our fathers we know always some fact, some distinction. They were soldiers or they were sailors; they filled that office or they made that law. But of our mothers, our grandmothers, our great-grandmothers, what remains? *Nothing but a tradition.* One was beautiful; one was red-haired; one was kissed by a Queen. We know nothing of them except their names and the dates of their marriages and the number of children they bore.
>
> — Virginia Woolf, "Women and Literature"

Nothing but a tradition. This fragment brings drama to Woolf's statement, arresting readers' attention in a way that a complete sentence would not, giving added emphasis to the word *nothing* and thus to Woolf's point.

Sentence fragments pose potential problems for you as a student writer, however, for although you will read them in literature, hear them in conversation, and see them everywhere in advertising, they are usually considered "errors" in most academic prose. This chapter will provide you with practice at recognizing and revising them.

EXERCISE 16.1

Look at the Toyota advertisement on p. 275. Go through it, identifying every sentence fragment. Then rewrite the advertisement, making all sentences complete. Finally, compare your version to the original, and to other classmates' versions. Which do you find most effective, and why?

BACKGROUND

Many instructors simply ban fragments outright. However, certain students will discover in their reading and writing just how effectively fragments can be used. In their research, Charles R. Kline, Jr., and W. Dean Memering quote fragments from a number of "formal" writings.

> "They then determined the number of these unrelated words and the sequence of words. 'The more words recalled, the less memory used to store the sentence. The fewer words recalled, the more memory used to store the sentence.' " — NOAM CHOMSKY, "Language and Mind"

> "Emily Dickinson's poems . . . are more authentically in the metaphysical tradition than Emerson's are. Not, however, that many of his values were not hers also— especially where they concerned the integrity of the mind and the sufficiency of inner resources." — F. O. MATTHIESEN, *American Renaissance*

What distinguishes these "professional" fragments from those of our students? Often nothing. Were teachers not so attuned to locating "errors" in student papers, they might find some fragments acceptable on rhetorical or stylistic grounds. Unacceptable fragments are those that (1) lack a close relationship to other sentences; (2) create noncontinuous thought; or (3) confuse the reader.

A writer is not someone who expresses his thoughts, his passion or his imagination in sentences but someone who thinks sentences. A Sentence-Thinker.
—ROLAND BARTHES

USEFUL READING

Kline, Charles R., Jr., and W. Dean Memering. "Formal Fragments: The English Minor Sentence." *Research in the Teaching of English* 11 (Fall 1977): 97–110. Rpt. in *Rhetoric and Composition: A Sourcebook for Teachers and Writers.* Ed. Richard L. Graves. Upper Montclair, NJ: Boynton, 1984. 148–61. Kline and Memering report that in their analysis of fifty books and magazines representing educated adult writers they found a wide variety of sentence fragments—none of which resulted in confusing or incoherent prose. They conclude that fragments that function effectively should be considered "minor sentences," and they offer a few general rules for the use of such sentences.

Noguchi, Rei R. *Grammar and the Teaching of Writing: Limits and Possibilities.* Urbana, IL: NCTE, 1991. Noguchi streamlines the teaching of grammar by focusing only on those problems that are amenable to instruction and by taking advantage of what all native speakers of English already know. Chapter 5 deals specifically with fragments.

➤ *Checking for sentence fragments*

If you have a tendency to write fragments, you should check for them in every piece of writing that you do. A group of words must meet the following three criteria to be a complete sentence. If it does not meet all three, it is a fragment and must be revised.

1. It must have a subject. (7c1)
2. It must have a finite verb, not just a verbal. (7c3)
3. Unless it is a question, it must have at least one clause that does *not* begin with a subordinating word. Some common subordinating words:

although	if	when
as	since	where
because	that	whether
before	though	who
how	unless	why

(For other subordinating words, see 7b3 for a list of relative pronouns and 7b7 for a list of subordinating conjunctions.)

Two methods of eliminating fragments

In general, a fragment can be revised by combining it with an independent clause or by turning it into an independent clause.

FRAGMENT	The beaver dam holding back the shallow pond.
REVISED	I saw the beaver dam holding back the shallow pond. [combined with independent clause *I saw*]
REVISED	The beaver dam was holding back the shallow pond. [turned into independent clause by adding *was* to participle *holding,* making verb finite]
FRAGMENT	Barely seven inches long, with nothing but a barrel, a handle, and a trigger.
REVISED	He was holding a gun barely seven inches long, with nothing but a barrel, a handle, and a trigger.
REVISED	It was barely seven inches long, with nothing but a barrel, a handle, and a trigger.

Everyday use

If you pay close attention to advertisements, you will find sentence fragments in frequent everyday use. Look, for instance, at an excerpt from a recent Toyota advertisement:

Our Lifetime Guarantee may come as a shock.

Or a strut. Or a muffler. Because once you pay to replace them, Toyota's Lifetime Guarantee covers parts and labor on any dealer-installed muffler, shock, or strut for as long as you own your Toyota! So if anything should ever go wrong, your Toyota dealer will fix it. Absolutely free.

Browse through a few magazines, or look at billboards and other signs, noting the use of fragments. Why do you think they are so often used in advertising? What effects do they create?

16a

Revising phrase fragments

Phrases, groups of words lacking either a subject, a finite verb, or both, appear frequently as fragments. Most common are verbal phrases, prepositional phrases, noun phrases, and appositive phrases.

Verbal-phrase fragments

A verbal phrase includes a gerund, an infinitive, a present participle, or a past participle, and any objects or modifiers (see 7c3). Verbal-phrase fragments lack a finite verb and often a subject. To revise, combine them with an independent clause or make them a separate sentence.

FRAGMENT	Vivian stayed out of school for three months after Laurel was born. *To recuperate and to take care of her.*
REVISED	Vivian stayed out of school for three months after Laurel was born to recuperate and to take care of her. [combined with independent clause]
REVISED	Vivian stayed out of school for three months after Laurel was born. She did so to recuperate and to take care of her. [turned into complete sentence]

TEACHING PRACTICE

As rhetorical devices, sentence fragments should not be overused lest they lose their effect. But, first of all, students need to be able to recognize unacceptable sentence fragments, those discontinuous ones that confuse the reader. Introduce the ineffective fragment to them by speaking to them in fragments: "Today. Chapter 16. Frequently used. Understand?" Naturally, your students won't know what you mean and will try to get more information from you. Write what you said on the board. Eventually, your students will tell you that your statements are incomplete. Then, drop your mask and announce that they've just given you the definition of "sentence fragment." Ask them to complete your statements. Once they demonstrate their ability to recognize and revise unacceptable fragments, introduce the concept of acceptable "nonsentences." On the board, write this famous quote from Mark Twain: "Man is the only animal that blushes. Or needs to." Ask your students to "correct" this fragment, no doubt an easy task for them: "Man is the only animal that blushes or needs to." Some of your students may be bothered by this revision and may suggest other forms of punctuation in an attempt to recapture the emphasis lost in the revision, while others may be content. You may want to ask what is wrong with the original. Is it confusing? Does the second part connect with the preceding sentence? Were they bothered or confused when they first read it?

From here, you can explain the difference between acceptable and unacceptable fragments, emphasizing the criteria of clarity and continuity. Point out that fragments of any kind should be used rarely and that acceptable fragments do not validate those that should be corrected.

BACKGROUND

What is a sentence? In *A Dictionary of Modern English Usage,* H. W. Fowler claims that modern writers "show greater freedom than was once customary" and that the word *sentence* has "broken the bounds" once set for it (546). He lists ten definitions for *sentence,* the first seven "popular," the eighth and ninth grammatical, and the tenth a combination of the two:

1. A group of words followed by a pause and revealing an intelligible purpose.

2. A group of words which makes sense.

3. A combination of words which is complete as expressing a thought.

4. A collection of words of such kind and arranged in such manner as to make complete sense.

5. A meaningful group of words that is grammatically independent.

6. A complete and independent unit of communication, the completeness and independence being shown by its capability of standing alone, i.e., of being uttered by itself.

7. A group of words, or in some cases a single word, which makes a statement, or a command (or expression of wish), or a question or an exclamation.

8. A number of words making a complete grammatical structure.

9. A combination of words that contains at least one subject and one predicate.

10. A set of words complete in itself, having either expressed or understood in it a subject or question or command or exclamation; if its subject or predicate or verb (or more) is understood, it is an elliptical sentence.

Prepositional-phrase fragments

A prepositional phrase consists of a preposition, its object, and any modifiers of the object (see 7c3). Prepositional-phrase fragments contain neither subjects nor finite verbs. Usually you can best revise them by simply joining them to the independent clause containing the word they modify.

FRAGMENT	Several civic groups are sponsoring public debates. *With discussions afterward.*
REVISED	Several civic groups are sponsoring public debates with discussions afterward.

Noun-phrase fragments

A noun phrase consists of a noun together with any adjectives, phrases, or clauses that modify it (see 7c3). Noun-phrase fragments contain a subject but no finite verb, and they frequently appear before fragments containing a verb but no subject. You can best revise such fragments by combining them into one sentence containing both a subject *and* a verb.

FRAGMENTS	*His editorial making a plea for better facilities for severely handicapped children. Pointed out that these facilities are always located in poor areas.*
REVISED	In his editorial making a plea for better facilities for severely handicapped children, he pointed out that these facilities are always located in poor areas.
REVISED	His editorial making a plea for better facilities for severely handicapped children pointed out that these facilities are always located in poor areas.

Appositive-phrase fragments

An appositive phrase is a noun phrase that renames or describes another noun (see 7c3). You can revise appositive-phrase fragments by joining them to the independent clause containing the noun to which the appositive phrase refers.

FRAGMENT	One of our nation's most cherished dreams may be in danger. *The dream of a good education for every child.*
REVISED	One of our nation's most cherished dreams, the dream of a good education for every child, may be in danger.
REVISED	One of our nation's dreams may be in danger: the dream of a good education for every child. [In this revision, the use of the colon creates greater emphasis.]

16b

Revising compound-predicate fragments

A compound predicate consists of two or more verbs, along with their modifiers and objects, that have the same subject (see 7c2). Compound-predicate fragments occur when one part of this predicate is punctuated as a separate sentence although it lacks a subject. These fragments usually begin with a conjunction. You can revise them by attaching them to the independent clause that contains the rest of the predicate.

FRAGMENT   They sold their house. *And moved into an apartment.*

REVISED   They sold their house and moved into an apartment.

EXERCISE 16.2

Revise each of the following items to eliminate any sentence fragments, either by combining fragments with independent clauses or by rewriting them as separate sentences. Example:

Zoe looked close to tears. Standing with her head bowed.

Standing with her head bowed, Zoe looked close to tears.

Zoe looked close to tears. She was standing with her head bowed.

1. Small, long-veined, fuzzy green leaves. Add to the appeal of this newly developed variety of carrot.
2. Living with gusto. That is what many Americans yearn for.
3. The region has dry, sandy soil. Blown into strange formations by the ever-present wind.
4. The climbers had two choices. To go over a four-hundred-foot cliff or to turn back. They decided to make the attempt.
5. Connie picked up the cat and started playing with it. It scratched her neck. With its sharp little claws.
6. Bush promoted one tax change. A reduction in the capital gains tax.
7. Trying to carry a portfolio, art box, illustration boards, and drawing pads. I must have looked ridiculous.
8. Organized crime has been able to attract graduates just as big business has. With good pay and the best equipment money can buy.
9. The workers sanded the floors. And installed the appliances.
10. Wollstonecraft believed in universal public education. Also, in education that forms the heart and strengthens the body.

EXERCISE 16.2: Suggested Answers

1. Small, long-veined, fuzzy green leaves add to the appeal of this newly developed variety of carrot.
2. Many Americans yearn to live with gusto.
3. The region has dry, sandy soil, blown into strange formations by the ever-present wind.
4. The climbers had two choices: to go over a four-hundred-foot cliff or to turn back. They decided to make the attempt.
5. Connie picked up the cat and started playing with it. It scratched her neck with its sharp little claws.
6. Bush promoted one tax change in particular: a reduction in the capital gains tax.
7. I must have looked ridiculous trying to carry a portfolio, art box, illustration boards, and drawing pads.
8. Offering good pay and the best equipment money can buy, organized crime has been able to attract graduates just as big business has.
9. The workers sanded the floors and installed the appliances.
10. Wollstonecraft believed in universal public education and in education that forms the heart and strengthens the body.

TEACHING PRACTICE

When speaking impromptu, President George Bush has often shown a tendency to speak in sentence fragments, characteristically omitting subjects—so much so that replicating this syntactic habit is a standard device of comedians and cariacaturists lampooning him. If you point this out to students, some may reply that it shows you can use fragments and still become president; perhaps the only response to this is that if you do both, a lot of people will make jokes about your speech patterns.

EXERCISE 16.3: Suggested Answers

1. *subordinate-clause fragment.* When Rick was in the fifth grade, his parents often left him with his sister.

2. *verbal-phrase fragment.* The protagonist comes to a decision to leave his family.

3. *noun-phrase fragment.* Fear is one of the basic emotions people have experienced throughout time.

4. *prepositional-phrase fragment.* We were thankful for a hot shower after a week in the wilderness.

5. *relative-clause fragment.* I plan to buy a computer, which will help me organize my finances.

6. *appositive-phrase fragment.* Forster stopped writing novels after *A Passage to India,* one of the greatest novels of the twentieth century.

7. *verbal-phrase fragment.* This battery never runs out of water, eliminating the possibility of ruined clothing from battery acid.

8. *compound-predicate fragment.* I loved *Beloved* and thought Toni Morrison deserved the Pulitzer prize.

9. *relative-clause fragment.* The president appointed five members who drew up a set of bylaws.

10. *subordinate-clause fragment.* Because the younger generation often rejects the ways of its elders, one might say that rebellion is normal.

16c

Revising dependent-clause fragments

Unlike phrases, dependent clauses contain both a subject and a finite verb. Because they *depend* upon an independent clause to complete their meaning, however, they cannot stand alone as grammatically complete sentences (see 7c4). Such clauses usually begin with a subordinating conjunction—such as *after, even though, if, whereas* (see 7b7)—or a relative pronoun—such as *who, which, that* (see 7b3). You can usually revise dependent clause fragments by either combining the dependent clause with the independent clause that precedes or follows it, or by deleting the subordinating word to create an independent clause.

FRAGMENT	*If a woman chooses a less demanding career track.* She sacrifices some earning potential.
REVISED	If a woman chooses a less demanding career track, she sacrifices some earning potential.
FRAGMENT	Eudora Welty grew up in Mississippi. *Whereas Alice Walker's childhood was spent in Georgia.*
REVISED	Eudora Welty grew up in Mississippi, whereas Alice Walker's childhood was spent in Georgia.
FRAGMENT	Injuries in automobile accidents occur in two ways. *When an occupant is hurt by something inside the car, or when an occupant is thrown from the car.*
REVISED	Injuries in automobile accidents occur in two ways: when an occupant is hurt by something inside the car, or when an occupant is thrown from the car.
REVISED	Injuries in automobile accidents occur in two ways. An occupant is hurt by something inside the car, or an occupant is thrown from the car.

EXERCISE 16.3

Identify all of the sentence fragments in the following items, and explain why each is grammatically incomplete. Then revise each one in at least two ways.

> *Controlling my temper. That has been one of my goals this year.*
> *Controlling my temper has been one of my goals this year.*
> *One of my goals this year has been controlling my temper.*

1. When Rick was in the fifth grade. His parents often left him with his sister.

2. The protagonist comes to a decision. To leave his family.

3. Fear, one of the basic emotions people have experienced throughout time.

4. We were thankful for a hot shower. After a week in the wilderness.

5. I plan to buy a computer. Which will help me organize my finances.

6. Forster stopped writing novels after *A Passage to India*. One of the greatest novels of the twentieth century.

7. This battery never runs out of water. Eliminating the possibility of ruined clothing from battery acid.

8. I loved *Beloved*. And thought Toni Morrison deserved the Pulitzer Prize.

9. The president appointed five members. Who drew up a set of bylaws.

10. One might say that rebellion is normal. Because the younger generation often rejects the ways of its elders.

EXERCISE 16.4   Reading with an Eye for Fragments

Identify the fragments in the passage below. What effect does Angelou achieve by using fragments rather than complete sentences?

Every child I knew had learned [the Negro national anthem] with his ABCs, along with "Jesus Loves Me This I Know." But I personally had never heard it before. Never heard the words, despite the thousands of times I had sung them. Never thought they had anything to do with me.
— MAYA ANGELOU, *I Know Why the Caged Bird Sings*

EXERCISE 16.5   Taking Inventory: Fragments

Read through some essays you have written. Using the guidelines on p. 274, see if you find any sentence fragments. If you find any, can you recognize any patterns? Do you write fragments when you're attempting to add emphasis? Are they all dependent clauses? phrases? Note any patterns you discover (in your writing log, if you keep one), and make a point of checking your writing for them routinely. Finally, revise any fragments you found to form complete sentences.

EXERCISE 16.4: Answers will vary.

TEACHING PRACTICE

To help your students better understand the role of context in determining the acceptability of comma splices and sentence fragments, bring in texts from outside the classroom as bases for exercises. Advertisements are a prime source, as are song lyrics. Rap lyrics are especially interesting in this regard, as they often contain a range of constructions, from extremely long and elaborate sentences to the briefest fragments. Ask students to identify and revise the sentence-level "errors" in the ads or lyrics and discuss the effects of punctuation in the originals and the revisions.

FOR COLLABORATIVE WORK

Ask students to bring to class any essays in which they find fragments. Choose several fragments, and put them on the board for class discussion. Ask students to identify the missing element in each and then, after supplying necessary context from the essay, to decide on the *best* means of revision.

17

Placing Modifiers Appropriately

Modifiers—adjectives, adverbs, and the various kinds of phrases and clauses used as adjectives and adverbs—enrich writing by making it more concrete, vivid, and memorable. As a writer, you want to take full advantage of them. Look, for example, at the following sentence:

> She wore the kind of clothes he liked, simple, unadorned and yet completely feminine, white gloves on Sundays, small black leather pocketbooks, carefully polished shoes, pretty small hats, a feather the only gay note on her best felt hat, and the seams in her stockings always straight.
> — ANN PETRY, *The Narrows*

This sentence could have stopped after the first clause: "She wore the kind of clothes he liked." Everything that follows is built on modifiers, and it is the modifiers that bring the sentence to life and help readers picture the clothes she wore.

To be effective, modifiers must be carefully placed and must refer clearly and unambiguously to some word or words in the sentence. In the above sentence, for example, *completely* modifies *feminine;* if it were placed elsewhere in the sentence, we would have a different statement: "completely unadorned and yet feminine," perhaps. And look at the difference if *only* were placed somewhere else: white gloves "only on Sundays," for instance—or even "only white gloves on Sundays"!

Columnist James J. Kilpatrick recently offered this humorous and enlightening demonstration of just how many ways the modifier *only* could be placed. He started with the sentence *She told me that she loved me.*

> Let us count the ways:
>
> *Only she told me that she loved me.* No one else has told me that.
> *She only told me that she loved me.* She did not provide any evidence of her love—she only told me about it.

She told only me that she loved me. Not the gabby type.

She told me only that she loved me. Pretty closemouthed. She had nothing more to say.

She told me that only she loved me. The lady is claiming exclusive rights.

She told me that she only loved me. She doesn't adore me, worship me, idolize me. She only loves me.

She told me that she loved me only. Ahhhh!

— JAMES J. KILPATRICK

We often see modifiers used ineffectively, however, even in the work of professional writers, for they are among the most difficult things to spot when editing. This chapter will examine three types of problem modifiers—misplaced, disruptive, and dangling—and ways of revising them.

EXERCISE 17.1

EXERCISE 17.1: Answers will vary.

Maya Angelou relies heavily on modifiers in the following description of herself at an awkward age.

I was too tall and raw-skinny. My large extroverted teeth protruded in an excitement to be seen, and I, attempting to thwart their success, rarely smiled. Although I lathered Dixie Peach in my hair, the thick black mass crinkled and kinked and resisted the smothering pomade to burst free around my head like a cloud of angry bees.

— MAYA ANGELOU, *Singin' and Swingin' and Gettin' Merry Like Christmas*

Think for a few minutes about some of the awkward stages you remember going through. Brainstorm a bit by completing these thoughts: "I was too . . ." or "What I remember most about being fifteen was . . ." Spend ten minutes or so writing a brief description about yourself then. Underline all the words you recognize as modifiers, then revise your passage by eliminating them all. Compare the two versions, and think about what modifiers add to your writing.

17a

Revising misplaced modifiers

Misplaced modifiers are words, phrases, and clauses that cause ambiguity or confusion because they are not placed as close to the words they modify as they might be or because they could modify the words either before or after them.

Where to use only *in a sentence is a moot question, one of the mootest questions in all rhetoric. The purist will say the expression "He only died last week" is incorrect, and that it should be "He died only last week." The purist's contention is that the first sentence, if carried out to a natural conclusion, would give us something like this: "He only died last week; he didn't do anything else; that's all he did." It isn't a natural conclusion, however, because nobody would say that. . . . The best way is often to omit* only *and use some other expression. Thus . . . one could say: "It was no longer ago than last Thursday that George L. Wodolgoffing became an angel."*

—JAMES THURBER

BACKGROUND

Although it is most clear to place a modifier either directly before or after the words it modifies, there are exceptions. For example, another possibility for the sample sentence could be: *I could hear the tumbleweeds rustling in the wind softly.* Sometimes, the writer's *emphasis* or *sense of rhythm* or *intention* determines the syntactic placement of the modifier in a sentence.

USEFUL READING

Williams, Joseph M. *Style: Ten Lessons in Clarity and Grace.* 3rd ed. Glenview, IL: Scott, 1989. See pp. 140–44, "Some Problems with Modifiers," where Williams discusses dangling and misplaced modifiers.

Everyday use

You will find modifiers in abundance at your local grocery store, urging you to choose fresh *strawberries,* new and improved *dishwashing liquid,* low-cholesterol *ice cream,* range-fed *chickens,* recyclable *paper products. The next time you go shopping, spend a few moments jotting down some of the more colorful or memorable modifiers you see and then bring them to class for discussion. What is the primary function of these modifiers—to provide information, to make the product sound more appealing, or something else?*

1

Misplaced words and phrases

In the sentence *Softly I could hear the tumbleweeds rustling in the wind,* the adverb *softly* seems to modify *could hear.* Yet the writer obviously meant it to modify *rustling* (because one cannot hear "softly"). Such confusion can be avoided by placing a modifier close to the word or words to which it actually refers.

I could hear the tumbleweeds *softly* rustling in the wind.

I could hear the tumbleweeds rustling *softly* in the wind.

Be especially careful with the placement of **limiting modifiers** like *almost, even, hardly, just, merely, nearly, only, scarcely,* and *simply.* In general, these modifiers should be placed right before the words they modify. As the example from James J. Kilpatrick on pp. 280–81 makes clear, putting such words in other positions may produce not just ambiguity but a completely different meaning. For example:

AMBIGUOUS	The court only hears civil cases on Tuesdays.
CLEAR	The court hears *only* civil cases on Tuesdays.
CLEAR	The court hears civil cases *only* on Tuesdays.

In the first sentence, placing *only* before the verb makes the meaning ambiguous. Does the writer mean that civil cases are the only cases heard on Tuesdays, or that those are the only days when civil cases are heard? The other sentences each express one of these meanings clearly.

Phrases also should ordinarily be placed close to the words they modify. The most common type of phrase modifier, the prepositional phrase, usually appears right after the word it modifies. In the following sentences, note how misplaced prepositional phrases cause confusion.

MISPLACED   The runners stood ignoring the crowd in their lanes. [This sentence implies that the crowd were in the lanes.]

REVISED   The runners *stood in their lanes* ignoring the crowd.

MISPLACED   She teaches a seminar this term on voodoo at Skyline College. [Surely the voodoo was not at the college.]

REVISED   She teaches *a seminar on voodoo* this term at Skyline College.

Participial phrases usually appear right before or after the words they modify. See how misplacing these phrases can lead to confusion:

MISPLACED   I pointed out the moose head to my guests mounted on the wall. [This sentence implies that the guests were mounted on the wall.]

REVISED   I pointed out the *moose head mounted on the wall* to my guests.

REVISED   I pointed out to my guests the *moose head mounted on the wall.*

MISPLACED   Billowing from every window, we saw clouds of smoke. [People cannot billow from windows.]

REVISED   We saw *clouds of smoke billowing from every window.*

2

Misplaced clauses

While you have more flexibility in the placement of dependent clauses than of modifying words and phrases, you should still try whenever possible to place them close to whatever you wish them to modify. If you do not, unintended meanings can result.

MISPLACED   The trees trimmed in the shapes of animals that line the walks delight visitors. [Do animals line the walks?]

REVISED   The *trees that line the walks* are trimmed in the shapes of animals and delight visitors.

MISPLACED   Nixon told reporters that he planned to get out of politics after he lost the 1962 gubernatorial race. [The sentence implies that Nixon planned to lose the race.]

REVISED   *After he lost the 1962 gubernatorial race,* Nixon told reporters that he planned to get out of politics.

EXERCISE 17.2: Suggested Answers

1. The audience applauded the comedian's slick and professional routine.
2. The city spent almost $2 million on the new stadium that opened last year.
3. On the day in question, the patient was not able to breathe normally.
4. The clothes that I was giving away were full of holes.
5. Elderly people and students live in the neighborhood full of identical tract houses which surrounds the university.
6. Doctors recommend a new, painless test for cancer.
7. In my mind, I went through the process of taxiing and taking off.
8. Before I decided to buy the stock, I knew the investment would pay off dramatically.
9. The bank offered flood insurance underwritten by the federal government to the homeowners.
10. The maintenance worker shut down the turbine that was revolving out of control.

EXERCISE 17.3: Suggested Answers

1. He vividly remembered enjoying the sound of Mrs. McIntosh singing. He remembered enjoying vividly the sound of Mrs. McIntosh singing.
2. The mayor promised that after her reelection she would not raise taxes. After her reelection, the mayor promised that she would not raise taxes.
3. The collector who originally owned the painting planned to leave it to a museum. The collector who owned the painting planned originally to leave it to a museum.
4. Doctors can now restore limbs that have been partially severed to functioning condition. Doctors can now restore limbs that have been severed to partially functioning condition.

EXERCISE 17.2

Revise each of the following sentences by moving any misplaced modifiers so that they clearly modify the words they are intended to. Example:

Aliens│are exploited by employers╱who are afraid of being deported│

1. Slick and professional, the audience applauded the comedian's routine.
2. The city almost spent $2 million on the new stadium that opened last year.
3. On the day in question, the patient was not normally able to breathe.
4. The clothes were full of holes that I was giving away.
5. Elderly people and students live in the neighborhood surrounding the university, which is full of identical tract houses.
6. Doctors recommend a new test for cancer, which is painless.
7. I went through the process of taxiing and taking off in my mind.
8. I knew that the investment would pay off in a dramatic way before I decided to buy the stock.
9. The bank offered flood insurance to the homeowners underwritten by the federal government.
10. Revolving out of control, the maintenance worker shut down the turbine.

3

Squinting modifiers

If a modifier could refer to *either* the word(s) before it *or* the word(s) after it, it is called a **squinting modifier**. For example:

SQUINTING   Students who practice writing *often* will benefit.

The modifier *often* might describe either *practice* or *will benefit*. That is, the sentence might have either of the following meanings:

REVISED   Students who *often practice* writing will benefit.
REVISED   Students who practice writing *will often* benefit.

If a sentence could be read more than one way because of your placement of a modifier, put the modifier where it clearly relates to only a single term.

EXERCISE 17.3

Revise each of the following sentences in at least two ways by moving the squinting modifier so that it unambiguously modifies either the word(s) before it or the word(s) after it. Example:

The course we hoped would engross us completely bored us.

The course we hoped would completely engross us bored us.

The course we hoped would engross us bored us completely.

1. He remembered vividly enjoying the sound of Mrs. McIntosh singing.
2. The mayor promised after her reelection she would not raise taxes.
3. The collector who owned the painting originally planned to leave it to a museum.
4. Doctors can now restore limbs that have been severed partially to functioning condition.
5. The speaker said when he finished his talk he would answer questions.

17b

Revising disruptive modifiers

Whereas misplaced modifiers confuse readers by appearing to modify the wrong word(s), **disruptive modifiers** cause problems because they interrupt the connections between parts of a grammatical structure or a sentence, making it hard for readers to follow the progress of the thought. Be careful not to place modifiers in such a way that they disrupt the normal grammatical flow of a sentence.

1

Modifiers splitting an infinitive

In general, do not split an infinitive by placing a modifier between the *to* and the verb. Doing so makes it hard for readers to recognize that the two go together.

DISRUPTIVE   Hitler expected the British to fairly quickly surrender.

REVISED   Hitler expected the British *to surrender* fairly quickly.

In some cases, however, a modifier sounds awkward in any position other than between the parts of the infinitive. To avoid a split infinitive in such cases, it may be best to reword the sentence to eliminate the infinitive altogether.

SPLIT   I hope this year *to* almost *equal* my last year's income.

REWRITTEN   I hope that this year I will earn almost as much as I did last year.

5. The speaker said he would answer questions when he finished his talk. When he finished his talk, the speaker said he would answer questions.

TEACHING PRACTICE

You may want to share the following examples of dangling, misplaced, and disruptive modifiers with your students:

1. Retrieving the duck, Kevin knew he could become a trainer.
2. I ate a hamburger wearing my tuxedo.
3. Soft and mushy, Albert baked a banana cake.
4. Big and noisy, Tom ran for his life away from the street gang.
5. Hanging from the telephone pole, Sally could not retrieve her kite.

You might have students work in small groups to see if they can deliberately generate some funny or ludicrous examples of their own.

2

Modifiers between the parts of a verb phrase

A verb phrase consists of a main verb together with one or more auxiliary verbs: *had studied, will be moving* (see 7c3). Modifiers consisting of one or even two or three adverbs can often appear between parts of a verb phrase without causing awkwardness: *He had very seldom actually fired a gun in the line of duty.* In general, however, do not interrupt a verb phrase with modifiers that are phrases or clauses.

DISRUPTIVE	Vegetables will, if they are cooked too long, lose most of their nutritional value.
REVISED	Vegetables *will lose* most of their nutritional value if they are cooked too long.
REVISED	If they are cooked too long, vegetables *will lose* most of their nutritional value.

3

Modifiers between a subject and verb

Adjective phrases and clauses often appear between a subject and verb: *The books that the librarians had decided were no longer useful were discarded.* In general, however, do not use an adverb clause or phrase in this position, because it disrupts the natural progression from subject to verb that readers expect.

DISRUPTIVE	The books, because the librarians had decided they were no longer useful, were discarded.
REVISED	The *books were discarded* because the librarians had decided they were no longer useful.

4

Modifiers between a verb and an object or subject complement

In general, do not place an adverb phrase or clause between a verb and a direct object or subject complement, because readers expect the object or complement to follow directly after the verb.

DISRUPTIVE	He bought with his first paycheck a secondhand car.
REVISED	He *bought a secondhand car* with his first paycheck.
REVISED	With his first paycheck, he *bought a secondhand car.*

EXERCISE 17.4

Revise each of the following sentences by moving the disruptive modifier so that the sentence reads smoothly. Example:

> *Rock festivals became/during the 1960s a form of political protest.*

1. Eastern North America was, when Europeans arrived, covered in forest.
2. The exhibit, because of extensive publicity, attracted large audiences.
3. The architect wanted to eventually design public buildings.
4. Bookstores sold, in the first week after publication, fifty thousand copies.
5. The singer had because of illness canceled her concert.

17c

Revising dangling modifiers

Dangling modifiers are words (usually adverbs), phrases (prepositional or participial), and elliptical clauses (clauses from which a word or words have been left out) that modify nothing in particular in the rest of a sentence. They often seem to modify something that is suggested or implied but not actually present in the sentence. Such modifiers are called dangling because they hang loosely from the rest of the sentence, attached to no specific element. They frequently appear at the beginnings or ends of sentences.

To revise dangling modifiers, you can change the subject of the main clause so that the modifier clearly refers to it, or you can change the dangling modifier itself into a phrase or a nonelliptical clause that clearly modifies an existing part of the sentence.

1

Dangling words and phrases

DANGLING	Reluctantly, the basset hound was given away to a neighbor. [Was the dog reluctant, or someone else who's not mentioned?]
REVISED	Reluctantly, *the family* gave away the basset hound to a neighbor.

DANGLING	As a young boy, his grandmother told stories of her years as a country schoolteacher. [His grandmother was never a young boy.]
REVISED	*As a young boy, he* heard his grandmother tell stories of her years as a country schoolteacher.
REVISED	*When he was a young boy,* his grandmother told stories of her years as a country schoolteacher.
DANGLING	Thumbing through the magazine, my eyes automatically noticed the perfume ads. [Eyes cannot thumb through magazines.]
REVISED	*In thumbing through the magazine,* I automatically noticed the perfume ads.
REVISED	My eyes automatically noticed the perfume ads *as I was thumbing through the magazine.*

EXERCISE 17.5

Revise each of the following sentences to correct the dangling phrases. Example:

   a viewer gets
Watching television news, ^ *an impression* ~~is given~~ *of constant disaster.*

1. High ratings are pursued by emphasizing fires and murders.
2. Interviewing grieving relatives, no consideration is shown for their privacy.
3. To provide comic relief, heat waves and blizzards are attributed to the weather forecaster.
4. Chosen for their looks, the newscasters' journalistic credentials are often weak.
5. As a visual medium, complex issues are hard to present in a televised format.

EXERCISE 17.5: Suggested Answers

1. Television news producers pursue high ratings by emphasizing fires and murders.
2. When interviewing grieving relatives, reporters show no consideration for their privacy.
3. To provide comic relief, newscasters attribute heat waves and blizzards to the weather forecaster.
4. Chosen for their looks, newscasters often have weak journalistic credentials.
5. As a visual medium, the televised format is not suited for presenting complex issues.

BACKGROUND

Cornelia and Bergen Evans tell us that the rule against the dangling modifier must sometimes be broken. In *A Dictionary of Contemporary American Usage* (New York: Random, 1957, 354–55), they discuss two types of participial phrases that are exceptions. First of all, some participles are often used independently either as prepositions or conjunctions: *concerning, regarding, providing, owing to, excepting,* and *failing.* Frequently, an unattached participle is meant to apply indefinitely to anyone or everyone, as in *Facing north, there is a large mountain on the right* and *Looking at the subject dispassionately, what evidence is there?* Constructed any other way, these idiomatic statements would seem unnatural and cumbersome.

2

Dangling elliptical clauses

DANGLING	A rabbit's teeth are never used for defense even when cornered. [Is it the teeth that are cornered?]
REVISED	*Even when cornered, a rabbit* never uses its teeth for defense.
REVISED	A rabbit's teeth are never used for defense, *even when the animal is cornered.*

DANGLING	Although a reserved and private man, everyone who met him seemed to like him. [The elliptical clause cannot refer to *everyone*.]
REVISED	*Although he was a reserved and private man*, everyone who met him seemed to like him.
REVISED	*Although a reserved and private man*, he seemed to be liked by everyone who met him.

EXERCISE 17.6

Revise each of the following sentences to correct any dangling elliptical clauses. Example:

 I was impressed by
While cycling through southern France, the Roman ruins ~~impressed me.~~

1. However unhappy, my part-time job is something I have to put up with.
2. While attending a performance at Ford's Theater, Booth shot Lincoln.
3. A waiter's job can become very stressful when faced with a busy restaurant full of hungry people.
4. Dreams are somewhat like a jigsaw puzzle; if put together in the correct order, organization and coherence become obvious.
5. No matter how costly, my family insists on a college education.

 Checking for misplaced or dangling modifiers

1. Identify all the modifying words, phrases, and clauses in each sentence, and draw an arrow from each modifier to the word it modifies.
2. If a modifier is far from what it modifies, try to move the two closer together.
3. Then check to see if any modifier could be misunderstood to refer to a word other than the one it is intended to modify. If so, move the modifier so that it refers clearly to only the intended word.
4. If you cannot find a word to which the modifier refers, revise the sentence to supply such a word, or revise the modifier itself so that it clearly refers to a word already in the sentence.

EXERCISE 17.6: Suggested Answers

1. However unhappy I am with my part-time job, I have to put up with it.
2. While attending a performance at Ford's Theatre, Lincoln was shot by John Wilkes Booth.
3. When waiters are faced with a busy restaurant full of hungry people, their jobs can become very stressful.
4. Dreams are somewhat like a jigsaw puzzle; when put together in the correct order, both dreams and puzzles have organization and coherence.
5. No matter how costly a college education may be, my family insists on it.

OPTIONAL EXERCISE

Have students revise each of the following sentences to eliminate the dangler (1) by providing a subject that tells who or what is being modified; (2) by rewording. One sentence is correct.

1. Diving into the lake, Bev's head struck the raft.
2. To be considered for a teaching job, your references must be top-notch.
3. Listening to the album, we forgot our worries.
4. Found guilty, the judge dismissed him.
5. At the age of two, my dad took me and my mom with him to Texas.

EXERCISE 17.7: Answers will vary.

OPTIONAL EXERCISE

Ask students to revise the following passage to eliminate any misplaced, disruptive, or dangling modifiers.

One day last December, before going to class, a blizzard forced the administration to, for the first time anyone could remember, announce that all classes would be until further notice suspended. After leaving the dorm, the first thing that we noticed was the silence. The snow that had been falling all night steadily covered the ground. Being the last day of the semester, we weren't very worried about classes, so we "arranged," with another dormitory, a snowball fight. While building up a stock of good snowballs near Lord Hall, our jackets began to get oppressively warm. Eventually, we peeled down to shirt sleeves, ready for a fight. The central lawn became the battleground for the great Stoke-Lord Snowball Fight, where the Stoke Hall people finally set up their forts. Our piles of snowballs almost reached the tops of our forts, which were well-packed and handy to be picked up and thrown. At last both sides were ready, and the first snowball flew through the air from the "Stoke stack." The bombardment was for a while fierce and deadly. I learned that when throwing a snowball, the standing position is very risky, getting a hard one in the mouth. Finally, having almost thrown all of our snowballs, the Stoke charge was met and resisted. The timing was measured with great accuracy, being sure not to countercharge until we saw that Stoke was low on snowballs. Then we all ran toward the enemy carrying three or four snowballs each and routed them.

EXERCISE 17.7 Reading with an Eye for Modifiers

E. B. White was a master of precise wording, choosing—and positioning—his words with great care. Read the following sentences by White, paying attention to the limiting modifiers italicized in each one. Identify which word or words each one modifies. Then try moving the modifier to some other spot in the sentence and consider how the meaning of the sentence changes as a result.

1. When we got back for a swim before lunch, the lake was exactly where we had left it, the same number of inches from the dock, and there was *only* the merest suggestion of a breeze.   – "Once More to the Lake"

2. Most of the time she *simply* rode in a standing position, well aft on the beast, her hands hanging easily at her sides, her head erect, her straw-colored ponytail lightly brushing her shoulders, the blood of exertion showing faintly through the tan of her skin.   – "The Ring of Time"

3. *Even* our new shoes seemed to be working out all right and weren't hurting much.   – "Twins"

4. It was, among other things, the sort of railroad you would occasionally ride *just* for the hell of it, a higher existence into which you would escape unconsciously and without hesitation.   – "Progress and Change"

EXERCISE 17.8 Taking Inventory: Modifiers

Look at two pages of a draft (or refer back to the description of yourself you did in Exercise 17.1), examining them for clear and effective modifiers. Can you identify any misplaced, disruptive, or dangling modifiers? Using the guidelines in this chapter, revise as need be. Then look for patterns—in the kinds of modifiers you use and in any problems you have placing them. Make a note of what you find—in your writing log, if you keep one.

18

Maintaining Consistent and Complete Grammatical Structures

About fifteen years ago, a writing instructor who had studied thousands of student essays came to a simple but profound conclusion about many of the sentences in them. Though at first glance the sentences seemed incoherent or nonsensical, they actually fell into certain patterns. They could be better characterized, the instructor decided, either as (1) unsuccessful attempts to combine sentence structures that did not fit together grammatically or sensibly or as (2) sentences missing some element necessary to complete meaning. In fact, many writers who produce garbled sentences do so in an attempt to use and master complex and sophisticated structures. What look like "errors," then, may be stepping stones on a writer's way to greater stylistic maturity. This chapter will provide practice in recognizing such mixed or incomplete structures and, more important, in revising or building on them.

18a

Making grammatical patterns consistent

In writing, inconsistent structures can pose problems for both writers and readers. One such inconsistency, a **mixed structure**, results from beginning a sentence with one grammatical pattern and then switching to another one. The following sentence, for instance, starts out one way and ends another.

MIXED   The fact that I get up at 5 A.M., which explains why I'm always tired in the evenings.

The sentence starts out with a subject (*fact*) followed by a dependent clause (*that I get up at 5 A.M.*). This structure should lead into a predicate to

BACKGROUND

In "The Uses—and Limits—of Grammar," Sarah D'Eloia explains "syntactically tangled sentences" as inconsistent and incomplete sentences that confuse the reader and that cannot be rhetorically justified in normal prose. Thus, these garbled sentences are the results of experiments in "logical and grammatical subordination, differential relation, and equivalence" (228), which students write for several reasons: (1) not knowing the "right" word or syntactic structure, the student may turn to the familiar (but inappropriate); (2) the student tries to juggle a number of subordinations at once; (3) unsure of the choice, the student may allow the alternatives to "contaminate" his or her decision; (4) the student lacks the academic self-confidence necessary to produce syntactically complex structures; (5) the student is unaware of the benefits that come with revision. Unfortunately, some of the most outgoing and sociable students lack confidence in academic situations: they do not believe their knowledge or opinions warrant development; their syntax is often tentative and qualifying. Worse, many of these students believe that "real" writers get it right the first time. When Mina Shaughnessy's writing students saw the messy pages of Richard Wright's novel *Native Son*, they concluded that Wright was not a good writer—he made too many mistakes.

FOR COLLABORATIVE WORK

We want our students to produce clear and consistent texts, yet we ask them to appreciate texts—canonized essays and stories—that often do not incorporate those same qualities. Critically acclaimed writer Toni Cade Bambara, for instance, frequently uses sentence structures that fall short of our classroom standards. Ask your students to listen for purpose and effect as you read aloud the following passage from "My Man Bovanne," a story of a woman and a blind man at a benefit dance. Then ask them to work in groups to revise the passage according to Edited American English. Did they improve the text? interfere with it? What were the specific effects of their revisions?

> But right away Joe Lee come up on us and frown for dancin so close to the man. My own son who knows what kind of warm I am about; and don't grown men all call me long distance and in the middle of the night for a little Mama comfort? But he frown. Which ain't right since Bovanne can't see and defend himself. Just a nice old man who fixes toasters and busted irons . . . and changes the lock on my door when my men friends get messy. Nice man. Which is not why they invited him. Grass roots you see. Me and Sister Taylor and the woman who does heads at Mamies and the man from the barber shop, we all there on account of we grass roots. And I ain't never been souther than Brooklyn Battery and no more country than the window box on my fire escape. And just yesterday my kids tellin me to take them countrified rags off my head and be cool. And now can't get Black enough to suit'em. So everybody passin sayin My Man Bovanne. . . . And him standin there with a smile ready case someone do speak he want to be ready. So that's how come I pull him on the dance floor and we dance. . . .

EXERCISE 18.1: Suggested Answers

All workers who do not work on Wednesday will receive their checks on Thursday.

complete the independent clause begun by *The fact,* but instead the writer shifts to another dependent clause (*which explains why I'm always tired in the evenings*). Thus the independent clause is never completed, and what results is a fragment. This fragment could be revised into a complete sentence in at least two ways.

REVISED	The fact that I get up at 5 A.M. explains why I'm always tired in the evenings. [Deleting *which* changes the second dependent clause into a predicate.]
REVISED	I get up at 5 A.M., which explains why I'm always so tired in the evenings. [Deleting *The fact that* makes the first dependent clause into an independent clause.]

EXERCISE 18.1

Assume you have been asked to edit the following notice (discovered in a New York grocery store). Look for at least two ways to make the sentences consistent.

For all workers who do not work on Wednesday will not receive their checks on Wednesday. Thursday is payday, and when you will receive your check. Thank you for your cooperation.   – MANAGEMENT

Although most listeners would have little difficulty in following a speaker's intended meaning, failure to maintain consistent grammatical patterns often leads to confusion, especially in writing. If you have ever had mixed sentences pointed out in your writing, proofread carefully for them. Look especially at the relationship between subject and predicate and between clauses. Here are some other examples of mixed sentences.

MIXED	Before the world as we know it was created, the universe was only chaos existed—a mass of nothing. [*Only chaos* must function in two different ways: as the subject complement of *universe* and as the subject of *existed*.]
REVISED	Before the world as we know it was created, the universe was only chaos—a mass of nothing. [Deleting *existed* leaves *only chaos* as a subject complement only.]
REVISED	Before the world as we know it was created, only chaos existed—a mass of nothing. [Deleting *the universe was* leaves *only chaos* as a subject only.]
MIXED	Because hope was the only thing left when Pandora finally closed up the mythical box explains why we never lose hope no matter how bad life gets. [The adverb clause beginning with *Because* is followed not by an independent clause but by a predicate beginning with *explains,* which lacks a subject.]
REVISED	Because hope was the only thing left when Pandora finally closed up the mythical box, we never lose hope no matter how bad life gets. [Deleting *explains why* changes the original predicate into an independent clause to which the adverb clause can be attached.]

18b

Matching subjects and predicates

Another kind of mixed sentence occurs when a subject and predicate do not fit together grammatically or simply do not make sense together. (See 7c1 and 7c2.) Such a mismatch, called **faulty predication**, often appears with the verb *be,* in which a subject complement and the subject do not make sense together. Many cases of faulty predication result from using forms of *be* when another verb would be stronger.

FAULTY	A characteristic that I admire is a person who is generous.

This sentence says that a person is a kind of characteristic. To make its subject and predicate consistent, you could change either the subject or the

USEFUL READING

D'Eloia, Sarah. "The Uses—and Limits—of Grammar." *The Writing Teacher's Source-book.* Ed. Gary Tate and Edward P. J. Corbett. New York: Oxford UP, 1981. 225–43.

BACKGROUND

The mismatch of the linking verb *be* and clauses opening with *when* or *because* is often termed "faulty predication." Linking verbs of course link a subject with a subjective complement, which renames or modifies the subject: *Sports courtesy is maturity in fast action. Sports courtesy is important to team players.* When a student uses *when* after *is,* he or she introduces an adverbial element, which no longer renames or modifies the subject, but modifies the verb: *Sports courtesy is when players treat one another with fairness and consideration.*

One of the best explanations of *reason . . . is because* can be found in Wilson Follett's *Modern English Usage* (New York: Hill, 1966, 275). Follett tells us that when we make *reason* the subject of a sentence, we tend to substitute *because* for *that.* Such a switch "besides being a breach of idiom, is an obvious redundancy: *because* = *for the reason that.*" Hence, *the reason is because* paraphrases as *the reason is for the reason that.*

complement to make them both refer to either persons or characteristics, or you could rewrite the sentence to change the verb.

REVISED   A *characteristic* that I admire is *generosity.*

REVISED   A *kind of person* that I admire is *one who is generous.*

REVISED   I *admire* a person who is generous.

The verb *be* also leads to faulty predication when it is used before an adverb clause opening with *when* or *where.*

FAULTY   A stereotype is when someone characterizes a group unfairly.

Although you will often hear constructions like this in conversation, an adverb clause used as a subject complement in academic or other formal writing is considered weak. To revise the sentence above, you can change the complement to a noun that will grammatically match the subject *stereotype,* or you can rewrite the sentence to change the verb.

REVISED   A *stereotype* is an unfair *characterization* of a group.

REVISED   A *stereotype characterizes* a group unfairly.

REVISED   *When someone characterizes a group unfairly,* he or she *creates* a stereotype.

Using *the reason (that) . . . is because* construction, which causes inconsistency between the subject and the subject complement, is another form of faulty predication.

FAULTY   The reason I like to play soccer is because it provides aerobic exercise.

REVISED   I like to play soccer *because* it provides aerobic exercise. [Deleting *the reason (that)* leaves an independent clause to which the *because* clause can be attached.]

REVISED   *The reason* I like to play soccer *is that* it provides aerobic exercise. [Changing *because* to *that* makes the adverb clause into a noun clause that can function as a subject complement. In other words, *that it provides aerobic exercise* renames *reason,* as a subject complement should.]

Faulty predication also occurs with verbs other than *be.* For example:

FAULTY   The rules of the corporation expect employees to be properly dressed. [*Rules* cannot expect anything.]

REVISED   As its rules state, the corporation expects employees to be properly dressed.

TEACHING PRACTICE

You may want to indicate to your students that the mismatch in the following sentence is equally one of word choice and meaning.

The rules of the corporation expect employees to be properly dressed.

As the handbook points out, rules cannot expect anything; corrections to this sentence depend on semantics or meaning. By usage, we give corporations "life," which is why a corporation can be said to expect something.

REVISED	The rules of the corporation require that employees be properly dressed.
FAULTY	The success of *Playboy* was widely imitated by other men's magazines. [*Success* cannot be imitated.]
REVISED	*Playboy* was widely imitated by other men's magazines.
REVISED	The success of *Playboy* led other men's magazines to imitate it.

EXERCISE 18.2

Revise each of the following sentences in two ways to make its structures consistent in grammar and meaning. Example:

> *The fact that our room was cold we put a space heater between our beds.*
>
> *Because our room was cold, we put a space heater between our beds.*
>
> *The fact that our room was cold led us to put a space heater between our beds.*

1. My interest in a political career would satisfy my desire for public service.
2. To find out if you need braces, your dentist will usually tell you.
3. The reason air pollution standards should not be relaxed is because many people would suffer.
4. By not prosecuting white-collar crime as vigorously as violent crime encourages white-collar criminals to think they can ignore the law.
5. Her age is a bit deceiving, with looks of a twenty-one-year-old but a true age of only fifteen.
6. A confluence is where two rivers join to form one.
7. Hawthorne's short stories are experiences drawn from his own life.
8. When Oedipus suddenly realizes he has killed his father and married his mother causes a "shock of recognition."
9. One controversial element of the curriculum has been colleges with a required course in Western culture.
10. The European discovery of Australia became a penal colony for Britain.

18c

Using elliptical structures carefully

Sometimes writers can avoid repetition and gain emphasis by using **elliptical structures**, in which they omit certain words or phrases in

EXERCISE 18.2: Suggested Answers

1. A political career would satisfy my desire for public service. My desire for public service makes me interested in a political career.

2. Your dentist will usually tell you if you need braces. To find out if you need braces, ask your dentist.

3. Many people would suffer if air pollution standards were relaxed. The reason air pollution standards should not be relaxed is that many people would suffer.

4. By not prosecuting white-collar crime as vigorously as we prosecute violent crime, we encourage white-collar criminals to ignore the law. We must prosecute white-collar crime as vigorously as violent crime unless we want to encourage white-collar criminals to ignore the law.

5. Although she looks twenty-one, she is only fifteen. She looks like a twenty-one-year-old, but she is only fifteen.

6. A confluence is a place where two rivers join to form one. A confluence joins two rivers to form one.

7. Hawthorne's short stories are drawn from his own life experiences. Hawthorne draws on his own life experiences to create his short stories.

8. Oedipus has the "shock of recognition" when he suddenly realizes that he has killed his father and married his mother. The "shock of recognition" comes when Oedipus suddenly realizes that he has killed his father and married his mother.

9. One controversial element of college curriculums has been a required course in Western culture. Required college courses in Western culture cause controversy.

10. Europeans discovered Australia, but the British made it into a penal colony. Although it was a European discovery, Australia became a British penal colony.

BACKGROUND

Elliptical structures omit certain *understood* words. For instance, when your students ask you when you plan to pass back their papers and you answer "Tomorrow," you have left out the understood words, "I will pass back your papers." And when you say to them, "If in doubt about the comments I've made on your papers, please see me," you've left out the understood information: "If *you are* in doubt." One student may say to another, "You'll probably get an A, but I won't (get an A)."

Although dependent on context, elliptical structures are the most convenient way to avoid repetition while providing conciseness and movement in speech and writing.

TEACHING PRACTICE

To better acquaint your students with the concept of ellipsis, you may want to turn to George Curmé's *English Grammar* (New York: Harper, 1947), which provides a list of different kinds of ellipses—the stylistic and syntactic omission of key words and phrases. Curmé explains the following kinds of omissions:

Clauses of comparison

That teacher cares for her students as a mother (cares for) her children.

Conditional sentences

She could easily win the contest (if she tried).

Clauses of exception

Nobody knew her except/but I (knew her).

Imperatives

Heads, eyes front. (Turn your heads and eyes to the front.)

Independent propositions

He cooks better than you do (better than you cook).

compound structures, as the following sentences by Eudora Welty demonstrate. Omitted words are in brackets.

> That bell belonged to the figure of Miss Duling as though it grew directly out of her right arm, as wings grew out of an angel or a tail [grew] out of the devil.

> Her gaze was in general sweeping, then suddenly at the point of concentration [it was] upon you.

These sentences are clear and effective because the omitted words match those in the other part. In the following sentence, however, the omitted verb does not match the one that occurs in the first part, and so the sentence is incomplete and must be revised to include both verbs.

INCOMPLETE   His skills are weak, and his performance only average.

REVISED   His skills *are* weak, and his performance *is* only average.

Checking for missing words

In the rush of composing, when the brain almost always runs ahead of the hand, writers sometimes accidentally leave out words, especially short ones like articles, pronouns, and prepositions. The best way to catch such inadvertent omissions is to proofread carefully, reading each sentence slowly—and aloud. If at all possible, read to someone else. If a word or phrase is missing, one of you should hear its omission.

INCOMPLETE   The professor's heavy German accent made difficult for the class understand her lectures.

REVISED   The professor's heavy German accent made *it* difficult for the class *to* understand her lectures.

Especially in speaking, we often omit *that* before a noun clause: *Yesterday, I realized* [that] *I was hopelessly behind in my work.* In this instance, the omission does not obscure meaning. If any possible confusion could arise, however, be sure to include the *that* in writing.

UNCLEAR   I noticed many motorcycles from the 1940s had become classics. [Readers at first assume *many motorcycles* is the object of *noticed* rather than the subject of the subordinate clause.]

REVISED   I noticed *that* many motorcycles from the 1940s had become classics.

Making comparisons complete, consistent, and clear

As you revise your writing, check comparative structures closely, remembering that when you compare two or more things, the comparison must be *complete, logically consistent,* and *clear.* (See 12d for more on comparative and superlative forms.)

Complete comparisons

INCOMPLETE	I was embarrassed because my parents were so different. [Different from what?]
REVISED	I was embarrassed because my parents were so different *from those of my friends.*

Logically consistent comparisons

ILLOGICAL	Woodberry's biography is better than Fields. [This sentence compares *biography,* a book, with *Fields,* a person.]
REVISED	Woodberry's biography is better than *the one by* Fields.
REVISED	Woodberry's biography is better than *Fields's is.*

Clear comparisons

UNCLEAR	Ted always felt more affection for his brother than his sister. [Did Ted feel more affection for his brother than his sister did or more affection for his brother than he felt for his sister?]
REVISED	Ted always felt more affection for his brother than *he did for* his sister.
REVISED	Ted always felt more affection for his brother than his sister *did.*

≫ *Checking comparisons*

1. Look through your draft for places where things are compared. Look for words like *different* or *prefer* as well as for comparative and superlative forms like *more, most, better, best, larger, oldest,* and so forth. Underline each comparison. *(Continued)*

TEACHING PRACTICE

"Incomplete" comparisons are common in spoken discourse. In practice, *A person who drives drunk is more dangerous* will probably make sense to most of your students; context will supply the missing information, or your students will effortlessly fill in the missing information. Ask your students if they can create a context for the incomplete comparisons on this page.

2. Are both things being compared specifically stated? If not, revise to include the one that is missing.

3. Are the things being compared logically consistent—for example, is the setting of a film compared with the setting of another film rather than with the other film itself? If the comparison is not logical, revise to make it so.

4. Could the comparison be misunderstood in any way? If so, revise to eliminate the ambiguity.

EXERCISE 18.3

Revise each of the following sentences to eliminate any inappropriate elliptical constructions; to make comparisons complete, logically consistent, and clear; and to supply any other omitted words that are necessary for meaning. Example:

Most of the candidates are bright, and one ⌄brilliant.

(i s)

1. My new stepmother makes my father happier.
2. Argentina and Peru were colonized by Spain, and Brazil by Portugal.
3. She argued that children are even more important for men than women.
4. Was the dictatorship in Iraq any worse than many other countries?
5. The personalities of marijuana smokers are different from nonsmokers.

EXERCISE 18.4 Revising for Consistency and Completeness

Revise to make every sentence grammatically and logically consistent and complete.

The reason I believe the United States should have a military draft is because draft would make us better citizens. By requiring the same sacrifice from every young person would make everyone feel part a common effort. In addition, a draft is fairer. When an army is made up of volunteers come mostly from the poor and minority groups. During the Persian Gulf War, news reports showed blacks were overrepresented among the troops, largely because their economic options were more limited than young whites and the military thus more attractive as a career. I also feel that women should be subject to the draft. A quality that the military needs is soldiers who are dedicated, and women soldiers have shown that they are more dedicated to their jobs than men. The requirements of a modern army also need skills that more women possess. Equality is when both sexes have equal responsibilities as well as equal opportunity.

EXERCISE 18.3: Suggested Answers

1. My new stepmother makes my father happier than the last one did.
2. Argentina and Peru were colonized by Spain, and Brazil was colonized by Portugal.
3. The speaker argued that children are even more important for men than they are for women.
4. Was the dictatorship in Iraq any worse than those in many other countries?
5. The personalities of marijuana smokers are different from those of nonsmokers.

EXERCISE 18.4: Suggested Answers

I believe the United States should have a military draft because it would make us better citizens. Requiring the same sacrifice from every young person would make everyone feel like a part of a common effort. In addition, a draft system is fairer than a volunteer one: most army volunteers tend to come from poor or minority groups. News reports during the Persian Gulf War showed the overrepresentation of blacks among the troops. The military is a more attractive career for young blacks largely because their economic options are more limited than those of young whites. I also feel that women should be subject to the draft. The military needs dedicated soldiers and women soldiers have shown that, if anything, they are more dedicated to their jobs than men are. Women also possess a variety of skills required in a modern army that men do not possess. Equality must mean equal responsibilities as well as equal opportunities for both sexes.

EXERCISE 18.5   Reading with an Eye for Inconsistent Structures

Mixed and inconsistent structures appear even in the writing of professionals. Read the following sentences carefully, identifying the problem in each and offering revisions.

The U.S. military attaché to Greece was killed today on the small street where he lived by a car bomb that blew his armor-plated car off the road as he was driving to work.   — ASSOCIATED PRESS

Inert, apparently harmless gases used in refrigeration deplete the protective ozone layer; they increase the amount of deadly ultraviolet radiation from the sun that reaches the surface of the Earth, destroying vast numbers of unprotected microorganisms that lie at the base of a poorly understood food chain—at the top of which precariously teeter we.   — CARL SAGAN

EXERCISE 18.6   Taking Inventory: Mixed or Incomplete Structures

Read over three or four paragraphs from a draft or completed essay you have written recently, checking for mixed sentences and incomplete or missing structures. Revise the paragraphs to correct any problems you find. If you find any, can you recognize any patterns? If so, make a note of them for future reference (in your writing log, if you keep one).

EXERCISE 18.5: Suggested Answers

The U.S. military attaché to Greece was killed today on the small street where he lived. A car bomb blew his armor-plated car off the road as he was driving to work.

Inert, apparently harmless gases used in refrigeration deplete the protective ozone layer, thereby increasing the amount of deadly ultraviolet radiation from the sun that reaches the surface of the Earth. This radiation destroys vast numbers of unprotected microorganisms that lie at the base of a poorly understood food chain—at the top of which precariously teeter we.

FOR COLLABORATIVE WORK

If students identify problem sentences in their own essays, they can profit by working in small groups to revise the passages, the writer explaining what he or she *meant* to say and the group working out various ways to convey that meaning.

Part Four

Sentences: Making Stylistic Choices

———— <> ————

19

Constructing Effective Sentences

BACKGROUND

In "Lexicon Rhetoricae" Kenneth Burke defines form as the "arousal and fulfillment of desire" (124). Burke describes five verbal forms, each with its own unique appeal.

1. *Syllogistic progressive form,* whereby the reader is advanced (by the text) step by step in cause-and-effect fashion, as in a mystery story

2. *Qualitative progressive form,* whereby the reader connects one quality to an earlier quality; the reader recognizes the rightness of one event to follow another, as in the death of Juliet after Romeo

3. *Repetitive form,* which involves the restatement of a theme with new details, as in the exemplifications of size discrepancy in *Gulliver's Travels*

4. *Conventional form,* whose appeal is that of form *per se,* as in a sestina, a sonnet

5. *Minor form,* which involves the natural appeal of the various figures of speech, such as metaphor, simile, synecdoche

Any form at whatever level of discourse, from the phrase and the sentence to the paragraph and the entire work, may inhabit any of these types. A writer may purposely suggest fulfillment of any of these formal appeals and then surprise the reader—by denying it.

Put most simply, effective sentences have two main characteristics:

- They emphasize ideas clearly
- They do so as concisely as possible

But how do writers create such sentences? One way is by carrying out what philosopher Kenneth Burke calls "the arousal and fulfillment of desire." Substituting the more mundane *expectations* for Burke's deliberately provocative *desire* illustrates what we mean: an **effective sentence** is one that creates or appeals to certain expectations and then either fulfills them or—as is sometimes the case—startles or amuses or alarms readers by *not* fulfilling them. Look at the following sentence:

> I sometimes think of the reader as a cat, endlessly fastidious, capable, by turns, of mordant indifference and riveted attention, luxurious, recumbent, and ever poised.   — Patricia Hampl, "Memory and Imagination"

This sentence fulfills expectations by following up on the image of the reader as cat with cat imagery ("endlessly fastidious," "luxurious"). In addition, the sentence is structured so as to pull its readers along, saving its most powerful image for the end: the catlike reader, "ever poised."

The writer of the following sentence, on the other hand, surprises readers by *breaking* expectations.

> He was a tall, dark, and handsome creep.

In this sentence, the writer plays on readers' expectations with the loaded words *tall, dark,* and *handsome*—only to undercut those expectations with the final *creep.*

You may want to try using such an element of surprise as one way to create effective sentences. The rest of this chapter, however, will focus on two basic devices writers use to fulfill rather than break expectations: *emphasis* and *conciseness*.

EXERCISE 19.1

Study Patricia Hampl's sentence, and then write a sentence of your own that imitates hers, beginning as she does: "I sometimes think of _____ as _____, . . ." Decide whether or not the sentences fulfill expectations set up by the opening words.

> *I sometimes think of the reader as a cat, endlessly fastidious, capable, by turns, of mordant indifference and riveted attention, luxurious, recumbent, and ever poised.*
>
> *I sometimes think of television as a shrew, incessantly noisy, demanding attention at all times to its advertising and mindless programming, insistently shrill, forever heckling.*

19a

Emphasizing main ideas

Effective sentences put the spotlight on main ideas, thus letting readers know which elements of the sentence are most important. We call this spotlighting of significant words and ideas **emphasis**. Careful control of

---

Everyday use

You can see the importance of emphasis and conciseness in directions, particularly those on medicines. Here, for instance, are some directions found on one common prescription drug.

Take one tablet daily. Some nonprescription drugs may aggravate your condition, so *read all labels carefully.* If any include a warning, check with your doctor. Refill prescription only until 12/12/92.

These directions aim to state their message as emphatically (to relay important information) and concisely (to fit on a small label) as possible. Look around for other directions that do the same — on health products, cigarettes, traffic signs, and so on. Bring the sentences you find to class to compare with those found by your classmates, and see if together you can draw any conclusions about what makes language concise and emphatic.

---

the emphasis in each sentence will make your writing both easier and more enjoyable to read. This section focuses on the ways you can emphasize main ideas by putting them in closing and opening positions and by arranging them in climactic order.

1

Using closing and opening positions for emphasis

When you read a sentence, what are you most likely to remember? Other things being equal, you remember the end. This is the part of the sentence that should move the writing forward by providing new information, as it does in the following example.

To protect her skin, she took *plenty of sun-block lotion.*

A less emphatic but still important position in a sentence is the opening, which hooks up the new sentence with what has come before.

When Rosita went to the beach, she was anxious not to get a sunburn. *To protect her skin,* she took plenty of sun-block lotion.

In this example, *to protect her skin* connects the new sentence to *anxious not to get a sunburn* in the sentence before. The second sentence would lose emphasis if the key words, *plenty of sun-block lotion,* were buried in the middle, as in the following version.

To protect her skin, she took *plenty of sun-block lotion,* and she also planned to stay under a beach umbrella most of the time.

Placing relatively unimportant information in the memorable closing position of a sentence can have the effect of undercutting proper emphasis or even of giving more emphasis to the closing words than you intend. Consider the following example:

She contributed $500,000 to the campaign last month.

Revised to emphasize the contribution, the sentence reads:

Last month she contributed $500,000 to the campaign.

To emphasize the amount of the contribution even more, the sentence could be reworded this way:

Last month she gave the campaign committee $500,000.

2

Using climactic order

Presenting ideas in **climactic order** means arranging them in order of increasing importance, power, or drama: building to climax. The following sentences show climactic order at work.

> Dissidents risk social rejection, forced relocation, long imprisonment, and almost certain death.

> After they've finished with the pantry, the medicine cabinet, and the attic, [neat people] will throw out the red geranium (too many leaves), sell the dog (too many fleas), and send the children off to boarding school (too many scuffmarks on the hardwood floors).
> — SUZANNE BRITT, "Neat People vs. Sloppy People"

Each of the preceding examples derives much of its power from the sequencing of its details. If the first sentence concluded with "long imprisonment" rather than "almost certain death," it would not make such an emphatic statement. Similarly, the second example saves its most dramatic item for last, making its point forcefully. The following sentence fails to achieve strong emphasis because its verbs are not sequenced in order of increasing power.

UNEMPHATIC	Soap operas assault our eyes, damage our brain cells, and offend our ears.
REVISED	Soap operas offend our ears, assault our eyes, and damage our brain cells.

 Checking for sentence emphasis

As you revise a draft, follow these steps to make sure that each sentence emphasizes the ideas you *want* emphasized.

1. Identify the word or words you want to receive special emphasis. If those words are buried in the middle of the sentence, revise the sentence to change their position, remembering that the end and the beginning are generally most emphatic.

2. Note any sentences that include a series of three or more words, phrases, or clauses. Check to see whether the items in the series could be arranged in climactic order and, if so, whether they are. If they could be but are not, decide whether the sentence would be stronger with climactic order, and rearrange if necessary.

(Continued)

FOR COLLABORATIVE WORK

To demonstrate climactic order, ask your class to suggest a topic (such as the qualities of a good friend, a good car, a popular campus restaurant). Brainstorm the topic, creating a list of associations on the board. Then, ask each student to write a one-sentence statement summarizing their ideas about the topic. Ask students to read their statements and comment on possible reasons for ordering their subtopics the way they did. You may want to take this opportunity to point out that climactic order reflects the relative importance the writer attaches to ideas.

OPTIONAL EXERCISE

Ask students to imitate the climactic form of the handbook example: *Soap operas offend our ears, assault our eyes, and damage our brain cells.* Then after reading aloud the following sentences and examining their climactic order, ask them to write imitations.

1. I have in my own life a precious friend, a woman of 65 who has lived very hard, who is wise, who listens well, who has been where I am and can help me understand it; and who represents not only an ultimate ideal mother to me but also the person I'd like to be when I grow up.
   —JUDITH VIORST

2. To assign unanswered letters their proper weight, to free us from the expectations of others, to give us back to ourselves—here lies the great, the singular power of self-respect.
   —JOAN DIDION

3. She loved the flat, she loved her life, she loved Herbie.
   —DOROTHY PARKER

4. I came, I saw, I conquered.
   —JULIUS CAESAR

USEFUL READING

Williams, Joseph M. *Style: Ten Lessons in Clarity and Grace.* 3rd ed. Glenview, IL.: Scott, 1989. In Lesson Four, "The Grammar of Emphasis," Williams demonstrates ways of shifting emphasis to the end of sentences (64–80), and in Lesson Seven, "Managing Long Sentences," Williams discusses how grammatical connections (particularly subject-verb-complement patterns) contribute to smooth prose (see 125–47).

EXERCISE 19.2: Suggested Answers

1. All sea-going vessels must be designed according to certain specifications, whether they are outrigger canoes, giant aircraft carriers, or run-of-the-mill cargo ships.

2. Also notable throughout the story is the image of chrysanthemums.

3. Despite hitting his head on the board during one of his dives, Louganis won the gold medal.

4. The presence of the Indian in these movies always conjures up destructive stereotypes of drunkenness, horse thieves, and bloodthirsty war parties.

5. Victorian women were warned that smoking would cause them to grow a mustache, contract tuberculosis, become sterile, or die young.

See how the sentence below can be revised using these steps:

For completely false "reasons," we in the Student Senate have for years been saddled with the burdens, which we're tired of, of low budgets, no real legislative power, and a depressing room to meet in.

The main point the writer wants to emphasize, that the Student Senate is tired of being saddled with poor conditions and no power, is obscured by unemphatic placement in the middle of the sentence.

REVISED FOR EMPHASIS

We in the Student Senate are tired of being saddled for years, for completely false "reasons," with the burdens of low budgets, no real legislative power, and a depressing room to meet in.

The items in the series at the end of the sentence do not seem to be in any particular order, even though they could be. If the meeting room is least important and the lack of power most important, the revision might read as follows.

REVISED FOR CLIMACTIC ORDER

We in the Student Senate are tired of being saddled for years, for completely false "reasons," with the burdens of a depressing room to meet in, low budgets, and no real legislative power.

EXERCISE 19.2

Revise each of the following sentences to highlight what you take to be the main or most important ideas. Example:

> Tobacco companies continue to fight the antismoking campaign—
> through ~~the highest courts of the land,~~ *local advertising,* through congressional lobbying, *the highest courts in the land.*
> through ~~local advertising.~~

1. All seagoing vessels, whether outrigger canoes, giant aircraft carriers, or run-of-the-mill cargo ships, must be designed according to certain specifications.

2. Also notable is the image of chrysanthemums throughout the story.

3. Louganis won the gold medal despite hitting his head on the board during one of his dives.

4. The presence of the Indian in these movies always conjures up destructive stereotypes of bloodthirsty war parties, horse thieves, and drunkenness.

5. Victorian women were warned that if they smoked, they would become sterile, grow a moustache, die young, or contract tuberculosis.

Being concise

In general, effective sentences are as **concise** as possible. More often than not, making a point in the fewest possible words is a hallmark of effective prose. Look at the following sentence:

> Her constant and continual use of vulgar expressions with obscene meanings indicated to her pre-elementary supervisory group that she was rather deficient in terms of her ability to interact in an efficient manner with peers in her potential interaction group.

Why write that when you could instead write the following?

> Her constant use of "four-letter words" told the day-care workers that she might have trouble getting along with other four-year-olds.

This example demonstrates how radical a change can be wrought by snipping away at the underbrush of *unnecessary* words. Doing so involves several kinds of changes: eliminating redundant words, eliminating "buzz-words," replacing wordy phrases, and simplifying grammatical structures.

1

Eliminating redundant words

Sometimes writers add words for emphasis, saying that something is large *in size* or red *in color*, or that two ingredients should be combined *together.* The italicized words are **redundant**, or unnecessary for meaning, as are the ones below.

REDUNDANT	*Compulsory* attendance at assemblies *is required.*
REVISED	Attendance at assemblies *is required.*
REDUNDANT	The auction featured *contemporary* "antiques" *made recently.*
REVISED	The auction featured *contemporary* "antiques."
REVISED	The auction featured "antiques" *made recently.*

TEACHING PRACTICE

To demonstrate that being concise may not always be preferable, discuss with your class the opening paragraph of Charles Dickens's *A Tale of Two Cities,* followed by a revision by the computer program *Workbench.* Read both versions aloud, and then get the class to decide which makes a more effective opening for the novel.

> It was the best of times, it was the worst of times, it was the age of wisdom, it was the age of foolishness, it was the epoch of belief, it was the epoch of incredulity, it was the season of Light, it was the season of Darkness, it was the spring of hope, it was the winter of despair, we had everything before us, we had nothing before us, we were all going direct to Heaven, we were all going direct the other way—in short, the period was so far like the present period, that some of its noisiest authorities insisted on being received, for good or for evil, in the superlative degree of comparison only.
> —CHARLES DICKENS

> The times were the best and worst, wise and foolish. The era was one of belief and disbelief, light and darkness, hope and despair. Before us lay everything and nothing. We were all going direct to heaven or straight to hell. The period was so much like today that its loudest critics could describe it only in superlatives.
> —WORKBENCH

USEFUL READING

Laib, Nevin. "Conciseness and Amplification." *CCC* 41 (1990): 443–59. Laib argues that carried to excess, conciseness can lean to "bluntness, opacity, and underdevelopment" and suggests that teachers of writing should encourage "profuseness" as well. According to Laib, "Elegant variation is an essential art of development, emphasis, and explanation."

2

Eliminating buzzwords

Another category of words that can usually be eliminated is known as **buzzwords**. These are words that might sound meaningful, perhaps even important, but that too often contribute no real meaning. In general, they should be deleted or replaced.

COMMON BUZZWORDS

angle, area, aspect, case, character, element, factor, field, kind, nature, scope, situation, type

Many modifiers are used in such an all-purpose way that they have become buzzwords, adding no meaning to a statement.

MEANINGLESS MODIFIERS

absolutely, awesome, awfully, central, definitely, fine, great, literally, major, quite, really, very

Taken together, buzzwords can build up whole sentences that say almost nothing at all.

The scope of this thing, the importance of this field, is so absolutely vital that I get really overwhelmed at the significance of the situation.

Because buzzwords tend to make your writing dull as well as wordy, use them very sparingly. When you cannot simply delete them, try to think of a more specific term that says what you mean.

WORDY	*The nature of the housing situation* can *have a really significant impact* on the quality of *the social aspect of a student's life.*
REVISED	*Housing* can *strongly influence* the quality of *a student's social life.*

3

Replacing wordy phrases

Many wordy phrases can be reduced to a single word or two. Doing so will make your writing more concise and thus easier to read.

WORDY	CONCISE
at the present time	now/today
at that point in time	then
in the event that	if

It is when I struggle to be brief that I become obscure. —HORACE

If you would be pungent, be brief. —SOUTHEY

WORDY	CONCISE
form a consensus of opinion	agree
exhibit a tendency to	tend to

WORDY   I see no reason at this point in time why we should not rely, as has often been the case in the past, on the good offices of the mayor.

REVISED   We should rely now, as we have in the past, on the help of the mayor.

Sometimes writers resort to this kind of wordiness because they think it sounds more formal, more official. Such might have been the case in what has come to be a classic story about the dangers of wordiness.

> A plumber wrote to the Federal Bureau of Standards that he had found hydrochloric acid did a fine job of clearing out his clogged drains.
> The Bureau answered: "The effectiveness and efficiency of hydrochloric acid is indisputable, but the corrosive or detrimental residue is incompatible with metallic permanence."
> The plumber replied he was delighted the Bureau agreed with him.
> Then the Bureau wrote: "We cannot and must not assume responsibility or admit to culpability in event of the production of toxic and noxious residue with hydrochloric acid and, therefore, recommend you use an alternate or secondary procedure."
> Again the plumber said he was delighted the Bureau agreed.
> At last the Bureau wrote, with admirable unity, emphasis, and concision, a reply that spoke volumes to the plumber: "Don't use hydrochloric acid. It eats the hell out of the pipes."

As this example indicates, corporate, bureaucratic, academic, and scientific writing is a major source of wordiness. Although the writer may think such language sounds impressive, it usually sounds only pompous. (See 27e5.)

4

Simplifying grammatical structures

Using the simplest grammatical structures possible will tighten and strengthen your sentences considerably. In the following example, notice how conciseness results from reducing an adjective clause to an appositive phrase, deleting a grammatically unnecessary *to be,* and reducing an adverb phrase to a one-word adverb.

WORDY   Kennedy, *who was only the second Roman Catholic to be nominated for the presidency by a major party,* had to handle the religion issue *in a delicate manner.*

OPTIONAL EXERCISE

Read aloud the following paragraph from a mystery novel by Amanda Cross (the heroine, Kate Fansler, is mapping out her mystery-solving plan), and then ask your students to revise it using the simplest grammatical structures.

> She felt, nonetheless, as she stood indecisively in the hall, like a knight who has set off to slay the dragon but has neglected to ask in what part of the world the dragon may be found. It was all very well to decide upon action, but what action, after all, was she to take? As was her habit, she extracted notebook and pen and began to make a list: see Janet Harrison's room, and talk to people who knew her in dormitory; find out about ten and twelve o'clock patients; find out who person in picture Janet Harrison had was (lists always had a devastating effect on Kate's syntax). —AMANDA CROSS, *In the Last Analysis*

REVISED   Kennedy, *only the second Roman Catholic nominated for the presidency by a major party,* had to handle the religion issue *delicately.*

In the following example, reducing an adverb clause to an elliptical form and combining two sentences produces one concise sentence.

WORDY   When she was questioned about her previous job, she seemed nervous. She also tried to change the subject.

REVISED   When questioned about her previous job, she seemed nervous and tried to change the subject.

Other ways to achieve conciseness by simplifying grammatical structures include using strong verbs and nouns, avoiding expletive constructions, and using the active rather than the passive voice. These methods are discussed in Chapter 23.

 Checking for conciseness

1. Read over your draft, looking for redundant words. If you are unsure about a word, read the sentence without it; if your meaning is not affected, leave the word out.

2. Look for buzzwords—words like *aspect* or *factor* or *type*—take them out. Does your meaning change? If so, can you replace the buzzword with a more meaningful term?

3. Look especially for meaningless modifiers—words like *definitely, quite,* and *very.* Take them out, and unless your meaning is not clear without them, leave them out.

4. Do you use any wordy phrases? See if you can replace them with a single word—instead of *because of the fact that,* try *because;* rather than *for the purpose of,* try *for.*

5. Finally, look for grammatical structures that might be simplified:

   Adjective clauses that could be reduced to appositive phrases
   Adverb phrases that could be reduced to one-word adverbs
   Expletive constructions that could be eliminated
   Consecutive sentences with the same subject or predicate that could be combined into one sentence

EXERCISE 19.3

Revise each of the following sentences to make it clear and concise by eliminating unnecessary words and phrases. Example:

summarize.

Let me ~~fill you in on the main points of the overall picture here.~~

1. At the present time, many different forms of hazing occur, such as various forms of physical abuse and also mental abuse.

2. Many people have a tendency toward the expansion of their sentences by the superfluous addition of extra words that are not really needed for the meaning of the sentences.

3. One of the major problems that is faced at this point in time is that there is world hunger.

4. After I stopped the practice of exercising regularly, I became ten pounds heavier in weight in a relatively short amount of time.

5. There are numerous theories that have been proposed by scientists as to why dinosaurs reached the point of becoming extinct.

EXERCISE 19.4   Revising for Emphasis and Conciseness

Revise the following paragraph so that each sentence emphasizes its main idea and is as concise as possible. Combine or divide sentences if necessary.

At the present time, one of the most serious problems that faces Americans in the area of public policy is the increasing rise in the cost of health care, which has occurred over an extended period of time. One major aspect of the severe crisis in health care costs is that more and more expensive medical technology is being developed and marketed to doctors and hospitals. Even hospitals that are small in size want the latest kind of diagnostic device. The high cost of this expensive equipment is passed on to consumers, who are the patients. It is then passed on to insurance companies. Therefore, many employers are charging their employees more for health insurance because they themselves are having to pay higher and higher premiums. Others are reducing the employees' coverage to a significant extent. Meanwhile, almost 40 million Americans suffer from the condition of a lack of any health insurance. In the event that they have an illness or an injury, they must go to a hospital emergency room. In large cities, emergency rooms are being overwhelmed by people seeking treatment for everything from life-threatening gunshot wounds to mysterious sniffles to broken bones.

EXERCISE 19.5   Reading with an Eye for Sentence Style

Here are two sentences from "A Sweet Devouring," Eudora Welty's essay about the pleasures of reading. Each sentence makes a powerfully emphatic statement. Read each one, and decide how Welty achieves such strong emphasis. Then read something by a favorite writer, looking for strong, emphatic sentences. Bring in one or two to compare with sentences chosen by your classmates.

EXERCISE 19.3: Suggested Answers

1. Many forms of hazing occur, such as physical and mental abuse.

2. Many people tend to expand their sentences by adding unnecessary words.

3. World hunger is a major problem.

4. I put on ten pounds immediately after I stopped exercising.

5. Scientists have proposed numerous theories on the extinction of dinosaurs.

EXERCISE 19.4: Suggested Answers

One of the most serious problems of public policy facing Americans today is the rising cost of health care. Expensive medical technology is being developed and marketed to doctors and hospitals, causing even small hospitals to want the latest diagnostic devices. The cost of this expensive equipment is passed on to patients and then to insurance companies. Because employers have to pay higher premiums, many are charging their employees more for health insurance and others are significantly reducing coverage. Meanwhile, almost 40 million Americans lack any health insurance and are forced to go to emergency rooms for illnesses or injuries. Emergency rooms in large cities are overwhelmed by people suffering everything from mysterious sniffles and broken bones to gunshot wounds.

OPTIONAL EXERCISE

Ask your students to read over Jennifer Gerkin's essay in 3i, paying attention to the sentences. Then have them choose a paragraph and evaluate its sentences in terms of emphasis and conciseness. Ask them to try to find a paragraph that they think might be made more emphatic or more concise and to revise accordingly.

EXERCISE 19.5 Answers will vary.

1. The pleasures of reading itself—who doesn't remember?—were like those of a Christmas cake, a sweet devouring.

2. And then I went again to the home shelves and my lucky hand reached and found Mark Twain—twenty-four volumes, not a series, and good all the way through.

EXERCISE 19.6　Taking Inventory: Sentence Effectiveness

Study two or three paragraphs you have written recently with an eye for buzzwords. Using 19b2 for guidance, eliminate meaningless words such as *aspect, factor, quite,* or *very.* Compare notes with one or two classmates to see what buzzwords, if any, you all tend to use. Finally, make a note of those you use (in your writing log, if you keep one) so that you can avoid them in the future.

20

Creating Coordinate and Subordinate Structures

Creating effective sentences calls on a writer to act as a conductor, directing the arrangement and flow of verbal passages just as the conductor of an orchestra does with musical passages. Such effective orchestration very often involves creating sentences that use *coordinate* and *subordinate* structures. **Coordinate structures** give essentially equal importance to two or more words, phrases, or clauses, often linking them together with coordinating conjunctions like *and* or *but*. **Subordinate structures**, on the other hand, create different levels of significance, stressing some ideas by expressing them in independent clauses or in key nouns or verbs and subordinating others by putting them into dependent clauses, phrases, or single words.

Learning to use different kinds of coordinate and subordinate structures will increase your sentence repertoire and allow you to write varied, interesting, and effective sentences. Look at the following sentences:

> Kit went through the new part of the library to the old.
> He walked around for a while.
> Then he went to the periodical section.
> He started looking at the *Times* on microfilm.

We could choose to combine these sentences in several ways.

USING COORDINATION

Kit went through the new part of the library to the old, and he walked around for a while; then he went to the periodical section and started looking at the *Times* on microfilm.

USING SUBORDINATION

After going through the new part of the library to the old and walking around for a while, Kit went to the periodical section, where he started looking at the *Times* on microfilm.

BACKGROUND

Current pedagogical theory values clarity and conciseness. Yet, composition researchers tell us that complex sentences indicate a writer's syntactic maturity. Are we sending our students mixed messages, then? No. The two concepts are not necessarily contradictory: Beginning writers often need practice in clarity and conciseness to make meaning; more mature writers can use those same qualities to grace their more complex sentence structures.

The notion that subordination and complex sentence structures indicate sophistication of thought and language ability, or maturity in the writer, needs some qualification, if only historical. In Old and Middle English, subordination was not expected, nor was it used to measure a writer's skill. In *Classical Rhetoric for the Modern Student,* 3rd ed., Edward P. J. Corbett tells us that "the history of the prose style of most Western languages reveals a gradual evolution from a paratactic syntax— stringing together a series of coordinate structures without conjunctions—to the most sophisticated of sentence patterns, subordination" (406).

USEFUL READING

Traugott, Lee Elizabeth Closs, and Mary Louise Pratt. *Linguistics for Students of Literature.* New York: Harcourt, 1980. See "Recursive Property of Language" for a transformational-linguistics perspective on coordination and subordination. Traugott and Pratt call subordination and coordination "linguistic creativity," that is, the ability to create complex sentences out of simple sentences by applying the generative principles of "recursiveness" (154–55).

BACKGROUND

In *Teaching English Grammar* (New York: Appleton, 1957), Robert C. Pooley cites passages from the King James Version (KJV) of the Bible as examples of the predominance of coordination over subordination in earlier English, not knowing that that particular translation reflects the sentence structure of the original Hebrew, not English. John B. Gabel and Charles B. Wheeler tell us that "in general [Hebrew] lacks our great variety of words that indicate logical connections between clauses and phrases. In Hebrew, sentence units tend to string out one after another in boxcar fashion and to be hooked together by means of a single, all-purpose connective that is usually translated 'and' in the KJV" (*The Bible as Literature: An Introduction* [New York: Oxford UP, 1986]). For example, Genesis 19:1–3 repeats that connective seventeen times in Hebrew; in the KJV, it appears as "and" sixteen of those times.

> (1) And there came two angels to Sodom at even; and Lot sat in the gate of Sodom: and Lot seeing *them* rose up to meet them; and he bowed himself with his face toward the ground; (2) And he said, Behold now, my lords, turn in, I pray you, into your servant's house, and tarry all night, and wash your feet, and ye shall rise up early, and go on your ways. And they said, Nay; but we will abide in the street all night. (3) And he pressed upon them greatly; and they turned in unto him, and entered into his house; and he made them a feast, and did bake unleavened bread, and they did eat.

In the example that uses coordination, the four actions of going through the new part of the library to the old, walking around, going to the periodical section, and looking at the *Times* are all given the same emphasis by being placed in three independent clauses, the last of which has a compound predicate.

The second combination gives a different emphasis, suggesting that Kit's destination, the periodical section, is most important. The action of his going there is expressed in an independent clause, whereas the other three actions are given less emphasis by being placed in a prepositional phrase (with compound gerund-phrase objects) and a dependent clause.

In addition to indicating emphasis, coordination and subordination can be used to create special, sometimes dramatic effects in writing. As a writer, you must often decide whether to use coordination, subordination, both, or neither, depending on which structure provides the emphasis and effect you want to achieve. This chapter will furnish you with some guidelines for using these structures appropriately.

Everyday use

If you think about how you use coordination and subordination every day, you may notice a difference in your spoken and written language. In speech, people tend to prefer coordination, often using and *and* and so *as all-purpose connectors. For instance:*

I'm going home now, *and* I'll see you later.

The relationship between these two clauses may be clear in speech, which occurs in some larger context and provides clues by voice, facial expressions, and gestures. But in writing, the relationship—and thus the meaning—might be less than perfectly clear. It could, for instance, have at least two rather different meanings.

Because I'm going home now, I'll see you later.
I'm going home now because I'll see you later.

The differences between these two sentences are expressed by subordination, and so they demonstrate well the reason subordinate structures are valued—and sometimes needed—in writing: as a way of making logical connections explicit.

Make a point of listening to yourself talk, and see if you rely on coordinate structures (listen for words like and, so, *and* but*). Jot down a few "coordinated" sentences, and then decide whether any of them would, in writing, be more appropriately phrased with subordination.*

EXERCISE 20.1

The following sentence uses coordination to link two ideas. Revise the sentence to use subordination instead. What effect does this change have on the sentence's meaning? Then compare your sentence with ones done by some classmates. Did you all subordinate the same clause?

Everything in the world dies, but we only know about it as a kind of abstraction.
— Lewis Thomas, "On Natural Death"

20a

Using coordination to relate equal ideas

What can you say about the following passage?

It was my birthday today, and I took cupcakes to school, and I wore a birthday crown, and we ate cupcakes, and we sang "Happy Birthday," and I sat in the middle, and I'm six years old.

We realize early on that the writer is a child—or someone writing from a child's point of view. Because the passage mentions cupcakes and school and a crown, we make this assumption even before we find out, in the last clause, that the writer is six years old. But the *style* of this passage, as well as its content, helps identify the writer. We get a clue from the seven short independent clauses strung together like beads with the coordinating conjunction *and,* a style typical of young writers who are learning to sequence events in a story. Note that aside from the clue "I'm six years old" at the very end of the sentence (generally an emphatic spot), we are given no grammatical signals to tell us how these clauses rank in importance. Were the cupcakes most significant to the writer? the birthday crown? We cannot tell, because the coordinate structure makes all the clauses grammatical equals.

Not all coordination must sound like "Run, Spot, run," however. When used well, coordinate structures relate separate but equal elements, making clear the emphasis given to different ideas. The precise relationship is stated in the element that links the ideas, usually a coordinating conjunction (*and, but, for, nor, or, so, yet*) or a semicolon. The following sentences by N. Scott Momaday all use coordination, but note that the precise relationship between clauses differs in each sentence, as expressed in the connecting element.

USEFUL READING

Lanham, Richard A. *Analyzing Prose.* New York: Scribner's, 1983. Lanham attacks the dominant theory of prose style, which values clarity, brevity, and sincerity. Instead, Lanham calls for use of a variety of different styles, depending upon the desired rhetorical effects.

Williams, Joseph M. *Style: Ten Lessons in Clarity and Grace.* 3rd ed. Glenview, IL: Scott, 1989. Chapter Six offers advice for the control of "sprawling" sentences, the result of a main clause connected to too many subordinate clauses.

They acquired horses, *and* their ancient nomadic spirit was suddenly free of the ground.

There is perfect freedom in the mountains, *but* it belongs to the eagle and the elk, the badger and the bear.

No longer were they slaves to the simple necessity of survival; they were a lordly and dangerous society of fighters and thieves, hunters and priests of the sun. — N. SCOTT MOMADAY, "The Way to Rainy Mountain"

Using coordination for special effect

Coordination can be used to create special effects, as in a passage by Carl Sandburg describing the reaction of the American people to Abraham Lincoln's assassination.

> Men tried to talk about it and the words failed and they came back to silence.
> To say nothing was best.
> Lincoln was dead.
> Was there anything more to say?
> Yes, they would go through the motions of grief and they would take part in a national funeral and a ceremony of humiliation and abasement and tears.
> But words were no help.
> Lincoln was dead. — CARL SANDBURG, *The War Years*

Together with the other short simple sentences, the coordinate clauses, phrases, and words in sentences 1 and 5 create a very powerful effect. Everything in the passage is grammatically equal, flattened out by the pain and shock of the death. In this way, the sentence structure and grammar mirror the dazed state of the populace. The short sentences and clauses are almost like sobs and illustrate the thought of sentence 1, that "the words failed."

The formal name for the conspicuous use of conjunctions is **polysyndeton**, from Greek *poly* ("many") and *syndeton* ("connectives"). Following are some additional examples.

> Satan pursues his way. And swims, or sinks, or wades, or creeps, or flies.
> — MILTON, *Paradise Lost*

Here the use of *or* between the verbs piles up images of movement, giving the impression that Satan can use *any* kind of movement and cannot be stopped.

> He [the writer] must teach himself that the basest of all things is to be afraid; and, teaching himself that, forget it forever, leaving no room in his

workshop for anything but the old verities and truths of the heart, the old universal truths lacking which any story is ephemeral and doomed—*love and honor and pity and pride and compassion and sacrifice.*
— WILLIAM FAULKNER, Nobel Prize Acceptance Speech

Here the repetition of *and* between lofty abstract nouns creates a solemn rhythm, almost like the tolling of a bell.

> Are you familiar with Motel 8? It's a chain of cheesy cheap motels across the South—twenty dollars a night gets you peeling beaverboard walls *and* thin pink blankets. There's no phone in the room, *but* a TV set that's always tuned to the Nashville Channel, *and* an air conditioner that's always got a screw or three loose *and* vibrates like a 747 on takeoff. You see piles of emptied cigarette butts in the parking lot, *and* always cigarette burns on the table, *and* more cigarette burns on the carpet, *and* a poorly repaired hole in the wall where some redneck put his fist through it in anger at his pregnant sixteen-year-old wife who didn't wanna go out to the Ponderosa.

Here the use of *and* and *but* results in a catalog of colorful, if somewhat unsavory, detail. By stringing together images in this way, the author presents them in a kind of heap, which contributes to the overall impression of the Motel 8.

 Checking your use of coordination

1. Identify all uses of *and, but, for, or, nor, so, yet,* and semicolons in your draft.
2. How many coordinate structures have you identified? If you find few, consider whether any other ideas or other elements should be linked in some way.
3. Now look on either side of each conjunction or semicolon. Do the words, phrases, or clauses that it links really need to be connected? Are they *equally important* ideas? If not, revise the sentence to eliminate the coordinate structure or to substitute a subordinate one.
4. Finally, is the relationship between any coordinate elements clear and logical? If not, try substituting a different coordinating structure. In sentences with semicolons, consider adding a conjunctive adverb (*certainly, however, incidentally, nevertheless, otherwise, therefore,* and so on—see 7b7 for a more complete list) to clarify the relationship between ideas.

USEFUL READING

Ong, Walter. *Orality and Literacy.* London: Methuen, 1982. 37. In Chapter 3, "Some Psychodynamics of Orality," Ong discusses the additive rather than subordinative nature of oral discourse.

Winterowd, Ross. "The Grammar of Coherence." *CE* 31 (1970): 328–35. Transformational grammar does not fully explain the coherence of units of discourse. Seven transitional relations account for coherence: coordinate expressed (*and*); obversive (*but*); causative (*for*); conclusive (*so*); alternative (*or*); inclusive (the colon); and sequential (*first . . . second*).

Revising for more effective coordination

See how the following passage can be analyzed and revised using the preceding guidelines.

> Watching television is a popular way to spend leisure time and makes viewers apathetic. Many people come home tired in the evenings, and so they turn on the TV to relax. They may intend to watch just the news, but then a game show comes on next, and they decide to watch a little of that, or they get too comfortable to get out of the recliner, and they end up spending the whole evening hypnotized by electronic sound and images. This pattern becomes a habit for too many Americans. These people become indifferent to their real lives. Their family members and friends come to seem less real to them than glamorous and vivid television personalities. Their daily' existence seems dull, too, compared with the dramatic or hilarious events on the screen.

REVISED

> Watching television is a popular way to spend leisure time, but excessive viewing makes viewers apathetic and indifferent to their real lives. Many people who come home tired in the evenings turn on the TV to relax. Although they may intend to watch just the news, then they decide to watch a little of the game show that comes on next, or they get too comfortable to get out of the recliner. Consequently, they end up spending the whole evening hypnotized by electronic sound and images. This pattern becomes a habit for too many Americans. Their family members and friends come to seem less real to them than glamorous and vivid television personalities; their daily existence seems dull compared with the dramatic or hilarious events on the screen.

In the first sentence, the relationship of the ideas connected by *and* is confusing. What does being a popular way to spend leisure time have to do with being apathetic? The revision better relates the clauses by changing *and* to *but* and also adds information from later in the paragraph to explain *apathetic*.

In the next sentence, *and* gives equal emphasis to coming home and turning on the TV. Subordinating the clause about coming home puts needed emphasis on the more important information, about the TV. Next, five independent clauses are connected with coordinating conjunctions. Although the ideas in these clauses are related, stringing them together in this way sounds jerky and monotonous and does not make clear to the reader that some of them are much more important than others. The revision turns two of the clauses into subordinate structures and the last one, the most important, into a separate sentence with a conjunctive adverb.

Finally, the last two sentences are very closely related, but the only signal of the relationship is the word *too*. The revision strengthens the connection by combining these sentences into one, with a semicolon between the clauses.

EXERCISE 20.2

Using the principles of coordination to signal equal importance or to create special emphasis, combine and revise the following twelve short sentences into several longer and more effective ones. Add or delete words as necessary.

The bull-riding arena was fairly crowded.
The crowd made no impression on me.
I had made a decision.
It was now time to prove myself.
I was scared.
I walked to the entry window.
I laid my money on the counter.
The clerk held up a Stetson hat filled with slips of paper.
I reached in.
I picked one.
The slip held the number of the bull I was to ride.
I headed toward the stock corral.

20b

Using subordination to distinguish main ideas

Subordination provides the means of distinguishing major points from minor points or bringing in supporting context or details. If, for instance, you put your main idea in an independent clause, you might then put any lesser ideas in dependent clauses, phrases, or even single words. Look at the following sentence, which shows the subordinated point in italics:

> Mrs. Viola Cullinan was a plump woman *who lived in a three-bedroom house somewhere behind the post office.*
> — MAYA ANGELOU, "My Name Is Margaret"

In this sentence, the dependent clause adds information about Mrs. Cullinan. While the information is important, it is grammatically subordinate to the independent clause, which carries the main idea: *Mrs. Viola Cullinan was a plump woman.*

Notice that the choice of what to subordinate rests with the writer and depends on the intended meaning. Angelou might have given the same basic

---

EXERCISE 20.2: Suggested Answers

The bull riding arena was fairly crowded, but this made no impression on me, for I had made a decision. It was now time to prove myself, and I was scared. I walked to the entry window, and I laid my money on the counter. The clerk held up a Stetson hat filled with slips of paper. I reached in and picked one. The slip held the number of the bull I was to ride, so I headed towards the stock corral.

BACKGROUND

In *Errors & Expectations,* Mina Shaughnessy describes subordination in terms of the demands it makes upon the student writer:

> If the dependent unit comes first in the sentence, the writer must suspend the independent unit in his mind while he qualifies it (as with introductory adverbial phrases and clauses). If the dependent unit comes between the subject and predicate of the base sentence (as with a relative clause after the subject), the writer must hold the main subject in his mind while he writes out the subject and predicate of the qualifying clause, and then he must return to the predicate of the base sentence. These operations require a memory for written words and grammatical structures that the inexperienced writer may not have. He hears what he says easily enough, but he does not as easily recall what he has written once his hand has moved on to another part of the sentence, and like the experienced writer, he is not in the habit of reviewing what he has written but instead moves headlong, as a speaker might, toward the open line, often forgetting the constraints he has set for himself a few words back.

Students react to these demands in different ways, of course. Some will shy away from the complexity and rely as much as possible on simple and compound structures. Others, motivated by a perceived need to write academic-sounding discourse, will produce what Shaughnessy calls "ruptured" or garbled sentences. Shaughnessy offers several options for the teacher: drills and grammatical explanations, sentence-combining exercises, and other types of exercises. But she concludes that the most improvement may occur when the student commits herself to communicating with her reader, despite "the exasperating literalism of the medium" (89).

BACKGROUND

Traditionally, teachers have assumed that grammar reflected logical thinking—that use of subordination should include subordinate ideas, with the most important ideas going in the main clause, and that coordination juxtaposed two ideas of equal rank. Linguists, however, hold that grammar is not necessarily logical. In "Coordination (Faulty) and Subordination (Upside Down)," James Sledd writes that "the traditional theory of clauses is simply untenable" (*CCC* 7 [1956]: 181–87). Subordinate ideas can and often do show up in main clauses, and main ideas can appear in subordinate clauses, as in the opening sentence of this note.

USEFUL READING

O'Hare, Frank. *Sentence Combining: Improving Student Writing without Formal Grammar Instruction*. Urbana, IL: NCTE, 1973. O'Hare studied sentence combining in seventh-grade classes. His book provides a full explanation of sentence combining and sample lessons.

information differently: *Mrs. Viola Cullinan, a plump woman, lived in a three-bedroom house somewhere behind the post office.* Subordinating the information about Mrs. Cullinan's size to that about her house would have resulted in a slightly different meaning, of course. As a writer, you must think carefully about where you want your emphasis to be and subordinate accordingly.

Besides adding information, subordination also helps establish logical relationships among facts. These relationships are often specified by subordinating conjunctions—words such as *after, because,* or *so* (see 7b7). Look, for example, at two more sentences from Maya Angelou, shown with the subordinate clauses italicized and the subordinating conjunctions underlined.

> I left the front door wide open *so all the neighbors could hear.* She usually rested her smile until late afternoon *when her women friends dropped in and Miss Glory, the cook, served them cold drinks on the closed-in porch.*
> – MAYA ANGELOU, "My Name Is Margaret"

Subordination can be used to combine short sentences in ways that signal logical relationships. For example:

SEPARATE SENTENCES

The children opened the cage.

The parrot flew out of the window.

I had forgotten to close it.

COMBINED SENTENCE

When the children opened the cage, the parrot flew out of the window, *which* I had forgotten to close.

Depending on what grammatical structures you use to subordinate, you can call attention to a less important element of a sentence in various ways, as the following series demonstrates.

The parks report was persuasively written. It contained five typed pages. [no subordination]

The parks report, *which contained five typed pages,* was persuasively written. [clause]

The parks report, *containing five typed pages,* was persuasively written. [participial phrase]

The *five-page* parks report was persuasively written. [adjective]

The parks report, *five typed pages,* was persuasively written. [appositive]

EXERCISE 20.3

Combine each of the following sets of sentences into one sentence that uses subordination to signal the relationships among ideas. Example:

> I was looking over my books.
> I noticed that *Burr* was missing.
> This book is a favorite of my roommate's.

> While I was looking over my books, I noticed that *Burr,* one of my roommate's favorite books, was missing.

1. I entered the hospital room.
   I was shocked.
   Tubes and life-support machines filled the room.
2. Madonna agreed to a film of her tour.
   The film was released in 1991.
   It was called *Truth or Dare.*
3. We had dug a seventy-foot ditch.
   My boss would pour gravel into the ditch.
   I would level the gravel with a shovel.
4. *Working* was written by Studs Terkel.
   It is an important book.
   It examines the situation of the American worker.
5. The scenery there is beautiful.
   The mountains have caps of snow.
   The lakes are deep and full of fish.
   The pastures are green.
   It is an ideal spot to spend spring break.

Using subordination for special effect

Carefully used subordination can create powerful effects. Some particularly fine examples come from Martin Luther King, Jr. In the following passage, he piles up dependent clauses to gain emphasis for his main statement, given in the independent clause. This emphasis is heightened by the repetition of the subordinating conjunction *when* to suggest forcefully "why we find it difficult to wait."

> Perhaps it is easy for those who have never felt the stinging darts of segregation to say, "Wait." But *when* you have seen vicious mobs lynch your mothers and fathers at will and drown your sisters and brothers at whim; *when* you have seen hate-filled policemen curse, kick, and even kill your black brothers and sisters; . . . *when* you have to concoct an answer

EXERCISE 20.3: Suggested Answers

1. When I entered the hospital room, I was shocked by the tubes and life-support machines everywhere.
2. *Truth or Dare,* a film of Madonna's tour, was released in 1991.
3. After my boss poured gravel into the seventy-foot-long ditch we had dug, I leveled the gravel with a shovel.
4. *Working,* an important book by Studs Terkel, examines the situation of the American worker.
5. The snow-capped mountains, green pastures, and deep, fish-filled lakes make the park a beautiful and ideal spot to spend spring break.

for a five-year-old son who is asking: "Daddy, why do white people treat colored people so mean?"; *when* you take a cross-country drive and find it necessary to sleep night after night in the uncomfortable corners of your automobile because no motel will accept you; . . . *when* your first name becomes "nigger," your middle name becomes "boy" (however old you are) and your last name becomes "John," and your wife and mother are never given the respected title "Mrs."; . . . *when* you are forever fighting a degenerating sense of "nobodiness"—then you will understand why we find it difficult to wait.

– MARTIN LUTHER KING, JR., "Letter from Birmingham Jail"

Look now at a student example that uses subordination in a similar way:

> *Though* dogs are messy and hard to train, *though* they chew up my shoes and give me the blues, *though* they howl like wolves but jump at their own shadows, *though* they eat me out of house and home—still, I love them all.

A dependent clause can also be used to create an ironic effect if it somehow undercuts the independent clause. Probably no American writer was better at using this technique than Mark Twain. In a tongue-in-cheek commencement address, Twain once opened a paragraph with this sentence (which you can see in context in 14e as an example of a shift in tone):

> Always obey your parents, *when they are present.*
>
> – MARK TWAIN, "Advice to Youth"

In undercutting the parental authority asserted in the independent clause, this dependent clause creates irony—and makes us laugh. Now look at a student writer's use of the same technique:

> Never eat fattening foods—*unless you are hungry.*

Like coordination, however, subordination can be used excessively. When too many subordinating structures, usually dependent clauses, are strung together, readers have trouble keeping track of the main idea expressed in the independent clause. Look, for example, at the following:

TOO MUCH SUBORDINATION

Philip II sent the Spanish Armada to conquer England, which was ruled by Elizabeth, who had executed Mary because she was plotting to overthrow Elizabeth, who was a Protestant, whereas Mary and Philip were Roman Catholics.

The long string of subordinate clauses at the end of this sentence makes the relationship of the ideas very hard to follow and also makes it hard for readers to remember the idea in the independent clause at the beginning. See how changing one of the dependent clauses to the independent clause of a new sentence and reducing two others to appositive phrases makes the relationship of ideas clearer:

REVISED

Philip II sent the Spanish Armada to conquer England, which was ruled by Elizabeth. She had executed Mary, a Roman Catholic like Philip, because Mary was plotting to overthrow Elizabeth, a Protestant.

 Checking your use of subordination

1. Underline the main ideas in each paragraph, perhaps underlining major ideas twice, lesser ones once.
2. If the "most important" ideas are not in independent clauses, try revising so that they are.
3. Try subordinating the less important ideas by putting them in dependent clauses or phrases.
4. Do any sentences contain more than three dependent clauses strung together? If so, does the main idea of the sentence get lost?
5. Examine any subordinating conjunctions you use—words like *although, if,* and *unless* (see 7b7)—to see that they express the correct relationship between clauses.

Revising for more effective subordination

Study the following passage about Edgar Allan Poe's "William Wilson," a strange tale about a young man who meets his double. Notice how it can be revised to connect and order its ideas more effectively.

In the years at the academy, <u>the two William Wilsons shared a bizarre relationship.</u> <u>The second Wilson established himself as equal to the first.</u> He was equal both in the classroom and on the playground. The first Wilson was used to feeling superior to his schoolmates, so <u>he was quite disturbed at the thought of having an equal.</u> He was especially disturbed that this equal had the same name and birthdate.

This passage depends heavily on simple sentences and use of simple coordination. Underlining the most important ideas gives the writer an idea of what might be subordinated to them, and the revision changes three of the less important ideas into prepositional phrases, an adjective clause, and an appositive phrase (shown here in italics).

EXERCISE 20.4: Suggested Answers

My friend Louise owns a huge mangy wolf, which is actually a seven-eighths wolf cross. The poor creature is allergic to everything, so it looks like a shabby, moth-eaten exhibit of a stuffed wolf in a third-rate museum. When Louise and Bill feed it rice and raw potatoes, it slavers all over everything. It never goes out of the house and it sleeps on the beds, which are covered with animal hair. It makes no sounds, looking at you with those sunken, wild eyes. It isn't dangerous or ferocious, just completely miserable. This animal is trying to tell you with every twitch that it should never have been born.

EXERCISE 20.5: Answers will vary.

FOR THE WRITING LOG

Ask students to use the analysis from Exercise 20.6 as the basis for a brief summary in their logs of (1) what they have learned about their own use of subordination and coordination, and (2) what plans or goals they have for using the two syntactic structures more effectively.

In the years at the academy, the two William Wilsons shared a bizarre relationship. The second Wilson established himself as equal to the first, *both in the classroom and on the playground.* The first Wilson, *who was used to feeling superior to his schoolmates,* was quite disturbed at the thought of having an equal, *especially one with the same name and birthdate.*

EXERCISE 20.4

Revise the following paragraph, using coordination and subordination where appropriate to clarify the relationships between ideas.

I stayed with my friend Louise. She owns a huge mangy wolf. It is actually a seven-eighths wolf cross. The poor creature is allergic to everything. It looks like a shabby, moth-eaten exhibit of a stuffed wolf in a third-rate museum. Louise and Bill feed it rice and raw potatoes. It slavers all over everything. It never goes out of the house. It sleeps on the beds. They are covered with animal hair. It makes no sounds. It just looks at you with those sunken, wild eyes. It is not dangerous or ferocious. It is just completely miserable. This animal should never have been born. It's trying to tell you that with every twitch.

EXERCISE 20.5 Reading with an Eye for Coordination and Subordination

Read over the first draft of "The Smart One," in 3f, with special attention to the coordination and subordination. Do you notice any patterns—is there some of each? more of one than the other? Analyze one paragraph, identifying the coordinate and subordinate phrases and clauses. Are they used appropriately? If not, revise the paragraph following the guidelines in this chapter.

EXERCISE 20.6 Taking Inventory: Coordination and Subordination

Analyze two paragraphs from one of your drafts for use of coordination and subordination. Do the independent clauses contain the main ideas? How many dependent clauses do you find? Should the ideas in the dependent clauses be subordinate to the ones in the independent clauses? Following the advice in 20a and 20b, revise the paragraphs to use coordination and subordination effectively. What conclusions can you draw about your use of coordination and subordination? Note them down (in your writing log, if you keep one).

21

Creating and Maintaining
Parallel Structures

Parallel grammatical structures form many of our most familiar phrases: *sink or swim, rise and shine, shape up or ship out.* But **parallelism**, expressing parallel elements in the same grammatical form, goes far beyond such clichés and, in fact, characterizes some of the most elegant passages in our language. Look, for example, at how E. B. White uses parallel structures to describe the enchantment of watching a bareback circus rider practicing her act:

> The enchantment grew *not out of anything that happened* or was performed *but out of something that seemed* to go round and around and around with the girl, attending her, a steady gleam in the shape of a circle—a ring *of ambition, of happiness, of youth.*
>
> — E. B. WHITE, "The Ring of Time"

Just as the young woman goes "round and around and around," balanced easily on her horse, so the sentence circles rhythmically too, balanced by a series of parallel phrases and clauses. Read the sentence aloud, and you will hear the effect of those parallel structures, rocking gently back and forth as does the horse in the ring.

This chapter will help you use parallelism to create pleasing rhythmic effects in your own writing.

21a

Using parallel structures in a series

All items in a series should be in parallel form—all nouns, all prepositional phrases, all adverb clauses, and so on. Such parallelism makes a series both graceful and easy to follow.

BACKGROUND

All successful rhetoricians recognize the power of parallel structures. The rhetorician Gorgias (c. 420 B.C.) was noted for his use of parallelism and antithesis. In his encomium (formal expression of enthusiastic praise) to Helen, he declares:

> Speech is a powerful lord which by means of the finest and most invisible body effects the divinest words: it can stop fear and banish grief and create joy and nurture piety.

By our contemporary standards, Gorgias's style is considered artificial and contrived—partially because of what we perceive as excessive parallelism.

In spite of our modern tendency to dislike excessive ornamentation of any kind, the appeal of parallel structures may be inherent in human psychology, or so argues Richard L. Graves in "Symmetrical Form and the Rhetoric of the Sentence." Graves notes that symmetry is everywhere—from our own physiology and self-expression to our art and architecture. Kenneth Burke, too, suggests that the concept of symmetry may be one of "the innate forms of the mind," along with comparison/contrast and repetition ("The Poetic Process," *Counter-Statement,* 1931 [Berkeley: U of California P, 1968], 46).

USEFUL READING

Graves, Richard L. "Symmetrical Form and the Rhetoric of the Sentence." *Classical Rhetoric and Modern Discourse.* Ed. Robert J. Connors, Lisa S. Ede, and Andrea A. Lunsford. Carbondale: Southern Illinois UP, 1984. 170–78. Graves identifies four major categories of parallelism: the repetition of key words; the use of opposite words (antithesis); repetition of grammatical elements; and various combinations of these three categories.

Lindemann, Erika. *A Rhetoric for Writing Teachers.* 2nd ed. New York: Oxford UP, 1987. Chapter 9 deals with teaching sentences. Especially useful is the discussion of sentence combining, backgrounding for understanding syntactic parallelism, repetition, and reduction.

BACKGROUND

Joseph Williams, echoing tradition, writes that "a common rule of rhetoric and grammar is that we can coordinate elements only of the same grammatical structure: clause and clause, predicate and predicate, prepositional phrase and prepositional phrase" (*Style: Ten Lessons in Clarity and Grace,* 3rd ed. [Glenview, IL: Scott, 1989], 128). Yet Williams concedes that the rule is often broken, on the grounds that clarity—not grammatical structure—measures the success or failure of parallel structures. Parallelism involves more than initially meets the eye. For instance, instead of looking at *She is tall, tanned, and very handsome* as a set of parallel adjectives, we might regard it as a combination of three separate but parallel sentences: *She is tall. She is tanned. She is very handsome.* In combining these sentences, the writer suppresses the repeated subject-verb cluster *She is,* expecting the reader to provide it mentally. When students see the source of parallel structures, they become more sensitive to their own parallel constructions.

EXERCISE 21.1: Answers will vary.

The quarterhorse *skipped, pranced,* and absolutely *sashayed* onto the track. [verbs]

Three subjects guaranteed to cause a fight are *politics, religion,* and *money.* [nouns]

The car rolled *down the hill, over the lawn,* and *into the swimming pool.* [prepositional phrases]

As more and more antismoking laws are passed, we see legions of potential nonsmokers *munching Nicorette, gnawing peppermints, chewing pencils, knitting sweaters,* or *practicing self-hypnotism.* [participial phrases]

Pushing a pen or pencil, pounding a typewriter, or *punching a word processor* just does not appeal to me. [gerund phrases]

When parallel elements are *not* presented in parallel grammatical form, the result can be awkward and even difficult to follow.

NONPARALLEL	The duties of the job included baby-sitting, house-cleaning, and the preparation of the meals.
PARALLEL	The duties of the job included *baby-sitting, house-cleaning,* and *preparing the meals.*

Lists

Items in a list should also be parallel in structure. Notice the lack of parallelism in the following list.

Observe the following regulations when using the library coffee service:

1. Coffee *to be made* only by library staff.
2. Coffee service *to be closed* at 4 P.M.
3. Doughnuts *to be kept* in cabinet.
4. No faculty members *should handle* coffee materials.

The fourth item on the list is not parallel with the others because it is a full sentence, not a phrase. Rewritten to maintain parallelism, this item could read: *Coffee materials not to be handled by faculty members.*

A formal outline should also be parallel in form (see 3e).

EXERCISE 21.1

Using two of the example sentences in 21a as models to imitate, write two sentences of your own that include a series of parallel phrases.

Everyday use

If you are in the habit of reading bumper stickers, you have probably seen parallelism at work in everyday language. Here are a couple of bumper sticker messages we've seen recently.

Children on board; parents on Valium.

Save the trees—axe the loggers.

Note down some such examples of parallel structures you see—on bumper stickers, T-shirts, wherever. Bring them to class, and compare them with those discovered by your classmates. Why do you think messages of this sort are often written in parallel form? A good way to explore this question might be by revising one of the parallel structures you find to make it not parallel. Does one version better catch your attention and stick in your mind?

21b

Using parallel structures with pairs

One common use of parallel structures occurs in the pairing of two ideas. The more nearly parallel the two structures are, the stronger the connection of ideas will be. Parallel structures are especially appropriate when two ideas are being compared or contrasted.

History became popular, and historians became alarmed.
— WILL DURANT

Writers are often more interesting on the page than in the flesh.

When two clauses in a sentence express compared or contrasted ideas in exactly or almost exactly parallel structures, they produce a **balanced sentence**, one with two parts that "mirror" each other. Balanced sentences create an especially forceful impression.

Mankind must put an end to war, or war will put an end to mankind.
— JOHN F. KENNEDY

There is much in your book that is original and valuable—but what is original is not valuable, and what is valuable is not original.
— SAMUEL JOHNSON

TEACHING PRACTICE

The following examples of parallel structures can be used to supplement those in the text:

Why is second base so important? Because when an easy grounder or a high pop-up is hit to that position, and you kick it away, or misjudge it and let it bounce on your head, the whole team gets demoralized. The shortstop comes over and says, Too bad the school bus didn't clip you this morning. The first baseman slaps his leg and laughs. The pitcher gives you the finger in front of everybody.
—LAURENCE SHEEHAN, "How to Play Second Base"

The dog has got more fun out of Man than Man has got out of the dog, for the clearly demonstrable reason that Man is the more laughable of the two animals. The dog has long been bemused by the singular activities and the curious practices of men, cocking his head inquiringly to one side, intently watching and listening to the strangest goings-on in the world. He has seen men sing together and fight one another in the same evening. He has watched them go to bed when it is time to get up, and get up when it is time to go to bed. He has observed them destroying the soil in vast areas, and nurturing it in small patches. He has stood by while men built strong and solid houses for rest and quiet, and then filled them with lights and bells and machinery. His sensitive nose, which can detect what's cooking in the next township, has caught at one and the same time the bewildering smells of the hospital and the munitions factory. He has seen men raise up great cities to heaven and then blow them to hell.
—JAMES THURBER, "A Dog's Eye View of Man"

OPTIONAL EXERCISE

Consider the following passage. Read it aloud, and ask students to try to identify the parallel structures.

> Let the word go forth from this time and place, to friend and foe alike, that the torch has been passed to a new generation of Americans—born in this century, tempered by war, disciplined by a hard and bitter peace, proud of our ancient heritage—and unwilling to witness or permit the slow undoing of those human rights to which this nation has always been committed, and to which we are committed today at home and around the world.
>
> —JOHN F. KENNEDY, Inaugural Address

What is the aural effect of the parallelism? Help your students break down each sentence into its root sentences, so they can see how beautifully those sentences were combined.

FOR THE WRITING LOG

Have your students comment in their logs on their analysis of the Kennedy passage.

EXERCISE 21.2: Suggested Answers

1. Live, drink, and be merry, for tomorrow we die.
2. My favorite pastimes include reading, exercising, and talking with friends.
3. We must either walk quickly or drive slowly.
4. I want not only hot fudge but also whipped cream.
5. The average teenager is willful, temperamental, and insecure.

With *coordinating conjunctions*

In general, use the same grammatical structure on both sides of any of the coordinating conjunctions—*and, but, or, nor, for, so, yet.*

We performed *whenever folks would listen* and *wherever they would pay.*

When elements connected by a coordinating conjunction are not parallel in form, the relationship of the elements can be hard to see.

NONPARALLEL	Ask a friend *in your class* or *who is good at math* to help you.
PARALLEL	Ask a friend *who is in your class* or *who is good at math* to help you.
PARALLEL	Ask a friend who *is in your class* or *is good at math* to help you.

With *correlative conjunctions*

Use the same structure after both parts of a correlative conjunction—*either . . . or, both . . . and, neither . . . nor, not . . . but, not only . . . but also, just as . . . so, whether . . . or.*

The organization provided both *scholarships for young artists* and *grants for established ones.*

NONPARALLEL	I wanted not only *to go away to school* but also *to New England.*
PARALLEL	I wanted not only *to go away to school* but also *to live in New England.*

EXERCISE 21.2

Complete the following sentences, using parallel words or phrases in each case. Example:

> The best teacher is one who <u>loves learning</u>, <u>respects students</u>, and <u>demands the best</u>.

1. _____, _____, and _____, for tomorrow we die.
2. My favorite pastimes include _____, _____, and _____.
3. We must either _____ or _____.
4. I want not only _____ but also _____.
5. The average teenager is _____, _____, and _____.

EXERCISE 21.3

Revise the following sentences to eliminate any errors in parallel structure.
Example:

Roger has studied archery, forestry, and ~~how to treat~~ *the treatment of* wild animals.

1. I remember the sticky, humid afternoons with the air as heavy as a wool blanket, my body dripping with sweat, how my sandy mouth yearned for an ice-cold glass of water.
2. I will always remember how the girls dressed in green plaid skirts and the boys wearing green plaid ties.
3. It was a question of either reducing their staff, or they had to somehow find new customers for their baked potatoes.
4. To need a new pair of shoes and not being able to afford them is enough to make anybody sensitive.
5. I'll never forget the good times we had—skiing, the swims, and especially that you taught me the basics of how to windsurf.
6. Too many students come to college only for fun, to find a husband or wife, or in order to put off having to go to work.
7. There are two types of wallflowers: the male wallflower is known as the nerd, and the female, who is known as the skeeve.
8. Her job was to show new products, help Mr. Greer with sales, and an opportunity to be part of advertising.
9. The Greek system not only provides the individual with a circle of friends but also it contributes to the development of leadership skills.
10. Stress can result in low self-esteem, total frustration, being unable to sleep, nervous breakdown, or eventually in suicide.

21c

Including all necessary words in parallel constructions

In addition to making parallel elements grammatically similar, be careful to include any words—prepositions, articles, verb forms, and so on—that are necessary for clarity, grammar, or idiom.

CONFUSING	We considered moving to a small town in the Southwest or Mexico. [To a small town in Mexico or to Mexico in general?]

EXERCISE 21.3: Suggested Answers

1. I remember the sticky, humid afternoons with the air as heavy as a wool blanket, my body dripping with sweat, my sandy mouth yearning for an ice-cold glass of water.
2. I will always remember how the girls dressed in green plaid skirts and the boys wore green plaid ties.
3. It was a question of either reducing their staff or somehow finding new customers for their baked potatoes.
4. Needing a new pair of shoes and not being able to afford them is enough to make anybody sensitive.
5. I'll never forget the good times we had— the skiing, the swimming, and especially the wind-surfing.
6. Too many students came to college to have fun, to find a husband or wife, or to put off having to go to work.
7. There are two types of wallflowers: the male, known as the nerd, and the female, known as the skeeve.
8. Her job was to show new products, to help Mr. Greer with sales, and to participate in advertising.
9. The Greek system not only provides the individual with a circle of friends but also contributes to the development of leadership skills.
10. Stress can result in low self-esteem, total frustration, sleeplessness, nervousness, or eventually suicide.

CLEAR	We considered moving *to a small town in the Southwest* or *to Mexico.*
CLEAR	We considered moving to a small town *in the Southwest* or *in Mexico.*
UNGRAMMATICAL	I had never before and would never again see such a sight. [*Had . . . see* is not grammatical.]
GRAMMATICAL	I *had never before seen* and *would never again see* such a sight.

21d

Using parallel structures for emphasis and effect

Parallel structures can help a writer emphasize the most important ideas in a sentence. Look at the following sentence:

> I would like to promise her that she will grow up with a sense of her cousins and of rivers and of her great-grandmother's teacups, would like to pledge her a picnic on a river with fried chicken and her hair uncombed, would like to give her *home* for her birthday, but we live differently now and I can promise her nothing like that.
>
> — JOAN DIDION, "On Going Home"

Notice that the first two parallel phrases, *would like to promise her . . . ,* *would like to pledge her . . . ,* provide a series of specific concrete details and images that lead up to the general statement in the last phrase, that Didion would like to give her daughter a sense of "home." Although Didion could have stated this general point first and then gone on to illustrate it with concrete details, she achieves far greater emphasis by making it the last in a series of parallel structures arranged in climactic order. (See 19a for more on emphasis.)

Besides emphasizing main ideas, parallel structures can create a number of different stylistic effects. One of these is orderliness, a sense of steady or building rhythm, as in the following sentence.

> Most police work is concerned with scared people who have been bitten by dogs, frantic people whose children have run away from home, old people who have no one to talk to, and impatient people whose first response to any situation is to "call the cops."

Note here how the repetition of the parallel phrases *scared people . . . ,* *frantic people . . . , old people . . . , impatient people . . .* builds a rhythm or beat that leads us to expect more of the same.

At work, he may have time to gulp down a cup of coffee if the dining halls are running smoothly, if all the workers show up, and if the boss is not asking questions.

This sentence creates an impression of somewhat desperate activity as it piles up the three parallel *if*-clauses.

> When [ants] are massed together, all touching, exchanging bits of information held in their jaws like memoranda, they become a single animal. Look out for that. It is a debasement, a loss of individuality, a violation of human nature, an unnatural act.
> — LEWIS THOMAS, "The Tucson Zoo"

The last sentence above comments on the image of the mass of ants; the comments are made more emphatic and intense by the parallelism.

 Checking your use of parallelism

1. Look for series of three or more items in the same sentence, and make all items parallel in structure. (21a) If there is some item you'd like to emphasize, try putting it at the end of the series. (21d)

2. Now look for places where two ideas are compared, contrasted, or otherwise paired in the same sentence. Often these ideas will appear on either side of a coordinating conjunction (*and, but, or, nor, for, so, yet*) or after both parts of a correlative conjunction (*both . . . and, either . . . or, neither . . . nor, not only . . . but also, whether . . . or, just as . . . so*). Revise if necessary to make both ideas parallel. (21b)

3. Be sure that you have included all words—articles, prepositions, the *to* of the infinitive, and so on—necessary for clarity. (21c)

4. Check for lists, and be sure all items are parallel in form.

EXERCISE 21.4

Underline the parallel structures in the following passage. Then use the passage as a model to imitate in creating a passage that uses parallelism in a similar way. You might begin such a passage with "At the _____ of the room, ..."

At the back of the room, standing on a furry white rug, was the long banquet table, dressed in damask, accented by groups of thin silver candlesticks bearing white candles, and laden with lovely food: cold chicken, lobster, candied ham fruit combinations, potato salad in a great golden dish, corn sticks, a cheese fluff in spiked tomato cups, fruit cake, angel cake, sunshine cake.
— GWENDOLYN BROOKS, *Maud Martha*

EXERCISE 21.4: Suggested Answers

At the back of the room, *standing on a furry white rug,* was the long banquet table, *dressed in damask, accented by groups of thin silver candlesticks bearing white candles,* and *laden with lovely food: cold chicken, lobster, candied ham fruit combinations, potato salad in a great golden dish, corn sticks, a cheese fluff in spiked tomato cups, fruit cake, angel cake, sunshine cake.*

Imitation passages will vary.

Using sources
Maintaining parallelism in headings

Parallel structures are particularly important in the headings and subheadings of reports, research projects, or long essays. In addition to serving as guideposts for your readers, headings divide complex or lengthy material into manageable segments. In adding headings, keep in mind the following details about parallelism:

- If you have more than one level of headings and subheadings, each level should be parallel in form. You might center one level, underline another, and so on. Whatever form you decide on, be sure that all the headings on each level have the same form.

- At each level, headings should also be parallel in wording—all nouns, all gerunds, all infinitive phrases, and so on.

EXERCISE 21.5   Revising for Parallelism

Revise the following paragraph to maintain parallelism and to supply all words necessary for clarity, grammar, and idiom in parallel structures.

> Growing up in a large city provides a very different experience from a suburban childhood. Suburban children undoubtedly enjoy many advantages over those who live in a city, including lawns to play ball on, trees for climbing, and often the schools are better. However, in recent years many people raised in the suburbs but who moved to large cities as young adults are deciding to bring up their own children in an urban setting. Their reasons for doing so include what they consider the cultural advantages of the city, the feeling that they will be able to spend more time with their children if they do not have to commute so far to work, and also they want to expose the children to a greater diversity of social and economic groups than most suburbs offer. Just as their own parents left the city for the space and calm of suburbia, so crowds and excitement are why today's parents are returning to it. Wherever they bring up their children, though, parents have never nor will they ever find utopia.

EXERCISE 21.6   Reading with an Eye for Parallelism

The following paragraph about a bareback rider practicing her circus act is laden with parallelism. (You will recognize the second sentence as the example used to open this chapter.) Read the paragraph, and identify all the parallel structures. Consider what effect they create on you as a reader, and try to decide why the author chose to put his ideas in such overtly parallel form. Try imitating the next-to-last sentence, the one beginning *In a week or two.*

EXERCISE 21.5: Suggested Answers

Growing up in a large city provides a very different experience from growing up in a suburb. Suburban children undoubtedly enjoy many advantages over city children, including lawns, trees, and better schools. However, in recent years many people who were raised in the suburbs but who moved to large cities as young adults are deciding to bring up their own children in an urban setting. Their reasons for doing so include being able to enjoy the cultural advantages of the city, being able to spend more time with their children if they do not have to commute so far to work, and being able to expose their children to a greater diversity of social and economic groups. Just as their own parents left the city for the space and calm of suburbia, so today's parents are returning to it for the crowds and excitement. Wherever they bring up their children, though, parents have never found nor ever will find utopia.

EXERCISE 21.6: Suggested Answers

The richness of the scene was in *its plainness, its natural condition—of horse, of ring, of girl,* even to the girl's bare feet that gripped the bare back of her proud and ridiculous mount. The

The richness of the scene was in its plainness, its natural condition—of horse, of ring, of girl, even to the girl's bare feet that gripped the bare back of her proud and ridiculous mount. The enchantment grew not out of anything that happened or was performed but out of something that seemed to go round and around and around with the girl, attending her, a steady gleam in the shape of a circle—a ring of ambition, of happiness, of youth. (And the positive pleasures of equilibrium under difficulties.) In a week or two, all would be changed, all (or almost all) lost: the girl would wear makeup, the horse would wear gold, the ring would be painted, the bark would be clean for the feet of the horse, the girl's feet would be clean for the slippers that she'd wear. All, all would be lost.

— E. B. WHITE, "The Ring of Time"

EXERCISE 21.7 Taking Inventory: Parallelism

Read over carefully several paragraphs from a draft you have recently written, noting any series of words, phrases, or clauses. Using the guidelines on p. 331, determine whether they are parallel, and if not, revise them for parallelism. Then reread the paragraphs, looking for places where parallel structures would add emphasis or clarity, and revise accordingly. Can you draw any conclusions about your use of parallelism? Make a note of them (in your writing log, if you keep one).

enchantment grew not *out of anything that happened or was performed* but *out of something that seemed to go round and around and around with the girl,* attending her, a steady gleam in the shape of a circle—a ring *of ambition, of happiness, of youth.* (And the positive pleasures of equilibrium under difficulties.) In a week or two, *all would be changed, all (or almost all) lost; the girl would wear makeup, the horse would wear gold, the ring would be painted, the bark would be clean for the feet of the horse, the girl's feet would be clean for the slippers that she'd wear.* All, all would be lost.

TEACHING PRACTICE

Ask students to bring their imitations *and* their revisions of their own paragraphs to class for discussion. Then divide the imitations and revisions into groups of five and ask students to work in groups to choose the one or two *most effective* uses of parallelism and to be prepared to report the reasons for their decisions to the rest of the class.

22

Varying Sentence Structures

Row upon row of trees identical in size and shape may appeal at some level to our sense of orderliness, but in spite of that appeal they soon become very boring. Constant unanimity in anything, in fact, soon gets tiresome; perhaps variety *is* the spice of life. Certainly that is true in sentence structures, where sameness can result in dull, listless prose.

The truth of this maxim was illustrated anew not long ago in a college classroom discussion of one student's essay. The group had worked on the essay for most of an hour, correcting errors, reorganizing paragraphs, clarifying the major points. Finally, one person said, "Okay, okay—but it's still BORING." All of the others, including the author, agreed. But they were stuck. The group could not come up with any new ideas and was about ready to give up when one student exclaimed, "I've got it! Look at these sentences. They all look about the same length!"

And they were. In fact, impossible as it may sound, every sentence in the essay was between twenty-two and twenty-five words long. Once the group realized this fact, they could begin to work again, carving some of the sentences into very short ones and combining others to create new rhythms. Through this revision, the essay took on new life as its boring sameness faded away.

This chapter will examine ways to use the traditional foes of boring sentences—variety in lengths, in openings, and in grammatical, functional, and rhetorical patterns.

EXERCISE 22.1: Answers will vary.

EXERCISE 22.1

Look at a piece of your writing. Count the words in each sentence to see how much your sentences vary in length. Choose one paragraph, and spend ten or fifteen minutes working to vary sentence length. Bring both versions to class.

22a

Varying sentence lengths

The situation described in the introduction illustrates perfectly the need for varying sentence length. Doing so not only makes prose more readable and interesting but also creates a pleasing rhythmic effect, what some students call "flow."

Deciding how and when to vary and balance sentence length is not always easy, however. How short is too short? How long is too long? Is there a "just right" length for a particular sentence or idea?

These questions are difficult to answer because the answers depend on, among other things, the writer's purpose, intended audience, and topic. A children's story, for instance, may call for mostly short sentences, while an article on nuclear disarmament in the *Atlantic* may call for considerably longer ones. In other words, in different situations either very long or very short sentences can be effective.

1

Using short sentences

Very short sentences can often pack a powerful punch. Study the following famous short sentences, and see if you agree that each owes much of its power to its brevity and that more words would detract.

Nice guys finish last.   Let them eat cake.

Love conquers all.   War is hell.

The following passage from a speech illustrates how effective a series of short sentences and other short structures—including sentence fragments—can be.

> What treaty that the whites have kept has the red man broken? Not one. What treaty that the white men ever made with us have they kept? Not one. When I was a boy the Sioux owned the world; the sun rose and set on their land; they sent ten thousand men to battle. Where are the warriors today? Who slew them? Where are our lands? Who owns them?
> — SITTING BULL, *Touch the Earth*

Notice how Sitting Bull's short questions, clauses, and fragments build a rhythm that gives power to his indictment of the white world. Repeated short sentences, if used with awareness of their effect, can go far beyond "See Spot run" into rhythmic beat and cadenced dignity.

TEACHING PRACTICE

Several techniques have been developed to help teach students to vary sentence structures, with sentence combining being perhaps the most well known and thoroughly studied. A lesser-known technique is Richard Larson's strategy of writing an essay on the board over several days, correcting and talking about the stylistic choices he makes as he writes. A third way to draw students' attention to varying sentence structures is Edward P. J. Corbett's method of stylistic analysis.

Whatever method you may choose, remember that stylistic choices about sentence structures depend upon the larger context of each individual sentence, the intended audience, and the purpose for writing.

USEFUL READING

Corbett, Edward P. J. *Classical Rhetoric for the Modern Student.* 3rd ed. New York: Oxford UP, 1990. See pages 398–423 for advice about analyzing sentence style.

Larson, Richard. "Back to the Board." *CCC* 29 (1978): 292–94. A further explanation of his composing technique.

Lindemann, Erika. *A Rhetoric for Writing Teachers.* 2nd ed. New York: Oxford UP, 1987. 133–39. A historical survey of sentence-combining research, from Hunt and O'Hare to Daiker and Morenberg.

FOR COLLABORATIVE WORK

Distribute the following paragraph. Ask half of your students to recast the information in the passage into a series of long sentences. Ask the other half to recast it into a string of short sentences. How do they compare? Reading the revisions aloud will help them "see" the difference.

As I said this I suddenly beheld the figure of a man, at some distance, advancing towards me with superhuman speed. He bounded over the crevices in the ice, among which I had walked with caution; his stature, also, as he approached, seemed to exceed that of man. I was troubled; a mist came over my eyes, and I felt a faintness seize me; but I was quickly restored by the cold gale of the mountains. I perceived, as the shape came nearer (sight tremendous and abhorred!) that it was the wretch whom I had created. I trembled with rage and horror, resolving to wait his approach and then close with him in mortal combat. He approached; his countenance bespoke bitter anguish, combined with disdain and malignity, while its unearthly ugliness rendered it almost too horrible for human eyes. But I scarcely observed this; rage and hatred had at first deprived me of utterance, and I recovered only to overwhelm him with words expressive of furious detestation and contempt.

—MARY SHELLEY, *Frankenstein*

Everyday use

Very short "capsule" reviews usually contain varied sentence structures, perhaps to keep readers' attention with a snappy, fast-paced description. A recent Newsweek *column included the following brief review.*

Thelma & Louise *looks like an* Easy Rider *for women. A good idea. But this isn't going to have men lining up in droves or cheering for more.*

The writer of this review varies sentence length by using a three-word fragment between two longer sentences and varies openings as well, beginning one sentence not with the subject but with but. *This variety helps make the brief synopsis easy to read and remember.*

Study some "capsule" reviews in a magazine or newspaper (or on TV), noting the variety of sentences used. Bring a few examples to class to compare with those found by classmates. Can you draw any conclusions about the effect of sentence variety on readers?

2

Using long sentences

In contrast to short sentences, long sentences are particularly useful for presenting a set of complex, interlocking ideas. The following paragraph shows how a series of long sentences can be used effectively in this way.

> Femininity pleases men because it makes them appear more masculine by contrast; and, in truth, conferring an extra portion of unearned gender distinction on men, an unchallenged space in which to breathe freely and feel stronger, wiser, more competent, is femininity's special gift. One could say that masculinity is often an effort to please women, but masculinity is known to please by displays of mastery and competence while femininity pleases by suggesting that these concerns, except in small matters, are beyond its intent. Whimsy, unpredictability and patterns of thinking and behavior that are dominated by emotion, such as tearful expressions of sentiment and fear, are thought to be feminine precisely because they lie outside the established route to success.
>
> — SUSAN BROWNMILLER, *Femininity*

Each of the three long sentences encapsulates the complex relationships between femininity and masculinity, and between women and men, that Brownmiller is seeking to explore. Short sentences would probably not work as effectively here because they could not adequately express the complexity of the ideas being presented.

3

Alternating short and long sentences

Although series of short and long sentences can both be effective in individual situations, frequent alternation in sentence length characterizes much memorable writing. After one or more long sentences that express complex ideas or images, the pith of a short sentence can be refreshing and arresting. For example:

> We are not so easily misled by vision. Most of the things before our eyes are plainly there, not mistakable for other things except for the illusions created by professional magicians and, sometimes, the look of the lights of downtown New York against a sky so black as to make it seem a near view of eternity. Our eyes are not easy to fool.
> — LEWIS THOMAS, "On Smell"

Similarly, a long sentence that follows a series of short ones can serve as a climax or summation that relaxes the tension or fulfills the expectation created by the series, giving readers a sense of completion. Here is an example.

> But it is under siege, too. Santa Fe, so recently hardly more than a remote and rather secretive village, is chic these days. The smart, the modish, the merely rich move in. The haven is embattled. The old hands watch thoughtfully as Santa Fe, *dear* Santa Fe, slowly but inexorably changes its character—as the condominiums spring up over the foothills, as the Soak Hot-Tub Club offers its twelve hot-tub suites with individual stereo and mood lighting, as downtown land reaches $100,000 an acre—as the triviality of things, the cuteness, the sham and the opportunism, spreads like a tinsel stain across the town.
> — JAN MORRIS, "Capital of the Holy Faith"

Notice the difference between these two passages, one of which contains sentences of fairly uniform length and the other of which varies sentence length. For example:

UNIFORM LENGTHS

The house is a fixer-upper, of course. For the past two days, I've been fixing things. It seems like the past two decades. I've been crawling about in the basement, which is dirt-floored, trying to learn to fix copper plumbing. The people renting the house last winter froze and burst the pipes. As a result, I have to put in all new stuff, learning as I go. With five-foot headroom, it's a real joy to be playing with torch and hot solder down there. I climb around oozing soilpipes from another era. I crouch Quasimodo-like, measuring, cutting, squatting, slouching, until my back

TEACHING PRACTICE

Consider the following paragraphs that include both long and short sentences used effectively. After your class has identified the variety of sentences according to length and type, ask them to write an imitation of these paragraphs on a topic of their own, such as participating in sports, giving birth, winning an award, or attending a concert. Finally, get your students to exchange and discuss their papers with at least three or four other students.

> Champion of the world. A Black boy. Some Black mother's son. He was the strongest man in the world. People drank Coca-Colas like ambrosia and ate candy bars like Christmas. Some of the men went behind the Store and poured white lightning in their soft-drink bottles, and a few of the bigger boys followed them. Those who were not chased away came back blowing their breath in front of themselves like proud smokers.
>
> It would take an hour or more before the people would leave the Store and head for home. Those who lived too far had made arrangements to stay in town. It wouldn't do for a Black man and his family to be caught on a lonely country road on a night when Joe Louis had proved that we were the strongest people in the world.
> —MAYA ANGELOU, "Champion of the World"

is permanently bent. I have been picking spiders out of my beard, and my clothes are indescribable.

VARIED LENGTHS

The house is a fixer-upper, of course, and so for the past two days (it seems like the past two decades), I've been fixing things, crawling about in the basement—dirt-floored, naturally—trying to learn to fix copper plumbing. What a nightmare! The people renting the house last winter froze and burst the pipes, and so I have to put in all new stuff. I'm learning as I go. With five-foot headroom, it's a real joy to be playing with torch and hot solder down there, climbing around oozing soilpipes from another era, crouching Quasimodo-like, measuring, cutting, squatting, slouching. My back is permanently bent. My beard is full of spiders. My clothes are indescribable.

In the second version, the writer uses coordination and subordination to combine the first four sentences of the first version into one long sentence that connects the main ideas of *a fixer-upper,* doing the fixing, and crawling about in the basement. He then adds a very short exclamatory sentence that both sums up the ideas in the first sentence and points ahead to the rest of the passage. Next, he combines two closely related ideas, about burst pipes and the installation of new ones, into one sentence of medium length, changing the participial phrase *learning as I go* into a separate short sentence. The next three sentences of the original version, all dealing with the ordeal of working in the basement, are combined into one long sentence. Finally, a dependent clause and the two short clauses of a compound sentence are separated into three short, parallel sentences (see Chapter 21), which give a blunt, hammering effect to the writer's expression of his complaints.

 Checking for varied sentence lengths

1. Count the words in each sentence, and underline the longest and shortest sentences in each paragraph.
2. If the difference between the longest and shortest sentences is fairly small—say, five words or fewer—consider revising the paragraph to create greater variety in length. Do not, however, change sentences arbitrarily. Think about the ideas you want to emphasize, and try to arrange your sentence lengths in a way that emphasizes them. Start by asking the questions in (3) and (4).
3. Do two or more short sentences in a row express closely related ideas? If so, could you make the relationship between these ideas

clearer or more precise by combining them into a single, longer sentence?

4. Is there a long sentence that contains two or three important ideas? Would these ideas be more emphatic if each was expressed in a short sentence of its own?

EXERCISE 22.2

The following paragraph can be improved by varying sentence length. Read it aloud to get a sense of how it sounds. Then revise it, creating some short emphatic sentences and combining other sentences to create more effective long sentences. Add words or change punctuation as you need to.

Before beginning to play bridge, it is necessary to have the proper materials, the correct number of people, and a knowledge of the rank of suits and cards. The necessary materials include a full deck of playing cards (minus the jokers) and a score pad, along with a pen or pencil. Bridge is played by four people divided into two partnerships, which are usually decided by drawing cards from a shuffled deck. The two players who draw the highest cards and the two who draw the lowest are partners, and the partners sit across from each other. The person who draws the highest card during partnership is the first dealer. Starting with the person on his or her left and going clockwise, the dealer deals each person one card at a time, face down. The deal continues until all four players have thirteen cards apiece. After the deal, the players sort their cards by suit, usually alternating black and red suits. The players then arrange the cards in ranking order from the highest, the ace, to the lowest, the deuce. The five highest cards, the ace, king, queen, jack, and ten, are referred to as honors. There is one suit that has great power and outranks every other one, the trump suit, which is designated at the start of the game.

22b

Varying sentence openings

In making prose readable and interesting, beginning sentences in different ways is just as important as making them of different lengths. For instance, when each sentence begins with the subject of an independent clause, a passage may seem to lurch or jerk along.

EXERCISE 22.2: Suggested Answers

To play bridge, you need to have the proper materials—a full deck of playing cards minus the jokers, a score pad, and a pen or pencil—and four players with a knowledge of suit and card ranking. The players are divided into two partnerships, which are usually decided by drawing cards from a shuffled deck; the two players who draw the highest cards and the two who draw the lowest are partners and sit across from each other. The person who draws the highest card during partnership is the first dealer. The dealer, starting clockwise with the person on the left, deals each player one facedown card at a time until all four players have thirteen cards apiece. After the deal, the players sort their cards by suit, usually alternating black and red suits, and then arrange the cards in ranking order, from the highest, the ace, to the lowest, the deuce. The five highest cards, the ace, king, queen, jack, and ten, are referred to as honors and the one suit that outranks every other one, which is designated at the start of the game, is called the trump suit.

BACKGROUND

In *Classical Rhetoric for the Modern Student,* Edward P. J. Corbett lists eleven sentence openers—all of which any beginning writer can learn to use in effective combination.

1. Subject—*John* broke the window; *The high cost* of living will offset . . .

2. Expletives—*It is plain that . . . There* are ten Indians. Exclamations: *Alas, Oh*

3. Coordinating conjunction—*And, But, Or, Nor, For, Yet, So*

4. Adverb word—*First, Thus, Moreover, Nevertheless, Namely.*

5. Conjunctive phrase—*On the other hand, As a consequence*

6. Prepositional phrase—*After the game, In the morning*

7. Verbal phrase—participial, gerundive, or infinitive phrase

8. Adjective phrase—*Tired but happy, we . . .*

9. Absolute phrase—*The ship having arrived safely, we . . .*

10. Adverb clause—*When the ship arrived, we . . .*

11. Front-shift (inverted word order)—*The expense we could not bear. Gone was the wind. Happy were they to be alive* (3rd ed., New York: Oxford UP, 1990, 422).

TEACHING PRACTICE

Ask your students to take out their latest piece of writing and analyze all the declarative sentences according to sentence openers. How many (and what percentage of) sentences begin with each of the above options? They may want to analyze a professional essay as well and then compare their results.

TEACHING PRACTICE

Some students have considerable trouble punctuating dependent clauses, especially introductory dependent clauses. They often turn them into sentence fragments by separating them from the main clause with a period. Outlined below is one possible method for helping students overcome this problem.

> I worked all summer at the car dealership. Although I really wanted to go to baseball camp.

1. You may want to point out the problem in meaning for the reader—the false or due expectation (Coming after a period, the *Although I really wanted* clause makes us think that another sentence is coming.)

2. Then, ask students to supply an alternative, relying on their competence to provide a solution. (They may want to erase the period and make the *A* of *Although* a lowercase letter. Or they may add more

The way football and basketball are played is as interesting as the players. *Football* is a game of precision. *Each play* is diagrammed to accomplish a certain goal, and a coach designs the plays the way an engineer would design a bridge. *Basketball* is a game of availability. A *basketball game* looks like a track meet; the team that drops of exhaustion first loses. *Basketball players* are also often compared to artists. *The players' moves and slam dunks* are their masterpieces.

Varying sentence openings can prevent this jerky effect. This section will focus on three ways of varying openings—transitional expressions; prepositional, verbal, and absolute phrases; and dependent clauses.

1

Using transitional expressions

See how transitions bring variety and clarity to this passage.

> In order to be alert Friday morning in New York, I planned to take the shuttle from Washington Thursday night. *On Thursday morning* it began to snow in Washington and to snow even harder in New York. *By mid-afternoon* I decided not to risk the shuttle and caught a train to New York. *Seven hours later* the train completed its three-hour trip. I arrived at Penn Station to find a city shut down by the worst blizzard since 1947.
>
> – LINDA ELLERBEE, *"And So It Goes"*

Here the transitional words establish chronology and help carry us along smoothly through the paragraph. Many other transitional expressions can be used to vary sentence openings. See 6c5 for a detailed list.

2

Using phrases

Prepositional, verbal, and absolute phrases can also provide variety in sentence openers.

PREPOSITIONAL PHRASES

At each desk, a computer printout gives the necessary data.

From a few scraps of wood in the Middle Ages to a precisely carved, electrified instrument in the 1980s, the guitar has gone through uncounted changes.

VERBAL PHRASES

Frustrated by the delays, the drivers started honking their horns.

To qualify for flight training, one must be in good physical condition.

ABSOLUTE PHRASES

Our hopes for snow shattered, we started home.

Baton raised in a salute, the maestro readied the orchestra.

3

Using dependent clauses

Dependent clauses are another way to open a sentence.

While the boss sat on his tractor, I was down in a ditch pounding in stakes and leveling out the bottom.

What they want is a place to call home.

Because the hills were dry, the fire spread rapidly.

 Checking for varied sentence openings

Underline the subject of each sentence. If most of your sentences begin with the subject, revise some of them to open in other ways. Consider the following suggestions.

1. Look for sentences that are related to the preceding sentence in a specific chronological, spatial, or logical way, which could be signaled by adding a transitional expression. (See 6c5 and 22b1.)

2. Try rewording some sentences to begin with a phrase. (See 7c3 and 22b2.)

3. If you have two related sentences, one after the other, see if it would be logical to combine them into one sentence, making the first a dependent clause. (See 7c4 and 22b3.)

Revising to vary sentence openings

The following passage uses only subject openings; see how varying the sentence openings makes the passage easier to read:

FIRST DRAFT

<u>Most marathon runners</u> find that running with another person is helpful. <u>They</u> must not be afraid to pass this person, though, in order to run as well as possible. <u>Runners</u> must realize furthermore that even if they do not win the race, they achieve a victory by pushing their bodies to finish.

information to the *Although* clause: *Although I really wanted to go to baseball camp, I needed to earn money, not spend it.*)

3. You can use this opportunity to suggest other alternatives that clarify or reiterate the meaning conveyed by the kernel sentence ([1] *Although I really wanted to go to baseball camp, I worked all summer at the car dealership.* [2] *I worked all summer at the car dealership although I really wanted to go to baseball camp instead.* [3] *I worked all summer at the car dealership. Although I really wanted to go to baseball camp, I needed to earn money, not spend it.*)

TEACHING PRACTICE

Consider sharing with your students the following passage. Point out to them the ways Rodriguez varies his sentence openers, including his use of dependent clauses.

Three months passed. Five. A half year. Unsmiling, ever watchful, my teachers noted my silence. They began to connect my behavior with the slow progress my brother and sisters were making. Until, one Saturday morning, three nuns arrived at the house to talk to our parents. Stiffly they sat on the blue living-room sofa. From the doorway of another room, spying on the visitors, I noticed the incongruity, the clash of two worlds, the faces and voices of school intruding upon the familiar setting of home. I overheard one voice gently wondering, "Do your children speak only Spanish at home, Mrs. Rodriguez?" While another voice added, "That Richard especially seems so timid and shy."
—RICHARD RODRIGUEZ,
"Aria: A Memoir of a Bilingual Childhood"

REVISED

Most marathon runners find that running with another person is helpful. In order to run as well as possible, though, *they* must not be afraid to pass this person. Furthermore, *runners* must realize that even if they do not win the race, they achieve victory by pushing their bodies to finish.

EXERCISE 22.3

Go back to the paragraph comparing football and basketball in 22b. Using transitional expressions, phrases, and/or dependent clauses, revise the paragraph to vary its sentence openings and thus make it smoother and more coherent.

22c

Varying sentence types

In addition to using different lengths and openings, you can help vary your sentence structures by using different *types* of sentences. Sentences can be classified in three different ways: grammatically, functionally, and rhetorically (see 7d).

1

Grammatical types

Grammatically, sentences fall into four categories—**simple, compound, complex,** and **compound-complex**—based on the number of independent and dependent clauses they contain. (See 7d1.) Varying your sentences among these grammatical types can go a long way toward creating readable, effective prose.

2

Functional types

Functional types of sentences include **declarative** (making a statement), **interrogative** (asking a question), **imperative** (giving a command), and **exclamatory** (expressing strong feeling). (See 7d2.) Most sentences in essays are declarative, but occasionally you may want to include a command, a question, or even an exclamation of some kind if such sentence types are appropriate for your purpose. (See 7d2.) Note how they are used in these examples.

EXERCISE 22.3: Suggested Answers

The way football and basketball are played is as interesting as the players. Because football is a game of precision, each play is diagrammed to accomplish a certain goal and a coach designs the plays the way an engineer would design a bridge. Basketball, however, is a game of availability. In fact, a basketball game looks like a track meet; the team that drops of exhaustion first loses. Basketball players are also often compared to artists because their moves and slam dunks are their masterpieces.

TEACHING PRACTICE

For quick reference, here are examples of each of the four grammatical types:

Simple: Later, Susan arrived.

Compound: People tried to reassure me, but they could not understand my fear.

Complex: While we walked over to the picnic, we talked about the problem of being roommates.

Compound-Complex: I told her about the courses I enjoyed most, and she told me about her current reading, including *The Sheep Look Up.*

COMMAND

Coal-burning plants undoubtedly harm the environment in various ways; among others, they contribute to acid rain. *But consider the alternatives.*

QUESTION

We kept pressing on into the park. *And why? Why would sixteen middle-aged people try to backpack thirty-seven miles?* At this point, I was not at all sure.

EXCLAMATION

Divorcés! They were everywhere! Sometimes he felt like a new member of an enormous club, the Divorcés of America, that he had never before even heard of.

3

Rhetorical types

Two rhetorical sentence types, periodic and cumulative, spotlight sentence endings and beginnings and can be especially helpful in achieving sentence variety. Although not all sentences can be classified as cumulative or periodic, these types can create strong effects when used in appropriate situations.

Periodic sentences

Periodic sentences postpone the main idea (usually in an independent clause) until the very end of the sentence. Effectively written periodic sentences are especially useful for creating tension or building toward a climactic or surprise ending. At their best, they keep us alert by holding information in a kind of "suspended animation" until the end. (See 7d3.) Note in each of the following examples how the writer holds back the main idea, thus using the end of the sentence to shock or inspire.

> Early one morning, under the arc of a lamp, carefully, silently, in smock and leather gloves, *old Doctor Manza grafted a cat's head onto a chicken's trunk.*
> — DYLAN THOMAS

> Even though large tracts of Europe and many old and famous states have fallen or may fall into the grasp of the Gestapo and all the odious apparatus of Nazi rule, *we shall not flag or fail.*   — WINSTON CHURCHILL

Look at the following sentence and its revision to see how periodic order can provide emphasis:

COMPLEX SENTENCE

The nations of the world have no alternative but coexistence because another world war would be unwinnable and because total destruction would certainly occur.

REVISED AS A PERIODIC SENTENCE

Because another world war would be unwinnable and because total destruction would certainly occur, the nations of the world have no alternative but coexistence.

Nothing is wrong with the first sentence, which conveys the information clearly. But to put greater emphasis on the idea in the independent clause of the sentence—no alternative but coexistence—the writer chose to revise using the periodic pattern.

Cumulative sentences

Cumulative sentences, which begin with an independent clause and then add details in phrases and other clauses, are the dominant rhetorical pattern today, far more common than periodic sentences. They are useful when you want to provide both immediate understanding of the main idea and a great deal of supporting detail. The writers of the following sentences use the cumulative pattern not only to add important detail but also to end with a strong word or image.

> From boyhood to manhood, *I have remembered him in a single image*— seated, asleep on the sofa, his head thrown back in a hideous corpselike grin, the evening newspaper spread out before him.
> — RICHARD RODRIGUEZ, "My Parents"

> *Powther threw small secret appraising glances at the coffee cup,* lipstick all around the edges, brown stains on the side where the coffee had dripped and spilled over, the saucer splotched with a whole series of dark brown rings.
> — ANN PETRY, *The Narrows*

EXERCISE 22.4

Revise the following sentences twice, as periodic and cumulative sentences.

1. The members of the crew team entered the shell house one by one. They were tired and weary. It was four o'clock on a cold, damp morning in Seattle, Washington.

2. I became the best salesperson in our store once I mastered the problems that I had encountered at the beginning and once I became thoroughly familiar with the stock.

EXERCISE 22.4: Suggested Answers

1. *Periodic:* At four o'clock on a cold, damp morning in Seattle, Washington, one by one, tired and weary, the members of the crew team entered the shell house. *Cumulative:* The members of the crew team entered the shell house one by one, tired and weary, at four o'clock on a cold, damp morning in Seattle, Washington.

2. *Periodic:* Once I mastered the problems that I had encountered at the beginning and once I became thoroughly familiar with the stock, I became the best salesperson in our store. *Cumulative:* I became the best salesperson in our store once I mastered the problems that I had encountered at the beginning and once I became thoroughly familiar with the stock.

Checking for varied sentence types

1. Mark each sentence as simple, compound, complex, or compound-complex. If any one or two patterns predominate, combine, divide, and otherwise revise sentences to vary the grammatical types in your draft. (22c1)

2. Next, note any sentences that are commands, questions, or exclamations. Consider whether the ideas in any declarative sentences might be emphasized effectively as commands, questions, or exclamations. (22c2)

3. Look for cumulative and periodic sentences. (See 22c3; many sentences will be neither.) Then look for ideas with much detail or with colorful images. Would they be best expressed as cumulative sentences? And look for ideas that could use greater emphasis—would they get such emphasis in periodic sentences?

Revising to vary sentence types

Study how the sentences in the following passage are identified and then revised.

FIRST DRAFT

The purpose of speech is most often to persuade. [simple] It is seldom to generate understanding or to stimulate thoughtful response. [simple] Speeches on television take advantage of this fact. [simple] A televised speech gives viewers the time only to receive information, to respond emotionally to it, to "feel" it. [simple/cumulative] Viewers can simply enjoy or deplore its impact. [simple] Unlike a televised speech, a written speech can be read, reread, and analyzed. [simple] The reader can thoroughly process and analyze it. [simple] For this reason, I prefer to read and study a speech, not watch and instantly swallow it. [simple] This preference is limited to speeches that may be of great importance to me. [simple]

REVISED

The purpose of speech is most often not to generate understanding or to stimulate thoughtful response; rather, its purpose is merely to persuade. [compound] A televised speech takes advantage of this merely persuasive purpose by giving viewers time only to receive information, to respond emotionally to it, to "feel" or simply enjoy or deplore it. [simple/cumulative] Unlike a televised speech, a written speech can be read and reread, thoroughly analyzed and processed. [simple/periodic] For this reason, I prefer to read and study, not watch and instantly "swallow," any speech that may be of great importance to me. [complex]

FOR COLLABORATIVE WORK

Have students, working in pairs or in groups of three, choose a topic of interest to all the members and then write passages of at least twenty-five short sentences (shorter than twelve words). After they have traded passages with another group or pair, ask each group to combine some of the twenty-five sentences into longer sentences, while retaining some short sentences for emphasis.

Naturally, each group will combine sentences differently, so you might want to make an opportunity to explain their choices and reasons for combining some sentences while keeping others short.

EXERCISE 22.5: Suggested Answers

When we arrived at the accident scene, I could tell that the injuries were not minor. (16 words; adverb clause; complex)

I walked up to the car nearest me to check the injuries of the people inside. (16 words; subject; simple)

I looked through the driver's window and saw the woman's body entangled in the steering wheel. (16 words; subject; simple)

I told dispatch, via two-way radio, to send medics "code red, lights and siren." (14 words; subject; simple)

I then went to see how the passenger in the car was. (12 words; subject; simple)

The passenger appeared to be in shock and had a broken leg. (12 words; subject; simple)

The officer walked over and checked the other vehicle. (9 words; subject; simple)

The driver of the other vehicle was drunk and had received no injuries at all. (15 words; subject; simple)

EXERCISE 22.6: Answers will vary.

EXERCISE 22.5 Revising for Sentence Variety

Following is an introductory paragraph from an essay. Analyze the paragraph carefully, noting for each sentence the length, the kind of opening, and the grammatical and rhetorical type. Then revise the paragraph to add variety in sentence lengths, sentence openings, and sentence types.

When we arrived at the accident scene, I could tell that the injuries were not minor. I walked up to the car nearest me to check the injuries of the people inside. I looked through the driver's window and saw the woman's body entangled in the steering wheel. I told dispatch, via two-way radio, to send medics "code red, lights and siren." I then went to see how the passenger in the car was. The passenger appeared to be in shock and had a broken leg. The officer walked over and checked the other vehicle. The driver of the other vehicle was drunk and had received no injuries at all.

EXERCISE 22.6 Reading with an Eye for Sentence Variety

Read with an eye for sentence variety something by an author you admire. Analyze two paragraphs for sentence length, opening, and type. Compare the sentence variety in these paragraphs with that in one of your paragraphs— perhaps the one you analyzed in Exercise 22.1. What similarities or differences do you recognize, and what conclusions can you draw about sentence variety?

EXERCISE 22.7 Taking Inventory: Sentence Variety

Choose several paragraphs of an essay you have written, and examine them very carefully for variety of sentence structure. For each sentence, note the length, the kind of opening, and the grammatical, functional, and rhetorical type. Then revise the paragraphs to achieve as wide a range of variation as possible in these qualities. Read the original and revised versions aloud, noting the differences in rhythm and impact. Note down any thoughts you have about sentence variety for future use (in your writing log, if you keep one).

23

Creating Memorable Prose

How many times have you read something so striking that you wanted immediately to share it with a friend? And how many times have you remembered the exact words of something you have read or heard? All of us recognize, and can even quote, certain passages from literature or history or music—the opening of *A Tale of Two Cities,* perhaps, or passages from "I Have a Dream" or lyrics to a well-known tune.

As students of writing, we would profit by taking the time to examine some of the elements that make pieces such as these so memorable. Consider, for instance, some lines from one of the most quoted speeches of our century, John F. Kennedy's Inaugural Address:

> Let every nation know, whether it wishes us well or ill, that we shall pay any price, bear any burden, meet any hardship, support any friend, oppose any foe to assure the survival and the success of liberty.
>
> In your hands, my fellow citizens, more than mine, will rest the final success or failure of our course.
>
> And so, my fellow Americans, ask not what your country can do for you; ask what you can do for your country.
>
> — JOHN F. KENNEDY, Inaugural Address

What strategies did Kennedy use to make these lines so very memorable? First would be his use of *repetition:* in the first sentence, the repetition of short verb phrases, each with the word *any,* creates a powerful, hammerlike rhythm. Second might be his use of *inverted word order:* saving the subject until the end of the second sentence adds dramatic emphasis to his statement. Third would be his use of *antithesis,* seen in the last sentence in the two parallel clauses that accentuate the contrast of self and country. Finally, Kennedy's reliance on *strong verbs* and the *active voice* results in prose that is lively and thus memorable.

TEACHING PRACTICE

The allusion to *A Tale of Two Cities* may stimulate the curiosity of students who are unfamiliar with its opening. You might follow up on the text's discussion of the Kennedy speech by reading Dickens's passage aloud and asking students to identify its memorable characteristics:

> It was the best of times, it was the worst of times, it was the age of wisdom, it was the age of foolishness, it was the epoch of belief, it was the epoch of incredulity, it was the season of Light, it was the season of Darkness, it was the spring of hope, it was the winter of despair, we had everything before us, we had nothing before us, we were all going direct to Heaven, we were all going direct the other way—in short, the period was so far like the present period, that some of its noisiest authorities insisted on being received, for good or for evil, in the superlative degree of comparison only.
>
> —CHARLES DICKENS, *A Tale of Two Cities*

USEFUL READING

Havelock, Eric A. "The Character and Content of the Code." *The Literate Revolution in Speech and Its Cultural Consequences* Princeton: Princeton UP, 1982. 140–44. Havelock identifies the characteristics of memorable oral speech: parataxis, echoes, correspondences and symmetries, foreshadowing, and repetition.

Lanham, Richard A. *Analyzing Prose.* New York: Scribner's, 1983. Lanham provides a full system for stylistic analyses.

Williams, Joseph M. *Style: Ten Lessons in Clarity and Grace.* 3rd ed. Glenview, IL: Scott, 1989. Williams deals with aspects of memorable prose style.

EXERCISE 23.1: Answers will vary.

TEACHING PRACTICE

In the midst of a relatively lifeless early draft of an essay on the Chernobyl nuclear disaster by a student writer, the reader suddenly comes across the following sentences:

> The force of the blast toppled the reactor's thousand ton lid. It shattered the sides and roof of the building as if they were glass. Tons of uranium dioxide fuel and other products used in the fission process detonated. The explosion sent heat, debris, and radiation nearly five kilometers into the sky.

The passage is not so different from the rest of the essay that we suspect plagiarism, but the strong verbs and nouns are striking and bring an otherwise dull essay alive momentarily.

Memorable writing can occur at all levels. Whole passages such as the one above may occur, or single words may jump out of an otherwise desert of weak, forgettable prose. Pointing out your recognition of what's good in a piece provides the student writer with a model, however brief, for later writing and boosts a student's self-esteem, something that may very well stimulate his or her commitment to writing.

Each of these strategies and devices can be used to good effect by all writers. This chapter will examine each one and offer practice to help you use them in your work, to make your writing not only worth reading—but worth remembering.

EXERCISE 23.1

Think of something in your current reading that sticks in your mind as particularly memorable. Then find that piece, and reread it to try to identify what makes the passage so memorable. Choose one sentence you especially like, and try imitating its structure in a sentence of your own.

Everyday use

Like the clothes we wear, the words we choose and the way we use them bring memorable qualities to our language. Nowhere are such choices more evident in daily life than it is in music. Every songwriter knows the importance of creating lyrics and rhythms that listeners will remember.

Rap music demands careful attention to stylistic choices, for its lyrics must be very concise as well as memorable. Here's an example from Queen Latifah and Monie Love's "Ladies First."

I'm conversating to the folks who have no whatsoever clue
So listen very carefully as I break it down for you
Merrily, merrily, merrily, merrily, hyper, happy, overjoyed
Pleased with all the beats and rhymes my sister has employed
Slick and smooth, throwing down, the sound totally a yes
Let me state the position: Ladies first, yes?

Yes!

Look at the words and structures the writer here has chosen to make the lyrics memorable: the active verbs (listen), the inversion of normal word order (no whatsoever clue), the powerful use of repetition (merrily, merrily, merrily, merrily), and especially the three yeses *that drive home both the rhythm and the point. What do you find most memorable about this particular rap?*

Think of some music and lyrics that you find particularly memorable. Listen to the song, and jot down its exact words. What has the writer done to make the lyrics memorable?

23a

Choosing strong verbs

The greatest writers in any language are those with a genius for choosing the precise words that will arrest and hold a reader's attention. In your own writing, you can help gain this attention by using precise nouns and adjectives instead of vague, catchall "buzzwords" (see 19b2). Perhaps even more important, however, you can use strong, precise verbs instead of weak, catchall verbs and instead of nouns.

1

Using strong, precise verbs

Verbs serve as the real workhorses of our language. Take a look, for instance, at the strong, precise verbs in the following passage:

> A fire engine, out for a trial spin, *roared* past Emerson's house, hot with readiness for public duty. Over the barn roofs the martens *dipped* and *chittered.* A swarthy daughter of an asparagus grower, in culottes, shirt, and bandanna, *pedalled* past on her bicycle.   – E. B. WHITE, "Walden"

Instead of the italicized verbs, White could have used more general verbs such as *drove, flew, called,* and *rode.* But the more precise verbs are stronger because they give readers vivid sensory impressions of the actions they express. In White's verbs, readers can hear the roar of the fire engine, see the martens swooping downward and hear them chirping shrilly, and feel the young woman pushing on the pedals of her bicycle.

Some of the most common verbs in English—especially *be, do,* and *have*—carry little or no sense of specific action, and many writers tend to overuse them in situations where more precise verbs would be clearer and more effective. Look at how the following sentences are strengthened by replacing them with more precise verbs:

WEAK	Constant viewing of rock videos *is* harmful to children's emotional development.
REVISED	Constant viewing of rock videos *stunts* and *distorts* children's emotional development.
WEAK	In front of the hotel, an artist would *do* your portrait on a framed sheet of glass.
REVISED	In front of the hotel, an artist would *etch* your portrait on a framed sheet of glass.

WEAK	We *had* basic training at Fort Ord.
REVISED	We *sweated* through basic training at Fort Ord.

The verb *be* is essential to writing; indeed, it appears in some of the most memorable English prose, such as the opening of the Gospel According to St. John.

> In the beginning was the Word, and the Word was with God, and the Word was God.

But as the three examples above illustrate, *be* can often be replaced by verbs that express action. As a general rule, if forms of *be* (*is, are, was, were, has been,* and so on) account for more than about a third of the verbs in a piece of writing, the writing may well seem static and flat.

Expletives

One potentially weak verb construction to watch out for is the **expletive**, which begins with *there* or *it* followed by a form of *be* (*there are, it is,* and so on). Expletives can offer effective ways of introducing an idea with extra emphasis, as Eudora Welty does in the following sentence.

> *It is* our inward journey that leads us through time—forward or back, seldom in a straight line, most often spiraling.
> — EUDORA WELTY, *One Writer's Beginnings*

Here the *it is* slows down the opening of the sentence and sets up a rather formal rhythm that adds emphasis to the main idea, "our inward journey." Often, however, writers do not use expletive openings to add emphasis. Instead, they merely overuse them, creating sentences that needlessly bury action in nouns, verbals, or dependent clauses. Notice how the following sentences are strengthened by deleting the expletives.

WEAK	*There are* many people who fear success because they believe they do not deserve it.
REVISED	Many people *fear* success because they believe they do not deserve it.
WEAK	*It is* necessary for a presidential candidate today to perform well on television.
REVISED	A presidential candidate today *must perform* well on television.

Memo:

1) The problem is, This is not very easy textbooks

2) However, educators must chose to deal w/ and come to grips with what is essentially a full-blown American Creole language that is not dying. Sociolinguists can help make explicit that today's Black linguistic usage represent a remarkable achievement — at everyone's way to hold on to one of the few aspects of Af culture that remains in the clearly

Style, retained from delivery.
Sophisticated must balance the
pause between thought + phrase more
explicit + made simpler. Must be
very good in for understanding that
in non-static, I'm sophistic while
being present + putting readers needs.

1) authentic conversant
2) Writers know The Cues ⟹ speaking
   knowing
   The Cues
3) Multiple intelligences —
   multiple (not dichotomous) doesn't
4) multi voices, literacies, discourses

2
Changing nouns to verbs

Much modern writing tends to express action by using nouns that are formed from verbs, a process called **nominalization**. Although nominalization can help make prose clearer and more concise—for example, using *abolition* instead of *the process of abolishing*—it can also produce the opposite effect, making a sentence unnecessarily wordy and hard to read. Nominalization reduces the *active* quality of a sentence, burying the action in an abstract noun and forcing the writer to use weak, generalized verbs and too many prepositional phrases. Too often, writers use nominalizations not to make a complex process easier to talk about but to make an idea *sound* more complex and abstract than it really is. Bureaucratic writing especially tends to use excessive nominalization in this way.

You can decide when to use a nominalized form and when to use the verb from which it derives by asking one question: which is most readily understandable? Look at the following sentence:

> The firm is now engaged in an assessment of its procedures for the development of new products.

This sentence scarcely impresses itself on our memories, and it sounds pretentious and stuffy as well. In contrast, note the more easily understood and forceful version.

> The firm is now assessing its procedures for developing new products.

⋙ *Checking your verbs and nouns*

1. First underline all the verbs, and look to see whether you are relying too much on *be, do,* and *have.* If so, try to substitute more specific verbs. (23a1)
2. Note nouns whose meaning could be expressed by a verb. Try revising using the verb instead of the noun. (23a2)
3. Identify all expletives, and delete any that are not used to create special emphasis. (23a1)
4. Look for passive verbs, and decide whether they obscure the performer of the action or dull the sentence. If so, revise them to be in the active voice. (23b)

BACKGROUND

In *Style: Ten Lessons in Clarity and Grace,* Joseph Williams offers four cases of useful nominalization:

1. Nominalizations can be subjects referring to previous sentences: *These arguments* all depend on a single unproven claim.
2. Nominalizations can name what would be the objects of their verbs: I do not understand *her meaning.*
3. *The fact that* typically can be reduced to a more succinct nominalization: *My denial* [replacing *the fact that I denied*] his accusations impressed the jury.
4. Some nominalizations serve as a conventional shorthand, referring to a well-established concept: *Taxation* without *representation* was not the central concern of the American *Revolution.* (19)

Williams also lists five common patterns of abstract nominalization and how to revise them:

1. When the nominalization is the subject of an empty verb, change the nominalization to a verb and find a new subject: "Our *intention* is" becomes "We *intend.*"
2. When the nominalization follows an empty verb, change the nominalization to a verb that can replace the empty verb; "The committee has no *expectation*" becomes "The committee does not *expect.*"
3. When the nominalization follows a *there is* or *there are,* change the nominalization to a verb that replaces the *is* or *are* and find a subject: "There is a *need* for further *study*" becomes "The staff *must study.*"
4. When a nominalization in a subject is linked to another nominalization in the predicate by a verb or a phrase that expresses some kind of logical connection such as cause and effect, condition and consequence, revise as follows: (a) Change

both abstractions to verbs, (b) find the subject of those verbs, and (c) link the new clauses with a word that expresses the logical connection: "the group's failure was the result of its chairman's resignation" becomes "the group failed because its chairman resigned."

5. When you have two nominalizations in a row, turn at least the first into a verb. Then either leave the second as it is or turn it into a verb in a clause beginning with *how* or *why*: "There was first a *review* of the evolution of the medial dorsal fin" becomes "First, she *reviewed* the *evolution* of the medial dorsal fin." (16–18)

EXERCISE 23.2: Suggested Answers

Those responsible for evaluating education have long resisted measuring the effectiveness of methods and teachers in terms of the results secured. They have emphasized teachers' procedures and have seldom examined their products, that is, what their pupils are able to do. However, we are beginning to see an increasing number of bold proposals that assume the American public expects the schools to show improved results. As public support of education increases, the taxpayers will increasingly insist on judging a teacher on his or her ability to enhance pupils' learning.

BACKGROUND

Both active and passive voices are natural to English speakers. When people are asked to recall a passage or sentence, they will regularly remember the verb as active even when it was passive in the original. Yet, occasions do occur when the passive is more natural and memorable. For instance, when relating something

Revising for verbs and nouns

Study how the following passage can be revised using these steps.

Last February, when I made the determination to buy a house, I opened a separate checking (and savings) account in order to give attention more easily to my household expenses. (There is a credit union policy that for every checking account there must be a matching savings account: thus the dormant savings account.) This new checking account was where the deposit of the inheritance from my grandmother occurred along with any other accumulation of money from outside sources.

REVISED

Last February, when I determined to buy a house, I opened a separate checking (and savings) account to deal more easily with household expenses. (Credit union policy demands a matching savings account for every checking account; thus the dormant savings account.) Into this new checking account I deposited the inheritance from my grandmother, along with any other money I accumulated from outside sources.

EXERCISE 23.2

Revise the following paragraph to eliminate weak verbs and unnecessary nominalizations and expletives.

There has long been resistance to the proposition that the effectiveness of educational methods and teachers must be measured in terms of the results secured. Those responsible for the evaluation of teachers have put emphasis on procedures in teaching and have seldom made an examination of the products, that is, the efficiency of the teacher as indicated by what his or her pupils can do following instruction. However, we are beginning to see an increasing number of bold proposals founded on the assumption that the American public has expectations of improved results from schooling. As public support of education increases, there will be greater insistence on making judgments about a teacher in the light of his or her ability to enhance the learning of pupils.

23b

Choosing between active and passive voice

In addition to choosing strong, precise verbs, you can help make your prose memorable by varying those verbs appropriately between active and passive voice. Look at the following paragraph:

A young man might go into military flight training believing that he was entering some sort of technical school in which he was simply going to acquire a certain set of skills. Instead, he found himself all at once enclosed in a fraternity. And in this fraternity, even though it was military, men were not rated by their outward rank as ensigns, lieutenants, commanders, or whatever. No, herein the world was divided into those who had it and those who did not. This quality, this *it,* was never named, however, nor was it talked about in any way.

— Tom Wolfe, *The Right Stuff*

In this paragraph, Wolfe introduces the indefinable quality that he has made the title of his book. Notice that in the first sentence, the focus is on someone *doing* things: going into flight training, entering a school, acquiring skills. All of the verbs are in the active voice.

In the second sentence, the verb is still active. But notice that because the subject and object are the same person, because the subject of the verb *found* also receives the action of the verb, the sentence almost has the *feel* of being in the passive voice, as if the verb were *was enclosed.* And in the independent clauses of the last three sentences, the focus clearly shifts to things *being done* (or not done): men not being rated, the world being divided, and a quality never being named or talked about. The persons doing these things are unimportant or unknown; in fact, like the quality itself, they are never named, and the verbs are in the passive voice. Notice, however, that Wolfe returns to the active voice when he again wants to emphasize the persons doing something: *those who had it and those who did not.*

Try to use the active voice whenever possible. Because the passive focuses attention away from the performer of an action and because it is usually wordier than the active, excessive use of it makes for dull and difficult reading.

But as the Wolfe paragraph indicates, the passive can be used very effectively in certain situations: when the performer is unknown, unwilling to be identified, or less important than the recipient of the action. In the last sentence, for example, Wolfe could have written *No one ever named this quality, this* it, *however, nor did anyone talk about it in any way.* By using the passive voice, however, he focuses attention on the quality itself rather than on the persons who do not name or talk about it; in fact, by not mentioning them, he heightens the sense of a mysterious quality that cannot be defined. (See Chapter 9 for further discussion of voice.)

EXERCISE 23.3

Look at the following sentences, in which some of the verbs are active and some passive. Then rewrite each sentence in the other voice, and decide which version you find preferable and why. Example:

that happened to ourselves, we use the passive voice as often as the active:

> I was bruised by the fall.
>
> The fall bruised me.

Otto Jespersen notes in *Essentials of English Grammar,* "As a rule the person or thing that is the centre of interest at the moment is made the subject of the sentence, and therefore the verb is in some cases put in the active, in others in the passive" (120).

As a rule of thumb, Joseph Williams, in *Style: Ten Lessons in Clarity and Grace,* suggests avoiding all "unnecessary" passive constructions (22). That is, when an active construction says exactly what the passive construction says and works as effectively (often more so), then the student ought to use the active voice. In choosing between active and passive, Williams says we ought to ask ourselves two questions. "First, must your audience know who is performing the action? Second, are you able to maintain a logical consistency in the subjects of your sentences?" (24). If the writer finds she is shifting from one subject to another from sentence to sentence in a passage, then she ought to try revising these sentences in the active voice.

The writing instructor needs to be aware that there are contexts in which the passive voice is expected and may even be preferred. A reporter protecting his or her source will write, "It is reported that. . . ." In such cases, the reader must be the final judge. However, in some academic settings, passive voice is not just expected; it is commanded by the conventions of the discipline. In scientific writing, for example, the writer is expected to remain objective; the third-person reflects that objectivity better than the first-person. Williams calls the voice used in such situations "the institutional passive" (26).

EXERCISE 23.3: Suggested Answers

1. In his research, Gower found that pythons often dwell in trees and live near rivers.

The active construction is preferable. It gives Gower the responsibility and recognition he deserves.

2. They started shooting pool, and before Cathy knew it, ten dollars was owed to the kid.

   Preference depends somewhat upon the context. The passive voice is unclear about who owes the kid ten dollars. Is Cathy alone? Are she and the kid the "they" of the sentence, or is someone else involved? The active is clearer if Cathy owes the kid money.

3. When I was eight, our family was uprooted from Florida to California by my father's crazy dreams.

   The active is preferred, since the passive doesn't add anything to the text.

4. I adjusted more easily to living in a dorm than to living in an apartment.

   Again, the active is preferred, since the passive adds nothing.

5. Hollywood totally distorts the image of native Americans in most of its films about the West.

   Again, much depends on context. Which is to be emphasized: native Americans? or Hollywood?

BACKGROUND

Linguistic special effects are not unlike the special effects produced for films; they can be spectacular and obvious or quiet and subtle; they ought to be meaningful, not simply ornamental. Of course, the choice of special effects—which to use, when to use them, whether to use them at all—depends upon the overall rhetorical effects sought. The style of James Joyce probably is not appropriate for a business report. Students need to recognize that different writing situations involve different reader expectations. Special effects may make for livelier prose, but not always more appropriate prose.

$\overset{I}{\text{You are}}$ hereby relieved $\overset{you}{\wedge}$ of your duties, by me.

1. In Gower's research, it was found that pythons often dwell in trees and live near rivers.

2. They started shooting pool, and, before Cathy knew it, she owed the kid ten dollars.

3. When I was eight, my father's crazy dreams uprooted our family from Florida to California.

4. For me, living in a dorm was more easily adjusted to than living in an apartment.

5. The image of native Americans has been totally distorted by Hollywood in most of its films about the West.

23c

Creating special effects

Contemporary movies often succeed or fail on the basis of their special effects. Similarly, special effects like repetition, antithesis, and inversion can animate your prose and often make it much more memorable.

1

Using repetition

Carefully used, repetition of sounds, words, phrases, or other grammatical constructions serves as a powerful stylistic device. Orators in particular have long known its power. Here is a famous use of repetition, from one of Sir Winston Churchill's addresses to the British people during World War II.

> We shall not flag or fail, we shall go on to the end. We shall fight in France, we shall fight on the seas and oceans, we shall fight with growing confidence and growing strength in the air, we shall defend our island, whatever the cost may be; we shall fight on the beaches, . . . we shall fight in the fields and in the streets, . . . we shall never surrender.
> — WINSTON CHURCHILL

In this passage, the constant, hammering *we shall,* accompanied by the repetition of *f* sounds (*flag, fail, fight, France, confidence, defend, fields*) had the effect of strengthening British resolve.

Though we may not be prime ministers, we can use repetition to equally good effect. Here are some examples.

So my dream date turned into a nightmare. Where was the quiet, considerate, caring guy I thought I had met? In his place appeared this jerk. He strutted, he postured, he preened—and then he bragged, he bellowed, he practically brayed—just like the donkey he so much reminded me of.

We need science, more and better science, not for its technology, not for leisure, not even for health or longevity, but for the hope of wisdom which our kind of culture must acquire for its survival.

— LEWIS THOMAS, "Medical Lessons from History"

Be careful, however, to use repetition only for a deliberate purpose. (See 19b.)

EXERCISE 23.4

Go through the examples in 23c1, identifying the uses of repetition. Using one example as a model, write a passage of your own that uses repetition effectively.

2

Using antithesis

Another special effect that can contribute to memorable writing is **antithesis**, the use of parallel structures to highlight contrast or opposition. Like other uses of parallelism (see Chapter 21), antithesis provides a pleasing rhythm that calls readers' attention to the contrast, often in a startling or amusing way. For example:

Love is an ideal thing, marriage a real thing.

The congregation didn't think much of the new preacher, and what the new preacher thought of the congregation she didn't wish to say.

It is a sin to believe evil of others—but it is not a mistake.

— H. L. MENCKEN

EXERCISE 23.5

Using one of the examples above, create a sentence of your own that uses antithesis. Then consider whether the antithesis makes the sentence more memorable or effective. You might begin by thinking of opposites you could build on: hope-despair, good-evil, fire-ice. Or you might begin with a *topic* you want to write about: success, greed, generosity, and so on.

EXERCISE 23.4: Answers will vary.

EXERCISE 23.5: Answers will vary.

BACKGROUND

Readers come to sentences with certain expectations, conditioned by familiarity to recognize typical patterns of language. For English speakers, one of these patterns is the subject-verb-object structure of the basic declarative sentence. Expectations change when we read a question or an imperative; we expect inversions then. But inversions in declarative sentences surprise us, and that surprise can be used to good effect.

As with any special effect, some inversions are less ornamental than others. Look at this sentence:

> Dolly she called Dollyheart, but Verena she called That One.
> —TRUMAN CAPOTE, *The Glass Harp*

This sentence is much clearer in emphasis in its inverted form than if structured conventionally:

> She called Dolly Dollyheart, but she called Verena That One.

Placement within a sentence alters the emphasis that a word gets. Look at this sentence:

> Gone are the potted plants, the Christmas cheeses, the toys for the children that were regularly issued by the old Francis Cleary.
> —MARY McCARTHY, *Cast a Cold Eye*

Note the drastic change in emphasis when we restructure the sentence into its conventional form:

> The potted plants, the Christmas cheeses, the toys for the children that were regularly issued by the old Francis Cleary are gone.

EXERCISE 23.6: Answers will vary.

EXERCISE 23.7: Answers will vary.

3

Using inverted word order

Inversion of the usual word order can make writing memorable by creating surprise or putting emphasis on a particular word or phrase. Word order in English is usually subject–verb–object / complement (if any). Inversion refers to any change in that order, such as putting the verb before the subject or putting the object before the subject and verb.

NORMAL	Two dead birds plummeted out of the tree.
INVERTED	Out of the tree plummeted two dead birds.

The inverted word order makes for a more dramatic sentence by putting the emphasis at the end, on *two dead birds*.

As with any unusual sentence pattern, inverted word order should be used sparingly, but it can indeed create special effects.

> Into this grey lake plopped the thought, I know this man, don't I?
> — DORIS LESSING

> In a hole in the ground there lived a hobbit. — J. R. R. TOLKIEN

> Into her head flowed the whole of the poem she had found in that book.
> — EUDORA WELTY

EXERCISE 23.6

After studying the examples of inversion above, look at something you have written, and find a sentence that might be more effective with inverted word order. Experiment with the word order, reading the results aloud and comparing differences in effect.

EXERCISE 23.7 Reading with an Eye for Prose Style

The last five chapters have presented many elements that mark effective prose. One amusing way to practice these elements lies in a special kind of imitation. Choose a writer you admire—Virginia Woolf, Chaucer, Maya Angelou, Stephen King, Dave Barry, Salt 'n' Pepa, whoever. Reread this writer's work, getting a "feel" for the rhythms, the structures, the special effects of the prose. Make a list of the elements that contribute to his or her distinctive style. Then choose a well-known story, and retell it in that style. Following is the opening of "The Three Little Pigs" written by one freshman as he imagined Edgar Allan Poe might have done.

It began as a mere infatuation. I admired them from afar, with a longing which only a wolf may know. Soon, these feelings turned to torment. Were I even to set eyes upon their porcine forms, the bowels of my soul raged, as if goaded by some festering poison. As the chilling winds of November howled, my gullet yearned for them. I soon feasted only upon an earnest and consuming desire for the moment of their decease.

EXERCISE 23.8

Prose can be memorable for reasons quite different from those presented in this chapter. The Bulwer-Lytton Competition, known less formally as the "Wretched Writing" contest, challenges writers to produce an opening sentence to a novel, one that will celebrate the possibilities of "deliberate wretchedness" without hurting anyone's feelings. Here are two finalists.

1. It was the eve of the yearly whale-slaughtering festival, thought Mamook as her horny fingers relentlessly pushed the whalebone needle through the sole of the mukluk; and suddenly, unaccountably, uncontrollably, she began to blubber.
2. When the last of the afterglow faded and the air was still, Josh liked to sit in the porch swing, in the dark, and test his night vision by spitting through the banisters.

Write an opening sentence for a story. Try to make it a "wonderfully bad" sentence. And why not enter it in the contest? Just send it to the Bulwer-Lytton Competition, c/o Professor Scott Rice, San Jose State University, San Jose, CA 95192.

EXERCISE 23.9   Taking Inventory: Memorable Sentences

Read over something you have written, looking for memorable sentences. If few sentences catch your eye, choose some that show promise—ones with strong verbs or a pleasing rhythm, perhaps. Using this chapter for guidance, try revising one or two to make them more effective and memorable. Finally, make some notes about ways your writing is effective and strategies for making it more effective. If you keep a writing log, put your notes there for future reference.

TEACHING PRACTICE

Students can produce remarkably effective and amusing imitations. Have them complete the "Three Little Pigs" or create completely new imitations of their own, and ask them to bring in several representative pieces by the author being imitated. Then ask students to identify the *precise* characteristics that are being imitated. How, for instance, do we *know* that the passage here imitates Poe?

EXERCISE 23.8: Answers will vary.

OPTIONAL EXERCISE

The Bulwer-Lytton Wretched Writing contest has now been joined by the Faulkner Write-Alike award for the "best" bad Faulkner in the land. The following sentence provides an example:

> The flags waved in the inexorable dust of the somnolent hamlet as the avaricious old avatar sought sanctuary from the sound and fury of mosquitoes swarming about the epicene body of his affable and profoundly unabashed comrade prone across the pagan catafalque as he lay dying.

Why not ask students to choose a favorite writer and try to produce a bad imitation sentence, or a more extended parody? If they are stuck for subject matter, they might get ideas, as in the example above, from trying to weave together the titles of some of the author's books.

Part Five

Selecting Effective
Words

————————— <> —————————

24

Mastering Spelling

BACKGROUND

In their research for this handbook, Lunsford and Connors found that spelling errors were the most common mistakes made by student writers. These findings suggest that spelling cannot—and should not—be overlooked by writing instructors.

The public unfortunately believes that the majority of students are bad spellers, but in fact, the results of recent research contradict this notion. For instance, Karl Taylor and Ede Kidder conclude that spelling errors generally decline from the first through the eighth grades. Only the "wrong words" category, primarily homonyms, increases ("The Development of Spelling Skills from First Grade through Eighth Grade." *Written Communication* 5 [April 1988]: 222–44). Their conclusion corroborates that of Lunsford and Connors, who found that the most frequent spelling errors involved problems with homonyms. As with other writing errors, spelling errors tend to fall into patterns which, once discovered, can be corrected.

The fact that English has come in contact with many other languages—German, Latin, Danish, Norse, Norman French, to name a few—during the course of its evolution makes English spelling a complex system. For example, English includes at least twelve different ways of representing the *sh* sound: *sh*oe, *s*ugar, o*c*ean, i*ss*ue, na*ti*on, *sch*ist, *ps*haw, suspi*ci*on, con*sci*ous, nau*se*ous, man*si*on, and fu*ch*sia. As everyone who has ever struggled to remember—or to find—a correct spelling knows, this complexity can lead to much frustration, and in fact, some have called for "spelling liberation." When a judge in Dickens's *Pickwick Papers* asks Sam Weller how to spell a particular word, for instance, Weller insists, "That depends entirely upon the taste and fancy of the speller, my Lord." Closer to home, President Andrew Jackson once exclaimed in exasperation: "It's a damn poor mind that can think of only one way to spell a word!"

Despite this tradition of complaint, modern linguists have demonstrated that English spelling is much more regular than is commonly thought and that this regularity relates not only to sound-letter connections but also to our stored visual memory of related words. We know that *president* is not spelled "presadent," for example, because we recognize its relation to *preside*. The good news, then, is simply this: careful attention to your own spelling patterns and attention to some fairly straightforward guidelines of English spelling can help you master spelling.

EXERCISE 24.1

Listen in on some of the conversations around you—on the bus or subway, in line for a movie, at a cafeteria, in a public park. Jot down some of one conversation, capturing it as accurately as possible. Then look carefully at the words and their spellings. Are any of the words "invented" or examples of dialect? If so, how did you decide how to spell them?

EXERCISE 24.1: Answers will vary.

24a

Mastering the most commonly misspelled words

Eudora Welty reports that she once failed to make 100 on a spelling test because she misspelled *uncle,* a mistake that her mother took very hard. "You couldn't spell *uncle*?" her mother said. "When you've got those five perfectly splendid uncles in West Virginia? What would *they* say to that?"

The three thousand first-year essays that were used in the research for this book revealed a fairly small number of persistently misspelled words, and Welty's mother would no doubt be glad to hear that *uncle* was not among them. A list of the fifty most common misspellings appears below. Look it over carefully and compare it with words you have trouble spelling correctly. (See 24f for ways to establish your own spelling inventory.)

 The fifty most commonly misspelled words

1. their/there/they're	18. through	35. business/es
2. too/to	19. until	36. dependent
3. a lot	20. where	37. every day
4. noticeable	21. successful/ly	38. may be
5. received/e/es	22. truly	39. occasion/s
6. lose	23. argument/s	40. occurrences
7. you're/your	24. experience/s	41. woman
8. an/and	25. environment	42. all right
9. develop/s	26. exercise/s/ing	43. apparent/ly
10. definitely	27. necessary	44. categories
11. than/then	28. sense	45. final/ly
12. believe/d/s	29. therefore	46. immediate/ly
13. occurred	30. accept/ed	47. roommate/s
14. affect/s	31. heroes	48. against
15. cannot	32. professor	49. before
16. separate	33. whether	50. beginning
17. success	34. without	

EXERCISE 24.2

Choose the correct spelling from the pair of words in the parentheses in each of the sentences below. After checking your answers, compare your misspellings with the list of fifty words most frequently misspelled. Enter the words you misspelled in your spelling log and keep them near your typewriter or computer.

BACKGROUND

In 1066, England was invaded for a fourth time. The Normans from France were led by William the Conqueror, and they overran the island in just a year. They declared their language, Norman French, to be the official language, and for the next two hundred years or so, business, education, and government were all conducted in French. Literature was written in either French or Latin. English was considered barbaric. However, the government could not—and didn't even bother to try to—control the language of the masses. Therefore, English continued to be spoken by most people in their daily lives.

As with the Norse invasion earlier, the Normans influenced the lexicon of the English language but little else. In *The Origins and Development of the English Language,* Thomas Pyles and John Algeo point out that French spelling conventions were borrowed along with French vocabulary.

Pyles and Algeo note, "Some of the apparent innovations in Middle English spelling were, in fact, a return to earlier conventions" (139). For instance, *th* was reintroduced. "Other new spellings were true innovations" (139); *g* entered English orthography for the first time.

The Normans were finally exiled from France entirely, and French was spoken less and less. English began to reappear in education, in business affairs, and in government documents. By the fifteenth century, English had once again been taken up by imaginative writers. Chaucer's *Canterbury Tales* was written in English.

USEFUL READING

Pyles, Thomas, and John Algeo. *The Origins and Development of the English Language.* 3rd ed. New York: Harcourt, 1982. The third edition of this history of the language contains a good deal of information on spelling.

EXERCISE 24.2: Answers

1. They're; their; there
2. to; too
3. beginning; a lot
4. noticeable; until
5. occurred; before
6. believe; lose
7. you're; definitely; your
8. affects; success; than; its
9. received; through
10. develop; truly; successful
11. cannot; separate
12. where; and
13. arguments; against; environment
14. businesses; dependent
15. Heroes; necessary
16. experience; exercise
17. professor; accept
18. categories; final
19. roommates; without
20. occasion; whether; weather
21. may be; therefore; immediately
22. woman's
23. occurrences; every day
24. It's; all right; sense
25. Apparently

1. (*Their/There/They're*) going to put (*their/there/they're*) new stereo system over (*their/there/they're*) in the corner.
2. My little brother wants (*to/too*) go swimming (*to/too*).
3. The (*begining/beginning*) of school is (*a lot/alot*) earlier this year than last.
4. The rise in temperature isn't (*noticable/noticeable*) (*until/untill*) the humidity rises.
5. The accident (*occured/occurred*) (*before/befour*) I could step aside.
6. We couldn't (*beleive/believe*) the national champions were expected to (*loose/lose*) the playoffs.
7. In making your major life decisions, (*your/you're*) (*definately/definitely*) on (*your/you're*) own.
8. Nothing (*affects/effects*) (*success/sucess*) more (*than/then*) self-confidence or (*its/it's*) absence.
9. We (*received/recieved*) our notice (*threw/through*) the mail.
10. The group hopes to (*develop/develope*) a (*truely/truly*) (*succesful/successful*) fast-food franchise.
11. We (*can not/cannot*) easily (*separate/seperate*) fact and opinion.
12. Please tell me (*wear/where*) (*an/and*) when we should meet.
13. Our (*argumants/arguments*) (*against/aginst*) continuing to pollute the (*enviroment/environment*) fell on deaf ears.
14. Local (*busines/businesses*) are (*dependant/dependent*) on the summer tourist trade.
15. (*Heroes/Heros*) are (*necesary/necessary*) to every culture's mythology.
16. Our first (*experiance/experience*) with aerobic (*exercise/exercize*) left us tired.
17. The (*professor/profesor*) agreed to (*accept/except*) our final research essays on Friday.
18. She qualified for three (*catagories/categories*) in the (*final/finel*) gymnastics competition.
19. The two (*roomates/roommates*) would be lost (*without/witout*) each other.
20. We intend to celebrate the (*ocasion/occasion*) (*weather/whether*) or not the (*weather/whether*) cooperates.
21. The plane to Chicago (*may be/maybe*) late; (*therefore/therfore*), we don't need to leave for the airport (*imediately/immediately*).
22. A (*woman's/women's*) place is now wherever she wants it to be.
23. Police departments report (*occurences/occurrences*) of more and more burglaries (*every day/everyday*).
24. (*Its/It's*) not (*all right/alright*) to forgo common (*since/sense*).
25. (*Aparently/Apparently*), the shipment of books never arrived.

Everyday use

Andrew Jackson's comment is just as true today as it was over a hundred years ago. A short drive along an interstate turned up the following examples of alternate spellings.

Kountry Kitchen

Drive Thru Food

Phat Phil's Phine Phood

These signs suggest the flexibility of English spelling, which allows for all kinds of inventive and playful uses. Keep an eye out for fanciful or amusing spellings. Find two or three examples, and decide what purpose the writer might have had for the misspelling (assuming it was intentional).

24b

Recognizing homonyms

Of the words most often misspelled by college students, the largest number are **homonyms**— words that sound alike but have different spellings and meanings. English has many homonyms, but a relatively small number of them—eight pairs or trios—cause student writers frequent trouble. If you tend to confuse any of these words, now is a good time to study them, looking for some twist of memory to help you remember the differences.

 The most troublesome homonyms

their (possessive form of *they*)	who's (contraction of *who is* or *who has*)
there (in that place)	
they're (contraction of *they are*)	whose (possessive form of *who*)
to (in the direction of)	its (possessive form of *it*)
too (in addition; excessive)	it's (contraction of *it is* or *it has*)
two (number between one and three)	your (possessive form of *you*)
	you're (contraction of *you are*)
weather (climatic conditions)	affect (noun: emotion)
whether (if)	(verb: to have an influence)
accept (to take or receive)	effect (noun: result)
except (to leave out)	(verb: to cause to happen)

In addition, Dorothy Thompson argues that short periods of spelling instruction are more effective than longer periods ("Spelling's Day in the Sun," *Instructor* 85 [1976]: 16). Ann Dobie suggests no more than fifteen or twenty minutes per class time.

Consider the following practice for each student's final draft:

1. Circle all misspelled words in the paper.
2. Ask the student to correct the misspelling himself or herself.
3. Ask the student to bring in two other related words and identify the shared core.

As their language evolves, children use longer, more complicated [syntactic] structures and more sophisticated vocabulary. As they begin to use less familiar words and to employ different structures, they make errors of all types from comma splices to misspellings. Error, then, is a sign of growth.

— KARL K. TAYLOR AND EDE B. KIDDER

Other homonyms and frequently confused words

advice (suggestion)
advise (to suggest [to])
allude (to refer)
elude (to avoid or escape)
allusion (reference)
illusion (false idea or appearance)
altar (sacred platform or table)
alter (to change)
are (form of *be*)
our (belonging to us)
bare (uncovered)
bear (animal; to carry or endure)
board (piece of lumber)
bored (uninterested)
brake (device for stopping)
break (to fragment)
buy (to purchase)
by (near; beside; through)
capital (principal city)
capitol (legislative building)
cite (to refer to)
sight (seeing; something seen)
site (location)
coarse (rough or crude)
course (plan of study; path)
complement (something that completes; to make complete)
compliment (praise; to praise)
conscience (feeling of right and wrong)
conscious (mentally aware)
council (leadership group)
counsel (advice; to advise)
dairy (source of milk)
diary (journal)
desert (dry area; to abandon)
dessert (sweet course of a meal)
device (something planned or invented)
devise (to plan or invent)
die (to expire)
dye (color; to color)

elicit (to draw forth)
illicit (illegal)
eminent (distinguished)
immanent (inherent)
imminent (expected in the immediate future)
fair (just or right; light in complexion; exposition)
fare (price of transportation; to go through an experience)
forth (forward; out into view)
fourth (between third and fifth)
gorilla (ape)
guerrilla (irregular soldier)
hear (to perceive with the ears)
here (in this place)
heard (past tense of *hear*)
herd (group of animals)
hoarse (sounding rough or harsh)
horse (animal)
know (to understand)
no (opposite of *yes*)
lead (a metal; to go before)
led (past tense of *lead*)
loose (not tight; not confined)
lose (to misplace; to fail to win)
meat (flesh used as food)
meet (to encounter)
passed (went by; received a passing grade)
past (beyond; events that have already occurred)
patience (quality of being patient)
patients (persons under medical care)
peace (absence of war)
piece (part)
personal (private or individual)
personnel (employees)
plain (simple, not fancy; flat land)
plane (airplane; tool; flat surface)

presence (condition of being)
presents (gifts; gives)
principal (most important; head of a school)
principle (fundamental truth)
rain (precipitation)
rein (strap to control a horse)
reign (period of rule; to rule)
right (correct; opposite of left)
rite (ceremony)
write (to produce words on a surface)
road (street or highway)
rode (past tense of *ride*)
scene (setting; view)
seen (past participle of *see*)
sense (feeling; intelligence)
since (from the time that; because)

stationary (unmoving)
stationery (writing paper)
than (as compared with)
then (at that time; therefore)
threw (past tense of *throw*)
thorough (complete)
through (in one side of and out the other; by means of)
waist (part of the body)
waste (to squander)
weak (feeble)
week (seven days)
wear (to put onto the body)
were (past tense of *be*)
where (in what place)
which (what; that)
witch (woman with supernatural power)

EXERCISE 24.3

Choose the appropriate word in parentheses to fill each blank.

If _____ (*your/you're*) looking for summer fun, _____ (*accept/except*) the friendly _____ (*advice/advise*) of thousands of happy adventurers: spend three _____ (*weaks/weeks*) kayaking _____ (*threw/thorough/through*) the inside passage _____ (*to/too/two*) Alaska. For ten years, Outings, Inc., has _____ (*lead/led*) groups of novice kayakers _____ (*passed/past*) some of the most breathtaking scenery in North America. _____ (*Their/There/They're*) goal is simple: to give participants the time of _____ (*their/there/they're*) lives. As one of last year's adventurers said, "_____ (*Its/It's*) a trip I will remember vividly, one that _____ (*affected/effected*) me powerfully."

1

Recognizing homonyms with more than one form

One special group of homonyms appearing in the list of words most often misspelled by college writers are words written sometimes as one word and other times as two words. The correct spelling depends on the meaning. Note the differences illustrated here.

Of course, they did not wear *everyday* clothes *every day* of the year.
Ideally, children *always* love their parents—in *all ways*.

EXERCISE 24.3: Answers

If *you're* looking for summer fun, *accept* the friendly *advice* of thousands of happy adventurers: spend three *weeks* kayaking *through* the inside passage *to* Alaska. For ten years, Outings, Inc., has *led* groups of novice kayakers *past* some of the most breathtaking scenery in North America. *Their* goal is simple: to give participants the time of *their* lives. As one of last year's adventurers said, "*It's* a trip I will remember vividly, one that *affected* me powerfully."

BACKGROUND

Never in the history of the English language was spelling more uniform than today. Spelling during the Middle Ages and early Renaissance was very relaxed. No prescriptions existed for spelling uniformity—not even within the same text. Orthographic conventions "were used with a nonchalance that is hardly imaginable in the era of the printing press" (Pyles and Algeo 142). A person might even spell his or her own name in different ways. Shakespeare, for instance, was spelled *Shakespeare, Shakespear,* and *Shake-spear,* and the "correct" spelling is still being argued.

Of course, most writers spelled words more or less consistently and people communicated with one another without great confusion. It is difficult to tell whether some spelling inconsistencies were products of the writers themselves or of the printers taking advantage of instability in spelling in order to easily "justify" a line. In spite of all the variety, Baugh and Cable tell us that "by 1550 a nucleus of common [spelling] practice" existed. In fact, the sixteenth century marked a distinct change in attitude toward spelling. Changing cultural values marked this period, and in their search for stability, scholars focused on stabilizing English spelling.

Throughout the sixteenth and seventeenth centuries, numerous attempts to standardize (and, in many cases, reform) spelling were made. The earliest one, *An A. B. C. for Children,* appeared sometime before 1558. Most of these attempts tried to develop an alphabet that corresponded to pronunciation.

The most important of these treatises is *Elementarie* (1582) by Richard Mulcaster. Mulcaster saw the futility of trying for an exact, scientific correspondence between spelling and pronunciation. Whether Mulcaster's work really influenced the stability of spelling or simply reflected that stability as it developed naturally is impossible to say, but English spelling did develop along the lines he called for.

USEFUL READING

Baugh, Albert C., and Thomas Cable. *A History of the English Language.* 3rd ed. Englewood Cliffs, NJ: Prentice, 1978. The authors cover the whole history of the language, including excellent sections on spelling.

By the time we were *all ready* for the game to begin, the coach's patience was *already* exhausted.

We *may be* on time for the meeting, or *maybe* we won't!

Nobody was surprised when the police announced that they had found *no body* at the scene of the crime.

The study of three thousand freshman essays mentioned earlier in this chapter revealed three particularly troublesome words that are often written in the wrong form. Two of them are always written as two words: *a lot* and *all right.* The third is written as one word: *cannot.* If you tend to misspell these words, take time now to commit the correct spelling to memory.

2

Recognizing American, British, and Canadian spellings

Spelling varies slightly among English-speaking countries. What is considered "correct" in Britain or Canada may be considered "incorrect" in the United States, and vice versa. Following are some words that are spelled differently in American and British English. If you have trouble spelling words like these—knowing, for example, whether a verb ends in *-ise* or *-ize*—consult a dictionary.

AMERICAN	BRITISH AND CANADIAN
center	centre
check	cheque
color	colour
criticize	criticise
judgment	judgement

24c

Linking spelling and pronunciation

Even for words without homonyms, pronunciation often leads spellers astray. Pronunciation can vary considerably from one region to another, and the informality of spoken English allows us to slur or blur other letters or syllables. The best way to link spelling and pronunciation is to learn to "pronounce" words mentally as they look, every letter and syllable included (so that, for example, you hear the *b* at the end of *crumb*) and to enunciate them slowly and clearly when you are trying to spell them.

1

Noting unpronounced letters or syllables

Learning to "see" words with unpronounced letters or syllables will help you spell them correctly. Here are some frequently misspelled words of this kind, with their unpronounced letters or syllables italicized.

can*d*idate	foreign	pro*b*ably
condem*n*	gover*n*ment	quan*t*ity
differ*e*nt	int*e*rest	rest*au*rant
drastica*l*ly	lib*r*ary	sep*a*rate (adjective)
envir*o*nment	mar*r*iage	sur*p*rise
Feb*r*uary	mus*c*le	We*d*nesday

2

Noting unstressed vowels

In English words, *a, i,* and *e* often sound alike in syllables that are not stressed. Hearing the word *definite,* for instance, gives us few clues as to whether the vowels in the second and third syllables should be *i*'s or *a*'s. In this case, remembering how the related word *finite* looks or sounds helps us know that the *i*'s are correct. If you are puzzled about how to spell a word with unstressed vowels, try to think of a related word that would give you a clue to the correct spelling. Then check your dictionary.

24d

Taking advantage of spelling rules

Fortunately, English spelling does follow some general rules that can be of enormous help to writers. This section focuses on those rules closely related to commonly misspelled words.

1

Remembering "i before e"

Most of you probably memorized the "i before e" rule long ago. Here is a slightly expanded version.

i before *e* except after *c*
or when pronounced "ay"
as in *neighbor* or *weigh*
or in *weird* exceptions like *either*
and *species*

BACKGROUND

One of the most controversial areas in the study of spelling remains the relationship of orthography to pronunciation. The Roman alphabet cannot phonetically represent the English language; for instance, the alphabet possesses only five vowel symbols, while the language has eleven, not including diphthongs and [r] modifications. Some language reformers call for refashioning spelling to conform to pronunciation. Yet good, practical reasons exist for differentiating the lexical and phonetic aspects of language.

Wilson Follett (*Modern American Usage: A Guide* [New York: Hill, 1966], 310) notes that pronunciations differ with dialects. Therefore, choosing the phonetic representation of words as a measure for spelling becomes a political decision as much as anything else.

William J. Stevens ("Obstacles to Spelling Reform," *The English Journal* 54 [1965]: 85–90) cites the problem of homonyms spelled alike under the above reform. We could not differentiate among *to, too,* and *two.*

More important, Carol Chomsky ("Reading, Writing, and Phonology," *Harvard Education Review* 40 [May 1970]: 287–309) argues that spelling corresponds less to surface features of the language (i.e., pronunciation) than to the underlying meanings of words. Spelling, she claims, retains lexical connections between words, connections that might be lost in pronunciation shifts. For instance, *nation* retains its semantic affiliation with *nationality* through their sharing of the same semantic core, represented orthographically as *nation* despite a different pronunciation of that core. On the other hand, such a connection does not exist between *nation* and *notion.* They share a common ending but not a semantic core. While variations in pronunciation, instigated by phonological rules such as the shifts in phonological stress with the addition of suffixes, may occur, semantic connections are retained through the spelling of the two words.

USEFUL READING

Anderson, Kristen F. "Using a Spelling Survey to Develop Basic Writers' Linguistic Awareness: A Response to Ann B. Dobie." *Journal of Basic Writing* 6 (1987): 72–78.

Dobie, Ann B. "Orthographical Theory and Practice, or How to Teach Spelling." *Journal of Basic Writing* 5 (1986): 41–48.

Dobie, Ann B. "Orthography Revisited: A Response to Kristen Anderson." *Journal of Basic Writing* (1988): 82–83.

EXERCISE 24.4: Answers

1. sleigh
2. conscience
3. ancient
4. leisure
5. pierce
6. caffeine
7. chief
8. receive
9. achieve
10. heiress

TEACHING PRACTICE

Although spelling can be very important in the creation of *ethos* for the writer, too much emphasis on spelling in the classroom might eventually paralyze some writers. It is important to emphasize to your students that spelling correction is a late-draft revision activity rather than an early-draft revision activity. Writers should not be concerned with spelling during early drafts that they know will be revised; they should get down on paper their ideas and the organization of those ideas before they need to be concerned with spelling. However, if student writers are bothered by the fact that they know some of the words

i BEFORE *e*

achi*e*ve	experi*e*nce	pi*e*ce
beli*e*ve	fi*e*ld	reli*e*ve
bri*e*f	fri*e*nd	thi*e*f
chi*e*f		

EXCEPT AFTER *c*

ceiling	deceive	perceive
conceive	receive	

OR WHEN PRONOUNCED "AY"

n*ei*ghbor	w*ei*gh	*ei*ghth

OR IN WEIRD EXCEPTIONS

either	seize	species
weird	foreign	ancient
neither	height	conscience
leisure	caffeine	science

EXERCISE 24.4

Insert either *ei* or *ie* in the blank in each of the following words.

1. sl___gh	5. p___rce	8. rec___ve
2. consc___nce	6. caff___ne	9. ach___ve
3. anc___nt	7. ch___f	10. h___ress
4. l___sure		

2
Adding prefixes

Prefixes are verbal elements placed at the beginnings of words to add to or qualify their meaning. The prefix *re-*, for example, adds repetition to the meaning of a word: *reappear* means "appear again." (See 26c for more information about prefixes.) Prefixes do not change the spelling of the words they are added to, even when the last letter of the prefix and the first letter of the word it is added to are the same. In such cases, keep both letters.

dis- + service = disservice   over- + rate = overrate

Some prefixes require the use of hyphens. For a discussion of such usage, see 38c. If you are in doubt about whether to hyphenate a word beginning with a prefix, always check your dictionary.

3

Adding suffixes

Suffixes are verbal elements placed at the *ends* of words in order to form related words. For example, we can build on the basic word *short* to get the following words:

short*age*, short*en*, short*er*, short*ly*, short*ness*

This section will provide guidance to spelling words with suffixes.

Dropping the final e

For words ending in an unpronounced *e* (*receive, lose, definite*), you must decide whether or not to drop the *e* when adding a suffix. In general, if the suffix starts with a vowel, *drop* the *e*.

explore + -ation = exploration	exercise + -ing = exercising
imagine + -able = imaginable	continue + -ous = continuous
future + -ism = futurism	productive + -ity = productivity

EXCEPTIONS

To distinguish homonyms or potentially confusing words

dye + -ing = dyeing (not *dying*)   singe + -ing = singeing
                                                              (not *singing*)

To clarify pronunciation

be + -ing = being (not *bing*)   shoe + -ing = shoeing
                                                          (not *shoing*)

To keep the sound of *c* or *g* soft

notice + -able = noticeable	marriage + -able = marriageable
peace + -able = peaceable	courage + -ous = courageous

Keeping the final e

If the suffix starts with a consonant, *keep* the *e*.

force + -ful = forceful	state + -ly = stately
excite + -ment = excitement	same + -ness = sameness

EXCEPTIONS

argue + -ment = argument	true + -ly = truly
judge + -ment = judgment	whole + -ly = wholly
due + -ly = duly	nine + -th = ninth

are misspelled, between writing drafts they should go through the text of the last draft, marking all the words the spelling of which they are unsure about. Then, before the next draft, they can look them up and write them out on a separate sheet of paper that they can refer to during the writing of the next draft.

FOR COLLABORATIVE WORK

Many "spelling" errors are actually errors of proofreading—or the lack thereof. We all commit "typos," but they indicate nothing more than our imperfect humanity, and they are easily corrected during proofreading. Genuine spelling errors are, of course, a different story. However, the reader has no way to distinguish between the two. Therefore, proofreading becomes a vitally important activity for the writer. To encourage students to proofread more carefully, you might consider the following practice.

Before taking up the final draft of the first paper, divide the class into groups of two or three. Have them exchange papers and check for words that they think might be misspelled. On a separate sheet of paper, they should note the page number and paragraph number, the misspelled word, and what they believe is the correct spelling of that word. After the papers have been returned to the authors, allow them time to go through their papers and make the corrections. They should be aware that there is no guarantee that their proofreaders are correct 100 percent of the time. The writers themselves must make the final choice about the spelling. Along with the paper, the separate sheet with the proofreader's notes on the spelling should be handed in. When grading this first paper, don't count off for any corrected spelling but do record the originally misspelled words pointed out by the proofreader.

Do the same for following papers, but call special attention—whether through grading sanctions or by a reminder to the student—to misspellings that are repeated from earlier work.

EXERCISE 24.5: Answers

1. futurism
2. wholly
3. argument
4. lonely
5. malicious
6. dyeing
7. hopeful
8. continuous
9. exercising
10. outrageous

EXERCISE 24.5

Combine each of the following words and suffixes, dropping the unpronounced *e* when necessary.

1. future + -ism
2. whole + -ly
3. argue + -ment
4. lone + -ly
5. malice + -ious
6. dye + -ing
7. hope + -ful
8. continue + -ous
9. exercise + -ing
10. outrage + -ous

Using -ally

Use *-ally* if the base word ends in *ic*.

drastic + -ally = drastically   tragic + -ally = tragically
basic + -ally = basically   frantic + -ally = frantically

Using -ly

Use *-ly* if the base word does not end in *ic*.

apparent + -ly = apparently   quick + -ly = quickly
certain + -ly = certainly   supposed + -ly = supposedly
conscious + -ly = consciously

EXCEPTION

public + -ly = publicly

Using -cede, -ceed, and -sede

The suffixes *-cede, -ceed,* and *-sede* are especially easy to master because almost all words ending in the sound pronounced "seed" use the spelling *-cede*. Use *-sede* with only one word: *supersede*. Use *-ceed* with only three words: *exceed, proceed, succeed*. Use *-cede* with all other words ending in the "seed" sound.

accede   intercede   recede
concede   precede   secede

Words ending in consonant and y

For words ending in *y*, you must sometimes change the *y* to *i* when you add a suffix. In general, if the *y* is preceded by a consonant, change the *y*.

bounty + -ful = bountiful   breezy + -ness = breeziness
try + -ed = tried   busy + -ily = busily
silly + -er = sillier

EXCEPTIONS

Keep the y before the suffix *-ing.*

dry + -ing = drying   carry + -ing = carrying
liquefy + -ing = liquefying   vary + -ing = varying

Keep the y in some one-syllable base words.

shy + -er = shyer   wry + -ness = wryness
dry + -ly = dryly

Keep the y if the base word is a proper name.

Kennedy + -esque = Kennedyesque

Words ending in vowel and y

If the y is preceded by a vowel, keep the y.

joy + -ous = joyous   employ + -ment = employment
play + -ful = playful   buoy + -ed = buoyed

EXCEPTIONS

day + ly = daily   gay + ly = gaily

EXERCISE 24.6

Combine each of the following words and suffixes, changing the final y to *i* when necessary.

1. lonely + -er   5. supply + -ed   8. obey + -ed
2. carry + -ing   6. duty + -ful   9. rainy + -est
3. defy + -ance   7. likely + -hood   10. coy + -ly
4. study + -s

Doubling the final consonant

When a word ends in a consonant, the consonant is sometimes doubled when a suffix is added. If the word ends in consonant + vowel + consonant, the suffix begins with a vowel, and the word contains only one syllable or ends in an accented syllable, double the final consonant.

EXERCISE 24.6: Answers

1. lonelier
2. carrying
3. defiance
4. studies
5. supplied
6. dutiful
7. likelihood
8. obeyed
9. rainiest
10. coyly

stop + -ing = stopping   begin + -ing = beginning
slap + -ed = slapped   occur + -ence = occurrence
hot + -est = hottest   refer + -ing = referring
run + -er = runner

DO NOT DOUBLE THE CONSONANT

If it is preceded by more than one vowel or by another consonant

bait + -ing = baiting   fight + -er = fighter
sleep + -ing = sleeping   start + -ed = started

If the suffix begins with a consonant

ship + -ment = shipment   fit + -ness = fitness

If the word is not accented on the last syllable

benefit + -ing = benefiting   fasten + -er = fastener

If the accent shifts from the last to the first syllable when the suffix is added

infer + -ence = inference   prefer + -ence = preference

If the last letter of the word and the first letter of the suffix are the same, keep both letters.

mortal + -ly = mortally   rotten + -ness = rottenness
room + -mate = roommate   usual + -ly = usually

EXERCISE 24.7: Answers

1. occurred
2. fastest
3. skipper
4. reference
5. commitment
6. regrettable
7. submitted
8. drastically
9. benefited
10. weeping

EXERCISE 24.7

Combine each of the following words and suffixes, doubling the final consonant when necessary.

1. occur + -ed   5. commit + -ment   8. drastic + -ally
2. fast + -est   6. regret + -able   9. benefit + -ed
3. skip + -er   7. submit + -ed   10. weep + -ing
4. refer + -ence

24e

Making words plural

Making singular nouns into plurals calls for using several different spelling guidelines.

Adding -s

For most words, add -*s*.

pencil, pencils   book, books   computer, computers

Adding -es

For words ending in *s, ch, sh, x,* or *z,* add -*es*.

Jones, Joneses   fox, foxes   flash, flashes
bus, buses   church, churches   buzz, buzzes

For words ending in *o,* add -*es* if the *o* is preceded by a consonant.

potato, potatoes   hero, heroes   veto, vetoes

EXCEPTIONS

memo, memos   piano, pianos
pro, pros   solo, solos

Add -*s* if the *o* is preceded by a vowel.

rodeo, rodeos   patio, patios
zoo, zoos   curio, curios

Words ending in f *or* fe

For some words ending in *f* or *fe,* change *f* to *v* and add -*s* or -*es*.

calf, calves   life, lives   leaf, leaves
half, halves   wife, wives   hoof, hooves
self, selves   shelf, shelves   knife, knives

Words ending in y

For words ending in *y,* change *y* to *i* and add -*es* if the *y* is preceded by a consonant.

theory, theories   huckleberry, huckleberries
eighty, eighties   sky, skies

EXCEPTIONS

Proper names

Henry, Henrys

Keep the y and add -s if the y is preceded by a vowel.

guy, guys   attorney, attorneys
delay, delays   alloy, alloys

Irregular plurals

For irregular plurals and nouns that have the same form in the singular and plural, memorize those you do not already know.

man, men	bacterium, bacteria	deer, deer
woman, women	locus, loci	sheep, sheep
child, children	alga, algae	moose, moose
foot, feet	basis, bases	series, series
tooth, teeth	datum, data	species, species

Compound words

For compound nouns written as one word, make the last part of the compound plural.

briefcase, briefcases
mailbox, mailboxes
bookshelf, bookshelves
grandchild, grandchildren

For compound nouns written as separate words or hyphenated, make the most important part of the compound plural.

brother-in-law, brothers-in-law
lieutenant governor, lieutenant governors
sergeant major, sergeants major
leap year, leap years
bus stop, bus stops

EXERCISE 24.8

Form the plural of each of the following words.

1. tomato	6. spoof	11. stepchild
2. hoof	7. beach	12. turkey
3. volunteer	8. yourself	13. mile per hour
4. baby	9. golf club	14. radio
5. dish	10. rose	15. phenomenon

EXERCISE 24.8: Answers

1. tomatoes
2. hooves
3. volunteers
4. babies
5. dishes
6. spoofs
7. beaches
8. yourselves
9. golf clubs
10. roses
11. stepchildren
12. turkeys
13. miles per hour
14. radios
15. phenomena

24f

Taking a personal spelling inventory

This chapter has surveyed general spelling rules and guidelines. You need now to tailor this advice to your own spelling patterns and problems. Doing so means becoming a detective of your own writing, looking for clues in as large and varied a sample of your prose as you have time to examine.

1

Identifying troublesome words and patterns

You can begin your inventory by looking through several pieces of your writing and making a list of every word misspelled. Whenever possible, identify the guideline in this chapter that deals with the misspellings. Here is the beginning of one student's inventory.

WORD	MISSPELLING	GUIDELINE
their	there	homonyms
receiving	recieving	"*i* before *e*"
hastiest	hastyest	suffix with final *y*
beginning	begining	double consonants
affect	effect	homonyms
sharing	shareing	unpronounced final *e*
environment	enviroment	unpronounced letters
theories	theorys	plural for words ending in *y*
dissatisfied	disatisfied	prefix

2

Using a spell checker

Some good news, perhaps, is that writers now have a special tool available to help with spelling: the spell checker, a program included on most word processors that helps find incorrect spellings. We say *perhaps* this is good news, however, for a reason. A comparison of spelling errors in first-year essays that were handwritten or typed with those in essays that were produced on a word processor either with or without a spell checker produced these interesting results:

handwritten or typed	1.74 errors per essay
word-processed *without* spell checker	3.81 errors per essay
word-processed *with* spell checker	1.60 errors per essay

These findings make an important point about writing on a word processor: seeing your words on screen or in nice neat typescript may make it difficult to "see" your spelling errors. Indeed, keyboarding often introduces new spelling errors, and the "clean" copy can, in a way, "conceal" these errors. If you use a word processor without a spell checker, then, you probably need to proofread for spelling more carefully than ever before.

These results also tell us that spell checkers alone won't correct spelling errors. Students using spell checkers misspelled almost as many words as did those who handwrote or typed their essays. To benefit from this tool, therefore, you must understand how to use a spell checker accurately and efficiently, and you must learn to adapt the spell checker to your own needs. And you must turn it on: just as a seat belt can save your life only if you wear it, so a spell checker can improve your spelling only if you use it.

➤ Using a spell checker

1. Use your spell checker. Check every word it calls to your attention.

2. Keep a dictionary near your computer, and look up *any* word the spell checker highlights that you aren't absolutely sure of.

3. Remember that spell checker dictionaries are limited; they don't recognize most proper names, foreign words, or specialized language. If your program has a "learn" option, enter any words you use regularly that you have trouble spelling into your spell checker dictionary. Add also your own spelling "demons."

4. Remember that spell checkers do not recognize homonym errors (misspelling *there* as *their,* for example; see 24b). If you know that you mix up certain words, therefore, you should check for them after running your spell checker. You may be able to use the search function on your word processor to identify words you need to check—every *there, their,* and *they're,* for instance.

5. Remember that spell checkers are not sensitive to capitalization. If you write "president bush," the spell checker won't question it.

6. Proofread carefully, even after you have used the spell checker.

3

Annotating your dictionary

For mastering particularly troublesome words, author John Irving recommends marking and dating words you look up in the dictionary. If you follow this advice, you will be able to identify words you look up frequently—and take steps to learn the correct spelling once and for all. Such words can then become part of your personal spelling inventory.

TEACHING PRACTICE

In addition to using the spell checker feature on their word-processing program, ask students who compose or type their papers on computers to use the *search* feature to check for homonym problems.

Instruct them to choose the homonyms and frequently confused words that they are unsure about (see the list in section 24b). Search for these in a draft, using the *search* feature. When the *search* stops at each instance of the word they are concerned about, they should double-check their use of it with the explanations from this handbook and with a dictionary.

4
Building on visualization and memory cues

Before the advent of printing, not to mention photocopying machines, people learned to train their memories extensively. You can activate your memory first by **visualizing** correct spelling or making mental pictures of how a word looks. You can also learn to use memory cues, or **mnemonic devices** (named for the Greek goddess of memory, Mnemosyne), in mastering words that tend to trip you up. Here are one student's memory cues.

WORD/MISSPELLING	CUE
a lot/alot	I wouldn't write *alittle*, would I?
government/goverment	Government should serve those it *governs*.
separate/seperate	*Separate* rates two *a*'s.
definitely/definately	There are a *finite* number of ways to spell *definitely*.

EXERCISE 24.9   Revising for Spelling

Correct each misspelling in the passage below. Whenever possible, classify the misspelling under one of the guidelines in this chapter. Then draw up three or four tips you could give this particular student on how to improve spelling.

For me, the ideel ocupation would be an arangement in which I could play with a band for six months and tour the other six months of the year. I wouldn't want to teach music because I would probly have to teach in a school where many students are forced to take music by there parrents. When children are forced to do something, its likly that they won't enjoy it. If I were able to both tour an teach, however, I would be happy.

I'm realy glad that I've gotten involved in music; it looks as if I'm destined to be a profesional musician. Surly I don't know what else I could do; I dout I'd be a good administrater or bussiness executive or lawyer. And the idea of being a doctor or denist and probing around people's bodys or looking at teeth that have huge, roting cavities isn't appealing to me. The more I think about it, the happyer I am with my music. I definately plan to pursue that career.

EXERCISE 24.10   Taking Inventory: Spelling

If you are keeping a writing log, devote a section of it to a personal spelling inventory. Choose a sample of your recent writing, and identify every misspelling. If you have any drafts in a word processor, use a spell checker. Then, following the format presented in 24f1, enter the word, your misspelling, and the guideline or pattern that relates to it. For persistent misspellings, create a memory cue (see 24f4), and enter it in the log along with the correct spelling.

FOR COLLABORATIVE WORK

Ask students to work together to create memory cues that they all can use to spell more effectively.

EXERCISE 24.9: Answers

For me, the *ideal occupation* would be an *arrangement* in which I could play with a band for six months and tour the other six months of the year. I wouldn't want to teach music because I would *probably* have to teach in a school, where many students are forced to take music by *their parents*. When children are forced to do something, *it's likely* that they won't enjoy it. If I were able to both tour *and* teach, however, I would be happy.

I'm *really* glad that I've gotten involved in music; it looks as if I'm destined to be a *professional* musician. *Surely* I don't know what else I could do; I *doubt* I'd be a good *administrator* or *business* executive or lawyer. And the idea of being a doctor or *dentist* and probing around people's *bodies* or looking at teeth that have huge, *rotting* cavities isn't appealing to me. The more I think about it, the *happier* I am with my music. I *definitely* plan to pursue that career.

The misspellings in this passage can be attributed to three causes:

1. The writer's reliance upon pronunciation as a guide for spelling, thus leading to leaving out unpronounced consonants and vowels and to additions and substitutions of wrong letters as in *ideel, occupation, arangement, probly, parrents, likly, an, realy, profesional, surly, dout, administrater, bussiness, denist,* and *definately.*

2. The writer's difficulty distinguishing homonyms as in *there* and *its.*

3. The writer's unfamiliarity with rules governing addition of suffixes to words ending in *y* as in *bodys* and *happyer.*

25

Using Dictionaries

BACKGROUND

The dictionary, as we know it, is comparatively modern. To the medieval scholar, a dictionary was a collection of "dictions" or phrases put together for the use of pupils studying Latin—the social elite. The earliest dictionaries in English (Robert Cawdray's *A Table Alphabetical* of 1604 is the first) consisted of *hard words*. Through the seventeenth and eighteenth centuries, dictionaries steadily increased in size as lexicographers gradually moved toward the principle of including all words, not just hard words, in dictionaries. By the time Samuel Johnson composed his dictionary, he could assume that he had to include all words in his dictionary. Johnson's contribution was his systematic inclusion of illustrative quotations to demonstrate proper usage. Noah Webster's *American Dictionary of the English Language* built on Johnson's use of quotations by including selections from the Founding Fathers of the Republic and by insisting on American spellings. In 1961 *Webster's Third International Dictionary of the English Language* caused an outcry because the editors, departing from Webster's practice, decided to let usage determine correctness rather than impose an external authority. In contrast to the prescriptive dictionaries of Johnson and Webster, most modern dictionaries tend to be descriptive.

In the opening scene of Rex Stout's *Gambit,* master sleuth Nero Wolfe is "in the middle of a fit," solemnly tearing the pages out of a large volume and dropping them into a fire. What is the book that Wolfe finds "subversive and intolerably offensive"? It is a dictionary—specifically, the third edition of *Webster's New International Dictionary.* Guilty of thousands of "crimes" and threatening the very "integrity of the English language," this dictionary must be destroyed, Wolfe declares, down to its very fine binding.

You may not have thought of dictionaries as the cause of violent controversy, but very often they have been. Such controversy usually relates to a tension between two basic and competing aims for dictionaries. One aim is to fix a standard of the language so that users of it can know what is "right" and what is "wrong." Before the advent of the printing press, English spelling in particular was far from fixed, and with good reason; few people had occasion to write words down. Even later, the author we designate as Shakespeare is known to have spelled his own name in several different ways. By the eighteenth century, however, writers such as Alexander Pope urged a codification of the language, which they felt had reached perfection. Enter Samuel Johnson, whose *English Dictionary* (1755) established an authoritative right and wrong for a long time.

The second and competing aim of a dictionary was articulated forcefully about one hundred years after Johnson: to record a full inventory of the language as it is used, without trying to prescribe "right" and "wrong." What enraged Wolfe was a particular dictionary's focus on this second aim rather than the first. These dual aims persist in our dictionaries today and may in fact influence your choice of which dictionary to use on which occasion. This chapter will map the territory covered by dictionaries and provide you with a means of choosing the dictionaries you want to work with.

Everyday use

A dictionary can be particularly handy when you are faced with signing—or preparing to sign—a contract. For many Americans, buying life insurance is a very important decision that calls for understanding and evaluating complex and competing plans. Reading such materials calls for a sharp eye and a clear knowledge of what words mean. Materials describing one such plan, for example, contain the following terms: semiannual, net cost, underwrite, waiver, conversion, incontestability, and incapacitated. How many of these terms do you understand? Which ones are generally familiar but may hold specific legal meanings in a contract? Which ones would you want to look up in a dictionary before signing your name to the contract?

EXERCISE 25.1

Without looking them up, try your hand at defining at least two of the unitalicized terms in the "Everyday use" box above. Compare your definitions with those of one or two other students. Then look up the terms in one of the dictionaries described in this chapter, and summarize briefly how your definitions differ from the ones in the dictionary.

25a

Exploring the dictionary

A good dictionary packs a surprising amount of information into a relatively small space, including much more than the correct spelling. Take a look, for instance, at this entry in *Webster's New World Dictionary*, Third College Edition:

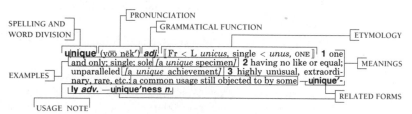

USEFUL READING

Baugh, Albert C., and Thomas Cable. *A History of the English Language*. 3rd ed. Englewood Cliffs, NJ: Prentice, 1978. See items 170, "Dictionaries of Hard Words"; 197, "Johnson's Dictionary"; and 246, "Noah Webster and an American Language."

Johnson, Samuel. "Preface to a Dictionary of the English Language." *Samuel Johnson: Rasselas, Poems, and Selected Prose* 3rd ed. Ed. Bertrand H. Bronson New York: Holt, 1971. Johnson describes his goals, the problems he encountered, and the limitations of the work.

Matthews, Mitford M. "The Freshman and His Dictionary." *About Language*. Ed. William H. Roberts and Gregoire Turgeon. Boston: Houghton, 1986. Matthews describes three categories of information freshmen need to know about dictionaries.

EXERCISE 25.1: Answers will vary.

FOR COLLABORATIVE WORK

Break the class into small groups, and either assign a word to each group or allow the group to pick a word they find interesting. Each person in the group should investigate the definition and usage of the word in one of the following dictionaries, usage books, or thesauruses. The group is responsible for presenting as rich a definition as possible for the word they research. The "product" of the research can take the form of a written report, but an oral presentation is often more valuable and interesting, particularly if the words the students choose contain surprises for them.

Here is a list of potential sources (not including the ones listed in the handbook).

Brewer's Dictionary of Phrase and Fable: Centenary Edition. New York: Harper, 1981.

Chapman, Robert L. *New Dictionary of American Slang.* New York: Harper, 1986.

Hall, John R. *A Concise Anglo-Saxon Dictionary.* Toronto: U of Toronto P, 1984.

Matthews, Mitford M. *A Dictionary of Americanisms on Historical Principles.* Chicago: U of Chicago P, 1951.

Partridge, Eric. *A Dictionary of Slang and Unconventional English.* 8th ed. New York: Macmillan, 1985.

Wentworth, Harold. *American Dialect Dictionary.* New York, 1944.

Wentworth, Harold, and Stuart B. Flexner. *Dictionary of American Slang.* 2nd ed. New York: Crowell, 1975.

TEACHING PRACTICE

To extend the ways students use dictionaries, devise assignments that require students to use a dictionary to complete the assignment. One such assignment might be an extended definition of a term (for example, *wife*), either of your own or of the students' choice. To have students define the term fully, you might require that they include all uses of the term, from formal to slang. You might also require that students examine how the term has changed over time (for example, *guy*), or you might require students to examine how the meaning of a certain word changes from country to country and region to region (*grill* and *barbeque*). The various requirements demand that students examine a variety of sources.

In fact, a dictionary entry may contain a dozen or more kinds of information about a word, the most common of which are listed below. The first six normally appear in all entries, the others only when necessary or relevant.

1. *Spelling,* including alternate spellings if they exist
2. *Word division,* with bars, dots, or spaces separating syllables and showing where a word may be divided at the end of a line
3. *Pronunciation,* including alternate pronunciations
4. *Grammatical functions and irregular forms,* including plurals of nouns, principal parts of verbs, and comparative and superlative forms of adjectives and adverbs
5. *Etymology,* the languages and words that the word comes from
6. *Meanings,* in order of either development or frequency of use
7. *Examples* of the word in the context of a phrase or sentence
8. *Usage labels and notes* (see explanation below)
9. *Field labels,* indicating that a word has a specialized meaning in a particular field of knowledge or activity
10. *Synonyms* and *antonyms*
11. *Related words* and their grammatical functions
12. *Idioms,* phrases in which the word appears and their meanings

Usage labeling and notes

For some words, many dictionaries include a kind of usage labeling, intended to let readers know that some or all meanings of the word are not considered appropriate in certain contexts. You can generally find such labels identified at the beginning of the dictionary. Here are some of the labels the *Webster's New World* uses.

1. *Archaic:* rarely used today except in specialized contexts
2. *Obsolete:* no longer used
3. *Colloquial:* characteristic of conversation and informal writing
4. *Slang:* extremely informal
5. *Dialect:* used mostly in a particular geographical or linguistic area, often one that is specified, such as Scotland or New England

In addition to labels, dictionaries sometimes include notes discussing usage in greater detail. In the *Webster's New World* entry for *unique,* notice that the third meaning includes a note that using the word with this meaning is "common" but is "still objected to by some."

EXERCISE 25.2

Look up the spelling, syllable division, and pronunciation of the following words in your dictionary. Note any variants in spelling and/or pronunciation.

1. process (noun)	5. whippet	8. hurrah
2. heinous	6. crayfish	9. greasy
3. exigency	7. macabre	10. theater
4. schedule		

EXERCISE 25.3

Look up the etymology of the following words in your dictionary.

1. rhetoric	5. apple	8. tortilla
2. student	6. sex	9. cinema
3. curry (noun)	7. okra	10. video
4. whine		

EXERCISE 25.4

Use your dictionary to find synonyms (and antonyms) for the following words.

1. coerce	3. parameter	5. awesome
2. prevaricate	4. odious	6. obfuscate

25b

Distinguishing among dictionaries

Since the time of Samuel Johnson's 1755 dictionary and Noah Webster's *American Dictionary of the English Language* (1828), the number and kinds of English-language dictionaries have multiplied many times over. While they all share the name *dictionary,* these numerous volumes differ considerably from one another. You may most often use an easily portable paperback dictionary, but you should be familiar with other kinds of dictionaries as well.

EXERCISE 25.2: Answers will vary.

EXERCISE 25.3: Answers

1. rhetoric: from ME *rethorike* < L *rhetorica* < Gr *rhetor,* orator < *eirein,* to speak

2. student: from ME < L *studere,* to study

3. curry: from Tamil *kari,* sauce

4. whine: from ME *whinen* < Indo-European *kwein,* to whiz, hiss, whistle

5. apple: from ME *appel* < OE *aeppel,* fruit, apple, eyeball, anything round

6. sex: from ME < L *sexus* < *secare,* to cut

7. okra: a word of West African origin

8. tortilla: from Sp, diminutive of *torta,* cake

9. cinema: from Fr *cinématographe* < Gr *kinema,* motion + *graphein,* to write

10. video: from L, I see < *videre,* to see

EXERCISE 25.4: Suggested Answers

1. *coerce:* (syn.) make, force, compel, constrain, oblige, drive.

2. *prevaricate:* (syn.) equivocate, lie, palter, fib.

3. *parameter:* (syn.) characteristic, element, factor.

4. *odious:* (syn.) disgusting, ghastly, hideous, unpleasant.

5. *awesome:* (syn.) impressive, overwhelming.

6. *obfuscate:* (syn.) darken, confuse.

OPTIONAL EXERCISE

Ask your students to copy the definitions of a word of their choice from three unabridged dictionaries: the *Oxford English Dictionary, Webster's Third New International Dictionary of the English Language,* and *The Random House Dictionary of the English Language.* Assign a short essay (250–500 words) that describes the changes in meaning their word has undergone. If you assign a word, make sure that the definitions include enough material for the length of assignment you expect. If the students choose their own words, take care to emphasize that they need to choose a word with enough information listed about that word. Ask students to append copies of the dictionary definitions to eliminate the need for extensive citations and to help build a file of words and definitions.

1

Abridged dictionaries

Abridged, or "abbreviated," **dictionaries** are the type most often used by college writers. Though they are not as complete as unabridged dictionaries, they are more affordable and more portable. Among the most helpful abridged dictionaries are *Webster's New World Dictionary, Random House Webster's College Dictionary,* and *The American Heritage Dictionary.*

Webster's New World Dictionary of the American Language, Third College Edition (New York: Simon, 1988). *Webster's New World* includes more than 170,000 entries; meanings are listed chronologically as they entered the language. Geographical and biographical names are included among the regular entries, and more than 800 drawings are provided.

Random House Webster's College Dictionary (New York: Random, 1991). The more than 180,000 entries in this dictionary include many words very new to the language, from *acquaintance rape* to *zouk.* This work is notable for its attempt to eliminate sexist language from definitions, its usage notes intended to warn users when terms may be offensive or disparaging, and its appendix on "Avoiding Sexist Language."

The American Heritage Dictionary, Second College Edition (Boston: Houghton, 1982). The more than 200,000 listings in this dictionary are augmented by 5,000 new scientific and technical terms and 3,000 new photographs supplementing the many photographs, drawings, and maps in the first edition. The *American Heritage* lists meanings in the order of most to least common. Notes on usage are extensive. Introductory essays provide a context for the usage notes in the form of a debate on the issue. Sections on biographical and geographical names, also liberally illustrated, follow the dictionary of general vocabulary, as does a section on abbreviations.

2

Unabridged dictionaries

Unabridged, or "unabbreviated," **dictionaries** are the royalty of their species—the most complete, richly detailed, and thoroughly presented dictionaries of English. Whereas good abridged dictionaries may include 175,000 items, unabridged dictionaries far more than double that figure. Because they are large and often multivolume—and hence expensive—you may not own an unabridged dictionary, but you will want and need to consult one on occasion in your library. Among the leading unabridged dictionaries are the *Oxford English Dictionary* and *Webster's Third New International Dictionary of the English Language.*

The Oxford English Dictionary, Second Edition, 20 volumes (New York: Oxford UP, 1989). The grandparent of unabridged dictionaries in English, the *OED* began in Britain in the nineteenth century as an attempt to give a full history of each English word, recording its entry into the language and illustrating the development of its various meanings with dated quotations in chronological order. Volunteers all over the English-speaking world contributed quotations, and the first edition was published piecemeal over a period of more than forty years. The second edition traces more than half a million words and is unparalleled in its historical account of changes in word meanings and spellings.

Webster's Third New International Dictionary of the English Language (Springfield, MA: Merriam, 1986). Containing more entries than any dictionary except the *OED*—more than 450,000 in all—this one-volume work stirred considerable controversy at its publication because of its tendency, as mentioned in the introduction to this chapter, to *describe* rather than to *prescribe* usage. In all, the editors collected 6,165,000 examples of recorded usage, on which they drew for their Usage Notes. *Webster's Third* lists meanings in order of their entry into the language and quotes from over 14,000 different authors to provide illustrations of words in context.

Here are the *Webster's Third* entries for *unique* as an adjective and as a noun. The adjective entry simply lists the meaning "unusual, notable" and examples of the use of *most unique*, without discussing the controversy over this usage. In addition, at the end of the entry, the notation **syn** refers to the entries for *single* and *strange*, where the shades of meaning that distinguish *unique* from its synonyms are explained. The phonetic symbols differ slightly from those in either the *OED* or the abridged dictionaries.

¹**unique** \yü'nēk, '₌₁₌\ *adj, sometimes* -ER/-EST [F, fr. L *unicus* sole, single, unique, fr. *unus* one + *-icus* -ic — more at ONE] **1 a :** being the only one **:** SOLE ⟨earning money whose ~ object could be nothing but Cyril's welfare —Arnold Bennett⟩ ⟨has thus preserved the original and often ~ records —G.B. Parks⟩ ⟨you are a miracle, a wonder, a mystery . . . one single ~ and inimitable living thing —J.C.Powys⟩ **b** *of a book* **:** known to exist in no other copy **2 :** being without a like or equal **:** single in kind or excellence **:** UNEQUALED ⟨they stand alone, ~, objects of supreme interest —A.B.Osborne⟩ ⟨as historian he knows that events, like persons, are ~ —J.M. Barzun⟩ ⟨remains singularly himself, a ~ lyrist of the first water —I.L.Salomon⟩ ⟨an almost ~ experience —Havelock Ellis⟩ ⟨tendencies present in our contemporary world which make our own times somewhat ~ —M.B.Smith⟩ ⟨story of his life is considerably more ~ than most autobiographies —Dorothy C. Fisher⟩ ⟨the more we study him, the less ~ he seems —Harry Levin⟩ — sometimes used with *to* ⟨the problem of what to do with surplus women is by no means ~ to our own society — Ralph Linton⟩ or *with* ⟨by no means ~ with the song sparrow —*Nature Mag.*⟩ **3 :** UNUSUAL, NOTABLE ⟨possessed ~ ability in the raising of funds —C.F.Thwing⟩ ⟨the wife of a career diplomat has a ~ opportunity to observe the world political scene —Ray Pierre⟩ ⟨a frankness ~ in literature —David Daiches⟩ ⟨~ peace and privacy —R.W.Hatch⟩ ⟨cheap, nourishing, and a ~ dining experience —T.H.Fielding⟩ ⟨the most ~ characteristic of that environment —R.A.Billington⟩ ⟨she's the most ~ person I ever met —Arthur Miller⟩ ⟨the most ~ theater in town —*advt*⟩ **4 :** capable of being performed in only one way ⟨the factorization of a number into its prime factors is ~⟩ **syn** see SINGLE, STRANGE
²**unique** \"\ *n* -S **:** something (as a specimen, thing, circumstance, or person) that is unique **:** the only one of its kind ⟨mistaking the ~ for the typical —W.J.Reilly⟩ ⟨the zest of the collector for possession of a ~ —Roy Bedichek⟩ ⟨a display of glass, including undercoated ~s —*Danish Foreign Office Jour.*⟩ ⟨the phoenix, the ~ of birds —Thomas De Quincey⟩

EXERCISE 25:5: Answers will vary.

EXERCISE 25.6: Suggested Answers

1. The *OED* lists a sixteenth-century definition of *dogmatism* as the preaching of new doctrine, the positive assertion of opinion, and a way of thinking based on principles that have not been tested by reflection.

   Webster's New World Dictionary gives both the idea of asserting opinion as well as the notion that this opinion usually occurs without reference to evidence.

2. The *OED* defines *alienate* as to make strange or turn away from, to transfer ownership, and to change or alter something.

   Webster's New World Dictionary adds two slightly different meanings: to cause to be withdrawn from society, and to transfer affection.

3. The *OED* defines *discriminate* as to make or constitute a difference, to distinguish with the mind or intellect, and to make a distinction.

   Webster's New World Dictionary also includes the notion of discernment or observing distinctions and adds the idea of showing partiality or prejudice.

4. The *OED* defines *hopefully* as an adverb: "In a hopeful manner; with a feeling of hope; with ground for hope, promisingly."

   Webster's New World Dictionary lists both adverb and adjective uses but notes that the adjectival use is "regarded by some as loose usage, but widely current."

5. The *OED* defines *humanism* as belief in the mere humanity of Christ, the quality of being human, a system of thought concerned with merely human interests, and the Renaissance study of Greek and Roman culture.

   Webster's New World Dictionary describes the philosophical basis of modern *humanism* in detail: "a modern, nontheistic, rationalist movement that holds that a man is capable of self-fulfillment, ethical conduct, etc. without the recourse to supernaturalism."

EXERCISE 25.5

See how Lewis Thomas uses *unique* in this sentence: "In a rose garden, a rose is a rose because of geraniol, a 10-carbon compound, and it's the geometric conformation of atoms and their bond angles that determine the unique fragrance." Compare the entries of *unique* on pp. 379 and 383, and decide whether Thomas's usage follows the advice of either one.

EXERCISE 25.6

Look up the following words in at least one abridged and one unabridged dictionary, and compare the entries. Record any differences or disagreements you find, and bring this record to class for discussion.

1. dogmatism	3. discriminate	5. humanism
2. alienate	4. hopefully	6. culture

EXERCISE 25.7

Look up one of the following words in the *OED,* and write a paragraph describing any changes in meaning it has undergone since its entry into English.

1. cheerful	3. vulgar	5. honest
2. machine	4. humor (noun)	6. romance

25c

Consulting specialized dictionaries

Abridged and unabridged dictionaries will provide you with an enormous amount of information. Sometimes, however, you will need to turn to additional sources for more specialized information. Such sources are available in dictionaries of usage, of synonyms, and of slang.

Dictionaries of usage

In cases where usage is disputed or where you feel unsure of your own usage, you may wish to consult a specialized dictionary of usage. The most widely used such work, although it is much more about British than about American usage, is H. W. Fowler's *Dictionary of Modern English Usage,* which was published in 1926 and revised by Sir Ernest Gowers in 1965.

Dictionaries of synonyms

All writers are sometimes stuck for just the right word, and at such times, a dictionary of synonyms or a thesaurus is a friend indeed. In these works, each entry is followed by words whose meanings are similar to that entry. A useful source is *Webster's Dictionary of Synonyms*.

A **thesaurus**, which comes from a word meaning "treasure" or "storehouse," provides lists of antonyms as well as synonyms. Two are particularly helpful: *Webster's Collegiate Thesaurus* and *The New Roget's Thesaurus of the English Language in Dictionary Form*.

Remember, however, to use dictionaries of synonyms and thesauruses very carefully, because rarely in English are two words so close in meaning that they can be used interchangeably in radically different contexts. As Mark Twain put it, the difference between the right word and the almost-right word is the difference between lightning and the lightning bug.

Dictionaries of etymology, regional English, and slang

On some occasions, you may want or need to find out all you can about the origins of a word, to find out about a term used only in one area of the country, or to see whether a term is considered to be slang or not. The following specialized dictionaries can help out.

> *The Oxford Dictionary of English Etymology.* Ed. C. T. Onions. New York: Oxford UP, 1966.
>
> *Dictionary of American Regional English.* Ed. Frederic G. Cassidy. Cambridge, MA: Belknap—Harvard UP, 1985.
>
> *Dictionary of American Slang,* 2nd supplemented edition. Ed. Harold Wentworth and Stuart Berg Flexner. New York: Crowell, 1978.

EXERCISE 25.8

Look up the following words in several specialized dictionaries, and find out as much as you can about their meanings, origins, and uses.

1. wazoo
2. tip
3. scam
4. jazz
5. whammy
6. advertorial

EXERCISE 25.9   Reading with Attention to Words

In his autobiography, Malcolm X says that he taught himself to write by reading and copying the dictionary. Certainly you can teach yourself to be a better writer by reading with very careful attention to the way other writers use words not very familiar to you. Choose a writer whose work you admire, and read that

6. Both the *OED* and *Webster's New World Dictionary* define *culture* as the cultivation of the soil, the production of a particular commodity, the growth of microorganisms in a prepared substance, the development of the intellect, and the ideas or customs of a group.

The *OED* includes two obsolete definitions: worship, and the training of the human body.

EXERCISE 25.7: Answers will vary.

OPTIONAL EXERCISE

Ask your students to look up *unique* in Fowler's *Modern English Usage,* in Bergen Evans and Cornelia Evans's *Dictionary of Contemporary American Usage,* and in Margaret M. Bryant's *Current American Usage* and write a brief description of how these three works agree and disagree on the usage of *unique.*

OPTIONAL EXERCISE

Ask your students to look up the entry *strange* in *Webster's New Dictionary of Synonyms* and read it carefully. Then ask them to write a brief summary of what the entry has to say about the relationship of *unique* to *strange.* Finally, have them look up *strange* in *The New Roget's Thesaurus,* and compare that entry with the one in *Webster's.*

EXERCISE 25.8: Answers will vary.

EXERCISE 25.9: Answers will vary.

FOR COLLABORATIVE WORK

Consider using an excerpt of Susan Brownmiller's book *Femininity* (New York: Fawcett, 1985) as an example of an extended definition of that term. Read the excerpt to your students, and ask them to work in small groups to identify each statement or partial definition that Brownmiller uses to build her complex definition and support her thesis. Then ask your students to use an invention technique, such as brainstorming or clustering, to find a word that they could define at length (perhaps *masculinity* might be a good place to start). Finally, ask them to write a short extended definition. This exercise could be extended by asking students to define a word using other texts, such as magazine advertisements, as sources and support for their extended definitions.

The following statements all appear in Brownmiller's work and help define her use of *femininity*:

> Femininity, in essence, is a romantic sentiment, a nostalgic tradition of imposed limitations. (215)

> Femininity functions as an effective antidote to the unrelieved seriousness, the pressure of making one's way in a harsh, difficult world. (217)

> Femininity operates as a value system of niceness, a code of thoughtfulness and sensitivity that in modern society is sadly in short supply. (218)

author's work for at least thirty minutes, noting down six or seven words that you would not ordinarily have thought to use. Do a little dictionary investigative work on these words, and bring your results to class for discussion.

EXERCISE 25.10   Taking Inventory: Your Own Words

Look back through the last several pieces of writing you have done, looking for two or three words you have used that interest you but that you know very little about. Then look up those words in at least one abridged and one unabridged dictionary and in any specialized dictionary that might give you further information. On the basis of what you have learned, check the way you have used these words in your writing. How accurately and appropriately have you used them? What synonyms could you have appropriately substituted?

26

Enriching Vocabulary

In one of the great heroic tales in English literature, Beowulf faces a series of difficult challenges. In the face of them, he calls not for weapons or for superhuman strength. Instead he says, quite simply, "I will unlock my word-hoard." Beowulf regards his "word-hoard," his vocabulary or language, as his greatest strength. Indeed, in the history of Western culture, the connection between language and creative power has been very close. In the Bible, for instance, how does God create the world? By calling it into existence through *naming* it.

Vocabulary comes from a Latin term for "name" (*vocabulum*), which in turn comes from the Latin verb for "call." The connection between vocabulary and calling into being is what led a famous philosopher to declare that "the limits of my language are the limits of my world." You can recognize what the philosopher means easily enough by remembering a time in your life when you learned the name of something new. Before that time, this thing did not exist for you; yet curiously enough, once you know its name, you begin to recognize it all around you. Such is the power of vocabulary in enriching not only our personal language but our lives as well.

26a

Considering your vocabulary

If you grew up speaking English, your English vocabulary is already extensive. At its largest, it includes all those words whose meanings you either recognize or can deduce from context. This, your **processing vocabulary**, allows you to interpret the meanings of many passages whose words you might not actively use yourself. Your **producing vocabulary** is more limited, made up of words you actually use in writing or speaking.

WORDS . . . are the wildest, freest, most irresponsible, most unteachable of all things. Of course, you can catch them and place them in alphabetical order in dictionaries. But words do not live in dictionaries; they live in the mind . . . all we can say about them, as we peer at them over the edge of that deep, dark and only fitfully illuminated cavern in which they live— the mind—all we can say about them is that they seem to like people to think and to feel before they use them, but to think and to feel not about them, but about something different.
— VIRGINIA WOOLF

Words are with us everywhere. In our erotic secrecies, in our sleep. We're often no more aware of them than our own spit, although we use them oftener than legs. So of course in the customary shallow unconscious sense, we comprehend the curse, the prayer, and the whoop.
— WILLIAM H. GASS

Words are all we have. —SAMUEL BECKETT

BACKGROUND
Studying how the English colonists in the New World confronted many new places, plants, animals, and experiences reveals how speakers of English have always developed new words. The colonists provided new names for new things in four ways.

1. By borrowing directly from another language, usually one of the native American languages. Native Americans spoke 350 different languages. The largest number of loan words came from the Algonquin languages. *Wigwam* is an example.

2. By translating foreign words (usually native American) and phrases into English. An example is *war path*.

3. By using an English word to serve as a label for something new. *Corn* and *robin* refer to different objects in England than they do in North America.

4. By coining a new word entirely, although such coinages were rare. The *bobwhite* and the *whipporwill* received names meant as imitations of the sounds they made. And *backwoods* is another colonial coinage.

Language continues to change. The process of adapting language to fit current needs never stops. Your students and their coinages are best seen as part of this process.

EXERCISE 26.1: Answers will vary.

Everyday use

Many years ago, the famous baseball player Dizzy Dean injured his leg sliding into second base. After examining the leg, the trainer announced with a serious expression that it looked as if the leg was fractured. "Fractured, hell!" cried Dean. "The damned thing's broken!" If fractured *wasn't a part of Dizzy Dean's active vocabulary before then, he surely figured it out quickly. So it is with all of us, for we meet new words every day; and with the help of context, word roots, and dictionaries, we figure them out and make them ours. Think of times recently when you learned the name of something new—a kind of plant, for example, or a computer term like* byte, *or an unfamiliar food like* fajitas. *How exactly did you discover its meaning?*

Part of what it means to mature intellectually is to broaden your mental horizons by learning how to name more things more accurately, to increase your own word-hoard. Doing so involves consciously strengthening the bridges between your processing vocabulary and your producing vocabulary by beginning to use in your own speaking and writing more of the words you recognize and can interpret in context. To accomplish this goal, you must become an investigative reporter of your own language and the language of others.

EXERCISE 26.1

Jot down two or three words you have heard or read lately that you would like to make part of your own vocabulary. Try defining them, and then write several sentences using each word.

Charting the history of English

Try to imagine a world without language. In fact, you probably cannot do so, for language is perhaps the most ancient heritage of the human race. Because language brings us together and indeed allows us to name and structure our experience of the world, it is well worth understanding how this heritage originated and has changed over the centuries. Knowing at least a little about the relationship of English to German, Norse, Latin, Greek, and French can help you learn more about any particular modern English word.

English has always been a hybrid language, what Daniel Defoe called "your Roman-Saxon-Danish-Norman English." Where did this hybrid come from, and how did it evolve? English, like one-third of all languages in the world, descends from Indo-European, a language spoken by a group of seminomadic peoples who almost certainly had domestic animals, worked leather, wove wool, and planted some crops. Where they lived is the subject of great controversy, though their original home must have been in some part of north-central Europe. Scholars began to argue for Indo-European as a "common source" and to try to identify its features when they noted more and more striking resemblances between words in a number of languages.

English	Latin	French	Greek	German	Dutch	Swedish	Danish
three	*tres*	*trois*	*treis*	*drei*	*drie*	*tre*	*tre*

A version of Indo-European was brought to Britain by the Germanic invasions following 449. This early language, called Anglo-Saxon or Old English, was influenced by Latin and Greek when Christianity was reintroduced into England beginning in 597, was later shaped by the Viking invasions beginning in the late 700s (the Danes feature prominently in *Beowulf*), and was transformed after the Norman Conquest (1066) by French.

Although English continued to evolve in the centuries after the conquest, Latin and French were the languages of the learned—of the church and court. (Indeed, lectures at Oxford University were delivered in Latin well into the nineteenth century.) It was Geoffrey Chaucer, in the late 1300s writing *The Canterbury Tales* in the language of the people, who helped establish what is now called Middle English as the political, legal, and literary language of Britain. And after the advent of printing in the mid-1400s, that language became more accessible and more standardized. By about 1600 it was essentially the Modern English we use today.

The following three versions of a Biblical passage will give you an idea of how much English had evolved up to this time.

ANGLO-SAXON GOSPELS, AROUND 1000 A.D.

And eft hē ongan hī æt þære sǣ lǣran. And him wæs mycel męnegu tō gęgaderod, swā þæt hē on scip ēode, and on bǣre sǣ wæs; and eall sēo męnegu ymbe þē sǣ wæs on lande.

WYCLIFFE BIBLE, ABOUT 1380

And eft Jhesus bigan to teche at the see; and myche puple was gaderid to hym, so that he wente in to a boot, and sat in the see, and al the puple was aboute the see on the loond.

KING JAMES VERSION, 1611

And he began again to teach by the seaside: and there was gathered unto him a great multitude, so that he entered into a ship, and sat in the sea: and the whole multitude was by the sea on the land.

USEFUL READING

Heath, Shirley Brice. *Ways with Words*. Cambridge: Cambridge UP, 1983. See Chapter 9, "Learners as Ethnographers," for more information about students as "investigative reporters."

Herndon, Jeanne H. *A Survey of Modern Grammars*. New York: Holt, 1976. See pp. 146–47 for a discussion of competence and performance, *la langue* and *la parole*.

BACKGROUND

English owes its hybrid nature to the various invasions of Britain—that is, to the fact that the earliest native peoples and their language, the Celts, and the later dominant peoples, the three Germanic tribes (the Jutes, the Angles, and the Saxons) intermixed with each other and other peoples invading the country. The Romans, who ruled Britain for almost four hundred years, contributed *castra,* the Latin word meaning "camp." It is evident in the names of such places as *Lancaster* and *Winchester.* Also, Latin words were brought over to Britain by the German invaders, whose language had borrowed them previously: *win* ("wine"), *ancor* ("anchor"), *weall* ("wall"). The Anglo-Saxons gave us the earliest ancestors of many modern English words, such as *hus* ("house"), *wulf* ("wolf"), and *faeder* ("father"). They also gave the island its permanent name, *Englaland* ("England"), the "land of the Angles." The Danes, who invaded Britain in the ninth century, added *skull, sky, band, egg, want,* and *low.* And they gave us our personal pronouns for the third person, *they, their,* and *them.* A tremendous number of new English words and new spellings originated with the Norman Invasion in 1066. *Service, castle, chancellor, army,* and *literature* all came from Norman French originally.

Renaissance scholars deliberately borrowed many Greek and Latin words. Also, many Greek and Latin prefixes, suffixes, and roots of words were borrowed and combined with other borrowings to form whole new words.

TEACHING PRACTICE

Old or Middle English may look remote to students, but if you read a Middle English text aloud, they will be surprised at how much they pick up. Provide your students with a copy of one of Chaucer's *Canterbury Tales,* and read part of it to them. Ask them to underline any words they cannot understand, and as a class, attempt to define these words. Here is a section from the Wife of Bath's tale:

Lo, here the wyse kind, dan Salomon
I towe he hadd wyves mo than oon.
As wolde God it level ful were to me
To be refressed half so ofte as he!
Which yifte of God hadde he for alle his wyvis!
No man hath switch, that in this world alyve is.

BACKGROUND

English continues to be a very democratic language, borrowing from almost every language it comes in contact with. From Spanish, we have *canyon, cafeteria,* and *taco.* From German, we borrowed *protein* and *bratwurst.* From Italian, we have *malaria,* but also *pasta* and *studio.* From Slavic, we have *robot* and *vampire.* From Arabic, we adopted *genie, candy, safari,* and *assassin* (originally meaning "hashisheater"). From Hebrew, we borrowed *amen, Sabbath,* and *Satan.* From Yiddish, we borrowed *kosher* and *matzo.* From Persian, we got *spinach, lilac,* and *bazaar.* From Sanskrit, we have *swastika* and *yoga.* From Hindustani, we got *dungaree, pajamas, jungle,* and *loot.* From Chinese, we adopted *tea* and *ketchup.* From Japanese, we borrowed *zen* and *karate.*

TEACHING PRACTICE

In *Classical Rhetoric for the Modern Student,* Edward P. J. Corbett notes that Samuel Johnson and Oliver Goldsmith identified themselves in their writing by stylistic choices, such as diction (405). Johnson's is described as "philosophical, polysyllabic, Latinate"; Goldsmith's as "concrete, familiar, colloquial."

Consider using examples of writing, either from these authors or from legalese and rock lyrics, to point out how vocabulary can restrict or free writers.

Note that in the Old English text, only a few words—*and, he, him, waes, on, lande*—look familiar. By the time of Chaucer and Wycliffe, however, many words are recognizable. And by the time of Shakespeare, the language is easily readable by us.

In the last four hundred years, as the extension of British and, later, American political and cultural influence has made English the second most widely spoken language in the world, continued borrowings from many languages have given it the world's largest vocabulary. Modern English, then, is a plant growing luxuriously in the soil of multiple sources.

26b

Recognizing word roots

As its name suggests, a **root** is a word from which other words grow, usually through the addition of prefixes or suffixes. From the Latin roots *-dic-* or *-dict-* ("speak"), for instance, grows a whole range of words in English: *contradict, dictate, dictator, diction, edict, predict, dictaphone,* and others. From the Greek root *-chrono-* ("time") come our words *chronology, synchronize, chronic,* and so on.

Here are some other Latin (L) and Greek (G) roots. Recognizing them will help you recognize networks of words.

ROOT	MEANING	EXAMPLES
-audi- (L)	to hear	audience, audio
-bene- (L)	good, well	benevolent, benefit
-bio- (G)	life	biography, biosphere
-duc(t)- (L)	to lead or to make	ductile, reproduce
-gen- (G)	race, kind	genealogy, gene
-geo- (G)	earth	geography, geometry
-graph- (G)	to write	graphic, photography
-jur-, -jus- (L)	law	justice, jurisdiction
-log(o)- (G)	word, thought	biology, logical
-luc- (L)	light	lucid, translucent
-manu- (L)	hand	manufacture, manual
-mit-, -mis- (L)	to send	permit, transmission
-path- (G)	feel, suffer	empathy, pathetic
-phil- (G)	love	philosopher, bibliophile
-photo- (G)	light	photography, telephoto
-port- (L)	to carry	transport, portable
-psych- (G)	soul	psychology, psychopath
-scrib-, -script- (L)	to write	inscribe, manuscript
-sent-, -sens- (L)	to feel	sensation, resent

ROOT	MEANING	EXAMPLES
-tele- (G)	far away	telegraph, telepathy
-tend- (L)	to stretch	extend, tendency
-terr- (L)	earth	inter, territorial
-vac- (L)	empty	vacuole, evacuation
-vid-, -vis- (L)	to see	video, envision, visit

EXERCISE 26.2

Using the list of roots above, try to figure out the meaning of each of the following words. Write a potential definition for each one, and then compare your dictionary's definition to yours.

1. terrestrial
2. scriptorium
3. geothermal
4. lucent
5. beneficent
6. audiology
7. vacuous
8. pathogenic
9. juridical
10. graphology

26c

Recognizing prefixes and suffixes

Originally individual words themselves, prefixes and suffixes are groups of letters added to words or to word roots to create new words. These word additions account for much of the flexibility of English, often allowing dozens of words to be built on one root.

1

Prefixes

Prefix appropriately demonstrates its own meaning: it is made up of a prefix (-*pre*-) and a root (-*fix*-) and means literally "fasten before." Fastened to the beginnings of words or roots, prefixes modify and extend meanings. Recognizing common prefixes can often help you decipher the meaning of otherwise unfamiliar words.

Prefixes of negation or opposition

PREFIX	MEANING	EXAMPLES
a-, an-	without, not	ahistorical, anemia
anti-	against	antibody, antiphonal
contra-	against	contravene, contradict

USEFUL READING

Mencken, H. L. *The American Language*. New York: Knopf, 1937. See "The Expanding Vocabulary," "The Making of New Nouns," and "American Slang."

EXERCISE 26.2: Suggested Answers

1. *terrestrial:* worldly, earthy, mundane; consisting of, living on, or growing on land.
2. *scriptorium:* a writing room, a room in a monastery for copying manuscripts, writing, and studying.
3. *geothermal:* having to do with the heat of the earth's interior.
4. *lucent:* giving off light, shining, translucent or clear.
5. *beneficent:* doing good, resulting in benefit.
6. *audiology:* the science of hearing, the evaluation of hearing defects.
7. *vacuous:* empty of matter, showing lack of intelligence, interest, or thought, characterized by lack of purpose.
8. *pathogenic:* producing disease.
9. *juridical:* of judicial proceedings, jurisprudence, or law.
10. *graphology:* the study of handwriting.

TEACHING PRACTICE

Consider asking your students to read and record inventive uses of vocabulary. To get them started, read some of Tom Wolfe's prose, such as "Pornoviolence" (the title coins a new word), "Hugh Hefner" (in which he coins the word *statusphere*), or "Las Vegas (What!) Las Vegas (Can't Hear You! Too Noisy) Las Vegas!!" (in which Wolfe names the signs on the strip: "Boomerang Modern, Palette Curvilinear, Flash Gordon Ming Alert Spiral, McDonald's Hamburger Parabola, Mint Casino Elliptical, Miami Beach Kidney"). Paul Fussell's "Notes on Class" uses the following terms to identify his classifications of society: "Top Out-of-Sight; Upper [class]; Upper Middle/Middle; High-Proletarian; Mid-Proletarian; Low-Proletarian/Destitute; Bottom Out-of-Sight," and a floating class "Class X."

PREFIX	MEANING	EXAMPLES
de-	from, take away from	demerit, declaw
dis-	apart, away	disappear, discharge
il-, im-, in-, ir-	not	illegal, immature, indistinct, irreverent
mal-	wrong	malevolent, malpractice
mis-	wrong, bad	misapply, misanthrope
non-	not	nonentity, nonsense
un-	not	unbreakable, unable

Prefixes of quantity

PREFIX	MEANING	EXAMPLES
bi-	two	bipolar, bilateral
milli-	thousand	millimeter, milligram
mono-	one, single	monotone, monologue
omni-	all	omniscient, omnipotent
semi-	half	semicolon, semiconductor
tri-	three	tripod, trimester
uni-	one	unitary, univocal

Prefixes of time and space

PREFIX	MEANING	EXAMPLES
ante-	before	antedate, antebellum
circum-	around	circumlocution, circumnavigate
co-, col-, com-, con-, cor-	with	coequal, collaborate, commiserate, contact, correspond
e-, ex-	out of	emit, extort, expunge
hyper-	over, more than	hypersonic, hypersensitive
hypo-	under, less than	hypodermic, hypoglycemia
inter-	between	intervene, international
mega-	enlarge, large	megalomania, megaphone
micro-	tiny	micrometer, microscopic
neo-	recent	neologism, neophyte
post-	after	postwar, postscript
pre-	before	previous, prepublication

PREFIX	MEANING	EXAMPLES
pro-	before, onward	project, propel
re-	again, back	review, re-create
sub-	under, beneath	subhuman, submarine
super-	over, above	supercargo, superimpose
syn-	at the same time	synonym, synchronize
trans-	across, over	transport, transition

EXERCISE 26.3

Using the list of prefixes above and the list of roots in 26b, try to figure out the meaning of each of the following words. Write a potential definition for each one, and then compare your dictionary's definition to yours.

1. remit
2. subterranean
3. translucent
4. monograph
5. distend
6. superscript
7. deport
8. neologism
9. inaudible
10. apathetic

2

Suffixes

Attached to the ends of words and word roots, **suffixes** modify and extend meanings, many times by altering the grammatical function or part of speech of the original word. Suffixes can, for example, turn the verb *create* into a noun, an adjective, or an adverb.

VERB	create
NOUNS	crea*tor*/crea*tion*/crea*tivity*/crea*ture*
ADJECTIVE	crea*tive*
ADVERB	crea*tively*

Noun suffixes

SUFFIX	MEANING	EXAMPLES
-acy	state or quality	democracy, privacy
-al	act of	rebuttal, refusal
-ance, -ence	state or quality of	maintenance, eminence
-dom	place or state of being	freedom, thralldom

EXERCISE 26.3: Suggested Answers

1. *remit:* send again or send back; release from the guilt or penalty of, refrain from, desist from an activity.
2. *subterranean:* beneath earth; of or relating to under the surface of the earth.
3. *translucent:* across or over light; permitting the passage of light, clear or transparent.
4. *monograph:* write a single writing; a learned treatise on a small area of learning.
5. *distend:* stretch apart or away; extend, enlarge from internal pressure.
6. *superscript:* write over or above; a distinguishing symbol written immediately above or above and to the right of another character.
7. *deport:* carry from; carry away, send out of the country by legal deportation, behave or comport oneself.
8. *neologism:* a recent word or thought; a word, usage, or expression that is often disapproved because of its newness or barbarousness.
9. *inaudible:* hear not; not capable of being heard.
10. *apathetic:* without feeling or not suffering; having or showing little or no feeling or emotion, having or showing little or no interest or concern.

SUFFIX	MEANING	EXAMPLES
-er, -or	one who	trainer, investor
-ism	doctrine or belief characteristic of	liberalism, Taoism
-ist	one who	organist, physicist
-ity	quality of	veracity, opacity
-ment	condition of	payment, argument
-ness	state of being	watchfulness, cleanliness
-ship	position held	professorship, fellowship
-sion, -tion	state of being or action	digression, transition

Verb suffixes

SUFFIX	MEANING	EXAMPLES
-ate	cause to be	concentrate, regulate
-en	cause to be or become	enliven, blacken
-ify, -fy	make or cause to be	unify, terrify, amplify
-ize	cause to become	magnetize, civilize

Adjective suffixes

SUFFIX	MEANING	EXAMPLES
-able, -ible	capable of being	assumable, edible
-al	pertaining to	regional, political
-esque	reminiscent of	picturesque, statuesque
-ful	having a notable quality	colorful, sorrowful
-ic	pertaining to	poetic, mythic
-ious, -ous	of or characterized by	famous, nutritious
-ish	having the quality of	prudish, clownish
-ive	having the nature of	festive, creative, massive
-less	without	endless, senseless

EXERCISE 26.4

Using the list of suffixes above, figure out the meaning of each of the following words. (Use your dictionary if necessary.) Then choose two of the words, and use each one in a sentence.

1. contemplative	5. barrenness	8. redden
2. fanciful	6. defiance	9. standardize
3. impairment	7. defiantly	10. satirist
4. liquefy		

Building a word-hoard

Making good use of prefixes or suffixes will increase the power of your vocabulary, but other methods will be even more helpful in creating a word-hoard that is a match for Beowulf's. These methods include analyzing word contexts, becoming an active reader, and becoming a collector of words.

1

Analyzing word contexts

If you have ever run into a person you knew but simply could not place—until you remembered the place where you normally saw the person (at the grocery store, say)—you know firsthand the importance of context in helping you identify people and things. The same principle holds true for words. So if a word is at first unfamiliar to you, look carefully at its context, paying attention to all the clues that context can give; often you will be able to deduce the meaning.

For instance, if the word *accouterments* is unfamiliar in the sentence *We stopped at a camping supply store to pick up last-minute accouterments*, the context—*a camping supply store* and *last-minute*—suggests strongly that *equipment* or some similar word fits the bill. And that is what *accouterments* means.

EXERCISE 26.5

Identify the contextual clues that help you understand any unfamiliar words in the following sentences. Then write paraphrases of three of the sentences.

1. Before Prohibition, the criminal fringe in the United States had been a self-effacing, scattered class with little popular support.
2. I felt ambivalent. I was angry with Sylvia, but I understood why she behaved so audaciously in asking for a raise after three days on the job.

(Chapter 1 provides you with guidelines to improve your reading.)

FOR COLLABORATIVE WORK

Ask students to choose a language to investigate: the language of rap, the language of parents, the language of doctors. As part of their investigation, ask students to draw up a "vocabulary," complete with definitions and examples, for the language they choose. A compendium of the language of freshmen could include words like *chill* (short for *chill out,* which means to cool it or calm down) and *yo* (a glottal vibration meant to indicate either "Give me your attention" or "Yes, you have my attention").

3. The community's reaction to the preternatural creature in Mary Shelley's *Frankenstein* shows that people are often more monstrous than a monster.

4. My fifth-grade teacher was the epitome of what I wanted to be, and I began to imitate him scrupulously.

5. Aristarchus showed that the sun is larger than the earth and proposed a heliocentric model of the solar system. During the second century A.D., however, Ptolemy challenged this theory with his geocentric model, which came to dominate astronomical thought for the next 1,400 years.

2

Becoming an active reader

As processors of information, we can read words alone, or we can read meanings. To read meanings means filling in blanks, making connections, leaping ahead, asking questions, taking mental notes. Active readers flex their mental muscles while reading; they exercise their own understanding and thereby stretch to greater knowledge. Out of such activity great word-hoards are born. (Chapter 1 provides you with guidelines to improve your reading.) Here are some additional tips for building your vocabulary through active reading.

- Make a habit of paraphrasing or summarizing unfamiliar words or phrases. Then check the dictionary to see how accurate you were.
- Practice naming the opposites of words. If you see *abbreviation,* for instance, try supplying its opposite—*enlargement, elaboration,* etc.
- Challenge authors by trying to come up with a better word or words than the ones they used.
- Read aloud to yourself from time to time, noting any words whose pronunciation you are unsure of. Check them out in the dictionary.

3

Becoming a collector of words

Collecting words is an important part of reading actively. Pay close attention to words, choosing those you like best and taking them home as part of your producing vocabulary. You are already a collector of words in one sense: you probably add words to your vocabulary on a fairly regular basis. All you need to do now is make that activity more conscientious and systematic. Begin by choosing a writer you admire and reading for as long as it takes to identify several words you like but would not use in speaking or writing. Your collection has started. Now analyze these words for what you like about them—for pronunciation, meaning, and usage. Next, try the words out on your friends and instructors. And then just continue to build your collection.

EXERCISE 26.6 Reading with Attention to Vocabulary

Read each of the following passages, paying particular attention to the italicized words. See if you can determine the meaning of any words you don't know by using the clues suggested in this chapter—context, prefixes, roots, suffixes. Check your understanding by then looking up each word in the dictionary.

1. Now, I doubt that the imagination can be suppressed. If you truly *eradicated* it in a child, he would grow up to be an eggplant. Like all our evil *propensities,* the imagination will win out.
   – URSULA LEGUIN, "Why Are Americans Afraid of Dragons?"

2. Science gets most of its information by the process of *reductionism,* exploring the details, then the details of the details, until all the smallest bits of the structure, or the smallest parts of the mechanism, are laid out for counting and scrutiny.   –LEWIS THOMAS, "THE TUCSON ZOO"

3. I think it is agreed by all parties, that this *prodigious* number of children in the arms, or on the backs, or at the heels of their mothers . . . is in the present *deplorable* state of the kingdom, a very great additional *grievance.* . . .   –JONATHAN SWIFT, "A Modest Proposal"

EXERCISE 26.7 Taking Inventory: Vocabulary

Read over a piece of writing you are working on or have recently completed. Underline any words you think could be improved on, and then come up with several possible substitutes. If you keep a writing log, list them there as a start on your own personal word-hoard.

EXERCISE 26.6: Suggested Answers

1. *eradicated:* tore out by the roots, got rid of, wiped out, destroyed.
   propensities: natural inclinations or tendencies.

2. *reductionism:* a theory or procedure that reduces complex data or phenomena to simple terms.

3. *prodigious:* enormous, huge.
   deplorable: lamentable, regrettable, very bad, wretched.
   grievance: a circumstance thought to be unjust or injurious and ground for complaint or resentment.

TEACHING PRACTICE

Students can build word power by trying to think of words to substitute for the italicized ones in the passages in the reading exercise. You can use these potential substitutes (*erased,* say, for *eradicated*) to reflect on nuances of connotation and on why a writer may have chosen one particular word over another.

27

Considering Diction

In writing of someone you work with, you might choose one or more of the following words: *accomplice, ally, associate, buddy, cohort, collaborator, colleague, comrade, co-worker, mate, partner, sidekick.* The choice you make is a matter of **diction**, which derives from the Latin word for "say" and means literally how you say or express something. Good diction involves many issues discussed elsewhere in this book, such as being concise (see Chapter 19), using parallel structures (see Chapter 21), choosing strong, precise verbs (see 23a), using dictionaries (see Chapter 25), strengthening vocabulary (see Chapter 26), and considering how your words can build common ground with readers (see Chapter 28).

This chapter will give you some guidance about aspects of good diction: using language appropriate to your purpose, topic, and audience; choosing words with the right denotations and connotations; balancing general and abstract words with specific and concrete ones; using figurative language; and choosing the appropriate register.

27a

Choosing appropriate language

Musing on the many possible ways to describe a face, Ford Madox Ford notes,

> That a face resembles a Dutch clock has been said too often; to say that it resembles a ham is inexact and conveys nothing; to say that it has the mournfulness of an old smashed-in meat tin, cast away on a waste building lot, would be smart—but too much of that sort of thing would become a nuisance.
> — FORD MADOX FORD, *Joseph Conrad*

Ford here implies a major point about diction: effective word choice can be made only on the basis of what is appropriate to the writer's purpose, to the topic, and to the audience. More specifically, he is suggesting that making appropriate word choices requires a writer to take into account a number of considerations.

What is appropriate may well vary from one region to another: the hard round object in the center of a cherry might be described as a stone, a pit, a pip, or a seed, depending on where the writer comes from. *Cherry pip* and *cherry stone* are examples of **regionalisms**, words or expressions peculiar to only one region or part of the country. Regionalisms are one frequent component of **dialects**, forms of a language that are distinctive to a particular region or social or ethnic group. In addition to distinctive words and expressions, dialects usually include distinctive pronunciations and grammatical constructions.

If you have never heard the phrase *cherry pip* used before, that particular choice of words will sound odd and perhaps puzzling to you. In other cases, especially in writing, a phrase or construction perfectly understandable and acceptable to users of one dialect will sound not only odd or puzzling but actually wrong to others. The verb constructions in *the car needs washed* or *the grass be dried up,* for example, would look wrong to many Americans, even though in certain American dialects these are standard ways of speaking.

Knowing what features of your dialect differ from the speech of many other Americans can help you decide how to make appropriate diction choices. In addition, you must also be alert to the level of formality, or register, that is appropriate for a particular topic and audience. Doing so requires that you recognize slang and colloquial language.

USEFUL READING

Corbett, Edward P. J. *Classical Rhetoric for the Modern Student.* 3rd ed. New York: Oxford UP, 1990. Corbett's discussion of ethical and emotional appeals provides a sound rationale for the importance of diction.

Weaver, Richard M. "Ultimate Terms in Contemporary Rhetoric." *Language is Sermonic: Richard M. Weaver on the Nature of Rhetoric.* Ed. Richard L. Johannesen et al. Baton Rouge: Louisiana State UP, 1970. See pp. 87–112, a discussion of the power of value-associated terms, particularly in the "ultimate" registers: those that Weaver calls "God terms" and "Devil terms."

Williams, Joseph M. *Origins of the English Language: A Social and Linguistic History.* New York: Macmillan, 1975. See pp. 204–07, a discussion of slang as a source of change in word meaning. Williams cites interesting historical instances of slang.

Everyday use

A good place to find diction at work is on restaurant menus. Here from two very different menus are descriptions of the same item—fried chicken.

Crispy-tender, finger-lickin', soul-satisfyin' good chicken. Choose regular or extra-spicy.

Succulent poulet frit, with a subtle hint of garlic.
Presented with steamed snow peas and potatoes lyonnaise.

What does the different diction tell you about the two restaurants? What do you think each of them would be like?

Any writer overwhelmingly honest about pleasing himself is almost sure to please others.
— MARIANNE MOORE

Slang is extremely informal language that is often confined to a relatively small group of people and usually becomes obsolete rather quickly. In the 1980s, examples of slang that gained fairly wide use included *yuppie, sleaze,* and *number-crunching.* **Colloquial language**, such as *a lot, in a bind,* or *snooze,* is less informal, more widely used, and longer-lasting than slang.

Like regional and dialectal words and constructions, slang and colloquial language can expose a writer to the risk of not being understood or of sounding wrong. If you are writing for a general audience about arms-control negotiations, for example, and you use the term *nukes* to refer to nuclear missiles, some readers may not know what you mean, and others may be distracted or irritated by what they see as a frivolous reference to a deadly serious subject.

Consider how choosing appropriate language works in the following set of sentences.

TO FRIENDS

I had to pull an incomplete in psych because I was barfing with that stomach flu all finals week and couldn't book it at all.

TO PARENTS

I had to take an incomplete in psychology because I had the stomach flu that was going around and couldn't study because I was throwing up all night before the final exam.

TO A COMMITTEE EVALUATING YOU FOR A SCHOLARSHIP

I was forced to request an incomplete in my Psychology 102 course because I had been violently ill with an intestinal virus for three days before the final examination (doctor's letter is enclosed) and was therefore unable to study.

What are the differences between these versions? Diction is the most obvious difference, but if you look more closely, you will see that each version reveals that choices of diction are related to definite judgments about purpose and audience. Consider how strange your friends would think you if you spoke to them in the language you might use to the scholarship committee. Your distant, formal tone, created by giving such full background, would confuse them. Similarly, if you wrote to the scholarship committee in the words you would use with friends, the committee would be equally confused. They would probably think either that you were trying to be funny at a serious time or that you did not know how to address people outside your personal circle. In either case, you would be less likely to achieve your purpose—to persuade the committee to give you the scholarship.

As this example indicates, the better you know the audience, the less **context**—background information—you must specify. (Note that the three examples get progressively longer as the speaker must supply more and more context.) Your friends know you well, know about incompletes, know about finals week, know about the flu. They know your context, and thus you can use slang and informal terms that are short and telegraphic. Your parents do not know as much of your context. You must be slightly more formal with them (they have always hated the word *barf*) in addition to explaining more of the situation. For the committee, you must be even more formal, supplying a detailed explanation that will show them your seriousness. This implicit knowledge about your purpose and audience leads you to use different diction for each version. (See Chapter 2 for discussion of using language appropriate to particular audiences.)

For most of the college writing you do, meeting the challenge of appropriateness means choosing words that will be most clear and most understandable to a wide range of educated readers. Edited American English (sometimes referred to as EAE) ordinarily fulfills this goal because it is *shared* by most writers throughout the country. In general, edited American English does not include regionalisms, dialect, slang, or colloquial language except when used deliberately for a special effect. So if you find instances of these in your writing, examine them very closely. Most often, they will be *inappropriate* for college writing; in Ford Madox Ford's words, "too much of that sort of thing" is not "smart."

EXERCISE 27.1

Choose something or someone to describe—a favorite cousin, a stranger on the bus, an automobile, a musical instrument, whatever strikes your fancy. Describe your subject using colloquial language and slang, regionalisms, or dialect. Then rewrite the description, this time using none of these. Read the two passages aloud, and note what different effects each creates.

27b

Denotation and connotation

Think of a stone tossed into a pool, and imagine the ripples spreading out from it, circle by circle. Or think of a note struck clear and clean, and the multiple vibrations that echo from it. In such images you can capture the distinction between **denotation**, the general meaning of a word, and

EXERCISE 27.1: Answers will vary.

USEFUL READING

Altick, Richard D., and Andrea A. Lunsford. *Preface to Critical Reading*. 6th ed. New York: Holt, 1984. Chapter 1 discusses the uses of connotation in advertising, political persuasion, and literature.

Why shouldn't we quarrel about a word? What is the good of words if they aren't important enough to quarrel over? Why do we choose one word more than another if there isn't any difference between them?

— G. K. CHESTERTON

connotation, the ripples, vibrations, and associations that accompany the word. As a writer, you want to choose words that are both denotatively and connotatively appropriate.

Words with similar denotations may have connotations that vary widely. The words *maxim, epigram, proverb, saw, saying,* and *motto,* for instance, all carry roughly the same denotation. Because of their different connotations, however, *proverb* would be the appropriate word to use in reference to a saying from the Bible; *saw* in reference to the kind of wisdom handed down to us anonymously; *epigram* in reference to a witty statement by someone like Woody Allen. *Dirt* and *soil* have roughly the same denotative meaning, and their connotations are close enough to allow us to use them interchangeably in most cases. *Pushy* and *assertive* also have much the same denotative meaning, but in this case their connotations suggest different attitudes on the part of the speaker or writer, one negative, the other neutral or positive.

Mistakes in denotation are bound to occur as we try out new words. To avoid mistakes, pay careful attention to the way words are used in context, and check your dictionary whenever you are unsure of meaning.

Because words with the wrong connotations for your intended meaning may not be as obvious as those with wrong denotations, take special care to avoid them. Good writers and readers are sensitive to the power of connotation for a number of reasons. In the first place, we do not want to be misunderstood: calling someone *skinny* rather than *slender,* for instance, might be taken as an insult or joke when such a meaning was unintended. And because connotation plays an important part in the language of politics and advertising (to name only the two most obvious fields), being alert to connotation and its power can help us read and listen more critically. Look, for instance, at the differences in connotation among the following three statements:

> Antiapartheid activists built a symbolic shanty on the green to protest the university's refusal to sell its investments in companies doing business in South Africa.

> Left-wing agitators threw up an eyesore right on the green to try to stampede the university into politicizing its investment policy.

> Supporters of human rights in South Africa challenged the university's investment in racism by erecting a protest shanty on campus.

As this example demonstrates, positive and negative connotations can shift meaning significantly. Take note of connotation in the writing of others. Even more important, however, examine the connotative power of your own writing, and try to use connotation to help make your meanings clear.

Many words carry fairly general connotations, evoking similar associational responses in most listeners or readers. But connotations can be personal or distinctive to a particular audience as well. If you ever became violently ill right after eating a particular food as a child, you know the power of personal connotation. The mere mention of, say, peanut butter cookies carries powerful negative connotations.

The power of connotations to a particular audience was well illustrated by the meeting between Michael Dukakis and Jesse Jackson at the 1988 Democratic National Convention. Jackson was offended that Dukakis, who had clinched the party's presidential nomination, had asserted his leadership by describing himself as "the quarterback on this team," a phrase that reminded blacks of the stereotype that they were not intelligent enough to play quarterback on football teams. For his part, Dukakis was upset by Jackson's having told the new voters he had brought into the party that they were being used to "carry bales of cotton" up to "the big house," because the connotations of this language suggested to blacks that Dukakis was like a white plantation owner profiting from the labor of black slaves. Whenever you write for a particular audience, try to be aware of the connotations your language will hold for that group of people.

 Checking for wrong words

"Wrong word" errors take so many different forms that it is very difficult to name any foolproof methods of checking for them. If you often find yourself using the wrong word, however, it will probably be well worth your time to go through each draft looking for them.

1. Circle every word you are not absolutely sure of. Check each one in a dictionary to see that you're using it properly.

2. Next, look for homonyms, words that sound like other words (such as *to, too,* and *two*). Using the information in 24b, make sure you are using the correct form.

3. Keep a list of any words you use incorrectly, including example sentences showing the way you've misused them. Make a point of proofreading carefully for them.

 Checking for wrong prepositions

Prepositions are among the most difficult words for writers of English to master, for their use is often governed not by an

(Continued)

easy-to-learn rule but by idiom. We meet someone "in an airplane," for instance, but "on a train (or bus)." Here are other confusing prepositions.

We'll arrive home *in* an hour or two—see you *at* five.

You see it *on* television but *at* the movies.

I was *at* the hospital to visit a friend; she was *in* the hospital for some minor surgery.

Because preposition usage in English is highly idiomatic, your best bet in an uncertain situation is to check a good dictionary to make sure you are following accepted usage. The *Oxford Advanced Learners* dictionary has especially good coverage of prepositions.

EXERCISE 27.2: Answers

1. attentively
2. rapturous
3. fragile
4. dramatically
5. frugal

EXERCISE 27.3: Suggested Answers

1. *racing:* charging, tearing, marching. These alternatives each connote a different context and set of circumstances, giving the reader a different impression of the Burmans' action. *Charging* suggests an attack, whereas *racing* gives the impression of the Burmans competing against one another and the author *me* to arrive at a destination. *Marching* suggests regimented, ordered, or determined movement, and *tearing* a frenzied, excited, wild, or uncontrolled pace. *Rise:* stand; *rattling:* heaving, pulsing; *mound:* mountain, hump

2. *tragic:* distressing, alarming, disturbing; *consumes:* defeats, feeds on, erodes; *displays:* champions, thrives on, builds up,

EXERCISE 27.2

Choose the word in parentheses whose denotative meaning makes sense in the context of the sentence. Use a dictionary if necessary.

1. She listened (*apprehensively/attentively*) to the lecture and took notes.
2. Going swimming on a hot day can be a (*rapturous/ravenous*) experience.
3. Please take good care of this antique photo album; it's very (*fractious/fragile*).
4. Bev improved her backhand (*dramatically/drastically*) with lessons.
5. Franklin advised his readers to be (*feudal/frugal*) and industrious.

EXERCISE 27.3

Study the italicized words in each of the following passages, and decide what each word's connotations contribute to your understanding of the passage. Think of a synonym for each word, and see if you can decide what difference the new word would make to the effect of the passage.

1. The Burmans were already *racing* past me across the mud. It was obvious that the elephant would never *rise* again, but he was not dead. He was breathing very rhythmically with long *rattling gasps,* his great *mound* of a side painfully rising and falling.

   — GEORGE ORWELL, "Shooting an Elephant"

2. If boxing is a sport, it is the most *tragic* of all sports because, more than any human activity, it *consumes* the very excellence it *displays*: Its very *drama* is this consumption. — JOYCE CAROL OATES, "On Boxing"

3. We caught two bass, *hauling* them in *briskly* as though they were mackerel, pulling them over the side of the boat in a *businesslike* manner without any landing net, and stunning them with a *blow* on the back of the head. — E. B. WHITE, "Once More to the Lake"

4. Then one evening Miss Glory told me to serve the ladies on the porch. After I set the tray down and turned toward the kitchen, one of the women asked, "What's your name, *girl*?" — MAYA ANGELOU, *I Know Why the Caged Bird Sings*

5. The Kiowas are a summer people; they *abide* the cold and keep to themselves; but when the season *turns* and the land becomes warm and *vital*, they cannot *hold still*. — N. SCOTT MOMADAY, "The Way to Rainy Mountain"

27c

Balancing general and specific diction

Good writers move their prose along and help readers follow the meaning by balancing **general words**, those that refer to groups or classes of things, with **specific words**, those that refer to individual things. One kind of general words, **abstractions**, are words or phrases that refer to qualities or ideas, things we cannot perceive through our five senses. Specific words are often **concrete words**; they name things we can see, hear, touch, taste, or smell. Most often, we cannot draw a clear-cut line between general or abstract words on the one hand and specific or concrete ones on the other. Instead, most words and phrases fall somewhere on a continuum between these two extremes.

GENERAL	LESS GENERAL	SPECIFIC	MORE SPECIFIC
book	dictionary	unabridged dictionary	my 1988 edition of *Webster's Dictionary*
furniture	bed	antique bed	1840 curly maple bedstead of my grandmother's

promotes; *drama:* excitement, tension, vitality

3. *hauling:* drawing; *briskly:* quickly; *businesslike:* efficient, effortless; *blow:* club, smack

4. *held:* breathed; *keenness:* coolness, crispness; *twitch:* perk up; *surprise:* adventure, enterprise; *tremors:* chills; *run:* jet

5. *abide:* tolerate; *turns:* changes; *vital:* alive; *hold still:* contain their energy

d

FOR COLLABORATIVE WORK

Moving from general to specific language often involves describing something so that it can be seen, heard, felt, experienced.

1. We had a good time.
2. We were bored and had nothing to do.
3. Their tiredness showed.
4. We weren't content to just sit there, frustrated, impatient, and annoyed.

Divide the class into groups, and ask them to expand each of these brief sentences into a paragraph. Ask them to work on showing the reader the good time or the frustration and annoyance. Suggest questions such as the following to help them develop the sentences into concrete descriptions. For example, to develop *We had a good time,* you might have them ask:

What were you doing?

With whom?

How did you do it?

What did it involve?

You can also ask them to apply the same questions to *Their tiredness showed.*

ABSTRACT	LESS ABSTRACT	CONCRETE	MORE CONCRETE
culture	visual art	painting	Van Gogh's *Starry Night*
winter	cold weather	icicles	fifteen-inch icicle hanging from the eaves of the dormitory

Because passages that contain mostly general terms or abstractions demand that readers supply most of the specific examples or concrete details with their imaginations, such writing is often hard to read. Taken to extremes, it is dull or boring. But writing that is full of specifics can also be tedious and hard to follow if the main point is not made clearly or is lost amid a flood of details. Strong writing must usually both provide readers with a general idea or overall picture and fill in that picture with specific examples or concrete details.

In the following passage, for instance, the author might have simply made a general statement—*their breakfast was always liberal and good*—or simply described the breakfast. Instead, he does both.

> There would be a brisk fire crackling in the hearth, the old smoke-gold of morning and the smell of fog, the crisp cheerful voices of the people and their ruddy competent morning look, and the cheerful smells of breakfast, which was always liberal and good, the best meal that they had: kidneys and ham and eggs and sausages and toast and marmalade and tea.
>
> – THOMAS WOLFE, *Of Time and the River*

Here are two student writers balancing general statements with illustrative specific details.

GENERAL	My neighbor is a nuisance.
SPECIFIC	My next-door neighbor is a nuisance, poking and prying into my life, constantly watching me as I enter and leave my house, complaining about the noise when I am having a good time, and telling my parents whenever she sees me kissing my date.
GENERAL	Central Texas has an unusual climate.
SPECIFIC	Few places in the United States display the wild climatic variations of central Texas: at one moment, the sky may be clear blue and the air balmy; at another, a racing flash flood may drown the landscape and threaten lives.

EXERCISE 27.4

Rewrite each of the following sentences to be more specific and concrete.

1. The entryway of the building was dirty.
2. The sounds at dawn are memorable.
3. Sunday dinner was good.
4. The attendant came toward my car.
5. The child played on the beach.

27d

Using figurative language

One good way to appeal to an audience is by using figurative language, or figures of speech. Such language paints pictures in our minds, allows us to "see" a point and hence understand more readily and clearly. Economists trying to explain the magnitude of the federal deficit use figurative language when they tell us how many hundred-thousand-dollar bills would have to circle the globe how many times to equal it. Scientists describing the way genetic data are transmitted use figurative language when they liken the data to a messenger that carries bits of information from one generation of cells to another. Far from being mere "decoration," figurative language plays a crucial role in helping us follow the writer's meaning, quickly and easily.

Particularly helpful in appealing to readers are figures that compare one thing to another—similes, metaphors, and analogies. Other figures include personification, hyperbole, understatement, irony, and allusion.

Similes

Similes (pronounced sim′ ə lēz) make explicit the comparison between two things by using *like, as, as if,* or *as though.*

> Buttresses flew like angels' wings against the exteriors.
> — BARBARA TUCHMAN, "Mankind's Better Moments"
> The comb felt as if it was raking my skin off.
> — MALCOLM X, "My First Conk"
> The migraine acted as a circuit breaker, and the fuses have emerged intact.
> — JOAN DIDION, "In Bed"

Metaphors

Metaphors (pronounced met′ ə fərz) are implicit comparisons, omitting the *like, as, as if,* or *as though* of similes.

EXERCISE 27.4: Suggested Answers

1. The entryway of the building looked like a garbage dump; paper was littered about, all kinds of bottles lay shattered, and rotting cantaloupe and chicken parts gave off an unbearable odor.

2. Cooing, singing, twittering—the early morning beckoning of birds outside my window make it a treat to get up.

3. The feast at mom's on Sunday was delicious as usual: roast chicken, garlic and sage stuffing, sweet garden peas, gallons of gravy, and half a fresh-baked apple pie each.

4. The valet stepped cautiously yet excitedly toward my Porsche.

5. Erin raced up, then retreated, then charged again, finally wetting her chubby toes in the surf.

TEACHING PRACTICE

To show your students that the use of figurative language occurs in our everyday reading and writing, encourage them to look at magazines, articles, and books that they read outside the classroom in their leisure time. Roger Angell's *Season Ticket: A Baseball Companion,* a collection of essays published in the *New Yorker* between 1983 and 1987, contains wonderful examples of simile, for example. Joel Conarroe, in a review in the *New York Times Book Review,* praises Angell: "This is a meticulous writer with an eye for the telling simile, the domestic image that can bring an observation vividly to life." Conarroe mentions Angell's description of "a slumping team" going through September "like an ember in a snowbank" and Steve Carlton's three-quarter-speed slider which "drops out of the strike zone like a mouse behind the sink."

Our plane landed at Cairo on a clear afternoon, and just beyond the windows, the Sahara was a rippling beige sea which had no shore.
— MAYA ANGELOU, *The Heart of a Woman*

Lee was tidewater Virginia, and in his backyard were family, culture, and tradition. — BRUCE CATTON, "Grant and Lee: A Study in Contrasts"

Analogies

Analogies compare similar features of two dissimilar things and are often extended to several sentences or paragraphs in length. The following sentence, for example, uses an analogy to help us understand the rapid growth of the computer industry.

If the aircraft industry had evolved as spectacularly as the computer industry over the past twenty-five years, a Boeing 767 would cost five hundred dollars today, and it would circle the globe in twenty minutes on five gallons of fuel.

The analogy in the next passage helps us "see" an abstract point.

One Hundred and Twenty-fifth Street was to Harlem what the Mississippi was to the South, a long traveling river always going somewhere, carrying something. — MAYA ANGELOU, *The Heart of a Woman*

Before you use an analogy, though, make sure that the two things you are comparing have enough points of similarity to justify the comparison and make it convincing to readers. (For more on analogies, see 5f3.)

Clichés and mixed metaphors

Just as effective use of figurative language can create the impression that the writer wants to create, so *ineffective* figures of speech can create the *wrong* impression by boring, irritating, or unintentionally amusing readers. Among the most common kinds of ineffective figurative language are clichés and mixed metaphors.

Cliché (pronounced klē shā′) comes from the French word for "stereotype," a metal plate cast from a page of type and used, before the invention of photographic printing processes, to produce multiple copies of a book or page without having to reset the type. So a **cliché** in language is an expression stamped out in duplicate to avoid the trouble of "resetting" the thought. Many clichés, like *busy as a bee* or *youth is the springtime of life,* are similes or metaphors.

By definition, we use clichés all the time, especially in speech, and many serve us quite usefully as familiar shorthand for familiar ideas. But as a writer, you should use them with caution for this reason: if your audience recognizes that you are using stereotyped, paint-by-numbers language, they are likely to conclude that what you are saying is not very new or interesting—or true. The person who tells you that you look "pretty as a picture" uses a clichéd simile that may well sound false or insincere. Compare it with a more original compliment a grandmother once paid to her grandchildren: "You all look as pretty as brand-new red shoes."

How can you check for clichés? While one person's trite phrase may be completely new to another, one rule of thumb will serve you well: if you can predict exactly what the upcoming word(s) in a phrase will be, it stands a very good chance of being a cliché.

Mixed metaphors are comparisons that are not consistent. Instead of creating a clear and dominant impression, they confuse the reader by pulling against one another, often in unintentionally funny ways, as in the announcement by a government official that "we must not drag our dirty linen through the eye of the public."

Here is a mixed metaphor revised for consistency.

MIXED

The lectures were like brilliant comets streaking through the night sky, showering the listeners with a blizzard of insight. [The conflicting images of streaking light and heavy precipitation produce humorous results.]

REVISED

The lectures were like brilliant comets streaking through the night sky, dazzling listeners with flashes of insight. [Now all images relate to light.]

Personification

Personification gives human qualities to animals, inanimate objects, or ideas, making them more vivid or understandable.

[Television] . . . stays in one corner of the room like a horrible electronic gossip.
— JONATHAN MILLER

In the meanwhile there came along a single red ant on the hillside of this valley, evidently full of excitement, who had either dispatched his foe, or had not yet taken part in the battle; . . . whose mother had charged him to return with his shield or upon it.
— HENRY DAVID THOREAU, "The Battle of the Ants"

Hyperbole

Hyperbole (pronounced hī pur′ bə lē), or **overstatement**, deliberately exaggerates to create special emphasis or humor.

OPTIONAL EXERCISE

Ask your students to evaluate the effectiveness of similes, metaphors, and analogies in the following sentences and to revise any that are mixed or clichés.

1. These children were brought up to eat, drink, and sleep tennis.
2. In presenting his alibi, the defendant chose the alley he was going to bowl on—and the jury wouldn't swallow it.
3. The president's economic plan is about as useful as rearranging the deck chairs on the *Titanic*.
4. The narrative was heavy as lead—it just flowed on and on and on.
5. For as long as I can remember, my mother has been the backbone for my father's convictions.

FOR COLLABORATIVE WORK

Ask students to work together in groups of three to five to complete the above Optional Exercise. In the case of identifying mixed metaphor and cliché especially, two (or more) heads are better than one. You also may want to ask students to write brief explanations of what they found wrong in the sentences and of how their revisions remedy the problems.

Under certain emotional circumstances, I can stand the spasms of a rich violin, but the concert piece and all wind instruments bore me in small doses and flay me in large doses.   — VLADIMIR NABOKOV

What a travesty of truth are those TV commercials in which we watch a family falling over themselves to reach the fast-food restaurant before they drown in their own drool!   — MAX WYMAN

Understatement

Like hyperbole, **understatement**, or **litotes** (pronounced li tō′ tēz), depends on a gap between statement and fact. But while hyperbole is loud and noisy, understatement turns the volume down to a whisper. Litotes can help create a very solemn tone, as it does when one of the characters in Stephen Crane's *The Open Boat,* faced with imminent death, remarks that if he drowns, it "will be a shame." It can also create humor and other effects.

Irony

Irony, language that suggests a meaning that contrasts with or undercuts the literal meaning of the words, can create a lighthearted, spoofing tone or a serious and bitter one. In probably the most famous piece of sustained irony in English literature, Jonathan Swift's "A Modest Proposal," Swift solemnly recommends the sale and consumption of children, a proposal intended to reveal the poverty and inhuman conditions in Ireland condoned by its British rulers at the time. The following "definition" of *writing principles* provides an example of more lighthearted irony.

Write hurriedly, preferably when tired. Have no plans; write down items as they occur to you. . . . Hand in your manuscript the moment it is finished.   — AMBROSE BIERCE

Irony can work well to gain an audience's attention and set a definite tone, but only if the audience can be expected to recognize and appreciate the irony. (See 33d on using quotation marks to convey irony.)

Allusion

Allusions, indirect references to cultural works, people, or events, can bring an entire world of associations to the minds of readers who recognize them. If, for instance, you tell a friend in a letter that you have to return to your herculean task of writing a research essay, you are expecting that your reader will understand, by your allusion to the Labors of Hercules in classical mythology, how big a job you think the essay is. If you choose to title an essay on the antiapartheid movement in the 1980s "A Terrible Beauty

Is Born," your allusion to William Butler Yeats's poem about the Irish Rebellion of 1916 will give readers the idea that you see important parallels between the two struggles.

You can draw allusions from history, from literature, from the Bible, from common wisdom, or from current events. Many current popular songs are full of allusions. Remember, however, that allusions work only if your audience recognizes them.

EXERCISE 27.5

Identify the similes and metaphors in the following passages, and decide how each contributes to your understanding of the passage it appears in.

1. John's mother, Mom Willie, who wore her Southern background like a magnolia corsage, eternally fresh, was robust and in her sixties.
   – MAYA ANGELOU, "The Heart of a Woman"

2. I was watching everyone else and didn't see the waitress standing quietly by. Her voice was deep and soft like water moving in a cavern.
   – WILLIAM LEAST HEAT MOON, "In the Land of 'Coke-Cola' "

3. My horse, when he is in his stall or lounging about the pasture, has the same relationship to pain that I have when cuddling up with a good murder mystery—comfort and convenience have top priority.
   – VICKI HEARNE, "Horses in Partnership with Time"

EXERCISE 27.6

Read through a magazine, an essay, a story, or some reading you have been assigned and find some examples of personification, hyperbole, understatement, irony, and allusion. Bring these examples to class for discussion.

Choosing the appropriate register

On the basis of the writer's relationship to the topic and the audience, we can distinguish three general levels of diction, or **registers**. In order of increasing distance from the writer, these levels are *familiar, informal,* and *formal.* Formal register is the one most often appropriate and useful for college writing.

EXERCISE 27.5: Suggested Answers

1. *like a magnolia corsage* (simile): this simile makes vivid and concrete Mom Willie's Southern heritage and suggests how positively she values it—and how proudly she "displays" it.

2. *deep and soft like water moving in a cavern* (simile): this simile compares the sound of her voice to water in a cavern

3. *lounging* (metaphor): compares the horse in pasture to people relaxing; *cuddling up* (metaphor): emphasizes the pleasure the writer has reading mysteries; *top priority* (metaphor): the reading is an activity of official importance

EXERCISE 27.6: Answers will vary.

1

Familiar register

Familiar register represents a very close relationship between writer and topic and between writer and audience—it is the language you probably use to talk to yourself or to those closest to you. It is the register found in diaries, journals, and personal letters; writers sometimes use it in essays, stories, plays, and novels to create a sense of intimacy between themselves and readers or between characters. Among the characteristics of familiar register are the frequent use of the first person (*I*) and first names, a lack of explicitly stated context (because the audience does not need it), and the use of sentence fragments, contractions, slang, colloquial language, regionalisms, dialect, and other grammatical constructions that disregard the "rules."

You will seldom, if ever, be called on to write in familiar register in college writing. You should, however, learn to recognize it as a reader. The following example is a letter from the English writer Virginia Stephen responding to a marriage proposal from her future husband, Leonard Woolf.

> My dear Leonard,
>   I am rushing for a train so I can only send a line in answer. There isn't anything really for me to say, except that I should like to go on as before; and that you should leave me free, and that I should be honest. As to faults, I expect mine are just as bad—less noble perhaps. But of course they are not really the question. I have decided to keep this completely secret, except for Vanessa; and I have made her promise not to tell Clive. I told Adrian that you had come up about a job which was promised you. So keep this up if he asks.
>   I am very sorry to be the cause of so much rush and worry. . . .
>   Yrs.
>   VS

Notice that Stephen assumes Woolf will know what her "line" is "in answer" to, what "this" is, and who Vanessa, Clive, and Adrian are. She uses a contraction (*isn't*) and abbreviations (*Yrs.,* her initials), as well as the colloquial expression *keep this up* to mean "pretend that this story is true." Because she was a professional writer living in a different time and a different culture, your familiar register is probably different from and less formal than hers. Nevertheless, you can see that she is writing to a very intimate audience (of one) on a very intimate topic.

2

Informal register

Informal register assumes a fairly close but not extremely close relationship between the writer and the audience and topic. It may use colloquial language, slang, and regionalisms or dialect (see 27a), as well as contractions and other grammatical constructions that are not considered appropriate in more formal writing. The register of most conversation and of much popular media, it is often found in short stories and novels as well, especially in dialogue. Some college classes—journalism, communications, or creative writing, for example—may call on you to use informal register. Here is an example.

> If I went through anguish in botany and economics—for different reasons—gymnasium work was even worse. I don't even like to think about it. They wouldn't let you play games or join the exercises with your glasses on and I couldn't see with mine off. I bumped into professors, horizontal bars, agricultural students, and swinging iron rings. Not being able to see, I could take it but I couldn't dish it out.
>
> — JAMES THURBER, "University Days"

Thurber is obviously closely involved with his topic, although the involvement is not as close as that of Virginia Stephen with Leonard Woolf's marriage proposal; Thurber is looking back at his college gymnasium work from the distance of years. Nor is he as intimately related to his audience, but his use of contractions (*don't, wouldn't, couldn't*) and the indefinite *They* and *you* create an informal tone of easy familiarity. Notice that in the last sentence he amuses the audience—a purpose for which informal register is often used—by coming up with a twist on a clichéd slang expression.

3

Formal register

Formal register is the language found in most academic, business, and professional writing and in serious nonfiction books and magazine articles. Because most of the writing you will do in college and probably throughout your working life should be in formal register, study carefully the following list of its characteristics.

1. Emotional distance between the writer and the audience: your stance should be courteous but not chummy or intimate.
2. Emotional distance between the writer and the topic: though you may know the topic very well and have strong feelings about it, your stance toward it should be somewhat restrained.
3. No colloquial language, slang, regionalisms, dialect, or contractions.
4. Careful attention to the conventions of edited American English, the grammatical "rules" like those presented in this book.
5. Attention to the logical relationships among words and ideas: phrases and sentences should be carefully structured, not just tossed out.

OPTIONAL EXERCISE

To give students practice in recognizing differences between registers, have them write a paragraph about something they might want to do at school—change their major, spend their junior year abroad, take a semester off, or something else. Have them first use familiar register, assuming their audience to be someone close—parents, spouse, good friend. Then ask them to rewrite their paragraphs to address their academic adviser, using formal register. Finally, suggest that they analyze each paragraph to identify the elements that create familiar or formal register.

Here is an example of formal register:

> "A people who mean to be their own governors," James Madison wrote, "must arm themselves with the power knowledge gives. A popular government without popular information or the means of acquiring it, is but a prologue to a farce or a tragedy, or perhaps both."
>
> Tragedy looms larger than farce in the United States today. Illiterate citizens seldom vote. Those who do are forced to cast a vote of questionable worth. They cannot make informed decisions based on serious print information. Sometimes they can be alerted to their interests by aggressive voter education. More frequently, they vote for a face, a smile, or a style, not for a mind or character or body of beliefs.
>
> – JONATHAN KOZOL, "The Human Cost of an Illiterate Society"

Notice that Kozol opens with an appeal to authority, citing a United States president who, in very strong and serious terms, warns against the effect of a populace without knowledge. Kozol repeats the key terms of Madison's warning, *tragedy* and *farce,* in the next sentence, and goes on to develop what he sees as one tragic aspect of illiteracy. His brief, straightforward sentences state the facts objectively, building up to the parallel structures of the last sentence, which contrasts voting for "a smile" with voting for "character." Though Kozol knows a great deal about his subject and feels strongly that illiteracy is a national tragedy, his tone throughout is restrained.

4

Register in technical writing

One special kind of language frequently found in formal register is the technical discourse used in particular fields that have created special vocabularies or given common words special meaning. Businesspeople talk about *greenmail* and *upside movement,* biologists about *nucleotides* and *immunodestruction,* and baseball fans about *fielder's choices* and *suicide bunts.* Such terms are understood by other specialists, but they can be very confusing to those outside the field. You need, then, to judge any use of technical language very carefully, making sure that your intended audience will understand your terms and replacing or defining those that they will not. Technical language can be divided into two overlapping categories: neologisms and jargon.

Neologisms

New words that have not yet found their way into dictionaries, **neologisms** can be very helpful to writers, especially in the sciences and applied disciplines, where new things and concepts appear every day and need names. Terms like *byte, thermosiphon, deconstruct,* and *neutrino,* for example, could not be easily replaced except by a much longer and more complex explanation. Some neologisms, however, do not meet a real need. Words like *deaccess* and *prioritization* could be easily replaced by existing words or phrases that general readers would understand.

Jargon

Jargon is the special vocabulary of a trade or profession, enabling members to speak and write concisely to one another. It should be reserved as much as possible for a specific technical audience. Here is an example of jargon used inappropriately in writing addressed to general readers, and then revised to eliminate some of the jargon and define.

JARGON

The VDT's in composition were down last week, so we had to lay out on dummies and crop and size the art with a wheel.

REVISED

The video display terminals were not working last week in the composing room, where models of the newspaper pages are made up for printing, so we had to arrange the contents of each page on a large cardboard sheet and use a wheel, a kind of circular slide rule, to figure out the size and shape of the pictures and other illustrations.

5

Pompous language, euphemisms, and doublespeak

In addition to avoiding inappropriate use of technical language, be alert to three other kinds of language sometimes found in formal register: pompous language, euphemisms, and doublespeak.

Pompous language is unnecessarily formal for the purpose, audience, or topic. Hence it often gives writing an insincere or unintentionally humorous tone, making the writer's idea seem less significant or believable rather than more so.

POMPOUS

Pursuant to the recent memorandum issued August 9 because of petroleum supply exigencies, it is incumbent upon us to endeavor to make maximal utilization of telephonic communication in lieu of personal visitation.

REVISED

As of August 9 shortages of petroleum require us to use the telephone rather than make personal visits whenever possible.

USEFUL READING

Orwell, George. "Politics and the English Language." *Shooting an Elephant and other Essays.* New York: Harcourt, 1974. A discussion of appropriate verbs and nouns, pretentious diction, and meaningless words.

Williams, Joseph M. *Origins of the English Language: A Social and Linguistic History.* New York: Macmillan, 1975. A brief discussion of the linguistic, psychological, and cultural reasons for jargon and euphemism.

To write simply is as difficult as to be good.
— W. SOMERSET MAUGHAM

Euphemisms are terms designed to make an unpleasant idea more attractive or acceptable. *Your position is being eliminated* seeks to soften the blow of being fired or laid off; the British call this being *declared redundant,* while Canadians refer to being *made surplus.* Other euphemisms include *pass on* for *die* and *sanitation engineer* for *garbage collector.*

Use euphemisms with great care. Although they can appeal to readers by showing that the writer is considering their feelings, they can also sound pompous or suggest a wishy-washy, timid, or evasive attitude. Moreover, when they are used to protect the writer rather than the readers, they cross the line into doublespeak.

The name given by George Orwell to the language of Big Brother in his novel *1984,* **doublespeak** is the use of language to hide or distort the truth. During the 1991 Persian Gulf War, for instance, many Americans were troubled by the military's use of the phrase *collateral damage* to refer to civilians killed as a result of bombings and other military activity. Although the military argued that it was useful and necessary jargon, many viewed it as an example of doublespeak.

Using Sources
Diction

As a researcher, you need to be particularly alert to the diction of any sources you use. Pay attention to the words the writer uses and to the connotations they carry, for they contribute to the impressions—either positive or negative—on you as a reader. Especially if you are using a source in support of an argument, you need to examine that source's diction carefully to determine the writer's point of view, and to note how he or she uses words to create a certain effect or support a conclusion.

- What dominant impression does the writing give—serious, sarcastic, lighthearted or something else?
- What words create that impression?
- Do these words have any special connotations? What do the connotations suggest about the writer's purpose?
- Do the word choices suggest any particular bias?

EXERCISE 27.7

Revise each of the following sentences to use formal register consistently. Example:

I can get all enthused about writing, but I sit down to write, and my mind goes right out to lunch.

Although I can be excited about writing, as soon as I sit down to write, my mind immediately goes blank.

1. Desdemona's attitude is that of a wimp; she just lies down and dies, accepting her death as inevitable.

2. All candidates strive for the same results: you try to make the other guy look gross and to persuade voters that you're okay for the job.

3. Often, instead of firing an incompetent teacher, school officials will transfer the person to another school in order to avoid the hassles involved in a dismissal.

4. The more she flipped out about his actions, the more he rebelled and continued doing what he pleased.

5. My family lived in Trinidad for the first ten years of my life, and we went through a lot, but when we came to America, we thought we had it made.

 Checking diction in your own writing

1. First, reconsider your topic, purpose, and audience. What kind of diction is most appropriate for these?

2. Choose a couple of paragraphs from different parts of a draft, and see if the words in them hold any special connotations—optimistic? sarcastic? pessimistic? Are these appropriate to your topic, purpose, and audience?

3. Look for general and abstract terms. Are they balanced by specific and concrete ones? Do you have more of the first than the second? Would adding more specific and concrete language help bring your prose to life?

4. Look for figures of speech. Do they help create vivid images for your readers? Can they be improved?

5. Look for clichés, and replace any you find with fresher language.

6. How would you characterize the register—familiar? informal? formal? Do you include slang or colloquial language? Do you use contractions? Is the register appropriate to your audience and purpose?

7. What, finally, would you say is the general attitude your writing conveys? Is it appropriate to your audience and purpose?

EXERCISE 27.8: Answers will vary.

EXERCISE 27.9: Answers will vary.

EXERCISE 27.8 Revising for Diction

Return to the description you wrote in Exercise 27.1. Note any words that carry strong connotations, and identify the concrete and abstract language as well as any use of figurative language. Then revise the description to make better use of diction.

EXERCISE 27.9 Reading with Awareness of Diction

Read the following brief poem. What dominant feeling or impression does the poem produce in you? Identify the diction, those specific words and phrases, that helps create that impression.

> What happens to a dream deferred?
>
> Does it dry up
> Like a raisin in the sun?
> Or fester like a sore—
> And then run?
> Does it stink like rotten meat?
> Or crust and sugar over—
> Like a syrupy sweet?
>
> Maybe it just sags
> Like a heavy load.
>
> Or does it explode?
> —LANGSTON HUGHES,
> "Dream Deferred (Harlem)"

TEACHING PRACTICE

Ask students to bring selections from their own work to class, choose several to duplicate or put on an overhead, and ask the class as a whole to discuss the diction of each piece. How would students describe the dominant impression given by the selection? How would they characterize its register? Which words seem most effective and memorable, and why? Are there any instances in which they might revise the diction for different effect?

EXERCISE 27.10 Taking Inventory: Diction in Your Own Writing

Read over a piece of your writing, underlining any words or phrases that are especially effective and any you think could be more vivid, appropriate, concrete —improved in any way. Then ask what kind of dominant impression you wanted to create in this piece of writing—amused? amusing? outraged? friendly? skeptical? How successful have you been? Do you see any patterns in your diction? Note down any strengths as well as any problems—in a writing log, if you keep one.

28

Considering Others: Building Common Ground

East is East, and West is West, and never the twain shall meet . . .

You say to-ma-to, and I say to-mah-to . . .

I did it my way.

United we stand, divided we fall.

We are the world.

These contrasting statements suggest one of the challenges every writer must face. . . . Many, many differences divide us. Each of us is, after all, unique—in genetic makeup and in total life experience. Each of us is an individual "I"—standing alone, doing it "my" way. As a result, we sometimes have difficulty understanding and caring for one another. And yet we also share common ground. We are, for instance, all part of a species inhabiting the same crowded, endangered planet. And as individuals, we are also part of numerous communities.

In the United States today, we are part of a richly diverse population representing just about every social, religious, linguistic, and cultural tradition imaginable and yet all bound by a common citizenship. How can such different people (East is East, and West is West . . .) ever build commonalities? Fortunately, language is here to help us out. The words we use can and do build common ground and help us understand that, with goodwill and effort, East can meet West, even if one continues to say "to-ma-to" and the other "to-mah-to."

As a writer, you will often be called on to appeal to many people who are in some—or many—ways different from you. When you are expressing *ideas* that readers may strongly disagree with, it is all the more important to use *language* that does not sharpen the disagreement—and that ideally makes readers *more* receptive to your argument. To be successful in this effort, you will need to understand as much as you can about the ways in

BACKGROUND

Your students may recognize Frank Sinatra's "I Did It My Way," and the popular artists' charity recording "We Are the World," which represent the two poles we focus on in this chapter—the unique individual and the shared community. For "United We Stand," see Aesop's "Union Gives Strength" ("The Bundle of Sticks"), John Dickinson's "By uniting we stand, by dividing we fall" ("The Liberty Song"), and George Pope Morris's "The Flag of Our Union."

"East is East, and West is West" ("and never the twain shall meet") is from Rudyard Kipling's "The Ballad of East and West." Finally, "You say to-ma-to," etc., is from Gershwin's "Let's Call the Whole Thing Off." Ask students for other examples from popular culture that suggest either the unique, solitary individual or the sense of shared community.

BACKGROUND

The thought of Kenneth Burke informs much contemporary work in rhetoric and composition, and it certainly informs this book in general and this chapter in particular. Burke's key term is *identification* (*Rhetoric of Motives* [Berkeley: U of California Press, 1969]):

> A is not identical with his colleague B. But insofar as their interests are joined, A is *identified* with B. Or he may *identify himself* with B even when their interests are not joined, if he assumes that they are, or is persuaded to do so. . . . To identify A with B is to make A "consubstantial" with B.
>
> . . . Here is perhaps the simplest case of persuasion. You persuade a man only insofar as you can talk his language by speech, gesture, tonality, order, image, attitude, idea, *identifying* your ways with his.(20,55)

Burke's concept of identification underlies the advice in this chapter, which is meant to remind student writers of the many ways that language can promote—or destroy—identification. Ironically, given the extensive attention Burke devotes to identification, his own texts exclude half of humankind with their consistent use of generic *he* and *man*.

TEACHING PRACTICE

Ask students to make a list of terms they would use to describe an attractive man or woman. Then ask them to make a second list of terms they would like to be used to describe *themselves*. Use these lists to generate discussion of the ways in which language can destroy or build common ground.

OPTIONAL EXERCISE

Ask students to think of a time when they have inaccurately characterized some group or person. Have them describe the occasion in a paragraph or two, trying to explain how they happened to realize their own inaccurate characterization and what they did to correct it.

Everyday use

We recently overheard a fourteen-year-old exclaim to his aunt: "I am not a 'kid' anymore, so please stop calling me that!" The nephew was objecting to a label he found both inaccurate and disrespectful, one that clearly built no common ground between him and his aunt. Can you think of situations when you've struggled to find just the right words to avoid offending someone: what salutation to use instead of "Dear Sir" when you're not sure who will read the letter, for instance, or how to describe an eighty-year-old without calling him or her "old," or what to call someone who delivers your mail instead of "mailman"—especially when that person is obviously not a man? These are choices we must make every day in trying to build common ground and communicate with others. Spend some time listening to people talking—or to television or radio broadcasters. Note any instances in which they seem to be making an effort to avoid language that might seem disrespectful or destroy common ground.

---

which others differ both from you and from one another. Knowing about and respecting these differences is the first step in building common ground with others.

Because the language we use influences perceptions in powerful ways, you need to pay special attention to how words include or exclude others, how they create or destroy common ground. This chapter will get you started in thinking about how your own language can work both to respect difference and to build common ground with others.

28a

Remembering the "golden rule"

As a young child, you may have learned to "do to others what you would have them do to you." To that "golden rule," we could add "say to others what you would have them say to you." Language has power. It can praise, delight, inspire. It can also hurt, offend, destroy. Language that insults or offends any group of readers breaks the golden rule of language use, preventing many readers from identifying with you and thus damaging your credibility as a writer.

In many instances, avoiding such language is simple enough. We can safely assume, for instance, that no readers respond well to being referred to disparagingly—for example, as "slobs" or "nerds." But other cases are more subtle and perhaps surprising. One student found, for example, that members of a group he had been referring to as "senior citizens" were irritated by that label. Similarly, a recent survey of people with physical disabilities reported that most of them resented euphemisms like "differently abled" and "physically challenged" because they saw these terms as trivializing their difficulties.

Because language usage changes constantly and people's preferences vary widely, few absolute guidelines exist for using language that will respect differences and build common ground in every instance. Two rules of thumb, however, can help: consider carefully the sensitivities and preferences of others, and watch for words that carry stereotypes and unintended assumptions.

1

Watching for stereotypes and other assumptions

Children like to play; citizens of the United States value freedom; people who do not finish high school tend to fare less well in the job market than those who graduate. These broad statements all contain **stereotypes**, standardized or fixed ideas about a group. To some extent, we all think in terms of stereotypes, and sometimes they can be helpful in making a generalization. Stereotyping any individual on the basis of generalizations about a group can be dangerous, however, for it can lead to inaccurate and even hurtful conclusions.

Stereotyping becomes especially evident in language, in the words we choose to refer to or describe others. Stereotyped language can and often does break the links between writers and readers—or between speakers and listeners. An instructor who notes a student's absence from class on the morning after a big fraternity party and says, "Ah, he must be a fraternity man," is stereotyping an individual on the basis of assumptions about "fraternity men." But such stereotyping may be far off the mark with this particular student—and with many other fraternity members. By indulging in it, this instructor may well be alienating some of her students and undermining her effectiveness as a teacher.

In an article in the *New Yorker* magazine, an executive who worked to find jobs for teenagers pointed up additional dangers of language that stereotypes others.

> When I hear the word *dropout,* I have this image in my mind of a kid sitting across from me in the subway car: he's smoking a cigarette; he has a radio the size of a grand piano, and he keeps turning up the volume; his legs are stretched out so nobody can pass; he is staring at me with a look I can only describe as hate. I know that's not fair or accurate because I've hired many of them. Still, I can't help thinking of that kid on the subway.

FOR THE WRITING LOG

To help students see that writing has powerful effects, ask them to write about a time when someone—a friend, parent, teacher, employer—wrote or said something about them that affected the way they thought or felt about themselves. Then ask them to write about a time when their words had an important effect on someone else.

BACKGROUND

Mike Rose, in his extraordinary *Lives on the Boundary* (NY: Penguin, 1989), talks about the sorts of sensitivity that will be necessary for many people to be well served by our schools.

> Democratic culture is, by definition, vibrant and dynamic, discomforting and unpredictable. It gives rise to apprehension; freedom is not always calming. And, yes, it can yield fragmentation, though often as not the source of fragmentation is intolerant misunderstanding of diverse traditions rather than the desire of members of those traditions to remain hermetically separate. A truly democratic vision of knowledge and social structure would honor this complexity. The vision might not be soothing, but it would provide guidance as to how to live and teach in a country made up of many cultural traditions.
>
> We are in the middle of an extraordinary social experiment: the attempt to provide education for all members of a vast pluralistic democracy. To have any prayer of success, we'll need many conceptual blessings: A philosophy of language and literacy that affirms the diverse sources of linguistic competence and deepens our understanding of the ways class and culture blind us to the richness of those sources. A perspective on failure that lays open the logic of error. An orientation toward the interaction of poverty and ability that undercuts simple polarities, that enables us to see simultaneously the constraints poverty places on the play of mind and the actual mind at play within those constraints. We'll need a pedagogy that encourages us to step back and consider the threat of the standard classroom and that shows us, having stepped back, how to step forward to invite a student across the boundaries of that powerful room. Finally, we'll need a revised

store of images of educational excellence, ones closer to egalitarian ideals—ones that embody the reward and turmoil of education in a democracy, that celebrate the plural, messy human reality of it. At heart, we'll need a guiding set of principles that do not encourage us to retreat from, but move us closer to, an understanding of the rich mix of speech and ritual and story that is America. (238)

TEACHING PRACTICE

Ask students to read the opening of the Declaration of Independence and to consider what groups of citizens are made invisible by the document's language:

> When in the Course of human events, it becomes necessary for one people to dissolve the political bands which have connected them with another, and to assume among the powers of the earth, the separate and equal station to which the Laws of Nature and of Nature's God entitle them, a decent respect to the opinions of mankind requires that they should declare the causes which impel them to the separation.—We hold these truths to be self-evident, that all men are created equal, that they are endowed by their Creator with certain unalienable Rights, that among these are Life, Liberty and the pursuit of Happiness.—That to secure these rights, Governments are instituted among Men, deriving their just powers from the consent of the governed.

A writer lives in awe of words, for they can be cruel or kind, and they can change their meanings right in front of you. They pick up flavors and odors like butter in a refrigerator.
—JOHN STEINBECK

In a world where language and naming are power, silence is oppression, is violence.
—ADRIENNE RICH

Note the ways in which the executive admits he stereotypes people on the basis of a label: *dropouts* are apparently all young and male—and all rude, noisy, and hostile. Like all stereotypes, his is the result of a stock response built up and maintained by many things in his experience—songs, books, movies, television shows, and news reports, as well as personal encounters with some individuals who have dropped out of school. The mass media are particularly powerful in creating stereotypes. But as the executive recognizes and points out, they are often not accurate or fair.

Very often based on half-truths, misunderstandings, and hand-me-down prejudices, stereotypes can lead to intolerance, irrational bias, and bigotry. Even apparently positive or neutral ones can hurt, for they inevitably ignore the uniqueness of an individual. As writers, we need to check carefully to make sure that our language doesn't stereotype any group *or* individual. Other kinds of unstated assumptions that enter into our thinking and writing destroy common ground by ignoring differences between others and ourselves. For example, a student whose paper for a religion seminar uses *we* to refer to Christians and *they* to refer to members of other religions had better be sure that all the class members and the instructor are Christian, or some of them may well feel left out of this discussion. assumption. In a letter to the editor of a newspaper about a current political issue, language implying that liberals are good and conservatives bad is likely to alienate some readers and prevent them from even considering the writer's argument about the specific issue.

Sometimes assumptions are so deeply ingrained that they have the effect of completely ignoring or "erasing" large groups of people. Such was the experience not too many years ago of black people in the United States who failed to see themselves mentioned in public documents, represented in the mass media, or treated as an important part of the populace. This denial of their existence is described eloquently in Ralph Ellison's 1952 novel, *Invisible Man.*

> I am an invisible man. No, I am not a spook like those who haunted Edgar Allan Poe; nor am I one of your Hollywood-movie ectoplasms. I am a man of substance, of flesh and bone, fiber and liquids—and I might even be said to possess a mind. I am invisible, understand, simply because people refuse to see me. Like the bodiless heads you see sometimes in circus sideshows, it is as though I have been surrounded by mirrors of hard, distorting glass. When they approach me they see only my surroundings, themselves, or figments of their imagination—indeed, everything and anything except me.
> —RALPH ELLISON, *Invisible Man*

Language can also serve to "erase," as students at the University of Kansas realized when they discovered that history books routinely reported only one survivor of General George Custer's Battle of Little Bighorn: Comanche, a horse (now stuffed and on display at their university). Several thousand

Sioux survived that battle, yet the history books simply ignored them, leaving them invisible to future readers.

On the other hand, stereotypes and other assumptions often lead writers to mention a group affiliation unnecessarily when it has no relation to the point under consideration, as in "a woman bus driver" or "a Jewish doctor." Decisions about whether to generalize about a group or whether to describe an individual as a member of a group are often very difficult for writers. The following sections invite you to think about how your language can build—rather than destroy—common ground.

2

Considering assumptions about gender

The feminist movement of the last three decades has done much to demonstrate how powerfully and often invisibly gender-related elements of language affect the ways we think and behave. We now know, for instance, that many young women at one time were discouraged from pursuing careers in medicine or engineering at least partially because our language, following stereotyped assumptions about gender roles in society, always referred to hypothetical doctors or engineers as "he" (and then labeled any woman who worked as a doctor a "woman doctor," as if to say, "She's an exception; doctors are normally male"). Equally problematic is the traditional use of *man* and *mankind* to refer to people of both sexes and the use of *he, him, his,* and *himself* to refer to people of unknown sex, as in "a lawyer must pass the bar exam before he can begin to practice." Because such usage ignores half the human race—or at least seems to assume that the other half is more important—it hardly helps a writer to build common ground. Similarly, labels like "male nurse" or "male secretary" may offend by reflecting stereotyped assumptions about proper roles for males.

Revising sexist language

Sexist language, those words and phrases that stereotype or ignore members of either sex or that unnecessarily call attention to gender, can usually be revised fairly easily. For example, here are some alternatives to the use of masculine pronouns to refer to persons of unknown sex.

- Use plural forms:
  Lawyers must pass the bar exam before *they* can begin to practice.
- Use *he or she, him or her,* and so on:
  A lawyer must pass the bar exam before *he or she* can begin to practice.
- Eliminate the pronouns:
  A lawyer must pass the bar exam before beginning to practice.

BACKGROUND

The harm done by sexist language is subtle but genuine, and it has been widely discussed in the literature over the past decade. That more than simple considerateness is ultimately at stake is argued by Francine Wattman Frank and Paula A. Treichler:

> [T]he sexist language question, seeming at first to represent a practical agenda, is a point of entry into the broader study of women and men as speakers, creators, and bearers of meaning within society and culture. Anyone who explores and seeks to change women's [and men's] place within texts must confront questions of women's place within both linguistic and material reality.

USEFUL READING

Carpenter, Carol. "Exercises to Combat Sexist Reading and Writing." *CE* 43 (1981): 293–300. Carpenter describes three activities designed to explore the implications of sexism while building reading and writing skills.

Frank, Francine Wattman, and Paula A. Treichler. *Language, Gender, and Professional Writing: Theoretical Approaches and Guidelines for Nonsexist Usage.* New York: Modern Language Assn., 1989. This book addresses the issue of linguistic sexism in scholarly and professional writing, presenting relevant ideas and research and a set of guidelines for nondiscriminary usage. The authors seek to demonstrate the importance and value of avoiding biased language and to stimulate readers to think about the matters discussed.

FOR THE WRITING LOG

Ask students to write an entry on the term *sexist language.* Ask them to try to define the term and to offer examples of terms that are or may seem to be sexist. These entries can be used to initiate class discussion.

USEFUL READING

Baron, Dennis. *Grammar and Gender.* New Haven: Yale UP, 1986. A critical history of the effects of sexism on theories of the origin of the English language, on attitudes toward women's language, and on prescriptions for the use of gender-specific nouns and generic male pronouns. Includes a survey of attempts to solve the third person singular pronoun problem.

Nilsen, Aileen Pace. "Winning the Great 'He'/'She' Battle." *CE* 46 (1984): 151–57. Currently co-editor of *English Journal,* Nilsen uses examples from manuscripts submitted for publication to illustrate the complexities involved in using "inconspicuous sex-fair language." Based on an analysis of these examples, she offers four principles for teachers and students who lack the sometimes considerable skill necessary for writing in a gender-neutral manner.

Publication Manual of the American Psychological Association. 3rd ed. Washington: American Psychological Assn., 1983. Included under "Expression of Ideas," the style manual lists thirty-one examples of nonsexist, nonbiased alternatives to so-called common usage constructions.

INSTEAD OF	TRY USING
anchorman, anchorwoman	anchor
chairman, chairwoman	chair, chairperson
coed	student
congressman	member of Congress, representative
mailman	mail carrier
male nurse	nurse
man, mankind	humans, human beings, humanity, the human race, humankind
manpower	workers, personnel
mothering	parenting
policeman, policewoman	police officer
steward, stewardess	flight attendant
woman engineer	engineer

(For more discussion of nonsexist pronouns, see 11d.)

 Checking your writing for sexist language

1. Have you used *man* or *men* or words containing them to refer to people who may be female? If so, consider substituting another word—instead of *fireman,* for instance, try *firefighter.*

2. If you mention the gender of someone identified in another way, is it necessary? If you identify someone as a female architect, for example, do you (or would you) refer to someone else as a "male architect"? And if you then note that the female is an attractive blond mother of two, do you mention that the male is a muscular, square-jawed father of three? Unless gender and related matters—looks, clothes, parenthood—are relevant to your point, consider leaving them unmentioned.

3. Do you use any occupational stereotypes? Watch for the use of female pronouns for nurses, male ones for engineers, for example.

4. Do you use language that in any way patronizes either sex?—referring to a wife as "the little woman," for instance, or to a husband as "her old man."

5. Have you used *he, him, his,* or *himself* to refer to people who may be female? Try revising with the help of the guidelines in 28a1.

6. Have you overused *he and she, him and her,* and so on? Frequent use of these pronoun pairs can be boring or even irritating to readers.

EXERCISE 28.1

The following excerpt is taken from the 1968 edition of Dr. Benjamin Spock's *Baby and Child Care*. Read it carefully, noting any language we today might consider sexist. Then try bringing it up to date by revising the passage, substituting nonsexist language as necessary.

What Makes Him Tick

399. Feeling his oats. One year old is an exciting age. Your baby is changing in lots of ways—in his eating, in how he gets around, in what he wants to do and in how he feels about himself and other people. When he was little and helpless, you could put him where you wanted him, give him the playthings you thought suitable, feed him the foods you knew were best. Most of the time he was willing to let you be the boss, and took it all in good spirit. It's more complicated now that he is around a year old. He seems to realize that he's not meant to be a baby doll the rest of his life, that he's a human being with ideas and a will of his own.

When you suggest something that doesn't appeal to him, he feels he **must** assert himself. His nature tells him to. He just says No in words or actions, even about things that he likes to do. The psychologists call it "negativism"; mothers call it "that terrible No stage." But stop and think what would happen to him if he never felt like saying No. He'd become a robot, a mechanical man. You wouldn't be able to resist the temptation to boss him all the time, and he'd stop learning and developing. When he was old enough to go out into the world, to school and later to work, everybody else would take advantage of him, too. He'd never be good for anything.

3

Considering assumptions about race and ethnicity

One good way to begin thinking about racial and ethnic stereotypes and the assumptions that accompany them is to consider the ways your life has been shaped by your own race or ethnicity. In thinking of yourself in terms of race and ethnicity, what images, qualities, ideas come to mind? What do you know about your ancestors and about their ethnic heritage? What has such a heritage meant to your own identity and to the way you typically relate to others? Have others ever made unfair or inaccurate assumptions about you or those important to you because of your ethnicity?

One student at Stanford University, an Irish American from Boston, realized that she had never even thought twice about her own ethnicity until she heard herself referred to by Mexican American dormmates as an "Anglo." Before that incident, she'd always considered ethnicity something affecting other people, but not herself. Recognizing how others viewed her ethnicity helped this student stop and think about the assumptions she had about them.

EXERCISE 28.1: Suggested Answers

Feeling their oats. One year old is an exciting age. Babies are changing in lots of ways—in their eating, in how they get around, in what they want to do, and in how they feel about themselves and other people. When they were little and helpless, you could put them where you wanted them, give them the playthings you thought suitable, feed them the foods you knew were best. Most of the time they were willing to let you be the boss, and took it all in good spirit. It's more complicated now that they are around a year old. They seem to realize that they're not meant to be baby dolls the rest of their lives, that they're human beings with ideas and wills of their own.

By 15 to 18 months, many children's behavior makes it clear that they're heading for what is often called "the terrible twos." When you suggest something that doesn't appeal to them, they feel they must assert themselves. Their nature tells them to. They just say "No" in words or actions, even about things that they like to do. The psychologists call it "negativism"; many parents call it "that terrible no stage." But stop and think what would happen to children who never felt like saying "No." They'd become robots. You wouldn't be able to resist the temptation to boss them all the time, and they'd stop learning and developing. When they were old enough to go out into the world, to school and later to work, everybody else would take advantage of them, too. They'd never be good for anything.

—BENJAMIN SPOCK, *Baby and Child Care* (1985)

TEACHING PRACTICE

You may want to get students working toward Exercise 28.4 at this point by asking them to write a paragraph or two about their own ethnic heritage. Some may want to talk with parents or grandparents about their own ethnicity. Such research would form the basis for class discussion and for a writing assignment about "where I come from," pieces that could lead to a class book.

TEACHING PRACTICE

You may want to ask students to spend a few minutes asking "what's in a name" and discussing the terms used to refer to their own ethnic group and, perhaps, their own names. Some students may not know, for instance, that Booker T. Washington long ago wrote that former slaves must change their slave names and that this impetus is related to the practice of taking names that reflect African or Islamic influence: Malcolm Little to Malcolm X and then to Malik Al-Shabazz; Cassius Clay to Muhammad Ali; Lew Alcindor to Kareem Abdul-Jabbar. What names might students choose to reflect their own ethnicity? What terms do they prefer to use when referring to their own ethnic group, and why?

TEACHING PRACTICE

Ask students to read the following excerpt from Carol Lee Sanchez's description of the language that white culture has used to characterize native Americans and to contrast these stereotypes with the native American perspective on themselves, their way of life, and the white culture that threatens them. Who is Sanchez's audience in this article? How does she build common ground with readers? Are students persuaded by her arguments?

As we all know only too well, generalizations about racial and ethnic groups can result in especially harmful stereotyping. Such assumptions can be seen in statements that suggest, for instance, that all African Americans are musically talented, that Asian Americans all excel in math and science, or that all Germans are efficiency experts. Negative stereotypes, of course, are even more damaging. In building common ground, writers must watch for any language that ignores not only differences among individual members of a race or ethnic group but among subgroups—for instance, the many nations to which native Americans belong or the diverse places from which Americans of Spanish-speaking ancestry have emigrated.

Using preferred terms

For writers, avoiding stereotypes and other assumptions based on race or ethnicity is only a first step. Beyond that lies the task of attempting to refer to any group in terms that its members actually desire. Doing so is sometimes not an easy task, for preferences change and even vary widely.

The word *colored,* for example, was once widely used in the United States to refer to Americans of African ancestry (in fact, it still appears in the name of the NAACP, the National Association for the Advancement of Colored People). By the 1950s, the preferred term had become *Negro;* in the 1960s, however, *black* came to be preferred by most, though certainly not all, members of that community. Then, toward the end of the 1980s, some leaders of the American black community urged that *black* in turn be replaced by *African American.* One such leader, the Reverend Jesse Jackson, argued that *African American* has "cultural integrity" because it designates "some land base, some historical cultural base," whereas *black* is a "baseless" designation.

Similarly, the word *Oriental,* which not too long ago was commonly used to refer to people of East Asian descent, is now often considered offensive. An example of how this usage has changed can be seen at the University of California at Berkeley, where the Oriental Languages department is now known as the East Asian Languages department. One advocate of the change explained that *Oriental* is appropriate for objects, like rugs, but not people.

Many of those once referred to as *American Indians* now prefer to be called *native Americans.* In Alaska and Canada, many of the native peoples once referred to as *Eskimos* now prefer *Inuit* (which is the official designated term in Canada). And among Americans of Spanish-speaking descent, the terms are many: *Chicano/Chicana, Hispanic, Latin American, Latino/Latina, Mexican American, Puerto Rican,* to name but a few.

Clearly, then, ethnic terminology changes often enough to challenge the most careful writer. The best advice may be just to consider your words carefully, to *listen* for the way members of groups refer to themselves (or *ask* for their preferences), and to check any term you're unsure of in a current dictionary. The 1991 edition of the *Random House Webster's College Dictionary* includes particularly helpful usage notes about racial and ethnic designations.

4

Considering other kinds of difference

Gender, race, and ethnicity are among the most frequent challenges for a writer seeking to find common ground with readers, but you will face many others as well. The following section discusses some of them.

Age

Mention age if it is relevant, but be aware that age-related terms can carry derogatory connotations (*matronly, teenybopper, well-preserved,* and so on). Although describing Mr. Fry as "elderly but still active" may sound polite to you, chances are that Mr. Fry would prefer being called "an active seventy-eight-year-old"—or just "a seventy-eight-year-old," which eliminates the unstated assumption of surprise that he would be active "at his age."

Class

Because you may not usually think about class as consciously as you do about age or race, for example, you should take special care to examine your words for stereotypes or assumptions about class. Such was the case in a recent *New York Times* column entitled "Young, Privileged, and Unemployed," written by a young woman who had lost her high-paying professional job. Unable to find other "meaningful work," the author wrote, she and others like her had been forced to accept "absurd" jobs like cleaning houses and baby-sitting.

The column provoked a number of angry letters to the *Times,* like this one: "So the young and privileged are learning what we of the working classes have always understood too well: there is no entitlement in life. We have always taken the jobs you label 'absurd.' Our mothers are the women who clean your mothers' houses. . . ." Thus did the writer destroy common ground with her readers by assuming that cleaning houses is an "absurd" way to make a living and that education or social standing entitles people to more "meaningful" occupations.

As a writer, then, do not assume that all your readers share your background or values—that your classmates' families all own their homes, for instance. And avoid using any words—*redneck, blueblood,* and the like—that might alienate anyone.

On the negative side, to be Indian is to be thought of as primitive, alcoholic, ignorant (as in "Dumb Indian"), better off dead (as in "the only good Indian is a dead Indian" or "I didn't know there was any of you folks still left"), unskilled, non-competitive, immoral, pagan or heathen, untrustworthy (as in "Indian-giver") and frightening. To be Indian is to be the primary model that is used to promote racism in this country.

How can that happen, you ask? Bad press. One hundred and fifty years of the most consistently vicious press imaginable. Newspapers, dime novels, textbooks and fifty years of visual media have portrayed and continue to portray Indians as savage, blood-thirsty, immoral, inhuman people. When there's a touch of social consciousness attached, you will find the once "blood-thirsty," "white-killer savage" portrayed as a pitiful drunk, a loser, an outcast or a mix-blood not welcomed by, or trusted by, either race. For fifty years, children in this country have been raised to kill Indians mentally, subconsciously through the visual media, until it is an automatic reflex. That shocks you? Then I have made my point. . . .

The Indian Way is a different way. It is a respectful way. The basic teachings in every Tribe that exists today as a Tribe in the western hemisphere are based on respect for all the things our Mother gave us. If we neglect her or anger her, she will make our lives very difficult and we always know that we have a hardship on ourselves and on our children. We are raised to be cautious and concerned for the *future* of our people, and that is how we raise our children—because *they* are *our* future. Your "civilization" has made all of us very sick and has made our mother earth sick and out of balance. Your kind of thinking and education has brought the whole world to the brink of total disaster, whereas the thinking and education among my people forbids the practice of almost everything Euro-Americans, in particular, value.

BACKGROUND

The *New York Times* recently reported on an experiment done by Smith College psychologist Dr. Fletcher Blanchard that led him to conclude that "a few outspoken people who are vigorously anti-racist can establish the kind of social climate that discourages racist acts." After asking 144 Smith College students for their reactions to a racist incident on campus, Dr. Blanchard found that students who heard others making racist remarks were more willing to make racist remarks themselves. These findings suggest that the peer group in the writing classroom could serve as an effective mechanism for encouraging students to consider the effect their language could have on others. ("New Ways to Battle Bias: Fight Acts, Not Feelings," *New York Times* 16 July 1991: B1,9.)

USEFUL READINGS

Matthews, Anne. "Brave, New 'Cruelty Free' World." *New York Times* 7 July 1991. A teacher of nonfiction writing at Princeton University, Matthews satirizes current expressions which, in attempting to be "cruelty-free," actually deny or trivialize difficult human conditions. She examines these terms: *vegan, zap,* and *challenged* (as in *physically challenged*).

A Media Guide to Disability. East Hartford, CT: Connecticut Disabilities Council, 1985. A discussion of language most often used in professional literature and most preferred by people with various disabilities.

Geographical areas

Though stereotypes related to geographical areas are not always insulting or even unpleasant, they are very often clichéd and exaggerated. New Englanders are not all thrifty and tight-lipped; Florida offers more than retirement and tourism; Texans do not all wear cowboy boots and Stetson hats; Midwesterners are not all hard-working; many Californians neither care about nor participate in the latest trends. Check your writing carefully to be sure it doesn't make these kinds of simplistic assumptions.

Check also that you use geographic terms accurately.

America, American. Although many people use these words to refer to the United States alone, you should be aware that such usage will not necessarily be acceptable to people from Canada, Mexico, and Central or South America.

British, English. British should be used to refer to the island of Great Britain, which includes England, Scotland, and Wales, or to the United Kingdom of Great Britain and Northern Ireland. In general, do not use *English* for these broader senses.

Russia(n), Soviet. Soviet should be used to refer to the Soviet Union, of which Russia is but one of many national republics. As this book goes to press, however, the usage—indeed, the existence—of the word *Soviet* is very much in flux, as many republics declare their independence. Do not use *Russia* to refer to the entire country.

Arab. This term refers only to people of Arabic-speaking descent. Note that Iran is not an Arab nation; its people speak Farsi, not Arabic. Note also that *Arab* is not synonymous with *Muslim* or *Moslem* (a believer in Islam). Most (but not all) Arabs are Muslim, but many Muslims (those in Pakistan, for example) are not Arab.

Physical ability or health

The most important question to ask yourself when writing about a person with a serious illness or other physical disability is whether to mention the disability at all if it is not in some respect relevant to what you are discussing. If you do refer to a disability, consider whether the words you use carry negative connotations. You might choose, for example, to say someone "uses" a wheelchair rather than to say he or she "is confined to" one, language that is both grammatically and physically passive. Similarly, you might note a subtle but meaningful difference between calling someone a "person with AIDS," rather than an "AIDS victim." Mentioning the person first, the disability second, such as referring to a "child with diabetes" rather than a "diabetic child" or a "diabetic," is always a good idea. On the other hand, the survey of people with disabilities that was mentioned earlier shows that you sometimes need to be careful not to minimize a disability.

Religion

Religious stereotypes are very often inaccurate and unfair. Roman Catholics hold a wide spectrum of views on abortion, for example, Muslim women do not all wear veils, and many Baptists are not fundamentalists. In fact, not all people believe in or practice a religion at all, so be careful of such assumptions. As in other cases, do not use religious labels without considering their relevance to your point, and make every effort to get them right—for example, *Reformed* churches but *Reform* synagogues.

Sexual orientation

Partly because sexual orientation was a topic "erased" from most public discourse until recent decades, the stereotypes and assumptions that surround it are particularly deep-seated and, often, unconscious. Writers who wish to build common ground, therefore, should not generally assume that readers all share any one sexual orientation—that everyone is attracted to the opposite sex, for example.

As with any label, reference to sexual orientation should be governed by context. Someone writing about Representative Barney Frank's economic views would probably have little if any reason to refer to his sexual orientation. On the other hand, a writer concerned with diversity in American government might find it important to note that Frank is one of the few members of Congress to have made his homosexuality public.

EXERCISE 28.2

Together with two or three classmates, look at the passage by James Thurber in 8c, and discuss whether you find any of its thinking or language stereotyped. If so, do you think Thurber's humorous purpose justifies inclusion of the stereotype(s)? If Thurber were a member of your class, would you advise him to make any revisions? What would they be?

28b

Taking time to listen

Eudora Welty once wrote about the importance of listening in her development as a writer, saying that long before she wrote stories, she "listened for stories," and that this listening led her eventually to scenes full of "things to find out and know about human beings." Listening carefully to

BACKGROUND

Students should be aware that people whose sexual orientation is not strictly heterosexual constitute a significant minority of our world and inhabit all walks of life. They should also be aware that, as with many other labels, the terms used to describe sexual orientation are in flux. *Sexual orientation* itself is the term preferred by many who view sexuality as genetically determined or as the result of very early socialization (or as some combination of the two). *Sexual preference,* on the other hand, is preferred by many who see sexuality as primarily a matter of personal or political choice.

It is also worth noting that style sheets for most organizations recommend using the term *gay* only as an adjective; *homosexual* and *lesbian* are used as both adjectives and nouns.

EXERCISE 28.2: Suggested Answers

Portraying a person with an Eastern European name as big and stupid, a football player as "dumb as an ox," and an economics professor as "thin, timid." (Also, though few students may recognize it, the Polish name, Bolenciecwcz, is deliberately misspelled.)

The stereotypes may add comic effect for some readers, but for others they will be insulting or degrading. Thurber's personal character is not at issue here, but in this instance he does uncritically employ clichés that perpetuate narrow and ungenerous thinking.

TEACHING PRACTICE

Give students a few paragraphs from Swift's *A Modest Proposal* and ask them to identify language that stereotypes certain groups—the Irish, women, or Americans, for example. Then ask them to consider such stereotyping in relation to Swift's *satiric purpose*. Particularly in the case of satire, such labeling may serve to argue for exactly the opposite of what it seems to be saying. In such cases, do the students find such stereotypes offensive—or useful? Ask them to find contemporary political satire and bring examples to class for further discussion.

others—taking time to hear where they are (perhaps literally) coming from—is a necessary step in finding common ground.

Listen especially for what makes those you are listening to unique, and look for common ground between you. Think of ways language can help create common ground—for example, by asking questions rather than making quick, possibly wrong assumptions. Finally, try to relate the experiences of the other person to your own. Look for ways, in short, not only to notice differences but also to make connections.

≫ *Checking for language that builds common ground*

1. Are your references to race, religion, gender, sexual orientation, and so on, relevant or necessary to your discussion? If not, consider leaving them out.
2. Are there any unstated assumptions that might come between you and your readers? Look, for instance, for language implying approval or disapproval of something and for the ways you use the pronouns *we, you,* and *they.*
3. Are the terms you use to refer to groups accurate and acceptable? Because group labels and preferences are always changing, you may need to take extra care to be sure you use the most current or widely accepted terms.
4. Does any language used to describe others carry offensive stereotypes or connotations?

Using sources
Building common ground

Whenever you refer to other sources, you have an opportunity to build common ground with readers. Citing sources your readers can be expected to recognize and respect, for example, can help strengthen the argument you present to those readers. And citing someone from the other side of the argument can at least demonstate that you've considered that side. (See 5g for more details on using authority to demonstrate fairness and attention to counterarguments.)

EXERCISE 28.3: Suggested Answers

Poet asserts his own individuality in lines 5, 6–14, 20–23. Poet forges common ground with his reader in lines 15–19 perhaps; lines 24–39 definitely.

EXERCISE 28.3   Reading with an Eye for Common Ground

The following poem is about finding common ground. Identify those places where the poet asserts his own individuality and those where he forges common ground with readers. How does he deal with issues of difference without insulting readers? How does this poem relate to your experience with others?

Theme for English B

The instructor said,

> Go home and write
> a page tonight.
> And let that page come out of you—
> Then, it will be true.

I wonder if it's that simple?

I am twenty-two, colored, born in Winston-Salem.
I went to school there, then Durham, then here
to this college on the hill above Harlem.
I am the only colored student in my class.
The steps from the hill lead down to Harlem,
through a park, then I cross St. Nicholas,
Eighth Avenue, Seventh, and I come to the Y,
the Harlem Branch Y, where I take the elevator
up to my room, sit down, and write this page:

It's not easy to know what is true for you or me
at twenty-two, my age. But I guess I'm what
I feel and see and hear. Harlem, I hear you:
hear you, hear me—we two—you, me talk on this page.
(I hear New York, too.) Me—who?

Well, I like to eat, sleep, drink, and be in love.
I like to work, read, learn, and understand life.
I like a pipe for a Christmas present,
or records—Bessie, bop, or Bach.

I guess being colored doesn't make me not like
the same things other folks like who are other races.
So will my page be colored that I write?
Being me, it will not be white.
But it will be
a part of you, instructor.
You are white—
yet a part of me, as I am a part of you.
That's American.

Sometimes perhaps you don't want to be a part of me.
Nor do I often want to be a part of you.
But we are, that's true!
As I learn from you,
I guess you learn from me—
although you're older—and white—
and somewhat more free.

This is my page for English B.

—LANGSTON HUGHES

EXERCISE 28.4 Taking Inventory: Common Ground

One good way to start thinking about differences and common ground is to look around the classroom and try to describe them in writing. Like you, generations of college students have found themselves in classes filled with people both like them and different from them. Here is Eudora Welty, describing her first year (1926) at Mississippi State College for Women.

> There I landed in a world to itself, and indeed it was all new to me. It was surging with twelve hundred girls. They came from every nook and corner of the state, from the Delta, the piney woods, the Gulf Coast, the black prairie, the red clay hills, and Jackson—as the capital city and the only sizeable town, a region to itself. All were clearly differentiated sections, at that time, and though we were all put into uniforms of navy blue so as to unify us, it could have been told by the girls' accents, by their bearings, the way they came into the classroom and the way they ate, where they'd grown up. This was my first chance to learn what the body of us were like and what differences in background, persuasion of mind, and resources of character there were among Mississippians—at that, among only half of us, for we were all white. I missed the significance of both what was in, and what was out of, our well-enclosed but vibrantly alive society.
>
> —EUDORA WELTY, *One Writer's Beginnings*

Take time now to examine where you've come from—your age, ethnicity, hometown, religion, and so on. Then do the same for one or more of your classmates. Write a paragraph about the differences *and* the common ground you see. Finally, study your paragraph for any assumptions your language reveals.

Part Six

Understanding Punctuation Conventions

<>

29

Using Commas

The first system of punctuation was introduced circa 260 B.C. by a librarian in Alexandria named Aristophanes. His system can be considered a forerunner of our own, but it was ignored in his own time, and Greek and Latin generally observed no punctuation at all until about the ninth century A.D. Aristophanes' system used three marks: the *periodos* (a dot set high on the line), the *kolon* (a dot set on the line), and the *komma* (a dot set halfway between the top and bottom of letters). Ancient Greece was, of course, preeminently an oral culture, and these marks signaled not grammatical units but places for the speaker to breathe. Punctuation took on grammatical functions, as opposed to performative ones, as a part of the emergence of a print culture. In "Historical Backgrounds of Elizabethan and Jacobean Punctuation Theory," Walter Ong notes that medieval grammarians

> *never* refer to the position of a punctuation mark in terms of grammatical structure. For the most part, they are content to indicate where a *distinctio* [period] may (not where it must or must not) occur, and if one wishes to breathe oftener than would be usual, there is no objection, apparently, to inserting the marks 'ex abundanti.' (351)

The concept of punctuation as breathing marks continued through the sixteenth and

The word *comma* comes from the Greek *komma,* meaning "cut" or "segment," and commas are used to separate parts of a sentence from one another. A clause, for example, is a segment of a sentence, and it is often set off from the rest of the sentence with a comma.

Commas also mark a pause in reading. In his essay "In Praise of the Humble Comma," Pico Iyer likens a comma to a flashing yellow light that asks the reader to slow down. You can see what he means by reading through the following sentences, first with the commas and then without.

> The hangman, a gray-haired convict in the white uniform of the prison, was waiting beside his machine.
>
> And then, when the noose was fixed, the prisoner began crying out to his god.
>
> The prisoner had vanished, and the rope was twisting on itself.
>
> "Well, that's all for this morning, thank God."
>
> —GEORGE ORWELL, "A Hanging"

Because the comma is the most frequently used punctuation mark in English, commas count in your writing. In fact, the study of student writing undertaken as part of the research for this book reveals that five of the twenty most common errors involve the comma. But reducing comma use to hard and fast rules is very difficult for several reasons. First, the comma can play a number of different roles in a sentence, making general rules hard to come by. More important, many decisions about commas relate to matters of purpose, rhythm, and style rather than grammar alone. As a result, conventions for using commas differ from one English-speaking country to another, even from one professional writer to another.

Getting full control of comma usage in your own writing thus involves not only learning some rules but also practicing the use of commas in writing and concentrating on the stylistic decisions you must learn to make as a writer. This chapter presents an opportunity for you to accomplish both these goals.

EXERCISE 29.1

The following paragraph from "Homeless," by Anna Quindlen, is reproduced without any of the commas Quindlen used. Add commas where you think they're necessary or helpful. Then look through this chapter to see if your comma usage is appropriate. Have you used any unnecessary commas? Can you see places where you need to add any? Compare your use of commas with a classmate's.

> They were not pictures of family or friends or even a dog or cat its eyes brown-red in the flashbulb's light. They were pictures of a house. It was like a thousand houses in a hundred towns not suburb not city but somewhere in between with aluminum siding and a chain-link fence a narrow driveway running up to a one-car garage and a patch of backyard. The house was yellow. I looked on the back for a date or a name but neither was there. There was no need for discussion. I knew what she was trying to tell me for it was something I had often felt. She was not adrift alone anonymous although her bags and her raincoat with the grime shadowing its creases had made me believe she was. She had a house or at least once upon a time had had one. Inside were curtains a couch a stove potholders. You are where you live. She was somebody.

Everyday use

Commas play a surprisingly important role in recipes. Study their use in the following recipe for sweet-potato pie.

1¼ c sweet potatoes, cooked and mashed	¼ t cinnamon
½ c brown sugar, firmly packed	1 T butter, melted
½ t salt	2 eggs, well beaten
	¾ c milk

Prepare pastry for a one-crust pie, and line an 8-inch pie pan; chill. Preheat oven to 400°. Combine sweet potatoes, brown sugar, salt, cinnamon, and butter. Mix together eggs and milk. Combine all ingredients. Pour into pie shell, and bake for 45 minutes.

One purpose commas serve here is to separate ingredients (sweet potatoes) from what the cook is supposed to do (cook and mash them). How else are they used? Look at some directions you use—for making pie crust, perhaps, or operating a tape recorder—and collect some examples of comma use. Where are they necessary, and where are they just helpful?

---

seventeenth centuries. Today, most handbooks define the proper uses of commas in grammatical terms, although this chapter does note the stylistic uses of commas (for rhythm, emphasis, and clarity).

EXERCISE 29.1: Suggested Answers

Here is the paragraph as published:

> They were not pictures of family, or friends, or even a dog or cat, its eyes brown-red in the flashbulb's light. They were pictures of a house. It was like a thousand houses in a hundred towns, not suburb, not city, but somewhere in between, with aluminum siding and a chain-link fence, a narrow driveway running up to a one-car garage and a patch of backyard. The house was yellow. I looked on the back for a date or a name, but neither was there. There was no need for discussion. I knew what she was trying to tell me, for it was something I had often felt. She was not adrift, alone, anonymous, although her bags and her raincoat with the grime shadowing its creases had made me believe she was. She had a house, or at least once upon a time had had one. Inside were curtains, a couch, a stove, potholders. You are where you live. She was somebody.

USEFUL READING

Ong, Walter. "Historical Backgrounds of Elizabethan and Jacobean Punctuation Theory." *PMLA* 59 (1944): 349–60. Despite the title, both the history of punctuation and Renaissance attitudes are treated equally.

Period Styles: A History of Punctuation. New York: Herb Lubalin Study Center of Design and Typography, Cooper Union for the Advancement of Science and Art, 1988. See the first essay, "Period Styles: A Punctuated History."

TEACHING PRACTICE

Ask students to bring in examples of sentences with introductory elements. (Have them look for sentences where introductory elements are set off by commas as well as ones where they're *not* set off by commas.) Put several examples up for discussion of how the comma (or the lack of a comma) affects readers' understanding of an author's intended meaning. You might also try repunctuating the examples, adding or deleting commas, and then considering the difference a comma makes.

EXERCISE 29.2: Answers

1. In one of his most famous poems,
2. Unfortunately,
3. Unable to make such a decision alone,
4. If you follow instructions carefully,
5. Therefore,
6. No comma needed.
7. Their bags packed,
8. No comma needed.
9. Like other young children,
10. Frightened by the firecrackers,

29a

Using commas after introductory elements

A comma usually follows an introductory word, expression, phrase, or clause. These introductory elements include adverbs (see 7b5); conjunctive adverbs (see 7b7); transitional expressions (see 6c5); participles, infinitives, and prepositional, participial, infinitive, and absolute phrases (see 7c3); and adverb clauses (see 7c4).

Slowly, she became conscious of her predicament. [adverb]

Nevertheless, the hours of a typist are flexible. [conjunctive adverb]

In fact, only you can decide. [transitional expression]

Frustrated, he wondered whether he should change careers. [participle]

In Fitzgerald's novel, the color green takes on great symbolic qualities. [prepositional phrase]

Sporting a pair of specially made running shoes, Jamie prepared for the race. [participial phrase]

To win the contest, Paul needed luck. [infinitive phrase]

Pens poised in anticipation, the students waited for the test to be distributed. [absolute phrase]

Since her mind was not receiving enough stimulation, she had to resort to her imagination. [adverb clause]

For certain introductory elements—adverbs, infinitives, prepositional and infinitive phrases, and adverb clauses—some writers omit the comma if the element is short and does not seem to require a pause after it.

At the racetrack Henry lost nearly his entire paycheck.

If the introductory element is followed by inverted word order, with the verb preceding the subject, do not use a comma.

From directly behind my seat came huge clouds of cigar smoke.

EXERCISE 29.2

Place a comma after the introductory element in any of the following sentences where the comma is needed.

1. In one of his most famous poems Frost asks why people need walls.
2. Unfortunately the door to the kennel had been left open.

3. Unable to make such a decision alone I asked my brother for help.
4. If you follow instructions carefully you will be able to install your radio.
5. Therefore answering the seemingly simple question is very difficult.
6. With the fifth century came the fall of the Roman Empire.
7. Their bags packed they waited for the taxi to the airport.
8. To become an Olympic competitor an athlete must train for years.
9. Like other young children Sam has trouble losing.
10. Frightened by the firecrackers the dog hid under the bed.

Using commas in compound sentences

A comma usually precedes a coordinating conjunction (*and, but, or, for, nor, so,* or *yet*) that joins two independent clauses in a compound sentence.

> The title may sound important, but *administrative clerk* is only a euphemism for *photocopier.*
> The climbers will reach the summit today, or they must turn back.
> The show started at last, and the crowd grew quiet.
> No one answered, so I left a message on the machine.

You may want to use a semicolon rather than a comma when the clauses are long and complex or contain other punctuation.

> When these early migrations took place, the ice was still confined to the lands in the far north; but eight hundred thousand years ago, when man was already established in the temperate latitudes, the ice moved southward until it covered large parts of Europe and Asia.
> — ROBERT JASTROW, *Until the Sun Dies*

With very short clauses, you can sometimes omit the comma before *and* or *or.*

> She saw her chance and she took it.

Always use the comma if there is any chance the sentence will be misread without it.

CONFUSING	The game ended in victory and pandemonium erupted.
REVISED	The game ended in victory, and pandemonium erupted.

Be careful not to use *only* a comma between independent clauses. Doing so is usually considered a serious grammatical error, called a comma splice. (See Chapter 15.) Either use a coordinating conjunction after the comma, or use a semicolon.

COMMA SPLICE	Do not thank "luck" for your new job, give yourself the credit you deserve.
REVISED	Do not thank "luck" for your new job, *but* give yourself the credit you deserve.
REVISED	Do not thank "luck" for your new job; give yourself the credit you deserve.

EXERCISE 29.3

Use a comma and a coordinating conjunction (*and, but, or, for, nor, so,* or *yet*) to combine each of the following pairs of sentences into one sentence. Delete or rearrange words if necessary. Example:

I had finished studying for the test, I went to bed.

1. Max Weber was not in favor of a classless society. He thought it would lead to the expansion of the power of the state over the individual.

2. Immigrants came here with high hopes. Their illusions were often shattered.

3. It felt good to be home. I had the odd feeling of being an outsider.

4. He wanted adventure. He moved to a cabin in the Alaskan wilderness.

5. Babies never have to feed themselves. They are not punished for misbehaving, either.

29c

Using commas to set off nonrestrictive elements

Nonrestrictive elements of a sentence—clauses, phrases, and words that do *not* limit or "restrict" the meaning of the words they modify—are set off from the rest of the sentence with commas. **Restrictive** elements *do* limit meaning and are *not* set off with commas.

RESTRICTIVE	Drivers *who have been convicted of drunken driving* should lose their licenses.
NONRESTRICTIVE	The two drivers involved in the accident, *who have been convicted of drunken driving,* should lose their licenses.

EXERCISE 29.3: Suggested Answers

1. Max Weber was not in favor of a classless society, *for* he thought it would lead to the expansion of the power of the state over the individual.

2. Immigrants came here with high hopes, *but* their illusions were often shattered.

3. It felt good to be home, *yet* I had the odd feeling of being an outsider.

4. He wanted adventure, *so* he moved to a cabin in the Alaskan wilderness.

5. Babies never have to feed themselves, *nor* are they punished for misbehaving.

USEFUL READING

Williams, Joseph M. *Style: Ten Lessons in Style and Grace.* 3rd ed. Glenview, IL: Scott, 1989. On pp. 178–79, Williams groups nonrestrictive modifiers under the heading loose or nonspecifying commentary.

In the first sentence, the clause *who have been convicted of drunken driving* is essential to the meaning of the sentence because it limits the word it modifies, *Drivers,* to only those drivers who have been convicted of drunken driving. Therefore, it is not set off by commas. In the second sentence, the same clause is not essential to the meaning because it does not limit what it modifies, *The two drivers involved in the accident,* but merely provides additional information about these drivers. Therefore, it *is* set off with commas.

Notice how using or not using commas to set off such an element can change the meaning of a sentence.

> The bus drivers rejecting the management offer remained on strike.

> The bus drivers, rejecting the management offer, remained on strike.

In the first sentence, not using commas to set off the participial phrase *rejecting the management offer* makes the phrase restrictive, limiting the meaning of *The bus drivers.* This sentence says that only some of the total group of bus drivers, the ones who rejected the offer, remained on strike, implying that other drivers went back to work. In the second sentence, using the commas around the participial phrase makes it nonrestrictive, implying that *The bus drivers* refers to all of the drivers and that all of them remained on strike.

To decide whether an element is restrictive or nonrestrictive, mentally delete the element, and then decide whether the deletion changes the meaning of the rest of the sentence or makes it unclear. If it does, the element is probably restrictive and should not be set off with commas. If it does not, the element is probably nonrestrictive and requires commas.

1

Using commas with adjective and adverb clauses

Adjective clauses begin with *who, whom, whose, which, that, when,* or *where.* (See 7c4.) Adverb clauses begin with subordinating conjunctions like *because, although,* or *before.* (See 7b7 and 7c4.) Adverb clauses are usually essential to the meaning of the sentence; in general, do not set them off with commas unless they precede the independent clause (see 29a) or begin with *although, even though, while,* or another conjunction expressing the idea of contrast.

NONRESTRICTIVE CLAUSES

I borrowed books from the rental library of Shakespeare and Company, *which was the library and bookstore of Sylvia Beach at 12 rue de l'Odeon.* [The clause describing Shakespeare and Company is not necessary to the meaning of the independent clause and therefore is set off with a comma.]
— ERNEST HEMINGWAY, *A Movable Feast*

The Indians, *who range in color from mocha to Dentyne,* are generally under five feet tall. [The central statement of this sentence is that the Indians are under five feet tall; the information about color does not limit this statement to only some of them but simply provides additional information.] — JOHN UPDIKE, "Venezuela for Visitors"

The park soon became a popular gathering place, *although some nearby residents complained about the noise.* [The adverb clause expresses the idea of contrast; therefore, it is set off with a comma.]

RESTRICTIVE CLAUSES

I grew up in a house *where the only regular guests were my relations.* [The information in the adjective clause is essential to the meaning of the sentence and therefore should not be set off with commas.] — RICHARD RODRIGUEZ, "Aria: A Memoir of a Bilingual Childhood"

The claim *that men like seriously to battle one another to some sort of finish* is a myth. [The adjective clause is necessary to the meaning of the sentence because it explains *which* claim is a myth.] — JOHN McMURTRY, "Kill 'Em! Crush 'Em! Eat 'Em Raw!"

An adjective clause that begins with *that* is always restrictive and is not set off with commas. An adjective clause beginning with *which* may be either restrictive or nonrestrictive; however, some writers prefer to use *which* only for nonrestrictive clauses.

2

Using commas with phrases

Participial phrases may be either restrictive or nonrestrictive. Prepositional phrases are usually restrictive but sometimes are not essential to the meaning of a sentence and are therefore set off with commas.

NONRESTRICTIVE PHRASES

Stephanie, amazed, stared at the strange vehicle. [The participle does not limit the meaning of *Stephanie.*]

The "synfuels" program, *launched at the height of the energy crisis,* languished with the drop in fuel prices. [The participial phrase does not limit the meaning of *The "synfuels" program* or change the central meaning of the sentence.]

Howard Hughes, *with all his billions,* lived a tortured life. [The prepositional phrase does not limit the meaning of *Howard Hughes.*]

RESTRICTIVE PHRASES

A penny *saved* is a penny *earned.* [Without the participles, the sentence has a very different meaning.]

Wood *cut from living trees* does not burn as well as dead wood. [The participial phrase is essential to the meaning.]

The wire *for the antenna* is the last one to be connected. [The prepositional phrase restricts the meaning of *wire*.]

3

Using commas with appositives

An appositive is a noun or noun substitute that renames a nearby noun or noun substitute. When an appositive is not essential to identify what it renames, it is set off with commas.

NONRESTRICTIVE APPOSITIVES

Ms. Baker, *my high school chemistry teacher,* inspired my love of science. [Ms. Baker's name identifies her; the appositive simply provides extra information.]

Beethoven's only opera, *Fidelio,* includes the famous "Prisoners' Chorus." [*Fidelio* is nonrestrictive because Beethoven wrote only one opera, so the name is not essential.]

RESTRICTIVE APPOSITIVES

The editorial cartoonist *Thomas Nast* helped to bring about the downfall of the Tweed Ring in New York City. [The appositive identifies *The editorial cartoonist* as a specific cartoonist.]

Mozart's opera *The Marriage of Figaro* was considered revolutionary in the eighteenth century. [The appositive is necessarily restrictive because Mozart wrote more than one opera.]

EXERCISE 29.4

Identify the restrictive and the nonrestrictive elements in the following sentences.

1. Teak, which has a beautiful grain, is used in veneers.
2. She who laughs last laughs best.
3. General Norman Schwarzkopf, who commanded U.S. forces in the field, became a national hero.
4. Salmon smoked over an alderwood fire has a unique flavor.
5. Thurgood Marshall, the first African American to serve on the U.S. Supreme Court, announced his retirement in 1991.

EXERCISE 29.4: Answers

1. *which has a beautiful grain* is a nonrestrictive clause because it provides additional, not essential, information.
2. *who laughs last* is a restrictive clause because only the *she* who has the last laugh can laugh best. Laughing best is restricted to the person who laughs last.
3. *who commanded U.S. forces in the field* is a nonrestrictive clause because it provides additional, not essential, information.
4. *smoked over an alderwood fire* is a restrictive participial phrase because the meaning of the sentence is not complete without it. That it is smoked over an alderwood fire is what gives the salmon *a unique flavor.*
5. *the first African American to serve on the U.S. Supreme Court* is a nonrestrictive appositive phrase because it provides nonessential information. Naming Thurgood Marshall is sufficient.

EXERCISE 29.5: Answers

1. No commas needed.
2. No commas needed.
3. I would feel right at home in the city dump, which bears a striking resemblance to my bedroom.
4. No commas needed.
5. No commas needed.
6. The Zunis, an ancient tribe, live in New Mexico.
7. The president, elected for a six-year term, acts as head of state.
8. Karl Marx, an important nineteenth-century sociologist, believed that his role as a social thinker was to change the world.
9. Birds' hearts have four chambers, whereas reptiles' have three.
10. No commas needed.

TEACHING PRACTICE

To develop your students' skills with commas in a series, challenge them to construct long sentences with multiple modifiers. Francis Christensen's analysis of cumulative sentences in "A Generative Rhetoric of the Sentence" contains some good models for students to imitate, including this one by William Faulkner: "Calico-coated, small-bodied, with delicate legs and pink faces in which their mismatched eyes rolled wild and subdued, they huddled, gaudy motionless and alert, wild as deer, deadly as rattlesnakes, quiet as doves."

You might give your students a few simple sentences—for example, *they huddled*—and ask them to expand them, either individually or collaboratively, into sentences like Faulkner's, paying close attention to punctuation as they go.

EXERCISE 29.5

Use commas to set off nonrestrictive clauses, phrases, and appositives in any of the following sentences that contain such elements.

1. Anyone who is fourteen years old faces strong peer pressure every day.
2. Embalming is a technique that preserves a cadaver for viewing.
3. I would feel right at home in the city dump which bears a striking resemblance to my bedroom.
4. The musical *West Side Story* was a modern version of Shakespeare's play *Romeo and Juliet.*
5. A house overlooking the ocean costs $500,000.
6. The Zunis an ancient tribe live in New Mexico.
7. The president elected for a six-year term acts as head of state.
8. Karl Marx an important nineteenth-century sociologist believed that his role as a social thinker was to change the world.
9. Birds' hearts have four chambers whereas reptiles' have three.
10. Britain and France agreed to aid each other if one of them was attacked.

29d

Using commas to separate items in a series

A comma is used between items in a series of three or more words, phrases, or clauses.

> I bumped into professors, horizontal bars, agricultural students, and swinging iron rings.
> — JAMES THURBER, "University Days"

> He has plundered our seas, ravaged our coasts, burnt our towns, and destroyed the lives of our people.
> — THOMAS JEFFERSON, Declaration of Independence

You may often see a series with no comma after the next-to-last item, particularly in newspaper writing, as in *The day was cold, dark and dreary.* Occasionally, however, omitting the comma can cause confusion, and you will never be wrong to include it.

When the items in a series contain commas of their own or other punctuation, separate them with semicolons rather than commas (see 30b).

Coordinate adjectives, those that relate equally to the noun they modify, should be separated by commas. In the sentence *They are sincere,* *talented, inquisitive researchers,* the three adjectives are coordinate: they each modify *researchers* and are therefore separated by commas. Here are some other examples of coordinate adjectives.

> The *long, twisting, muddy* road led to a shack in the woods.
>
> His *bizarre, outrageous* sense of humor endeared him to his friends.

In a sentence like *The cracked bathroom mirror reflected his face,* however, *cracked* and *bathroom* are not coordinate because *bathroom mirror* is the equivalent of a single word, which is modified by *cracked.* Hence they are *not* separated by commas.

> Byron carried an *elegant gold pocket* watch.
>
> *Outdated black nylon furniture* sat in dusty silence on the porch.

You can usually determine whether adjectives are coordinate by inserting *and* between them. If the sentence makes sense with the *and,* the adjectives are coordinate and should be separated by commas.

> They are sincere *and* talented *and* inquisitive researchers. [The sentence makes sense with the inserted *and*'s, so the adjectives *sincere, talented,* and *inquisitive* should be separated by commas.]
>
> Byron carried an elegant *and* gold *and* pocket watch. [In this instance, the sentence does not make sense with the *and*'s, so, the adjectives *elegant, gold,* and *pocket* should not be separated by commas.]

EXERCISE 29.6

Revise any of the following sentences that require commas to set off words, phrases, or clauses in a series.

1. They found employment in truck driving farming and mining.
2. We bought zucchini peppers and tomatoes at the market.
3. Members plant tend and harvest corn.
4. The daddy-long-legs's orange body resembled a colored dot amidst eight long black legs.
5. A prestigious car a large house and membership in an exclusive club are taken as signs of success.
6. Superficial observation does not provide accurate insight into people's lives—how they feel what they believe in how they respond to others.
7. The ball sailed over the fence across the road and through the window.
8. I timidly offered to help a loud overbearing lavishly dressed customer.
9. Ellen is an accomplished free-lance writer.

USEFUL READING

Christensen, Francis. "A Generative Rhetoric of the Sentence." *Rhetoric and Composition.* Ed. Richard Graves. Upper Montclair, NJ: Boynton, 1984. 110–18. The examples referred to above are on pages 113–16.

EXERCISE 29.6: Answers

1. They found employment in truck driving, farming, and mining.
2. We bought zucchini, peppers, and tomatoes at the market.
3. Members plant, tend, and harvest corn.
4. The daddy-long-legs's orange body resembled a colored dot amidst eight long, black legs.
5. A prestigious car, a large house, and membership in an exclusive club are taken as signs of success.
6. Superficial observation does not provide accurate insight into people's lives—how they feel, what they believe in, how they respond to others.
7. The ball sailed over the fence, across the road, and through the window.
8. I timidly offered to help a loud, overbearing, lavishly dressed customer.
9. No comma needed.
10. These Cosell clones insist on calling every play, judging every move, and telling everyone within earshot exactly what is wrong with the team.

10. These Cosell clones insist on calling every play judging every move and telling everyone within earshot exactly what is wrong with the team.

29e

Using commas to set off parenthetical and transitional expressions

Parenthetical expressions are added comments or information. Because they often interrupt or digress, they are usually set off with commas. Transitional expressions are also usually set off with commas. They include conjunctive adverbs like *however* and *furthermore* and other words and phrases used to connect parts of sentences. (For full lists, see 7b7 and 6c5.)

Some studies, *incidentally*, have shown that chocolate, *of all things*, helps to prevent tooth decay.

Roald Dahl's stories, *it turns out*, were often inspired by episodes from his own childhood.

Ceiling fans are, *moreover*, less expensive than air conditioners.

Ozone is produced by dry cleaning, *for example*.

29f

Using commas to set off contrasting elements, interjections, direct address, and tag questions

Contrasting elements

On official business it was she, *not my father*, one would usually hear on the phone or in stores.
   — RICHARD RODRIGUEZ, "Aria: A Memoir of a Bilingual Childhood"
The story is narrated objectively at first, *subjectively toward the end*.

Interjections

My God, who wouldn't want a wife?   — JUDY BRADY, "I Want a Wife"
We had hiked for, *say*, seven miles before stopping to rest.

FOR COLLABORATIVE WORK

Consider sharing the following passage with your students, asking them to work together in groups to identify the grammatical reasons for Mark Twain's commas. Then ask the groups to rewrite some or all of the passage, combining sentences or eliminating commas by shortening sentences. Finally, discuss Twain's stylistic reasons for punctuating this passage as he does. What effects have your students achieved by punctuating the passage differently?

The bull started up, and got along well for about ten feet, then slipped and slid back. I breathed easier. He tried it again—got a little higher—slipped again. But he came at it once more, and this time he was careful. He got gradually higher and higher, and my spirits went down more and more. Up he came—an inch at a time—with his eyes hot, and his tongue hanging out. Higher and higher—hitched his foot over the stump of a limb, and looked up, as much as to say, "You are my meat, friend." Up again—higher and higher, and getting more excited the higher he got. He was within ten feet of me! I took a long breath—and then said I, "It is now or never." I had the coil of the lariat all ready; I paid it out slowly, till it hung right over his head; all of a sudden I let go of the slack, and the slip noose fell fairly round his neck! Quicker than lightning I out with the allen and let him have it in the face, It was an awful roar, and must have scared the bull out of his senses. When the smoke cleared away, there he was, dangling in the air, twenty foot from the ground, and going out of one convulsion into another faster than you could count! I didn't stop to count, any-how—I shinned down the tree and shot for home.
                          —MARK TWAIN, *Roughing It*

Direct address

Ah, *swinging generation,* what new delights await?
— TOM WOLFE, "Pornoviolence"

My friends, I must say to you that we have not made a single gain in civil rights without determined legal and nonviolent pressure.
—MARTIN LUTHER KING, JR., "Letter from Birmingham Jail"

Tag questions

The homeless are our fellow citizens, *are they not?*

Seattle is not the capital of Washington, *is it?*

EXERCISE 29.7

Revise each of the following sentences, using commas to set off parenthetical and transitional expressions, contrasting elements, interjections, words used in direct address, and tag questions.

1. One must consider the society as a whole not just its parts.
2. The West in fact has become solidly Republican in presidential elections.
3. Her friends did not know about her illness did they?
4. The rescue team alas arrived too late.
5. Ladies and gentlemen I bid you farewell.

EXERCISE 29.7: Answers

1. One must consider the society as a whole, not just its parts.
2. The West, in fact, has become solidly Republican in presidential elections.
3. Her friends did not know about her illness, did they?
4. The rescue team, alas, arrived too late.
5. Ladies and gentlemen, I bid you farewell.

29g

Using commas with dates, addresses, titles, and numbers

Commas are used according to established rules with dates, addresses and place names, and numbers. Commas are also used to separate personal and professional titles from the name preceding them.

Dates

For dates, use a comma between the day of the week and the month, between the day of the month and the year, and between the year and the rest of the sentence, if any.

The war began on Thursday, *January 16, 1991,* with air strikes on Iraq.

Do not use commas with dates in inverted order or with dates consisting only of the month and the year.

> 18 October 1989

> Thousands of Germans swarmed over and through the wall in *November 1989* and effectively demolished it.

Addresses and place names

In addresses and place names, use a comma after each part, including the state if no ZIP code is given. In addresses that include the ZIP code, do not use a comma either before or after it.

> Forward my mail to the Department of English, Ohio State University, Columbus, Ohio 43210 until further notice.

> Portland, Oregon, is much larger than Portland, Maine.

Titles

Use commas to set off a title such as *Jr., M.D.,* and so on, from the name preceding it and from the rest of the sentence.

> James Siddens, *Ph.D.*

> Martin Luther King, *Jr.,* was one of this century's greatest orators.

Numbers

In numbers of five digits or more, use a comma between each group of three digits, starting from the right.

> The city's population rose to *17,126* at the 1990 census.

Do not use a comma within street numbers or ZIP codes.

> My parents live at *11311* Wimberly Drive, Richmond, Virginia 23233.

The comma is optional within numbers of four digits, except for years, where it is never used. Use a comma with numbers of more than four digits.

> The college has an enrollment of *1,789* (or *1789*) this semester.

> The French Revolution began in *1789*.

EXERCISE 29.8

Revise each of the following sentences, using commas appropriately with dates, addresses and place names, titles, and numbers.

1. People were cultivating crops before 10000 B.C.
2. Ithaca New York has a population of about 20000.
3. The ship was hit by two torpedoes on May 7 1915 and sank in minutes.
4. MLA headquarters are at 10 Astor Place New York New York 10003.
5. The nameplate read *Donald Good R.N.* and looked quite impressive.

29h

Using commas with quotations

Commas are used to set off quotations from words used to introduce or identify the source of the quotations. A comma following a quotation goes *inside* the closing quotation mark.

"No one becomes depraved all at once," wrote Juvenal.

A German proverb warns, "Go to law for a sheep, and lose your cow."

"Nothing has really happened," said Virginia Woolf, "until it has been recorded."

When a quoted question or exclamation is followed by explanatory words, do not use a comma after the question mark or exclamation point.

"What's a thousand dollars?" asks Groucho Marx in *Coconuts*. "Mere chicken feed. A poultry matter."

"Out, out, damned spot!" cries Lady Macbeth.

Do not use a comma when a quotation is introduced by *that* or when the rest of the sentence includes more than the words used to introduce or identify the source of the quotation.

The writer of Ecclesiastes concludes that "all is vanity."

People who say "Have a nice day" irritate me.

Do not use a comma before an indirect quotation, one that does not use the speaker's exact words.

Patrick Henry declared that he wanted either liberty or death.

Abigail Adams said that all men would like to be tyrants.

EXERCISE 29.9

Insert a comma in any of the following sentences that require one.

EXERCISE 29.9: Answers

1. No change.
2. Joseph Epstein admits, "I prefer not to be thought vulgar in any wise."
3. No change.
4. "Neat people are lazier and meaner than sloppy people," according to Suzanne Britt.
5. No change.

EXERCISE 29.10: Answers will vary.

The commas are the most useful and usable of all the stops. It is highly important to put them in place as you go along. If you try to come back after doing a paragraph and stick them in the various spots that tempt you you will discover that they tend to swarm like minnows into all sorts of crevices whose existence you hadn't realized and before you know it the whole long sentence becomes immobilized and lashed up squirming in commas. Better to use them sparingly, and with affection, precisely when the need for each one arises, nicely, by itself.

— LEWIS THOMAS

1. "The public be damned!" William Henry Vanderbilt was reported to have said. "I'm working for my stockholders."
2. Joseph Epstein admits "I prefer not to be thought vulgar in any wise."
3. Who remarked that "youth is wasted on the young"?
4. "Neat people are lazier and meaner than sloppy people" according to Suzanne Britt.
5. "Who shall decide when doctors disagree?" asked Alexander Pope.

29i

Using commas to facilitate understanding

Sometimes a comma is necessary to make a sentence much easier to read or understand.

CONFUSING	The members of the dance troupe strutted in in matching tuxedos and top hats.
REVISED	The members of the dance troupe strutted in, in matching tuxedos and top hats.
CONFUSING	Before I had planned to major in biology.
REVISED	Before, I had planned to major in biology.

EXERCISE 29.10

Read the following passage aloud, listening for the use of commas. Then read it again, mentally deleting the commas and noting how their absence affects meaning and rhythm. Finally, choose two of the sentences to use as a model for imitation, creating a similar pair of sentences of your own.

I ran across many words whose meanings I did not know, and I either looked them up in a dictionary or, before I had a chance to do that, encountered the word in a context that made its meaning clear. But what strange world was this? I concluded the book with the conviction that I had somehow overlooked something terribly important in life. I had once tried to write, had once reveled in feeling, had let my crude imagination roam, but the impulse to dream had been slowly beaten out of me by experience. Now it surged up again and I hungered for books, new ways of looking and seeing. It was not a matter of believing or disbelieving what I read, but of feeling something new, of being affected by something that made the look of the world different.

— RICHARD WRIGHT, "The Library Card"

29j

Checking for unnecessary commas

Just like insufficient use, excessive use of commas can spoil an otherwise fine sentence or passage.

1

Omitting commas around restrictive elements

Do not use commas to set off restrictive elements, which limit or restrict the meaning of the words they modify or refer to (see 29c).

UNNECESSARY	I don't let my children watch TV shows, that are violent.
REVISED	I don't let my children watch TV shows that are violent. [restrictive adjective clause]
UNNECESSARY	A law, requiring the use of seatbelts, was passed in 1987.
REVISED	A law requiring the use of seatbelts was passed in 1987. [restrictive participial phrase]
UNNECESSARY	My only defense, against my allergies, is to stay indoors.
REVISED	My only defense against my allergies is to stay indoors. [restrictive prepositional phrase]
UNNECESSARY	The actor, James Earl Jones, will speak on campus this fall.
REVISED	The actor James Earl Jones will speak on campus this fall. [restrictive appositive]

2

Omitting commas between subjects and verbs, verbs and objects or complements, and prepositions and objects

Do not use a comma between a subject and its verb, a verb and its object or complement, or a preposition and its object. This general rule holds true even if the subject, object, or complement is a long phrase or clause.

UNNECESSARY	*Watching movies on my VCR late at night,* has become an important way for me to relax. [comma between subject and verb]
REVISED	Watching movies on my VCR late at night has become an important way for me to relax.

UNNECESSARY	Parents *must decide, how much TV their children may watch.* [comma between verb and object]
REVISED	Parents must decide how much TV their children may watch.
UNNECESSARY	The winner *of, the trophy for outstanding community service* stepped forward. [comma between preposition and object]
REVISED	The winner of the trophy for outstanding community service stepped forward.

3

Omitting commas in compound constructions

Do not use a comma before or after a coordinating conjunction joining the two parts of a compound construction.

UNNECESSARY	*A buildup of the U.S. military, and deregulation of major industries* were the Reagan administration's goals. [compound subject]
REVISED	A buildup of the U.S. military and deregulation of major industries were the Reagan administration's goals.
UNNECESSARY	Mark Twain *trained as a printer and, worked as a steamboat pilot.* [compound predicate]
REVISED	Mark Twain trained as a printer and worked as a steamboat pilot.

4

Omitting commas in a series

Do not use a comma before the first item or after the last item in a series.

UNNECESSARY	The antiques auction included, furniture, paintings, and china.
REVISED	The antiques auction included furniture, paintings, and china.
UNNECESSARY	The swimmer took slow, powerful, strokes.
REVISED	The swimmer took slow, powerful strokes.

Checking for commas

Research has shown that five of the most common errors in college writing involve commas. Following are some brief guidelines for each of the five common comma errors, with examples from Lewis Thomas's "On the Need for Asylums."

AFTER INTRODUCTORY ELEMENTS

Check every sentence that doesn't begin with the subject to see whether it opens with an element that needs to be followed by a comma. In general, most introductory elements should be followed by a comma. Though some writers do not add commas after short introductory elements, you'll never be wrong to add one. Only when an introductory element is followed directly by a verb is it wrong to add a comma. (29a)

From time to time, medical science has achieved an undisputable triumph that is pure benefit for all levels of society and deserving of such terms as "breakthrough" and "medical miracle."

IN COMPOUND SENTENCES

Look at every sentence that contains a coordinating conjunction (*and, but, or, nor, for, so,* or *yet.*) In each one, examine the words before the conjunction. Could they function as a complete sentence, with a subject and a predicate? Could the words following the conjunction function as a sentence? If the answers to these questions are yes, you've got a compound sentence. Make sure the conjunction is preceded (not followed) by a comma. (29b)

It is not a long list, but the items are solid bits of encouragement for the future.

IN A SERIES

Circle every *and* and *or.* Then look at each one to see if it comes at the end of a series of three or more words, phrases, or clauses. Be sure that each item in a series (except the last) is followed by a comma. (29d)

The conquests of tuberculosis, smallpox, and syphilis of the central nervous system should be at the top of anyone's list.

TO SET OFF NONRESTRICTIVE ELEMENTS

Identify all adjective clauses beginning with *which, who, whom, whose, when,* or *where.* Consider each one, and decide whether it is

(Continued)

USEFUL READING

Shaughnessy, Mina. *Errors & Expectations: A Guide for the Teacher of Basic Writing.* New York: Oxford UP, 1977. See "Handwriting and Punctuation," particularly pp. 18–24 for a discussion of how basic writers use commas and periods.

essential to the meaning of the sentence. If so, it should not be set off by commas. Apply these same criteria to participial and prepositional phrases and to appositives: any that are essential to the meaning of the sentence should not be set off by commas. (29c)

For centuries the madhouses, as they were called, served no purpose beyond keeping deranged people out of the public view.

WITH RESTRICTIVE ELEMENTS

Identify all adjective clauses beginning with *that,* and make sure they are *not* set off with commas. Then, look for any adjective clauses beginning with *which, who, whom, whose, when,* or *where.* In each case, decide whether it is essential to the meaning of the sentence; if not, the clause should be set off with commas. Finally, look for participial and prepositional phrases and for appositives. Ask the same question of each of them, and set off with commas any that are not essential. (29j)

There was a time when many doctors were glad to volunteer their services.

EXERCISE 29.11: Answers

1. The four types of non-verbal communication are kinesic, haptic, proxemic, and dormant communication.

2. Observers watch facial expressions and gestures and interpret them.

3. There was nothing to do after we ate but go to bed.

4. Our supper that evening consisted of stale bologna sandwiches.

5. Clothes that had to be ironed were too much trouble.

6. As we sat around the campfire, we felt boredom and disappointment.

7. Magazines like *Modern Maturity* are aimed at retired people.

8. The photographer Edward Curtis is known for his depiction of the West.

9. We all took panicked, hasty looks at our notebooks.

10. Driving a car and talking on the car phone at the same time demand great care.

EXERCISE 29.11

Revise each of the following sentences, deleting unnecessary commas.

1. The four types of nonverbal communication are, kinesic, haptic, proxemic, and dormant, communication.

2. Observers watch facial expressions and gestures, and interpret them.

3. There was nothing to do, after we ate, but go to bed.

4. Our supper that evening, consisted of stale bologna sandwiches.

5. Clothes, that had to be ironed, were too much trouble.

6. As we sat around the campfire, we felt boredom, and disappointment.

7. Magazines, like *Modern Maturity,* are aimed at retired people.

8. The photographer, Edward Curtis, is known for his depiction of the West.

9. We all took panicked, hasty, looks at our notebooks.

10. Driving a car, and talking on the car phone at the same time demand care.

EXERCISE 29.12   Reading with an Eye for Commas

The following poem by Robert Frost uses commas to create rhythm and guide readers. Read the poem aloud, listening especially to the effect of the commas at the end of lines one and five. Then read it again as if those commas were omitted, noting the difference. What is the effect of Frost's decision *not* to use a comma at the end of line three?

> Some say the world will end in fire,
> Some say in ice.
> From what I've tasted of desire
> I hold with those who favor fire.
> But if it had to perish twice,
> I think I know enough of hate
> To say that for destruction ice
> Is also great
> And would suffice.
> — ROBERT FROST, "Fire and Ice"

EXERCISE 29.13   Taking Inventory: Commas

The following passage by Maya Angelou, from *I Know Why the Caged Bird Sings*, has had all of Angelou's commas removed. Punctuate the passage with commas as seems appropriate to you, and then explain in writing why you put commas where you did. Finally, check over your use of commas, consulting this chapter for guidance and noting any problems or observations (in your writing log, if you keep one).

The summer picnic gave ladies a chance to show off their baking hands. On the barbecue pit chickens and spareribs sputtered in their own fat and a sauce whose recipe was guarded in the family like a scandalous affair. However in the ecumenical light of the summer picnic every true baking artist could reveal her prize to the delight and criticism of the town. Orange sponge cakes and dark brown mounds dripping Hershey's chocolate stood layer to layer with ice-white coconuts and light brown caramels. Pound cakes sagged with their buttery weight and small children could no more resist licking the icings than their mothers could avoid slapping the sticky fingers.

Proven fishermen and weekend amateurs sat on the trunks of trees at the pond. They pulled the struggling bass and the silver perch from the swift water. A rotating crew of young girls scaled and cleaned the catch and busy women in starched aprons salted and rolled the fish in corn meal then dropped them in Dutch ovens trembling with boiling fat.

On one corner of the clearing a gospel group was rehearsing. Their harmony packed as tight as sardines floated over the music of the county singers and melted into the songs of the small children's ring games.

TEACHING PRACTICE

Write the Frost poem on the board, and read it aloud. Then try changing its comma structure—perhaps by ending line 4 with a comma instead of a period, or by adding commas in line 7 after *that* and *destruction.* Read the poem aloud each way, and ask students to describe the different effects. Finally, ask them to decide which one they prefer, and why.

Popping in a comma can be like slipping on the necklace that gives an outfit quiet elegance, or like catching the sound of running water that complements, as it completes, the silence of a Japanese landscape.
— PICO IYER

30

Using Semicolons

In classical Greek, groups of words comparable to what we call sentences were set off and called *colons*. A semicolon, therefore, is literally half of a colon, or half of a sentence divided by the punctuation mark we call a **semicolon**. Lewis Thomas demonstrates effective use of the semicolon as he defines it, noting that

> The semicolon tells you that there is still some question about the preceding full sentence; something needs to be added. . . . It is almost always a greater pleasure to come across a semicolon than a period. The period tells you that is that; if you didn't get all the meaning you wanted or expected, you got all the writer intended to parcel out and now you have to move along. But with a semicolon there you get a pleasant little feeling of expectancy; there is more to come; read on; it will get clearer.
> — LEWIS THOMAS, "Notes on Punctuation"

As Thomas suggests, semicolons have the effect of creating a pause stronger than that of a comma but not as strong as the full pause of a period. Their primary uses are to link coordinate independent clauses and to separate items in a series.

30a

Using semicolons to link independent clauses

You can join independent clauses in several ways: with a comma and a coordinating conjunction (see 29b), with a colon (see 34d), with a dash (see 34c), or with a semicolon. Semicolons provide writers with subtle ways of signaling closely related clauses. The second clause often restates an idea expressed in the first, as it does in the first sentence of the Lewis Thomas passage above, or it sometimes expands on or presents a contrast to the first. As a writer, you must choose when and where to use semicolons to signal such relationships. Note, for instance, the following examples.

> Immigration acts were passed; newcomers had to prove, besides moral correctness and financial solvency, their ability to read.
>
> — MARY GORDON, "More Than Just a Shrine"

> The problem, of course, is that it is one thing to urge somebody else to take on those anxiety-producing challenges; it is quite another to get ourselves to do it.
>
> — JAMES LINCOLN COLLIER, "Anxiety: Challenge by Any Other Name"

In the first sentence, Gordon uses a semicolon to lead to a clause that expands on the statement made in the first clause. She might have joined the two clauses with *and* or *so,* but not using a conjunction gives the sentence a more abrupt, clipped rhythm that suits the topic: laws that imposed strict requirements. She might also have used a period to separate the two clauses into two sentences, but then the two ideas would not be so clearly linked. In the second example, the semicolon links two contrasting clauses; the logical connection between them is far more subtle and more immediate than it would be had Collier instead used *but.*

The sentences above contain only two independent clauses, but semicolons can also join more than two such clauses.

> On Mother's Day, Good Souls conscientiously wear carnations; on St. Patrick's Day, they faithfully don boutonnieres of shamrocks; on Columbus Day, they carefully pin on miniature Italian flags.
>
> — DOROTHY PARKER, "Good Souls"

Everyday use

Although semicolons are among the more formal punctuation marks, you can sometimes spot them working quite well in informal settings — on bumper stickers, for example Here are two seen recently.

Careful! Baby on board; driver on edge.

Vote for Espy; he means business!

Try replacing these semicolons with commas, periods, or exclamation points, and you'll see how useful they are. Keep your eyes open for everyday uses of semicolons — in ads, on billboards, wherever — and bring them to class to compare with ones discovered by your classmates.

A semicolon can also be used to link independent clauses joined by conjunctive adverbs such as *therefore, however,* or *indeed* or transitional expressions such as *in fact, in addition,* or *for example.* (See 7b7 and 6c3.)

> The circus comes as close to being the world in microcosm as anything I know; in a way, it puts all the rest of show business in the shade.
> — E. B. WHITE, "The Ring of Time"

If two independent clauses joined by a coordinating conjunction contain commas, use a semicolon instead of a comma before the conjunction to make the sentence easier to read.

> Every year, whether the Republican or the Democratic Party is in office, more and more power drains away from the individual to feed vast reservoirs in far-off places; and we have less and less say about the shape of events which shape our future.
> — WILLIAM F. BUCKLEY, JR., "Why Don't We Complain?"

EXERCISE 30.1

Choose one of the five examples shown in 30a, and use it as a model for a sentence of your own. Bring your sentence to class to compare it with those done by your classmates.

EXERCISE 30.2

Combine each of the following pairs of sentences into one sentence by using a semicolon. Example:

The exam begins in two hours; Please be on time.

1. If you are preoccupied, your game will suffer. An opportunity for a relaxing afternoon will turn into a frustrating experience.
2. City life offers many advantages. In many ways, however, life in a small town is much more pleasant.
3. Florida's mild winter climate is ideal for bicycling. In addition, the terrain is very flat.
4. Physical education forms an important part of a university's program. Nevertheless, few students and professors clearly recognize its value.
5. The debate over "political correctness" affects more than the curriculum. It also affects students' social relationships.
6. Voltaire was concerned about the political implications of his skepticism. He warned his friends not to discuss atheism in front of the servants.

EXERCISE 30.1: Answers will vary.

EXERCISE 30.2: Answers

1. If you are preoccupied, your game will suffer; an opportunity for a relaxing afternoon will turn into a frustrating experience.
2. City life offers many advantages; in many ways, however, life in a small town is much more pleasant.
3. Florida's mild winter climate is ideal for bicycling; in addition, the terrain is very flat.
4. Physical education forms an important part of a university's program; nevertheless, few students and professors clearly recognize its value.
5. The debate over "political correctness" affects more than the curriculum; it also affects students' social relationships.
6. Voltaire was concerned about the political implications of his skepticism; he warned his friends not to discuss atheism in front of the servants.

7. Kerosene, solar power, and electricity are popular sources of energy for heating homes in New England. The most popular, however, is wood.

8. My high school was excessively competitive. Virtually everyone went on to college, many to the top schools in the nation.

9. Pittsburgh was once notorious for its smoke and grime. Today its skies and streets are cleaner than those of many other American cities.

10. Propaganda is defined as the spread of ideas to further a cause. Therefore, propaganda and advertisement are synonymous terms.

Using semicolons to separate items in a series

Ordinarily, commas separate items in a series (see 29d). But when the items themselves contain commas or other punctuation, using semicolons will make the sentence clearer and easier to read. Such a series is best used at the *end* of a sentence.

> Anthropology encompasses archaeology, the study of ancient civilizations through artifacts; linguistics, the study of the structure and development of language; and cultural anthropology, the study of the way of life of various peoples, especially small, nonindustrialized societies.

> I recognized the film as a political document, expressing the worst sentiments of America in the cold war: its hero, a tough military man who wants only to destroy the enemy utterly; its villain, a naively liberal scientist who wants to learn more about it; the carrot and its flying saucer, a certain surrogate for the red menace; the film's famous last words—a newsman's impassioned plea to "watch the skies"—an invitation to extended fear and jingoism.
> — STEPHEN JAY GOULD, *Ever Since Darwin*

Note that a semicolon never *introduces* a series (see 30d).

Checking for overused semicolons

If semicolons are used too often, they distract readers in the same way unnecessary repetition does, by calling attention to themselves instead of to what the writer is saying. In addition, sentence upon sentence punctuated with semicolons will sound monotonous and jerky.

7. Kerosene, solar power, and electricity are popular sources of energy for heating homes in New England; the most popular, however, is wood.

8. My high school was excessively competitive; virtually everyone went on to college, many to the top schools in the nation.

9. Pittsburgh was once notorious for its smoke and grime; today, its skies and streets are cleaner than those of many other American cities.

10. Propaganda is defined as the spread of ideas to further a cause; therefore, propaganda and advertisement are synonymous terms.

BACKGROUND

Bergen and Cornelia Evans claim that the semicolon is most appropriate for formal writing. "If a writer wishes to use an informal narrative style he should avoid semicolons as much as possible" (*A Dictionary of Contemporary American Usage* [New York: Random, 1957], 440).

However, George Summey, Jr., in *American Punctuation,* argues against thinking of the semicolon as "a stiff and formal mark that ought to be seldom used": "It is actually used by good current writers today and might well be used oftener if our writers would take the trouble to drop some of their *and's* and *but's* and use patterns that take a semicolon and no conjunction." The problem is not with the semicolon, Summey says, but with the "awkward patterns" and "stiff wording" with which it has been associated (98).

William and Mary Morris suggest that one reason for the lack of use of the semicolon is "the trend toward short, trenchant sentences" in journalism (*Harper Dictionary of Contemporary Usage* [New York: Harper, 1975], 547). But, in fact, the absence of the semicolon in less formal writing is changing. Still, the tendency to use the semicolon remains a stylistic choice. Some writers like Annie Dillard, whose *Pilgrim at Tinker Creek* is definitely not a formal piece, seem fond of the semicolon, while other writers, like John McPhee, rarely use it. Donald Barthelme's short story "Sentence" (*City Life* [New York: Farrar, 1970], 107–14) consists of one long sentence (or actually of a part of one sentence). While it includes numerous instances of dashes, parentheses, quotation marks, question marks, exclamation points, and commas, it has only one semicolon. The reason might be that the semicolon seems too close to being end punctuation, and the story is meant to give us the feeling of continuousness and endlessness. The period, incidentally, doesn't appear at all.

EXERCISE 30.3: Answers will vary.

BACKGROUND

One can imagine writers getting away with never using semicolons, except perhaps the rare use with a series of items. From this perspective, the semicolon becomes more a stylistic device than a grammatical one, which is not something you can say about the period, for instance. Clearly, then, the choice of a semicolon over another punctuation mark is often a rhetorical choice.

George Summey, Jr., offers these flexible guidelines for when to choose the semicolon.

> What mark should be used in a given case— comma or semicolon, semicolon or period— will depend only in part on the length of the groups. Circumstances that may make the semicolon preferable to the comma are length and complexity of the groups, the absence of a connective, or a shift of grammatical subject. And any of these same circumstances may make the period better than the semicolon. Each case must be settled by the writer according to the immediate situation. The more important a group is in its context, the more reason for preferring semicolon to comma or period to semicolon. (*American Punctuation* 99)

OVERUSED	Like many people in public life, he spoke with confidence; perhaps he even spoke with arrogance; yet I noted a certain anxiety; it touched and puzzled me; he seemed too eager to demonstrate his control of a situation and his command of the necessary data.
REVISED	Like many people in public life, he spoke with confidence, perhaps even with arrogance; yet I noted a certain anxiety that touched and puzzled me. He seemed too eager to demonstrate his control of a situation and his command of the necessary data.

EXERCISE 30.3

Revise the following passage, substituting other punctuation for some of the semicolons. Add or delete words if necessary.

Remember when the neighborhood kids played football out in the vacant lot; they were there every Saturday, having a good time. Whatever happened to just playing for a good time? Now, uniformed coaches yell at young players to win; they put more and more pressure on them; and parents join in the chant of win, win, win; in fact, if the child is not a winner, he or she must be—that's right—a loser. The young athlete is constantly told that winning is everything; what used to be fun is now just like a job; play to win, the adults say, or do not play at all.

30d

Checking for misused semicolons

A comma, not a semicolon, should separate an independent clause from a dependent clause or a phrase.

MISUSED	The police found a set of fingerprints; which they used to identify the thief.
REVISED	The police found a set of fingerprints, which they used to identify the thief.

A colon, not a semicolon, should introduce a series.

MISUSED	The tour includes visits to the following art museums; the Prado, in Madrid; the Louvre, in Paris; and the Rijksmuseum, in Amsterdam.
REVISED	The tour includes visits to the following art museums: the Prado, in Madrid; the Louvre, in Paris; and the Rijksmuseum, in Amsterdam.

> *Checking for effective use of semicolons*

> 1. Note all the semicolons. If you find few or none, look at each sentence together with the one that follows. Are there any pairs of sentences that express closely related ideas that would be strengthened by being combined into one sentence using a semicolon?
>
> 2. Make sure semicolons are used only between independent clauses or between items in a series. If you have used a semicolon between an independent clause and a dependent clause or a phrase, change it to a comma. If you have used a semicolon before the *first* item in a series, change it to a colon.
>
> 3. Are semicolons used to separate more than three independent clauses in a sentence or to separate clauses in more than two consecutive sentences? If so, would making some clauses into separate sentences sound smoother or less monotonous?

EXERCISE 30.4

Revise each of the following sentences to correct the misuse of semicolons.

> *The new system would encourage high school students to take more academic*
>
> *courses⟋ thus strengthening college preparation.*

1. We accept the following forms of payment; cash, check, or credit card.
2. If the North had followed up its victory at Gettysburg more vigorously; the Civil War might have ended sooner.
3. He left a large estate; which was used to endow a scholarship fund.
4. Our uniforms were unbelievably dingy; stained from being splattered with food and often torn here and there.
5. Verbal scores have decreased more than 54 points; while math scores have decreased more than 36.

EXERCISE 30.4: Answers

1. We accept the following forms of payment: cash, check, or credit card.
2. If the North had followed up its victory at Gettysburg more vigorously, the Civil War might have ended sooner.
3. He left a large estate, which was used to endow a scholarship fund.
4. Our uniforms were unbelievably dingy, stained from being constantly splattered with food and often torn here and there.
5. Verbal scores have decreased more than 54 points, while math scores have decreased more than 36.

30e

Using semicolons with quotation marks

Ordinarily, a semicolon goes *outside* closing quotation marks.

Jackson's most famous story is "The Lottery"; it is a horrifying allegory about the power of tradition and the search for scapegoats.

OPTIONAL EXERCISE

The writer of the following paragraph chose not to use any semicolons, although there are several places where she might have. Ask students to read the paragraph carefully to find at least two such places and then decide whether they would have used a semicolon.

> It is appropriate, I think, that Bob's Surplus has a communal dressing room. I used to shop only in places where I could count on a private dressing room with a mirror inside. My impulse then was to hide my weaknesses. Now I believe in sharing them. There are other women in the dressing room at Bob's Surplus trying on blue jeans who look as bad as I do. We take comfort from one another. Sometimes a woman will ask me which of two items looks better. I always give a definite answer. It's the least I can do. I figure we are all in this together, and I emerge from the dressing room not only with a new pair of jeans but with a renewed sense of belonging to a human community. —PHYLLIS ROSE, "Shopping and Other Spiritual Adventures"

EXERCISE 30.5: Answers will vary.

EXERCISE 30.5 Reading with an Eye for Semicolons

In the following paragraph, Annie Dillard describes a solar eclipse in elaborate detail, using semicolons to separate each part of her description. Read the paragraph with attention to the use of semicolons. What different effect would the paragraph have if Dillard had used periods instead of semicolons? Imagine also if she had used commas and coordinating conjunctions. What is the effect of all the semicolons?

> You see the wide world swaddled in darkness; you see a vast breadth of hilly land, and an enormous, distant, blackened valley; you see towns' lights, a river's path, and blurred portions of your hat and scarf; you see your husband's face looking like an early black-and-white film; and you see a sprawl of black sky and blue sky together, with unfamiliar stars in it, some barely visible bands of cloud, and over there, a small white ring. The ring is as small as one goose in a flock of migrating geese—if you happen to notice a flock of migrating geese. It is one 360th part of the visible sky. The sun we see is less than half the diameter of a dime held at arm's length. — ANNIE DILLARD, "Solar Eclipse"

EXERCISE 30.6 Taking Inventory: Semicolons

Think of something you might take five or ten minutes to observe—a football game, a brewing storm, an ant awkwardly carrying a crumb—and write a paragraph describing your observations point by point and using semicolons to separate each point, as Annie Dillard does in the paragraph above. When you have finished, look at the way you used semicolons. Are there places where a period or a comma and a coordinating conjunction would better serve your meaning? Revise appropriately. What can you conclude about effective ways of using semicolons? If you keep a writing log, record your thoughts there, along with any interesting examples you found.

31

Using End Punctuation

A period, question mark, or exclamation point tells readers they have reached the end of one unit of thought and can pause and take a mental breath before moving on to the next one. As a writer, you are most often guided by meaning in your choice of end punctuation. Sometimes, however, you can use it for special effect. Look, for instance, at the way end punctuation guides readers in the following three sentences:

> Am I tired.
> Am I tired?
> Am I tired!

The end punctuation tells us how to read each sentence: the first as a dry, matter-of-fact statement; the second as a puzzled or perhaps ironic query; the last as a note of exasperation. This chapter will explain how you can use these three kinds of end punctuation.

Everyday use

We see periods, question marks, and exclamation points constantly in advertising, often used to create special effects. Look at the following ads, and consider how each one would be different without these marks:

Toshiba laptops: the desktop alternative.

Get Microsoft Word now, and receive this kit FREE!

So you think you can't afford a new PC?

Look for some ads that use these marks of punctuation for special effect, and bring them into class to compare with those of your classmates.

TEACHING PRACTICE

In order to use end punctuation of any kind, the student must first have a sense of what a sentence is. As Mina Shaughnessy points out in *Errors & Expectations,* end punctuation requires "a familiarity with the sentence as a grammatical unit and with the process whereby simple sentences are enlarged so as to include various types of subordinate structures" (27). Beginning writers will have been producing sentences orally for a long time before they come to produce them in writing, but writing is an abstract operation, not a natural operation like speaking. We speak, producing whole thoughts in subjects and predicates, without reflection; writing requires a great deal of reflecting on what we are doing. Thus, you may want to review the handbook chapter on sentence production (Chapter 7).

You may also encounter "a psychological resistance to the period" (Shaughnessy 18). The period imposes an end to the thought that the student may have had difficulty in beginning. The period tells the writer that he or she must begin again, a task that the inexperienced writer may find fearful.

Also, students sometimes become overly concerned with end punctuation. Shaughnessy believes that such concern suggests a perception of the sentence as a whole unit that ought not to be divided or modified in any way.

USEFUL READING

Shaughnessy, Mina. *Errors & Expectations: A Guide for the Teacher of Basic Writing.* New York: Oxford UP, 1977. Chapter 2, "Handwriting and Punctuation," focuses on end punctuation.

Thomas, Lewis. "Notes on Punctuation." *New England Journal of Medicine* 296 (1977): 1103–05. This witty personal essay is remarkable for its erudition—perhaps more so because it is written by a medical researcher (turned essayist) and published originally in a medical journal.

EXERCISE 31.1: Answers will vary.

For many beginning writers, the need to mark off sentences inhibits the progress of their thoughts. In speech, they can produce sentences as easily and unconsciously as they can walk; in writing, they must stop to deliberate over what is and what is not a sentence.

— MINA SHAUGHNESSY

EXERCISE 31.1

Imagine that you work for a company that is preparing to launch a new product. First decide what the product is—some sort of food or drink, an automobile, the latest laptop computer, or something else—and what its name should be. Then write a headline and some copy for the product's first advertisement. Note the way you have used periods, question marks, and exclamation points, and compare your advertisement with those of several classmates.

Using periods

Use a period to close sentences that make statements or give mild commands.

> All I know about grammar is its infinite power.
>
> — JOAN DIDION, "Why I Write"

> Never use a foreign phrase, a scientific word or a jargon word if you can think of an everyday English equivalent.
>
> — GEORGE ORWELL, "Politics and the English Language"

A period also closes indirect questions, which report rather than ask questions.

> I asked how old the child was.
>
> We all wonder who will win the election.
>
> Many parents ask if autism is an inherited disorder.

In American English, periods are also used with most abbreviations:

Mr.	Jr.	Ph.D.
Ms.	B.C.	M.D.
Mrs.	A.D.	M.B.A.
A.M./a.m.	ibid.	R.N.
P.M./p.m.	Dr.	Sen.

Some abbreviations do not require periods. Among them are the two-capital-letter postal abbreviations of state names, such as *FL* and *TN* (though note that the traditional abbreviations of state names, such as *Fla.* or *Tenn.,* do call for periods), and most groups of initials that are pronounced separately or as words (*GE, CIA, PCB, AIDS, SALT, UNICEF*). If you are not sure whether a particular abbreviation should include periods, check a dictionary. (See Chapter 36 for more information about abbreviations.)

EXERCISE 31.2

Revise each of the following sentences, inserting periods in appropriate places. Example:

Ms. Maria Jordan received both a Ph.D. in chemistry and an M.Ed.

1. Please attend the meeting on Tuesday at 10 AM in the Board Room
2. Cicero was murdered in 43 BC
3. "What's the matter, Darryl?" I asked
4. She asked whether Operation PUSH had been founded by Jesse Jackson
5. A voluntary effort by the AMA could help contain hospital costs

31b

Using question marks

A question mark closes sentences that ask direct questions.

If you own things, what's their effect on you?
— E. M. FORSTER, "My Wood"

How would you feel if you became an incorrigible juvenile delinquent by proxy, at the age of fifty-five?
— LEWIS THOMAS, "On Cloning a Human Being"

Question marks do not close *indirect* questions, which report rather than ask questions. Indirect questions close with a period (see 31a).

She asked if I opposed his nomination.

Do not use a comma or period after a question mark that ends a direct quotation.

"Am I my brother's keeper?" Cain asked.
Cain asked, "Am I my brother's keeper?"

Polite requests phrased as questions can be followed by periods rather than question marks.

Would you please close the door.

Questions in a series may have question marks even when they are not separate sentences.

EXERCISE 31.2: Answers

1. Please attend the meeting on Tuesday at 10 A.M. in the Board Room.
2. Cicero was murdered in 43 B.C.
3. "What's the matter, Darryl?" I asked.
4. She asked whether Operation PUSH had been founded by Jesse Jackson.
5. A voluntary effort by the AMA could help contain hospital costs.

BACKGROUND

The question mark appeared in the eighth century. Lewis Thomas, in his "Notes on Punctuation," claims the question mark is not, "strictly speaking," a stop, but rather an "indicator of tone." Yet question marks also indicate grammatical meaning. A sentence like *Joseph danced the boogaloo* may be either declarative or interrogative, depending on the context.

Joseph danced the boogaloo.

Joseph danced the boogaloo?

John Wilson, in *The Elements of Punctuation* (Boston, 1856), describes the dual function of the question mark, along with the exclamation point, parenthesis, and dash.

They are rhetorical, so far as they help to exhibit the force and intensity of a style which is rhetorical in its structure; but they are also grammatical, because they often serve to indicate, in connection with other marks, the nature, construction, and sense of the passages in which they occur. (92)

The exclamation point has been variously called the note of admiration, the shriek of surprise, the astonisher or paralyzer, the period that blew its top. — GEORGE SUMMEY, JR.

I often confronted a difficult choice: should I go to practice? finish my homework? spend time with my friends?

A question mark in parentheses can be used to indicate that a writer is unsure about a date, figure, or word.

> Quintilian died in A.D. 95 (?).
> The meeting is on Oleonga (?) Street.

EXERCISE 31.3: Answers

1. Social scientists face difficult questions: should they use their knowledge to shape society? merely describe human behavior? try to do both?
2. Are people with so many possessions really happy?
3. "Can I play this?" asked Manuel.
4. Correct; indirect question.
5. The judge asked, "What is your verdict?"

EXERCISE 31.3

Revise each of the following sentences, adding question marks and substituting them for other punctuation where appropriate. One of the sentences does not require any question marks. Example:

> *She asked the travel agent, "What is the air fare to Greece/"*

1. Social scientists face difficult questions: should they use their knowledge to shape society, merely describe human behavior, try to do both.
2. Are people with so many possessions really happy.
3. "Can I play this" asked Manuel.
4. I looked at him and asked what his point was.
5. The judge asked, "What is your verdict."

BACKGROUND

The exclamation point was rarely used before the Renaissance. It differs fundamentally from the other two end punctuation marks. While the period and the question mark function grammatically (as well as "rhetorically"—that is, phonologically—in the case of the question mark), the exclamation point functions almost entirely to indicate a change in voice. While it does mark the end of a sentence, it does not do so always, and when it does, it could be replaced with a period or question mark.

31c

Using exclamation points

Exclamation points close sentences that show surprise or strong emotion: emphatic statements, interjections, and emphatic commands.

> In those few moments of geologic time will be the story of all that has happened since we became a nation. And what a story it will be!
> — JAMES RETTIE, "But a Watch in the Night"

> Ouch!

> Look out!

Use exclamation points very sparingly because they can distract your readers or suggest that you are exaggerating the importance of what you are saying. Do not, for instance, use them with mild interjections or to suggest sarcasm or criticism. In general, try to create emphasis through diction (see Chapter 27) and sentence structure (see 19a) rather than exclamation points.

Do not use a comma or a period after an exclamation mark that ends a direct quotation.

"We shall next be told," exclaims Seneca, "that the first shoemaker was a philosopher!"
— THOMAS BABINGTON MACAULAY, "Francis Bacon"

EXERCISE 31.4

Revise each of the following sentences, adding or deleting exclamation points where appropriate and removing any other unnecessary punctuation. Example:

Look out!* The tide is coming in fast*!*

1. This university is so large, so varied, that attempting to tell someone everything about it would take three years!
2. I screamed at Jamie, "You rat. You tricked me."
3. "This time we're starting early!," she shouted.
4. Stop, thief.
5. Oh, no. A flash flood warning.

 Checking your use of end punctuation

1. Go through your draft, looking to see how many sentences end with periods. If you find that all or almost all of them do, see if any of them might be more effective phrased as questions or exclamations.
2. Have you used any exclamation points? If so, consider carefully whether they are justified. Does the sentence actually call for extra emphasis? If in doubt, use a period instead.

EXERCISE 31.5 Revising for End Punctuation

Look at the passage by Tom Wolfe that opens Chapter 34, and you will see that Wolfe has punctuated it as one very long sentence. Revise the sentence by breaking it into several shorter ones, using periods, question marks, and exclamation points to try to achieve the same rhythm that Wolfe has. Change the wording as necessary but as little as possible.

EXERCISE 31.4: Suggested Answers

1. This university is so large, so varied, that attempting to tell someone everything about it would take three years.
2. I screamed at Jamie, "You rat! You tricked me!"
3. Correct.
4. Stop, thief!
5. Oh no! A flash flood warning!

BACKGROUND

Attitudes toward the exclamation point have ranged from disgust to simple tolerance. Rarely has anyone exclaimed the praises of the exclamation point. At best, commentators describe it neutrally, as did the author of *A Treatise of Stops, Points, or Pauses* in 1680, calling it "a Note of Admiration, wondering, or crying out." Typically, we encounter descriptions like that of George Summey, Jr., who notes that, at the time he was writing *American Punctuation* (1949), typewriters did not possess exclamation point keys. Instead, the mark was made by striking a period, backspacing, and then striking an apostrophe. Summey calls this procedure "more trouble than the mark is likely to be worth" (90).

EXERCISE 31.5: Answers will vary.

EXERCISE 31.6: Answers will vary.

EXERCISE 31.6   Reading with an Eye for End Punctuation

Consider the use of end punctuation in the following paragraph. Then experiment with changing some of the end punctuation. What would be the effect of deleting the exclamation point from the quotation by Cicero or of changing it to a question mark? What would be the effect of changing Cicero's question to a statement?

> To be admired and praised, especially by the young, is an autumnal pleasure enjoyed by the lucky ones (who are not always the most deserving). "What is more charming," Cicero observes in his famous essay *De Senectute,* "than an old age surrounded by the enthusiasm of youth! . . . Attentions which seem trivial and conventional are marks of honor—the morning call, being sought after, precedence, having people rise for you, being escorted to and from the forum. . . . What pleasures of the body can be compared to the prerogatives of influence?" But there are also pleasures of the body, or the mind, that are enjoyed by a greater number of older persons.
> — MALCOLM COWLEY, *The View from 80*

EXERCISE 31.7   Taking Inventory: End Punctuation

Look through something you have written recently, noting its end punctuation. Using the guidelines on p. 465, see if your use of end punctuation follows any patterns. Try revising the end punctuation in a paragraph or two to emphasize (or de-emphasize) some point. What conclusions can you draw about ways of using end punctuation to draw attention to (or away from) a sentence? If you keep a writing log, put your thoughts there for future use.

32

Using Apostrophes

As a mark of the possessive case, the punctuation mark we call the apostrophe has an unusual history. In Old English, the endings of nouns changed depending on their grammatical function—a noun used as a subject, for example, had a different ending from the same noun used as a direct object. By the fourteenth century, Middle English had dropped most of this complicated system except for possessive and plural endings: *Haroldes* (or *Haroldis* or *Haroldys*) *sword* was still used to mean "the sword of Harold." Then, in the sixteenth century, scholars concluded that the ending *-es* and its variant forms were actually contractions of *his*. Believing that *Haroldes sword* meant "Harold his sword," they began using an apostrophe instead of the *e: Harold's sword*.

Even though this theory was later discredited, the possessive ending retained the apostrophe because it was a useful way to distinguish between possessive and plural forms in writing. Today, we use the apostrophe primarily to signal possessive case, contractions and other omissions of words and letters, and certain plural forms. This chapter presents the conventions governing its use.

BACKGROUND

One of the difficulties in teaching students to use apostrophes is tied to the differences between speaking and writing. Our students will often omit apostrophes in writing because they do not hear them in oral discourse. Though it can be argued that indeed we *do* hear some punctuation (through intonation, rhythm, pauses, and breathing), the apostrophe is decidedly "silent"; based on sound alone, there is no way to distinguish *cant* from *can't, isnt* from *isn't, Joes* from *Joe's*. A student may be very adept at spoken discourse (as most are), but less practiced with the conventions of written English and, hence, have difficulty remembering to insert apostrophes.

USEFUL READING

Hashimoto, Irwin. "Pain and Suffering: Apostrophes and Academic Life." *Journal of Basic Writing* 7.2 (1988): 91–98. Hashimoto humorously discusses students' frequent problems with apostrophes. He places "a large chunk of the blame" on a handbook tradition that leads us to look for simple, clear rules and overlook "the ugly truth" that the rules for apostrophes are really quite messy.

32a

Using apostrophes to signal possessive case

The possessive case denotes ownership or possession of one thing by another (see Chapter 8). Use an apostrophe to form the possessive case of nouns and indefinite pronouns—*Fran's coat, nobody's fault*.

> *Everyday use*
>
> *The little apostrophe can sometimes make a big difference in meaning. A friend of ours found that out when he agreed to look after a new neighbor's apartment while she was out of town for a few days. "I'll leave instructions on the kitchen counter," the neighbor said as she gave him her key. Here are the instructions he found: "(1) Please water the plants in the living room—once will be fine. (2) The cat's food is on the counter. Once a day on the patio, please. Thanks. I'll see you Friday."*
>
> *Because the note said* cat's, *he expected one cat—and when he saw one, he put it and the food outside on the patio. When the neighbor returned, she found one healthy cat—and a second, very weak one that had hidden under the bed. The difference between* cat's *and* cats' *in this instance almost cost his neighbor a cat.*

BACKGROUND

Although there is some disagreement over adding just an apostrophe rather than an apostrophe and -s to singular nouns ending in -s, the most authoritative sources on usage recommend using an apostrophe and an -s with all singular nouns, including those words ending with -s. Here are some additional examples.

Nogales's hot and dry summers

Cass's research into the squash melon

the *princess's* last visit

Exceptions, however, are proper names that end in a "eez" sound—often Greek or hellenized names.

Aristophanes' comedies

B. F. Yerkes' research

1

Forming the possessive case of singular nouns and indefinite pronouns

Add an apostrophe and -s to form the possessive of most singular nouns, including those that end in -s, and of indefinite pronouns.

John Wayne's first westerns are considered classics.

The reading list included *Keats's* poem.

Anyone's guess is as good as mine.

Apostrophes are *not* used with the possessive forms of *personal* pronouns: *yours, his, hers, its, ours, theirs.*

2

Forming the possessive case of plural nouns

For plural nouns not ending in -s, add an apostrophe and -s.

Robert Bly helped to popularize the *men's* movement.

The *children's* first Christmas was spent in Wales.

For plural nouns ending in -s, add only the apostrophe.

The *clowns'* costumes were bright green and orange.

Fifty dollars' worth of groceries filled only two shopping bags.

3

Forming the possessive case of compound words

For compound words, make the last word in the group possessive.

The *secretary of state's* speech was televised.
Her *daughters-in-law's* birthdays both fall in July.
My *in-laws'* disapproval dampened his enthusiasm for the new house.

4

Forming the possessive case with two or more nouns

To signal individual possession by two or more owners, make each noun possessive.

There are great differences between *John Wayne's* and *Henry Fonda's* westerns. [Wayne and Fonda appeared in different westerns.]

To signal joint possession, make only the last noun possessive.

MacNeil and Lehrer's program focuses on issues.

 Checking for possessive apostrophes

1. Circle all the nouns that end in -*s*. Then, check each one that shows ownership or possession to see that each has an apostrophe in the right place, either before or after the -*s*.
2. Then underline all the indefinite pronouns, such as *someone* and *nobody*. (See 7b3 for a list.) Any that end in -*s* should have an apostrophe before the -*s*.

EXERCISE 32.1

Write a brief paragraph, beginning "I've always been amused by my neighbor's _____." Then, go through your paragraph, noting every use of an apostrophe.

EXERCISE 32.2

Complete each of the following sentences by inserting 's or an apostrophe alone to form the possessive case of the italicized words.

EXERCISE 32.1: Answers will vary.

EXERCISE 32.2: Answers

1. Grammar is *everybody's* favorite subject.
2. *Malcolm Forbes's* flamboyant lifestyle celebrated his wealth.
3. I was having a good time at *P.J.'s*, but my friends wanted to go to *Sunny's*.
4. *Carol and Jim's* income dropped drastically after Jim lost his job.
5. Parents often question their *children's* choice of friends.
6. Many smokers disregard the *surgeon general's* warnings.
7. The restaurant management took a percentage of *everyone's* tips.
8. The *governors'* attitudes changed after the convention.
9. This dog has a *beagle's* ears and a *St. Bernard's* nose and feet.
10. *My friend's* and my *brother's* cars have the same kind of stereo system.

BACKGROUND

Typically, contractions have a less formal tone than the combined words written out in full. As a general rule, writers are probably wise to limit the use of contractions in formal settings, including letters of application, business letters, legal documents, and papers for college courses. Yet even in formal contexts, contractions may sometimes be appropriate where the alternative would sound overly contrived. The rhetorical considerations of purpose, content, context, and audience should guide the writer's use of contractions. Fred Astaire would have sounded somewhat stiff singing "Is it not romantic?" while Abraham Lincoln would have struck an incongruously chatty tone had he said, "With firmness in the right, as God gives us to see the right, let's strive on to finish the work we're in."

1. Grammar is *everybody* favorite subject.
2. *Malcolm Forbes* flamboyant lifestyle celebrated his wealth.
3. I was having a good time at *P.J.*, but my friends wanted to go to *Sunny*.
4. *Carol and Jim* income dropped drastically after Jim lost his job.
5. Parents often question their *children* choice of friends.
6. Many smokers disregard the *surgeon general* warnings.
7. The restaurant management took a percentage of *everyone* tips.
8. The *governors* attitudes changed after the convention.
9. This dog has a *beagle* ears and a *St. Bernard* nose and feet.
10. *My friend and my brother* cars have the same kind of stereo system.

32b

Using apostrophes to signal contractions and other omissions

Contractions are two-word combinations formed by leaving out certain letters, which are indicated by apostrophes. For example:

it is/it's	would not/wouldn't
was not/wasn't	do not/don't
I am/I'm	does not/doesn't
he is, he has/he's	will not/won't
you will/you'll	let us/let's
I would/I'd	who is, who has/who's
he would/he'd	cannot/can't

Contractions are common in conversation and informal writing. Most academic work, however, calls for greater formality.

Distinguishing it's *and* its

Do not confuse the possessive pronoun *its* with the contraction *it's*. *Its* is the possessive form of *it*. *It's* is a contraction for *it is*.

This disease is unusual; *its* symptoms vary from person to person.
It's a difficult disease to diagnose.

(See 24b for other commonly confused pairs of possessive pronouns and contractions—*their/they're, whose/who's,* and *your/you're*.)

Checking for misuse of its *and* it's

1. Circle each *its*. Check to see that it shows possession; if not, add an apostrophe before the *s*.
2. Check each *it's*. Does it mean "it is"? If not, remove the apostrophe.

USEFUL READING

Flesch, Rudolf. *The ABC of Style: A Guide to Plain English*. New York: Harper, 1964. See pp. 29–30 on the use of contractions in writing.

Signaling omissions

An apostrophe signals omissions in some common phrases:

ten of the clock	rock and roll	class of 1992
ten o'clock	rock 'n' roll	class of '92

In addition, writers can use an apostrophe to signal omitted letters in approximating the sound of speech or some specific dialect. Note the way Mark Twain uses the apostrophe to form contractions and signal omitted letters in the following passage, in which Huckleberry Finn tells Jim about King Henry the Eighth.

> S'pose people left money laying around where he was—what did he do? He collared it. S'pose he contracted to do a thing; and you paid him, and didn't set down there and see that he done it—what did he do? He always done the other thing. S'pose he opened his mouth—what then? If he didn't shut it up powerful quick, he'd lose a lie, every time. That's the kind of a bug Henry was; and if we'd 'a' had him along 'stead of our kings, he'd 'a' fooled that town a heap worse than ourn done.
> — MARK TWAIN, *The Adventures of Huckleberry Finn*

32c

Using apostrophes to form the plural of numbers, letters, symbols, and words used as terms

An apostrophe and *-s* are used to form the plural of numbers, letters, symbols, and words referred to as such.

The gymnasts need marks of *8*'s and *9*'s to qualify for the finals.

Many *Ph.D.*'s cannot find jobs as college teachers.

The computer prints *e*'s whenever there is an error in the program.

I marked special passages with a series of three ***'s.

The five *Shakespeare*'s in the essay were spelled five different ways.

Note that numbers, letters, and words referred to as words are usually italicized; but the plural ending is not, as in the examples above.

The plural of years can be written with or without the apostrophe (*1990's* or *1990s*). Whichever style you follow, be consistent.

EXERCISE 32.3: Answers

1. There was a big revival at my Auntie *Reed's* church.

2. I heard the songs and the minister saying: "Why *don't* you come?"

3. Finally Westley said to me in a whisper: "*I'm* tired *o'* sitting here. *Let's* get up and be saved."

4. So I decided that maybe to save further trouble, *I'd* better lie. . . .

5. That night, . . . I cried, in bed alone, and *couldn't* stop.

EXERCISE 32.4: Answers will vary.

TEACHING PRACTICE

Ask students to practice reading this rhyme aloud, first with all the contractions written out and omitted letters restored and then as Hurston wrote it. Ask them then to work together to describe the difference, considering, for example, which version sounds more like speech and which version sounds more formal.

EXERCISE 32.3

The following sentences, from which all apostrophes have been deleted, appear in Langston Hughes's "Salvation." Insert apostrophes where appropriate. Example:

> *"Sister Reed, what is this child's name?"*

1. There was a big revival at my Auntie Reeds church.

2. I heard the songs and the minister saying: "Why dont you come?"

3. Finally Westley said to me in a whisper: "Im tired o sitting here. Lets get up and be saved."

4. So I decided that maybe to save further trouble, Id better lie. . . .

5. That night, . . . I cried, in bed alone, and couldnt stop.

EXERCISE 32.4 Reading with an Eye for Apostrophes

In the following rhyme, Zora Neale Hurston uses apostrophes to form contractions and signal omitted letters. They help create the rhythms and cadences of a spoken dialect. To get a sense of how the apostrophes have this effect, try reading the lines aloud with the missing letters filled in.

> Ah got up 'bout half-past fo'
> Forty fo' robbers wuz 'round mah do'
> Ah got up and let 'em in
> Hit 'em ovah de head wid uh rollin' pin.
> —ZORA NEALE HURSTON, *Jonah's Gourd Vine*

EXERCISE 32.5 Taking Inventory: Apostrophes

As a tool for presenting contractions and omitted letters, apostrophes play a larger role in informal writing than in formal writing. One thing that many students need to learn is to write with few or no contractions, a task that requires some effort because we all use contractions in conversation. To get an idea of the difference between spoken and written language, try transcribing a "paragraph" or so of your own spoken words. Make a point of using apostrophes whenever you use a contraction or otherwise omit a letter. Look over your paragraph to see how many apostrophes you used, and then revise the piece to make it more formal, eliminating all or most apostrophes. Can you draw any conclusions about ways you should and should not use apostrophes? Note down any thoughts you have—in your writing log, if you keep one.

33

Using Quotation Marks

BACKGROUND

Lewis Thomas offers the following advice for using quotation marks: (1) quote exact words; (2) do not string together thoughts that the author did not intend to be connected; (3) do not use quotation marks to qualify ideas that you would like to disown; (4) do not put them around clichés to avoid your responsibility in using them.

USEFUL READING

Shaughnessy, Mina. *Errors & Expectations: A Guide for the Teacher of Basic Writing.* New York: Oxford UP, 1977. See Chapter 2, an insightful discussion of punctuation. In particular, Shaughnessy claims that basic writers rarely use quotation marks.

Thomas, Lewis. "Notes on Punctuation." *New England Journal of Medicine* 296 (1977): 1103–05.

"By necessity, by proclivity,—and by delight, we all quote," wrote Ralph Waldo Emerson. Quotation marks, which tell readers that certain words were spoken or written by someone other than the writer, have been a convention of written English since before the time of the printing press. As printing techniques evolved and became standardized, quotation marks came to signal not only direct quotations but also certain titles, definitions, and words used ironically or invented by the writer. This chapter presents the conventions governing their use.

33a

Using quotation marks to signal direct quotation

In written American English, double quotation marks signal a direct quotation.

> Bush called for a "kinder, gentler" America.

> He smiled and said, "Son, this is one incident that I will never forget."

Single quotation marks enclose a quotation within a quotation. Open and close the passage you are quoting with double quotation marks, and change any quotation marks that appear *within* the quotation to single quotation marks.

> In "The Uses of the Blues," Baldwin says, "The title 'The Uses of the Blues' does not refer to music; I don't know anything about music."

Do not use quotation marks for *indirect* quotations, which do not use someone's exact words.

> Father smiled and said that he would never forget the incident.

1
Quoting longer passages

If the passage you wish to quote exceeds four typed lines, set it off from the rest of the text by starting it on a new line and indenting each line ten spaces from the left margin. This format, known as **block quotation**, does not require quotation marks.

> In *Winged Words: American Indian Writers Speak,* Leslie Marmon Silko describes her early education, saying:
> > I learned to love reading, and love books, and the printed page, and therefore was motivated to learn to write. The best thing . . . you can have in life is to have someone tell you a story . . . but in lieu of that . . . I learned at an early age to find comfort in a book, that a book would talk to me when no one else would.

2
Quoting poetry

The same general rules apply to quoting poetry as to quoting prose. If the quotation is brief (fewer than four lines), include it within your text, enclosed in double quotation marks. Separate the lines of the poem with slashes, each preceded and followed by a space.

> In one of his best-known poems, Robert Frost remarks, "Two roads diverged in a yellow wood, and I— / I took the one less traveled by / And that has made all the difference."

If the poetic quotation is longer, start it on a new line, indent each line ten spaces from the left margin, and do not use quotation marks.

> The duke in Robert Browning's "My Last Duchess" is clearly a jealous, vain person, whose arrogance is illustrated through his statement:
> > She thanked men—good! but thanked
> > Somehow—I know not how—as if she ranked
> > My gift of a nine-hundred-years-old name
> > With anybody's gift.

When you quote poetry, take care to follow the indentation, spacing, capitalization, punctuation, and other features of the original passage.

EXERCISE 33.1

Quoting someone else's words can contribute authority and texture to your writing, adding other voices and images to your own. See how Gretel Ehrlich uses a quotation in the following passage about Wyoming:

BACKGROUND

As a general rule, a writer can decide whether or not to use a comma or colon before a quotation by reading aloud the sentence or passage containing the quotation. If the quotation follows smoothly from the text that precedes it, no comma or colon is necessary. For instance, the quotation in the following sentence needs no comma or colon:

> Mannes argues that television commercials "contribute to the diminution of human worth and the fragmenting of our psyches."

However, if the quoted words do not fit syntactically into the larger sentence, then they should be preceded by a comma or colon, as in the following sentence:

> When Ralph Waldo Emerson was asked to take part in directly promoting abolition, he said: "I have my own spirits in prison—spirits in deeper prisons—whom no man visits if I do not."

EXERCISE 33.1: Answers will vary.

Most characteristic of the state's landscape is what a developer euphemistically describes as "indigenous growth right up to your front door"—a reference to waterless stands of salt sage, snakes, jackrabbits, deerflies, red dust, a brief respite of wildflowers, dry washes, and no trees.

—GRETEL EHRLICH, *The Solace of Open Spaces*

Spend a few minutes reading a newspaper or magazine to find an article of interest on a topic you know something about. Then, write a paragraph of your own about that topic, quoting the article at least once. Choose something worded in a very memorable way or someone whose voice will lend weight to your own words. Finally, check your use of quotation marks against the guidelines in this chapter.

33b

Using quotation marks to signal dialogue

When you write dialogue or quote a conversation, enclose the words of each speaker in quotation marks, and mark each shift in speaker by beginning a new paragraph, no matter how brief the quoted remark may be.

> "But I can see you're bound to come," said his father. "Only we ain't going to catch us no fish, because there ain't no water left to catch 'em in."
> "The river!"
> "All but dry."
> "You been many times already?"
> "Son, this is my first time this year."
>
> — EUDORA WELTY, "Ladies in Spring"

Everyday use

Some people seem to find quotation marks so visually appealing that they use them as a kind of verbal makeup, dabbing them in anywhere they feel a word or phrase could use a bit of sprucing up. Like cosmetics, though, quotation marks can have unfortunate effects if applied too freely. What is the effect of the quotation marks in the following advertisements?

On a movie marquee: Coming "Attractions"

In a supermarket: "Fresh" Asparagus

Look around you for similar misguided uses of quotation marks, and bring them to class for comparison with those found by your classmates.

FOR COLLABORATIVE WORK

Divide the class into groups of three. Using one of the following sentences as an opener, have two members of each group take on the roles involved and produce a dialogue. The third person of the group records the dialogue, and together afterwards, they decide on how it should be punctuated.

1. One roommate asks the other, "What should we do tonight?"

2. One sibling says to the other, "Oh no you don't."

3. As I turned the corner, I heard someone say "Stop right there."

Beginning a new paragraph with each change in speaker helps readers follow the dialogue. In the Welty example on the previous page, we know when the father is speaking and when the son is speaking without the author's having to repeat "said his father" and so on.

33c

Using quotation marks to signal titles and definitions

Quotation marks are used to enclose the titles of short poems, short stories, articles, essays, songs, sections of books, and episodes of television and radio programs.

- "Dover Beach" moves from calmness to sadness. [poem]

  Alice Walker's "Everyday Use" is about more than just quilts. [short story]

  In "The Iks," Lewis Thomas describes a small tribe in Uganda. [essay]

  Both the *Atlantic* and the *New York Review of Books* carried articles entitled "Illiberal Education." [articles]

  In the chapter "Complexion," Rodriguez describes his sensitivity about his skin color. [section of book]

Use italics rather than quotation marks for the titles of longer works, such as books and magazines (see 37a). Do not use either for the titles of your own writing, unless your title is or includes another title or a quotation.

Definitions are sometimes set off with quotation marks.

The French phrase *idée fixe* means literally "fixed idea."

33d

Using quotation marks to signal irony and coinages

One way of showing readers that you are using a word or a phrase ironically is to enclose it in quotation marks.

The "banquet" consisted of dried-out chicken and canned vegetables. [The quotation marks around the word *banquet* suggest that the meal was anything but a banquet.]

Quotation marks are also used to enclose words or phrases made up by the writer, as is *forebirth* in the following example.

FOR COLLABORATIVE WORK

Divide the class into groups of three, and ask each group to compose a one- or two-page passage that includes as many of the following as possible: direct quotations, quotations within quotations, dialogue, titles, definitions, and special-emphasis words or phrases.

Your whole first paragraph or first page may have to be guillotined in any case after your piece is finished: it is a kind of "forebirth."

— JACQUES BARZUN, "A Writer's Discipline"

EXERCISE 33.2

Revise each of the following sentences, using quotation marks appropriately to signal titles, definitions, irony, or coinages.

1. Kowinski uses the term mallaise to mean physical and psychological disturbances caused by mall contact.
2. In Flannery O'Connor's short story Revelation, colors symbolize passion, violence, sadness, and even God.
3. The little that is known about gorillas certainly makes you want to know more, writes Alan Moorehead in his essay A Most Forgiving Ape.
4. The fun of surgery begins before the operation ever takes place.
5. Wolfe's article Radical Chic satirized wealthy liberals.
6. Big Bill, the first section of Dos Passos's *U.S.A.*, opens with a birth.
7. Amy Lowell challenges social conformity in her poem Patterns.
8. Pink Floyd's song Time depicts the impact of technology on society.
9. My dictionary defines *isolation* as the quality or state of being alone.
10. In the episode Driven to Extremes, *48 Hours* takes a humorous look at driving in New York City.

Checking for misused quotation marks

Use quotation marks only when there is a reason for them. Do not use them just to emphasize particular words or phrases, as in the following sentence.

MISUSED   Some of the boys, not including Travis, of course, would take "stingers" off wasps and bees and then put the insects "down" others' shirts.

REVISED   Some of the boys, not including Travis, of course, would take stingers off wasps and bees and then put the insects down others' shirts.

Do not use quotation marks around slang or colloquial language that you think is inappropriate for formal register (see 27e3); they create the

---

EXERCISE 33.2: Answers

1. Kowinski uses the term "mallaise" to mean physical and psychological disturbances caused by mall contact.
2. In Flannery O'Connor's short story "Revelation," colors symbolize passion, violence, sadness, and even God.
3. "The little that is known about gorillas certainly makes you want to know more," writes Alan Moorehead in his essay "A Most Forgiving Ape."
4. The "fun" of surgery begins before the operation ever takes place.
5. Wolfe's article "Radical Chic" satirized wealthy liberals.
6. "Big Bill," the first section of Dos Passos's *U.S.A.,* opens with a birth.
7. Amy Lowell challenges social conformity in her poem "Patterns."
8. Pink Floyd's song "Time" depicts the impact of technology on society.
9. My dictionary defines *isolation* as "the quality or state of being alone."
10. In the episode "Driven to Extremes," *48 Hours* takes a humorous look at driving in New York City.

BACKGROUND

Sir Ernest Gowers offers this advice on the overuse of quotation marks to indicate the irregular use of terms: "If the word is the right one, do not be ashamed of it: if it is the wrong one, do not use it."

impression that you are apologizing for using such language. In general, try to express your idea in formal language. If you have a good reason to use a slang or colloquial term, use it without quotation marks.

MISUSED   After their twenty-mile hike, the campers were "wiped out" and ready to "hit the sack."

REVISED   After their twenty-mile hike, the campers were exhausted and ready to go to bed.

33f

Using quotation marks with other punctuation

1

Periods and commas go *inside* closing quotation marks.

"Don't compromise yourself," said Janis Joplin, "you are all you've got."

2

Colons and semicolons go *outside* closing quotation marks.

Everything is dark, and "a visionary light settles in her eyes"; this vision, this light, is her salvation.

I felt only one emotion after finishing "Eveline": pity.

3

Question marks, exclamation points, and dashes go *inside* closing quotation marks if they are part of the quotation, *outside* if they are not.

PART OF QUOTATION

Gently shake the injured person while asking, "Are you all right?"

"Jump!" one of the firefighters shouted.

"Watch out—watch out for—" Jessica began nervously.

NOT PART OF QUOTATION

What is the theme of "The Birth-Mark"?

How tired she must be of hearing "God Save the Queen"!

"Break a leg"—that phrase is supposed to bring good luck to a performer.

4

Footnote numbers go *outside* closing quotation marks.

Tragedy is defined by Aristotle as "an imitation of an action that is serious and of a certain magnitude."[1]

(For more information on footnotes and for examples of quotation marks used with bibliographical references, see Chapters 43 and 44.)

⟩⟩ *Checking for quotation marks*

1. *Use quotation marks around*
   - direct quotations
   - titles of short works
2. *Do not use quotation marks around*
   - indirect quotations
   - titles of long works
   - words you want to emphasize
   - block quotations
3. *Check other punctuation used with closing quotation marks:*
   - periods and commas should be *inside* the marks
   - colons, semicolons, and footnote numbers should be *outside*
   - question marks, exclamation points, and dashes should be inside if they are part of the quoted material, outside if they are not

EXERCISE 33.3

Revise each of the following sentences, deleting quotation marks used inappropriately, moving those placed incorrectly, and using more formal language in place of slang expressions in quotation marks. Example:

> *In Herman Melville's "Bartleby the Scrivener" Bartleby states time and again "I would prefer not to."*

1. The grandmother in O'Connor's story shows she is still misguided when she says, "You've got good blood! I know you wouldn't shoot a lady"!
2. What is Hawthorne telling the readers in "Rappaccini's Daughter?"
3. You could hear the elation in her voice when she said, "We did it".

EXERCISE 33.3: Suggested Answers

1. The grandmother in O'Connor's story shows she is still misguided when she says, "You've got good blood! I know you wouldn't shoot a lady!"
2. What is Hawthorne telling the readers in "Rappaccini's Daughter"?
3. You could hear the elation in her voice when she said, "We did it."
4. This "typical American" is Ruby Turpin, who in the course of the story receives a message that brings about a change in her life.
5. Being overweight is a problem because excess pounds are hard to lose and can be dangerous to a person's health.

4. This "typical American" is Ruby Turpin, who in the course of the story receives a "message" that brings about a "change" in her life.

5. Being "overweight" is a problem because "excess pounds" are hard to lose and can be "dangerous" to a person's health.

6. One of Jackson's least-known stories is "Janice;" this story, like many of her others, leaves the reader shocked.

7. Macbeth "bumps off" Duncan to gain the throne for himself.

8. In his article "The Death of Broadway", Thomas M. Disch writes that "choreographers are, literally, a dying breed[1]".

9. "Know thyself—" this is the quest of the main characters in both Ibsen's *Peer Gynt* and Lewis's *Till We Have Faces.*

10. One thought flashed through my mind as I finished *"In Search of Our Mothers' Gardens:"* I want to read more of this writer's work.

6. One of Jackson's least-known stories is "Janice"; this story, like many of her others, leaves the reader shocked.

7. Macbeth murders Duncan to gain the throne for himself.

8. In his article "The Death of Broadway," Thomas M. Disch writes that "choreographers are, literally, a dying breed."[1]

9. "Know thyself"—this is the quest of the main characters in both Ibsen's *Peer Gynt* and Lewis's *Till We Have Faces.*

10. One thought flashed through my mind as I finished *In Search of Our Mothers' Gardens:* "I want to read more of this writer's work."

EXERCISE 33.4   Revising for Quotation Marks

Revise the following paragraph to use quotation marks appropriately.

In his poem "The Fly, William Blake uses the image of the poet as a fly to make a "profound statement" about the fragility of human life and thought. "Addressing" the fly, the poet regrets that "he has killed it as it was playing" and goes on to ask "whether he is not a fly, too": "For I dance, / And drink, & sing / Till some blind hand / Shall brush my wing." This image "echoes" Shakespeare's play *King Lear,* in which the character Gloucester says, "As flies to wanton boys are we to th' gods; / They kill us for their sport". Apparently, Blake is less "stressed out" by the thought of himself as a helpless "bug", since he concludes the poem, "Then am I / A happy fly, / If I live / Or if I die. But in his essay "Moral Vision in "The Fly"," Sylvester Pritchard argues that "Blake's closing image of death suggests a despair no less deep than that of Gloucester in his terrible blind sight[2]".

EXERCISE 33.5   Reading with an Eye for Quotation Marks

Read the following passage from an essay by Joan Didion about the painter Georgia O'Keeffe, paying particular attention to the use of quotation marks. What effect is created by Didion's use of quotation marks around the words *hardness, crustiness,* and *crusty*? How do the quotations by O'Keeffe help to support Didion's description of her?

"Hardness" has not been in our century a quality much admired in women, nor in the past twenty years has it even been in official favor for men. When

EXERCISE 33.4: Suggested Answers

In his poem "The Fly," William Blake uses the image of the poet as a fly to make a profound statement about the fragility of human life and thought. Addressing the fly, the poet regrets that he has killed it as it was playing and goes on to ask whether he is not a fly, too: "For I dance, / and drink, & sing / Till some blind hand / Shall brush my wing." This image echoes Shakespeare's play *King Lear,* in which the character Gloucester says, "As flies to wanton boys are we to th' gods; / They kill us for their sport." Apparently, Blake is less disturbed by the thought of himself as a helpless insect, since he concludes the poem, "Then am I / A happy fly, / If I live / Or if I die." But in his essay "Moral Vision in 'The Fly,'" Sylvester Pritchard argues that "Blake's closing image of death suggests a despair no less deep than that of Gloucester in his terrible blind sight."[2]

EXERCISE 33.5 Answers will vary.

hardness surfaces in the very old we tend to transform it into "crustiness" or eccentricity, some tonic pepperiness to be indulged at a distance. On the evidence of her work and what she has said about it, Georgia O'Keeffe is neither "crusty" nor eccentric. She is simply hard, a straight shooter, a woman clean of received wisdom and open to what she sees. This is a woman who could early on dismiss most of her contemporaries as "dreamy," and would later single out one she liked as "a very poor painter." (And then add, apparently by way of softening the judgment: "I guess he wasn't a painter at all. He had no courage and I believe that to create one's own world in any of the arts takes courage.") This is a woman who in 1939 could advise her admirers that they were missing her point, that their appreciation of her famous flowers was merely sentimental. "When I paint a red hill," she observed coolly in the catalogue for an exhibition that year, "you say it is too bad that I don't always paint flowers. A flower touches almost everyone's heart. A red hill doesn't touch everyone's heart."

— JOAN DIDION, "Georgia O'Keeffe"

EXERCISE 33.6 Taking Inventory: Quotation Marks

Choose a topic that is currently of interest to students on your campus, and interview one of your friends about it for ten or fifteen minutes. On the basis of your notes from the interview, write two or three paragraphs about your friend's views on the topic, using as many direct quotations as possible. Then look at what you have written to see how closely you followed the conventions for quotation marks that have been explained in this chapter. Note any usages that caused you problems—in your writing log, if you keep one.

FOR COLLABORATIVE WORK

Ask students to bring their interviews to class. Then ask them to work in pairs, trading interviews and reading them with special attention to use of quotation marks. Are they used accurately throughout? Are any uses of quotation marks confusing or unclear? What suggestions could they give each other for revision?

34

Using Other Punctuation Marks

Parentheses, brackets, dashes, colons, slashes, and ellipses are marks that allow writers to punctuate sentences so that readers can best understand their meaning. Following is a sentence that demonstrates the use of most of these punctuation marks.

> Likewise, "hassling"—mock dogfighting—was strictly forbidden, and so naturally young fighter jocks could hardly wait to go up in, say, a pair of F-100s and start the duel by making a pass at each other at 800 miles an hour, the winner being the pilot who could slip in behind the other one and get locked in on his [never *her* or *his or her!*] tail ("wax his tail"), and it was not uncommon for some eager jock to try too tight an outside turn and have his engine flame out, whereupon, unable to restart it, he has to eject . . . and he shakes his fist at the victor as he floats down by parachute and his million-dollar aircraft goes *kaboom!* on the palmetto grass or the desert floor, and he starts thinking about how he can get together with the other guy back at the base in time for the two of them to get their stories straight before the investigation: "I don't know what happened, sir. I was pulling up after a target run, and it just flamed out on me."
>
> — TOM WOLFE, *The Right Stuff*

Here Wolfe uses dashes, parentheses, an ellipsis, and a colon to create rhythm and build momentum in a very long (178-word) sentence that starts with a definition of *hassling* set off by dashes and builds to the pilot's "story" after the colon: "I don't know what happened, sir." The editorial comment inserted in brackets calls attention to the fact that the "right stuff" was, in the world Wolfe describes, always male. This chapter will guide you in deciding when to use these marks of punctuation to signal relationships among sentence parts, to create particular rhythms, and to help readers follow your thoughts.

BACKGROUND

Parentheses, brackets, dashes, and slashes developed well after the technology of the written word first appeared, but the colon was one of the first punctuation marks used. Since most discourse was oral rather than written, punctuation evolved to mark places where speakers paused or breathed rather than grammatical units. The first system of punctuation, created by Aristophanes in the second century B.C., used only three marks: the period, colon, and comma. Six centuries later, St. Jerome (A.D. 400) punctuated his translation of the Vulgate Bible using a rhetorical system of colons and commas to mark breathing points. The elocutionary nature of punctuation developed further during the tenth to thirteenth centuries with the addition of marks to denote places where the speakers should raise their voices (the *punctus elevatus, punctus interrogativus,* and *punctus circumflexus*) and confirmed the use of the colon as a breathing stop, particularly between verses of the Psalms. However, over time, written discourse became less connected to oral discourse, especially after the invention of printing, and punctuation began to take on more rhetorical or grammatical functions. Parentheses, brackets, dashes, and slashes function primarily to indicate grammatical divisions. Parentheses began to appear around 1500, and dashes by 1700, but the slash (also called a virgule or solidus) has been with us a little longer. Virgules first appeared in the thirteenth and fourteenth centuries as a form of light stop; after about 1450 the virgule, which was originally placed high, began to appear on the base line and developed a curve. Today we know this mark as a comma.

EXERCISE 34.1: Answers will vary.

BACKGROUND

The term *parentheses* derives from the classical Greek figure of speech *parenthesis,* which denotes the act of inserting a verbal unit (a word, phrase, or sentence) into a position that interrupts the sentence flow. Such material can be punctuated with dashes or commas as well as with parentheses.

Everyday use

Though you may never have paid much attention to them before, parentheses, brackets, dashes, colons, slashes, and ellipses are all around us. Pick up the TV Guide, *for instance, and you will find all those punctuation marks in abundance, helping viewers preview programs in the most clear and efficient way possible. For example:*

9 PM Movie (CC)—▶Biography: 2 hrs. A thoughtful screenplay by *China Beach* creator John Sacret Young and a moving performance by Raul Julia distinguish "Romero," a fact-based 1989 film about the heroic Salvadoran archbishop. [Time approximate after baseball.]

A good way to see how helpful these various punctuation marks are is to take them all out and then to decide how much extra work you have to do to read without them. Then look around to see where you find these marks. Which ones do you see often? Which ones less often?

EXERCISE 34.1

Try revising the use of punctuation in the Tom Wolfe passage on the opening page of this chapter, replacing dashes with parentheses (or vice versa). Compare the original and your revision. What conclusions can you draw about the emphasis each mark brings?

Using parentheses

Parentheses are used to enclose material that is of minor or secondary importance in a sentence—material that supplements, clarifies, comments on, or illustrates what precedes or follows it. Parentheses are also used around numbers or letters that precede items in a list.

Enclosing less important material

Normal children do not confuse reality and fantasy—they confuse them much less often than we adults do (as a certain great fantasist pointed out in a story called "The Emperor's New Clothes").
— URSULA LEGUIN, "Why Are Americans Afraid of Dragons?"

Boxing is a purely masculine world. (Though there are female boxers— the most famous is the black champion Lady Tyger Trimiar with her shaved head and tiger-striped attire—women's role in the sport is extremely marginal.) — Joyce Carol Oates, "On Boxing"

As the examples above demonstrate, a period may be placed either inside or outside a closing parenthesis, depending on whether the text inside the parentheses is a complete sentence. A comma, on the other hand, is always placed *outside* a closing parenthesis (and never before an opening one).

Gene Tunney's single defeat in an eleven-year career was to a flamboyant and dangerous fighter named Harry Greb ("The Human Windmill"), who seems to have been, judging from boxing literature, the dirtiest fighter in history. — Joyce Carol Oates, "On Boxing"

If the material in parentheses is a question or an exclamation, use a question mark or exclamation mark inside the closing parenthesis.

Our laughing (so deep was the pleasure!) became screaming. — Richard Rodriguez, "Aria: A Memoir of a Bilingual Childhood"

Use parentheses judiciously, because they break up the flow of a sentence or passage, forcing readers to hold the original train of thought in their minds while considering a secondary one. As a writer, you often have a choice of setting off material in three ways: with commas, with parentheses, or with dashes. The choice is partially one of how interruptive the material is and partially one of personal style. In general, use commas when the material is least interruptive (see 29c and f), parentheses when it is more interruptive, and dashes when it is the most interruptive (see 34c). One other consideration is whether the material ends in an exclamation point or question mark (as does the last example above); if so, you can use *only* parentheses or dashes.

Enclosing numbers or letters in a list

Five distinct styles can be distinguished: (1) Old New England, (2) Deep South, (3) Middle American, (4) Wild West and (5) Far West or Californian. — Alison Lurie, *The Language of Clothes*

34b

Using brackets

Brackets are used to enclose parenthetical elements in material within parentheses and to enclose explanatory words or comments inserted into a

A parenthesis is a convenient device, but a writer indulges his own convenience at the expense of his readers' if his parenthesis is so long that a reader, when he comes to the end of it, has little chance of remembering where he was when it began. — H. W. Fowler

The created world is but a small parenthesis in eternity. — Sir Thomas Browne

for life's not a paragraph and death i think is no parenthesis. — E. E. Cummings

USEFUL READING

The Chicago Manual of Style. 13th ed. Chicago: U of Chicago P, 1982. See Chapter 5, "Punctuation," which discusses colons, dashes, parentheses, brackets, and hyphens.

Palacas, Arthur L. "Parentheticals and Personal Voice." *Written Communication* 6 (1989): 506–27. Based on a sample of professional writing, Palacas argues that one clear source of "voice" is appositive and parenthetical structures.

Brackets need not detain us long; their use is almost self-evident and should need but little illustration. They introduce into a context something that has a bearing upon it in a purely subordinate way, and their effect is to keep the words that they enclose "out of the light," as it were, so that the words that precede and follow them may run on with the least possible interruption.
— G. V. CAREY

quotation. If your typewriter does not include keys for brackets, draw them in by hand.

Setting off material within parentheses

Eventually the investigation had to examine the major agencies (including the previously sacrosanct National Security Agency [NSA]) that were conducting covert operations.

Inserting material within quotations

In the following sentence, the bracketed words replace the words *he* and *it* in the original quotation.

As Curtis argues, "[Johnson] saw [the war] as a game or wrestling match in which he would make Ho Chi Minh cry 'uncle.'"

In the following sentence, the bracketed material explains what the *that* in the quotation means.

In defending his station's inferior children's programs, a network executive states, "If we were to do that [supply quality programs in the afternoon, one of the demands of ACT], a lot of people might say: 'How dare they lock the kids up for another two and a half hours.'"
— MARIE WINN, *The Plug-In Drug: Television, Children, and the Family*

In the quotation in the following sentence, the artist Gauguin's name is misspelled. The bracketed word *sic,* which means "so," tells readers that the person being quoted—not the writer—made the mistake.

One admirer wrote, "She was the most striking woman I'd ever seen—a sort of wonderful combination of Mia Farrow and one of Gaugin's [sic] Polynesian nymphs."

EXERCISE 34.2: Answers

1. One incident of cruelty was brought to public attention by the Animal Liberation Front (ALF).

2. During my research, I found that a flat-rate income tax (a single-rate tax with no deductions) has its problems.

3. The leaflet urged voters to "defend the rights that are represented by the Statute [sic] of Liberty."

4. Many researchers used the Massachusetts Multiphasic Personal Inventory (MMPI) for hypnotizability studies.

5. Some of the alternatives suggested include (1) tissue cultures, (2) mechanical models, (3) *in vitro* techniques and (4) mathematical and electrical models.

EXERCISE 34.2

Revise the following sentences, using parentheses and brackets correctly. Example:

She was in fourth grade (or was it third?) when she became blind.

1. One incident of cruelty was brought to public attention by the Animal Liberation Front ALF.

2. During my research, I found that a flat-rate income tax a single-rate tax with no deductions has its problems.

3. The leaflet urged voters to "defend the rights that are represented by the Statute sic of Liberty."

4. Many researchers used the Massachusetts Multiphasic Personal Inventory the MMPI for hypnotizability studies.

5. Some of the alternatives suggested include 1 tissue cultures, 2 mechanical models, 3 *in vitro* techniques, and 4 mathematical and electrical models.

34c

Using dashes

Pairs of dashes allow a writer to interrupt a sentence to insert a comment or to highlight particular material. In contrast to parentheses, dashes give more rather than less emphasis to the material they enclose. On most typewriters and with most word-processing software, a dash is made with two hyphens (and *no* spaces before, between, or after).

Inserting a comment

The pleasures of reading itself—who doesn't remember?—were like those of Christmas cake, a sweet devouring.
— EUDORA WELTY, "A Sweet Devouring"

Emphasizing explanatory material

Mr. Angell is addicted to dashes and parentheses—small pauses or digressions in a narrative like those moments when the umpire dusts off home plate or a pitcher rubs up a new ball—that serve to slow an already deliberate movement almost to a standstill.
— JOEL CONARROE, *New York Times Book Review*

A single dash is used to set off a comment or emphasize material at the end of a sentence. It is also used to mark a sudden shift in tone, to introduce a summary or explanation of what has come before, or to indicate hesitation in speech.

Emphasizing material at the end of a sentence

In the twentieth century it has become almost impossible to moralize about epidemics—except those which are transmitted sexually.
— SUSAN SONTAG, *AIDS and Its Metaphors*

The dash is a handy device, informal and essentially playful, telling you that you're about to take off on a different tack but still in some way connected to the present course—only you have to remember that the dash is there, and either put in a second dash at the end of the notion to let the reader know that he's back on course, or else end the sentence, as here, with a period.
— LEWIS THOMAS

Marking a sudden change in tone

Under democracy, one party always devotes its chief efforts to trying to prove that the other is unfit to rule—and both commonly succeed and are right.   — H. L. MENCKEN, "Minority Report"

Introducing a summary or explanation

In walking, the average adult person employs a motor mechanism that weighs about eighty pounds—sixty pounds of muscle and twenty pounds of bone.   — EDWARD WAY TEALE

Indicating hesitation in speech

As the officer approached his car, the driver stammered, "What—what have I done?"

In introducing a summary or explanation, the difference between a single dash and a colon is a subtle one. In general, however, a dash is less formal. In fact, you should use dashes sparingly in college writing, not only because they are somewhat informal but also because they cause an abrupt break in reading. Too many of them create a jerky, disconnected effect that makes it hard for readers to follow your thought.

 Checking for effective use of dashes and parentheses

1. Be sure that any material set off with dashes or enclosed in parentheses requires special emphasis.
2. Then check to see that the dashes or parentheses don't make the sentence difficult to follow.
3. Finally, decide whether the punctuation you've chosen creates the proper emphasis: parentheses tend to de-emphasize material they enclose; dashes add the most emphasis.

EXERCISE 34.3

Punctuate the following sentences with dashes where appropriate. Example:

> *He is quick, violent, and mean—they don't call him "Dirty Harry" for*
>
> *nothing—but appealing nonetheless.*

1. Many people would have ignored the children's taunts but not Ace.

EXERCISE 34.3: Answers

1. Many people would have ignored the children's taunts—but not Ace.
2. Even if smoking is harmful—and there is no real proof of this assertion—it is unjust to outlaw smoking while other harmful substances remain legal.
3. I recall thinking to myself, "I'm going—I'm going to—oh, I don't know!"
4. Union Carbide's plant in Bhopal, India, sprang a leak—a leak that killed over 2,500 people and injured 150,000 more.
5. Fair-skinned people—and especially those with red hair—should use a strong sunscreen.

2. Even if smoking is harmful and there is no real proof of this assertion it is unjust to outlaw smoking while other harmful substances remain legal.

3. I recall thinking to myself, "I'm going I'm going to oh, I don't know!"

4. Union Carbide's plant in Bhopal, India, sprang a leak a leak that killed over 2,500 people and injured 150,000 more.

5. Fair-skinned people and especially those with red hair should use a strong sunscreen.

34d

Using colons

Colons are used to introduce something that is an explanation, example, or appositive of what precedes it and to introduce a series, list, or quotation. They are also used to separate elements such as hours, minutes, and seconds; biblical chapter numbers; and titles and subtitles.

Introducing an explanation, example, or appositive

And we are all on our own when it comes to keeping those lines open to ourselves: your notebook will never help me, nor mine you.
— JOAN DIDION, "On Keeping a Notebook"

The men may also wear the getup known as Sun Belt Cool: a pale beige suit, open collared shirt (often in a darker shade than the suit), cream-colored loafers and aviator sunglasses.
— ALISON LURIE, *The Language of Clothes*

Introducing a series, list, or quotation

The glossary of physics is an enchantment in itself: "chain," "strangeness," "strong" and "weak" forces, "quarks."   — LEWIS THOMAS, "An Apology"

We began a series of workshops on nonviolence, and we repeatedly asked ourselves: "Are you able to accept blows without retaliation?"
— MARTIN LUTHER KING, JR., "Letter from Birmingham Jail"

Separating elements

HOURS, MINUTES, AND SECONDS

4:59 P.M.

2:15:06

BIBLICAL CHAPTERS AND VERSES

Deuteronomy 17:2–7

I Chronicles 3:3–5

TITLES AND SUBTITLES

"Grant and Lee: A Study in Contrasts"

The Joy of Insight: Passions of a Physicist

Checking for misused colons

Except when it is used to separate the standard elements discussed in the preceding section, a colon should be used only at the end of an independent clause. Do not put a colon between a verb and its object or complement, between a preposition and its object, or after such expressions as *such as, especially,* or *including.*

MISUSED	The major natural fibers are: cotton, wool, silk, and linen.
REVISED	The major natural fibers are cotton, wool, silk, and linen.
MISUSED	In poetry, additional power may come from devices such as: simile, metaphor, and alliteration.
REVISED	In poetry, additional power may come from devices such as simile, metaphor, and alliteration.

EXERCISE 34.4

Insert a colon in each of the following items that needs one. Some of the items do not require a colon. Example:

> Canada : *A Story of Challenge* is required reading for the course.

1. The sonnet's structure is effective in revealing the speaker's message love has changed his life and ended his depression.

2. Another example is taken from Psalm 139 16.

3. Nixon claims that throughout the Watergate investigation he believed it was his duty to stay on as president "to make every possible effort to complete the term of office to which you elected me."

4. Shifting into German, Kennedy declared "Ich bin ein Berliner."

5. Education can alleviate problems such as poverty, poor health, and the energy shortage.

6. Gandhi urged four things tell the truth even in business, adopt more sanitary habits, abolish caste and religious divisions, and learn English.

7. Some of the improvements included the establishment of after-school recreation programs and a consumer cooperative, the opening or expansion of health clinics, and changes in the content of school curricula.

8. *Signs of Trouble and Erosion A Report on Education in America* was submitted to Congress and the president in January 1984.

9. Even more important was what money represented success and prestige.

10. The eclipse will peak in Los Angeles at 1128 A.M.

Using slashes

Slashes are used to mark line divisions in poetry quoted within text (see 33a2), to separate two alternative terms, and to separate the parts of fractions. When used to separate lines of poetry, the slash should be preceded and followed by a space.

Marking line divisions in poetry

In "Sonnet 29," the persona states, "For thy sweet love rememb'red such wealth brings, / That then I scorn to change my state with kings."

Separating alternatives

"I'm not the typical wife/girlfriend of a baseball player — those women you see on TV with their hair done up and their Rose Bowl Parade wave to the crowds." — ROGER ANGELL, "In the Country"

Separating parts of fractions

The child did not start talking until she was 3½ years old.

34f

Using ellipses

Ellipses, or ellipsis points, are three equally spaced dots. Most often used to indicate that something has been omitted from a quoted passage, they can also be used to signal a pause or hesitation in the same way that a dash can (see 34c).

Indicating omissions

Just as you should be very careful to use quotation marks around any material that you quote directly from a source, so you should use an ellipsis to indicate that you have left out part of a quotation that appears to be a complete sentence. Look at the following example:

ORIGINAL TEXT

The quasi-official division of the population into three economic classes called high-, middle-, and low-income groups rather misses the point, because as a class indicator the amount of money is not as important as the source. — PAUL FUSSELL, "Notes on Class"

WITH ELLIPSES

As Paul Fussell argues, "The quasi-official division of the population into three economic classes . . . rather misses the point. . . ."

In this example, the ellipses are used to indicate two different omissions—one in the middle of the sentence and one at the end of the sentence. When you omit the last part of a quoted sentence, add a period before the ellipsis—for a total of four dots. Be sure a complete sentence comes before and after the four points. If your quotation ends with a source documentation (such as a page number, a name, or a title), follow these steps:

1. Use three ellipsis points but no period after the quotation.
2. Add the closing quotation mark, closed up to the third ellipsis point.
3. Add the source documentation in parentheses.
4. Use a period to indicate the end of the sentence.

Hawthorne writes, "My friend, whom I shall call Oberon—it was a name of fancy and friendship between him and me . . ." (575).

Indicating a pause or hesitation

What you get is . . . the view from Oswald's rifle.
— TOM WOLFE, "Pornoviolence"

Then the voice, husky and familiar, came to wash over us—"The winnah, and still heavyweight champeen of the world . . . Joe Louis."
—MAYA ANGELOU, *I Know Why the Caged Bird Sings*

EXERCISE 34.5: Answers will vary.

EXERCISE 34.5

Complete the following sentence by incorporating two parts of one of the sentences in the passage below, using ellipsis points to indicate what you omit:

"In 'Shopping and Other Spiritual Adventures,' Phyllis Rose says of Americans' attitudes toward shopping, ⸺⸺⸺⸺⸺⸺⸺⸺⸺."

We Americans are beyond a simple, possessive materialism. We're used to abundance and the possibility of possessing things. The things, and the possibility of possessing them, will still be there next week, next year. So today we can walk the aisles calmly.

— PHYLLIS ROSE, "Shopping and Other Spiritual Adventures"

EXERCISE 34.6

The following sentences use the punctuation marks presented in this chapter very effectively. Read the sentences carefully; then choose one, and use it as a model for writing a sentence of your own, making sure to use the punctuation marks in the same way in your sentence.

1. The dad was—how can you put this gracefully?—a real blimp, a wide load, and the white polyester stretch-pants only emphasized the cargo.
   — GARRISON KEILLOR, "Happy to Be Here"

2. I took exercise daily (as I still do), did not smoke (and still don't), and though excessively fond of wine, seldom drank spirits, not much liking the taste of them. — JAN MORRIS, "To Everest"

3. Not only are the distinctions we draw between male nature and female nature largely arbitrary and often pure superstition: they are completely beside the point. — BRIGID BROPHY, "Women"

4. One day a man would be ascending the pyramid at a terrific clip, and the next—bingo!—he would reach his own limits in the most unexpected way. — TOM WOLFE, *The Right Stuff*

5. A few traditions, thank heaven, remain fixed in the summer state of things—the June collapse of the Giants, Gaylord Perry throwing (or not throwing) spitballs, Hank Aaron hitting homers, and the commissioner . . . well, commissioning. — ROGER ANGELL, *Five Seasons*

EXERCISE 34.7 Revising for Parentheses and Dashes

The following paragraph uses a considerable number of parentheses and dashes. Using the guidelines in this chapter, revise the paragraph to make it flow more smoothly and emphasize appropriate elements by deleting some of the parentheses and dashes, replacing one with the other, or substituting other punctuation.

By the time we reached Geneva, we had been traveling more than seven weeks—it seemed like seven months!—and were getting rather tired of one

EXERCISE 34.6: Answers will vary.

EXERCISE 34.7: Answers will vary.

another's company. (We had been only casual acquaintances before the trip.) Since there was not a great deal to see in the city—especially on Sunday—we decided to take the train to Chamonix (France) to see Mont Blanc—Europe's second-highest mountain (a decision that proved to be a disaster). After an argument about the map (the kind of argument we were having more and more often), we wandered around endlessly before finding the train station, only to discover that it was the wrong one. So we had to walk even farther—back to the other train station. Despite an exhausting pace, we just missed the train—or so we thought—until we learned that there was no train to Chamonix that day—because it was Sunday. I have never (for obvious reasons) gone back to Geneva.

EXERCISE 34.8   Reading with an Eye for Punctuation

Although Emily Dickinson's poems are characteristically punctuated with dashes, the first editor of her work systematically eliminated them. Here is a brief Dickinson poem—with her original dashes restored. Read it twice, first ignoring the dashes and then using them to guide your reading. What effect does the final dash have? Finally, try composing a four-line poem that uses dashes to guide reading and meaning.

> Much Madness is divinest Sense—
> To a discerning Eye—
> Much Sense—the starkest Madness—
> 'Tis the Majority
> In this, as All, prevail—
> Assent—and you are sane—
> Demur—you're straightway dangerous—
> And handled with a Chain—
> — EMILY DICKINSON

EXERCISE 34.9   Taking Inventory: Punctuation

Look through a draft you have recently written or are working on, and check your use of parentheses, brackets, dashes, colons, slashes, and ellipses. Have you followed the conventions presented in this chapter? If not, revise accordingly. Then, read through the draft again, looking especially at all the parentheses and dashes. Are there too many? Check the material in parentheses to see if it could use more emphasis and thus be set off instead with dashes. Then, check any material in dashes to see if it could do with less emphasis and thus be punctuated with commas or parentheses. If you keep a writing log, enter some examples of this work in your log.

EXERCISE 34.8: Answers will vary.

BACKGROUND

Emily Dickinson published very few poems during her lifetime. But privately, she bound her manuscripts into packets or "fascicles," folded sheets of paper sewn together by hand, which give the impression of being little "books," meant to be read by others. Yet her capitalization and punctuation were very unconventional. Especially curious is her use of dashes as an almost universal punctuation mark, sometimes occurring in places that break up sentences into ungrammatical units.

Until the middle of this century, editors always normalized her mechanics. In 1950, Edith Perry Stamm proposed a theory to explain Dickinson's dashes. She claims that Dickinson's system of dashes indicated various spoken intonations. Most experts discount Stamm's theory, because it seems likely that if Dickinson had wanted to indicate intonation, she would have made her marks clearer to distinguish.

OPTIONAL EXERCISE

Ask students to read some other poems with dashes and to study the effects they bring to the poem. They might even try repunctuating the poem, replacing dashes with colons or parentheses, for instance, to appreciate the difference. You could refer them to Langston Hughes's "Dream Deferred (Harlem)" on page 418; other poems with dashes you might suggest include:

"Birches" and "Mending Wall," Robert Frost

"The Love Song of J. Alfred Prufrock," T. S. Eliot

"The Ruined Maid," Thomas Hardy

"Daddy," Sylvia Plath

Part Seven

Understanding Mechanical Conventions

<>

35

Using Capitals

AT ONE TIME, ALL LETTERS WERE WRITTEN AS CAPITALS, LIKE THIS. By the time that movable type was invented, a new system had evolved, and printers used a capital letter only for the first letter of any word they felt was particularly important. Today, the conventions of capitalization are fairly well standardized, although they vary from language to language.

EXERCISE 35.1: Answers will vary.

EXERCISE 35.1

Spend a few minutes writing a letter to someone you haven't seen for sometime. If nothing else comes to mind, tell him or her about your classes. Then look over your letter. How many words have you capitalized—and why?

35a

Capitalizing the first word of a sentence or of a line of poetry

Capitalize the first word of a sentence.

Posing relatives for photographs is a challenge.
Could you move to the left a little?
Smile, and say cheese!

If you are quoting a full sentence, capitalize its first word.

Everyone was asking, "What will I do after I graduate?"

USEFUL READING

Period Styles: A History of Punctuation. New York: Herb Lubalin Study Center of Design and Typography in the Cooper Union for the Advancement of Science and Art, 1988. See the first essay, "Period Styles: A Punctuated History."

Capitalization of a sentence following a colon is optional.

> Gould cites the work of Darwin: The [*or* the] theory of natural selection incorporates the principle of evolutionary ties between all animals.

A sentence that is set off within another sentence by dashes or parentheses should not be capitalized. Note, however, that a sentence within parentheses that stands by itself *is* capitalized.

> Those assigned to transports were not humiliated like washouts— *somebody* had to fly those planes—nevertheless, they, too, had been *left behind* for lack of the right stuff.
>
> It *heaved,* it moved up and down underneath his feet, it pitched up, it pitched down, it rolled to port (this great beast *rolled!*) and it rolled to starboard, as the ship moved into the wind and, therefore, into the waves, and the wind kept sweeping across, sixty feet up in the air out in the open sea, and there were no railings whatsoever.
>
> Or a man could go for a routine physical one fine day, feeling like a million dollars, and be grounded for *fallen arches*. It happened!—just like that! (And try raising them.)
>
> — TOM WOLFE, *The Right Stuff*

The first word of each line in a poem is also traditionally capitalized.

> Loveliest of trees, the cherry now
> Is hung with bloom along the bough,
> And stands about the woodland ride
> Wearing white for Eastertide.
> – A. E. HOUSMAN, "Loveliest of Trees"

Some poets do not capitalize each line, however. When citing poetry, therefore, be careful to follow the original capitalization.

Everyday use

Writers often capitalize words or even whole passages to add a special emphasis (WOW! ZAP!). The writer Dave Barry uses this technique in his humorous newspaper columns: "Today, I saw a chicken driving a car. (I AM NOT MAKING THIS UP.)" Look through your own local newspaper, noting examples of capital letters used for emphasis. Bring some examples to class for comparison with those found by classmates.

BACKGROUND

Originally, a large letter usually marked the beginning of a sentence, and that letter could be either upper- or lowercase. The *Codex Alexandrinus* (a fifth century copy of the Bible) is one of the first documents that uses large letters to mark off each sentence. A full lowercase set of characters existed as early as A.D. 510, and the mixing of lowercase and uppercase characters developed from this date. By the time printing became established (in the mid-1500s), capital letters always signaled the start of a sentence (as in the Gutenberg Bible), but they were also liberally scattered throughout manuscripts at the printer's discretion. By the seventeenth century, the use of capital letters had become more or less standardized; they were used at the beginning of sentences and for proper names and titles. The *Encyclopaedia Britannica* (1975) notes that standardizing the usage of uppercase and lowercase letters was a crucial development:

> Three of the most important components [of a system of punctuation] are the space left blank between words; the indentation of the first line of a new paragraph; and the uppercase, or capital, letter written at the beginning of a sentence and at the beginning of a proper name or a title.

Today, we take blank space and paragraph indentation for granted. However, our elaborate conventions for the use of capital letters take more time and effort for students to recognize and adhere to.

TEACHING PRACTICE

For examples of how a writer of more serious intentions may use capitalization for different kinds of emphasis, refer your students to the excerpt from Cynthia Ozick's "We Are the Crazy Lady" on p. 517.

Morning sun heats up the young beech tree
leaves and almost lights them into fireflies

I wish I could dig up the earth to plant apples
pears or peaches on a lazy dandelion lawn

I am tired from this digging up of human bodies
no one loved enough to save from death
— JUNE JORDAN, "Aftermath"

35b

Capitalizing proper nouns and proper adjectives

Capitalize **proper nouns** (those naming specific persons, places, and things) and **proper adjectives** (those formed from proper nouns). In general, do not capitalize **common nouns** (those naming general classes of people, places, and things) unless they begin a sentence or are used as part of a proper noun. Do not capitalize articles (*a, an,* or *the*), or prepositions preceding or within such terms.

PROPER	COMMON
Alfred Hitchcock, Hitchcockian	a director, directorial
Brazil, Brazilian	a nation
Golden Gate Bridge	a bridge

 Some commonly capitalized terms

NAMES OF INDIVIDUALS

Martin Luther King, Jr.	Eleanor Roosevelt
Morgan Freeman	Willie Mays
Lewis Thomas	Louise Erdrich
Aristotelian logic	Petrarchan sonnet form

GEOGRAPHICAL NAMES

Asia	Pacific Ocean
Nepal	Sugarloaf Mountain
St. Louis	Michigan Avenue
African art	Parisian fashions

STRUCTURES AND MONUMENTS

Flatiron Building	Gateway Arch
Fort McHenry Tunnel	Coit Tower

BACKGROUND

The eighteenth century saw a movement to begin proper nouns with lowercase letters. In a letter to his son, dated April 13, 1752, Lord Chesterfield denounced the fashion:

> It offends my eyes to see *rome, france, caesar, henry the fourth,* etc. begin with small letters; and I do not conceive that there can be any reason for doing it half so strong as the reason of long usage to the contrary. This is an affectation of Voltaire.

However, in the first draft of the Declaration of Independence, Thomas Jefferson did not capitalize words that usually received capitalization in the eighteenth century, including *nature, creator,* and even *god.*

USEFUL READING

The Chicago Manual of Style. 13th ed. Chicago: U of Chicago P, 1982. See Chapter 7, "Names and Terms," for a discussion of when to use capital letters; section 7.123 comments on articles in titles.

SHIPS, TRAINS, AIRCRAFT, AND SPACECRAFT

S.S. *Titanic*	*Metroliner*
Spirit of St. Louis	*Challenger*

INSTITUTIONS, ORGANIZATIONS, AND BUSINESSES

Library of Congress	Kiwanis Club
St. Martin's Press	United Auto Workers
General Motors Corporation	Democratic Party

HISTORICAL EVENTS, ERAS, AND CALENDAR ITEMS

Shays's Rebellion	Saturday
Great Depression	July
Middle Ages	Memorial Day

RELIGIONS AND RELIGIOUS TERMS

Buddhism, Buddhists	Allah
Catholicism, Catholics	Jesus Christ
Islam, Muslims or Moslems	God
Judaism, Jews	the Bible
United Methodist Church,	the Koran
Methodists	the Bible

ETHNIC GROUPS, NATIONALITIES, AND LANGUAGES

African American	English
Chicano/Chicana	Chinese
Slavic	Iraqi
Arab	Latin

TRADE NAMES

Reeboks	Huggies
Xerox	Levi's
Cheerios	Walkman

BACKGROUND

The use of capitals may seem simply conventional, but the conventions involved have rhetorical functions. In *Modern Punctuation* (New York: Oxford UP, 1919), George Summey, Jr., lists three general functions of capitalization:

1. "As an aid to clearness." (Capitalizing proper nouns to distinguish them from common nouns and capitalizing the first letter of a sentence aid the *logos* of the writer's work.)

2. "For courtesy or reverence." (Capitalizing names and titles aid the writer's *ethos*.)

3. "For emphasis." (Although generally out of fashion nowadays, capitalizing words such as *Nature* can possibly aid a writer's *logos* or *pathos*.) (165)

TEACHING PRACTICE

Consider encouraging your students to act as researchers by asking them to bring to class examples of how capitalization rules are used and abused. Direct them to student newspapers, print advertisements, labels on bottles and cans, and billboards for examples, and ask them to determine what they feel are appropriate and inappropriate uses (when capitals *should* be used), and effective and ineffective uses (when capitals help focus attention). Try to direct attention to the context of language use; what may be appropriate in an advertisement may be inappropriate in a formal paper for your class.

1

Capitalizing titles of individuals

Capitalize titles used before a proper name. When used alone or following a proper name, most titles are not capitalized. The only exceptions are titles of some very powerful officials—for example, many writers capitalize the word *president* when it refers to the President of the United States.

Justice O'Connor	Sandra Day O'Connor, the justice
Governor Ann Richards	Ann Richards, governor of Texas
Professor Lisa Ede	Lisa Ede, an English professor
Doctor Edward A. Davies	Edward A. Davies, our doctor

2

Capitalizing academic institutions and courses

Capitalize the names of specific schools, departments, or courses, but not the common nouns for institutions or subject areas.

University of California (*but* a California university)
History Department (*but* a history major)
Political Science 102 (*but* a political science course)

Capitalizing titles of works

Capitalize most words in titles of books, articles, stories, essays, plays, poems, documents, films, paintings, and musical compositions. Articles (*a, an, the*), prepositions, conjunctions, and the *to* of an infinitive are not capitalized unless they are the first or last words in a title or subtitle.

Walt Whitman: A Life	"Lovely to Look At"
"June Recital"	Magna Carta
"Shooting an Elephant"	*Thelma & Louise*
Our Town	*The Magic Flute*

Remember to capitalize the titles of your own compositions.

Capitalizing *I* and *O*

Always capitalize the pronoun *I* and the interjection *O*. Be careful, however, to distinguish between the interjections *O* and *oh*. *O* is an older form that is usually used for direct address in very formal speech. It is always capitalized, whereas *oh* is not unless it begins a sentence or is part of a title.

In fact, I don't know the answer.

Grant us peace, O Lord.

35e

Checking for unnecessary capitalization

1

With compass directions, unless the word designates a specific geographic region

John Muir headed west, filled with the need to explore.

The nation was at that time divided into three competing economic sections: the Northeast, the South, and the West.

2

With family relationships, unless the word is used as part of the name or as a substitute for the name

When she was a child, my mother shared a room with my aunt.

I could always tell when Mother was annoyed with Aunt Rose.

The train on which Uncle Charlie arrived spewed out thick black smoke, foreshadowing a disastrous visit.

3

With seasons of the year and parts of the academic year

spring	fall semester
winter	winter term
autumn	spring quarter

EXERCISE 35.2

Capitalize words as needed in the following sentences. Example:

t. s. eliot, who wrote the waste land, was an editor at faber and faber.

1. the town in the south where i was raised had a statue of a civil war soldier in the center of main street.

2. we had a choice of fast-food, chinese, or italian restaurants.

3. the keynote address was given by governor bill clinton of arkansas.

4. the council of trent was convened to draw up the catholic response to the protestant reformation.

5. in *home before dark,* cheever tells how her father once panicked when driving east on the tappan zee bridge over the hudson river.

EXERCISE 35.2: Answers

1. The town in the South where I was raised had a statue of a Civil War soldier in the center of Main Street.

2. We had a choice of fast-food, Chinese, or Italian restaurants.

3. The keynote address was given by Governor Bill Clinton of Arkansas.

4. The Council of Trent was convened to draw up the Catholic response to the Protestant Reformation.

5. In *Home before Dark,* Cheever tells how her father once panicked when driving east on the Tappan Zee Bridge over the Hudson River.

6. I wondered if my new Levi's were faded enough and if I could possibly scuff up my new Keds just a little more before I arrived for spring term.

7. Accepting an award for his score for the film *The High and the Mighty,* Dmitri Tiomkin thanked Beethoven, Brahms, Wagner, and Strauss.

8. In this essay, I will be citing the works of Vladimir Nabokov, in particular his novels *Pnin* and *Lolita* and his story "The Vane Sisters."

9. The Battle of Lexington and Concord was fought in April 1775.

10. My favorite song by Cole Porter is "You'd Be So Nice to Come Home To."

6. i wondered if my new levi's were faded enough and if i could possibly scuff up my new keds just a little more before i arrived for spring term.

7. accepting an award for his score for the film *the high and the mighty,* dmitri tiomkin thanked beethoven, brahms, wagner, and strauss.

8. in this essay, i will be citing the works of vladimir nabokov, in particular his novels *pnin* and *lolita* and his story "the vane sisters."

9. the battle of lexington and concord was fought in april 1775.

10. my favorite song by cole porter is "you'd be so nice to come home to."

EXERCISE 35.3: Answers will vary.

TEACHING PRACTICE

Ask your students to read the poem by e. e. cummings on page 191, paying particular attention to capitalization. Discuss how cumming's placement of capitals helps them to understand the poem.

EXERCISE 35.3 Reading with an Eye for Capitalization

The following poem uses capitalization in an unconventional way. Read it over a few times, at least once aloud. What effect does the capitalization have on your understanding and recitation of the poem? Why do you think the poet chose to use capitals as she did?

> A little Madness in the Spring
> Is wholesome even for the King,
> But God be with the Clown—
> Who ponders this tremendous scene—
> This whole Experiment of Green—
> As if it were his own!
> — EMILY DICKINSON

EXERCISE 35.4 Taking Inventory: Capitalization

Read over something you have written recently with an eye for capitalization. Have you capitalized all proper nouns and adjectives? Have you used capitals properly with dashes and parentheses? Have you capitalized sentences following colons, and if so, have you done so consistently? If you keep a writing log, enter notes and examples of any problems you have with capital letters.

36

Using Abbreviations and Numbers

In his essays and by the example of his life, Henry David Thoreau urged us to "simplify, simplify." Two of the tools that help writers reach that goal are abbreviations and numerals. Both serve to speed up prose and thus to allow readers to process information efficiently. As with other elements, there are certain conventions for using abbreviations and numerals, especially in academic work. This chapter will explain these conventions to help you use abbreviations and numbers appropriately and correctly.*

EXERCISE 36.1

Take a few moments to write directions to someplace you know well—to your home from the edge of town, for example. Then read over what you've written, noting any use of abbreviations and numbers. Finally, check the guidelines in this chapter to see whether you've used them correctly.

ABBREVIATIONS

Abbreviating titles and academic degrees

When used before or after a name, some personal and professional titles and academic degrees are abbreviated, even in academic writing.

---

*For rules on using abbreviations and numbers in a particular discipline, the *MLA Handbook for Writers of Research Papers* or *The Chicago Manual of Style* is usually followed in the humanities; the *Publication Manual of the American Psychological Association,* in the social sciences; and the *CBE Style Manual,* in the natural sciences.

BACKGROUND

The controversy over whether to abbreviate or spell out a word can become heated. On the one hand, commentators William and Mary Morris take the conservative approach: "Generally speaking, *abbreviations* are to be avoided in formal writing . . ." (2). On the other hand, commentators like Rudolf Flesch take a different view: "It's a superstition that abbreviations shouldn't be used in serious writing and that it's good style to spell everything out. Nonsense: use abbreviations whenever they are customary and won't attract the attention of the reader" (3).

Flesch's statement points to an important aspect of abbreviation usage: choosing whether to use abbreviations or spell out the words is a rhetorical decision. As the authors of *Words into Type* note, "An abbreviation that can be used in certain branches of writing might be poor form in others" (100). For instance, *vs.* for *versus* is acceptable in legal writing, but not, to conservative taste, in other formal writing. The writer must once again recognize and evaluate her or his audience. One rule of thumb, however, does apply across disciplines: when in doubt, spell it out.

EXERCISE 36.1: Answers will vary.

abb

504 **36a** USING ABBREVIATIONS AND NUMBERS

BACKGROUND

Writers have always used abbreviations, whether on stone, paper, or computer screens. *SPQR, Senatus Populusque Romanus,* the insignia of Rome, was the most famous abbreviation of antiquity. For the several centuries preceding our own, the use of abbreviations declined, but since World War II, we have experienced a veritable flood of abbreviated words, especially in technical writing—and more especially in the United States. We abbreviate much more than other cultures. Just looking at the way some companies and products are spelled will indicate the extent to which people in the United States like to abbreviate:

> *EZ* for *easy* as in EZ Sleep Motel.
>
> *X* for *ex-* as in X-cel Optical Co.
>
> *Hi* for *high* as in Hi-Lo Oil Co.

Also, our abbreviations, taking the general meaning of that word, involve much more than this chapter suggests. *Laser, radar, scuba, snafu,* and *sonar* are among the acronyms that are now integral parts of the English lexicon. Abbreviations as well as acronyms can become pronounceable words themselves. Abbreviating has become an important way of coining new words: *ad* for *advertisement; auto* for *automobile; bra* for *brassiere; exam* for *examination; lab* for *laboratory; phone* for *telephone; photo* for *photograph.*

USEFUL READING

Morris, William and Mary. *Harper Dictionary of Contemporary Usage.* New York: Harper, 1975. This usage guide differs somewhat from others by relying on a panel of writers to discuss problems of usage.

Ms. Steinem	Henry Louis Gates, Jr.
Mr. Guenette	Paul Irvin, M.D.
Dr. C. William McCurdy	Jamie Barlow Kayes, Ph.D.

Other titles, including religious, military, academic, and government titles, should always be spelled out in academic writing. In other writing, they may be abbreviated when they appear before a full name but should be spelled out if they appear before only a surname.

Gen. Norman Schwarzkopf	General Schwarzkopf
Prof. Beverly Moss	Professor Moss
Sen. Barbara Mikulski	Senator Mikulski

Academic degrees may be abbreviated when used alone, but never abbreviate personal or professional titles used alone.

ACCEPTABLE	She received her *Ph.D.* this year.
INAPPROPRIATE	He was a rigorous *prof.,* and we worked hard.
REVISED	He was a rigorous *professor,* and we worked hard.

Use either a title or an academic degree, but not both, with a person's name.

INAPPROPRIATE	Dr. James Dillon, Ph.D.
REVISED	Dr. James Dillon
REVISED	James Dillon, Ph.D.

Everyday use

Any time you use a telephone book, you will see abbreviations and numbers in abundance, helping readers find their ways to the proper information quickly and efficiently. If you look up the American Automobile Association in Chicago, for example, here's what you find.

AAA—CHICAGO MOTOR CLUB
  Emergency 24 Hr. Road Service
    Toll Free. 800–262–6327
  Membership Services and Insurance
    68 E. Wacker Pl. 372–1818

Here abbreviations and figures obviously allow the publisher to include a great deal of information in a small amount of space—imagine the phone book without them! Look around you for some other uses of abbreviations and figures. How do you normally use them?

36b

Using abbreviations with years and hours

The following abbreviations are acceptable used with numerals.

399 B.C. ("before Christ"; follows date)
A.D. 49 (*anno Domini,* Latin for "year of our Lord"; precedes date)
11:15 A.M. *or* a.m. (*ante meridiem,* Latin for "before noon")
9:00 P.M. *or* p.m. (*post meridiem,* Latin for "after noon")

36c

Using acronyms and initial abbreviations

Abbreviations that can be pronounced as words are called **acronyms**: OPEC, for example, is the acronym for the Organization of Petroleum Exporting Countries. **Initial abbreviations** are those that are pronounced as separate initials: NRA for National Rifle Association, for instance. Many of the most common abbreviations of these types come from business, government, and science: NASA, PBS, DNA, GE, UNICEF, AIDS, SAT.

As long as you can be sure your readers will understand them, you can use such abbreviations in much of your college writing. If you are using a term only once or twice, you should spell it out; but when you need to use a term repeatedly, abbreviating it will serve as a convenience for you and your readers alike. If the abbreviation may be unfamiliar to your readers, however, you should "define" it for them. Spell out the full term at the first use, and give the abbreviation in parentheses. After that, you can use the abbreviation by itself.

The Comprehensive Test Ban (CTB) Treaty was first proposed in the 1950s. For those nations signing it, the CTB would bring to a halt all nuclear weapons testing.

36d

Using other kinds of abbreviations

The following guidelines will help you use some other very common abbreviations. In general, you should not use any type of abbreviation not discussed in this chapter in the body of an academic writing assignment. For example:

BACKGROUND

Most of us don't always remember that while B.C. follows a date, A.D. precedes it. Even columnist and conservative grammarian William Safire admits an infamous mistake regarding the use of A.D. As a speechwriter at the White House, he approved of the wording of the plaque left on the moon by the first American astronauts to land there. It reads, "July 1969, A.D." Safire expresses the wish that "some descendant of mine will take a sharp stylus on some weekend rocket to the moon and, while awaiting a transfer rocket to Mars, will draw a little arrow placing it in front of the word *July.* This will show that human beings in the early days of space were grammatically fallible; that mankind . . . is forever editing, and that a little precision is a dangerous thing."

USEFUL READING

The Chicago Manual of Style. 13th ed. Chicago: U of Chicago P, 1982. Provides complete information on the standard form and punctuation of abbreviations.

Mencken, H. L. *The American Language.* New York: Knopf, 1937. The author provides a readable discussion of abbreviations.

Skillin, Marjorie E. et al., *Words into Type.* Englewood Cliffs: Prentice, 1974.

abb

506 **36d** USING ABBREVIATIONS AND NUMBERS

| INAPPROPRIATE | The bio lab was deserted on Fri. nights. |
| REVISED | The biology laboratory was deserted on Friday nights. |

Company names

Use such abbreviations as *Inc., Co.,* and *Corp.* and the ampersand symbol (&) if they are part of a company's official name. You should not, however, use them in most other contexts.

Sears, Roebuck & Co. was the only store in town.

Reference information

Though it is conventional to abbreviate such words as *chapter* (ch.), *page* (p.), or *pages* (pp.) in source citations, it is not acceptable to do so in the body of a paper.

| INAPPROPRIATE | The preface to the 1851 *ed.* of *Twice-Told Tales* states that the stories are not autobiographical. |
| REVISED | The preface to the 1851 *edition* of *Twice-Told Tales* states that the stories are not autobiographical. |

Latin abbreviations

In general, avoid the following Latin abbreviations except when citing sources.

cf.	compare (*confer*)
e.g.	for example (*exampli gratia*)
et al.	and others (*et alii*)
etc.	and so forth (*et cetera*)
i.e.	that is (*id est*)
N.B.	note well (*nota bene*)

| INAPPROPRIATE | Many firms have policies to help working parents—*e.g.,* flexible hours, parental leave, day care. |
| REVISED | Many firms have policies to help working parents—*for example,* flexible hours, parental leave, day care. |

Geographical terms and months

Many place names and most months of the year should be abbreviated in source citations, but they should always be written out within sentences.

BACKGROUND

In presenting the form of common abbreviations, this handbook conforms with *The Chicago Manual of Style.* However, you may want to take note that in some instances *The MLA Style Manual* prescribes different usages. For example, the MLA editors use no periods with *AD, BC,* or *NB* (Walter S. Achtert and Joseph Gibaldi, *The MLA Style Manual* [New York: Modern Language Assn., 1985], 210, 218).

BACKGROUND

Two Latin abbreviations, *e.g.* and *i.e.,* can easily be confused, although their meanings are rarely interchangeable. *E.g.* means "for example" (from the Latin *exempli gratia*). It introduces an instance or examples of that to which it relates. *I.e.* means "that is" (from the Latin *id est*). It introduces a repetition in different words, a restatement or amplification of ideas that just precede it.

INAPPROPRIATE	In *Feb.* 1990 we moved from Cloverdale, *Calif.*, to *L.A.*
REVISED	In *February* 1990 we moved from Cloverdale, *California,* to *Los Angeles.*

Common exceptions are *Washington, D.C.; USSR;* and *U.S.,* which is acceptable as an adjective but not as a noun.

UNACCEPTABLE	The exchange student enjoyed the *U.S.*
ACCEPTABLE	The *U.S. delegation* negotiated the treaty.

Symbols

Symbols such as ¢, @, #, %, +, and = should not be used in the body of a paper, though they are commonly used in graphs and tables. One common exception is the dollar sign ($), which is acceptable before specific figures.

INAPPROPRIATE	Only *50%* of applicants are accepted.
REVISED	Only *50 percent* of applicants are accepted.

Units of measurement

Except for scientific and technical writing, most units of measurement should not be abbreviated in the body of a paper.

INAPPROPRIATE	The ball sailed 425 *ft.* over the fence.
REVISED	The ball sailed 425 *feet* over the fence.

 Checking for appropriate use of abbreviations

1. Circle all the abbreviations you've used. One by one, be sure you've used the correct form. If in doubt, check each one in this chapter or in a dictionary.
2. Do you use any abbreviation more than once? If so, be sure that you use it consistently.
3. Double-check to see that any words you've abbreviated shouldn't be spelled out instead.
4. Do you use any abbreviations your readers might not understand? If so, spell them out on first use, with the abbreviation following in parentheses.

EXERCISE 36.2: Answers

1. The hit NBC show is set in a fictional Los Angeles law firm.

2. An MX missile, which is 71 feet long and 92 inches around, weighs 190,000 pounds.

3. The morning shift is easier because customers usually just order coffee, tea, doughnuts, and so forth.

4. In 1991, Representative William Gray gave up his seat in Congress to serve as president of the United Negro College Fund.

5. A large corporation like AT&T may help to finance an M.B.A. for an employee.

6. Like black-and-white television, the five-cent candy bar is a relic of the past.

7. Founded in 1966, the National Organization for Women fights discrimination against women.

8. The local National Public Radio station has a broadcast range of seventy-five miles.

9. After less than a year at the University of Virginia, Poe left and joined the United States army.

10. Dostoyevsky was influenced by many European writers—for example, Dickens, Stendhal, and Balzac.

EXERCISE 36.2

Revise each of the following sentences to eliminate any abbreviations that would be inappropriate in academic writing. Example:

The population of the ~~U.S.~~ grew about 10~~%~~ in the 1980s.

(*United States* ... *percent*)

1. The hit NBC show is set in a fictional L.A. law firm.

2. An MX missile, which is 71 ft. long and 92 in. around, weighs 190,000 lbs.

3. The A.M. shift is easier because customers usually just order coffee, tea, doughnuts, etc.

4. In 1991, Rep. William Gray gave up his seat in Congress to serve as pres. of the UNCF.

5. A large corp. like AT&T may help to finance an M.B.A. for an employee.

6. Like black-and-white TV, the 5¢ candy bar is a relic of the past.

7. Founded in 1966, NOW fights discrimination against women.

8. The local NPR station has a broadcast range of 75 mi.

9. After less than a yr. at U.Va., Poe left and joined the U.S. army.

10. Dostoyevsky was influenced by many European writers—e.g., Dickens, Stendhal, and Balzac.

NUMBERS

36e

Spelling out numbers of one or two words

If a number can be written as one or two words, spell it out.

The victim's screams were heard by *thirty-eight* people, none of whom called the police.

Police arrested the assailant *six* days later.

36f

Using figures for numbers longer than two words

Numbers that cannot be written in one or two words should be expressed in figures.

Did you know that a baseball is wrapped in 174 yards of blue-gray wool yarn and is held together by 216 red stitches?

If one of several numbers of the same kind in the same sentence needs to be expressed in figures, they all should be expressed that way.

INCONSISTENT | A complete audio system can range in cost from one hundred dollars to $2,500; however, a reliable system can be purchased for approximately five hundred dollars.

CONSISTENT | A complete audio system can range in cost from $100 to $2,500; however, a reliable system can be purchased for approximately $500.

36g

Spelling out numbers that begin sentences

When a sentence begins with a number, either spell out the number or rewrite the sentence.

INAPPROPRIATE | 277,000 hours (or 119 years) of CIA labor cost taxpayers $16 million.

HARD TO READ | Two hundred seventy-seven thousand hours (or 119 years) of CIA labor cost taxpayers $16 million.

REVISED | Taxpayers spend $16 million for 277,000 hours (or 119 years) of CIA labor.

36h

Using figures according to convention

ADDRESSES

23 Main Street; 175 Fifth Avenue, New York, NY 10010

DATES

September 17, 1951, 4 B.C., the 1860s, the sixties

DECIMALS, FRACTIONS, AND PERCENTAGES

65.34, 8½, 77 percent (*or* 77%)

(Continued)

TEACHING PRACTICE

You might be asked to specify relatedness as a factor in deciding whether to use a numeral or spell out the number. *The Chicago Manual of Style* states:

> Numbers applicable to the same category should be treated alike within the same context, whether paragraph or series of paragraphs; do not use figures for some and spell out others (234).

Here is an example.

> The English Department has 75 graduate students in six major areas: 29 in literature; 25 in rhetoric and composition; 8 in literary theory; 6 in linguistics; 4 in folklore; and 3 in film.

In this sentence, all the numerals relate to student population. However, the spelled-out number (*six*) relates to *major areas*. Therefore, the writer is permitted to spell out numbers and use numerals in the same sentence. The key factor in deciding whether to spell it out or not is rhetorical: which way would cause less confusion? Spelling out the one number that is unrelated to the seven other numbers distinguishes it so that the reader will not confuse it with the others.

DIVISIONS OF BOOKS AND PLAYS

volume 5, pages 81–85 (*not* 81–5)
Act III, Scene ii (or Act 3, Scene 2), lines 3–9

SPECIFIC AMOUNTS OF MONEY

$7,348, $1.46 trillion, $2.50, thirty-five (*or* 35) cents

SCORES AND STATISTICS

an 8–3 Red Sox victory, a verbal score of 600
an average age of 22, a mean of 53, a ratio of 3 to 1

TIME OF DAY

6:00 A.M., 5:45 p.m., 12:01
without A.M. or P.M.: five in the morning, four o'clock

EXERCISE 36.3: Suggested Answers

1. Three hundred and seven miles long and eighty-two miles wide, the island offered little of interest.

2. Some call it the handbook for the nineties.

3. You can travel around the city for only sixty-five cents.

4. The invasion of Kuwait began on August 2, 1990.

5. The department received 1,633 calls and 43 letters.

6. Cable TV is now available to 72 percent of the population.

7. Correct.

8. In the thirty-five to forty-four age group, the risk is estimated to be about 1 in 2,500.

9. The parents considered twenty-five cents enough for a five-year-old.

10. The amulet measured 1⅛ by 2⅖ inches.

EXERCISE 36.3

Revise the numbers in the following sentences as necessary for correctness and consistency. If a sentence is correct, circle its number. Example:

> twenty first
> Does the 21st century begin in 2000 or 2001?

1. 307 miles long and 82 miles wide, the island offered little of interest.

2. Some call it the handbook for the 90s.

3. You can travel around the city for only 65 cents.

4. The invasion of Kuwait began on August second, 1990.

5. The department received 1,633 calls and forty-three letters.

6. Cable TV is now available to seventy-two percent of the population.

7. Walker signed a three-year, $4.5 million contract.

8. In the 35 to 44 age group, the risk is estimated to be about 1 in 2,500.

9. The parents considered 25 cents enough for a five-year-old.

10. The amulet measured one and one-eighth by two and two-fifths inches.

EXERCISE 36.4 Reading with an Eye for Abbreviations and Numbers

Read the following passage adapted from an essay by Jean Shepherd ("Hairy Gertz and the Forty-Seven Crappies"), and revise to make its treatment of abbreviations and numbers correct and consistent.

And in the middle of the lake, several yds. away, are over 17,000 fishermen, in wooden rowboats rented at a buck and a ½ an hr. It is 2 A.M. The temp is 175, with humidity to match. And the smell of decayed toads, the dumps at the far end of the lake, and an occasional soupçon of Std. Oil, whose refinery is a couple of mi. away, is enough to put hair on the back of a mud turtle. 17 thousand guys clumped together in the middle fishing for the known 64 crappies in that lake. . . . Each boat contains a minimum of 9 guys and 14 cases of beer. And once in a while, in the darkness, is heard the sound of a guy falling over backward into the slime: SSSSGLUNK!

EXERCISE 36.5 Taking Inventory: Abbreviations and Numbers

Look over an essay or two that you have written, noting your uses of abbreviations and numbers. Check your usage for correctness, consistency, and appropriateness. If you discover anything you have done wrong, make a note of it (in your writing log, if you are keeping one) so that you will do it correctly the next time.

EXERCISE 36:4: Answers

Here is the passage as published.

And in the middle of the lake, several *yards* away, are over *17,000* fishermen, in wooden rowboats rented at a buck and a *half* an hour. It is 2 A.M. The *temperature* is 175, with humidity to match. And the smell of decayed toads, the dumps at the far end of the lake, and an occasional soupçon of *Standard Oil,* whose refinery is a couple of *miles* away, is enough to put hair on the back of a mud turtle. *Seventeen thousand* guys clumped together in the middle fishing for the known *sixty-four* crappies in that lake. . . . Each boat contains a minimum of *nine* guys and *fourteen* cases of beer. And once in a while, in the darkness, is heard the sound of a guy falling over backward into the slime: SSSSGLUNK!

37

Using Italics

After the invention of printing, most type-carvers produced type that printed letters with the vertical strokes straight up and down, as in this sentence. Today such type is called **roman**. Early Italian type designers, however, came to specialize in a slanted type, *like this,* known today as **italic**. Italics are used to set off material of certain kinds or for special emphasis. As with other formal devices in writing, italic usage is governed by conventions, which this chapter presents.

If you have a fairly sophisticated word processor and printer, you may be able to print italic type. Otherwise, you can indicate italics by <u>underlining</u> the words you wish to treat in that way.

37a

Using italics for titles

In general, italics are used to signal the titles of long or complete works; shorter works or sections of works are set off with quotation marks. Use italics for the following kinds of works.

BOOKS	
A Tale of Two Cities	*The Color Purple*
CHOREOGRAPHIC WORKS	
Martha Graham's *Frontier*	Agnes De Mille's *Rodeo*

BACKGROUND

Italic is one of the three families of type that have dominated Western typography since the invention of printing. The other two are roman and **black letter** (also referred to as Old English or Gothic but not to be confused with newer Gothic typefaces). Black letter type is used today almost exclusively for decoration. Roman is the name for the kind of type that is used predominantly in printing in the West today. Italic falls in between, having both technical uses (to indicate titles, etc.) and rhetorical uses (to indicate emphasis). Each of the three major types has its origins in calligraphy.

Black letter type developed out of decorative handwriting usually associated with Germany and England. Roman letters developed first as capitals—in Rome, of course. Italic letters were based on the cursive writing used by chancery scribes in Italy to speed up their work.

The preferred type of the earliest printers was black letter. However, the first printers in Italy, Konrad Sweynheim and Arnold Pannartz, found it inappropriate for the Humanist movement that was sweeping fifteenth-century Italy. They searched calligraphic history for a more "Humanistic" type and developed what

FILMS AND VIDEOS

Black Orpheus   *Gone with the Wind*

JOURNALS

New England Journal of Medicine   *Daedalus*

LONG MUSICAL WORKS

Brandenburg Concertos   The Grateful Dead's *American Beauty*

LONG POEMS

The Odyssey   *Hiawatha*

MAGAZINES

Time   the *New Yorker*

NEWSPAPERS

the *New York Times*   the Cleveland *Plain Dealer*

PAMPHLETS

Thomas Paine's *Common Sense*

PAINTINGS AND SCULPTURE

Picasso's *Three Musicians*   O'Keeffe's *Black Iris*

PLAYS

Long Day's Journey into Night   *Gypsy*

TELEVISION AND RADIO PROGRAMS

Late Night with David Letterman *All Things Considered*

RECORDINGS

R.E.M.'s *Out of Time*   Bonnie Raitt's *Luck of the Draw*

Several exceptions are worth noting. Sacred books, such as the Bible or the Koran, and public documents, such as the Constitution or the Magna Carta, are *not* italicized. Notice also with magazines and newspapers that an initial *the* is neither italicized nor capitalized, even if it is part of the official name.

they called "Antiqua." In time, Antiqua became what we know of as "roman." For many years, black letter continued to be used for non-Humanist texts, ecclesiastical writings, and legal works.

The first printer to use italic type was Aldus Manutius, who worked in Venice in the late fifteenth century. His type designer, Francesco Griffo of Bologna, modeled his italic design on the cursive letters used in the papal chanceries of the time. Italic type first appeared in a series of Latin pocketbook-size texts, aimed at the new audience of Renaissance readers who had the Humanist love for Latin writers. The series succeeded immediately. The first volume, the "Aldine Virgil," appeared in 1501.

BACKGROUND

Newspapers provide an inexpensive, always available source of writing on which students can model much of their own use of conventions. However, in some cases, a newspaper may not be a good resource for models of italics usage. Traditionally, they have used quotation marks in place of italics. Today, many major newspapers, including the *New York Times,* the *Washington Post,* the *Chicago Tribune,* and the *Los Angeles Times,* italicize their headlines. They use a number of different typefaces in order to produce variety, especially on front pages which are full of different news stories. However, they continue to use quotation marks to indicate any titles, including those of books, plays, and magazines, despite style manuals that say these titles ought to be italicized.

USEFUL READING

The Chicago Manual of Style. 13th ed. Chicago: U of Chicago P, 1982. Provides full guidance in the use of italics.

"Printing, Typography, and Photoengraving." *The New Encyclopaedia Britannica: Macropaedia.* 1987. This article provides a brief history and discussion of the nature of typography.

37b

Using italics for words, letters, and numbers referred to as words

Italicize words, letters, or numbers referred to as words.

What's vulgar? Some people might say that the contraction of the words *what* and *is* itself is vulgar.　　　　— JOSEPH EPSTEIN, "What Is Vulgar?"

The first four orbitals are represented by the letters *s, p, d,* and *f.*

On the back of his jersey was the famous *24.*

Italics are also sometimes used to signal a word that is being defined.

Learning to play the flute depends mostly on *embouchure*—the way in which the lips are positioned over the mouthpiece.

37c

Using italics for foreign words and phrases

Italicize words and phrases from other languages unless they are so frequently used by English speakers that they have come to be considered a

---

Everyday use

Look around, and you'll see italics used in many ways: on signs, in pamphlets, on the sides of trucks. On a recent visit to Chicago, a student looking for good cheap food found this listing in a visitors' guide.

Gold Coast Dogs (418 North State). Chicago is serious about hot dogs. A good Chicago hot dog is an all-beef critter with natural casing, in a steamed bun and topped with your choice of the following (aka *everything*): yellow mustard, relish, raw chopped onion, tomato wedges, a dill pickle sliced lengthwise, maybe jalapeno peppers if you're perverse, and celery salt. A good Chicago hot dog *never* touches catsup, brown mustard, cooked onions, cheese, or sauerkraut.

For what purposes are the italics used? Look around you for some examples of italics in use, and bring in two or three interesting examples to compare with those discovered by your classmates.

part of English. The French word "bourgeois" or the Italian "pasta," for instance, do not need to be italicized. If you are in doubt about a particular word, most dictionaries offer guidelines.

> At last one of the phantom sleighs gliding along the street would come to a stop, and with gawky haste Mr. Burness in his fox-furred *shapka* would make for our door. — VLADIMIR NABOKOV, *Speak, Memory*

> I was *un católico* before I was a Catholic.
> — RICHARD RODRIGUEZ, *Hunger of Memory*

Note that Latin genus and species names are always italicized.

> The caterpillars of *Hapalia,* when attacked by the wasp *Apanteles machaeralis,* drop suddenly from their leaves and suspend themselves in air by a silken thread. — STEPHEN JAY GOULD, "Nonmoral Nature"

37d

Using italics for the names of vehicles

Italicize names of specific aircraft, spacecraft, ships, and trains. Do not italicize types and classes, such as "Learjet," "space shuttle," "airbus," or "Bonanza."

AIRCRAFT AND SPACECRAFT

Spirit of St. Louis   *Discovery*

SHIPS

the *Santa Maria*   U.S.S. *Iowa*

TRAINS

the *Orient Express*   Amtrak's *Silver Star*

37e

Using italics for special emphasis

Italics can be used to help create emphasis in writing.

> *Now* is the time to make real the promises of democracy.
> — MARTIN LUTHER KING, JR., "I Have a Dream"

> Gil's homer pulled the cork, and now there arose from all over the park a full, furious, happy shout of "Let's go, *Mets!* Let's go, *Mets!*" There were

BACKGROUND

Writers may want to emphasize with italics parts of a work for a variety of different reasons. Fowler suggests several:

1. To emphasize the main point of the phrase or clause or sentence.
2. To stress a contrast with reader expectations (and, of course, reveal the writer's awareness of the contrast).
3. To stress a contrast with another word, phrase, etc., within proximity (with both words, phrases, etc., usually italicized).
4. To suggest a stress upon a word or phrase, if it were spoken aloud.
5. To suggest that that which is being emphasized deserves more consideration or "thinking over" than the reader would normally give it. As Fowler says, "They pull up the reader and tell him not to read on, or he will miss some peculiarity in the italicized word. The particular point he is to notice is left to his own discernment . . ." (*A Dictionary of Modern English Usage,* 2nd ed. [New York: Oxford UP, 1965], 313).

Whether or not to use italics for emphasis is still being debated and probably will continue to be debated as long as some writers feel the need for that special emphasis. Fowler calls it "a primitive way of soliciting attention" (313). Yet, as *The Chicago Manual of Style* states, "Writers have probably always felt the need for devices to give special expression . . ." (140).

TEACHING PRACTICE

Providing your students with models can help them to see both how italics are used and how use of italics for emphasis is a rhetorical decision, thus varying from writer to writer.

Consider having your class read extensively (for more than just a few paragraphs) in the work of a writer or writers who use italics regularly. (J. D. Salinger and Tom Wolfe might be examples.) Ask your students to consider whether the writer overuses italics.

EXERCISE 37.1: Answers

1. Hawthorne's story "My Kinsman, Major Molineux" bears a striking resemblance to Shakespeare's play *A Midsummer Night's Dream.*

2. An excerpt from his book *Waiting for the Weekend* was published in the *Atlantic.*

3. Georgetown offers a potpourri of cultures and styles.

4. The word *veterinary* comes from the Latin *veterinarius.*

5. Niko Tinbergen's essay "The Bee-Hunters of Hulshorst" is a diary of experiments on *Philanthus triangulum Fabr,* the bee-killer wasp.

6. Flying the *Glamorous Glennis,* named for his wife, Chuck Yeager was the first pilot to fly faster than the speed of sound.

7. The *Washington Post* provides extensive coverage of Congress.

8. *The Waste Land* is a long and difficult but ultimately rewarding poem.

9. If you have seen only a reproduction of Picasso's *Guernica,* you can scarcely imagine the impact the original painting makes.

10. Seven astronauts were killed when the *Challenger* exploded.

EXERCISES 37.2: Answers will vary.

wild cries of encouragement before every pitch, boos for every called strike. . . . The fans' hopes, of course, *were* insane.

— ROGER ANGELL, *The Summer Game*

Mother's little brothers used to delight in hiding in the hay where they could listen to Grandpa pray, and he on his side would be sure to get all their names in when he was asking for forgiveness and beg the Lord to be patient with them, whatever had been their sinful ways, and lead them into righteousness *before it was too late.*

— EUDORA WELTY, *One Writer's Beginnings*

Although italic emphasis is useful on occasion, especially in informal writing, use it sparingly. It is usually better to create emphasis with sentence structure and word choice.

EXERCISE 37.1

In each of the following sentences, underline any words that should be italicized and circle any italicized words that should not be. Example:

> *Critics debated whether* <u>Thelma & Louise</u> *was a feminist film.*

1. Hawthorne's story *My Kinsman, Major Molineux* bears a striking resemblance to Shakespeare's play A Midsummer Night's Dream.

2. An excerpt from his book Waiting for the Weekend was published in the Atlantic.

3. Georgetown offers a *potpourri* of cultures and styles.

4. The word veterinary comes from the Latin *veterinarius.*

5. Niko Tinbergen's essay *The Bee-Hunters of Hulshorst* is a diary of experiments on *Philanthus triangulum Fabr,* the *bee-killer wasp.*

6. Flying the Glamorous Glennis, named for his wife, Chuck Yeager was the first pilot to fly faster than the speed of sound.

7. The Washington Post provides extensive coverage of Congress.

8. The Waste Land is a long and difficult but ultimately rewarding poem.

9. If you have seen only a reproduction of Picasso's Guernica, you can scarcely imagine the impact the original painting makes.

10. Seven astronauts were killed when the Challenger exploded.

EXERCISE 37.2 Reading with an Eye for Italics

The following passage about a graduate English seminar uses italics in several different ways—for emphasis, for a foreign phrase, and for a title. Read the passage carefully, particularly noting the effects created by the italics. How would it differ without any italic emphasis? What other words or phrases might Ozick have italicized?

> To get into this seminar, you had to submit to a grilling wherein you renounced all former allegiance to the then-current literary religion, New Criticism, which considered that only the text existed, not the world. I passed the interview by lying—cunningly, and against my real convictions. I said that probably the world *did* exist—and walked triumphantly into the seminar room.
>
> There were four big tables arranged in a square, with everyone's feet sticking out into the open middle of the square. You could tell who was nervous, and how much, by watching the pairs of feet twist around each other. The Great Man presided awesomely from the high bar of the square. His head was a majestic granite-gray, like a centurion in command; he *looked* famous. His clean shoes twitched only slightly, and only when he was angry.
>
> It turned out he was angry at me a lot of the time. He was angry because he thought me a disrupter, a rioter, a provocateur, and a fool; also crazy. And this was twenty years ago, before these things were *de rigueur* in the universities. Everything was very quiet in those days: there were only the Cold War and Korea and Joe McCarthy and the Old Old Nixon, and the only revolutionaries around were in Henry James's *The Princess Casamassima*.
>
> – CYNTHIA OZICK, "We Are the Crazy Lady"

EXERCISE 37.3   Taking Inventory: Italics

Write a paragraph or two describing the most eccentric person you know. Make a point to italicize some words for special emphasis. Read your passage aloud to see what effect the italics bring. Consider italicizing any other words you wish to emphasize. Now, explain each use of italics, stating in words the reason for the special attention. If you find yourself unable to give a reason, ask yourself whether the word should in fact be italicized at all.

Then revise the passage to eliminate *all but one* use of italics. Try revising sentences and choosing more precise words to convey emphasis without italics. Compare the two versions, and decide which is more effective. Can you make any conclusions about using italics for emphasis? If you keep a writing log, add to it any thoughts, with examples from this exercise. In addition, you might keep your eye open for italics in your reading and copy down in your log any examples that impress you.

38

Using Hyphens

the lady whose odd smile is the merest hyphen — KARL SHAPIRO

The "merest" hyphen is used to divide words at the end of a line and to link words or word parts (such as *hand-me-down* or *bye-bye*). As such, it serves purposes both mechanical and rhetorical. Its mechanical ones are fairly straightforward, with simple rules that tell us when and where we can divide a word at the end of a line. The rhetorical ones, however, are somewhat more complicated, for though they are governed in some cases by rules, they are defined in other cases by the needs of readers. Stewart Beach points out the rhetorical usefulness of a hyphen in the following anecdote.

> I came across a word I thought was a series of typos for *collaborators.* Reading it again, I realized the word was *colaborers.* But a hyphen would have [prevented] all the confusion. — STEWART BEACH

Indeed, had the word included a hyphen—*co-laborers*—its meaning would have been instantly clear.

Sometimes the dictionary will tell you whether to hyphenate a word. Other times, you will have to decide. This chapter will help you with the decisions and the rules that go along with using hyphens.

USEFUL READING

Teall, Edward N. *Meet Mr. Hyphen and Put Him in His Place.* New York: Funk, 1937. See Chapter 1 for a short history of hyphens.

Webb, Robert A. *The Washington Post Deskbook on Style.* New York: McGraw, 1978. See the entry under "hyphens" for rules and illustrative examples.

38a

Using hyphens to divide words at the end of a line

It is best not to divide words between lines, but when you must do so, remember to break words *between syllables.* The word *metaphor,* for instance, is made up of three syllables (*met-a-phor*), and you could break it after either the *t* or the *a.* All dictionaries show syllable breaks, so the best advice for dividing words correctly is simply to look them up. In addition, you should follow certain other conventions, including the following.

- *Never divide one-syllable words,* even relatively long words such as *drought* or *through.*

- *Divide compound words only between the parts.* Words such as *headache* or *mother-in-law* should be broken between their parts (*head-ache*) or at their hyphens (*mother-in-law*).

- *Divide words with prefixes or suffixes between the parts.* The word *disappearance,* then, might be broken after its prefix (*dis-appearance*) or before its suffix (*disappear-ance*). Prefixed words that include hyphens, such as *self-righteous,* should be divided at the hyphen.

- *Never divide abbreviations, contractions, or figures.* Though such "words" as *NASA, didn't,* and *250,000* have audible syllables, it is not permissible to divide them in writing.

- *Leave at least two letters on each line when dividing a word.* Words such as *acorn* (*a-corn*) or *scratchy* (*scratch-y*), therefore, cannot be divided at all, and a word such as *Americana* (*A-mer-i-can-a*) can be broken only after *r* or *i.*

EXERCISE 38.1

Divide each of the following words into syllables, first referring to your dictionary. Then indicate with a hyphen the places where you might break each word at the end of a line. Indicate any words that cannot be divided into syllables or broken at the end of a line.

1. passable
2. retract
3. stripped
4. military
5. antechamber
6. inner-directed
7. haven't
8. dimming
9. anonymous
10. attitude

EXERCISE 38.1: Answers

1. pass*able; pass-able
2. re*tract; re-tract
3. stripped; do not break one-syllable words
4. mil*i*tar*y; mil-i-tary
5. an*te*cham*ber; ante-chamber
6. in*ner*di*rect*ed; inner-directed
7. have*n't; do not break contractions
8. dim*ming; dim-ming
9. a*non*y*mous; anon-y-mous
10. at*ti*tude; at-ti-tude

Everyday use

Hyphens play a number of roles in our everyday lives. On any day we might make a left-hand turn, order a medium-sized Coke, wear a Dodgers T-shirt, buy gasoline at a self-service station, drop in at the campus writing center for some one-on-one tutoring, worry about a long-term relationship, listen to some fifties rock-and-roll, or go out for Tex-Mex food. Jot down some of the hyphens you run across in a day.

38b

Using hyphens with compound words

Compound words are words, such as *rowboat* or *up-to-date,* that are made up of more than one word. Some of them are written as one word, some as separate words, and some with hyphens.

ONE WORD	housefly, textbook, flowerpot
SEPARATE WORDS	high school, parking meter, floppy disk
WITH HYPHENS	city-state, sister-in-law, jack-of-all-trades

It is often difficult to remember whether a particular compound word is one word, separate words, or hyphenated. Even compounds that begin with the same word are often treated every which way—*blueberry, blue-green,* and *blue cheese,* for instance. In general, then, consult the dictionary if you have any doubt about how to spell a compound. There are, in addition, some conventions that can guide you in using hyphens with compound words.

1

Hyphenating compound adjectives

Often you will use adjectives made up of word combinations that are not listed in a dictionary. The guiding principle then is to hyphenate most compound adjectives that precede a noun but not those that follow a noun.

a *hard-nosed* boss, a *six-foot* plank

My boss is extremely *hard nosed.*

The plank was *six feet* long.

In general, the reason for hyphenating such compound adjectives is to facilitate reading. Notice, for example, how the hyphen affects your understanding of the following two sentences.

The designers used potted palms as living room dividers.

The designers used potted palms as *living-room* dividers.

In the first sentence, the word *living* may seem to modify *room dividers;* in the second, the hyphen makes clear that it is part of a compound adjective. But commonly used compound adjectives do not need to be hyphenated for clarity—*income tax reform* or *first class mail* would seldom if ever be misunderstood. Never hyphenate a combination of an adverb ending in *-ly* and an adjective: *a radically different approach.*

2

Hyphenating coined compounds

You may sometimes want to use hyphens to link a group of words that would not normally be hyphenated but that you are using in an unexpected way, especially as an adjective. Such combinations are called **coined compounds**.

> She sat . . . with her "get-out-of-my-kitchen" and "come-here-do-you-realize-what-you've-done" [look]. . . .
> — EUDORA WELTY, "Music from Spain"

> I've had people tell me that waiting for *life-or-death* news they've stood in front of an open refrigerator eating anything in sight—cold boiled potatoes, chili sauce, bowls of whipped cream.
> — ALICE MUNRO, "The Moons of Jupiter"

3

Hyphenating fractions and compound numbers

To write out fractions, use a hyphen to join the numerator and denominator. Also use hyphens to spell out whole numbers from twenty-one to ninety-nine, both when they stand alone and when they are part of larger numbers. (Usually such larger numbers should be written as numerals.)

one-seventh	thirty-seven
seven-sixteenths	three hundred fifty-four thousand

4

Using suspended hyphens

A series of compound words that share the same base word can be shortened by the use of suspended hyphens.

Each student should do the work *him-* or *herself*.

38c

Using hyphens with prefixes and suffixes

Most words with prefixes or suffixes are written as one word, without hyphens: *antiwar, misinform, gorillalike*. Only in the following cases do you need a hyphen.

WITH CAPITALIZED BASE WORDS

pro-Democratic, un-American, non-Catholic

WITH FIGURES

pre-1960, post-1945, the over-65 age group

WITH CERTAIN PREFIXES AND SUFFIXES

all-state, ex-husband, self-possessed, quasi-legislative, mayor-elect, fifty-odd, twenty-some

Note that hyphens are used with *ex-* and *-some* only when these mean "former" and "approximately," respectively.

WITH COMPOUND WORDS

pre-high school, pro-civil rights, post-cold war

FOR CLARITY OR EASE OF READING

re-cover, anti-inflation, troll-like

Re-cover means "cover again"; the hyphen distinguishes it from *recover* meaning "get well." In *anti-inflation* and *troll-like,* the hyphens separate confusing clusters of vowels and consonants.

EXERCISE 38.2

Using the dictionary as a reference, insert hyphens as needed.

1. deescalate
2. pre World War II
3. pre and post-Wall Berlin
4. happily married couple
5. a what we worry look
6. self important
7. president elect
8. seven hundred thirty three
9. a hard working farmer
10. a politician who is quick witted

EXERCISE 38.3

Insert or delete hyphens as necessary, and correct any incorrect word divisions in the following sentences. Use your dictionary if necessary.

1. Stress can lead to hypertension and ulcers.
2. McKuen began to write as an escape from his on the move life, which included various odd jobs ranging from ditchdigging to cookiecutting.
3. The carpenter asked for a two pound bag of three quarter inch nails.

EXERCISE 38.2: Answers

1. de-escalate
2. pre-World War II
3. pre- and post-Wall Berlin
4. Correct
5. a what-me-worry look
6. self-important
7. president-elect
8. seven hundred thirty-three
9. a hard-working farmer
10. a politician who is quick-witted (Quick-witted is commonly found in dictionaries; thus hyphenation is correct even though the compound adjective comes after the noun.)

4. Suicide among teen-agers has tripled in the past thirty five years.
5. We urged him to be open minded and to temper his insensitive views.
6. The Soviets were divided between pro and antiGorbachev factions.
7. One of Mikhail Baryshnikov's favorite dancers was none other than Fred A-staire.
8. The government declared an all-out war on poverty and homeless-ness.
9. The governor elect joked about the preelection polls.
10. The beautifully-written essay earned high praise.

EXERCISE 38.4 Reading with an Eye for Hyphenation

The following paragraph uses many hyphens. Read it carefully, and note how the hyphens make the paragraph easier to read. Why do you think *semi-pro* is hyphenated? Why is *junior-college* hyphenated in the last sentence?

All semi-pro leagues, it should be understood, are self-sustaining, and have no farm affiliation or other connection with the twenty-six major-league clubs, or with the seventeen leagues and hundred and fifty-two teams . . . that make up the National Association—the minors, that is. There is no central body of semi-pro teams, and semi-pro players are not included among the six hundred and fifty major-leaguers, the twenty-five hundred-odd minor-leaguers, plus all the managers, coaches, presidents, commissioners, front-office people, and scouts, who, taken together, constitute the great tent called organized ball. (A much diminished tent, at that; back in 1949, the minors included fifty-nine leagues, about four hundred and forty-eight teams, and perhaps ten thousand players.) Also outside the tent, but perhaps within its shade, are five college leagues, ranging across the country from Cape Cod to Alaska, where the most promising freshman, sophomore, and junior-college ballplayers . . . compete against each other. . . .

—ROGER ANGELL, "In the Country"

EXERCISE 38.5 Taking Inventory: Hyphenation

The difference between *re-sign* and *resign* is a hyphen.   —JIM PALMER

The above statement, heard on a televised baseball game, shows how important a hyphen can be. Look through some of your own writing to see if you ever use hyphens in a way that affects meaning or clarity. Have you followed the conventions governing use of hyphens in compound words, with prefixes and suffixes, with fractions and numbers? If you find you are misusing hyphens or are unclear about how to use them in certain situations, check those instances against this chapter. Note down any rules or thoughts about hyphenation for future use—in your writing log, if you keep one.

EXERCISE 38.3: Answers

1. Correct.
2. McKuen began to write as an escape from his on-the-move life, which included various odd jobs ranging from ditch-digging to cookie-cutting.
3. The carpenter asked for a two-pound bag of three-quarter-inch nails.
4. Suicide among teenagers has tripled in the past thirty-five years.
5. We urged him to be open-minded and to temper his insensitive views.
6. The Soviets were divided between pro- and anti-Gorbachev factions.
7. One of Mikhail Baryshnikov's favorite dancers was none other than Fred Astaire.
8. The government declared an all-out war on poverty and homelessness.
9. The governor-elect joked about the pre-election polls.
10. The beautifully written essay earned high praise.

EXERCISE 38.4: Answers will vary.

TEACHING PRACTICE

Ask students to bring examples of their own use of hyphens in writing to class for discussion, using these examples as a way to talk about using hyphens effectively and correctly.

Part Eight

Doing Research
and Using Sources

——————— ≪≫ ———————

39

Becoming a Researcher

BACKGROUND

The fifteenth edition of the *New Encyclopaedia Britannica (NEB)* (1987) attributes the dominance of human beings on earth to the "innate ability to communicate and to store, retrieve, and use knowledge so that each generation does not have to relearn the lessons of the past in order to act effectively in the present." The *NEB* points out that this ability to pass on information from generation to generation has transformed human beings into the composite beneficiaries of the ideas and experiences of our ancestors.

Research is the activity that enables us to process, create, and communicate knowledge. But research goes beyond simply gathering data and passing it on. In its most beneficial sense, research is the process of investigating information or data for a purpose: to make decisions about our lives, to understand our world, or to create or advance understanding. Research, then, is the use of information in "decision making" that responds to specific situations, times, and needs. Far from being restricted to work on a college "research essay," research informs much of what we do throughout our lives.

The English word *research* derives not only from the French *chercher,* which means "search," but also from the Late Latin *circare,* which means "circle around, explore." **Research**, then, is a way of exploring a subject by circling carefully around and around it, a process that the editors of the eleventh edition of the *Encyclopaedia Britannica* identify as all "investigations . . . based on sources of knowledge." Without research, they go on, "no authoritative words could have been written, no scientific discoveries or inventions made, no theories of any value propounded."

Work in many professions—engineering, news reporting, law, medicine, police detection—relies heavily on research. But this process of investigating sources, compiling data, and drawing conclusions based on what we find pervades our personal lives as well as our work. We find something out, and then we act on it. This chapter thus rests on the assumption that we are all researchers. From this basic assumption come five important premises.

1. *You already know how to do research.* You act as a researcher whenever you investigate something—whether a college, a course, a cosmetic, a computer, or a car—by reading up on it, discussing its features with your friends or experts, or checking several stores to see what is in stock, how much it costs, and what it can do.

In addition, you already possess many essential research skills. You know how to combine experience, observation, and new information when you try to solve a problem, answer a question, make a decision, or analyze a situation. You know how to seek out pieces of information, evaluate their usefulness, fit them all together, and then use them to make an "educated guess." Such basic research methods are important skills for working and living. These are the very skills you will build on as you become more familiar with academic research.

2. *Good research makes you into a genuine expert.* If you approach your research with serious intent, you may gradually become someone who knows more than anyone else on campus about Wordsworth's "Lucy poems," new uses of metal hybrids, or Jackie Robinson's place in sports history. You will be truly knowledgeable, and you will be able to add your knowledge to the conversation of educated people that goes on all about you, not only in college but also in the media, in community groups, and in the workplace.

3. *Research is usually driven by a purpose.* Whether for common everyday needs or in an academic setting, researchers seek out facts and opinions for a reason—wanting to make a discovery; to answer a question, solve a problem, or prove something; to teach; to correct an error; or to advocate a position. Research is rarely an end in itself. Instead, it is a process or method, used in many situations and fields, for systematically discovering, testing, and sharing new ideas.

Your main purpose in college research will most often be to fulfill a specific assignment: for example, to compare literary texts, to trace the causes of the Civil War, or to survey and summarize students' feelings about mandatory drug testing of athletes. Sometimes, however, you may be asked to determine your own purpose for research.

4. *Your purpose influences the research you do, which in turn refines your purpose.* When you begin any research, it is impossible to know exactly what you will find out. You begin with a question you want to answer or a general idea that you want to explore, but you may find that your specific purpose shifts as you learn more about your subject. The evidence you have gathered, for example, may prove so startling that it calls for you to persuade—to advocate a solution to a problem—when you originally had meant only to explain the problem. In turn, as you refine your purpose, that purpose will help guide you in choosing additional sources and organizing material.

5. *Research rarely progresses in a neat line from start to finish.* You begin with a question that may or may not be explorable or supportable. Then you do some background research and perhaps some writing. Your initial investigation, however, may lead you to start all over again—or to modify your idea and then to refer to other, more specific sources. This additional research focuses your idea even more, leading you to more and more specific sources. Writing is an important part of this investigative process, for it forces you to sharpen your ideas and perhaps to turn back to your sources for more information. Wherever the process of research takes you, however, your overriding goal remains the same: to develop a strong critical understanding of the information you are gathering.

FOR COLLABORATIVE WORK

To show your students that they do indeed know how to do research, ask your students to give you advice and help in deciding on your purchase of a stereo system or a bicycle; or have them help you decide whether to live on the north side of campus or the south side. You might ask them to help you draw up a list of things you would need to find out in deciding whether to accept job offers in the Pacific Northwest, on the East Coast, or in the Midwest.

In each of these cases, having your students work together brainstorming questions and generating information and criteria that will help you decide shows them that they already have ways of researching. They'll ask questions. They'll rely on their own experiences. They'll consult other people or other sources, such as consumer magazines or encyclopedias. By investigating your choices and reporting their findings back to you, they'll help you make your choice. These activities will help reinforce the fact that all research is purposeful.

FOR THE WRITING LOG

As preparation for a discussion of the nature and process of college-level research, have students write a page or so in their logs about their previous experiences with researching and research papers.

USEFUL READING

Emig, Janet. "Writing as a Mode of Learning." *CCC* 28 (1977): 122–28. Emig's view of writing as a means of learning informs the interconnection among researching, writing, and learning.

Langer, Judith A. "Learning through Writing: Study Skills in the Content Areas." *Journal of Reading* 29 (1986): 400–06. Langer reports that writing essays encourages content learning more effectively than taking notes and answering questions.

BACKGROUND

Regardless of the field of study, researching, writing, and learning are interconnected. James Britton's distinction between *expressive* and *transactional* writing helps to explain this interconnection. We write in order to learn; that is, we think on paper, using writing to process information and to probe ideas. This function of writing, a form of self-expression and exploration, Britton calls *expressive*. It serves the writer; it enables him or her to learn and understand information. We also write to communicate learning. We use language to inform, to persuade, or to help someone else understand. This function Britton calls *transactional* to emphasize the exchange or transmission of information for an audience's learning purposes. See James Britton, et al., *The Development of Writing Abilities, 11–18* (London: Macmillan, 1975).

TEACHING PRACTICE

Ask students to discuss the research process they might use for each of the situations listed in "Everyday use."

Essays do, in a way, resemble scientific writing: they report experiments in thought.

–LEWIS THOMAS

Everyday use

The following situations suggest the number of roles research plays in our everyday lives.

Your employer tells you that the company needs a new intercom system and asks you to recommend the best system for the money.

You have an opportunity to visit Tokyo for a week. You need to plan that week—to find out where to stay, what to see, what to do.

You are on a tight budget and want to find the local grocery with the lowest prices.

Take a few minutes to think of occasions in the last month when you conducted some kind of research. Then decide if there were any times you didn't *do any research but might—or should—have done so.*

One student's experience illustrates how ideas can change and develop during the research process. Assigned to write an essay on a topic of current interest to him, he began by puzzling over whether modern rock guitar styles could be traced to the electric guitar styles developed in the 1940s and 1950s by Chicago blues groups. This beginning was a good one; the student liked the subject and already knew something about it. Starting with background sources about modern rock guitarists like Eric Clapton and Pete Townshend, he found repeated references to Muddy Waters, Howlin' Wolf, Buddy Guy, Albert King, and other Chicago blues artists. He listened to a number of records and found repeated riffs (musical phrases) and clear derivations. Based on the information he found and his understanding of the records themselves, he began to make notes toward an essay.

This student's research might have ended at the point of drafting, but it did not. In several sources on the Chicago electric blues tradition, he found references to "country blues" and Southern "race records" as influences on the Chicago artists. He was not sure what these terms meant but wanted to find out. As he continued his research, he discovered that blues music harks back to nineteenth-century slave songs and chants, that the country blues was nearly always played on a single acoustic guitar, and that the well-documented history of country blues guitar styles was easily traced back to the 1920s.

Clearly the story was older and the traditions much deeper than he had imagined. He decided to get more books about Southern and country blues musicians of the 1920s and 1930s in order to learn all he could about the guitar styles of musicians like Charley Patton, Robert Johnson, Leadbelly, Mississippi John Hurt, and Lightnin' Hopkins. In addition, he began to consider the differences between electric and acoustic instruments. Finally, he looked for records still available by some of the very early country blues musicians. To his amazement, he heard on these very early records some of the exact riffs and techniques he so admired by contemporary guitarists.

Thus, this writer arrived at this point of his research with a stronger and deeper idea for development, a far better grasp of musical history, and more and better research sources. And he had accumulated enough information and evidence to begin crafting a fine essay.

Research for writing

For college work, research may range from a couple of hours spent gathering background about a topic or evidence for an argument for a brief essay to weeks or months of full-scale exploration for a term paper centered on the results of your investigation. Chapters 39–44 provide guidelines to help you with *any* research done for the purpose of writing. In addition, these chapters show examples of work by student Daniel Taffe, whose complete essay appears in Chapter 43. An additional complete essay appears in Chapter 44.

39a

Understanding research assignments and topics

In college, most research you do responds to a writing assignment. Before you do anything else, therefore, be sure that you understand the requirements and limits of the assignment.

For his Introduction to Writing course, Daniel Taffe received the following assignment:

> Choose a topic—a subject, a person, or an event—that you want to know more about, and use it as the topic for a research essay that makes and substantiates a claim about your topic. *Note:* Because you have only one month to complete the essay, be careful that your topic is not too broad and that information about the topic is available to you.

1

Analyzing a research assignment

Begin your research by paying close attention to the exact wording of the assignment. If it is not handed out in printed form, copy it carefully, word for word. Note whether it specifies a topic or asks you to choose your own. Consider any requirements for essential purpose, audience, scope of research, length, and deadline, and use these factors to help you choose a topic if one has not been specified. (See 39a2 for more on choosing topics.) When you have a topic, consider your rhetorical stance—your own perspective on the topic. Then try to map out a rough schedule for your research, consulting the schedule on p. 532.

Upon questioning, Daniel Taffe's instructor clarified some requirements of his research assignment: the essay should use information from multiple sources to support the claim; it should be roughly seven to ten pages in length; and it should be written for members of his writing class.

Identifying the purpose

Read through the assignment for **cue words**, such as *describe, survey, analyze, explain, classify, compare,* or *contrast,* that specify the pattern the instructor expects the essay to follow. What do such words mean in this particular field or discipline? What do these meanings suggest about the purpose(s) of the assignment? Keeping these meanings in mind as you begin researching will help you identify sources that fulfill that purpose. (See 2c for a discussion of ways to assess purpose.)

Identifying the audience

Find out if your assignment specifies an audience other than the instructor. Then consider what they and your instructor will expect you to provide, by answering the following questions.

- Who will be interested in the information you gather, and why?
- What do you know about their backgrounds?
- What will they want to know?
- What will they already know?
- What response do you want to elicit from them?
- What assumptions might they hold about the topic?
- What kinds of evidence will you need to present to convince them?
- What will your instructor expect in a strong essay on this topic?

(See 2e for additional questions to consider about your audience.)

Considering your rhetorical stance

When you have at least a broad topic, think about your own attitude toward it, your rhetorical stance. Are you primarily just curious about it? Do you approve of it? dislike it? find it bewildering? Monitoring where you stand on the topic will help you understand your purpose, your audience, and your relationship to your sources. (See 2d.)

Gauging the scope of research

Next consider any information about the kind of research you will need to do. Does the assignment specify anything about how many or what kind of library sources you can or should use? Does it require or suggest any field research—interviewing, surveying, or observing? If your assignment includes such requirements, keep them in mind as you plan your research.

Noting the length

Does your assignment specify the length of the final draft? The amount of research and writing time you must budget for a five- to seven-page essay differs markedly from that needed for one of fifteen to twenty pages. And whatever your preliminary estimate, you may need more time if materials are not readily available or if you discover after a first draft that you need to do more research. The best plan is to begin work as soon as possible.

Working toward the deadline

What is your deadline for the completed project? Are any preliminary materials—a working bibliography, a research thesis, an outline, or a first draft—due before this date?

Keeping a research log

You might want to set up a **research log** for keeping track of your work. If you already keep a writing log, you might set off a special section of it for your research project. Use the log to jot down thoughts about your topic, lists of things to do, ideas about possible sources or connections between information or to keep track of library materials you need to get (or return). Such notes may help you proceed more efficiently and give you a sense of the progress—or the need for progress—in your research.

FOR THE WRITING LOG

A research log (or a section of the writing log set off for such a purpose) is a good place to keep track of reading, note-taking, and writing progress, to ask questions, and to attempt tentative syntheses or conclusions. But no less important, it is a good place to write about the blocks, obstacles, or challenges any researcher inevitably faces.

TEACHING PRACTICE

In the following passage, astronomer Carl Sagan describes the excitement of the kind of research in which he is engaged, research that makes you "*really* think" and consequently "experience a kind of exhilaration." Ask students to read Sagan's description carefully. Have they done any research that fits his description? What kind of research would allow them to experience "exhilaration?"

. . . the main trick of [doing research in] science is to *really* think of something: the shape of clouds and their occasional sharp bottom edges at the same altitude everywhere in the sky; the formation of a dewdrop on a leaf; the origin of a name or a word—Shakespeare, say, or "philanthropic"; the reason for human social customs—the incest taboo, for example; how it is that a lens in sunlight can make paper burn; how a "walking stick" got to look so much like a twig; why the Moon seems to follow us as we walk; what prevents us from digging a hole down to the center of the Earth; what the definition is of "down" on a spherical Earth; how it is possible for the body to convert yesterday's lunch into today's muscle and sinew; or how far is up—does the universe go on forever, or if it does not, is there any meaning to the question of what lies on the other side? Some of these questions are pretty easy. Others, especially the last, are mysteries to which no one even today knows the answer. They are natural questions to ask. Every culture has posed such questions in one way or another. Almost always the proposed answers are in the nature of "Just So Stories," attempted explanations divorced from experiment, or even from careful comparative observations.

But the scientific cast of mind examines the world critically as if many alternative worlds might exist, as if other things might be here which are not. Then we are forced to ask why what we see is present and not something else. Why are the Sun and the Moon and the planets spheres? Why not pyramids, or cubes, or dodecahedra? Why not irregular, jumbly shapes? Why so symmetrical, worlds? If you spend any time spinning hypotheses, checking to see whether they make sense, whether they conform to what else we know, thinking of tests

➤ Scheduling a research project

Assignment date _____   Try to complete by

Analyze assignment; decide on primary purpose and
   audience; choose topic if necessary. _____
Arrange library tour; develop search strategy. _____
Do background reading; narrow topic if necessary. _____
Decide on research question, tentative hypothesis. _____
Start working bibliography; track down sources. _____
Develop working thesis and rough outline. _____
If necessary, conduct interviews or observations, or
   distribute and collect questionnaires. _____
Send for needed materials by mail. _____
Read and evaluate sources; take notes. _____
Draft explicit thesis and outline. _____
Prepare first draft. _____
Obtain and evaluate critical responses. _____
Do more research if necessary. _____
Revise draft. _____
Prepare list of works cited. _____
Edit revised draft; use spell checker, if available. _____
Prepare final draft. _____
Do final proofreading. _____

Final draft due _____

2

Choosing a topic

Sometimes a research topic may choose you: it so fascinates or compels you that you simply *must* explore it. Other times, a specific topic is assigned, or the choice is limited in some way. Even in these cases, however, you will probably have some leeway in tailoring the topic to your interests.

If your assignment does not specify a topic, you can best begin articulating one by keeping in mind any specifications about purpose, audience, scope, length, and deadline (see 39a1) and asking yourself the following questions:

- What subjects do you know something about?
- What subjects might you like to become an expert on?
- What subjects evoke a strong reaction from you—intense attraction, puzzlement, or skepticism?

In addition, skim through your textbooks or class notes, current magazines or journals, or standard reference works (such as *Editorial Reports, Library of Congress Subject Headings,* or periodical indexes), looking for some topic or question that intrigues you. You may find the techniques presented in 3a for exploring a topic—brainstorming, freewriting, looping, clustering, and questioning—useful for discovering one. Even if your instructor has assigned a broad topic—such as animal rights or the role of the United States after the cold war—you may find these questions and methods useful in deciding on what aspect of it to research.

Daniel Taffe, for example, began his research by deciding to find out about artist Diego Rivera, whose work he had seen while on vacation. His first look in the library circulation computer yielded Rivera's autobiography, *My Art, My Life.* In skimming this text, however, what really caught his imagination were the discussions about Frida Kahlo, Rivera's wife. Because he had not progressed far in his research, he decided to shift his topic and find out more about Kahlo.

Getting response to your topic

As soon as you come up with a topic, draft several sentences that describe it. Then try to get some response—from your instructor and perhaps from some classmates. Ask them to consider the following questions.

- Would you be interested in reading about this topic?
- Is the topic manageable?
- Can you suggest any interesting angles or approaches?
- Can you suggest any good sources of information on this topic?

Narrowing and focusing a topic

Any topic you choose to research must be manageable—must suit the scope, audience, length, and time limits for your assignment. Making a topic manageable often requires narrowing it, but narrowing is not always sufficient in itself. "World War II" may be too general, but "the Battle of Midway" will probably not be any easier to manage. Rather than simply reducing a large subject to a smaller one, then, it may be more useful to *focus* on a particular slant, looking for a governing question to guide your research. One good way to work toward such a question is to brainstorm a series of questions you might ask about your topic. You can then evaluate them and choose one or two that seem most interesting and manageable.

you can pose to substantiate or deflate your hypotheses, you will find yourself doing science. And as you come to practice this habit of thought more and more you will get better and better at it. To penetrate into the heart of the thing—even a little thing, a blade of grass, as Walt Whitman said—is to experience a kind of exhilaration that, it may be, only human beings of all the beings on this planet can feel. We are an intelligent species and the use of our intelligence quite properly gives us pleasure. In this respect the brain is like a muscle. When we think well, we feel good. Understanding is a kind of ecstasy. —CARL SAGAN, *Broca's Brain*

FOR COLLABORATIVE WORK

One way of working toward a manageable topic or question is to have students brainstorm together on a topic. After students have explored a topic using some of the techniques presented in Chapter 3, have them individually explain their interest in a topic, briefly giving some background or other information on it. Open the discussion up to the class, encouraging them to ask questions and to respond to the topic.

By fielding the class's questions and responses, students develop a sense of the possible directions their topics can have. This informal class brainstorming session helps them identify perspectives that interest others in the topic. Limit each session to fifteen minutes, five minutes for the student to present his or her topic, ten minutes for the class to respond and ask questions. At the end of the fifteen minutes, have each student freewrite for ten to fifteen minutes, noting (1) suggestions for focusing, narrowing, or phrasing the research question, (2) a statement on his or her own interest in or possible approach to the topic, or (3) remarks on matters of purpose, audience, scope, or length.

To make the most of the activity, have at least four individual sessions, with no more than two presented in any one class. Then break up the class into groups of four or five to work through this activity. The small group activity gives the entire class practice at working out possible topics.

Asking a research question and developing a hypothesis

The result of this focusing process is a **research question** that can be answered or considered through research data. The research question may be tentatively answered by a **hypothesis**, a statement of what you anticipate your research might show. (If the research question you pose has an obvious answer or requires technical knowledge beyond your grasp, refocus your question.)

Like a working thesis (see 3b), a hypothesis must be not only manageable, but interesting and specific. In addition, it must be arguable, a debatable proposition that can be proved or disproved by research evidence (see 5b). For example, a statement like this one cannot be disproved: "Senator Joseph McCarthy attracted great attention with his anti-Communist crusade during the 1950s." No one would argue against this fact, and its statement is not a hypothesis. On the other hand, this statement is debatable: "Roy Cohn's political views and biased research while he was an assistant to Senator Joseph McCarthy during the 1950s were largely responsible for McCarthy's anti-Communist crusade." Such a statement would have to be proved or disproved; thus, it is a hypothesis.

In most cases, you will want to explore your topic by doing background reading in general reference books and making notes before you can formulate a research question or develop a hypothesis. In moving from a general topic of interest, such as Senator Joseph McCarthy's anti-Communist crusade of the 1950s, to a useful hypothesis, such as the one in the previous paragraph, you first focus on a single manageable issue within the field, such as Roy Cohn's role in the crusade. After background reading, you then raise a question about that issue ("To what extent did Cohn's political views and research contribute to McCarthy's crusade?") and put forward a possible answer, your hypothesis. Throughout this process, you will profit by trying to articulate your thoughts in writing.

The following example outlines Daniel Taffe's movement from general topic to hypothesis.

TOPIC	Frida Kahlo's art
ISSUE	Influences on Kahlo's art
RESEARCH QUESTION	What were the major influences on Kahlo's work?
HYPOTHESIS	The events of her own life were the central influence on Kahlo's work.

The hypothesis that tentatively answers the research question is precise enough to be supported or challenged by a manageable amount of research.

39c

Investigating what you know about your topic

Once you have narrowed and focused a topic, you need to marshal everything you already know about it. In practice, this step calls for what computer scientists call a "data dump": you try to "dump" all your immediate thoughts about the topic onto paper. Here are some useful strategies for doing so.

- *Brainstorming.* Take five minutes to list, in words or phrases, everything you think of or wonder about your hypothesis. You may find it helpful to do this as a group with other students.
- *Freewriting in favor of your hypothesis.* For five minutes, write about every reason that you believe your hypothesis is true. As in any freewriting (see 3a2), do not stop writing for any reason.
- *Freewriting against your hypothesis.* For five minutes, write down every argument you can think of, no matter how weak or improbable, that someone opposed to your hypothesis might make.
- *Freewriting on your audience.* Write for five minutes about your audience, including your instructor. What do they currently believe about your topic? What sorts of evidence will convince them to accept your hypothesis? What sorts of sources will they respect?
- *Tapping your memory for sources.* List, in the form of short notes, everything you can remember about *where* you learned about your topic: books, magazines, courses, conversations, television. Much of what you know may seem "common knowledge," but common knowledge comes from somewhere, and "somewhere" can serve as a starting point for investigation.

(For more information on these strategies, see 3a.)

39d

Moving from hypothesis to working thesis

As you gather information and begin reading sources (see Chapters 40 and 41), your research question is likely to be refined and your hypothesis to change significantly. Only after you have explored it, tested it, and sharpened it through your reading and writing does the hypothesis become a **working thesis.**

BACKGROUND

Scientist and writer Lewis Thomas recommends taking alternate routes to exploring a question or research topic, including going the opposite direction to what seems most natural or just "fiddling around." "Fiddle around," he says, ". . . but never with ways to keep things the same, no matter who, not even yourself."

A person observing the occurrence of certain facts and phenomena asks, naturally enough, what process, what kind of operation known to occur in Nature applied to the particular case, will unravel and explain the mystery? Hence you have the scientific hypothesis; and its value will be proportionate to the care and completeness with which its basis has been tested and verified. It is in these matters as in the commonest affairs of practical life: the guess of the fool will be folly, while the guess of the wise man will contain wisdom. In all cases, you see that the value of the result depends on the patience and faithfulness with which the investigator applies to his hypothesis every possible kind of verification.
—THOMAS HUXLEY

The hypothesis mentioned in 39b, for instance, might be focused further, or even completely changed, once research begins. The writer might find that the influences on McCarthy's crusade are so difficult to trace that he or she would decide to refocus the essay on why the crusade found such widespread public support or why it ended when it did. In Daniel Taffe's case, he found that the autobiographical influences on Kahlo's work were so well established that they could not be considered a hypothesis. Therefore, he shifted his attention to other influences and developed the following working thesis: "Frida Kahlo's unique style results not only from autobiographical influences but also from her knowledge of European and Mexican art."

In doing your own research, you may find that your interest shifts, that a whole line of inquiry is unproductive, that a journal you need to complete an argument is not available, or that your hypothesis is simply wrong. In each case, the process of research pushes you to know more and more about your hypothesis, to make it more focused and precise, to become an expert on your topic. You are, in short, becoming a researcher.

EXERCISE 39.1   Taking Inventory: Research

If you have done research for an essay before, now is a good time to go back and evaluate the work you did both as a researcher and as a writer in light of the principles developed in this chapter. What was the purpose of that research? Did you have any audience other than your instructor? How was your topic focused? What kinds of sources did you use? What were you most pleased with about your research, and about your essay? What pleased you least? What advice would you give yourself if you were to revise that essay?

40

Conducting Research

As Indiana Jones's exploits suggest, research and adventure go hand in hand. Scientist June Goodfield speaks of research in the following way.

> The reason why [research] is so absorbing and exciting is that every new fact may be important, and so every new day may be important. As you go through the process, there is no way you can tell beforehand which fact, or which day, is going to be the golden one.

This passage captures one of the essential pleasures of conducting research: the anticipation and excitement of learning something new. This chapter describes two kinds of research that can lead to such learning—library research and field research.

Everyday use

A few moments' thought may bring to mind some piece of everyday research you have done that required both reading and some kind of field work, like interviewing someone or taking a survey. An enterprising pair of writers with a passion for ice cream, for instance, wanted to write an article for a local magazine on the best ice cream in Pittsburgh. Their guiding research questions (who has the best ice cream, and what makes it the best?) led them first to the library, where they did background reading on the history of ice cream and the way it is made. Then they went into the field, systematically tasting ice cream all over the city and interviewing ice-cream makers. Along the way to preparing their article, these researchers got to eat their fill of free ice cream.

> *Think of a topic close to your home that you'd like to find out more about, and imagine how you'd go about doing so. Would you go to a library? ask friends? go and observe something directly?*

BACKGROUND

According to Charles Bazerman, "gathering convincing data is not easy." The method that a researcher uses greatly determines the evidence that supports the research, the conclusions the researcher is able to draw, and ultimately the effectiveness with which the research will influence others to accept its claims. In other words, the way a researcher explores and produces data will affect how an audience responds to the research. Will it be believable? Is it accurate? reasonable and reliable? thorough? careful? appropriate? significant?

Bazerman advises researchers that "method is so central to the understanding and evaluation of the final written product that in many disciplines a writer is obliged to describe as part of the statement the method used to produce and analyze the data. In this way, many articles contain stories of how they were made" (331).

To appreciate the importance of choosing the methods appropriate to different research projects, researchers need to know that methods vary across disciplines and within them, and that they often change with time. For example, in linguistics, many sociolinguists believe that understanding the way words change in meaning is most accurately explained by observing the way words are used in different social contexts. Historical linguists, on the other hand, prefer to explain meaning changes in terms of the historical origins of words and language groups.

TEACHING PRACTICE

Have your students list the sources of the information they would use to help you decide on the stereo system to buy. They will probably mention their own experiences or their family's experience with a reliable or unreliable system. They will probably mention consumer guides. They'll also likely mention popular stereo magazines or newspaper and television advertisements. Have them classify these sources as either primary or secondary and explain their classifications. For example, their own experience is a primary source. The fact that they have owned a particular system for many years and that they have recommended it to relatives and friends who've had trouble-free experiences is a form of raw data. If they mention an article in *Stereo Review* that speaks praisingly of their system, the magazine is a secondary source.

USEFUL READING

Bazerman, Charles. *The Informed Writer: Using Sources in the Disciplines.* 2nd ed. Boston: Houghton, 1985. See Chapters 11–15 for an extensive, in-depth discussion of the ways different disciplines gather data for research. Bazerman describes the various methods of data gathering in the social and natural sciences and in the humanities and theoretical disciplines.

McCartney, Robert. "The Cumulative Research Paper." *Teaching English in the Two-Year College* 12 (1985): 198–202. This article provides a model for allowing students to research in depth on one topic through several assignments.

Using primary and secondary sources

Samuel Johnson once remarked that "knowledge is of two kinds: we know a subject ourselves, or we know where we can find information upon it." In this sentence, Johnson has summed up the distinction between primary sources, or firsthand knowledge, and secondary sources, knowledge available from the work of others.

Primary sources represent the basic sources of raw information. Primary sources include laboratory experiments you conduct, notes you take in the field, surveys or interviews you conduct, objects or art works you examine, literary works you read, and performances you attend. Other primary sources are diaries, letters, firsthand accounts of events by eyewitnesses, contemporary news reports, historical documents, or raw data from experiments conducted by others.

Secondary sources are accounts of phenomena produced by others. They include reports and analyses by scholars, experts, and researchers of other people's laboratory work, field experiences, surveys, and so forth. Secondary sources also include various sorts of critical writing, such as biographies or reviews.

Sometimes, what constitutes a primary or secondary source depends on your purpose or your field of study. A critic's evaluation of a painting, for instance, serves as a secondary work if you are writing an essay on that painting, but as a primary work if you are conducting a study of that critic's writings.

Most research writing depends on both primary and secondary sources. The primary sources ground the project in facts from firsthand accounts and your own discoveries, while the secondary sources provide background for your investigation and support for your conclusions. Daniel Taffe, for example, eventually refocused his research on imagery in the paintings of Frida Kahlo, which he traced to imagery in a number of Renaissance paintings and to Mexican art and culture—all primary sources. In discussing these works, he cited biographies, works of art criticism, and articles on the Kahlo museum and recent sales of Kahlo's work—all secondary sources.

Unlike his essay, some research projects, such as a background survey or a review of the literature on a given topic, may require no primary sources at all. Secondary sources, on the other hand, are necessary for most research projects; even a report of a laboratory experiment is sometimes prefaced by a discussion of what other researchers have done previously. Research very often builds on secondary sources in this way. You read to find out what is known or not known about a problem; you formulate a question based on what needs to be found out; then you devise a research method to answer that question.

40b

Exploring library resources

The library is one of a researcher's best friends, for answering a research question and exploring and testing a hypothesis most often begin there. Libraries provide two necessary kinds of information: general background, which will give you an overview of your topic and place your research question in context, and particular support, which helps answer your research question and develop your hypothesis.

1

Beginning your library research

Start by reviewing your research question, hypothesis, and knowledge you already have about your topic (see 39b–c). Where did that knowledge come from? Do you own any books about your topic? Have you recently read any magazine articles about it? Do your textbooks help? This is the time to begin to list possible sources (see 41a).

Next, turn to acquaintances who may be able to point you in useful directions. If, for instance, you are writing about computers and a student down the hall knows a lot about them, go and talk to her. What books does she recommend? Does she have any computer magazines?

Finally, talk to your instructor. Even if you are researching a topic you selected, the instructor may be able to suggest where to begin looking for sources. If he or she has not arranged a library orientation tour for your class, find out about regularly scheduled tours, go along, and ask about sources on your topic.

Developing a research strategy

At this point, you are ready to begin your library research. The chart that follows will help you explore library resources in a systematic way, describing where to look to find various categories of information.

BACKGROUND

When the inventions of writing and paper enabled people to accumulate information, efforts were put into keeping and presenting the new written information. Constructed in about 600 B.C., the royal library at Nineveh, capital of the Assyrian empire, may have been among the world's first great libraries. Historians and archeologists believe that it contained tens of thousands of works on the arts, the sciences, and religion. Its grand achievement of cataloguing all contemporary knowledge made it the early ancestor of today's huge information systems and scientific databases.

TEACHING PRACTICE

Set up a meeting for your class with the reference librarian (or ask the librarian to attend your class) to discuss the resources in your particular library and how best for students to get access to them.

But the intellect which has been disciplined to the perfection of its powers, which knows, and thinks while it knows, which has learned to leaven the dense mass of facts and events with the elastic force of reason, such an intellect cannot be partial, cannot be exclusive, cannot be impetuous, cannot be at a loss, cannot but be patient, collected, and majestically calm, because it discerns the end in every beginning, the origin in every end, the law in every interruption, the limit in each delay; because it ever knows where it stands, and how its path lies from one point to another.

—JOHN HENRY NEWMAN

BACKGROUND

It is often when we dare to write beyond the edges of our own discipline, when we cross the border into another realm, perhaps not quite so familiar, that the real surprises occur. Astronomer-writer Carl Sagan delights in living on the edge. "Such insights as I've been able to achieve have been at the borders of the sciences, where different disciplines overlap. That's where the excitement is and where I want to be."

WHERE TO FIND GENERAL BACKGROUND MATERIAL
- Guides to Reference Books
- Encyclopedias
- Biographical Dictionaries and Indexes
- Sources for Current Events, Statistics, and Atlases
- Book Indexes

WHERE TO FIND SPECIFIC INFORMATION IN PERIODICALS
- Periodical Indexes
- Abstracts and Citation Indexes
- Computer Databases

WHERE TO FIND SPECIFIC INFORMATION IN BOOKS
- Library Catalog

WHERE TO FIND OTHER MATERIALS
- Vertical File
- Special Collections
- Interlibrary Loans

Because Daniel Taffe found very little about the topic he wanted to research—Frida Kahlo's life and art—in general reference books, he moved on to his college library catalog, where he found some books about Kahlo. He also checked InfoTrac, a periodicals database on CD-ROM that he could access through computer terminals in the library; there he found a few recent articles about Kahlo, her paintings, and Mexican art. Noticing that a frequently cited biography was published in 1983, he checked periodical indexes for that year and found reviews of the biography through *The Readers' Guide to Periodical Literature* and *The Humanities Index*. Because he was interested in the autobiographical elements in Kahlo's work, he also checked the psychology database PsycLIT, which yielded a few additional sources.

After doing some reading in the materials he had found, he spoke again with his instructor, who brainstormed with him about the ideas he was exploring and then suggested that he interview an art historian. The interview helped him decide which of his ideas to pursue and which to drop. He then returned to the library and, after locating some more sources, felt he had enough material to support a working thesis.

Identifying key words

Looking through card catalogs, indexes, or databases will go more efficiently if you have identified **key words** to look for—synonyms for your topic, broader terms that would include it, or appropriate subtopics. Information on ice cream, for instance, might appear under the heading of frozen desserts, dairy products, or sherbet.

A good place to check for key words is the *Library of Congress Subject Headings,* which lists the headings under which books are cataloged in most libraries. As you search a particular print index or computer database, check its list of key words, or **descriptors**, because many indexes and databases use terms peculiar to their systems. Also check the glossary and index of appropriate textbooks. When Daniel Taffe searched a computer database, he entered three key terms: *Frida Kahlo, Diego Rivera,* and *Mexican artists.*

Finding sources

Where to start? You may decide to follow the research strategy from the beginning, with an overview, looking first at an encyclopedia, for example. This approach may be especially useful if you need a better focus on a research question or want to check for basic bibliographies. On the other hand, you may already have ideas about where to begin and prefer to go right to the library catalog and periodical indexes. Before you plunge in, however, ask yourself a few questions.

- *How much time do you have to spend?* If you have only two weeks to do your research, you will want to be selective. If you have several months, however, you can follow a broader course, perhaps even consulting materials beyond those available in your library.

- *How current do your sources need to be?* If you must investigate the very latest findings in a field, you will want to check periodicals. On the other hand, if you want broader, more detailed coverage and background information, you will look more to books.

- *Do you need to consult sources contemporary with an event or a person's life?* If your research deals with a specific time period, you may need to examine newspapers, magazines, and books written during that period.

- *What kinds of sources do you need to consult?* Check your assignment to see if you are required to consult different kinds of sources. If you need to use primary sources, find out if they are readily available or if you will need to make special arrangements. If you need to locate nonprint sources or items in special collections, find out where they are kept in the library and if you need special permission for access to them.

- *How many sources should you consult?* You can expect to look over many more sources than you actually end up using. Your best guideline is to make sure you have enough sources to support your hypothesis or to prove your thesis. Check to see if your assignment specifies a minimum or maximum number of sources.

Consulting the library staff

Your most valuable source at the library is the highly trained staff, especially the reference librarians. To get the most helpful advice from them, pose *specific* questions: not "Where can I find information about computers?" but "Where can I find information on the history of computers?" The more precise your question, the more useful an answer you will get.

If you find yourself unable to ask clear and precise questions, you probably need to do some general background research into your topic. Then work again on narrowing and focusing, defining a clearer issue, asking a more specific research question, and finding a sharper hypothesis. On your second trip to the library, you will be ready to ask more specific questions and to find appropriate sources.

2

Selecting reference materials

Your library's reference collection includes two broad types of **reference materials**: those that are general in scope and those that deal with specific disciplines (music, zoology, political science, and so on). Guides to reference books can help you identify the ones that suit your purpose. Your research question can then help you choose the best sources to use. Among the types most often consulted are encyclopedias, biographical dictionaries, sources for current events, and book indexes.

Guides to reference books

Whether your interest is in nuclear physics, baseball history, or agricultural economics, you can probably find it in one of the two guides to reference books listed below. Because these guides list other reference books—not actual sources—a few minutes with them can be a shortcut to the books that match your interests and purposes.

> *Guide to Reference Books.* 10th ed. 1986. Edited by Eugene P. Sheehy, this large book is usually just called "Sheehy." It supplies annotated lists of general reference works and specialized bibliographies and is divided into five sections: General Reference; Humanities; Social and Behavioral Sciences; History and Area Studies; and Science, Technology, and Medicine. Each of these sections is further subdivided into areas and then into special approaches. Full bibliographic in-

formation, including the Library of Congress call number, is provided for each entry.

Walford's Guide to Reference Material. 4th ed. 1980–86. "Walford" consists of three volumes: Volume 1—Science and Technology; Volume 2—Social and Historical Sciences, Philosophy, and Religion; and Volume 3—Generalities, Languages, the Arts, and Literature.

Encyclopedias

For general background on a subject, **encyclopedias** are a good place to begin, particularly because many include bibliographies that could lead you to valuable sources. Though some encyclopedias do provide in-depth information, more often they serve as a place to start, not as a major source of information.

GENERAL ENCYCLOPEDIAS

Collier's Encyclopedia. 24 vols. 1990. Designed to meet the needs of student research.

Encyclopedia Americana. 30 vols. 1990. Pays particular attention to American public figures, institutions, and places.

New Encyclopaedia Britannica. 32 vols. 1989. In three parts: the *Micropaedia,* which contains brief articles for quick reference, the *Macropaedia,* which contains longer entries that treat selected subjects in depth, and the *Propaedia,* which outlines the material covered in the *Micropaedia* and *Macropaedia.* For fine essays in the classics and humanities, see if your library has the eleventh edition of the *Britannica,* published in 1911 and considered by many to be the most thoughtful and scholarly encyclopedia ever produced.

SPECIALIZED ENCYCLOPEDIAS

Compared with general encyclopedias, **specialized encyclopedias** usually provide more detailed articles by authorities in the field as well as extensive bibliographies for locating sources. Again, you should rely on these books more for background material as you familiarize yourself with your topic than as major sources of information. These volumes are often located in the reference area for the particular discipline. Here are some examples.

Cambridge Ancient History. 12 vols. 1939–70, with later revisions.

Cambridge History of Africa. 8 vols. 1975–86.

Cambridge Medieval History. 9 vols. 1911–67.

Encyclopedia of Anthropology. 1976.

Encyclopedia of Asian History. 4 vols. 1988.

Encyclopedia of Banking and Finance. 1983.

Encyclopedia of Bioethics. 2 vols. 1982.

Encyclopedia of Biological Sciences. 1981.

Encyclopedia of Chemistry. 1983.

Encyclopedia of Computer Science and Technology. 15 vols. 1975–80.

Encyclopedia of Crime and Justice. 4 vols. 1983.

Encyclopedia of Economics. 1982.

Encyclopedia of Education. 10 vols. 1971.

Encyclopedia of Management. 1982.

Encyclopedia of Philosophy. 4 vols. 1973.

Encyclopedia of Physical Education, Fitness and Sports. 3 vols. 1980.

Encyclopedia of Physics. 1983.

Encyclopedia of Religion. 16 vols. 1986.

Encyclopedia of Social Work. 3 vols. 1989.

Encyclopedia of World Architecture. 2 vols. 1988.

Encyclopedia of World Art. 15 vols. 1959–83, and supplements.

Encyclopedia of World History. 1972.

Harvard Guide to American History. 2 vols. 1974.

International Encyclopedia of the Social Sciences. 8 vols. 1977, and supplements.

McGraw-Hill Dictionary of Earth Sciences. 1984.

McGraw-Hill Dictionary of Modern Economics. 1984.

McGraw-Hill Encyclopedia of Science and Technology. 20 vols. 1987.

McGraw-Hill Encyclopedia of World Drama. 5 vols. 1984.

New Cambridge Modern History. 14 vols. 1957–70.

New Grove Dictionary of Music and Musicians. 20 vols. 1980.

Oxford Classical Dictionary. 1970.

Oxford Companion to American Literature. 1983.

Oxford Companion to English Literature. 1985.

Consult a reference librarian for any other specialized encyclopedias related to your discipline.

Biographical dictionaries and indexes

The lives and historical settings of famous people are the topics of **biographical dictionaries** and **indexes**. Before you use these sources, consider whether you need a volume covering people who are living or people who are dead. If the latter, decide if you want a current volume covering deceased people or an older volume covering living people that was published during the person's lifetime. Here are a few examples of biographical reference works; many others, particularly volumes specialized by geographic area or field, are available.

> *Biography Index.* 1946–; quarterly. Lists biographical material found in current books and over 2,600 periodicals. Online and CD-ROM databases cover July 1984–present (see 40b3).
>
> *Current Biography.* 1940–; monthly, with annual cumulations. Informative articles on people in current events. Includes photographs and short bibliographies.
>
> *Contemporary Authors.* 1967–; annual. Short biographies of authors who have published works during the year.
>
> *Dictionary of American Biography.* 1927–37, and supplements. Contains biographies of over 15,000 deceased Americans from all phases of public life since colonial days. Entries include bibliographies of sources.
>
> *Dictionary of National Biography.* 1885–1900, and supplements through 1985. Covers deceased notables from Great Britain and its colonies (excluding the postcolonial United States).
>
> *Notable American Women: 1607–1950.* 3 vols. 1972. Supplement: *Notable American Women: The Modern Period.* 1980. Contains biographies (with bibliographies) of women who contributed to American society. The supplement covers women who died between 1951 and 1975.
>
> *Who's Who.* 1849–; annual. Covers well-known living British people. *Who Was Who,* with volumes covering about a decade each, lists British notables who died between 1897 and the present.
>
> *Who's Who in America.* 1899–; biannual. Information about famous living Americans. Notable Americans no longer living are in *Who Was Who in America,* covering from 1607 to the present. Similar specialized works include *Who's Who of American Women, Who's Who of Black Americans, Who's Who in Government,* and so on.
>
> *International Who's Who.* 1935–; annual. Contains biographies of persons of international status.

Sources for current events, statistics, and maps

Almanacs, yearbooks, atlases, and other sources provide information on current events and statistical and geographical data. In addition to the following works, each of the general encyclopedias listed earlier in this section publishes an annual yearbook surveying events and developments of the preceding year in various fields.

ALMANACS, YEARBOOKS, NEWS DIGESTS

World Almanac and Book of Facts. 1868–; annual. Presents data and statistics on business, education, sports, government, population, and many other topics. Includes institutional names and addresses and reviews important public events of the year.

Information Please Almanac. 1947–; annual. Includes many charts, facts, and lists as well as short summaries of the year's events and accomplishments in various fields.

Statesman's Year-Book. 1863–; annual. Contains facts and helpful current statistics about agriculture, government, population, development, religion, and other topics in countries of the world.

Statistical Abstracts of the United States. 1878–; annual. Published by the Bureau of the Census; presents government data on population, business, immigration, and other subjects. Also available on CD-ROM: STATPACK (1987–) (see 40b3).

Facts on File: News Digest. 1941–; weekly. Summarizes and indexes facts about current events. Also available online (1975–) and on CD-ROM (1980–) (see 40b3).

ATLASES

In addition to physical maps of all parts of the world, the following **atlases** contain maps showing population, food distribution, mineral concentrations, temperature and rainfall, and political borders, as well as many other facts and statistics.

Hammond Medallion World Atlas. 1982.

National Geographic Atlas of the World. 1990.

The New International World Atlas. 1986.

The New York Times Atlas of the World. 1983.

Book indexes

Other useful sources located in the reference room are **book indexes**, which can be helpful for quickly locating complete information on a book when you know only one piece of it—the author's last name, perhaps, or the title. They can also be valuable for alerting you to other works by a particular author or on a particular subject.

Books in Print. 1948–; annual. Lists by author, subject, and title all books distributed in the United States that are currently in print. Also available online and on CD-ROM (see 40b3).

Cumulative Book Index. 1898–; monthly. Lists by author, subject, and title books in English distributed in the United States and internationally. Also available on CD-ROM (see 40b3).

Paperbound Books in Print. 1955–; semiannual. Lists by author, subject, and title all paperback books distributed in the United States that are currently in print. Also available on CD-ROM (see 40b3).

3

Using periodical indexes and computer databases

Because periodicals—journals, magazines, and newspapers—are published frequently and more quickly, they can lend an immediacy to your research that books cannot. In addition, while an entire book may not be devoted to your specific topic, a number of articles may be. You can locate articles in periodicals by searching periodical indexes and computer databases.

Once you have located articles to examine, check your library's **serials catalog** or **serials list**, usually kept in the periodicals reading room. This catalog names all the periodicals available in the library and notes their form—original publications, bound volumes, microform. As you search indexes, check the serials catalog often to make sure you aren't noting down periodicals that aren't available in your library or through interlibrary loan.

Periodical indexes

Periodical indexes are guides to articles published in periodicals. Each index covers a specific group of periodicals, usually identified at the beginning of the index or volume. In addition to printed indexes, your library may own microform indexes that cover many of the same entries. Microform indexes cover only the past three or four years, however, so if you are searching for earlier material, check printed indexes. Microforms are rolls of film (microfilm) or sheets (microfiche) that must be read on motorized projection machines. Ask the librarian for help in locating the microforms and using the machines.

Many libraries also offer access to the online and CD-ROM computer database versions of many periodical indexes. What these databases are and how to use them are discussed in the next section. Those indexes discussed here that are available in computer databases are so noted. Check with a reference librarian to see what databases are available at your library.

GENERAL INDEXES

General indexes for periodicals—usually located in the periodicals reading room—list articles from current general-interest magazines (such as *Time* and *Newsweek*), newspapers, or a combination of these. General indexes will usually provide current sources on your topic, though these may not treat the topic in sufficient depth for your purposes.

Readers' Guide to Periodical Literature. 1900–; semimonthly, with quarterly and annual cumulations. Indexes articles from over 170 magazines. Particularly helpful for social trends, popular scientific questions, and contemporary political issues. Entries are arranged by author and subject, with cross-references leading to related topics. Also available online and on CD-ROM (both 1983–). Here is a *Readers' Guide* entry for the subject heading *Frida Kahlo*.

Kahlo, Frida, 1907-1954
about
Frida Kahlo: the Chicana as art heroine. B. Rose. il
  pors *Vogue* 173:152+ Ap '83
Making an art of pain. H. Herrera. il pors *Psychol Today*
  17:86 Mr '83
A Mexican Georgia O'Keeffe. K. Larson. il por *N Y*
  16:82-3 Mr 28 '83
A painter's passion. H. Herrera. il pors *House Gard*
  155:98-109+ Ag '83
The ribbon around the bomb. M. Newman. bibl il pors
  Art Am 71:160-9 Ap '83

The New York Times Index. 1851–; bimonthly, with annual cumulations. Lists, by subject, every article that has appeared in the *New York Times.* For most articles of any length, short summaries are given as well. Also available online through NEXIS (1980–).

Magazine Index. Updated monthly. Analyzes over 400 general-interest magazines. Available only on microfilm (1988–), online (1973–), and on CD-ROM, separately and as part of InfoTrac (see below).

National Newspaper Index. Updated monthly. Covers the *New York Times, Los Angeles Times, Wall Street Journal, Washington Post,* and *Christian Science Monitor.* Available only on microfilm (1989–), on-line (1979–), and on CD-ROM, separately and as part of InfoTrac (see below).

InfoTrac. Updated monthly. Available only on CD-ROM, InfoTrac includes three indexes: the *General Periodicals Index* (current year and past four), which covers over 1,100 general-interest publications, incorporating the *Magazine Index* and including the *New York Times* and *Wall Street Journal;* the *Academic Index* (current year and past four), which covers over 900 scholarly and general-interest publications, including the *New York Times;* and the *National Newspaper Index* (current year and past three). Some entries include a summary or even the entire article. Here is an example of an entry from the *General Periodicals Index.*

                                    General Periodicals Index-A
KAHLO, FRIDA
    1.   "Women in Mexico." (22 women artists active in Mexico in
          the 20th century) (exhibition at the National Academy of
          Design, New York) by Ronny Cohen il v29 ArtForum Jan '91
          p127(2)

NewsBank. 1970–; updated monthly. Includes over one million articles from 500 U.S. newspapers. Available only on microfiche and CD-ROM.

Book Review Digest. 1905–; annual. Contains excerpts from reviews of books along with information for locating the full reviews in popular and scholarly periodicals. Be sure to check not only the year of a book's publication but also the next year. Also available online and on CD-ROM (both 1983–).

Access: The Supplementary Index. 1979–; monthly. Indexes magazines not covered by the *Readers' Guide,* such as regional and particular-interest magazines (the environment, women's issues).

Alternative Press Index. 1970–; monthly. Indexes alternative and radical publications.

The Times Index (London). 1913–; bimonthly. Lists articles and summaries of stories published in the London *Times.*

Nineteenth Century Readers' Guide to Periodical Literature. 1890–99.

Poole's Index to Periodical Literature. 1802–1907. Indexes nineteenth-century British and American periodicals.

SPECIALIZED INDEXES

Many disciplines have **specialized indexes** to help researchers find information in great depth. In general, such indexes list articles in scholarly journals for that discipline, but they may include other publications as well; check the beginning of the volume. Indexes available in computer databases are labeled O (for online) and CD-ROM. The name of any database different from that of the print index is also given. For most efficient use of these resources, ask a reference librarian to help you identify those indexes most likely to address your topic.

America: History and Life. 1955–. (O)

Applied Science and Technology Index. 1958–. Formerly *Industrial Arts Index.* 1913–57. (O, CD-ROM)

Art Index. 1929–. (O, CD-ROM)

Biological and Agricultural Index. 1964–. Formerly *Agricultural Index.* 1916–63. (CD-ROM)

Business Periodicals Index. 1958–. Formerly *Industrial Arts Index.* 1913–57. (O, CD-ROM)

Central Index to Journals in Education. 1969–. (O)

Education Index. 1929–. (O, CD-ROM)

Essay and General Literature Index. 1900–.

General Science Index. 1978–. (O, CD-ROM)

Humanities Index. 1974–. Formerly *International Index.* 1907–65; *Social Sciences and Humanities Index.* 1965–74. (O, CD-ROM)

Index Medicus. 1960–; 1899–1926. Formerly *Quarterly Cumulative Index Medicus.* 1927–59. (O, CD-ROM: MEDLINE)

Index to Legal Periodicals. 1908–. (O, CD-ROM: LEXIS)

MLA Bibliography of Books and Articles in the Modern Languages and Literature. 1921–. (O, CD-ROM)

Music Index. 1949–.

Philosopher's Index. 1967–. (O)

Public Affairs Information Service (PAIS). 1915–. (O, CD-ROM)

Social Sciences Index. 1974–. Formerly *International Index.* 1907–65; *Social Sciences and Humanities Index.* 1965–74. (O, CD-ROM)

United States Government Publications. 1895–. (O, CD-ROM)

Abstracts and citation indexes

Abstracts are specialized indexes that also briefly summarize entries, thus helping you better judge an item's potential usefulness. **Citation indexes** list sources cited in an article as well as information about the article. Here is a list of some specialized and citation indexes.

Biological Abstracts. 1926–. (CD-ROM)

Chemical Abstracts. 1907–. (O: *Chemical Abstracts Service Source Index*)

Dissertation Abstracts International. 1938–. (O, CD-ROM)

Historical Abstracts. 1955–. (O)

Physics Abstracts. 1898. (O: INSPEC)

Psychological Abstracts. 1927–. (O: PsycINFO, CD-ROM: PsycLIT)

Science Citation Index. 1955. (O, CD-ROM: SciSearch)

Sociological Abstracts. 1952–. (O, CD-ROM: Sociofile)

Social Sciences Citation Index. 1969. (O, CD-ROM: Social SciSearch)

Searching computer databases

Your college library may subscribe to **online** databases that are accessed through a computer network and may own **CD-ROM (compact disc—read only memory)** machines that are connected to the library's computer terminals. These databases are specialized electronic indexes listing thousands of books and articles by authors, titles, and subjects.

One common computer service is DIALOG, with information on more than a million sources. DIALOG is divided into smaller databases, such as

ERIC, which indexes education journals, and PsycINFO, which indexes psychology publications.

Many printed and microform indexes are available in database versions, some through DIALOG. Most of these database versions include only articles published since the late 1970s or early 1980s.

You may be able to access a database on CD-ROM yourself, but you will probably need a librarian to conduct an online search for you. To use a database, you provide a list of authors, titles, or other key words, and the computer searches the database for references to them and prints out a list of every reference it finds. Because you may be charged for access time and printing for an online search or given a time limit for using a terminal and CD-ROM database, you may want to ask a librarian about available services and any costs before deciding to consult a database.

Sometimes the key words you use to conduct a database search will be authors or titles, but more often they will be subject headings. Computer databases contain so much information that your most difficult task will usually be choosing key words precise enough to cut down the number of items you have to consider. Most databases include a thesaurus of key words, or **descriptors**, that can help you.

You might, for instance, type the key word "bulimia" into the database PsycLIT, and the computer would tell you that it could show you 1,365 items. How do you know which to consult? You must narrow the search by using more key words, usually by using *and* between them. Depending on the way your thesis is developing, you might try "bulimia and treatments" (47 items), "bulimia and treatments and group therapy" (14 items), or

SilverPlatter 2.00   PsycLIT (1/83 - 6/91)   1 of 1

TI   DOCUMENT TITLE: Frida Kahlo and Diego Rivera: The transformation of
catastrophe to creativity.
AU   AUTHOR(S): Natchez,-Gladys
IN   INSTITUTIONAL AFFILIATION OF FIRST AUTHOR: Private practice, New
York, NY, US
JN   JOURNAL NAME: Psychotherapy-Patient; 1987 Vol 4(1) 153-174
IS   ISSN: 07386176
LA   LANGUAGE: English
PY   PUBLICATION YEAR: 1987
AB   ABSTRACT: Describes the development of creativity in the lives of
Diego Rivera and Frida Kahlo, 2 Mexican artists who were married to each
other. The factors that led to their particular creativity are examined
as well as those that promote creativity in general. (PsycLIT Database
Copyright 1989 American Psychological Assn, all rights reserved)
KP   KEY PHRASE: development of creativity in lives of Mexican artists D.
Rivera & F. Kahlo
DE   DESCRIPTORS: ARTISTS-; CREATIVITY-; PERSONALITY-DEVELOPMENT
CC   CLASSIFICATION CODE(S): 2740
PO   POPULATION: Human
UD   UPDATE CODE: 8904
AN   PSYC ABS. VOL. AND ABS. NO.: 76-11344
JC   JOURNAL CODE: 2344

TEACHING PRACTICE

Ask students to brainstorm together on the best key words to use in a database search on the following topics: AIDS, computer viruses, white-collar crime.

"bulimia and agoraphobia" (5 items). The narrower you can make your search, the more specific the sources you find will be.

After you have narrowed your search to a reasonable number of items, look at the references to them on the screen and choose which ones you wish to print out. Using the printouts, you will be able to read the abstract attached to each reference and determine whether you need to find the actual article for further information.

When Daniel Taffe typed the key word *Frida Kahlo* into PsycLIT, the database told him it contained only one reference with this word in it. After looking at this reference on the screen, he printed it out. His printout is shown at the bottom of p. 551.

4

Using the library catalog

A **library catalog** lists all the library's materials, or holdings. The traditional format for the library catalog is the **card catalog**. Today, some libraries have a **microfiche catalog**, and many have transferred (or are in the process of transferring) the holdings to a **circulation computer**, which allows patrons to use public terminals to search for material. Most libraries

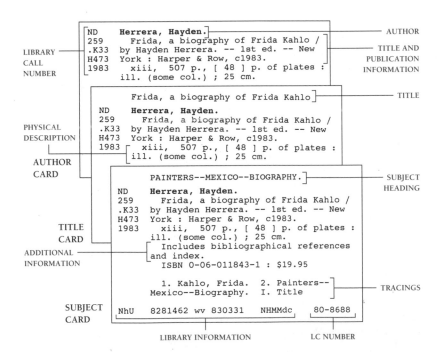

res

with circulation computers, however, maintain card catalogs as well. If your library is still in the process of computerizing its catalog, ask a reference librarian which catalog to check for recently published materials.

In whatever form, library catalogs follow a standard organization. Each holding in the library is identified by three kinds of entries for each item—one headed by the author, one by the title, and one or (usually) more by the subject. If you look up a book under one of these headings and don't find it, try the others; sometimes cards get lost or computer systems misfile information.

At the bottom of the facing page, you will find examples of author, title, and subject cards.

Using the circulation computer

With a circulation computer, you can find listings for sources more quickly than in the card catalog and can experiment a bit with different subject headings without spending much time. Most circulation computers have detailed instructions for using them, and many give you clear instructions for how and when to type in information. As with the card catalog, you search for holdings by author, title, or subject. The screen displays entries similar to those in the card catalog. Here is an example of a circulation computer entry.

```
AUTHOR:        Herrera, Hayden
TITLE:         Frida, a biography of Frida Kahlo / by Hayden Herrera.
EDITION:       1st ed.
PUBLISHER:     New York : Harper & Row, c1983.
PHYSICAL DESC:iii, 507 p., [48] p. of plates : ill. (some col.) ; 25 cm.

NOTES:         Includes bibliographical references and index.
SUBJECTS:      Kahlo, Frida.
                 Painters - Mexico - Biography.


LOCATION           CALL#/VOL/NO/COPY           STATUS

UNH/STACK          ND259.K33 H47 1983 c.1      Available
```

Note that many circulation computers, like the one in the example, indicate whether a book is available or has been checked out and, if so, when it is due to be returned.

Identifying subjects

Subjects in the library catalog are usually identified and arranged according to the system presented in *Library of Congress Subject Headings* (LCSH). This three-volume reference may be kept at the reference desk or near the catalog so that you can check the exact wording of subject headings and define key terms of interest to you. The LCSH can be useful because it identifies headings that might not readily occur to you. For most headings, you'll find other subjects that are treated under that heading (identified by *UF,* "use for"), broader headings that include the subject (*BT,* "broader topic"), and narrower headings that might be relevant (*NT,* "narrower topic"). These abbreviations are new to the most recent edition of LCSH and replace a system that used *sa* ("see also") and *xx* ("broader topic") and listed subdivisions without labels.

Searching only subject entries is likely to be inefficient, however, because the headings are so broad. If the best Library of Congress heading you can identify does not match your particular needs or is so broad that it lists many books but only a few that will be useful to you, use other leads. Look to bibliographies, book indexes, reference books, periodical indexes, and notes in other publications to identify potentially useful authors and titles. Such leads are likely to be much more specific and helpful.

Using tracings

The **tracings** listed at the bottom of catalog entries identify the subject cards under which the book is listed. Keep in mind that searching only subject cards can be inefficient and follow up on these tracings only if they seem relevant to your topic.

Using call numbers

Besides identifying a book's author, title, subject, and publication information, each catalog entry also lists a **call number**—the book's identification number. For these numbers, most academic libraries now use the Library of Congress System, which begins call numbers with letters of the alphabet. Some libraries, however, still use the older Dewey Decimal System, with all numerals, while others combine both systems. Once you have written down the complete call number, look for a library map or shelving plan to tell you where your book is housed. When you find it, take the time to browse through the books around it. Very often you will find the immediate area a more important treasure trove than any bibliography or index.

If your book is not on the shelf, ask about it at the circulation desk. The book may not circulate, or it may not have been used by anyone lately and thus be in an area closed to the public. You may be able to find out if someone has checked it out and if it is due soon. Very often a library will recall a book when another person needs it. Allow for the time required for the library to notify the borrower to return the book and then to notify you that it is available. Your deadline will determine whether it is realistic to request a recall.

5

Using other library resources

In addition to books and periodicals, libraries hold other useful materials that might be appropriate for your research. For example:

- *Vertical file.* Pamphlets and brochures from government and private agencies, usually kept in file cabinets.
- *Special collections.* Manuscripts, rare books, local literature and memorabilia.
- *Audio collections.* Records, audiocassettes, and compact discs of all kinds of music, readings, and speeches.
- *Video collections.* Slides, filmstrips, and videocassettes.
- *Art collections.* Drawings, paintings, engravings, and photographs.
- *Interlibrary loans.* Many libraries will borrow books from another library for you; be aware that interlibrary loans often take some time and may involve some cost to you.

40c

Collecting data in the field

For many research projects, particularly in business and the social sciences, you will need to collect data "in the field"—whether that field is an ice cream parlor, your hometown, a laboratory, a day-care center, or the corner grocery store. As a field researcher, you will become a detective not only of books and journals but also of the world. You must discover where you can find relevant information, decide on the best ways to gather it, and find the best people to inform you about it. Three useful techniques for field research include observing, interviewing, and surveying opinions.

1

Observing

Much professional writing depends on careful direct observation: a doctor's diagnostic notes, a reporter's news article, a social worker's case study. Sometimes called naturalistic research, **observation** calls on you to look at phenomena without trying to alter them in any way, keeping yourself out of the picture as much as possible. You can observe anything in this way, from the use of bicycle paths on campus to the kinds of products advertised during Saturday morning television shows to the growth of chicks in an agriculture lab.

FOR COLLABORATIVE WORK

Though you will often assign research to be carried out individually, you might ask students to work as a team or group on a project. As one possibility, ask students to work in research teams to gather information for a report on the condition, the level of use, and any needed changes of the bike paths on campus. Allow a week or so for them to organize their efforts and to decide what kind of observations, interviews, and other data gathering they will need to do. Then ask them to write together a brief summary of how they have proceeded, noting problems they have encountered and projecting ways to solve them.

Encourage your students to benefit from their colleagues' feedback, input, contributions, responses, and constructive criticism when they are, for example, working out an observation schedule. Or encourage them to brainstorm in groups to generate the most purposeful, specific questions for a survey.

Careful observation can supply support for a hypothesis or working thesis. For example, one student, mentioned in Chapters 2 and 3, decided to try to persuade the traffic and parking division of his college to provide more motorcycle parking space in his dormitory parking lot. Because he wanted to show the need for such space, he set aside an eight-hour period to sit in the lot, recording the number of cars and motorcycles unable to find space. When he found that the ratio of motorcycles to cars was roughly two to one, direct observation paved the way for his request by helping to demonstrate a need.

Preparing for observation

Before you go out into the field to observe, decide exactly what you want to find out and try to anticipate what you are likely to see. Are you going to observe an action repeated by many people (such as pedestrians crossing a street) or a sequence of actions (such as a medical procedure)? Are you observing a situation that might produce many different reactions—a child crying in a grocery store, for example? Try to decide exactly what you want to record and how to do so. In the grocery store, for instance, decide whether to observe the crying child, his or her parents, other shoppers, or store employees, and what you want to note—what they say, or what they do.

 ### Conducting observation

- Determine the purpose of the observation, and review your research question and hypothesis to see that they relate to it.
- Set a definite period of time for the observation.
- If necessary, make an appointment.
- Develop an appropriate system for recording your information. (The student studying motorcycle parking, for instance, decided to use lined paper with three vertical columns to tabulate cars, motorcycles, and times.)
- Take materials for keeping notes.
- Consider using a camera, tape recorder, or videocassette recorder.
- Assume the role of reporter, using the *who, what, when, where, why,* and *how* questions to note down what you see and hear (see 3a5).

2

Interviewing

Sometimes you will need information that is best sought by **interviewing**, or asking direct questions of other people. If you can talk with an expert, in person or on the telephone, you might get information you could not get through any other kind of research. In addition to getting "expert opinion," you might ask for firsthand accounts, for biographical information, or for suggestions of other places to look or people to consult.

Finding people to interview

How do you go about identifying people to interview? Check first to see whether your research thus far names any people you might contact directly. Next, take a few minutes to brainstorm for names. In addition to authorities on your topic, consider people in your community who might be knowledgeable—faculty members, lawyers, librarians, local government officials, alumni of your college. Once you identify promising possibilities, either write or telephone to see whether an interview might be arranged.

Composing questions

To prepare useful questions, you need to know your topic well and to know a fair amount about your interviewee. Try to learn as much as you can about his or her experience and opinions. You will probably want to ask several kinds of questions. **Factual questions** ask for specific answers, ones that do not invite expansion or opinion.

> How many firebases was your unit posted to in Vietnam?
>
> What flavors of ice cream does your company produce?
>
> How many people contributed to this year's United Way campaign?

In contrast, **open-ended questions** ask the interviewee to think out loud, to go in directions that interest him or her, and to give additional details or anecdotes.

> How would you characterize the atmosphere of the Watergate hearings?
>
> How does public acceptance of modern art today compare with the situation forty years ago? How would you account for the change?
>
> How do you feel now about your decision to go to Canada in 1968 rather than be drafted?

Avoid questions that encourage vague or rambling answers ("What do you think of youth today?") or yes/no answers ("Should the Indian Point reactor

TEACHING PRACTICE

Ask students to work in pairs, first preparing tentative interview questions, and then practicing these questions on their partners. Each partner, in turn, provides a critique of the questions. As an alternative, set up one mock interview for your class. Then lead a class discussion on the strengths and weaknesses of the interview.

TEACHING PRACTICE

Ask students to choose a professor in a field of study that interests them and interview that person about the research he or she tends to do. Encourage them to draw up a list of questions they would like answered about the kind of research questions asked in that field, the most typical methods of answering them, and the kinds of sources most often used. After the interview, have students summarize in two or three paragraphs what they have learned.

be closed?"). Instead of the latter, ask questions that require answers with support ("Why should the Indian Point reactor be closed?").

 Planning an interview

- Determine your exact purpose, and check it with your research question and hypothesis to be sure they all relate.
- Set the interview up well in advance, specifying the amount of time it will take and asking permission to tape if you wish to do so.
- Prepare a written list of questions you can use to structure the interview. Brainstorming or freewriting techniques can help you come up with questions (see 3a).
- If possible, try out your questions on one or two people to determine how best to sequence them, how clear and precise they are, and how long answers will take.
- Prepare a final copy of your questions, leaving plenty of space for notes after each one.
- Check out all equipment beforehand—pens, tape recorder, and so on. Record the subject, date, time, and place of interview at the beginning of all tapes.
- Take or have ready several pencils or pens and a notebook.

Conducting an interview

Be prompt, and dress appropriately if you are meeting with the person. If you want to use a tape recorder, ask the interviewee again for permission to record your conversation. Even if you use a recorder, have a notebook ready with your questions, and write down the answers and any other notes you wish to make. Do not feel bound to your prepared questions, as long as the interview proceeds in a direction that seems fruitful. Be flexible. Note the time, and be careful not to take up more time than you said you would. End the interview with a thank you—and follow up with a letter thanking the person for taking the time to meet with you. (See 47c3.)

3

Surveying opinion

Surveys can take the form of interviews (see 40c2), but more often they depend on **questionnaires**. The student investigating campus parking for motorcycles surveyed his dormitory's residents to learn how many owned motorcycles and how many of these had difficulty finding parking spaces. Though he sent questionnaires to everyone in the dorm, such extensive surveying is often unwieldy and even unnecessary. All you need is a representative sample of people and a questionnaire whose questions will elicit the information necessary to accomplish your purpose.

Questions should be clear and easy to understand and designed so that you will be able to analyze the answers easily. For example, questions that ask respondents to say yes or no or to rank something on a five-point scale of most to least desirable are easy to tabulate.

 Designing a questionnaire

1. Write out your purpose, and review your research question and hypothesis to determine the kinds of questions to ask.
2. Determine the audience for your questionnaire, and figure out how you will reach them.
3. Using brainstorming, freewriting, or another strategy from 3a, draft some potential questions.
4. Check each question to see that it calls for a short, specific answer.
5. Test the questions on several people—including your instructor, if possible. Note which questions are hard to answer and why, and how much time the answers require. Revise the questions as necessary.
6. If the questionnaire is to be mailed, draft a cover letter explaining the purpose of it and asking the recipient to complete it. Provide an addressed, stamped envelope.
7. Be sure to state a deadline as well as a place for returning the form.
8. Consider adding a question that asks for any other comments.
9. Type the questionnaire, leaving adequate space for all answers.
10. Proofread your questionnaire.

EXERCISE 40.1   Taking Inventory: Your Research

Return to the inventory you completed on p. 536. Add to that inventory by examining the ways in which you conducted research: What use did you make of primary and secondary sources? What library and field work did you carry out? What about the process of conducting research was most satisfying to you? What was most disappointing or irritating? What sources were most (and least) useful? What tips might you offer yourself on how to conduct research more efficiently in the future? If you are keeping a writing log, or a research log as part of your writing log, record your answers there.

41

Using Sources

All research builds on the astute, judicious, and sometimes inspired use of sources—that research work done by others. As Isaac Newton noted, those researchers who see the farthest do so because they "stand on the shoulders of giants." And while researchers cannot always count on a giant's shoulders to stand on, the quality of their insights is often directly related to how well they have understood and used the source materials—the shoulders—they have relied on. As a reader, you will want to make the most of your sources, using the insights you gain from them in creating powerful prose of your own. This chapter will guide you in your use of sources in research.

41a

Choosing sources

Experienced researchers know that all sources are not created equally useful, that some are much more helpful or provocative than others. One of your goals, therefore, is to learn to judge, in Francis Bacon's words, which are to be tasted, which swallowed, and which chewed and digested. The following sections will provide some guidance to help you make such judgments.

1

Building a working bibliography

One important result of choosing sources for research is the creation of a **working bibliography**—a list of books, articles, and other sources that seem likely to address your research question. The emphasis here is on *working*—for this list will include materials that may end up *not* being

---

Everyday use

Every time you turn the dial to At the Movies *to help you decide whether to see a new film or pick up* Consumer Reports *to check out its evaluation of an appliance you're thinking of buying, you are calling on source materials for help. Spend a few minutes thinking of other everyday source materials you use—manuals or guidebooks, for instance. Make a list of these sources, and bring it to class for discussion. How do you go about evaluating these source materials? How do you know which ones to trust?*

---

useful. As you use reference books, bibliographic sources, periodical indexes, the card catalog, or the circulation computer, make a bibliography entry for *every source* you think you *might* use.

Before you begin a working bibliography, check your assignment or ask your instructor to determine what system you are required to follow for documenting the sources you use (see Chapters 43 and 44). If you familiarize yourself with the system now and follow it carefully, you will have, in the proper format, all the information necessary to prepare your final list of sources cited.

 Keeping a working bibliography

1. Decide on a format: use index cards (one for each source), a notebook, or a computer file. If you use cards or notebook pages, record information on one side only so that you can arrange entries alphabetically when preparing the list of sources cited. Many word-processing programs will sort the entries for you. Whatever system you use, follow it consistently and completely.

2. For each book, record the following:
   - Call number or other location information
   - Author and/or editor
   - Title and subtitle, if any
   - Publisher's name and location
   - Year of publication
   - Other information—translator, volume number, edition, etc.
   - Inclusive page numbers for chapters or short works

   (Continued)

USEFUL READINGS

Kennedy, Mary Lynch. "The Composing Process of College Students Writing from Sources." *Written Communication* 2 (1985): 434–56. Based on a protocol analysis of six students writing from sources, Lynch found that fluent readers read the sources "with pencil-in-hand," doing more planning, re-reading, and note-taking prior to writing than the less able readers.

Quantic, Diane. "Insights into the Research Process from Student Logs." *Journal of Teaching Writing* 5 (1986): 211–25. This article discusses writing blocks related to research papers and suggests strategies to overcome these blocks.

Sherrard, Carol. "Summary Writing: A Topographical Study." *Written Communication* 3 (1986): 324–43. In studying paragraph-length summaries written by university students, Sherrard found that most of the summaries were "remarkably mechanical." Summary strategies most favored included omitting text sentences, mapping existing sentences into summary sentences, and combining only those sentences that were next to each other.

3. For each article, list the following:
   - Author and/or editor
   - Article title and subtitle, if any
   - Periodical name, volume number, and date
   - Inclusive page numbers for the article

4. For entries from bibliographic or periodical indexes, list the name of the index in case you need to check the information again, and add the call number or other location information when you find the source in your library catalog.

5. For entries from database searches, use printouts. You will need to convert the entries of any sources you use to the correct documentation style, but the printout can save you the time of copying the information by hand.

6. For nonprint sources, list the information required by the documentation system you are using and note where you found the information.

7. When you examine the actual sources, check the accuracy of your information by consulting the title and copyright pages of a book and the table of contents and first page of an article in a journal or magazine.

For his research essay on Frida Kahlo, Daniel Taffe, who was using the Modern Language Association style of documentation (see Chapter 43), decided to record his sources on index cards. Here are two of the cards he created—the first for a book and the second for a periodical article.

BOOK

ND 259. K 33
H 47
1983

Herrera, Hayden. *Frida: A Biography of Frida Kahlo.* New York: Harper, 1983.

ARTICLE

> Jenkins, Nicholas. "Calla Lilies and Kahlos:
> The Frida Kahlo Museum in Mexico
> City." ARTnews Mar. 1991: 104-05.
>
>
>
> General Periodicals Index (InfoTrac)

2

Assessing the usefulness of a source

Examining the following characteristics of a book or an article with your research question and assignment requirements in mind can help you assess its usefulness.

- *Relevance.* Is the source closely related to your research question?
- *Author's credentials and stance.* Is the author an expert on the topic? Where does the author stand on the issues involved—and does this stance support or challenge your own views?
- *Date of publication.* How current is the material? Recent sources are often more useful than older ones, particularly in the sciences. However, the most authoritative works are often older ones.
- *Level of specialization.* Does the source provide a general or specialized view? General sources may be helpful as you begin your research, but you may then need the authority or up-to-dateness of more specialized sources. Extremely specialized works, on the other hand, may be too hard to understand.
- *Publication background.* If a book was published not by a commercial publishing house or academic press but by a corporation, government agency, or interest group, what is the publisher's position on the topic? What kind of periodical published an article? popular? academic? alternative?

- *Intended audience.* For what audience was the source written? general readers? specialists? advocates of something? opponents of something? a particular group?
- *Cross-referencing.* Is the source cited in other works?
- *Length.* Is the source long enough to provide adequate detail?
- *Availability.* Do you have access to the source?

You can determine many of these characteristics just by quickly looking at the parts of a source that are listed below. If you then want to explore the source more thoroughly, these elements can also help you decide how to do so most efficiently.

- *Title and subtitle.* If you are investigating coeducation in the nineteenth century and find a book called *Women in Education,* the subtitle *The Challenge of the 1970s* will tell you that you probably do not need to examine the book.
- *Copyright page.* In a book, this page will show you when the book was originally published, whether it is a revised edition, and who published it.
- *Abstract.* Abstracts are concise summaries of articles or books. They routinely precede articles in some journals and are included in certain periodical or bibliographic guides. Abstracts can help you decide whether to read the entire work, so use them accordingly.
- *Table of contents.* Part and chapter titles can often give you a good idea of what a book contains. Try to determine whether the chapter topics seem *specific* enough to be useful to you. In a periodical, the table of contents often includes brief descriptions of articles and can also give you a general impression of the periodical if it is unfamiliar to you.
- *Preface or foreword.* Very often these preliminary pages of a book specify in detail the writer's purposes, range of interests, intended audience, topic restrictions, research limitations, and thesis.
- *Subheadings.* Subheadings in the text can give you an idea of how much detail is given on a topic and whether that detail would be helpful to you.
- *Conclusion or afterword.* Some books and articles end with a summary of the contents and a statement of significance that could help you decide how appropriate that source is for your project.
- *Note on the author.* Check the dustcover of a book, the first and last few pages of a book or article, or an article itself for author information.
- *Index.* Check the index for words and topics key to your project; then see whether they seem to have much importance in the book. Are the listings for your key terms many or few?
- *Bibliography and/or footnotes.* Lists of references, usually at the end of a book or article, show how carefully a writer has investigated the subject. In addition, they may help you find other sources.

Reading sources with a critical eye

Research calls for active, aggressive reading. Active readers take up conversation with the books they read, responding to the text with questions and comments. The more attentively you read, and the more you respond to what you read, the better your research will be. This section will help you become an active, questioning reader.

Researchers read with a strong sense of purpose: how does this source relate to my research goals? does it support my ideas, develop them further, or challenge them? Reading with a purpose calls for examining your sources with an astute, critical eye. Because of time constraints and the wealth of material available on most topics, you probably will not have time to read completely through all of your potential material. Thus, reading with a critical eye can make your research process more efficient. The following considerations can guide your critical reading.

Reading with your research question in mind

A good way of focusing your attention on the information most necessary to your research is to read with your research question in mind. Use the index and the table of contents to zero in on the parts of books that will help you answer your research question. Consider the following questions as you read.

- How does this material address your research question?
- In what ways does it provide support for your hypothesis?
- How might particular quotations help support your thesis?
- Does the source include counterarguments to your hypothesis that you will need to answer? If so, what answers can you provide?

Identifying the author's stance and tone

Every author holds opinions that affect his or her discussion of an issue, opinions that you as a reader must try to recognize and understand. Even the most seemingly factual report, such as an encyclopedia article, is necessarily filled with judgments, often unstated. Read with an eye for the author's overall rhetorical stance, or perspective on the topic (see 2d), as well as for facts or explicit opinions. This stance is closely related to the author's tone, the way his or her attitude toward both topic and audience is conveyed in the writing. Alertness to perspective and tone will help you

Conclusions result from the interpretive analysis of data.

For a striking example, see Anne Fausto-Sterling, *Myths of Gender: Biological Theories About Women and Men* (New York: Basic, 1987). Fausto-Sterling, a biologist, demonstrates that many of the questionable distinctions between males and females that scientists have "proven" derive from their research methods and the kinds of questions they have asked. For instance, male superiority in athletic performance can be "proven" when it is measured by muscle strength rather than other criteria such as resiliency or endurance.

more fully understand a source and, as a result, better decide how (or whether) to use it. The following questions can help you read for perspective and tone.

- What is the author's stance or perspective? Is he or she an enthusiastic advocate of something, a strong opponent, a skeptical critic, an amused onlooker, a confident specialist in the field?
- Are there any clues to why the author takes this stance?
- How does this stance affect the author's presentation?
- If the author has a professional affiliation, how might the affiliation affect his or her stance?
- In what ways do you share—or not share—the author's stance?
- What is the author's tone? Is it cautious, angry, flippant, serious, impassioned? What words express this tone?

In the following paragraph, which appeared in a *Parade* magazine essay about nuclear war, the author's stance is obvious from the first sentence: he sees his topic, the possibility of nuclear war, as "an unprecedented human catastrophe." His dismissal of those who disagree with him as "fools and madmen" indicates the depth of his feelings, but his overall tone is restrained and objective because he assumes ("everyone knows") that the great majority of his readers share his view.

> Except for fools and madmen, everyone knows that nuclear war would be an unprecedented human catastrophe. A more or less typical strategic warhead has a yield of 2 megatons, the explosive equivalent of 2 million tons of TNT. But 2 million tons of TNT is about the same as all the bombs exploded in World War II—a single bomb with the explosive power of the entire Second World War but compressed into a few seconds of time and an area 30 or 40 miles across. . . .
> —Carl Sagan, "Nuclear War and Climatic Catastrophe: A Nuclear Winter"

Assessing the author's argument and evidence

Just as every author has a point of view, every piece of writing has what may be called an argument, a position it takes. Even a report of scientific data implicitly "argues" that we should accept it as reliably gathered and reported. As you read, then, try to identify the author's argument, the reasons given in support of his or her position. Then try to decide *why* the author takes this position. Considering the following questions as you read can help you recognize—and assess—the points being argued in your sources.

- What is the author's main point?
- How much and what kind of evidence supports that point?

- How persuasive do you find the evidence?
- Can you offer any counterarguments or refutations to the evidence?
- Can you detect any questionable logic or fallacious thinking? (See 5e.)

Questioning your sources

Because all sources make an explicit or implicit argument, they often disagree with one another. Disagreements among sources arise sometimes from differences about facts, sometimes from differences about how to interpret facts. For instance, if an authoritative source says that the chances of a nuclear power plant melting down are 1 in 100,000, two different commentators could interpret that statistic very differently. A critic of nuclear power could argue that nuclear accidents are so terrible that this chance is too much to take, while a supporter of nuclear power could argue that such a small chance is essentially no chance at all.

The point is that all knowledge must be interpreted subjectively, by people. As a result, a writer may well tell the truth and nothing but the truth, but he or she can never tell the *whole* truth because people are not all-knowing. Thus you must build your own informed opinion, your own truth, by seeking out and assessing many viewpoints as you read. Not all disputes can be solved by appealing to "neutral facts" because facts are seldom neutral. You must examine all sources critically, using them not as unquestioned authorities but as contributions to your own interpretation.

41c

Taking notes

After you have decided that a source is useful, you will need to take careful notes on it. Doing so most efficiently calls for approaching a source with some general questions in mind. What do you expect to learn about the topic? What can the source help you demonstrate? To what part of your research is the source most relevant?

Note-taking methods vary greatly from one researcher to another. Whatever method you adopt, however, your goals will include (1) getting down enough information to help you recall the major points of the source; (2) getting down the information in the form in which you are most likely to want to incorporate it into your essay (see 42d); and (3) getting down all the information you will need to cite the source accurately. Taking careful and complete notes will not only help you digest the source information as you read but will also help you incorporate the material into your essay without inadvertently plagiarizing the source.

Taking accurate notes

1. Using index cards, notebook pages, or a computer file, list the author's name and a shortened form of the title of the source. Your working bibliography entry for the source (see 41a1) should contain full publication information, so you need not repeat it in your notes.

2. Record exact page references. If the note refers to more than one page, indicate page breaks so that if you decide to use only part of the note, you will know which page to cite.

3. Label each note with a subject heading.

4. Identify the note as a quotation, a paraphrase, a summary, a combination of these forms, or some other form—such as your own critical comment—to avoid any confusion later. Mark quotations accurately with quotation marks, and paraphrase and summarize completely in your own words to be sure you do not inadvertently plagiarize the source. (See 41d.)

5. Read over each completed note carefully to recheck quotations, statistics, and specific facts for accuracy.

Most of your notes will take the form of direct quotation, paraphrase, or summary. Deciding what material to include in your notes and whether to quote, paraphrase, or summarize it is an outgrowth of reading with a critical eye. You may use some sources for background information and others as support for your thesis, and these different purposes may guide you to take one kind of note rather than another—summarizing background information, for example, but quoting statements that support your views. Likewise, as you read, you will want to evaluate the usefulness of the source to your project and begin to assign the role a particular source will play in your paper.

 Deciding whether to quote, paraphrase, or summarize

QUOTE

- Wording that is so memorable or expresses a point so perfectly that you cannot improve or shorten it without weakening the meaning you need
- Authors' opinions you wish to emphasize

- Respected authorities whose opinions support your own ideas
- Authors whose opinions challenge or vary greatly from those of others in the field

PARAPHRASE

- Passages that you do not wish to quote but whose *details* you wish to note *fully*

SUMMARIZE

- Long passages whose *main points* you wish to record *selectively*

1

Quoting

Quoting involves noting down a source's *exact words*. Direct quotations can be effective for catching your readers' attention—for example, including a well-turned phrase in your introduction or giving an eyewitness's account in arresting detail. In a research essay, quotations from respected authorities can help establish your credibility as a researcher by showing that you've sought out experts in the field. In addition, allowing authors to speak for themselves, particularly if they hold opinions counter to yours or to those of other experts, helps demonstrate your fairness (see 5d).

Finally, well-chosen quotations can broaden the appeal of your essay by drawing on emotion as well as logic, appealing both to the reader's mind and heart. A student writing on the ethical issues involved in bullfighting, for example, might introduce an argument that bullfighting is not a sport by quoting Ernest Hemingway's striking comment that "the formal bull-fight is a tragedy, not a sport, and the bull is certain to be killed." (See 5e and 5f for more on logical and emotional appeals.)

Here is an example of an original passage and Daniel Taffe's notecard recording a quotation from it. Notice how he uses ellipses to mark where he omitted some of the author's words and brackets to show that he changed capitalization.

ORIGINAL SOURCE

But Frida was also the product of a bold and brilliant generation that looked back with devotion to its Mexican roots and valued the reality it found there, uncontaminated by foreign influences. She admitted to having a great admiration for her husband's work, as well as that of José Guadalupe Posada, José María Velasco, and Gerardo Murillo (Dr. Atl), and she found great beauty in the highly developed pre-Conquest indigenous arts. — MARTHA ZAMORA, *Frida Kahlo: The Brush of Anguish* (110)

> Mexican cultural influences
>
> Zamora, _Frida_, p. 110
>
> "...Frida was...the product of a bold and brilliant
> generation that looked back with devotion to its
> Mexican roots and valued the reality found there,
> uncontaminated by foreign influences....[S]he
> found great beauty in the highly developed
> pre-Conquest indigenous arts."

Quoting accurately

- Copy quotations *carefully,* with punctuation, capitalization, and spelling exactly as in the original.
- Use brackets if you introduce words of your own into the quotation or make changes in it, and use ellipses if you omit material (see 33b and 33f). Remember to use the brackets and ellipses if you incorporate the quotation into your essay.
- Enclose the quotation in quotation marks; don't rely on your memory to distinguish your own words from those of the source.
- Record the author, shortened title, and page number(s) on which the quotation appeared.
- Make sure you have a corresponding working bibliography entry with complete source information (see 41a1).
- Label the note with a subject heading.

2
Paraphrasing

A **paraphrase** accurately states all the relevant information from a passage *in your own words and phrasing,* without any additional comments or elaborations. A paraphrase is useful when the main points of the passage, their order, and at least some details are important but—unlike passages worth quoting—their particular wording is not. Unlike a summary, a paraphrase always restates *all* the main points of the passage in the same order and in about the same number of words.

BACKGROUND

Paraphrasing is a skill that has twofold value. It helps us to communicate. But it also helps us do something else that isn't always readily apparent to students: it helps us in our learning. Because a paraphrase requires us to put someone else's meaning into our own words, we have to understand the meaning of the original. If we have trouble with the paraphrase, our difficulty likely indicates that we don't have an adequate grasp of the original passage. The measure of how well we understand what we've read is the paraphrase (or the summary). We don't understand what we read as well as we think we do unless we can express that understanding with our own words. In expressing our understanding we are involved in a process of learning.

Paraphrasing material helps you digest a passage, because chances are you can't restate the passage in your own words unless you grasp its full meaning. When you incorporate an accurate paraphrase into your essay, you show readers your understanding of that source.

In order to paraphrase without plagiarizing inadvertently, *use your own words and sentence structures;* do not simply substitute synonyms, and do not imitate the author's style. If you wish to cite some of the author's words within the paraphrase, enclose them in quotation marks. A good way of assuring your originality is to paraphrase without looking at the source. When you have finished, turn back to the source and check to see that the paraphrase accurately presents the author's meaning and that it uses your own words and phrasing.

Writing *acceptable paraphrases*

Looking at the following examples of paraphrases that resemble the original too closely will help you understand how to write acceptable paraphrases. Be aware that even for acceptable paraphrases you must include a citation in your essay identifying the source of the information.

ORIGINAL

But Frida's outlook was vastly different from that of the Surrealists. Her art was not the product of a disillusioned European culture searching for an escape from the limits of logic by plumbing the subconscious. Instead, her fantasy was a product of her temperament, life, and place; it was a way of coming to terms with reality, not of passing beyond reality into another realm.   — HAYDEN HERRERA, *Frida: A Biography of Frida Kahlo* (258)

UNACCEPTABLE PARAPHRASE: USING THE AUTHOR'S WORDS

As Herrera explains, Frida's vision *differed vastly from* the Surrealists' outlook, which grew out of a *disillusioned European culture* hoping to *escape* the confines *of logic*. Her fantasy was due to her own personality and life, including her Mexican roots, and she used it to *come to terms with reality* rather than to move *beyond reality* (258).

Because the italicized language is either borrowed from the original without quotation marks or changed only superficially, this paraphrase plagiarizes.

UNACCEPTABLE PARAPHRASE: USING THE AUTHOR'S SENTENCE STRUCTURES

As Herrera explains, Frida's vision was completely unlike the vision of the Surrealists. Her paintings were not the result of a disenchanted European civilization looking for a release from the confines of logical thinking by probing beneath the conscious mind. Rather, her dream was the result of her personality, situation, and location; it was a means of dealing with the real world, not of moving past it to a new dimension (258).

TEACHING PRACTICE

Have students paraphrase (and summarize) their reading assignments on a regular basis.

FOR COLLABORATIVE WORK

Whenever students paraphrase (or summarize), have them compare versions and explain similarities and differences. Collaborating on a second version will help them appreciate not simply where their troubles lie but also the learning effectiveness of collaboratively talking out, working out, and writing out material they are studying.

FOR COLLABORATIVE WORK

Divide the class into groups of six, and present them with these instructions: choose for paraphrasing a short passage of about one hundred words from a text, an essay, or an article. Each member of the group should first individually restate the original in his or her own words. Keep in mind that the paraphrase requires a writer to include all major and supporting details. Once you have produced your paraphrase, break into three groups of two, and, working together, co-write a paraphrase of the original excerpt. Then discuss the similarities or differences of the three versions. Try to explain them, especially the differences, focusing on the following guiding questions:

1. Working in pairs, did you disagree over terms and their meaning in the original passage?
2. Was it easy to agree on synonyms or on paraphrases of ideas and concepts?
3. Did you agree on the information to include? to leave out?
4. How similar are the three coauthored versions? Why, or why not?
5. What does trying to agree on a paraphrase tell you about how different people read and interpret a passage? About how they choose to rephrase it?

TEACHING PRACTICE

The importance of paraphrasing cannot be overestimated. Make sure to point out to students that:

1. Often a paraphrase may seem to make sense to the writer but that it may not to a reader because of the writer's familiarity with the original passage and because the paraphrase is in his or her choice of language.

2. There are at least two purposes of paraphrasing, one to help the writer himself or herself understand, and another to present the information to another person to understand.

3. Much research involves paraphrasing or explaining ideas in the researcher's own words.

4. Having others respond to their writing helps them learn how to judge and use language for different audiences, different in their levels of understanding and expertise with a subject.

While this paraphrase does not rely on the words of the original, it does follow the sentence structures too closely. Substituting synonyms for the major words in a paraphrase is not enough to avoid plagiarism. The paraphrase must represent your own interpretation of the material, and thus must show your own thought patterns.

Now look at two examples of paraphrases of the same passage that express the author's ideas accurately and acceptably, the first completely in the writer's own words and the second including quotations from the original.

ACCEPTABLE PARAPHRASE: IN THE WRITER'S OWN WORDS

As Herrera explains, Frida's surrealistic vision was unlike that of the European Surrealists. While their art grew out of their disenchantment with their society and their desire to explore the subconscious mind as a refuge from rational thinking, Frida's vision was an outgrowth of her own personality and life experiences in Mexico. She used her surrealistic images to understand better her actual life, not to create a dreamworld (258).

ACCEPTABLE PARAPHRASE: QUOTING SOME OF THE AUTHORS WORDS

As Herrera explains, Frida's surrealistic vision was unlike that of the European Surrealists. While their art grew out of their "disillusioned European culture" and their desire "for an escape from the limits of logic" through an exploration of the subconscious, Frida's dream was an outgrowth of her own personality and life experiences in Mexico. She used her surrealistic images to understand better her actual life, not to "[pass] beyond reality into another realm" (258).

Notice that in the last sentence of the second paraphrase, *passing* needed to be changed to *pass* for the quotation to fit smoothly into the sentence. This change is indicated by using brackets (see 34b and 42d).

Here is an example of an original passage and Daniel Taffe's notecard recording a paraphrase of the first paragraph. (Compare a summary of the full passage, p. 574.)

ORIGINAL SOURCE

Although largely self-taught, and considered by many to be a naive painter, Frida was actually very sophisticated. Intelligent, well-read, and well-informed, she was acquainted with the traditional schools of painting. More important, she recognized the vanguard of Mexican and foreign art not only through her travels but through direct contact with the artists. Direct influences show up in some cases, as in *Magnolias* (1945), reminiscent of the work of Georgia O'Keeffe, or in *Four Inhabitants of Mexico City* (1938), recalling de Chirico. Her earliest works showed an acquaintance with art books; in her first self-portrait for Gómez Arias, she described herself as "your Botticelli," and in letters to him she expressed interest in Modigliani and Piero della Francesca. Her use of suffocating background vegetation is similar to that of Henri Rousseau, the small figures in *What the Water Gave Me* (1938) like something out of Hieronymus Bosch, and the written legends in others like those of the Mexican painter Hermenegildo Bustos.

But Frida was also the product of a bold and brilliant generation that looked back with devotion to its Mexican roots and valued the reality it found there, uncontaminated by foreign influences. She admitted to having a great admiration for her husband's work, as well as that of José Guadalupe Posada, José María Velasco, and Gerardo Murillo (Dr. Atl), and she found great beauty in the highly developed pre-Conquest indigenous arts. — MARTHA ZAMORA, *Frida Kahlo: The Brush of Anguish* (110)

Artistic influences

Zamora, *Frida*, p. 110

Frida mostly taught herself to paint, but she was not as unsophisticated as many thought her to be. She was bright and knowledgeable, familiar with the history of painting, acqainted with contemporary Mexican and foreign artists and their work. Some of her paintings show the influence of O'Keeffe and de Chirico. She referred to her first self-portrait as "your Botticelli" and mentioned Modigliani and della Francesca in letters to Arias. She depicts flora like Rousseau and uses small figures like Bosch and captions like Bustos.

(Paraphrase)

 Paraphrasing accurately

- Include all main points and any important details from the original, in the same order in which they were presented.
- State the meaning in your own words and sentence structures. If you want to include especially memorable language from the original, enclose it in quotation marks.
- Leave out your own comments, elaborations, or reactions.
- Record the author, shortened title, and the page number(s) on which the original material appeared.

(Continued)

- Make sure you have a corresponding working bibliography entry.
- Label the note with a subject heading, and identify it as paraphrase to avoid confusion with a summary.
- Recheck the paraphrase against the original to be sure that the words and sentence structures are your own and that they express the author's meaning accurately.

3

Summarizing

A **summary** is a significantly shortened version of a passage, a section, or even a whole chapter or work that *captures main ideas in your own words.* Unlike paraphrasing, a summary uses just enough information to record the main points or the points you wish to emphasize. You needn't include all the author's points or any details, but be sure not to distort his or her meaning. The length of a summary depends on how long the original is and how much information you will need to use. Your goal is to keep the summary as brief as possible, capturing only the gist of the original.

For a short passage, try reading the passage carefully and, without looking at the text, writing a one- or two-sentence summary. For a long passage or an entire chapter, skim the headings and topic sentences and make notes of each before writing your summary in a paragraph or two. For a whole book, you may want to refer to the preface and introduction as well as chapter titles, headings, and topic sentences—and your summary may take a page or more.

Artistic influences

Zamora, <u>Frida</u>, p. 110

Although Frida was well acquainted with historical and contemporary artists from Europe and America, whose influence is evident in her works (particularly in her images of flora and her rendering of many scenes in a painting), she was deeply aware of her Mexican heritage.

(Summary)

On the facing page is a notecard recording a summary of the passage whose first paragraph is paraphrased by Daniel Taffe on p. 573. Notice that it states the author's main points selectively—and without using her words.

 Summarizing accurately

- Include just enough information to recount the main points you wish to cite. A summary is usually much shorter than the original.
- Use your own words. If you want to include language from the original, enclose it in quotation marks.
- Record the author, shortened title, and page number(s) on which the original material appeared.
- Make sure you have a corresponding working bibliography entry.
- Label the note with a subject heading, and identify it as a summary to avoid confusion with a paraphrase.
- Recheck any material you plan to use against the original to be sure you have captured the author's meaning and that your words are entirely your own.

Combination notes

Often your reading will lead you to take a **combination note**—perhaps a paraphrase with some quotations, like the one on p. 572, or a summary of an entire chapter with a paraphrase of a key paragraph. If you combine forms, be sure to follow the guidelines for each kind of note, and label clearly what material is in which form.

Other kinds of notes

Many researchers take notes that do not fall into the preceding categories. Some take **key term notes**, which may include names, dates, short statements—anything that may jog their memory when they begin drafting. Others record **personal or critical notes**—thoughts, questions, disagreements, criticisms—striking ideas that come to mind as they read. Still others adopt systems peculiar to their research project. Daniel Taffe, for example, kept a separate note for each of Frida Kahlo's paintings that dealt with the themes he pursued in his essay. By labeling these notes with subject headings, he could quickly determine how frequently each theme appeared in her work.

You may find reason to keep notes of various kinds in addition to those described here. Whatever form your notes take, always list the source's title, author, and page number(s) to document the material accurately. In addition, check that you have carefully distinguished your own thoughts and comments from the source's.

Photocopying source material

Nearly all libraries provide photocopying machines that you can use to copy pages or even whole articles or chapters. You can then annotate the photocopies with thoughts and questions, highlight interesting quotations, and call out key terms. Try not to rely on photocopying too heavily, however. Remember that you still need to read the material carefully, and resist the temptation to treat photocopied material as notes, an error that could lead to inadvertent plagiarizing as well as to wasting time looking for information you only vaguely remember having read. If you have read and taken careful notes on your sources rather than relying primarily on photocopies, your drafting will be more efficient.

If you do photocopy material, write out on the photocopy all the information you need to cite the material in your list of sources cited. (And check that page numbers are clearly legible on copies.)

41d

Recognizing plagiarism, acknowledging sources

"There is," in the words of Ecclesiastes, "no new thing under the sun." In a way, the biblical saying is true of research as well as of life in general: whatever research we do is influenced and affected by everything we have already read and experienced. If you try, for instance, to trace the origins of every idea you have had just *today,* you will quickly see the extent to which we are all indebted to others as the sources of information.

Giving full acknowledgment to those sources presents a challenge, but doing so is important for several reasons. First, acknowledging your sources allows you to thank those whose work you have built on and thus to avoid plagiarism. Second, it helps readers by placing your research into a *context* of other thinking and research; it shows in what ways your research is part of a larger conversation and lets readers know where *they* can find more information. Finally, acknowledging your sources helps you critically examine your own research and thinking. How timely and reliable are those sources? Have you used them accurately?

Acknowledging sources fully and generously, then, provides a means of establishing your *ethos,* or credibility, as a researcher. (See 5d.) Failure to credit sources breaks trust both with the research "conversation" and with readers; as a sign of dishonesty, it can easily destroy the credibility of both researcher and research.

1

Recognizing plagiarism

Plagiarism, the use of someone else's words or ideas as your own without crediting the original writer, can result in serious consequences. At some colleges, students who plagiarize fail the course automatically; at others, they are expelled. Outside academic life, eminent political, business, and scientific leaders have been stripped of candidacies, positions, and awards following charges of plagiarism.

You are probably already aware of cases of deliberate plagiarism—handing in a paper that a friend wrote for a similar course, copying passages directly from source materials. In addition, however, you need to know about unintended plagiarism—a quotation accidentally used without quotation marks, a paraphrase that too closely resembles the original, background details gleaned from a source but used without acknowledgment in the mistaken belief that none was necessary. By understanding what material you must document, taking systematic, accurate notes, and giving full credit to sources in both parenthetical citations and your list of sources cited, you can avoid unintended plagiarism. Doing so for every idea you build on, however, is an impossible task. In practical terms, where do you draw the line?

2

Knowing which material requires acknowledgment

Some of the information you use does not need to be credited to another source because it is well known or because you gathered the data yourself. The following lists should help you discern which materials you need to credit and which ones you can use without credit.

Materials not requiring acknowledgment

Common knowledge. If most readers like yourself would be likely to know something, you need not cite it. You do not need to credit a source for a statement that George Bush was elected president in 1988, for example. If, on the other hand, you give the exact number of popular votes he received in the 1988 election, you should cite the source for that figure.

BACKGROUND

In a lecture called "Why Is Plagiarism Wrong?" given at DePauw University on November 11, 1987, Barry M. Kroll outlined the five different approaches instructors take to discourage plagiarism. The most traditional—and apparently least effective—approach involves *prohibitions.* The instructor simply tells students, typically in moralistic terms, that plagiarism is wrong. Kroll warns us, "Virtually all college students already 'know' that plagiarism is a prohibited act. But despite that knowledge, a significant number of students do not appear to take the prohibition seriously enough to be dissuaded from plagiarizing in their college papers."

The second approach involves *prevention,* an attempt to make it difficult to plagiarize. Some strategies of this approach include assigning different textbooks and paper topics from term to term and not using books for which *Cliffs Notes* exist. Unfortunately, this approach does little to teach the student not to plagiarize.

Some instructors and institutions try to deter students from plagiarizing by establishing *penalties* for those caught plagiarizing. This approach gains effectiveness when supported by the institution. However, it turns instructors into police, and most instructors dislike such a role. Such a role tends to undermine instructor-student rapport.

Other instructors and institutions reject the notion that without penalties cheating would increase. Their remedy for plagiarism is to provide students with *practice* in using source material. This perspective assumes that most plagiarism is caused by unfamiliarity with the conventions of citation, sloppiness and neglect, and insufficient practice in citing sources. Unfortunately, we have ample evidence that students often do plagiarize intentionally.

The fifth approach to plagiarism—and the one that Kroll recommends—consists of teaching the *principles* behind society's attitudes toward plagiarism. In a separate study of how freshmen actually view plagiarism, Kroll discovered that students understood what it was and took it seriously, and that they could explain the wrongness of plagiarism with reference to three principles: fairness to authors; responsibility to one's education; and ownership of ideas. The latter two principles, Kroll argues, are inadequate, and the first incomplete. Kroll found no reference by students to the idea that plagiarism is wrong because it is deception. Yet, Kroll recommends that principle as being the best argument against plagiarism. Such deception is morally unacceptable and is detrimental to the institution, to the community, and to the character of the individual. Moreover, this principle is the basis for the other approaches: "For unless our students understand the reasons that plagiarism is wrong and destructive, they are likely to see our prohibitions as outmoded, to see the practices of careful documentation as merely tedious exercises, and to see the penalties for plagiarism as irrationally punitive."

In the final analysis, plagiarism can be both personally and rhetorically devastating. Whatever the personal consequences, plagiarism inevitably undermines the writer's *ethos*. The writer who plagiarizes loses all authority, and thus persuasion becomes an impossibility.

USEFUL READING

Kroll, Barry M. "How College Freshmen View Plagiarism." *Written Communication* 5 (1988): 203–21. Kroll describes the results of a study in which 150 college freshmen wrote their explanations of why plagiarism is wrong, rated five standard explanations, and responded to statements about the seriousness and possible consequences of plagiarism.

Facts available in a wide variety of sources. If a number of encyclopedias, almanacs, or textbooks include the information, you need not cite a specific source. For instance, you would not need to cite a source for the fact that the Japanese bombing of Pearl Harbor on December 7, 1941, destroyed most of the base except for the oil tanks and submarines. You would, however, need to credit a source that argued that the failure to destroy the submarines meant that Japan was destined to lose the Pacific War.

Your own findings from field research. If you conduct field research—observation, interviews, surveys—and produce results, simply announce those results as your own.

Materials requiring acknowledgment

For material that does not fall under the above three headings, credit sources as fully as possible, using quotation marks and citing the source parenthetically and listing it in a list of sources (see Chapters 43 and 44).

Direct quotations. Whenever you use another person's words directly, credit the source. (If two quotations from the same source appear close together, you can use one parenthetical citation placed after the second quotation.) Even if you are quoting in the middle of a paraphrase whose source you intend to acknowledge, set off in quotation marks and *separately* acknowledge the direct use of the author's words.

Facts that are not widely known or assertions that are arguable. If your readers would be unlikely to know a fact, or if an author presents as fact an assertion that may or may not be true, cite the source. To claim, for instance, that Switzerland is amassing an offensive nuclear arsenal would demand citing a source, because Switzerland has long been an officially neutral state. If you are not sure whether a fact is familiar to your readers or a statement is debatable, citing the source is advisable.

Judgments, opinions, and claims of others. Whenever you summarize or paraphrase anyone else's opinion, give the source for that summary or paraphrase. Even though the wording should be completely your own, you need to acknowledge the source.

Statistics, charts, tables, and graphs from any source. Credit all statistical and graphical material not derived from your own field research, even if you yourself create the graph from data in another source.

Help provided by friends, instructors, or others. A conference with an instructor may give you the idea you need to clinch an argument. Give credit. Friends may help you conduct surveys, refine questionnaires, or think through problems. Credit them, too.

If your working bibliography contains complete entries that you double-checked *as you examined the source,* and if your notes clearly identify direct quotations, paraphrases, and summaries that you double-checked for accuracy *as you took the notes,* the task of acknowledging the source of the information incorporated into your essay will be much easier.

 Recognizing plagiarism, acknowledging your sources

- Maintain an accurate and thorough working bibliography. (See 41a1.)
- Establish a consistent note-taking system, listing sources and page numbers and identifying clearly all quotations, paraphrases, summaries, statistics, and graphics. (See 41c.)
- Identify all quotations with quotation marks—both in your notes and in your essay.
- Be sure that your summaries and paraphrases are in your own words and sentence structures.
- In your essay, give a parenthetical citation for each quotation, paraphrase, summary, arguable assertion or opinion, statistic, and graph from a source. (See 43a and 44a.)
- Prepare an accurate and complete list of sources cited according to the required documentation style. (See 43c and 44c.)

41e

Interpreting sources

Your task as a reader is to identify and understand sources and sets of data as completely as possible. As a writer, your aim must be to present data and sources *to other readers* so that they can most readily understand the point you are making. Doing so calls for careful thinking on your part, as you work to interpret sources.

Turning data into information

Computer scientists sometimes distinguish between **data,** bits of facts or strings of statements, and **information,** the meaning attached to the data. As a researcher, you will gather a great deal of data, probably more than you need or can use. But those data become information only when their meaning is made clear. You may have gathered two dozen facts about a city's finances, for example, but turning them into information calls for pointing out their significance as a group—that, for instance, the city is on the brink of bankruptcy.

Synthesizing data and drawing inferences

You can begin turning data into information by **synthesizing**—grouping similar pieces of data together; looking for patterns or trends, identifying the gist, or main point, of the data. Most often, finding the gist of a source or set of data will call for drawing **inferences**—conclusions that are not explicitly stated but that follow logically from the data given. For example, you may have data indicating severe drought in every Midwestern state. Other data report very low levels of crop production in those states. From these data, you draw the inference that farmers in the Midwest face financial crisis. As a researcher, you have turned data into information.

Recording your thoughts and ideas

Perhaps the most exciting part of research occurs when the materials you are reading spark something in your mind and new ideas take hold. As you read, your mind is busy processing all the materials you are discovering with those you have previously discovered, seeking connections and similarities, making distinctions, synthesizing in the ways discussed above. Ideas will occur to you that can become part of your thesis or argument. *Don't let them get away.* Jot them down, perhaps in a special section of your writing log or research log if you are keeping one.

Do not worry about whether an idea is true or right or even useful—just get it down, and think about it later. Some ideas may be thrown away because they do not suit the final shape your essay takes, but others will likely *provide* that shape. Disagreements among sources can provide particularly fruitful areas to consider and may provoke you to new insights all your own. Consequently, you need to pay close attention to the arguments put forth by all your sources—those you agree with as well as those you do not.

EXERCISE 41.1   Taking Inventory: Paraphrases and Summaries

If you are working on a research essay, choose an important source and prepare a paraphrase of two or three paragraphs of it, using your own words and sentence structures. Analyze your paraphrase using the guidelines on pp. 573–74. Then try summarizing the same passage and checking to see how well you followed the guidelines on p. 575. Take note of any mistakes you made in paraphrasing or summarizing, and list ways you can avoid such mistakes in the future. Record these notes along with the revised paraphrase and summary in your writing log or research log, if you are keeping one.

42

Writing a Research Essay

A nineteenth-century author once remarked that "in research the horizon recedes as we advance. . . . And research is always incomplete." Indeed, we might slightly alter a line from Samuel Johnson and say that a person who is tired of research is tired of living. For in many ways, the process of living constantly demands research. But while you may continue to pursue a research question for a long time, there comes a time to draw the strands of research together and to articulate your conclusions in writing. This chapter will help you at that point.

The processes of research and writing are intimately linked. While you conduct research, you will also be coming up with ideas, considering organizational possibilities, recognizing connections among your materials, making notes, and perhaps beginning to draft. From these thoughts, you will eventually choose the final form in which to cast your own conclusions.

You will probably do most of your final organizing and drafting when your research is largely complete and you have most of the facts, evidence, quotations, and other data you think you need. For most college research essays, the process of drafting a final version should begin *at least* two weeks before the deadline, to allow for response to the draft, for further research, and for revision and editing.

42a

Refining your plans

Throughout your research, you have been generating notes that answer your research question and reflect on your hypothesis. Your growing understanding of the subject, in turn, has no doubt led you to gather other information, which may have altered your original question. This somewhat

USEFUL READING

Dinitz, Susan, and Jean Kiedaisch. "The Research Paper: Teaching Students to Be Members of the Academic Community." *Exercise Exchange* 31 (1986): 8–10. The authors suggest that rhetorical concerns— purpose and voice—should be primary concerns for research papers.

Jeske, Jeff. "Borrowing from the Sciences: A Model for the Freshman Research Paper." *Writing Instructor* 6 (Winter 1987): 62–67. A helpful four-part model for writing the research essay that encourages students to reflect on the research process itself while they are producing a research project.

TEACHING PRACTICE

To help your students appreciate the value of the questions in 42a1, point out that they help students:

1. Identify their intended audience.

2. Judge whether to define basic terms or to take for granted that their audience already has a basic familiarity with the subject or field. For example, they wouldn't have to define the concept *regeneration* for an audience of senior-level students working in molecular genetics. Nor would they have to define a term such as *apartheid* for senior-level political science students. But in a paper examining economic disparity in South Africa that they are writing for a composition class, they might want to define and explain the term fully.

3. Evaluate the sources they will use and how to use them. If the audience is not a specialized one, students will not want to assume that a simple mention of some researcher's claims will give an audience sufficient understanding. If the source involves an advanced level of understanding, and the audience is not a professor or some other well-informed, advanced audience, then sources will have to be carefully explained.

4. Decide on how to present themselves, to identify their relationship to the audience, and to judge how they want to appear to the audience.

5. Consider further how they see their subject. What are they trying to prove? What are they trying to explain? What is their purpose in relation to their potential audience?

6. Reconsider their thesis with the audience in mind. Is the thesis new to the audience? a restatement? a reexamination of something they already assume or accept?

Everyday use

Everyday decisions we must make often call for some research and writing. A student confirmed this fact recently when she needed to decide whether to take a full-time summer job or go to summer school full time and work only a few hours a week. Because money was tight, her decision was important. To make it, she first gathered information on how much money she could earn—and save—that summer and on how that figure compared with the amount she might save if she attended summer school and thus graduated a term early, when she could pursue a permanent job. In addition, she checked out all summer course offerings and met with her adviser to talk about whether the job experience she might gain in summer work would make her more marketable. Once she had gathered all this information, she drafted a list of advantages and disadvantages for each choice and discussed them with her adviser and friends. Only then did she make a final decision. Can you remember a decision you have made that called for some research and writing?

---

circular process, a kind of research spiral, is at the heart of all research-based writing.

You should by now have a fair number of notes containing facts, opinions, paraphrases, summaries, quotations, and other material of all kinds. You probably also have thoughts about the connections among the many pieces of information you found. And you should have some sense of whether your hypothesis has been established sufficiently to serve as the thesis of an essay. At this point, you should reconsider your purpose, audience, stance, and thesis.

1

Reconsidering your purpose, audience, stance, and thesis

Given what you now know about your research question, reconsider questions such as the following.

1. What is your central purpose? What other purposes, if any, do you have?

2. What stance do you take toward your topic? Are you an advocate, a critic, a reporter? (See 2d.)

3. Are you addressing an audience other than your instructor?

4. How much about your research question does your audience know already? How much background will they need to be given?

5. What sorts of supporting information are they likely to find convincing—examples? precedents? quotations from authorities? (See 5e.)

6. What tone will most appeal to them and help them understand your points? Should you present yourself as a colleague, an expert, or a student?

7. How can you establish common ground with them and show consideration of points of view other than your own? (See 5d and Chapter 28.)

8. What is your thesis trying to establish? How likely is your audience to accept it?

2

Developing an explicit thesis

A useful means of relating your purpose, audience, and thesis before you begin a full draft is to write out an **explicit thesis statement**. Such a statement forces you to articulate all your major lines of argument and to see how well those arguments carry out your purpose and appeal to your audience. At the drafting stage, your explicit thesis statement might take the following form.

In this essay, I plan to (explain, argue, demonstrate, analyze, and so on) for an audience of _____
that _____
because or if (1) _____, (2) _____,
(3)_____.

For example, Daniel Taffe developed the following explicit thesis.

In this essay, I plan to demonstrate for an audience of classmates from my Introduction to Writing class that Frida Kahlo's unique style results not only from autobiographical influences but also from her knowledge of earlier European art, including traditional Christian imagery and Mexican culture.

3

Testing your thesis

Writing out an explicit thesis will often confirm the research you have been doing and support your hypothesis. It may, however, reveal that your hypothesis is invalid, inadequately supported, or insufficiently focused. In such cases, you must then rethink your original research question, perhaps do further research, and work toward a revised hypothesis and eventually a revised thesis. To test your thesis at this point, consider the following list of questions.

FOR COLLABORATIVE WORK

To make fuller use of the thesis statement form, call on a student to present his or her statement on the board. Open the class up to respond to the statement. To get things started, ask the writer to clarify or define terms or vague points. Ask the student why he or she has picked the subject. In other words, open the class up to a brainstorming session in which the writer is required to answer the class's questions and make clearer the thesis and purpose. In fielding the class's responses, the writer will likely clarify the project in his or her own mind. The writer will see where his or her difficulties lie, where his or her command of the subject is lacking, or where he or she will need to elaborate. The writer may find that the project is too large or may find a way of refining the thesis.

Once you have demonstrated this activity for the whole class, break them up into groups of four or five and have them work on each other's thesis statements.

1. How can you state the topic of your thesis or your comment about the topic more precisely or more clearly? (See 3b.)

2. In what ways will your thesis interest and appeal to your audience? What can you do to make that interest grow? (See 5f.)

3. How could the wording of your thesis be more specific? Could you use more concrete nouns (see 27c) or stronger verbs (see 23a)? Should you add qualifying adjectives or adverbs (see Chapter 12)?

4. Is your thesis going to be manageable, given your limits of time and knowledge? What might you do to make it more manageable?

5. What research evidence do you have to support each aspect of your thesis? What additional evidence do you need?

Organizing information

In discussing her own process of writing, Marie Winn talks about the challenge of transforming a tangle of ideas and information "into an orderly and logical sequence on a blank piece of paper." This is the task of organization, of grouping information effectively. Experienced writers differ considerably in the ways they go about this task, and you will want to experiment until you find an organizational method that works well for you. This section will discuss two organizing strategies—grouping material by subject headings and outlining.

1

Grouping notes by subject headings

During your research, you have been taking notes and keeping lists of ideas. To organize these materials using a grouping strategy, examine them for connections, finding what might be combined with what, which notes will be more useful and which less useful, which ideas lend support to the thesis and which should be put aside. Brainstorm about your research question one last time, and add the resulting notes to your other materials, looking to see if they fit with any of the materials you already have.

If you have been keeping notes on cards, you can arrange the cards in stacks by subject headings, putting the ones with your main topics in the center and arranging any related cards around them. If you have been taking notes in a notebook, you can cut the pages apart and group the slips of paper. If your notes are in a computer file, see if your program can sort them by subject headings or search for particular headings.

Grouping your notes in this way will help you identify major ideas and see whether you have covered all the necessary areas. It will also help you decide whether you have too many ideas to manage—or whether you need to do more research in some area. Most important, it will allow you to see how the many small pieces of your research fit together and result in the larger structure of a complete essay.

Once you have these initial groups, skim through the notes looking for connections you can use to organize your draft. Daniel Taffe noticed that the notes on one of his main topics—early European art—seemed to be related to another set of notes—on Kahlo's retablo-like paintings. He thus decided to see whether he could show how traditional European religious imagery was echoed in the distinctly Mexican work of Kahlo.

2

Outlining

Outlines can be used in various ways. Some writers group their notes, draft, and then outline the draft to study its tentative structure. Others develop a working outline from their notes, listing the major points in a tentative order with support for each point. Such a working outline may see you through the rest of the process, or you may decide to revise it as you go along. Still other writers prefer to plot out their organization early on in a formal outline. (See 3e for further discussion of outlines.)

Because Daniel Taffe's instructor asked that he submit a formal outline with his research essay, he decided to move early on from the informal topic outline he made as he grouped his notes to a formal one. His formal outline appears on pp. 621–23.

42c

Drafting your essay

When you are ready to draft your essay, set yourself a deadline, and structure all your tasks with that deadline in mind. Gather your notes, outline, and any sources you may need to consult. Most writers find that some sustained work (perhaps two or three hours) at this point pays off. Begin drafting where you feel most confident. If you have a good idea for an introduction, begin there. If you are not sure exactly how you want to introduce the essay but do know how you want to approach some particular point, begin with that, and return to the introduction later. The most important thing is to get started.

The drafting process itself varies considerably among researchers, and much about the way you draft will be up to you. Some writers try to make the first draft as perfect as possible, working meticulously paragraph by paragraph. Others draft as fast as they can, getting all their material down in whatever form and smoothing it out later. Some follow an outline from start to finish; others draft sections separately and arrange them later. Your writing process is your own, and no one else can tell you what works best for you. The tips offered in 3f, however, may help.

1

Drafting a working title and introduction

The title and introduction play special roles, for they set the context for what is to come. Ideally, the title announces the subject of the essay in an intriguing or memorable way. The introduction should draw readers into the essay and provide them with any background they will need to understand the discussion. You can find general advice on titles in 4f1 and on introductions in 4f2 and 6e1, but some specific things you should consider in drafting an introduction for a research essay include the following.

- It is often effective to *open with a question,* especially your research question. Then you might explain what you will do to answer the question and *end with your thesis* (in essence, the answer).

- Because in your essay you will be bringing together several distinct points from various sources, you will probably want to *forecast your main points,* to help readers get their bearings.

- You will want to *establish your own credibility* as a research writer by showing your experience and demonstrating what you have done to become an expert on your topic.

- In general, you may *not* want to open with a quotation—though it can be a good attention-getter, giving any one source such prominence is probably not a good idea. In a research essay, you may want to quote several sources to support your ideas. Opening with a quotation from one source may give the impression that you will be presenting that writer's ideas rather than using them in support of your own.

Because Daniel Taffe knew that most of his readers had probably never heard of his topic, he decided to open his introduction, shown on p. 624, with the simple question "Who is Frida Kahlo?" After briefly answering this question in a way that builds common ground with readers by implying that their ignorance of Kahlo is not unexpected, he piques their interest with facts about recent sales of her paintings to a celebrity and for a record price. He then builds his credibility as a researcher by discussing the preeminent role

FOR COLLABORATIVE WORK

Have students working in groups of five brainstorm a list of purposes that they think the introduction and conclusion should serve. Ask them to be as specific as possible. Once they've compiled lists, ask them to seek out major journals in various fields and to identify and compare the actual purposes of introductions and conclusions. Here are some possibilities they may come up with:

1. Introductions
   State the problem or topic to be explored
   Give briefly the background or context for the question or topic
   Get readers interested
   Give briefly the reason for discussing or researching a topic
2. Conclusions
   Answer the question initially raised in the introduction
   Confirm the hypothesis
   Repeat the main idea or point that the paper has worked to explain
   Confirm the importance of the question or subject
   Suggest areas for further research

of Hayden Herrera in Kahlo scholarship. Finally, he forecasts one of his main points, autobiographical elements in Kahlo's work, in leading up to the other one, Christian and Mexican elements, which forms the basis of his thesis.

2

Drafting your conclusion

A good conclusion to a research essay helps readers know what they have learned. Its job is not to persuade (the body of your essay should already have done that), but it *can* contribute to the overall effectiveness of your argument. General advice on writing conclusions can be found in 4f3 and 6e2, but following are some specific strategies especially appropriate for research essays.

- A specific-to-general pattern is frequently appropriate, opening with a reference to your thesis and then expanding to a more general conclusion that reminds readers of the significance of your discussion.

- If you have covered several main points, you may want to remind readers of them. Be careful, however, to provide more than a mere summary.

- Try to end with something that will have lasting impact—a provocative quotation or question, a vivid image, a call for action, or a warning. Remember, however, that most readers don't like to be preached to in an obvious way.

- Tailor your conclusion to the needs of your readers, in terms of both the information you include and the tone and style you adopt.

Daniel Taffe's conclusion, shown on p. 636, summarizes the main points of his essay and then ends with an assertion of his topic's importance that is based on an anecdote about Kahlo's life and art. His use of the pronouns *us* and *we* invokes a kinship with his audience and the possibility that they, too, are or will become students of her work.

42d

Incorporating source materials

Once you are at the point of drafting your essay, a new task awaits: weaving your source materials into your own writing. The challenge is to use your sources yet to remain the author—to quote, paraphrase, and summarize other voices while at the same time remaining the single dominant voice in your essay.

You tentatively decided to quote, paraphrase, or summarize material when you read your sources critically and took notes (see 41b–c). As you choose which sources to use in your essay and how to use them, however, you may want to reevaluate those decisions. For example, you may decide to summarize in your essay what you paraphrased in your notes, to use only the quotation you included in the midst of a summary, or not to use a particular quotation at all. To avoid plagiarizing, document any material you do include from a source with a parenthetical citation (see 43a and 44a) and an entry in your list of sources.

1

Using direct quotations

Your essay must be your own work, and you should depend on other people's words as little as possible, limiting quotations to those *necessary* to your argument or *memorable* for your readers. Reasons to use direct quotations include the following.

- To incorporate a statement expressed so effectively by the author that it cannot be paraphrased without altering meaning
- To contribute to your own credibility as a writer by quoting an authority on your topic
- To allow an author to defend his or her position in his or her own words
- To use a striking quotation for effect

Once you have decided to use a quotation, you need to consider how to work it into your text

Enclosing brief quotations within your text

Quotations of no more than four lines (MLA style) or no more than forty words (APA style) should be worked into your text, enclosed by quotation marks. For example:

> In Miss Eckhart, Welty recognizes a character who shares with her "the love of her art and the love of giving it, the desire to give it until there is no more left" (10).

> In Russia, however, the men who took control had hardly any experience in military or administrative fields at all. As Edward Crankshaw explained, "They were a disciplined set of revolutionary conspirators who had spent most of their adult lives in exile in Russia or abroad" (44).

Notice that both of the preceding examples alert readers to the quotations by using **signal phrases** that include the author's name. When you cite a quotation in this way, you need put only the page number in the parentheses.

When you introduce a quotation without mentioning the author's name, place the name in the parentheses before the page number. Be sure, however, that you always distinguish for your readers where someone else's words begin. For example:

> In *The Third Life of Grange Copeland*, Grange's inability to respond to his son is evident "even in private and in the dark and with his son, presumably sleep" when he "could not bear to touch his son with his hand" (Walker 121).

These are but two ways of introducing a quotation. Both the MLA and the APA styles dictate conventions for what should appear in parenthetical citations in what circumstances and how it should be punctuated. See 43a and 44a for guidelines.

Setting off long quotations

Quotations longer than four lines (MLA style) or forty words (APA style) should be set off from the regular text. Begin such a quotation on a new line, and indent each line of it ten spaces (MLA) or five spaces (APA) from the left margin. This indentation sets off the quotation clearly so that quotation marks are unnecessary. Type the quotation to the regular right margin, and double-space it like regular text. Long quotations are usually introduced by a signal phrase or a sentence followed by a colon.

> A good seating arrangement can prevent problems; however, "withitness," as defined by Woolfolk, works even better:
>> Withitness is the ability to communicate to students that you are aware of what is happening in the classroom, that you "don't miss anything." With-it teachers seem to have "eyes in the back of their heads." They avoid becoming too absorbed with a few students, since this allows the rest of the class to wander. (359)
> This technique works, however, only if students actually believe that their teacher will know everything that goes on.

While long quotations are often necessary in research essays, use them cautiously. Too many of them may suggest to your readers that you did not rely on your own thinking in writing the essay. In addition, long quotations can make an essay seem choppy, and they can distract attention from your analysis of the material. If you think you may be overusing them, substitute paraphrases or summaries for some of them.

res

Integrating quotations into your text

Quotations have to be carefully integrated into your text so that they link smoothly and clearly with the surrounding sentences. In most cases, you need to use a signal phrase to provide such a link. For example:

WITHOUT A SIGNAL PHRASE

In *Death of a Salesman,* Willy Loman dreams the wrong dreams and idealizes the wrong ideals. "He has lived on his smile and on his hopes, survived from sale to sale, been sustained by the illusion that he has countless friends in his territory, that everything will be all right . . ." (Brown 97).

It is possible to figure out the connection between the quotation and text, but see how the following revision uses a signal phrase to make the link far easier to recognize. Note also the slightly awkward shift in verb tenses from text to quotation, which is smoothed out in the revision.

WITH A SIGNAL PHRASE

In *Death of a Salesman,* Willy Loman dreams the wrong dreams and idealizes the wrong ideals. His misguided perceptions are well captured by Brown: "He has lived on his smile and on his hopes, survived from sale to sale, been sustained by the illusion that he has countless friends in his territory, that everything will be all right . . ." (97).

Introducing a quotation with the author's name and a **signal verb** is a clear and simple way of integrating it into your text. Remember, however, that the verb must be appropriate to the idea you are expressing.

As Eudora Welty notes, "Learning stamps you with its moments. Childhood's learning," she continues, "is made up of moments. It isn't steady. It's a pulse." (9)

In this example, two signal verbs—*notes* and *continues*—integrate the quotations appropriately for the sense of the sentence. Here are some other possible signal verbs. Some of them, like *notes* and *continues,* can be used by themselves with the author's name; others, like *interprets* or *opposes,* require more complex phrasing.

 Signal verbs

acknowledges	answers	claims
advises	asserts	concludes
agrees	believes	concurs
allows	charges	confirms

criticizes	interprets	reports
declares	lists	responds
describes	objects	reveals
disagrees	observes	says
discusses	offers	states
disputes	opposes	suggests
emphasizes	remarks	thinks
expresses	replies	writes

Indicating changes with brackets and ellipses

Sometimes, for the sake of clarity or length, you will wish to alter a direct quotation in some way—to make a verb tense fit smoothly into your text, to replace a pronoun with a noun, to eliminate unnecessary detail, to change a capital letter to lowercase or vice versa. Enclose any changed or added words in brackets, and indicate any deletions with ellipsis points. Because most quotations that you integrate into your essay come from longer passages, you need not use ellipses at the beginning of a quotation nor end, unless the last sentence of the quotation as you cite it is incomplete.

> A farmer, Jane Lee, spoke to the Nuclear Regulatory Commission about the occurrences. "There is something wrong in the [Three Mile Island] area. It is happening within nature itself," she said, referring to human miscarriages, stillbirths, and birth defects in farm animals ("Legacy" 33).

> Economist John Kenneth Galbraith has pointed out that "large corporations cannot afford to compete with one another. Their survival is predicated upon . . . market segmentation. In a truly competitive market someone loses. . . . American big business has finally learned that everybody has to protect everybody else's investment" (Key 17).

Be especially careful that any changes you make in a quotation do not alter its essential meaning. Even if an error occurs in the original passage, do not correct it, but alert readers to it by inserting "sic" ("thus") in brackets after it.

> As the reviewer for *Gumshoe* remarks, "This absorbing mystery offers an attractively sardonic heroin [sic] and a humdinger of a plot" (31).

In any event, use brackets and ellipses sparingly, for too many of them make for difficult reading and can even suggest to readers that you have changed the meaning by removing some of the context. (For more on brackets and ellipses, see 34b and 34f.)

2

Using paraphrases and summaries

When you want to use ideas from sources but have no need to quote their exact words, use paraphrases or summaries. Reasons for using paraphrases and summaries include the following.

- To present background information and other facts that your readers may not know
- To explain various positions on your topic

Integrating paraphrases and summaries

As with quotations, you need to introduce paraphrases and summaries clearly, usually by using a signal phrase that includes the name of the author of the material. Using the author's name also helps lend authority to the material. Sometimes, in fact, you will want to highlight the source even more prominently. Notice in the following example how the writer focuses on one authority, first introducing her by name and title and then both quoting and summarizing her work.

> On the other hand, some observers of the battle of the sexes are trying to arrange cease-fires. Professor of linguistics Deborah Tannen says that she offers her book *That's Not What I Meant!* to "women and men everywhere who are trying their best to talk to each other" (19). Tannen goes on to illustrate how communication between women and men breaks down and then to suggest that a full awareness of "genderlects" can improve relationships (297).

In the following example, on the other hand, the writer focuses more on the information paraphrased, identifying the authors only parenthetically.

> Three areas of established differences in cognitive abilities are recognized by the majority of researchers: verbal ability, mathematical ability, and spatial ability (Block 517). As shown by current research, a specific cognitive sex difference exists in verbal ability; in general, females are superior to males in this area starting in early childhood (Weitz 99).

Remember that indicating the sources of paraphrases and summaries is important. Even unintentional failure to cite sources for materials that are not in quotation marks but that you could not have known or arrived at by yourself constitutes plagiarism. Make certain that you record the sources of general background information as well as specific quotations, facts, viewpoints, and so forth. If your notes are incomplete or your source is unclear, relocate and reread the original to clarify the information. If you are unable to do so, you would be wise to leave out the material rather than risk plagiarism. (See Chapters 41, 43, and 44.)

Incorporating quotations, paraphrases, and summaries

1. In general, use signal phrases or other clues to indicate where the cited material begins.
2. Identify quotations by enclosing ones of up to four lines (MLA style) or forty words (APA style) in quotation marks and setting off longer ones.
3. Check that you reproduced the wording, spelling, punctuation, and capitalization of quotations accurately and that you indicated changes by brackets and ellipses. If your notes are unclear, look again at the original.
4. Document every quotation, paraphrase, and summary with a citation in your text and a corresponding entry in your list of sources cited. If you use some of the author's words within a paraphrase or summary, enclose them in quotation marks, and give a separate citation for them after the closing quotation mark.

3

Checking for excessive use of source material

Exactly how much you should use sources in an essay has to depend on your purpose, your audience, and the section of the essay. In general, however, your essay should not give the impression of being a patchwork of quotations, paraphrases, and summaries from other people. If it does, you will have merely accumulated data; you won't have actually presented information in your own way (see 41e). You need a rhetorical stance, a perspective that represents you as the author. If you are over-quoting and over-citing, your own voice will disappear. The following passage illustrates this problem:

> The United States is one of the countries with the most rapid population growth. In fact, rapid population increase has been a "prominent feature of American life since before the founding of the republic" (Day 31). In the past, the cause of the high rate of population growth was the combination of large-scale immigration and a high birthrate. As Day notes, "Two facts stand out in the demographic history of the United States: first, the single position as a receiver of immigrants; second, our high rate of growth from natural increase" (31).
>
> Nevertheless, American population density is not as high as in most European countries. Day points out that the Netherlands, with a density of 906 persons per square mile, is more crowded than even the most densely populated American states (33).

FOR COLLABORATIVE WORK

Ask students to work in pairs and select an article from a major journal in a field of interest to them. Have them identify each occurrence of paraphrase, summary, or quotation and the function that each serves. These may include:

1. To provide background information
2. To define terms
3. To provide a position for rebuttal
4. To explain quoted material
5. To illustrate a point
6. To show disagreements among sources
7. To cite authorities and, hence, to reinforce claims or statements
8. To state a point more precisely, powerfully, or accurately than with a paraphrased version

Once the group has identified the functions, have them exchange their article with another group. Have them repeat the exercise and then compare versions and findings.

Most readers would think that the source, Day, was much too prominent here. If this passage were a background discussion or a survey of the literature on a topic, with each source being different, such a large number of citations might be acceptable. But all these citations are from the same source, and readers are likely to conclude that the source is primary and the author only secondary.

42e

Reviewing your draft

Because a research essay involves a complex mix of your thoughts and materials from outside sources, it calls for an especially careful review before you begin revising. As with most kinds of writing, however, taking a break after drafting a research essay is important. Get away from the draft, and try to put it out of your mind. Stay away from it for as long as you can, so that when you reread it you can bring a fresh eye to the task.

When you return to the draft, read it straight through without stopping. Then, read it again slowly, reconsidering four things: purpose, audience, thesis, and support. You might find that outlining your draft helps you to analyze it at this point (see 3e).

- From your reading of your draft, what do you now see as its *purpose*? How does this compare with your original purpose? Does the draft do what your assignment requires?
- What *audience* does your essay address?
- What is your *stance* toward the topic?
- What is your *thesis*? Is it clearly stated?
- What *evidence* supports your thesis? Is the evidence thorough and compelling?

Answer these four questions as best you can, since they are the starting point for revision. Next, you need a closer reading of your essay. At this point, you might benefit from the comments of other readers. Consider asking friends or classmates to read your draft and respond to the questions for reviewing a draft in 4b. You can also use these questions yourself as you analyze your own essay in greater detail.

You may also get helpful advice if you ask questions specific to your essay. If you are unsure about whether to include a particular point, how to use a certain quotation, or where to add more examples, ask readers specifically what they think you should do. (For more on getting critical responses to a draft, see 4c.)

FOR THE WRITING LOG

Suggest to students that they copy these questions into their log in a prominent place so that they can turn easily to them at any point in the drafting process. The log is a good place to reflect on the current state of any draft they may be working on.

42f

Revising and editing your draft

Using any responses you have gathered and your own analysis of your draft, turn now to your final revision. It is advisable, at this stage, to work in several steps.

- *Considering any responses.* Have readers identified any problems you need to solve? If so, do they make any specific suggestions about ways to revise? Have they identified any strengths that might suggest ways of revising? For example, if they showed great interest in one point but no interest at all in another point, consider expanding the first and deleting the second.

- *Reconsidering your original purpose, audience, and stance.* From the above analysis, do you feel confident that you have achieved your purpose? If not, what is missing? Have you made your strongest possible appeal to your readers? How have you established common ground with them? How have you satisfied any special concerns they may have? Has your rhetorical stance toward your topic changed in any way? If so, what effect has that change had on your essay?

- *Gathering any additional material.* If you need to strengthen any points, go back to your notes to see if you have the necessary materials. If not, consider whether you need to do any more research. If you failed to consider adequately any opposing viewpoints, for instance, you may need to find more material.

- *Deciding on any changes you need to make.* Figure out everything you have to do to perfect your draft, and write it out. With your deadline firmly in mind, plan your revision.

- *Rewriting your draft.* Do the major work first—changes in content, added examples or evidence, paragraph-level concerns. Then turn to sentence-level work, and finally to individual words. Revise for clarity and to sharpen the dominant impression of the essay as a whole. (See 4g.)

- *Reconsidering your title, introduction, and conclusion.* In light of your reevaluation and revision of your draft, reread these important parts to see whether they still serve their purpose. Does the introduction accurately predict and the conclusion accurately restate what the body of the final essay discusses? If not, do you need to forecast your main points in the introduction or to summarize them in the conclusion? Does your introduction capture readers' attention? Does your conclusion help them see the significance of your argument? Is your title specific enough to let your readers know about your research question and engaging enough to make them want to read *your* answer to it?

I am strongly in favor of intelligent, even fastidious revision, which is, or certainly should be, an art in itself. . . . —JOYCE CAROL OATES

I rewrite so much that the first chapter of a book sometimes may be rewritten forty or fifty times. . . . It's this way, see—when a writer first starts out, he gets a big kick from the stuff he does, and the reader doesn't get any; then, after a while, the writer gets a little kick and the reader gets a little kick; and finally, if the writer's any good, he doesn't get any kick at all and the reader gets everything. —ERNEST HEMINGWAY

I love spending an hour or two with a dictionary and a thesaurus looking for a more nearly perfect word. Or taking my pen and ruthlessly pruning all the unnecessary adjectives, or fooling around with the rhythm of a sentence or a paragraph by changing a verb into a participle or making any number of little changes that a magazine editor I work with calls "mouse milking." —MARIE WINN

- *Checking your documentation.* Have you included a citation in your text for every quotation, paraphrase, and summary you incorporated, following consistently the required style? (See 41d and Chapters 43 and 44.)
- *Editing your draft.* Now is the time to attend carefully to any remaining problems in grammar, usage, spelling, punctuation, and mechanics. If you are writing on a computer, take the time to use the spell checker. Check for any patterns you have identified as problems in your own writing. It may be fruitful as well to turn to Taking a Writing Inventory (pp. I-1–I-27) and to consult the editing checklist in 4h.

Preparing your list of works cited or references

Once you have a final draft with your source materials in place, prepare your list of works cited (MLA) or references (APA). Follow the guidelines for your required style carefully, creating an entry for each source used in your essay. Double-check your draft against your list of sources cited to see that you have listed every source mentioned in the parenthetical citations and that you have not listed any sources not cited in your essay. (See Chapters 43 and 44 for guidelines.)

Preparing and proofreading your final copy

Your final rough draft may end up looking very rough indeed, filled with cross-outs, additions in the margins, circles, and arrows. So your next task is to create a final, carefully typed, painstakingly prepared clean copy. This is the version of the paper that you will submit, the one that will represent all your work and effort. (For information on preparing a final manuscript, see Chapter 49.)

Proofreading is a time for celebration. At this point, you are making your research essay as perfect as possible, your very best effort. Many writers look forward to this final reading, often taking time to read through once backwards in order to catch every word-level typographical error. So after proofreading, congratulate yourself and savor the rewards of a job well done. You have produced a solid piece of research, clearly written and cogently argued. You have become a researcher.

EXERCISE 42.1   Reading with an Eye for Research

The research essays at the end of Chapters 43 and 44 were written by two students, the first of whom you've followed through Chapters 39 to 42. This essay, which follows MLA style, was written for a composition class; the second, which follows APA style, for a psychology class. Read these essays carefully, and study the marginal annotations. Compare your research essay with these, noting differences in approach, style, format, and use of sources.

EXERCISE 42.2   Taking Inventory: Your Research Essay

Pause now to reflect on the research essay you have written. How did you go about organizing your information? What would you do to improve this process? What problems did you encounter during drafting? How did you solve these problems? How many quotations did you use, and how did you integrate them into your text? When and why did you use summaries and paraphrases? What did you learn from revising? Record your findings in your writing or research log, if you keep one.

43

Documenting Sources, MLA Style

BACKGROUND

Writers document their sources for four reasons.

1. Careful documentation gives credit for words or ideas to the original writer or speaker, and relieves the writer of any indictment of plagiarism.

2. Documentation lends the writer authority as a researcher. It says to the reader, "I am honest and open to anyone wishing to retrace the steps in my research." Documentation is an important element in the *ethos* of the writer presenting research. Undocumented (plagiarized) sources—or sources imprecisely documented, even if only slightly—suggest that this writer is careless or even dishonest.

3. Documentation is a courtesy to later writers on the subject who may want to use some of the material. Documentation provides them with directions for finding it.

4. Documentation allows others to follow up on a writer's research in order to test its validity. Not only should writers tolerate such a procedure; they should welcome it. To have others look so carefully at one's work implies that such work is important.

> Adam was the only man who, when he said a good thing, knew that nobody had said it before him.
> —MARK TWAIN

Adam, in other words, had the luxury of not having to document his sources, but no writer since Adam has been able to make that claim. In your writing, full and accurate documentation is important because it helps build your credibility as a writer and researcher by giving credit to those people whose works influenced your own ideas.

Documentation styles vary among disciplines, with one format favored in the humanities, for instance, another in the social sciences, and another in engineering, but they all require the same basic information. Thus you will want to use the conventions of documentation appropriate to a particular course and field. Following these rules of punctuation and format ensures consistency and helps protect you from plagiarizing because of omitted source information (see 42d).

Everyday use

"Says who?!" is an insistent question we have all had to answer at one time or another. The question usually follows some claim: Kevin Costner's Robin Hood *is an insult to the viewer's intelligence; a Yugo isn't worth the cost of a good bicycle, let alone a car. "Says who?" calls on the speaker to document his or her sources by referring to several reviews of* Robin Hood, *for example, or to an article in* Consumer Reports *on the Yugo—or maybe by simply relying on personal experience and replying, "Says me!" When have you needed to document your sources in this way? Has the ability to provide such documentation helped you make your points?*

This chapter discusses the basic format for the **Modern Language Association (MLA) style**, widely used in literature and languages as well as other fields, and shows examples for various kinds of sources. For further reference, consult the following:

> Gibaldi, Joseph, and Walter S. Achtert. *MLA Handbook for Writers of Research Papers*. 3rd ed. New York: Modern Language Assn., 1988.

 Directory to MLA style

43a. Parenthetical citations

Author named in a signal phrase, *601*

Author named in a citation, *601*

Two or three authors, *601*

Four or more authors, *601*

Corporate author, *602*

Unknown author, *602*

Author of two or more works, *602*

Two or more authors with the same surname, *602*

Multivolume work, *602*

Literary work, *603*

Bible, *603*

Indirect source, *603*

Two or more sources in the same citation, *603*

Entire work or one-page article, *604*

Nonprint source, *604*

43b. Explanatory and bibliographic notes

43c. List of works cited

1. BOOKS

One author, *606*

Two or three authors, *606*

Four or more authors, *606*

Corporate author, *606*

Unknown author, *607*

Two or more books by the some author(s), *607*

Editor or editors, *607*

Author and editor, *608*

Selection in an anthology or chapter in a book with an editor, *608*

Two or more items from an anthology, *609*

Translation, *609*

Edition other than the first, *609*

One volume of a multivolume work, *610*

Two or more volumes of a multivolume work, *610*

Preface, foreword, introduction, or afterword, *610*

Article in a reference work, *610*

Book that is part of a series, *611*

Republication, *611*

(Continued)

> *Plagiarists are always suspicious of being stolen from.* —SAMUEL TAYLOR COLERIDGE

BACKGROUND

While MLA and APA styles of documentation are widely used in the humanities and social sciences, other disciplines typically use other styles. In addition to the manuals listed in the text, the following style manuals provide documentation styles for disciplines other than English.

Geology
Suggestions to Authors of the Reports of the United States Geological Survey. 6th ed. Washington: GPO, 1978.

Law
A Uniform System of Citation. 14th ed. Cambridge, MA: Harvard Law Review Assn., 1986.

Linguistics
LSA Bulletin, Dec. issue, annually.

Mathematics
A Manual for Authors of Mathematical Papers. 7th ed. Providence: American Mathematical Soc., 1980.

Medicine
International Steering Committee of Medical Editors. "Uniform Requirements for Manuscripts Submitted to Biomedical Journals." *Annals of Internal Medicine* 90 (Jan. 1979): 95–99.

Huth, Edward J. *Medical Style and Format: An International Manual for Authors, Editors, and Publishers*. Philadelphia: ISI P, 1987.

Other style manuals
John Bruce Howell. *Style Manuals of the English-Speaking World*. Phoenix: Oryx, 1983.

BACKGROUND

The practice of documenting sources developed out of the larger movement toward bibliography and documentation that has become one of the great contributions of the twentieth century. Documentation arose out of the increase of information and the growth of information systems.

In ancient times, information storage and retrieval was accomplished for the most part by individuals mnemonically and by societies through rituals. With the rise of literacy came the desire to classify information systematically in the form of writing. Libraries are the most familiar information systems. The first libraries were built simply to preserve but not to make available their information. That intention really did not begin to change until the late nineteenth century.

Of course, there were earlier attempts at systematic classification of information, but only at a local level. In the second century A.D., the Greek physician Galen compiled a catalog of his works. In A.D. 731 or 732, Bede the Venerable provided a bibliography in his *Ecclesiastical History of the English People*. The most ambitious bibliography was produced in the sixteenth century by the Swiss scientist Conrad Gesner, who compiled a twenty-volume bibliography of world literature.

The invention of the printing press and the great increase in the desire for knowledge during the Renaissance helped to increase the flow of information via books and the need and desire for some way to classify such information in order to make it more readily available. Many different and individualized systems of classification and organization of information developed until, in the late nineteenth century, American librarian Melvil Dewey invented the Dewey Decimal System of Classification, which libraries quickly adopted.

43d. A sample research essay, MLA style

43a

MLA format for parenthetical citations

MLA style uses **parenthetical citations** in the text of an essay to document every quotation, paraphrase, summary, or other material from a source. Parenthetical citations correspond to full-information bibliographic entries in an alphabetical list of works cited at the end of the text. Usually the author's name is mentioned in a signal phrase that introduces the material, and the page number of the original source is given in parentheses after the material. Be sure to use an author's full name the first time you cite him or her. For later citations, use the author's last name. In general, make your parenthetical citations as short as possible, but include enough information for your readers to locate the material in your works-cited list.

Place a parenthetical citation as near to the material as is possible without disrupting the flow of the sentence, usually before the punctuation mark at the end of the sentence or phrase that contains the material. Place any punctuation mark *after* the closing parenthesis. If your citation refers to a quotation, place it *after* the closing quotation mark but *before* any punctuation mark. For long quotations typed as a block, place the parenthetical citation two spaces after the final punctuation mark. Here are examples of the various ways to cite sources.

AUTHOR NAMED IN A SIGNAL PHRASE

Ordinarily, use the author's name in a signal phrase to introduce the material, and simply cite the page number(s) in parentheses.

```
Herrera indicates that Kahlo believed in a ''vitalistic
form of pantheism'' (328).
```

AUTHOR NAMED IN A CITATION

When you do not name the author in the text, include the author's last name before the page number(s) in the parenthetical citation, with no comma between them.

```
In places, de Beauvoir ''sees Marxists as believing in
subjectivity as much as existentialists do''
(Whitmarsh 63).
```

TWO OR THREE AUTHORS

Use all the authors' last names in a signal phrase or parenthetical citation.

```
Gortner, Hebrun, and Nicolson maintain that ''opinion
leaders'' influence other people in an organization
because they are respected, not because they hold high
positions (175).
```

FOUR OR MORE AUTHORS

Use the first author's name and "et al." ("and others") or name all the authors in a signal phrase or parenthetical citation.

```
Similarly, as Belenky et al. assert, examining the lives
of women expands our understanding of human
development (7).
```

BACKGROUND

Another important development in the history of documentation was the change during the late Middle Ages and Renaissance in the notion of authorship. Medieval authors did not view their work as necessarily theirs alone; there was little sense of knowledge as somehow owned or its origins as deserving acknowledgment. However, in modern times, authorship became more personalized; writers began to think in terms of original ideas and to believe that they had a right to be acknowledged as the author of such ideas.

The form of such acknowledgment, whether it is MLA style or APA style or any of the many other documentation styles, derives from bibliographical description. Such description is meant to record various characteristics of each book thereby revealing the uniqueness of each. Citation of a source is not nearly as detailed as a true bibliographical description, which records physical qualities of each book as well as author, title, place of publication, and so on.

BACKGROUND

In "Shakespeare in Quotation," Margareta de Grazia offers the following insights:

> In Shakespeare's time, quotation marks (" ") were never used to enclose passages. Commas and inverted commas, single and double, were generally placed only at the onset of a passage. They were used interchangeably with the pointing index finger (☞) that directed the reader's eye to passages of special note, pointing the reader to a special point. Both signals appeared in the margin rather than within the text itself, the space where aids to the reader were supplied . . . . They thus indicated not that a passage originated elsewhere, but rather simply that it was important. . . . Quotes now mark off private property; before the eighteenth century, they signalled communal gound or commonplaces. They marked material to be copied by each reader in his copy-book or commonplace book, thereby assuring that the commonplaces would become more common still. By simply perusing the margins of a text, readers might lift material for their own personalized storehouse of wise and therefore widely applicable sayings.

CORPORATE AUTHOR

Give the name of a corporate author, if brief, or a shortened form of it in a signal phrase or parenthetical citation.

In fact, one of the leading foundations in the field of higher education supports the recent proposals for community-run public schools (Carnegie Corporation 45).

UNKNOWN AUTHOR

Use the title, if brief, or a shortened version in a signal phrase or parenthetical citation.

''Hype,'' by one analysis, is ''an artificially engendered atmosphere of hysteria'' (''Today's Marketplace'' 51).

AUTHOR OF TWO OR MORE WORKS

For a work by an author of two or more works in your list of works cited, include a shortened version of the title in a signal phrase or parenthetical citation.

Gardner presents readers with their own silliness through his description of a ''pointless, ridiculous monster, crouched in the shadows, stinking of dead men, murdered children, and martyred cows'' (<u>Grendel</u> 2).

TWO OR MORE AUTHORS WITH THE SAME SURNAME

If your list of works cited includes works by different authors with the same surname, always include the author's first name in signal phrases or parenthetical citations for those works.

Children will learn to write if they are allowed to choose their own subjects, James Britton asserts, citing the Schools Council study of the 1960s (37-42).

MULTIVOLUME WORK

Name the author in a signal phrase or parenthetical citation. Note the volume number and page number(s), with a colon and one space between them, in the parentheses.

```
Modernist writers prized experimentation and gradually
even sought to blur the line between poetry and prose,
according to Forster (3: 150).
```

If you name only one volume of the work in your list of works cited, you need include only the page number in the parenthetical citation.

LITERARY WORK

For literary works available in many editions, cite the page number(s) from the edition you used, followed by a semicolon and such information as part or chapter in a novel (175; ch. 4) or act and/or scene in a play (37; sc. 1). For poems, cite only the line number(s), using the word "line(s)" in the first reference to alert readers that the numbers do not refer to pages (lines 33–34). For verse plays, give only the act, scene, and line numbers, separated by periods.

```
As Macbeth begins, the witches greet Banquo as ''Lesser
than Macbeth, and greater'' (1.3.65).
```

BIBLE

Identify biblical quotations by chapter and verse. For books whose names are longer than five letters, use an abbreviation in a parenthetical citation (*Gen.* for *Genesis; Matt.* for *Matthew*). Spell out all books named in your text. If you use the King James Version, you do not need to include a works-cited entry. If you use any other version, treat it as you would a book in the works-cited list (see 43c).

INDIRECT SOURCE

Use the abbreviation "qtd. in" to indicate that you are quoting from an indirect source—that is, someone else's report of a conversation, statement, interview, letter, or the like.

```
As Arthur Miller says, ''When somebody is destroyed
everybody finally contributes to it, but in Willy's
case, the end product would be virtually the same''
(qtd. in Martin and Meyer 375).
```

TWO OR MORE SOURCES IN THE SAME CITATION

If you refer to more than one source in parentheses, include the information for each of them, separated by semicolons.

Recently, however, some economists have recommended that
<u>employment</u> be redefined to include unpaid domestic labor
(Clark 148; Nevins 39).

ENTIRE WORK OR ONE-PAGE ARTICLE

To cite a whole work rather than a specific passage, or a one-page
article, include the reference in the text without any page numbers or
parentheses.

Thomas Hardy's tragic vision is given full vent in his
<u>Jude the Obscure</u>, a bleaker novel than <u>The Return of the
Native</u>.

NONPRINT SOURCE

Give enough information in a signal phrase or parenthetical citation
for readers to locate the source in the list of works cited. Usually, use the
name or title under which you listed the source.

Kahlo is seated with a Judas doll, identified in the
film <u>Portrait of an Artist: Frida Kahlo</u> as a papier–mâché
doll stuffed with firecrackers to be exploded on the day
before Easter.

43b

MLA format for explanatory and bibliographic notes

MLA style allows **explanatory notes** for information or commentary
that would not readily fit into the text but is needed for clarification or
further explanation. In addition, MLA style permits **bibliographic notes** for
citing several sources for one point and for offering information about or
evaluation of a source. Superscript numbers are used in the text to refer
readers to the notes, which may appear as endnotes (typed under the
heading Notes on a separate page after the text but before the Works Cited)
or as footnotes at the bottom of the page (typed four lines below the last text
line). For example:

SUPERSCRIPT NUMBER IN TEXT

Stewart emphasizes the existence of social contracts in
Hawthorne's life so that the audience will accept a

different Hawthorne, one more attuned to modern times
than the figure in Woodberry.[3]

NOTE

    [3] Woodberry does, however, show that Hawthorne <u>was</u>
often an unsociable individual. He emphasizes the
seclusion of Hawthorne's mother, who separated herself
from her family after the death of her husband, often
even taking meals alone (28). Woodberry seems to imply
that Mrs. Hawthorne's isolation rubbed off onto her son.

For other examples, see the Notes page of Daniel Taffe's essay (p. 637).

MLA format for a list of works cited

    A list of **Works Cited** is an alphabetical list of the sources actually cited in your essay. (If your instructor asks that you list everything you have read as background, call the list Works Consulted.) Start your list on a separate page after the text of your essay and any notes (see 43b). Number the page as you did those in your text. Type the heading Works Cited, neither underlined nor in quotation marks, centered one inch from the top of the page. Double-space and begin your first entry. Start each entry flush with the left margin; indent any subsequent line of the entry five spaces. Double-space the entire list.

    List your sources alphabetically by authors' last names. If a source is by an unknown author, alphabetize it by the first major word of the title after any initial *a, an,* or *the.*

    On the following pages, you will find sample entries that follow the MLA specifications for various kinds of sources.

1

Books

The basic entry for a book includes the following elements:

1. *Author.* List the author by last name first followed by a comma and the first name.
2. *Title.* Underline the title and any subtitle and capitalize all major words. (See 35c for more on capitalizing titles.)

3. *Publication information.* Give the city of publication (and country or postal abbreviation for the state if the city is unfamiliar), and add a colon, a space, and a shortened version of the publisher's name—dropping *Press, Publishers, Inc.,* and so on (*St. Martin's* for *St. Martin's Press, Inc.*), using only the first surname (*Harcourt* for *Harcourt Brace Jovanovich*), and abbreviating *University Press* (*Oxford UP* for *Oxford University Press*)—a comma, and the year of publication.

These elements are separated from one another by a period and two spaces, and the entry ends with a period. Here is an example of a basic entry for a book.

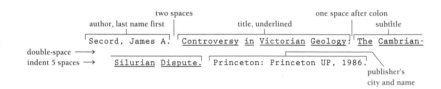

ONE AUTHOR

Herrera, Hayden. <u>Frida: A Biography of Frida Kahlo</u>.
    New York: Harper, 1983.

TWO OR THREE AUTHORS

List the first author last name first; then list the name(s) of the other author(s) in regular order, with a comma between authors and an *and* before the last one.

McNeill, John T., and Helena M. Gamer. <u>Medieval</u>
    <u>Handbooks of Penance</u>. New York: Octagon, 1965.

FOUR OR MORE AUTHORS

Give the first author listed on the title page, followed by a comma and "et al." ("and others"), or list all the names.

Belenky, Mary Field, et al. <u>Women's Ways of Knowing</u>.
    New York: Basic, 1986.

CORPORATE AUTHOR

Give the name of the group listed on the title page as the author, even if the same group published the book.

American Chemical Society. <u>Handbook for Authors of</u>
    <u>Papers in the American Chemical Society Publi-</u>
    <u>cations</u>. Washington: American Chemical Soc., 1978.

UNKNOWN AUTHOR

Start the entry with the title, and list the work alphabetically by the
first major word of the title after any initial *a, an,* or *the.*

<u>The New York Times Atlas of the World</u>. New York: New
    York Times Books, 1980.

TWO OR MORE BOOKS BY THE SAME AUTHOR(S)

If you cite two or more works by the same author(s), arrange the
entries alphabetically by title. List the name(s) of the author(s) in the first
entry, but in subsequent entries use three hyphens followed by a period
instead.

Lasswell, Harold D. <u>The Analysis of Political</u>
    <u>Behaviour: An Empirical Approach</u>. New York:
    Oxford UP, 1948.
---. <u>The Future of Political Science</u>. American
    Political Science Association Series. New York:
    Atherton, 1963.

If you cite a work by a single author who is also listed as the first coauthor
of another work you cite, list the single-author work first, and repeat the
author's name in the entry for the coauthored work. Also repeat the author's
name if you cite a work in which that author is listed as the first of a different
set of coauthors. Use three hyphens only when the work is by *exactly* the
same author(s) as the previous entry.

EDITOR OR EDITORS

Treat an editor as an author, but add a comma and "ed." (or "eds." for
more than one editor).

Woodward, C. Vann, ed. <u>Mary Chestnut's Civil War</u>. New
    Haven: Yale UP, 1981.

AUTHOR AND EDITOR

To cite a book that has both an author and an editor, start the entry with the author's name if you cite the body of the text, and list the editor's name, introduced by "Ed.," in regular order after the title.

```
James, Henry.  Portrait of a Lady.  Ed. Leon Edel.
     Boston: Houghton, 1963.
```

If you cite the editor's work, start the entry with his or her name, followed by a comma and "ed.," and list the author's name, introduced by the word "By," in regular order after the title.

```
Edel, Leon, ed.  Portrait of a Lady.  By Henry James.
     Boston: Houghton, 1963.
```

**SELECTION IN AN ANTHOLOGY OR CHAPTER
IN A BOOK WITH AN EDITOR**

List the following items of information, separated from one another by a period and two spaces: the author(s) of the selection or chapter; its title, with titles of essays, short stories, poems, and chapters in quotation marks and those of plays and long poems underlined; the title of the book in which the selection or chapter appears, underlined; "Ed." and the name(s) of the editor(s) in regular order; the publication information; and the inclusive page numbers of the selection.

```
Gordon, Mary.  ''The Parable of the Cave.''  The Writer
     on Her Work.  Ed. Janet Sternburg.  New York:
     Norton, 1980.  27-32.
```

If the selection was originally published in a periodical and you are asked to supply information for this original source, use the following format:

```
Didion, Joan.  ''Why I Write.''  New York Times Book
     Review.  9 Dec. 1976: 22.  Rpt. in The Writer on
     Her Work.  Ed. Janet Sternburg.  New York: Norton,
     1980.  3-16.
```

For inclusive page numbers up to 99, note all digits in the second number. For numbers above 99, note only the last two digits and any others that change in the second number (115–18, 1378–79, 296–301).

TWO OR MORE ITEMS FROM AN ANTHOLOGY

If you cite two or more selections in an anthology, include the anthology on your list of works cited.

Spender, Dale, and Janet Todd, eds. <u>British Women</u>
    <u>Writers: An Anthology from the Fourteenth Century</u>
    <u>to the Present</u>. New York: Bedrick, 1989.

Also list each selection you cite by its author and title, followed by a cross-reference to the anthology. The cross-reference consists of the last name(s) of the editor(s) and the inclusive page numbers of the selection.

Behn, Aphra. <u>The Rover</u>. Spender and Todd 32—152.

Linton, Eliza Lynn. ''The Mad Willoughbys.'' Spender
    and Todd 536—86.

TRANSLATION

Start the entry with the author's name, and give the translator's name, preceded by "Trans.," after the title.

Zamora, Martha. <u>Frida Kahlo: The Brush of Anguish</u>.
    Trans. Marilyn Sode Smith. San Francisco:
    Chronicle, 1990.

If you cite a translated selection in an anthology, add the translator's name with "Trans." before the title of the anthology.

Horace. <u>The Art of Poetry</u>. Trans. Burton Raffel. <u>The</u>
    <u>Critical Tradition: Classic Texts and Contemporary</u>
    <u>Trends</u>. Ed. David H. Richter. New York:
    Bedford—St. Martin's, 1989. 66—77.

EDITION OTHER THAN THE FIRST

To cite a book identified on its title page as an edition other than the first, add this information, in abbreviated form, after the title.

Kelly, Alfred H., Winfred A. Harbison, and Herman Belz.
    <u>The American Constitution: Its Origins and</u>
    <u>Development</u>. 6th ed. New York: Norton, 1983.

ONE VOLUME OF A MULTIVOLUME WORK

Give the volume ("Vol.") number after the title, and list the number of volumes ("vols.") in the complete work at the end of the entry.

```
Foner, Philip S., and Ronald L. Lewis, eds.  The Black
     Worker.  Vol. 3.  Philadelphia: Lippincott, 1980.
     8 vols.
```

TWO OR MORE VOLUMES OF A MULTIVOLUME WORK

If you cite two or more volumes of a multivolume work, note the number of volumes ("vols.") in the complete work before the publication information.

```
Foner, Philip S., and Ronald L. Lewis, eds.  The Black
     Worker.  8 vols.  Philadelphia: Lippincott, 1980.
```

PREFACE, FOREWORD, INTRODUCTION, OR AFTERWORD

List the author of the item, then the item title, neither underlined nor in quotation marks. After the title of the book, give its author's name in regular order, preceded by the word "By." (If the same person wrote both the book and the cited item, use just the last name after "By.") List the inclusive page numbers of the item at the end of the entry.

```
Schlesinger, Arthur M., Jr.  Introduction.  Pioneer
     Women: Voices from the Kansas Frontier.  By Joanna
     L. Stratton.  New York: Simon, 1981.  11-15.
```

ARTICLE IN A REFERENCE WORK

List the author of the article, often identified by initials corresponding to full names in a list of contributors. If no author is identified, begin with the title. For a well-known encyclopedia, just note any edition number and date. If the encyclopedia entries are arranged in alphabetical order, no volume or page numbers are needed.

```
''Traquair, Sir John Stewart.''  Encyclopaedia
     Britannica.  11th ed.  1911.
Johnson, Peder J.  ''Concept Learning.''  Encyclopedia
     of Education.  1971.
```

BOOK THAT IS PART OF A SERIES

To cite a book that is part of a series (as noted on the title page or the page before), add the series name, neither underlined nor in quotation marks, and any series number after the title.

```
Bloom, Harold, ed. Ralph Waldo Emerson. Modern
     Critical Views. New York: Chelsea, 1985.
```

REPUBLICATION

To cite a modern edition of an older book, a paperback edition, or other republication, add the original publication date, with a period, right after the title. Then give the publication details for the edition you used.

```
Scott, Walter. Kenilworth. 1821. New York: Dodd,
     1956.
```

GOVERNMENT DOCUMENT

Begin with the author, if identified. If no author is given, start with the name of the government followed by the agency and any subdivision. Use abbreviations if they can be readily understood. Then list the title, underlined. For congressional documents, cite the number, session, and house of Congress (using S for Senate or HR for House of Representatives), and the type (Report, Resolution, Document in abbreviated form) and number of the material. If you cite the *Congressional Record,* give only the date and page number. End with the publication information—which is often the Government Printing Office (GPO)—as for a book.

```
New Hampshire. Dept. of Transportation. Right of Way
     Salinity Reports, Hillsborough County, 1985. Con-
     cord: New Hampshire Dept. of Transportation, 1986.
United States. Cong. House. Report of the Joint
     Subcommittee on Reconstruction. 39th Cong., 1st
     sess. H. Rept. 30. 1865. New York: Arno, 1969.
U.S. Bureau of the Census. Historical Statistics
     of the United States, Colonial Times to 1870.
     Washington: GPO, 1975.
```

PAMPHLET

Treat a pamphlet as a book.

<u>Why</u> <u>Is</u> <u>Central</u> <u>America</u> <u>a</u> <u>Conflict</u> <u>Area?</u> Opposing View-
points Pamphlets. St. Paul, MN: Greenhaven, 1984.

PUBLISHED PROCEEDINGS OF A CONFERENCE

Treat the proceedings as a book, but add information about the conference if it is not part of the title.

Martin, John Steven, and Christine Mason Sutherland,
eds. <u>Proceedings</u> <u>of</u> <u>the</u> <u>Canadian</u> <u>Society</u> <u>for</u> <u>the</u>
<u>History</u> <u>of</u> <u>Rhetoric</u>. Calgary, Alberta: Canadian
Soc. for the History of Rhetoric, 1986.

PUBLISHED BEFORE 1900

Omit the publisher's name, and add a comma between the place of publication and the date.

Randolph, Peter. <u>From</u> <u>Slave</u> <u>Cabin</u> <u>to</u> <u>the</u> <u>Pulpit</u>.
Boston, 1893.

PUBLISHER'S IMPRINT

If a book was published by a publisher's imprint (indicated on the title page), hyphenate the imprint and the publisher's name.

Rose, Phyllis. <u>Parallel</u> <u>Lives:</u> <u>Five</u> <u>Victorian</u>
<u>Marriages</u>. New York: Vintage-Random, 1984.

TITLE WITHIN THE TITLE

Do not underline the title of a book within the title of a book you are citing. Underline and enclose in quotation marks a title of a short work within a book title.

Gilbert, Stuart. <u>James</u> <u>Joyce's</u> Ulysses. New York:
Vintage-Random, 1955.

2

Periodicals

The basic entry for a periodical includes the following elements:

1. *Author*. List the author by last name first, followed by a comma and the first name.

2. *Article title.* Enclose the title and any subtitle in quotation marks and capitalize all major words. (See 35c for more on capitalizing titles.)

3. *Publication information.* Give the periodical title (excluding any initial *a, an,* or *the*), underlined and with all major words capitalized; the volume number and issue number, if appropriate; and the date of publication. For journals, list the year in parentheses followed by a colon, a space, and the inclusive page numbers. For magazines and newspapers, list the month (abbreviated, except for May, June, and July) or the day and month before the year, and do not use parentheses. Do not use "p." or "pp." before the inclusive page numbers. For inclusive page numbers, note all digits for numbers 1 to 99 and note only the last two digits and any others that change for numbers above 99 (24–27, 134–45).

These elements are separated from one another by a period and two spaces, and the entry ends with a period. Here is an example of a basic entry for an article in a journal.

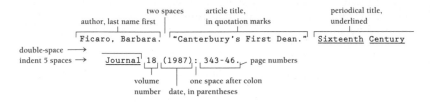

ARTICLE IN A JOURNAL PAGINATED BY VOLUME

If a periodical numbers pages continuously from one issue to the next within each year, follow the title of the publication with the volume number in arabic numerals.

```
Norris, Margot.  ''Narration under a Blindfold: Reading
     Joyce's 'Clay.' ''  PMLA 102 (1987): 206-15.
```

ARTICLE IN A JOURNAL PAGINATED BY ISSUE

Put a period and the issue number after the volume number.

```
Loffy, John.  ''The Politics at Modernism's Funeral.''
     Canadian Journal of Political and Social Theory 6.3
     (1987): 89-96.
```

ARTICLE IN A MONTHLY MAGAZINE

Put the month (or months, hyphenated) before the year. Do not include volume or issue numbers.

```
Said, Edward.  ''Through Gringo Eyes.''  Harper's Apr.
     1988: 70-72.
```

ARTICLE IN A WEEKLY MAGAZINE

Include the day, month, and year in that order, with no commas between them. Do not include volume or issue numbers.

```
Holden, Ted.  ''Campbell's Taste of the Japanese Market
     is Mm-Mm Good.''  Business Week 28 Mar. 1988: 42.
```

ARTICLE IN A NEWSPAPER

After the author and article title, give the name of the newspaper, underlined, as it appears on the front page but without any initial *a, an,* or *the.* Add the city in brackets after the name if it is not part of the title. Then give the date, the edition if one is listed, and add a colon and the page number(s). If the article appears on discontinuous pages, give the first page followed by a plus sign.

```
Cooper, Chester.  ''Fateful Day in Vietnam.''
     Washington Post 11 Feb. 1968, late ed.: 4+.
```

EDITORIAL OR LETTER TO THE EDITOR

Use the label "Editorial" or "Letter," neither underlined nor in quotation marks, after the title, or after the author's name if there is no title.

```
Magee, Doug.  ''Soldier's Home.''  Editorial.  Nation 26
     Mar. 1988: 400-01.
Stewart, Francis James.  Letter.  Economist 19-25 Mar.
     1988: 4.
```

UNSIGNED ARTICLE

Begin with the article title, alphabetizing the entry according to the first word after any initial *a, an,* or *the.*

```
''The Odds of March.''  Time 15 Apr. 1985: 20+.
```

REVIEW

List the author, if identified, and the title, if the review has one. Then add "Rev. of" and the title of the work being reviewed. If no author or title of the review is given, begin the entry with "Rev. of," and alphabetize the entry according to the title of the work.

```
Block, J. H.  ''Debatable Conclusions about Sex
     Differences.''  Rev. of The Psychology of Sex
     Differences, by E. E. Maccoby and C. N. Jacklin.
     Contemporary Psychology Aug. 1976: 517-22.
```

ARTICLE WITH A TITLE WITHIN THE TITLE

Enclose in single quotation marks the title of a short work within an article title. Underline the title of a book within an article title.

```
Frey, Leonard H.  ''Irony and Point of View in 'That
     Evening Sun.' ''  Faulkner Studies 2 (1953): 33-40.
```

3

Other sources

UNPUBLISHED DISSERTATION

Enclose the title in quotation marks. Add the identification "Diss.," the name of the university or professional school, a comma, and the year the dissertation was accepted.

```
Hennig, Margaret.  ''Career Development for Women
     Executives.''  Diss.  Harvard Business School,
     1970.
```

PUBLISHED DISSERTATION

Cite a published dissertation as a book, adding the identification "Diss." and the university. If the dissertation was published by University Microfilms International, list the UMI number at the end of the entry.

```
Botts, Roderic C.  Influences in the Teaching of
     English, 1917-1935: An Illusion of Progress.  Diss.
     Northeastern U, 1970.  Ann Arbor: UMI, 1971.
     71-1799.
```

MATERIAL FROM AN INFORMATION SERVICE OR A DATABASE

Cite previously published material as a book, adding the information service number at the end. For unpublished material, list the information service and date before the reference number.

> Daly, John. ''Writing Apprehension and Writing
> Competency.'' <u>Journal of Educational Research</u> 72
> (1978): 566—72. ERIC EJ 482 107.

ARTICLE FROM A MICROFORM

Treat the article as a printed work, identifying the name of the microform and information for locating it and placing "Microform" in brackets.

> Sharpe, Lora. ''A Quilter's Tribute.'' <u>Boston Globe</u> 25
> Mar. 1989. NewsBank [Microform], Social Relations,
> 1989, fiche 6, grids B4—6.

INTERVIEW

List first the person who has been interviewed. Then list the title, if the interview has one, in quotation marks (or underlined if it is the complete work). If it does not have a title, use the label "Interview," neither underlined nor in quotation marks, and identify the source. If you were the interviewer, use the label "Telephone interview" or "Personal interview," and give the date.

> Schorr, Daniel. Interview. <u>Weekend Edition</u>. Natl.
> Public Radio. WEVO, Concord. 26 Mar. 1988.
> Honeywell, Richard. Telephone interview. 15 Apr. 1991.

LETTER

If the letter was published, cite it as a selection in a book, noting the date and any identifying number after the title.

> Frost, Robert. ''Letter to Editor of the <u>Independent</u>.''
> 28 Mar. 1894. <u>Selected Letters of Robert Frost</u>.
> Ed. Lawrance Thompson. New York: Holt, 1964. 19.

If the letter was sent to you, follow the form below.

> Diaz, Gloria. Letter to the author. 12 Feb. 1989.

If the letter is from an archival collection, identify the writer and the recipient, give the date, and then give the name of the collection and the name and city of the institution that houses the collection.

Hones, William. Letter to John and Joseph Le Conte. 14

    Jan. 1868. Le Conte Family Papers. Bancroft

    Library, U of California, Berkeley.

SOFTWARE PROGRAM

List the writer of the program, if identified. Then add the title of the software, underlined, followed by the version number ("Vers. 4.2," for example) and the words "Computer software." Next identify the company that distributes the software, and the date. Note the computer type, memory required, operating system, format, and any other details.

Nota Bene. Vers. 3.0. Computer software. Dragonfly

    Software, 1988. MS-DOS 2.0, 512 KB, disk.

FILM OR VIDEOTAPE

Start with the title, underlined; then name the director; the company distributing the film or videotape; and the date. Other contributors, such as writers or actors, may follow the director's name. If you cite a particular person's work, such as the director's, start the entry with that person's name.

The Night of the Hunter. Dir. Charles Laughton. With

    Robert Mitchum, Shelley Winters, and Lillian Gish.

    United Artists, 1955.

TELEVISION OR RADIO PROGRAM

Begin with the title of the program, underlined. Add other details (such as narrator, director, actors) after the title as necessary. Then identify the network, the local station and city, and the date. If you cite the work of a particular person, begin the entry with that person's name. If you cite a particular episode with a title, start the entry with that title in quotation marks.

Hill Street Blues. Writ. Michael Kozoll and Stephen

    Bochco. With Daniel J. Travanti, Joe Spano, and

    Charles Haid. NBC. WNBC, New York. 15 Jan. 1981.

RECORDING

Your research interest determines whether the name of the composer, artist, or conductor precedes the title of the recording, which is underlined, or of the composition recorded, which is not underlined. If you are using a medium other than a record, give the medium after the title. Then add the names of any other pertinent people. End with the name of the manufacturer, the catalog number, and the date, all separated by commas.

```
Vega, Suzanne.  Solitude Standing.  A & M, SP 3156,
     1987.
Grieg, Edvard.  Concerto in A-minor, op. 16.  Compact
     disc.  Cond. Eugene Ormandy.  Philadelphia Orch.
     RCA, Red Seal LSC 3065, 1989.
```

WORK OF ART

List the artist followed by the work's title, underlined. Add the name of the museum or other location, a comma, and the city.

```
Kahlo, Frida.  Self-Portrait with Cropped Hair.  Museum
     of Modern Art, New York.
```

LECTURE OR SPEECH

List the speaker, the title in quotation marks, the name of the sponsoring institution or group, the place, and the date. If the speech is untitled, use a descriptive label ("Lecture," "Keynote Address," etc.).

```
Stern, Virginia.  ''Sir Stephen Powle as Adventurer in
     the Virginia Company of London.''  Seminar on the
     Renaissance.  Columbia University.  New York.  15
     Oct. 1985.
```

PERFORMANCE

List the title, other appropriate details (such as composer, writer, director), the place, and the date. If you cite a particular person, start the entry with that person's name.

```
Frankie and Johnny in the Clair de Lune.  By Terrence
     McNally.  Dir. Paul Benedict.  Westside Arts
     Theater, New York.  18 Jan. 1988.
```

MAP OR CHART

Cite a map or chart as a book with an unknown author, adding the label "Map" or "Chart."

```
     Pennsylvania.  Map.  Chicago: Rand, 1985.
```

CARTOON

List the cartoonist's name, the title (if any) of the cartoon, the label "Cartoon," and the usual publication information.

```
Trudeau, Gary.  ''Doonesbury.''  Cartoon.  Philadelphia
     Inquirer.  9 Mar. 1988: 37.
```

EXERCISE 43.1 Taking Inventory: Documentation

Take time to look carefully at the parenthetical citations and/or notes and the list of works cited you have prepared for a research essay. Using the guidelines in this chapter, check each citation, note, and list entry, noting (1) any whose form is incorrect and (2) any source you are still unsure of how best to document. If you are keeping a writing log or a research log, enter your findings there. For those sources you need help on documenting, check with your instructor.

43d

A sample research essay, MLA style

Daniel Taffe's final essay appears on the following pages. In preparing this essay, he followed the MLA guidelines described in this chapter. He was required to prepare a title page. Had he not needed a separate title page, he would have followed MLA instructions for a heading at the top of the first page of his essay (see Chapter 49 for an example).

Frida Kahlo: More Than a Life

Heading centered
one-third down
the page

by Daniel Taffe

English 231
Professor Connors
15 May 19XX

Taffe i

Roman numerals used for outline pages

Heading centered

Outline

Thesis statement: Frida Kahlo's
unique style results not only from
autobiographical influences but also
from her knowledge of earlier European
art, traditional Christian imagery,
and Mexican culture.

I. Autobiographical influences play a
large part in Kahlo's work.

  A. The events of her life were
exciting and often painful.

    1. She was stricken with polio
at age six.

    2. She was almost killed in a
traffic collision in 1925.

    3. She began to paint while
convalescing.

    4. She married Diego Rivera in
1929.

    5. Their relationship stormy,
she and Rivera divorced in
1939 but remarried in 1940.

    6. She suffered many medical
problems.

    7. She died in 1954.

  B. Some of her works refer to her
physical pain.

  C. Some paintings depict the pain
of her marriage.

II. Earlier European art, traditional Christian imagery, and Mexican culture also strongly influenced Kahlo's work.

A. Her background acquainted her with a wide range of European and Mexican art.

1. She was educated at the elite National Preparatory School.

2. She had access to her father's collection of German literature and philosophy books.

3. She studied many art books, particularly in Italian Renaissance painting.

4. Her relationship with Rivera and her travels in Europe increased her awareness of art.

B. Some of her stylistic conventions seem derived from earlier European painters.

1. The facial ''mask'' in her self-portraits echoes Bosch.

2. The landscape in <u>The Broken Column</u> and <u>Tree of. Hope</u> echo Traini.

C. Religion provided her with a number of themes and subjects.

　1. She professed no organized religion but held pantheistic beliefs.

　2. Her most directly religious work was <u>Moses</u>.

　3. <u>The Wounded Table</u> reflects the Christian theme of the Last Supper.

　4. <u>The Broken Column</u> and <u>The Little Deer</u> show her identification with the martyrdom of St. Sebastian.

D. Her Christian imagery often shows a Mexican influence.

　1. She and Rivera saw <u>Henry Ford Hospital</u> as a retablo.

　2. <u>My Birth</u> is based on a well-known Aztec sculpture.

TEACHING PRACTICE

After reading the introduction, direct your students to pp. 582–83 and use the eight questions under "Reconsidering your purpose, audience, stance, and thesis" as a basis for discussing how Daniel Taffe establishes his rhetorical stance.

TEACHING PRACTICE

Note that Daniel Taffe uses a question to introduce his subject. Ask students to brainstorm about other possible ways to open this research essay.

TEACHING PRACTICE

Direct students' attention to the discussion of accurate and effective paraphrasing on pp. 570–74. Then ask them to decide how well Daniel Taffe has followed the guidelines given there.

↓ 1″   Taffe 1

Title: Announces topic, arouses readers' interest

Frida Kahlo: More Than a Life   Title centered

Who is Frida Kahlo? Ten or fif-   Double-space
teen years ago, few people would have
known. Today, however, Kahlo is being
recognized as a major figure in
twentieth-century art. Her paintings,
primarily self-portraits, continue to
gain popularity in the United States
as well as in her native Mexico. <u>My</u>
<u>Birth</u>, for example, was re cently pur-
chased by Madonna, and <u>Self-Portrait</u>
<u>with Loose Hair</u> sold in the spring of
1991 for $1.65 million, a record price
for any Latin American artist (Plagens
et al. 54).

Introduction: Invites readers to learn about Kahlo, provides background

Facts cited—author named in citation

Much of the scholarship on Kahlo
and her art has been produced by Hayden Herrera, author of <u>Frida: A Biog-</u>
<u>raphy of Frida Kahlo</u> and numerous pe-
riodical articles about the artist.
Indeed, it is nearly impossible to
read anything about Kahlo without encountering a reference to Herrera's
research. Although her biography was
published almost thirty years after
Kahlo's death, her information comes,
as Angela Carter notes in her review,
from sources remarkably close to the
subject. In addition to Kahlo's journal, numerous letters, and medical

Taffe 2

records, Herrera was able to consult a number of lovers, friends, and relatives, as well as former wives of Kahlo's husband, the artist Diego Rivera (33).

Paraphrase — author named in signal phrase

Notes the biographical focus of most Kahlo criticism

Herrera's interpretation of Kahlo's painting is primarily biographical, as is that of nearly every other Kahlo critic. For example, Herrera describes Kahlo's work as ''autobiography in paint'' and goes on to label this autobiographical work original, specific, and personal (xii).

Brief quotation incorporated in text—author named in signal phrase

Suggests that the focus of criticism should be expanded

While this view is certainly not incorrect, it seems limited in important ways. For Frida Kahlo's unique style results not only from autobiographical influences but also from her knowledge of earlier European art, traditional Christian imagery, and Mexican culture.

Explicit thesis stated

First major point: Establishes autobiographical elements in Kahlo's work by citing major events of her life

The autobiographical aspect of Kahlo's work is undoubtedly important and thus worth examining. Her life was eventful, exciting, and often painful. Born in 1907 in a suburb of Mexico City, she was stricken with polio at age six. After a nearly complete recovery, she entered the National Preparatory School to pursue

TEACHING PRACTICE

Refer students to the discussion of direct quotations on pp. 569–70 and then ask them to examine the use of direct quotation in this paragraph. What in these quotations is particularly necessary and/or memorable?

TEACHING PRACTICE

Point out the formal features of long quotations, such as rules for indentation, and then reread "Setting off long quotations" (pp. 589) with the class, noting that long quotations must be introduced in some clear and explanatory way.

Taffe 3

medical training. Tragedy struck
again in 1925, however, when a bus she
was riding on was crushed by a trolley
car. As Carter describes:

> She almost died, and hurt
> herself so badly she never
> got over it. Her spine,
> collarbone, pelvis and a
> number of ribs were broken;
> her right leg was shattered,
> her left foot crushed; and
> . . . the steel handrail of
> the bus . . . pierced her
> left side and emerged
> through her vagina. (33)

While convalescing, Kahlo began
to paint, and soon painting became her
career. A few years later, in 1929,
she married Diego Rivera, twice her
age and already a well-known muralist.
Their relationship was volatile; they
fought when together and were miserable when apart. Both carried on many
well-publicized affairs, and they divorced in 1939 only to remarry in
1940. Throughout the years, Kahlo
continued to suffer medical problems
stemming from the accident. After
many operations, in 1953 her right leg

Long quotation set off—ellipses indicate omissions

TEACHING PRACTICE

This paragraph contains much factual information about Kahlo but no references.
Ask students to refer to the discussion of
materials not requiring acknowledgment
(pp. 577–78). Then ask them to look back
at this paragraph and assess whether any of
the information provided should be attributed to a source.

Taffe 4

was amputated below the knee. She was devastated, and her health declined rapidly. She died less than a year later, in 1954.

As Herrera details in her biography, much of Kahlo's art grows out of these dramatic personal experiences. Self-portraits such as The Broken Column (Herrera, pl. XXVIII),[1] which portrays Kahlo encased in a steel orthopedic corset, nails embedded painfully in her body, her spine replaced with a broken marble column, or Remembrance of an Open Wound (fig. 40), in which a seated Kahlo displays a bandaged left foot and a large gash on her left thigh, refer to the physical aftermath of her accident.

Likewise, The Two Fridas (pl. XIV) and A Few Small Nips (pl. VIII) directly depict the pain of her relationship with Rivera. The first shows two self-portraits, one in Victorian dress and the other in the Tehuana (Mexican peasant) costume that Kahlo often wore. Each Frida has her heart exposed, and an artery connects the two. The artery originates at a picture of Rivera held by the Tehuana

Builds on first major point by relating details of her life to particular paintings

Examines two works in detail for their autobiographical elements

Explanatory note indicates source of paintings

Taffe 5

Frida, thus linking the lives of the
three. But the Victorian Frida's
heart is broken because she does not
have Rivera. She holds the other,
open end of the artery in her hand and
tries to pinch it shut with medical
tweezers, but the red blood drips onto
her dress. This portrait provides a
graphic example of the connection
Kahlo felt to Rivera and of her
devastating sense of loss because of
his infidelity.

Shortly after a separation pre-
cipitated by Rivera's affair with her
sister, Kahlo completed <u>A</u> <u>Few</u> <u>Small</u>
<u>Nips</u> (pl. VIII). The work is her most
violent, the clearest expression of
the pain she suffered in her marriage.
The painting, as Martha Zamora notes,
is based on a true story: a man
stabbed his girlfriend to death and
when confronted with the murder said,
''But I only gave her a few small
nips'' (50). Kahlo's painting portrays a young woman lying in bed, na-
ked but for one sock and shoe. Her
body is covered with bleeding gashes,
and her face has a pale, almost bluish
tint; she is clearly dead. Splashes
of blood spatter the bed, the floor,

Paraphrase and
brief quotation—
author identified
in signal phrase

Taffe 6

even the frame of the painting. And
they spatter the man standing over
her. A ribbon bearing the words
''unos cuantos piquetitos'' (''a few
small nips'') is held at the top of
the painting by two birds, one black
and one white. Although not an exact
likeness, the man's features suggest
that he represents Rivera, and the
woman Kahlo.

Reiteration of the-
sis and second
major point: In-
fluenced by ear-
lier art

If Kahlo's work is often personal, however, it is also clearly
influenced by earlier art, including
traditional Christian and Mexican imagery. Indeed, it would be surprising, given her background, if she had
not been acquainted with a wide range
of art, both European and Mexican.
Kahlo was well educated--the National
Preparatory School she attended
spawned some of Mexico's greatest
minds. Herrera identifies Kahlo's
father as a scholarly European who
emigrated to Mexico, where he became a
photographer (5-7), and says that
Kahlo studied her father's collection
of German literature and philosophy
books (19) as well as many art books,
particularly those reproducing Italian
Renaissance paintings (64). And

Summary of long
passage—author
named in signal
phrase

TEACHING PRACTICE

After reading this paragraph of the essay,
point out Daniel Taffe's use of summary.
Refer students to the discussion of summaries on pp. 574–75 and ask them to assess
the effectiveness of the summary provided
here.

Taffe 7

Second source
cited to corrobo-
rate main point

Zamora notes that Kahlo referred to
her first self-portrait, given to a
close friend, as ''your Botticelli''
(110). Her relationship with Rivera
and her travels in Europe no doubt
served further to broaden her awareness of contemporary art and its roots
in earlier styles and themes.

Subpoint: First
stylistic influ-
ence—"masks"
like Bosch's

A careful study of her art reveals both stylistic and larger thematic influences on Kahlo's work. One
of her striking conventions is the use
of a stylized facial ''mask'' like
that in her first self-portrait,
Self-Portrait Wearing a Velvet Dress
(pl. I). In this painting, the mask
is simply a blank stare devoid of any
evidence of emotion. As Kahlo sits
facing the viewer, she does not smile,
but neither does she appear overly
sad. In many of her later self--
images, however, the mask is streaked
by tears, which, combined with the ex-
pressionless face, tell far more about
the subject than would any realistic
expression.

Certainly, there is autobiographical basis for the mask; it hides the
subject's pain much as Kahlo hid her
pain from her friends during her life.

Taffe 8

But as Professor Richard Honeywell points out, the mask also suggests the influence of a painting by Hieronymus Bosch (1450—1516), <u>Bearing of the Cross</u> (reproduced in Delavoy 59).[2] The masks of the figures in Bosch's painting, which depicts Christ being led to the site of his crucifixion, are horrid grimaces. As Delavoy explains, Bosch realized that a mask could ''never convey the human quality of a real face treated expressively'' (58). The effect of the masks is perhaps greater than that of actual faces, however, because of the horror they evoke. In much the same way, Kahlo's mask creates an effect, albeit a different one. Her mask hides emotion, yet in doing so shows her pain powerfully.

    Another stylistic influence appears in Kahlo's use of landscape. In both <u>The Broken Column</u> and <u>Tree of Hope</u> (pl. XXX), Kahlo's physical suffering, depicted as cuts in her chest and back and in the nails embedded in her flesh, is mirrored in the gouges scarred into the barren terrain in the backdrop, which projects an aura of pain and hopelessness. This use of

Information from interview cited

Bibliographic note acknowledges help

"Reproduced in" shows that citation is for painting, not Delavoy's text

Subpoint: Second stylistic influence— Traini's landscape

Taffe 9

landscape, according to Honeywell, is
a familiar element in paintings such
as The Triumph of Death, by Francesco
Traini (reproduced in Gardner 59),
paintings Kahlo would have undoubtedly
seen. Traini's violent, ragged landscape, featuring tall cliffs dropping
out of sight, augments the power of
his elaborate depiction of several
young aristocrats confronting three
corpses.

Subpoint: The-
matic influence—
religion

     Another major influence on Kah-
lo's work, religion, provided her
with a number of themes and subjects.
Her own religious upbringing was
mixed. Herrera indicates that her
mother was devoutly Catholic and her
father, ''by birth Jewish,'' was ''by
persuasion an atheist'' (6); she says
that Kahlo herself, while professing
no organized religion (283), nevertheless believed in a ''vitalistic form
of pantheism'' (328). Although most
of her religious imagery is specifically Christian, her most directly religious subject is Moses (fig. 69),
which Zamora identifies as having been
commissioned by José Domingo Lavin in
1945 (102). A complex work detailing
the birth of its subject, it resembles

Taffe 10

in composition Bosch's Garden of Earthly Delights (reproduced in Delavoy 88—89) and Traini's The Triumph of Death, both of which contain many little scenes to help tell the whole story.

First religious theme—the Last Supper

    The story of the Last Supper has been depicted by many artists, the most famous version being that of Leonardo da Vinci (reproduced in Hartt 452—53). In 1940, Kahlo contributed to this tradition The Wounded Table (fig. 55), painted after Kahlo and Rivera's divorce. As explained in the film Portrait of an Artist: Frida Kahlo, it depicts, from left to right, a young boy and girl (her sister's children), a Judas doll (a papier--mâché figure stuffed with firecrackers to be exploded on the day before Easter), Kahlo, a skeleton, and a young deer. Kahlo thus occupies the central position of Jesus, with a symbol of betrayal on her right, of death on her left, and of innocence at either end of the table. Blood on the floor underneath her skirt reveals that she has already been wounded.

Film cited by title

    It is not surprising that another Christian theme explored by Kahlo is

TEACHING PRACTICE

Reread the section on "Integrating quotations into your text" (pp. 590—91) and then discuss how Daniel Taffe integrates the quotations from Herrera into his own sentences.

Second religious theme—martyrdom of St. Sebastian

martyrdom, particularly the martyrdom of St. Sebastian. A popular Renaissance subject, Sebastian's death was depicted by, among others, Antonio del Pollaiuolo and Antonello da Messina, both in 1475. In both portrayals, Sebastian has been tied to a post and shot full of arrows. Kahlo uses the St. Sebastian theme in two paintings, again substituting herself for the central character. In The Broken Column, described previously, Kahlo is passive, almost fatalistically calm as she stands bound to her column by her metal corset, her flesh pierced by nails. In The Little Deer (pl. XXXI), a deer with Kahlo's head and a body pierced with arrows runs through a wood. Together, the two images suggest that Kahlo found echoes of her physical and emotional torment in the tradition of Christian martyrdom.

Subpoint: Mexican influence—retablos

In Mexico, as Herrera notes, this tradition is powerfully influenced by the ''bloodiness and self-mortification'' of the Aztec tradition (283). Indeed, in much of Kahlo's work the Christian imagery shows a Mexican influence. Rivera and Kahlo owned a collection of nineteenth-

---

TEACHING PRACTICE

Ask students to review "Checking for excessive use of sources" (pp. 593–94). Because Herrera's book is so central to work on Kahlo, Daniel Taffe found himself relying on it extensively. He was aware that he might be overusing this one source and sought to balance it with others whenever possible. Ask students to read through the essay again with this question in mind. Do they think that Taffe relies too much on one source? If so, what alternatives can they suggest?

Taffe 12

century retablos, described by Nicholas Jenkins as ''votive paintings on
tin, each about the size of a post-
card, melodramatically relating the
facts of an intercession by God: here
a child rescued from a burning bed,
there a man rescued from drowning''
(105). In 1932, Kahlo completed <u>Henry
Ford Hospital</u> (pl. IV), her first work
on a metal surface. Although the
painting does not adhere to the strict
characteristics of a retablo, Herrera
argues that both Rivera and Kahlo
viewed it as one (151). Instead of a
divine deliverance, the painting tells
the story of a calamity: Kahlo's mis-
carriage.

Yet another example of Christian
imagery filtered through Mexican culture is <u>My Birth</u> (pl. VI). In this
painting, the Virgin Mary gazes out of
a framed portrait above a bed covered
in white. On the bed is a woman giving birth, her head and shoulders covered, suggesting that she is dead.
The child being born——Kahlo——also appears to be dead. According to Herrera, this painting is based on a
well-known Aztec sculpture of a woman
giving birth to a man's head, a sculp-

Additional exam-
ple of Mexican
influence

Taffe 13

ture and a tradition with which Kahlo
was well acquainted (158).

Conclusion: Summary of argument and echo of thesis

Thus, despite a desire on the
part of my critics and admirers to see
her as an almost entirely original
artist, evidence suggests that Kahlo's
art strongly reflects a number of influences from earlier paintings and
from her own Mexican culture. While
her work is clearly informed by her
life experience, she had a deep understanding of European and Mexican artistic traditions, an understanding
that powerfully shaped her creation of
what the art world has come to identify as uniquely Kahlo. Just eight
days before she died, Herrera tells
us, Kahlo wrote in bright red paint on
her last painting ''VIVA LA VIDA''
[LONG LIVE LIFE] (440). Those who
study her art are increasingly likely
to answer ''VIVA LA KAHLO.''

TEACHING PRACTICE

Ask students to refer to "Drafting your conclusion" (p. 587). Then ask them to identify the strategy Daniel Taffe has used in his conclusion. How effective do they find his conclusion? What alternative conclusions can they offer?

Taffe 14

1″

Notes

[1] All cited Kahlo paintings are reproduced in Herrera and identified by the plate or figure number assigned by Herrera. Color plates (pl.) follow p. 162 and p. 290; black-and-white illustrations (fig.) follow p. 130 and p. 226.

[2] I wish to thank Professor Honeywell, who in our interview suggested that I consult several standard histories of Western art, such as Gardner, Janson, and Hartt.

1" ↓ Taffe 15

Heading centered → Works Cited ←————— Double-space

Weekly periodical

Carter, Angela. ''A Ribbon around a
Bomb.'' <u>New Statesman & Society</u>
12 May 1989: 32—33.

First line of each entry flush with left margin

Translation

Delavoy, Robert L. <u>Bosch</u>. Trans.
Stuart Gilbert. Cleveland, OH:
World, 1984.

Gardner, Helen. <u>Art through the Ages</u>.

One volume of multivolume work

Subsequent lines indented five spaces →

Vol. 2. 7th ed. New York:
Harcourt, 1980. 3 vols.

Hartt, Frederick. <u>History of Italian
Renaissance Art</u>. Englewood
Cliffs, NJ: Prentice, 1981.

Herrera, Hayden. <u>Frida: A Biography
of Frida Kahlo</u>. New York:
Harper, 1983.

Honeywell, Richard. Telephone interview. 15 Apr. 1991.

Interview

Janson, H. W. <u>Key Monuments in the
History of Art</u>. New York:
Abrams, 1959.

Jenkins, Nicholas. ''Calla Lilies and
Kahlos: The Frida Kahlo Museum,
Mexico City.'' <u>ARTnews</u> Mar.
1989: 104—05.

Monthly periodical

Plagens, Peter, et al. ''Frida on Our
Minds.'' <u>Newsweek</u> 27 May 1991:
54—55.

Article by more than four authors

Taffe 16

<u>Portrait</u> <u>of</u> <u>an</u> <u>Artist:</u> <u>Frida</u> <u>Kahlo</u>.   Film
      Dir. Eila Hershon. RM Arts/
      Hershon/WDR, 1983.
Zamora, Martha. <u>Frida</u> <u>Kahlo:</u> <u>The</u>
      <u>Brush</u> <u>of</u> <u>Anguish</u>. Trans. Marilyn
      Sode Smith. San Francisco:
      Chronicle, 1990.

44

Documenting Sources, APA and Other Styles

The current *Publication Manual of the American Psychological Association* (APA) has evolved over the years from a seven-page 1929 article offering general guidelines for stylistic standards to a book of over two hundred detail-filled pages. Now followed by writers in a number of fields throughout the social sciences, the APA guidelines, like those of other style manuals, aim to foster clear communication and easy reference. This chapter illustrates **APA style** and guides you in using such documentation in your own writing. For further reference, consult the following:

> American Psychological Association. *Publication Manual of the American Psychological Association.* 3rd ed. Washington: American Psychological Assn., 1983.

In addition, this chapter presents brief guidelines for two other styles: the **number style**, used frequently in the natural sciences, and the **note-and-bibliography style**, used frequently in the humanities.

 Directory to APA style

44a

APA format for parenthetical citations

In APA style, **parenthetical citations** in the text identify each quotation, paraphrase, summary, or other material from a source. Parenthetical citations correspond to full-information bibliographic entries in a list of references at the end of the text. Generally, the author's name is used in a signal phrase to introduce the cited material, and the date in parentheses immediately follows the author's name. For a quotation, the page number, preceded by "p.," appears in parentheses after the quotation. Following are examples of ways to cite various kinds of sources.

AUTHOR NAMED IN A SIGNAL PHRASE

Key (1983) argues that the placement of women in print advertisements is subliminally important.

As Briggs (1970) observes, parents play an important role in building their children's self-esteem because ''children value themselves to the degree that they have been valued'' (p. 14).

AUTHOR NAMED IN A PARENTHETICAL CITATION

When you do not name the author in your text, give the name and the date, separated by a comma, in parentheses at the end of the cited material.

One study has found that only 68% of letters received by editors were actually published (Renfro, 1979).

TWO AUTHORS

Use both names in all citations. Join the names with "and" in a signal phrase, but use an ampersand (&) instead in a parenthetical reference.

Murphy and Orkow (1985) reached somewhat different conclusions by designing a study that was less dependent on subjective judgment than were previous studies.

A recent study that was less dependent on subjective judgment resulted in somewhat different conclusions than had previous studies (Murphy & Orkow 1985).

THREE TO FIVE AUTHORS

List all the authors' names in a signal phrase or parenthetical citation for the first reference.

Belenky, Clinchy, Goldberger, and Tarule (1986) suggest that many women rely on observing and listening to others as ways of learning about themselves.

In any subsequent references, use just the first author's name plus "et al." ("and others"). Note that all the authors' names should appear in the entry in the list of references.

From this experience, observe Belenky et al. (1986),
women learn to listen to themselves think, a step toward
self-expression.

SIX OR MORE AUTHORS

Use the first author's name and "et al." ("and others") in every citation, including the first. Note that all the authors' names should appear in the entry in the list of references.

As Mueller et al. (1980) demonstrated, television holds
the potential for distorting and manipulating consumers
as free-willed decision makers.

CORPORATE AUTHOR

Generally, spell out the name of a corporate author each time you cite it. If the organization's name is long, spell out the name the first time you use it and indicate in parentheses the abbreviation you will use in subsequent citations. If you name the organization in a parenthetical citation the first time you use it, add the abbreviation in brackets within the parentheses.

The Centers for Disease Control (CDC) released new
figures. . . . Later, the CDC announced . . .

(The Centers for Disease Control [CDC], 1990)
(CDC, 1990)

UNKNOWN AUTHOR

Use the title or the first few words of it in a signal phrase or parenthetical citation.

The school profiles for the county substantiate this
trend (<u>Guide to Secondary Schools</u>, 1983).

TWO OR MORE AUTHORS WITH THE SAME SURNAME

If your list of references includes works by different authors with the same surname, include the author's first or first two initial(s) in each citation.

```
G. Jones (1984) conducted the groundbreaking study of
retroviruses.
```

TWO OR MORE SOURCES IN THE SAME PARENTHETICAL CITATION

If you cite more than one source in the parentheses, list all the sources in the order in which they appear in the list of references. That is, list works by different authors in alphabetical order (separated by semicolons) and works by the same author in chronological order (separated by commas).

```
(Chodorow, 1978; Gilligan, 1982)
(Gilligan 1977, 1982)
```

SPECIFIC PARTS OF A SOURCE

Use abbreviations ("chap.," "sec.," and so on) in the parenthetical citation to name the part you are citing.

```
Montgomery (1988, ch. 9) argues that his research
yielded the opposite results.
```

PERSONAL COMMUNICATION

Cite any personal letters, telephone conversations, or interviews in your text with the person's name, the identification "personal communication," and the date. Because your readers would not be able to recover these sources, you do not need to include them in your list of references.

```
J. L. Morin (personal communication, October 14, 1990)
supported the claims made in her recent article with new
evidence.
```

APA format for content notes

APA style allows content notes for information you wish to include to expand or supplement your text. Notes are indicated in the text by superscript numerals in consecutive order throughout the text, and the notes themselves are typed on a separate page after the last page of the text, under the heading Footnotes, centered at the top of the page. Double-space all entries. Indent the first line of each note five spaces, but begin subsequent lines at the left margin.

SUPERSCRIPT IN TEXT

The age of the children involved was an important factor in the selection of items for the questionnaire.[1]

FOOTNOTE

[1]Marjorie Youngston Forman and William Cole of the Child Study Team provided great assistance in identifying appropriate items.

APA format for a list of references

The alphabetical list of the sources actually cited in your essay is called **References**. (If your instructor asks that you list everything you have read as background, call the list Bibliography.) Start your list on a separate page *after* the text of your essay and any notes (see 44b) but *before* any appendices that explain your research procedures or results. Number the page as you did those in your text. Type the heading References, neither underlined nor in quotation marks, centered one and one-half inches from the top of the page. Double-space and begin your first entry. Start each entry flush with the left margin; indent any subsequent lines of the entry three spaces. Double-space the entire list.

List your sources alphabetically by authors' last names. If a source is by an unknown author, alphabetize it by the first major word of the title after any initial *a, an,* or *the.*

The APA style specifies treatment and placement of four basic elements—author, publication date, title, and publication information—as follows. These elements are separated from one another by a period and two spaces, and the entry ends with a period.

1. *Author.* List all authors last name first, and use only initials for first and middle names. Separate multiple authors with commas, and use an ampersand before the last author.

2. *Publication date.* Enclose the date in parentheses. Use only the year for books and journals; use the year, a comma, and the month or month and day for magazines. Do not abbreviate the month.

3. *Title.* Underline titles and subtitles of books and periodicals, but do not enclose titles of articles in quotation marks. For books and articles, capitalize only the first word of the title and subtitle and any proper nouns

or proper adjectives. Capitalize all major words in a periodical title. (See 35c for information on capitalization.)

4. *Publication information.* For a book, list the city of publication (and the country or postal abbreviation for the state if the city is unfamiliar), a colon, and the publisher's name, dropping any *Inc., Co.,* or *Publishers.* For a periodical, follow the periodical title with a comma, the volume number (underlined), the issue number (if appropriate) in parentheses, a comma, and the inclusive page numbers of the article. For newspapers and magazines, include the abbreviations "p." ("page") or "pp." ("pages").

Consult the various sample entries below for information on where in an entry you should place other information. Here are examples of basic book and periodical entries.

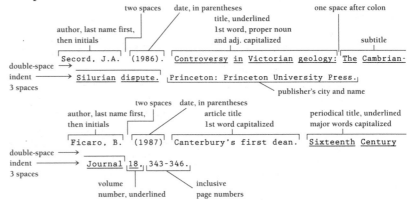

BOOK BY ONE AUTHOR

Coon, D. (1980). <u>Introduction to psychology:
Exploration and application</u>. New York: West
Publishing.

BOOK BY TWO OR MORE AUTHORS

Newcombe, F., & Ratcliffe, G. (1978). <u>Defining
females—The nature of women in society</u>. New York:
Wiley.

BOOK BY A CORPORATE AUTHOR

Institute of Financial Education. (1983). <u>Income
property lending</u>. Homewood, IL: Dow Jones—Irwin.

BOOK BY AN UNKNOWN AUTHOR

National Geographic Atlas of the World. (1988).
   Washington: National Geographic Society.

BOOK PREPARED BY AN EDITOR

Solomon, A. P. (Ed.). (1980). The prospective city.
   Cambridge, MA: MIT Press.

SELECTION IN A BOOK WITH AN EDITOR

Taylor, R. C. R. (1982). The politics of prevention.
   In P. Conrad & R. Kern (Eds.), The sociology of
   health and illness (pp. 471–483). New York: St.
   Martin's.

TRANSLATION

Durkheim, E. (1957). Suicide. (J. A. Spaulding &
   G. Simpson, Trans.). Glencoe, IL: Free Press of
   Glencoe.

EDITION OTHER THAN THE FIRST

Kohn, M. L. (1977). Class and conformity: A study in
   values (2nd ed.). Chicago: University of Chicago
   Press.

ONE VOLUME OF A MULTIVOLUME WORK

Baltes, P., & Brim, O. G. (Eds.). (1980). Life–span
   development and behavior (Vol. 3). New York: Basic
   Books.

REPUBLICATION

Piaget, J. (1952). The language and thought of the
   child. London: Routledge & Kegan Paul. (Original
   work published 1932)

GOVERNMENT DOCUMENT

U.S. Bureau of the Census. (1975). <u>Historical
Statistics of the United States, Colonial Times to
1870</u>. Washington: Government Printing Office.

ARTICLE IN A JOURNAL PAGINATED BY VOLUME

Shuy, R. (1981). A holistic view of language.
<u>Research in the Teaching of English, 15</u>, 101—111.

ARTICLE IN A JOURNAL PAGINATED BY ISSUE

Maienza, J. G. (1986). The superintendency:
Characteristics of access for men and women.
<u>Educational Administration Quarterly, 22</u>(4), 59—79.

ARTICLE IN A MAGAZINE

Ferguson, T., & Rogers, J. (1986, May). The myth of
America's turn to the right. <u>Atlantic</u>, pp. 48—51.

ARTICLE IN A NEWSPAPER

Browne, M. W. (1988, April 26). Lasers for the
battlefield raise concern for eyesight. <u>The New York
Times</u>, pp. C1, C8.

UNSIGNED ARTICLE

What sort of person reads creative computing? (1985,
August). <u>Creative Computing</u>, pp. 8, 10.

EDITORIAL OR LETTER TO THE EDITOR

Burney, P. S. (1985, May). Cryptographic message
sending [Letter to the editor]. <u>Byte: The Small
Systems Journal</u>, p. 14.

REVIEW IN A PERIODICAL

Larmore, C. E. (1989). [Review of <u>Patterns of Moral
Complexity</u>]. <u>Ethics, 99</u>, 423—426.

MATERIAL FROM AN INFORMATION SERVICE OR A DATABASE

Belenky, M. F. The role of deafness in the moral
     development of hearing impaired children. In
     A. Areson & J. De Caro (Eds.), Teaching, learning and
     development. Rochester, NY: National Institute for
     the Deaf, 1984. (ERIC Document Reproduction Service
     No. ED 248 646)

PUBLISHED INTERVIEW

McCarthy, E. (1968, December 24). [Interview with
     Boston Globe Washington staff]. Boston Globe, p.
     B27.

SOFTWARE PROGRAM

SuperCalc3 Release 2.1. (1985). [Computer program].
     San Jose, CA: Computer Associates, Micro Products
     Division.

FILM OR VIDEOTAPE

Hitchcock, A. (Producer & Director). (1954). Rear
     window [Film]. Los Angeles, CA: MGM.

TWO OR MORE WORKS BY THE SAME AUTHOR(S)

List two or more works by the same author in chronological order.
Repeat the author's name in each entry.

Macrorie, K. (1968). Writing to be read. New York:
     Hayden.
Macrorie, K. (1970). Uptaught. Rochelle Park, NY:
     Hayden.

TWO OR MORE WORKS BY THE SAME AUTHOR(S) IN THE SAME YEAR

List two or more works by the same author published in the same year
alphabetically, and place lowercase numbers (*a, b,* etc.) after the dates in
parentheses.

Murray, F. B. (1983a). Equilibration as cognitive
conflict. <u>Developmental Review</u>, <u>3</u>, 54–61.

Murray, F. B. (1983b). Learning and development
through social interaction. In Liben, L. (Ed.),
<u>Piaget and the foundations of knowledge</u>. Hillsdale,
NJ: Lawrence Erlbaum.

44d

Number style

Number-style documentation is used in many of the natural sciences. In this style, each parenthetical citation is a number that corresponds to a full citation in a list of sources, usually called Literature Cited. The literature-cited entries are made up of author, title, and publication information. Requirements for arranging and punctuating these three elements vary greatly among disciplines, so be sure to ask your instructor which style you should follow. Some common style manuals include the following:

American Chemical Society. *Handbook for Authors of Papers in the American Chemical Society Publications.* Washington: American Chemical Soc., 1978.

American Institute of Physics. *Style Manual for Guidance in the Preparation of Papers.* 3rd ed. New York: American Inst. of Physics, 1978.

Council of Biology Editors. *CBE Style Manual: A Guide for Authors, Editors, and Publishers in the Biological Sciences.* 5th ed., rev. and exp. Bethesda, MD: CBE, 1983.

The following discussion pertains to the style advocated by the Council of Biology Editors (CBE). In CBE style, the literature-cited list includes only works actually cited in the essay. The list is arranged either alphabetically by authors' last names, with each entry assigned a number in sequence, or in the order in which the sources are cited in the text.

Citations in the text are identified by a number in parentheses following any quotation, paraphrase, summary, or other reference from a source. Each number corresponds to a literature-cited entry. If a citation refers to a specific page, it includes the entry number, a comma, the abbreviation "p.," and the page number (1, p. 245). Here are a sample text reference and two literature-cited entries, one for a book and one for a periodical, that conform to CBE style.

TEXT REFERENCE

First, Freidson argues, the doctor is in the autonomous position of having a monopoly on the applied uses of medical scientific knowledge (1).

LITERATURE CITED

1. Freidson, E. Profession of medicine. New York: Dodd—Mead; 1972.
2. Finkel, M. J. Drugs of limited commercial value. New Engl. J. Med. 302:643—44; 1980.

Note-and-bibliography style

The note-and-bibliography style was the standard format preferred by the Modern Language Association (MLA) until 1984 and thus is sometimes referred to as old MLA style. (See Chapter 43 for current MLA guidelines.) This style is still used in some fields, particularly in the humanities.

1

Note-and-bibliography format for bibliography entries

The format for entries in the bibliography is the same as the current MLA format for entries in a works-cited list (see 43c). The bibliography appears on a separate page at the end of the essay, after the list of notes (see 44e2).

2

Note-and-bibliography format for notes

The note-and-bibliography style uses superscript numbers ([1]) to mark citations in the text. Citations are numbered sequentially throughout the text and correspond to notes that contain complete publication information about the sources cited.

In the text, the superscript number for each note is placed near the cited material—at the end of the quotation, sentence, clause, or phrase. The number is typed after any punctuation, and no space is left between it and the preceding letter or punctuation mark.

As Glueck says, ''Most addicts have had dealings with some type of crime before they became acquainted with narcotics.''[5]

Notes can be footnotes (typed at the bottom of the page on which the citation appears in the text) or endnotes (typed on a separate page under the heading Notes). The first line of each note is indented five spaces and begins with a superscript number and one space before the first word of the entry. All remaining lines of the entry are typed flush with the left margin. A note usually begins with the author's name, in normal order, followed by a comma, the title of the source, the publication information in parentheses, and the page number(s). The first note for a source gives full information about it. Subsequent notes use a shortened reference, usually the author's name and the page number(s).

Examples of some variations in first notes are shown below. Corresponding bibliographic entries for these examples appear in 43c.

Books

ONE AUTHOR

[1] Hayden Herrera, <u>Frida: A Biography of Frida Kahlo</u> (New York: Harper, 1983) 356.

MORE THAN ONE AUTHOR

[2] John T. McNeill and Helena M. Gamer, <u>Medieval Handbooks of Penance</u> (New York: Octagon, 1965) 139.

UNKNOWN AUTHOR

[3] <u>The New York Times Atlas of the World</u> (New York: New York Times Books, 1980) 67.

EDITOR OR EDITORS

[4] C. Vann Woodward, ed., <u>Mary Chestnut's Civil War</u> (New Haven: Yale UP, 1981) 214.

SELECTION IN AN ANTHOLOGY OR CHAPTER IN A BOOK WITH AN EDITOR

[5] Mary Gordon, ''The Parable of the Cave,'' <u>The Writer on Her Work</u>, ed. Janet Sternburg (New York: Norton, 1980) 30.

EDITION OTHER THAN THE FIRST

⁶ Alfred H. Kelly, Winfred A. Harbison, and Herman Belz, The American Constitution: Its Origins and Development, 6th ed. (New York: Norton, 1983) 187.

MULTIVOLUME WORK

⁷ Philip S. Foner and Ronald L. Lewis, eds., The Black Worker, vol. 3 (Philadelphia: Lippincott, 1980) 134.

Periodicals

ARTICLE IN A JOURNAL PAGINATED BY A VOLUME

⁸ Margot Norris, ''Narration under a Blindfold: Reading Joyce's 'Clay,' '' PMLA 102 (1987): 206.

ARTICLE IN A JOURNAL PAGINATED BY ISSUE

⁹ John Loffy, ''The Politics at Modernism's Funeral,'' Canadian Journal of Political and Social Theory 6.3 (1987): 88.

ARTICLE IN A MAGAZINE

¹⁰ Edward Said, ''Through Gringo Eyes,'' Harper's Apr. 1988: 71.

ARTICLE IN A NEWSPAPER

¹¹ Chester Cooper, ''Fateful Day in Vietnam,'' Washington Post 11 Feb. 1968: 4+.

Subsequent notes to the same source

If you use two works by the same author, add a comma and a shortened version of the title after the author's name so that a reader will know which source you are citing.

¹² Herrera 32.

¹³ Lewis, Reconstruction 59.

¹⁴ Lewis, Postwar Era 204.

EXERCISE 44.1 Taking Inventory: Documentation

Take time to look carefully at the parenthetical citations and/or notes and list of references cited you have prepared for a research essay. Using the guidelines in this chapter, check each citation, note, and list entry, noting (1) any whose form is incorrect, and (2) any source you are still unsure of how best to document. If you are keeping a writing log or a research log, enter your findings there. For those sources you need help on documenting, check with your instructor.

A sample research essay, APA style

Leah Clendening's final essay appears on the following pages. In preparing this essay, she followed the APA guidelines described in sections 44a–44c.

Content Analysis

Short title and
page number

1

A Content Analysis of Letters

Heading centered
and double-spaced

to the Editor

Leah Clendening

Professor Garrett

Psychology 201

May 20, 19XX

Content Analysis

2

Abstract

No paragraph indent

This study analyzed the content of 624 letters to the editor in two newspapers—one published in a city of over 500,000, the other in a city of about 15,000—in order to explore the relationship between community size and subject matter of letters. A researcher read all of the letters printed in the newspapers on the weekdays of three nonconsecutive months in late 1987 and early 1988, then classified them according to whether they dealt with local or national issues and recorded the findings on a category sheet. Results indicate a significant difference: letters in the smaller community concentrated almost entirely on local issues, while those in the larger community concentrated more frequently on national than on local issues.

Content Analysis

3

A Content Analysis of Letters
to the Editor

Research has indicated that the
average person who writes letters to
an American newspaper tends to be a
conservative, well-adjusted white male
who is middle-aged or older and a
longtime resident of his community
(Singletary & Cowling, 1979). One
study concluded that 71.4% of the
letters printed were written by people
who wished to inform or persuade by
writing their letters. Most of the
remainder, 27.0%, wished only to use
the letter as a means of self-
expression; the other 1.6% wished
to arouse readers to action (Lemert &
Larkin, 1979).

Problem

But what are the major concerns
of these letter writers? Are they
more concerned about events in their
local communities or about national
issues? Does the size of the
community have some influence on the
subjects of letters its members write?
These questions led to the following
hypothesis: people living in a small
community (with a population of about

Paragraphs indented five spaces

Passive voice used to focus on the research rather than the researcher

Previous work surveyed

First-level heading centered

Research question stated

Hypothesis stated

TEACHING PRACTICE

Refer students to the discussion of introductions on pp. 586–87. Then ask them to evaluate the effectiveness of this introduction to an essay in the social sciences. How does it differ from Daniel Taffe's introduction to his essay on p. 624?

TEACHING PRACTICE

Ask students to compare the organizational format of this essay to the one by Daniel Taffe on pp. 620–39. What similarities and differences can they identify?

Content Analysis

4

15,000) tend to be concerned more with local than with national issues. People living in a large community (with a population over 500,000) show more concern for national than for local issues.

Method

Second-level heading under-lined and flush left

Newspapers

The two newspapers that served as data sources, the <u>Mount Vernon News</u> and the Cleveland <u>Plain Dealer</u>, were chosen mainly for convenience and availability. Cleveland has a population of 573,822 and a weekly distribution of the <u>Plain Dealer</u> of 482,564. Mount Vernon has a population of 14,380 and a weekly distribution of the <u>Mount Vernon News</u> of 10,936 (<u>1985 IMS/Ayer Directory</u>, 1985). Each newspaper's letters were read for the weekdays of October 1987, December 1987, and February 1988. Sunday issues were not taken into account.

A category sheet of possible subjects for the letters to the editor was adapted from the coding sheet of Donohew's study on Medicare (Budd, Thorp, & Donohew, 1967, p. 41). One

Subjects of study identified

Short title used to identify source with no author

Materials described

Content Analysis

5

column recorded national issues, and a
second local issues. The sheet was
constructed with a space for the
newspaper's abbreviation, the date,
and the letter number(s). The Mount
Vernon News was given the abbreviation
MVN, and the Cleveland Plain Dealer
the abbreviation CPD.

Procedure

After the category sheet was
finished and approved, observation
began. The letters were read and
marked for content in a library
setting. Each letter was then
classified on the category sheet that
had been titled with the proper
abbreviations, date, and letter
number. As observation progressed,
constraints of time demanded a change
from filling out a separate sheet for
each letter to recording each day's
letters on the same category sheet.
The space left for recording the
letter number was used to record the
total number of letters for each
particular day. After all observation
was finished, the counts for each of
the newspapers were totaled for each
month and overall.

Page noted for specific source

Steps in carrying out research explained

TEACHING PRACTICE

Consider providing students with several letters to the editor of your local newspaper and asking them to follow the procedures described in this paragraph of the essay. Use their experiences to generate discussion on how effectively this paragraph is organized and on how well they were able to replicate the procedure.

TEACHING PRACTICE

As a focus for discussion of these "Results," ask students to reread "Reconsidering your purpose, audience, stance, and thesis" (pp. 582–84). What audience is Leah Clendening addressing? How likely is it that this audience will be convinced by the results of the Chi-square test?

TEACHING PRACTICE

Depending on their needs and interests, some of your students may want to do a bit of research on how best to present information in graphic form. Most technical writing textbooks include a section on graphs and tables. See, for example, Deborah Andrews and Margaret Blickle, *Technical Writing: Principles and Forms* (New York: Macmillan, 1982), pp. 151–85.

Content Analysis

6

Results

During the three months, 60 letters were read from the Mount Vernon News. Fifty-three pertained to local issues, while seven pertained to national issues. A Chi-square test with an adjustment for continuity was used on these data to find if there was a statistically significant difference between concern with local and national issues. Results showed an overwhelming difference between issues, even at the .01 probability level. A graph (Figure 1) was also constructed to show the number of national and local issues for each month for the MVN.

Results from first newspaper analyzed statistically

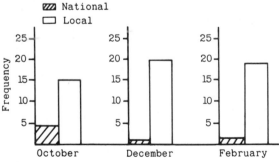

Graph used to show results

Frequency of national and local issues for MVN

Figure 1. Frequency of national and local issues for WVN

Content Analysis

7

Of a total of 564 letters read
from the Cleveland Plain Dealer, 248
pertained to local issues and 316 to
national issues. A Chi-square test
with an ajustment for continuity was
also used on these data and, once
again, showed a statistically
significant difference. A graph
(Figure 2) was constructed to show
the frequency of national and local
issues for each month for the CPD.

Results from
second newspaper
analyzed
statistically

Graph used to
show results

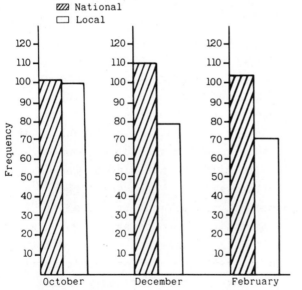

Frequency of national and local issues for CPD

Figure 2. Frequency of national and
local issues for CPD

Content Analysis

8

One interesting side note is that   Findings counter
                                         to previous
21.6% of the letters from the   research noted
Plain Dealer expressed grievances or
appreciation, compared to 36% of the
letters from the Mount Vernon News.
These findings differ considerably
from those of Lister, who found that
only 5% of letters to the editor were
of this particular type (Lister, 1985).

Discussion

The findings of this study
generally supported the hypothesis,
especially in the smaller community,
where letters concentrated
overwhelmingly on local issues.
Perhaps residents of such a community
do not see themselves as strongly
affected by national politics and
events. For the larger community, the   Results
                                           interpreted
findings were not as clear; one
possibility is that many of the
letters were not from the larger
community itself but from smaller
communities surrounding it.

If more time had been permitted,   Biases and
                                           possible
an entire year's letters could have   improvements in
been categorized, perhaps yielding   the study listed
more representative information. In
addition, use of a second reader could

Content Analysis

9

have reduced bias on the part of a
single reader in the categorization of
letters. It was found as the study
progressed that a few categories could
have been added, such as religion and
local and state elections; the lack of
these categories, however, did not
severely affect the study. Another
bias that would be difficult to
account for is editorial bias: one
study found that only 68% of letters
received by editors were published
(Renfro, 1979). The only way to
eliminate this bias would be to read
all the letters received instead of
only those that were printed.

Conclusion

The study raises some interesting
questions that further study would
probably help to answer. Does gender
or age seem to influence whether
people are interested in local or
national issues? What is the causal
relationship between residence in
small towns and apparent greater
interest in local affairs? Future
studies may answer such questions,
building on the information here.

Larger questions
noted in
conclusion

TEACHING PRACTICE

Ask students to use the strategies on p. 587
under "Drafting your conclusion" as a means
of evaluating the conclusion of this essay.

Content Analysis

10

References

Budd, R. W., Thorp, K., & Donohew, L. (1967). <u>Content analysis of communications</u>. New York: Macmillan.

Lemert, J. B., & Larkin, J. P. (1979). Some reasons why mobilizing information fails to be in letters to the editor. <u>Journalism Quarterly</u>, <u>56</u>, 504–512.

Lister, L. (1985). An analysis of letters to the editor. <u>Social Work</u>, <u>30</u>, 77–78.

The <u>1985 IMS/Ayer Directory of Publications</u> (117th ed.). (1985). Fort Washington, PA: IMS Press.

Renfro, P. C. (1979). Bias in selection of letters to the editor. <u>Journalism Quarterly</u>, <u>56</u>, 822–826.

Singletary, M. W., & Cowling, M. (1979). Letters to the editor of the non-daily press. <u>Journalism Quarterly</u>, <u>56</u>, 165–168.

Heading centered on new page

First line of each entry flush with left margin

Subsequent lines indented three spaces

Entries alphabetical by author, last names first; use initials for first and middle names

Part Nine

Academic and Professional Writing

—————————— ◇ ——————————

45

Writing in Different Disciplines

How is writing used in various professions? A recent survey asked that question of two hundred members of professional organizations serving the following seven groups: chemists, psychologists, technical writers, city planners and managers, engineers, business executives, and teachers of language and literature. As you might guess, the great majority (98 percent) report that writing is very important to doing their jobs well. More surprising is just how *much* time these professionals devote to writing—an average of 46 percent of their working hours. Other surprises emerged in comparing results by profession; for instance, engineers report spending more time writing than do English teachers. But overall, this survey confirmed that good writing plays an important role in almost every profession, and in some it is crucial to success. As one MBA wrote, "Those who advance quickly in my company are those who write and speak well."

Everyday use

While you encounter the language of different fields all the time—in signing a contract or making a will (the language of law), for example, or in examining an estimate for major car repairs (the language of automotive engineering)—you probably use the language of different disciplines most often in the notes you take for your college classes. Take a minute to look carefully at the notes you have taken recently in two classes—one in the humanities or social sciences, perhaps, the other in the sciences. What words or phrases or other symbols in your notes do you associate with the language of each discipline? What other differences can you find in the two sets of class notes? Compare your findings with those of some classmates.

This chapter will lead you to think about the different ways writing works in various disciplines. You may begin to get a sense of such differences as you prepare essays or other written assignments for various other courses. Certainly by the time you choose a major, you should be ready to familiarize yourself with the expectations, vocabularies, styles, methods of proof, and conventional formats used in your field.

EXERCISE 45.1

Consider how the following topics might be approached in the specified disciplines or fields. What issues might each field see? What approach might each take? How might each investigate and write about the topic? Choose one topic and write a paragraph or two about how it might be approached by the different disciplines.

1. first-grade reading abilities—as seen by reading teachers, librarians, eye doctors, or reading-test designers

2. soccer—as seen by sports physicians, psychologists, recreation directors, or historians

3. ancient Egyptian mythology—as seen by comparative literature specialists, anthropologists, archaeologists, or art historians

4. a sunken ship—as seen by engineers, marine biologists, economists, or journalists

45a

Analyzing academic assignments and expectations

Assignments vary widely from course to course and even from professor to professor. You may be asked to prepare one-sentence answers to study questions in history or physics, detailed laboratory reports in biology, case studies in psychology or sociology, or even film scripts in a visual media course. Thus the directions this section offers can only be general, based on experience and on discussions with professors in many disciplines. The best advice is really very simple: make sure you are in control of the assignment rather than the assignment's being in control of you. To take control, you need to understand the assignment fully and to understand what professors in the particular discipline expect in an effective response to the assignment.

When you receive an assignment in *any* discipline, your first job is to make sure you understand what that assignment is asking you to do. Some differ in scope and practice, but all of them aim to improve student writing by showing faculty from across the disciplines how to use writing regularly and thoughtfully in their classrooms.

USEFUL READING

Bean, John C., Dean Drenk, and F. D. Lee. "Microtheme Strategies for Cognitive Skills." *New Directions for Teaching and Learning: Teaching Writing in the Disciplines.* Ed. C. W. Griffin. San Francisco: Jossey, 1982. The authors describe how to use a series of short assignments to improve thinking and writing skills.

CCC 36 (1985). This entire issue is devoted to the role of writing in the academic and professional disciplines. Two essays of special interest are "Learning to Write in the Social Sciences" (140–49) and "A Freshman Writing Course in Parallel with a Science Course" (160–65).

Young, Art, and Toby Fulwiler. *Writing across the Disciplines: Research into Practice.* Upper Montclair, NJ: Boynton, 1986. An informative collection of research on writing-across-the-discipline-programs from four perspectives: purpose, evaluation, writing and learning connections, politics and the effectiveness of these programs.

assignments may be as vague as "Write a five-page essay on one aspect of the Civil War." Others, like this psychology assignment, will be fairly specific: "For your first research assignment, you are to collect, summarize, and interpret data drawn from a sample of letters to the editor published in two newspapers, one in a small rural community, and one in an urban community, over a period of three months. Organize your research report according to APA requirements." (See the end of Chapter 44 for one student's essay in response to this assignment.) In any case, you must take charge of analyzing the assignment. Answering the following questions can help you do so.

 Analyzing an assignment

1. *What is the purpose of the assignment?* Does it serve an informal purpose—as a basis for class discussion or as a way to brainstorm about a topic? Or is the purpose more formal, a way to demonstrate your mastery of certain material and your competence as a writer?

2. *What is the assignment asking you to do?* Are you to summarize, explain, evaluate, interpret, illustrate, define? If the assignment asks you to do more than one of these things, does it specify the order in which you are to do them? (Note that the psychology assignment above does specify the activities to be carried out and the general topic to be covered in the report.)

3. *Do you need to ask for clarification of any terms?* Students responding to the psychology assignment might well ask the instructor, for instance, to discuss the meaning of *collect* or *interpret* and perhaps to give examples. Or they might want further clarification of the term *urban community* or the size of a suitable *sample*.

4. *What do you need to know or find out to do the assignment?* Students doing the psychology assignment need to develop a procedure—a way to analyze or categorize the letters to the editor. Furthermore, they need to know how to do simple statistical analyses of the data.

5. *Do you understand the professor's expectations regarding background reading and preparation, method of organization and development, format, and length?* The psychology assignment mentions no background reading, but in this field an adequate statement of a problem usually requires setting that problem in the context of other research. A student might well ask how extensive this part of the report is to be.

6. *Can you find an example of an effective response to a similar assignment?* If you can, you can analyze its parts and use it as a model for developing your own response. One psychology student,

when asked to describe what constituted a "good" essay in that discipline, said, "Well, for the first two assignments I basically summarized the relevant research data as clearly and briefly as I could and then pointed out weaknesses in the research and implications of it. Since I got A's on both papers I decided I must be doing something right." And indeed she was. By trial and error, she had fixed on an approach to the assignments, a method of organization, and a format that fit into what was accepted as "good" writing in her psychology courses.

7. *Does your understanding of the assignment fit with that of other students?* Talking over an assignment with classmates is one good way to test your understanding.

EXERCISE 45.2

Here is an assignment from a communications course. Read it carefully, and then use the list of seven questions in 45a to analyze the assignment.

Assignment: Distribute a questionnaire to twenty people (ten male, ten female) asking these four questions: (1) What do you expect to say and do when you meet a stranger? (2) What don't you expect to say and do when you meet a stranger? (3) What do you expect to say and do when you meet a very close friend? (4) What don't you expect to say and do when you meet a very close friend? When you have collected your twenty questionnaires, read them over and answer the following questions:

1. What, if any, descriptions were common to all respondents' answers?

2. How do male and female responses compare?

3. What similarities and differences were found between the responses to the stranger and to the very close friend situations?

4. What factors (environment, time, status, gender, and so on) do you feel have an impact on these responses?

5. Discuss your findings, using concepts and theories explained in your text.

45b

Understanding disciplinary vocabularies

The rhetorician Kenneth Burke describes the way people become active participants in the "conversation of humankind" in the following way. Imagine, he says, that you enter a crowded room in which everyone is

What is it that brings about such an intimate connection between language and thinking? Is there no thinking without the use of language, namely in concepts and concept-combinations for which words need not necessarily come to mind? Has not everyone of us struggled for words although the connection between "things" was already clear? —ALBERT EINSTEIN

FOR COLLABORATIVE WORK

Ask students to work in groups of three. Each student should bring to class two copies of a short passage of approximately one hundred words taken from an article, an essay, or a textbook in a field with which he or she is familiar. Have students give a copy to each of their partners and ask them to list terms, phrases, or concepts that seem to involve specialized or highly technical language. Ask them to define and explain these terms. Have students retrieve their articles and their partners' lists, check their efforts, and then in discussion, clarify the terms for them. Discuss their confusion or lack of it.

This exercise gives students familiar with a particular field practice explaining basic terms to an audience unfamiliar with that field. For example, the term *blastema* is basic knowledge to students in molecular genetics, as is *Cyrillic alphabet* to Slavic language majors. *Morpheme* is a basic concept to linguistics students, as is *hypotenuse* to geometry students. Thus, this exercise serves two purposes:

1. It helps students develop an awareness of how to adapt their language and explanations to audiences with different degrees of expertise or familiarity with a field's vocabulary.

2. It also allows students to test their own understanding of terms and concepts. One way we determine how well we ourselves understand these is to explain them to someone else.

FOR COLLABORATIVE WORK

Divide the class into groups of no more than three students who are working in the same major field or some fairly closely related field. Ask each group to compile a glossary of twenty key terms that are essential to a field or that overlap related fields. Have students alphabetize the terms and give a definition and explanation of each.

talking and gesturing animatedly. You know no one there and cannot catch much of what is being said. Slowly you move from group to group listening, and finally you take a chance and interject a brief statement into the conversation. Others listen to you and respond. Thus, slowly but surely, do you come to *participate* in, rather than to observe, the conversation.

Entering into an academic discipline or a profession is much like entering into such a conversation. At first you feel like an outsider, and you do not catch much of what you hear or read. You may be experiencing this situation right now. Indeed, everyone experiences the same thing when entering a brand-new field. Trying to enter the new "conversation" takes time and careful attention. Eventually, however, the vocabulary becomes familiar, and participating in the conversation seems easy and natural.

Of course, this chapter cannot introduce you to the vocabulary of every field, nor would it be helpful to do so. The point is that *you* must make the effort to enter into the conversation, and that again means taking charge of the situation. To get started, one of the first things you need to do is to study the vocabulary.

Determine how much of what you are hearing and reading depends on specialized or technical vocabulary. Try highlighting key terms in your reading or your notes to help you distinguish the specialized vocabulary of the field from the larger discussion. If you find little specialized vocabulary, try to master the new terms quickly by reading your textbook carefully, by asking questions of the instructor and other students, and by looking up a few key words or phrases.

If you find a great deal of specialized vocabulary, however, you may want to familiarize yourself with it somewhat methodically. Any of the following procedures may prove helpful.

- Keep a log of unfamiliar or confusing words *in context*. To locate definitions or explanations, review past reading or check the terms in your textbook's glossary or index.

- Review your class notes each day after class. Underline important terms, review their definitions, and identify anything that is unclear. Use your textbook or ask questions to clarify anything confusing before the class moves on to a new topic.

- Check to see if your textbook has a glossary of terms or sets off definitions in italics or boldface type. If so, study pertinent sections carefully to master the terms.

- Try to start using or working with key concepts. Even if they are not yet entirely clear to you, working with them will help you formulate questions that will help you come to understand them. For example, in a statistics class, try to work out (in words) how to do an analysis of covariance, step by step, even if you are not sure you could come up with your own precise definition of the term. Or try to plot the narrative progression in a story even if you are still not entirely sure of the definition of *narrative progression.*

■ Find the standard dictionaries or handbooks of terms for your field. Students beginning the study of literature, for instance, can turn to several guides such as *A Dictionary of Literary, Dramatic, and Cinematic Terms,* or *A Handbook to Literature.* Those entering the discipline of sociology may refer to the *Dictionary of the Social Sciences,* while students beginning statistical analysis may turn to *Statistics without Tears.* Ask your instructor or a librarian for help finding the standard references in your field.

Whatever your techniques for learning a specialized vocabulary, begin to use the new terms whenever you can—in class, in discussion with instructors and other students, and in your assignments. This ability to *use* what you learn in speaking and writing is crucial to your full understanding of and participation in the discipline.

Identifying the style of a discipline

Becoming familiar with technical vocabulary is one important way of initiating yourself into a discipline or field of study. Another method is to identify stylistic features of the writing in that field. You will begin to assimilate these features automatically if you take time simply to immerse yourself in reading and thinking about the field. To speed up this process, however, study some representative pieces of writing in the field. Consider them with the following questions in mind.

■ How would you describe the overall *tone* of the writing? Is it very formal, somewhat formal, informal?

■ In general, how long are the sentences? How long are the paragraphs?

■ Are verbs generally active or passive—and why? Do active or passive verbs seem to be part of a characteristic manner of speaking used by writers and researchers in the field?

■ Do the writers use first person (*I*) or prefer terms such as *one* or *the investigator*? What is the effect of this stylistic choice?

■ Does the writing use visual elements such as graphs, tables, charts, or maps? How are these integrated into the text?

■ What bibliographical styles (such as MLA, APA, note-and-bibliography, or number style) are used? (See Chapters 43 and 44.)

Of course, writings within a single discipline may have different purposes and different styles. Although a research report is likely to follow a conventional form, a published speech greeting specialists at a convention may well be less formal and more personal no matter what the field. Furthermore, answering questions such as those on the previous page will not guarantee that you can produce a piece of writing similar to the one you are analyzing. Nevertheless, looking carefully at writing in the field brings you one step closer not only to producing similar writing but to producing more effective writing as well.

45d

Understanding the use of evidence

"Good reasons" form the core of any writing that argues a point, for they provide the *evidence* for the argument. Chapter 5 explains how to formulate good reasons. However, what is acceptable and persuasive evidence in one discipline may be more or less so in another. Observable, quantifiable data may constitute the very best evidence in, say, experimental psychology, but the same kind of data may be less appropriate—or even impossible to come by—in a historical study. As you grow familiar with any area of study, you will gather a sense of just what it takes to prove a point in that field. You can speed up this process or make it more efficient, however, by doing some investigating and questioning of your own. As you read your textbook and other assigned materials, make a point of noticing the use of evidence. The following questions are designed to help you do so.

- How do writers in the field use precedent and authority? What or who counts as an authority in this field? How are the credentials of an authority established?

- What use is made of empirical data (things that can be observed and measured)? What kinds of data are used? How are such data gathered and presented?

- How are statistics used? How is numerical information used and presented? Are tables, charts, or graphs common? How much weight do they seem to carry?

- How is logical reasoning used? How are definition, cause and effect, analogies, and examples used in this discipline?

- How does the field use primary and secondary sources? What are the primary materials—the firsthand sources of information—in this field? What are the secondary materials—the sources of information derived from others? How is each type of source likely to be presented?

USEFUL READINGS

Hemmeter, Thomas, and David Connors. "Research Papers in Economics: A Collaborative Approach." *Journal of Advanced Composition* 7 (1987): 81–91. Hemmeter and Connors describe their collaboratively taught course combining writing instruction in an advanced-level economics course. The essay focuses especially on the writing of the "end-of-the-term research paper."

Powell, Alfred. "A Chemist's View of Writing, Reading, and Thinking across the Curriculum." *CCC* 36 (1985): 414–18. Powell, a chemistry professor, outlines numerous discipline-based writing and reading projects that he assigns in a two-semester course sequence in organic chemistry.

Shamoon, Linda K., and Robert A. Schwegler. "Sociologists Reading Student Texts: Expectations and Perceptions." *Writing Instructor* 7 (Winter 1988): 71–81. Examines the expectations and perceptions that instructors have of their students' writing. A group of sociology instructors are asked two questions: (1) to what extent are instructor expectations and perceptions discipline specific? (2) what features of good expository writing do college instructors look for—thesis statements? topic sentences? paragraph coherence?

- In writing about literature, what kinds of textual evidence are cited? examples? information about its author? information about other texts the work refers to? dialogue? lines of verse?
- How are quotations used and integrated into the text?

In addition to carrying out your own investigation of the way evidence is used in your discipline, you may want to raise this issue in class. Ask your instructor how you can best go about making a case in that field.

EXERCISE 45.3

Do some reading in books and journals associated with your prospective major or a discipline of particular interest to you, using the questions above to study the use of evidence in that discipline. If you are keeping a writing log, make an entry in it summarizing what you have learned.

45e

Using conventional patterns and formats

You can gather all the evidence in the world and still fail to produce effective writing in your discipline if you do not know the field's conventions, the generally accepted format for organizing and presenting evidence. Again, these formats vary widely from discipline to discipline and sometimes from instructor to instructor, but patterns do emerge. In fact, disciplines may share similar conventions for similar types of studies. The typical laboratory report, for instance, follows a fairly standard organizational framework whether it is in botany, chemistry, or parasitology. A case study in sociology or education or anthropology likewise follows a typical organizational plan. And many disciplines share a conventional format for problem-solution reports: statement of problem, background for the problem's formulation, review of the literature on the subject, findings and possible solution, conclusions, and recommendations.

Your job in any discipline is to discover its conventional formats and organizing principles so that you can practice using them. This task is easy enough to begin. Ask your instructor to recommend some excellent examples of the kind of writing you will do in the course. Then analyze these examples in terms of format and organization. You might also look at major scholarly journals in your field, checking to see what types of formats seem most common and how each is organized. Study these examples, keeping in mind these questions about organization and format.

Everyone lives on the assumptions that a great deal of knowledge is not worth bothering about; though we all know that what looks trivial in one man's hands may turn out to be earth-shaking in another's, we simply cannot know very much, compared with what might be known, and we must therefore choose. What is shocking is not the act of choice which we all commit openly but the claim that some choices are wrong. Especially shocking is the claim that there is some knowledge that a [person] must have.
—WAYNE C. BOOTH

- What types of essays or reports are common in this field? What is the purpose of each type?
- What can a reader expect to find in each type of essay or report? What does each type assume about its readers?
- How is a particular type of essay or report organized? What are its main parts? Are they labeled with conventional headings? What logic underlies this sequence of parts?
- How does a particular type of essay or report show the connections among ideas? What assumptions of the discipline does it take for granted? What points does its organization emphasize?

The following sections illustrate three general patterns common in research essays—surveying literature, reporting experimental or field research, and interpreting sources.

Surveying literature in the social sciences

An introductory psychology class was given the assignment to write a brief literature review related to one aspect of child development, summarizing three journal articles addressing the topic, and drawing some conclusions based on their findings. Following are the notes Laura Brannon made analyzing first the assignment and then the vocabulary, style, evidence, and organizational pattern appropriate for the field of psychology. These notes correspond to the appropriate questions for analysis presented in 45a–45e.

ANALYZING THE ASSIGNMENT

1. I guess the purpose is to familiarize myself with some aspect of child development and to see several viewpoints in the field.
2. Assignment says to summarize three journal articles. Then, evaluate and interpret their findings.
3. *Literature review* is defined in the assignment.
4. The articles I plan to review each focus on a particular study, so I need to be able to see the strengths and weaknesses of each study. (I also must be able to understand their use of statistics to be able to evaluate the data and then must be able to draw conclusions based upon this evaluation.)
5. No specific format is specified.
6. By examining previous responses to similar assignments, I can determine an acceptable format—will ask professor for some.

FOR COLLABORATIVE WORK

If your students can provide assignments from various disciplines, have them carry out a similar analysis to the one here. Let them work in groups to analyze the assignments and their expectations.

USEFUL READING

Bazerman, Charles. *The Informed Writer: Using Sources in the Disciplines.* 2nd ed. Boston: Houghton, 1985. See pp. 293–300 for a brief discussion and example of literature reviews.

ANALYZING THE SPECIALIZED VOCABULARY

1. Articles will have technical vocabulary from psychology and statistics.
2. I will need to know terms such as *variables, inter-rater agreement,* and so on to understand the readings.
3. Terms showing reliability of research need to be in my summary.

ANALYZING THE STYLE

1. Sentences and paragraphs tend to be short.
2. Many passive verbs are used, especially in the sections presenting data (resembles newspaper style).
3. Overall tone is very formal (sometimes less so in the introduction).
4. First person is used very little.
5. Visual elements are used when necessary to clarify the findings. They are first mentioned in text (i.e., *see Table 1*) and then table follows (i.e., at end of paragraph).
6. Professor says journals use APA style; must find out what this means.

ANALYZING THE USE OF EVIDENCE

1. Psychology relies heavily on previous findings. Credentials are often based upon data alone.
2. Experimental data are very important. Experiments are devised to control for all variables other than the one being manipulated. (If extraneous variables are not controlled, the data will probably be rejected as worthless.)
3. Statistics are very important—results must be within the 0.05 level of significance (only a 5 percent possibility that the results were caused by chance). Probabilities must be presented with results, but tables and graphs are used as necessary.
4. Cause-effect logic is important. Frequently, generalizations are made concerning the "real" world based on current research findings.
5. All three articles report on primary research.
6. Quotations are used to help make a point.

ANALYZING CONVENTIONAL PATTERNS

1. In a literature survey, the three articles can be discussed in separate sections. Label each one with a heading. Change to new section for each article discussed, and introduce each.
2. Arrange articles in chronological order.
3. Summarize each article and include quotations as appropriate to make my main points clear.
4. End with my conclusions about what articles show and about what may happen in the future.

After browsing through her textbook and thinking about the assignment, Laura Brannon decided to focus on child abuse. A trip to the library turned up many articles on this subject, and she chose three. She summarized the three articles, worked through a draft, and analyzed it, following the revision guidelines in Chapter 4. Here is the opening and closing of her essay, a literature survey reviewing three articles and drawing conclusions about what they show and mean.

Note that she first presents the subject of her literature review and acknowledges the complexity of the issue—child abuse—as a means of leading in to the three articles she intends to survey. She then summarizes the first article, giving pertinent information about the subjects of the study, the size of the study, and the methods used before presenting significant results and reporting on shortcomings noted by the authors. Her summaries of the other two articles have been omitted in the excerpt printed here.

In her conclusion, she moves on to offer her own interpretation of the significance of the three articles and draws out the implications of these studies for those who seek to prevent child abuse. Note that her citations and references follow APA style guidelines throughout (see Chapter 44).

                    Early Detection of Child Abuse

     There is no simple one-word answer to the question
of what causes child abuse. The abuse of children
results from a complex interaction among parent, child,
and environmental factors. This complexity does not
necessarily mean, however, that potential victims and
abusers cannot be identified before serious damage is
done. Researchers have examined methods of detecting
potential or actual child abuse.

            Prediction of Child Abuse: Interviews

     In a study by Altemeier, O'Connor, Vietze, Sandler,
and Sherrod (1984), 1,400 women between 9 and 40 weeks
pregnant were interviewed to test their abusive
tendencies. Four researchers were present (with an
inter-rater agreement of 90% or better). The Maternal
History Interview included questions about the mother's
own childhood, self-image, support from others,
parenting philosophy, attitudes toward pregnancy, and
health-related problems (including substance abuse).

Maternal and paternal stresses during the preceding year were measured with a modified Life Stress Inventory. Any information not included in the standard interview but felt by the researchers to make the mother a high risk for abuse of her child––for example, being overtly untruthful––was also recorded. When the infants were 21 to 48 months old, the Juvenile Court and the Department of Human Services were checked for reports of their abuse or neglect.

Although the interview predicted abuse (p < .0001), its ability to predict decreased with time; for example, although ''six of seven families reported for abuse within the first nine months following the interview were high risk, . . . after 24 months only one of seven had been assigned to this group'' (Altemeier et al., p. 395). The researchers point out some shortcomings of their study, particularly the high rate of false positives. (Only 6% of the high-risk population was reported for abuse, 22% if failure to thrive and neglect were included.) Although many incidents of abuse may go unreported (which could account for some of the false positives), this false-positive percentage should be reduced. Also, it would be preferable if the role of subjective judgments in the method for prediction could be reduced as well.

[Brannon's review of two additional studies follows.]

Conclusions

Overall, the findings of these studies seem to indicate that tests can be devised to predict potential child abusers. The study by Murphy, Orkow, and Nicola (1985), which relies less on subjective judgments, has a significantly lower false positive rate than the earlier

TEACHING PRACTICE

Ask students to identify the tone of Laura Brannon's conclusion and discuss its appropriateness. What difference could another tone— for example, angry—make in this essay?

study by Altemeier et al. (1984). Therefore, although such tests have not yet been perfected, they appear to be improving.

The two studies tried to integrate the complex relationships between child, parent, and environmental factors that are involved in child abuse. Ideally, if potential abusers could be identified early enough, they could undergo treatment even before the child is born. Of course, a parent could not be separated from a child on the basis of one test, and therefore, the results should remain confidential to avoid any potential for abuse of the test itself.

Whereas the tests look carefully at the parent's situation, the injury variables analyzed in the Johnson and Showers study (1985) focus attention on the child. If teachers, neighbors, relatives, or other people notice that children have frequent injuries (especially with the locations, types, and causes associated with different ages and races), abuse can be detected early and perhaps stopped.

References

Altemeier, W. A., O'Connor, S., Vietze, P., Sandler, H., & Sherrod, K. (1984). Prediction of child abuse: A prospective study of feasibility. <u>Child</u> <u>Abuse</u> <u>and</u> <u>Neglect:</u> <u>The</u> <u>International</u> <u>Journal</u>, <u>8</u>, 393–400.

Johnson, C. F., & Showers, J. (1985). Injury variables in child abuse. <u>Child</u> <u>Abuse</u> <u>and</u> <u>Neglect:</u> <u>The</u> <u>International</u> <u>Journal</u>, <u>9</u>, 207–215.

Murphy, S., Orkow, B., & Nicola, R. (1985). Prenatal prediction of child abuse and neglect: A prospective study. <u>Child</u> <u>Abuse</u> <u>and</u> <u>Neglect:</u> <u>The</u> <u>International</u> <u>Journal</u>, <u>9</u>, 225–235.

45g

Reporting research in the natural sciences

A biology class was asked to write a report analyzing a genetic question about a particular species of crayfish: when a female heterozygous for red claws was mated with a male with black claws, the resulting offspring included 154 red claws, 235 black claws, and 43 blue claws. Students were to explain the results by constructing hypotheses and evaluating them through the use of the Chi-square test, to elaborate on gene expression, and to refer to at least two scientific journals. Excerpts from Julie Slater's response to this assignment follow. Note that her report follows the format recommended by her science instructor: the Introduction explains the principles on which the experiment was conducted; the Methods and Materials section offers a brief description of the experiment; and the Results section explains what the experiment produced. In the Summary section (which follows the omitted Discussion section), she presents the crosses she made in determining the male genotype and explains what factors her procedures could not take into account. Note too that her citations and Literature Cited use the number style (see 44d).

Determining the Genotype of One Parent—
When the Other Is Known—by Evaluation
of the Offspring Frequencies

INTRODUCTION

The purpose of this experiment was to determine the genotype of a male crayfish with black claws that was mated with a red-clawed female known to be heterozygous for claw color. This determination was made by evaluating the frequencies of three different claw colors observed in the offspring. Hypotheses involving Mendelian principles of genetics and various possible hybrid crosses were proposed and either proven false or recognized as probable by meeting the given stipulations of a black mated to a heterozygous red and the offspring frequencies (1).

METHODS AND MATERIALS

Two crayfish of a particular species complex were mated. The female, known to be heterozygous for the phenotype of red claws, was mated with a male that expressed black claws. The offspring were grouped according to claw color and counted. The data were analyzed statistically using a Chi-square test.

RESULTS

In the 432 offspring produced, three phenotypes were noted: 235 crayfish with black claws, 154 with red, and 43 with blue. The observed ratio was 5.4 : 3.6 : 1.

DISCUSSION

[Slater's seven-paragraph discussion follows.]

CONCLUSION

The genotype of the male crayfish was determined as rrBb. This determination was made by using a dihybrid cross of RrBb x rrBb, where epistasis was taken into account, with an expected ratio of 4:3:1. It does not take into account the possibility that the offspring frequencies have been altered by interference during gene replication, transcription, or translation. Other knowledge that should be considered is the evidence that coloring of body surfaces is governed by at least three to five loci and that genes can actually ''cheat'' to ensure self-survival. Each of these possibilities could create a result that would require further extensive study into the chromosomal makeup of the species. Despite these possibilities, however, the genotype of the male was proposed and accepted as rrBb.

MONOHYBRID CROSSES

    <u>Figure 1</u>

    Rr x rr →   1 Rr red

    f,red m,black   1 rr black

    f=female, m=male

    <u>Figure 2</u>

    Rr x Rr → 3 R_ ?

    f,?   m,?   1rr ?

DIHYBRID CROSSES

    <u>Figure 3</u>

    RrBb x RrBb →   9/16 R_B_ ?

    f,?   m,?   3/16 R_bb ?

                       3/16 rrB_ ?

                       1/16 rrbb ?

    <u>Figure 4</u>

    RrBb x rrBb →   3/8 R_B_   red

    f,red m,black   1/8 R_bb ?

                       3/8 rrB_ black

                       1/8 rrbb ?

    <u>Figure 5</u> (involving epistasis)

    RrBb x rrBb →   3/8 R_B_ red

     f,red m,black 1/8 R_bb black

                       3/8 rrB_ black

                       1/8 rrbb blue

CENTRAL DOGMA

    <u>Figure 6</u>

    replication

       DNA →   mRNA   → Protein

           transcription translation

                     involving

                     tRNA

LITERATURE CITED

1. Strickberger, M. W. Genetics. New York: Macmillan; 1968.

2. Branda, R. F.; Eaton, J. W. Skin color and nutrient photolysis: An evolutionary hypothesis. Sci. 8:625-626; 1978.

3. Gardner, E. J. Principles of genetics. New York: Wiley; 1965.

4. Crow, J. F. Genes that violate Mendel's rules. Sci. Amer. 237(3): 134-146; 1979.

5. Purves, W. K.; Orians, G. H. Life: The science of biology. Sunderland: Sinauer Associated Inc.; 1987.

45h

Interpreting sources in the humanities

In a time of rapid and radical change such as ours, those disciplines that help us think carefully and critically about what it means to be human. Of these, the study of literature offers a wealth of insight into people's motives, character, and potential. Reading and writing about literature thus offer powerful means of exploring the human condition. Such explorations can help us not only understand other people more completely but also take the pulse of our own humanity.

1

Understanding the language of literary interpretation

In writing about literature, you may need to use a number of special terms to help focus your discussion. In doing so, you might raise questions about the intentions, sources, or influences of the writer; the arrangement of the work; the nature of the work's readers; or its relationship to the larger social and cultural context. The following list includes terms that are frequently used in the close reading of literary works to analyze their structure and style.

To analyze the system of sounds in a work, you might use the following terms:

BACKGROUND

Although the word *humanities* originally referred to the classical works of Greek and Latin—and in some English-speaking countries still denotes the study of Latin texts—the humanities in American education generally refer to learning about human culture. What does it mean to be human? Scientist Donna Haraway suggests that answering this question may today be more difficult than ever before. In "A Manifesto for Cybourgs," she demonstrates how two boundaries—one between humans and the natural world, another between humans and machines—are increasingly blurred, resulting in "gray areas" where it is extremely difficult if not impossible to say which is which.

USEFUL READING

Holman, C. Hugh, and William Harman. *A Handbook to Literature.* 5th ed. New York: Macmillan, 1986. A useful and convenient reference guide to literary terminology.

Alliteration the repetition of sound to create special emphasis or rhythm, as in this sectence from Eudora Welty: "Monsieur Boule inserted a delicate dagger in Mademoiselle's left side and departed with a posed immediacy."

Meter the rhythm of verse, as determined by the kind—iambic, dactylic, and so on—and number of feet (groups of syllables)—pentameter, tetrameter—in a line. Iambic pentameter indicates five feet of two syllables, with the stess falling on the second of the two, as in the following line: An Aged Man is but a paltry thing.

Rhythm the beat or pattern of stresses in a line of poetry, including traditional metrical patterns or the movement of free verse, and in prose, created by repetition, parallelism, and a variation of sentence length and structure. Robert Frost's "Fire and Ice" (in Chapter 29) uses a basic iambic rhythm, with every other syllable stressed: ˇ/ˇ/ˇ/.

Rhyme scheme the pattern of end rhymes in a poem, usually designated by the letters *a, b, c*. The Emily Dickinson poem (in Chapter 35) has a rhyme scheme of *aabccd*. A Shakespearean sonnet typically follows a rhyme scheme of *abab cdcd efef gg*.

Stanza a division of a poem: a four-line stanza is called a *quatrain;* a two-line stanza, a *couplet*. Robert Francis's poem (in Chapter 13) contains five two-line stanzas.

Literary language is sometimes distinguished from the nonliterary by its purposeful use of imagery, often to "make strange" or defamiliarize the ordinary so that we can look at it in new ways. The following terms may find use in any discussion of imagy.

Analogy a comparison of two things that are alike in some respect, often to explain one of the things or to represent it more vividly by relating it to the second. A simile is an explicit analogy, a metaphor an implied one. In his essay "The World's Biggest Membrane" Lewis Thomas draws an analogy between earth's atmosphere and a giant membrane.

Figurative language the use of metaphor, simile, personification, and other figures of speech that enrich description. (See 5f3 and 27d.)

Imagery the vivid descriptions and figures of speech that evoke a picture in the reader's mind or appeal to the other senses. The running sore in "Dream Deferred (Harlem)" (in Chapter 27) creates such a vivid image.

Symbolism the use of one thing to represent other things or ideas, as the flag symbolizes patriotism or as ice symbolizes hate in Frost's "Fire and Ice" (in Chapter 29).

The codes and structures of narrative are very important to literary interpretation. You might want to examine the complexities which arise from representations of the author, the characters and their relationships, or the structures of time and space in a work. Some helpful terms for doing so include the following.

Character   the people in a story, who have different motivations and who may act, react, and change accordingly during the course of a story. In Amy Dierst's essay on *The Third Life of Grange Copeland*, she examines the characters in the story as one way of interpreting its meaning.

Dialogue   the conversation among characters, which can show how they interact and suggest why they act as they do. The passage from Eudora Welty in 33b demonstrates the use of dialogue in a short story.

Implied author   the "author" that is inferred or implied by the text, as distinct from the real person/author. In *The Adventures of Huckleberry Finn*, for example, the real author is Samuel Clemens (or Mark Twain); the implied author is the "author" we imagine as Clemens presents himself in the text.

Intertextuality   the system of references in one text to other texts. You might think of texts as being part of a vast intertextual conversation, with one text echoing one or many others through quotations, allusions, parodies, or thematic references. Gary Larson's Far Side Frankenstein cartoons, for example, refer intertextually to Mary Shelley's original novel (*Frankenstein*) as well as to many movie versions and to other works that treat the theme of the dangers or limits of science.

Irony   the use of language to suggest the opposite, or nearly the opposite, of what the words usually mean, as in saying that being caught in a freezing downpour is "delightful." See 27d.

Narrator   the person telling a story. In a short story, poem, or novel, the narrator may be a character or may adopt an omniscient viewpoint outside the story. In *The Adventures of Huckleberry Finn*, for example, the narrator is Huck Finn himself.

Parody   an imitation intended for humorous or satiric effect, as in Dana Carvey's parodic imitations of George Bush. Exercise 23.7 shows an example of a student parody of Edgar Allan Poe's style.

Plot   the events selected by the writer to reveal the conflicts among or within the characters, often arranged in chronological order but sometimes including flashbacks to past events. In her essay on *The Third Life of Grange Copeland* (see 45h3), Amy Dierst describes events of the plot.

Point of view   the perspective from which the work is presented—in fiction, by a narrator outside the story or a character speaking in first or third person; in poetry, by the poet or a role assumed by the poet. In "Theme for English B" (in Chapter 28), the point of view is that of the student.

Protagonist   the hero, heroine, or main character, often opposed by an *antagonist,* as Othello is opposed by Iago.

Setting   the scene of the literary work, including the time, physical location, and social situation. "Theme for English B" (in Chapter 28) is set in Harlem during the 1950s.

Style   the writer's choice of words and sentence structures. Two devices characteristic of John F. Kennedy's style are repetition and inverted word order. (See the beginning of Chapter 23 for an example from his Inaugural Address.)

Theme   a major and often recurring subject or topic. Amy Dierst discusses the theme of conflict between men and women in her essay about *The Third Life of Grange Copeland* (see 45h3). The predominant theme often reveals the larger meaning of the work, including any thoughts or insights about life or people in general.

Tone   the writer's attitude, conveyed through specific word choices and structures. In her essay arguing in favor of Clarence Thomas for the U.S. Supreme Court (in Chapter 5), Maya Angelou's tone is solemn and serious. 18

Looking for the features identified in the special vocabulary of literary study is one way to begin training yourself to read, interpret, and criticize literary works—to join the conversation of English studies.

2

Developing a critical stance

As a reader of literature, you are not a neutral observer, not an empty cup into which the "meaning" of a literary work is poured. If such were the case, literary works would have exactly the same meanings for all of us, and reading would be a fairly boring affair. If you have ever gone to a movie with a friend and each come away with a completely different understanding or response, you already have ample evidence that literature never has just one meaning.

Just as all your reading is based to some extent on your personal history and knowledge and reasons for reading, so your writing about literature is based to some extent on your own critical stance, what you've read and where you're coming from as a writer. What perspective do you bring? How do you approach the text you're writing about? In literary studies today, such stances vary widely, and you may encounter in your professors a number of different approaches.

In general, student writers tend to adopt one of three primary stances: a *text-based stance* that builds an argument by focusing on specific features of the literary text in question; a *context-based stance* that builds an argument by focusing on the context in which a literary text exists; a *reader-based stance* that focuses on the response of a particular reader to the text and an interpretation that grows out of his or her personal response; or some combination of these approaches. The rest of this chapter introduces three student writers, each of whom takes one of these three critical stances.

USEFUL READING

Lynn, Stephen. "A Passage into Critical Theory." *CE* 52 (1990): 258–71. A brief guide for teachers to some schools of critical theory including new criticism, structuralism, deconstruction, psychological criticism, and feminist criticism. Lynn offers concrete examples of these critical approaches by applying each of them to the same passage.

3

A text-based stance

The writer of the following essay, Amy Dierst, responded to an assignment for an introductory literature class that asked her to "analyze some aspect of one of the works read this term." This is a fairly open-ended assignment, and so she checked with her instructor to make sure that her chosen focus, "the role of men," would qualify as an "aspect" of a work to be analyzed. Note that because the assignment called for an analysis of a work read by the entire class, the writer did not need to review the plot. As a student in a literature class, she could assume that analyzing characters and themes was an appropriate form of interpretation.

This kind of literary interpretation, based largely on specific evidence from the literary text itself, is the approach most students take in writing about literature. Amy Dierst makes a claim about the role of men in *The Third Life of Grange Copeland* that she then substantiates by citing passages from the primary source, the novel itself, as well as from secondary sources, other interpretations of the novel.

```
      The Role of Men in The Third Life of Grange Copeland
           Many observers of American society charge that it
      has created a distorted definition of manhood and
      produced men who, in their need to assert control of
      their lives, release their frustration at the expense of
      women.  In her novel The Third Life of Grange Copeland,
      Alice Walker addresses this theme from the point of view
      of black men and women, for whom racism heightens the
      distortion and its consequences.  She suggests that by
      stifling black men's sense of freedom and control, a
      racist society creates frustrations that are released in
      family violence and inherited by their children.
      Because his wife and children are the only aspect of the
      black man's life that he can control, they become the
      scapegoat upon which his frustrations are released.  As
      Walker's title suggests, she sees redemption, or
      spiritual rebirth into a new life, as the best defense
      against society's injustice.  Though Walker's male
      characters have been labeled by some as either
```

heartlessly cruel or pathetically weak (Steinem 89), many of them, like Grange Copeland, do change during the course of a work. Individual transformation stimulates the potential for change in the social system as a whole.

In this novel, Walker shows how the social and economic system of the 1920s offered a futile existence to Southern black families. Grange Copeland, like most Southern black men of his era, lived and worked on a farm owned and operated by a white man. This system, called sharecropping, did not allow for future planning or savings, for everything earned was returned to the white man's pocket for rent. Thus sharecropping, like slavery before it, contributed to the black man's feelings of powerlessness. In his desperation and helplessness, Grange turns to exert power in the one place he is dominant, his home. He releases his frustration by abusing his family in a weekly cycle of cruelty:

> By Thursday, Grange's gloominess reached its peak and he grimaced respectfully, with veiled eyes, at the jokes told by the man who drove the truck [the white farm owner, Mr. Shipley]. On Thursday night, he stalked the house from room to room pulled himself up and swung from the rafters. Late Saturday night Grange would come home lurching drunk, threatening to kill his wife and Brownfield [his son] stumbling and shooting his shotgun. (Walker 12)

At other times, Grange displays his frustration through neglect, a more psychologically disturbing device that later affects Brownfield's emotional stability. Grange's inability to rise above his own discontent with his life and express feeling toward his

TEACHING PRACTICE

Call students' attention to the way quotations and examples from the novel are used as evidence in this essay and ask them to compare this kind of evidence with the evidence presented in the previous student essays.

TEACHING PRACTICE

One of the difficulties students often have in writing essays about literature is weaving quotations smoothly into the text of their own. Refer students back to the discussion of quotations in Chapter 42 and ask them to evaluate the use of quotations in this essay. Are they introduced clearly? Do they "fit in" to the preceding sentence? Does the student writer comment sufficiently on their significance?

son becomes his most abusive act. Eventually, he
abandons his family completely for a new life in the
North. Even when he says good-bye, ''even in private
and in the dark and with his son, presumably asleep,
Grange could not bear to touch his son with his hand''
(Walker 121).

Brownfield picks up where Grange left off, giving
his father's violent threats physical form by beating
his own wife and children regularly. Although he, too,
blames the whites for driving him to brutality, Walker
suggests that his actions are not excusable on these
grounds. By the time he reaches adulthood, sharecropping is not a black man's only option and cannot be
used as a scapegoat. Nevertheless, he chooses to
relinquish his freedom and work for Mr. Shipley.

By becoming the overseer on Mr. Shipley's
plantation, Brownfield positions himself for the same
failure that ruined his father. As Trudier Harris
notes, over time Brownfield's loss of control of his
life turns his feelings of depression and lost pride
into anger, and his own destructive nature turns him
toward violence and evil (240). Unable or unwilling to
take responsibility for himself, Brownfield blames his
own inadequacies on his wife, Mem, who bears the brunt
of his anger:

> Brownfield beat his once lovely wife now,
> regularly, because it made him feel briefly
> good. Every Saturday night he beat her,
> trying to pin the blame for his failure on her
> by imprinting it on her face, and she . . .
> repaid him by becoming a haggard . . . witch.
> (Walker 55)

Brownfield demonstrates his power by stripping Mem,
a former schoolteacher, of anything that would threaten

his manhood. Reasoning that her knowledge is a power that he cannot have and therefore she does not deserve, he wants her to speak in her old dialect so that she will not appear to be more intelligent than he does. He also wants her to be ugly because her ugliness makes it easier for him to justify beating her. He wants her to reach a state of ultimate degradation where any strength of her character will be quickly extinguished by a blow to the face or a kick in the side. In fact, ''he rather enjoyed her desolation because in it she had no hopes. She was totally weak, totally without view, without a sky'' (Walker 59). In a final attempt to release his frustration, as Paul Theroux suggests, Brownfield kills Mem, literally and symbolically obliterating the remainder of her identity––her face (2).

But in the face of this brutality and degradation, Walker raises the possibility of a different fate for black men and women. While in the North, Grange undergoes a spiritual rebirth and, as Karen Gaston notes, comes to understand that white injustice is not alone responsible for the cruelty of black men toward their families (278). He also realizes that to weaken and destroy a wife and family is not a sign of manhood, saying:

> You gits just as weak as water, no feeling of doing nothing yourself, you begins to destroy everybody around you, and you blame it on crackers [whites]. Nobody's as powerful as we make out to be, we got our own souls, don't we? (Walker 207)

Grange redeems his spirit in his ''third life'' with his granddaughter, Ruth. His objective now is not to destroy what he loves but to cherish it. When a judge orders Ruth to go back to live with Brownfield after his

---

TEACHING PRACTICE

Ask students to identify the tone—or dominant impression—the writer of this essay creates and discuss how persuasive and effective they find the tone to be.

release from prison, Grange kills him before this horror becomes a reality. Although he is shot to death as he tries to escape the police, he dies a redeemed man and passes his inner strength of hope on to his granddaughter.

The impact of the racist system of the South unquestionably pervades the lives of Walker's black characters. Nevertheless, she does not portray as justifiable the destructive need of black men to exert their strength at the expense of the weak. It is necessary to be aware of societal injustices and their effects but not to use them as excuses for individual cruelty. Through her characters, Walker gives us faith that cruelty turns back on itself. Some meet tragic endings, but the redemption of Grange shows Walker's faith in change. She envisions the children of tomorrow inheriting not hatred and selfishness but compassion and honesty. Her affirmative voice demonstrates the potential for social change through individual transformation.

Here is Amy Dierst's list of works cited in her essay.

Works Cited

Gaston, Karen C. ''Women in the Lives of Grange
    Copeland.'' <u>College Language Association Journal</u>
    24 (1981): 276-86.

Harris, Trudier. ''Violence in <u>The Third Life of Grange</u>
    <u>Copeland</u>.'' <u>College Language Association Journal</u>
    19 (1975): 238-47.

Steinem, Gloria. ''Do You Know This Woman? She Knows
    You--A Profile on Alice Walker.'' <u>Ms</u>. June 1982:
    89-94.

Theroux, Paul. Rev. of <u>The Third Life of Grange Copeland</u>, by Alice Walker. <u>Bookworld</u> 4 Sept. 1970: 2.

Walker, Alice. <u>The Third Life of Grange Copeland</u>. New York: Harcourt, 1970.

4

A context-based stance

The following essay was written for a literature class focusing on the Renaissance, and students were given a free hand in choosing topics as long as they wrote about one of the works studied in the class. Faye Purol decided to investigate some of the performance history of Shakespeare's *Othello*, and in doing so she found that this play was among the most frequently produced plays in the antebellum South. Interested to find that this play should be so popular in a time of legally sanctioned racial inequality, she decided to investigate this context for *Othello*, a decision that led her to consider elements *outside* the text of the play and to draw on other sources—like contemporary reviews and playbills—that usually do not appear in a text-based essay like the one on *Grange Copeland*. Here is the opening of Faye Purol's essay.

Shakespeare's Moor in the Old South

The first performance of a Shakespearean work in the Old South took place in Williamsburg, Virginia, in 1751. That play was <u>Richard III</u>, and from then until the Civil War began in 1861, Shakespeare was the most popular dramatist in the New World. From the first, <u>Othello</u> was among the most frequently performed plays, somewhat remarkable in a time and place in history where slavery was legally sanctioned. <u>Othello</u>, with its then-shocking theme of miscegenation, was in most every theater's repertoire, and while sometimes altered and a few times banned, it was usually performed just as Shakespeare wrote it, to favorable audience receptions. I will examine the circumstances under which <u>Othello</u> was

TEACHING PRACTICE

Refer students to the discussion of introductory paragraphs on pp. 586–87. Then ask them to consider Faye Purol's introduction: In what ways does it engage readers' interest and focus attention on the topic? Ask students to offer alternative strategies for opening this essay.

FOR COLLABORATIVE WORK

Faye Purol was particularly interested in this approach to her topic because she herself is from the South and wanted to explore her own background more thoroughly. Consider asking students to spend five or ten minutes brainstorming in small groups about where they come from and the relationship those backgrounds might have to any literary work they are studying. You may want to ask students to explore possible connections in a journal entry or to discuss the results of their brainstorming with you. The object is to help them make some personal connection with the work in question.

TEACHING PRACTICE

Call students' attention to the kinds of evidence used in this context-based essay: historical data about performances of the play, information about the audiences attending the performances, contemporary newspaper articles about performances, letters to the editor. Ask them to compare this evidence with the kinds used in Amy Dierst's essay on *The Third Life of Grange Copeland* (pp. 686–90). Doing so will help students understand the relationship between the critical stance a writer takes toward a literary work and the kinds of evidence he or she looks for.

performed; instances when the script was altered or the play banned completely; and possible reasons why, at a time and place least expected, performances of Othello were consistently popular events.

Like the Globe and other theaters in England, American theaters attracted all levels of people; as James H. Dorman observes, landed gentry, who were familiar with books and well-versed in art, enjoyed the pageantry alongside less educated riverboat captains and crews, shopkeepers, laborers, bonded and free citizens, American Indians, and strangely enough, members of that euphemistically named ''peculiar institution,'' slaves (233). Financial circumstances necessitated that theaters cater to all classes, and persons of color were admitted to theater galleries along with everyone else. Hence, Dorman notes, black people, both slave and free, were always a part of the audience.

> [E]vidence of theatre attendance by Negroes abounds in the sources of the period. A letter in the Richmond Compiler as early as November of 1819 complained that the theatre was likely to [be] a corrupting influence on slaves, not only because it took them from their work, but because of ''the scenes they witness, and the society they mix with in the gallery.'' (234)

No doubt, slaves who saw Othello had opinions about what they saw. No accounts have been found that describe what any of them thought about the play, however, which can certainly be attributed to the fact that few slaves had been taught to read or write. . . .

The Virginia Gazette reported an incident which occurred when the emperor and empress of the Cherokee Nation attended a performance of Othello:

> During the performance the fighting with naked
> swords on the stage caused such great surprise
> that the empress ordered her attendants to go
> and prevent the actors from killing one
> another. (Dunn 74)

Presumably, the empress was impressed with the action
rather than with any racial implications, and history
reveals little evidence that many American Indians
attended the theater. Still, audiences viewing Othello
could be said to be as varied in social strata as
America itself. . . .

Investigating a certain context in which *Othello* was performed led this
writer to performance data, newspaper accounts, and letters to the editor. In
addition, she might have looked at many other things—contemporary
reviews, advertisements, theater programs, actors' journals. Though drama
especially lends itself to analysis of context, because it's performed in various
contexts, you can investigate the context of most any literary work. Looking
at accounts of the Great Depression, for example, could yield insights into
the characters in John Steinbeck's *Grapes of Wrath*. Here is a partial list of
works cited in Faye Purol's complete essay.

Works Cited

Dorman, James H., Jr. Theatre in the Ante Bellum South.
    Chapel Hill: U of North Carolina P, 1967.

Dunn, Esther Cloudman. Shakespeare in America. New
    York: Macmillan, 1939.

Holbein, Woodrow L. ''Shakespeare in Charleston,
    1800—1860.'' Shakespeare in the South: An
    Overview. Ed. Philip C. Kolin. Jackson: UP of
    Mississippi, 1983. 88—111.

Shockley, Martin S. ''The Richmond Theatre, 1780—1790.''
    Virginia Magazine of History and Biography July
    1952: 421—22.

——. ''Shakespeare's Plays in the Richmond Theatre,
    1819—1838.'' Shakespeare Association Bulletin Apr.
    1940: 88—94.

TEACHING PRACTICE

If you are interested in using reading journals in your class, you might want to look at almost any issue of *Reader: Essays in Reader-Oriented Theory, Criticism, and Pedagogy,* edited by Elizabeth Flynn and published by Michigan Technological University. Many teachers find that keeping such journals on a regular basis gives students valuable practice in writing about literature and often leads to insights that can be developed in a critical essay.

TEACHING PRACTICE

Note that this student is writing in her reader-response journal and, as a result, is at times informal and almost always centered on her own response. Ask students to read the journal entry, looking for each instance of Amy Lewis's personal response and each reference to her own personal experience. Refer students to Hughes's poem on p. 431. Then ask them to prepare a journal entry of their own, responding either to Hughes's poem or to Amy Lewis's response to it.

TEACHING PRACTICE

Call students' attention to the way in which Amy Lewis works a quotation from the poem smoothly into the first sentence of her second paragraph. Ask students to offer alternative versions of this sentence.

5

A reader-based stance

The following except by Amy Lewis was written in a class that used reading journals as a means of capturing and analyzing personal responses to the literary works studied. The assignment asked students to "choose one of the poems read in class and record in your journal your responses to the poem, beginning with your dominant or overall response, tracing the causes of that response, and moving from your response to an interpretation of the poem." Note that this journal assignment allows for a slightly more informal tone as well as for references to the reader's personal life and history. Note also that it does not call for any sources other than the text and the reader's own response to it.

As specified in the assignment, this essay begins with the student's personal response to the poem, looks to see what might account for this response, and then moves to her interpretation of the poem. If a context-based analysis looks outside the work as a way to illuminate its meaning, a reader-based analysis looks *inside*, to the unique responses of one reader.

```
Theme for Emerson, Thoreau, Whitman, Melville--and Me
     My first response to ''Theme for English B'' was a
sense of empathy with the speaker's feelings of
alienation from the university--specifically, from the
educated white man's university.  Hughes makes this
alienation clear by describing the student's lonely,
tedious journey from school down the hill to his
solitary room in another world, the ''Harlem Branch Y.''
As a woman, I suffer a similar sense of alienation at
school when a middle-aged, white, male professor hands
me his syllabus for a nineteenth-century American
literature course: Emerson, Thoreau, Whitman, and
Melville--no women, no people of color, nothing but
white males.  I like Emerson, but the lopsidedness of
the syllabus almost makes me not want to get close to
any of the other authors.  For whatever reason, nothing
in their writing motivates me to write.
```

As the student in ''Theme for English B''
questions, so do I: It's <u>not</u> that simple to ''let that
page come out of you.'' Does the instructor really want
to hear about the pages this student might have inside
him, writing in his room at the Harlem Y? I too wonder,
how can I express my isolation from those white male
writers in my responses <u>to</u> them? By thinking about who
he is and what he likes to do, Hughes's student reaches
some understanding of himself and of what he might write
for his English theme. He realizes that while Harlem is
a part of him, so too is the world of New York City,
which surrounds Harlem. The student defines himself by
focusing on what he enjoys in life (''I like to eat,
sleep, drink, and be in love, / I like to work, read,
learn, and understand life.'') and then recognizes these
to be experiences he and his white instructor share.

How then can I respond to the male authors, the
male professor? For me, the pages are colored by my
struggle to respond in the same way that Hughes's
student says his page ''will not be white.'' Just as
what he writes is composed of himself, but also partly
of the white instructor, so it is for me: The pages that
I write for my American literature course contain parts
of me <u>and</u> of my white, male professor since I certainly
internalize some of his lectures, some class discussion.
And at the same time, as I speak up in class, as I
respond to those authors, so too are those around me,
including the professor, touched by what I think and
say. As the student in the poem points out, we are all
a part of everyone we come into contact with—and they,
a part of us. By virtue of our interaction, we are
constantly learning from one another, which is how we
grow. Maybe that is what Hughes means when he says
''That's American.''

FOR COLLABORATIVE WORK

Amy Lewis concludes her journal entry by focusing on how we are all part of one another's experience. Ask students to read over her response to this poem and then to spend ten minutes working in groups to answer the following questions: 1) What other conclusion might Amy Lewis have drawn in her journal? 2) In one or two sentences, how might you word that conclusion?

EXERCISE 45.4   Reading with an Eye for Critical Stance

Find a review of a book, and read it carefully. What is the writer's claim about the book, and how does he or she substantiate that claim? What critical stance(s) does he or she take in interpreting the work: one based on the text, one based on the context, or one based on the reader's own response?

FOR COLLABORATIVE WORK

Ask students to bring the results of their examinations of their essays to class. Then group them according to discipline—all engineers together, sociology majors together and so forth. Ask them to compare notes and, as a group, to prepare a brief description of the conventions of writing in their particular discipline. Then ask each group to report to the class as a whole.

EXERCISE 45.5   Taking Inventory: Writing in a Discipline

Choose a piece of writing you have produced for a particular discipline—an essay on literature, a laboratory report, a review of the literature in the discipline, or any other assignment. Examine it closely for its use of that discipline's vocabulary, style, methods of proof, and conventional format. How comfortable are you in writing a piece of this kind? In what ways are you using the conventions of the discipline easily and well? What conventions of the discipline give you difficulty, and why? If you are keeping a writing log, make an entry in it on what you need to know about how to write effectively in this discipline. Use this entry as the basis for interviewing an instructor in this field.

46

Writing Essay Examinations

"If you can't write it," says author and former college dean Arthur Adams, "you don't know it." While Adams's statement is debatable in some circumstances, it certainly applies to essay examinations, where writing is the way to demonstrate what you know.

Writing an effective essay examination requires two important abilities: recalling information and organizing the information in order to draw relevant conclusions from it. These conclusions form the thesis of the essay while the information serves as support. While this process sounds simple, writing an effective essay examination under pressure in limited time can be a daunting task. This chapter suggests ways to turn this sometimes daunting task into a perfectly manageable one.

EXERCISE 46.1

Create a question you think you might be likely to encounter on an essay examination in a class you are currently taking. Then write a paragraph or two about what you would need to know in order to write an A+ answer.

Preparing for essay examinations

In getting ready for an essay examination, nothing can take the place of knowing the subject well. You can, in other words, prepare for an essay examination throughout the term by taking careful notes of lectures, texts, and other assigned reading. You may want to outline a reading assignment,

FOR THE WRITING LOG

Ask students to write a journal entry about their previous experiences with essay exams. What strategies do they commonly use in preparing for and writing essay exams? Under what circumstances do they do well on them? Start your class discussion with their perceptions and responses.

TEACHING PRACTICE

In their book *Facts, Artifacts, and Counterfacts,* David Bartholomae and Anthony Petrosky suggest that asking students to write essay examinations is antithetical to the teaching of a drafting process of writing. Yet they hesitate to reject essay writing entirely. Exam writing "requires students to consolidate much of what they have learned in the course and to use their knowledge efficiently." But the emphasis can shift from ideas and organization to error control (101).

Given this hesitation, you may well wonder whether you should require essay exams. In many cases, however, exams are institutionally required and may even be institutionally composed, with the individual instructor having little choice in what goes into the test or how it is given—or sometimes even how it is graded. If the exams are institutionally imposed, you should find out as much as you can as early as you can in order to schedule preparation time, if needed.

If you are allowed the decision of whether or not to test a class, you need to clarify for yourself exactly what you expect your students to get out of it.

There are two reasons for giving such an exam. First, you may want to test your students' knowledge and abilities. In such a case, you will want to make sure that you either limit the topic or extend the time given so that students can complete the process—discover, narrow, and organize the topic; write, revise, and proofread the essay. Second, you may simply want to give your students experience writing under such conditions as practice for future exams in other college courses. In that case, you will want to spend class time on how to write under such conditions and then to simulate those conditions in an exam. In fact, essay writing is being used more frequently and in more and more disciplines. Instructors view essay examinations as better indicators of knowledge than multiple-choice tests and short-answer definitions.

list its main points, list and define its key terms, or briefly summarize its argument or main points. A particularly effective method is to divide your notes into two categories. In a notebook, label the left-hand pages "Summaries and Quotations." Label the right-hand pages "Questions and Comments." Then as you read your text or other assigned material, use the left-hand page to record brief summaries of the major points made, the support offered for each point, and noteworthy quotations. On the right-hand page, record questions that your reading has not answered, ideas that are unclear or puzzling to you, and your own evaluative comments. This form of notetaking encourages active, hardheaded reading and, combined with careful class notes, will do much to prepare you. Here is an entry from one student's notes, on Chapter 5 of this book.

Summaries and Quotations	Questions and Comments
Rhetoric—art of language (Aristotle) All language is argumentative— purpose is to persuade	Maybe all language *is* persuasive, but if I greet people warmly, I don't *consciously* try to persuade them that I'm glad to see them. I just respond naturally (unless they're having an insecure day).
To identify an *argument,* ask: 1. Does it try to persuade me? 2. Does it deal with a problem without a clear-cut answer? 3. Could I actually disagree with it?	Of all the statements that can be debated, I think the less absolute the possible answers, the more important the question (such as nuclear disarmament) and the harder to solve (otherwise the answer would be obvious—no problem).

USEFUL READING

Bartholomae, David, and Anthony Petrosky. *Facts, Artifacts, and Counterfacts: Theory and Method for a Reading and Writing Course.* Upper Montclair, NJ: Boynton, 1986.

Berlin, James A. *Rhetoric and Reality: Writing Instruction in American Colleges, 1900–1985.* Carbondale: Southern Illinois UP, 1987.

Everyday use

You will probably need to write the equivalent of an "essay exam" at various times in your life. Some health insurance companies ask for a personal statement to accompany applications, as do many applications for loans, including those for student loans. One recent graduate we know found herself writing a very important "exam" as part of her efforts to adopt a child when she was asked for a lengthy biographical essay that included an analysis of personal strengths and goals. Can you think of a time when you have needed to write the equivalent of an essay examination?

In addition to taking careful, detailed notes, you can prepare for an essay examination by writing out essay answers to questions you think are likely to appear on the examination. Practicing ahead of time is much more effective than last-minute cramming. On the day of the exam, do ten to fifteen minutes of writing just before you go into the examination to get your thinking muscles "warmed up" and prepare you to do your best job of writing the examination.

46b

Analyzing essay examination questions

Before you begin writing, read the question over carefully several times, and *analyze* what it asks you to do. Most essay examination questions contain two kinds of terms, **strategy** terms that describe your task in writing the essay and **content** terms that define the scope and limits of the topic.

STRATEGY ┌──────── CONTENT ────────┐
Analyze Jesus' Sermon on the Mount.

STRATEGY ┌──────── CONTENT ──────────────┐
Describe the major effects of reconstruction.

STRATEGY ┌─────────── CONTENT ───────────┐
Discuss the function of the river in *Huckleberry Finn*.

STRATEGY ┌──────────── CONTENT ────────────┐
Explain the advantages of investing in government securities.

Words like *analyze, describe, discuss,* and *explain* tell what logical strategy to use and often set the form your answer takes. Since not all terms mean the same thing in every discipline, be sure you understand *exactly* what the term means in context of the material covered on the examination. In general, however, the most commonly used strategy terms have standard meanings, shown on the following chart.

 Common strategy terms

> **ANALYZE** Divide an event, idea, or theory into its component elements, and examine each one in turn: *Analyze Milton Friedman's theory of permanent income.*
>
> *(Continued)*

BACKGROUND

Instructors have always wanted to assess the progress of their students, but writing tests are a rather new phenomenon in the history of education. Not until the mid-nineteenth century did writing tests become widespread. In 1874, Harvard led the way by introducing the first written entrance examination. Before that date, candidates were "promoted" on the basis of oral examinations. In the new test, students were required in an hour to produce a carefully thought out, carefully revised, unified, error-free essay on subjects such as a Shakespearean play, a novel like Scott's *Ivanhoe,* or dueling in the age of Queen Anne. Needless to say, many failed.

Ironically, before the institution of this exam, composition was not primarily considered a lower-level college or secondary school subject. Previously, it had been an upper-division course that the student took for three years. James Berlin suggests that the new entrance exam was one of several related events caused by the shift in educational priorities from rhetoric to poetics (*Rhetoric and Reality* 23). After 1874, essay exams proliferated in the schools and colleges.

TEACHING PRACTICE

How you give an essay exam depends upon how you view the function of exams. Before scheduling an exam, determine why you want to examine your students in this way. If you are interested in testing your students' writing abilities, consider these alternatives:

> Schedule the exam over two class periods. Students come to class on the first exam day with nothing but a pen; you provide test booklets. The assignment includes several topic choices. The student spends the first day deciding upon a topic and a thesis, discovering support for that thesis, and writing a first draft. Take up all the exam booklets at the end of the period. On the second day, return the booklets

to the students and have them rewrite and proofread and correct their essays. At the end of the second day, they turn in the exams.

Hand out topics several days ahead of time, assigning your students the task of deciding upon a topic, finding a thesis, and discovering support for that thesis before the time of the exam. On the day before the day of the exam, take up all of their preliminary work in order to insure that a student does not arrive with a fully written essay. On the day of the exam, they should arrive with nothing but a pen. You return their preliminary work to them with an exam booklet, and they write their essay during class.

TEACHING PRACTICE

If your intention in giving an essay exam is to give your students practice in taking such exams, you will want to simulate the conditions of such exams in as many ways as possible. Therefore, you will want to limit the exam to one class period.

No matter how you give an essay exam, you ought to prepare your class in two ways. First, you should make your expectations very clear to your students. A pre-exam class discussion of successful strategies, perhaps with reference to model exam essays, could help build confidence and calm fears. Second, you should allow your students practice runs. You might provide short in-class writings. You might even provide ungraded practice writings simulating exam conditions. If you give more than one exam, you might consider making the first one short and its grade less of the percentage of the overall grade.

TEACHING PRACTICE

Choosing topics for an essay examination in a composition course can be tricky. Unless you specifically authorize your students to research the exam topic before the day of the writing, you must choose a topic with which they will be familiar. Also, you might consider looking for overlapping interests in your students' writings. Indeed, if you are ambitious, you

COMPARE AND/OR CONTRAST Demonstrate similarities or dissimilarities between two or more events or topics: *Compare the portrayal of women in* Beloved *with that in* Their Eyes Were Watching God.

DEFINE Identify and state the essential traits or characteristics of something, differentiating it clearly from other things: *Define Hegelian dialectic.*

DESCRIBE Tell about an event, person, or process in detail, creating a clear and vivid image of it: *Describe the dress of a knight.*

EVALUATE Assess the value or significance of the topic: *Evaluate the contribution of black musicians to the development of an American musical tradition.*

EXPLAIN Make a topic as clear and understandable as possible by offering reasons, examples, and so on: *Explain the functioning of the circulatory system.*

SUMMARIZE State the major points concisely and comprehensively: *Summarize the major arguments against using animals in laboratory research.*

Strategy terms give you important clues for the thesis of your answer. Sometimes, however, strategy terms are not explicitly stated in an essay question. In these cases, you need to infer a strategy from the content terms. For example, a question that mentions two groups working toward the same goal may imply comparison and contrast, or a question referring to events in a given time period may imply summary. Once you understand which strategy to follow, make sure you understand the meanings of all content terms. Particularly in technical or advanced courses, specialized language may need to be clarified. *Romanticism,* for instance, means one thing in the context of eighteenth-century literature and something else in modern art. Do not hesitate to ask for such clarification.

Thinking through your answer and taking notes

You may be tempted to begin writing an essay examination at once. Time is precious—but so too are organizing and planning. You will profit, therefore, by spending some time—about 10 percent of the allotted time is a good rule of thumb—thinking through your answer.

Begin by deciding which major points you need to make and in what order to present them. Then jot down support or evidence for each point. Craft a clear, succinct *thesis* that satisfies the strategy term of the exam question. While in most writing situations you start from a working thesis in outlining your topic, when writing under pressure you will probably find it easier and more efficient to outline (or simply jot down) your ideas and craft your thesis from your outline. Suppose you were asked to define the three major components of personality according to Freud. This is a clear question, and you should be able to make a brief outline as a framework for your answer.

> Id
> basic definition—what it *is* and *is not*
> major characteristics
> functions
>
> Ego
> basic definition—what it *is* and *is not*
> major characteristics
> functions
>
> Superego
> basic definition—what it *is* and *is not*
> major characteristics
> functions

From this outline, you can develop a thesis: *According to Freud, the human personality consists of three major and interlocking elements: the id, the ego, and the superego.*

Drafting your answer

Your goal in producing an essay examination answer is twofold: to demonstrate that you have mastered the course material and to communicate your ideas and information clearly, directly, and logically. During the drafting stage, follow your outline as closely as you can. Once you depart from it, you will lose time and perhaps have trouble returning to the main discussion. As a general rule, develop each major point into at least one paragraph. And make clear the connections among your main points by using transitions: <u>The last element</u> *of the human personality, according to Freud, is the superego.*

Besides referring to your outline for guidance, pause and read what you have written before going on to a new point. This kind of rereading may remind you of other ideas while you still have time to include them; it

could provide individualized exam questions for your students.

Responding to essay examinations is not the same as responding to a paper. Generally speaking, you cannot expect as much, both in quality and quantity, from in-class writings. Probably you will want to read generously in terms of mechanics and grammar unless the errors seriously affect the meaning of the writing. You can expect a clear thesis, clear support for that thesis, a fair amount of thoroughness in covering the topic, clear organization of the essay, and readable prose. The style may not be extraordinarily good; it may not even be up to the student's usual quality; but it still should be readable.

FOR COLLABORATIVE WORK

After the examination but before you have returned these essays to your students, make sure that they have recorded the process by which they wrote their exam, perhaps in their writing logs. Consider having each of your students share his or her process with the rest of the class. Ask each student what he or she will do differently the next time. Are there invention strategies the student would use that he or she didn't use? After each student has shared his or her process, consider dividing the class into groups of three or four and having each group decide upon what they consider to be the best processes for each of the exam topics. Have each group share their ideal processes with the rest of the class. Finally, as a class, try to come to some sort of consensus on what the best processes would be.

TEACHING PRACTICE

Students react in a variety of ways to exams. Naturally, most become anxious at the thought of being tested, but in some, the pressure can cause such an emotional distress that a person may become physically ill and intellectually paralyzed. Such a condition is often referred to as "test anxiety," and it is much more common among students than instructors sometimes realize. Allen J. Ottens, a psychological counselor and author of numerous papers and a book on test anxiety, writes that such anxiety "is a significant problem affecting a substantial number of students" (1).

Of course, instructors cannot read their students' minds, and often those who suffer from such anxiety are not readily apparent. However, you should become aware of the following symptoms of test anxiety:

1. Frequent panicky talk by a student about the exam and its terrible consequences.

2. Frequent self-belittling by the student and comparisons of himself or herself with other students.

3. Reminiscences of previous tests in which the student performed badly.

4. Performing of irrelevant tasks that appear to be avoidance of tasks relevant to the test.

5. Attendance to what other students are doing during the test rather than attending to the student's own writing.

6. Too much clock-watching during an exam.

7. Physiological indicators, like trembling hands, unexplainable sweating, complaints of illness (which may be very real, by the way) on days when exams are scheduled.

8. Expressions or indications of embarrassment at asking questions.

9. Rushing through the exam so that the student misinterprets directions and/or does significantly worse than you expected.

10. Any other unusual behavior related to the exam.

11. And, of course, the student's explicit expression of fear of the exam.

Instructors themselves should not attempt to cure test anxiety in their students. It is a

should also help you establish a clear connection with whatever follows. Write neatly, skip lines, and leave ample margins so you have space for changes or additions when you revise.

Revising and editing your answer

Leave enough time (at least five to ten minutes) to read through your essay answer carefully. Consider the following questions.

- Is the thesis clearly stated? Does it answer the question?
- Are all the major points covered?
- Are the major points adequately developed and supported?
- Is each sentence complete?
- Are spelling, punctuation, and syntax correct?
- Is the handwriting legible?

Considering a sample essay answer

See how one student handled an essay and short-answer examination in a first-year American history course. She had fifty minutes to answer two of three essay questions and three of five short-answer questions. She chose to answer the following question first.

> Between 1870 and 1920, blacks and women both struggled to establish certain rights. What did each group want? Briefly analyze their strategies for improvement, and indicate the degree of their success.

This student began her exam with this question because she knew the most about this topic. With another essay and three short answers to write, she decided to devote *no more than twenty minutes* to this essay.

First, she analyzed what the question asked her to do, especially noting the strategy terms. She decided that the first sentence of the question strongly *implied* comparison and contrast of the two struggles. The second sentence asked for an explanation of the goals of each group, and in the third sentence, she took *analyze* and *indicate* to mean "explain what each group did and how well it succeeded." As it turned out, this was a very shrewd reading of the question. In a post-exam discussion, the instructor remarked that those who had included a comparison and contrast produced better answers than those who did not. Note that, in this instance, the strategy the instructor expected is not stated explicitly in the question. Instead, class members were expected to read between the lines to infer the strategy.

The student then identified content terms around which to develop her answer: the groups—blacks and women—and their actions—goals, strategies, and degrees of success. Using these terms, she spent about three minutes producing the following outline.

Introduction
goals, strategies, degree of success

Blacks
want equality
two opposing strategies: Du Bois and Washington
even with vote, great opposition

Women
many goals (economic, political, educational), but focus on vote
use male rhetoric against them
use vote to achieve other goals

Conclusion
educational and economic differences between groups

From this outline, the student crafted the following thesis: *In the years between 1870 and 1920, blacks and women were both fighting for equal rights, but in different ways.* She then wrote the following answer.

The years between 1870 and 1920 saw two major groups—blacks and women—demanding more rights, but the two groups approached the problem of inequality in different ways. Initially, women wanted the vote, equality within the family, and equal job and education opportunities. Their attempts to achieve all these goals at once were unsuccessful, as men countered by accusing them of attacking the sanctity of the family institution. (Demanding equality in the family meant confronting traditional Christianity, which subordinated women to men.) With the lead of Carrie Chapman Catt, women narrowed their goal to a focus on the vote. They emphasized that they would vote to benefit middle-class Americans (like themselves), reduced the stridency of their rhetoric, and said that they would clean up an often corrupt govenment (they turned the men's strategy against them here by *emphasizing* their own purity and virtue). They also invited Wilson to talk at their conventions and won him to their side. Because of their specific focus and reorganization, women did finally

THESIS

WOMEN

GOALS

STRATEGY

DEGREE OF SUCCESS

psychological problem, best dealt with by the student and a psychologist or psychoanalyst. However, instructors can help the student.

Your reassurance that the student can perform up to his or her abilities can go a long way in building self-confidence in the face of the exam. Of course, you must also be honest as well as supportive; you should not tell the student he or she can perform better than you really think he or she can.

If you believe a student to have test anxiety, set up a private conference. You will want to talk to students about any problems they have without others around. In the conference, you can approach the subject directly, presenting the reasons you are concerned, and asking the student if he or she is aware of any cause for concern. A student might already be aware of and dealing with test anxiety. If not, you will want to suggest that the student see a school counselor. You should make it clear that while test anxiety is serious, it is also a common problem, and one that can be resolved. You might also suggest that the student check the library or local bookstores for books on test anxiety, such as Allen J. Ottens' *Coping with Academic Anxiety.* Finally, be reassuring, but honest. You cannot dismiss any student from work required of all other students in the class, but you might be able to compromise. Would the student cope with the exam better if he or she took it alone? In that case, you should be able to arrange a time and room in the same way you would a make-up exam. Perhaps further conferences to discuss improvements in his or her writing generally and strategies for dealing with exams would help. Perhaps the tests count little in the overall grade the student will receive; you could reassure the student of that. In addition, preparing for an exam in a peer group can help to reassure the student that he or she is able to contribute and do the work.

USEFUL READING

Ottens, Allen J. *Coping with Academic Anxiety.* New York: Rosen, 1984. This book is one of several that describe what is usually referred to as "test anxiety," and offer suggestions for coping with it.

If a liberal education should teach students "how to think," not only in their own fields but in fields outside their own—that is, to understand "how the other fellow orders knowledge," then bulling, even in its purest form, expresses an important part of what a pluralist university holds dear, surely a more important part than the collecting of "facts that are facts" which schoolboys learn to do. Here, then, good bull appears not as ignorance at all but as an aspect of knowledge. It is both relevant and "true." In a university setting good bull is therefore of more value than "facts," which, without a frame of reference, are not even "true" at all.

—WILLIAM G. PERRY, JR.

receive the vote which then gave them the power to work toward their other reform goals.

Less well organized and less formally educated than middle-class women, American blacks often were unable to dedicate their full effort to the cause of equality because of severe economic problems. In addition, their leaders disagreed over strategy. Washington told the blacks to work hard and earn the vote and equality, while Du Bois maintained that blacks, like all other Americans, deserved it already. The blacks also had to overcome fierce racial prejudice. Even after they finally won the vote, whites passed laws (literacy tests and grandfather clauses) and used force (particularly through the Ku Klux Klan) to keep blacks from voting. Therefore, even after the blacks got the vote in name, they had to fight to keep and use it. — BLACKS / GOAL / STRATEGY (SPLIT) / DEGREE OF SUCCESS

Thus both blacks and women fought for (and are still fighting for) equal rights, but the women were more successful in late nineteenth-century America. Educated, organized, and financially secure, they concentrated their efforts on getting the vote as a means to higher political objectives, and they got it. Blacks, on the other hand, had to overcome great financial barriers that reduced access to education and worked against strong organization. Even after they received the vote, prejudicial laws and practices kept these Americans subjugated. — TWO GROUPS CONTRASTED

Although this essay answer is not perfect, as the commentary and analysis in 46g makes clear, it responded accurately and fully enough to receive a mark of A and only one criticism at the end: "No advances at all for blacks?—e.g. education."

Analyzing and evaluating your answer

Although you will not have time to analyze your answers during an examination, you can improve your essay examination abilities by analyzing your own answers later. When the student who wrote the answer in 46f did so, she decided to go through her answer sentence by sentence to see how well she followed the guidelines in 46e and what additional points she might have covered. Last, she analyzed her answer with her instructor's comments in mind.

- *Thesis.* I think my thesis worked, but it might have been clearer if I had named specific rights rather than just saying "certain rights."

- *Major points.* I included all the points in my outline, but I should have developed more the term *equality* in discussing the blacks' struggle.

- *Spelling, punctuation, usage.* Would have been better to skim essay over for spelling and punctuation errors (as in the sixth sentence).

- *Additional points.* I could have talked much more about individual women's contributions—no time.

- *Response to instructor's comments.* I should have listed black advances, which I knew—my interpretation was too negative. I also know much more about Washington and Du Bois than I showed on the exam.

Analyzing her answer in this way allows her to see whether she tends to stray from the topic and whether she could improve certain elements—such as thesis and topic sentences—in future exams.

EXERCISE 46.2 Reading an Essay Answer with a Critical Eye

Here is question 3 on the examination described in this chapter, followed by the same student's answer. Using the checklist in 46e and the suggestions in 46g, analyze and evaluate her answer.

The United States, one might argue, entered the world arena in 1899 and moved to center stage in 1918. What were the landmarks of American entry into the world arena and what, according to George Kennan, were the major mistakes the United States made during those entry years?

The United States grew in power and land during the early twentieth century. We proved our strength in the War with Spain, and in the process, we acquired, at least temporarily, Cuba and the Philippines and tried to shape their governments. We also asserted ourselves in Hawaii, Guam, and Puerto Rico. Our entry into World War I showed our concern with, and entry into, World politics. The war probably would have been lost had we not entered when we did. We provided fresh soldiers who inspired the Europeans. We also provided financial assistance and military equipment to the allies throughout the war (although, initially we sold amunnitions to the Central Powers as well). According to Kennan, the Americans made many mistakes in their approach to the war. First, we did not recognize the importance of European affairs to our own safety. We said that WWI was none of our concern until the neutral rights issue came to a head. When we finally entered the war, we were unprepared. Kennan also states that Americans have a terrible approach to war. Democracies are slow to anger, but once they fight, they go for the kill, forgetting political objectives and focusing on hatred. Also, Kennan feels that we should not have gotten trapped into a war with Spain because of our involvement in Cuba. Finally, Kennan criticizes the Open Door Policy concerning China's regions of influence as being the work of a few elite men. By saying that all of the countries agreed, we took a big gamble. In conclusion, Kennan criticizes American politics because we fail to see the implications of world problems to ourselves; we are never prepared when we enter war; we focus on hatred rather than political objectives; and we take too many risks. Kennan wants us to learn from these mistakes and change our attitudes because, when you're dealing with nuclear war, you can't afford to make *any* mistakes.

EXERCISE 46.3 Taking Inventory: Your Own Essay Answers

Choose at least two of your recent answers to essay examination questions. Review each question, and then read your answer carefully. How could you improve the organization, content, and accuracy of your answer? Make an entry in your writing log, if you are keeping one, noting any new strategies you can use for improving your essay exam answers.

47

Writing Professional and Business Correspondence

Principles of professional and business communication are rooted in ideas as old as civilization. In fact, archaeologists now believe that the very earliest forms of Western writing record business transactions. Today, much of the world's commerce is conducted in writing—in proposals and reports, and especially in letters and memos—electronically, by e-mail or fax, or on paper. Such correspondence is at its best when it observes the "6Cs" of effective professional communication: Be clear, be concise, be courteous, be correct, be consistent, and be complete. This chapter presents guidelines for effective business and professional correspondence: letters, memos, résumés, and electronic communication.

EXERCISE 47.1

Spend half an hour or so brainstorming materials for your résumé, using the following headings to organize your notes: education; honors, awards, and prizes; work experience; special skills; school and community activities.

47a

Writing for readers

Professional and business communications are intended to achieve specific results. An effective business letter is clear and concise, in language its reader will readily understand. It is, in addition, polite, intended to build goodwill. Before you start writing, you should have a clear picture of your readers, your purposes for writing, and the situation in which you are

BACKGROUND

Since their inception, English departments have privileged belles lettres, and composition courses, until recently, have focused nearly exclusively on academic writing: personal essays, scholarly research papers, and literary interpretation. Modern rhetoric studies, however, have expanded the realm of rhetoric to include all forms of persuasion (Chaim Perelman), all speech acts (J. L. Austin and John Searle), and all acts of identification (Kenneth Burke). Rhetoricians like these have taught us that writing for nonacademic audiences is no less a matter for study than are the genres and forms traditionally taught in English departments—and certainly, much of the writing your students will do after they graduate will address nonacademic audiences (prospective employees and clients, co-workers, friends). Writing outside the academy may be less immediately important to either you or your students, but it will dominate most of your students' writing for most of their lives.

USEFUL READING

Keene, Michael L. "Technical Information in the Information Economy." *Perspectives on Research and Scholarship in Composition.* Ed. Ben W. McClelland and Timothy R. Donovan. New York: Modern Language Assn., 1985. Keene reviews recent research in technical communication.

What is our subject matter? In this broad context [an essay proposing to reform English department curriculums] the answer to the question should be equally broad: everything in writing is the product of the verbal imagination . . . the written word in all its forms.

—JOHN C. GERBER

Everyday use

We recently asked a group of people if they had written any business or professional correspondence outside of work during the last couple of weeks. Here is some of the correspondence they mentioned: a letter to a credit bureau asking for a copy of the writer's credit file, a letter to the principal of a child's school, a letter asking that a credit card be canceled, and a letter thanking a community group for assistance with home care for a relative. While business and professional correspondence is most often written at work, these examples suggest that such correspondence plays a part in our everyday lives as well. Can you remember any times when you wrote some such correspondence in your everyday life? What situations required such correspondence?

---

writing. Only then can you decide what information you need to include and how to design your letter or memo for greatest readability.

The "6Cs" of business and professional communication help you focus on your reader—the person you need to inform or persuade.

- *Be Clear.* Use simple words and straightforward sentences with active verbs. Try to keep paragraphs short—in general, six lines or less—and to use topic sentences to help readers follow your points.

- *Be Concise.* Use the words you need to make your point, but no more. Don't give readers information they don't need.

- *Be Courteous.* You catch more flies with honey than with vinegar. Write in a friendly, conversational tone. Imagine how you would respond if you were the reader.

- *Be Correct.* Use a spell checker, and then proofread carefully. Just one misspelled word can make readers think you (or your ideas) are sloppy.

- *Be Consistent.* If you refer to someone as *Susan* in one sentence, don't switch to *Sue* in the next. If you use kilograms in one part of a letter, don't switch to pounds in another.

- *Be Complete.* Be sure to include all the information readers need. You don't want them to have to call or write you for important, but missing, details.

47b

Using conventional formats

The most common professional and business correspondence formats are memos and letters.

1

Writing memos

Memos are the most common form of printed correspondence sent within an organization. They tend to be brief because they generally deal with one subject only. Keep in mind the following guidelines.

- State your topic in a subject line.
- Initial your memo next to your name.
- Begin with the most important information, and move on from there.
- Try to involve readers in your opening paragraph, and make some attempt to build goodwill in your conclusion.
- Focus each paragraph on one idea.
- Emphasize specific action, making clear exactly *what* you want readers to do, and *when*.

SAMPLE MEMO

```
Date:       December 10, 19XX
To:         Members of the Shipping Department
From:       Willie Smith   W. S.
Subject:    Scheduling Holiday Time

With orders running 25% higher than average this holiday
season, I can give everyone in the department an
opportunity for overtime as well as for the company's
traditional half day off for holiday shopping.  The
schedule needs to be completed by tomorrow at 5 pm,
however, so let me know your preferences.

Please fill out the attached form with the days and
hours you can work overtime and your first, second, and
third choices for time off.  Return it to me before you
leave today.

I will try to accommodate everybody's preferences,
relying on seniority in case of conflicts.  If we work
together, December should be good for all of us--on and
off the job.
```

BACKGROUND

Toward the end of "What Survey Research Tells Us about Writing at Work," Paul V. Anderson lists the implications for teaching that these surveys suggest. Career-related writing courses should do the following:

1. Explain to students that writing will probably play a large and important role in the students' careers, regardless of the students' majors
2. Focus on general writing strategies that students can apply in a variety of work-related rhetorical situations
3. Teach students to write communications that people in the workplace will perceive to be clear, concise, well-organized, and grammatically correct
4. Provide students with instruction and practice in writing for a variety of kinds of readers
5. Provide students with instruction and practice in writing a variety of kinds of communications

USEFUL READING

Anderson, Paul V. "What Survey Research Tells Us about Writing at Work," *Writing in Nonacademic Settings.* Ed. Lee Odell and Dixie Goswami. New York: Guilford, 1986. See pp. 75–77 where Anderson discusses the implications his research has for teaching career-related courses.

Redish, Janice C., Robbin M. Battison, and Edward S. Gold. "Making Information Accessible to Readers." *Writing in Nonacademic Settings.* Ed. Lee Odell and Dixie Goswami. New York: Guilford, 1986. The authors argue that students need more experience revising organization rather than work on revising at the sentence level.

BACKGROUND

In "Making Information Accessible to Readers," Janice C. Redish, Robbin M. Battison, and Edward S. Gold argue that students need to develop overall organizational skills rather than sentence-level stylistic skills to improve nonacademic writing. As a result of their research, they argue that to help students produce documents in which information is easy to locate, instructors can

> have students write or revise a reference document. They can have students work on documents that are long enough to need informative headings, context-setting paragraphs, and other features that make information accessible. They can teach students general skills rather than ways to write within a prescribed format. They can provide more realistic assignments—ones that have consequences for readers other than themselves. They can send students out of the classroom to find documents that people need to have written or revised.

2
Writing letters

Letters are generally sent outside an organization. Whether you're writing a letter of praise or complaint, giving or asking for information, your letter should follow certain conventions. In general, it should always be written to a specific person. Begin by briefly explaining the context for the letter, and close with a specific action that you are taking or want your reader to take. Consider also the following tips.

- Open cordially, and maintain a polite tone—even if you have a complaint.
- State the reason for your letter (a request, a problem, whatever) clearly and specifically. Include whatever details will help your reader see your point and be able to respond.
- Make clear what you hope your reader will do.
- Express appreciation for your reader's attention. Close positively, and with thanks.
- Make response as simple as possible by including your telephone or fax number, and, if appropriate, a self-addressed, stamped envelope.

In many organizations, writers are expected to follow a set letter format. Most frequent is the **block format**, shown on p. 711, in which everything aligns at the left margin.

47c

Applying for a job

Although a job application may contain a number of elements (writing samples, portfolios, and so on), the résumé and the letter of application are part of nearly all applications. Also a good idea, though not a requirement, is a follow-up letter, sent after a job interview.

1
Writing résumés

Résumé comes from the French word for "summary." A **résumé** summarizes your experience and qualifications and provides support for your letter. A **letter of application** or **cover letter**, on the other hand, emphasizes specific parts of the résumé, telling how your background is suited to a particular job.

Sample letter, block format

return address	1432 Coventry Lane Newton, MA 02135
date	November 7, 19XX
one space	
inside address	Professor Margaret Dorner Chair, Department of Biology Fillmore University Fillmore, NE 68508
one space	
salutation	Dear Professor Dorner:
one space	

Professor Mark Spencer, my adviser at Newton College, has suggested I write to you regarding opportunities for graduate students at Fillmore University.

I will graduate next June with a B.S. in biological sciences. My senior thesis examines the ecology of a small stream system here in Massachusetts, and I hope to continue my studies in a department with a reputation for investigating riparian communities. Professor Spencer has told me that Fillmore might be ideal.

double-space between paragraphs

Could you please send me an application for your graduate school and any brochures or other information about your master's program. Thank you for your attention. I look forward to hearing from you.

one space

Sincerely yours,

four spaces

Pat McIntyre

Pat McIntyre

Pat McIntyre
1432 Coventry Lane
Newton, MA 02135

Professor Margaret Dorner
Chair, Department of Biology
Fillmore University
Fillmore, NE 68508

TEACHING PRACTICE

Consider asking students to prepare two résumés rather than one to emphasize how résumés can be changed to suit the position they are applying for. Allow students to select positions they want to apply for, or to choose want advertisements from a newspaper. Ask them to try to select advertisements that vary by duration of employment (full time versus part time) or by depth of experience needed (technical knowledge of a computer system versus keyboarding skills). Two contrasting advertisements are listed below:

OFFICE MANAGER
Immediate need—wants to hire this week. Meet and greet patients. Be the one who handles insurance and moderate secretarial duties. Small, stable office with very nice co-workers. Excellent benefits include free parking, health, pension, merit reviews.

CHILD CARE CENTER
Needs mature, energetic individual for part-time position from 2–6 P.M. with pre-school children. HS diploma required. Child care or early childhood development experience preferred.

An effective résumé is brief—one or two carefully planned pages will usually suffice. Begin by brainstorming and taking notes, answering the following questions.

- What skills have you acquired in school, at work, and from your hobbies? Try to find a common thread in all these experiences.
- What can you do well: draw, write, speak other languages, organize, lead, instruct, sell, solve problems, think creatively?
- Are you good at making decisions?
- Are you good at original thinking, at taking the initiative, or at following directions?
- Are you looking for security, excitement, money, travel, power, prestige, or something else?

Research reports that employers usually spend less than sixty seconds scanning a résumé. Remember that they are interested not in what they can do for you, but what you can do for them. They expect a résumé to be typed or printed neatly on high-quality paper; to read easily, with clear headings, adequate spacing, and a conventional format; and to provide all the information necessary to make an interviewing decision.

Your résumé may be arranged chronologically or functionally (around skills or expertise). Either way, you will probably include the following.

1. *Name, address, and phone,* usually centered at the top.
2. *Career objective(s).* List career goals and specific jobs for which you realistically qualify.
3. *Educational background.* Start with your most recent school, and list the others in reverse chronological order. Include degrees, diplomas, majors, and special programs or courses that pertain to your field of interest. Consider including your grade-point average if it is high. List notable honors and scholarships.
4. *Work experience.* List any jobs in reverse chronological order, identifying each with dates, names of employers, and the nature of your duties. If a job is related to the one for which you are applying, give full details. Otherwise, be brief. Include any military experience in this category.
5. *Personal interests, activities, awards, and skills.* If space permits, list hobbies, offices held, dates and types of volunteer work, and any recognition for outstanding achievement.
6. *References.* Choose references who know your work well and for whom you have worked successfully. Then ask these people if they are willing to serve as a reference. On your résumé, list the name, full title, and address of each reference.

Look at the résumé on pp. 713–14, noting in particular the use of space-saving phrases instead of full sentences.

Andrew Saunders
837 Sluslaw Highway
Corvallis, OR 97330
(503) 555-1763

CAREER OBJECTIVE:

A challenging public relations position in the travel and tourism industry

EDUCATION:

B.A., Journalism (to be awarded June 19XX)
Oregon State University
Major: Public Relations
Minor: Psychology
Major G.P.A.: 3.4/4.0

Core Courses:
- Writing for public relations
- Magazine production and design
- News writing and editing

PUBLIC RELATIONS
EXPERIENCE:

<u>Public Relations Intern</u>
Willamette Valley Visitor's Association
Eugene, OR
April-December 19XX
- Wrote and placed news releases.
- Served as liaison with West Coast newspapers.
- Assisted in production of monthly newsletter.
- Developed and managed campaign for annual Willamette Valley Winery Tour.

<u>Publicity Chairperson</u>
Oregon State University Coalition for the Homeless
September 19XX-June 19XX
- Planned successful food drive.
- Developed public-awareness campaign.

Andrew Saunders   2

OTHER WORK
EXPERIENCE: <u>Supervisor</u>
                        Sherwin-Williams Company
                        Portland, OR
                        June 19XX-June 19XX
                        ▪ Supervised warehouse
                          operations and eight-person
                          staff.
                        ▪ Worked with computerized
                          order system.

                        <u>Inside Salesperson</u>
                        Sherwin-Williams Company
                        Eugene, OR
                        Summers 19XX-XX

PROFESSIONAL
ORGANIZATIONS: Public Relations Student
                          Society of America
                        ▪ Vice President, Oregon State
                          University chapter, 19XX

                        Society of Professional
                          Journalists/Sigma Delta Chi

REFERENCES: Martin Anderson
                        Manager
                        Willamette Valley Visitor's
                          Association
                        4281 Valley River Rd.
                        Eugene, OR 97403
                        (503) 555-6333

                        Professor Shirley Sinclair
                        Department of Journalism
                        Oregon State University
                        Corvallis, OR 97330
                        (503) 555-2000 ext. 541

                        Professor Stuart Goldberg
                        Department of Journalism
                        Oregon State University
                        Corvallis, OR 97330
                        (503) 555-2000 ext. 237

2

Writing letters of application

Your letter of application is the first "version" of you that a prospective employer will see. As your personal ambassador, it should be absolutely flawless—in format, spelling, grammar, punctuation, mechanics, and usage. Whenever possible, send it to a specific individual.

A sample letter of application, modified block style

```
                                    837 Sluslaw Highway
                                    Corvallis, OR 94330
                                    February 10, 19XX


Suzanne Camdon
Director of Public Information
Northern California Bureau of Tourism
1421 Fairfax St.
San Francisco, CA 94120

Dear Ms. Camdon:

        I would like to be considered for the opening
you listed at Oregon State's placement office for a
public relations writer.  I will receive my degree in
journalism this June, and I think my education as well
as my professional experience might be appropriate for
the position.

        I recently completed an internship with the
Willamette Valley Visitor's Association.  Details of
my work there are on the enclosed résumé, but I
learned, in general, how to develop a good travel
story, meet deadlines for print and electronic media,
and work with members of the hospitality industry.

        Of special interest to you may be my work on
the Willamette Spring Winery Tour (some samples of
which are attached).  With the campaign I developed,
wineries reported a 27 percent increase over the
previous year.

        I will phone in a week or so to see if I might
talk with you more about this position.  In the
meantime, I can be reached at (503) 555-1763.  I
look forward to talking with you soon.

                            Sincerely yours,

                            *Andrew Saunders*

                            Andrew Saunders

enc.
```

TEACHING PRACTICE

Point out to your students that there are two kinds of letters of application: invited letters (either personally or through an advertisement), and prospecting letters. In a prospecting letter the applicant does the following:

1. Demonstrates familiarity with the company

2. Expresses a sincere desire to work for that company

3. Usually states that the applicant is willing to travel and relocate

4. Distinguishes the applicant from others, perhaps by linking experience to that employer's primary business

5. Requests an interview

An invited letter identifies where the advertisement and job description appeared, states the applicant's desire to be considered for the position, links the needs of the employer to the qualifications of the applicant (and usually refers to the résumé), and requests an interview.

USEFUL READING

Barnett, Marva T. *Writing for Technicians.* Albany: Delmar, 1982. Section six includes chapters on various kinds of letters, and also discusses résumés and application letters in detail.

You may want to begin by reviewing your résumé, deciding which areas to emphasize and what information to add. Although each letter will take a somewhat different form, in most letters of application you will want to do the following:

- State your reason for writing, and name the position you seek. If appropriate, mention how you learned about the job.
- Describe, as specifically as possible, your educational and/or work experience.
- Emphasize your interest in the position, and request an interview. Say when you will follow up with a telephone call if you plan to do so.

EXERCISE 47.2   Taking Inventory: Correspondence

If you have recently written a letter for business or professional reasons, evaluate it using the guidelines presented in this chapter. If not, identify a job that might interest you, and draft a job application letter. Review your letter, and revise accordingly. What would you say is the most important detail in such writing? Note down your thoughts in your writing log, if you keep one.

Part Ten

Working with Your Text

<><>

48

Writing with a Computer

USEFUL READING

Daiute, Colette. *Writing and Computers*. Reading, MA: Addison-Wesley, 1985. See "Writers in College and Graduate School" for a discussion of how computers can be used in freshman composition.

Imagine this scene: preparing to draft an essay, you begin gathering equipment. First a quill pen or two. Then penknives for trimming and sharpening the quill, ink, ink pots, blotting materials and containers, a stack of paper—which is *very* expensive—and perhaps a stationery stand. Finally you begin. But the ink blots and runs, the quill splits and must be mended, you misspell a word. You will have to start all over again.

Until fairly recently, this scene described the plight of writers and explains why so many tended to concentrate on neatness, on getting things right the first time. Producing or recopying drafts were very messy, very

---

Everyday use

Since the microchip made computer use easier, faster, and cheaper, it has been hard to go through even part of a day without encountering someone writing with a computer. Most offices are now computerized, and employees communicate electronically over local area networks. You probably know someone who works in such an office, or you may work in one yourself. At a large discount store such as Service Merchandise, the clerk types your order into a computer and then hands you a printout of your order. If you phone in an order to Pizza Hut, your order is entered onto a computer as you speak; if you call again, the computer will know what you ordered, when you ordered it, and where you live. Even at a museum you are likely to encounter a computer that invites you to ask questions—and receive answers on the spot. For a day or two, note down every example you run into of someone using a computer.

time-consuming tasks. Then came such advances as ballpoint pens, typewriters, copy machines, and—most recently and spectacularly—the computer. Today, writers can modify and revise drafts with the touch of a key, design as well as write their documents, and turn out multiple neat, clean copies in a twinkling.

This chapter offers some answers to the questions students most frequently ask about writing on a computer.

EXERCISE 48.1

Make a list of all the things that computers help you do better in your writing. Then make a second list, of all those things you *wish* the computer could help you with in writing. Bring your "wish list" to class for discussion. Some of your wishes may, in fact, already be attainable.

48a

How is a computer useful?

Word-processing programs like *MacWrite II, MicrosoftWord,* and *WordPerfect,* which are used on computers and stand-alone word-processing computers, take the drudgery out of writing, giving writers the freedom to create texts efficiently and professionally, without needing to erase errors or retype drafts. With a computer, you can integrate the various steps of the writing process—brainstorming, outlining, drafting, revising. If a new idea comes to you while you're in the middle of drafting, you can simply type that idea in to work on later, or you can stop to work on it and then easily move it to another part of your text.

Storing your writing, notes, and bibliographies on disks, you'll also find that your work is easier than ever to organize and easier to keep track of. You can, in addition, keep an extra copy of your work on a small, easily transportable disk, eliminating the need to copy and keep track of many pieces of paper.

Other word-processing applications you may find useful include designing and writing brochures and newsletters; maintaining mailing lists and sending multiple letters; or writing and producing long documents with computer-created tables of contents, indexes, chapter headings, and footnotes or endnotes.

USEFUL READING

Halpern, Jeanne, and Sarah Liggett. *Computers & Composing: How the New Technologies Are Changing Writing.* Carbondale: Southern Illinois UP, 1984. See Chapter 3, "Teachers Can Use Research about the New Systems in Freshman and Advanced Composition Courses."

Nancarrow, Paula, Donald Ross, and Lillian Bridwell. *Word Processors and the Writing Process.* Westport, CT: Greenwood, 1984. An excellent annotated bibliography of research on computers and composition.

Phillips, Martin. "CALL [computer assisted language learning] in its educational context." *Computers in English Language Teaching and Research.* London: Longman, 1986. Phillips discusses some ways computers challenge present theories of how we organize learning.

Schwartz, Helen J. "Monsters and Mentors: Computer Applications for Humanistic Education." *CE* 44 (1982): 141–52. This article provides guidance on how to use computers to develop ideas and work collaboratively.

Schwartz, Helen J., and Lillian S. Bridwell-Bowles. "A Selected Bibliography on Computers in Composition: An Update." *CCC* 38 (1987): 453–57. This article is a useful, annotated bibliography of computer programs for writing classes that extends the earlier one published in *CCC* 35 (1984): 71–77.

Selfe, Cynthia L. *Computer-Assisted Instruction in Composition: Create Your Own.* Urbana: NCTE, 1986. The introduction discusses the history, possibilities, and limitations of computers in the classroom.

TEACHING PRACTICE

To help students adjust to using a computer, concentrate early in the term on making learning relaxed, not rushed; require that students write, but ask for informal rather than evaluated assignments. In your teaching, do not rely on a computer manual and program to present information—teach in person. To help students adjust to the machines, provide simple, straightforward handouts so that students can find technical answers easily. Keep working sessions on the computer brief and focused at the very start of the term so that students don't get frustrated. Finally, make sure that students know how to handle disks safely and that students save their files frequently.

Do I need to write directly on a computer?

Some writers prefer to draft by hand and recopy their work on a computer. Others prefer to use what they see as a less complicated typewriter. But most professional writers find that writing directly on a computer is the more efficient system. No matter how many drafts they write, they only need to keyboard their document once. Most computers also allow the flexibility of choosing different typefaces—**bold** or *italic,* for example—options not available on a typewriter.

48c

How can I use a computer to plan, organize, and draft?

Simply sit down at the keyboard and type in ideas as they come to you, in whatever order. Later on, you can move them around, combine them, or expand them.

If you know the main topics you want to cover, type them in and number them I, II, III. Then add details beneath each point. The organization you set out to follow is *not* carved in stone: if you realize that a subpoint deserves more emphasis, a couple of keystrokes makes it number IV (or II or III).

Perhaps you prefer starting with the six well-known journalists' questions. Just type in *who, what, when, where, why,* and *how,* skipping some lines between each. As you develop the answers, you fill the blanks. If one answer to *why* suggests another *who,* simply scroll back to that place in your text and type in your thoughts.

Your ideas may come in words or phrases or sentences. Simply type them in as they come, and worry about developing them more fully later. Just getting them up on the screen will help you see where you need to do some more research. You can then type in the questions needing answers and print them out to take to the library.

You might simultaneously work with notes, an outline, the start of a draft, even questions for further research. A computer lets your writing processes remain fluid, working as your mind works rather than as paper and pen allow.

48d

How can I revise with a computer?

All computers let you insert, move, and delete words, sentences, or even paragraphs. These are the basic steps writers take to revise. But you can also keep different versions of your text in your computer so that you can compare the effectiveness of the changed and unchanged text. You can also insert material from other files—library notes, for example, or some text you wrote for another purpose—into the body of your text document without rekeyboarding.

Some writers do all their revising on-screen, but many prefer to print out and work on hard-copy versions of their drafts. With hard copy, you can see the entire draft spread out before you, work on it, and then return to the screen to enter your revisions.

Computers also facilitate work you do with others. If you work in a computer-laboratory class, a computer network may permit your instructor or your classmates to respond to your drafts directly on the computer. Even without this facility, however, you can still print multiple copies of your drafts for response from others.

48e

How can I edit and proofread with a computer?

Once you have revised your draft and are ready to edit and proofread, a number of word-processing functions can help you make needed changes. Most writers find spell checkers invaluable (see 24f). No spell checker can tell if you've used the wrong word, however—such as *their* for *there*—or identify a word as misspelled if misplaced letters have created a new real word—such as *realty* for *reality*. Nothing substitutes for your own vigilance—or the eyes of a careful friend.

Computerized style checkers and grammar checkers are also available to use in conjunction with word-processing programs. These can help you identify misplaced punctuation, count prepositional phrases, or recognize passive constructions or long sentences. No style checker, however, can judge shades of meaning, tone, or style. These are things that only you, the writer, can resolve.

Yet even the basic functions of a word-processing program can help you become your own style and spelling checker. The search command lets

I wondered how this [impersonal, on-line editing] would affect the subtle relationship between writers and editors. I thought of all the times when a Herald Tribune *editor brought over a piece of my copy to discuss changes he had made or wanted to make, and of all the times when I—as an editor or a teacher—had gone over my changes with a young writer or a student. To be apprenticed to a good editor is the best way to learn how to write. What would happen when all the editing was done on film by successive editors? Who would know who had done what? Who would remember what the original copy said? And who would be accountable for what had been changed?*

—WILLIAM ZINSSER

you identify words or constructions you use to excess. Finding all instances of the word *of* throughout your text may serve as a cue to eliminating prepositional phrases. Having the computer identify sentences that begin *there is* or *there are* can help you identify—and replace—these weak constructions. Using your computer's search-and-replace sequence, you can change a misspelled name throughout the text.

48f

What formats can a computer provide?

Most word-processing programs include a variety of typefaces and readily permit you to <u>underline</u>, *italicize,* and **boldface** portions of your text. Most also permit easy insertion of superscript figures or symbols [*], such as those used to indicate footnotes, or subscript numbers such as those in chemical compounds [H_2O]. They even allow you to change typesize in the middle of a page.

While word-processing programs allow you to justify your text (squaring off both margins, as on this page), use justification carefully. The preferred style for most business communication is "ragged right," with the right margin uneven rather than squared off. Before printing your academic papers, find out if your instructor prefers a justified or ragged right margin; single-, double-, or line-and-a-half spacing; or a specific kind of typeface.

Many varied typefaces are now available for most word-processing programs, but varied typography should be used sparingly. Standard, readable fonts are always the best choice for correspondence and academic work. Finally, some programs can create boxes, rules, and bullets [•], which you can use to highlight sections of text or lists, to set off examples or headings, and more.

48g

What other ways can a computer be useful for writing?

Word-processing programs can let you store formats you use frequently so that you need not set margins, spacing, and tabs every time you write. Some programs have predesigned formats for letters, memos, and other kinds of text.

You can also get various reference works in computerized form—a thesaurus, for example, or an encyclopedia or almanac. Such works make available on-screen much information formerly obtainable only at a library.

Special programs allow you to get answers or help on-line, saving you the trouble of going to find a reference book. *The St. Martin's Hotline,* for example, an on-line version of this handbook, enables you to pop up answers to questions about grammar, style, punctuation, or mechanics right on your screen. Similarly, *The St. Martin's MindWriter/Descant* program provides prompts to help you generate and revise text—again, on-screen. Both of these programs are available, free of charge, from your instructor.

Finally, graphics programs allow you to add design elements to your writing—graphs, drawings, symbols, and more.

48h

What do I need to know about printing with a computer?

There are essentially two forms of computer printers: laser printers and dot-matrix printers. Laser printers produce high-quality text that can look like commercial typography. The less expensive dot-matrix printers form letters with lines of dots, which are thus somewhat harder to read than laser-printed text. Letters and résumés should always be produced on a high-quality printer. Your instructor will probably announce any requirements about printing assigned work, but always use good quality white paper. Erasable paper is usually unacceptable because the text rubs off too easily.

EXERCISE 48.2 Taking Inventory: Computers and Writing

Take the time to reflect on your use of technology in writing. If you do not yet use a computer, make a list of those things a computer might help with in your writing. If you are using a computer, spend some time now analyzing how efficient that use is. What does the computer help most with? What does it help least with? In what ways has using a computer changed the way you go about writing?

49

Preparing Your Manuscript

BACKGROUND

When addressing an audience, a speaker's presence is judged visually and aurally. The speaker's appearance, tone of voice, the degree to which he or she meets the audience's eyes, all create an impression. Our rhetorical sense tells us that we ought to dress appropriately when we go before a committee to be interviewed for a scholarship. Classical rhetoricians viewed this aspect of our behavior as one aspect of rhetoric's five arts or canons, *actio* (or *pronunciatio*), which we translate today as "delivery."

In classical rhetoric, *actio* referred exclusively to the delivery of a speech to an audience. In our literate culture, however, rhetoric must also include written communications, where the audience is removed from the writer's immediate proximity. The writer has a different set of cues than the speaker on which to rely to get his or her image across to the reader. The primary cues, of course, must come from the writing itself: what it says, how it presents the writer's ideas and feelings, how it reflects him or her. But the physical appearance of the message also creates an impression. A manuscript that is carelessly typed on paper that is difficult to read gives the impression of someone who cares little if the reader really

In preparing your manuscript, you should make it your goal to present your work in a clean, neat, easy-to-read package, one you are happy to identify as your own.

49a

Following guidelines

Follow your instructor's guidelines carefully, and ask for more information if these are not clear to you. Most instructors expect word-processed or typewritten manuscripts, but some may accept neat, legible handwritten papers.

1

Word-processing or typing your manuscript

A typewritten manuscript is far easier to read than a handwritten one. You should, therefore, type or print out a word-processed paper whenever possible, even if your instructor does not require you to do so.

Selecting paper

Type or print your paper on medium-grade $8\frac{1}{2}'' \times 11''$ bond paper. Do not use legal-sized paper ($8\frac{1}{2}'' \times 14''$), notebook paper, or mismatched, odd-sized sheets. Onionskin or "erasable" paper is usually unacceptable because it is difficult for your instructor to write on. If you must use erasable paper, submit a photocopy of your finished paper.

Use a good quality of paper if you use a computer printer. Inexpensive grades are often too flimsy, and many leave stubs when the sheets are separated and the tractor holes are torn off. (Always tear computer-printed pages apart, and remove the tractor holes from the sides.)

Selecting typeface

Use a standard typeface, either **pica** (10-point) or **elite** (12-point). Because special typefaces, such as simulated script, are hard to read, avoid using them. If you use a computer, a letter-quality printer is best. Check with your instructor before using a dot-matrix printer because some readers strongly object to reading low-quality dot-matrix print.

2

Handwriting your manuscript

If for some reason you cannot type your manuscript, write as clearly and legibly as you can, forming each word with care. Handwritten papers tend to contain more mechanical errors than do typed papers because they are more difficult to proofread. Thus you should devote extra care to the actual writing.

Selecting paper

Use white, ruled, 8½″ × 11″ loose-leaf notebook paper. Do not use spiral notebook paper, unlined paper, or paper with very narrow lines. Write on only one side of each piece of paper; ask your instructor whether you should write on every other line.

Everyday use

Many occasions call for preparing a manuscript with the greatest care you can muster: a résumé for an important job interview, an application for your first mortgage, a will. One couple who wrote their own wedding vows printed copies of the vows on handmade paper as gifts for all their guests; this was one manuscript they wanted to be perfect. Take a moment to reflect on pieces of writing—letters, applications, whatever—you wanted to be perfectly presented. What occasioned these pieces of writing, and why was it so important that they be perfect?

---

reads his or her work. Manuscript preparation, then, is another aspect of *ethos*, the persuasive appeal of the character of the writer. Seen in this light, its importance cannot be denied.

USEFUL READING

Achtert, Walter S., and Joseph Gibaldi. *The MLA Handbook for Writers of Research Papers*. 3rd. ed. New York: The Modern Language Assn., 1988.

The Chicago Manual of Style. 13th ed. Chicago: U of Chicago P, 1982. Two of the best and most commonly used style manuals.

Connors, Robert J. "*Actio*: A Rhetoric of Manuscripts." *Rhetoric Review* 2 (September 1983): 64–73. Connors equates manuscript preparation with the last of the five lesser arts or canons of rhetoric. He discusses the rhetorical effects of typefaces, paper, and format.

Selecting ink

Write neatly in dark blue or black ink, using a medium- or fine-point pen. Do not use pencil; it is hard to read and smears.

3

Positioning title and page numbers

The styles recommended for papers written in certain disciplines (MLA for many of the humanities; APA for many of the social sciences) specify the format for the title page. (See pp. 620 and 655 for examples of title pages for each style.) If your instructor does not specify a style, follow the standard format for the first page of a typed paper. One inch down from the top of the paper, type your name at the left margin, followed by the course number, your instructor's name, and the date, each on a separate line. Double-space each line as well as your title, which is centered. Capitalize each major word in the title, but don't underline it or enclose it in quotation marks. If the title is very long, divide it into two double-spaced lines, and center each one. Double-space between the title and the first line of the essay.

If your paper is longer than two pages, number each page consecutively, beginning with the first page. Place page numbers in the upper right-hand corner, one-half inch from the top and flush with the right-hand margin. Use arabic numerals, and do not use periods, slash marks, or parentheses with the page numbers. Type your name before each page number in case some of the pages are misplaced.

4

Including documentation and notes

Credit any sources you researched in writing your essay according to the style required by your instructor. (See 43c and 44c for examples of common documentation and note formats.)

49b

Using a readable page format

If your instructor asks you to follow a specific style manual in writing and preparing your paper, consult it for more specific details about format. Otherwise, use the following format.

Setting margins

White space helps readers. Standard guidelines call for one-inch margins top and bottom, left and right. (More generous margins, even one and one-half inches, make the page easier to read.) Begin each new page by measuring down one inch from the top of the paper.

Indenting paragraphs

Indent each new paragraph five spaces from the left margin. Do *not* leave an extra double-space between paragraphs. If you have only one line left at the bottom of a page, go to a new page to begin a new paragraph.

Double-spacing

Papers for college courses should be double-spaced unless you are specifically asked to do otherwise. Double-spaced type is much easier to read and proofread, and it leaves room for your instructor to make comments and suggestions. (See 33a1 for information about inserting long quotations.)

Binding your manuscript

Unless your instructor asks you to use a binder, a folder, or staples, use only a paper clip to secure the pages of your paper.

49c

Putting your best product forward

Your final copy deserves care; proofread and correct it meticulously. A computer facilitates this job, allowing you to proofread from hard copy or on the screen, make changes, and then print out a clean draft. If you are typing your paper, however, try to make corrections as you go along, using white correction fluid or lift-off tape if your typewriter has a self-correcting mechanism. After you finish typing, go back and proofread each page. If possible, set the manuscript aside and look at it later with fresh eyes.

Correct minor typographical errors by applying correction fluid and retyping. If there is not enough room for the correction, delete the error with a single pen stroke. Then add the correction above the line, marking where it belongs with a caret (∧).

BACKGROUND

Beyond the questions of unity, coherence, and paragraph development in general, paragraph breaks are also an element of *actio*. H. W. Fowler writes, "Paragraphing is also a matter of the eye. A reader will address himself more readily to his task if he sees from the start that he will have breathing-spaces from time to time than if what is before him looks like a marathon course" (434–35).

USEFUL READING

Fowler, H. W. *A Dictionary of Modern English Usage.* 2nd ed. Rev. by Sir Ernest Gowers. New York: Oxford UP, 1965.

FOR COLLABORATIVE WORK

Before allowing your students to hand in the final drafts of their papers, have them exchange these drafts for one final peer response, focusing purely on *actio*. In order to ensure that your students bring in a final typed draft, don't tell them ahead of time. Provide each student with a pencil and eraser. Proofreading marks should be made in pencil lightly so that the author of the paper can erase them, if he or she chooses. It is important that your students realize that making or not making the suggested corrections is their choice. If a student finds substantial changes need to be made, then he or she should be permitted to turn the paper in the next day.

```
                                        sequence
    What Meredith, or any author of a sonnet tries to do, is
                                             ^
    to create a whole world of feelings.
```

If you must make more than two or three such corrections on a page, retype or reprint the page. Add any brackets, accent marks, or other symbols neatly in ink if they are not on your keyboard.

Finally, handle the finished product carefully, following those well-known directions: *do not fold, mutilate, or spindle.*

EXERCISE 49.1   Taking Inventory: Your Finished Manuscript

Take a critical look at some writing you have recently finished or submitted. Using the guidelines in this chapter, assess your use of format and typing conventions. Note particularly those that you have not generally followed or those that are unfamiliar to you. Then annotate your writing, making corrections or noting the appropriate conventions in the margins or above the lines. Keep this annotated copy with your writing log, noting which conventions you need to check carefully when you next begin preparing a manuscript.

A Look at
Three Writers

This handbook asks you to think of yourself as a writer, one who inquires deeply into the world of ideas and people and things. Along the way, this text introduces you to many other writers; both student and professional. In every case, you see writers using the tools of their trade—words, grammatical structures, punctuation—to communicate ideas to their readers.

Running like a thread throughout this text are examples from three writers in particular: Maya Angelou, Lewis Thomas, and Eudora Welty. Each is a contemporary writer and noted stylist whose writing is widely admired and often anthologized. In addition, the three offer widely varying perspectives on experience and on language; they write out of very different traditions and address very different topics. Finally, each is deeply reflective about the act of writing and willing to share those reflections with others.

The examples from these writers offer you, first of all, a wealth of material to draw on in exercising your own writing muscles and in reflecting on your own writing. You can, in fact, improve your writing by practicing conscious imitation of the various sentences from Angelou's, Thomas's, and Welty's work. In addition, a close look at their words may well whet your appetite for more. If so, the following brief sketches suggest ways to satisfy that appetite. You will also find, in the Index to Authors and Titles at the end of this book, page numbers for every example shown from each of their writings.

Maya Angelou [b. 1928]

Maya Angelou once spoke of her own writing process, saying: "I write on the bed lying down—one elbow is darker than the other, really black from leaning on it—and I write in longhand on yellow pads." While her habits may be unusual, they have produced remarkable results. Born in St. Louis, Angelou spent her youth in Arkansas and California, a period described evocatively in her autobiographical volume *I Know Why the Caged Bird Sings*. She has published four other volumes of autobiographical writing: *Gather Together in My Name* (1974), *Singin' and Swingin' and Gettin' Merry Like Christmas* (1976), *The Heart of a Woman* (1981), and *All God's Children Need Traveling Shoes* (1986).

In addition to her work as a writer, Maya Angelou has been a Creole cook, a cocktail waitress, a dancer, a singer, a streetcar conductor, and a coordinator for the Southern Christian Leadership Conference; and she is currently a professor of American studies at Wake Forest University. She says that she quite simply loves writing, loves "the sense of achievement" when you've "almost got the sentence right." As the many examples in this book demonstrate, Maya Angelou makes a habit of getting her sentences right.

Lewis Thomas [b. 1913]

In writing, Lewis Thomas often finds himself surprised by ideas, which, he says, is "a little bit like being in a laboratory," including the fact that "the outcome in writing essays, like the outcome in a laboratory, often enough turns out to be a dud." Often enough, however, Thomas's essays turn out to be anything but duds: his very first collection, *The Lives of a Cell* (1974), won the National Book Award. That collection, like *The Medusa and the Snail* (1979), *Late Night Thoughts on Listening to Mahler's Ninth* (1983), and his memoir *The Youngest Science* (1983), reflects his wide experience as a scientist, medical researcher, hospital administrator, and meticulous observer of life. Most of his writing presents scientific and medical issues in a way that makes them accessible—and even captivating—to readers like us.

Eudora Welty [b. 1909]

"I am a writer," says Eudora Welty, "who came of a sheltered life. A sheltered life can be a daring life as well. For all serious daring starts from within." For Welty, all serious writing also starts from within, in the inner puzzles that lead to unexpected connections, new insights, startling discoveries.

Eudora Welty was born and raised in Jackson, Mississippi, where she still lives. Her early life is chronicled in her autobiographical memoir, *One Writer's Beginnings* (1984). Her novels include *The Ponder Heart* (1967), *The Robber Bridegroom* (1978), and *Delta Wedding* (1979); her short stories can be found in *Collected Stories* (1980).

Welty speaks often of her passion for words, for the "imaginative meaning of words in our minds," and for the power she feels in the "beautiful, sober accretion of a sentence." In this handbook, you will find many examples of Eudora Welty's own powerful way with words and sentences.

Glossary of Grammatical Terms

absolute phrase   See *phrase*.

abstract noun   See *noun*.

acronym   A word, usually a noun, formed from the first letter(s) of several words, such as RADAR for *radio detecting and ranging*.

active voice   See *voice*.

adjective   A word that modifies, quantifies, identifies, or describes a word or words acting as a noun. An **attributive** adjective precedes while a **predicative** (or *predicate*) adjective follows the noun or pronoun that it modifies (*a good book, the book is good*). Of the overlapping types of adjectives, **descriptive adjectives** identify a quality that is *common,* such as a type, color, or weight (*research paper, yellow paper, heavy paper*) or *proper,* derived from a proper noun (*English history, Jacobean drama, Homeric epic*). **Demonstrative adjectives** (*this, that, these,* and *those*) specify particular nouns (*this paper, those papers*). **Indefinite adjectives** indicate quantity (*some research, any research, such research*). **Relative adjectives** qualify words bound directly to a modifying clause (*I know which research is yours*). **Interrogative adjectives** ask questions about the words they modify (*Whose research is finished? What research is she doing? Which research is in progress?*). **Limiting adjectives** are the articles *a, an,* and *the.* **Numerical adjectives** modify words with *cardinal* (*two girls*) or *ordinal* numbers (*tenth year*). **Participial adjectives** are verbals that act as adjectives (*a waiting car, a damaged package*). **Possessive adjectives** include *my, your, his, her, its, one's, our, your, their* (*her research, our research*) as well as proper possessives formed by adding an *-'s* to a proper noun (*Einstein's research, America's coastline*). See 7b4, 11a, 11b, and 11d.

adjective clause   See *clause*.

adjective forms   Changes in an adjective from the **positive** (simply *tall, good*) to **comparative** (comparing two—*taller, better*) or the **superlative** (comparing

731

more than two—*tallest, best*). Short regular adjectives (*tall*) add -*er* and -*est,* but irregular adjectives (*good*) do not follow this pattern. Most adjectives of two syllables or more form the comparative by adding *more* or *less* (*more beautiful, less beautiful*) and the superlative by adding *most* and *least* (*most beautiful, least beautiful*). Some adjectives (*only, forty*) do not change form.

adverb   A word that qualifies, modifies, limits, or defines a verb, an adjective, another adverb, or a clause, frequently answering the questions *where?, when?, how?, why?, to what extent?,* or *under what conditions?* Adverbs derived from adjectives and nouns commonly end in the suffix -*ly. She will soon travel south and probably visit her very favorite sister.* See also *conjunction.* See 7b5, 11c, and 11d.

adverb clause   See *clause.*

adverb forms   Changes in an adverb from the **positive** (*eagerly*) to the comparative (comparing two—*more eagerly*) or the **superlative** (comparing more than two—*most eagerly*). The forms of some adverbs and adjectives are identical (*fast, faster, fastest; little, less, least*). Most adverbs, however, add *more* or *less* in the comparative and *most* or *least* in the superlative (*quickly, more quickly, most quickly*).

agreement   The correspondence of a pronoun with its antecedent in person, number, and gender or of a verb with its subject in person and number. *Tina sings, and her fans go wild; the band members play, and the crowd goes wild.* See also *antecedent, gender, number, person.* See Chapters 10 and 11.

antecedent   The specific noun that a pronoun replaces and to which it refers. The two must agree in person, number, and gender. *Fred Astaire moved his feet as no else has.* The antecedent can sometimes follow the pronoun that refers to it. *Moving his feet as no one else has, Fred Astaire was an amazing dancer.* See 7b3, 12a and b.

appositive   A noun or noun phrase that identifies or adds identifying information to a preceding noun phrase. *Magic Johnson, the best player in the NBA, scored thirty-one points. The cruelest month, April, is my favorite.* See 7c3 and 29c3.

article   *A, an* or *the,* the most common adjectives. *A* and *an* are **indefinite** and do not specifically identify the nouns they modify. *A strange feeling came over me as an awful specter arose. The* is **definite** or specific. *The awful figure of my long-lost grandfather stood before me.*

auxiliary verb   A verb that combines with the base form or with the present or past participle of a main verb to form a verb phrase and to determine tense. The **primary** auxiliaries are *do, have,* and *be* (*Did he arrive? We have eaten. She is writing.*) **Modal** auxiliaries such as *can, may, shall, will, could, might, should, would,* and *ought* [*to*] have only one form and show possibility, necessity, obligation, ability, capability, and so on. See 7b1 and 9a.

cardinal number   A number that answers the question *how many?—seven, one hundred fifty.* See also *ordinal number.*

case   The form of a noun or pronoun that reflects its grammatical role in a sentence. Nouns and indefinite pronouns can be **subjective, possessive,** or **objective,** but they change form only in the possessive case. *The dog* (subjective) *barked. The dog's* (possessive) *tail wagged. The mail carrier called the dog* (objective). The personal pronouns *I, he, she, we,* and *they,* as well as the relative or interrogative pronoun *who,* change form in all three cases. *We* (subjective) *will take the train to Chicago. Our* (possessive) *trip will last a week. Dr. Baker will meet us* (objective) *at the station.* See also *person; pronoun.* See Chapter 8.

clause   A group of words containing a subject and a predicate. An **independent** clause can stand alone as a sentence. *The car hit the tree.* A **dependent clause,** as the name suggests, is grammatically subordinate to an independent clause, linked to it by a subordinating conjunction or a relative pronoun. The dependent clause can function as an adjective, an adverb, or a noun. *The car hit the tree that stood at the edge of the edge of the road* (adjective clause). *The car, when it went out of control, hit the tree* (adverb clause). *The car hit what grew at the side of the road* (noun clause). See also *nonrestrictive element, restrictive element.* See 7c4.

collective noun   See *noun.*

comma splice   An error resulting from joining two independent clauses with only a comma. See Chapter 15 for ways of revising comma splices.

common noun   See *noun.*

comparative   See *adjective forms, adverb forms.*

complement   A word or group of words completing the predicate in a sentence. A **subject complement** follows a linking verb and renames or describes the subject. It can be a **predicate noun** (*Anorexia is an illness.*) or a predicate adjective (*Karen Carpenter was anorexic.*). An object complement renames or describes a direct object (*We considered her a baby and her behavior infantile.*) See 7c2.

complete predicate   See *predicate.*

complete subject   See *subject.*

complex sentence   See *sentence.*

compound adjective   A combination of words (of whatever parts of speech) that function as a single adjectival unit (*blue-green sea, ten-story building, get-tough policy, supply side economics, north by northwest journey*). Most, but not all, compound adjectives need hyphens to separate their individual elements.

compound-complex sentence   See *sentence.*

compound noun   A combination of words forming a unit that can function as a single noun (*go-getter, in-law, Johnny-on-the-spot, oil well, southeast*).

compound predicate   See *predicate*.

compound sentence   See *sentence*.

compound subject   See *subject*.

concrete noun   See *noun*.

conjunction   A word or words that join words, phrases, clauses, or sentences. *Coordinating conjunctions* (such as *and, but, or,* or *yet*) join elements that are grammatically comparable (*Marx and Engels wrote* [two nouns]; *Marx writing one essay, but Engels writing the other* [two phrases]; *Marx wrote one essay, yet Engels wrote the other* [two independent clauses]). **Correlative conjunctions** (such as *both, and; either, or;* or *not only, but also*) are used in pairs to connect elements that are grammatically equivalent (*neither Marx nor Engels; not only Marx, but also Engels*). A **subordinating conjunction** (such as *although, because, before, if, that, when, where,* or *why*) introduces a dependent clause, which it subordinates to an independent clause. *Marx wrote at the British Museum, where he did most of his work. Before his association with Marx, Engels was already a social theorist.* A **conjunctive adverb** (such as *consequently, moreover,* or *then*) modifies one independent clause following another independent clause. A conjunctive adverb generally follows a semicolon or colon and precedes a comma. *Thoreau lived simply at Walden; however, he regularly joined his aunt for tea in Concord.* See 7b7 and 15b.

coordination   The grammatical equality of two or more sentence elements. When elements are coordinate, they seem to express equally significant ideas. *She wanted both to stay and to go.* See also *subordination*. See 20a.

coordinating conjunction   See *conjunction*.

correlative conjunction   See *conjunction*.

count noun   See *noun*.

dangling modifier   A word, phrase, or clause that cannot logically modify the sentence element to which it is syntactically related. *Studying Freud, the meaning of my dreams became clear* (incorrect; the subject of the sentence must be capable of the action represented by the participle, but *the meaning* could not have been *studying Freud*). *Studying Freud, I began to understand the meaning of my dreams* (revised; *I* was doing the studying). As the incorrect example illustrates, dangling modifiers often occur in passive sentences.

declension   See *case, inflection, number, person*.

degree   See *adjective forms, adverb forms*.

demonstrative adjective   See *adjective*.

demonstrative pronoun   See *pronoun*.

denotation   The literal meaning of a term, as opposed to its **connotation** or associations. See 27b.

dependent clause   See *clause.*

descriptive adjective   See *adjective.*

determiner   See *article.*

direct address   A construction that uses a noun or pronoun naming whoever is spoken to. *Hey, Jack. You, get moving.*

direct discourse   Quotation that reproduces a speaker's exact words, marked with quotation marks. Jesse Jackson has often said, "I was born in the ghetto, but the ghetto wasn't born in me." See 33a and b.

direct object   A noun or pronoun receiving the action of a **transitive verb** in an **active** construction. *McKellan recited Shakespearean soliloquies.* See also *indirect object.* See 7c2.

double comparative   The incorrect use of a comparative to modify another comparative (*more better; less longer*). See also *adjective forms, adverb forms.* See 12d3.

double negative   The incorrect use of more than one negative word to communicate a single negative idea. *Nobody couldn't do nothing; I couldn't hardly do anything.*

double superlative   The incorrect use of a superlative to modify another superlative (*most unkindest cut; least profoundest thought*). See also *adjective forms, adverb forms.* See 12d3.

expletive   A construction that introduces a sentence with *there* or *it*, usually followed by a form of *be.* (*There are four excellent candidates for this job. It was on this day in 1952 that she was born.*)

finite verb   A verb that can join with a subject to form an independent clause without adding any auxiliary verb. *I breathe.* See 7c3, 9d–g.

fused sentence   An error in which two main clauses are run together without a coordinating conjunction or suitable punctuation. Also known as a *run-on* sentence. See Chapter 15.

future   See *tense.*

gender   The classification of a noun or pronoun—*god, he* (masculine); *goddess, she* (feminine); *godliness, it* (neuter)—according to its sex.

gerund   A verbal identical in form to the present participle but functioning as a **noun.** *Studying is a bore* (gerund subject). *I enjoy studying* (gerund object). See 7c3.

gerund phrase   See *phrase.*

helping verb   An auxiliary verb. See *auxiliary verb.*

imperative mood   The form of a verb expressing a command or urging an action. An imperative may or may not have a stated subject. *Leave. You be quiet. Let's go.*

inconsistent structure   The joining of two or more logically and grammatically incompatible elements in a single sentence.

indefinite adjective   See *adjective.*

indefinite pronoun   See *pronoun.*

independent clause   See *clause.*

indicative mood   The form of a verb expressing a fact, questioning a fact, or voicing an opinion or probability. *Washington crossed the Delaware on Christmas Eve. Did he defeat the Hessians?* See also *mood.*

indirect discourse   A paraphrased quotation that does not repeat another's words verbatim and hence is not enclosed in quotation marks. *Coolidge said that, if nominated, he would not run.*

indirect object   A noun or pronoun identifying to or for whom or what a transitive verb's action is performed. The indirect object almost always precedes the direct object; it is usually the personal recipient of verbs of giving, showing, telling, and the like. *I handed the dean my application and told him that I needed financial aid.* See also *direct object.* See 7c2.

indirect question   A sentence pattern in which a question is the basis of a subordinate clause. *Everyone wonders why young people continue to take up smoking.* (The question, phrased directly, is "Why do young people continue to take up smoking?")

infinitive   The base form of a verb (*go, run, hit*), preceded by *to* (*to go, to run, to hit*). The *to* form is a verbal that can serve as a noun, adverb, or, occasionally, an adjective. *To go would be unthinkable* (noun, subject). *I do not wish to go* (noun, object). *I shall go to beg, to borrow, or to steal* (adverbs). *I'd like my sandwich to go* (adjective). An infinitive can be active (*to hit*) or passive (*to be hit*). Further, an infinitive can be present (*to [be] hit*) or perfect (*to have [been] hit*). An infinitive may be modified or take objects or complements as an **infinitive phrase**. See *phrase.* See 7b1, 7c3, and 9a.

inflection   Changes in word forms to indicate person, number, gender, and case in pronouns; number, gender, and case in nouns; comparative and superlative forms in adjectives and adverbs; and person, tense, voice, and mood in verbs.

intensifier   A modifier that increases the emphasis of the word or words that it modifies. *I should very much like to go. I'm so happy.* Despite their name, intensifiers are stylistically weak; they are best avoided in formal writing.

intensive pronoun   See *pronoun.*

interjection   A grammatically independent word or group of words that is usually an exclamation of surprise, shock, dismay, or the like. *Help! We're losing control. My word, what do you think you're doing?*

interrogative adjective   See *adjective.*

interrogative pronoun   See *pronoun.*

intransitive verb   A verb that does not need a direct object to complete its meaning. *The children raced up the path.* See also *verb.* See 7c2.

irregular verb   A verb with a past tense and past participle that does not follow the usual *-ed* or *-d* pattern, but marks these forms in other ways. For example, *see, saw, seen; bring, brought, brought; go, went, gone.* See also *regular verb.* See 9b.

limiting adjective   See *adjective.*

linking verb   A linking verb joins a subject with a subject complement or complements. Common linking verbs are *appear, be, become, feel,* and *seem. The argument appeared sound. It was an exercise in logic.* See also *verb.* See 7c2.

main clause   An independent clause. See *clause.*

mass noun   See *noun.*

misplaced modifier   A word, phrase, or clause confusingly positioned so that it fails to apply clearly to the expression intended. *With a credit card, the traveler paid for the motel room and opened the door. The traveler paid for the motel room and opened the door with a credit card.* Unless the writer intended to indicate that the traveler broke into a room already paid for, *with a credit card* should follow *paid* or *room.* See 17a.

modal auxiliaries   See *auxiliary verb.*

modifier   A word, phrase, or clause that acts as an adjective or an adverb and qualifies the meaning of another word, phrase, or clause. See also *adjective, adverb, clause, phrase.*

mood   The form of a verb used to indicate whether an action or a state is a possible fact or to ask a question (*indicative*), to give a command (*imperative*), or to express a wish or describe a condition contrary to fact (*subjunctive*). In other words, mood reflects the writer or speaker's attitude toward the idea expressed by the verb. *The sea is turbulent* (indicative). *Be still, ye seas* (imperative). *Would that the sea were calm* (subjunctive). See also *imperative mood, indicative mood, subjunctive mood.* See pp. 213–15.

nominal   A word, phrase, or clause that acts as a noun.

nonfinite verb   See *verbal.*

nonrestrictive element   A word, phrase, or clause that modifies but does not limit or change the essential meaning of a sentence element. A nonrestrictive element is set off from the rest of the sentence with commas, dashes, or parentheses. *Quantum physics, a difficult subject, is fascinating. He addressed, acerbically, the failure of the system.* See also *restrictive element.* See 29c.

noun   A noun names a person, place, tangible object, concept, quality, action, or the like. Nouns serve as subjects, objects, complements, and appositives. Most nouns form the plural with the addition of *-s* or *-es* and the possessive with the addition of 's (see *number, case*). **Common nouns** name one (*rock, child, box*) or more (*rocks, children, boxes*) in a class or general group. **Proper nouns** begin with capital letters and name specifics such as a particular person, place, religion, time period, holiday, movement, or thing (*Angelou, Caesar, Florida, Jefferson Memorial, Elizabethan Age, July, Rosicrucianism, Ramadan*). Some proper nouns can form plurals (*Adamses, Caesars*). **Abstract nouns** name intangible qualities, concepts, actions, or states (*virtue, Virtue, peace, violence, evil, health, haste, time, inertia*). Some abstract nouns may be common or proper, depending on the sense that the writer wishes to communicate. Many abstract nouns have plural forms (*virtues, evils*), and as plurals they become increasingly *concrete*. **Concrete nouns** name people, places, or things and may be common or proper. In addition, **collective nouns** name coherent groups. In its singular form, a collective noun names a body or group of related elements; in its plural form, it names several such bodies or groups (*pride, prides* [of lions]; *family, families; Congress, Congresses*). **Count nouns** name people, places, and things that can be counted (*one woman, two women; one park, three parks; one tree, four trees; one Smith, five Smiths*). **Mass nouns** name concrete things that are not usually counted although their plural forms may occur (*sand, sands* [of Waikiki]; *rain,* [summer] *rains*). See 7b2.

noun clause   See *clause.*

noun phrase   See *phrase.*

number   The form of a noun, pronoun, demonstrative adjective, or verb that indicates whether it is singular or plural: *oak* is singular, *oaks* plural; *I* and *me* are singular, *we* and *us* plural; *he buys* is singular, *they buy* plural; *this book* is singular, *these books* plural. See 7b1–2, Chapter 10, and Chapter 11.

object   A word or words, acting as a noun or pronoun, influenced by a transitive verb, a verbal, or a preposition. See also *direct object, indirect object, object of a preposition.* See 7c2.

object complement   See *complement.*

objective case   See *case.*

object of a preposition   A noun or pronoun connected to a sentence by a preposition, thus completing a **prepositional phrase.** *Johnson went to Pembroke College at Oxford. Thank you for coming.* See 7b6 and 7c3.

ordinal number   The form of a number that expresses order or sequence (*first, seventeenth, twenty-third, two hundredth*). See also *cardinal number.*

participial adjective   See *adjective.*

participial phrase   See *phrase.*

participle   A verbal with properties of both an adjective and a verb. Like an adjective, a participle can modify a noun or pronoun; like a verb, it has present and past tenses and can take an object. The **present** participle usually ends in

-ing, the **past** participle in -ed, d, -en, or an irregular form. Without any auxiliary verbs, the present participle is active, the past participle passive. *Reeling, Spinks hit the canvas. The torn page was a clue.* See 7c3. With auxiliary verbs, present participles form the progressive tenses (I *am making,* I *was making,* I *will be making,* I *have been making,* I *had been making,* I *will have been making*). Past participles form the perfect tenses (I *have made,* I *had made,* I *will have made*). Further, past participles, with auxiliary verbs, are used to form the passive voice (I *am beaten,* I *was beaten*). These compound tenses are known as verb phrases. See also *adjective, phrase, tense, verbal, voice.*

parts of speech   The eight grammatical categories into which words can be grouped depending on how they function in a sentence. Many words act as different parts of speech in different sentences. The parts of speech are *adjectives, adverbs, conjunctions, interjections, nouns, prepositions, pronouns,* and *verbs.* See 7b.

passive voice   See *voice.*

past participle   See *participle.*

past perfect tense   See *tense.*

past tense   See *tense.*

perfect tenses   See *participle, tense, verb.*

person   The relation between a subject and its corresponding verb, indicating whether the subject is speaking about itself (first person *I* or *we*), being spoken to (second person *you*), or being spoken about (third person *he, she, it,* or *they*). *Be* has several forms depending on the person (*am, is,* and *are* in the present tense plus *was* and *were* in the past). Other verbs change form in the present tense indicative with a third-person singular subject (*I fall, you fall, she falls, we fall, they fall*). See 7b1, Chapter 9, and Chapter 10. **Personal pronouns** also change form as subjects, objects, and possessives. See 7b3.

personal pronoun   See *pronoun.*

phrase   A group of words that functions as a single unit but lacks a subject, a finite verb in a predicate, or both. Phrases can be grouped not only by the parts of speech that govern or introduce them but also by their grammatical functions as adjectives, adverbs, nouns, or verbs. An **absolute phrase** modifies an entire sentence and thus is grammatically divorced from the sentence. It uses a noun or pronoun as its subject and a participle (possibly implied) or participial phrase as its predicate. *The party being over, everyone left. The party over, everyone left* (participle implied). A **gerund phrase** serves as a noun, acting as a subject, a complement, or an object. It contains a gerund, the -ing form of a verb acting as a noun. *Exercising regularly and sensibly is a key to good health* (subject). *I dislike exercising regularly and sensibly* (direct object). *I am bored with exercising regularly and sensibly* (object of a preposition). An **infinitive phrase** may serve as an adjective, an adverb, or a noun and is governed by an infinitive. *The Pacific Coast is the place to be* (adjective). *She went to pay her taxes* (adverb). *To be young again is all I want* (noun). A **noun phrase**, including a noun and its modifiers, may serve as a subject, a complement, or an object. *A long, rough road* (subject) *crossed the barren desert* (object). *A raccoon is a resourceful animal* (complement). A **participial phrase** is governed by a present or past participle and functions as an adjective. *Breaking his leg, he stumbled. Having broken his leg, he stumbled.* A **prepositional phrase** is introduced by a preposition and may act as an adjective, an adverb, or a noun. *The gas in the laboratory is leaking* (adjective). *The firefighters went to the lab to check* (adverb). *Out of season is the least crowded time* (noun). A **verb phrase** is composed of a main verb and one or more auxiliaries, acting as a single verb in the sentence predicate. *I should have come to the review session.* See 7c3.

positive degree   See *adjective forms, adverb forms.*

possessive adjective   See *adjective, case.*

possessive case   See *case.*

predicate   The actual or implied finite verb and related words in a sentence. The predicate expresses what the subject does, experiences, or is. A **simple predicate** is the verb or verb phrase related to the subject. *For years the YMHA has been a cultural center in New York City.* A **compound predicate** has more than one simple predicate. *The athletes swam, cycled, and ran in the triathlon competition.* A **complete predicate** includes the simple predicate and any associated modifiers and objects. *I gave Sarah an engagement ring.* See 7c2.

predicate adjective   See *complement.*

predicate noun   See *complement.*

prefix   An addition (often derived from a Latin preposition or negative) to the beginning of a root word to alter its meaning (*preview, undress*). See 26c1.

preposition   A part of speech that indicates the position of a noun or pronoun in space or time and links it to other sentence elements. *He was at the top of the ladder before the other contestants had climbed to the fourth rung.* See *phrase.* See 7b6.

present participle   See *participle.*

present perfect   See *participle, tense, verb, verbal.*

present progressive   See *participle, tense, verb, verbal.*

present tense   See *tense, verb.*

progressive forms   See *participle, tense, verb.*

pronoun   A single-word noun substitute that refers to an actual or logical antecedent. **Demonstrative pronouns** (*this, that, these,* and *those*) point out particular nouns. *This is the article I read. Those are the books I bought.* **Indefinite**

pronouns do not refer to specific nouns and include *any, each, everybody, everyone, some,* and similar words. *Never in the field of human conflict was so much owed by so many to so few.* Some indefinite pronouns have a possessive case. *Everyone's best interests will be served by a cure for AIDS.* **Intensive** (or **emphatic**) **pronouns** (*myself, yourself, himself, herself, oneself, itself, ourselves, yourselves, themselves*) emphasize their antecedent nouns or personal pronouns, agreeing with them in person, number, and gender. *She herself knew that we ourselves were blameless. The fire did not damage the house itself.* **Interrogative pronouns** (*who, which,* and *what*) ask questions. *Which would you like? What is going on?* **Personal pronouns** (*I, you, he, she, it, we, you,* and *they*) observe number, gender, and case as they refer to particular people or things. *He knew what was his and also what was best for him.* See also *case, gender, number.* **Reciprocal pronouns** (*each other, one another*) refer to the individuals included in a plural antecedent. *Holmes and Frazier fought each other. The candidates debated one another.* **Reflexive pronouns**, identical in form to intensive pronouns, refer back to the subject of the sentence or clause. *I washed myself* (direct object). *I gave myself a pat on the back* (indirect object). **Relative pronouns** (*who, whom, which, that, what, whoever, whomever, whichever,* and *whatever*) connect a dependent clause to a sentence. *I wonder who will win the prize.* See 7b3.

proper adjective See *adjective.*

proper noun See *noun.*

reciprocal pronoun See *pronoun.*

reflexive pronoun See *pronoun.*

regular verb A verb with a past tense and past participle ending in *-d* or *-ed* (*care, cared, cared; look, looked, looked*). See also *irregular verb.* See 9b.

relative adjective See *adjective.*

relative pronoun See *pronoun.*

restrictive element A word, phrase, or clause that limits the essential meaning of the sentence element it modifies or provides necessary identifying information about it. The restrictive element is not set off from the element that it modifies with commas, dashes, or parentheses. *The tree that I hit was an oak. The oak at the side of the road was a hazard.* See also *nonrestrictive element.* See 28c and 28il.

run-on sentence See *comma splice, fused sentence.*

sentence A group of words containing a subject and a finite verb and expressing a complete thought. In writing, a sentence begins with a capital letter and ends with a period, a question mark, or an exclamation point. A sentence may be **declarative** and make a statement (*The sun rose.*), **interrogative** and ask a question (*Did the sun rise?*), **exclamatory** and indicate surprise or other strong emotion (*How beautiful the dawn is!*), or **imperative** and express a command (*Get* *up earlier tomorrow.*). Besides having these functions, sentences are classified grammatically. A **simple** sentence is a single independent clause without dependent clauses. *I left the house.* Its subject, predicate, or both may be compound. *Sears and Roebuck founded a mail-order house and a chain of stores.* A **compound** sentence contains two or more independent clauses linked with a coordinating conjunction, a correlative conjunction, or a semicolon. *I did not wish to go, but she did. I did not wish to go; she did.* A **complex** sentence contains an independent clause and one or more dependent clauses. *After he had cleaned up the kitchen, Tom fell asleep in front of the television.* A **compound-complex** sentence contains at least two independent clauses and one or more dependent clauses. *We had hoped to go climbing, but the trip was postponed because she sprained her ankle.* See also *clause.* See Chapter 7.

sentence fragment   A group of words that is not a grammatically complete sentence, usually because it lacks a subject or a finite verb. Often fragments are dependent clauses, introduced by a subordinating word but punctuated as sentences. In formal writing, fragments should be revised to be complete sentences. See Chapter 16 for ways of correcting sentence fragments.

simple predicate   See *predicate.*

simple sentence   See *sentence.*

simple subject   See *subject.*

simple tense   See *tense.*

split infinitive   The often awkward intrusion of an adverb between *to* and the base form of the verb in an infinitive construction (*to better serve* rather than *to serve better*). See 17b1.

squinting   A misplaced word, phrase, or clause that could refer equally, but with different meanings, to words preceding or following it. *Playing poker often is dangerous.* The position of *often* fails to indicate whether frequent poker playing is dangerous or whether poker playing is often dangerous. See 17a3.

subject   The noun, pronoun, and related words that indicate who or what a sentence is about. A **simple** subject is a single noun or pronoun. *Owls are nocturnal birds.* A **complete** subject is the simple subject and its modifiers. *The timid gray mouse fled from the owl.* (*Mouse* is the simple subject; *the timid gray mouse* the complete subject.) Further, a subject may be **compound**: *The mouse and the owl heard the fox.*

subject complement   See *complement.*

subjective case   See *case.*

subjunctive mood   The form of a verb used to express a wish, a request, or a condition that does not exist. The *contrary-to-fact subjunctive* using *were* is the most common. *If I were president, I would change things.* The dependent *that* clause expressing a command, demand, necessity, request, requirement, or suggestion is also common. *I asked that he come.* The subjunctive also survives in many time-honored expressions. *Be that as it may. Long live the Queen!* See 9h.

subordinate clause   A dependent clause. See *clause.*

subordinating conjunction   See *conjunction.*

subordination   The grammatical dependence of one sentence element on another. *Because that town's schools are excellent, its taxes are steep.* Although a subordinate clause is grammatically dependent on the independent clause it modifies, the information it contains may be very important to the text in which it occurs. See also *clause, coordination.* See 20b.

substantive   A word, phrase, or clause that serves a noun.

suffix   An addition to the end of a word that alters the word's meaning or part of speech—as in *migrate* (verb) and *migration* (noun) or *late* (adjective or adverb) and *lateness* (noun). See 26c2.

superlative   See *adjective forms, adverb forms.*

syntax   The arrangement of words in a sentence in order to reveal the relation of each to the whole and each to the other.

tense   The verb forms that indicate the time at which an action takes place or a condition exists. The times expressed by tense are basically present, past, and future. Verbs have **simple** (I love), **perfect** (I have loved), **progressive** (I am loving), and **perfect progressive** (I have been loving) forms that show tense and, used in sequences, show the time relationships of actions and events. See 9d–g.

transitive verb   A verb that directs action toward a direct object and may express action done to or for an indirect object. A transitive verb may be in the active or passive voice. *The artist gave me the sketch.* See also *verb.* See 7c2.

verb   A word or group of words, essential to a sentence, that expresses what action the subject takes or receives, what the subject is, or what the subject's state of being is. Verbs change form to show tense, number, voice, and mood. A **transitive** verb takes an object or has passive forms. *Edison invented the incandescent bulb. The incandescent bulb was invented by Edison.* An **intransitive** verb does not take an object. *The bulb glowed.* **Linking** verbs join a subject and its complement. *Edison was pleased.* Depending upon its use in a sentence, a verb may sometimes belong to all three groups. *Evans grew oranges* (transitive). *The oranges grew well* (intransitive). *The oranges grew ripe* (linking). See also *auxiliary verb, irregular verb, mood, person, regular verb, tense, verbal, voice.* See 7b1 and Chapter 9.

verbal   A **gerund, participle,** or **infinitive** serving as a noun, an adjective, or an adverb. *Running is excellent exercise* (gerund/noun). A *running athlete is an exhilarating sight* (participle/adjective). *We went to the track to run* (infinitive/adverb). See also *gerund, infinitive, participle.* See 7c3.

verbal phrase   A phrase using a gerund, a participle, or an infinitive. See *phrase.*

verb phrase   A main verb and its auxiliary verbs. A verb phrase can act only as a predicate in a sentence. *She should have won the first race.* See *phrase.*

voice   The form of a transitive verb that indicates whether the subject is acting or being acted on. When a verb is **active**, the subject is the doer or agent. *Parker played the saxophone fantastically.* When a verb is **passive**, the subject and object of the active sentence are transposed. Then the grammatical subject receives the action of the verb, action taken by the object of a preposition. *The saxophone was played fantastically by Parker.* The passive voice is formed with the appropriate tense of the verb *be* and the past participle of the transitive verb. See also *verb.* See pp. 210–13.

Glossary of Usage

This glossary provides usage guidelines for some commonly confused words and phrases. Conventions of usage might be called the "good manners" of discourse. Just as our notions of good manners vary from culture to culture and time to time, so do conventions of usage. The word *ain't,* for instance, now considered inappropriate in formal discourse, was once widely used by the most proper British speakers and is still used normally in some spoken American dialects. So usage matters, like other choices you must make in writing, depend on what your purpose is and what is appropriate for a particular audience at a particular time. Matters of usage, especially those which are controversial or which seem to be changing, are treated in the body of this textbook. In addition, this glossary provides you, in brief form, with a guide to generally accepted usage in college writing and with a guide for distinguishing between words whose meanings are similar or which are easily confused. For fuller discussion of these matters, you may want to consult one of the usage guides listed in 25c.

a, an   Use *a* with a word that begins with a consonant (*a forest, a book*), with a sounded *h* (*a hemisphere*), or with another consonant sound such as "y" or "w" (*a euphoric moment, a one-sided match*). Use *an* with a word that begins with a vowel (*an umbrella*), with a silent *h* (*an honor*), or with a vowel sound (*an X-ray*).

accept, except   The verb *accept* means "receive" or "agree to." *Melanie will accept the job offer.* Used as a preposition, *except* means "aside from" or "excluding." *All the plaintiffs except Mr. Sneath decided to accept the settlement offered by the defendant.*

advice, advise   The noun *advice* means an "opinion" or "suggestion"; the verb *advise* means "offer or provide advice." *Charlotte's mother advised her to become a secretary, but Charlotte, who intended to become a dancer, ignored the advice.*

affect, effect   As a verb, *affect* means "influence" or "move the emotions of"; as a noun used by psychologists, it means "emotions or feelings." *Effect* is a noun meaning "result" or, less commonly, a verb meaning "bring about." *A nuclear war would have far-reaching effects. Many people are deeply affected by this realization, and some join groups aimed at effecting arms reduction.*

aggravate   Colloquially, *aggravate* means "irritate" or "annoy," but this usage should be avoided in formal writing. The formal meaning of *aggravate* is "make worse." *Having another mouth to feed aggravated their poverty.*

all ready, already   *All ready* means "fully prepared." *Already* means "previously." *We were all ready for Lucy's party when we learned that she had already left.*

all right   *All right* is always two words, not one.

all together, altogether   *All together* means "all in a group" or "gathered in one place." *Altogether* means "completely," "in all," or "everything considered." *When the students were all together in the room, it was altogether filled.*

allude, elude   *Allude* means "refer indirectly." *Elude* means "avoid" or "escape from." *The candidate frequently alluded to his immigrant grandparents who had come here to elude political oppression.*

allusion, illusion   An *allusion* indirectly refers to something, as when a writer mentions or hints at a well-known event, person, story, quotation, or other information, assuming that the reader will recognize it (*a literary allusion*). An *illusion* is a false or misleading appearance (*an optical illusion*).

a lot   *A lot* is not one word but two. Do not use it in formal writing to express "a large amount" or "a large number."

already   See *all ready, already.*

alright   See *all right.*

altogether   See *all together, altogether.*

among, between   In referring to two things or people, use *between.* In referring to three or more things or people, use *among. The relationship between the twins is different from that among the other three children.*

amount, number   Use *amount* for quantities (mass nouns) that you cannot count (singular nouns such as water, light, or power). Use *number* for quantities that you can count (usually plural nouns such as objects or people). *A small number of volunteers cleared a large amount of brush within a few hours.*

an   See *a, an.*

and/or   *And/or* should be avoided except in business or legal writing, where it is a short way of saying that one or both of two items apply. In other formal writing, take time and space to write out *X, Y, or both* rather than *X and/or Y.* If you mean *and* or *or,* use just that word.

any body, anybody, any one, anyone   *Anybody* is an indefinite pronoun, as is *anyone. Although anyone could enjoy carving wood, not just anybody could make a sculpture like that. Any body is two words, an adjective modifying a noun. Any body of water has its own distinctive ecology. Any one* is two adjectives or a pronoun modified by an adjective. *Customers were allowed to buy only two sale items at any one time.*

anyplace, anywhere   In formal writing, use *anywhere*, not *anyplace. She walked for an hour, not going anywhere in particular.*

anyway, anyways   Use *anyway*, not *anyways*, in writing.

anywhere   See *any place, any where.*

apt, liable, likely   *Likely to* means "probably will," and *apt to* means "inclines or tends to," but either word will do in many instances. *During an argument, he is apt to yell while she is likely to slam doors. Liable to* is often used in a more negative sense. *He is liable to get angry if he strikes out. Liable* is also a legal term meaning "obligated" or "responsible for." *The dog's owners are liable for any damage that he causes.*

as   Avoid using *as* for *because* or *when* in sentences where its meaning is not clear. For example, does *Carl left town as his father was arriving* mean *at the same time as his father was arriving* or *because his father was arriving?*

as, as if, like   These expressions are used when making comparative statements. Use *as* when comparing two qualities that people or objects possess. *The box is as wide as it is long.* Also use *as* to identify equivalent terms in a description. *Gary served as moderator at the town meeting.* Use *like* to indicate similarity but not equivalency: *Hugo, like Jane, was a detailed observer.* In such instances, *like* acts as a preposition, followed by a noun or noun phrase, while *as* may act either as a preposition or as a conjunction introducing a clause. *The dog howled like a wolf, just as if (not like)* she were a wild animal.

assure, ensure, insure   *Assure* means "convince" or "promise," and its direct object is usually a person or persons. *The candidate assured the voters he would not raise taxes. Ensure* and *insure* both mean "make certain," but *insure* is usually used in the specialized sense of protection against financial loss. *When the city began water rationing to ensure that the supply would last, the Browns found that they could no longer afford to insure their car wash business.*

as to   *As to* should not be used as a substitute for *about. Phoebe was unsure about (not as to) Bruce's intentions.*

at, where   See *where.*

awful, awfully   The formal meanings of *awful* and *awfully* are "awe-inspiring" and "in an awe-inspiring way" respectively. Colloquial speech often dilutes *awful* to mean "bad" (*I had an awful day*) and *awfully* to mean "very" (*It was awfully cold*). In formal writing, avoid these casual usages.

awhile, a while   The adverb *awhile* can be used to modify a verb. *A while,* however, is an article and a noun and can be the object of a preposition such as *for, in,* or *after. We drove awhile and then stopped for a while.*

bad, badly   *Bad* is an adjective, used to modify a subject or an object or to follow a linking verb such as *be, feel,* or *seem. Badly* is an adverb, used to modify a verb. *The guests felt <u>bad</u> because the dinner was so <u>badly</u> prepared.*

because of, due to   Both phrases are used to describe the relationship between a cause and an effect. Use *due to* when the effect (a noun) is stated first and followed by the verb *be. His illness was <u>due to</u> malnutrition.* (*Illness,* a noun, is the effect.) Use *because of,* not *due to,* when the effect is a clause, not a noun. *He was sick <u>because of</u> malnutrition.* (*He was sick,* a clause, is the effect.)

being as, being that   These expressions are used colloquially as substitutes for *because;* avoid them in formal writing. *<u>Because</u>* (not *<u>being as</u>*) *Romeo killed Tybalt, he was banished to Padua.*

beside, besides   *Beside,* a preposition, means "next to." *Besides* is either a preposition meaning "other than" or "in addition to" or an adverb meaning "moreover." *No one <u>besides</u> Francesca knows whether the tree is still growing <u>beside</u> the house.*

between   See *among, between.*

breath, breathe   *Breath* is the noun, and *breathe* is the verb. *"<u>Breathe</u>," said the dentist, so June took a large <u>breath</u> of laughing gas.*

bring, take   *Bring* is comparable to *come; take* is comparable to *go.* Use *bring* when an object is moved from a farther place to a nearer one; use *take* when the opposite is true. *Please <u>take</u> my prescription to the pharmacist, and <u>bring</u> my medicine back to me.*

but, yet   Use these words separately, not together. *He is strong-minded <u>but</u>* (not *<u>but yet</u>*) *gentle.*

but that, but what   Avoid using these as substitutes for *that* in expressions of doubt. *Hercule Poirot never doubted <u>that</u>* (not *<u>but that</u>*) *he would solve the case.*

can, may   *Can* refers to ability and *may* to possibility or permission to do something. *Since I <u>can</u> ski the slalom well, I <u>may</u> win the race. <u>May</u>* (not *<u>can</u>*) *I leave early to practice?*

can't, couldn't   These are the contractions for *cannot* and *could not.* Avoid them, like other contractions, in formal writing. *If I <u>couldn't</u> complete it during the break, I certainly <u>can't</u> now.*

can't hardly, can't scarcely   Both *hardly* and *scarcely* are negatives; therefore, the expressions *can't hardly* and *can't scarcely* are redundant double negatives. *Tim is claustrophobic and <u>can</u>* (not *<u>can't</u>*) *<u>hardly</u> breathe in elevators.*

can't help but   This expression is wordy and redundant. Use the more formal *I cannot but go* or the less formal *I can't help going* instead of *I can't help but go.*

can't scarcely   See *can't hardly, can't scarcely.*

censor, censure   *Censor* means to remove material that is considered offensive for political, moral, personal, or other reasons. *Censure* means "formally reprimand." *The public* censured *the newspaper for* censoring *negative letters to the editor.*

center around   This idiom rarely if ever appears in formal writing. Use *center on* instead. *Their research* centers on *the disease-resistant hybrid varieties.*

compare to, compare with   *Compare to* means "describe one thing as similar to another." *Hillary* compared *the noise* to *the roar of a waterfall. Compare with* is the more general activity of noting similarities and differences between objects or people. *The detective* compared *the latest photograph* with *the old one, noting how the man's appearance had changed.*

complement, compliment   *Complement* means "go well with" or "enhance." *Compliment* means "praise." *Several guests* complimented *Julie on her marmalade, which* complemented *the warm, buttered scones.*

comprise, compose   *Comprise* means "contain" (the whole *comprises* the parts). *Compose* means "make up" (the parts *compose* the whole). *The class* comprises *twenty students. Twenty students* compose *the class.*

conscience, conscious   *Conscience,* a noun, means "a sense of right and wrong." *Conscious,* an adjective, means "awake" or "aware." *After the angry argument, Lisa was* conscious *of her troubled* conscience.

consensus of opinion   Use *consensus* instead of this redundant phrase. *The family* consensus *was to sell the old house.*

consequently, subsequently   *Consequently* means "as a result" or "therefore." *Subsequently* just means "afterwards." *Roger lost his job, and* subsequently *I lost mine.* Consequently, *I was unable to pay my rent.*

continual, continuous   *Continual* describes an activity that is repeated at regular or frequent intervals. *Continuous* describes either an activity that is ongoing without interruption or an object that is connected without break. *The damage done by* continuous *erosion was increased by the* continual *storms.*

couple of   *Couple of* is used informally to mean either "two" or "a few." Avoid it in formal writing, and say specifically what you mean.

could of   See *have, of.*

criteria, criterion   *Criterion* means "a standard of judgment" or "a necessary qualification." *Criteria* is the plural form. *Many people believe that public image is the wrong* criterion *for choosing the next president of the United States.*

data   *Data* is the plural form of the Latin word *datum,* meaning "a fact" or "a result collected during research." Although *data* is used colloquially as either singular or plural, in formal writing it should be treated as plural. *These* data *indicate that fewer people smoke today than ten years ago.*

different from, different than *Different from* is generally preferred in formal writing although both phrases are used widely. *Her lab results were no differ-ent from his.*

differ from, differ with *Differ from* means "be unlike" in identity, appearance, or actions. *Differ with* means "disagree with" in opinion or belief. *Mr. Binns differs with Ms. White over the importance of class discussion. Therefore, the way Mr. Binns conducts his class differs from the way she conducts hers.*

discreet, discrete *Discreet* means "tactful" or "prudent." *Discrete* means "distinct" or "separate." *The dean's discreet encouragement brought representatives of all the discrete factions to the meeting.*

disinterested, uninterested *Disinterested* means "unbiased" or "impartial." *It was difficult to find disinterested people for the jury. Uninterested means "not interested" or "indifferent." Cecile was uninterested in the outcome of the trial.*

distinct, distinctive *Distinct* means "separate" or "well defined." *The experiment involved separating the liquid into its five distinct elements. Distinctive means "distinguishing from others" or "characteristic." Even from a distance, everyone recognized Greg's distinctive way of walking.*

doesn't, don't *Doesn't* is the contraction for *does not* and should be used with *he, she, it,* and singular nouns. *Don't* is the contraction for *do not* and should be used with *I, you, we, they,* and plural nouns. In formal writing, however, avoid these and other contractions.

due to See *because of, due to.*

each other, one another *Each other* is preferred in sentences involving two subjects, and *one another* in those involving more than two subjects.

effect See *affect, effect.*

elicit, illicit The verb *elicit* means "to draw out" or "evoke." The adjective *illicit* means "illegal." *The police tried to elicit from the criminal the names of others involved in his illicit activities.*

elude See *allude, elude.*

emigrate from, immigrate to, migrate *Emigrate from* means "move away from one's country." *Immigrate to* means "move to a foreign country and settle there." *My family emigrated from Norway in 1957. We immigrated to the United States. Emigration and immigration are generally permanent actions; migration suggests movement that is temporary or seasonal and either to or from a place. Every winter, whales off the Pacific coast migrate south from Alaska toward warmer water.*

ensure See *assure, ensure, insure.*

enthused, enthusiastic *Enthused* is used colloquially to mean "enthusiastic about." Avoid it in formal writing. *The students remained enthusiastic despite the rain and the mud that threatened to flood the excavation.*

equally as good   Replace this redundant phrase with either *equally good* or *as good as*. *The two tennis players were equally good, each as good as the other.*

especially, specially   *Especially* means "very" or "particularly." *Specially* means "for a special reason or purpose." *The audience especially enjoyed the new composition, specially written for the holiday.*

every day, everyday   *Everyday* is an adjective used to describe something as ordinary or common. *Every day* is an adjective modifying a noun, specifying which particular day. *I ride the subway every day even though pushing and shoving are everyday occurrences.*

every one, everyone   *Everyone* is an indefinite pronoun. *Every one* is a noun modified by an adjective, referring to each member of a group. *Because he began the assignment after everyone else, David knew that he could not finish every one of the selections.*

except   See *accept, except.*

explicit, implicit   *Explicit* means "directly or openly expressed." *Implicit* means "indirectly expressed or implied." *The explicit message of the ad urged consumers to buy the product while the implicit message promised popularity.*

farther, further   *Farther* refers to physical distance. *How much farther is it to Munich? Further* refers to time or degree. *I want to avoid further delays and further misunderstandings.*

fewer, less   Use *fewer* with objects or people that can be counted (plural nouns). Use *less* with amounts that cannot be counted (countable mass nouns). *The world would be safer with fewer bombs and less hostility.*

finalize   *Finalize* is a pretentious way of saying "end" or "make final." *We closed (not finalized) the deal.*

firstly, secondly, thirdly   These are common in British English; more common in American English are *first, second,* and *third.*

flaunt, flout   *Flaunt* means "show off." *Flout* means "mock" or "scorn." *The teens flouted convention by flaunting their multicolored wigs.*

former, latter   *Former* refers to the first and *latter* to the second of two things previously introduced. *Anna and Kim are both excellent athletes; the former plays tennis, and the latter has won several marathons.* See also *later, latter.*

further   See *farther, further.*

good, well   *Good* is an adjective and should not be used as a substitute for the adverb *well. Gabriel is a good host who cooks quite well.*

good and   *Good and* is colloquial for "very"; avoid it in formal writing. *After Peter lost his sister's camera, he was very (not good and) sorry.*

half a, a half, a half a   Both *half a* and *a half* are standard. *A half a* is wordy. *She ate half a (or a half but not a half a) sandwich.*

hanged, hung Of these two past forms of the verb *hang*, only *hanged* refers to executions while *hung* is used for all other meanings. *The old woman hung her head as she passed the tree where the murderer was hanged.*

hardly See *can't hardly, can't scarcely.*

have, of *Have*, not *of*, should follow *could, would, should,* or *might. We should have (not of) invited them.*

herself, himself, myself, yourself Do not use these reflexive pronouns as subjects or as objects unless they are necessary. Compare *John cut him* with *John cut himself. Jane and I* (not *myself*) *agree. They invited John and me* (not *myself*).

he/she, his/her *He/she* and *his/her* are ungainly ways to avoid sexism in writing. Other solutions are to write out *he or she* or to alternate using *he* and *she*. Perhaps the best solutions are to eliminate the pronouns entirely or to make the subject plural (*they*), thereby avoiding all reference to gender. For instance, *Everyone should carry his/her driver's license* could be revised to *Drivers should carry driver's licenses at all times* or *People should carry their driver's licenses.*

himself See *herself, himself, myself, yourself.*

his/her See *he/she, his/her.*

hisself Replace *hisself* with *himself* in formal writing.

hopefully *Hopefully* is widely misused to mean "it is hoped," but its correct meaning is "with hope." *Sam watched the roulette wheel hopefully,* not *Hopefully, Sam will win.*

hung See *hanged, hung.*

if, whether Use *whether* or *whether or not* to express an alternative. *She was considering whether or not to buy the new software.* Reserve *if* for the subjunctive case. *If it rains tomorrow, our Tai Chi class will meet in the gym.*

illicit See *elicit, illicit.*

illusion See *allusion, illusion.*

immigrate to See *emigrate from, immigrate to, migrate.*

impact As a noun, *impact* means "a forceful collision." As a verb, it means "pack together." *Because they were impacted, Jason's wisdom teeth needed to be removed.* Avoid the colloquial use of *impact* or *impact on* as a weak and vague verb meaning "affect." *Population control may reduce (not impact) world hunger.*

implicit See *explicit, implicit.*

imply, infer To *imply* is to suggest. To *infer* is to make an educated guess. Speakers and writers *imply*; listeners and readers *infer. Beth and Peter's letter implied that they were planning a very small wedding; we inferred that we would not be invited.*

incident, instance *Incident* refers to a specific occurrence. It should not be confused with *instance*, which is an overused, though correct, word for "example" or "case." *The violent incident was just one instance of John's fiery temper.*

incredible, incredulous   *Incredible* means "unbelievable." *Incredulous* means "not believing." *When townspeople attributed the incredible events in their town to the presence of a UFO, Marina was incredulous.*

infer   See *imply, infer.*

inside, inside of, outside, outside of   Drop *of* after the prepositions *inside* and *outside. The class regularly met outside (not of) the building.*

instance   See *incident, instance.*

insure   See *assure, ensure, insure.*

interact with, interface with   *Interact with* is a vague phrase meaning "doing something that somehow involves another person." *Interface with* is computer jargon for "discuss" or "communicate." Avoid these colloquial expressions in formal writing.

irregardless, regardless   *Regardless* is the correct word because *irregardless* is a double negative.

is when, is where   These vague and faulty shortcuts should be avoided in definitions. *Schizophrenia is a psychotic condition in which (not when or where) a person withdraws from reality.*

its, it's   *Its* is a possessive adjective, even though it, like *his* and *her*, does not have an apostrophe. *It's* is a contraction for *it is*; avoid *it's* and other contractions in formal writing. *It's (more formally, it is) important to begin each observation just before the rat has its meal.*

kind, sort, type   As singular nouns, *kind, sort*, and *type* should be modified by *this* and followed by singular nouns. The plural forms, *kinds, sorts*, and *types* should be modified by *these* and followed by plural nouns. Write *this kind of dress* or *these kinds of dresses*, not *these kind of dress.* Use such phrases to classify or categorize, but leave them out otherwise.

kind of, sort of   Avoid using these colloquial expressions as substitutes for "rather" or "somewhat." *Laura was somewhat (not kind of) tired after painting for several hours in the studio.*

later, latter   *Later* means "more late" or "after some time." *Latter* refers to the last of two items mentioned and can be used to avoid repeating a subject twice. *Jackson and Chad won all their early matches, but the latter was injured later in the season.* See also *former, latter.*

latter   See *former, latter* and *later, latter.*

lay, lie   *Lay* means "place" or "put." Its forms are *lay, laid, laying, laid*, and *laid.* It generally has a direct object, specifying what has been placed. *She laid her books on the desk. Lie* means "recline" or "be positioned," and does not take a direct object. Its forms are *lie, lay, lain, lying. She lay awake until two, worrying about the exam.*

leave, let *Leave* means "go away" or "depart." *Let* means "allow." The expressions *leave alone* and *let alone,* however, are generally considered interchangeable. *Let me leave now, and leave* (or *let*) *me alone from now on!*

lend, loan In formal writing, use *loan* as a noun and *lend* as a verb. *Please lend me your pen so that I may fill out this application for a loan.*

less See *fewer, less.*

let See *leave, let.*

liable See *apt, liable, likely.*

lie See *lay, lie.*

like See *as, as if, like.*

like, such as Both *like* and *such as* may be used in a statement giving an example or a series of examples. *Like* means "similar to"; use *like* when comparing the subject mentioned to the examples. *A hurricane, like a flood or any other major disaster, may strain a region's emergency resources.* Use *such as* when the examples represent a general category of things or people. *Such as* is often an alternative to *for example. A destructive hurricane, such as Gilbert in 1988, may drastically alter an area's economy.*

likely See *apt, liable, likely.*

literally *Literally* means "actually" or "exactly as it is written" and may be used to stress the truth of a statement that might otherwise be understood as figurative. *Literally* should not be used as an intensifier in a figurative statement. *Sarah was literally at the edge of her seat* may be accurate, but *Sarah is so hungry that she could literally eat a horse* is probably not.

loan See *lend, loan.*

loose, lose *Lose* is a verb meaning "misplace." *Loose,* as an adjective, means "not securely attached." *Sew on that loose button before you lose it.*

lots, lots of These informal expressions, meaning "much" or "many," should be avoided in formal writing.

man, mankind In the past, *man* and *mankind* were used to represent all human beings, but many people now consider these terms sexist because they do not mention women. Replace such words with *people, humans, humankind, men and women,* or similar all-encompassing phrases. Replace occupational terms ending with *-man* with gender-free phrasing such as *fire fighter* for *fireman, letter carrier* for *mailman,* and *minister, clergy* or *cleric* for *clergyman.*

may See *can, may.*

may be, maybe *May be* is a verb phrase. *Maybe,* the adverb, means "perhaps." *He may be the president today, but maybe he will lose the next election.*

media *Media,* the plural form of *medium,* takes a plural verb. *The media are* (not *is*) *going to cover the council meeting.*

might of See *have, of.*

migrate See *emigrate from, immigrate to, migrate.*

moral, morale A *moral* is a succinct lesson. *The unstated moral of the story is that generosity eventually is rewarded. Morale* is the spirit or mood of an individual or a group of people. *Office morale was low.*

Ms. A term invented in the 1960s to give women a title comparable to *Mr.* for men. Formerly, a woman was called either *Miss* or *Mrs.,* each term defining her in terms of her marital status, which is a private matter. Use *Ms.* unless the woman specifies another title. *Ms.* should appear before a woman's name, not before her husband's name: *Ms. Jane Tate* or *Ms. Tate,* not *Ms. John Tate.*

myself See *herself, himself, myself, yourself.*

nor, or Use *either* with *or* and *neither* with *nor. Cindy hopes to study abroad either next year or the year after. Neither her mother nor her father is very encouraging.*

number See *amount, number.*

of See *have.*

off of Use *off* rather than *off of. The spaghetti slipped off* (not *off of*) *the plate.*

OK, O.K., okay All are acceptable spellings, but do not use the term in formal writing. Replace it with more exact language. *The performance was unpolished but enthusiastic* (not *OK*).

on, upon *Upon* is an overly formal substitute for *on. My grade will depend on* (not *upon*) *how well I do on my final examination.*

on account of Use this substitute for *because of* sparingly or not at all. See also *because of, due to.*

one another see *each other, one another.*

or See *nor, or.*

outside, outside of See *inside, inside of, outside, outside of.*

owing to the fact that Avoid this and other unnecessarily wordy expressions for *because.*

per Use the Latin *per* only in standard technical phrases such as *miles per hour.* Otherwise, find English equivalents. *As mentioned in* (not *as per*) *the latest report, our town's average food expenses every week* (not *per week*) *are $40 per capita.*

percent, percentage These words identify a number as a fraction of one hundred. Because they show exact statistics, these terms should not be used casually to mean "portion," "amount," or "number." *Last year, 80 percent of the club's members were female.* Use *percent* after a figure. In formal writing, spell out *percent* rather than using its symbol (%). *Percentage* is not used with a specific number. *A large percentage of sales representatives are single.*

plenty   *Plenty* means "enough" or "a great abundance." *Many immigrants consider America a land of plenty.* In formal writing, avoid its colloquial usage, meaning "very." *He was very* (not *plenty*) *tired.*

plus   *Plus,* a preposition meaning "in addition to," often is used in the context of money. *My inheritance is enough to cover my debts plus yours.* Avoid using *plus* as a transitional adverb meaning "besides," "moreover," or "in addition." *That dress does not fit me. Besides* (not *plus*), *it is the wrong color.*

precede, proceed   Both verbs, *precede* means "come before," and *proceed* means "continue" or "go forward," as in the related word *procession. Despite the storm that preceded the hallway flooding, we proceeded to class.*

pretty   Avoid using *pretty* in formal writing as a substitute for *rather, somewhat,* or *quite. Bill was quite* (not *pretty*) *disagreeable.*

principal, principle   These words are unrelated but are often confused because of their similar spellings. *Principal,* as a noun, refers to a head official or an amount of money loaned or invested. When used as an adjective, it means "most significant." The word meaning "a fundamental law, belief, or standard" is *principle. When Albert was sent to the principal, he defended himself with the principle of free speech.*

proceed   See *precede, proceed.*

quotation, quote   *Quote* is a verb, and *quotation* is a noun. In colloquial usage, *quote* is sometimes used as a short form of *quotation.* In formal writing, however, use *quotation* as the noun form. *He quoted the president, and the quotation was preserved in history books.*

raise, rise   *Raise* means "lift" or "move upward." In the case of children, it means "bring up" or "rear." As a transitive verb, it takes a direct object— someone raises something. *The guests raised their glasses in good cheer. Rise* means "go upward." It is not followed by a direct object; something rises by itself. *She saw the steam rise from the pan just as the soup bubbled into a boil.*

rarely ever   In formal writing, use *rarely* by itself, or use *hardly ever. When we were poor, we rarely went to the movies.*

real, really   The adjective *real* means "true" or "not artificial." The adverb *really,* in informal usage, means "very" or "extremely." Do not substitute *real* for *really. The old man walked really* (not *real*) *slowly.* In formal writing, avoid using *really* altogether. *The old man walked very* (not *really*) *slowly.*

reason is because   This expression mixes *the reason is that* and *because.* Use one or the other but not both together. In general, use the less wordy *because* unless you want to give a statement the air of an explanation. *The reason the copier stopped is that* (not *is because*) *the paper jammed.*

regardless   See *irregardless, regardless.*

relate to   Avoid this vague colloquial expression in formal writing. *Relate to* loosely means "understand" or "appreciate." Write *I like the Rolling Stones* and explain why rather than writing *I can relate to the Rolling Stones.* Also see *regarding, in regard to, with regard to, relating to.*

respectfully, respectively   *Respectfully* means "with respect." *Respectively* means "in the order given." *The brothers, respectively a juggler and an acrobat, respectfully greeted the audience.*

rise   See *raise, rise.*

scarcely   See *can't hardly, can't scarcely.*

secondly   See *firstly, secondly, thirdly.*

set, sit   *Set* means "put" or "place," and it is followed by a direct object—the thing that is placed. *Sit* does not take a direct object and refers to the action of taking a seat. *Amelia sat in the armchair and set her teacup on the table next to her.*

sexist language   See *man/mankind; he/she, his/her.*

shall, will   Today *shall* is used much more in British English than in American English. Use *shall* for polite questions in the first person ("*Shall we buy it?*" "*Shall I call a taxi?*"). Use *will* in all other cases involving the future tense.

should of   See *have, of.*

since   *Since* has two meanings. The first meaning shows the passage of time (*I have not eaten since Tuesday*); the second and more informal meaning is "because" (*Since you are in a bad mood, I will go away*). Be careful not to write sentences in which *since* is ambiguous in meaning. *Since I broke my leg, I have been doing nothing but sleeping.* (*Since* here could mean either "because" or "ever since." In order to avoid such problems some writers prefer not to use *since* to mean "because.")

sit   See *set, sit.*

so, so that   In formal writing, avoid using *so* by itself as an intensifier, meaning "very." Instead, follow *so* with *that* to show how the intensified condition leads to a result. *Aaron was so tired that he fell asleep at the wheel of his car.*

some body, somebody, some one, someone   *Somebody* is an indefinite pronoun, as is *someone.* When *somebody comes walking down the hall, I always hope that it is someone I know. Some body* is two words, an adjective modifying a noun, while *some one* is two adjectives or a pronoun modified by an adjective. *In dealing with some body like the senate, arrange to meet consistently some one person who can represent the group.*

someplace, somewhere   *Someplace* is informal for *somewhere;* use the latter in formal writing.

some time, sometime, sometimes   *Some time* means "a length of time." *Please leave me some time to use the computer. Sometime* means "at some indefinite later time." *Sometime I will take you to the Orkney Islands. Sometimes* means "occasionally." *Sometimes I see him on my way to class.*

somewhere   See *someplace, somewhere.*

sort   See *kind, sort, type.*

sort of   See *kind of, sort of.*

so that   See *so, so that.*

specially   See *especially, specially.*

stationary, stationery   *Stationary* is an adjective meaning "standing still." *Stationery* is a noun meaning "writing paper or materials." *When the bus was stationary at the light, Karen took out her stationery and wrote a quick note to a friend.*

subsequently   See *consequently, subsequently.*

such as   See *like, such as.*

supposed to, used to   Both of these expressions require the final *-d* indicating the past participle. *He is supposed to bring his calculator to class.*

sure, surely   Avoid using *sure* as an intensifier in formal writing. Replace this colloquial expression with "certainly" or "without a doubt," or use the adverb *surely,* which means "it must be so." *Surely* is often used to express a hoped-for situation. *Surely, John will go to a doctor.* It is also used persuasively. *We cannot go on a picnic. Surely, it will rain.*

take   See *bring, take.*

than, then   Use the conjunction *than* in comparative statements. *The cat was bigger than the dog.* Use the adverb *then* when referring to a sequence of events or emotions. *Jim finished college, and then he joined the Peace Corps.*

that, which   *That,* always followed by a restrictive clause, singles out or identifies the object being described. *The trip that you took in Japan was expensive.* ("That you took to Japan" singles out the specific trip). *Which* may be followed by either a restrictive or a nonrestrictive clause but often is used only with the latter. The *which*-clause may simply add more information about a noun or noun clause, and it is set off by commas. *The book, which is on the table, is a good one.* (This *which*-clause simply adds extra, nonessential information about the book—its location. In contrast, *The book that is on the table is a good one* specifies or singles out the book on the table as opposed to the book on the chair or the book in some other particular place.)

their, there, they're *Their* is a pronoun, the possessive form of *they. The gardeners held onto their hats as the helicopter flew over. There* refers to a place. *There, birds sing even at night. There* also is used with the verb *be* in expletive constructions (*there is, there are*). *There is only a short line at the cafeteria right now. They're* is a contraction of *they* and *are* and, like all contractions, it should be avoided in formal writing. *They're* (more formally, *they are*) *living in Japan.*

theirselves, themselves Use *themselves* rather than *theirselves.*

then See *than, then.*

thirdly See *firstly, secondly, thirdly.*

'til, till, until *Till* and *until* are both acceptable in formal writing, but some writers prefer the full word *until.* The older form *'til,* like all contractions, should be avoided in formal writing.

to, too, two *To* is a preposition, generally showing direction or nearness. *Stan flew to Cleveland.* Avoid using *to* after *where. Where are you flying* (not *flying to*)? *Too* means "also." *I am flying there too. Two* is the number. *We, too, are going to the meeting in two hours.*

to, where See *where.*

toward, towards *Toward* is generally preferred, but either word is acceptable.

try and, try to *Try and* is colloquial for *try to;* use *try to* in formal writing. *Try to have an expressive face.*

two See *to, too, two.*

type See *kind, sort, type.*

uninterested See *disinterested, uninterested.*

unique *Unique* means "the one and only." It describes an absolute state and therefore should not be used with adjectives that suggest degree, such as *very* or *most. Malcolm's hands are unique* (not *very unique*).

until See *'til, till, until.*

upon See *on, upon.*

used to See *supposed to, used to.*

very Avoid using *very* to intensify a weak adjective or adverb; instead, replace both words with one stronger, more precise, or more colorful word. Instead of *very nice,* for example, use *kind, warm, sensitive, endearing,* or *friendly,* depending on your precise meaning. Replace *very interesting* with a word such as *curious, fascinating, insightful, lively, provocative,* or *absorbing.*

way, ways When referring to distances, use *way,* not *ways. The Trivia Bowl championships were a long way* (not *ways*) *off.*

well See *good, well.*

when, where   See *is when, is where*.

where   Use *where* alone, not with prepositions such as *at* or *to*. *Where are you going?* (not *Where are you going to?*) *Where do you shop?* (not *Where do you shop at?*)

whether   See *if, whether*.

which   See *that, which*.

which, who   When referring to ideas or things, use *which* (or *that*). When referring to people, use *who*, not *which*. *My aunt, who was irritated, pushed on the door, which was still stuck.*

who, whom   In relative clauses, use *who* if the following clause begins with a verb. *Monica, who smokes incessantly, is my godmother.* (Who is followed by the verb *smokes.*) *Monica, who is my godmother, smokes incessantly.* (Who is followed by the verb *is.*) Use *whom* if the following clause begins with a noun or pronoun. *I have heard that Monica, whom I have not seen for ten years, wears only purple.* (Whom is followed by the pronoun *I*). An exception occurs when a verbal phrase such as *I think* comes between *who* and the following clause. Ignore such a phrase as you decide which form to use. *Monica, who [I think] wears nothing but purple, is my godmother.* (Ignore *I think; who* is followed by the verb *wears.*)

who's, whose   *Who's* is the contraction of *who* and *is*. Avoid *who's* and other contractions in formal writing. *Who's* (more formally, *Who is*) *in the garden? Whose* is a possessive form; it may be followed by the noun it modifies. *Whose sculpture is in the garden? Whose is on the patio?*

will   See *shall, will*.

would of   See *have, of*.

yet   See *but, yet*.

your, you're   *Your* shows possession. *Bring your sleeping bags along. You're* is the contraction of *you* and *are*. Avoid it and all other contractions in formal writing. *You're* (more formally, *You are*) *in the wrong room.*

yourself   See *herself, himself, myself, yourself*.

Answers to
Even-numbered Exercises

To help you check your progress as you work, here are answers to some exercises in Chapters 7–38. Specifically, you will find answers to even-numbered items of those exercises with predictable answers. Exercises with many possible answers—those asking you to imitate a sentence or to revise a paragraph, for example—are not answered here.

EXERCISE 7.2: Answers

The subject is set in italics; the predicate is set in boldface.

2. *He* **was an army doctor, with a gray toothbrush moustache and a gruff voice.**

4. *The dog* **answered the sound with a whine.**

EXERCISE 7.3: Answers

2. ran, ran over (two-word verb)

4. can collect; might run; should finish

6. announced

8. will extend

10. smelled

EXERCISE 7.4: Answers

Nouns are set in italics; articles are set in boldface.

2. *plagiarism*

4. *Henderson's story;* **a**; *tale; theft; violation*

EXERCISE 7.5: Answers

Pronouns are set in italics; antecedents are set in boldface.

2. **crowd**; *that; one; I*

4. *They; themselves*

EXERCISE 7.6: Answers

Adjectives are set in italics; adverbs are set in boldface.

2. **Anxiously**; *my; the; long*

4. *Twenty; Italian; the; strong*

6. *That*; **too**; *easily*; *our*; *first*
8. *the*; *the*; **more**; *pessimistically*
10. *the*; *personal*; *a*; *political*; *not*; *the*

EXERCISE 7.7: Suggested Answers

2. The beautiful, athletic heroine marries the charming, bookish prince.
4. The tall, white candles gleamed brightly on the well-scrubbed tabletop.

EXERCISE 7.8: Answers

2. through; across; into
4. During; down; between

EXERCISE 7.9: Answers

2. nevertheless; as
4. but
6. not only . . . but also
8. until
10. neither . . . nor; therefore

EXERCISE 7.10: Answers

Complete subjects are set in italics; simple subjects are set in boldface.

2. *a two-foot* **snowfall**
4. *A* **house** *that faces west*

EXERCISE 7.11: Answers

Predicates are set in italics.

2. *made us a nation*: trans-made; do-us; oc-nation
4. *will never die*: intrans-will . . . die

EXERCISE 7.12: Answers

2. in his vocabulary
4. of the dugout

EXERCISE 7.13: Suggested Answers

2. Without fear, Socrates faced death.
4. Except for a few of his followers, everyone thought Socrates was crazy.

EXERCISE 7.14: Answers

2. gerund-careful saving: n, object of prep
4. part-Raised in Idaho: adj, modifying "I" part-exploring nature: adj, obj compl

EXERCISE 7.15: Answers

2. inf-To listen to Bruce Springsteen; prep-to Bruce Springsteen
4. part-Floating on my back; prep-on my back

6. app-a sensitive child; prep-with a mixture of awe and excitement; prep-of awe and excitement

8. part-Basking in the sunlight; prep-in the sunlight; prep-in reminiscence of birch trees; prep-of birch trees

10. prep-of recreation; gerund-taking a nap

EXERCISE 7.16: Suggested Answers

2. After soaking up the sun and eating good food, she looked healthy when he saw her the second time.

4. The Sunday afternoon dragged to an absolute halt.

6. In addition to kissing babies, posing for pictures, and eating boiled chicken, the candidates shook hands with the voters.

8. A late bloomer, Ben often thought regretfully about the past.

10. A young couple and their children, they lived in a trailer, crowded together like sardines.

EXERCISE 7.17: Suggested Answers

2. Waiting to go through customs, we clutched our passports in our hands.

4. To annoy his parents, Michael had his ear pierced.

EXERCISE 7.18: Answers

2. dep-As a potential customer entered the store; sub conj-As; ind-Tony nervously attempted to retreat to the safety of the back room

4. dep-When she was deemed old enough to understand; sub conj-when; ind-she was told the truth; ind-she finally knew why her father had left home; rel-why

6. ind-I decided to bake a chocolate cream pie; dep-which was Lynn's favorite; rel-which

8. ind-The trip was longer; dep-than I had remembered; rel-than

10. ind-I could see that he was very tired; rel-that; ind-I had to ask him a few questions

EXERCISE 7.19: Suggested Answers

2. After many changes and upheavals, the German government dismantled the Berlin wall, which had become a symbol of oppression.

4. Rob, who was a collector of jazz records, always borrowed money from his friends.

6. We stood outside for an hour while the opening band played.

8. Because she was willing to stay home on weekends and study, Erin won the translation contest.

10. A man, whose memorial plaque hangs in the lobby, was killed in that mill in 1867.

EXERCISE 7.20: Answers

(The entire sentences are independent clauses.)

2. prep p-in our bare skins; n p-our bare skins

4. prep p-in a zoo; n p-a zoo; n p-the ticket; prep p-for some animals and birds; n p-some animals and birds

6. inf p-to read Thoreau; inf p-to enjoy him; n p-his enthusiasms; n p-his acute perception

8. n p-no sensible writer; inf p-to develop; n p-a style; v p-do have; n p-distinguishing qualities; n p-very evident; dep cl-when you read the words; n p-the words

10. prep p-of Charlotte's descendants; v p-still live; prep p-in the barn; n p-Charlotte's descendants; n p-the barn; dep cl-when the warm days of spring arrive; n p-the warm days; prep p-of spring; n p-tiny spiders; part p-emerging into the world; n p-the world

EXERCISE 7.21: Answers

2. complex, declarative, periodic

4. simple, declarative, cumulative

6. complex, declarative

8. compound-complex, declarative

10. complex, declarative, periodic

EXERCISE 8.2: Answers

2. hers

4. his

EXERCISE 8.3: Answers

2. whoever: subject of *faces*

4. whom: object of preposition, *with*

EXERCISE 8.4: Answers

2. whom

4. he

6. she

8. whoever

10. whom, who

EXERCISE 8.5: Answers

2. I⟶me

4. correct

6. him⟶he

8. me⟶I

10. whomever⟶whoever

EXERCISE 9.2: Answers

2. have⟶has

4. correct

6. be⟶is

8. don't⟶doesn't

10. is running

EXERCISE 9.3: Answers

2. come, found

4. lost; took

6. grew

8. met, taken

10. met, thought, known

EXERCISE 9.4: Answers

2. sang⟶sung; begun⟶began

4. went⟶gone

EXERCISE 9.5: Answers

2. laid

4. lying

6. sat

8. raise

10. rose

EXERCISE 9.6: Answers

2. have predicted/have been predicting—action begun in past continues

4. arrived/has arrived—started in past, may continue today

6. rode/was riding—past action, completed

8. will have watched—future action, completed by a certain time

10. rises—general truth

EXERCISE 9.8: Answers

2. *Having left* England in December, the settlers *arrived* in Virginia in May.

4. *Having cut off* all contact with family, he *did* not *know* whom to ask for help.

EXERCISE 9.9: Answers

2. Such things as elevators, subways, and closets *were avoided* by Marianne.

4. The first snow of winter *covered* the lawns and rooftops.

EXERCISE 9.11: Answers

2. was——→were

4. was——→were

EXERCISE 10.1: Suggested Answers

2. Visiting relatives *are* treacherous. ["relatives" is the subject.]

EXERCISE 10.2: Answers

2. am

4. supplies

6. were

8. holds

10. leaves

EXERCISE 10.3: Answers

2. correct; "talking and getting up" are considered a single unit

4. correct

6. display——→displays; "neither/nor"

8. correct; "most" refers to a quantity

10. seem——→seems; "either/or" calls for a singular verb

12. correct; "only one" is singular

14. was (second verb)——→were; "that" refers to "countries"

EXERCISE 11.2: Suggested Answers

2. Roommates do not always get along, but they can usually manage to tolerate each other temporarily.

4. Both Tom and Teresa are willing to lend us a car.

6. Every house and apartment has its advantages and its drawbacks.

8. Correct

10. I often turn on the fan and the light and neglect to turn them off.

EXERCISE 12.3: Answers

2. negatively⟶acts

4. really⟶cold

6. well⟶eating

8. surely⟶have made

10. strictly⟶brought up

EXERCISE 12.5: Suggested Answers

2. According to the article, walking is more healthful [not healthy] than jogging.

4. Women tend to live longer than men; hence, more of the elderly are women.

6. A research scientist from the Lunar and Planetary Laboratory, University of Arizona, argues that mining asteroids may well prove economically important.

8. The student cafeteria is operated by a college food service, part of a chain.

10. I think *Oedipus Rex* is a more successful play than *The Sandbox*.

EXERCISE 13.2: Suggested Answers

2. Lear divides his kingdom between the two older daughters, Goneril and Regan, whose extravagant professions of love are more flattering than the simple affection of the youngest daughter, Cordelia. The consequences of this error in judgment soon become apparent, as the older daughters prove neither grateful nor kind to him.

4. New England helped to shape many aspects of American culture, including education, religion, and government. As New Englanders moved west, they carried their institutions with them.

6. James told Allen that his own mother was ill. James told Allen that Allen's mother was ill.

8. When drug therapy is combined with psychotherapy, the patients relate better and are more responsive to their therapists, and they are less vulnerable to what disturbs them.

10. If guns cause crimes, outlaw guns.

EXERCISE 13.3: Suggested Answers

2. Texans often hear about the influence of big oil corporations.

4. After recently having a conversation with a veteran, my friend saw the Persian Gulf War differently.

6. The chair was delivered three weeks late, which, according to the store management, is a normal practice.

8. Many employees resented smoking, so the company policy prohibited it.

10. In his lyrics, Tom Jobim often describes the beaches of Rio.

EXERCISE 14.2: Suggested Answers

2. Then, suddenly, the big day *arrived*. The children were still a bit sleepy, for their anticipation had kept them awake.

4. A cloud of snow powder rose as skis and poles *flew* in every direction.

EXERCISE 14.3: Suggested Answers

2. I think it better that Grandfather die painlessly, bravely, and with dignity than that he *continue* to live in terrible pain.

4. The consultant recommended that the candidates tell more jokes and *smile* more during their speeches.

EXERCISE 14.4: Suggested Answers

2. No change

4. The first thing *we see* as we start down the slope is a large green banner.

EXERCISE 14.5: Suggested Answers

2. Workers with computer skills were in great demand, and a programmer could almost name *his or her* salary.

4. New parents often find it hard to adjust to having a baby around; *they* can't just get up and go someplace.

EXERCISE 14.6: Suggested Answers

2. According to the article, the ozone layer is rapidly dwindling, *and the lives of future generations are endangered.*

4. Oscar Wilde wrote that books cannot be divided into moral and immoral categories, *and that books are either written well or badly.*

EXERCISE 15.2: Suggested Answers

2. Reporters today have no choice but to use computers.

4. My mother taught me to read, but my grandmother taught me to *love* to read.

6. Lincoln called for troops to fight the Confederacy; as a result, four more Southern states seceded.

8. Jim grew beautiful tulips; however, he had less luck with strawberries.

10. As the music lifted her spirits, she stopped sighing and began to sing.

EXERCISE 16.2: Suggested Answers

2. Many Americans yearn to live with gusto.

4. The climbers had two choices: to go over a four-hundred-foot cliff or to turn back. They decided to make the attempt.

6. Bush promoted one tax change in particular: a reduction in the capital gains tax.

8. Offering good pay and the best equipment money can buy, organized crime has been able to attract graduates just as big business has.

10. Wollstonecraft believed in universal public education and in education that forms the heart and strengthens the body.

EXERCISE 16.3: Suggested Answers

2. *verbal-phrase fragment.* The protagonist comes to a decision to leave his family.

4. *prepositional-phrase fragment.* We were thankful for a hot shower after a week in the wilderness.

6. *appositive-phrase fragment.* Forster stopped writing novels after *A Passage to India,* one of the greatest novels of the twentieth century.

8. *compound-predicate fragment.* I loved *Beloved* and thought Toni Morrison deserved the Pulitzer prize.

10. *subordinate-clause fragment.* Because the younger generation often rejects the ways of its elders, one might say that rebellion is normal.

EXERCISE 17.2: Suggested Answers

2. The city spent almost $2 million on the new stadium that opened last year.

4. The clothes that I was giving away were full of holes.

6. Doctors recommend a new, painless test for cancer.

8. Before I decided to buy the stock, I knew the investment would pay off dramatically.

10. The maintenance worker shut down the turbine that was revolving out of control.

EXERCISE 17.3: Suggested Answers

2. The mayor promised that after her reelection she would not raise taxes. After her reelection, the mayor promised that she would not raise taxes.

4. Doctors can now restore limbs that have been partially severed to functioning condition. Doctors can now restore limbs that have been severed to partially functioning condition.

EXERCISE 17.4: Suggested Answers

2. The exhibit attracted large audiences because of extensive publicity.

4. Bookstores sold fifty thousand copies in the first week after publication.

EXERCISE 17.5: Suggested Answers

2. When interviewing grieving relatives, reporters show no consideration for their privacy.

4. Chosen for their looks, newscasters often have weak journalistic credentials.

EXERCISE 17.6: Suggested Answers

2. While attending a performance at Ford's Theatre, Lincoln was shot by John Wilkes Booth.

4. Dreams are somewhat like a jigsaw puzzle; when put together in the correct order, both dreams and puzzles have organization and coherence.

EXERCISE 18.2: Suggested Answers

2. Your dentist will usually tell you if you need braces. To find out if you need braces, ask your dentist.

4. By not prosecuting white-collar crime as vigorously as we prosecute violent crime, we encourage white-collar criminals to ignore the law. We must prosecute white-collar crime as vigorously as violent crime unless we want to encourage white-collar criminals to ignore the law.

6. A confluence is a place where two rivers join to form one. A confluence joins two rivers to form one.

8. Oedipus has the "shock of recognition" when he suddenly realizes that he has killed his father and married his mother. The "shock of recognition" comes when Oedipus suddenly realizes that he has killed his father and married his mother.

10. Europeans discovered Australia, but the British made it into a penal colony. Although it was a European discovery, Australia became a British penal colony.

EXERCISE 18.3: Suggested Answers

2. Argentina and Peru were colonized by Spain, and Brazil was colonized by Portugal.

4. Was the dictatorship in Iraq any worse than those in many other countries?

EXERCISE 19.2: Suggested Answers

2. Also notable throughout the story is the image of chrysanthemums.

4. The presence of the Indian in these movies always conjures up destructive stereotypes of drunkenness, horse thieves, and blood-thirsty war parties.

EXERCISE 19.3: Suggested Answers

2. Many people tend to expand their sentences by adding unnecessary words.

4. I put on ten pounds immediately after I stopped exercising.

EXERCISE 20.3: Suggested Answers

2. *Truth or Dare,* a film of Madonna's tour, was released in 1991.

4. *Working,* an important book by Studs Terkel, examines the situation of the American worker.

EXERCISE 21.2: Suggested Answers

2. My favorite pastimes include reading, exercising, and talking with friends.

4. I want not only hot fudge but also whipped cream.

EXERCISE 21.3: Suggested Answers

2. I will always remember how the girls dressed in green plaid skirts and the boys wore green plaid ties.

4. Needing a new pair of shoes and not being able to afford them is enough to make anybody sensitive.

6. Too many students came to college to have fun, to find a husband or wife, or to put off having to go to work.

8. Her job was to show new products, to help Mr. Greer with sales, and to participate in advertising.

10. Stress can result in low self-esteem, total frustration, sleeplessness, nervousness, or eventually suicide.

EXERCISE 22.4: Suggested Answers

2. *Periodic:* Once I mastered the problems that I had encountered at the beginning and once I became thoroughly familiar with the stock, I became the best salesperson in our store. *Cumulative:* I became the best salesperson in our store once I mastered the problems that I had encountered at the beginning and once I became thoroughly familiar with the stock.

EXERCISE 23.3: Suggested Answers

2. They started shooting pool, and before Cathy knew it, ten dollars was owed to the kid.
   Preference depends somewhat upon the context. The passive voice is unclear about who owes the kid ten dollars. Is Cathy alone? Are she and the kid the "they" of the sentence, or is someone else involved? The active is clearer if Cathy owes the kid money.

4. I adjusted more easily to living in a dorm than to living in an apartment.
   The active is preferred, since the passive adds nothing.

EXERCISE 24.2: Answers

2. to; too	14. businesses; dependent
4. noticeable; until	16. experience; exercise
6. believe; lose	18. categories; final
8. affects; success; than; its	20. occasion; whether; weather
10. develop; truly; successful	22. woman's
12. where; and	24. It's; all right; sense

EXERCISE 24.4: Answers

2. conscience	8. receive
4. leisure	10. heiress
6. caffeine	

EXERCISE 24.5: Answers

2. wholly	8. continuous
4. lonely	10. outrageous
6. dyeing	

EXERCISE 24.6: Answers

2. carrying	8. obeyed
4. studies	10. coyly
6. dutiful	

EXERCISE 24.7: Answers

2. fastest	8. drastically
4. reference	10. weeping
6. regrettable	

EXERCISE 24.8: Answers

2. hooves

4. babies

6. spoofs

8. yourselves

10. roses

12. turkeys

14. radios

EXERCISE 25.3: Answers

2. student: from ME < L *studere,* to study

4. whine: from ME *whinen* < Indo-European *kwein,* to whiz, hiss, whistle

6. sex: from ME < L *sexus* < *secare,* to cut

8. tortilla: from Sp, diminutive of *torta,* cake

10. video: from L, I see < *videre,* to see

EXERCISE 25.4: Suggested Answers

2. *prevaricate:* (syn.) equivocate, lie, palter, fib.

4. *odious:* (syn.) disgusting, ghastly, hideous, unpleasant.

6. *obfuscate:* (syn.) darken, confuse.

EXERCISE 25.6: Suggested Answers

2. The *OED* defines *alienate* as to make strange or turn away from, to transfer ownership, and to change or alter something.
   Webster's New World Dictionary adds two slightly different meanings: to cause to be withdrawn from society, and to transfer affection.

4. The *OED* defines *hopefully* as an adverb: "In a hopeful manner; with a feeling of hope; with ground for hope, promisingly."
   Webster's New World Dictionary lists both adverb and adjective uses but notes that the adjectival use is "regarded by some as loose usage, but widely current."

6. Both the *OED* and *Webster's New World Dictionary* define *culture* as the cultivation of the soil, the production of a particular commodity, the growth of microorganisms in a prepared substance, the development of the intellect, and the ideas or customs of a group.
   The *OED* includes two obsolete definitions: worship, and the training of the human body.

EXERCISE 26.2: Suggested Answers

2. *scriptorium:* a writing room, a room in a monastery for copying manuscripts, writing, and studying.

4. *lucent:* giving off light, shining, translucent or clear.

6. *audiology:* the science of hearing, the evaluation of hearing defects.

8. *pathogenic:* producing disease.

10. *graphology:* the study of handwriting.

EXERCISE 26.3: Suggested Answers

2. *subterranean:* beneath earth; of or relating to under the surface of the earth.

4. *monograph:* write a single writing; a learned treatise on a small area of learning.

6. *superscript:* write over or above; a distinguishing symbol written immediately above or above and to the right of another character.

8. *neologism:* a recent word or thought; a word, usage, or expression that is often disapproved because of its newness or barbarousness.

10. *apathetic:* without feeling or not suffering; having or showing little or no feeling or emotion, having or showing little or no interest or concern.

EXERCISE 26.4: Suggested Answers

2. *fanciful:* full of fancy, indulging in fancies, imaginative in a playful way, whimsical.

4. *liquefy:* to change into a liquid.

6. *defiance:* the act of defying, bold resistance to authority or opposition.

8. *redden:* to make red, to become red.

10. *satirist:* a writer of satires.

EXERCISE 26.6: Suggested Answers

2. *reductionism:* a theory or procedure that reduces complex data or phenomena to simple terms.

EXERCISE 27.2: Answers

2. rapturous   4. dramatically

EXERCISE 27.3: Suggested Answers

2. *tragic:* distressing, alarming, disturbing; *consumes:* defeats, feeds on, erodes; *displays:* champions, thrives on, builds up, promotes; *drama:* excitement, tension, vitality

4. *held:* breathed; *keenness:* coolness, crispness; *twitch:* perk up; *surprise:* adventure, enterprise; *tremors:* chills; *run:* jet

EXERCISE 27.4: Suggested Answers

2. Cooing, singing, twittering—the early morning beckoning of birds outside my window make it a treat to get up.

4. The valet stepped cautiously yet excitedly toward my Porsche.

EXERCISE 27.5: Suggested Answers

2. *deep and soft like water moving in a cavern* (simile): this simile compares the sound of her voice to water in a cavern

EXERCISE 27.7: Suggested Answers

2. All candidates strive for the same results: to discredit the opposition and to persuade the majority of voters that they are qualified for the position.

4. The more angry she became over his actions, the more he rebelled and continued doing what he pleased.

EXERCISE 29.2: Answers

2. Unfortunately,
4. If you follow instructions carefully,
6. No comma needed.
8. No comma needed.
10. Frightened by the firecrackers,

EXERCISE 29.3: Suggested Answers

2. Immigrants came here with high hopes, *but* their illusions were often shattered.
4. He wanted adventure, *so* he moved to a cabin in the Alaskan wilderness.

EXERCISE 29.4: Answers

2. *who laughs last* is a restrictive clause because only the *she* who has the last laugh can laugh best. Laughing best is restricted to the person who laughs last.
4. *smoked over an alderwood fire* is a restrictive participial phrase because the meaning of the sentence is not complete without it. That it is smoked over an alderwood fire is what gives the salami *a unique flavor.*

EXERCISE 29.5: Answers

2. No commas needed.
4. No commas needed.
6. The Zunis, an ancient tribe, live in New Mexico.
8. Karl Marx, an important nineteenth-century sociologist, believed that his role as a social thinker was to change the world.
10. No commas needed.

EXERCISE 29.6: Answers

2. We bought zucchini, peppers, and tomatoes at the market.
4. The daddy-long-legs's orange body resembled a colored dot amidst eight long, black legs.
6. Superficial observation does not provide accurate insight into people's lives—how they feel, what they believe in, how they respond to others.
8. I timidly offered to help a loud, overbearing, lavishly dressed customer.
10. These Cosell clones insist on calling every play, judging every move, and telling everyone within earshot exactly what is wrong with the team.

EXERCISE 29.7: Answers

2. The West, in fact, has become solidly Republican in presidential elections.
4. The rescue team, alas, arrived too late.

EXERCISE 29.8: Answers

2. Ithaca, New York, has a population of about 20,000.
4. MLA headquarters are at 10 Astor Place, New York, New York 10003.

EXERCISE 29.9: Answers

2. Joseph Epstein admits, "I prefer not to be thought vulgar in any wise."

4. "Neat people are lazier and meaner than sloppy people," according to Suzanne Britt.

EXERCISE 29.11: Answers

2. Observers watch facial expressions and gestures and interpret them.

4. Our supper that evening consisted of stale bologna sandwiches.

6. As we sat around the campfire, we felt boredom and disappointment.

8. The photographer Edward Curtis is known for his depiction of the West.

10. Driving a car and talking on the car phone at the same time demand great care.

EXERCISE 30.2: Answers

2. City life offers many advantages; in many ways, however, life in a small town is much more pleasant.

4. Physical education forms an important part of a university's program; nevertheless, few students and professors clearly recognize its value.

6. Voltaire was concerned about the political implications of his skepticism; he warned his friends not to discuss atheism in front of the servants.

8. My high school was excessively competitive; virtually everyone went on to college, many to the top schools in the nation.

10. Propaganda is defined as the spread of ideas to further a cause; therefore, propaganda and advertisement are synonymous terms.

EXERCISE 30.4: Answers

2. If the North had followed up its victory at Gettysburg more vigorously, the Civil War might have ended sooner.

4. Our uniforms were unbelievably dingy, stained from being constantly splattered with food and often torn here and there.

EXERCISE 31.2: Answers

2. Cicero was murdered in 43 B.C.

4. She asked whether Operation PUSH had been founded by Jesse Jackson.

EXERCISE 31.3: Answers

2. Are people with so many possessions really happy?

4. Correct; indirect question.

EXERCISE 31.4: Suggested Answers

2. I screamed at Jamie, "You rat! You tricked me!"

4. Stop, thief!

EXERCISE 32.2: Answers

2. *Malcolm Forbes's* flamboyant lifestyle celebrated his wealth.

4. *Carol and Jim's* income dropped drastically after Jim lost his job.

6. Many smokers disregard the *surgeon general's* warnings.

8. The *governors'* attitudes changed after the convention.

10. *My friend's and my brother's* cars have the same kind of stereo systems.

EXERCISE 32.3: Answers

2. I heard the songs and the minister saying: "Why *don't* you come?"

4. So I decided that maybe to save further trouble, *I'd* better lie. . . .

EXERCISE 33.2: Answers

2. In Flannery O'Connor's short story "Revelation," colors symbolize passions, violence, sadness, and even God.

4. The "fun" of surgery begins before the operation ever takes place.

6. "Big Bill," the first section of Dos Passos's *U.S.A.*, opens with a birth.

8. Pink Floyd's song "Time" depicts the impact of technology on society.

10. In the episode "Driven to Extreme," *48 Hours* takes a humorous look at driving in New York City.

EXERCISE 33.3: Suggested Answers

2. What is Hawthorne telling the readers in "Rappaccini's Daughter"?

4. This "typical American" is Ruby Turpin, who in the course of the story receives a message that brings about a change in her life.

6. One of Jackson's least-known stories is "Janice"; this story, like many of her others, leaves the reader shocked.

8. In his article "The Death of Broadway," Thomas M. Disch writes that "choreographers are, literally, a dying breed."[1]

10. One thought flashed through my mind as I finished *In Search of Our Mothers' Gardens:* "I want to read more of this writer's work."

EXERCISE 34.2: Answers

2. During my research, I found that a flat-rate income tax (a single-rate tax with no dedutions) has its problems.

4. Many researchers used the Massachusetts Multiphasic Personal Inventory (MMPI) for hypnotizability studies.

EXERCISE 34.3: Answers

2. Even if smoking is harmful—and there is no real proof of this assertion—it is unjust to outlaw smoking while other harmful substances remain legal.

4. Union Carbide's plant in Bhopal, India, sprang a leak—a leak that killed over 2,500 people and injured 150,000 more.

EXERCISE 34.4: Answers

2. Another example is taken from Psalm 139:16.

4. Shifting into German, Kennedy declared: "Ich bin ein Berliner."

6. Ghandi urged four things: tell the truth even in business, adopt more sanitary habits, abolish caste and religious divisions, and learn English.

8. *Signs of Trouble and Erosion: A Report on Education in America* was submitted to Congress and the president in January 1984.

10. The eclipse will peak in Los Angeles at 11:28 A.M.

EXERCISE 35.2: Answers

2. We had a choice of fast-food, Chinese, or Italian restaurants.

4. The Council of Trent was convened to draw up the Catholic response to the Protestant Reformation.

6. I wondered if my new Levi's were faded enough and if I could possibly scuff up my new Keds just a little more before I arrived for spring term.

8. In this essay, I will be citing the works of Vladimir Nabokov, in particular his novels *Pnin* and *Lolita* and his story "The Vane Sisters."

10. My favorite song by Cole Porter is "You'd Be So Nice to Come Home To."

EXERCISE 36.2: Answers

2. An MX missile, which is 71 feet long and 92 inches around, weighs 190,000 pounds.

4. In 1991, Representative William Gray gave up his seat in Congress to serve as president of the United Negro College Fund.

6. Like black-and-white television, the five-cent candy bar is a relic of the past.

8. The local National Public Radio station has a broadcast range of seventy-five miles.

10. Dostoyevsky was influenced by many European writers—for example, Dickens, Stendhal, and Balzac.

EXERCISE 36.3: Suggested Answers

2. Some call it the handbook for the nineties.

4. The invasion of Kuwait began on August 2, 1990.

6. Cable TV is now available to 72 percent of the population.

8. In the thirty-five to forty-four age group, the risk is estimated to be about 1 in 2,500.

10. The amulet measured by 1⅛ by 2⅔ inches.

EXERCISE 37.1: Answers

2. An excerpt from his book *Waiting for the Weekend* was published in the *Atlantic*.

4. The word *veterinary* comes from the Latin *veterinarius*.

6. Flying the *Glamorous Glennis*, named for his wife, Chuck Yeager was the first pilot to fly faster than the speed of sound.

8. *The Waste Land* is a long and difficult but ultimately rewarding poem.

10. Seven astronauts were killed when the *Challenger* exploded.

EXERCISE 38.1: Answers

2. re*tract; re-tract

4. mil*i*tar*y; mil-i-tary

6. in*ner*di*rect*ed; inner-directed

8. dim*ming; dim-ming
10. at*ti*tude; at-ti-tude

EXERCISE 38.2: Answers

2. pre-World War II
4. Correct
6. self-important
8. seven hundred thirty-three
10. a politician who is quick-witted (Quick-witted is commonly found in dictionaries; thus hyphenation is correct even though the compound adjective comes after the noun.)

EXERCISE 38.3: Answers

2. McKuen began to write as an escape from his on-the-move life, which included various odd jobs ranging from ditch-digging to cookie-cutting.
4. Suicide among teenagers has tripled in the past thirty-five years.
6. The Soviets were divided between pro- and anti-Gorbachev factions.
8. The government declared an all-cut war on poverty and homelessness.
10. The beautifully written essay earned high praise.

Acknowledgments (continued)

e. e. cummings. "Me up at does" is reprinted from *Complete Poems, 1913–1962*, by e. e. cummings, by permission of Liveright Publishing Corporation. Copyright © 1923, 1925, 1931, 1935, 1938, 1939, 1940, 1944, 1945, 1946, 1947, 1948, 1949, 1950, 1951, 1952, 1953, 1954, 1955, 1956, 1957, 1958, 1959, 1960, 1961, 1962 by the Trustees for the e. e. cummings Trust. Copyright © 1961, 1963, 1968 by Marion Morehouse Cummings.

Emily Dickinson. "A Little Madness in the Spring" and "Much Madness Is Divinest Sense" reprinted by permission of the publishers and the Trustees of Amherst College from *The Poems of Emily Dickinson*, Thomas H. Johnson, ed., Cambridge, MA: The Belknap Press of Harvard University Press, Copyright 1951, © 1955, 1979, 1983 by the President and Fellows of Harvard College.

Robert Francis. "The Pitcher" is reprinted from *The Orb Weaver*, © 1960 by Robert Francis, Wesleyan University Press. By permission of University Press of New England.

Robert Frost. "Fire and Ice" and "The Road Not Taken" from *The Poetry of Robert Frost* edited by Edward Connery Lathem. Copyright 1923, © 1969 by Holt, Rinehart, and Winston. Copyright 1951 by Robert Frost. Reprinted by permission of Henry Holt and Company, Inc.

Greenpeace advertisement courtesy of Greenpeace USA, 1436 U Street, NW, Washington, DC.

A. E. Housman. "The Loveliest of Trees" from "A Shropshire Lad"—Authorised edition. From *The Collected Poems of A. E. Housman*. Copyright 1939, 1940 © 1965 by Holt, Rinehart, and Winston. Copyright © 1967, 1968, by Robert E. Symons. Reprinted by permission of Henry Holt and Company, Inc.

Langston Hughes. "Theme for English B," copyright 1951 by Langston Hughes. Copyright renewed 1979 by George Houston Bass. Reprinted by permission of Harold Ober Associates Incorporated. "Dream Deferred (Harlem)," from *The Panther and the Lash* by Langston Hughes. Copyright 1951 by Langston Hughes. Reprinted by permission of Alfred A. Knopf, Inc.

June Jordan. "Aftermath," from the book *Naming Our Destiny: New and Selected Poems* by June Jordan. Copyright © 1989 by June Jordan. Used by permission of the publisher, Thunder's Mouth Press.

Dana Owens, Simone Johnson, Anthony Peaks, Mark James. "Ladies First," © 1989 T-Boy Music Publishing, Inc. (ASCAP) c/o Lipservices. International Copyrights Secured. All Rights Reserved. Used by Kind Permission.

Readers' Guide to Periodical Literature, Page 890, Volume 43, March 1983–1984. Copyright © 1984 by The H. W. Wilson Company. Material reproduced with permission of the publisher.

Lewis Thomas. "The Attic of the Brain," copyright © 1980 by Lewis Thomas. From Late Night Thoughts on Listening to Mahler's Ninth by Lewis Thomas. Used by permission of Viking Penguin, a division of Penguin Books USA Inc.

Webster's New World Dictionary, Third College Edition, © 1988 by Simon and Schuster, New York. Used by permission of the publisher.

Webster's Third New International Dictionary © 1986 by Merriam-Webster Inc., publisher of the Merriam-Webster ® dictionaries. Reprinted by permission.

Eudora Welty. Excerpts reprinted by permission of the publishers of *One Writer's Beginnings* by Eudora Welty, Cambridge, MA: Harvard University Press, Copyright © 1983, 1984 by Eudora Welty.

Index of
Authors and Titles

Subject Index

Name Index to Annotations

➤ CHECKING FOR KEY ELEMENTS IN YOUR WRITING

Broad Content Issues

Organization and Presentation

The Twenty Most Common Surface Errors